W9-CII-116

New England

Mara Vorhees,
Glenda Bendure, Ned Friary, Richard Koss, John Spelman,
Regis St. Louis

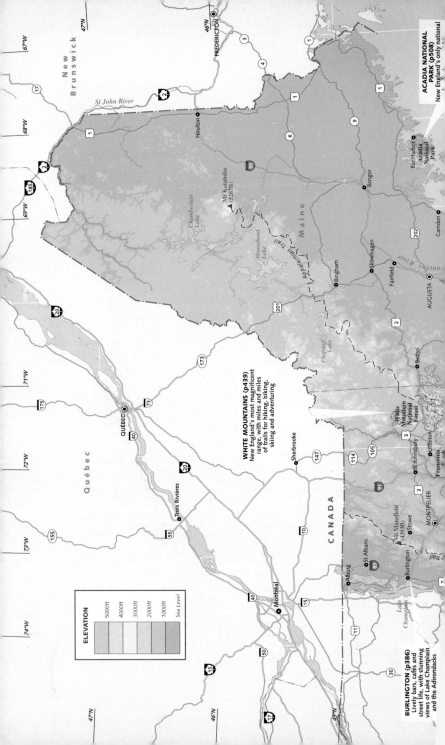

ACADIA NATIONAL
PARK (p508)
New England's only national

WHITE MOUNTAINS (p439)
New England's most magnificent
range, with miles and miles
of trails for hiking, biking,
skiing and adventuring

BURLINGTON (p386)
Lively bars, cafés and
street life, with stunning
views of Lake Champlain
and the Adirondacks

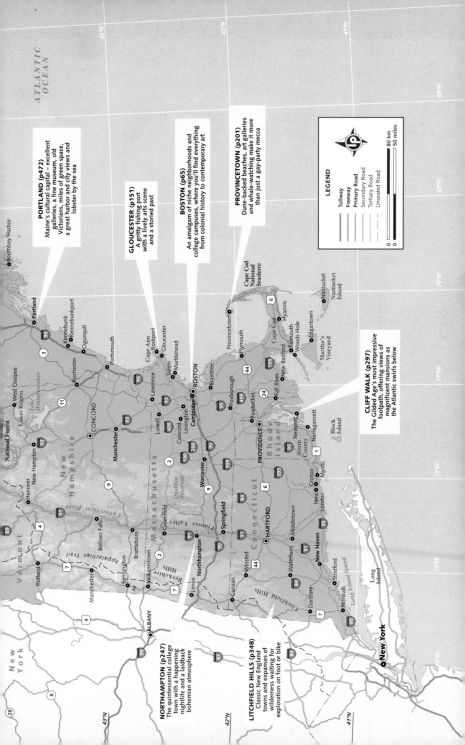

PORTLAND (p472)
Maine's cultural capital – excellent galleries, a fine museum, old Victorians, miles of green space, a great harbor and city views and lobster by the sea

GLOUCESTER (p151)
A gritty fishing port with a lively arts scene and a storied past

BOSTON (p65)
An amalgam of niche neighborhoods and college campuses, where you'll find everything from colonial history to contemporary art

PROVINCETOWN (p201)
Dune-backed beaches, art galleries and whale-watching make it more than just a gay-party mecca

CLIFF WALK (p297)
The Gilded Age's most impressive footpath, offering views of magnificent mansions as the Atlantic swirls below

NORTHAMPTON (p247)
The quintessential college town with a happening nightlife and a laidback bohemian atmosphere

LITCHFIELD HILLS (p348)
Classic New England towns and expanses of wilderness waiting for exploration on foot or bike

LEGEND
Tollway
Freeway
Primary Road
Secondary Road
Tertiary Road
Unsealed Road

0   80 km
0   50 miles

ATLANTIC OCEAN

On the Road

MARA VORHEES
Coordinating Author
I met this red rooster at the De-Cordova Sculpture Park, where he was participating in an exhibit on Confronting Animals in Contemporary Art. As you can see, I am taking the theme very seriously.

GLENDA BENDURE Years ago the first place I stopped on my very first visit to Cape Cod was right here in Sandwich. A centuries-old grist mill sits at the edge of a swan-filled pond where children play. It's still one sweet introduction to the Cape.

NED FRIARY Anyone who thinks the Cape is overdeveloped needs to hit the Cape Cod Rail Trail. Here it's cranberry bogs worked by hand, untouched conservation land, quiet ponds and screeching hawks. Pedaling along this trail I'm awed by how this slice of Cape Cod has barely changed in a hundred years.

RICHARD KOSS Driving along one of the dirt roads threading Vermont's pristine Northeast Kingdom, I paused one afternoon by this stream. For half an hour, I completely vegged out and blocked out all thoughts of my travel itinerary. Twenty seconds after this photo, I took a false step and found myself knee-deep in mud.

JOHN SPELMAN Ralph's Chadwick Square Diner has two items on its menu: burgers, which people actually order, and the more mysterious chili. These, and beer, become delicious thanks to the fabulous diner in which you consume them. On my visit Worcester's only three hipsters debated the toughness of Vikings and samurai. A rock show followed.

REGIS ST. LOUIS On my long odyssey across Maine and New Hampshire, my furry-faced friend Cosmic made an excellent traveling companion. Here we are in picturesque Acadia National Park, taking a break along the western shores of Somes Sound during a hike up St Sauveur Mountain.

See full author bios page 545

New England Highlights

You can choose your own adventure in New England, cradle of the American experiment and home to countless nooks and crannies. Big-city Boston serves as the hub linking the region's varied flavors: idyllic Vermont farmlands yielding savory syrups and cheeses; rugged Maine coastlines, weathered and emotive; expansive Cape Cod beaches dotted by clam shacks and rental cottages; heady, energetic college towns. Whatever your interests – art galleries, winter sports, farmers markets, tiny bookstores – New England's bounty will reward.

Bring an inquisitive mind and hearty appetite – but leave the Yankees cap at home.

JOHN ELK III

1 **MOUNT DESERT ISLAND, MAINE**

When visiting Mt Desert Island in Maine (p501), my friends and I were trying to find the perfect viewing spot for the sunset. We arrived at Indian Point Reserve 10 minutes before sunset. The sign told us that it was a mile through the woods to reach the shore. We started running, our feet pounding on the moss, taking care not to trip over the gnarled pine roots that covered the ground. At the end of the path was a patch of green grass and three red Adirondack chairs. Hot and sweaty from our run, we jumped in the surprisingly warm water and then settled into the chairs to watch the sun set into the water.

Rana Freedman, Lonely Planet staff, Oakland

FENWAY PARK, BOSTON, MASSACHUSETTS

A trip to Fenway Park (p121) is a time warp to 1912. From antique wooden seats to the manual score-board afoot the Green Monster, the magic of Fenway sustains legions of Red Sox fans nationwide. Even the uninitiated will appreciate this cathedral of baseball. Before their own success compels the Red Sox to upgrade, catch a game at Fenway!

Chris Howard, traveler, Boston

LOU JO

IZZET KERIBAR

VERMONT LEAVES & BACKROADS

Vermont is gorgeous year round, but the fall leaf-peeping season is the jewel in its crown. Manchester (p369) is a classic Vermont town and a great starting point. From there you can loop on back roads through the russet-colored foli-age, maple-tapping houses, horse farms, wood craft shops, steepled churches and village inns. Hike or drive to the summit of Mt Equi-nox (p370) for sweeping views of the Green Mountains and upstate New York. Finish with a mulled cider on the front porch of the stately, cozy Equinox Inn (p372) overlooking the marble paved sidewalks and colonial buildings of Manchester Village.

Christina Margarita Tunnah, Lonely Planet staff, Oakland

PROVINCETOWN & MARTHA'S VINEYARD, MASSACHUSETTS

Oh, how we would love to have stayed longer. That's the feeling my wife and I had after just a few hours in P-town (p201), the gay mecca and fun capital of Cape Cod. Wander the streets and wharf area, people-watch from one of the many eateries on Commercial St, and don't miss the view from atop the 252ft Pilgrim Monument. If you're staying on the upper Cape, pop over to one of the nearby islands. We paid a visit to Martha's Vineyard (p219), a laid-back place of technicolor gingerbread houses surrounding Trinity Park in Oakbluffs (p223), and captain's cottages and easy strolling streets in orderly Edgartown (p226).

Glenn van der Knijff, Lonely Planet staff, Melbourne

GLENN VAN DER KN

NEW ENGLAND BEER

With beers like Berkshire Brewing Company, McNeils, Magic Hat, Carrabasett, Geary's, Gritty McDuffs etc, New England makes the best beer (at least porters and stouts) in the world.

Chris Deliso, Lonely Planet author, Kumanovo

KIM GRANT

EOIN CLARKE

5

SKIING NEW ENGLAND

Stowe Mountain (p395), Sugarbush (p384), Mad River Glen (p384), Loon Mountain (p444) – these are the names that perk the ears of East Coast skiers and snowboarders each autumn, when gear sales rev up and visions of first runs on powder days dance in their heads.

Jay Cooke, Lonely Planet staff, Oakland

6

KIM GRANT

7

BEN & JERRY'S & THE VERMONT GOVERNOR'S MANSION

We went to make the Ben & Jerry's pilgrimage (p401), to get the free scoop. Well the state courthouse in Montpelier (p402) wasn't too far, so we went to the governor's office and asked to meet her. Looking about as bad as a couple of college kids could look, arriving after just camping in Baxter State Park (p519) in Maine with a lobster crate on top of my crappy old Honda Prelude, Governor Kunin came out of her office to meet us. That she met us at all? That to me is what makes Vermont the best state in the Union.

Todd Sotkiewicz, Lonely Planet staff, Oakland

APPALACHIAN TRAIL

A 2174-mile trail carving along the length of the eastern US? How cool is that? New England hikers have five states in which they can access the Appalachian Trail (p24), the most famous in America.

Gary Aldridge, traveler, Seoul

8

LEE FOSTER

MAINE LOBSTER

9

Until you've had fresh lobster served up beachside after a Windjammer cruise (p495) off the rocky coast of Maine, you've not tasted one of New England's greatest treats.

Jay Cooke, Lonely Planet staff, Oakland

CORINNE HUMP

RICHARD CUMM

NEW ENGLAND SEACOAST

10

I love the seacoast of New England – the old harbors with wooden schooners, seaside crab shacks, salty air and squawking seagulls, and the stately old lighthouses that once brought sailors safely home.

Eric Beck, traveler, Austin

Contents

Regional Map Contents

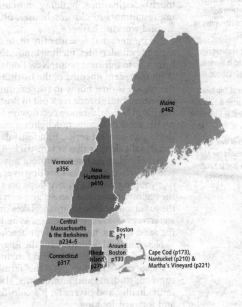

Destination New England

You're likely to return from New England with an album of images: white-clapboard churches on well-manicured greens; red-brick buildings on leafy college campuses; granite mountains majestically ablaze with fall colors; paint-peeling fishing boats bobbing at their mores. New England is all that, and more.

It's a politically liberal region. Look at voting records, elected officials and enacted policies: the liberal status is undeniable. The most conspicuous example? Five out of six states have legalized some form of same-sex union (an act that other states in the union are outlawing). But – as always – the situation is more nuanced than the image implies. Case in point: of the region's two homegrown candidates in the 2008 presidential election, the frontrunner was a Massachusetts Republican.

New England is increasingly international. It has long been a destination for immigrants from Ireland, Italy and Portugal, and the mixture is becoming even more diverse. Chinatown is expanding in Boston, while Brazilian flags are strewn about the suburbs. Hartford and Springfield are havens for Haitians, while Vietnamese and Cambodians are settling in Lowell. The result is a richer, spicier and more complex blend of cultures.

Besides rural charm, New England is also about urban grit. Industrial and port cities around the region were built on the backs of factory workers, mill girls and sailors. Today towns like Salem, Mystic, Lowell, Providence and Portland are remaking themselves as trendsetters and tourist destinations, building museums out of former factories, opening restaurants in old warehouses, offering cruises on canals and walks around working harbors.

No matter what new identity these cities take on, however, they retain their edgy undersides, fuelling innovative art and nonstop nightlife. Which brings us to our next point: New England is at the cutting edge of culture. With the recent opening of the Institute of Contemporary Arts in Boston, the region is now home to two exciting, experimental contemporary art museums. Indie bands rock out in Boston, Portland, Providence and Burlington. The world-renowned Boston Symphony Orchestra takes its show on the road in summer, delighting audiences in the Berkshires. Around the region concert series, film festivals and theater productions make for a cultural calendar that is jam-packed and jaw-dropping.

New England is big on outdoor adventure: you'll find a sport for every season. Whether you're hurdling over carriage roads on a mountain bike or swooping down a snowy slope on a snowboard, the rounded peaks of the region's mountain ranges give everyone a rush. While you're paddling the luxuriously languid inland lakes or rafting down a rippling river, her waterways awaken your senses. Whether you're bird-watching or building sand castles, her windswept beaches are beguiling.

New England is history. It's the Pilgrims who came ashore at Plymouth Rock and the minutemen who fought for American independence. But it's also contemporary. It's the farmers and fishermen struggling for survival; students and immigrants, always adapting. New England oozes individuality and diversity; it's colorful and controversial, free-thinking and forward-looking.

FAST FACTS

Population of six New England states: 14.3 million

Total area of New England states: 72,000 sq miles

Miles of coastline in New England: 4965

Lobster sheds its shell in the first five years of life: 25 times

Unemployment rate in six New England states: 4.5%

Number of tea crates emptied into Boston Harbor on December 16, 1773: 342

Gallons of maple syrup produced in Vermont annually: 430,000

Number of thru-hikers who started the Appalachian Trail in Springer Mt, Georgia in 2007: 1125

Number of thru-hikers who finished the Appalachian Trail in Katahdin, Maine in 2007: 159

Getting Started

Although New England is geographically small, it contains an unlimited array of outdoor adventures, culinary treats, cultural diversions and artistic masterpieces. The main challenge in planning a trip may be deciding between them! So here is our first word of warning: don't try to pack too much into too little (and we're not talking about your suitcase). If you find yourself with some unprogrammed time on your hands, there is no shortage of spontaneous pursuits to engage you on the spur of the moment.

That said, it's worth making a few advance arrangements if you are combing the beaches of Cape Cod in summer, leaf-peeping in the Green or White Mountains in October, or celebrating with the students during graduation week in Boston. Reserving a room in advance is advisable, especially if you have your heart set on staying somewhere in particular.

For the most flexibility and freedom of travel, consider renting a vehicle or bringing your own. Except for the city of Boston, New England is prime road-trip country. Driving your own car (or bicycle!) will ensure that you explore more back roads, browse more antique shops, devour more diner specials and engage in more of what New England has to offer.

See Climate Charts (p524) for more information.

WHEN TO GO

With four distinct seasons, travel in New England presents four different faces. If you're prepared to roll with abrupt and dramatic weather changes, you can explore New England year-round. Although many travelers think of New England primarily as a summer destination, that would unduly discount the entire catalog of winter sports (see p62) and the peak fall foliage season, when the drama of leaf-peeping reaches its zenith (see p24 and p53).

If temperate spring weather lasts a while, traveling from late April to early June can be glorious, with apple and cherry trees in bloom and farmers out tapping maple trees for sap (see the boxed text, p359). If spring is short, as it usually is, it may arrive on a Tuesday, and be followed on Wednesday by the heat and humidity of summer.

In July and August, summer resort areas are very busy, accommodations are fully booked and restaurants are crowded. With the exception of the coast or mountains, summers can be uncomfortably humid. Unless your heart is

---

DON'T LEAVE HOME WITHOUT ...

- Checking the visa situation (see p531)
- Checking the updated security regulations at the airport. Remember to put Swiss army knives and toiletries (over 5 oz) in your suitcase, as you won't be allowed to carry them on the airplane.
- Drivers license and car insurance (see p537)
- A jacket or sweater (even in summer!) if you're lingering on the coast or in northern mountains
- Lightweight rain gear for spring and fall
- A demure bathing suit (remember, New England is full of Puritans)
- Binoculars for whale- and bird-watching
- An insatiable appetite, a pleasure-seeking palate and a taste for boutique ice cream

set on swimming, time your travel to occur between mid-May and mid-June, before local schools close and families hit the road (but avoid Boston at the end of May when the city is packed for college graduations).

Another great time is early September – after the big summer rush but before the 'leaf-peepers' (foliage tourists) arrive. The weather in these shoulder seasons is generally warm and sunny. Autumn harvest time means fresh cranberries on sale in the markets, pick-your-own fruit days and cider-making at orchards (see p51).

Early November is a serene, almost haunting, time before the snows hit and icy winds blow. Winter can be severe or moderate, but it's rarely mild. December to March is ski season in the mountains. Almost all of interior New England experiences harsh weather with lakes 'iced in' until April. When it's not snowing, however, you'll likely find winter in New England to be bright and sunny.

For more details, see the Climate sections in individual regional chapters.

COSTS & MONEY

The cost of living in New England is similar to the rest of the eastern seaboard, which is higher than the rest of the US. Travelers will find that urban areas – especially Boston – are particularly pricey for hotels and restaurants (although there are plenty of options for the budget traveler). In recent years, the floundering dollar has made the US an attractive destination for European and Canadian travelers, and New England is no exception.

Travel costs are highest in the summer and during fall foliage; in the mountains, rates go up during ski season. Of course, costs vary widely depending on your mode of travel. If you camp, drive your own car and pack picnics, your daily expenses can be as low as $50 per person per day. A traveler staying in budget motels and hostels and eating in budget restaurants can expect to spend between $80 and $100 per person per day.

Midrange travelers can expect to spend between $100 and $150 per day, which includes staying at a midrange hotel, paying admission for parks and museums, eating at restaurants and paying for transportation. This does not account for the occasional splurge on shopping, dining or accommodation!

Many discounts are available; see p525. Most state tourism centers publish brochures that include discount coupons for places to eat and stay; also look for travel coupons online. Discounts on car rentals and accommodations are often available to members of auto clubs affiliated with the American Automobile Association (AAA; p538).

Parents should inquire about reduced rates on meals and activities for children. Often museums will have a free family day or family discounts. For our Top Ten picks for kids, see p16. For more information on traveling with children, see p524.

TRAVEL LITERATURE

New England's reverence for the written word started with the Puritans, and has been nurtured over the centuries by the area's great universities and literary societies. Here are a few local literary lights to consider when you are selecting your reading material.

Start with *Walden; Or, Life in the Woods* (1854) by Henry David Thoreau, a quiet and searching story of his 26 months in a small cabin on Walden Pond (p139). Compare that with *A Walk in the Woods* (1999) by Bill Bryson, who hikes the Appalachian Trail with his friend – both of them gloriously middle-aged and out-of-shape explorers.

In *Land's End* (2002), Pulitzer Prize–winner Michael Cunningham, a frequent visitor to Provincetown over the past two decades, explores its

HOW MUCH?

Bike rental (24 hours): $25

Cappuccino: $3.50

Cover charge Abbey Lounge: $8-12

T-ride: $1.70

Red Sox ticket bleacher seat (face value): $23

LONELY PLANET INDEX

Gallon of gas: $2.80

Liter of water: $2.50

Pint of Sam Adams: $5

'Boston: Wicked Pissah' T-shirt: $20

Bowl of clam chowder: $5

artistic history and its alternative lifestyle – which in Provincetown is not the alternative but the norm. (The book is only 172 pages and makes a good beach read.)

For many years, Linda Greenlaw lived on Monhegan Island and worked as a captain of a swordfish boat – a rarity in the male-dominated fishing industry. She wrote several *New York Times* bestselling books based on her experiences, including *The Lobster Chronicles* (2003) and *The Hungry Ocean* (2000).

The Wapshot Chronicle (1957), John Cheever's debut novel, is a sardonic account of an old eccentric Massachusetts family whose steady decline is hastened by the ribald activities of Moses Wapshot and his brother Coverely.

Many of John Irving's novels are set in New England. Fans muse about which novel is his best, but perennial favorites include *A Prayer for Owen Meany* (1989) and *Hotel New Hampshire* (1981), both hilarious coming-of-age stories set in New Hampshire.

A cause célèbre when it appeared in 1992, Donna Tartt's *The Secret History* still resonates. It explores the amusing (and ultimately murderous) hijinks of a clique of classical studies students at a New England college based on Bennington, Vermont.

INTERNET RESOURCES

Boston Globe's New England Guide (www.boston.com/travel/newengland/) Vast listings of travel tips and itineraries.

Lonely Planet (www.lonelyplanet.com) What better place to start?

National Parks Service (www.nps.gov/parks) Features fast facts about national parks, recreation areas and historic sites across the US, including New England.

New England Lighthouses (www.lighthouse.cc) A comprehensive list of lighthouses by state.

Visit New England (www.visitnewengland.com) One of many online travel resources, including a comprehensive listing of hotels and attractions.

Yankee Magazine (www.yankeemagazine.com) An excellent general interest site with classic things to see, great destination profiles and events.

TRAVELING RESPONSIBLY

Like the rest of the country, New England is slowly but surely becoming more environmentally aware. With hundreds of square miles of national forest and protected parkland, the region values its natural resources. Major cities are also getting in on the game, purchasing fuel-efficient buses, constructing bike paths and hosting farmers markets. (See p79 for more information about the 'greening' of Boston.)

What does this mean for you? It gives you more ways to minimize your impact as a traveler. Besides the suggestions listed here, check out the GreenDex at the back of this book.

Getting There & Away

If you wish to avoid flying to New England, you do have some more environmentally friendly options. The East Coast of the United States is served by an excellent network of trains and buses, so it's easy to get to Providence, Boston and other major New England cities from anywhere on the eastern seaboard. **Amtrak** (www.amtrak.com) runs frequent trains between New York City and Boston. The region is also well served by the national bus company **Greyhound** (www.greyhound.com) as well as by regional company **Peter Pan** (www.peterpanbus.com). Trains and buses between Boston and New York (four to five hours), for example, run frequently throughout the day. If you are coming from another part of the country, you'll have to spend a

TOP PICKS

NEW ENGLAND
VT
UNITED STATES NH
OF AMERICA MA — Boston

For Foodies

The feast isn't confined to Thanksgiving, as New England's bountiful food options make all seasons ripe for culinary exploration:

- **Carmen** (p107) Boston, Massachusetts
- **Wellfleet OysterFest** (p198) Wellfleet, Massachusetts
- **Brewster Fish House** (p190) Brewster, Massachusetts
- **Boulevard Diner** (p237) Worcester, Massachusetts
- **River Tavern** (p341) Chester, Connecticut
- **Al Forno** (p292) Providence, Rhode Island
- **Eli's** (p310) Block Island, Rhode Island
- **Simon Pearce Restaurant** (p378) Quechee, Vermont
- **Pangea** (p369) North Bennington, Vermont
- **Cook's Lobster House** (p488) Bailey Island, Maine

Only in New England

In a world of seeming sameness, New England is still remarkably and refreshingly defined by regional characteristics. Here are a few of our favorite unique, off-beat and exclusively New England experiences:

- **Head of the Charles** (p98) Boston, Massachusetts
- **Lobster ice cream** (p177) Falmouth, Cape Cod
- **Montague Bookmill** (p255) Montague, Massachusetts
- **Brimfield Antique Show** (p239) Sturbridge, Massachusetts
- **Cliff Walk** (p297) Newport, Rhode Island
- **Gillette Castle** (p341) East Haddam, Connecticut
- **Bread and Puppet Museum** (p405) Northeast Kingdom, Vermont
- **Covered Bridge Museum** (p367) Bennington, Vermont
- **Pumpkin Festival** (p425 and p98) Keene, New Hampshire or Boston, Massachusetts
- **Lobster Festival** (p494) Rockland, Maine

New England for Kids

Your kids can playfully and pleasantly pass their entire vacation at the beach (take your pick which one). But if you want to broaden their horizons, here are a few more opportunities to entertain and educate:

- **Plimoth Plantation** (p165) Plymouth, Massachusetts
- **Haunted Happenings** (p147) Salem, Massachusetts
- **Whale-watching cruise** (p205 and p154)
- **Lobstering cruise** (p467)
- **Flying Horses Carousel** (p224) Oak Bluffs, Massachusetts
- **Higgins Amory Museum** (p235) Worcester, Massachusetts
- **Magic Wings Butterfly Conservatory & Gardens** (p254) Deerfield, Massachusetts
- **Roger Williams Park & Zoo** (p280) Providence, Rhode Island
- **Mystic Aquarium & Institute for Exploration** (p320) Mystic, Connecticut
- **New England Aquarium** (p83) Boston, Massachusetts
- **Stepping Stones Museum for Children** (p336) Norwalk, Connecticut
- **Children's Museum** (p85) Boston, Massachusetts
- **Children's Museum of Maine** (p476) Portland, Maine

bit more time. It takes about 3½ days to travel by train from San Francisco to Boston, but there is plenty to see along the way.

Slow Travel

Within New England, there is a reliable network of regional buses that serve the bigger towns. **Concord Trailways** (www.concordtrailways.com) plies routes from Boston to New Hampshire and Maine, while **C&J Trailways** (www .ctrailways.com) goes to the coastal towns of Newburyport and Portsmouth. **Plymouth & Brockton Street Railway Co** (www.p-b.com) connects Boston to the South Shore and Cape Cod. **Vermont Transit** (www.vermonttransit.com) has routes all around Vermont, New Hampshire and Maine, as well as connections to Montreal and Boston. The **MBTA commuter rails** (www.mbta.com) run to some towns around Boston, while ferries run to Cape Cod and the islands, as well as to some coastal towns.

If you don't want to be tied to bus and boat schedules, consider riding a bike. Bike rental is available in all of New England's bigger towns, as well as in major tourist destinations like Provincetown and Newport. You can also bring bikes on ferries and trains. For information about the region's best bike trails, see p59.

Accommodation

No accommodation is more environmentally sound than camping (assuming your camp stove does not start a forest fire). Here are some other options for relatively eco-friendly lodging:

Vanessa Noel Hotel Green (p214) Nantucket, Massachusetts
Copley Square Hotel (p101) Boston, Massachusetts
AMC Highland Center (p457) Crawford Notch, New Hampshire
Albert B Lester Memorial HI-AYH Hostel (p452) North Conway, New Hampshire
Pinestead Farm Lodge (p449) Franconia, New Hampshire
Four Columns Inn (p362) Newfane, Vermont

Food

Locally grown, organic, in-season food is one of the big draws to the region and it doesn't take a lot to find a restaurant serving this kind of fare. Check out p50 for excellent farmers markets and other places to purchase fresh produce straight from the source. Our top picks for restaurants using local and organic produce:

Ten Tables (p111) Boston, Massachusetts
Naked Oyster (p184) Hyannis, Massachusetts
Juice (p199) Wellfleet, Massachusetts
Al Forno (p292) Providence, Rhode Island
Fire & Ice (p383) Middlebury, Vermont
Smokejacks (p393) Burlington, Vermont
Shaker Table (p423) Concord, New Hampshire
Canoe Club (p432) Hanover, New Hampshire

Events Calendar

With a calendar jam-packed full of historical, cultural, culinary and otherwise celebratory events, there's never a dull moment in New England.

JANUARY–FEBRUARY

MOBY-DICK: THE MARATHON January 3
The 25-hour marathon reading of the Melville classic takes place at the New Bedford Whaling Museum (p169) at noon on the anniversary of the writer's departure on a whaling ship from the New Bedford, Massachusetts, port.

MARCH–APRIL

BOSTON MARATHON 3rd Monday in April
The country's 'longest-running' marathon (p98), when tens of thousands of spectators watch runners cross the finish line at Copley Plaza in Boston.

PATRIOTS DAY April 19
Companies of minutemen and regulars don colonial dress and re-enact the historic battles on Patriots Day (p135) on the greens in Lexington and Concord, Massachusetts. Arrive just after dawn.

MAY–JUNE

FIELDS OF LUPINE FESTIVAL early June
This little-known floral festival (p449) celebrates the annual bloom of delicious lupine with garden tours, art exhibits and concerts in Franconia, New Hampshire.

BUNKER HILL DAY Sunday nearest June 19
Residents re-enact the fateful Battle of Bunker Hill (1775) in Charlestown (Boston, Massachusetts) and then commemorate the event with a local parade (p98).

JULY

INDEPENDENCE DAY July 4
Independence Day celebrations take place all around the region.

HARBORFEST week of July 4
This week-long festival (p98) is an extension of the Fourth of July weekend in Boston, Massachusetts. Kids' activities, chowder-tasting and

other events culminate in the annual fireworks and Pops concert on the Esplanade.

MASHPEE WAMPANOAG POW WOW weekend nearest July 4
Native Americans from around the country join the Mashpee Wampanoag for a big three-day heritage celebration (p179) in Mashpee, Massachusetts, that includes Native American dancing, crafts, competitions and after-dark fireball.

GAY PRIDE PARADE mid-June
Drawing tens of thousands of participants and spectators, this mid-month parade (p98) culminates in a big party on Boston Common.

NEWPORT MUSIC FESTIVAL mid-July
Classical music lovers come from far and wide to hear the concerts (p301) that are hosted in Newport's famous mansions.

REVOLUTIONARY WAR FESTIVAL 2nd Sunday after July 4
Exeter, New Hampshire, celebrates Independence Day a little late, with reenactments, colonial cooking, road races and free concerts (p419).

NORTH ATLANTIC BLUES FESTIVAL mid-July
The little town of Rockland in Maine gets the summertime blues (p494), attracting musicians from around the region for a weekend-long jam session.

BARNSTABLE COUNTY FAIR 3rd week In July
Cape Cod hosts an old-fashioned agricultural fair (p177) at Falmouth, with garden displays, farm animals, carnival rides, music and fireworks.

INTERNATIONAL TENNIS HALL OF FAME CHAMPIONSHIPS July
Although the Hall of Fame is always in Newport, Rhode Island, it is only the championship tournament (p289) that attracts the biggest names in tennis to come play on the grass courts.

AUGUST

NEWPORT FOLK FESTIVAL early August
One of the region's most exciting music events, this folk festival (p301) at Newport, Rhode Island,

attracts national stars as well as new names to perform all weekend long.

MAINE LOBSTER FESTIVAL　1st week August
If you love lobster like Maine loves lobster, why not come along for the week-long Lobster Festival (p494) held in Rockland, Maine? King Neptune and the Sea Goddess oversea a week full of events, from live music to children's activities to fireworks, and – of course – as much lobster as you can eat.

FEAST OF THE BLESSED SACRAMENT　1st weekend in August
For almost 100 years, the local Portuguese community has been celebrating this four-day feast (p169) in New Bedford, Massachusetts; it's now the country's largest.

RHODE ISLAND INTERNATIONAL FILM FESTIVAL　2nd week in August
The region's largest public film festival (p289) in Providence, Rhode Island, attracts interesting, independent films and sophisticated film-savvy audiences.

JVC JAZZ FESTIVAL　mid-August
This, Newport's second music festival (p301) is an equally enticing event, with big names in jazz music.

SEPTEMBER

BLUES TRUST　3rd weekend in September
If you got the blues, you won't want to miss this weekend in September, when Blues Trust (p116) sponsors two days of (free) live jazz music at the Hatch Shell in Boston.

BEANTOWN JAZZ FESTIVAL　last weekend in September
The Berklee College of Music sponsors this free two-day music festival (p116) in Boston's South End. Three stages, panel discussions, food vendors, kids' activities and all that jazz.

BIG E　2nd half of September
Officially known as the Eastern States Exposition (p243), this fair in West Springfield, Massachusetts, features animal shows, carnival rides, cheesy performances and more.

OCTOBER

WELLFLEET OYSTERFEST　weekend after Columbus Day
Who can be surprised that a food festival (p198) in Wellfleet celebrates oysters? Come to this huge event for plenty of eating, drinking and slurping.

HAUNTED HAPPENINGS　October
The 'Witch City' of Salem celebrates Halloween (p147) all month long, with special exhibits, parades, concerts, pumpkin carvings, costume parties and trick-or-treating.

HEAD OF THE CHARLES　3rd weekend in October
This, the world's largest rowing event (p98), takes place in Boston on the River Charles, attracting thousands of rowers and thousands more spectators.

LIFE-IS-GOOD PUMPKIN FESTIVAL　3rd Saturday in October
On the Saturday before Halloween, good-deed-doers and good gourd-carvers descend on the Boston Common to carve pumpkins for a cause (p98). Boston currently holds the record for the most lit jack-o'-lanterns, although Keene, New Hampshire, is vying for the record.

KEENE PUMPKIN FESTIVAL　3rd Saturday in October
Help Keene win back its title by building a tower of jack-o'-lanterns as high as the sky. The size of the town triples for this annual festival (p425).

NOVEMBER–DECEMBER

BOSTON TEA PARTY REENACTMENT　Sunday before December 16
New Englanders take their reenactments seriously. In the case of the Tea Party (p98), they dress up like Mohawk Indians and dump tea into the Boston Harbor, just like their forebears in 1773.

FIRST NIGHT　December 31
It actually starts on the 'last night', on New Years Eve, and continues into the wee hours of the New Year. Activities, performances and other events are held at venues all around Boston (p98). Buy a button and attend as many as you can (but dress warmly and be prepared to stand in line).

Itineraries
CLASSIC ROUTES

CAPE COD ROUTE 6A
Three Days/Sandwich to Provincetown

Only have three days to spare? Welcome to the club. Bostonians head down to the Cape for long weekends throughout the year. After you've successfully fought the bridge traffic (in summer and on holiday weekends), stop in **Sandwich** (p174) to chill out at the tranquil Shawme Pond, poke around the oldest house on the Cape and visit a renowned glass museum. Slide slowly down Rte 6A, popping into antique shops and turning left toward Cape Cod Bay wherever it suits your fancy. Stop in **Yarmouth Port** (p184) to walk the Grey's Beach boardwalk across a marsh to broad views of sand and sea. In **Brewster** (p188), stop at the Brewster Store and Nickerson State Park and walk the tidal flats. Have a picnic lunch overlooking Rock Harbor or at Nauset Beach in **Orleans** (p194).

If you have fantasies about finding the perfect beach, spend an afternoon at the **Cape Cod National Seashore** (p196). Bayside or oceanside, the artsy **Wellfleet** (p197) is a charmer. At night there's only one place to be: **Provincetown** (p201). Stay for a whale watch and learn about the painters and authors who continue to summer here.

From salt marshes and seals to antique and art galleries, Cape Cod offers diversions for every palate. This 121-mile route, manageable in three or four days, takes you to pristine beaches and little-known lobster shacks, tourist attractions and the notorious nightlife of Provincetown.

COASTAL NEW ENGLAND   Two Weeks/Mystic to Bar Harbour

New England is intrinsically tied to the sea – historically, commercially and emotionally. To see this connection firsthand, just follow the coastline. Begin in **Mystic** (p319), where the unmissable Mystic Seaport Museum brings to life a 19th-century maritime village. Nearby, in quaint **Stonington** (p323), the Old Lighthouse Museum is perched on the peninsula's tip.

Bike around **Block Island** (p306), greet some piping plovers and hit the beach. Then head for **Newport** (p294), take the Cliff Walk, explore ye olde downtown and spend the evening on Thames St.

Dip into Cape Cod briefly at **Falmouth** (p176) and **Woods Hole** (p178) to check out a lovely lighthouse, plenty of historic houses surrounding a picture-perfect town green and a world-famous oceanographic institute.

Stop at **Plymouth** (p164) to relive the Pilgrims' transatlantic voyage. Then head north to **Boston** (p65) the region's cultural and intellectual capital. Continue northward to **Marblehead** (p149) and **Salem** (p143), both rich in maritime history. To glimpse New England's fishing industry at work (and to sample its culinary treats), journey to **Cape Ann** (p151).

The New Hampshire seacoast is scant, but not without merit: frolic among the waves and visit historic **Portsmouth** (p411).

Explore the handsome buildings of **Portland** (p472), as well as the Portland Head Light and the Portland Museum of Art. Venture into the lovely (but crowded) **Boothbay Harbor** (p490) for a harbor cruise. Stop in **Camden** (p496) to take a windjammer cruise and clamber to the top of Camden Hills State Park for fine views. Beautiful **Bar Harbor** (p503) and **Acadia National Park** (p508) are the northernmost and overall highlights of the New England coast.

New England is inextricably tied to seafaring rhythms. This tour takes about two weeks and links historic and active seaports with beautiful and vibrant coastal communities. It's about 575 miles, but you'll drive more than 700 miles if you start in New York City.

MOUNTAIN MEANDER   One Week/Boston to Stowe

Drive up I-93 from Boston to **Franconia Notch State Park** (p445), where you can hike down the Flume, ride a tramway up Cannon Mountain and see what little remains of the Old Man of the Mountain. Spend the night at one of many welcoming inns in **Franconia** or **Bethlehem** (p447).

From here, journey east on Rte 302, enjoying spectacular views of the White Mountains all around. Stop at the historic Mount Washington Hotel at **Bretton Woods** (p455). This is the base for a ride on the **Cog Railway** (p456) to the top of Mt Washington, New England's highest peak. Or, if you prefer to make the climb on your own two feet, continue on Rte 302 to **Crawford Notch State Park** (p456), the trailhead for countless hikes in the area.

To give your legs a break, drive west across the White Mountain National Forest on the spectacular **Kancamagus Highway** (p443), and hook up with I-89, which will take you across the border into Vermont.

Expansive vistas unfold with abandon as you approach the Green Mountains. Cut over to **Killington** (p378), great for wintertime skiing and summertime mountain biking. Continue north on VT100, which is often called 'the spine of the state.' Snaking north through the mountains, this classic route feels like a backcountry road, littered with cow-strewn meadows and white-steepled churches. Take your pick of any number of tiny towns along the way, but don't miss **Warren** and **Waitsfield** (p384), excellent for browsing art galleries and antique shops.

Outdoor enthusiasts should sidle on up to **Stowe** (p395), as its looming Mt Mansfield is the outdoor capital of northern Vermont. After exerting yourself sledding or skiing, biking or hiking, indulge in some Ben & Jerry's ice cream from the factory in **Waterbury** (p401).

With presidential peaks, rushing waterfalls and swirling flumes, the mountains offer New England's best in outdoor sports, as well as accessible vistas and solitary sojourns. This 400-mile meander takes in the best of the White and Green Mountains in about two weeks.

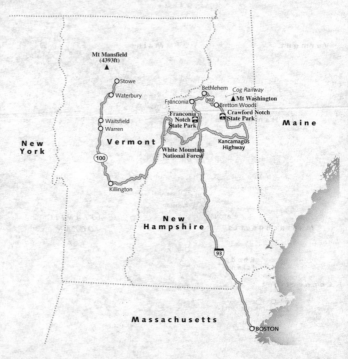

NEW ENGLAND LOOP   Three Weeks

Spend a few days strolling the historic streets of **Boston** (p65). Then head up the coast, stopping for witch history and maritime lore in **Salem** (p143) or hitting the beaches on **Cape Ann** (p151) or **Plum Island** (p161). Your next destination is **Portland** (p472), a hot spot for live music and live lobsters.

After a few days on the coast, head inland to New Hampshire. Use **North Conway** (p450) as a base for exploring Mt Washington Valley, then drive west along the scenic **Kancamagus Highway** (p443), stopping along the way for a hike in the White Mountains. You will eventually hit **Franconia Notch State Park** (p445), which is packed with opportunities for hiking, skiing or ogling the spectacular scenery.

Take Rte 25 northwest to **Montpelier** (p401), the country's quaintest capital. Continue northwest on I-89 all the way to **Burlington** (p386), a lively town with stunning views of Lake Champlain and the Adirondacks. Head south, stopping in **Middlebury** (p381), a precious college town with buildings bathed in marble.

Crossing into Western Massachusetts, stop in **Williamstown** and neighboring **North Adams** (p271) to admire the contemporary art at MASS MoCA; and in **Lenox** (p264) to hear some tunes at Tanglewood. Make your way through Connecticut's lovely **Litchfield Hills** (p348). In **Hartford** (p342), you can see the old stomping grounds of two of America's most celebrated authors. Then continue east to **Providence, Rhode Island** (p276) for progressive politics, excellent art, rockin' good music and creamy, cool cabinets. Hop on I-95 north and you're back in Boston quicker than you can say 'That was wicked awesome.'

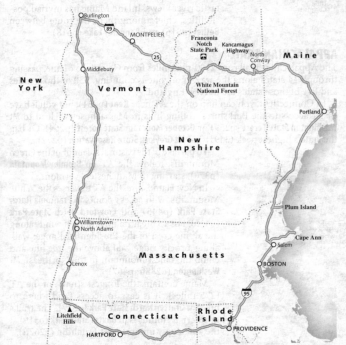

Urban or rural? Mountains or sea? New England offers a little bit of everything. This route loops through all six New England states, covering 715 miles. You'll want at least three weeks to savor all the sights and enjoy the adventures on the way.

TAILORED TRIPS

LEAF-PEEPING

It's a major event, one approaching epic proportions in this region: watching leaves change color. You can do it just about anywhere – all you need is one brilliant tree. But if you're like most people, you want lots and lots of trees. Right in Boston, the greens of the **Boston Common** (p70) and the **Charles River Esplanade** (p86) become multicolored tapestries in October. Or bike the **Minuteman Commuter Bikeway** (p93) to see the changing colors in the northwestern suburbs.

In Connecticut, the **Litchfield Hills** (p348) offer a clutch of rolling hills between Cornwall Bridge and Salisbury. **Little Compton** (p305) is a forgotten Rhode Island seaside town of old estates and village greens that are ablaze with color in autumn.

In Vermont, take US 91 north from St Johnsbury to the Canadian border for long vistas of dairy farms and sugar maples, typical of the **Northeast Kingdom** (p403). Practically anywhere in **central Vermont** (p374) yields blazes of jaw-dropping color.

The **Kancamagus Highway** (p443), a breathtakingly beautiful drive across New Hampshire's White Mountains, features spectacular vistas, while the scenic Upper Connecticut River Valley from **Keene** (p424) to **Hanover** (p428) yields fantastic river views. Inland Maine has myriad possibilities, chief among them the route between **Bethel** (p516) and **Rangeley Lake** (p518).

APPALACHIAN TRAIL

The Appalachian Trail runs 2100-plus miles from Georgia to Maine, passing through 14 states along the way. If anyone is counting, 730 of those miles and five of those states are in New England.

In Connecticut, you can hop on the AT near **Kent** (p351), but you'll have easier access to the Berkshires' rolling hills in Massachusetts. Head to **Mt Washington State Forest** (p259) or **October Mountain State Forest** (p264). Or bag the state's highest peak (3491ft) at **Mt Greylock State Reservation** (p272).

To partake of the pastoral splendor of the Green Mountains, follow the AT up **Bromley Mountain** (p370), starting in Manchester, Vermont.

In New Hampshire, the AT traverses the White Mountains, with access points in **Franconia Notch State Park** (p445) and **Crawford Notch State Park** (p456). For 13 breathtaking miles, it winds along the alpine crest of the Presidential Range: walk along a rocky ridge well above the tree line and climb the tallest mountain in the Northeast, **Mt Washington** (6288ft; p457).

Maine contains the longest stretch of the AT (275 miles). It is easy to access (and tough to hike) at **Grafton Notch State Park** (p517). The trail's northern terminus is in **Baxter State Park** (p519) at the amazingly untamed Mt Katahdin (5267ft).

COLLEGE TOWNS

From the Five Colleges to the Seven Sisters (well, four of them), New England is crowded with colleges and overrun with universities, making for a dynamic, diverse student scene. Hundreds of institutions of higher education are located in Boston, including **Boston University** and **Boston College** (see p120), while neighboring Cambridge is home to academic authorities **Harvard University** (p91) and **Massachusetts Institute of Technology** (MIT; p92). But Boston is only the beginning of this college tour.

Besides the mighty Crimson, as Harvard is known, New England is home to three Ivy League institutions. **Yale University** (p331) is the centerpiece of the gritty city of New Haven; **Dartmouth University** (p429) dominates Hanover, making it the quintessential New England college town; and **Brown University** (p279) lends its progressive viewpoints to Providence.

In a league of its own, the **Rhode Island School of Design** (p278) is also in Providence, making the city one of the edgiest and artiest in the region.

In Central Massachusetts, the Pioneer Valley is also known as Five Colleges, it's home to **Amherst** (p251), **Hampshire** (p251), **Mount Holyoke** (p246) and **Smith College** (p247), as well as **UMass Amherst** (p251).

Other highly regarded liberal arts colleges with lively, leafy campuses include **Middlebury College** (p382) in Middlebury; **Bowdoin College** (p486) in Brunswick; and **Keene State College** (p424) in Keene.

REVOLUTIONARY HISTORY

Revolutionary history begins in Boston. Follow the **Freedom Trail** (p94) to learn about the lead-up to the War for Independence. Then go west to **Lexington** (p132) and **Concord** (p135), where the first battles took place. Further west, in Springfield, the **Armory National Historic Site** (p243) commemorates the inexhaustible federal armory that dates to the American Revolution.

It started in Boston but it spread throughout the region. The first naval 'engagement' took place in **Machiasport** (p512), while another Maine battle took place in **Castine** (p498), where the remains of a fort still stand.

Connecticut experienced its first major battle at **Stonington** (p323), which has exhibits about the battle in its Lighthouse Museum. More famously, **Fort Griswold State Park** (p326), in Groton, is where colonial troops were massacred in the Battle of Groton Heights. **Essex** (p340) is home to many 18th-century buildings, including the historic Griswold Inn.

Vermont residents – known as the Green Mountain Boys – played a major role in the Battle of Bennington, commemorated by the **Bennington Monument** and **Battlefield Historic Site** (p366). The gang's leader lived in Burlington, where you can now visit the **Ethan Allen Homestead** (p387).

The only Revolutionary War battle fought in New Hampshire was in **Portsmouth** (p411), which is rich with 18th-century architecture. New Hampshire established the first state constitution and independent seat and government in early 1776 in **Exeter** (p418).

History Gerald Easter

WHEN NEW WORLDS COLLIDE

When the first European explorers arrived in the New World, they found a patchwork of diversity and abundance. Along the shore, tidal flats and salt marshes were rich with shellfish and waterfowl, while the cold waters just offshore teemed with ground fish, especially the mighty cod. In the interior, ice-age glaciers had worn down the mountains, leaving a rolling hilly terrain, dappled with ponds and lakes. The forests of pine, maple, birch and oak were home to moose, deer, bear and beaver. The rivers filled with spawning fish in early spring, while the riverbanks sprouted colorful berries in late summer.

The Europeans also found about 100,000 Native American inhabitants, mostly Algonquians, organized into small regional tribes. The feisty northern tribes were solely hunter-gatherers, while the more sociable southern tribes hunted and practiced primitive slash-and-burn agriculture, growing corn, squash and beans. Their subsistence economy involved seasonal migration, following food sources between the coast and the interior, and gift exchange between villages.

Before the English Pilgrims arrived (see the boxed text, opposite), the Native Americans were already acquainted with Portuguese fishermen, French fur traders, English explorers, Dutch merchants and Jesuit missionaries. The Europeans were welcomed as a source of valued manufactured goods, but they were also feared; and for good reason – in the Great Sadness of 1617, a smallpox epidemic had devastated the Native American population in the southeast. The Pilgrims were notable as the first Europeans to make a successful settlement in New England. Chief Massasoit of the Wampanoag tribe did not view this scrawny band of settlers as a threat and even hoped that they might be useful allies against his tribal rivals.

But the clash of cultures soon proved fatal to the Native American way of life. English coastal encampments spread as seemingly unoccupied lands were claimed for the King and commodity export – John Winthrop, the first governor of the Massachusetts Bay Colony, declared 'God hath hereby cleared our title to this place.' In less than a hundred years, the indigenous population was reduced by 90% by disease, war and forced migration.

A SHINING CITY ON A HILL

Seventeenth-century England was torn by religious strife. The Protestant Pilgrims were assailed by the Catholic-leaning King James I, who vowed to 'harry them out of the country.' In 1620, the Pilgrims – led by Separatist devotee William Bradford – crossed the Atlantic to establish a community dedicated to religious austerity.

James Mayer and Byron Dix provide detailed, illustrated descriptions of Native American archeological sites around New England in *Manitou: The Sacred Landscape of New England's Native Civilization.*

Several tribes of the Wampanoag nation continue to be active in Massachusetts, including in Mashpee (www .mashpeewampanoag tribe.com), Gay Head (www.wampanoagtribe .net) and Chappaquiddick (www.chappaquiddick -wampanoag.org).

TIMELINE

1497	1614	1620
John Cabot claims New England for his patron, King Henry VII of England	At the behest of future King Charles, Capt John Smith braves the frigid north Atlantic, makes his way from Maine to Cape Cod, maps the coastline and dubs the region 'New England'	The Pilgrims establish Plymouth Colony, the first permanent European settlement in the New World

THE FIRST THANKSGIVING

Plymouth is known for one thing most of all – Pilgrims. And the Pilgrims are known mostly for Thanksgiving (and big-buckled shoes). While footwear styles come and go, Thanksgiving remains a time-honored tradition for American families.

The first Thanksgiving was held in the early fall of 1621. The Pilgrims were thankful, but not for a bountiful harvest – they were thankful simply to be alive. (Of the 100 passengers aboard the *Mayflower*, only half survived the first year in the wilderness.) There may have been a wild turkey on the table, but the plates more likely featured venison, lobster and squirrel…mmmmm. There was no pumpkin pie, alas – the Pilgrims did not have any ovens.

True to legend, the Native Americans were on hand for the first feast. Chief Massasoit of the Wampanoags had no problems with the pathetic Pilgrims, since he had set them up on the land of a rival tribe, the Patuxet, which had been wiped out by smallpox a year earlier. The Wampanoag, in fact, provided most of the food. The Pilgrims were really not very good hosts.

Although there were no Lions or Cowboys, games were played that weekend. The Pilgrim menfolk competed against the Native Americans in shooting, archery and a crude colonial version of croquet.

Thanksgiving with the Pilgrims pretty much ended there. The fall festival was not repeated in subsequent years. The Pilgrims were pious, not partyers. The Wampanoag came to reconsider their stance on the newcomers. Over the years a fall harvest feast was common in some colonies, especially in New England. In 1789 George Washington called for a national Thanksgiving day to honor the new constitution, but again this did not become a widespread annual event.

The Thanksgiving celebrated today has more to do with 19th-century nationalism than with 17th-century settlers. In 1863, in the midst of civil war, Abraham Lincoln proclaimed the last Thursday in November as a national Thanksgiving holiday. The popular depiction of the Pilgrims in harmony with natives and nature was meant to emphasize the common heritage of a people at war with itself. The Thanksgiving tradition is the celebration of a myth, but a myth that unifies the nation.

Oh, and by the way, the Pilgrims did not really wear big-buckled shoes either.

Trouble arose when the badly off-course *Mayflower* weighed anchor in Cape Cod Bay. A group of nonreligious passengers had booked their fares expecting to strike out on their own in Virginia; they threatened a mutiny when they realized they would have to spend the winter with the Separatists. The resulting Mayflower Compact brokered a deal in which both parties would have an equal say in matters of governance. Under Bradford's capable leadership, Plymouth Colony maintained a religious focus and grew modestly over the next decade. Today, you can visit a historically accurate re-creation of this first settlement at Plimoth Plantation (p165).

In 1630, the merchant vessel *Arbella* delivered another group of Protestant separatists, the Puritans, 50 miles north of Plymouth. The Puritans were better prepared: they were well financed, well equipped and 1000 strong, and

1628	1675	1686
The Puritans settle the Massachusetts Bay Colony at the future site of Boston	Wampanoag chief King Philip terrorizes the colonists. Twenty-five towns are destroyed and thousands are killed before he is shot, ending King Philip's War	King James II establishes the Dominion of New England, instituting more rigorous controls over the colonies

included those of high social rank. At the head of their party, John Winthrop stood atop the Shawmut peninsula of present-day Boston and proclaimed the founding of 'a shining city on a hill.'

The Massachusetts Bay Colony was a product of the Puritan gentry ambition to build a Christian community of personal virtue and industriousness – a community purified of pompous ceremony and official corruption, and disdainful of tyranny. Theirs was a kind of legalistic Calvinism, enforced Old Testament style. Anyone who missed church without good cause was apt to catch a whipping. Governor Winthrop constructed centralized institutions to maintain unity among the settlers, who dispersed to choice locations around the harbor and along the rivers. The General Court, an assembly of propertied men, became the principal mechanism of government. Church membership was a prerequisite for political and property rights.

The Puritan theocracy did not go unchallenged. In Boston, Anne Hutchinson started a women's Bible circle, promoting the idea of salvation through personal revelation. The popularity of this individualist-inspired view was threatening to the colony's patriarchal elders, who arrested the heretic Hutchinson and banished her to an island. One of Hutchinson's arch defenders was her brother-in-law, the Reverend John Wheelwright, who led a group to resettlement in New Hampshire. This was the beginning of a trend in which independent folk, exasperated by encroachments on individual liberty by the Massachusetts state, would found their own settlements.

From his pulpit in Salem, Roger Williams sermonized for religious tolerance, separation of church and state, and respect for Native American rights. In 1636, Williams and a small group of backers founded a new settlement, Providence, along Narragansett Bay. The Rhode Island Colony welcomed Anne Hutchinson, declared religious freedom and made peace with the Native Americans.

Meanwhile, Bay Colony officials exiled yet another 'heretic' parson, Thomas Hooker, who suggested that nonpropertied men should not be excluded from political affairs. Hooker relocated to Hartford, amid the growing farm communities of the Connecticut River Valley.

Over time, the Puritan gentry were less effective in compelling others to embrace their vision of an ideal Christian community. The incessant pull of individual interests and the rise of a secular commercial culture proved to be the undoing of Winthrop's vision.

CRADLE OF LIBERTY

The Stuart kings were no friends of the Protestant separatists in New England. When the English Civil War ended, they attempted to impose a greater degree of imperial control, which was fiercely resisted by the free-spirited colonists.

An extensive archive of colonial history, including resources for genealogical research, are at www.mayflowerfamilies.com.

Winona Ryder and Daniel Day-Lewis star in *The Crucible*, a 1996 adaptation of Arthur Miller's play about the Salem witch fiasco.

The Internet Modern History Sourcebook (www.fordham.edu/halsall/mod/modsbook07.html) is an online archive of colonial documents, including the Mayflower Compact, William Bradford's *History of Plymouth Plantation* and the colonial charters.

1692	1754–1763	1765
Twenty villagers in Salem are killed as a result of witch hysteria	New Englanders are drawn into the French and Indian War, in which the British fought the French in the New World. The king levies taxes on the colonies to pay for war efforts	The Stamp Act incites protests among colonists, leading to the formation of the Sons of Liberty

In 1686, King James II reorganized the colonies into a Dominion of New England and appointed Sir Edmund Andros as royal governor. Andros acted quickly to curb colonial independence. He suspended the General Court, levied new taxes, forbade town meetings and Anglicized the church. When he tried to revoke the land-grant charters, the colonists openly defied the king's agent.

When King James was deposed in the Glorious Revolution, the colonists rose in rebellion, seizing the obnoxious Andros and shipping him back to England. Although local autonomy was restored, New England from this time was effectively incorporated into the imperial administration.

In the late 18th century, New England and the British throne clashed over the issue of taxation, exposing the conflicting strains of royal subject and personal liberty.

In 1765, the British Parliament passed the Stamp Act to finance colonial defense. Massachusetts colonists were first to object. Local businessman Sam Adams, to safeguard colonial autonomy, formed the Sons of Liberty, which incited a mob to ransack the royal stamp office. The actions were defended in a treatise written by a local lawyer, Sam's cousin John Adams, who cited the Magna Carta's principal of no taxation without consent. Eastern Connecticut and Rhode Island joined the protest. When New England merchants threatened a boycott of British imports, the measure was repealed.

The British government devised new revenue-raising schemes. Again, they were met with hostile noncompliance, and Boston emerged as the center of conflict. Parliament closed the Massachusetts General Assembly and dispatched two armed regiments to the city, which only inflamed local passions.

Forced underground, the Sons of Liberty set up a covert correspondence system to agitate public sentiment and coordinate strategy with sympathizers. In December 1773, the Sons of Liberty disguised themselves as Mohawks and dumped a cargo of taxable tea into the harbor. The Boston Tea Party enraged King George, whose retribution was swift and vengeful (see p85). The port was blockaded and the city placed under direct military rule.

The conflict tested the region's political loyalties. Tory sympathizers included influential merchants, manufacturers and financiers, while the rebels tended to be drawn from lesser merchants, artisans and yeoman farmers. The colonial cause was strongly supported in Rhode Island, Hartford and New Hampshire, where local assemblies voted to provide economic assistance to Boston. Aroused Providence residents even set fire to the British warship *Gaspee* when it ran aground in Narragansett Bay while chasing suspected smugglers. New Hampshire instigators seized Fort William & Mary when the panicky loyalist governor attempted to enlist more British reinforcements.

In April 1775, the British again attempted to break colonial resistance, this time arresting rebel ringleaders Sam Adams and John Hancock and seizing

Governor Andros journeyed to Hartford to confiscate its charter, but during the confrontation the assembly hall suddenly went dark and the charter was whisked outside and hidden in an oak tree.

David Hackett Fischer's tome, *Paul Revere's Ride*, provides an in-depth look at the events leading up to the American Revolution and the mythical figure of Revere.

1770	1775	1776
Provoked by a local gang throwing snowballs, British troops fire into a crowd in Boston and kill five people, an incident dubbed the Boston Massacre	War for Independence breaks out with the Battles of Lexington and Concord	Colonial leaders sign the Declaration of Independence

a secret store of gunpowder and arms. As the troops assembled, Paul Revere slipped across the river into Charlestown, where he mounted his famous steed Brown Beauty and galloped off into the night to spread the alarm. By next morning, armed local militias began converging on the area. The incident sparked a skirmish between imperial troops and local farmers on the Old North Bridge in Concord (p135) and the Lexington Green (p132), leaving over a hundred dead. The inevitable had arrived: war for independence.

After the Green Mountain Boys captured Fort Ticonderoga, they hauled its heavy artillery cannon all the way to Boston. Its strategic position overlooking the harbor forced the British fleet to retreat.

Other colonies soon joined ranks, heeding the advice of Boston-born Benjamin Franklin, who said 'if we do not hang together, we will surely hang separately.' New Hampshire, Connecticut and Maine (then part of Massachusetts) wholeheartedly supported the revolutionary cause. The Green Mountain Boys, led by Ethan Allen, were a bandit gang, resisting the advances of the New York colony into northwest New England. They used the colonial rebellion as an opportunity to declare Vermont's independence.

The war did not go well at first for the feisty but ill-prepared colonists, but the tide turned when the French were finally persuaded to ally with the rebellion. In 1781, the American army and French navy cornered the main British army on the Yorktown peninsula in Virginia and forced their surrender. British rule had come to an end in the American colonies.

OF SAILS & WHALES

New England port cities flourished during the Age of Sail. In the 17th century, the infamous 'triangular trade route' was developed, involving West

---

WHO WAS FIRST?

Everyone is always eager to be first. Both Rhode Island and New Hampshire make claims about being the first colony to declare independence from Great Britain. But there is only one 'first.' So whose claim is legit?

The New Hampshire Provincial Government was kicked out of Portsmouth in 1774, so it moved up the road to Exeter (p418), thus establishing the *first* independent government in the colonies. In January 1776, this local body ratified a constitution, the *first* colony to do so. But the document was explicit in 'declaring that we never sought to throw off our dependence upon Great Britain, but felt ourselves happy under Her protection while we could enjoy our constitutional rights and privileges, and that we shall rejoice if such a reconciliation between us and our parent state can be affected.' The local governance was a temporary provision, put in place until the dispute with Britain could be resolved. Not exactly a declaration of independence.

In May of that same year, still two months before the unveiling of *the* Declaration of Independence, Rhode Island issued its formal statement. With none of the stipulations and explanations of New Hampshire's constitution, Rhode Island was the first to declare outright independence.

Several colonies followed suit. New Hampshire finally came around six weeks later, resolving that 'the Thirteen United Colonies should be declared a free and independent state.'

1789	1790	1791
New Hampshire ratifies the US Constitution, providing the ninth and final vote needed to execute it	The construction of the Brown-Slater textile mill in Rhode Island spurs New England's industrial revolution	Vermont becomes the first new state to join the Union after the original 13

Indian sugar, New England rum and West African slaves. Merchants who chose not to traffic in human cargo could still make large profits by illicitly undercutting European trade monopolies.

In the 18th century, Britain's stricter enforcement of trade monopolies and imposition of higher tariffs squeezed the merchants' profits. But after the American Revolution, New England merchants amassed fortunes by opening up trade routes to the Far East. Shipbuilding thrived in Massachusetts, Maine and Connecticut, and cities such as Salem, Newburyport and Portsmouth were among the richest trading cities in the world. Visit the Salem Maritime National Historic Site (p144) or Newburyport's Custom House Maritime Museum (p160) to see this history firsthand.

The whaling industry also thrived. Even today, the rich feeding grounds of Stellwagen Bank off Cape Cod attract whales to the region. In the preindustrial period, whales provided commodities such as oil for lamps, teeth and bone for decorative scrimshaw, and other material for hoop skirts, umbrellas and perfume.

The whalers in New England were strategically placed to pursue the highly sought-after sperm whales along Atlantic migratory routes. Buzzards Bay, Nantucket Island (p209) and New Bedford (p168) were all prominent whaling centers. In the mid-19th century, New Bedford hosted a whaling fleet of over 300 ships, employing over 10,000 people directly and indirectly, and cashing in at over $12 million in profits. Today, visitors can relive the whaling heyday at the New Bedford Whaling National Historical Park (p168).

In the late 17th century, Rhode Island provided safe haven for pirates; indeed, Captain Kidd and Blackbeard were on a first-name basis with most Newport proprietors.

INDUSTRIAL REVOLUTION

New England's industrial revolution began in Rhode Island when Quaker merchant Moses Brown contracted English mechanic Samuel Slater to construct a water-powered cotton-spinning factory. The Brown-Slater partnership was a brilliant success. Their mills sprouted up along the Blackstone River, driving a vibrant Rhode Island textile industry.

Thirty miles northwest of Boston, along the Merrimack River, a group of wealthy merchants built one of the wonders of the industrial age: a mile-long planned city of five-story red-brick factories, lining the river for nearly a mile, driven by a network of power canals. Named for the project's deceased visionary, Francis Cabot Lowell, the city counted over 40 mills and employed over 10,000 workers; machines hummed 12 hours a day, six days a week.

This was not the grimy squalor of Manchester. Lowell was an orderly city. The workforce at first was drawn from the region's young farm women, who lived in dormitories under paternalistic supervision. The 'mill girls' were gradually replaced by cheaper Irish immigrant labor. The Lowell

Britain was so protective of its industrial technology that skilled workers were prohibited from leaving the country, so mechanic Samuel Slater disguised himself as a farmer to gain passage on a boat heading west.

1820	1831	1837
Maine gains independence from Massachusetts, becoming the 23rd state to enter the Union	Abolitionist agitator William Lloyd Garrison first publishes the *Liberator*	An Irish funeral procession meets a volunteer fire company on the streets of Boston. A melee ensues, leaving a row of Irish flats burned to the ground.

National Historical Park (p141) recalls the city's role as the instigator of the industrial revolution.

By the mid-19th century, steam power and metal machines had transformed New England. Railroads crisscrossed the region, hastening industrialization and urbanization. Brawny textile mills arose along rivers in Lawrence, Nashua, Concord and Fall River. Leather works and shoe-making factories appeared near Boston. Springfield and Worcester became centers for tool- and dye-making, southern Connecticut manufactured machinery, and the Maine woods furnished paper mills. Even Paul Revere abandoned his silversmith shop in the North End and set up a rolling copper mill and foundry 15 miles southwest along the Neponset River.

NEW ENGLAND MELTING POT

The rapid rise of industry led to social as well as economic changes. The second half of the 19th century brought a wave of immigrant laborers to New England, throwing the world of English-descended Whig Protestants into turmoil.

The first Irish immigrants arrived to work in the mills in the 1820s. Disparaged by native New Englanders, the Irish were considered an inferior race of delinquents, whose spoken brogue suggested that one had a 'shoe in one's mouth'. They undercut local workers in the job market and, worse yet, brought the dreaded papist religion from which the Puritans had fled. Tensions ran high, occasionally erupting in violence.

A potato famine back home spurred an upsurge in Irish immigration to Boston. Between 1846 and 1856, more than 1000 new immigrants stepped off the boat per month, a human floodtide that the city was not prepared to absorb. Anti-immigrant and anti-Catholic sentiments were shrill. As a political expression of this rabid reaction, the Know Nothing Party swept into office in Massachusetts, Rhode Island and Connecticut, promising to reverse the flow of immigration, deny the newcomers political rights and mandate readings from the Protestant Bible in public school.

Subsequent groups of Italian, Portuguese, French Canadian and East European Jewish immigrants suffered similar prejudices and indignities. By the end of the 19th century, the urban landscape of New England resembled a mosaic of clannish ethnic enclaves. Sticking together became an immigrant survival strategy for finding work, housing and companionship. Neighborhoods took on the feel of the old country with familiar language, cuisine and customs. The New England melting pot was more like a stew than a puree.

In the early 20th century, when new southern and Eastern European immigrants began preaching class solidarity, they were met with renewed fury from New England's ruling elite. Labor unrest in the factories mobilized a harsh political reaction against foreigners and socialism.

In 1834, rumors of licentiousness and kidnapping led a Boston mob to torch the Ursuline Convent in present-day Somerville, Massachusetts.

Local history professor, Thomas O'Connor, recounts the history of the Irish enclave in *South Boston: My Home Town*.

Anthony Hopkins is John Quincy Adams in *Amistad*, the true story of a runaway slave ship that runs aground off the coast of Connecticut.

1851	1853	1863
Built in an East Boston shipyard, Donald McKay's *Flying Cloud* sails from New York to San Francisco with a damaged mast in just 21 days, shattering all previous records.	Franklin Pierce becomes US president, the only New Hampshire native to do so	Massachusetts native Robert Gould Shaw leads the 54th Regiment of black troops into battle in the Civil War. Colonel Shaw is killed in action and buried in a common grave next to the fallen black soldiers.

REFORM & RACISM

The legacy of race relations in New England is marred by contradictions. Abolitionists and segregationists, reformers and racists have all left their mark.

The first slaves were delivered to Massachusetts Bay Colony from the West Indies in 1638. By 1700, roughly 400 slaves lived in Boston. In the 18th century, Rhode Island merchants played a leading role in the Atlantic slave trade, financing over 1000 slave ventures and transporting more than 100,000 Africans.

A number of New England's black slaves earned their freedom by fighting against the British in the Revolution. Crispus Attucks, a runaway slave of African and Native American descent, became a martyr by falling victim in the Boston Massacre. Salem Poor, an ex-slave who bought his freedom, was distinguished for heroism in the Battle of Bunker Hill.

In the early 19th century, New England became a center of the abolition movement. In Boston, William Lloyd Garrison, a newspaper publisher, Theodore Parker, a Unitarian minister, and Wendell Phillips, an aristocratic lawyer, launched the Anti-Slavery Society to agitate public sentiment. New England provided numerous stops along the Underground Railroad, a network of safe-houses that helped runaway slaves reach freedom in Canada.

The New England states still maintained their own informal patterns of racial segregation with African Americans as an underclass. Although Massachusetts was the first state to elect an African American to the US Senate by popular vote in 1966, race relations were fraught. In the 1970s Boston was inflamed by racial conflict when a judge ordered the city to desegregate the schools through forced busing. The school year was marked by a series of violent incidents involving students and parents.

In *Common Ground*, J Anthony Lucas examines the Boston busing crisis from the perspective of three different families. Winner of the Pulitzer Prize and the National Book Award.

20TH-CENTURY TRENDS

The fears of the Yankee old guard were finally realized in the early 20th century when ethnic-based political machines gained control of city governments in Massachusetts, Rhode Island and Connecticut.

While the Democratic Party was originally associated with rural and radical interests, it became the political instrument of the recently arrived working poor in urban areas. Flamboyant city bosses pursued a populist and activist approach to city politics. Their administrations were steeped in public works and patronage. According to Providence boss Charlie Brayton, 'An honest voter is one who stays bought.'

The Republican Party in New England was cobbled together in the mid-19th century from the Whigs, the Know Nothings and the antislavery movement. In the 20th century, it became the political vehicle for the old English-descended elite, which envisioned a paternalistic and frugal government and preached self-help and sobriety.

The Last Hurrah is a 1958 film based on the life of James Curley, the corrupt but beloved mayor of Boston.

1919	1927	1929
Boston police go out on strike; chaos reigns until the military reserve arrives	Two Italian anarchists, Nicola Sacco and Bartolomeo Vanzetti, are executed on trumped-up murder charges, revealing the persistence of class and ethnic animosities in Boston	The New Bedford–based *Wanderer* returns home for the last time, bringing New England whaling to an end, overtaken by industrial technology and changes to social attitudes

---

HISTORY-MAKERS AMONG US

One person really can change history. It's happening all around us in New England:

■ **Ben & Jerry** – Vermont hippies who popularized conscientious capitalism and Chunky Monkey (see p401)

■ **Jim Koch** – successful Boston brewer (unlike his beer's namesake, Sam Adams) who launched the microbrew revolution (see the boxed text, p113)

■ **JCR Licklidder** – Massachusetts Institute of Technology (MIT) computer scientist who first conceived of a 'galactic network' that would later spawn the internet (see p92)

■ **Theo Epstein** – boy genius baseball executive who ended 80-plus years of grief by bringing the World Series championship to Boston (p121)

Economically, New England has experienced its share of booms and busts over the past century. The good times of the early 20th century crashed down in the Great Depression. After a brief recovery, the region began to lose its textile industry and manufacturing base to the south. With the mills shut down and the seaports quieted, the regional economy languished and its cities fell into disrepair.

But entrepreneurial spirit and technological imagination combined to revive the region, sustained by science, medicine and higher education. Boston, Providence and Hartford were buoyed by banking, finance and insurance. The biggest boost came from the technological revolution, which enabled local high-tech companies to make the 'Massachusetts Miracle,' an economic boom in the 1980s. Even with stock-market corrections and bubble bursts, technological developments continue to reinvigorate New England.

Sarah Messer's youth in the historic Hatch house in Marshfield, Massachusetts inspired her to write *Red House: Being a Mostly Accurate Account of New England's Oldest Continuously Lived-in House* (2004).

NEW ENGLAND, NEW CENTURY

Economic change continues to affect social and political trends in the 21st century. Notably, the decline of manufacturing in the north and the advent of air-con in the south have lured people away from New England in the early 21st century. New waves of immigrants from East Asia, the Caribbean and Brazil have steadied population numbers, though its various factions are in flux.

After several generations of moving away, New Englanders are returning to the cities. Downtowns are being revitalized as mills, and warehouses are converted into living spaces, restaurants and retail spaces. Long-lost neighborhoods in Boston, Providence and Portsmouth are undergoing processes of gentrification as yuppies transform urban blight into urban chic.

Long-existing ethnic enclaves have begun to break up. Access to higher education has sent second and third generations into prestigious professions and posh suburbs, fostering assimilation and dilution of New England's elite

1946	1954	1960
Massachusetts scientist Percy Spenser accidentally melts his chocolate bar and invents the microwave oven	General Dynamics Shipyard in Groton, Connecticut launches the *Nautilus*, the world's first nuclear-powered submarine	Massachusetts native John F Kennedy is elected president, ushering in the era of Camelot

culture. Meanwhile, high real-estate values mean that property is sold to the highest bidder, no matter where they come from.

A lasting strain of independent politics is evident in New England's northern states, sustained by a healthy suspicion of politics, fiscal conservatism and social libertarianism. New England continues to provide a supportive political climate for social reformers, carrying on a legacy that includes 19th-century abolitionists, 20th-century suffragettes and 21st-century gay-rights advocates.

In recent years, New England has been at the forefront of countless 'progressive' issues, including antismoking legislation (smoking in the workplace is illegal in all six states) and health care (as of 2007, health care is required of all Massachusetts residents and subsidized for low-income qualifiers). In 2008, New Hampshire became the fifth New England state to legalize and recognize same-sex unions.

The new century continues to bring changing circumstances and opportunities to New Englanders. The Vermont farmer has gone organic; the Gloucester fisherman is conducting whale-watching tours; the Mohegan Native American is a gaming executive; the Boston Irish order chardonnay with their sushi; and the New England Yankee is still voting Independent.

1966	1970s	2000
Edward Brooke of Massachusetts is the first African American popularly elected to the US Senate	Boston attempts to racially integrate schools by busing students between neighborhoods, inciting violent reactions from all sides.	Vermont becomes the second state in the union to legalize same-sex civil unions

The Culture

REGIONAL IDENTITY

New England is an assemblage of diverse ethnic and racial communities. Despite this multitude of backgrounds, there is a strong regional identity, defined mainly by its Yankee roots. A powerful work ethic was at the heart of Puritan beliefs and has been a hallmark of the New England Yankee since the days of the first colonists. Today, this stereotype persists, especially in the fast-paced cities.

The region's history also comes into play in the characteristic Yankee independence and individuality. 'Live Free or Die' is the motto stamped on New Hampshire license plates, and plenty of New Englanders cherish the sentiment.

This idea plays out in politics, where New England is synonymous with the 'liberal east coast.' The region strongly supports Democratic and Independent candidates and has been at the forefront of countless 'liberal' issues (see p34). Conservatives argue that these progressive values are out of touch with mainstream America. New Englanders, for their part, have come to accept this, but when they consider what's going on in mainstream America, they're OK with that.

LIFESTYLE

In a geography characterized by individuality, there is no such thing as a 'typical' lifestyle. Diverse ethnic backgrounds and education levels result in widely divergent belief systems and home life, as does the urban–rural divide.

Recent social and political trends have drawn New England gays and lesbians out of the closet and into the limelight. With civil unions legal in Vermont, Connecticut, Maine and New Hampshire – plus marriage equality in Massachusetts – the movement has made enormous strides in defending and defining gay civil rights. It is not unusual for gay couples to set up households and raise children (though the highly pampered pet is still more common). Indeed, in places like Provincetown, Northampton and Boston's South End, it is straight individuals who might feel out of place.

GLAD (www.glad.org) is a New England human rights organization dedicated to ending discrimination based on sexual orientation.

The student population is significant, overlapping on its fringes with other groups. Students are almost always single, living alone in apartments or in group houses. They may think they are poor, but they often have outside sources of financial support (read: parents). By definition, they are educated, which means they have job prospects and will soon join the ranks of the professional class.

Which brings us to the 'yuppies.' New England has more than its fair share of young urban professionals, thanks to the strong economy and the endless supply from the area's universities. Yuppies are often blamed for driving up real-estate prices, diluting communities and contributing to suburban sprawl.

Many people in the old enclaves welcome newcomers, recognizing the advantages of diversity and development. But others resent being invaded by outsiders, whether immigrants or yuppies: and who needs development if it means you can't afford the rent?

ECONOMY

New England has one of the healthiest, fastest-growing and diverse regional economies in the US, with a combined gross state product of $623 billion in 2005. In recent years, the technology and biotechnology industries have spawned from local university research labs (Massachusetts Institute of Technology researchers developed the first computer in 1928). Boston is a major center for financial services, while Hartford is the insurance capital of the country. Much of this white-collar industry developed in the 1980s and 1990s, breathing new life into a region that was suffering from the decline of its manufacturing sector (this was dubbed the 'Massachusetts Miracle' in the region's most populous state). While the fishing industry has suffered as a result of declining stocks, cod and lobster continue to be important regional products. Tourism, education and medicine are all major players.

The result today is a robust economy that continues to grow. The downside of the region's prosperity, of course, is its high cost of living. New England is consistently rated as one of the country's most expensive places to live. Housing prices are prohibitively high. This concerns companies and schools that want to attract talent from elsewhere. Recruiters lament the low- and moderate-income family being frozen out of the housing market, as do the families themselves.

Mark Kurlansky's fascinating book, *Cod: A Biography of the Fish that Changed the World*, traces the impact of this fish, and its dangerous decline, on the development of New England.

POPULATION

New England is home to over 14 million people, or about 5% of the US population. Three quarters of this total live in southern New England, home to the region's biggest cities. Rhode Island, Massachusetts and Connecticut are three of the country's four most densely populated states, with 80% to 90% of their populations living in urban areas. By contrast, New Hampshire (51% urban), Vermont (32%) and Maine (45%) are much more sparsely populated.

New England is one of the best educated regions in the US; this is not surprising, considering the number of colleges and universities here. About 36% of New Englanders have a higher education, significantly higher than the 24% nationwide.

SPORTS

There might as well be a sign on every single New England highway that borders the region: 'Entering Red Sox Nation.' The intensity of fans has only grown since the Boston Red Sox (p121) broke its agonizing 86-year losing streak and won the 2004 World Series. This band of scruffy players came to symbolize overcoming adversity for folks around the country. With a follow-up victory in 2007, the Sox permanently ditched their underdog status and Red Sox Nation rejoiced.

Erudite Massachusetts is home to more than 64 colleges and universities.

The Red Sox has sold out every home game since 2003, which means tickets are hard to come by and expensive. A more manageable alternative is to see the AAA Pawtucket Paw Sox (p293), which is in the Red Sox farm system. Alternatively, Cape Cod hosts the country's oldest and most active amateur baseball league (see the boxed text, p179), which also sends players into the majors.

Sports fanaticism is not limited to baseball. This is evident from the face painters and beer bellies that brave subzero temperatures to watch the New England Patriots (p121) play football. Super Bowl champions in 2002, 2004 and 2005 – that's a 'three-peat' for football fans – the Pats put individualism aside and pull together to beat other teams that might look better on paper. College football fans can follow the competitive Boston College Eagles (see p121) in the prestigious Atlantic Coast Conference (ACC) competition.

After spending a summer with the Chatham A's, Jim Collins wrote *The Last Best League* about baseball players trying to go from the smalltime to the big leagues.

The Boston Celtics (p121) have won more basketball championships than any other NBA team, especially during the years when Larry Bird dominated the court. After a long period of downtime, the team's recent rebound has reminded fans of these glory days.

Hockey is also historically huge in Boston, though the Bruins (p121) have underperformed in recent years. Harvard, Boston College and Boston University hockey teams earn the devotion of spirited fans. The competition culminates in April, when local teams play in hockey's premier college event, the Bean Pot Tournament.

Sports mavens will want to visit the New England Sports Museum (p80) in Boston. Stop in Springfield, Massachusetts to see the Naismith Memorial Basketball Hall of Fame (p243), or mosey on down to Newport, Rhode Island for the International Tennis Hall of Fame (p299).

MULTICULTURALISM

Irish, Italian and Portuguese communities have been well established in the urban areas since the 19th century. In more recent years, New England cities have continued to attract immigrants from non-European origins: you can hear Caribbean rhythms in Hartford, Connecticut and Springfield, Massachusetts, smell Vietnamese and Cambodian cookery in Cambridge and Lowell, and see Brazilian flags waving in Somerville.

Immigrants continue to confront obstacles of adaptation, including language barriers, financial limitations and legal hazards. In December 2006, federal officials raided a leather manufacturing company in New Bedford, Massachusetts, arresting hundreds of purported illegal immigrants, leaving many detainees' children without proper care and resulting in mass deportations. Criticized as inhumane and ineffective, the raid highlighted the enduring contradiction between the 'American Dream' and an immigrant's reality.

Meanwhile, cities such as Cambridge, Somerville and Orleans, Massachusetts have declared themselves 'sanctuary cities' for immigrants, meaning they do not enforce immigration law. New Haven, Connecticut has gone so far as to issue municipal identification cards to immigrants who are otherwise undocumented. The policy is obviously controversial, and critics argue that it leads to increased crime. But these cities recognize that they depend on immigrant labor to keep their economies running.

America's first newspaper, the unauthorized *Publick Occurrences, Both Foreign and Domestick*, was published in Boston in 1690, then immediately suppressed.

MEDIA

The fourth estate is alive and well in New England and busy with the standard newsworthy events. The widely read and widely respected *Boston Globe* is the region's top media organization. In the early 2000s, Globe reporters were instrumental in uncovering the Catholic Church abuse scandal, for which they were awarded a Pulitzer Prize. Like all respectable newspapers, the Globe is sometimes accused of having a liberal bias. Other media outlets are more local in nature, focusing especially on the antics of politicians and their entourages. **New England News** (www.newenglandnews.org) is a website dedicated to promoting independent and accountable journalism. The site contains news blurbs and blogs by professional and 'citizen' journalists.

RELIGION

The colonists who founded the Massachusetts Bay Colony were Puritans, adherents to a strict form of Calvinism that sought to 'purify' the church of the excesses of ceremony acquired over the centuries. The Puritans had little tolerance for differing beliefs, and settlements spread throughout New England as dissenters departed to found their own (often more tolerant) colonies. Rhode Island, for example, was founded by Roger Williams after he was banished from the Massachusetts Bay Colony. Few traces of these fundamentalist beliefs are found in New England today. The Puritans' spiritual heirs – the Congregationalists – tend to be more tolerant than their forebears.

Believers who questioned the concept of the trinity split off to found the first Unitarian Church at King's Chapel in Boston (p79). Transcendentalism flourished in Boston and Concord in the 19th century. The belief that God 'transcended' all people and things attracted the era's greatest philosophers, including Emerson, Thoreau, Hawthorne and Melville. Its modern incarnation is Unitarian-Universalism. In 1866, Mary Baker Eddy founded the Christian Science Church (p87), which professes personal healing through prayer.

The immigrants that arrived in droves throughout the 19th century changed Boston's religious makeup. They were mostly Irish, Italian and Portuguese, and all strongly Catholic. Nowadays, about 42% of the region's residents identify as Catholic (more than all other religious groups combined).

ARTS

From high culture to low-down blues, the New England arts scene has something for everyone. New England developed as an artistic center in the 19th century. Almost all of the region's illustrious cultural institutions date to this Golden Age.

These days, the region's intellectual atmosphere and artistic tradition attract writers, musicians, artists and architects. Artists hang their masterpieces at galleries and museums in Cape Cod, the Berkshires and Boston. Actors strut their stuff on stages around the region. Vibrant music scenes rock the house in Boston, Providence, Burlington and Portland. World-renowned design schools, art colleges, music programs and conservatories continue to train young talent, and the region's artistic tradition inspires creative types to keep creating.

Literature

By the 19th century, New England's universities had become a magnet for writers, poets and philosophers, with Boston, Cambridge and Concord, Massachusetts fertile breeding grounds for ideas (see the boxed text, p41).

Ralph Waldo Emerson (1803–82) promulgated his teachings from his home in Concord (p137). Emerson's friend and fellow Concordian Henry David Thoreau (1817–62) is best remembered for his journal of observations written in a log cabin at Walden Pond (p139). Louisa May Alcott (1832–88) later moved to Boston, but she wrote her largely autobiographical novel *Little Women* while living at Orchard House (see p137) in Concord. Nathaniel Hawthorne also spent time with this crowd in Concord although he was born in Salem, which is the setting for *House of Seven Gables* (p146).

Henry Wadsworth Longfellow lived up the road in Cambridge, where he penned such famous poetry as *Paul Revere's Ride* and *The Song of Hiawatha*. His estate on Brattle St is now the Longfellow National Historic Site (p92).

Few New England authors were more prominent than Mark Twain (born Samuel Clemens; 1835–1910). Born in Missouri, Twain settled in Hartford, Connecticut, where his homestead is now the Mark Twain House & Museum (p345).

Harriet Beecher Stowe (1811–96) was born in Litchfield, Connecticut and lived in Brunswick, Maine before she eventually moved to Hartford. Today the Harriet Beecher Stowe House (p345) remembers the abolitionist and author, whose influential book *Uncle Tom's Cabin* recruited thousands to the anti-slavery cause.

One of the Beat Generation's defining authors was Jack Kerouac, born in Lowell, Massachusetts. His hometown features prominently in many of his novels (see p141), but he eventually decamped to New York. Henry James,

Prominent writers have deep connections to New England that are plumbed through www .literarytraveler.org.

WRITING NEW ENGLAND

John Sedgwick is the author of five books, four of which are set in New England. His latest, *In My Blood*, is a sort of family memoir about the Sedgwick line, a Brahmin (upper-class) family from Stockbridge, Massachusetts. We spoke with John at his home in Cambridge.

Tell me about your own family history and how it led you into the literary field. The Sedgwick literary tradition goes back at least five generations. In the mid-19th century, Catharine Maria Sedgwick was a very distinguished author, considered the first notable female novelist in America. Her grand-nephew – my grandfather – was Henry Dwight Sedgwick, who wrote 38 books – erudite biographies of people like Edward the Black Prince, La Fayette, Henry of Navarre. He had a nice life: travel in Europe to research in summer; return to Massachusetts to write in winter; repeat. I did not really know him, but he cast a long shadow. And his brother Ellery was the owner and editor of the *Atlantic Monthly* for 30 years.

Did you always know that you would follow in your grandfather's footsteps? It clicked in for me when I was studying at Harvard and I fell under the influence of a woman named Anne Fadiman. She would later go on to write *The Spirit Catches You When You Fall Down* and to edit *American Scholar*. She was a fellow student, the daughter of Clifton Fadiman, who had written for the *New Yorker*. She is the one who informed me about this occupation called 'freelance writer,' which I had never heard of before. She taught me how to write more than any other single person.

You have spent your whole life in New England, so maybe you are not qualified to answer this question, but how does it compare to other regions of the country, as a place for writers to live and work? Boston – as a city – is the perfect size for fostering young talent and creating a community of writers. In New York, there are too many writers competing with each other, so they end up beating each other with sticks. Boston writers are just happy to meet other people that are going through the same creative processes. Pen New England (www.pen-ne.org) has done a lot to encourage literary fellowship. And of course the universities are constantly pumping out new writers and instructors.

How does the region's literary history play into it? Yes, the region's literary history plays a role, especially during the period that FO Matthiessen called the American Renaissance. In the mid-19th century, Boston was the undisputed literary capital. It has not really been the same since then, but that history does provide a nice backdrop. It's a well that we all draw from. Even in my own work, I stumble over these guys. Any discourse on the physical landscape somehow references Thoreau, and on the moral landscape, Emerson.

As related to Mara Vorhees

ee cummings, TS Eliot and Robert Lowell all hailed from New England, but did their most definitive work after leaving the region.

America's favorite poet, Robert Frost (1874–1963), was an exception to this trend. He moved from California and lived on farms in Shaftsbury, Vermont (now the Robert Frost Stone House Museum; p367) and Franconia, New Hampshire (now Frost Place; p447), where he wrote poems including *Nothing Gold Can Stay* and *The Road Not Taken*.

In the late 20th century – and continuing into contemporary times – New England has regained its reputation as a literary center. Stephen King, author of horror novels such as *Carrie* and *The Shining*, lives and sets his novels in Maine (see the boxed text, p516). Other noteworthy regional authors include Annie Proulx, John Irving, Donna Tartt, Jhumpa Lahiri, David Foster Wallace and John Cheever.

Listen to audio recitations and read interviews and poems by America's favorite poet on http://robertfrostoutloud.com.

Film & TV

With small, independent industries in Boston and Providence, New England is an exciting venue for film. A great resource for moviemakers and movie-lovers is **NE Film** (www.newenglandfilm.com), publishing inter-

TOP 10 LITERARY LIGHTS

■ **Ralph Waldo Emerson** (1803–82) Essayist with a worldwide following and believer in the mystical beauty of all creation; founder of transcendentalism.

■ **Henry David Thoreau** (1817–62) Best remembered for *Walden; Or, Life in the Woods*, his journal of observations written during his solitary sojourn from 1845 to 1847 in a log cabin at Walden Pond.

■ **Mark Twain** (born Samuel Clemens; 1835–1910) Born in Missouri, Twain settled in Hartford, Connecticut and wrote *The Adventures of Tom Sawyer* and *The Adventures of Huckleberry Finn*.

■ **Emily Dickinson** (1830–86) This reclusive 'Belle of Amherst' crafted beautiful poems, mostly published after her death.

■ **Edith Wharton** (1862–1937) This Pulitzer Prize–winning novelist's best-known work, *Ethan Frome*, paints a grim portrayal of emotional attachments on a New England farm.

■ **Eugene O'Neill** (1888–1953) From New London, Connecticut, O'Neill wrote the play *A Long Day's Journey into Night*.

■ **Robert Frost** (1874–1963) New England's signature poet, whose many books of poetry use New England themes to explore the depths of human emotions and experience.

■ **Stephen King** (b 1947) Maine horror novelist; wrote *Carrie* and *The Shining*.

■ **Annie Proulx** (b 1935) New England–born award-winning author of *The Shipping News*.

■ **John Irving** (b 1942) New Hampshire native writes novels set in New England, including *The World According to Garp, The Hotel New Hampshire* and *A Prayer for Owen Meany*.

esting articles, industry events and a comprehensive directory of locally made films.

Film festivals are hosted around the region, including in Boston (see the boxed text, p118), Concord (www.snobfilmfestival.org) and Providence (p289). As well, Boston has provided a setting for some well-loved TV shows, including *Cheers, Boston Public, The Practice, Spenser for Hire, Ally McBeal* and *St Elsewhere*.

Music

The most famous symphony orchestra in the area is the Boston Symphony Orchestra (BSO; see p118). In summer, the orchestras move outdoors: the BSO heads for its season at the Tanglewood estate in Lenox, Massachusetts (see the boxed text, p266), and the Boston Pops play an annual July 4 concert on the Charles River Esplanade.

Good chamber music series are also at Tanglewood, as well as in Great Barrington, Massachusetts (p233); Newport, Rhode Island (p301); Marlboro, Vermont (p361); and Blue Hill, Maine (p500), among other venues.

When it comes to modern music, New England has an equally excellent tradition of grooving to great tunes. Back in the day, bands like Aerosmith, the Cars and the J Geils band exemplified the Boston beat. More recently, the city has punked out with the Mighty Mighty Bosstones, the Pixies and the wildly popular Dropkick Murphys. Even small towns have spawned some big names: indie rockers Phish got started at Nectar's in Burlington, Vermont (p394). Portland, Providence, North Hampton and New Haven all have vibrant music scenes. Boston hosts the annual NEMO Music Festival (see the boxed text, p116), which showcases hundreds of independent musicians.

Jazz and blues are not quite as widespread, although the Berklee College of Music (p117) ensures that these genres jive in Boston. The Blues Trust

---

TOP 10 NEW ENGLAND FILMS

- *Jaws* (1975) is an improbable but still terrifying story of a great white shark attacking swimmers on New England beaches; it's set on Martha's Vineyard.

- *On Golden Pond* (1981), the story of two lovers in their declining years, was filmed at New Hampshire's Squam Lake and features fine performances by Henry Fonda and Katharine Hepburn.

- *Glory* (1989), starring Denzel Washington and Matthew Broderick, tells the true story of the first Civil War black volunteer infantry unit.

- *Little Women* (1994) is based on Louisa May Alcott's wonderful book about girls growing up in 19th-century Concord. The movie stars Susan Sarandon as Marmie and Winona Ryder as Jo.

- *The Crucible* (1996) is an adaptation of Arthur Miller's play about the Salem witch trials, and stars Daniel Day-Lewis and Winona Ryder.

- *Amistad* (1997), with an all-star cast directed by Stephen Spielberg, tells the true story of an 1839 mutiny aboard a slave ship and the ensuing legal battle to vindicate and free the mutineers.

- *Good Will Hunting*, with local-boys-turned-stars Ben Affleck and Matt Damon, is the 1998 hit that tells the story of a blue-collar boy from South Boston who becomes a math/physics savant at the Massachusetts Institute of Technology (MIT).

- *The Cider House Rules* won Michael Caine an Academy Award in 2000 for his role as a doctor in an orphanage in rural Maine.

- *Mystic River* (2006) earned Academy Awards for Sean Penn (Best Actor) and Tim Robbins (Best Supporting Actor). Based on the novel by Dennis Lehane, it's the dark story of three childhood friends who are thrown together in adulthood when one of their daughters is murdered. Lehane followed up with another Boston-based detective novel, *Gone Baby Gone*, which was made into a movie by Ben Affleck in 2007.

- Matt Damon co-stars with Leonardo DiCaprio in *The Departed* (2006), which takes place in Boston. This suspense-filled mob movie won the Best Picture Oscar in 2007.

---

and Beantown Jazz Fest (see the boxed text, p116) both take place in Boston, while Newport hosts the JVC Jazz Festival (p301).

New England is also home to a thriving folk tradition, thanks to the venerable Club Passim in Cambridge (p117) and the high-profile Newport Folk Festival (p301) and Lowell Folk Festival (p142).

Architecture

New England is not eager to break with architectural tradition. Nonetheless, the region has its share of dramatic contemporary structures (all of them controversial at the time of construction): the John F Kennedy Library & Museum (p90) in Boston, by IM Pei; the Ray & Maria Strata Center (p92) in Cambridge, by Frank Gehry; and the new ICA (p85) in Boston, by Diller Scofidio + Renfro.

Even more impressive than its new architecture is the creative way in which the region is converting its old architecture. The most dramatic example is Mass MoCA (p271), the contemporary art museum that once was an electrical power plant. Former mills in Manchester, New Hampshire (Amoskeag Mills; p420) and textile factories in Lowell, Massachusetts (p141) now house historical museums, condos and commercial enterprises. In Boston, the infamous Charles St Jail is now a luxury hotel (see the boxed text, p99).

This trend grows out of a 20th-century movement to restore and recast old industrial buildings, especially in the port cities along the coast. Preservationists reclaimed the sturdy granite warehouses along Boston's

PORTRAYING BOSTON

Michelle Fornabai is an architect and designer who uses materials and technology to explore the link between self and surroundings. She teaches at the Columbia School of Architecture and the Rhode Island School of Design (RISD). We talked to Michelle at her home in Boston.

You live in Boston, and you teach in Providence and New York. How does New England compare with other regions as a place to live and be an artist? Boston does not have the number of artists that New York has, but that gives us more of a sense of community. I think the art community is younger here, with recent grads from RISD and MassArt living in the South End and Fort Point. It's definitely closer-knit. At an event like First Fridays, or the annual Open Studios (see the boxed text, p86), you can see the emergent art and really get a sense of Boston's art scene. On the one hand, that means it is small. On the other hand, it means you can track it in a way that's not possible in New York.

What does the region offer for artists and art-lovers? Boston has some really strong collections – amazing Asian art at the MFA (Museum of Fine Arts; p88), for example. The ICA (Institute of Contemporary Art; p85) has a vital collection, and it is growing. They are focusing on solid contemporary art, mixed with emergent and local artists, which is particular to the ICA and very exciting.

RISD (p278) often has seasonal shows where you can buy works by the students, from jewelry to handbags to textiles and glassblowing. Their museum is really good. There is also a store called RISD Works, featuring faculty works and alumni works.

Massachusetts Institute of Technology (MIT; p92) is making an effort to put a visual face on what they do, through their galleries and museums. This is exciting because their things are 'in process'. The chance to look at technology and art – that is unique to Boston.

What does the opening of the ICA mean for the region as an artistic center? The ICA started with this small collection in a little building in Back Bay. Now it is this amazing building with exponentially more visitors. So they are adjusting to this new scale. And the administration has also rethought what the museum should do. They are offering media tech, film series, performance space, there is a huge wall for billboard-sized works.

The ICA has received criticism because the collection is a small percentage of the space. But I think it's crucial that they considered contemporary art practices, instead of just objects and paintings. Now that the ICA is running all these programs, I am optimistic about the future of contemporary art in Boston.

But I may be biased, because I just participated in an exhibit there.

Tell us about the exhibit. My friend Terri was commissioned to participate in an exhibit on the Boston Harbor Islands (see the boxed text, p84). So she did a sound piece on Spectacle Island. But then she decided that she wanted to have a presence in the museum, so she asked me to help her. We created, in the Founders Gallery, a huge 100ft-long sculpture that was tactile and kids could climb on it and it emitted sound. It was part of an effort to get people to visit the Harbor Islands.

As related to Mara Vorhees

waterfront (p83) for apartments, offices, shops and restaurants. Ports in Portland, Portsmouth, Newburyport and Providence – once gritty, dirt-under-the-fingernails places – were transformed into quaint old towns, lined with boutiques, galleries and restaurants. Indeed, during the final decades of the 20th century, historic preservation became a Yankee obsession, and the well-protected and restored historic cores of towns and cities provide examples of the many architectural styles that once flourished here.

Named for the reigning monarchs in the 18th century, Georgian architecture is prevalent on university campuses at Harvard (Harvard Yard; p91), Dartmouth (p429) and many other New England schools. The quintessential New England architecture – the classic white-steepled church – is also a ubiquitous Georgian element.

ANTIQUES ROADSHOW

Is it any wonder that the PBS TV series *Antiques Roadshow* is a smash hit in New England? Yankees are crazy about antiques. Considering that in the 18th century there wasn't much more to the US than New England, they have a better inventory, let's face it. New England craftsmen dominated well into the 1800s, making beautiful furniture, functional and well-made tools, and goods and artifacts of daily living.

'Our readers are passionate about antiques and collectibles,' says Michael Carlton, editor of *Yankee Magazine. Yankee* runs a regular antiques and collectibles column, frequently featuring the work of Skinner, Inc, headquartered in Boston. Skinner is one of the nation's leading auction houses for antiques, and is the premier auction house in New England. Skinner appraisers appear frequently on *Antiques Roadshow.* The company conducts nearly 60 auctions a year, giving art and antiques enthusiasts the opportunity to bid on lots of rare and desirable objects.

Top spots for antiquing in New England include Beacon Hill in Boston (p122), Route 6A on Cape Cod (p188) and of course the famous Brimfield Antique Show (p239) in Sturbridge, Massachusetts. Rural routes in Vermont, New Hampshire and Maine are veritable treasure troves.

State capitols typify 19th-century neoclassicism, with domes, colonnades and arcades. The best example may be the Massachusetts State House (p75), designed by Charles Bulfinch (1763–1844), but the New Hampshire State Capitol (p422) also follows this design.

Painting, Sculpture & Visual Arts

For all its wealth, 19th-century New England society could not fully nurture its renowned artists, including Henry Sargent (1770–1845) of Gloucester, James Abbott McNeill Whistler (1834–1903) of Lowell, and John Singleton Copley (1738–1815) of Boston, all of whom left Massachusetts to pursue training and artistic fulfillment abroad. An exception was Winslow Homer (1836–1910), who pursued a career as an illustrator for the popular press but later dedicated his talents to painting. Homer is famous for his scenes of the New England coast.

By the 20th century, New England had matured as a venue for artists. John Singer Sargent (1856–1925) painted his telling portraits of Boston's upper class, and Childe Hassam (1859–1935) used Boston Common and other New England cityscapes and landscapes as subjects for his impressionist works. All of these painters are well represented at the Museum of Fine Arts (p88).

New England's most famous artist was Norman Rockwell (1894–1978). His magazine illustrations, particularly the covers for the *Saturday Evening Post,* cemented US popular culture and helped define the nation's concept of 'American.' He lived and worked in Arlington, Vermont (p367) and Stockbridge, Massachusetts (p262).

Highly regarded for her 'American primitive' paintings of rural life, Anna Mary Robertson Moses (1860–1961) didn't begin painting until she was in her late seventies. Work by 'Grandma Moses' resides in Bennington's museum (p366), Vermont.

New England has produced its share of sculptors. Daniel Chester French (1850–1931) designed the Minute Man memorial in Concord (p137), and the seated John Harvard in Harvard Yard (see the boxed text, p91). Augustus Saint-Gaudens did similarly monumental pieces, such as the Shaw Memorial opposite the Massachusetts State House (p75). His estate in New Hampshire is now the Saint-Gaudens National Historic Site (p430). Alexander Calder (1898–1976) made many of his world-famous mobiles and stabiles at his studio in Roxbury, Connecticut.

Contemporary art is no less exciting, thanks to schools like Rhode Island School of Design (RISD; p278) in Providence and the Massachusetts College of Art (MassArt; see the boxed text, p120) in Boston. Mass MoCA (p271) in North Adams and the Institute of Contemporary Art (ICA) (p85) in Boston are relatively new but daring enterprises, exhibiting the best of regional and national artists. Lively gallery scenes exist around the region, including Boston (see the boxed text, p86), Provincetown (p204), Portland (p476), New London (p327) and Brattleboro (p359).

Small theater companies are active in nearly every village and hamlet. Visit the New England Entertainment Digest (www.jacneed.com) to find a community theater near you.

Theater & Dance

In the 18th century, the Puritanical cultural miasma in New England gave churchgoing Yankees a marked suspicion of plays and show folk. But even then, interest in the stage was intense, and every ship that arrived from England came with stories of the plays and entertainment in London.

In later years, when the puritanical fervor subsided, New England became a center for summer theater productions. Most famously, Eugene O'Neill founded the Provincetown Players (although his experimental plays were still banned from Boston stages). This tradition continues today at venues such as the Provincetown Theater (p208) and the American Repertory Theater (p117) in Cambridge.

Food & Drink

New England is the land of the first Thanksgiving and of bountiful autumnal harvests. It is America's seafood capital, home of the mighty cod, whose role in culture and cuisine has earned the fish a place of honor in the Massachusetts State House, and the boiled lobster, which is celebrated at local 'Lobsterfests' around the region.

This regional cuisine has deep cultural roots; and like all things cultural, it is dynamic and developing. Advances in culinary culture have changed the dining landscapes of cities around the region, including Boston, Providence and Portland. In the last decade, these cities have developed multifaceted local cuisines, drawing on unique New England traditions and varied international influences.

Indeed, you'll be hard-pressed to find the old stand-bys – Boston baked beans or New England boiled dinner – on any menu. But do not despair: you will find local specialties like maple syrup, artisan cheeses and, of course, fresh seafood.

STAPLES & SPECIALTIES

'New England is America's seafood capital, home of the mighty cod'

Old-fashioned New England cuisine is a blend of Anglo-American, European and Native American food traditions. It combined established English recipes with local offerings from the earth and sea. For a taste of ye olde New England, head to Ye Olde Union Oyster House (p108) or Durgin Park (p107).

The influx of immigrants in the 19th century had a profound impact on local cuisine. Seafood was still prominently featured, but now it was served under Italian tomato sauces and in spicy Portuguese stews. The southern Europeans, who had inherited the tomato from the Americas, now brought it back to the New World in unrecognizable but undeniably delicious forms.

Today, eating habits vary widely between communities, families and individuals. Breakfast is popularly considered 'the most important meal of the day,' but is nonetheless sometimes skipped, as busy professionals run off to work. Otherwise, it often features toast and cereal, egg dishes or stacks of pancakes, possibly drenched in blueberries and the New England specialty – maple syrup. The quintessential Boston breakfast is coffee and a doughnut from Dunkin' Donuts.

Weekend brunch is an increasingly popular tradition in the city. Otherwise, lunch centers on that all-American omnipresent staple, the sandwich. In New England, unlike many European countries, alcohol is not often drunk at lunchtime (another holdover from the Puritans).

Dinner is the biggest meal of the day, whether eaten at home or in a restaurant. In recent years, dining out has become a form of entertainment and the most common venue for socializing.

Seafood & Shellfish

First things first: ask 10 locals about New England's best chowder and you're likely to get 10 different answers. The thick, cream-based soup is chock full of clams or fish, though clam chowder is more prevalent. Usually, the meaty insides of giant surf clams are used to make the famous concoction.

Other varieties of clams include soft-shelled clams, or 'steamers' (so-called because they are steamed to eat). Any self-respecting raw bar will have a selection of hard-shelled clams or 'quahogs', often including littlenecks and cherrystones. Other raw-bar specialties include oysters, the best being

---

CLAM CHOWDER

4lb chopped clams
46oz clam juice
6 tsp celery salt
6 tsp white pepper
6 tsp Worcestershire sauce
3 tsp Tabasco sauce
4 to 6 whole potatoes
1lb butter
1lb flour
1 qt half-and-half

Place the clams and clam juice in a stockpot. Add the celery salt, white pepper, Worcestershire sauce and Tabasco sauce. Peel and dice potatoes. Add to the clams. Bring to a boil, lower the heat to simmer, and cook slowly. In a small saucepan melt the butter. Add the flour to make a white roux. Cook for 15 to 20 minutes on low heat. Whisk the roux into the clam mixture, and add the half-and-half. Cook slowly to blend all the ingredients. Makes four to six servings.

Courtesy of Durgin Park (p107)

Wellfleet oysters from Cape Cod (see p197). Littlenecks, cherrystones and oysters are usually eaten raw with a dollop of cocktail sauce and a few drops of lemon.

New England is a mecca for seafood lovers who come to get their fix of fresh lobster (see p464). The lobster gets steamed or boiled, then the fun begins; see p48 for tips on how to eat one.

Scrod (which might be any white-fleshed fish) is often broiled or fried, and served with french fries, in the classic fish-and-chips combo. The venerable Omni Parker House (p100) in Boston claims responsibility for coining the term 'scrod'. Apparently, sailing captains would pick out the best of the day's catch and store it in a container marked 'select catch remains on deck', or SCROD. Other fish making regular appearances on menus include bluefish and mackerel, as well as swordfish, tuna steaks and striped bass.

The New England Clam Shack Cookbook, by Brooke Dojny, has recipes from the region's best clam shacks. Take a road trip down the coast and sample them all!

Fruits & Vegetables

Fruit grows in abundance throughout New England. Apples, peaches and berries are available at roadside stands, farmers markets (see p50) and pick-your-own farms (p51). The most adored of New England fruits is the tiny but tasty Maine blueberry. In the fall, bogs on Cape Cod yield crimson cranberry crops, spectacular to look at and tart to taste. With a healthy dose of sugar, cranberries make delicious juices, muffins and pies. Thanksgiving dinner is not complete without cranberry sauce.

Corn, beans and squash – dubbed the 'life-giving sisters' – are staple foods in New England. They are the ingredients of another traditional Thanksgiving dish, succotash. The single food item most associated with Boston is certainly baked beans, thanks to the city's nickname Beantown. Boston baked beans are white or navy beans, molasses, salt pork and onions slow-cooked in a crock. Baked beans were a traditional Sunday meal, since they could be made in advance and the Puritans did not cook on Sundays.

Maine grows 98% of America's blueberries – a whopping 30 million lb annually.

Cheese & Dairy

New England's largest dairy is Hood, known even to non-milk-drinkers, thanks to the iconic Hood milk bottle near the Children's Museum (see p85).

HOW TO EAT A LOBSTER

Eating a lobster is a messy affair (as you may have guessed when you were provided with a bib).

At lobster pounds, live lobsters are cooked to order. They range in size from 1lb (chicken lobsters, or 'chicks') and 1.25lb to 1.5lb (selects) to large lobsters weighing from 2lb to 20lb. Culls – lobsters missing a claw – are sold at a discount, as the claw meat is considered choice. Anything smaller than a chick is a 'short' and does not meet the legal minimum size for harvesting.

Besides the bib, a lobster comes with a cracker for breaking the claws, a small fork or pick for excavating, a container of drawn butter and a slice of lemon.

Start by twisting off the skinny legs and sucking out the slender bits of meat inside. Then move on to the claws: twist the claws and knuckles off the body, break them with the cracker and dip the tender meat in butter before eating.

Pick up the lobster body in one hand and the tail in the other. Twist the tail back and forth to break it. Tear off each flipper at the end of the tail and suck out the meat. Then use your finger or an implement to push the bigger pieces of meat out of the tail.

There is delicious meat in the body as well, but it takes extra work (and many people just discard it). Tear off the carapace (back shell), then split the body in two lengthwise. Use a pick to dig out the meat from behind the spot where the skinny legs were attached.

Now it's finally safe to remove your bib; and here's where you'll need that towelette to wipe your hands.

New Englanders are benefiting from a regional interest in returning to organic, hormone-free milk and dairy products, and Vermont is leading this movement. Dozens of family farms and small producers are making artisan cheeses from goat, sheep and cow milk. The great variety and high quality of New England cheeses (see www.newenglandcheese.com) will thrill the most discriminating gourmet – the old standby Vermont cheddar is still the most popular. Sample the goods at Sugarbush Farm (p375) or the Grafton Village Cheese Company (p363).

Cheeses of Vermont (2002), Henry Tewksbury's delightfully passionate guide to artisan and farmstead cheesemakers, directs explorers to out-of-the-way cheesemaking operations.

Desserts

Old-fashioned New England meals are sometimes followed by Indian pudding (a baked pudding made from milk, molasses and cornmeal), a soupy gingerbread, or bread pudding. In autumn, menus feature seasonal pies like pumpkin, apple and squash (often considered the most important part of Thanksgiving dinner). Apple crisp and apple cobbler are delicious variations on the theme, especially when topped with homemade ice cream. In June and July, strawberries and rhubarb are in season, making it prime time for strawberry-rhubarb pie.

DRINKS

Although the region's northeast is not as fertile as the Napa Valley, grape wine is produced in eastern Massachusetts, southeastern Rhode Island and northwestern Connecticut. Even if they're not great, New England wines are generally drinkable. Sample them at Haight Vineyards (p349) or Hopkins Vineyard (p351), both in Connecticut.

Bostonians take beer seriously and there are microbreweries and brew pubs in town (see p113). Although New England's breweries don't often distribute beyond their local communities, Sam Adams and the Boston Beer Co have achieved national and international recognition.

In western Massachusetts, toss back a cold one at Northampton Brewery (p250) or Hyland Orchard & Brewery (p239) in Sturbridge. In Vermont, check out Otter Creek Brewing (p382) in Middlebury, Magic Hat (p389) in

Boston-based writer Andy Crouch blogs about beer on www.beerscribe .com. He also wrote *The Good Beer Guide to New England* (2006).

EAT YOUR WORDS

When it comes to food and drink, sometimes New Englanders have a funny way of expressing themselves:

bubbler	water fountain
cabinet	milkshake (Rhode Island only)
frappe	milkshake
grinder	a heated submarine sandwich
half-and-half	a very light cream (between 10% and 18% butterfat), typically used in coffee
jimmies	chocolate sprinkles (on ice cream)
order	groceries
packie	liquor store
scrod	white-fish catch of the day
steamers	steamed clams
tonic	carbonated soft drink; soda

When ordering coffee:

black	no sugar, no cream
light	cream only
regular	cream and sugar, and lots of it
sweet	sugar only

Burlington or the Long Trail Brewing Company (p377) in Woodstock. Head to Red Hook Brewery (p414) or Portsmouth Brewery (p416) in Portsmouth, New Hampshire, or Woodstock Station & Brewery (p443) in Woodstock. When in Maine, you can drink at Federal Jack's Restaurant & Brew Pub (p472) in the Kennebunks or Bar Harbor Brewing Company (p504) in the town of the same name.

The hometown secret in New England is cider and it occupies pride of place on the drink list. Even though it's quite alcoholic, settlers allowed their children to drink it, and clergymen who abstained from harder liquors relished the sweet-tasting drink.

CULINARY CALENDAR & FOOD FESTIVALS

Boston Vegetarian Food Festival (www.bostonveg.org) Veggie products, recipes and speakers, including lots of free samples. In mid-October.

Harwich Cranberry Festival (www.harwichcranberryfestival.org) Harwich, Massachusetts (p190) hosts lots of berry-themed events in mid-September, including a craft fair and fireworks.

Ludlow Zucchini Festival (☎ 802-228-5830) This quirky event in mid-August features size contests, cook-offs and an only-in-Vermont 'Zacapult' competition.

Maine Lobster Festival (☎ 207-596-0376; www.mainelobsterfestival.com) In early August, over 12 tons of lobsters are prepared in the world's largest lobster cooker in Rockland, Maine (p494).

Norwalk Oyster Festival (☎ 203-838-9444; www.seaport.org) Norwalk, Connecticut (p336) celebrates the region's seafaring (and seafood-eating) past in September.

Restaurant Week (www.restaurantweekboston.com) Participating restaurants all around Boston offer excellent-value prix-fixe menus at the end of August – $20 for lunch, $30 for dinner.

Vermont Maple Festival (www.vtmaplefestival.org) St Albans hosts a week of antiques and exhibitions, carnivals and crafts, music and maple-sugar sweets at the end of April. The highlight is the Sunday morning 'Sap Run', an 8.5-mile road race.

Wellfleet OysterFest (www.wellfleetoysterfest.org) A weekend of oyster shucking and slurping on Cape Cod (p198) in mid-October.

Yarmouth Clam Festival (☎ 207-846-3984; www.clamfestival.com) Going strong for 43 years, this annual July event in Yarmouth, Maine, features clam-shucking contests, canoe races and a festival parade.

Learn where to pick apples on www.apples-ne.com, which also extols the virtues of varieties grown in New England.

WHERE TO EAT & DRINK

Unless you are deep in the forest, you're never far from a food source in New England.

Almost every New England town has an old-fashioned diner that is open early and often serves breakfast throughout the day. The same goes for a local pub, always good for a cold beer, filling fare and a bit of local color (and particularly welcoming for solo travelers). Many towns also have at least one upscale restaurant, often catering to tourists passing through. In every coastal town you will find a seafood shack to serve you a lobster roll or a bowl of chowder.

Urban areas, obviously, have a much wider selection of eateries. Most cities are packed with fancy restaurants, cozy coffee shops, simple sandwich joints and eclectic ethnic eateries. Boston, Providence and Portland have particularly vibrant culinary scenes.

Most restaurants are open for lunch from about 11:30am until 2:30pm, and for dinner from 5pm until 9pm or 10pm (later on weekends, especially in urban areas). Some places might serve breakfast from about 7am until 10am. There is obviously lots of variation. In this guide, specific opening hours are listed only when they differ radically from the norm.

As for costs, breakfast will run $5 to $15, depending on whether you're at a diner or a culinary hot spot. Lunch will be in this same range. A satisfying dinner in a pleasant, not-too-fancy restaurant costs $15 to $25 per person, not including tax, tip or drinks. In large cities and upscale resorts, it is not unusual to see a bill of $50 to $75 per person, especially if drinks are consumed.

VEGETARIANS & VEGANS

New Englanders take pride in the fact that this is one of the most socially conscious regions of America. As a result, many restaurants offer vegetarian options, and they do it with panache. Of course, it is easier to find vegetarian options in cosmopolitan areas than in tiny towns, but, usually, even at the local diner you can find something healthy and meat-free. Natural food markets and grocery stores are popping up throughout New England faster than weeds in a compost pile. In the restaurant reviews in this guide, look for the vegetarian icon (**V**) to indicate that a place is veggie-friendly.

EATING WITH KIDS

Everyone gets cranky when they are hungry, especially children. To keep your kids happy on the road, try not to disrupt their eating schedule; don't force unfamiliar foods on them; and try to give them some room to move. See p524 for more information on traveling in New England with children. You might also plan to picnic outdoors so the little ones don't have to sit still. Consider staying at a hotel with a kitchenette, especially if you have spawned picky eaters.

Mystic Pizza (1988), a celebrated and sappy coming-of-age flick that was primarily shot in Stonington, Connecticut, features Julia Roberts in her breakout role as a waitress at a pizza parlor.

Connecticut's Northeast Organic Farms site (www .ctnofa.org) offers farm tours and promotes locally sustainable agriculture and ecologically sound farming and gardening.

The Boston Vegetarian Society (www.bostonveg .org) publishes a complete calendar of events, as well as listings of veggie restaurants and inns around New England.

TO MARKET, TO MARKET

When you want it fresh, there's no better place to look than the regional farmers markets. See also the boxed texts on p260 and p359.

- Haymarket, Boston (p103)
- Mid-Cape Farmers Market (p183)
- Orleans Farmers Market (p195)
- Monument Square, Portland (p479)
- Brattleboro Farmers Market (p359)

PICK YOUR OWN

Do-It-Yourselfers will appreciate the chance to go get their own apples, berries, cherries, pumpkins and more:

- Atwood Orchards (p382)
- Hyland Orchard & Brewery (p239)
- Atkins Farms Country Market (p251)
- Windy Hill Farm (p258)
- Woodstock Orchards (p329)

HABITS & CUSTOMS

The duration of meals, table manners and etiquette change with different dining situations, but here are a few tips. In fast-food restaurants, you are expected to clear your own tray. Meals at midrange to upper-end eateries require a 15% to 20% tip for your server (added to the bill; cash preferred). Smoking is forbidden in restaurants. If you are having dinner with an American family, it's polite to bring a bottle of wine or something to share. Be sensitive about when it is time to leave: depending upon the age of your hosts, it may be earlier than you are used to.

COOKING COURSES

Patron saint of food Julia Child, alumna of Smith College (p247) and longtime resident of Cambridge, spent four decades teaching people to cook before she died in 2004. She was active in the Cambridge and Boston community and supported a scholarship program for aspiring culinary arts students. If you want to embody Julia's bon vivant, bon appétit spirit, take a class at the New England Culinary Institute (p403), one of the country's top cooking schools; the Cambridge School of Culinary Arts (p95); or the Rhode Island School of Design (p278), where you can also tour markets and restaurants with reputable chefs.

The New England Confectionery Company (NECCO), which makes little pastel-colored wafers, was established in 1847 and is the oldest continuously operating candy company in the world.

Join legions of amateur foodies who turn to the mysterious www .phantomgourmet.com, a site based on UPN 38's 'Phantom Gourmet' TV show.

Environment

About 400,000 years ago, a mile-high glacier ground inexorably across New England, leaving the region with a natural playground of clefts and rubble and sheared-off mountainsides, filled as much with stone as with soil. The soil's richness enabled early, flinty New Englanders to scrape a living out of this rugged countryside, even as the frost-buckled earth exhumed new scatterings of stone into the fields every spring.

THE LAND

Not all of the region's magnificent old-growth forests were cleared by settlers in the 1800s and 1900s. The *Sierra Club Guide to Ancient Forest of the Northeast* (2004) by Bruce Kershner and Robert T Leverett leads you to over 130 of these inspiring regional locales.

Several hundred million years ago, the earth thrust the bedrock of New England up into a spine of craggy mountains, running roughly northeast to southwest. Over the ages, erosion and the ebb and flow of geologic pressures reduced these early alpine peaks to lower heights, so that by eight million years ago they achieved the appearance that they have today.

Just one million years ago, the earth's surface temperature dropped inexplicably. Glaciers ground their way down through New England, blanketing the region with a river of ice a mile thick. Pushed ever southward by the pressure of ice buildup at the North Pole, these glaciers dredged up millions of tons of soil and rock and moved it to the southern New England states. Deposits of soil and rock formed the islands of Nantucket and Martha's Vineyard.

As the earth warmed again some 10,000 to 20,000 years ago, the ice retreated from New England. As it moved away it scooped out holes that became glacial ponds (Walden Pond, p139, for example). Rivers turned into cataracts of raging glacial melt-water, grinding out round potholes and carving huge bowls and contorted shapes out of solid stone. To see some stunning examples, visit New Hampshire's Franconia Notch (p445), which runs by the Pemigewasset River, or visit Lost River Gorge in North Woodstock (p442). The retreating glacier deposited rock and debris in oblong hills called drumlins (for a good example see Bunker Hill, p83), and left huge granite boulders called erratics in fields and streams.

The resulting landscape has verdant, winding valleys, abundant forests and a rocky coastline sculpted into coves and sprinkled with sandy beaches. The mountains lack the dramatic height of the Rockies, but they are no less rugged and beautiful. Farmers may complain that New England's rock-strewn soil 'grows boulders' (they're actually pushed up by the succession of freezing winters), but outdoors enthusiasts find the New England topography a perfect place for biking, hiking, canoeing, kayaking and boating (see p58).

WILDLIFE

Once chlorophyll (the substance that makes green leaves green) is no longer produced in the autumn, leaves revert to their underlying color.

Many critters make their home in New England. A year-round profusion of food fattens them up for the big migration, the long winter's nap, or just to survive the harsh winter. You don't have to mount an expedition to the deepest reaches of the forest to see a magnificent moose. By the same token, even the rarest blossoms can be found by quiet roadsides as well as deep in the forests, and any open field dazzles with a palette of blooms.

Animals

LAND MAMMALS

The moose is loose! While it may not be possible to spot one in every corner of New England, you have a pretty good chance if you know where to look. You're more likely to spot a moose the further north you look. The

LEAF-PEEPING

One of New England's greatest natural resources is change. No, not the serious kind that requires you to re-examine your life – we mean the kind that causes the lush nimbus of trees to fling off that staid, New England green and deck their boughs with flaming reds, light-bending yellows and ostentatious oranges. We're talking about the changing of the guard from summer to fall, better known as New England's seventh season (after mud season and black-fly season): foliage season.

Peak times vary by latitude and altitude, with the best bets for late September to mid-October. If your holiday is scheduled for a couple of weeks before your destination region's peak foliage moment, bend time back into your favor by traveling north a bit, or even higher in altitude, where the season hits earlier. Even after the party's over, the colorful confetti catches in streams and fades into more hues of rust and brown than could fill a paint-chip booklet.

Lest you think that leaf-peeping is only for tourists, you should know that even crusty old Yankees find reasons to take to the back roads during the fall. Weekends bear witness to bumper-to-bumper traffic on the most popular routes. If communing with nature is what you have in mind, head for the wilds on a midweek morning and find a hiking trail.

Prime driving routes include the Mohawk Trail (MA 2) in the northern Berkshires (p258), the Kancamagus Hwy in the White Mountains (p443) and VT 100 from Wilmington (p363) to Stowe (p395). See also our Leaf-Peeping itinerary on p24.

Yankee Foliage (www.yankeefoliage.com) is a great website covering the whole region. Otherwise, you can pinpoint peak autumn foliage on any given September or October day by calling these numbers:

Connecticut (☎ 800-282-6863; www.ct.gov/dep)
Maine (☎ 800-777-0317; www.maine.gov/doc/foliage)
Massachusetts (☎ 800-227-6277; www.massvacation.com/scienceNature/fall-foliage.php)
New Hampshire (☎ 800-258-3608; http://foliage.visitnh.gov.ns1www.silvertech.net)
Rhode Island (☎ 800-556-2484)
Vermont (☎ 802-837-6668; www.vermont.com/foliage.cfm)

Kancamagus Hwy (p443) in New Hampshire's White Mountains is prime moose-spotting territory, as is the aptly named Moosehead Lake region in Maine (p519). Both places are brimming with bogs, which is where moose like to browse. As with most wildlife, they favor twilight and nighttime. Consider taking a tour with Pemi Valley Excursions (p442) or venture into the Northern Forest Heritage Park (p459) in New Hampshire.

White-tailed deer are everywhere, as are squirrels (red and grey), chipmunks, raccoons, porcupines and rabbits. Bears tend to keep to areas with large, thick stretches of forest, except where there are backyard birdfeeders or sloppy campsites to raid. For beavers, look for their telltale domed lodges at the edge of a pond (muskrat houses are flatter). Tree stumps chewed to pencil-points are good clues that you're looking in the right place.

MARINE MAMMALS

Whales, dolphins and seals play in New England's coastal waters, and ecotourism provides an alternative livelihood for some fishing crews put out of work by the closing of fishing grounds. The whales seem to truly enjoy sporting for the boats; the captains of whale-watching cruises know their 'regulars' by name. Take one from Gloucester (p154) or Provincetown (p205).

BIRDS

Thanks to environmental clean-up efforts, bald eagles are making a comeback in the northeast and can be seen cruising at altitude over large lakes or diving

Everything you ever wanted to know about moose – and more – is online at Mooseworld (www.mooseworld.com). The site includes loads of photos and stories of sightings.

New England Sea Birds (www.neseabirds.com) devotes itself to birds and animals found off this coastline, and it includes tips on locating rare species and breeding colonies.

for dinner. Just about any large- to medium-size lake or bog will have a rookery of great blue herons, which roost in May, and Canada geese are everywhere. Find a high point along the Connecticut River Valley (p338) in the fall and watch the annual hawk migration. There's nowhere like the Parker River National Wildlife Refuge on Plum Island (p160) or the Felix Neck Wildlife Sanctuary in Martha's Vineyard (p227), both off the coast of Massachusetts, to take in sea birds, including a healthy population of fish hawks (osprey).

Loons – large, buoyant, black-and-white-speckled waterfowl with a lonesome wail – are usually found on large lakes where the water's edge has not been ransacked by development. Once you hear their yodeling cry, you'll never forget it.

Plants

The New England Wildflower Society (www.newenglandwild .org) is compiling an online database of native plant species, called *Flora Novae Angliae*.

New England forests are thick with beech, birch, hemlock, maple, oak, pine and spruce. The hills are alive with wildflowers, with colors that reflect the passing of the seasons. Springtime's first flower, the dandelion, is spread in exuberant blankets of yellow, the first blossoms available to bees coming out of a long, hive-bound winter. From there, blue and purple blossoms of all kinds signal that summer is around the corner. Visit Franconia, New Hampshire for the annual Fields of Lupine Festival (p449), when the hillsides are blanketed in purple blossoms. Blooms warm into reds and yellows as the days lengthen, and the trend skews orange as fall approaches.

Maples are the mascots of the region, yielding not only color in the fall (see p53, and p24 for fall foliage routes), but sap in springtime. Balsam sweetens the air in higher-altitude forests, and birches jut out like inverted lightning strikes with greater frequency and thicker trunks the further north you go.

The foraging is good all summer, with a succession of herbs, fruits, roots, shoots, berries and mushrooms. On the cusp of April and May, fiddleheads (young fern shoots) explain the occasional New Englander bent over on the roadsides, filling plastic bags. After a good, soaking rain, shroomers take to the hills. June brings the strawberries, August the blueberries, and September heralds the cranberry harvests.

NATIONAL & STATE PARKS

Whether it's old buildings or open space, preservation is alive and well in New England. Almost a century ago, in 1911, 800,000 acres were set aside for the White Mountain National Forest (p439) of New Hampshire and Maine. Thus New England's first national forest was born. Twenty years later, in 1932, 400,000 acres in Vermont were designated Green Mountain National Forest (p371). Both efforts stemmed from reaction to rapacious logging practices that denuded land and left behind a tinderbox of felled timber, which fueled catastrophic wildfires throughout the region. Now, the two extensive swaths of land are packed with a playground of natural features and a relatively contiguous ecosystem lending shelter and protection to wildlife.

Acadia National Park's 57 miles of hand-constructed carriage roads, built in the early 1930s, are the best broken stone roads in the US.

The two forests are traversed by the northernmost section of the Appalachian Trail (AT; see p58), which terminates in Maine.

Volunteers work at the **White Mountain National Forest** (☎ 603-528-8796; www .fs.fed.us/r9/forests/white_mountain) maintaining campgrounds and trailheads, implementing education programs, assisting with scientific research, restoring fire-damaged areas and doing administrative work. Interested volunteers should refer to the website or call for further information. Otherwise, refer to the US government's volunteer website at www.volunte er.gov/gov.

New England's only national park is sited on the rugged, northeastern coast of Maine; Acadia National Park (p508) contains 7000 acres of granite-domed mountains, 45 miles of carriage roads, 40 miles of sandy beaches, 115

NEW ENGLAND MAJOR PARKS & NATURAL AREAS

Park or natural area	Features	Activities	Page
Baxter State Park	the wildest wilderness in New England, studded with rocky peaks & cross-country skiing	hiking, mountaineering, rock climbing, ice climbing	p519
Blue Hills Reservation	miles of rolling hills with city skyline views from their peaks	hiking, rock climbing, mountain biking & cross-country skiing	p163
Boston Harbor Islands	more than 30 offshore islands, within minutes of downtown Boston	swimming, boating, camping & bird-watching	p84
Camden Hills State Park	a mountain-peaked park with exquisite views of Penobscot Bay	hiking & cross-country skiing	p496
Crawford Notch State Park	a steep valley with stunning vistas over the Presidentials	hiking & cross-country skiing	p456
Franconia Notch State Park	raging rivers, forested hillsides & glacial lakes	hiking, kayaking & skiing	p445
Grafton Notch State Park	traversed by the AT & splashed with waterfalls	hiking	p517
Hammonasset Beach State Park	2 miles of flat, sandy beach with a fun-filled boardwalk	camping, swimming & bird-watching	p329
Monomoy National Wildlife Refuge	an uninhabited island that is an important Atlantic seaboard flyway for migrating birds	swimming & bird-watching	p192
Mt Greylock State Reservation	the highest point in Massachusetts, with great mountain views & a lodge	hiking & wildlife-watching	p272
Mt Monadnock State Park	a lone peak in southern New Hampshire	hiking, cross-country skiing & camping	p427
October Mountain State Forest	Massachusetts' largest tract of green space, bisected by the AT	hiking, fishing & boating	p264
Parker River National Wildlife Refuge	sandy beaches surround acres of dunes & wetlands	swimming & bird-watching	p160
Quechee Gorge State Park	trails winding through fields, forests & along a lake	hiking, swimming, camping & cross-country skiing	p376
Quoddy Head State Park	one of the easternmost points in the US, with volcanic bedrock & subarctic bogland	hiking & whale-watching	p512
Walden Woods	acres of woodlands with historic Walden Pond at its center	walking, biking, kayaking & swimming	p139

miles of hiking trails, and a sunset view off Cadillac Mountain. At Acadia, there are volunteer opportunities to interact with visitors and maintain trails and campgrounds. If your interest is short-term, **Friends of Acadia** (☎ 207-288-3934; www.friendsofacadia.org) also organizes work crews that go out three times a week in summer months.

The other granddaddy of nationally preserved lands in New England is the Cape Cod National Seashore (p196), a 44,600-acre stretch of rolling dunes and stunning beaches, laced with salt marshes, pitch-pine and scrub-oak forests and freshwater kettle ponds. Potential volunteers should call the volunteer coordinator (☎ 508-349-3785) to learn how they can support the Cape Cod National Seashore by working at the visitor centers, assisting with natural research projects and protecting shorebirds.

State parks are everywhere, even in urban locations, and offer access to some of the area's best natural wonders. Most allow camping, and each offers facilities for its own unique blend of activities. A selection of some of the most interesting parks follows, but you can also consult the New England Outdoors chapter (p58).

The Atlantic coastline of the Cape Cod National Seashore was dubbed an 'ocean graveyard' because so many ships ran afoul of the shoals. Between Truro and Wellfleet alone, almost 1000 ships were lost.

ENVIRONMENTAL ISSUES

Protecting air, land and water are the fundamentals of environmental conservation in New England; but intangibles – such as aesthetics, sustainability and energy independence – are joining the list of protection-worthy concepts. Tourism is one of New England's most lucrative industries; for information on traveling in a sustainable manner, see p15.

Pollutants from around the country are funneled into New England air, courtesy of the jet stream weather pattern. Pollution from incinerators, coal- and oil-fired power plants, dirty manufacturing facilities, auto emissions – you name it, and here it comes. Consequently, rain and snow contain heavy metals and acidic compounds, and mercury. Every New England state has issued advisories restricting or condemning consuming fish caught in its waters.

Forest protection butts directly up against an entrenched way of life in northern sections of the region. On heavily traveled roads, loggers leave a buffer of trees shielding horrific, clear-cut sections; but venture beyond and the pretense is dropped, revealing a denuded land. The good news is that more land is falling under environmental easement protection and landowners are requiring more balanced logging practices to reduce the impact of extraction. Conservation groups are lobbying for larger roadless tracts to knit together entire ecosystems once divided.

Urban sprawl creates an ugly blight, consuming rich land that once supported family farms. If that's not enough, it is the origin of the latest, major source of pollution in our rivers and streams: storm-water runoff. As more land is paved, rainwater, rich with oils and pollutants picked up from heavy traffic areas, is no longer filtered by the earth before finding its way into New England's water tables and streams.

Too often, environmental protection is ignored until it impacts the pocketbook. Hence, the dire conditions of the oceans are only now stimulating large-scale management and reclamation efforts. Dragnet fishing is so called because it involves dragging a weighted net across the ocean floor, devastating everything in its path. Decades of this practice – along with overfishing and increasingly poisonous pollution and dumping – have created something close to a desert on the ocean floor. Now there is a movement toward establishing Marine Protected Areas to restore habitats and create preserves that are off-limits to fishing.

Needless to say, there is strong opposition to this from fishing interests. Conservationists argue that they lack a vision of sustainability; fishers argue

---

Richly descriptive and leaving you longing for the lush and mossy backwoods, Henry David Thoreau's *The Maine Woods* (1854) is essentially one of the first travelogues published in the USA.

Jonathan Harr's *A Civil Action* (1996), made into a popular movie starring John Travolta, follows the true story of a legal case that turned on the connection between industrial polluters and the deaths of children in Woburn, Massachusetts.

ON WALDEN POND

When Henry David Thoreau decided to spend two years living in the woods on his friend's pond-side property, little did he know he would spawn a social movement. Thoreau's sanctuary at Walden Pond (p139) was a secluded cove owned by his close friend Ralph Waldo Emerson. He moved there with a specific intent to live with studied deliberateness and simplicity, seeking a transcendental truth through an intimate relationship with nature.

Thoreau's legacy is large. His book, *Walden; Or, Life in the Woods,* has raised the eco-awareness of many generations of nature-lovers; and Walden Pond is sometimes considered the birthplace of the conservation movement.

In 1990, recording artist Don Henley founded the **Walden Woods project** (www.walden.org) to preserve the forest lands that surround the pond. The project raised money to purchase land that was threatened by development and, in 1998, the Thoreau Institute was founded to preserve and promote the writer's philosophical and environmental teachings. The Walden Woods Project continues to advocate and educate on behalf of Concord's natural world and Thoreau's legacy. For volunteer opportunities, see the website.

that even moderate retooling costs can be enough to sink many small enterprises. Once again, the conflict sets those who make a marginal living against those who would protect the long-term ability for them to do so.

Ocean- and ridgeline-based wind farms promise a step towards energy independence. Yet they're still new enough to cause confusion – testing one's ability to navigate through anti-wind fear tactics and pro-wind assurances to arrive at something close to the truth. A proposed farm off the coast of Nantucket is spiking aesthetic protests, as owners of zillion-dollar summer manses foresee plunging property values due to a 'diminished view.'

There are local organizations around the region doing environmental work (see p79 for some examples). Other local organizations include:

Island Institute (www.islandinstitute.org) Rockland, Maine.

Marine Environmental Research Institute (☎ 207-374-2135; www.meriresearch.org) Blue Hill, Maine.

Society for the Protection of New Hampshire Forests (www.forestsociety.org)

Woods Hole Oceanographic Institute (www.whoi.edu) Woods Hole, Massachusetts.

For more information and volunteer opportunities around the region, contact the following organizations:

Appalachian Mountain Club (☎ 617-523-0655; www.outdoors.org)

Conservation Law Foundation (☎ 617-350-0990; www.clf.org)

Natural Resources Defense Council (☎ 212-727-2700; www.nrdc.org)

Nature Conservancy (☎ 703-841-4850; www.nature.org)

Sierra Club (☎ 415-977-5799; www.sierraclub.org)

Trustees of Reservations (☎ 978-921-1944; www.thetrustees.org)

What Love Can't Do, by Kitty Beer, is a dramatic futuristic account of three generations of women living in a New England wracked by global warming.

New England Outdoors

Rolling hills and rocky peaks; steep slopes covered with snow; rushing rivers and glass-like lakes; windswept beaches and sandy dunes: this is what draws millions of outdoor adventurers to New England.

The White Mountains of New Hampshire and Maine, the Green Mountains in Vermont and the Berkshires in Western Massachusetts are all highpoints for hiking, rock climbing and camping. Thousands of miles of rugged coastline entice travelers with endless sailing, canoeing, sea kayaking, windsurfing, whale-watching and scuba diving opportunities. Hundreds of glacial lakes and pretty ponds provide opportunities for swimming, canoeing, boating, fishing and water-skiing.

Hunting is also a time-honored tradition in New England. Seasons are defined by weapon and/or game and vary by state and locality. Check with a dependable source, such as a hunting shop, the state Fish and Wildlife departments, and tourism bureaus, before setting out.

HIKING & WALKING
Walking

Freud said that sometimes a walk is just a walk; but here in New England, we have walks, and then we have *walks*.

The blissfully undisturbed landscape of Rhode Island's Block Island (p306), dubbed 'one of the last great places in the western hemisphere' by the Nature Conservatory, is perfect for gadding about on foot. Monhegan Island, Maine (p493), is another place to enjoy gorgeous coastal scenery in the absence of cars.

If you like edgier walks, try the famed cliff walks that run along the rocky bluffs in Newport, Rhode Island (p297), or in Ogunquit, Maine (p467). Either way, the ocean surges on one side and mansions rise in grandeur on the other. For a more transcendental stroll, try circling Thoreau's Walden Pond (p139) in Concord, Massachusetts.

Even urban areas enjoy little oases of green, which are perfect for biking, walking or jogging. See p92 for Boston and p477 for Portland.

In the White Mountains of New Hampshire, head to Franconia Notch State Park (p375) to stroll alongside swimming holes carved by glacial meltwater, wind through stands of birch trees in brilliant color and follow the route of the rushing water of the flume. Otherwise, there's a lovely walk in the Lakes Region that starts in Wolfeboro (p436) and skirts the lakes along an old rail line.

Most of New England's state forests, parks and reservations have walking or hiking trails of varying levels of difficulty (see the Parks & Wildlife sections in the introductions to individual state chapters).

Mountain Hiking

You won't go wrong deciding which rearing peaks deserve the effort of lugging your knapsack, backpack or climbing gear. The **Appalachian Trail** (☎ 304-535-6331; www.nps.gov/appa; PO Box 807, Harpers Ferry, WV 25425-0807) runs through all the New England states except for Rhode Island, with plenty of access points all along the way. See p24.

The White Mountains in New Hampshire throw back some of the foulest weather on record, but still draw everyone from day-hikers to ice and rock climbers to multiday technical mountaineers. There are access

New England's paths and peaks – and myriad ways to have fun in them – are detailed at www .mountainwanderer.com.

The *AMC White Mountain Guide* (2003) features the most complete trail information for hiking in New Hampshire; *Hiking Maine* (2002) offers maps and trail information for 72 hikes in the northernmost New England state.

For dramatic photos, weather reports and virtual tours of New England's fiercest peak, browse www.mount washington.org.

points all along the Kancamagus Hwy (p443) and around Crawford Notch (p455) or Pinkham Notch (p457).

New Hampshire's utterly accessible Mt Monadnock (p427) is a 'beginners' mountain,' a relatively easy climb up a bald granite batholith. Much less traveled, Moosilauke Ravine Lodge (p444) offers great views and few crowds on its miles of trails.

Maine's sublimely remote Mt Katahdin (p519) remains relatively untouched by tourism. Those who make it across the infamous 1.1-mile Knife Edge – 3ft wide in places with a sheer, 1500ft drop on both sides – will remember the experience for life. Acadia National Park (p508) and Grafton Notch State Park (p517) have miles of groomed trails for all skill levels.

Vermont's Green Mountains are seamed with hiking trails, particularly Vermont's own end-to-ender, the Long Trail (p371), with both easy and challenging hikes. Many excellent trails radiate out of the Stowe (p395) area, which also sports world-class ice climbing.

Mt Greylock (p272) in the Berkshires of western Massachusetts makes an excellent goal for a day's walk from Williamstown.

ORGANIZED HIKES

The **Appalachian Mountain Club** (AMC; ☎ 617-523-0636; www.outdoors.org; 5 Joy St, Boston, MA 02108) offers great outings in every New England state. **AMC Pinkham Notch Camp** (☎ 603-466-2727; www.outdoors.org; Pinkham Notch, NH 16; ⏰ 6:30am-10pm) in the White Mountains of New Hampshire is an excellent source of information on gear, courses and outings.

CAMPING & BACKPACKING

Camping in New England is safe and plentiful. With common-sense precautions, encounters with bear (no grizzlies here), cranky moose and snakes are unusual. It's the nibbling chipmunks, persistent raccoons and tip-toeing deer that are more common. With generous tracts of woodland, New England has plenty of tent sites, yurts, lean-tos and cabins for everyone from car campers to trekkers.

Huts and primitive campsites line the major mountain trail systems, but these can fill quickly during summer, fall and winter weekends. The Appalachian Mountain Club maintains huts throughout the White Mountains. Other options for camping are along the Kancamagus Hwy (p443), in Franconia Notch State Park (p445) and in Crawford Notch State Park (p456). The cabins and lean-tos in Maine's Baxter State Park (p519) provide nice drive-in sites.

Keep in mind that peaks such as Mt Washington and Mt Katahdin are their own biomes, with vastly different weather between base camp and summit. These peaks are known for thrashing winds and hard-core weather swings. Even in the most civilized of forests, the weather can change swiftly. Bring raingear, plenty of layers of clothing and provisions for more days than you need them in case something happens.

For camping details, see Sleeping sections of regional chapters, and p522.

BIKING & MOUNTAIN BIKING

With thousands of miles of back roads and an increased presence of bike lanes in metropolitan areas, it's safer than ever to cycle through open country and pretty villages, and to explore cities on your own two wheels. Visibility and predictability are the keys to safe city riding, and the more closely you hew to a driver's rules of the road, the better.

Mt Monadnock (3165ft), with 12 trails to the summit affording views of all six New England states, is the world's most-climbed peak.

Dedicated to camping in New England, Around the Campfire (www .aroundthecampfire .homestead.com) includes reviews of campsites, as well as camp songs, games, recipes and scary tales.

Bicycle Touring

Rails-to-Trails (www
.railtrails.org) details all
the nice (mostly) flat
railroad beds that have
been converted to hiking
and biking trails.

From Boston to Lexington, follow part of Paul Revere's midnight ride to the birthplace of the Revolutionary War on the Minuteman Commuter Bikeway (p134). Use *Pocket Rides*, by **Rubel BikeMap** (www.bikemaps.com), to help choose from more than 50 streetwise rides in and around Boston; some feature excellent beach and lighthouse tours. Refer also to p92.

On Cape Cod in Massachusetts, tool around the Cape Cod Canal (p174), Shining Sea Bikeway (p177), the Cape Cod Rail Trail (p188), and the Cape Cod National Seashore bike paths near Provincetown (p205).

In Rhode Island, take a spin on the beautiful 14.5-mile East Bay Bicycle Path (p289), which follows the waterfront out of Providence and weaves past picnic-worthy state parks.

The Burlington Recreation Path (p389) follows the shore of Lake Champlain for 7.5 miles of smooth riding. It links up with the 13-mile Island Line Trail that takes cyclists out to the Colchester causeway. During inn-to-inn excursions (see p375), you can cover the back roads and teeny towns of central Vermont.

Islands are particularly well-suited for great biking. Rent wheels for Block Island (p308), Rhode Island; for the carriage roads of Mt Desert Island (p505), Maine; for the beachy trails of Nantucket (p213) and Martha's Vineyard (p224 and p227), Massachusetts; and for the long loop around Isleboro, Maine (p496).

One of the best companies that offers bicycle-touring packages and excursions is Bike Vermont (p375).

Mountain Biking

The New England Moun-
tain Biking Association
(www.nemba.org) is a
wealth of information
about places to ride, trail
conditions and ways to
connect with other riders.

Fire roads, snowmobile trails and hairy drops at ski areas are fair game for mountain bikers. New England embraces the sport more and more each year as resorts and private facilities add miles of single-track to their offerings. Foliage season is prime time for gallivanting through psychedelic forests. Springtime thaws in April and early May are recuperative times for the trails, freshly exposed after a long winter's nap. Local bike shops will gladly reveal their favorite haunts.

In Stowe (p398), Vermont, the hills are alive with whoops and hollers as riders roam the slopes on some of the most challenging terrain around. Several shops rent wheels.

The Loon Mountain ski area (p444) of New Hampshire zooms daredevils up the mountain in a handy gondola for a white-knuckle, tooth-rattling trip back down. As usual, ask their bike shop dudes for the lowdown on cool local rides.

Western Maine's Bethel Outdoor Adventure & Campground (p517) will set your wheels in motion in that stunning countryside, home of the Sunday River Ski Area.

ROCK CLIMBING

Ropes used in mountain
and ice climbing can hold
up to 6000lb of weight.

New Hampshire is known as 'the granite state,' a big clue that there's going to be great climbing somewhere nearby, no matter where you are. The same goes for much of the rest of New England, which is crammed with ledges and giant glacial erratics – huge boulders left by receding glaciers, seemingly apropos of nothing. Bring your crash pad, your rack and your climbing buddy and trawl the local gear shops and climbing walls, and you'll find someone to deliver the beta on the local climbing scene.

In New Hampshire, Cathedral Ledge (p451) is probably the most famous rock- and ice-climbing spot in New England. On any given day, climbers can be seen inching up its face. While beginners are literally learning the ropes, seasoned climbers rope up and climb onward and upward.

In North Conway the **International Mountain Climbing School** (☎ 603-356-7064; www.ime-usa.com) offers mountaineering and ice- and rock-climbing courses and outings, as does the Eastern Mountain Sports Climbing School (p451).

In Stowe, Vermont, hook up at the Inn at Turner Mill (p399) with inn-keeper and veteran climber Greg Speer for area guidance on the swaths of world-class rock- and ice-climbing pitches.

Acadia National Park (p509) offers dramatic routes on cliffs that rise straight up out of the pitching sea. Acadia Mountain Guides climbing school in Bar Harbor (p509) offers climbing and mountaineering trips, courses and clinics. Remote Mt Katahdin (p519), in the state's interior, offers an alpine feel with long routes.

SWIMMING & SAILING

The ocean never really heats up in New England, but that doesn't stop hoards of hardy Yankees from spilling onto the beaches and into the sea on hot summer days. But it's not just the Atlantic where heels can be cooled. Thanks to a mile-high glacier that covered New England about 30,000 years ago, New England is blessed with a generous scattering of crystal-clear lakes and rivers; surely it's the swimming-hole capital of the world.

For accurate, locally derived information on surfing in New England, visit www.nesurf.com.

Protected from the arctic currents, Rhode Island's beaches tend to be the warmest, particularly at Block Island (p308) and Newport (p300).

Plum Island (p161), just barely off the coast of Massachusetts, offers a nice combination of dunes, a wide beach and a wildlife sanctuary harboring more than 800 species of plants and wildlife. In Ipswich, Crane Beach (p159) is a wonderful, pristine stretch of sand in the heart of a wildlife refuge, with trails traversing its dunes. Beaches on Cape Cod, Nantucket and Martha's Vineyard are legendary. Bring your surfboard and hang ten at Good Harbor (p158) and Long Beach in Gloucester.

New Hampshire's short coastline is hemmed in with condos, but Rye Beach (p417) is an old favorite, drawing crowds from all corners.

Maine has a scattering of coastal beaches, including Ogunquit (p467), Kennebunkport (p469) and Bar Harbor (p503).

Lakes and rivers are great fun for a dip, from the serpentine Saco River that runs alongside the Kancamagus Hwy (p443) in New Hampshire to a dozen spots along the Cascade Trail in Franconia Notch State Park (p445). Rangeley Lake (p518) in Maine and New Hampshire's Lake Winnipesaukee (p432) are two of New England's largest inland lakes; the former is quite isolated, but the latter is bursting with resorts, shops and services.

In Vermont, the West River, which runs southeast from Londonderry to Brattleboro (p357), and the Battenkill, which runs south from Manchester (p369), offer many spots where locals come to frolic.

For maritime sails, options are wonderfully varied: pluck lobster from their traps on a boat out of Ogunquit (p467), Maine; hop aboard a research vessel out of Norwalk (p336), Connecticut, and learn about the inhabitants of the sea. Inherit the wind aboard a windjammer out of Camden (p497), Maine, or a 19th-century-style schooner in Mystic (p321), Connecticut. Holler 'thar she blows' from whale-watching boats that depart from Gloucester (p154), Provincetown (p205), Boston (p84) and Plymouth (p166), all in Massachusetts.

FISHING

In addition to its renown for deep-sea fishing, New England has become a true fly-fishing destination. Because of the famous Orvis (p370) and LL Bean

The angler's guide to New England is on-line at www.onthewater.com.

SKIING & SNOWBOARDING

New England has no shortage of snow. And there is no better way to enjoy it than to strap on some skis. These days, the downhill variety takes all forms, including free-heeling telemarking and snowboarding. Nordic skiing – whether racing, backcountry or recreational – is equally popular. Whatever your mode for enjoying the gravity of the situation, here are some top locations to savor the snow.

Killington Ski Area Known throughout New England for the earliest and latest runs of the season due to the unbelievably extensive snowmaking apparatuses here. With 200 runs on seven mountains, lifts with heated cars and top-notch facilities, the area works hard to earn its high ticket price. The steepest mogul field in the east, acres of glades and miles of cross-country trails are pure heaven for snow sportsters. See p378.

- Nearest town: Killington, Vermont
- One-day lift ticket: $76-79
- Information: ☎ 802-422-3261, 800-621-6867; www.killington.com

Mad River Glen The motto here is: 'ski it if you can.' Proud of its proletarian roots, this rough-and-ready spot still sports one of the country's last single-chair chairlifts, refuses admittance to boarders and offers some of the most exhilarating, hard-core skiing around. Every year, in March or April, the place explodes with telemark skiers for one of the oldest telemark festivals in the country. See p384.

- Nearest town: Waitsfield, Vermont
- One-day lift ticket: $35-56
- Information: ☎ 802-496-3551; www.madriverglen.com

Gunstock Ski Area This is one of the sweetest, family-style resorts in New England. Most trails in this area are intermediate, though there are some advanced trails that are nice and hair-raising. Tubing trails are a delight, as are the 30 miles of cross-country trails that pass through beautiful forests. See p433.

- Nearest town: Gilford, New Hampshire
- One-day lift ticket: $49-59
- Information: ☎ 802-496-3551, 800-gunstock; www.gunstock.com

(p484) fly-fishing schools in Vermont and Maine, respectively, and because of an abundance of rivers, lakes and ocean.

Manchester, Vermont, has become a fly-fishing mecca because of the trout-sweetened Batten Kill River and Orvis, the granddaddy of the craft with a retail store, rod-building workshop and the American Museum of Fly Fishing (p370).

Connecticut's Housatonic Meadows State Park (p352) has a two-mile stretch of the Housatonic River set aside exclusively for fly-fishing. Head for the Mountain Goat (p270) in the Berkshires for fly-fishing gear and the best advice on where to use it.

On Block Island (p308), charter a boat and bring back a marlin, or try your luck off Rockport (p156) or Plymouth (p166), Massachusetts. Opportunities abound in Orleans (p194), where Cape Cod's largest charter fishing fleet is docked.

Maine might as well be fishing heaven with isolated lakes and wild rivers everywhere. It also has a sturdy tradition of excellent guides and pontoon-plane access for some of the most exquisite locations, especially the centrally located Moosehead Lake (p519) region.

When engaging in cold-weather outdoor activities, sprinkle your socks with hot-pepper powder to keep your feet warm

Sunday River Ski Resort Zigzagging across the face of eight peaks can take all day. From the top, you can almost hear its namesake whispering through the valley – and yet you'll also be surrounded with every possible luxury in the lodges, spas and condos below. See p517.

■ Nearest town: Bethel, Maine

■ One-day lift ticket: $67

■ Information: ☎ 207-824-3000; www.sundayriver.com

Sugarloaf Maine's second-highest peak, Sugarloaf resort, is a 4237ft beauty with 54 miles of trails. The lift goes above the tree-line, so the views from the summit are expansive and spectacular. Black diamond skiers will scoot down the steep slopes of Central Mountain and jump to the bumpy, natural terrain at King Pine Bowl. See p518.

■ Nearest town: Kingfield, Maine

■ One-day life ticket: $64

■ Information: ☎ 207-237-2000; www.sugarloaf.com

Stowe This place hosts the largest connected cross-country ski trail network in the East and its downhill trails are pretty extensive too. The upper trail system, situated at 2100ft with fabulous views, is great for snowshoeing as well. Stowe (the town) is completely given over to Stowe (the mountain) in the winter. See p397.

■ Nearest town: Stowe, Vermont

■ One-day lift ticket: $79-84; cross-country: $17-19

■ Information: ☎ 800-253-4754, 802-253-3000; www.stowe.com

Craftsbury Outdoor Center Located in the wooded hills of the Northeast Kingdom, Craftsbury sports 50 miles of groomed trails where families cruise, speedy skate-skiers whoosh and back-country skiers ply the additional 30 miles of ungroomed trails. This is one of the most renowned cross-country ski centers in the country with a decidedly international draw. See p404.

■ Nearest town: Craftsbury, Vermont

■ One-day lift ticket: $16

■ Information: ☎ 802-586-7767; www.craftsbury.com

At the northern tip of New Hampshire's brief seacoast, find a sweet, hidden spot at Odiorne Point State Park (p417), or head for the high seas out of Hampton Beach (p417). For excellent salmon fishing, head inland to the Lakes Region (p432).

CANOEING, KAYAKING & RAFTING

You'll see more kayaks and canoes atop cars speeding down the byways of New England than you can shake a paddle at. The coast and inland areas are thick with kayaking opportunities for serious sea-kayakers or Sunday-afternoon duffers.

The region's enormous inland lakes – such as Vermont's Champlain (p389), New Hampshire's Winnipesauke (p437), and Maine's Moosehead (p519) – create their own, swift-moving weather patterns, wild currents and swells that challenge the technique, navigational skills and adrenaline demands of expert kayakers. The key is getting the lowdown on local tides, currents and weather prognostications from the locals themselves. Local boat purveyors always have tide charts and advice you would do well to heed.

The Maine islands are great fun to thread through and, when the water is frisky, sea kayakers love playing in the rolling chop. LL Bean (p484) in Freeport will set you up with a boat, tours, lessons and a list of prime locations for beginners and experts alike. Or ferry out from Casco Bay (p477) to Peaks Island for a frolic. Paddle past ospreys, eagles and bear (oh my!) at Sears Island (p498), just outside of Bath. Wiggle through cranberry bogs or swing with the swells just off Acadia National Park (p509).

Heading into the remote Maine woods to go canoeing, dogsledding, fishing, ice climbing or kayaking? Locate an expert through www .maineguides.com.

The Sakonnet River in Rhode Island feeds into the sea, with estuaries for recreational kayakers and big swells with big fish for experts. Meanwhile, you can serenely paddle between interconnected salt ponds on Block Island (p308), communing with the land, sea and sky.

Plum Island (p161), north of Boston, is a sweet spot for all levels, rife with seals and birds galore. Watch the tides, though, or you'll be dragging your yak through sneaker-sucking mud and scootching across sandbars at low tide.

The Norwalk Islands (p337) off the coast of Connecticut are a half-mile out and make for a nice, watery ramble.

The Deerfield River (p258) in the Berkshires of Massachusetts gives a thrilling ride. For one of the best floats, with a slow but steady current and some slight riffles, paddle down Vermont's Battenkill (p368) from Bennington.

Boston

The Cradle of Liberty. The Hub of the Universe. The Athens of America. These are big words for a mid-sized city. But Boston lives up to them. With its rich history, grand architecture and world-renowned academic and cultural institutions, the city retains and radiates the glory it has garnered over the last four centuries.

It all started with the Puritans, who set out in search of religious freedom and founded Boston as their 'shining city on a hill.' In the following century the Sons of Liberty caroused and rabble-roused until the colonies found themselves in the midst of a War for Independence. A hundred years later it was Boston's poets and philosophers who were leading a cultural revolution – pushing progressive causes like abolitionism, feminism and transcendentalism.

Today's Boston is among the country's most forward-thinking and barrier-breaking cities. This is most evident politically, as Boston is at the forefront of controversial issues like same-sex marriage and universal healthcare. It's also visible in the changing landscape of the city, as it is now home to some of the country's most cutting-edge architecture and innovative urban planning projects. Culturally, Boston is shedding its staid and stodgy reputation as artists, literati, thespians and filmmakers rediscover the city's rich resources and create new ones.

No single element has influenced the city so profoundly as its educational institutions. Their scholars, scientists, philosophers and writers have thrived on and contributed to the city's evolution. Contemporary Boston is no exception, drawing students from around the world who serve as a renewable source of cultural and intellectual energy.

HIGHLIGHTS

- Exploring Fort Warren, picking berries, swimming and sunbathing on the **Boston Harbor Islands** (p84)
- Admiring the artistic and architectural innovation at the new **ICA** (p85)
- Bargaining for trash and treasures at the **South End Open Market** (p122)
- Saving room for a cannoli or gelato after dinner in the Italian **North End** (p106)
- Packing a picnic and settling in for a free outdoor concert at the **Charles River Esplanade** (p86)

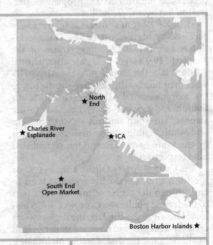

★ North End

★ Charles River Esplanade

★ ICA

★ South End Open Market

Boston Harbor Islands ★

- TELEPHONE CODE: 617
- POPULATION: 597,000
- AREA: 48 SQ MILES

CLIMATE

Here's a promise: at least once during your visit to Boston somebody will say 'If you don't like the weather, wait a minute!' With the ocean to the east and mountains to the north and west, Boston's weather is subject to extremes.

Besides the day-to-day (or minute-to-minute) fluctuations, Boston enjoys wonderful seasonal variations. Spring brings temperate weather and blooming trees, usually in April. This mild weather often lasts until mid-June, but it is also accompanied by plenty of rain. July and August are hot and humid, with temperatures ranging from 68°F to 75°F.

Autumn is Boston's most glorious season. Weather usually remains warm throughout September, while cooler temperatures in October bring out the colorful foliage. Winter lasts too long for most people's tastes, stretching from December to April. During this period, visitors can expect temperatures between 28° and 38°F and plenty of snow.

ORIENTATION

For a city of its stature, Boston is geographically small and logistically manageable. The sights and activities of principal interest to travelers are contained within an area that's only about 1 mile wide by 3 miles long. It's bounded on the eastern edge by Boston Harbor and the Atlantic Ocean, on the north by the Charles River and Cambridge. Boston proper has almost 600,000 people; 'greater' Boston has over three million.

Most of Boston's attractions are easily accessed by Massachusetts Bay Transportation Authority (MBTA) subway trains, or 'the T' (see p129). To get to Logan International Airport, take the Blue Line to the Airport T-stop, then hop on the fast, free shuttle bus to the terminal; or take the Red Line to South Station and ride the Silver Line bus to the airport. The train stations – North Station and South Station – have dedicated T-stops by the same name (Green/Orange and Red Line respectively).

The Central Artery (also known as I-93 or the John F Fitzgerald Expressway) used to cut through the center of the city. As a part of the largest public works project in US history, known as the Big Dig, the highway was recently widened and rerouted underground to alleviate the persistent traffic nightmares. Closed roads and construction are now giving way to parks and open space known as the Rose Kennedy Greenway. In any case, Boston is much easier to navigate on foot than by car, especially during busy traffic times.

Downtown streets are winding, one way and narrow, especially in the oldest part of the city. Expect to get a bit lost as you wander around Downtown Crossing, the Italian North End and Brahmin Beacon Hill. Abutting downtown, the area of Beacon Hill is bounded by Cambridge and Beacon Sts and extends west to the Charles River. Two large parks – the Boston Common and Public Garden – lie adjacent to it to the south.

Back Bay, created thanks to a mid-19th-century landfill project, is more orderly than the rest of the city. Its streets are laid out east to west in alphabetical order: Arlington, Berkeley, Clarendon and so on to Hereford. Commonwealth Ave (referred to as 'Comm Ave') is Boston's grandest boulevard, with a grassy promenade running the length of it. The Back Bay ends at Massachusetts Ave (known simply as 'Mass Ave'), which runs northwest across the Charles River and into Cambridge and Harvard Sq.

West of Massachusetts Ave lies Kenmore Sq and the Fenway. The Fenway includes a 4-mile-long grassy byway that weaves through the city. South of Back Bay is, appropriately, the South End. It lies between Berkeley St in the east and Massachusetts Ave in the west, with Huntington and Shawmut Aves defining its northern and southern boundaries.

The Charles River, with a popular grassy esplanade along both its banks, separates Boston and Cambridge, the latter home to Harvard University and Massachusetts Institute of Technology (MIT). The best views of the Boston skyline and Beacon Hill are from the northern banks of the Charles River near the Longfellow Bridge.

INFORMATION
Bookstores

Calamus Bookstore (Map pp72-3; ☎ 617-338-1931; www.calamusbooks.com; 92B South St; ☷ 9am-7pm Mon-Sat, noon-6pm Sun; ☻ South Station) Boston's biggest and best LGBT bookstore, hosting author talks, art exhibits and other community events.

The Coop (Harvard Cooperative Society; Map p78; ☎ 617-499-2000; 1400 Massachusetts Ave; ☷ 9am-10pm Mon-Sat, 10am-9pm Sun; ☻ Harvard) Three floors of books, music and every other 'essential' item a student

MASSACHUSETTS

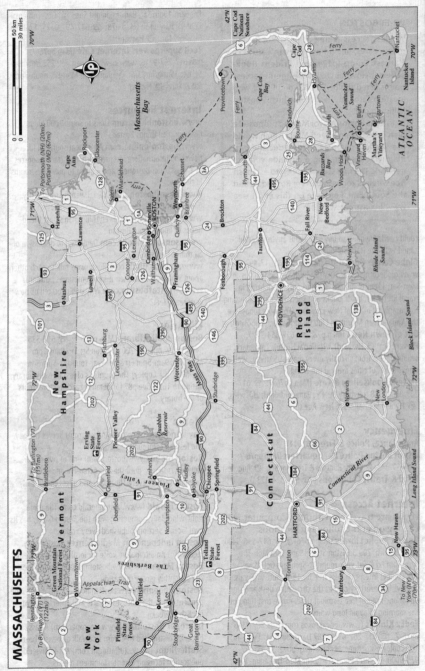

WI-FI BOSTON

Wireless access is free at most hotels and many cafés, including **Darwin's** (p111), **Harvest Co-op** (p124) and **Trident Booksellers** (below), as well as the internet access points listed (below). For a long list of wi-fi locations around the city, see http://boston .wifimug.org.

In 2006 Boston Mayor Menino proposed a plan called 'Main Streets WiFi', which would use wireless technology to bridge the digital divide by installing a citywide wireless network. The first step has been to establish free wireless zones in parts of Roslindale and the South End. For more on this effort, see www.mainstreetswifi.com.

could need. Anyone can buy just about anything emblazoned with the Harvard logo.

Globe Corner Bookstore (Map p78; ☎ 617-497-6277; www.globecorner.com; 90 Mt Auburn St; ☺ 9:30am-9pm Mon-Sat, 11am-6pm Sun; ◉ Harvard) Specializing in travel literature, guide books and specialty maps, including topographical maps of New England. (For more topos, see the Appalachian Mountain Club Headquarters, opposite).

Out of Town News (Map p78; ☎ 617-354-7777; Harvard Sq; ◉ Harvard) A National Historic Landmark, selling papers from virtually every major US city, as well as from dozens of cities around the world.

Trident Booksellers & Cafe (Map pp76-7; ☎ 617-267-8688; 338 Newbury St; ☺ 9am-midnight; 🖳 wi-fi; ◉ Hynes) Specializes in New Age titles.

Emergency

Ambulance, Police & Fire (☎ 911)
City of Boston Police Headquarters (Map pp76-7; ☎ 617-343-4200; cnr Ruggles & Tremont Sts; ◉ Ruggles)
Road & Traffic Conditions (☎ 617-374-1234)

Internet Access

If you are traveling without a computer, you can log on at the following locations:
Boston Public Library (Map pp76-7; ☎ 617-536-5400; www.bpl.org; 700 Boylston St; ☺ 9am-9pm Mon-Thu, 9am-5pm Fri & Sat year-round, 1-5pm Sun Oct-May; ◉ Copley) Internet access free for 15-minute intervals. Or get a visitor courtesy card at the circulation desk and sign up for one hour of free terminal time. Arrive first thing in the morning to avoid long waits.
FedEx Kinko's (www.fedexkinkos.com) Back Bay (Map pp76-7; ☎ 617-262-6188; 187 Dartmouth St; ☺ 24hr; ◉ Copley); Government Center (Map pp72-3; ☎ 617-973-9000; 2 Center Plaza; ☺ 24hr Mon-Thu, 6am-10pm

Fri, 6am-10pm Sat, 8am-midnight Sun; 🚇 Government Center); Harvard Sq (Map p78; ☎ 617-497-0125; 1 Mifflin Pl; ☺ 24hr; ◉ Harvard)
Tech Superpowers Internet Café (Map pp76-7; ☎ 617-267-9716; www.newburyopen.net; 252 Newbury St; per 15min/hr $3/5; ☺ 9am-8pm Mon-Fri, noon-7pm Sat & Sun; ◉ Hynes)

Internet Resources

www.bostonblogs.com Links to some 1000 blogs discussing all things Boston.
www.boston-online.com An offbeat source of local news and information; includes such important resources as a glossary of Bostonese and a guide to public restrooms in the city.
www.cityofboston.gov Official website for the city government.
www.dogboston.com Everything man's best friend needs to know about Boston
www.sonsofsamhorn.com Dedicated to discussion of all things Red Sox.
www.universalhub.com Bostonians talk to each other about whatever is on their mind (sometimes nothing).
www.worstofboston.com Why don't you tell us how your really feel?

Libraries

Boston Public Library (Map pp76-7; ☎ 617-536-5400; www.bpl.org; 700 Boylston St; ☺ 9am-9pm Mon-Thu, 9am-5pm Fri & Sat year-round, 1-5pm Sun Oct-May; ◉ Copley) The country's oldest free city library, dating to 1852. See p87 for details of architectural tours of the library.

Media

Bay Windows (www.baywindows.com) Serves the gay and lesbian community.
Boston Globe (www.boston.com) One of two major daily newspapers; publishes an extensive and useful Calendar section every Thursday, and a less useful daily *Sidekick*.
Boston Herald (www.bostonherald.com) The more right-wing daily, competing with the *Boston Globe;* has its own 'Scene' section, published every Friday.
Boston Independent Media Center (boston.indy media.org) An alternative voice for local news and events.
Boston Magazine (www.bostonmagazine.com) The city's monthly glossy magazine.
Boston Phoenix (www.bostonphoenix.com) A free independent paper that focuses on arts and entertainment; published weekly.
Improper Bostonian (www.improper.com) A sassy biweekly distributed free from sidewalk dispenser boxes.
Stuff@Night (www.stuffatnight.com) A free biweekly publication focusing on entertainment events.

Medical Services & Pharmacies

In case of a medical emergency, the failsafe response is to go to the emergency room at any local hospital, where staff are required to treat everyone that shows up. Unfortunately, if your life is not threatened, ER waits can be excruciating long and the cost is exorbitant. Therefore, the ER should be reserved for true emergencies.

CVS Pharmacy Government Center (Map pp72-3; ☎ 617-523-3653; 2 Center Plaza; ⏱ 6am-7pm Mon-Fri, 9am-6pm Sat & Sun; ⊕ Government Center); Harvard (Map p78; ☎ 617-354-4420; 1446 Massachusetts Ave, Cambridge; ⏱ 24hr; ⊕ Harvard); Newbury St (Map pp76-7; ☎ 617-236-4007; 240 Newbury St; ⏱ 7am-midnight; ⊕ Hynes)

Massachusetts General Hospital (MGH; Map pp72-3; ☎ 617-726-2000; 55 Fruit St; ⊕ Charles/MGH) Arguably the city's biggest and best; can refer you to smaller clinics and crisis hotlines.

MGH Traveler's Clinic (Map pp72-3; ☎ 617-724-1934; Cox Bldg, 5th fl, cnr Blossom & Charles Sts; ⏱ 4:30-7:30pm Mon, 8:30am-5pm Tue, 8:30-11:30am Wed, 12:30-3pm Thu, 8:30am-12:30pm Fri; ⊕ Charles/MGH) Offers immunization services.

Money

There are Cirrus and Plus ATMs all around the city. Not all banks will exchange foreign currency, but the following full-service branches do:

Bank of America (☎ 800-841-4000) Copley Sq (Map pp76-7; 557 Boylston St; ⊕ Copley); Downtown (Map pp72-3; 100 Federal St; ⊕ Downtown Crossing); Government Center (Map pp72-3; ⊕ Government Center); Harvard Sq (Map p78; ☎ 877-353-3939; 1414 Massachusetts Ave, Cambridge; ⊕ Harvard); Kenmore Sq (Map pp76-7; 540 Commonwealth Ave; ⊕ Kenmore)

Post

Boston's **main post office** (Map pp72-3; ☎ 800-275-8777; 25 Dorchester Ave; ⏱ 24hr; ⊕ South Station) is just one block southeast of South Station. Mail can be sent to you here marked c/o General Delivery, Boston, MA 02205, USA. Post offices are generally open from 8am to 5pm weekdays and 9am to 3pm on Saturday, but it all depends on the branch. Some convenient branches:

Back Bay (Map pp76-7; ☎ 617-267-8162; 800 Boylston St, Prudential Center; ⏱ 8am-7pm Mon-Fri, 8am-2pm Sat; ⊕ Prudential)

Beacon Hill (Map pp72-3; ☎ 617-723-1951; 136 Charles St; ⏱ 8am-5:30pm Mon-Fri, 8am-noon Sat; ⊕ Charles/MGH)

Harvard Sq (Map p78; 125 Mt Auburn St; ⏱ 7:30am-6:30pm Mon-Fri, 7:30am-3:30pm Sat; ⊕ Harvard)

Toilets

There are new-fangled self-cleaning toilets near several of Boston's tourist spots, including Faneuil Hall, the New England Aquarium, the Boston Public Library and Constitution Pier. The toilets will cost you a quarter, but when they work, it's worth it! For an online guide to public restrooms (including cleanliness ratings) in Boston, see www.boston online.com/restrooms.html. Some restrooms that receive a four-roll rating:

Borders Bookstore (p122; Cambridgeside Galleria Mall)
Charles Hotel (p103; Harvard Sq)
Lenox Hotel (p101; Back Bay)
Mary Baker Eddy Library (p87; Back Bay)

Tourist Information

Appalachian Mountain Club Headquarters (AMC; Map pp72-3; ☎ 617-523-0636; www.outdoors.org; 5 Joy St; ⏱ 8:30am-5pm Mon-Fri; ⊕ Park St) The resource for outdoor activities in Boston and throughout New England.

Boston Common Information Kiosk (Map pp72-3; ☎ 617-426-3115; Tremont & West Sts; ⏱ 8:30am-5pm; ⊕ Park St)

Cambridge Visitor Information Booth (Map p78; ☎ 617-441-2884, 800-862-5678; www.cambridge-usa .org; Harvard Sq; ⏱ 9am-5pm Mon-Sat, 1-5pm Sun; ⊕ Harvard) Detailed information on current Cambridge happenings and self-guided walking tours.

Greater Boston Convention & Visitors Bureau (GBCVB; off Map pp72-3; ☎ 617-536-4100, 800-888-5515; www.bostonusa.com; 2 Copley Place, Suite 105, Boston, MA 02116) Write in advance for an information pack.

Massachusetts Office of Travel & Tourism (Map pp72-3; ☎ 617-973-8500, 800-227-6277; www.massvacation.com, State Transportation Bldg, 10 Park Plaza, Suite 4510, Boston, MA 02116; ⏱ 9am-5pm Mon-Fri; ⊕ Boylston)

National Park Service Visitor Center (NPS; Map pp72-3; ☎ 617-242-5642; 15 State St; ⏱ 9am-5pm; ⊕ State) Plenty of historical literature, a short slide show and free walking tours of the Freedom Trail (see p94).

Prudential Center Visitor Center (Map pp76-7; 800 Boylston St; ⏱ 9am-6pm; ⊕ Prudential)

DANGERS & ANNOYANCES

As with most big US cities, there are run-down sections of Boston in which crime is a problem. These are primarily in Roxbury, Mattapan and Dorchester (where tourist attractions are limited). Parts of the South End border Roxbury: avoid walking around in areas southeast of Washington St and southwest of

BOSTON

BOSTON IN...

Two Days

Spend one day reliving revolutionary history by following the **Freedom Trail** (p94). Take time to lounge on the **Boston Common** (below), peek in the **Old State House** (p80) and visit the **Paul Revere House** (p81). Afterwards, stroll back into the **North End** (p106) for dinner at an atmospheric Italian restaurant. On your second day, pack a picnic, rent a bike and ride along the **Charles River Route** (p92). Go as far as **Harvard Square** (p91) to cruise the campus and browse the bookstores.

Four Days

Follow the two-day itinerary then, on your third day, head out to the **Harbor Islands** (p84) to visit **Fort Warren** (p84) or go berry picking on **Grape Island** (p84). Spend your last day discovering **Back Bay** (p86). Window-shop and gallery-hop on **Newbury St** (p86), go to the top of the **Prudential Center** (p87) and browse the **Boston Public Library** (p87).

One Week

If you have a week to spare, you can see all the sights listed in the two previous itineraries, plus you have time to peruse the impressive American collection at the **Museum of Fine Arts** (p88), catch a **Red Sox game** (p121) and tour the **Massachusetts State House** (p75).

Massachusetts Ave after dark. You might find a few vestiges of skankiness along Washington and Essex Sts in Chinatown, where one or two X-rated shops are hanging on by the thread of a G-string. Avoid parks such as Franklin Park and the Back Bay Fens after dark. The same goes for streets and subway stations that are otherwise empty of people.

SIGHTS
Beacon Hill & Boston Common

When the local news reports the day's events 'on Beacon Hill' it's usually referring to goings-on in the Massachusetts State House, the focal point of politics in the Commonwealth, the building famously dubbed 'the hub of the solar system.' The State House is an impressive jewel that crowns Beacon Hill; but that is not what makes this neighborhood the most prestigious in Boston.

Perhaps what makes Beacon Hill is its history, as this enclave has been home to centuries of great thinkers. In the 19th century it was the site of literary salons and publishing houses, as well as the center of the abolitionist movement.

Or perhaps the appeal of Beacon Hill is the utter loveliness of the place: the narrow cobblestone streets lit with gas lanterns; the distinguished brick townhouses decked with purple windowpanes and blooming flowerboxes. These residential streets are reminiscent of London, and streets such as stately

Louisburg Square capture the grandeur that was intended. Or perhaps it is the charm of **Charles Street**, the commercial street that traverses the flat of the hill.

BOSTON COMMON

The 50-acre Boston Common (Map pp72–3) is the country's oldest public park. If you have any doubt, refer to the plaque emblazoned with the words of the treaty between Governor Winthrop and William Blaxton, who sold the land for £30 in 1634. The Common occupies a pentagonal swathe of land between Beacon Hill, Downtown and the Theater District, accessible by two T-stops: Park St at the northern end and Boylston at the southern end.

The Common has served many purposes over the years, including as a campground for British troops during the American Revolution and as green grass for cattle grazing until 1830. Although there is still a grazing ordinance on the books, the Common today serves picnickers, sunbathers and people-watchers. In winter the **Frog Pond** attracts ice skaters (p93), while summer draws theater lovers for **Free Shakespeare on the Common** (☎ 617-532-1252; www.freeshakespeare.org; admission free) for a week in July.

For a free tour of the Boston Common and the Public Garden, inquire at the information kiosk (p69).

(Continued on page 75)

METROPOLITAN BOSTON

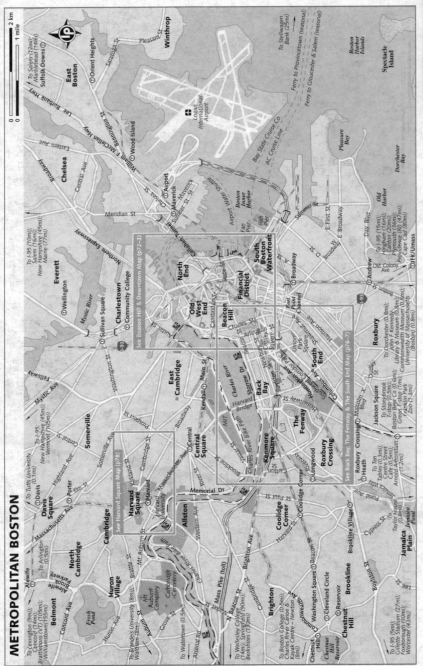

BOSTON

BEACON HILL & DOWNTOWN

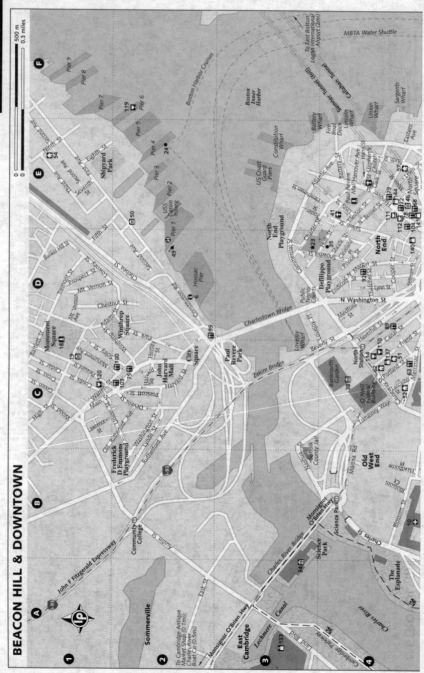

500 m
0.3 miles

MBTA Water Shuttle

To East Boston/
Logan International
Airport (2m)

Boston Harbor Cruises

Boston
Inner
Harbor

Sargents
Wharf

Union
Wharf

Eastern
Ave

Lincoln
Wharf

Battery
Wharf

Fire
Boat
Dock

Condition Wharf

US Coast
Guard
Piers

Pier 9
Pier 8
Pier 7
Pier 6
Pier 5
Pier 4
Pier 3
Pier 2
Pier 1

Shipyard
Park

Ninth St
Eighth St
Seventh St
Fifth St

Second Ave
Third Ave

North End

Hoosac
Pier

North
End
Playground

DeFillipo
Playground

N Washington St

Charlestown Bridge

Paul
Revere
Park

Zakim Bridge

Lovejoy
Wharf

North
Station

Banknorth
Garden

O'Neill
Federal
Building

Old
West
End

Monument
Square

Winthrop
Square

Chestnut St

City
Square

John Harvard
Mall

Frederick
D Emmons
Playground

Rutherford Ave

Community
College

Charlestown

Sommerville

John F Fitzgerald Expressway

To Cambridge Antique
Market Shop (0.1mi);
Charles River
Boat Co (0.5mi)

East
Cambridge

Lechmere

Science
Park

The
Esplanade

Charles River

Cambridge Parkway

Charles River Bridge

Monsignor O'Brien Hwy

Science Park

Suffolk
County Jail

Beverly St

Nashua St

Lomasney Way

Martha Rd

Blossom St

Staniford St

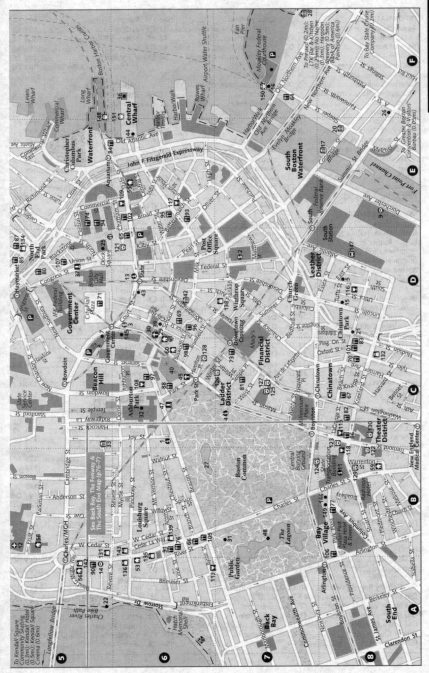

BOSTON

(Continued from page 70)

PUBLIC GARDEN

The Public Garden (Map pp72–3) is a 24-acre botanical oasis of Victorian flowerbeds, verdant grass and weeping willows shading a tranquil lagoon. Until it was filled in the early 19th century it was (like the rest of Back Bay) a tidal salt marsh. Now, at any time of year, it is an island of loveliness, awash in seasonal blooms, gold-toned leaves or untrammeled snow.

Taking a ride on the **Swan Boats** (Map pp72-3; ☎ 617-522-1966; www.swanboats.com; adult/senior/child $2.75/2/1.25; ♥ 10am–4pm mid-Apr–mid-Sep; ♿) ; ◉ Arlington) in the lagoon has been a Boston tradition since 1877. And don't miss the famous statue **Make Way for Ducklings**, based on the characters in the beloved book by Robert McKloskey.

MASSACHUSETTS STATE HOUSE

High atop Beacon Hill, Massachusetts leaders and legislators attempt to turn their ideas into concrete policies and practices within the golden-domed **State House** (Map pp72-3; ☎ 617-727-3676; www.sec.state.ma.us; cnr Beacon & Bowdoin Sts; admission free; ♥ 9am-5pm, tours 10am-4pm Mon-Fri; ◉ Park). Charles Bulfinch designed the commanding state capitol building, but it was Oliver Wendell Holmes who first dubbed it 'the hub of the solar system' (thus earning Boston the nickname 'the Hub').

Knowledgeable 'Doric Docents' lead free 40-minute tours covering the history, artworks, architecture and political personalities, as well as a visit to the legislative chambers when it's in session.

Across the street on the corner of Beacon and Park Sts, the **Robert Gould Shaw Memorial** (Map pp72–3) honors the white Civil War commander of the 54th Massachusetts Regiment, the African American unit celebrated in the film *Glory*.

MUSEUM OF AFRO-AMERICAN HISTORY

Beacon Hill was never the exclusive domain of blue-blood Brahmins. Waves of immigrants, and especially African Americans, free from slavery, settled here in the 19th century. Housed in the old African Meeting House and the Abiel Smith School, the **Museum of Afro-American History** (Map pp72-3; ☎ 617-725-0022; www.afroammuseum.org; 46 Joy St; suggested donation $5; ♥ 10am-4pm Mon-Sat; ◉ Park) offers exhibits on Boston's African American roots, as well as an extensive library and interactive computer kiosks. In honor of the bicentennial of

the African Meeting House, in 2007 the museum announced a renovation and expansion project that will allow for the opening of a nearby education center in the coming years.

The **Black Heritage Trail** is a 1.6-mile walking tour that explores this history further. See p97 for details.

Downtown

It's hard to tell that this area was once the domain of cows. The 17th-century well-trodden paths eventually gave rise to the maze of streets occupied by today's high-rises. But the remnants of Colonial architecture are vivid reminders that this is where Boston grew up.

Although vestiges of 17th-century Boston are not uncommon in this part of town, the atmosphere of these streets is hardly historic. Downtown is a bustling commercial center, its streets lined with department stores and smaller shops.

The Freedom Trail cuts through Downtown, highlighting the historic spots from the 17th and 18th centuries (see p94). But this neighborhood is all about commerce in the 21st century; and you won't need to follow the redbrick road to find it.

PARK ST CHURCH & GRANARY BURYING GROUND

Shortly after the construction of **Park St Church** (Map pp72-3; ☎ 617-523-3383; www.parkstreet.org; 1 Park St; ♥ 9:30am-3:30pm Tue-Sat Jul & Aug; ◉ Park), powder for the war of 1812 was stored in the basement, earning this location the moniker 'Brimstone Corner.' But that was hardly the most inflammatory event that took place here. Noted for its graceful, 217ft steeple, this Boston landmark has been hosting historic lectures and musical performances since its founding. In 1829 William Lloyd Garrison railed against slavery from the church's pulpit. And on Independence Day in 1831 Samuel Francis Smith's hymn 'America' (My Country 'Tis of Thee) was first sung. These days, Park St is a conservative congregational church.

Dating to 1660, the adjacent **Granary Burying Ground** (Map pp72-3; ☎ 617-635-4505; Tremont St; admission free; ♥ 9am-5pm; ◉ Park) is crammed with historic headstones, many with evocative – if not creepy – carvings. This is the final resting place of all your favorite heroes from the American Revolution, including Paul Revere, Samuel Adams, John Hancock and James Otis. Benjamin Franklin is missing, as

BOSTON

BACK BAY, THE FENWAY & THE SOUTH END

Massachusetts Institute of Technology

INFORMATION
Bank of America...................................1 C3
Bank of America...................................2 G3
Boston Public Library......................(see 17)
City of Boston Police
  Headquarters..................................3 D6
CVS Pharmacy.....................................4 F3
FedEx Kinko's......................................5 F3
Post Office...6 F3
Prudential Center Visitors Center...7 E3
Tech Superpowers Internet Cafe...8 E3
Trident Booksellers & Cafe............9 E3

SIGHTS & ACTIVITIES
Arlington St Church.........................10 G2
Back Bay Yoga Studio.....................11 D3
Baptiste Power Vinyasa Yoga........12 G3
Beacon Hill Skate.............................13 H3
Boston Bicycle..................................14 B3
Boston Center for Adult
  Education.......................................15 G2
Boston Duck Tours......................(see 98)
Boston Marathon Monument.......16 F3
Boston Public Library......................17 F3
Christian Science Church...............18 E4

Fenway Studios................................19 D3
Hatch Memorial Shell......................20 G1
Isabella Stewart Gardner
  Museum..21 C5
John Hancock Tower.......................22 G3
Mapparium....................................(see 23)
Mary Baker Eddy Library................23 E4
Museum of Fine Arts......................24 C5
Old South Church...........................25 F3
Skywalk Observatory.......................26 F3
South End Yoga...............................27 G5
Trinity Church..................................28 G3
Urban Adventours.......................(see 14)

The Esplanade

Boston University Bridge
BU Boathouse
To Scullers Jazz Club (1mi)

Soldiers Field Rd
Charles River Bike Path
To Worcester (50mi);
Springfield (95mi)
Boston University

Granite St

Commonwealth Ave
BU Central
Bay State Rd
Boston University
To Agganis Arena (0.4mi);
Eastern Mountain Sports (0.5mi);
Paradise Lounge (0.5mi);
Great Scott (1mi); Brighton (2mi);
New Balance Factory Store (2.2mi)
Babbit St
BU East
Blandford
Commonwealth Ave
Kenmore
Cummington St

Back St
Charlesgate West
Charlesgate Overpass
Marlborough Ave

Storrow Dr

Beacon St
Massachusetts Turnpike
Newbury St

SLEEPING
463 Beacon St.................................29 E2
Berkeley Residence YWCA.............30 G4
Buckminster Hotel...........................31 C3
Chandler Inn.....................................32 G3
Charlesmark at Copley....................33 F3
College Club.....................................34 G2
Colonnade..35 F4
Commonwealth Court Guest
  House...36 E3
Copley House...................................37 F4
Copley Inn..38 F4
Copley Square Hotel.......................39 F3
Encore...40 F5
Fenway Summer Hostel..................41 C3
Gryphon House................................42 D3
Hostelling International – Boston..43 D3
Lenox Hotel......................................44 F3
Midtown Hotel.................................45 E4
Newbury Guest House.....................46 E3
Oasis Guest House...........................47 E4
YMCA of Greater Boston................48 E5

Hall Pond

Mountfort St
To Coolidge Corner
Theater (1mi);
John F Kennedy
National Historic Site
(1.5mi)

Lansdowne St
Ipswich St
Berklee College of Music

Fenway Park

Fenway Park

The Fenway

Community Victory Gardens

Muddy River

EATING
B&G Oysters Ltd..............................49 G4
Bangkok Blue...................................50 F3
BarLola...51 F2
Bertucci's..52 G3
Bob's Southern Bistro.....................53 E5
Brasserie Jo..................................(see 35)
Brown Sugar Café...........................54 C4
Eastern Standard.............................55 C3
Farmers Market...............................56 G3
Flour...57 G5
Franklin Café....................................58 H4
Hamersley's Bistro..........................59 G4
India Quality....................................60 D3
La Verdad...61 C3
Legal Sea Foods (Copley Place)....62 F3
Legal Sea Foods (Prudential
  Center)...63 F3
Meyers & Chang.............................64 H4
Mike's City Diner.............................65 G6
Parish Café & Bar............................66 G2
Petit Robert Bistro...........................67 F4
Petit Robert Bistro...........................68 D3
Piattini..69 F3
Toro...(see 65)
Trident Booksellers & Cafe........(see 9)

Fullerton St

Boylston St
Van Ness St
Peterborough St
Queensberry St
Agassiz Rd
Park Dr

Kilmarnock St

Kelleher Rose Garden

Ave Louis Pasteur

The Fenway

Palace Rd
Museum Rd
Huntington Ave
Museum

Northeastern
Northeastern University

Roxbury Crossing
MassArt
Longwood Ave

DRINKING
28 Degrees.......................................70 H3
Boston Beer Works..........................71 C3
Cask 'n Flagon.................................72 C3
Cottonwood Café............................73 G3
Delux Café & Lounge......................74 G4
Jillian's..75 C3
Vox Populi..76 F3

ENTERTAINMENT
Beehive..(see 80)
Berklee Performance Center..........77 E3
Bill's Bar...78 C3
BosTix...79 F3
Boston Center for the Arts.............80 G4
Boston Symphony Orchestra..........81 E3
Club Café..82 G3
Fritz...(see 32)
Huntington Theater Company........83 E4
Jacques...84 H3
New England Conservatory.............85 E5
Wally's Café......................................86 E5

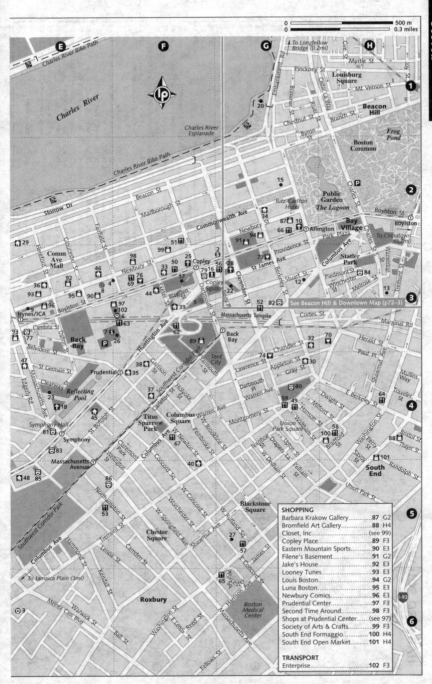

HARVARD SQUARE

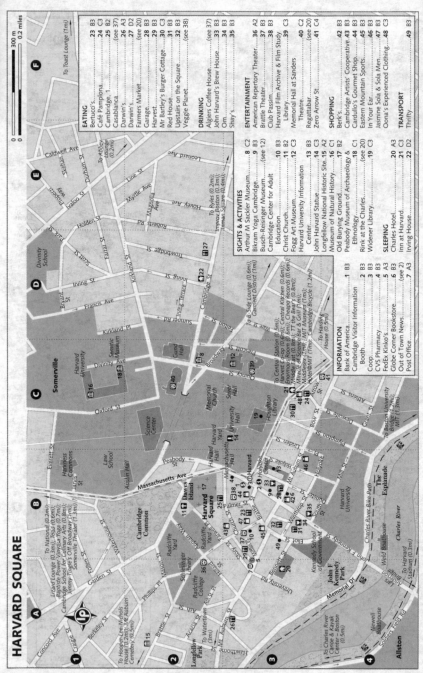

INFORMATION
Bank of America.................................1 B3
Cambridge Visitor Information
  Booth.......................................2 B3
Coop..3 B3
CVS Pharmacy..................................4 B3
FedEx Kinko's.................................5 B3
Globe Corner Bookstore.................(see 2)
Out of Town News..............................6 B3
Post Office...................................7 A3

SIGHTS & ACTIVITIES
Arthur M Sackler Museum.......................8 C2
Bikram Yoga Cambridge.........................9 B3
Busch-Reisinger Museum................(see 12)
Cambridge Center for Adult
  Education..................................10 B3
Christ Church................................11 B2
Fogg Art Museum..............................12 C3
Harvard University Information
  Center....................................13 B3
John Harvard Statue..........................14 B3
Longfellow National Historic Site...15 A2
Museum of Natural History...........16 C1
Old Burying Ground...........................17 B2
Peabody Museum of Archaeology &
  Ethnology.................................18 C1
Rink at the Charles...................(see 20)
Widener Library..............................19 B3

SLEEPING
Charles Hotel................................20 A3
Inn at Harvard...............................21 C3
Irving House.................................22 D2

EATING
Bertucci's...................................23 B3
Café Pamplona................................24 C3
Cambridge, 1.................................25 B2
Casablanca.............................(see 37)
Darwin's.....................................26 A3
Darwin's.....................................27 D2
Farmers Market........................(see 20)
Garage.......................................28 B3
Harvest......................................29 B3
Mr Bartley's Burger Cottage..................30 C3
Red House....................................31 B3
Upstairs on the Square.......................32 B3
Veggie Planet.........................(see 38)

DRINKING
Algiers Coffee House..................(see 37)
John Harvard's Brew House....................33 B3
Om...34 B3
Shay's.......................................35 B3

ENTERTAINMENT
American Repertory Theater...................36 A2
Battle Theater...............................37 B3
Club Passim..................................38 B3
Harvard Film Archive & Film Study
  Library...................................39 C3
Memorial Hall at Sanders
  Theatre...................................40 C2
Regattabar............................(see 20)
Zero Arrow St................................41 C4

SHOPPING
Berk's.......................................42 B3
Cambridge Artists' Cooperative...............43 B3
Cardullo's Gourmet Shop......................44 B3
Eastern Mountain Sports......................45 B3
In Your Ear..................................46 B3
Jasmine Sola & Sola Men......................47 B3
Oona's Experienced Clothing..................48 C3

TRANSPORT
Thrifty......................................49 B3

GREEN BOSTON

Bostonians have the great fortune to witness the greening of their city, quite literally. The Central Artery is underground, out of sight, soon to be replaced by the Rose Kennedy Greenway (see the boxed text, p81). The new park will provide a pleasant counterpart to the Charles River Esplanade (p86), on the south shore of the river, and the Emerald Necklace (p93), stretching from Boston Common to Franklin Park. And certainly, after 15 years of construction, the greenway is a welcome addition to an otherwise concrete landscape.

Other ongoing environmental initiatives are also coming to fruition. For hundreds of years the Boston Harbor was a dumping site for sewage, earning its reputation as the most polluted waterfront in the country. In the mid-1980s the Environmental Protection Agency (EPA) ordered the city to clean up its act. The 11-year effort is finally reaping benefits. For the first time in over a century, water quality in the harbor is safe for swimming, beaches are clean and enjoyable places to play and, thanks to the HarborWalk (p93), the waterfront is a wonderful area for strolling.

A similar effort is under way in the Charles River, inspiration for the Standell's song 'Dirty Water.' Improvements have been significant. In 2007, a local advocacy group saw fit to celebrate the progress by organizing the first-ever **Charles River Swim** (www.charlesriverswimmingclub.org), a tradition which will hopefully continue as water quality continues to improve.

Another green goal in Boston is reducing the number of cars on the roads, thus diminishing greenhouse gas emissions. Boston-based **Zipcar** (www.zipcar.com)– the country's largest car-sharing company – encourages urbanites to shed cars, drive less and use other forms of transportation. This trend complements the city's long-term transportation plans to extend the subway and build more bike paths ('long-term' being the operative word).

For volunteer opportunities, contact the following:

Boston Harbor Association (www.tbha.org)
Charles River Clean-up Boat (www.rbcant.us/cleanupboat)
Friends of the Community Paths (www.pathfriends.org)
MassBike (www.massbike.org)

---

he is buried in Philadelphia, but the Franklin family plot contains his parents. The five victims of the Boston Massacre share a common grave. Other noteworthy permanent residents include Peter Faneuil, of Faneuil Hall fame, and Judge Sewall, the only magistrate to denounce the hanging of the so-called Salem witches.

KING'S CHAPEL & BURYING GROUND

Bostonians were not pleased at all when the original Anglican church was erected on this site in 1688. (Remember, it was from the Anglicans – the Church of England – that the Puritans were fleeing.) The granite **chapel** (Map pp72-3; ☎ 617-227-2155; www.kings-chapel.org; 58 Tremont St; admission by donation $2; ⊙ 10am-4pm Mon-Sat, 1:30-4pm Sun Jun-Aug, Sat & Sun only Sep-May; ⊙ Park St or Government Center) standing today was built in 1754 around the original wooden structure. Unfortunately, building funds ran out before completion; thus, the missing spire. The church houses the largest bell ever made by Paul Revere, as well as a sonorous organ. Services are held at 11am

Sunday and 12:15pm Wednesday; recitals are at 12:15pm Tuesday.

The adjacent **burying ground** is the oldest in the city. Famous graves include John Winthrop, the first governor of the fledgling Massachusetts Bay Colony; William Dawes, who rode with Paul Revere; and Mary Chilton, the first European woman to set foot in Plymouth.

OLD SOUTH MEETING HOUSE

No tax on tea! That was the decision on December 16, 1773, when 5000 angry colonists gathered at the Old South Meeting House to protest British taxes, leading to the Boston Tea Party. These days the graceful **meeting house** (Map pp72-3; ☎ 617-482-6439; www.oldsouthmeetinghouse .org; 310 Washington St; adult/senior & student/child $5/4/1; ⊙ 9:30am-5pm Apr-Oct, 10am-4pm Nov-Mar; ⊙ Downtown Crossing) is still a gathering place for discussion, although not so much rabble-rousing goes on here any more. Instead, the meeting house hosts concerts, theater performances and lecture series, as well as walking tours, reenactments and other historical programs.

When you visit, you can listen to an audio of the historic pre–Tea Party meeting. Ask about scavenger hunts and other activities for kids.

OLD STATE HOUSE & MASSACRE SITE

Dating to 1713, the **Old State House** (Map pp72-3; ☎ 617-720-3290; www.bostonhistory.org; 206 Washington St; adult/senior & student/child $5/4/1; ☺ 9am-5pm; ♿; ☻ State) is Boston's oldest surviving public building, where the Massachusetts Assembly used to debate the issues of the day. The building is perhaps best known for its balcony, where the Declaration of Independence was first read to Bostonians in 1776. Operated by the Bostonian Society, the museum depicts Boston's role in the American Revolution, including videos on the Boston Massacre and the history of the Old State House. The NPS (National Park Service) Visitor Center is across the street on State St.

Encircled by cobblestones, the **Boston Massacre site** (Map pp72-3) marks the spot where the first blood was shed for the American independence movement. On March 5, 1770, an angry mob of colonists swarmed the British soldiers guarding the State House. Sam Adams, John Hancock and about 40 other protesters hurled snowballs, rocks and insults. Thus provoked, the soldiers fired into the crowd and killed five townspeople, including Crispus Attucks, a former slave. The incident sparked enormous anti-British sentiment in the lead-up to the revolution.

OLD CITY HALL

A monumental French Second Empire building, **Old City Hall** (Map pp72-3; ☎ 617-523-8678; www.old cityhall.com; 45 School St; ☻ State) is now office space with one fancy restaurant, but this site has seen its share of history. Out front, a plaque commemorates the **site of the first public school**, Boston Latin, founded in 1635 and still operational in the Fenway. The hopscotch sidewalk mosaic, *City Carpet,* marks the spot where Benjamin Franklin, Ralph Waldo Emerson and Charles Bulfinch were educated.

Statues of Benjamin Franklin, founding father, and Josiah Quincy, second mayor of Boston, stand inside the courtyard. They are accompanied by a life-size replica of a donkey, symbol of the Democratic party. ('Why the donkey?' you wonder. Read the plaque to find out.) Two bronze footprints 'stand in opposition.'

Government Center & West End

Government Center sits on the site of the notorious Scollay Sq of yesteryear, while the West End is sometimes called the 'Old West End' because there's not much left of this formerly vibrant neighborhood. What few vestiges remain are found in the little byways between Merrimac and Causeway Sts (Map pp72-3).

The massive institutions that now dominate this neighborhood include Boston City Hall and other government facilities, as well as the many annexes of Mass General Hospital. Of more interest to travelers is the Banknorth Garden, home of the Boston Celtics and the Boston Bruins (see p121), and site of Boston's biggest crowd-drawing concerts.

MUSEUM OF SCIENCE

The educational playground at the **Museum of Science** (Map pp72-3; ☎ 617-723-2500; www.mos.org; Science Park, Charles River Dam; adult/senior/child $16/14/13; ☺ 9am-5pm Sat-Thu Sep-Jun, 9am-7pm Jul-Aug, 9am-9pm Fri year-round; ♿; ☻ Science Park) has more than 600 interactive exhibits. Favorites include the world's largest lightning-bolt generator, a full-scale space capsule, a World Population Meter and a virtual fish tank. The amazing array of exhibits explores computers, technology, complex systems, algae, maps, models, dinosaurs, birds and much more. Live science demonstrations involve animals and experiments taking place before your eyes, while the Discovery Center offers other hands-on fun that's cool for kids.

The museum also houses the **Hayden Planetarium & Mugar Omni Theater** (per show adult/child/senior $9/7/8, 1 show & museum admission $20/17.50/16). The planetarium boasts a state-of-the-art projection system that casts a heavenly star show, programs about black holes and other astronomical mysteries, and evening laser light shows with rock music.

NEW ENGLAND SPORTS MUSEUM

Nobody can say that Bostonians are not passionate about their sports teams. The **New England Sports Museum** (Map pp72-3; ☎ 617-624-1234; www.sportsmuseum.org; Banknorth Garden; adult/child $6/4; ☺ 11am-2pm game days, 11am-3pm non-game days; ☻ North Station) is not the best place to witness this deep-rooted devotion (that would be Fenway Park), but sports fans might enjoy the tribute to the retired members of the Boston Celtics or the dramatic stories of Red

BIG DIG = BIG PARK

The Big Dig has finally been dug. After two decades of construction and $15 billion in cost, the infamous Central Artery/Tunnel project is complete at last. The project involved the dismantling of the Central Artery, the perpetually congested raised highway that cut through Downtown. In its place, the Big Dig built more than 40 miles of subterranean superhighway. To undertake a massive public works project in the heart of the city, according to the former project director, was like 'performing bypass surgery on a patient while he continues to work and play tennis.'

Besides the free-flowing traffic and the quicker trip to the airport, the Big Dig has major implications for the city above ground, reclaiming about 27 acres of industrial wasteland for parks and civic plazas. Where the hulking Central Artery once created barriers and shadows, Bostonians will soon enjoy a tree-lined open space, the Rose Kennedy Greenway. Some of the parks:

- **North End Park** (Map pp72–3) Between Blackstone St and Cross St, this little strip of green space reconnects the North End to its Downtown neighbors, acting as a critical link between the historic neighborhood and the modern city center.

- **Wharf District Parks** Between State St and High St, four parks will define the landscape where the city meets the sea. Harbor Park Pavilion (a gateway to the Harbor Islands) and Rings Fountain are only two of the planned features, which also include open-air performance space and sculpture gardens.

- **Chinatown Park** (Map pp72–3) Between Chinatown and the Leather District, this new Asian-accented park opened to much fanfare in 2007. See p85.

- **Boulevard** Traversing the Downtown corridor, a new tree-lined boulevard will be studded with plazas, parks and public art.

It sounds lovely, and Bostonians look forward to the day when they can walk along a ribbon of green from North Station to South Station. That said, if they've learned anything from the Big Dig, it's to not hold their breath.

Sox Century. Unfortunately, the exhibits are strong on photographs and jerseys and not much else, though they do cover all of the major professional sports. The highlight is the penalty box from the old Boston Garden.

This museum is actually in the concourse area of the box seats at the Banknorth Garden. The good news is that, if you go on a game day, you may see the Celtics or the Bruins warming up. The bad news is that it often closes for special events at the garden; and even when it is open, admission is only at designated times (call to confirm).

North End

One of Boston's oldest neighborhoods, the North End has a history that is rich with diversity and drama. These days, the North End's Italian flavor is the strongest. Old-timers still carry on passionate discussions in Italian and play bocce in the parks. Others complete their ritual shopping at specialty stores selling fresh flowers, handmade pasta, cannoli or biscotti, fragrant spices and fresh-baked bread.

But the neighborhood's rich history is not forgotten. Paul Revere's famous ride was kicked off right here. Walk the Freedom Trail past his house to the storied Old North Church. Then follow up with a heaping plate of pasta and you'll have a pretty good sense of what the North End is all about.

With the recent completion of the Big Dig and the opening of the North End Park (see above), the quaint old quarter is more vibrant than ever, benefiting from its reintegration into the city.

PAUL REVERE HOUSE

On the night of April 18, 1775, silversmith Paul Revere set out from his home on North Sq; he was one of three horseback messengers who carried advance warning on this night of the British march into Concord and Lexington. The small clapboard **house** (Map pp72-3; ☎ 617-523-2338; www.paulreverehouse.org; 19 North Sq; adult/senior & student/child $3/2.50/1; ☒ 9:30am-5:15pm mid-Apr–Oct, 9:30am-4:15pm Nov–mid-Apr; ☉ Haymarket) was built in 1680, which makes it the oldest house in Boston.

LENNY ZAKIM & BUNKER HILL

Driving north from Boston on the Central Artery, your car emerges from the Tip O'Neill Tunnel into the open air, where you are surrounded on all sides by the Boston city skyline and the crisp white cables of the Leonard P Zakim Bunker Hill Bridge. Capped with obelisks that mirror its namesake monument, it is the widest cable-stayed bridge in the world. And against the clear blue or dark night, it is stunning.

Lenny Zakim was a local human rights activist who spent years railing against racism in the second half of the 20th century. His goal – appropriately – was to 'build bridges between people.' Bunker Hill was the battle where the patriots first proved their potency in the War for Independence. As Mayor Menino said at the dedication: 'The Leonard P Zakim Bunker Hill Bridge will showcase the diversity and the unity of race, religion and personal background that exist in Boston today, because of the work of community leaders like Lenny Zakim and because patriots fought long ago in Charlestown to make our country independent.' It's a stretch, but he managed to merge these disparate dedicatees.

The name is nonetheless unwieldy, so don't be afraid to take short cuts. Either the Zakim Bridge or the Bunker Hill Bridge will do.

A self-guided tour through the house and courtyard gives a glimpse of what life was like for the Revere family (which included 16 children!). Also on display are some examples of his silversmith and engraving talents, as well as an impressive bell that was forged in his foundry.

OLD NORTH CHURCH

On the same night that Paul Revere rode forth to warn of the onset of British soldiers, the sexton of the Old North Church hung two lanterns in the church steeple to signal that they would come by sea. Today the 1723 **Old North Church** (Map pp72–3; ☎ 617-523-6676; www.old north.com; 193 Salem St; ☽ 9am-6pm Mon-Fri, 9am-5pm Sat & Sun; ☻ Haymarket) is Boston's oldest active church. Tall white box-pews, many with brass nameplates of early parishioners, occupy the graceful interior.

Behind the church, lovely terraces and gardens beautify the exterior. Heading down the hill, shady **Paul Revere Mall** (Map pp72–3) perfectly frames the Old North Church. Often called 'the prado' by locals, it is a lively meeting place for North Enders of all generations.

COPP'S HILL

Dating to 1660, the city's second-oldest cemetery is **Copp's Hill Burying Ground** (Map pp72–3), named for William Copp, who originally owned this land. The oldest graves here belong to his children. An estimated 10,000 souls occupy this small plot of land, including more than a thousand free black people, many of whom lived in the North End. Find the grave

of Daniel Malcolm, whose headstone commemorates his rebel activism. British soldiers apparently took offense at these claims and used the headstone for target practice.

Across the street is Boston's **narrowest house** (Map pp72–3; 44 Hull St; ☻ North Station), measuring a whopping 9½ft wide. The circa-1800 house was reportedly built out of spite to block light from the neighbor's house and to obliterate the view of the house behind it.

Charlestown

The Charlestown Navy Yard was a thriving shipbuilding center throughout the 19th century. Although the navy yard was closed in 1974, the surrounding neighborhood has been making a comeback ever since. The impressive granite buildings have been transformed into shops, condos and offices, which enjoy a panoramic view of Boston. The narrow streets immediately surrounding Monument Sq are lined with restored 19th-century Federal and Colonial houses, and Main St has a handful of trendy restaurants.

USS CONSTITUTION & MUSEUM

'Her sides are made of iron!' So cried a crewman as he watched a shot bounce off the thick oak hull of the USS *Constitution* during the war of 1812. This bit of irony earned the legendary ship her nickname, Old Ironsides. The **USS Constitution** (Map pp72–3; ☎ 617-242-2543; www.uss constitution.navy.mil; Charlestown Navy Yard; admission free; ☽ 10am-6pm Tue-Sun Apr-Oct, 10am-4pm Thu-Sun Nov-Mar; ♿ ; ☻ North Station) is still the oldest commissioned US Navy ship, dating to 1797. And she is taken out onto Boston Harbor every Fourth of July in order to maintain her commissioned status. Navy personnel give 30-minute guided tours of the top deck, gun deck and cramped quarters (last tour 3:30pm).

For a play-by-play of the USS *Constitution's* various battles, as well as her current role as the flagship of the US Navy, head indoors to the **museum** (Map pp72-3; ☎ 617-426-1812; www.uss constitutionmuseum.org; Charlestown Navy Yard, bldg 22; admission free; ⊙ 9am-6pm May-Oct, 10am-5pm Nov-Apr; ⊛ ; ◉ North Station). More interesting is the exhibit on the Barbary War, which explains the birth of the US Navy during this relatively unknown conflict, America's first war at sea. Upstairs, kids can experience what it was like to be a sailor on the USS *Constitution* in 1812.

Also on the grounds you will find the **Charlestown Navy Yard Visitors Center** (Map pp72-3; ☎ 617-242 5601; bldg No 5; ⊙ 9am-5pm; ◉ North Station), a good source of information about the Freedom Trail and other NPS Sights.

MONUMENT SQUARE

'Don't fire until you see the whites of their eyes!' came the order from Colonel Prescott to revolutionary troops on June 17, 1775. Considering the ill-preparedness of the revolutionary soldiers, the bloody battle that followed resulted in a surprising number of British casualties. Ultimately, however, the Redcoats prevailed (an oft-overlooked fact). The so-called Battle of Bunker Hill is ironically named, as most of the fighting took place on Breed's Hill, where the **Bunker Hill Monument** (Map pp72-3; ☎ 617-242-5641; www.nps .gov/bost; Monument Sq; admission free; ⊙ 9am-4:30pm late Sep-early Jun, 9am-5pm late Jun-early Sep; ◉ North Station or Community College) stands today. The 220ft granite hilltop obelisk rewards physically fit visitors with fine Boston views at the top of its 295 steps.

Across the street, the **Bunker Hill Museum** (Map pp72-3; ☎ 617-242 7275; 43 Monument Sq; admission free; ⊙ 9am-5pm; ◉ North Station or Community College) has new digs in the redbrick building that used to house the public library. Two floors of exhibits include a few artifacts and a 360-degree mural depicting the battle. If you can find where the artist signed his masterpiece, you win a prize.

Waterfront

Long gone are the days when sailing ships brought exotic spices, tea and coffee into these docks. While some remnants of this maritime trade are still visible in the architecture (especially on Long Wharf), the Waterfront is now a center for a new industry: tourism. Tourists and residents stroll the **HarborWalk**; ferries shuttle visitors between historic sights; and alfresco diners enjoy the breeze off the harbor. Christopher Columbus Park and the Wharf District Parks (coming soon; see p81) offer a shady place for tired tourists.

For the ultimate escape from the city, hop on a ferry and go out to sea: specifically to one of the Boston Harbor Islands for a day of berrypicking, beachcombing or sunbathing.

FANEUIL HALL MARKETPLACE & QUINCY MARKET

Constructed in 1740 as a market and public meeting place, **Faneuil Hall** (Map pp72-3; ☎ 617-242-5642; www.faneuilhall.com; Congress & North Sts; admission free; ⊙ 9am-5pm; ◉ Haymarket or Aquarium) is the brick Colonial building topped with the beloved grasshopper weathervane. Although the hall was supposed to be exclusively for local issues, the Sons of Liberty called many meetings here, informing public opinion about their objections to British taxation without representation, thus earning Faneuil Hall its nickname, the 'Cradle of Liberty.' Out front, Sam Adams sits astride his horse.

Behind Faneuil Hall three long granite buildings make up the rest of the marketplace, the center of the city's produce and meat industry for almost 150 years. In the 1970s **Quincy Market** (Map pp72–3) was redeveloped into today's touristy, festive shopping and eating center, so it still serves its original purpose, albeit with all the modern trappings.

The six luminescent glass columns of the **New England Holocaust Memorial** (Map pp72-3; ☎ 617-457-0755; btwn Union & Congress Sts) are engraved with six million numbers, symbolizing the Jews killed in the Holocaust. Each tower – with smoldering coals sending plumes of steam up through the glass corridors – represents a different Nazi death camp.

Two lifelike bronzes of Boston's former Mayor Curley, a cherished but controversial Irish American politician, pose on North St between Union and Congress Sts.

NEW ENGLAND AQUARIUM

Teeming with sea creatures of all sizes, shapes and colors, the **New England Aquarium** (Map pp72-3;

BOSTON

URBAN ADVENTURE

Boston Harbor is sprinkled with 34 islands, many of which are open for bird-watching, trail walking, fishing and swimming. The **Boston Harbor Islands** (☎ 617-223-8666; www.bostonislands .org; admission free) offer a range of ecosystems – sandy beaches, rocky cliffs, fresh and salt-water marsh and forested trails – only 45 minutes from downtown Boston. Since the massive multi-million-dollar clean-up of Boston Harbor in the mid-1990s, the islands are one of the city's most magnificent natural assets.

The transportation hub for the islands is **Georges Island**, as the inter-island shuttle leaves from here. It is also the site of **Fort Warren**, a 19th-century fort and Civil War prison. While NPS rangers give guided tours of the fort, it is largely abandoned, with many dark tunnels, creepy corners and magnificent lookouts to discover.

Recently revamped, **Spectacle Island** has a brand new marina ($15 to $25 per day), visitor center, snack bar and supervised beaches. Five miles of walking trails provide access to a 157ft peak overlooking the harbor.

Islands with walking trails, campsites and beach access include **Bumpkin**, **Grape** and **Lovells**. Open for camping from Memorial Day to Labor Day, each island has 10 to 12 individual sites and one large group site. You must bring all of your own water and equipment, and facilities are primitive. Make **reservations** (☎ 877-422-6762; www.reserveamerica.com) in advance.

The new Harbor Pavilion in Wharf Park will serve as an information center and gateway to the Harbor Islands when it opens. In the meantime, stop by the **Boston Harbor Islands Information Center** (Map pp72-3; Moakley Federal Courthouse; ⊙ South Station) for more information.

To get to most of the islands, **Harbor Express** (Map pp72-3; ☎ 617-222-6999; www.harborexpress .com; 1 Long Wharf, off Atlantic Ave; round trip adult/senior/child $10/8/7 Mon-Wed, $12/9/7 Thu-Sun; ⊙ service 9am-5pm May-early Oct) offers a seasonal ferry service from Long Wharf. Purchase a round-trip ticket to Georges Island or Spectacle Island, where you catch a free water taxi to the smaller islands.

Some handy information if you are camping here:

■ Bring your own water and supplies.

■ Hang your food high in the trees out of reach of animals.

■ Expect rather primitive sites and composting toilets.

☎ 617-973-5200; www.neaq.org; Central Wharf, off Old Atlantic Ave; adult/child $18/10; ⊙ 9am-5pm Mon-Fri, 9am-6pm Sat & Sun, extended hr Jun-Aug; ♿ ; ⊙ Aquarium) was the first step Boston took to reconnect the city to the sea. Harbor seal and sea otter frolic in a large observation tank at the entrance, but the main attraction is a three-story, cylindrical saltwater tank. It swirls with more than 600 creatures great and small, including turtle, sharks and eel. At the base of the tank, the penguin pool is home to three species of fun-loving penguin. Countless side exhibits explore the lives and habitats of other underwater oddities, including exhibits on ethereal jellyfish and rare, exotic sea dragons. Daily programs include tank dives, penguin presentations, harbor-seal training exhibits and puppet shows.

The aquarium's **3-D IMAX theater** (adult/child $10/8; ⊙ 10am-10pm) features films with aquatic themes. The aquarium also organizes **whale-watching cruises** (adult/child $36/30; ⊙ 9:30 or 10am & 1:30 or 2pm May-Oct). Combination tickets are also available.

Seaport District

Separated from Boston proper by the jelly fish-laden Fort Point Channel, this area has always afforded spectacular views of downtown Boston. But until recently it had been neglected by city officials and ignored by developers. Such prime waterside real estate can only go unexploited for so long, however. The Seaport is now the target of an ambitious development project, as evidenced by the huge convention center, several luxury hotels and – the centerpiece – the new ICA on the water's edge (see opposite).

Following the **HarborWalk**, it's a pleasant stroll across Northern Ave Bridge to the Seaport District. While there is still a disproportionate amount of unused space, much of this area is targeted for condos, parks and shopping malls. Indeed, construction may well be under way by the time you are reading this.

INSTITUTE OF CONTEMPORARY ART
Boston is poised to become a focal point for contemporary art, with the highly touted opening of the new **ICA** (Map pp72-3; ☎ 617-927-6613; www .icaboston.org; 100 Northern Ave; adult/senior & student/child $12/10/free; ☑ 10am-5pm Tue-Sun, 10am- 9pm Thu & Fri; ⊕ South Station) in its dramatic new quarters. The building is a work of art in itself – a striking glass structure cantilevered over a waterside plaza. The spacious light-filled interior allows for multimedia presentations, educational programs and studio space. More importantly, it provides the venue for the development of the ICA's permanent collection of 21st-century art. Exhibits showcase national and international artists working in a wide variety of media, from painting and sculpture to audio and video. Thursday nights are free for all after 5pm, while families enjoy free admission on the second Saturday of the month.

CHILDREN'S MUSEUM
The interactive, educational exhibits at the delightful **Children's Museum** (Map pp72-3; ☎ 617-426-8855; www.bostonchildrensmuseum.org; 300 Congress St; adult/infant/child & senior $9/1/7; ☑ 10am-5pm Sat-Thu, 10am-9pm Fri; ☑ ; ⊕ South Station) keep kids entertained for hours. Highlights include a bubble exhibit, a two-story climbing maze, a rock-climbing wall, a hands-on construction site and intercultural immersion experiences. In 2006 the museum underwent major expansion, with the addition of a new light-filled atrium featuring an amazing climbing structure, bridges and glass elevators. In nice weather kids can enjoy outdoor eating and playing in the waterside park. Look for the iconic Hood milk bottle on Fort Point Channel. Admission on Friday evenings costs only $1.

BOSTON TEA PARTY SHIP & MUSEUM
On the cold evening of December 16, 1773, a group of fiery colonists disguised as Mohawks burst from the Old South Meeting House and headed to Griffin's Wharf, where they clambered aboard the three ships harbored there. Armed with axes and hatchets, the colonists destroyed 342 crates of British tea, defiantly dumping the precious cargo into the sea. Today the **Boston Tea Party Ship & Museum** (Map pp72-3; ☎ 617-269-7150; www.bostonteapartyship .com; Congress St Bridge; ⊕ South Station) is testimony to the spirited rebels who refused to pay the levy imposed on their beloved beverage.

At the time of research the museum was closed for rebuilding after suffering extensive fire damage. Re-opening – currently set for fall 2008 – has been delayed for years due to lack of funding.

Chinatown & Theater District
These side-by-side neighborhoods are home to Boston's lively theater scene, its most hip-hop-happening nightclubs and its best international dining. Ethnically and economically diverse, they border Boston's Downtown districts, but they are edgier and artsier.

Although tiny by New York standards, Boston's **Theater District** (Map pp72–3) has long served as a pre-Broadway staging area. In the 1940s Boston had over 50 theaters. Many landmark theaters have recently received long-needed facelifts, and their colorful marquees and posh patrons have revived the aura of 'bright lights, big city.' See p117 for information about specific theaters.

Chinatown is overflowing with ethnic restaurants, live poultry and fresh produce markets, teahouses and textile shops. In addition to the Chinese, who began arriving in the late 1870s, this tight-knit community also includes Cambodians, Vietnamese and Laotians. The official entrance is **Chinatown Gate** (Map pp72-3; cnr Beach St & Surface Rd; ⊕ Chinatown), a gift from the city of Taipei. Surrounding the gate and anchoring the southern end of the Rose Kennedy Greenway is the new **Chinatown Park** (see the boxed text, p81). Incorporating elements of feng shui, the park design is inspired by the many generations of Asian immigrants who have passed through this gate.

South End
What the Castro is to San Francisco, what Dupont Circle is to Washington DC, so the South End is to Boston: a once-rough neighborhood that was claimed and cleaned up by the gay community, and now everyone wants to live there.

And why not? The South End boasts the country's largest concentration of Victorian row houses, many of which have been painstakingly restored by gay residents. It offers Boston's most innovative and exciting options for dining out, especially along trendy **Tremont St**. And now, the area south of Washington St has earned the moniker **'SoWa'** for the artistic

OPEN STUDIOS

Newbury St in Back Bay and Charles St on Beacon Hill are Boston's traditional venues for gallery-hopping. Art connoisseurs, however, may find them rather staid. To experience the cutting edge of Boston's burgeoning art scene, look for open-studio events in the South End, the Seaport District and Jamaica Plain.

The old brick warehouses on the southeast side of Fort Point Channel were the center of the nation's wool trade until the 1960s, when they were converted to art studios. The **Fort Point Arts Community** (Map pp72-3; ☎ 616-423 4299; www.fortpointarts.org; 300 Summer St; Ⓢ South Station) continues to be an active, energetic group of artists that includes painters, designers, photographers and mixed-media artists. The community has a gallery; or you can visit during its seasonal two-day Open Studios event.

In the South End the area south of Washington St has been dubbed SoWa. Out of the former warehouses and factories, artists have carved out studios and gallery space. Many of these artists exhibit on a weekly basis at the **South End Open Market** (p122), an open-air arts and crafts market. Its seasonal opening in May coincides with the annual **SoWa Art Walk** (www.sowaartwalk.com). In the fall, **United South End Artists** (www.useaboston.org) hosts another open studios weekend. During these two-day events, artists invite the community into their studios and show off the painting, sculpture, film and multimedia work that was produced here. There is also a vibrant scene on the first Friday of every month (dubbed 'First Fridays'), when local galleries stay open late to welcome visitors and host openings.

Fenway Studios (Map pp76-7; www.friendsoffenwaystudios.org; 30 Ipswich St; Ⓡ Hynes), housed in a historic early-20th-century Arts & Crafts building, is home to 25 artists who live and work on site. It's worth attending their occasional open-studios events just to see the amazing interior, modeled on the ateliers of 19th-century Paris.

In Jamaica Plain, a local community groups sponsor **First Thursdays** (www.jpcentresouth.org), when shops and restaurants along the main drag are transformed into galleries where local artists can exhibit their works. Otherwise, check out the annual **JP Open Studios** (www.jpopenstudios .com), held in the fall.

For complete information about open-studios events around the city, check out the **Boston Open Studios Coalition** (www.bostonopenstudios.org).

community that is converting the old warehouses into studio and gallery space (see above). And the green strip of **Southwest Corridor Park** is a beautiful paved and landscaped walkway (see p93 for more information).

But the most enticing corners of the South End are those with exquisite London-style row houses with steep stoops and tiny ornamental gardens. Several sweet streets run between Tremont St and Shawmut Ave, particularly the lovely elliptical **Union Park** and intimate **Rutland Square**.

Back Bay

During the 1850s Back Bay (Map pp76–7) was an uninhabitable tidal flat. Boston was experiencing a population and building boom, so urban planners embarked on an ambitious 40-year project: filling in the marsh, laying out an orderly grid of streets, erecting magnificent Victorian brownstones and designing high-minded civic plazas. So Back Bay was born.

The grandest of Back Bay's grand boulevards is **Commonwealth Avenue** (more 'commonly' Comm Ave). Boston's Champs Élysées, the dual carriageway connects the Public Garden to the Back Bay Fens, a green link in Olmsted's Emerald Necklace (see p93).

North of here is lovely **Marlborough Street**, its brick sidewalks lit with gas lamps and shaded by blooming magnolias. South is swanky **Newbury Street**, destination for the serious shopper or gallery-hopper. And **Copley Square** represents the best of Back Bay architecture, as it gracefully blends disparate elements from all eras.

CHARLES RIVER ESPLANADE

The southern bank of the Charles River Basin is an enticing urban escape, with grassy knolls and cooling waterways, all designed by Frederick Law Olmsted. The park – known as the Charles River Esplanade (Map pp76–7) – is dotted with public art, including an oversized bust of **Arthur Fiedler**, the long-time conductor of the Boston Pops. The **Hatch Memorial Shell** (Map pp76–7) hosts free outdoor concerts and movies, including the famed Fourth of July concert by the Boston Pops.

The paths along the river are ideal (though sometimes crowded) for bicycling, jogging or walking. The Esplanade stretches almost 3 miles along the Boston shore of the Charles River, from the Museum of Science to the BU (Boston University) Bridge. For a great view of Boston, walk – or take the T Red Line between Charles/MGH and Kendall – across the **Longfellow Bridge**, nicknamed the 'Salt and Pepper' bridge because of its towers' resemblance to the condiment shakers.

COPLEY SQUARE

High-minded Copley Sq is surrounded by historic buildings. A masterpiece of American architecture, **Trinity Church** (Map pp76–7; ☎ 617-536-0944; www.trinitychurchboston.org; 206 Clarendon St; adult/senior & student/child $5/4/free; ☷ 9am-6pm Tue-Sat, 7am-7pm Sun; ☉ Copley) is the country's ultimate example of Richardsonian Romanesque. The granite exterior uses sandstone in colorful patterns, while the interior displays an awe-inspiring array of vibrant murals and stained glass. In the west gallery, the jeweled window *Christ in Majesty* is considered one of America's finest examples of stained-glass art.

Across the street, the 62-story **John Hancock Tower** (Map pp76–7; 200 Clarendon St; ☉ Copley), constructed with more than 10,000 panels of mirrored glass, stands in stark contrast to Trinity Church. The observatory on the 60th floor was closed for security reasons in the aftermath of September 11.

With eyes constantly drifting upward, it's easy to miss the square's plebeian-sized, down-to-earth elements. The city's most famous annual event, the Boston Marathon, finishes right here. Runners are commemorated by the **Boston Marathon Monument** (Map pp76–7; cnr Boylston & Dartmouth Sts). Paying tribute to the runners who subscribe to the 'slow and steady' strategy is Nancy Schon's sculpture **Tortoise & Hare**.

BOSTON PUBLIC LIBRARY

Dating from 1852, the esteemed **Boston Public Library** (BPL; Map pp76–7; ☎ 617-536-5400; www.bpl.org; 700 Boylston St; admission free; ☷ 9am-9pm Mon-Thu, 9am-5pm Fri & Sat year-round, 1-5pm Sun Oct-May; ☉ Copley)

lends credence to Boston's reputation as the 'Athens of America.' The old McKim building is notable for its magnificent facade and exquisite interior art.

Pick up a free brochure and take a self-guided tour, noting the murals by Puvis de Chavannes and John Singer Sargent, as well as sculpture by Augustus Saint-Gaudens and Domingo Mora. Alternatively, free guided tours depart from the entrance hall (times vary).

Besides this amazing artistry, the library holds untold treasures in its special collections, including John Adams' personal library. Frequent exhibits showcase some of the highlights – check the BPL website for details. An inviting café, Novel, overlooks the enchanting Italianate courtyard, which is a peaceful place to read.

PRUDENTIAL CENTER SKYWALK OBSERVATORY

This landmark Boston building is a not much more than a fancy shopping mall, technically called the Shops at Prudential Center (see p121). But it does provide a bird's-eye view of Boston from its 50th-floor **Skywalk Observatory** (Map pp76–7; ☎ 617-859-0648; www.prudentialcenter.com; adult/child/student & senior $11/7.50/9; ☷ 10am-10pm Mar-Oct, 10am-8pm Nov-Feb; ☉ Prudential). Completely enclosed by glass, the skywalk offers spectacular 360-degree views of Boston and Cambridge, accompanied by an entertaining audio tour. You can also peruse the *Dreams of Freedom* immigration exhibit and watch a fun film called *Wings over Boston* (not for acrophobes). Alternatively, enjoy the same view from Top of the Hub for the price of a drink.

CHRISTIAN SCIENCE CHURCH & MAPPARIUM

Known to adherents as the 'Mother Church,' this **Christian Science Church** (Map pp76–7; ☎ 617-450-3790; www.tfccs.org; 175 Huntington Ave; ☷ 10am-4pm Mon-Sat; ☉ Symphony) is the international home base for the Church of Christ, Scientist, founded by Mary Baker Eddy in 1866. Tour the grand classical revival basilica, which can seat 3000 worshippers, listen to the 14,000-pipe organ and linger on the expansive plaza with its 670ft-long reflecting pool.

Right next door, the **Mary Baker Eddy Library for the Betterment of Humanity** (Map pp76–7; ☎ 617-450-7000; www.marybakereddylibrary.org; 200 Massachusetts Ave; adult/child, student & senior $6/4; ☷ 10am-4pm Tue-

WORTH THE TRIP: BROOKLINE

Although it seems to be part of Boston proper, Brookline is a distinct entity with a separate city government. It is a 'streetcar suburb,' a historical term describing its development after electric trolleys were introduced in the late 1800s. Off the beaten tourist path, it combines lovely, tranquil residential areas with lively commercial zones, including Coolidge Corner and Brookline Village. Both have deeply rooted Jewish and Russian populations, as you will notice from the synagogues and kosher delis on every corner. Take the Green 'C' Line to Coolidge Corner or 'D' Line to Brookline Village.

The **John F Kennedy National Historic Site** (off Map pp76-7; ☎ 617-566-7937; www.nps.gov/jofi; 83 Beal St; adult/child $3/free; ⏱ 10am-4:30pm Wed-Sun May-Oct; ⊙ Coolidge Corner) occupies the modest three-story house that was JFK's birthplace and boyhood home. Matriarch Rose Kennedy oversaw its restoration and furnishing in the late 1960s; today her narrative sheds light on the Kennedys' family life. Guided tours allow visitors to see furnishings, photographs and mementos that have been preserved from the time the family lived here. Walk north on Harvard St from Coolidge Corner.

Sun; ♿ ; ⊙ Symphony) is odd amalgam, housing the offices of the internationally regarded newspaper, the **Christian Science Monitor**, as well as one of Boston's hidden treasures, the intriguing **Mapparium**, which is a room-size stained-glass globe that visitors walk through on a glass bridge. It was created in 1935, which is reflected by the globe's geopolitical boundaries. The acoustics, which surprised even the designer, allow everyone in the room to hear even the tiniest whisper.

Second-floor galleries deal with the 'search for the meaning of life,' both on a personal and global level. From here, you can also peer into the newsroom of the *Monitor*, which Eddy founded when she was 87.

BACK BAY CHURCHES

The **Arlington St Church** (Map pp76-7; ☎ 617-536-7050; www.ascboston.org; 351 Boylston St; ⏱ noon-6pm Wed-Sun May-Oct; ⊙ Arlington) was the first public building to be erected in Back Bay, in 1861. The graceful church features extraordinary commissioned Tiffany windows and 16 bells in its steeple, which was modeled after London's well-known church St Martin-in-the-Fields.

The magnificent Venetian Gothic church on Copley Sq is called the 'new' **Old South Church** (Map pp76-7; ☎ 617-536-1970; www.oldsouth.org; 645 Boylston St; ⏱ 9am-7pm Mon-Thu, 9am-5pm Fri, 10am-4pm Sat, 9am-4pm Sun; ⊙ Copley) because, up until 1875, the congregation worshiped in the Old South Church on Milk St (now the Old South Meeting House; see p79). The congregation boasts many founding fathers among its historic members, including Samuel Adams and Paul Revere.

Kenmore Square & the Fenway

West of Back Bay, Beacon St and Comm Ave converge at Kenmore Sq, the epicenter of student life in Boston. In addition to the behemoth Boston University, more than a half-dozen colleges are in the area. Kenmore Sq has a disproportionate share of clubs, inexpensive but nondescript eateries and dormitories disguised as brownstones. You'll know you're in Kenmore Sq when you spot the landmark **Citgo sign**.

The Fenway refers to an urban residential neighborhood south of Kenmore Sq, attractive to students for its low-cost housing and dining. Fenway is also the name of a road that runs through here. Not least, Fenway Park is where the Boston Red Sox play baseball. But when people refer to 'the Fenway,' they're generally talking about the **Back Bay Fens**, a tranquil and interconnected park system that's an integral link in the Emerald Necklace (p93).

Kenmore Sq and the Fenway are a bit off the beaten tourist track, but they are home to some celebrated cultural institutions – Boston Symphony Orchestra, the Museum of Fine Arts and the Boston Red Sox.

MUSEUM OF FINE ARTS

The highlight of the **Museum of Fine Arts** (MFA; Map pp76-7; ☎ 617-267-9300; www.mfa.org; 465 Huntington Ave; adult/child/student & senior $17/6.50/15; ⏱ 10am-4:45pm Sat-Tue, 10am-9:45pm Wed-Fri, West Wing only Thu & Fri evening; ♿ ; ⊙ Ruggles or Museum) is undoubtedly its American collection, including American painting and decorative arts. Major works include paintings by John Singleton Copley, Winslow Homer, Edward Hopper and the

BOSTON

ART HEIST OF THE CENTURY

On March 18, 1990, two thieves disguised as police officers broke into the Isabella Stewart Gardner Museum. They left with nearly $200 million worth of artwork. The most famous painting stolen was Vermeer's *The Concert*, but the loot also included three works by Rembrandt and others by Manet and Degas, not to mention French and Chinese artifacts. The crime was never solved.

Mrs Jack's will stipulated that the collection remain exactly as it was at the time of her death. So the walls where these paintings hung remain barren, even today. Meanwhile, the Isabella Stewart Gardner Museum continues to offer a $5 million reward for information leading to the recovery of the artwork. So if you have any leads, please let us know.

Hudson River School, not to mention the fantastic murals by John Singer Sargent in the main stairwell.

The museum has an incredible collection of European paintings, including many by French impressionists. The recent acquisition of *Duchessa di Montejasi with Her Daughters* makes the MFA's Degas collection one of the richest in the world. The museum also boasts excellent exhibits of Japanese art, including Buddhist and Shinto treasures.

The MFA is undergoing an extensive renovation and expansion, with the construction of a new visitors center, new galleries and – most notably – a new American Wing. The Sharf Visitors Center is expected to open in 2008, while other projects are longer term. The museum will remain open throughout.

Children under the age of 17 are admitted free after 3pm on weekdays and all day on weekends – a fantastic family bargain. Admission on Wednesday evenings is free for everyone.

ISABELLA STEWART GARDNER MUSEUM

The magnificent Venetian-style palazzo that houses this **museum** (Map pp76-7; ☎ 617-278-5166; www.gardnermuseum.org; 280 The Fenway; adult/student/senior/child $10/5/7/free; ⊙ 11am-5pm Tue-Sun; ⊙ Museum) was home to 'Mrs Jack' Gardner herself until her death in 1924. A monument to one woman's taste for acquiring exquisite art, the Gardner is filled with almost 2000 priceless objects, primarily European, including outstanding tapestries and Italian Renaissance and 17th-century Dutch paintings. The palazzo itself, with a four-story greenhouse courtyard, is a masterpiece, a tranquil oasis which alone is worth the price of admission.

Jamaica Plain

Jamaica Plain, or 'JP' as it is fondly known, centers on its namesake **Jamaica Pond** (Map p71; ☎ a spring-fed pond that is pleasant for strolling or running. This lovely body of water surrounded by park is another link in the Emerald Necklace (p93), as are Arnold Arboretum and Franklin Park.

JP has strong Irish immigrant roots but in recent years the population has diversified. The area has attracted Spanish-speaking populations from Cuba and Dominican Republic, Asian immigrants from China and Vietnam, and black families from neighboring Roxbury. In the 1990s, as real-estate values soared around the city, JP became a destination for artists, political activists and lesbians. Now **Centre St** is lined with ethnic eateries, vegetarian restaurants and funky coffee shops. Take the Orange Line to Green St for Centre St and Jamaica Pond.

ARNOLD ARBORETUM

Under a public-private partnership with the city and Harvard University, the 265-acre **Arnold Arboretum** (off Map p71; ☎ 617-524-1718; www.arboretum.harvard.edu; 125 Arborway, Jamaica Plain; admission free; ⊙ dawn-dusk; ☯ ; ⊙ Forest Hills) is planted with over 13,000 exotic trees, flowering shrubs and other specimens. This gem of a spot is pleasant year-round, but it's particularly beautiful in the spring. Dog walking, Frisbee throwing, cycling, sledding and general contemplation are encouraged (but picnicking is not allowed). A **visitors center** (⊙ 9am-4pm Mon-Fri, 10am-4pm Sat, noon-4pm Sun) is located at the main gate, where brochures for self-guided walking tours are available. Otherwise, free guided tours are offered occasionally between April and November; see the website for details.

FRANKLIN PARK ZOO

The 70-acre Franklin Park is surrounded by one of the city's sketchier neighborhoods, but the **zoo** (off Map p71; ☎ 617-541-5466; www.zoonewengland.com; 1 Franklin Park Rd; adult/child/senior $11/6/9.50; ⊙ 10am-5pm Mon-Fri, 10am-6pm Sat & Sun Apr-Sep, 10am-4pm daily Oct-Mar; ☯ ; ⊙ Forest Hills) itself is safe. The well-designed Tropical Forest pavilion comes complete with lush vegetation, waterfalls, ring-tailed lemurs, ocelot, mandrills (a type of baboon) and a newly renovated indoor gorilla exhibit. The nearby Bird's World exhibit showcases indigenous wetland and swampland birds. Don't miss the magical **Butterfly Landing** (admission additional $1; ⊙ 10am-4:30pm Mon-Fri, 10am-5:30pm Sat & Sun Apr-Sep, closed Oct-Mar), where you can stroll among blooming perennials, gushing waterfalls and 1000 fluttering butterflies in free flight. Take the Orange Line to Forest Hills, then ride bus 16 to the Franklin Park Zoo.

South Boston & Dorcester

Columbia Point juts into the harbor south of the city center in Dorchester, one of Boston's edgier neighborhoods. The location is unlikely, but it does offer dramatic views of the city and a pleasant place to stroll. The museums – associated with the University of Massachusetts (UMass) Boston – are a part of ongoing revitalization efforts. The **HarborWalk** now connects this area to South Boston and Boston.

JOHN F KENNEDY LIBRARY & MUSEUM

The legacy of John F Kennedy is ubiquitous in Boston, but the official memorial to the 35th president is the **John F Kennedy Library & Museum** (off Map p71; ☎ 617-514-1600; www.jfklibrary .org; Columbia Point, Dorchester; adult/child/student & senior $10/7/8; ⊙ 9am-5pm; ⊕ JFK/UMass). The striking modern marble building – designed by IM Pei – was dubbed 'the shining monument by the sea' soon after it opened in 1979. Its architectural centerpiece is the magnificent glass pavilion, with soaring 115ft ceilings and floor-to-ceiling windows overlooking Boston Harbor.

The museum is a fitting tribute to JFK's life and legacy. The effective use of video recreates history for visitors who may or may not remember the early 1960s. A highlight is the museum's treatment of the Cuban Missile Crisis: a short film explores the dilemmas and decisions that the president faced, while an archival exhibit displays actual documents and correspondence from these gripping 13 days. Family photographs and private writings – of both John and Jacqueline – add a personal but not overly sentimental dimension to the exhibits.

COMMONWEALTH MUSEUM

This **museum** (off Map p71; ☎ 617-727-9268; www .commonwealthmuseum.org; 220 Morrissey Blvd, Columbia Point; admission free; ⊙ 9am-5pm Mon-Fri, 9am-3pm alternating Sat; ⊕ JFK/UMass) exhibits documents dating back to the first days of colonization. Rotating exhibits showcase various aspects of state history, ranging from the archaeology of the Big Dig (p81) to the lives of 18th-century Acadian exiles in Massachusetts.

Cambridge

Boston's neighbor to the north was home to the country's first college and first printing press. Thus Cambridge established early on its reputation as fertile ground for intellectual and political thought – a reputation that has been upheld over 350 years (and counting). This is due primarily to its hosting of the two academic heavyweights Harvard University and MIT. No less than seven presidents of the USA and countless cabinet members have graduated from Harvard University; 59 MIT faculty, staff and alums have won the Nobel Prize for chemistry, physics, economics, medicine and peace. Most noticeably, Cambridge's thousands of student residents ensure the city's continued vibrancy and diversity.

Cambridge is fondly called the 'People's Republic' for its progressive politics. In this vein, Cambridge City Hall was the first to issue marriage licenses to gay and lesbian couples, when same-sex marriages became legal in Massachusetts in 2004.

Life on the 'other side' is all about squares (pardon the pun). **Harvard Square** is overflowing with cafés, bookstores, restaurants and street musicians. Although many Cantabrigians (residents or natives of Cambridge) rightly complain that the square has lost its edge – once independently owned shops are continually gobbled up by national chains – Harvard Sq is still a vibrant, exciting place to hang out. Further east, grittier Central Sq is the stomping ground of MIT students.

CAMBRIDGE COMMON

There's a lot to Harvard Sq besides the university: it's a hotbed of Colonial and revolutionary history. Opposite the main entrance to Harvard Yard, **Cambridge Common** (Map p78; ⓰; ⊕ Harvard) is the village green where General Washington took command of the Continental Army on July 3, 1775. The traffic island at the south end, known as **Dawes**

THE STATUE OF THREE LIES

In Harvard Yard, the sculpture by Daniel Chester French is inscribed with 'John Harvard, Founder Of Harvard College, 1638' and is known as the statue of three lies:

- It does not actually depict Harvard (since no image of him exists), but a student chosen at random.
- John Harvard was not the founder of the college, but its first benefactor in 1638.
- The college was actually founded two years earlier, in 1636.

This Harvard symbol hardly lives up to the university's motto, *Veritas* (truth).

Harvard). It exhibits Western art from the Middle Ages to the present, including decorative arts. Set around an Italian Renaissance courtyard, the Fogg has one of the country's finest collections of impressionist and post-impressionist works. Entered through the Fogg, the **Busch-Reisinger Museum** (tours 1pm Mon-Fri) specializes in Central and Northern European art.

Across the street, the **Arthur M Sackler Museum** (Map p78; 617-495-9400; 485 Broadway; tours 2pm Mon-Fri; Harvard) is devoted to Asian and Islamic art. It boasts the world's most impressive collection of Chinese jade, as well as fine Japanese woodblock prints. One ticket covers admission to all three art museums; admission is free on Saturday morning.

HARVARD SCIENCE MUSEUMS

The **Museum of Natural History** (Map p78; 617-495-3045; www.hmnh.harvard.edu; 24 Oxford St; adult/child/student & senior $9/6/7; 9am-5pm; ; Harvard) is coming around to catering to the casual science buff, in addition to the botanists, zoologists and geologists that are its normal audience. The highlight is the famous botanical galleries, which feature more than 3000 lifelike pieces of handblown-glass flowers and plants. Also on site: zoological galleries (stuffed animals) and mineralogical galleries (shiny rocks).

Founded in 1866, the **Peabody Museum of Archaeology and Ethnology** (Map p78; 617-496-1027; www.peabody.harvard.edu; 11 Divinity Ave; adult/child/student & senior $9/6/7; 9am-5pm; Harvard) is one of the world's oldest museums devoted to anthropology. Rotating exhibits showcase pieces from its impressive collection, which focuses on artifacts from Native Americans and other indigenous groups. The Hall of the North American Indian traces how native peoples responded to the arrival of Europeans from the 15th to the 18th centuries.

One ticket covers admission to both science museums.

Island, pays tribute to the 'other rider' William Dawes, who rode through here on April 18, 1775, to warn that the British were coming (look for bronze hoof prints embedded in the sidewalk).

Across the street, **Christ Church** (Map p78) was used as barracks after its loyalist congregation fled. The adjacent **Old Burying Ground** (Map p78) is a tranquil Revolution-era cemetery, where Harvard's first eight presidents are buried.

HARVARD YARD

The geographic heart of **Harvard University** (Map p78; www.harvard.edu; Harvard) – where the brick buildings and leaf-covered paths exude academia – is Harvard Yard (through Anderson Gates from Massachusetts Ave). The focal point of the yard is the **John Harvard statue** (Map p78; see above), where every Harvard hopeful has a photo taken. The massive building with Corinthian columns and steep stairs is **Widener Library**, which contains more than 5 miles of books.

Learn many fun facts when you take a free campus tour, which departs from the **Harvard University Information Center** (Map p78; 617-495-1573; www.harvard.edu; Holyoke Center, 1350 Massachusetts Ave; Harvard). Check the website for details of the schedule.

HARVARD ART MUSEUMS

Harvard's oldest museum is the **Fogg Art Museum** (Map p78; 617-495-9400; www.artmuseums.harvard.edu; 32 Quincy St; adult/student/senior/child $9/6/7/free; 10am-5pm Mon-Sat, 1-5pm Sun, tours 11am Mon-Fri;

TORY ROW

Heading west out of Harvard Sq, Brattle St is the epitome of Colonial posh. Lined with mansions that were once home to royal sympathizers, the street earned the nickname Tory Row. The **Hooper-Lee-Nichols House** (off Map p78; 617-547-4252; www.cambridgehistory.org; 159 Brattle St; adult/student & senior $5/3; 2-4pm Tue-

Thu; ⊕ Harvard) is a 1685 Colonial that is open for architectural tours.

Brattle St's most famous resident was Henry Wadsworth Longfellow, whose stately manor is now known as the **Longfellow National Historic Site** (Map p78; ☎ 617-876-4491; www.nps.gov/long; 105 Brattle St; adult/child $3/free; ⊙ house 10am-4:30pm Wed-Sun May-Oct, grounds dawn-dusk year-round; ⊕ Harvard). The poet lived here for 45 years, writing many of his most famous poems including *Hiawatha*. Now under the auspices of the NPS, the Georgian mansion contains many of Longfellow's belongings and lush period gardens. The site also offers poetry readings and historical tours.

Brattle St ends at **Mt Auburn Cemetery** (off Map p78; ☎ 617-547-7105; 580 Mt Auburn St; admission free, guided tour $5; ⊙ 8am-5pm; ⊟ 71 or 73), the first 'garden cemetery' in the US. Maps pinpoint the rare botanical specimens and notable burial plots, including those of Mary Baker Eddy (founder of the Christian Science Church), Isabella Stewart Gardner (socialite and art collector), Winslow Homer (19th-century American painter), Oliver Wendell Holmes (US Supreme Court Justice) and Henry W Longfellow (19th-century writer).

MASSACHUSETTS INSTITUTE OF TECHNOLOGY (MIT)

The MIT campus near Central Sq offers a completely novel perspective on Cambridge academia: proudly nerdy, but not quite so tweedy as Harvard. The **MIT Information Center** (off Map p78; ☎ 617-253-4795; Lobby 7, 77 Massachusetts Ave, Cambridge; ⊙ 9am-5pm, tours 10:45am & 2:45pm Mon-Fri; ⊕ Central) offers excellent guided campus tours, where you can learn all about MIT's amazing contributions to the sciences.

Alternatively, get an up-close look at robots, holograms, strobe photography, kinetic sculptures and other scientific wonders at the **MIT Museum** (off Map p78; ☎ 617-253-4444; http://web .mit.edu/museum; 265 Massachusetts Ave; adult/child, student & senior $5/2; ⊙ 10am-5pm Tue-Fri, noon-5pm Sat & Sun; ⊕ Central).

A stroll around campus is proof that MIT supports artistic as well as technological innovation. Download a map of the **public art** (http:// web.mit.edu/lvac/www/collections/map.pdf) that bejewels the East Campus (east of Massachusetts Ave). The nearby **List Visual Arts Center** (☎ 617-253-4680; Weisner Bldg, 20 Ames St; suggested donation $5; ⊙ noon-6pm Tue-Thu, Sat & Sun, noon-8pm Fri; ⊕ Central) mounts sophisticated shows of contemporary art across all media. Don't miss the funky **Ray & Maria Strata Center** (32 Vassar St), an avant-garde building designed by architectural legend Frank Gehry.

ACTIVITIES
Biking & Running

More than 50 miles of bicycle trails originate in the Boston area. While riding through the downtown streets can be tricky, these mostly off-road trails offer a great opportunity for cyclists to avoid traffic and explore the city on two wheels. You can take your bike on any of the MBTA subway lines except the Green and Silver Lines, but you must avoid rush hours (7am to 10am and 4pm to 7pm weekdays) and always ride on the last train car.

MassBike (☎ 617-542-2453; www.massbike.org) is an excellent nonprofit organization with loads of information about bike trails, tours and other events, as well as details about biking laws in Massachusetts and tips for riding in the city.

Rubel BikeMaps (☎ 617-776-6567; www.bikemaps .com) produces laminated 'Pocket Rides,' 50 different loop rides in greater Boston or from area commuter rail stations. For the metro Boston area, look for the 'BU Bridge Bike Pack,' in which all tours start from the BU Bridge. See also p96.

Try the following outfits for bicycle rental:
Boston Bicycle (Map pp76-7; ☎ 617-236-0752; 842 Beacon St; per day/week $25/125; ⊙ 10am-7pm Mon-Sat, noon-6pm Sun; ⊕ St Mary's) Offers customized bike tours through the affiliate Urban Adventours (see p96). This is a convenient place to pick up a bike for riding along the Emerald Necklace. Keep in mind that you cannot bring your bike on the Green Line.
Cambridge Bicycle (off Map p78; ☎ 617-876-6555; www.cambridgebicycle.com; 259 Massachusetts Ave; per day/week $25/125; ⊙ 10am-7pm Mon-Sat, noon-6pm Sun; ⊕ Central) The Cambridge affiliate of Boston Bicycle. Convenient for biking along the Charles River.

CHARLES RIVER BIKE PATH

One of the most popular circuits runs along both sides of the Charles River between the bridge near the Museum of Science (p80) and the Mt Auburn St Bridge in Watertown Center (about 5 miles west of Cambridge). The round trip is 17 miles, but 10 bridges in between offer ample opportunity to turn around and shorten the trip. This trail isn't particularly well maintained (be careful of roots and narrow passes) and is often crowded with pedestrians. On Sunday from mid-April to mid-November, Memorial Dr

(Cambridge) is closed to cars between the Eliot Bridge and River Rd, which helps to relieve some of the traffic.

HARBORWALK

In theory, **HarborWalk** (Map pp72-3; www.boston harborwalk.com; ❻ Aquarium) extends for almost 47 miles, following the perimeter of Boston Harbor north through Charlestown and south through South Boston and Dorchester, as well as across the harbor in East Boston. In realty, the most accessible and best-marked portion of HarborWalk is along the Waterfront between Lewis Wharf and Fort Point Channel. The paved or boardwalk path weaves around the wharfs and marinas, affording many magnificent harbor views.

EMERALD NECKLACE

Designed by Frederick Law Olmstead, the **Emerald Necklace** (www.emeraldnecklace.org) is a chain of parks running through the middle of the city, from the Back Bay Fens to Jamaica Way to Arnold Arboretum. The packed dirt is fine for mountain bikes and hybrids, but not really suitable for road bikes. This shady path is not as crowded as the Charles River route, but beware of a few dangerous intersections and road crossings.

MINUTEMAN COMMUTER BIKEWAY

The best of Boston's bicycle trails starts in Arlington (near Alewife T station) and leads 10 miles to historic Lexington center (p132), then traverses an additional 4 miles of idyllic scenery and terminates in the rural suburb of Bedford. The wide, straight, paved path is in excellent condition, though it also gets crowded on weekends. The Minuteman Bikeway is also accessible from Davis Sq in Somerville via the 2-mile Community Path to Arlington.

SOUTHWEST CORRIDOR PARK

Almost 5 miles long, the **Southwest Corridor** (Map pp76–7) is a beautiful paved and landscaped walkway, running between and parallel to Columbus and Huntington Aves. The path leads from Back Bay, through the South End and Roxbury, to Forest Hills in Jamaica Plain. Take the Orange Line to any stop between Back Bay and Forest Hills. Forest Hills Cemetery is also a pleasant place to pedal.

Boating & Kayaking

The **Charles River Canoe & Kayak Center** (www.ski-paddle.com; adult per hr $14-20, child per hr $7) has two outlets offering canoe and kayak rental: **Newton** (off Map p71; ☎ 617-965-5110; 2401 Commonwealth Ave; ⏰ 10am-8pm Mon-Fri, 9am-8pm Sat & Sun Apr-Oct) and **Boston** (off Map p78; ☎ 617-462-2513; Soldiers Field Rd; ⏰ 4pm-7:45pm Thu, 1pm-7:45pm Fri, 10am-7:45pm Sat & Sun May–mid-Oct; ❻ Harvard). Daily rental rates are also available.

Community Boating (Map pp72-3; ☎ 617-523-1038; www.community-boating.org; Charles River Esplanade; rental per 2 days kayak/sailboat $50/$100; ⏰ 1pm-dusk Mon-Fri, 9am-dusk Sat & Sun Apr-Oct; ❻ Charles/MGH) offers experienced sailors unlimited use of sailboats and kayaks, but you'll have to take a test to demonstrate your ability. Located between the Hatch Memorial Shell and the Longfellow Bridge.

In Charlestown, **Courageous Sailing** (Map pp72-3; ☎ 617-242-3821; www.courageoussailing.org; 1 First Ave, Charlestown; half-day $95; ⏰ noon-dusk Tue-Fri, 10am-dusk Sat & Sun May-Oct; ❐ North Station) offers nonmembers, for a fee, the opportunity to take a Rhodes 19 out for a four-hour sail around the harbor.

Skating

All of the routes listed under Biking are also suitable for in-line skating (with the exception of some sections of the Emerald Necklace that are not paved). But the most popular spots are the Charles River Esplanade and – on Sundays – Memorial Dr in Cambridge. You can rent skates from **Beacon Hill Skate** (Map pp76-7; ☎ 617-482-7400; 135 Charles St S; per hr/day $10/25; ⏰ 11am-5:30pm Mon & Wed-Sat, noon-4pm Sun; ❻ New England Medical Center).

The **Inline Club of Boston** (ICB; www.sk8net.com) is a local group that hosts organized group skates for all different skill levels. Participants must sign a waiver before participating in the free events.

For ice skating:

Boston Common Frog Pond (Map pp72-3; ☎ 617-635-2120; www.bostoncommonfrogpond.org; Boston Common; adult/child $4/free, skate rental $8/5; ⏰ 10am-5pm Mon, 10am-9pm Tue-Sun mid-Nov–mid-Mar; ❻ Park St)

Kendall Square Community Skating (off Map pp72-3; ☎ 617-492-0941; www.paddleboston.com; 300 Athenaeum St, Cambridge; adult/child/student & senior $3/2/1, rental $5; ⏰ noon-5pm Mon, noon-8pm Tue-Thu, noon-9pm Fri, 11am-9pm Sat, 11am-6pm Sun; ❻ Kendall).

Rink at the Charles (Map p78; ☎ 617-661-5096; Elliot St, Cambridge; adult/child $5/3, skate rental $5; ⊙ 2-8pm Mon-Fri, 10am-8pm Sat & Sun Dec-Mar; ⊕ Harvard) In front of the Charles Hotel.

WALKING TOUR: FREEDOM TRAIL

The best introduction to revolutionary Boston is the Freedom Trail (Map p94). The redbrick path winds its way past 16 sites that earned this town its status as the cradle of liberty. The 2.5-mile trail follows the course of the conflict, from the Old State House, where Redcoats killed five men marking the Boston Massacre, to the Old North Church, where the sexton hung two lanterns to warn that British troops would come by sea. Visit the Boston Common information kiosk (p69) to pick up a free map or to hook up with a 90-minute guided tour led by the **Freedom Trail Foundation** (☎ 617-357-8300; www.thefreedomtrail.org; adult/child/senior $12/6/10; ⊙ 11am, noon & 1pm).

Start at **Boston Common** (1; p70), America's oldest public park. On the northern side of the park, you can't miss the gold-domed **Massachusetts State House** (2; p75) sitting atop Beacon Hill. On the eastern side of the Common, **Park St Church** (3; p75) stands on the corner of Tremont and Park Sts. Walk north on Tremont St, where you will pass the Egyptian Rival gates of the **Granary Burying Ground** (4; p75), the final resting place of many notable patriots.

Continue north to School St, where the stately, columned **King's Chapel** (5; p79) overlooks the adjacent burying ground. If it's open, take a peek at the interior, which is considered one of the finest examples of Georgian architecture. Turn east on School St, and take note of the bronze statue of Benjamin Franklin outside the Old City Hall. A plaque commemorates this spot as the **site of the first public school** (6; p80).

Continue down School St to Washington St, where the little brick building on the corner is known – appropriately as the **Old Corner Bookstore** (7). Built in 1718, this building was leased to a bookseller in 1829, when it commenced a 75-year run as a bookstore and literary and intellectual hotspot. It now houses the headquarters of Historic Boston, a nonprofit company that organizes efforts to preserve the city's historic buildings. Diagonally opposite this, the **Old South Meeting House** (8; p79) saw the beginnings of one of the American Revolution's most vociferous protests, the Boston Tea Party.

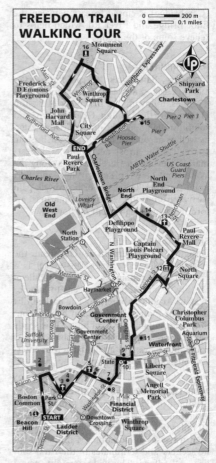

Further north on Washington St, the **Old State House** (9; p80) was the scene of more historic drama: the first reading of the Declaration of Independence. Outside the Old State House a ring of cobblestones marks the **Boston Massacre site** (10; p80), yet another uprising that fueled the revolution. Cross the traffic-filled intersection and head north on Congress St. Historic **Faneuil Hall Marketplace** (11; p83) has served as a public meeting place and marketplace for over 250 years. This is a choice spot to stop for lunch at the food court or from one of the nearby eateries.

From Faneuil Hall, make your way to the North End. The route is always subject to change, due to ongoing construction related to the Big Dig (see p81). Head north on Union

St, crossing in between the row of bars and restaurants and the Holocaust Memorial. Turn right on tiny Hanover St, weaving through the fruit and vegetable stalls of Haymarket, and walk across the North End Park. You will pop out at the base of the North End's main thoroughfare, Hanover St. Continue north for a block or two, before heading east on Richmond St. You will find yourself in charming North Sq, which is also the site of **Paul Revere's House** (**12**; p81).

Back on Hanover St, walk two blocks north to Paul Revere Mall. Besides a dramatic statue of the patriot himself, this park also provides a lovely vantage point to view your next destination, the **Old North Church** (**13**; p82). From the church, head west on Hull St to **Copp's Hill Burying Ground** (**14**; p82), with grand views across the river to Charlestown.

Continue west on Hull St to its end. Turn left on Commercial St and walk across the Charlestown Bridge. Turning right on Constitution Rd brings you to the Charlestown Navy Yard, home of the world's oldest commissioned warship, the **USS Constitution** (**15**; p82).

Now wind your way through the historic streets of Charlestown center to your final destination. Cut up to Chelsea St, then head north on Chestnut St. Take a quick left on Adams St, which leads past Winthrop Sq. Then turn north and walk one block to **Bunker Hill Monument** (**16**; p83), site of the devastating American Revolution battle.

From here, you can grab a bite to eat and recuperate in one of Charlestown's trendy or traditional eating establishments. The nearest T-station is across the bridge, North Station.

COURSES

The local adult education centers in Boston are incredible sources for courses, from walking historical tours to writing workshops hosted by local authors, to massage for couples. Most of the classes take place once a week over the course of a semester or season. But the centers also offer many short courses and one-day workshops on just about any subject. Try the following centers:

Boston Center for Adult Education (Map pp76-7; ☎ 617-267-4530; www.bcae.org; 5 Commonwealth Ave; ☼ 9am-6pm Mon-Thu, 9am-5pm Fri; ☻ Arlington)

Cambridge Center for Adult Education (Map p78; ☎ 617-547-6789; www.ccae.org; 42 Brattle St; ☼ 9am-9pm Mon-Thu, 9am-7pm Fri, 9am-2pm Sat; ☻ Harvard)

Boating

Charles River Canoe & Kayak Center (off Map p71; ☎ 617-965-5110; www.ski-paddle.com; 2401 Commonwealth Ave, Newton) Offers introductory kayaking classes for two or three sessions, as well as day-long introductory trips.

Community Boating (Map pp72-3; ☎ 617-523-1038; www.community-boating.org; Charles River Esplanade; ☻ Charles/MGH) Offers a wide variety of courses for paddlers, windsurfers and sailors, ranging from beginners to racers.

Cooking

The recreation division of the **Cambridge School of Culinary Arts** (off Map p78; ☎ 617-354-2020; www.cambridgeculinary.com; 2020 Massachusetts Ave, Cambridge; courses $70-95; ☻ Porter) offers one-time courses that focus on seasonal meals and crucial cooking skills. The most popular option is a series of courses for 'Cooking Couples' ($140).

Yoga

For detailed listings of Boston's yoga schools, see www.bostonyoga.com.

Back Bay Yoga Studio (Map pp76-7; ☎ 617-375-0785; www.backbayyoga.com; 1112 Boylston St; 90min class $15; ☻ Hynes) Offers massage, meditation and all forms of yoga.

Baptiste Power Vinyasa Yoga (www.baronbaptiste.com; 90min class adult/student $14/12) Boston (Map pp76-7; ☎ 617-423-9642; 139 Columbus Ave; ☻ Arlington); Cambridge (off Map p78; ☎ 617-661-9642; 2000 Massachusetts Ave; ☻ Porter) Courses take place in a room where temperatures reach 90°F, allowing for greater flexibility and lots of sweating.

Bikram Yoga (www.bikramyoga.com; 90min class adult/senior & student $20/15) Boston (Map pp72-3; ☎ 617-555-9926; 108 Lincoln St; ☻ South Station); Cambridge (Map p78; ☎ 617-556-9926; 30 John F Kennedy St; ☻ Harvard) Another option for heat yoga. The price includes two towels: you'll need them both.

South End Yoga (Map pp76-7; ☎ 617-247-2716; www.southendyoga.com; 11 W Concord St; 90min class $15-17; ☻ Back Bay) Offering courses in a variety of yoga forms, including ashtanga, mysore and vinyasa. The number of classes is limited and the schedule of classes varies, so check the website to see what fits in your schedule.

BOSTON FOR CHILDREN

Boston is a giant living history museum, the setting for many educational and lively field trips. In our listings, look for the child-friendly icon (👶) for Boston's top spots for kids. A handy reference book is *Kidding Around Boston* by Helen Byers (Avalon; $9). Most importantly, don't forget to think outside the box; many adult-oriented museums and historic sites have special programs geared toward kids. Check the following websites in advance to make the most of your visit with your child.

Boston Public Library (p87; www.bpl.org) BPL offers an incredible Kid's Page, including reading lists, tutorials and homework help for research projects, as well as some other fun and games. A similar site called the Teen Lounge exists for older kids.

Freedom Trail (p94; www.thefreedomtrail.org) Download a scavenger hunt or a reading list for your child before setting out. Also consider 'Boston by Little Feet' a walking tour designed especially for children. See Boston by Foot, opposite.

Massachusetts State House (p75; www.sec.state .ma.us) Check out the Kid's Zone. It features word games, trivia quizzes and the priceless *Ladybug Story*, a tale about how a group of kids used the legislative process to make the ladybug the official bug of Massachusetts. Also 'What's under the Gold Dome?' is the kid's guide to the State House.

Museum of Fine Arts (p88; www.mfa.org) Provides information on loads of programs offered by the MFA for kids of all ages. For example, Family Place (open Tuesday and Thursday) teaches children over the age of four to use art, music and poetry to explore the gallery's collections.

Paul Revere House (p81; www.paulreverehouse.org) Features a page 'Just for Kids' that allows children to learn about the Revere family kitchen (including a recipe for a Colonial snack: dried apples), play old-fashioned games, read age-specific articles and complete a crossword puzzle about the historic house.

Playgrounds

We're not sure if America's first public park is home to its first playground, but the **Boston Common** (p70) has a huge playscape with swings, jungle gyms and all the rest. Across the river, the **Cambridge Common** (p90) has the same.

Child Care

If you must leave the kids behind, a few agencies offer temporary babysitting services. Most upscale hotels also offer babysitting services or referral.

Boston Best Babysitter (☎ 617-268-7148; www .bbbabysitters.com; 1 child per hr $13-15 plus per additional child $1, per day $40, transportation fee $10)

In Search of Nanny, Inc (☎ 978-921-1735; www .insearchofnanny.com) For a fee, offers an updated list of recommended caregivers available on a one-time basis. Registration costs $40 plus $40 per day. An additional $14-18 per hour is paid directly to the caregiver.

Nanny Poppins (☎ 617-227-5437; www.nannypop pins.com; per hr $10-18 plus placement fee $30-50)

TOURS
Bike Tours

Boston Bike Tours (☎ 617-30-5902; www.boston biketours.com; with/without bike rental $30/24; 🕚 11am Fri-Sun) Every weekend Boston Bike Tours follows a different route, whether it's Paul Revere's Ride, the Freedom Trail or the Emerald Necklace.

Urban Adventours (Map pp76-7; ☎ 617-233-7595; www.urbanadventours.com; 842 Beacon St; tours $50-75; 🕚 10am, 2pm & 6pm; 🚇 St Mary's) Founded by avid cyclists who believe the best views of Boston are from a bicycle. The City View Ride provides a great overview of how to get around by bike. Other more specialized tours are for photographers and art and architecture buffs. Prices include bikes and helmets; reservations required.

Boat Tours

Boston Duck Tours (☎ 617-723-3825; www.boston ducktours.com; adult/child/student & senior $27/18/24; 🕚 9am-dusk Apr-Nov; 👶); Museum of Science (Map pp72-3; 🚇 Science Park) Prudential Center (pp76-7; 🚇 Copley) Land and water tours using modified amphibious vehicles from WWII depart from the Prudential Center and the Museum of Science. Rain or shine, the 90-minute narrated tour splashes around the Charles River, then takes to Boston city streets. Buy tickets in advance.

Boston Harbor Cruises (Map pp72-3; ☎ 617-227-4320; www.bostonharborcruises.com; 1 Long Wharf; adult/child/senior & student $19/15/17; 🕚 11am, 1pm & 3pm daily Jun-Aug, Sat & Sun Sep; 🚇 Aquarium) Narrated sightseeing trips around the harbor, as well as sunset cruises and trips through the Charles River locks.

Charles River Boat Co (Off Map pp72-3; ☎ 617-621-3001; http://charlesriverboat.com; Cambridgeside Galleria; adult/child/senior $13/6/10; 🕚 11:30am-4:30pm daily Jun-Aug, Sat & Sun Apr-May & Sep; 🚇 Lechmere) The 75-minute narrated trip travels the Charles River Basin between Harvard and the Boston Harbor locks.

Gondola di Venezia (Map pp72-3; ☎ 617-876-2800; www.bostongondolas.com; Community Boating, Charles River Esplanade; tours per couple $99-229; 🚇 Charles/ MGH) Make no mistake about it, the Charles River is not the Grand Canal. But the gondolier's technique and the craftsmanship of the boat make these private gondola rides a romantic treat. The basic one-hour gondola ride is $99, but there are a whole range of more extravagant tours, featuring breakfast ($119) or live accordian music

($139). The most romantic ride is the *bellissimo* ($229), which includes roses, photographs and a lithograph of the gondola.

Trolley Tours

Overheard on a Duck Tour: 'Trolleys can go in the water too… Once.' Nonetheless, trolley tours offer great flexibility because you can hop off at sites along the route and hop on the next trolley that comes along. There is little to distinguish the various companies (besides the color of the trolley).

Beantown Trolley (☎ 781-986-6100, 800-343-1328; www.brushhilltours.com; adult/child/senior $29/12/27; ◷ 9:30am-4:30pm) The only trolley that offers service to the Museum of Fine Arts and the Seaport District. The price includes hotel pickup and a harbor cruise from the New England Aquarium. Trolley color: red.

Discover Boston Tours (Map pp72-3; ☎ 617-742-1440; www.discoverbostontours.com; 66 Long Wharf; adult/child/senior 1 day $28/15/26, 2 days $38/25/35; ◷ 9am-5pm; ◉ Aquarium) Audio tapes available in Spanish, French, German and Japanese. Trolley color: white.

Old Town Trolley Tours (Map pp72-3; ☎ 617-369-800-868-7482; www.historictours.com; Old Atlantic Ave; adult/child/student & senior 1 day $29/9/25, 2 days $43/18/40; ◷ 9am-4pm Nov-Apr, 9am-5pm May-Oct; ◉ Aquarium) Price includes admission to the Old State House. Also offers a special 'Ghosts & Graveyards' tour by night. Trolley color: orange.

Walking Tours

The granddaddy of walking tours is the Freedom Trail, a 2.5-mile trail that traverses the city from the Boston Common to Charlestown. For details see p94. Most walking tours depart from the Boston Common Information Kiosk.

Black Heritage Trail (☎ 617-742-5415; www.nps.gov /boaf; tours free; ◷ 10am, noon & 2pm Mon-Sat Jul-Aug; ◉ Park St) A 1.6-mile walking tour that explores the history of the abolitionist movement and African American settlement on Beacon Hill. The NPS conducts guided tours in summer, but maps and descriptions for self-guided tours are available at the Museum of Afro-American History (p75). Tours depart from the Boston Common Information Kiosk.

Boston by Foot (☎ 617-367-3766; www.bostonbyfoot .com; tours $8-14; ⅙) This fantastic nonprofit offers 90-minute walking tours of Boston's neighborhoods. Specialty tours include Literary Landmarks, Boston Underfoot (with highlights from the Big Dig and the T) and Boston for Little Feet – a kid-friendly version of the Freedom Trail. Check the website to find out when and where.

Boston Movie Tour (☎ 866-668-4345; www.boston movietours.net; 147 Tremont St; adult/child/student & senior $20/10/17; ◷ 2pm Fri-Mon Jun-Sep; ◉ Park St) It's not Hollywood, but Boston has hosted its share of famous movie scenes. Stroll along the Movie Mile, site of famous scenes from *Good Will Hunting*, *A Civil Action* and *The Departed*.

Michele Topor's North End Market Tours (☎ 617-523-6032; www.northendmarkettours.com; per person $48) This 3½-hour tour around the North End includes shopping in a *salumeria* (delicatessen), sampling pastries at the local *pasticcerias* (cake and pastry shops) and touring an *enoteca* (wine shop). The sights and smells of the North End provide a great introduction to Italian cuisine and culture. Reservations required.

My Town Tours (☎ 617-536-8696; www.mytowninc .org; adult/child $15/10; ⅙) If you've had your fill of white men like Paul Revere and John Hancock, head to the South End to hear stories about immigrants, people of color and other working-class heroes.

Photo Walks (☎ 617-851-2273; www.photowalks.com; adult/youth $25/12; ◷ 10am & 1pm daily May-Sep, less often Oct-Apr) A walking tour combined with a photography lesson. Visit Boston's most scenic spots and get some picture-taking tips along the way. Reservations required.

Secret Tour (☎ 617-720-2283; www.northendboston .com/secrettours; per person $30; ◷ 10am, 1pm & 4pm Fri & Sat; ◉ Haymarket) This two-hour tour begins at Old North Sq – opposite Paul Revere's House – and explores the North End's hidden courtyards and passageways, thus uncovering the neighborhood's checkered past.

Tales of Olde Cambridge (☎ 617-354-3344; www .livelylore.com; per person $15) A husband-wife team – an actor and an educator – has developed an interactive, entertaining tour of historic Harvard Sq. Hear 'true tales of witches, patriots, heroes, heretics, revolutionaries, spies and (gasp) liberals.'

Unofficial Tours (☎ 203-305-9735; www.harv .unofficialtours.com; suggested donation adult & senior $20; ◷ 10:30am, 11:30am, 12:30pm, 1:30pm & 2:30pm; ◉ Harvard) This unofficial Harvard tour was founded by two dynamic students – 'a New England liberal and a conservative Texan' – who give the inside scoop on Harvard's history and student life at the university. Tours depart from the visitor information booth (p69) outside the Harvard Sq T-stop.

FESTIVALS & EVENTS

For information on events, the *Boston Globe* publishes a weekly calendar that comes out on Thursday. Prior to your arrival, check with the GBCVB (p69) or visit its website www .bostonusa.com. Remember that accommodations are much harder to secure during big events.

GAY & LESBIAN BOSTON

Out and active gay communities are visible all around Boston, especially in the South End and Jamaica Plain. Pick up the weekly *Bay Windows* (www.baywindows.com) and monthly *Sojourner* at **Calamus Bookstore** (Map pp72-3; ☎ 617-338-1931; www.calamusbooks.com; 92B South St; ☼ 9am-7pm Mon-Sat, noon-6pm Sun; ④ South Station), which is also an excellent source of information about community events and organizations. **Edge** (www.edgeboston.com) is an informative e-zine with lots of news, entertainment and commentary targeting gay audiences.

The biggest event of the Boston gay and lesbian community is **Boston Pride** (☎ 617-262-9405; www.bostonpride.org), a week of parades, parties, festivals and flag-raisings, held in mid-June.

There is no shortage of entertainment options catering to LGBTs. From drag shows to dyke nights, this sexually diverse community has something for everybody. The places reviewed below are some of our favorites:

For a glossy gay dance club, stop in **Club Café** (Map pp76-7; ☎ 617-536-0966; www.clubcafe.com; 209 Columbus Ave; ☼ noon-2am; ④ Arlington), a Boston mainstay where you can admire the fellas as you listen to the Madonna dance remix of the moment.

Fritz (Map pp76-7; ☎ 617-482-4428; www.fritzboston.com; 26 Chandler St; ④ Arlington) is inside the Chandler Inn. Enjoy a long bar full of chatty men and lots of bottles of booze, all dimly lit by pink Christmas lights.

Boston's most beautiful ladies put on quite a show at drag cabaret **Jacques** (Map pp76-7; ☎ 617-426-8902; www.jacquescabaret.com; 79 Broadway; admission $6-10; ④ Arlington).

On Friday night, **Toast Lounge** (off Map p78; ☎ 617-923-9211; www.toastlounge.com; 70 Union Sq, Somerville; ☼ 5pm-1am Sun-Thu, 9pm-2am Fri, 5pm-2am Sat; ④ Central), a basement martini lounge, is Boston's premier club for women. The place has two smallish dance floors, dim lights and a cozy bar. Take bus 91 from Central Sq or bus 87 from Lechmere.

Spring

Boston Marathon (☎ 617-236-1652; www.boston marathon.org) On the third Monday in April, thousands of runners compete in the 26.2-mile run that has been an annual event for more than a century.

Summer

Bunker Hill Day On June 17, includes a parade and battle re-enactment at Charlestown's Bunker Hill Monument (p83).

Harborfest (☎ 617-227-1528; www.bostonharborfest .com) This week-long festival is an extension of the Fourth of July weekend.

Independence Day (☎ 888-484-7677; www.july4th .org) On July 4, Boston hosts a line-up of free performances on the Esplanade, culminating with the Boston Pops playing Tchaikovsky's 1812 Overture, complete with brass cannon and synchronized fireworks.

Patron Saints' Feasts (www.northendboston.com) In the North End, Italian festivals honoring patron saints are celebrated with food and music on the weekends in July and August.

Restaurant Week (www.restaurantweekboston.com) At the end of August, participating restaurants around the city offer prix-fixe menus: $20 for lunch, $30 for dinner – an awesome opportunity to sample some restaurants that are otherwise out of your price range.

Fall

Head of the Charles (☎ 617-868-6200; www.hocr .org) The world's largest rowing event. The mid-October regatta draws more than 3000 collegiate rowers, while preppy fans line the banks of the river.

Pumpkin Festival (www.lifeisgood.com) The third Saturday in October is also the Saturday before Halloween. The local company Life is Good (which operates the store Jake's House, p123) invites everyone to bring a pumpkin to the Boston Common and carve it for a cause.

Winter

Boston Tea Party Reenactment (www.oldsouth meetinghouse.org) On the Sunday prior to December 16, costumed actors march from Downtown to the waterfront and dump bales of tea into the harbor.

First Night (www.firstnight.org) New Years Eve celebrations begin early on December 31 and continue past midnight, culminating in fireworks over the harbor. Buy a special button that permits entrance to many events.

SLEEPING

From poor student backpackers to high-class business travelers, Boston's tourist industry caters to all types of visitors. That means the city offers a complete range of accommodations, from backpacker-style dorms and hostels, to inviting guesthouses

DOING TIME IN A LUXURY HOTEL

For almost 140 years, the guests were not happy to be staying here. The conditions were not exactly welcoming (one former resident recalls sharing his cell with giant water bugs). The rooms were miniscule and the views were blocked by bars. 'It was a dungeon,' the resident insisted.

So it is with intended irony that the notorious Charles St Jail has been converted into the luxurious **Liberty Hotel** (Map pp72-3; ☎ 617-224-4000; www.libertyhotel.com; 225 Charles St; r from $375; P ⊠ 🖵 ﴾ﺥ﴿; ⦿ Charles/MGH).

When the Charles St Jail was built in 1851, its granite construction and cruciform shape were innovative architecture: the building became a prototype for prisons across the country. But more than a century passed and little was done to maintain the facility. In 1973 lawyers sued the city on behalf of the inmates. Conditions were so bad that the court declared they violated the constitutional rights of the incarcerated people. The city promised to make repairs, but instead the jail was shut down. The last inmate moved out in 1990.

Today, the space is exquisite. The spectacular lobby soars to a 90ft ceiling (it used to be an indoor exercise space). Some of the interior walls are the same red bricks that inmates used to stare at; bars remain on some windows for effect. The restaurant, Clink, preserves some old observation cells. For the most part, this place remembers its former incarnation as a prison in a playful way. But amid this sumptuousness, some wonder if it is conscionable to capitalize on the misfortune and misery of the inmates who lived here in such squalor.

in historic quarters, to swanky hotels with all the amenities you would expect.

A few agencies maintain databases of B&Bs in the area:

Bed & Breakfast Agency of Boston (☎ 617-720-3540, 800-248-9262, free from UK 0800-89-5128; fax 617-523-5761; www.boston-bnbagency.com; B&B s $70-90, d $100-160, studio apt $90-140, 1-bedroom apt $120-180) Lists over 100 different properties, including B&Bs and furnished apartments.

Bed & Breakfast Associates Bay Colony (☎ 781-449-5302, 888-486-6018, from UK 08-234-7113; www .bnbboston.com) A huge database of furnished rooms and apartments.

Beacon Hill

John Jeffries House (Map pp72-3; ☎ 617-367-1866; www.johnjeffrieshouse.com; 14 David Mugar Way; s/d $99/129, ste $155-165; P ⊠ 🖵 ﴾ﺥ﴿; ⦿ Charles/MGH) Reproduction furnishings, original molding, hardwood floors and mahogany accents warmly recall the era when Dr John Jeffries founded what is now the world-renowned Massachusetts Eye and Ear Infirmary. Many patients reside here when they come to town for treatment, as do travelers. While the parlor is a lovely spot to enjoy your complimentary breakfast, you can also whip up your own meal in your in-room kitchenette (available in most rooms).

Charles Street Inn (Map pp72-3; ☎ 617-314-8900, 877-772-8900; www.charlesstreetinn.com; 94 Charles St; r $350-400 Mon-Fri, $375-425 Sat & Sun; ⊗ 9am-9pm; ⊠ 🖵 ;

⦿ Charles/MGH) Built in 1860 as a showcase home, this Second Empire Victorian inn is now a model for how to meld the best of the 19th and 21st centuries. Ornate plaster cornices, ceiling medallions and window styles grace the nine rooms and common areas, where you're never vying for space or staff attention. Rooms are fitted with Victorian fabrics, handmade Turkish rugs, whirlpool tubs and working fireplaces. For added romance, a complimentary continental breakfast is served in your room.

Downtown

ourpick Harborside Inn (Map pp72-3; ☎ 617-723-7500; www.harborsideinnboston.com; 185 State St; r $189; P ⊠ 🖵 ﴾ﺥ﴿; ⦿ Aquarium or State) In its former life as a mercantile building, this structure played an integral role in the bustling waterfront port. Fortunately, renovations preserved historic details. Guest rooms have original exposed-brick and granite walls and hardwood floors. They're offset perfectly by Oriental carpets, sleigh beds and reproduction Federal-era furnishings. Add $20 for a city view.

Nine Zero (Map pp72-3; ☎ 617-772-5800; www.ninezero .com; 90 Tremont St; r from $249; P ⊠ 🖵 ﴾ﺥ﴿; ⦿ Park St) Chic. Boutique. The Kimpton Group's latest acquisition caters to a diverse audience. Deluxe rooms have high-speed internet access and all sorts of business-friendly high-tech gadgets. Bold splashes of color and mod bathrooms appeal to urbanites, while Egyptian cotton bedding tempts upper-crust doyennes. All of the above enjoy the marvelous views of the State House and the Granary (if they are willing to pay for them).

Omni Parker House (Map pp72-3; ☎ 617-227-8600; www.omnihotels.com; 60 School St; r Apr-Oct $289-389; P ⊠ 🖳 🕭; ☻ Park St or Government Center) Even though cold facts won't keep you warm at night, history and Parker House go hand in hand like JFK and Jackie O (who got engaged here). To wit: Malcolm X was a busboy here; Ho Chi Minh was a pastry chef here; and Boston Cream Pie, the official state dessert, was created here. As for the rooms, they're handsome and elegant, furnished with cherry furniture and antique heirlooms, but they do not lack modern amenities either.

Government Center & West End

Boston Backpackers' Youth Hostel (Map pp72-3; ☎ 617-723-0800, 774-287-9602; www.bostonbackpackers .com; 234 Friend St; dm $25; 🖳; ☻ North Station) Rising rents drove out two other hostels that were housed on this block. Enter the new Boston Backpacker's Youth Hostel. The space is architecturally appealing, with wide-plank floors, exposed-brick walls and sky-high ceilings. Six rooms on two levels are furnished with sturdy bunk beds. Tiled showers and bathrooms are spotless. Laundry facilities are available, as are discounts at the pub downstairs.

Shawmut Inn (Map pp72-3; ☎ 617-720-5544, 800-350-7784; www.shawmutinn.com; 280 Friend St; r/ste $99/189; ⊠ 🖳; ☻ North Station) This small hotel offers just the basic goods in each room: cable/satellite TV and dial-up internet access. Kitchenettes have a refrigerator, microwave and coffee/tea maker. Rooms can be on the smallish and darkish side, but the price is right.

Bulfinch Hotel (Map pp72-3; ☎ 617-624-0202; www .bulfinchhotel.com; 107 Merrimac St; d $199-249; P ⊠ 🖳 ☻ North Station) Exemplifying the up-and-coming character of this once-downtrodden district, the namesake hotel occupies a fully restored 19th-century flat-iron building on the western edge of the Bulfinch Triangle. This place oozes understated sophistication.

North End & Charlestown

La Cappella Suites (Map pp72-3; ☎ 617-523-9020; www.lacappellasuites.com; 290 North St; ste courtyard view $130-190, city view $150-210; ⊠ 🖳; ☻ Haymarket) 'La Cappella' refers to the small chapel of *La Societá di San Calogero di Sciacca* that previously occupied this redbrick building

in the North End. Now it is a private home with three spacious guest suites on the upper floors, topped off by a shared roof deck. Look for Italian marble flooring, panoramic views of the skyline and the harbor, and access to kitchen and common areas.

Constitution Inn & Fitness Center (Map pp72-3; ☎ 617-241-8400, 800-495-9622; www.constitutioninn.org; 150 Second Ave; d $170-180; P ⊠ 🖳 🕭; ☻ North Station) Housed in a granite building in the historic Charlestown Navy Yard, this excellent hostelry and YMCA-run fitness center caters to military personnel. But luckily the Y also accepts civilian guests. You'll find, among other things, crisp, modern rooms with all the basics (some with kitchenettes), plus an Olympic-class fitness center. It's no surprise that service is excellent: this place is run like a tight ship.

Chinatown & Theater District

Milner Hotel (Map pp72-3; ☎ 617-426-6220, 800-453-1731; www.milner-hotels.com; 78 Charles St S; d $140-175; P 🖳; ☻ Boylston) Some folks find the golden filigree, faux marble and chandeliers in the lobby at the Milner to be on the gaudy side. Get over that and you'll enjoy the spirit that infuses the youthful yet professional staff with a sense of fun. As for the rooms, they are small and darkish, with plain but passable decor. As Mr Milner said back in 1918, 'A bed and a bath for a buck and a half.' (Prices have gone up a little since 1918.)

South End

Berkeley Residence YWCA (Map pp76-7; ☎ 617-375-2524; www.ywcaboston.org/berkeley; 40 Berkeley St; s/d/tr $60/90/105, weekly $280/430/495; ☻ Back Bay) Most of the 200 rooms at this Y are open only to female guests, although one floor is for men. Bathrooms are shared, as are other useful facilities such as the telephone, library, TV room and laundry. It's a safe, friendly and affordable place for travelers. All rates include breakfast; dinner is also included in long-term rates.

Chandler Inn (Map pp76-7; ☎ 617-482-3450; www .chandlerinn.com; 26 Chandler St; r $151; ☻ Back Bay) This building's original use as a dormitory for the Coast Guard shows through in the spare design and furnishings of the rooms. The Chandler Inn may offer spartan quarters, but the location posits you within roll-me-home range of some of Boston's hottest spots. Gay travelers will feel right at home.

Encore (Map pp76-7; ☎ 617-247-3425; www.encore bandb.com; 116 W Newton St; r $180-210; P 🅧 🖵; 🖢 Back Bay or Massachusetts Ave) Co-owned by an architect and a set designer, this 19th-century townhouse sets a stage for both of their passions. Exposed-brick walls are adorned with exotic masks, interesting art and theatrical posters; bold colors and contemporary pieces furnish the spacious guestrooms. Each of the three rooms has a sitting area or private deck that offers a spectacular skyline view.

Back Bay
BUDGET & MIDRANGE

463 Beacon Street (Map pp76-7; ☎ 617-536-1302; www .463beacon.com; 463 Beacon St; d with shared bathroom $79, with private bathroom $149-164; P; 🖢 Hynes) What's more 'Boston' than a handsome historic brown stone in the Back Bay? This gorgeous guesthouse lets you live the blue-blood fantasy – and save your cash for the chichi boutiques and martini bars of Newbury St.

Copley House (Map pp76-7; ☎ 617-236-8300, 800-331-1318; www.copleyhouse.com; 239 W Newton St; studio apt $85-135, 1-bedroom apt $135-165; 🖵; 🖢 Prudential) With a full kitchen in each room, Copley House offers a comfortable spot to hole up for some well-deserved peace and quiet. The simple apartment-style rooms are located in four different buildings, straddling the Back Bay and the South End. A judicious use of antique wood and big windows beaming with light make this Queen Anne–style inn a place of respite and a handy base for exploring Boston.

Commonwealth Court Guest House (Map pp76-7; ☎ 617-424-1230, 888-424-1230; www.commonwealthcourt .com; 284 Commonwealth Ave; r $99-140; 🖢 Hynes) The Euro-style guesthouse is housed in a turn-of-the-century brownstone in the heart of Back Bay. Once a private residence, it retains a homey feel and lots of lavish architectural details. Service is pleasant but not overly attentive (maid service occurs only twice a week).

College Club (Map pp76-7; ☎ 617-536-9510; www .thecollegeclubofboston.com; 44 Commonwealth Ave; s with shared bathroom $99-105, d with private bathroom $170-190; 🖵; 🖢 Arlington) Originally a private club for female college graduates, the College Club has 11 enormous rooms with high ceilings, now open to both sexes. After a recent renovation, the place looks wonderful. Period details, typical of the area's Victorian brownstones, include claw-foot tubs, ornamental fireplaces and bay windows. Rates include continental breakfast.

our pick Newbury Guest House (Map pp76-7; ☎ 617-437-7666, 800-437-7668; www.hagopianhotels.com; 261 Newbury St; s/d from $120/135; P 🅧 🖵; 🖢 Hynes or Copley) Dating to 1882, these three interconnected brick and brownstone buildings offer big bang for the buck. Details like molded ceilings, carved mantles and bay windows are still visible. A complementary continental breakfast is laid out next to the marble fireplace in the salon.

Copley Inn (Map pp76-7; ☎ 617-236-0300, 800-232-0306; www.copleyinn.com; 19 Garrison St; r $155; 🖢 Prudential) Although much of the old brownstone's character has been rehabbed right out of it, the Copley Inn is still a very nice, comfortable and convenient establishment. Equipped with kitchens, rooms in this four-storey walk-up are relatively spacious. As such, there's plenty of pay-off in sacrificing atmosphere for sweet elbow room.

Charlesmark at Copley (Map pp76-7; ☎ 617-247-1212; www.thecharlesmark.com; 655 Boylston; r $159-189; P 🅧 🖵; 🖢 Copley) This hip hostelry sits at the crossroads of Euro-style luxury and ingenious functionality. The design is classic modernism. And the effect is upscale, urbane and surprisingly affordable. The downstairs lounge spills out onto the sidewalk where the people-watching is tops.

Midtown Hotel (Map pp76-7; ☎ 617- 262-1000, 800-343-1177; www.midtownhotel.com; 220 Huntington Ave; r $159-239; P 🅧 🖵 🖳; 🖢 Symphony) This low-rise motel looks like it belongs by the side of the highway, instead of in the shadow of the Prudential Center. But its spacious rooms fill up with families, businesspeople and tour groups. That's because the price is right and the location is unbeatable. Service is friendly and efficient; rooms are plain but clean.

TOP END

Copley Square Hotel (Map pp76-7; ☎ 617-536-9000, 800-225-7062; www.copleysquarehotel.com; 47 Huntington Ave; s/d $189/219; P 🅧 🖵; 🖢 Copley or Back Bay) It's downright heroic when a fine hotel wins awards for its environmental vision. Everything from how the hotel does its laundry (no chlorine) to the fuel used in its vans (compressed natural gas) diminishes the environmental footprint without diminishing the elegance that pervades the Copley. This superlative attention to environmental impact goes hand-in-green-hand with superior attention to its guests.

Lenox Hotel (Map pp76-7; ☎ 617-536-5300, 800-225-7676; www.lenoxhotel.com; 61 Exeter St; r $255-425, deluxe $315-455, ste $375-515; (P) (X) (Q); (θ) (Copley) The Lenox bundles together good service, great location and nice rooms. What more can you hope for? Guest rooms are comfortably elegant (with chandeliers and crown molding) without being stuffy. If your pockets are deep enough, it's worth splurging for a junior suite, which boast the best views. Prices vary according to the time of year, so check the cost when booking.

Colonnade (Map pp76-7; ☎ 617-424-7000; www.col onnadehotel.com; 120 Huntington Ave; r $429; (P) (X) (Q) (G); (θ) Prudential) Of all the many reasons to stay at the Colonnade, from the handsome guestrooms to the vibrant Parisian bistro to the prime location, none is more compelling than its enticing rooftop pool. Known as RTP, the pool is a glamorous place to see and be seen; and it's also optimal for alfresco dining, sunbathing and yes, even swimming.

Kenmore Square & Fenway

BUDGET

YMCA of Greater Boston (Map pp76-7; ☎ 617-536-7800; www.ymcaboston.org; 316 Huntington Ave; s/d/tr/q $46/66/$81/$96; (Q); (θ) Northeastern) The Village People were right: It *is* fun to stay at the YMCA. You can use the gyms, indoor track, basketball and squash courts and swimming pool; you get a hearty breakfast and free passes to various programs. Rooms (rented to both genders May to August but only to men the rest of the year) are small; stark, battered furnishings are on a par with local hostels. But the place is pretty clean, in a locker-room sort of way.

Hostelling International – Boston (Map pp76-7; ☎ 617-536-1027; www.bostonhostel.org; 12 Hemenway St; dm $28-45, d $70-100; (X) (Q); (θ) Hynes) Same-sex and coed dorm-style bunk rooms hold four to six people each, plus there are some private rooms for couples. The price includes sheets, towels, soap and shampoo, as well as breakfast. The 200 beds are almost always full, so reserve as far in advance as possible; book online for the cheapest rate. The best feature of this hostel is the daily activities arranged by the events coordinator: walking tours, museum visits and comedy clubs, all at discounted (if not free) rates.

Fenway Summer Hostel (Map pp76-7; ☎ 617-267-8599, reservations 617-536-1027; www.bostonhostel.org; 575 Commonwealth Ave; dm/r $35/89, nonmembers $38/92; (X) (Q); (θ) Kenmore) This former Howard Johnson hotel turned HI (Hostelling International)

youth hostel doubles as a Boston University dorm, so it's only open for travelers from June to August. Rooms have three beds each: rent the bed or rent the room. Each room has its own bathroom, which allows plenty of privacy in hostel-hopping terms.

MIDRANGE

ourpick **Oasis Guest House** (Map pp76-7; ☎ 617-267-2262, 800-230-0105; www.oasisgh.com; 22 Edgerly Rd; s with shared bathroom $89-99, d with shared bathroom $89-119, with private bathroom $109-159; (P) (X) (Q); (θ) Hynes or Symphony) True to its name, this homey guesthouse is a peaceful, pleasant oasis in the midst of Boston's chaotic city streets. Thirty-odd guest rooms occupy four attractive, brick, bow-front townhouses on this tree-lined lane. The modest, light-filled rooms are tastefully and traditionally decorated, most with queen beds and nondescript prints.

Buckminster Hotel (Map pp76-7; ☎ 617-236-7050, 800-727-2825; www.bostonhotelbuckminster; 645 Beacon St; r from $120; (P) (X); (θ) Kenmore) The Buckminster offers 100 nearly affordable rooms, some with views into Fenway Park. Euro-style rooms and suites are quite roomy, with all the tools and toys of comfort and convenience.

Gryphon House (Map pp76-7; ☎ 617-375-9003; www .innboston.com; 9 Bay State Rd; r $189-205; (P) (X) (Q); (θ) Kenmore) A premier example of Richardson Romanesque, this beautiful five-storey brownstone is a paradigm of artistry and luxury overlooking the picturesque Charles River. Eight spacious suites have different styles – Victorian, Gothic, Arts & Crafts, etc – but they all have 19th-century period details. Inquire about discounts for Red Sox fans (seriously!). Rates may increase when special events are being held.

Jamaica Plain

Taylor House (off Map p71; ☎ 617-983-9334; www .taylorhouse.com; 50 Burroughs St; s $125-159, d $145-220; (P) (X) (Q); (θ) Green St) Sitting pretty pond-side, this gracious Italianate Victorian mansion has undergone a loving restoration – apparent from the ornamental details throughout the house and the gorgeous gardens outside. The three spacious guest rooms have dark polished-wood floors, sleigh beds and plenty of sunshine. Dave and Daryl are your designers, decorators and amazing hosts. P.S. Must love dogs (two friendly golden retrievers live here too).

FARMERS MARKETS

Touch the produce at **Haymarket** (Map pp72-3; Blackstone St; ☉ 8am-5pm Fri & Sat; ⊙ Haymarket), you risk the wrath of the vendors ('They're a friggin' dollar – quit looking at the strawberries and just buy 'em!'). But no-one else in the city matches these prices on ripe-and-ready fruits and vegetables.

Most neighborhoods have a seasonal farmers market from mid-May to late November. In addition to just-picked fruit and local vegetables, you might find Vermont farmstead and artisanal cheese, crusty loaves and tempting fruit tarts, all fresh, fresh, fresh. Some locations (☎ 617-626-1700 for further inforemation):

- **City Hall Plaza** (Map pp72-3; ☉ 11am-6pm Mon & Wed; ⊙ Government Center)
- **Downtown Crossing** (Map pp72-3; Washington & Summer Sts; ☉ 9am-5pm; ⊙ Downtown Crossing)
- **Copley Sq** (Map pp76-7; ☉ 11am-6pm Tue & Fri May-Oct; ⊙ Copley)
- **Charles Hotel** (Map p78; 1 Bennett St, Cambridge; ☉ 10am-3pm Sun; ⊙ Harvard)

Cambridge

Irving House (Map p78; ☎ 617-547-4600, 877-547-4600; www.irvinghouse.com; 24 Irving St; s/d with shared bathroom $100/165, s/d/q with private bathroom $135/185/215; P ⊠ ☐ ; ⊙ Harvard) Call it a big B&B or a homey hotel, this property behind Harvard Yard welcomes even the most world-weary traveler. The 44 rooms range in size, but every bed is covered with a quilt and big windows let in plenty of light. Perks include museum passes and laundry facilities.

Harding House (off Map p78; ☎ 617-876-2888, 877-489-2888; www.cambridgeinns.com/harding/; 288 Harvard St; s/d with shared bathroom $100/125, s/d/q with private bathroom from $155/225/240; P ⊠ ☐ ; ⊙ Central) This delightful treasure blends refinement and comfort, artistry and efficiency. Rooms are spacious and bright. Old wooden floors toss back a warm glow and sport gorgeous throw rugs. Lovely antique furnishings complete the inviting atmosphere.

Kendall Hotel (off Map pp72-3; ☎ 617-577-1300; www.kendallhotel.com; 350 Main St; r $175-485; P ⊠ ☐ ; ⊙ Kendall) Once the Engine 7 Firehouse, this city landmark is now a cool and classy all-American hotel. The 65 guest rooms retain a firefighter riff, without a whiff of 'cutsie.' Bold color choices include mustard yellow, burnt orange and deep-sea blue. There's no scrimping at the breakfast table, either, with a full buffet included. Prices vary widely according to the time of year.

Hotel@MIT (off Map p78; ☎ 617-577-0200, 800-222-8733; www.hotelatmit.com; 20 Sidney St; r $179-259; P ⊠ ☐ ; ⊙ Central) The Hotel@MIT near Central Sq fuses art, design and science. Rooms and suites are awash with wood, chrome and ergonomically designed furniture. Computer boards equipped with high-speed internet con-

nections are built into wood armoires. Guests may be world-famous geneticists or Nobel Prize-winning technologists, so this hip Hilton hotel doesn't skimp on providing them all the high-tech and luxury amenities they expect.

Charles Hotel (Map p78; ☎ 617-864-1200; www.charleshotel.com; 1 Bennett St; r from $269; P ☐ ; ⊙ Harvard) 'Simple, Stylish, Smart.' Harvard Sq's most illustrious hotel lives up to its motto. Overlooking the Charles River, this institution has hosted the university's most esteemed guests, from Bob Barker to the Dalai Lama. Decor at the Charles – including rooms and restaurants – is surprisingly sparse, but the facilities include the luxuries and amenities one would expect from a highly rated hotel.

Inn at Harvard (Map p78; ☎ 617-491-2222; www.theinnatharvard.com; 1201 Massachusetts Ave; d $289-319; P ⊠ ☐ ; ⊙ Harvard) The inn's collegiate atmosphere is appropriate for its setting, just outside the gates of Harvard Yard. All guest rooms are decorated with contemporary colors, cherry-wood furniture and original artwork. Onsite services are limited – this is not a full-service hotel after all – but guests are allowed to use the university gym and all the resources of Harvard Sq are at your doorstep.

EATING

These days you'll have to look hard to find the old standards of New England cuisine: boiled dinner (Irish-style corned beef, potatoes and cabbage); seafood Newburg (seafood dish with a heavy cream sauce); and – of course – Boston baked beans (navy beans and salt pork in molasses). Some chefs might prepare these dishes on a cold winter's day

BOSTON

STRAIGHT FROM THE CHEF'S MOUTH

Gordon Hamersley is the chef and proprietor at Hamersley's Bistro (p110), in the South End. He began cooking as a student at Boston University in the early 1970s. After receiving formal training in Los Angeles and in France, he moved back to Boston and opened Hamersley's in 1987.

What was it about Boston that made you decide to move back and open your restaurant here? A conversation with Julia Child convinced me that coming back to Boston was a great idea. She mentioned Jasper White, Lydia Shire, Moncef Meddeb and others that were doing good food here and a young restaurant scene with potential. I also hated rooting for the Red Sox from the West Coast. That was it really. We decided to move back here – the place I began cooking…

What is unique about Boston cuisine or dining? The natural products from New England set us apart from other states. Our great shellfish and ground fish, small farms raising high-quality animals… and a vibrant vegetable farm scene very close to the city really make Boston a unique place to cook.

What would you recommend from the menu at Hamersley's Bistro for a visitor to our city? I guess items in that season that represent New England and my particular style of cooking. For example, tonight we're doing a halibut and clam roast with black trumpet mushrooms and bacon. It typifies the New England products and is cooked in a way that shows off my style.

How has Boston's restaurant 'scene' changed over the past decade? It has gone from a very formal dining scene with fancy rooms, high prices and stuffy service to one where we are more casual now. What seems to be important for diners is the quality of the food and wine lists and a relaxed (not necessarily less expensive) atmosphere.

But the food here is really quite diverse now too. As a diner you can find a vast array of food styles that are really top notch. French, Italian, Thai, Japanese, Chinese, Spanish and American cooking really shines now more than ever and it is cooked by well-trained and dedicated chefs.

What trends and changes can diners look forward to in the future? I think the trend of small, privately owned, high-quality places is going to continue to grow here. I'm really pleased that new young chefs are emerging and that the chain types are being successfully kept at bay. The trend toward more organic food is here to stay, I think, and you'll find it making inroads into less expensive places as the price of organic produce comes down.

As related to Mara Vorhees

under the trendy label of 'comfort food,' but they no longer define dining in Boston.

Seafood still reigns supreme (and foodies are well advised to take advantage of every opportunity to eat it). It's still frequently fried, but also grilled, pan-seared or prepared in any number of creative ways.

Boston obviously presents some fine opportunities to feast on Italian and Chinese fare, but other more exotic ethnic cuisines are also well represented, especially Korean, Thai, Portuguese and Indian. In recent years Mediterranean influences have become more pronounced, and Middle Eastern food is becoming mainstream. Whether it's called tapas or meze, 'small plates' are gaining popularity, as diners recognize the benefit of sampling lots of different menu items.

Eating cheaply does not mean eating badly. But if you want to splurge, you will find some of the country's most highly regarded chefs in Boston. Expect to pay less than $15 per person

for a meal at a budget eatery, and from $15 to $30 per person at midrange establishments (not including drinks). Top-end restaurants will set you back at least $30 per person.

Beacon Hill

For an afternoon of people-watching and coffee-drinking or a night of starry eyes and sweet nothings, Beacon Hill's old-world ambiance lends romance, and there are some gems hidden away amid these cobblestone streets. Climbing up Charles St, you'll find a mix of cute cafés, quick bites and gourmet delicatessens, plus no shortage of swanky spots.

BUDGET

Try either of these places for a taste of Beacon Hill's best pizza.

Upper Crust (Map pp72-3; ☎ 617-723-9600; 20 Charles St; meals $8-12; ☯ lunch & dinner; Ⓥ ⓖ; ◉ Charles/ MGH) Neapolitan-style pizza features crispy thin crust and fresh, straightforward toppings.

Order your pie as you like it or sample the 'slice of the day.'

Figs (Map pp72–3; ☎ 617-742-3447; 42 Charles St; meals $15-30; ⏰ lunch & dinner; Ⓥ ; Ⓞ Charles/MGH) Brainchild of celebrity chef Todd English. Enjoy whisper-thin crusts topped with interesting, exotic toppings. Case in point: the namesake fig and prosciutto with gorgonzola cheese. There is another location (the original) in Charlestown (Map pp72–3).

MIDRANGE

Panificio (Map pp72–3; ☎ 617-227-4340; 144 Charles St; meals $8-25; ⏰ breakfast, lunch & dinner; Ⓥ ⏰ ; Ⓞ Charles/MGH) It's not easy to snag a spot in this cozy, sun-filled bistro. By day, regulars stop in for fresh soups and sandwiches, buttery pastries and piping hot coffee. In the evenings, the menu expands to include homemade pastas and hot meat dishes. Don't miss the weekend Italian brunch, featuring toasted bread with decadent toppings.

Paramount (Map pp72–3; ☎ 617-720-1152; 44 Charles St; meals $8-30; ⏰ breakfast, lunch & dinner; Ⓥ ; Ⓞ Charles/MGH) Basic diner fare includes pancakes, steak and eggs, burgers and sandwiches, and big, hearty salads. For dinner, add table service and candlelight and the place goes upscale without losing its down-home charm. The menu is enhanced by homemade pastas, a selection of meat and fish dishes and an impressive roster of daily specials.

Scollay Square (Map pp72–3; ☎ 617-742-4900; 21 Beacon St; meals $15-30; ⏰ lunch & dinner; Ⓞ Park St) Down the road from the former Scollay Sq, the retro restaurant hearkens back to the glory days of its namesake. Old photos and memorabilia adorn the walls, including a series of burlesque beauties peering out from behind the bar, where suits sip martinis to big-band music. The classic American fare is reliably good, while service – formally dressed in black and white – is excellent.

TOP END

Bin 26 Enoteca (Map pp72–3; ☎ 617-723-5939; 26 Charles St; meals without wine $25-40; ⏰ lunch & dinner Mon-Sat, dinner Sun; Ⓞ Charles/MGH) If you are into your wine, you'll be into the bin. With big windows overlooking Charles St and wine bottles lining the walls, the interior is decidedly minimalist. The extensive wine list includes some fancy bottles that are out of many travelers' price range, as well as a moderately priced house wine that is bottled in Italy just for the restau-

rant. The food is seasonal and simple, focusing on antipasti, cheese, charcuterie and pasta.

No 9 Park (Map pp72–3; ☎ 617-742-9991; 9 Park St; dinner $60; ⏰ lunch & dinner Mon-Fri, dinner Sat; Ⓞ Park) Set in a 19th-century mansion, this swanky place tops many lists for fine dining in Boston. Chef-owner Barbara Lynch has been lauded by food and wine magazines for her delectable French and Italian culinary masterpieces (featured in a daily changing tasting menu, $135 with wine) and her first-rate wine list.

Downtown

The streets east of Boston Common (also known as the Ladder District) boast some of Boston's finest fine dining. The nearby Financial District is the workaday world for thousands of bankers, lawyers and office managers, so there is no shortage of sandwich shops and lunch spots. The cheapest eats in Boston are hawked at Downtown Crossing, on Summer between Washington and Chauncy Sts, where lunch-cart vendors offer tasty, inexpensive fast food like burritos, sandwiches and hot dogs.

BUDGET

Chacarero (Map pp72–3; ☎ 617-367-1267; 26 Province St; meals $5-10; ⏰ 11am-7pm Mon-Fri; ⏰ ; Ⓞ Downtown Crossing) A *chacarero* is a traditional Chilean sandwich made with grilled chicken or beef, Muenster cheese, fresh tomatoes, guacamole and the surprise ingredient: steamed green beans. Stuffed into homemade bread, these sandwiches are the hands-down favorite for lunch around Downtown Crossing.

Pressed (Map pp72–3; ☎ 617-482-9700; 2 Oliver St; meals $8-12; ⏰ breakfast & lunch Mon-Fri; Ⓥ ; Ⓞ Downtown Crossing) The simple, straightforward menu features almost 20 different sandwiches, all made on fresh bread and pressed in a heated grill. Our favorite is the Cuban (pork, ham, cheddar and pickles on *ciabatta*) but there are many authentic Italian options and loads of ideas for vegetarians. Another outlet is in the Seaport District (off Map pp72–3).

Sam La Grassa's (Map pp72–3; ☎ 617-357-6861; 44 Province St; meals $10-15; ⏰ 11am-5pm; Ⓞ Downtown Crossing) Step up to the counter and place your order for one of Sam La Grassa's signature sandwiches, then find a spot at the crowded communal table. You won't be disappointed by the famous Rumanian pastrami or the 'fresh from the pot' corned beef.

MIDRANGE & TOP END

Sakurabana (Map pp72-3; ☎ 617-542-4311; 57 Broad St; meals $12-30; ⏰ lunch & dinner; 🚇 Downtown Crossing) The surroundings aren't too snazzy, but the fish is fresh and tasty at this hole-the-wall sushi bar. The place gets packed at lunchtime as white collars descend from the surrounding office buildings to fill up on sashimi, teriyaki and tempura.

Silvertone (Map pp72-3; ☎ 617-338-7887; 69 Bromfield St; meals $15-30; ⏰ lunch & dinner; 🚇 Park St) B&W photos and retro advertisement posters create a nostalgic atmosphere at this still-trendy pub and grill. The old-fashioned comfort food is always satisfying (mac and cheese comes highly recommended), as is the cold beer drawn from the tap.

our pick **Ivy** (Map pp72-3; ☎ 617-451-1416; 49 Temple Place; meals $20-30; ⏰ lunch & dinner; 🚇 Park St) Ivy is the rare place that manages to combine all the elements: chic, urban decor; a cool but unpretentious vibe; and excellent, innovative food and drink. All this, and it won't break your bank. The menu is mostly small plates – pastas, salads and seafood – meaning more *piatti* (dishes) to sample and share. Afterwards, all guests receive a complementary scoop of organic gelato – a fine finish to your meal.

Government Center & West End

After the massive redevelopment of the 1950s and more recent construction related to the Big Dig (p81), this neighborhood is suffering from a shortage of eating options. If you are looking for someplace to chow down before an event at the Banknorth Garden, head to the Bullfinch Triangle, southeast of the arena.

Osteria Rustico (Map pp72-3; ☎ 617-742-8770; 85 Canal St; meals $10-15; ⏰ breakfast & lunch Mon-Sat; 🚇 North Station) Open only for breakfast and lunch, this family-run Italian joint is one of Boston's best-kept secrets. But those in the know keep coming back for more – staff seem to know everyone by name, or at least by their favorite sandwich. Pastas, salads and subs are all highly recommended.

Anthem (Map pp72-3; ☎ 617-523-8383; 138 Portland St; lunch $15-20, dinner $15-40; ⏰ lunch & dinner Mon-Fri, dinner Sat; 🚇 North Station) This sophisticated restaurant exudes a cool, quirky Goth ambiance. The menu is mod, offering upscale comfort food, like mighty meatloaf, *tasso* (a kind of Cajun ham), mac and four cheeses, and baked-tuna-and-noodle casserole. Reservations recommended on event nights.

North End

The streets of the North End are lined with *salumerie* and *pasticcerie* and more restaurants per block than anywhere else in Boston. Hanover St is the main drag, but the southern end of Salem St is loaded too. Many do not take reservations, so arrive early or be prepared to wait.

For dessert, head to **Maria's Pastry** (Map pp72-3; ☎ 617-523-1196; 46 Cross St; ⏰ 7am-7pm; 🚻; 🚇 Haymarket) for Boston's most authentic Italian pastries, or to the **Gelateria** (Map pp72-3; ☎ 617-720-4243; 272 Hanover St; ⏰ 10am-midnight; 🚻; 🚇 Haymarket) for a dish of gelato, ice cream's Italian cousin.

BUDGET

The North End's best pizza can be found at the places listed here.

Galeria Umberto (Map pp72-3; ☎ 617-227-5709; 289 Hanover St; meals $2-5; ⏰ lunch Mon-Sat; 🚇 Haymarket) This lunchtime legend closes as soon as the slices are gone. Loyal patrons line up early so they are sure to get theirs.

Pizzeria Regina (Map pp72-3; ☎ 617-227-0765; 11½ Thatcher St; meals $8-15; ⏰ lunch & dinner; 🚻; 🚇 Haymarket) Famous for brusque but endearing waitresses and crispy, thin-crust pizza.

MIDRANGE

Giacomo's Ristorante (Map pp72-3; ☎ 617-523-9026; 355 Hanover St; meals $15-30; ⏰ dinner; 🚇 Haymarket) Customers usually line up before the doors open so they are guaranteed a spot in the first round of seating at this North End favorite. Enthusiastic and entertaining waiters, plus cramped quarters, ensure that you get to know your neighbors. The cuisine is no-frills southern Italian fare, served in unbelievable portions.

Pomodoro (Map pp72-3; ☎ 617-367-4348; 319 Hanover St; meals $20-30; ⏰ dinner; 🚇 Haymarket) This cozy hole-in-the-wall place on Hanover is one of the North End's most romantic settings for delectable Italian cuisine. The food is simply but perfectly prepared: fresh pasta, spicy tomato sauce, grilled fish and meats, and wine by the glass. Credit cards are not accepted and the toilet is across the street, but that's all part of the charm.

Daily Catch (Map pp72-3; ☎ 617-523-8567; 323 Hanover St; meals $20-30; ⏰ lunch & dinner; 🚇 Haymarket) Although owner Paul Freddura long ago added a few tables and an open kitchen, this shoebox fish joint still retains the atmosphere of a retail fish market; fortunately, it also retains the freshness of the fish. There's not much room to maneuver but you can certainly keep an eye on how your monkfish marsala or lobster *fra diavolo* is being prepared. The specialty is calamari, fried to tender perfection.

our pick Trattoria Il Panino (Map pp72-3; ☎ 617-720-5720; 11 Parmenter St; meals $20-30; ⏱ lunch & dinner; ⊕ Haymarket) A rare opportunity for alfresco dining, this charming trattoria offers seating in the ever-pleasant garden during summer months. When weather is foul, settle into a cozy corner of the dimly lit dining room. It's a romantic rendezvous, only enhanced by your sweet-talking, Italian-accented waiter. Budget-minded travelers can head across the street, where Il Panino's express outlet sells some of the same exquisite pasta dishes.

TOP END

Neptune Oyster (Map pp72-3; ☎ 617-742-3474; 63 Salem St; meals $30-40; ⏱ lunch & dinner; ⊕ Haymarket) Neptune's menu hints at Italian, but you'll also find elements of Mexican, French Cajun and old-fashioned New England. The daily seafood specials and impressive raw bar (featuring three kinds of oysters, plus little-necks, crabs and mussels) confirm that this newcomer is not your traditional North End eatery. The retro interior offers a convivial – if crowded – setting.

Carmen (Map pp72-3; ☎ 617-742-6421; 33 North Sq; meals $30-40; ⏱ dinner Tue & Wed, lunch & dinner Thu-Sun; ⊕ Haymarket) Exposed brick and candlelit tables make this tiny wine bar cozy yet chic. The innovative menu offers a selection of small plates providing a fresh take on seasonal vegetables; mains like roast Cornish hen and seared tuna sit alongside classic pasta dishes. Reservations recommended.

Charlestown

Traditionally, Charlestown has not been a major stop for Boston foodies. In recent years, however, the neighborhood's gentrification has attracted the attention of some of the city's top chefs. Now Charlestown's best restaurants draw patrons from all over the city.

Sorelle Bakery Café (Map pp72-3) City Sq (☎ 617-242-5980; 100 City Sq; ⏱ 7:30am-8pm; ⓐ ; ⊕ North Station); Monument Ave (☎ 617-242-2125; 1 Monument Ave; ⏱ 6:30am-5pm Mon-Fri, 8am-3pm Sat & Sun; ⊕ North Station) Now at two locations, Sorelle's has earned a loyal following of regulars who take coffee at the counter, feast on fresh sandwiches ($5 to $8) and scones, and bus their own tables.

Tangierino (Map pp72-3; ☎ 617-242-6009; 83 Main St; meals $30-50; ⏱ 5:30-11:30pm; ⊕ North Station) This unexpected gem transports guests from a Colonial townhouse in historic Charlestown to a sultan's palace in the Moroccan desert. The menu features North African specialties, like *harira* (lamb and lentil soup), couscous and *tajine* (Moroccan stew). But the highlight is the exotic interior, complete with thick Oriental carpets, plush pillows and rich, jewel-toned tapestries.

Waterfront

Faneuil Hall and its environs are packed with touristy places touting baked beans, live lobsters and other Boston specialties. It's hard to get off the beaten track, but that doesn't mean you won't find some fun, funky and delicious places to eat.

BUDGET

Quincy Market (Map pp72-3; ☎ 617-338-2323; ⏱ 10am-9pm Mon-Sat, noon-6pm Sun; ⓐ ; ⊕ Haymarket) Northeast of Congress and State Sts, this food hall is packed with about 20 restaurants and 40 food stalls. Choose from chowder, bagels, Indian, Greek, baked goods and ice cream, and take a seat at one of the tables in the central rotunda.

Sultan's Kitchen (Map pp72-3; ☎ 617-570-9009; 116 State St; meals $8-12; ⏱ 11:30am-8:30pm Mon-Fri, 11am-4pm Sat; Ⓥ ; ⊕ State) Seasonal vegetables, whole grains, legumes and olive oil are among the ingredients that go into the healthful and delicious dishes at this Turkish deli. The kebabs are the house specialty, especially *kofta*, made from lean ground lamb. Counter service and scattered tables don't make for the most atmospheric setting, but the photos of Istanbul help.

MIDRANGE

Durgin Park (Map pp72-3; ☎ 617-227-2038; North Market, Faneuil Hall; meals $8-30; ⏱ lunch & dinner; ⓐ ; ⊕ Haymarket) Known for no-nonsense service and sawdust on the floorboards, Durgin Park hasn't changed much since the restaurant opened in 1827. Nor has the menu, which features New England standards like prime rib, fish chowder, chicken pot pie and Boston baked beans.

Bertucci's (Map pp72-3; ☎ 617-227-7889; 22 Merchants Row; meals $10-20; ⏱ lunch & dinner; Ⓥ ⓐ ; ⊕ State) Despite its nationwide expansion, Bertucci's remains a Boston favorite for brick-oven pizza.

The location near Faneuil Hall Marketplace is one of several in the Boston area; others are in the Back Bay (Map pp76–7) and in Harvard Sq (Map p78). Lunch is a real bargain: all mains ($8 to $10) come with unlimited salad and fresh, hot rolls.

Legal Sea Foods (Map pp72-3; ☎ 617-227-3115; 255 State St; meals $10-40; ☺ lunch & dinner; ◉ Aquarium) With a reputation and now-national empire built on the motto 'If it's not fresh, it's not Legal,' Legal Sea Foods has few rivals. The menu is simple: every kind of seafood, broiled, steamed, sautéed, grilled or fried. Some think Legal's clam chowder is New England's best. This outlet on the waterfront is one of many around town.

Ye Olde Union Oyster House (Map pp72-3; ☎ 617-227-2750; 41 Union St; meals $25-40; ☺ lunch & dinner; ◉ Haymarket) The oldest restaurant in Boston has been serving seafood in this historic red-brick building since 1826. Countless history-makers have propped themselves up at this bar, including Daniel Webster and John F Kennedy. Apparently JFK used to order the lobster bisque, but the raw bar is the real draw. Order a dozen on the half-shell and watch the shucker work their magic.

TOP END

Sel de la Terre (Map pp72-3; ☎ 617-720-1300; 255 State St; meals $10-40; ☺ lunch & dinner; ◉ Aquarium) Local produce and seafood – plus fresh-baked bread from the attached *boulangerie* – are the focus of the country French menu at this gem of a bistro on the waterfront. The atmosphere is rustic and relaxed, but service is always attentive. If you are hungry during off-hours, the *boulangerie* is open early for breakfast, while the bar offers a late-night menu (until 12:30am) from Wednesday to Saturday.

Seaport District

There was a time when hanging around the Seaport District meant you were eating seafood, because there was no other reason to be here. With the opening of the convention center and the ICA, this district is quickly developing as a hotspot for new restaurants. It's still mostly seafood, but check out the hotel restaurants for a change of pace.

Barking Crab (Map pp72-3; ☎ 617-426-2722; 88 Sleeper St; meals $15-25; ◉ South Station) Big buckets of crabs (Jonah, blue, snow, Alaskan, etc, depending what's in season), steamers dripping in lemon and butter, paper plates piled high

with all things fried… the Barking Crab is everything a clam shack should be. The food is plentiful, the picnic tables are communal and the beer flows freely.

No Name (off Map pp72-3; ☎ 617-338-7539; 151/2 Fish Pier; meals $15-25; ☺ lunch & dinner; ◉ South Station) The location on the fish pier lends credence to the motto 'Where the fresh are so fresh, they jump out of the water and onto your plate.' This place has lost some of its charm since being discovered by outsiders, but that doesn't stop dock workers from showing up for fried clams and fish chowder.

LTK Bar & Kitchen (off Map pp72-3; ☎ 617-330-7430; 255 Northern Ave; meals $20-30; ☺ lunch & dinner; wi-fi; ◉ South Station) LTK stands for Legal Test Kitchen: this is where Legal Sea Foods is exploring 'dining in the 21st century.' The idea here is to incorporate technology into the dining room, offering computerized menus, wireless internet access and iPod docks. Foodwise, LTK has incorporated multicultural cuisine into the menu, like sushi, pho and tempura.

Chinatown & Theater District

The most colorful part of Chinatown is overflowing with authentic restaurants (many open until 4am), bakeries and markets. This is some of Boston's best budget eating. The Theater District has no shortage of restaurants catering to hungry, showgoing crowds.

BUDGET & MIDRANGE

Jumbo Seafood (Map pp72-3; ☎ 617-542-2823; 5-7-9 Hudson St; meals $6-30; ☺ 11am-1am Sun-Thu, 11am-4am Fri & Sat; ♿; ◉ Chinatown) You know the seafood is fresh when you see the huge tanks of lobster, crabs and fish that constitute the decor at this Chinatown classic. But it's not only seafood on the menu, which represents the best of Hong Kong cuisine. Lunch specials ($4.75 to $6.25, including soup and fried rice) are a bargain.

Finale Desserterie (Map pp72-3; ☎ 617-423-3184; 1 Columbus Ave; desserts $9-14; ☺ lunch & dinner Mon-Fri, 6pm-midnight Sat, 4-11pm Sun; ◉ Arlington) Choose from a long list of tempting treats, from crème brulée to chocolate soufflé, and enjoy them with coffee, wine or port. Mirrors over the pastry chefs' workstation allow patrons to watch their magic.

Peach Farm (Map pp72-3; ☎ 617-482-3332; 4 Tyler St; meals $10-20; ☺ 11am-3am; ◉ Chinatown) Popular wisdom says that if you don't know where to eat in Chinatown, you should ask some locals where *they* like to eat. Chances are they will direct you to the Peach Farm, a Chinatown haunt where the focus is on the food. It's not much to look at, but fried noodles and rice, moo shi and Szechuan dishes are plentiful and cheap. Bonus: late-night hours.

China Pearl (Map pp72-3; ☎ 617-426-4338; 9 Tyler St; meals $10-20; ☺ breakfast, lunch & dinner; ⊕ Chinatown) The dull roar at China Pearl (the sound of a restaurant packed with patrons) is a good indication that this place is the best of the bunch for dim sum. Choose your treats as the carts cruise past your table or – if you don't know what's what – copy the Chinese people at the next table.

Buddha's Delight (Map pp72-3; ☎ 617-451-2395; 3 Beach St, 2nd fl; meals $10-20; ☺ lunch & dinner; V ; ⊕ Chinatown) Non–meat-eaters will be thrilled with the low-as-they-go prices and the staggering number of vegetarian options at this hole-in-the-wall place. The many imitation meat dishes – from roast pork to meatballs – are made exclusively from soy. While the taste and texture get mixed reviews, it's safe to say that no animals were harmed in the making of this food.

Montien (Map pp72-3; ☎ 617-338-5600; 63 Stuart St; meals $12-30; ☺ lunch & dinner; ⊕ Boylston) Popular with neighborhood residents and theater patrons, this quiet Thai restaurant is perfect for grabbing a bite before the show. You can't go wrong with the red curry or tried and true pad thai. Montien has another newer outlet in Inman Sq in Cambridge.

Suishaya (Map pp72-3; ☎ 617-423-3848; 2 Tyler St; meals $15-25; ☺ 11:30am-2am; ⊕ Chinatown) Serving the best Korean food this side of the river, Suishaya is also recommended for sushi and sashimi. Late-night hours make it popular with the clubbing crowd. As with many Chinatown joints, it's not the prettiest place to look at, but at 2am who notices the decor?

Jacob Wirth (Map pp72-3; ☎ 617-338-8586; 31-37 Stuart St; meals $20-30; ☺ 11:30am-8pm Sun & Mon, 11:30am-10pm Tue-Thur, 11:30-midnight Fri, 11:30am-11pm Sat; ☺ ; ⊕ Boylston) Boston's second-oldest eatery is this atmospheric Bavarian beer hall. The menu features wiener schnitzel, sauerbraten, potato pancakes and pork chops, but the highlight is the beer – almost 30 different drafts, including Jake's House Lager and Jake's Special Dark. On Friday nights, Jake hosts a singalong that rouses the *haus*.

TOP END

Via Matta (Map pp72-3; ☎ 617-422-0008; 79 Park Plaza; meals $20-40; ☺ 11:30am-1am; ⊕ Arlington) Via Matta tries to recreate your finest memories of Italy – the ambiance, the romance and of course the flavors. Sample the chef's whims in the tastefully trendy dining room or better yet in the dark, sexy *enoteca* (meals $20 to $30).

South End

Much like the neighborhood itself – where the up-and-coming live next door to the down-and-out – the South End boasts an eclectic mix of trendy, high-end eateries and old-school neighborhood cafés.

BUDGET

Flour (Map pp76-7; ☎ 617-267-4300; 1595 Washington St; meals $6-12; ☺ 7am-9pm Mon-Fri, 8am-6pm Sat, 9am-5pm Sun; V ☺ ; ⊕ Back Bay) Flour implores patrons to 'make life sweeter… eat dessert first!' It's hard to resist at this pastry-lover's paradise. But dessert is not all: sandwiches, soups, salads and pizzas are also available. And just to prove there's something for everybody, Flour sells homemade dog biscuits for your canine friend.

Mike's City Diner (Map pp76-7; ☎ 617-267-9393; 1714 Washington St; meals $10-15; ☺ breakfast & lunch; ☺ ; ⊕ Massachusetts Ave) Start the day with a big breakfast of eggs, bacon, toast and other old-fashioned goodness, topped with a bottomless cup of coffee. Or if you need to refuel at lunchtime, go for classics like meatloaf and mashed potatoes or fried chicken and biscuits. Service is friendly and fast, part of the appeal of this South End institution.

MIDRANGE

Meyers & Chang (Map pp76-7; ☎ 617-542-5200; www .myersandchang.com; 1145 Washington St; meals $15-25; ⊕ New England Medical Center) The South End's latest and greatest offering is this super-hip Asian spot that blends Thai, Chinese and Vietnamese. That means delicious dumplings, spicy stir-fries and oodles of noodles. Chef Alison Hearns does amazing things with a wok. The vibe is casual but cool, international and independent. Very South End.

Franklin Café (Map pp76-7; ☎ 617-350-0010; 278 Shawmut Ave; meals $20-30; ☺ 5:30pm-1:30am; ⊕ Back Bay) Once a favorite neighborhood restaurant (and that's saying something in this restaurant-rich neighborhood), the Franklin has been discovered by outsiders. It's still friendly and hip – a fantastic spot for people-watching (especially the beautiful boys in the 'hood). The menu is New American comfort food prepared by a gourmet chef.

Toro (Map pp76-7; ☎ 617-536-4300; 1704 Washington St; meals $20-30; ☷ dinner; **V**; ☻ Massachusetts Ave) Much anticipated and highly lauded, this cool tapas bar was opened to much fanfare by celebrity chef Ken Oringer. True to its Spanish spirit, this place is bursting with energy, from the open kitchen to the lively bar, to the communal butcher-block tables. The menu features simple but sublime tapas; for accompaniment, take your pick from rioja or sangria or any number of spiced-up mojitos and margaritas.

TOP END

B&G Oysters Ltd (Map pp76-7; ☎ 617-423-0550; 550 Tremont St; per oyster $2, meals $30-40; ☷ lunch & dinner; ☻ Back Bay) This casually cool oyster bar bustles, as patrons flock to the South End to indulge in a wide selection of the freshest oysters from local waters. An extensive list of wines and a modest menu of mains and appetizers (mostly seafood) are ample accompaniment for the oysters. Meat-lovers should head across the street to the Butcher Shop, another endeavor by local celebrity chef Barbara Lynch.

Hamersley's Bistro (Map pp76-7; ☎ 617-423-2700; 553 Tremont St; dinner $40-60; ☷ dinner Mon-Sat, brunch & dinner Sun; ☷ Back Bay) Consistently at the top of every 'best restaurants' list, Hamersley's serves perfectly prepared French and country American cuisine. The seasonal menu is diverse, but the house specialty is a simple, delicious roast chicken with garlic, parsley and lemon ($25). The ambiance is warm and inviting, now featuring lovely terrace seating.

Back Bay

Boston's swankiest neighborhood is also one of its finest dining spots. Newbury St is lined with trendy bars, classy grills and cozy cafés. The abundance of students guarantees that some of these eateries are actually affordable.

BUDGET & MIDRANGE

Legal Sea Foods (Map pp76-7; meals $8-24; ☷ lunch & dinner) Copley Pl (☎ 617-266-7775; 100 Huntington Ave; ☻ Copley); Prudential Center (☎ 617-266-6800; 800 Boylston St; ☻ Prudential) For the classic New England dinner, visit one of the Back Bay outlets of Legal Sea Foods, Boston's most famous restaurant. (Also see p108.)

Parish Café & Bar (Map pp76-7; ☎ 617-247-4777; 361 Boylston St; meals $10-20; ☷ noon-2am; ☻ Arlington) Sample the creations of Boston's most famous chefs without exhausting your expense account. The menu at Parish features an impressive roster of sandwiches, each designed by a local celebrity chef, including Lydia Shire, Ken Oringer, Barbara Lynch and Jasper White. Despite the creative fare, this place feels more 'bar' than 'café.'

Bangkok Blue (Map pp76-7; ☎ 617-266-1010; 651 Boylston St; meals $10-20; ☷ lunch & dinner; ☻ Copley) Cash-strapped travelers with the Back Bay blues will find the cure at Bangkok Blue, where the spicy Thai staples will sate your appetite without busting your bank. This understated eatery does a brisk lunchtime business, as hearty portions draw a regular clientele and efficient service ensures quick turnover.

Trident Booksellers & Cafe (Map pp76-7; ☎ 617-267-8688; 338 Newbury St; meals $10-30; ☷ 9am-midnight; ☐ wi-fi **V** ☻ Hynes) Is Trident a bookstore with an amazingly eclectic menu or a café with a super selection of reading material? The food menu is varied, ranging from the comforting (muffins, soups, smoothies) to the daring (spinach *arancini*, Tibetan dumplings). Vegetarians rejoice over vegan cashew chili.

BarLola (Map pp76-7; ☎ 617-266-1122; 160 Commonwealth Ave; meals $20; ☷ 4pm-1am Mon-Fri, 10am-1am Sat & Sun; ☻ Copley) This authentic Spanish eatery is tucked into a subterranean space on residential Comm Ave. The menu is exclusively tapas, prepared by a team of chefs trained in Spain, plus an impressive list of Spanish wines, including cava and sangria.

TOP END

Brasserie Jo (Map pp76-7; ☎ 617-425-3240; 120 Huntington Ave; meals $15-30; ☷ 7am-1am Sun-Thu, 7am-1:30am Fri & Sat; ☻ Prudential) Both classy and convivial, this French brasserie is a prime place to catch a bite before the symphony. The kitchen stays open late so you can also stop by afterwards, when you might see the Maestro himself feasting on classic French fare like steak-frites, mussels *marinière* and croques monsieur. Regulars crow about the coq au vin.

Piattini (Map pp76-7; ☎ 617-536-2020; 226 Newbury St; meals $20-30; ☷ lunch & dinner; ☻ Copley) If you're having trouble deciding what to order, Piattini can help. The name means 'small plates,' so you don't have to choose just one dish. The list of wines by the glass is extensive, with each accompanied by tasting notes and fun facts. This intimate enoteca is a delightful setting to sample the flavors of Italy, and you might just learn something while you are here.

Kenmore Square & Fenway

Most places in Kenmore Sq are targeting the large local student population, meaning cheap ethnic eats and divey sandwich shops. The square's recent revitalization means that upscale restaurants are finding their way here too. The quiet streets between the Back Bay Fens and Fenway Park are home to a few neighborhood favorites: indeed, Peterborough St is one of the best streets in Boston for cheap eats.

our pick La Verdad (Map pp76-7; ☎ 617-351-2580; 1 Landsdowne St; meals $10-20; ☽ 11:30am-2am; **V** ⑥; ⓡ Kenmore) We can thank celebrity chef Ken Oringer for this excellent, affordable addition to the Landsdowne St scene. These tacos are the real deal: warm flour tortillas filled with chicken, beef, beans or (our personal favorite) chorizo. Pitchers of margaritas and sidewalk seating guarantee a good time.

Brown Sugar Café (Map pp76-7; ☎ 617-266-2928; 129 Jersey St; meals $10-20; ☽ lunch & dinner; **V**; ⓔ Museum) This crowded, unassuming neighborhood joint is often lauded for the best Thai food in the city. The delectable dishes are beautifully presented – try the mango curry.

India Quality (Map pp76-7; ☎ 617-267-4499; 484 Commonwealth Ave; meals $10-20; ☽ lunch & dinner Mon-Fri, dinner Sat & Sun; **V**; ⓔ Kenmore) India Quality has been serving chicken curry and shrimp *saag* (shrimp cooked with spinach and herbs) to hungry students, daytime professionals and baseball fans since 1983. The place is rather nondescript but the food is anything but, especially considering the reasonable prices. Service is reliably fast and friendly.

Petit Robert Bistro (Map pp76-7; ☎ 617-375-0699; 468 Commonwealth Ave; meals $10-30; ☽ lunch & dinner; ⓔ Kenmore) Once upon a time the legendary Maison Robert represented the finest dining in Boston. That ultra-chic institution has closed, but chef Jacky Robert has reapplied his talents to this welcoming working-class bistro. The French fare is straightforward and hearty, with daily specials posted on the blackboard. Another outlet is in the South End (Map pp76–7).

Eastern Standard (Map pp76-7; ☎ 617-532-9100; 528 Commonwealth Ave; meals $20-30; ☽ lunch & dinner;

ⓔ Kenmore) Whether you choose to sit in the sophisticated, brassy interior or on the heated patio (open year-round), you're sure to enjoy the upscale atmosphere at this Kenmore Sq restaurant bar. French bistro fare, with a hint of New American panache, caters to a pre-game crowd that prefers wine and cheese to peanuts and crackerjacks.

Jamaica Plain

Funky, progressive Jamaica Plain hosts an ever-growing restaurant scene. The neighborhood's diverse population enjoys a variety of spunky cafés and international eateries, most of which are lined up along Centre St. The atmosphere is informal, so fine dining is limited.

Centre Street Cafe (off Map p71; ☎ 617-524-9217; 669 Centre St; meals $15-30; ☽ lunch & dinner Mon-Sat, brunch Sun; ⓔ Green St) This artistic, eclectic restaurant embodies the essence of Jamaica Plain. It's not particularly fancy fare, but ingredients are organic and locally grown, and the outcome is – as the menu promises – 'outrageously good!' A highlight is Sunday brunch, when patient would-be patrons wait in lines that stretch down the block.

Ten Tables (off Map p71; ☎ 617-524-8810; 597 Centre St; meals $20-30; ☽ dinner; ⓔ Green St) True to its name, this gem has only ten tables. The emphasis is on simplicity – appropriate for a restaurant that specializes in traditional cooking techniques. The menu is short but changes frequently to highlight local, organic produce, handmade pastas, fresh seafood and homemade sausages.

Cambridge

Head across the Charles for more bustling neighborhoods. The most famous, Harvard Sq, has coffee houses, sandwich shops, ethnic eateries and upscale restaurants to suit every budget and taste. Some regulars complain that rising rents have caused H-Square to lose its edge, but you won't hear that about neighboring Central Sq. Even post-industrial Kendall Sq boasts Boston's best pizza. For more eating adventures, get off the beaten track in Inman Sq or Davis Sq up the road in Somerville.

BUDGET

Darwin's (Map p78; ☎ 617-354-5233; 148 Mt Auburn St; meals $8-12; ☽ 8am-5pm; ⑤ wi-fi; ⓔ Harvard) Punky staff serve fat sandwiches, fresh soup and salads, and delicious coffee and pastries, all with a generous helping of attitude. The limited seating is often occupied by students who are in for the long haul (thanks to wireless access). So unless you intend to surf, take your lunch to enjoy at JFK Park or Radcliffe Yard. A new location is on Cambridge St near Irving House (p78).

Mr Bartley's Burger Cottage (Map p78; ☎ 617-354-6559; 1246 Massachusetts Ave; meals $10-12; ⊗ lunch & dinner; ♿ ; ◉ Harvard) Packed with small tables and hungry college students, this burger joint has been a Harvard Sq institution for more than 40 years. Bartley's offers at least 40 different burgers; if none of those suits your fancy, create your own 7oz juicy masterpiece with the toppings of your choice. Sweet potato fries, onion rings, thick frappes and raspberry-lime rickeys complete the classic American meal.

Veggie Planet (Map p78; ☎ 617-661-1513; 47 Palmer St; meals $10-15; ⊗ lunch & dinner; Ⓥ ♿ ; ◉ Harvard) Vegetarians and vegans can go nuts on creative interpretations of pizza (literally nuts: try the peanut curry pizza with tofu and broccoli). Oddly shaped pies call on all the ethnic cuisines – but none of their animals – for their tantalizing tastes. This place is for the pure of body and spirit (2% of the profit is donated to feed the hungry, so order away!).

Café Pamplona (Map p78; 12 Bow St; meals $10-15; ⊗ 11am-1am Mon-Sat, 2pm-1am Sun; ◉ Harvard) Located in a cozy cellar on a backstreet, this decidedly no-frills European café is the choice among old-time Cantabrigians. In addition to tea and coffee, Pamplona has light snacks like gazpacho, sandwiches and biscotti. The tiny outdoor terrace is a delight in summer.

With about a dozen places to eat under one roof, you're bound to find something fast, filling and cheap at the food court in the **Garage** (Map p78; cnr John F Kennedy & Mt Auburn Sts; ◉ Harvard).

MIDRANGE

Miracle of Science Bar & Grill (off Map p78; ☎ 617-868-2866; 321 Massachusetts Ave; meals $15-20; ⊗ 11:30am-1am; ◉ Central) With all the decor of your high-school science lab, this bar and grill is still pretty hip, and popular among MIT student types. Join them for burgers and other tasty grilled fare.

ourpick Cambridge, 1 (Map p78; ☎ 617-576-1111; 27 Church St; meals $20-30; ⊗ noon-midnight; ◉ Harvard) Set in the old fire station, this pizzeria's interior is sleek, sparse and industrial, with big windows overlooking the Old Burying Ground in the back. The menu is equally simple: nine pizzas, five salads and one dessert. These pizzas are delectable, with oddly shaped crispy crust and creative topping combos.

Red House (Map p78; ☎ 617-576-0605; 98 Winthrop St; meals $20-30; ⊗ noon-midnight; ◉ Harvard) Formerly known as the Cox-Hicks house, this quaint clapboard house dates to 1802. In summer, the draw is the patio overlooking a quiet corner of Harvard Sq. The menu is varied, but always includes a good selection of seafood and pasta. Almost all mains come in half-portions – a boon for your budget.

Casablanca (Map p78; ☎ 617-876-0999; 40 Brattle St; meals $20-30; ⊗ food served noon-1am or 2am Mon-Sat; Ⓥ ; ◉ Harvard) Below the Brattle Theater, this Harvard Sq classic has long been the hangout of film fans, local literati and other arty types. Regulars skip the formal dining room and slip in the back door to the boisterous bar where food is also served. A colorful mural depicting Rick's Café sets the stage for innovative Mediterranean delights, including a great selection of meze (appetizers).

Central Kitchen (off Map p78; ☎ 617-491-5599; 567 Massachusetts Ave; meals $20-30; ⊗ dinner; ◉ Central) Serving rustic Mediterranean fare in a gritty urban setting. Look for bistro classics like mussels *marinière*, pan seared foie gras and cassoulet. If you think this place is cool, head upstairs to the lounge, the Enormous Room.

TOP END

Harvest (Map p78; ☎ 617-868-2255; 44 Brattle St; meals $20-50; ⊗ lunch & dinner; ◉ Harvard) A Harvard Sq classic. This place is simple but sophisticated, a description that applies to the menu as well as the space. The modern American fare allows for some regional influences, such as the seductive raw bar. Local luminaries, especially Harvard faculty, are often spotted here.

Upstairs on the Square (Map p78; ☎ 617-864-1933; 91 Winthrop St; meals $40-60; ⊗ 11am-1am; ◉ Harvard) Pink and gold hues, zebra and leopard-skin rugs, and lots of glamour and glitz: such is the decor that defines this restaurant, the successor to once-renowned Upstairs at the Pudding. The creative menu and carefully chosen wine list have earned high praise. The downstairs Monday Club Bar is open for lunch, offering a more casual atmosphere, a slightly cheaper menu and a wall of windows overlooking Winthrop Park.

BREWPUBS & BREWERY TOURS

Bostonians take beer seriously. In the past decade a number of microbreweries have sprung up. While all those listed here are recommended for beer and snacks, some serve noteworthy, moderately priced meals.

Boston Beer Co (off Map p71; ☎ 617-368-5080; www.samadams.com; 30 Germania St, Jamaica Plain; ꙮ noon-3pm Tue-Thu, noon-5:30pm Fri, 11am-3pm Sat; admission by donation $2; ◉ Stony Brook) Also known as the Samuel Adams brewery and Boston Beer Museum, Boston Beer Co produces the only local brew that's achieved international fame.

Boston Beer Works (www.beerworks.net) Fenway (Map pp76-7; ☎ 617-536-2337; 61 Brookline Ave; ꙮ 10:30am-1am; ◉ Kenmore); West End (Map pp72-3; ☎ 617-896-2337; 112 Canal St; ꙮ 10:30am-1am; ◉ North Station) This brewery has seasonal concoctions brewed in exposed tanks and pipes. About 16 different kinds of beer, including Boston Red, IPA and Buckeye Oatmeal Stout, are usually available and the food isn't bad either. If you don't like sporting crowds, avoid the Fenway branch on the night of a Sox game.

Harpoon Brewery (off Map pp72-3; ☎ 617-574-9551; www.harpoonbrewery.com; 306 Northern Ave; ꙮ tastings 4pm Tue-Sat, 2pm Fri & Sat, noon Sat; ◉ South Station) This brewery is the largest facility in the state. Complimentary tastings take place in a newly renovated room overlooking the brewery. From South Station, walk over the Northern Ave Bridge (about 20 minutes) to the Marine Industrial Park.

John Harvard's Brew House (Map p78; ☎ 617-868-3585; www.johnharvards.com; 33 Dunster St, Cambridge; ꙮ 11:30am-12:30am Sun-Thu, 11:30am-1:30am Fri & Sat; ◉ Harvard) This subterranean venue feels like an English pub and has perhaps the best beer among the crowded microbrewery field. You'll find ales and stouts here, plus a sampler rack. Above-average pub grub is available at lunch and dinner, and for Sunday brunch.

Rock Bottom (Map pp72-3; ☎ 617-742-2739; www.rockbottom.com; 115 Stuart St; ꙮ lunch & dinner; ◉ Boylston) This is part of a national brewpub chain, although each outlet brews different beers using ingredients to customize the product. Traditional beer styles are offered alongside more distinctive specialty ales and lagers.

DRINKING

Boston is a drinking city, due in no small part to the hordes of Irish immigrants and their descendents who have opened up Erin-themed pubs around the city. Not to mention the staunch sports fans who flock to bars with blaring TVs to watch the Red Sox and the Pats. But this town has something for every palate: microbreweries, swanky martini lounges and stylish wine bars… it just depends what your poison is. Keep in mind that the T stops running at 12:30pm, 90 minutes before closing time.

Beacon Hill

21st Amendment (Map pp72-3; ☎ 617-221-7100; 150 Bowdoin St; ꙮ noon-1am; ◉ Park St) Across from the Massachusetts State House, this is the favorite watering hole for politicos and staffers. Named for the ever-important amendment repealing Prohibition laws, the place attracts a consistent lunch crowd, as well as regulars who stop by for a pint on their way home from work.

Cheers (Map pp72-3; ☎ 617-227-9605; 84 Beacon St; ꙮ 11am-2am; ◉ Arlington) The Bull & Finch was an authentic English pub (dismantled in England, shipped to Boston and reassembled in a Beacon Hill townhouse). But that's not why hundreds of tourists descend on the place daily: the pub inspired the TV sitcom *Cheers*, and has been thus renamed. Most visitors are disappointed that the interior bears no resemblance to the TV set. More importantly, tourists are the main clientele, so nobody knows your name (or anybody else's).

Downtown

Last Hurrah (Map pp72-3; ☎ 617-227-8600; 60 School St; ꙮ 11:30am-12:30am Sun-Fri, 4:30-11:30pm Sat; ◉ Park St) Having been a haunt for Boston's 19th-century intelligentsia and politicians, the beautiful lobby bar of the Omni Parker House is a throwback to old Boston. Enjoy a dish of hot nuts, drink bourbon and don't wear shorts.

Mr Dooley's Boston Tavern (Map pp72-3; ☎ 617-338-5656; 77 Broad St; ꙮ 11:30am-2am; ◉ State) With Irish bands playing traditional tunes several nights a week, and a decent list of appropriate beers, this cozy bar is one of the best bets in the area. Sit in a booth and linger over a copy of the *Irish Immigrant* or *Boston Irish Reporter* to learn about current events on the other side of the Atlantic.

Government Center & West End

Quite a few of the city's most popular rowdy sports bars are concentrated around the Banknorth Garden, especially on Canal St and Friend St.

Fours (Map pp72-3; ☎ 617-720-4455; 166 Canal St; ☽ 11am-1am; ◉ North Station) All sports, all the time, this makes a great place to appreciate Bostonian's near-fanatical obsession with sporting events. In addition to the game of your choice, admire the loads of pictures depicting legendary events in Boston's sporting history.

North End

Caffè Vittoria (Map pp72-3; ☎ 617-227-7606; 296 Hanover St; ◉ Haymarket) An atmospheric old-world café that has been here since the 1930s; undoubtedly, so have some Italian-speaking patrons. Complete with wrought-iron furniture and old photographs, this is a charming place to have a drink before or after your Italian feast. To get the full effect, wait for a table in the original dining room.

Caffè dello Sport (Map pp72-3; ☎ 617-523-5063; 308 Hanover St; ◉ Haymarket) A primo place for watching any sporting event, especially soccer. This place gets packed with old Italian guys cheering on the Boston Red Sox or the Italian football team of their choice.

Charlestown

Warren Tavern (Map pp72-3; ☎ 617-241-8142; 2 Pleasant St; ☽ 11:15am-1am; ◉ Bunker Hill Community College) One of the oldest pubs in Boston, the Warren Tavern has been pouring pints for its customers since George Washington and Paul Revere drank here. It is named for General Joseph Warren, a fallen hero of the Battle of Bunker Hill (shortly after which – in 1780 – this pub was opened).

Tavern on the Water (Map pp72-3; ☎ 617-242-8040; 1 8th St, Pier 6; ☽ 11:30am-9pm Sun & Mon, 11:30am-10pm Tue-Thu, 11:30am-11pm Fri & Sat ◉ North Station) Set at the end of the pier behind the Navy Yard, this understated tavern offers one of the finest views of the Boston harbor and city skyline. The food is not so memorable, but

it's a fine place to go to catch some rays on your face, the breeze off the water, and an ice cold one from behind the bar.

Waterfront & Seaport District

Faneuil Hall and Quincy Market are packed with bars, most with an uninspired tourist vibe. Just north of Faneuil Hall you'll find Union St, with an assortment of popular pubs that look very 1770 on the outside and very 1989 once you pass the threshold.

Black Rose (Map pp72-3; ☎ 617-742-2286; 160 State St; ☽ 11:30am-2am; ◉ State) The most famous – or perhaps that's infamous – of Boston Irish pubs. Back in the day, rumors ran rampant that a percentage of Black Rose proceeds went to support the IRA. These days the place is not so radical, focusing on hearty food, slow-drawn draughts and boisterous Irish music nightly.

Chinatown & Theater District

Intermission Tavern (Map pp72-3; ☎ 617-451-5997; 228 Tremont St; ☽ 10:30am-2am; ◉ Boylston) Enter beneath the emotive masks of Comedy and Tragedy into the cozy interior, where show posters adorn the brick walls. Reasonable prices and late hours attract clubbers, theatergoers and other night owls for an after-hours drink to end the evening.

Les Zygomates (Map pp72-3; ☎ 617-542-5108; 129 South St; ☽ 11:30am-1am Mon-Fri, 6pm-1am Sat; ◉ South Station) This late-night Parisian bistro serves up live jazz music alongside classic cocktails and contemporary French cuisine. Daily prix -fixe menus and weekly wine tastings attract a clientele that is sophisticated but not stuffy. The tempting selection of starters and cocktails make it a perfect pre- or post-theater spot.

South End

Delux Cafe & Lounge (Map pp76-7; ☎ 617-338-5258; 100 Chandler St; ☽ 5pm-1am Mon-Sat; ◉ Back Bay) If Boston has a laidback hipster bar, this is it. The small room on the 1st floor of a brownstone comes covered in knotty pine paneling, artwork from old LPs and Christmas lights. A small TV in the corner plays silent cartoons and a noteworthy kitchen serves incredible grilled-cheese sandwiches and inspired comfort food.

28 degrees (Map pp76-7; ☎ 617-728-0728; 1 Appleton St; ☽ 5:30-11pm; ◉ Back Bay) 'Over 23,582 bellinis served,' boasts this super-slick cocktail bar on the edge of the South End. The cocktail of champagne, peaches and vodka is just one on the list of perfectly chilled treats, which change seasonally. The sexy interior is a perfect spot to impress a date. Don't leave without checking out the loo.

Back Bay

Cottonwood Café (Map pp76-7; ☎ 617-247-2225; 222 Berkeley St; ⏰ 11:30am-2am; ⊙ Copley) Boston's best margaritas. The setting is appropriately southwestern and slightly upscale, with a pleasant patio that is open most of the year. Beware the food; we've found that the quality varies greatly.

Vox Populi (Map pp76-7; ☎ 617-424-8300; 755 Boylston St; ⏰ 11:30am-1am; ⊙ Copley) 'Urban chic' is the goal of this bistro and martini bar. The effect is inviting, especially in the 1st-floor fireplace lounge. The eclectic menu represents fusion at its most extreme; if you just come for drinks, you're bound to find something you like on the list of creative martinis and classic cocktails.

Kenmore Square & Fenway

Behind Fenway Park near Kenmore Sq, clubs are lined up like ducks in a row on Brookline Ave and Lansdowne St.

Jillian's (Map pp76-7; ☎ 617-437-0300; 145 Ipswich St; ⏰ 11am-2am; ⊙ Kenmore) Although this three-story club has more than 50 billiard tables, people also come here to play darts, snooker, table tennis and over 250 virtual reality games. The 3rd floor has a sleek bowling alley ($4.50 11am to 5pm, $6 5pm to 2am), completely decked out with a multiscreen video show playing above the lanes. This vast 70,000-sq-ft place has no less than six bars and a full-service restaurant downstairs.

Cask 'n Flagon (Map pp76-7; ☎ 617-536-4840; 62 Brookline Ave; ⏰ 11:30am-2am; ⊙ Kenmore) Boston's iconic sports bar has long served the Fenway faithful and it occupies a conspicuous site opposite the Green Monster. What this means, if you are early enough to score a pre-game sidewalk seat, is that you'll have a prime spot from which to watch Lansdowne St reach its frenzied best. Otherwise, come to watch an away game with the diehards.

Cambridge

Shay's (Map p78; ☎ 617-864-9161; 58 John F Kennedy St; ⏰ noon-midnight; ⊙ Harvard) Harvard's favorite student bar. It's crowded, cozy and cheap: what's not to love? Out the front is a small

patio full of smokers jockeying for one of the few tables.

Algiers Coffee House (Map p78; ☎ 617-492-1557; 40 Brattle St; ⏰ 8am-midnight; ⊙ Harvard) Although the pace of service can be glacial, the palatial Middle Eastern decor makes this an inviting rest spot. The one good thing about the relaxed service is that you won't be rushed to finish your pot of Arabic coffee or mint tea. Bonus: roof deck seating.

B-Side Lounge (off Map p78; ☎ 617-354-0766; 92 Hampshire St; ⏰ 11:30am-2am Mon-Sat, 11am-2am Sun; ⊙ Kendall) Sliding into a booth at the B-Side feels like sitting in the back of a 1962 Cadillac – a really nice one that someone took great care of. The casually stylish place makes good mint juleps and plays rockabilly.

Enormous Room (off Map p78; ☎ 617-491-5599; 567 Massachusetts Ave; ⏰ 5:30pm-midnight; ⊙ Central) Enter through the door marked with an elephant to find a harem-like room with people draped on cushions. Plush Oriental rugs and richly colored pillows create an exotic North African ambience, which is complemented by world music and expensive drinks.

Om (Map p78; ☎ 617-576-2800; 57 John F Kennedy St; ⏰ 5pm-1am Sun-Wed, 5pm-2am Thu-Sat; ⊙ Harvard) Almost too trendy for Harvard Sq, this fashionable lounge attracts a well-dressed crowd to sit on plush couches and sip fancy cocktails. Eerie illumination and interior waterfalls creates a chic decor to match the clientele.

ENTERTAINMENT

From high culture to low-down blues, Boston's entertainment scene has something for everyone. The vibrant university culture enhances the breadth and depth of cultural offerings on both sides of the river. For up-to-the-minute listings, check out local media publications (p68).

Live Music

The vibrant music scene in Boston ranges from contemplative folk to lively alternative to snazzy jazz. All of these modes (and more) appear at the city's larger venues.

Bank of America Pavilion (off Map pp72-3; ☎ 617-728-1600; www.bankofamericapavilion.com; 290 Northern Ave; ⊙ South Station) A white sail-like summertime tent with sweeping harbor views. Shuttle buses run from South Station.

Memorial Hall at Sanders Theater (Map p78; ☎ 617-496-2222; www.harvard.edu/arts; Holyoke

BOSTON

MUSIC FESTIVALS

Fall in Boston means not only colorful leaves and rowing boats, but also great music. Check out these music festivals that take place in September.

Blues Trust (www.bluestrust.com) Feeling blue? Don't miss this weekend when Blues Trust sponsors two days of (free) live jazz music at the Hatch Shell.

Beantown Jazz Festival (☎ 617-747-2261; www.beantownjazz.org) The Berklee College of Music sponsors this free two-day festival in the South End. Three stages, panel discussions, food vendors, kids' activities and all that jazz.

NEMO Music Festival (www.nemoboston.com) On the last weekend in September, NEMO is dedicated to showcasing up-and-coming indie and alt-rock artists. Hundreds of musicians perform at venues around the city; buy one badge and hear them all.

Center, Cambridge; ◉ Harvard) This beautiful 1166-seat wood-paneled theater is known for its acoustics.

Orpheum Theater (Map pp72-3; ☎ 617-679-0810; 1 Hamilton Pl; ◉ Park) A slightly worn but relatively intimate venue with great acoustics.

ROCK & INDIE

From legends like Aerosmith and the Cars to modern rockers like the Mighty Mighty Bosstones and the Drop Kick Murphys, plenty of nationally known bands trace their roots back to Boston clubs. To help you figure out who's playing where, check out the listings in the *Boston Phoenix* or the *Weekly Dig*.

Great Scott (off Map pp76-7; ☎ 617-566-9014; www .greatscottboston.com; 1222 Commonwealth Ave; cover $5-12; ◉ Harvard Ave) The current 'it' place for rock and indie, Great Scott has recently been transformed into a music palace, thanks to the efforts of booker Ben Sistoe. The place rarely gets uncomfortably crowded and the stage is well raised.

Abbey Lounge (off Map p78; ☎ 617-441-9631; www .abbeylounge.com; 3 Beacon St, Cambridge; cover $5-10; ◉ Central) This loveable dive in Inman Sq doubles as a venue where a lot of local bands get their first gigs. Expect zero frills and cheap beer.

Middle East (off Map p78; ☎ 617-354-8238; www .mideastclub.com; 472 Massachusetts Ave, Cambridge; cover $10-15; ◉ Central) While the Middle East sometimes gets itself together to book top rock acts, the two stages of this club spend much of their time under the feet of a protracted battle of the bands.

TT the Bear's (off Map p78; ☎ 617-492-2327; www .ttthebears.com; 10 Brookline St, Cambridge; cover $7-10; ◔ 6pm or 7pm-midnight or 1am; ◉ Central) A dirty dive with two bars in two rooms, one of which provides refuge for those who know

that not all local bands are actually worth listening to.

Lizard Lounge (off Map p78; ☎ 617-547-0759; 1667 Massachusetts Ave, Cambridge; ◉ Porter) Surprisingly big acts get booked in a room that can't fit more than a hundred. It doubles as a jazz and rock venue and the bar stocks an excellent list of New England beers.

Toad (off Map p78; ☎ 617-497-4950; 1920 Massachusetts Ave, Cambridge; admission free; ◉ Porter) This tiny, ultracasual place has music every night and it never charges a cover. The remaining members of Morphine play here regularly, as do some other local faves.

Paradise Lounge (off Map pp76-7; ☎ 617-562-8800; www.thedise.com; 967 Commonwealth Ave; admission $10-30; ◉ Pleasant St) One of Boston's most legendary rock clubs, where you can get up close and personal with some big names. The newly opened lounge has a hip, cozy atmosphere and a limited menu.

BLUES & JAZZ

Scullers Jazz Club (off Map pp76-7; ☎ 617-642-4111; www .scullersjazz.com; 400 Soldiers Field Rd, Doubletree Hotel; tickets $15-45; ◉ Central) Boston's top jazz venue is this intimate setting that books big names and serves stiff drinks (and dinner, if you like). Though it enjoys impressive views over the Charles, the room itself lacks the grit you might hanker for in a jazz club; rather, it feels like it sits inside a Doubletree Hotel (which it does).

Regattabar (Map p78; ☎ 617-661-5500, tickets 617-395-7757; www.regattabarjazz.com; 1 Bennett St, Cambridge; tickets $15-30; ◔ Tue-Sat; ◉ Harvard) Like Scullers (see above), the Regattabar looks like a conference room in a hotel – in this case the Charles Hotel. As it only has 225 seats, you are guaranteed a good view and high-quality sound.

Berklee Performance Center (Map pp76-7; www .berkleebpc.com; ☎ 617-747-2261; 136 Massachusetts Ave; admission $20-25; ◉ Hynes) For high-energy jazz recitals and smoky-throated vocalists, the performance hall at the notable music college marks a unique spot on Boston's musical landscape. Often features students and faculty from the college.

Beehive (Map pp76-7; ☎ 617-423-0069; www.bee hiveboston.com; 541 Tremont St; admission free; ⏰ 5pm-2am; ◉ Copley) The Beehive has transformed the basement of the Boston Center for the Arts into a 1920s Paris jazz club. This place is more about the scene than the music, which is often provided by Berklee students. But the food is good and the vibe is definitely hip. Reservations required if you want a table.

Wally's Café (Map pp76-7; www.wallyscafe.com; ☎ 617-424-1408; 427 Massachusetts Ave; admission free; ⏰ 9pm-2am Mon-Sat, 3-7pm & 9pm-2am Sun; ◉ Massachusetts Ave) Gritty, storied and small, Wally's is the kind of place where someone on stage will recognize a high-caliber out-of-town musician in the crowd and convince them to play. It's been an institution since the 1960s. The highlight is the Sunday afternoon jam session, especially popular with Berklee students.

Ryles (off Map p78; ☎ 617-876-9330; www.ryles.com; 212 Hampshire St, Cambridge; cover $10-15; ⏰ 7pm-1am Tue-Thu, 7pm-2am Fri & Sat, 10am-3pm Sun; ◉ Central) Upstairs is a dance hall with early-evening instructions for would-be swing and salsa dancers. Downstairs you'll find a dining room with a natty, jazz-inspired decor. Each has its own stage, which draws local and national talent. The music is free during the popular Sunday brunch, but you may need a reservation.

FOLK & WORLD

For a full calendar of music events featuring artists from around the world, see **World Music** (www.worldmusic.org).

Club Passim (Map p78; ☎ 617-492-7679; www .clubpassim.com; 47 Palmer St, Cambridge; admission $5-15; ◉ Harvard) This club is a legendary Boston institution. Though Boston folk music seems to be endangered outside of Irish bars, Club Passim does such a great job booking top-notch acts that it practically fills the vacuum by itself. The place does not serve alcohol, but it does serve food from the on-site restaurant Veggie Planet (p112).

Theater

Though it lives in the shadow of New York, Boston's theatrical culture is impressively strong for a city of its size. Multiple big-ticket venues consistently book top shows, produce premieres and serve as testing grounds for many plays that eventually become hits on Broadway.

Tickets are available online or at the individual theater box offices. **BosTix** (www.bos tix.com; ⏰ 10am-6pm Tue-Sat, 11am-4pm Sun) offers discounted tickets to productions citywide. Discounts up to 50% are available for same-day purchase: check the website to see what's available, but purchases must be made in person in cash at outlets at **Faneuil Hall** (Map pp72-3; ◉ Haymarket) or **Copley Square** (Map pp76-7; ◉ Copley).

THEATER DISTRICT

Opera House (Map pp72-3; ☎ 617-880-2442; 539 Washington St; ◉ Downtown Crossing) After more than a decade of neglect, the Opera House reopened its doors in 2004 for a highly acclaimed production of Disney's *Lion King*. The lavish theater has been restored to its 1928 glory, complete with mural-painted ceiling, gold-gilded molding and plush velvet curtains. It regularly hosts productions from the Broadway Across America series, as well as the Christmastime performance of *The Nutcracker* by the Boston Ballet.

Wang Center for the Performing Arts (Map pp72-3; ☎ 617-482-9393, tickets 800-447-7400; www.wangcenter .org; 270 Tremont St; ◉ Boylston) The opulent and enormous Wang Theater, built in 1925, has one of the largest stages in the country. The Boston Ballet performs here, but the Wang also hosts extravagant music and modern dance productions, as well as occasional giant-screen movies (the center was originally built as a movie palace). It also houses the more intimate Shubert Theater, known as the 'Little Princess' of the Theater District.

OTHER VENUES

American Repertory Theater (ART; Map p78; ☎ 617-547-8300; www.amrep.org; 64 Brattle St, Cambridge; tickets $45-75; ◉ Harvard) There isn't a bad seat in Harvard University's theater. The prestigious ART stages new plays and experimental interpretations of classics. It also has new, additional performance space at Zero Arrow St. Student 'rush' tickets for both venues are sold for $12 on the day of the performance.

BOSTON

Huntington Theater Company (Map pp76-7; ☎ 617-266-0800; www.bu.edu/huntington; 264 Huntington Ave, Boston University Theater; ☻ Symphony) For award-winning theater, it's tough to outdo the Huntington, where the trophy cabinet has long been full. It stages many shows before production is transferred to Broadway (at least three of which have won Tonys). The company's credentials also include over 50 world premieres. Plays occur in the fine Boston University Theater as well as the Calderwood Pavilion at the Boston Center for the Arts.

Boston Center for the Arts (BCA; Map pp76-7; ☎ 617-426-7700; www.bostontheaterscene.com; 539 Tremont St; ☻ Copley) There's rarely a dull moment here. Each year over 20 companies present more than 45 separate productions ranging from comedies to drama and modern dance to musicals.

Classical Music

Boston Symphony Orchestra (BSO; Map pp76-7; ☎ 617-266-1200; www.bso.org; 301 Massachusetts Ave; tickets $30-120; ☻ Symphony) Near-perfect acoustics match the ambitious programs of the world-renowned BSO, which performs at Symphony Hall from October to April. The Boston Pops plays popular classical music and show tunes from May to July and offers a popular holiday show in December. Same-day discounted 'rush' tickets are sold at 5pm on Tuesday and Thursday and at 10am on Friday.

New England Conservatory (NEC; Map pp76-7; ☎ 617-585-1270; www.newenglandconservatory.edu; Jordan Hall, 30 Gainsborough St; ☻ Symphony) Founded in 1867, the NEC is the country's oldest music school and hosts professional and student chamber and orchestral concerts in the acoustically excellent Jordan Hall.

Opera & Dance

Dancers and prancers, take note. If you are here in January, you won't want to miss **Dance Across the City** (☎ 617-532-1263; www.danceacrossthecity.org). Sponsored by the Wang Center, the one-day event includes free classes and performances in every genre of dance, held at venues around the Theater District on the first Saturday in January.

Boston Ballet (Map pp72-3; ☎ 617-695-6950; www.bostonballet.org; tickets $25-100) Boston's skillful ballet troupe performs both modern and classic works at the Wang Center (p117). Student and child 'rush' tickets are available for $20 two hours before the perform-

ance; seniors get the same deal, but only for Saturday matinees.

Boston Lyric Opera (Map pp72-3; ☎ 617-542-6772; 265 Tremont St, Shubert Theater; tickets $33-112; ☻ Boylston) This longstanding company stages classic performances in the Shubert Theater, where you might see *Madame Butterfly*, *The Little Prince* or *The Barber of Seville*.

Boston Opera (Map pp72-3; ☎ 617-451-3388; www.operaboston.org; 219 Tremont St, Cutler Majestic Theater; tickets $25-100; ☻ Boylston) Playing out of the gilded Cutler Majestic Theater, this acclaimed opera company has been impressing Boston for almost three decades. Expect intelligently selected shows that bring to life the rarely heard works of masters, pus innovative repertoires of more recent vintage.

Cinemas

Films are shown regularly at several venues that you might not expect. Besides the cinemas listed here, check out a few other venues: films followed by panel discussions at the **Boston Public Library** (BPL; Map pp76-7; ☎ 617-536-5400; www.bpl.org; 700 Boylston St; ☻ Copley); arty films in the Remis Auditorium at the **Museum of Fine Arts** (MFA; Map pp76-7; ☎ 617-267-9300; www.mfa.org; 465 Huntington Ave;

FILM FESTIVALS

Film festivals are all the rage in Boston, with local interest groups organizing events to showcase films catering to their people, be they bikers or bisexuals. Here are some of our favorites.

■ During the last week in April, venues around the city host the **Independent Film Festival of Boston**, which includes shorts, documentaries and drama produced locally and nationally. Check out www.iffboston.org for details.

■ For 10 days in mid-September all Bostonians become film critics, as they are invited to screenings of some 50 different films at theaters around the city during the **Boston Film Festival**. Find out how to become one of them at www.bostonfilmfestival.org.

■ The **Boston Underground Film Festival** is held over three days in March to celebrate the bizarre, demonic and insane. More information can be found at www.bostonundergroundfilmfestival.com.

Ruggles or Museum); and free family flicks (June to August only) at the **Hatch Memorial Shell** (Map pp76-7; www.mass.gov/dcr/ hatch_events.htm).

Brattle Theater (Map p78; www.brattlefilm.org; ☎ 617-876-6837; 40 Brattle St, Cambridge; Ⓣ Harvard) The Brattle is a film lover's 'cinema paradiso.' Film noir, independent films and series that celebrate directors or periods are shown regularly in this renovated 1890 repertory theater.

Coolidge Corner Theater (off Map pp76-7; ☎ 617-734-2500; www.coolidge.org; 290 Harvard St, Brookline; Ⓣ Coolidge Corner) The area's only not-for-profit cinema shows documentaries, foreign films and first-run movies on two enormous screens in a grand art-deco theater.

Somerville Theatre (off Map p78; ☎ 617-625-5700; www.somervilletheatreonline.com; Davis Sq, Somerville; Ⓣ Davis) A classic movie house that survived the megaplex invasion, this theater alternates second-run films with live musical performances.

Kendall Square Cinema (off Map pp72-3; ☎ 617-494-9800; www.landmarktheaters.com; 1 Kendall Sq, Cambridge; Ⓣ Kendall) Kendall has nine screens showing foreign films and lesser-known artsy flicks. The concession stand sits alongside a coffee counter that is well equipped with espresso machines and pastries.

Harvard Film Archive & Film Study Library (Map p78; ☎ 617-495-4700; www.harvardfilmarchive.org; 24 Quincy St, Cambridge; Ⓣ Harvard) From the offbeat to the classic, at least two films per day are screened at the Carpenter Center for the Visual Arts at Harvard University. Directors and actors are frequently on hand to talk about their work.

Comedy Clubs

Comedy Connection (Map pp72-3; ☎ 617-248-9700; www.comedyconnectionboston.com; Quincy Market, Faneuil Hall Marketplace; tickets $15-40; Ⓣ Haymarket) On the 2nd floor of Quincy Market, this is Boston's premier comedy club, the one attracting the biggest names.

Improv Boston (off Map p78; ☎ 617-576-1253; www.improvboston.com; 1253 Cambridge St, Cambridge; tickets $5-12; Ⓣ Central) This witty, long-running ensemble performs at the Back Alley Theater in Inman Sq from Wednesday to Saturday and makes things up as they go along; often audience members throw out ideas and the cast is off and running. The show redefines itself with every fast-paced performance. The early Saturday show (6pm) is family oriented.

Jimmy Tingle's Off Broadway (off Map p78; ☎ 617-591-1616; www.jimmytingle.com; 255 Elm St, Somerville; tickets $10-15; Ⓣ Davis) Boston's homegrown but nationally known funny man, Jimmy Tingle, performs as well as hosting other comedians at this club in Davis Sq. Like the true Cantabrigian that he is, Jimmy's humor is laced with serious social and political commentary.

Dance Clubs

The thriving club scene is fueled by the constant infusion of thousands of American and international students. Clubs are fairly stable, but the nightly lineup often changes. Check the *Boston Phoenix, Improper Bostonian* or *Stuff@Night* (p68) for up-to-the-minute information. Clubs along Lansdowne St near Kenmore Sq cater to a university crowd, while those in the Theater District are favored by young professionals. Cover charges vary widely, from free (if you arrive early) to $20, but the average is usually $10 to $15 on weekends. Most clubs are open 10pm to 2am and require proper dress.

THEATER DISTRICT

Felt (Map pp72-3; ☎ 617-350-5555; http://feltclubboston.com; 533 Washington St; ☽ 4:30pm-2am Tue-Sun; Ⓣ Boylston) A nightclub, lounge and billiards club all in one. There are only 14 pool tables, so there's usually a wait, but there is plenty of people-watching to do in the meantime. The dance floor is upstairs.

The Estate (Map pp72-3; ☎ 617-651-7000; 1 Boylston Pl; ☽ 10pm-2am Thu, Fri & Sun, 9pm-2am Sat; Ⓣ Boylston) Tucked into 'the Alley,' this place used to be an infamous din of iniquity called the Big Easy (or more often, the 'Big Sleazy'). But now the club has gone upscale, with plush furniture and sparkling chandeliers surrounding a dancefloor packed with pretty people. The bouncers are in charge of admitting only Boston's beautiful (and they take this job a little too seriously, we have heard). So dress to impress and be prepared to wait in line.

Venu (Map pp72-3; ☎ 617-338-8061; www.venuboston.com; 100 Warrenton St; ☽ 11:30pm-2am Tue & Thu-Sun; Ⓣ Boylston) To signal your insider status at this superchic club, pull out your best designer knockoff and arrive fashionably late for DJ-spun tunes. Fun features include Carnival Sunday with music from Brazil, and the hottest Asian night in town (www.asiannight411.com; reservations recommended) on Saturday.

Mojitos (Map pp72-3; ☎ 617-988-8123; 48 Winter St; cover $5; ☽ 9am-2am Thu-Sun; Ⓣ Downtown Crossing)

BOSTON

BOSTON: COLLEGE TOWN

The greater Boston area has many, many college campuses – too many to mention here. The vibrancy of the student population is one of the defining characteristics of this youthful city. Cultural and sporting events are often open to the public.

- **Berklee College of Music** (Map pp76-7; ☎ 617-747-2222; www.berklee.edu; 921 Boylston St; Ⓗ Hynes) One of the country's finest music schools. For performance information, see p117.

- **Boston College** (BC; off Map p71; ☎ 617-552-8000; www.bc.edu; 140 Commonwealth Ave/MA 30, Chestnut Hill; Ⓗ Boston College or Cleveland Circle) BC's neo-gothic campus has a good art museum and excellent Irish and Catholic ephemera collections in the library. Its basketball and football teams are usually high in national rankings.

- **Boston University** (BU; Map pp76-7; ☎ 617-353-2000, 617-353-2169; www.bu.edu; 881 Commonwealth Ave; Ⓗ BU Central) West of Kenmore Sq, enrolls about 30,000 graduate and undergraduate students, and has a huge campus and popular sports teams.

- **Brandeis University** (off Map p71; ☎ 781-736-2000; www.brandeis.edu; South St, Waltham) A small campus that includes the Rose Art Museum, specializing in New England art. Take the MBTA commuter rail from North Station to the Brandeis/Roberts stop.

- **Harvard University** (Map p78; ☎ 617-495-1573; www.harvard.edu; Holyoke Center, 1350 Massachusetts Ave; Ⓗ Harvard) Harvard has so much to offer it's overwhelming. Aside from the museums (p91 and pp91, look for concerts and speakers at Memorial Hall at Sanders Theater (p115) and films at the Harvard Film Archive (p119).

- **Massachusetts Institute of Technology** (off Map p78; ☎ 617-253-4795; Lobby 7, 77 Massachusetts Ave, Cambridge; Ⓨ 9am-5pm, tours 10:45am & 2:45pm Mon-Fri; Ⓗ Central) It's probably no surprise that MIT has an interesting museum about science and technology; but who knew it also boasts a world-class collection of public art, not to mention some of the city's most innovative architecture? See p92 for details.

- **MassArt** (Map pp76-7; ☎ 617-879-7333; www.massart.edu; 621 Huntington Ave; admission free; Ⓨ 10am-6pm Mon-Fri, 11am-5pm Sat; Ⓗ Longwood Ave) More formally known as the Massachusetts College of Art, this is the country's first and only four-year independent public art college (most art degrees are two-year programs). There are always some thought-provoking or sense-stimulating exhibits to see.

- **Northeastern University** (Map pp76-7; ☎ 617-373-2000; www.northeastern.edu; 360 Huntington Ave; Ⓗ Ruggles or Northeastern) Boasts one of the country's largest work-study cooperative programs.

- **Tufts University** (off Map p71; ☎ 617-628-5000; www.tufts.edu; College Ave, Medford; Ⓗ Davis) Home to the acclaimed Fletcher School of International Affairs.

- **University of Massachusetts, Boston** (off Map p71; UMass; ☎ 617-287-5000; www.umb.edu; 100 Morrissey Blvd; Ⓗ UMass/JFK) Host to the John F Kennedy Library & Museum (see p90).

- **Wellesley College** (off Map p71; ☎ 781-283-1000; www.wellesley.edu; 106 Central St, Wellesley) A Seven Sisters women's college that also sports a hilly, wooded campus and the excellent Davis Museum & Cultural Center. Take the commuter rail to Wellesley.

This large Latin-inspired club is two-in-one. On one level, find a lounge where house bands play salsa and timba tunes (free salsa lessons most nights). In the basement, a club caters to the scantily clad, with hip-hop, reggaeton and sounds from the Tropic of Capricorn.

OTHER VENUES

Bill's Bar (Map pp76-7; ☎ 617-421-9678; www.billsbar.com; 5½ Lansdowne St; admission $8-12; Ⓨ Wed-Sun; Ⓗ Kenmore) The self-mocking 'bastard child of Lansdowne St,' this smaller club, with live music and DJs, is packed with Boston University students who live by alternative music. Specialized nights include Reggae Sunday and Karaoke Wednesday, but otherwise Bill's got live music and DJs working the wax.

Middlesex (off Map p78; ☎ 617-686-6739; www .middlesexlounge.com; 315 Massachusetts Ave, Cambridge; cover $5; ☻ Central) Sleek and sophisticated, Middlesex brings the fashionable crowd to the Cambridge side. Black modular furniture sits on heavy casters, allowing the cubes to be rolled aside when the place transforms from lounge to club, making space for the beautiful people to become entranced with DJs experimenting with French pop and electronica.

Sports

Boston loves its sports teams. And why not, with the three-time world champion New England Patriots and the long-overdue World Series–winning Red Sox? Emotions run high around every sports season, especially baseball. There is no better way to strike up a spirited conversation than to inquire about the Sox. For sports talk radio all the time, tune into 850AM.

Boston Red Sox (☎ tickets 617-267-1700; www.red sox.com; 4 Yawkey Way; tickets bleachers $18-20, regular seats $25-55; ☻ season early Apr-late Sep; ☻ Kenmore) The Sox play in Fenway Park (Map pp76–7), the nation's oldest and most storied ballpark, built in 1912. Unfortunately, it is also the most expensive. During sold-out games there are often first-come, first-served standing-room-only tickets sold at 9am for same-day games; head to the ticket windows on Yawkey Way.

Boston Celtics (☎ info 617-523-3030, tickets 617-931-2000; www.celtics.com; Banknorth Garden, 150 Causeway St; tickets $10-95; ☻ season late Oct-Apr; ☻ North Station) The Celtics, who've won more basketball championships than any other NBA team, play at Northbank Garden (Map pp72–3) above North Station. Tickets start at $10, but you won't be able to see anything from those seats.

Boston Bruins (☎ info 617-624-1900, tickets 617-931-2000; www.bostonbruins.com; Banknorth Garden, 150 Causeway St; tickets $25-85; ☻ season mid-Oct–mid-Apr; ☻ North Station) The Bruins, under the former star power of Bobby Orr, Phil Esposito and Ray Bourque, play ice hockey at Banknorth Garden (Map pp72–3). That is, when they are not involved in a labor dispute.

New England Patriots (☎ 508-543-8200, 800-543-1776; www.patriots.com; Gillette Stadium, Foxborough; standing-room tickets $39; ☻ season late Aug-late Dec) The three-time Super Bowl champs play football in a new state-of-the-art stadium that's just 50 minutes south of Boston, but it's hard to get a ticket (most seats are sold to season-ticket holders). From I-93, take I-95 south to Rte 1. Otherwise, direct trains go to Foxborough (off Map p71) from South Station.

New England Revolution (☎ 877-438-7387; www .revolutionsoccer.net; Gillette Stadium, Foxborough; tickets $20-40; ☻ season mid-Apr–early Oct) The local soccer team also plays in Foxborough (off Map p71).

Many colleges also have teams worth watching, and spirited, loyal fans. In April look for the annual Bean Pot Tournament, college hockey's premier event.

Boston University (☎ 617-353-4628; www.aggan isarena.com; Agganis Arena, Commonwealth Ave; ☻ St Paul St) In January 2005 BU opened a brand-new fancy arena to host its basketball and hockey teams. Take the Green Line 'B' branch to St Paul St for Agganis Arena (off Map p76–7).

Boston College (off Map p71; ☎ 617-552-3000; www .bceagles.com; Conte Forum, 140 Commonwealth Ave/MA 30, Chestnut Hill; ☻ Boston College) BC is competitive in hockey, football and basketball. Fans are devoted, so tickets are often impossible to get. Take the Green Line 'B' branch to the end.

Harvard University (Map p78; ☎ 617-495-2211; http://gocrimson.ocsn.com; N Harvard St & Soldiers Field Rd; ☻ Harvard) Harvard's sports teams play across the river in Allston. Staunch Ivy League rivalries bring out alumni and fans.

SHOPPING

Boston may not be alluring for bargain-hunters but it boasts its fair share of bohemian boutiques, distinctive galleries and offbeat shops. For shopping the old-fashioned way, head to Downtown Crossing. Two large department stores and lots of smaller practical retail outlets cater to everyday Bostonians. For chic boutiques and artsy galleries, you can't beat **Newbury St** (great for window shopping if not the real deal). Also in the Back Bay, the **Shops at Prudential Center** (Map pp76-7; ☎ 617-267-1002; 800 Boylston St; ☻ Prudential) and **Copley Place** (Map pp76-7; ☎ 617-369-5000; 100 Huntington Ave; ☻ Back Bay) are both vast, light-filled shopping malls replete with pricey shops.

Across the river in Cambridge, Harvard Sq has spirited street life with plenty of musicians and performance artists. Unfortunately, most of the independent stores have been replaced by national chains due to rising rents. Just beyond the Museum of Science, **Cambridgeside**

Galleria (Map pp72-3; ☎ 617-621-8666; 100 Cambridgeside Pl, Cambridge; ⊖ Lechmere) is a three-story mall with 100 shops, including several moderately priced department stores.

Antiques

Beacon Hill is a treasure trove for antique hunters. At least a dozen shops are packed onto Charles and River Sts. Don't expect to find any bargains in this tony neighborhood, however.

Boston Antique Co-op (Map pp72-3; ☎ 617-227-9810; www.bostonantiqueco-op.com; 119 Charles St; ⊖ Charles/ MGH) This cooperative antique market is a collection of 40 dealers under one roof. Most of the merchandise comes from area estates, so there is a good collection of furniture and household accessories, especially fine porcelain and textiles.

Eugene Galleries (Map pp72-3; ☎ 617-227-3062; 76 Charles St; ⊖ Charles/MGH) This tiny shop has a remarkable selection of antique prints and maps, especially focusing on old Boston. Follow the history of the city's development by examining 18th- and 19th-century maps; witness the filling-in of the Back Bay and the greening of the city. Historic prints highlight Boston landmarks.

Cambridge Antique Market (off Map pp72-3; ☎ 617-868-9655; 201 Monsignor O'Brien Hwy, Cambridge; ⊖ Lechmere) This old brick warehouse looks foreboding from the outside, but inside is an antiquer's paradise. With over 150 dealers on five floors, this antique market is a trove of trash and treasures. The constant turnover of dealers lends a flea-market feel, guaranteeing that you never know what you will find.

Arts & Crafts

While Newbury St has the densest concentration of galleries, a few others allow you to support local artists without losing your shirt. There's a number of avant-garde galleries in the Leather District and the South End. For information on open studios, see p86.

South End Open Market (Map pp76-7; ☎ 617-481-2257; www.southendopenmarket.com; 500 Harrison Ave; ☽ 10am-4pm Sun May-Oct; ☒ New England Medical Center) Part flea market and part artists' market, this weekly outdoor event is a fabulous opportunity for strolling, shopping and people-watching. Over 100 vendors set up shop under white tents: it's never the same two weeks in a row, but it always has plenty of arts and crafts, as well as edgier art, vintage clothing, jewelry, antiques, local farm produce and homemade sweets.

Bromfield Art Gallery (Map pp76-7; ☎ 617-451-3605; www.bromfieldgallery.com; 450 Harrison Ave; ☽ noon-5pm Wed-Sun; ⊖ Back Bay) The city's oldest cooperative, this South End gallery hosts solo shows by its members, as well as the occasional visiting artists. The work runs the gamut in terms of media, but you can always expect something challenging or entertaining.

Barbara Krakow Gallery (Map pp76-7; ☎ 617-262-4490; www.barbarakrakowgallery.com; 10 Newbury St; ⊖ Arlington) The catalogue of artists represented by this well-established gallery (since 1964) reads like something you would expect from a museum, including Ellsworth Kelly, Sol LeWitt and Jasper Johns. Though it's very much the domain of modernists, the gallery sometimes displays the work of emerging artists.

Society of Arts & Crafts (Map pp76-7; ☎ 617-266-1810; 175 Newbury St; ⊖ Copley) Founded in 1897, the nonprofit gallery promotes emerging and established artists and encourages innovative handicrafts. The collection changes constantly, but you'll find high-quality weaving, leather, ceramics, glassware, furniture and other hand-crafted items.

Cambridge Artists' Cooperative (Map p78; ☎ 617-868-4434; 59a Church St, Cambridge; ⊖ Harvard) Owned and operated by Cambridge artists, this three-floor gallery displays an ever-changing exhibit of their work. The pieces are crafty – handmade jewelry, woven scarves, leather products and pottery. The craftspeople double as sales staff, so you may get to meet the creative force behind your souvenir.

Clothing & Accessories
NEW CLOTHING

Boston's sweetest boutiques are on Charles St in Beacon Hill and – of course – along Newbury St in Back Bay, with some up-and-coming spots in the South End and the North End. Despite claims that Harvard Sq has turned into an outdoor shopping mall, a few unique boutiques continue to thrive, offering stylish simplicity and casual comfort.

Filene's Basement (Map pp76-7; ☎ 617-424-5520; 497 Boylston St; ⊖ Copley) The granddaddy of bargain stores, Filene's Basement carries overstocked and irregular items at everyday low prices. But the deal gets better: items are automatically marked down the longer they remain in the store. With a little bit of luck and lots of determination you could find a $300 designer jacket for $30. The original store used to be a mainstay of shopping in Downtown Crossing; since its closing in 2007, bargain-hunters must go across town to the new Back Bay store, which somehow seems incongruous. But that's where the bargains are!

Louis Boston (Map pp76-7; ☎ 617-262-6100; 234 Berkeley St; ⏰ 11am-6pm Mon, 10am-6pm Tue & Wed, 10am-7pm Thu-Sat; ⓐ Arlington) This beautiful four-story townhouse occupies the entire block between Newbury and Boylston Sts. So you know there is plenty of room inside for ultratrendy (and pricey) clothing and cool, contemporary housewares. The 1st floor is filled with gift items like gourmet foods, fancy bath accessories, nostalgic books and sweet pet gear. Upstairs, you'll find the fashion: Louis caters disproportionately to the male of the species, but somebody's got to.

Jake's House (Map pp76-7; ☎ 617-262-5068; 285 Newbury St; ⓐ Copley) Life *is* good for this locally designed brand of T-shirts, backpacks and other gear. Styles depict the fun-loving stick figure Jake engaged in guitar-playing, dog-walking, coffee-drinking, mountain-climbing and just about every other good-vibe diversion you might enjoy. Jake's activity and message vary, but his 'life is good' theme is constant.

VINTAGE CLOTHING

Garment District (off Map p78; ☎ 617-876-5230; 200 Broadway, Cambridge; ⏰ 11am-9pm Sun-Fri, 9am-9pm Sat; ⓐ Kendall) If your memories of the fashion-conscious '60s and '70s have faded like an old pair of jeans, entering this store will bring it all back with a vengeance. Downstairs, Dollar-a-Pound has different merchandise and different pricing methods. Like a flea market gone berserk, piles of clothing are dumped on the warehouse floor and folks wade through, looking for their needle in the haystack. Upon checkout, your pile is weighed and you pay 'by the pound.'

Closet, Inc (Map pp76-7; ☎ 617-536-1919; 175 Newbury St; ⓐ Copley) For shoppers with an eye for fashion but without a pocketbook to match. The Closet (and it does feel like some fashion maven's overstuffed closet) is a second-hand clothing store that carries high-quality suits, sweaters, jackets, jeans, gowns and other garb by acclaimed designers. Most items are in excellent condition.

Second Time Around (Map pp76-7; ☎ 617-247-3504; 219 Newbury St; ⏰ 11am-7pm Mon-Fri, 10am-7pm Sat,

10am-6pm Sun; ⓐ Copley) Come early and come often, because you never know what you're going to find; but you can be sure it will have a designer label. Merchandise is all in perfect condition and no more than two years old. An additional outlet is on Beacon Hill (Map pp72–3).

Oona's Experienced Clothing (Map p78; ☎ 617-491-2654; 1210 Massachusetts Ave, Cambridge; ⓐ Harvard) Oona's sells kitschy clothes from all eras. Dress-up dandies come here for Halloween costumes, drag wear, retro attire from any decade and outfits for every theme. Not that you need an excuse to go vintage: Oona's merchandise is cheap enough that you can buy it just for fun.

Boston Costume (Map pp72-3; ☎ 617-482-1632; 69 Kneeland St; ⏰ 9:30am-6pm Mon-Sat; ⓐ New England Medical Center) Perfectly placed to cater to the actors in the Theater District and the drag queens in the South End. In addition to costume rental, this vintage clothing store has fishnet stockings and feather boas.

SHOES & ACCESSORIES

Helen's Leather (Map pp72-3; ☎ 617-742-2077; 110 Charles St; ⏰ 10am-6pm Mon-Sat, 10am-8pm Thu, noon-6pm Sun; ⓐ Charles/MGH) You probably didn't realize that you would need your cowboy boots in Boston. Never fear, you can pick up a slick pair right here on Beacon Hill. Helen also carries stylish dress boots and work boots, as well as other leather goods.

Moxie (Map pp72-3; ☎ 617-557-9991; 51 Charles St; ⓐ Charles/MGH) 'No outfit is complete without that perfect pair of shoes.' And 'Why have one bag when you can have a collection?' These bits of wisdom are what inspire Moxie, which entices shoppers with unique styles, designer labels and top-notch service.

Luna Boston (Map pp76-7; ☎ 617-262-3900; 286 Newbury St; ⏰ 11am-7pm; ⓐ Hynes) If you have a thing for handbags then Luna has a thing for you. With a mile-long list of designers, Luna will have no problem finding you the perfect tote, clutch or satchel. Also: laptop carriers, beach bags, backpacks and baby bags.

Berk's (Map p78; ☎ 617-492-9511; 50 John F Kennedy St; ⏰ 10am-9pm Mon-Sat, 11am-7pm Sun; ⓐ Harvard) Berk's is a little store with a great selection of shoes – half for your sensible feet and half for your fancy feet. Prices can be prohibitively high, unless you hold out for the awesome end-of-season sales. Look for the tables on the sidewalks piled high with shoes.

BOSTON

Food & Drink

Savenor's (Map pp72-3; ☎ 617-723-6328; 160 Charles St; ⊕ Charles/MGH) Famous for catering to the likes of Julia Child when she lived in Cambridge. This gourmet shop is small, but packed to the brim with fancy selections of cheese, deli meats, freshly baked bread and pastries, fruit and vegetables.

Dairy Fresh Candies (Map pp72-3; ☎ 617-742-2639; www.dairyfreshcandies.com; 57 Salem St; ☸ 9am-7pm Mon-Fri, 8am-7pm Sat, 11am-6pm Sun; ⊕ Haymarket) Walking through the doors of this tiny storefront is like entering Willy Wonka's Chocolate Factory, with its unsurpassed selection of nuts, chocolates, candies and dried fruit.

Polcari's Coffee (Map pp72-3; ☎ 617-227-0786; 105 Salem St; ☸ 10am-6pm Mon-Sat; ⊕ Haymarket) Since 1932, this corner shop is where North Enders stock up on their beans. Look for 27 kinds of imported coffee, over 150 spices and an impressive selection of legumes, grains, flours and loose teas. Don't bypass the chance to indulge in a fresh Italian ice.

Salumeria Italiana (Map pp72-3; ☎ 617-523-8743; www.salumeriaitaliana.com; 151 Richmond St; ⊕ Haymarket) Shelves stocked with extra virgin olive oil and aged balsamic vinegar; cases crammed with cured meats, hard cheeses and olives of all shapes and sizes; boxes of pasta, jars of sauce: this little store is the archetype of North End shops. Shopping tip: inquire about the specialty Rubio aged balsamic vinegar.

Wine Bottega (Map pp72-3; ☎ 617-227-6607; 341 Hanover St; ⊕ Haymarket) This relative newcomer has a large choice of wines packed into a small space. The owner is enthusiastic about little-known wineries, so the selection is eclectic – perfect for the adventurous oenophile.

South End Formaggio (Map pp76-7; ☎ 617-350-6996; 268 Shawmut Ave; ☸ 9am-8pm Mon-Fri, 9am-7pm Sat, 11am-5pm Sun; ⊕ Back Bay) The smallish cheese case is virtually overflowing with artisanal cheeses: hard cheeses, soft cheeses, pungent cheeses, mild cheeses, spreadable cheeses, shredded cheeses. To really get to know your cheeses, join the cheesemongers for a Sunday-night wine and cheese pairing ($35 per person).

Cardullo's Gourmet Shop (Map p78; ☎ 617-491-8888; 6 Brattle St; ⊕ Harvard) We've never seen so many goodies packed into such a small space. The excellent selection of New England products is a good source for souvenirs. Cardullo's newest gourmet 'treat' is flavored Edible Bugs – that's right, crickets,

---

BEST BOSTON SOUVENIRS

Remember the good times with a super Boston souvenir:

- Funky, fun, feel-good, Life-is-good t-shirt from **Jake's House** (p123)

- 'Wicked Good Boston Bands,' a CD produced inhouse at **Newbury Comics** (below)

- New running shoes, purchased at massive discount from the **New Balance Factory Store** (opposite)

- *Make Way for Ducklings,* the famous children's book by Robert McCloskey, from the **Coop** (p66)

- Complete lobster dinner (packed in dry ice to ship or take home) from **Legal Sea Foods** (p108)

---

scorpions and ants, organically grown and charmingly packaged. That's got to be a good source of protein.

Harvest Co-Op (off Map p78; ☎ 617-661-1580; 581 Massachusetts Ave; ☸ 8am-10pm; ⌨ wi-fi; ⊕ Central) Socially conscious shoppers will appreciate this cooperative market. Besides being community owned, Harvest also supports sustainable agriculture, certified organic, fair trade, and local and small family farms. In front of the store, the Café@Harvest is a pleasant place to stop for lunch (and offers free wi-fi).

Music

Newbury Comics (Map pp76-7; ☎ 617-236-4930; 332 Newbury St; ⊕ Hynes) Any outlet of this local chain is usually jam-packed with teenagers clad in black and sporting multiple piercings. Apparently these kids know where to find cheap CDs and DVDs. The newest alt-rock and the latest movies are on sale here, plus comic books, rock posters and other silly gags. No wonder everyone is having such a wicked good time. Another outlet is in the Garage in Harvard Sq.

For used discs and records:

Cheapo Records (off Map p78; ☎ 617-354-4455; 645 Massachusetts Ave; ☸ 10am-6pm Mon-Wed, 10am-9pm Thu-Sat, 11am-5pm Sun; ⊕ Central) With tunes blasting out from its basement digs, Cheapo Records lures in music-lovers to browse through its huge selection of vinyl and decent selection of CDs. And yes, they really are cheap-o.

In Your Ear (Map p78; ☎ 617-491-5035; 72 Mount Auburn St; ◉ Harvard) The albums on the wall will catch your eye, but they are expensive; look down below for unbelievable bargains.

Looney Tunes (Map pp76-7; ☎ 617-247-2238; 1106 Boylston St; ⏱ 10am-9:30pm Mon-Sat, noon-8pm Sun; ◉ Kenmore) The rotating collection of hundreds of thousands of records is not all packed into this tiny store near Berklee School of Music (though it feels like it): there is another store in Harvard Sq and a huge stock of items in storage.

Sporting Goods

Eastern Mountain Sports (Map pp76-7; ☎ 617-236-1518; 855 Boylston St; ⏱ 10am-8pm Mon-Sat, noon-6pm Sun; ◉ Copley) Once an exclusive retailer of rock-climbing equipment, this local chain now sells camping gear, kayaks, snowboards and all the special apparel you need to engage in the aforementioned activities. Additional stores are in Harvard Sq (Map p78) and on Commonwealth Ave near BU (off Map pp76–70).

Hilton's Tent City (Map pp72-3; ☎ 617-227-9242; 272 Friend St; ⏱ 9am-9pm Mon-Fri, 9am-6pm Sat, noon-6pm Sun; ◉ North Station) It's dusty and musty, but it boasts four floors of tents (set up to test out), as well as outdoor apparel, camping gear, backpacks and other outdoor accessories. Prices are competitive and staff helpful (they have to be because it's nearly impossible to find anything on your own).

New Balance Factory Store (off Map pp76-7; ☎ 877-623-7867; 40 Life St, Brighton; 🚌 64) Factory seconds and overruns of running shoes, fleece jackets and synthetic clothing made by New Balance. You may have to search for your size, but you can easily save 25% to 50% on any given item. Look for the automatic 20% reduction when you trade in an old pair of shoes. This place is not so easy to get to: hop on the bus in Central Sq heading west and get off at the corner of Beacon and Life Sts

Travel Goods

London Harness Company (Map pp72-3; ☎ 617-542-9234; 60 Franklin St; ⏱ 9:30am-6pm Mon-Fri, 10am-4pm Sat; ◉ Downtown Crossing) The history of the London Harness Company goes back to 1776, when a local saddlemaker joined forces with a well-established trunkmaker. This historic partnership claimed Ben Franklin as a customer, and today the London Harness Company is the country's oldest luggage retailer (you can't buy saddles here any more).

GETTING THERE & AWAY

Air

In East Boston, **Logan International Airport** (Map p71; ☎ 800-235-6426; www.massport.com; ◉ Airport) has five separate terminals that are connected by a frequent shuttle bus (11). Public information booths are located in the baggage claim areas of Terminals A, B, C and E. See p533 for further information.

Boat

Boats operate on a reduced schedule in September and October but run daily in the months shown here.

Bay State Cruise Company (off Map pp72-3; ☎ 617-748-1428; www.boston-ptown.com; Commonwealth Pier; adult/child/senior $44/28/40, bike $5; ⏱ depart Boston 8am, 1pm & 5:30pm, depart Provincetown 10am, 3pm & 7:30pm mid-May–Sep; ◉ South Station) Operates boats from the World Trade Center in the Seaport District to Provincetown at the tip of Cape Cod.

Boston Harbor Cruises (Map pp72-3; ☎ 617-227-4321; www.bostonharborcruises.com; Long Wharf; adult/child/senior $45/35/40, bike $5; ⏱ depart Boston 9am & 2pm, depart Provincetown 11am & 4pm mid-Jun–mid-Sep; ◉ Aquarium) Ferries to Provincetown departing from Long Wharf.

Salem Ferry (Map pp72-3; ☎ 978-741-0220; www.salemferry.com; Central Wharf; round trip adult/child/senior $22/14/18; ⏱ depart Boston 9am-9pm mid-Jun–Aug; ◉ Aquarium) A new service between Boston Central Wharf (at the New England Aquarium) and Salem.

Bus

For inter-city travel, Boston has a modern, indoor, user-friendly **bus station** (Map pp72-3; 700 Atlantic Ave; ◉ South Station), at Summer St, conveniently adjacent to the South Station.

Greyhound (☎ 617-526-1800, 800-231-2222; www.greyhound.com) buses travel across the country. A seven-day advance purchase on one-way tickets often beats all other quoted fares.

All of these regional lines operate out of the South Station bus station:

Concord Trailways (☎ 617-426-8080, 800-639-3317; www.concordtrailways.com) Plies routes from Boston to New Hampshire (Concord, Manchester, and as far up as Conway and Berlin) and Maine (Portland and Bangor). Its partner Dartmouth Coach goes to Hanover, New Hampshire.

C&J Trailways (☎ 603-430-1100, 800-258-7111; www.cjtrailways.com) Provides daily service to Newburyport, Massachusetts, as well as Portsmouth and Dover, New Hampshire. Kids free when accompanied by a full-paying adult.

Peter Pan Bus Lines (☎ 800-343-9999; www.peterpanbus.com) Serves 52 destinations in the northeast, as far north as Concord, New Hampshire and as far south as Washington DC, as well as western Massachusetts. Fares are comparable to Greyhound.

Plymouth & Brockton Street Railway Co (☎ 508-746-0378; www.p-b.com) Provides frequent service to the South Shore and to most towns on Cape Cod, including Hyannis and Provincetown.

Vermont Transit (☎ 800-552-8737; www.vermont transit.com) The route from Boston goes via Manchester and Concord, New Hampshire to White River Junction, Montpelier and Burlington, Vermont, then all the way to Montreal, Québec in Canada. Another route runs up the coast to Newburyport, Massachusetts; Portsmouth, New Hampshire; and Portland, Augusta, Bangor and Bar Harbor, Maine.

The cheapest way to get to New York city is on one of the **Chinatown Buses** (www.chinatown -bus.com; tickets $15). These are bus companies that run between the major cities on the east coast, from Chinatown to Chinatown. It's crowded, it's confusing, but it sure is cheap. This rock-bottom price is already more expensive than it used to be, but the buses actually leave from South Station (Map pp72–3), which makes life easier for the non-Chinese traveler. Buses depart daily at the top of every hour.

Fung Wah Bus Company (☎ 212-925-8889; www .fungwahbus.com; ⏰ 7am-10pm & 11:30pm) Fung Wah started the Chinatown service eight years ago.

Lucky Star Bus (☎ 800-881-0887; www.luckystarbus .com; ⏰ 7am-8pm & 11:30pm) Arrive 30 minutes before your scheduled departure to assure that your seat is not given away.

Car & Motorcycle

From western Massachusetts, the Massachusetts Turnpike ('Mass Pike' or I-90, a toll road) takes you right into Downtown. After paying a toll in Newton (the amount varies depending on how many miles you have driven on the pike; it's $2.70 if you are coming all the way from Stockbridge), drive east 10 more minutes on the pike and pay another toll ($1); then the fun begins.

There are three exits for the Boston area: Cambridge, Copley Sq (Prudential Center) and Kneeland St (Chinatown). Then, the turnpike ends abruptly. At that point you can head north or south of the city on the I-93 Expressway (the Central Artery) or right past South Station, into downtown.

From New York and other southerly points, take I-95 north to MA 128 to I-93, which cuts through the heart of the city. From northerly points, take I-93 south across the Leonard Zakim Bunker Hill Bridge.

A few sample distances from Boston to various points around New England:

Destination	Distance (miles)	Duration (hr)
Burlington, Vermont	220	4½
New York City, New York	227	4½
Portland, Maine	108	2¼
Portsmouth, New Hampshire	57	1
Providence, Rhode Island	45	1

Train

Amtrak (☎ 800-872-7245; www.amtrak.com) trains leave from South Station (Map pp72–3), located on the corner of Atlantic Ave and Summer St, but also stop at Back Bay Station (Map pp76–7) on Dartmouth St. Service to New York City's Penn Station costs $78 one way and takes four to 4½ hours. Service to Manhattan on the high-speed Acela train (3½ hours) is a lot more expensive ($102 to $117 one way); reservations are required. Amtrak's online 'Rail Sale' program offers substantial discounts on many reserved tickets.

MBTA commuter rail (☎ 617-222-3200, 800-392-6100; www.mbta.com) trains heading west and north of the city, including to Concord, leave from bustling North Station (Map pp72–3) on Causeway St. Catch the 'beach trains' to Salem, Gloucester and Rockport here. Trains heading south, including to Plymouth, leave from South Station (Map pp72–3).

GETTING AROUND
To/From the Airport

Downtown Boston is just a few miles from Logan International Airport and is accessible by subway (the 'T'), water shuttle, van shuttle, limo, taxi and rental car.

The T, the **MBTA subway** (☎ 617-222-3200, 800-392-6100; www.mbta.com; per ride $2; ⏰ 5:30am-12:30am), is normally the fastest and cheapest way to reach the city from the airport. From any terminal, take a free, well-marked shuttle bus (22 or 33) to the Blue Line T-station called Airport and you'll be downtown within 30 minutes.

The Silver Line is the MBTA's new 'bus rapid transit service'. It travels between Logan International Airport and South Station (which is the railway station as well as a Red Line T-station), with stops in the Seaport District. Silver Line buses pick up directly at the airport terminals. This is the most

BOSTON TRANSPORT MAP

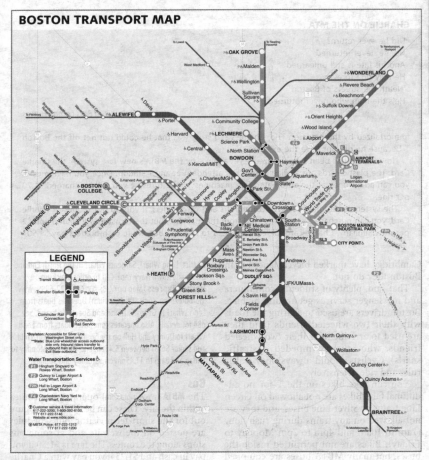

convenient way to get into the city if you are staying in the Seaport District, Theater District or South End, or anywhere along the Red Line.

Taxis are plentiful but pricey; traffic snarls can translate into a $25 fare to Downtown. The regional bus lines (Concord Trailways, Peter Pan and Plymouth & Brockton; see p125) operate **Logan Direct** (☎ 800-235-6426; tickets $8), which provides direct bus service between Logan airport and the South Station Transportation Center.

Several water shuttles operate between Logan and the waterfront district in Boston. **City Water Taxi** (☎ 617-422-0392; www.citywatertaxi .com; one way/round trip $10/17; ☻ 7am-10pm Mon-Sat, 7am-8pm Sun) Serves 15 destinations in Boston

Harbor, including Long Wharf, the Seaport District and the North End. Use the checkerboard call box at Logan dock to summon the water taxi.

Rowes Wharf Water Taxi (☎ 617-406-8584; www .roweswharfwatertaxi.com; one way/round trip $10/17; ☻ 7am-7pm) Serves Rowes Wharf near the Boston Harbor Hotel, the Moakley Federal Courthouse on the Fort Point Channel and the World Trade Center in the Seaport District. Taxis also go to the North End and Charlestown for a higher fare (one way $20).

Bicycle

Boston has been rated 'Worst City for Cycling' by *Bicycle* magazine. That is because the city streets are old and narrow, and often overcrowded with cars. Many roads in

BOSTON

CHARLIE ON THE MTA

Did he ever return?
No, he never returned
And his fate is still unlearned
He may ride forever
'Neath the streets of Boston
He's the man who never returned.

Jacqueline Steiner and Bess Lomax Hawes

Immortalized by the Kingston Trio, Charlie's sad story was that he could not get off the Boston T because he did not have the exit fare.

Now Charlie has been immortalized – yet again – by the MBTA's new fare system: the Charlie Card. The plastic cards are available from the attendant at any T station. Once you have a card, you can add money at the automated fare machines; at the turnstile you will be charged $1.70 per ride.

The system is designed to favor commuters and cardholders. If you do not request a Charlie Card, you can purchase a paper fare card from the machine, but the turnstile will charge you $2 per ride. Similarly, Charlie-cardholders pay $1.25 to ride the bus, while cash-holders pay $1.50.

Cambridge have marked bicycle lanes but in Boston they do not.

That said, plenty of students, commuters and messenger services get around by bike. Boston drivers are used to sharing the roads with their two-wheeled friends (and they are used to arriving *after* their two-wheeled friends, who are less impeded by traffic snarls). Cyclists should always obey traffic rules and ride defensively.

You can take bikes on the T for no additional fare. Bikes are not allowed on Green Line trains or Silver Line buses, and they are not allowed on any trains during rush hour (7am to 10am and 4pm to 7pm Monday to Friday). Bikes are not permitted inside the buses, but many MBTA buses are equipped with bicycle racks on the outside. For information about off-road bicycle trails and bike rental, see p92.

Boat

For information on the water taxi to the airport, see p126. For information on cruises, see p96.

Boston Harbor Cruises (Map pp72-3; ☎ 617-227-4321; www.bostonharborcruises; Long Wharf; ☉ Aquarium) Commuter service to Charlestown Navy Yard (adult/child $1.70/0.80) Ferries run from 6:30am to 8pm Monday to Friday, and 10am to 6pm Saturday and Sunday).

City Water Taxi (☎ 617-422-0392; www.citywatertaxi .com; fares $10-20; ☉ 7am-10pm Mon-Sat, 7am-8pm Sun) Makes on-demand taxi stops at about 15 waterfront points, including the airport, the Barking Crab, the Seaport

District, Long Wharf, Sargents Wharf in the North End and the Charlestown Navy Yard. Call to order a pick-up.

Harbor Express (Map pp72-3; ☎ 617-222-6999; www .harborexpress.com; ☉ Aquarium) Operates boats from Long Wharf to George's Island and Spectacle Island. See p84 for details. Also operates commuter boats from Long Wharf to Quincy and Hull on the South Shore (adult/child and senior $6/3) between 5:45am and 11:45pm Monday to Friday and 8am to 11:45pm on Saturday and Sunday.

Bus

The **MBTA** (www.mbta.com) operates bus routes within the city. These can be difficult to figure out for the short-term visitor, but schedules are posted on the website and at some bus stops along the routes. The fare is $1.50 if you pay in cash and $1.25 if you pay with a Charlie Card (see above).

Car & Motorcycle

With any luck you won't have to drive in or around Boston. Not only are the streets a maze of confusion, choked with construction and legendary traffic jams, but Boston drivers use their own set of rules. Driving is often considered a sport – in a town that takes its sports very seriously.

Two highways skirt the Charles River: Storrow Dr runs along the Boston side and Memorial Dr (more scenic) parallels it on the Cambridge side. There are exits off Storrow Dr for Kenmore Sq, Back Bay and Government Center. Both Storrow Dr and Memorial Dr are accessible from the Mass Pike and the I-93.

CAR RENTAL

All major car rental agencies are represented at the airport; free shuttle vans will take you to their nearby pick-up counters. When returning rental cars, you'll find gas stations on US 1 north of the airport. These rental companies have offices downtown:

Avis (Map pp72-3; ☎ 617-534-1400, 800-331-1212; www.avis.com; 3 Center Plaza; ☺ Government Center)

Budget (Map pp72-3; ☎ 617-497-1800, 800-527-0700; www.budget.com; 24 Park Plaza; ☺ Arlington)

Enterprise (Map pp76-7; ☎ 617-262-8222, 800-736-8222; Prudential Center, 800 Boylston St; ☾ 7am-6pm Mon-Fri, 9am-3pm Sat, 9am-1pm Sun; ☺ Prudential)

Hertz (Map pp72-3; ☎ 617-338-1500, 800-654-3131; www.hertz.com; 30 Park Plaza; ☾ 7am-7pm Sun-Thu, 7am-8pm Fri, 7am-6pm Sat; ☺ Arlington)

National (off Map p78; ☎ 617-661-8747, 800-227-7368; www.nationalcar.com; 1663 Massachusetts Ave, Cambridge; ☾ 8am-5:30pm Sat-Thu, 8am-7pm Fri; ☺ Porter) Between Harvard Sq and Porter Sq.

Thrifty (Map p78; ☎ 617-876-2758; www.thrifty.com; 110 Mt Auburn St, Harvard Square Hotel, Cambridge; ☺ Harvard)

PARKING

Folks on Beacon Hill pony up $150,000 to own a space at the Brimmer Street Garage. The explanation is simple economics: supply and demand. Since on-street parking is limited, you could end up paying $25 to $35 daily to park in a lot. Some cheaper options:

Boston Common Garage (Map pp72-3; ☎ 617-954-2096; ☺ Park St) Park for $10 after 4pm Monday to Friday and all day Saturday and Sunday.

Center Plaza Garage (Map pp72-3; ☎ 617-742-7807; One Center Plaza; ☺ Government Center) Charges $8 after 4pm weekdays and all day Saturday and Sunday. Great option for Garden events.

Parcel 7 Garage (Map pp72-3; cnr New Sudbury & Congress Sts; with validation 2/3hr $1/3; ☺ Haymarket) Convenient for dining in the North End. Be sure to get your ticket validated at the restaurant where you eat.

Prudential Center (Map pp76-7; ☎ 617-236-3100; 800 Boylston St; up to 4 hr/per day $10/20; ☺ Prudential) Requires a $10 purchase from the Shops at Prudential Center (save your receipts). Discounted rates available for Red Sox games ($15) and other special events ($13).

South Boston Fan Pier (Map pp72-3; all day $7; ☺ South Station)

State Street Parking (Map pp72-3; ☎ 617-742-7275; 75 State St; ☺ State) Park for $12 after 5pm Monday to Friday, all day Saturday and Sunday.

Taxi

Cabs are plentiful (although you may have to walk to a major hotel to find one) but expensive. Rates are determined by the meter, which calculates miles. Expect to pay about $10 to $15 between most tourist points within the city limits, without much traffic. You'll have lots of trouble hailing a cab during bad weather and between 3:30pm and 6:30pm weekdays. Again, head to major hotels or Faneuil Hall. Recommended taxi companies include **Independent** (☎ 617-426-8700) and **Metro Cab** (☎ 617-242-8000).

The T (Subway)

The **MBTA** (☎ 617-222-3200, 800-392-6100; www.mbta .com) operates the USA's oldest subway, which was built in 1897. It's known locally as 'the T' and has four lines – Red, Blue, Green and Orange – that radiate out from the principal downtown stations. These are Park St (which has an information booth), Downtown Crossing, Government Center and State. When traveling away from any of these stations, you are heading outbound.

Tourist passes with unlimited travel (on subway, bus or water shuttle) are available for periods of one week ($15) and one day ($9). Kids aged five to 11 ride for free. Passes may be purchased at the following T stations: Park St, Government Center, Back Bay, Alewife, Copley, Quincy Adams, Harvard, North Station, South Station, Hynes and Airport. For longer stays, you can buy a monthly pass allowing unlimited use of the subway and local bus ($59). Otherwise, buy a paper fare card ($2 per ride) or a Charlie Card ($1.70 per ride) at all stations. See opposite for details.

The T operates from approximately 5:30am to 12:30am. The last Red Line trains pass through Park St at about 12:30am (depending on the direction), but all T stations and lines are different: check the posting at the station.

Around Boston

From the moment the Pilgrims stepped ashore at Plymouth Rock, this area was on the map – both geographically and historically. Today, the towns surrounding Boston include destinations that represent every aspect of New England history.

Plymouth was New England's first permanent settlement – its history has been carefully recreated by Plimoth Plantation and Mayflower II. Here, travelers are invited to experience first-hand the life of the country's earliest settlers. The American Revolution's first battles took place on the historic greens at Lexington and Concord – these momentous events are reenacted every year on Patriot's Day, so you can see for yourself how the war unfolded.

National Historic Sites and heritage centers all around eastern Massachusetts recall the innovation and industriousness of the new postrevolutionary nation. Gawk at the treasures that traders brought back from afar, now on display in Salem and Newburyport; climb aboard the fishing boats and whaling ships in Gloucester and New Bedford to imagine life on the sea; work the looms in Lowell, just like the mill girls who kept the place running in its heyday.

But the region around Boston isn't living in the past. Today these areas are teeming with tourists attracted to lively art scenes, including the Peabody Essex Museum in Salem and the Rocky Neck artist colony in Gloucester. Miles of pristine coastline draw beachcombers and sunbathers (not to mention piping plovers). Hikers and cyclists, canoeists and kayakers, bird-watchers and whale-watchers have myriad opportunities to engage with the local active lifestyle.

HIGHLIGHTS

- Getting spooked at Haunted Happenings Halloween festival in **Salem** (p147)
- Biking the **Minuteman Commuter Bikeway** (p134) from Cambridge to Lexington, then continuing on to Concord for a cooling dip in **Walden Pond** (p139)
- Catching sight of a breeching whale from the deck of a whale-watching tour off the coast of **Gloucester** (p154)
- Tracing the footsteps of Beat-generation author Jack Kerouac in **Lowell** (p142)
- Catching some rays on **Plum Island** (p161) then downing a lobster roll from Starboard Galley (p162) in **Newburyport**
- Witnessing the Pilgrims' earliest settlement at **Plimoth Plantation** (p165)

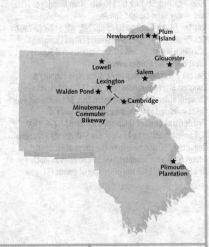

■ TELEPHONE CODES: 781, 978, 508	■ POPULATION: 4.4 MILLION	■ AREA: 3000 SQ MILES

AROUND BOSTON

Information

Greater Boston Convention & Visitors Bureau
(GBCVB; www.bostonusa.com) Offers lots of information, not only on Boston, but on much of eastern Massachusetts.
Mass Tourist (www.masstourist.com) Includes links to towns and major sights around Massachusetts.
Massachusetts Office of Travel & Tourism (☎ 617-973-8500, 800-227-6277; www.massvacation.com; 10 Park Plaza, Suite 4510, Boston) The state's official tourism agency.

History

The original inhabitants of Massachusetts belonged to several different Algonquian tribes, including the Wampanoag and the Pennacook. After running aground off the coast of Cape Cod, the Pilgrims established their permanent settlement at Plymouth Colony in 1620. The Puritans followed them in 1628, establishing the Massachusetts Bay Colony on the sites of present-day Boston and Salem. In the following years, daring souls in search of religious freedom or economic opportunity would settle right along the coast of Massachusetts. When these colonies finally broke free from Mother England, the War for Independence started with the Battles of Lexington and Concord.

Eastern Massachusetts played a crucial role in the country's economic development. In the early 19th century, during the age of sails and whales (p30), towns such as Salem, Newburyport and New Bedford amassed great wealth from maritime trade, shipbuilding and whaling. At the same time, Lowell was an exemplary textile town, instigating the industrial revolution (p31). Villages on Cape Ann – especially Gloucester – were leaders in the fishing industry.

With the decline of these sectors in the 20th century, the area has turned to tourism to pick up the economic slack, with varying degrees of success. In an attempt to revitalize their aging city centers, Salem, Lowell and New Bedford have created National Historic Sites, turning old industrial buildings into museums and opening restaurants and cafés to cater to tourists. Gloucester, too, touts its working waterfront as a heritage center, where visitors can book a whale-watching tour or learn about marine life.

The Culture

As the name of the chapter implies, the towns 'Around Boston' function as suburbs of the state capital. More than four million people reside in the greater Boston area, compared to 591,000 in the city proper. For the traveler, these destinations boast their own unique histories and intriguing tourist attractions; for the resident, however, life is often centered on the big city. Many people commute into Boston from its surrounding areas for well-paying jobs; well-to-do families inhabit houses with well-groomed lawns; and well-trained dogs romp with well-dressed children. These are the yuppies who have ditched the urban and gone suburban.

Land & Climate

Eastern Massachusetts has a humid continental climate, much like the rest of New England. It consists mostly of flat uplands, so it is not usually subject to the fierce winds and harsh weather of the mountains. Indeed, the warm air off the ocean often has a moderating effect on coastal temperatures. That said, the state sees its fair share of Nor'easters – powerful storms with infamous torrential downpours and high winds.

National & State Parks

The region around Boston includes several diverse sites – significant to the region's revolutionary, mercantile and industrial past – that have been designated as National Historical Parks by the National Park Service (NPS). The Minute Man National Historical Park (p134) incorporates Battle Rd between Lexington and Concord, where the first skirmishes of the American Revolution developed into full-blown fighting. This area remains much as it was 200 years ago. Other National Historical Parks are less pristine, but still capture a significant piece of the nation's history,' they include the Lowell National Historic Park (p141), Salem Maritime National Historic Site (p144) and the New Bedford Whaling National Historical Park (p168).

State, county and private efforts have made great strides toward limiting intrusive development and preserving ecosystems, especially on the North Shore: much of Cape Ann is protected, as are vast swathes of land further north. Sandy Point (p161) is a lovely state park, while Halibut Point Reservation (p158), Crane Wildlife Refuge (p159) and Parker River National Wildlife Refuge (p160) are managed by the ever-attentive Trustees of Reservations. Walden Pond (p139) is an inspirational, wonderful natural resource, also managed by Massachusetts state, while the acres of undisturbed woods around it are protected by the efforts of private institutions. Just a few miles south of Boston, the Blue Hills Reservation (p163) is the little-known but much appreciated result of the Massachusetts Department of Conservation and Recreation.

Getting There & Away

Many of the sights around Boston are accessible by the **Massachusetts Bay Transportation Authority commuter rail** (MBTA; ☎ 617-722-3200, 800-392-6100; www.mbta.com). Trains depart from Boston's North Station to destinations on the North Shore, including a line to Gloucester and Rockport, and another line to Newburyport. Salem is served by both of these train lines. North Station is also the departure point for trains heading west to Concord and Lowell. Plymouth is served by trains departing from South Station in Boston. Other destinations can be reached by bus, but it's really preferable to use a private vehicle to get the most from a trip out of the city.

WEST OF BOSTON

Some places might boast about starting a revolution, but Boston's western suburbs can actually make the claim that two revolutions were launched here. Most famously, the American Revolution – the celebrated War for Independence that spawned a nation – started with encounters on the town greens at Lexington and Concord. And the industrial revolution – the economic transformation that would turn this new nation from agriculture to manufacturing – began in the textile mills of Lowell.

LEXINGTON

pop 30,355

This upscale suburb, about 18 miles from Boston's center, consists of a bustling village of white churches and historic taverns, with tour buses surrounding the village green. Here, the skirmish between patriots and British troops jump-started the War for Independence. Each year on April 19 historians and patriots don their 18th-century costumes and grab their rifles for an elaborate reenactment of the events of 1775 (see p135).

While this history is celebrated and preserved, it is in stark contrast to the peaceful, even staid, community that is Lexington today. If you stray more than a few blocks from the green, you could be in Anywhere, USA, with few reminders that this is where it all started. Nonetheless, it is a pleasant enough Anywhere, USA, with restaurants and shops lining the main drag, and impressive Georgian architecture anchoring either end.

Orientation & Information

MA 4 and MA 225 follow Massachusetts Ave through the center of Lexington. The Battle Green is at the northwestern end of the business district, which sits around the corner of Mass Ave and Waltham St. Minute Man National Historical Park is about two miles west of Lexington center on Route 2A.

Bank of America (1761 Massachusetts Ave; ✆ 8:30am-4pm Mon-Fri, 9am-3pm Sat) ATM and exchange facilities.

Lexington Chamber of Commerce & Visitor Center (☎ 781-862-2480; www.lexingtonchamber .org; 1875 Massachusetts Ave; ✆ 9am-5pm Apr-Nov, 10am-4pm Dec-Mar) Opposite Battle Green, next to Buckman Tavern.

Lexington Historical Society (☎ 781-862-1703; www.lexingtonhistory.org; 13 Depot Sq; ✆ 8:30am-2:30pm Mon-Fri)

Post Office (1661 Massachusetts Ave; ✆ 8am-6pm Mon-Fri, 8am-2pm Sat)

Sights & Activities

BATTLE GREEN

Paul Revere, William Dawes and Samuel Prescott set out on their midnight ride on April 18, 1775. They were riding to warn the communities west of Boston that a British expeditionary force was coming to search for arms rumored to be stockpiled at Concord. When 700 Redcoats marched up to Lexington Green just after daybreak on April 19, they found Capt John Parker's company of 77 minutemen in formation ready to meet them.

Clearly outnumbered, Capt Parker ordered his men to disperse peaceably. A shot rang out – the side from which it came has never been clear – and then other shots followed, and soon eight minutemen lay dead on the green, with 10 others wounded. The skirmish was the first organized, armed resistance to British rule in a colonial town, and marked the beginning of the Revolutionary War.

Today, Lexington Green (now called Battle Green) remembers this huge event. The

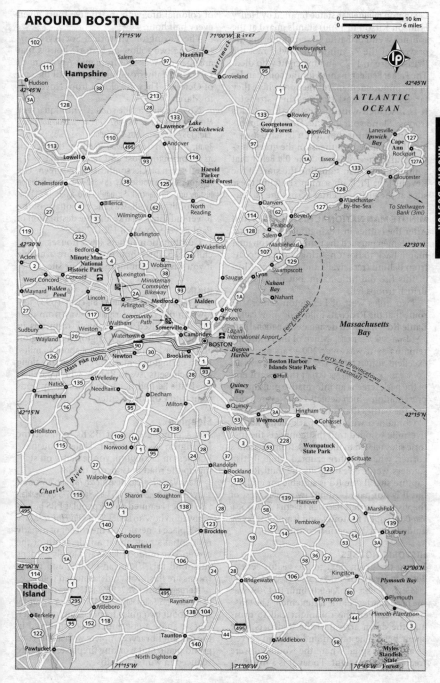

AROUND BOSTON

AROUND BOSTON

Lexington **minuteman statue** (crafted by Henry Hudson Kitson in 1900) stands guard at the southeast end of Battle Green, honoring the bravery of the 77 minutemen who met the British here in 1775 and the eight who died. The **Parker Boulder**, named for the commander of the minutemen, marks the spot where they faced a force almost 10 times their strength. It is inscribed with his instructions to his troops: 'Stand your ground. Don't fire unless fired upon. But if they mean to have a war, let it begin here.' Southeast of the green, history buffs have preserved the **Old Belfry** that sounded the alarm signaling the start of the Revolution. Pick up a map showing these sites at the visitors center across the street.

MINUTE MAN NATIONAL HISTORICAL PARK
After the battles in Lexington and Concord, minutemen pursued the British troops on their march back to Boston, firing at the Redcoats from behind trees, walls and buildings. Most of this fire did little harm, but occasionally British troops fell.

Two miles west of Lexington center, the route that the Redcoats followed – now called Battle Rd – has been designated a **national park** (dawn-dusk year-round). Much of the landscape remains as it was over 200 years ago. The excellent **visitors center** (☎ 978-862-7753; www.nps .gov/mima; 9am-5pm Apr-Oct) at the eastern end of the park screens an informative multimedia presentation which depicts Paul Revere's ride and the battles that followed.

Contained within the park, **Battle Rd** is a five-mile wooded trail that connects the historic sites related to the battles, from Meriam's corner, where gunfire erupted while British soldiers were retreating, to the Paul Revere capture site. Battle Rd is suitable for cycling, but it is not paved. About two miles west of the visitors center, **Hartwell Tavern** (9am-5pm May-Oct) is open for tours, and features talks by guides dressed in period costume.

HISTORIC HOUSES
Facing the green next to the visitor center, **Buckman Tavern** (☎ 781-862-5598; 1 Bedford St; adult/ child $5/3; 10am-4pm Apr-Oct), built in 1709, was the headquarters of the minutemen. The tense hours between the midnight call to arms and the dawn arrival of the Redcoats were spent here. The tavern and inn also served as a field hospital where the wounded were treated after the fight. Today it is a museum

of colonial life, with instructive tours given every half hour.

The Lexington Historical Society maintains the two following historic houses that are open on weekends from mid-April to mid-June, and daily from mid-June until the end of October. They are closed from November to March.

Now serving as the society's headquarters, **Munroe Tavern** (☎ 781-862-1703; www.lexingtonhistory .org; 1332 Massachusetts Ave; adult/child $5/3; 1:30-3pm), built in 1695, was used by the British as a command post and field infirmary. It's about seven blocks southeast of the green. The **Hancock-Clarke House** (☎ 781-862-1703; www.lexington history.org; 36 Hancock St; adult/child $5/3; 11am-2pm), built in 1698, was the parsonage of the Reverend Jonas Clarke and the destination of Paul Revere on April 19, 1775.

Combination tickets (two houses adult/ child $8/5, three houses $10/6) are available if you wish to visit more than one site.

BIKING
The **Minuteman Commuter Bikeway** (p93) follows an old railroad right-of-way from near the Alewife Red Line subway terminus in Cambridge, through Arlington to Lexington and Bedford, a total distance of about 14 miles. From Lexington center, you can also ride along Massachusetts Ave to Rte 2A, which parallels the **Battle Rd Trail** (left), and eventually leads right into Concord Center.

Sleeping
For a complete list of B&Bs, contact the Lexington visitor center. Unless you have business in Lexington, you're better off staying up the road in Concord (p138).

Mary Van's My Old House (☎ 781-861-7057; www .maryvansmyoldhouse.com; 12 Plainfield St; r $75-85, breakfast $10;) Featured on the popular PBS home-renovation how-to series *This Old House*, Mary Van's place is nestled on the corner of a shady residential street, about a mile south of the center. Two outdoor decks and lovely gardens surround this Victorian beauty, and inside rooms are flush with old-fashioned frill.

Morgan's Rest (☎ 781-652-8018; www.morgansrest bandb.com; 205 Follen Rd; r $105-125;) A friendly B&B about two miles from Lexington center. Guests enjoy a gourmet breakfast served in the elegant library, complete with a gorgeous grand piano and working fireplace. Rates are reduced in winter months.

Eating & Drinking

More than a dozen eateries lie within a five-minute walk of the Battle Green. Most are open for lunch and dinner daily.

Rancatore's (☎ 781-862-5090; 1752 Massachusetts Ave; ☺ 10am-11pm; **V**) Cool off with a scoop of homemade ice cream or sorbet from this family-run place. The hot-fudge sundaes are legendary.

our pick **Vila Lago Gourmet Foods** (☎ 781-861-6174; 1845 Massachusetts Ave; meals $5-10; ☺ lunch & dinner; **V**) This café has high ceilings, intimate tables, a scent of fresh-roasted coffee and a great deli case. You'll often see cyclists in here kicking back with the daily paper, a cup of exotic java or tea, and a sandwich of roasted turkey, Swiss and sprouts.

Upper Crust (☎ 781-274-0089; 41 Waltham St; meals $8-10; ☺ lunch & dinner; **V**) Crispy, Neapolitan pizza with tangy garlic, fresh tomatoes and spicy pepperoni, served up in a clean, no-frills setting.

Lexx (☎ 781-674-2990; 1666 Massachusetts Ave; meals $8-30; ☺ lunch & dinner) This contemporary kitchen takes things upscale, with a decor that is sophisticated but not stuffy. The new American menu boasts 'Wholesome Food,' which in this case means fresh, seasonal and creative.

Getting There & Away

Take MA 2 west from Boston or Cambridge to exit 54 (Waltham St) or exit 53 (Spring St). From I-95 (MA 128), take exit 30 or 31. **MBTA** (☎ 800-392-6100) buses 62 (Bedford VA Hospital) and 76 (Hanscom Field) run from the Red Line Alewife subway terminus through Lexington center at least hourly on weekdays, and less frequently on Saturday; no buses on Sunday.

The most enjoyable way to get to Lexington – no contest – is to come by bicycle via the Minuteman Commuter Bikeway. See p93 for details. From there you can follow the bikeway another 4 miles west to its terminus in Bedford, or ride the Battle Rd Trail to Concord.

CONCORD
pop 16,993

Tall, white church steeples rise above ancient oaks, elms and maples in colonial Concord, giving the town a stateliness that belies the American Revolution drama that occurred centuries ago. Indeed, it is easy to see how

---

PATRIOTS' DAY

Only in Massachusetts is Patriots' Day an official holiday. And only in Lexington and Concord is it a historic event (www .battleroad.org). Every year around April 19, minuteman companies in colonial dress, bearing colonial matchlock firearms, reenact the battle on Lexington Green. The British heavies – somewhat fewer than their original force of 700 – come dressed authentically as well, and the air is again filled with the tramp of hobnailed boots, barked commands, explosions of musket fire and clouds of gun smoke. Authenticity is pursued with some vigor, so the reenactment starts at the same time as the original event: just after dawn.

---

writers such as Ralph Waldo Emerson, Nathaniel Hawthorne, Henry David Thoreau and Louisa May Alcott found their inspiration here. Concord was also the home of famed sculptor Daniel Chester French (who went on to create the Lincoln Memorial in Washington DC).

These days travelers can relive history in Concord. Indeed, every year on Patriot's Day history buffs re-enact the minutemen's march to Concord, commemorating the battle with a ceremony at the Old North Bridge and a parade later in the day. Literary mavens might still experience Thoreau's Garden of Eden at Walden Pond; and French's legacy lives on at the DeCordova Sculpture Park. The homes of literary figures such as Ralph Waldo Emerson, Nathaniel Hawthorne, and Louisa May Alcott are also open for visitors. For the less culturally inclined, the placid Concord River and the country roads are excellent for canoeing and cycling.

Orientation

Concord lies about 22 miles northwest of Boston along MA 2. The center of this sprawling, mostly rural town is Monument Sq, marked by its war memorial obelisk. The Colonial Inn stands on the square's north side.

Main St runs westward from Monument Sq through the business district to MA 2. Walden and Thoreau Sts run southeast from Main St and out to Walden Pond some 3 miles away. The MBTA commuter rail train

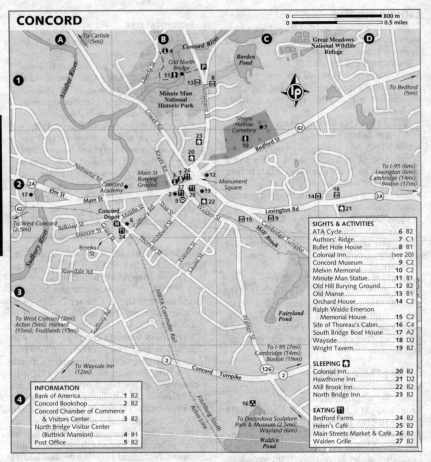

CONCORD

0 ———— 800 m
0 ———— 0.5 miles

INFORMATION	
Bank of America...................1	B2
Concord Bookshop.................2	B2
Concord Chamber of Commerce	
& Visitors Center................3	B2
North Bridge Visitor Center	
(Buttrick Mansion)..............4	B1
Post Office........................5	B2

SIGHTS & ACTIVITIES	
ATA Cycle.........................6	B2
Authors' Ridge....................7	C1
Bullet Hole House................8	B1
Colonial Inn...................(see 20)	
Concord Museum.................9	C2
Melvin Memorial.................10	C2
Minute Man Statue...............11	B1
Old Hill Burying Ground.........12	B2
Old Manse........................13	B1
Orchard House...................14	C2
Ralph Waldo Emerson	
Memorial House...............15	C2
Site of Thoreau's Cabin.........16	C4
South Bridge Boat House.........17	A2
Wayside...........................18	D2
Wright Tavern....................19	B2

SLEEPING	
Colonial Inn......................20	B2
Hawthorne Inn...................21	D2
Mill Brook Inn....................22	B2
North Bridge Inn.................23	B2

EATING	
Bedford Farms...................24	B2
Helen's Café......................25	B2
Main Streets Market & Café......26	B2
Walden Grille.....................27	B2

station, Concord Station ('the Depot'), is on Thoreau St at Sudbury Rd, a mile west of Monument Sq.

Information

Bank of America (52 Main St; ☿ 8:30am-4pm Mon-Fri, 9am-1pm Sat)

Concord Bookshop (☎ 978-369-2405; 65 Main St) An independent bookstore packed with good reads.

Concord Chamber of Commerce & Visitors Center (☎ 978-369-3120; www.concordchamberofcommerce .org; 58 Main St; ☿ 9:30am-4:30pm daily Apr-Oct)

Concord Magazine (www.concordma.com) A quarterly publication focusing on history and current events of the town. The associate website is replete with information, including historical and artistic goings-on.

North Bridge Visitor Center (☎ 978-369-6993; www.nps.gov/mima; Liberty St; ☿ 9am-5pm Apr-Oct, 9am-4pm Nov-Mar)

Post Office (34 Walden St; ☿ 9am-5pm Mon-Fri, 9am-noon Sat)

Sights & Activities
MONUMENT SQUARE

The grassy center of Monument Sq is a favorite resting and picnicking spot for cyclists touring Concord's scenic roads. At the southeastern end of the square is **Wright Tavern**, one of the first places the British troops searched in their hunt for arms on April 19, 1775. It became their headquarters for the operation. At the opposite end of the square is the **Colonial Inn** (p138), the center of Concord socializing,

BULLET HOLE HOUSE

On your way up to the Old North Bridge from Monument Sq, keep an eye out for the yellow house on the east side of Monument St. British troops fired at the owner of the house as they retreated from the engagement at North Bridge, and a hole made by one of their bullets can still be seen in the wall of the shed attached to the house.

now as then. **Old Hill Burying Ground**, with graves dating from colonial times, is on the hillside at the southeastern end of Monument Sq.

OLD NORTH BRIDGE

When the Redcoats arrived in Concord, three companies remained to secure the North Bridge. The Yankee minutemen mustered on Punkatasset Hill, northeast of the town center, and awaited reinforcements, which came steadily from surrounding towns. From their perch the minutemen saw smoke rising from the town.

The British searchers were burning the gun carriages they had found, but the minutemen assumed the worst. 'Will you let them burn the town down?' shouted their commander, Lieutenant Joseph Hosmer. Enraged minutemen responded by firing on the British troops, wounding half of their officers and forcing them back across the North Bridge. Soon the British were on their way out of Concord. The battle, called 'the shot heard 'round the world' by Ralph Waldo Emerson, was the first successful armed resistance to British rule.

The wooden span of Old North Bridge, now part of Minute Man National Historical Park (p134), has been rebuilt many times, but still gives a good impression of what it must have looked like at the time of the first battle of the Revolution. Daniel French's first statue, the **Concord Minute Man**, presides over the park from the opposite side of the bridge. Up the hill, the Buttrick Mansion houses the park's visitors center and a quaint café.

CONCORD MUSEUM

Southeast of Monument Sq, this **museum** (☎ 978-369-9609; www.concordmuseum.org; 200 Lexington Rd; adult/child/senior & student $10/5/8; ☉ 9am-5pm Mon-Sat & noon-5pm Sun Apr-Dec, 11am-4pm Mon-Fri & 1-4pm Sun Jan-Mar) brings together the town's diverse history under one roof. The museum's prized

possession is one of the 'two if by sea' lanterns that once hung in the steeple of the Old North Church (p82) in Boston as a signal to Paul Revere. It also has the world's largest collection of Henry David Thoreau artifacts, including his writing desk from Walden Pond.

RALPH WALDO EMERSON HOMES

Ralph Waldo Emerson (1803–82) was the paterfamilias of literary Concord, one of the great literary figures of his age and the founding thinker of the Transcendentalist movement. He lived in Concord from 1835 to 1882, and the **Ralph Waldo Emerson Memorial House** (☎ 978-369-2236; 28 Cambridge Turnpike; adult/child/senior & student $7/free/5; ☉ 10am-4:30pm Thu-Sat, 1-4:30pm Sun mid-Apr–Oct) is open for guided tours. The house often hosted his renowned circle of friends and still contains many original furnishings.

Right next to Old North Bridge, the **Old Manse** (☎ 978-369-3909; www.thetrustees.org; 269 Monument St; adult/child/senior & student $8/5/7; ☉ 10am-5pm Mon-Sat, noon-5pm Sun mid-Apr–Oct) was built in 1769 by Ralph Waldo's grandfather, the Reverend William Emerson, and was owned by the Emerson family for several following generations.

Nathaniel and Sophia Hawthorne also lived here for three years following their marriage. The author describes the house in *Mosses from an Olde Manse,* a book of short stories he wrote while he lived here.

One of the highlights of Old Manse is the lovely **grounds** (admission free; ☉ dawn-dusk). The fabulous organic garden was planted by Henry David Thoreau as a wedding gift to the Hawthornes.

LOUISA MAY ALCOTT HOMES

Louisa May Alcott (1832–88) was a junior member of Concord's august literary crowd, but her work proved to be durable: *Little Women* is one of the most popular books ever written. The mostly autobiographical novel takes place in Concord.

Her childhood home, **Orchard House** (☎ 978-369-4118; www.louisamayalcott.org; 399 Lexington Rd; adult/senior & student/child/family $8/7/5/20; ☉ 10am-4:30pm Mon-Sat, 1-4:30pm Sun Apr-Oct, 11am-3pm Mon-Fri, 10am-4:30pm Sat, 1-4:30pm Sun Nov-Mar), is about 1 mile east of Monument Sq. Alcott's father, Bronson, bought the property in 1857 and lived here with his family until his death in 1888. Louisa wrote *Little Women* here in 1868 and died here 20 years later. The house, furnishings and Bronson's Concord School of Philosophy, on the hillside behind the house, are all open to visitors by guided tour.

Another house that Alcott lived in and wrote about is right next door. Now called **The Wayside: House of Authors** (☎ 978-318-7826; www.nps .gov/mima; 455 Lexington Rd; adult/child $5/free; ☽ tours 11am, 1pm, 3pm & 4:30pm Fri-Sun mid-Apr–Oct), it was also at various times the home of Nathaniel Hawthorne and of children's author Margaret Sidney. Life-size sculptures and audio programming depict all three of these famous authors (and their families) during the times that they lived here. Now operated by the National Park Service, it is open by guided tour only.

SLEEPY HOLLOW CEMETERY

The most famous Concordians rest in spacious **Sleepy Hollow Cemetery** (Bedford St). Though the cemetery is only a block east of Monument Sq, the most interesting part, **Authors' Ridge**, is a 15-minute hike along Bedford St (MA 62).

Henry David Thoreau and his family are buried here, as are the Alcotts and the Hawthornes. Ralph Waldo Emerson's tombstone is a large uncarved rose quartz boulder, an appropriate Transcendentalist symbol. Down the hill a bit is the tombstone of Ephraim Bull, developer of the famous Concord grape.

Nearby is the **Melvin Memorial**, a much photographed monument to the memory of three Concord brothers who died in the Civil War. It's the work of Daniel French, who is also buried in Sleepy Hollow.

CANOEING

A mile west of Monument Sq, **South Bridge Boat House** (☎ 978-369-9438; www.concordcanoerentalsand cruises.com; 502 Main St; canoes per hr/day Mon-Fri $12.50/60, Sat & Sun $14/66, s/d kayaks per hr $14/17; ☽ 10am-dusk Mon-Fri & 9am-dusk Sat & Sun Apr-Oct) rents canoes for cruising the Concord and Assabet Rivers. The favorite route is downstream to Old North Bridge, and back past the many fine riverside houses and the campus of prestigious Concord Academy – a paddle of about two hours.

BIKING

The country roads around Concord are beautiful for biking – if you don't mind battling a few tough hills. The roads around Walden Pond, in particular, boast picturesque countryside and a lack of car traffic. Rent bikes at **ATA Cycle** (☎ 978-369-5960; www.atabike.com; 93 Thoreau St; per day $25; ☽ 10am-7pm Mon-Fri, 9am-6pm Sat & noon-5pm Sun). Alternatively, sign up with Concord Bike Tours.

Tours

Concord Bike Tours (☎ 978-371-3969; www.concord biketours.com; adult $35-50, child $26-30) Bike tours ranging from one to three hours follow routes of historic significance and natural beauty.

Concord Guides (☎ 978-287-0897; www.concord guides.com; adult/under 5yr/6-10yr/11-18yr/senior $19/ free/7/12/15; ☽ 2-4pm Sat & Sun) Two-hour customized walking tour led by local teachers, authors and historians. Reservations required.

Concord Walking Tours (☎ 978-369-3120; www.con cordchamberofcommerce.org; adult/child/senior $18/7/12; ☽ 11am Mon & Fri, 11am & 1pm Sat & Sun Apr-Oct) The Chamber of Commerce offers tours of both revolutionary and literary Concord. Tours depart from the visitors center.

Liberty Ride (☎ 781-862-0500, ext 702; www .libertyride.us; adult/child $20/10; ☽ 10am-4:30pm) The two-hour bus route covers the major minuteman sites in Lexington and Concord, as well as some of Concord's places of literary importance.

Sleeping

While there is a paucity of hotels and motels in Concord, travelers will find dozens of B&Bs in the area. Get a complete list from the Concord Chamber of Commerce.

Mill Brook Inn (☎ 978-369-5515; www.bedand breakfast.com/concord-massachusetts.html; 69 Walden St; r $110-145; ▨) This tiny B&B in the center of Concord has only two guest rooms, so you are guaranteed personalized service. The 18th-century house boasts amazing architectural details, including fireplaces and beehive ovens in the guest rooms, high-tank toilets and soapstone sinks in the bathrooms, and a wonderful stenciled floor in the foyer. Continental breakfast, afternoon tea and evening sherry hour are included.

Colonial Inn (☎ 978-369-9200, 800-370-9200; www .concordscolonialinn.com; 48 Monument Sq; r $149-229; ▨) Dating from 1716, the Colonial Inn boasts a role in the events of April 19, 1775: a part of the inn was used as a storehouse for colonial arms and provisions. The oldest part of the inn houses 12 of the more expensive guest rooms, a lobby, dining rooms and tavern (featuring afternoon tea). The other less expensive 48 guest rooms are in a modern brick annex known as Prescott Wing. Special arrangements are available for longer-term guests.

Wayside Inn (☎ 978-443-1776; www.wayside.org; 76 Wayside Inn Rd, Sudbury; s/d $125/160; 🐾) The inn was made famous by Longfellow's poems *Tales from a Wayside Inn*, and now offers 10 period rooms and lovely landscaped grounds. Also on-site is an extensive archive of the history of the inn, which has been operating since 1700. It's 13 miles south of Concord on US 20.

Hawthorne Inn (☎ 978-369-5610; www.concordmass .com; 462 Lexington Rd; r $185-245) Owned and operated by a couple of artists, this inn claims to be 'where history, literature and artistic whimsy entwine.' By 'artistic whimsy,' they mean gardens filled with flowers and figures, china cabinets packed with kitschy collectibles, furniture adorned with colorful coverlets and breakfast served on hand-painted pottery. You'll find it about a mile southeast of Monument Sq, across the street from the Wayside (p137), which was of course Hawthorne's house.

North Bridge Inn (☎ 978-371-0014; www.north bridgeinn.com; 21 Monument St; ste $190-250; 🐾) Just up the road from the Colonial Inn, this inn offers a more intimate experience. Six suites are decked out with down comforters, plush pillows, tiled bathrooms and kitchenettes. The gourmet breakfast is served in a flower-filled dining room. Rates are for double occupancy, but the suites are large enough to accommodate families and small groups.

Eating

Bedford Farms (☎ 978-341-0000; 68 Thoreau St; 🕑 noon-9pm; 🅥) Dating to the 19th century, this local dairy specializes in delectable ice cream and frozen yogurt. Conveniently located next to the train depot.

Main Streets Market & Cafe (☎ 888-493-3981; 42 Main St; meals $6-30; 🕑 6:30am-6pm daily, dinner Tue-Sat; 🅥) This longstanding family-owned market has recently expanded its operation. Always a favorite for breakfast and lunch, it now stays open into the evening, offering an eclectic menu of full dinners with live local musicians playing in the background. The spicy signature chili is hard to beat.

Helen's Café (☎ 978-369-9885; 17 Main St; meals $10-15; 🕑 7am-9pm) This popular breakfast and lunch spot hums with the sound of plates hitting the Formica table tops and staff jawing with regular customers. Hungry patrons come looking for cheese-stuffed omelets, homemade soups and grinders, and thick frappes from the ice-cream counter.

Walden Grille (☎ 978-371-2233; 24 Walden St; meals $10-30; 🕑 lunch & dinner) Set in a former firehouse, this popular spot is a tavern-restaurant with soft lighting, exposed brick walls and lyrical landscape paintings. The New American menu gets mixed reviews, but the atmosphere is welcoming.

Getting There & Away

Driving west on MA 2 from Boston or Cambridge, it's some 20 miles to Concord. Coming from Lexington, follow signs from Lexington Green to Concord and Battle Rd, the route taken by the British troops on April 19, 1775.

MBTA commuter rail (☎ 617-722-3200, 800-392-6100; www.mbta.com; Concord Depot, 90 Thoreau St) trains run between Boston's North Station and Concord Depot eight times a day ($6.50, 40 minutes) in either direction on the Fitchburg/South Acton line.

AROUND CONCORD
Walden Pond

'I went to the woods because I wished to live deliberately, to front only the essential facts of life, and see if I could not learn what it had to teach, and not, when I came to die, discover that I had not lived.' So wrote Henry David Thoreau about his time at **Walden Pond** (☎ 978-369-3254; www.mass.gov/dcr/parks/northeast/wldn .htm; 915 Walden St; admission free, parking $5; 🕑 dawn-dusk). Thoreau took the naturalist beliefs of Transcendentalism out of the realm of theory and into practice when he left the comforts of the town and built himself a rustic cabin on the shores of the pond. His famous memoir of his time spent there, *Walden; or, Life in the Woods* (1854), was full of praise for nature and disapproval of the stresses of civilized life – sentiments that have found an eager audience ever since.

The glacial pond is now a state park, surrounded by acres of forest preserved by the Walden Woods project, a nonprofit organization. It lies about 3 miles south of Monument Sq, along Walden St (MA 126) south of MA 2. There's a swimming beach and facilities on the southern side, and a footpath that circles the large pond (about a half-hour stroll). The **site of Thoreau's cabin** is on the northeast side, marked by a cairn and signs. The park gets packed when the weather is warm; the number of visitors is restricted, so arrive early in summer.

WORTH THE TRIP: TRANSCENDENTALIST FRUITLANDS

Transcendentalism was a 19th-century social and philosophical movement that flourished in the mid-19th century in Boston and Concord. Though small in numbers, the Transcendentalists had a significant effect on American literature and society. Ralph Waldo Emerson, Henry David Thoreau and Margaret Fuller all turned away from their Unitarian tradition to pursue Transcendentalism.

The core of Transcendentalist belief was that each person and element of nature had within them a part of the divine essence, that God 'transcended' all things. The search for divinity was thus not so much in scripture and prayer, nor in perception and reason, but in individual intuition or 'instinct.' By intuition we can know what is right and wrong according to divine law. By intuition we can know the meaning of life. Living in harmony with the natural world was very important to Transcendentalists.

Bronson Alcott (1799–1888), educational and social reformer and father of Louisa May Alcott, joined this group of Concordians in pursuing Transcendental ideals. Toward this end, he founded Fruitlands, an experimental vegetarian community in Harvard, Massachusetts.

Fruitlands Museums (☎ 978-456-3924; 102 Prospect Hill Rd, Harvard; adult/child/senior & student $10/2/8; ☼ 11am-4pm Mon-Fri, 10am-5pm Sat & Sun May-Oct) is now open to the public. The original hillside farmhouse was actually used by Alcott and his utopian 'Con-Sociate' (communal) family.

Other museums have since been moved to the 200-acre estate, including the 1794 Shaker House, a Native American museum, and a gallery featuring paintings by 19th-century itinerant artists and Hudson River School landscape painters. One of the highlights of a visit is the **Fruitlands Tearoom** (lunch $11-14, brunch buffet $20; ☼ 11am-3pm Wed-Sat, brunch 10am-1pm Sun). Dine alfresco, and soak up the fresh air and fabulous scenery.

Fruitlands is in Harvard, about 30 miles west of Boston. Take Rte 2 to exit 38A, Rte 111. From here take the first right onto Old Shirley Rd, which becomes Prospect Hill Rd after 2 miles. The museum entrance is at the top of the hill on the right.

DeCordova Museum & Sculpture Park

The magical **DeCordova Sculpture Park** (☎ 781-259-8355; www.decordova.org; 51 Sandy Pond Rd, Lincoln; adult/senior, student & child $9/6; ☼ dawn-dusk) encompasses 35 acres of green hills, providing a spectacular natural environment for a constantly changing exhibit of outdoor artwork. As many as 75 pieces are on display at any given time. The entry fee includes admission to the onsite **museum** (☼ 10am-5pm Tue-Sun), which hosts rotating exhibits of contemporary sculpture, painting, photography and mixed media. Note that admission to the sculpture garden is free when the museum is closed.

From Concord center, drive east on Rte 2 and turn right on Bedford Rd. From Walden Pond, it is a breathtakingly beautiful and heartachingly hilly drive (or bike ride) from Rte 126 on Baker Bridge Rd. Turn right when the road dead-ends at Sandy Pond.

Discovery Museums

The **Discovery Museums** (☎ 978-264-4200; www.discoverymuseums.org; 177 Main St, Acton; ♿) consist of two unique side-by-side museums –

both great for children. Occupying an old Victorian house, the **Children's Museum** (adult & child/senior $9/8; ☼ 9am-4:30pm Tue-Sun) invites kids to play make-believe, cooking up some eats in a bite-size diner, hunting for wildlife on safari, conducting a toy train and more. The **Science Museum** (adult & child/under 5yr $9/5; ☼ 1-4:30pm Tue, Thu & Fri, 1-6pm Wed, 9am-4:30pm Sat & Sun) is for slightly older kids, but it's equally playful with hands-on exhibits such as earth science and an inventor's workshop. You can get admission to both museums for $13/12 per adult or child/senior.

LOWELL
pop 105,000

Twenty-five miles northwest of Boston, Lowell is a textile mill town located at the confluence of the Concord and Merrimack Rivers. In the early 19th century, factories here churned out cloth by the mile, driven by the abundant waterpower of Pawtucket Falls. Today, the city's economy is no longer so robust, but its historic center recalls the industrial revolution glory days – a working textile mill, canal boat tours and trolley rides evoke the birth of America as an industrial giant.

Besides being the birthplace of the textile industry, Lowell was also the birthplace of two American cultural icons, painter James Abbott McNeill Whistler and writer Jack Kerouac.

In modern Lowell, high-tech and other industries have diversified the economic base. And an influx of Southeast Asian immigrants has diversified the culture (and cuisine) of this classic New England mill town. A short walk away from the historic center into the ethnic neighborhood known as the Acre reveals that Lowell has definitely changed from the city it was 150 years ago.

Orientation & Information

From I-495, follow the Lowell Connector to its end at exit 5-C to reach the city center. Trains from Boston terminate at the Gallagher Transportation Terminal on Thorndike St, a 15-minute walk southwest of the city center. A shuttle bus runs every 30 minutes to the Downtown Transit Center in the heart of the city.

Once in the city center, most of the sights are within walking distance. Merrimack St is the main commercial thoroughfare, holding the Downtown Transit Center, the chamber of commerce office and several restaurants.

The historic multiethnic neighborhood known as The Acre lies West of the Merrimack Canal and north of Broadway St.

City of Lowell (www.lowellma.org) Extensive information about the city's resources.

Greater Merrimack Valley Convention & Visitors Bureau (☎ 978-459-6150, 800-443-3332; www .merrimackvalley.org; 9 Central St; ☒ 8:30am-5pm Mon-Fri)

Market Mills Visitors Center (☎ 978-970-5000; www .nps.gov/lowe; 246 Market St, Market Mills; ☒ 9am-5pm) Starting place for the Lowell National Historic Park.

Sights & Activities

LOWELL NATIONAL HISTORICAL PARK

The historic buildings in the city center – connected by the trolley and canal boats – comprise the national park, which gives a fascinating peek at the workings of a 19th-century industrial town. Stop first at the Market Mills Visitors Center to pick up a map and check out the general exhibits. An introductory multimedia video on historic Lowell is shown every half-hour.

Five blocks northeast along the river, the **Boott Cotton Mills Museum** (☎ 978-970-5000; 115 John St; adult/child/student $6/3/4; ☒ 9:30am-4:30pm) has exhibits that chronicle the rise and fall of the industrial revolution in Lowell, including technological changes, labor movements and immigration. The highlight is a working weave room, with 88 power looms. A special exhibit on **Mill Girls & Immigrants** (☎ 978-970-5000; 40 French St; admission free; ☒ 1:30-4:30pm) examines the lives of working people, while other seasonal exhibits are sometimes on display in other historic buildings around town.

Canal Tours (☎ 978-970-5000; adult/child $8/6) are offered throughout the summer, but the schedule varies according to season and water levels.

JACK KEROUAC SITES

Dedicated in 1988, the **Jack Kerouac Commemorative** (Bridge St) features a landscaped path where excerpts of the writer's work are posted, including opening passages from his five novels set in Lowell. They are thoughtfully displayed with Catholic and Buddhist symbols, representing the belief systems that influenced him. The memorial is northeast of the visitors center along the Eastern Canal.

Two miles south of Lowell center, Kerouac is buried in the Sampas family plot at **Edson Cemetery** (cnr Gorham & Saratoga Sts). His gravesite remains a pilgrimage site for devotees who were inspired by his free spirit.

For more insight into Kerouac's life in Lowell, catch a screening of *Lowell Blues*, a film at the Market Mills Visitors Center shown daily at 4pm. The NPS also offers walking tours of the sights associated with Kerouac, see p142.

WHISTLER HOUSE MUSEUM OF ART

In 1834 Anna Mathilda (McNeill) Whistler, wife of the local agent for the Locks and Canals Corporation, gave birth to future artist James Abbott McNeill Whistler (1834–1903). The coming of the railroad made locks and canals less important, and the Whistlers moved away from Lowell in 1837. Young James went on to become one of America's greatest 19th-century painters.

Whistler's **birthplace** (☎ 978-452-7641; www .whistlerhouse.org; 243 Worthen St; adult/senior, student & child $5/4; ☒ 11am-4pm Wed-Sun), built in 1823, is now the home of the Lowell Art Association. It contains a permanent collection of the

---

THE TOWN & THE CITY OF JACK KEROUAC

One of the most influential American authors of the 20th century, Beat Generation writer Jack Kerouac (1922–69) was born in Lowell at the mill town's industrial peak. He graduated from Lowell High School and wrote for the *Lowell Sun*. It is not surprising, then, that the author used Lowell as the setting for five of his novels that drew on his youth in the 1920s, '30s and '40s.

Kerouac is remembered annually during the Lowell Celebrates Kerouac (LCK) festival (below). LCK – in conjunction with the Jack Kerouac Subterranean Information Society – has also compiled a fantastically detailed **walking tour** (http://ecommunity.uml.edu/jklowell/) of Lowell, based on places that Kerouac wrote about and experienced.

Of course, Kerouac is most famous for his classic novel *On the Road*. With it, he became a symbol of the spirit of the open road. In 2007, in honor of the 50th anniversary of this ground-breaking book, Lowell hosted a summer-long festival of the Beats. The highlight was the original manuscript of *On the Road*, which was on display at the Boott Cotton Mills Museum. For more information on Kerouac's life in Lowell, see www.ontheroadinlowell.org.

---

artist's works, and hosts exhibits of works by his contemporaries and modern New England artists. Outside, an 8ft bronze statue of the artist, completed by sculptor Mico Kaufman, is the centerpiece of the Whistler Park and Gardens.

Whistler House is on the west side of the Merrimack Canal, two blocks west of the Market Mills Visitors Center.

OTHER MUSEUMS

The **American Textile History Museum** (☎ 978-441-0400; www.athm.org; 491 Dutton St; adult/senior, student & child $8/6; ⊙ 9am-4pm Thu-Fri, 10am-5pm Sat & Sun) features vintage spinning wheels and looms that continue to operate in the weave shed. It's located a block south of the Whistler House.

The **New England Quilt Museum** (☎ 978-452-4207; www.nequiltmuseum.org; 18 Shattuck St; adult/senior & student $5/4; ⊙ 10am-4pm Tue-Sat year-round, noon-4pm Sun May-Dec) has a collection of over 150 antique and contemporary quilts from around New England, as well as an extensive library and a lovely gift shop. It's located a half-block from the Lowell National Historic Park visitors center.

The edgy, artist-run **Revolving Museum** (☎ 978-937-2787; www.revolvingmuseum.org; 22 Shattuck St; admission free; ⊙ 11am-4pm Tue-Sun) has fun and funky exhibits and special events.

Tours

Exploring Lowell Tours (☎ 978-970-5000; www.nps.gov/lowe; ⊙ 2:30pm Sat & Sun) The Lowell National Historic Park rangers offer free tours of Lowell Cemetery, the Acre and the Riverwalk. There are also tours focusing on the Lowell 'mill girls' and the sights associated with Jack Kerouac. Reservations required.

Festivals & Events

Lowell Celebrates Kerouac (LCK; ☎ 877-537-6822; lckorg.tripod.com) Every October, this local nonprofit organization hosts four days of events dedicated to Beat writer Jack Kerouac, featuring tours of many places in his novels, as well as panel discussions, readings, music and poetry. Literature buffs travel from around the world for this unique event.

Lowell Folk Festival (☎ 978-970-5000; www.lowell folkfestival.org) Three days of food, music (on six stages!), parades and other festivities honoring the diverse multicultural community Lowell has become. It takes place every year at the end of July.

Sleeping

There are not many places to stay in Lowell, or reasons to stay here. However, if you must spend the night, a few options meet standard needs.

Doubletree Lowell (☎ 978-452-1200; http://double tree.hilton.com; 50 Warren St; r from $89; ⊠) Located in the heart of downtown Lowell overlooking the canals. Some rooms have scenic views of the Merrimack, and all rooms are modern with standard amenities.

Courtyard Lowell (☎ 978-458-7575; http://marriott .com; 50 Industrial Ave E; r $94-109; ⊠) Although it's a Marriott Hotel, the Courtyard Lowell manages to maintain a bit of New England charm with its colonial-style building. Rooms and service are up to snuff, as you would expect.

Eating & Drinking

Arthur's Paradise Diner (☎ 978-452-8647; 112 Bridge St; meals $6-10; ☺ breakfast & lunch) The epitome of 'old school,' this place is open only for breakfast and lunch and specializes in something called the Boot Mill sandwich (egg, bacon, cheese and home fries on a grilled roll). Expect long waits, testy service and an atmosphere as authentic as it comes. In other words, paradise.

Southeast Asian Restaurant (☎ 978-452-3182; 343 Market St; meals $7-12; ☺ lunch & dinner; **V**) Aficionados of Lao, Thai, and Vietnamese cuisines come here from all over New England to feast on authentic Asian fare, including the legendary 'bowl of fire' (Lao spicy beef). In the heart of the Acre, the restaurant and associated market are a beacon of culture for Lowell's Southeast Asian immigrants.

Athenian Corner (☎ 978-458-7052; 207 Market St; meals $8-25; ☺ lunch & dinner) Across the street from the Market Mills Visitors Center, this restaurant is a hallmark of Lowell's immigrant Greek community. The Panagiotopoulis family offers real-deal Greek specialties, such as *faki* (lentil soup), souvlaki and moussaka; finish it off with sticky sweet baklava or creamy rice pudding. Authentic Athens right in Lowell's center.

Worthen House (☎ 978-459-0300; 141 Worthen St; meals $12-20; ☺ lunch & dinner) This old brick tavern is famed for its amazing, pulley-driven fan system (which is still operational). The pressed tin ceiling and wooden bar remain from the early days, giving this place an old-fashioned neighborhood feel. Stop by for a pint of Guinness and a burger.

La Boniche (☎ 978-458-9473; 143 Merrimack St; meals $15-30; ☺ lunch & dinner Tue-Sat) This little bistro inspires patrons to rave about the delectable food, even if service is sometimes spotty. The two dining rooms in this restored storefront nook fill with scents of French nouvelle cuisine, attracting an upscale crowd for lunch and dinner. The excellent selection of paté gets top reviews.

Entertainment

The Class A **Lowell Spinners** (☎ 978-459-1702; www .lowellspinners.com; tickets $3.50-7.50) are a Red Sox feeder-team. Locally, they play at LeLacheur Park, which is north of the center on the Merrimack River.

Getting There & Around

Lowell is at the end of the Lowell Connector, a spur road that goes north from MA 3 and I-495.

MBTA commuter rail (☎ 617-722-3200, 800-392-6100) trains depart Boston's North Station for Lowell ($6.75). Trains go in either direction 10 times a day during the week, four times on weekends.

The **Lowell Regional Transit Authority** (☎ 978-452-6161) operates the bus system, including the downtown shuttle buses that link the Gallagher Transportation Terminal and the Downtown Transit Center.

NORTH SHORE

The entire coast of Massachusetts claims a rich history, but no part offers more recreational, cultural and dining diversions than the North Shore of Boston. Salem was among America's wealthiest ports during the 19th century; Gloucester is the nation's most famous fishing port; and Marblehead remains one of the premier yachting ports in the United States. Trade and fishing have brought wealthy residents, sumptuous houses, and great collections of art and artifacts to the area. Explore the region's rich maritime history and spectacular coastal scenery, and don't miss the opportunity for a seafood feast.

SALEM

pop 40,400

This town's very name conjures up images of diabolical witchcraft and women being burned at the stake. Indeed, in the late 17th century it was widely believed that anyone could make a pact with the devil in order to gain evil powers.

In March 1692, some local girls began pulling pranks. Other children copied their antics, and their parents came to believe that the devil had come to Salem. The girls accused a slave named Tituba of being a witch, and the accused was tortured until she confessed. In order to save her own life, Tituba accused two other women of being accomplices. Soon the accusations flew thick and fast, as local women and men confessed to riding broomsticks, having sex with the devil and participating in witches' sabbaths. They implicated others in an attempt to save themselves.

AROUND BOSTON

By September 1692, 156 people stood accused, 55 people had pleaded guilty and implicated others to save their own lives, and 14 women and five men who would not confess had been hanged. The frenzy died down when the accusers began pointing at prominent merchants, clergy and even the governor's wife.

The famous Salem witch trials of 1692 are engrained in the national memory. Indeed, the town of Salem goes all out at Halloween (see p147), when the whole town dresses up for parades and parties, and shops sell all manner of wiccan accessories. More appropriately, the Salem Witch Trials Memorial, a modest monument off Charter St, honors the innocents who died.

These incidents obscure Salem's true claim to fame: its glory days as a center for clipper-ship trade with China. The responsible party, Elias Hasket Derby, benefited enormously from his enterprise, eventually becoming America's first millionaire. Derby built half-mile-long Derby Wharf, which is now the center of the Salem Maritime National Historic Site (right).

Many Salem vessels followed Derby's ship *Grand Turk* around the Cape of Good Hope, and soon the owners founded the East India Marine Society to provide warehousing services for their ships' logs and charts. The new company's charter required the establishment of 'a museum in which to house the natural and artificial curiosities' brought back by members' ships. The collection was the basis for what is now the world-class Peabody Essex Museum (right), and has grown to a half-million artifacts.

Today Salem is a middle-class commuter suburb of Boston with an enviable location on the sea. And its rich history and culture, from witches to ships to art, continue to cast a spell of enchantment on all those who visit.

Orientation & Information

Commercial Salem centers around Essex St, a pedestrian mall running east to west from Washington St to the historic Salem Common. To the southeast, Derby Wharf stretches out into Salem Harbor. The train station is a short walk north of Essex St.

The 1.7 mile Heritage Trail is a route connecting Salem's major historic sites. Follow the red line painted on the sidewalk.

Bank of America (193 Washington St; ⏰ 9am-4pm Mon-Fri, 9am-2pm Sat)

Central Wharf Visitor Center (☎ 978-740-1660; www.nps.gov/sama; 193 Derby St; admission free; ⏰ 9am-5pm)

Destination Salem (☎ 978-744-0004; www.salem .org; 63 Wharf St) The local chamber of commerce visitor center.

Hawthorne in Salem (www.hawthorneinsalem.org) An extensive site with loads of articles about Nathaniel Hawthorne, his life in Salem and his writings about the town.

Historic Salem, Inc (☎ 978-745-0799; www.historic salem.org) A nonprofit organization dedicated to architectural preservation in Salem by maintaining a record of 'endangered' architectural resources in the city.

NPS Regional Visitor Center (☎ 978-740-1650; 2 Liberty St; ⏰ 9am-5pm)

Post Office (2 Margin St; ⏰ 8am-5pm Mon-Fri, 8am-1pm Sat)

Salem Public Library (☎ 978-744-0860; 370 Essex St; ⏰ 9am-9pm Mon-Thu, 9am-5pm Fri & Sat year-round, 9am-5pm Sun Jun-Aug) Free internet access.

Sights & Activities
SALEM MARITIME NATIONAL HISTORIC SITE

This site comprises the custom house, the wharves and the other buildings along Derby St that are remnants of the shipping industry that once thrived along this stretch of Salem. In all, the site comprises 10 different historic locations within a two-block area. Start at the visitors center to pick up a map and to see the informative film *To the Farthest Ports of the Rich East*.

Of the 50 wharves that once lined Salem Harbor, only three remain, the longest of which is **Derby Wharf**. Visitors can stroll out to the end and peek inside the 1871 **lighthouse**. The most prominent building along Derby St is the **Custom House**, where permits and certificates were issued and, of course, taxes paid. Other buildings at the site include warehouses, the scale house, and Elias Hasket Derby's 1762 home. Stop by at the **West India Goods Store**, a working store with spices and other items similar to those sold two centuries ago. You can also board the replica of the **tall ship Friendship** (adult/child & senior $5/3) to see how the sailors lived.

PEABODY ESSEX MUSEUM

All of the art, artifacts and curiosities that Salem merchants brought back from the Far East were

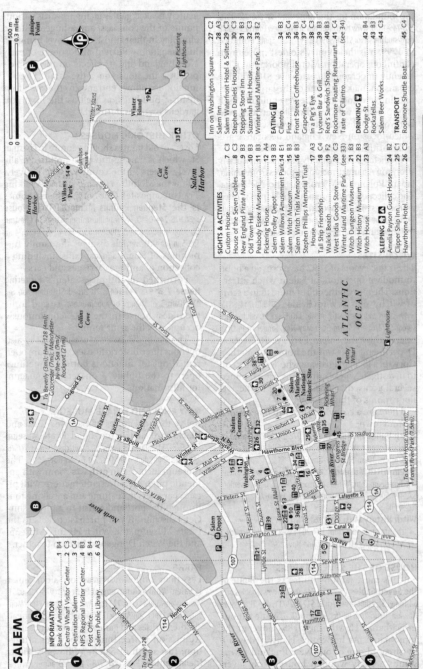

SALEM

the foundation for this **museum** (☎ 866-745-1876, 978-745-1876; www.pem.org; Essex St Mall, New Liberty St; adult/child/student/senior $13/free/9/11; ☻ 10am-5pm). Founded in 1799, it is the country's oldest museum in continuous operation. More importantly, it has recently undergone an extensive $100 million expansion, making it one of the largest museums in New England. The new building itself is impressive, with a light-filled atrium, and is a wonderful setting for the vast collections, which focus on New England decorative arts and maritime history.

Predictably, the Peabody Essex is particularly strong on Asian art, including pieces from China, Japan, Polynesia, Micronesia and Melanesia. The collection from preindustrial Japan is rated as the best in the world. **Yin Yu Tang** (adult/child $4/free) is a Chinese house that was shipped to the museum from Huizhou province.

WITCH SITES
The tragic events of 1692 have proved a boon to modern operators of Salem witch attractions. The most authentic of more than a score of witchy sites is **Witch House** (☎ 978-744-8815; www.salemweb.com/witchhouse; 310 Essex St; adult/child/senior $8/4/6; ☻ 10am-5pm May-Nov, longer hr in Oct), operated by the Salem Parks & Recreation Department. This was the home of Jonathan Corwin, a local magistrate who was called on to investigate witchcraft claims. He examined several accused witches, possibly in the 1st-floor rooms of this house.

There are a covey of other witch museums around town:

Witch Dungeon Museum (☎ 978-741-3570; www.witchdungeon.com; 16 Lynde St; adult/child/senior $7/5/6; ☻ 10am-5pm Apr-Nov)

Salem Witch Museum (☎ 978-744-1692; www.salemwitchmuseum.com; Washington Sq N; adult/6-14yr/senior $7.50/6.50/5; ☻ 10am-5pm Sep-Jun, 10am-7pm Jul-Aug)

Witch History Museum (☎ 978-741-7770; www.witchhistorymuseum.com; 197-201 Essex St; adult/child/senior $7/5/6; ☻ 10am-5pm Apr-Nov)

HOUSE OF THE SEVEN GABLES
Salem's most famous house is the **House of the Seven Gables** (☎ 978-744-0991; www.7gables.org; 54 Turner St; adult/senior/child $12/7.25/11; ☻ 10am-5pm Nov-Jun, 10am-7pm Jul-Oct, longer hr Oct), made famous in Nathaniel Hawthorne's 1851 novel of the same name. As he wrote: 'Halfway down a by-street of one of our New England towns stands a rusty wooden house, with seven

acutely peaked gables facing towards various points of the compass, and a huge clustered chimney in their midst.' The novel brings to life the gloomy Puritan atmosphere of early New England and its effects on the people's psyches; the house does the same. The admission fee allows entrance to the site's four historic buildings, as well as the luxuriant gardens on the waterfront.

OTHER HISTORIC HOUSES
Lovers of old houses should venture to **Chestnut St**, which is among the most architecturally lovely streets in the country. (Alternatively, follow the McIntire Historic District Walking Trail on opposite). One of these stately homes is the **Stephen Phillips Memorial Trust House** (☎ 978-744-0440; www.phillipsmuseum.org; 34 Chestnut St; adult/child/senior & student $5/2.50/4; ☻ 10am-4pm Tue-Sun Jun-Oct), which displays the family furnishings of Salem sea captains, including a collection of antique carriages and cars.

Furnished in antiques, Salem's **Pickering House** (☎ 978-744-1647; 18 Broad St; admission $4; ☻ 10am-3pm Mon, or by appointment) is said to be the oldest house in the USA continuously occupied by the same family.

The Peabody Essex Museum (p144) also operates three historical houses, which are often rented out for functions but are sometimes open to the public. Contact the museum for information.

NEW ENGLAND PIRATE MUSEUM
Relive the adventures of Captains Kidd and Blackbeard at the fun-filled **Pirate Museum** (☎ 978-741-2800; 274 Derby St; adult/child/senior $7/5/6; ☻ 10am-5pm daily May-Oct, Sat & Sun Nov; ♿). The museum includes an artifacts room with authentic pirate treasures, interactions with pirate characters in costume and a walking tour through the port and a visit to a pirate ship. Get a discount if you purchase tickets to the Pirate Museum, the Witch History Museum and the Witch Dungeon Museum together.

PARKS
Less than 2 miles northeast of Salem center is **Salem Willows Amusement Park** (☎ 978-745-0251; www.salemwillows.com; 171 Fort Ave; ☻ 10am-11pm Mon-Sat, 11am-11pm Sun Apr-Oct), with beaches, cheap children's rides and games, and harbor cruises. Admission is free but you pay per attraction. Just south of Salem Willows is **Winter Island Maritime Park** (☎ 978-745-9430; admission free;

HAUNTED HAPPENINGS

Everyone in Salem celebrates Halloween, not just the witches. And they celebrate for much of the month of October, during the annual **Haunted Happenings Halloween festival** (☎ 877-725-3662; www .hauntedhappenings.org), featuring special exhibits, parades, concerts, pumpkin carvings, costume parties and trick-or-treating. It all culminates on October 31, with the crowning of the King and Queen of Halloween. Oooh, that's scary.

☉ dawn-dusk; ℗ weekday/weekend $5/10), the site of Fort Pickering and its lighthouse. It is now a public park with a campground and the tiny **Waikiki Beach** (don't get too excited by the name: it's really just wishful thinking). Two miles south of the town center, **Forest River Park** has two beaches, picnic areas and a saltwater swimming pool.

Tours

Pick up a map and description of the following walking tours from any of the visitors centers.

Bowditch's Salem A self-guided walking tour of the Great Age of Sail, this route traces the lifelong footsteps of Nathaniel Bowditch, a Salem sailor and author of *The New American Practical Navigator*.

McIntire Historic District Walking Trail A 1-mile route that highlights some of Salem's architectural gems, especially the Federal-era homes designed by architect Samuel McIntire.

Salem Historical Tours (☎ 978-745-0666; www .salemhistoricaltours.com; 8 Central St) Did somebody say murder? This series of spooky tours tell tales of witchcraft and haunted houses. Thematic walking tours include Cemetery 101 (adult/child/senior $10/6/8; ☉ 1pm), Haunted Footsteps Ghost Tours (adult/child/senior $14/8/10; ☉ 8pm) and the Salem Witchcraft Walk (adult/child/ senior $10/6/8; ☉ 3pm).

Salem Trolley (☎ 978-744-5469; www.salemtrolley .com; 8 Central St; all-day ticket adult/child/senior $12/3/10; ☉ 10am-5pm daily Apr-Oct, Sat & Sun weather permitting Mar & Nov) This tour follows a figure-eight route, with a running commentary, past most of the town's places of interest.

Sleeping

Many of Salem's historic houses have been converted into B&Bs and guesthouses. Breakfast is included unless otherwise stated.

Winter Island Maritime Park (☎ 978-745-9430; 50 Winter Island Rd; RV sites/campsites $40/25; ☉ May-Oct; ℗) Less than 2 miles east of the center of town, this little park has space for 25 tents and 30 RVs. The park is pleasant, but it gets packed in summer. Bring your own breakfast: you're camping, after all.

Inn on Washington Square (☎ 978-741-4997; www .washingtonsquareinn.com; 53 Washington Sq N; r $100-200, ste $150-225) This tiny place has only three rooms, which are decorated with canopy beds and other period furnishings. The most romantic room is the Honeymoon Suite, fully equipped with a Jacuzzi. Breakfast – which means a basket of homemade muffins – is served in your room.

Hawthorne Hotel (☎ 978-744-4080, 800-729-7829; www.hawthornehotel.com; 18 Washington Sq W; r $104-309; ℗ ✕ 🗐 wi-fi) This historic Federalist-style hotel is at the very heart of Salem's center. For years it was the only full-service hotel, with 89 double rooms, a fancy (if staid) restaurant and a cozy pub. Rooms are decked out with reproduction 18th-century furnishings, so you can feel like a wealthy merchant from Salem's glory days. It also operates the Suzannah Flint House (www. suzannahflinthouse.com), a small B&B in an 1808 federal house.

Clipper Ship Inn (☎ 978-745-8022; www.clipper shipinn.com; 40 Bridge St; d $105-125, tw $125-145; ℗ ✕ 🕭) If you prefer anonymity over homey ambiance, this red-brick motel is an excellent option. Crisp, clean rooms and efficient service make it a comfortable place to lay your head, even if it's not in a historic home. Breakfast not included.

Coach House Inn (☎ 978-744-4092, 800-688-8689; www.coachhousesalem.com; 284 Lafayette St; r $105-185, 2-r ste $165-240; ℗ ✕) This beautiful 1870 Victorian mansion was once the home of a successful sea captain. Now it contains 11 guest rooms, each with a private bath, a four-poster bed and other period details. It's located about a mile south of the town center on MA 1A/MA 114.

Stepping Stone Inn (☎ 978-741-8900; www.the steppingstoneinn.com; 19 Washington Sq N; r $105-150; ☉ Apr-Nov; ℗ ✕) Just off Salem Common, this restored house was built for naval officer Benjamin True in 1846. The eight unique rooms are simply decorated, but they have hardwood floors and some have four-post beds.

our pick Stephen Daniels House (☎ 978-744-5709; 1 Daniels St; r $115-135; ℗) Two blocks north of the waterfront, this must be Salem's oldest lodging, with parts dating from 1667 – before the witch trials. Two walk-in fireplaces grace the common area, and the rooms are filled with period antiques. It is appropriate in this spooky town that such an old house be haunted: rumor has it that a ghost cat roams the ancient halls and has even been known to jump in bed with guests.

Amelia Payson Guest House (☎ 978-744-8304; www.ameliapaysonhouse.com; 16 Winter St; d $115-145; ☼ Apr–mid-Nov; ℗ 🖳 wi-fi) This Greek Revival home is decorated with a lot of floral wallpaper, Oriental rugs, rich drapes and ornamental fixtures. It's just steps from Salem Common.

Salem Inn (☎ 978-741-0680, 800-446-2995; www.saleminnma.com; 7 Summer St; d $129-179, ste $179-219) Thirty-three rooms are located in three different historic houses including the Captain West House, a large brick sea captain's home from 1834. The rooms vary greatly, but they are all individually decorated with antiques, period detail and other charms.

Salem Waterfront Hotel & Suites (☎ 978-740-8788; www.salemwaterfronthotel.com; 225 Derby St; r $159-189; ℗ 🛏 🖳 wi-fi🐾) This newish property has a prime location overlooking Pickering Wharf and Salem Harbor. Eighty-six spacious rooms (some of them suites) have graceful decor and all the expected amenities, but breakfast is not included.

Eating

Pickering Wharf has a nice selection of cafés and restaurants, all overlooking the Salem waterfront.

Front Street Coffeehouse (☎ 978-740-6697; 20 Front St; ☼ 7am-7pm; 🖳 wi-fi) A cool place to sip a caffe latte or munch on a giant sandwich. This is where multipierced urban youths, well-groomed soccer moms and out-of-town visitors all find common ground.

Red's Sandwich Shop (☎ 978-745-3527; 15 Central St; dishes $3-9; ☼ breakfast & lunch Mon-Sat, 6am-1pm Sun) This Salem institution has been serving eggs and sandwiches to faithful customers for over 50 years. The food is hearty and basic, but the real attraction is Red's old-school decor, complete with counter service and friendly faces. It's housed in the old London Coffee House building (1698).

A Taste of Cilantro (☎ 978-745-8928; 282R Derby St; meals $6-10; ☼ lunch & dinner) Located just around

the corner from Cilantro (below), this is great for a quicker, less expensive bite.

Lyceum Bar & Grill (☎ 978-745-7665; 43 Church St; meals $6-25; ☼ lunch & dinner) This historic building has hosted some of America's foremost orators in its lecture halls, from Daniel Webster to Henry David Thoreau. Today the elegant dining room is one of Salem's top dining spots. The New England fare is traditional but not tired, and service is always excellent.

Cilantro (☎ 978-745-9436; 282 Derby St; meals $9-22; ☼ lunch & dinner) The North Shore goes south of the border. This is not your mama's Mexican food, though. Cilantro's menu uses inventive dishes like sea bass *al naranjo* (seabass with oranges) or *albondigas al chipotle* (cheese-stuffed meatballs) to draw out the subtle textures and flavors that sometimes get lost in your average taco.

Rockmore Floating Restaurant (☎ 978-740-1001; Pickering Wharf; meals $10-20; ☼ 11am-9pm Jun-Aug) That's right: floating. Set on a barge in the middle of Salem Harbor, this clam shack is the ultimate place to refuel on a hot summer day. The food is mediocre at best, but no place else offers an ocean breeze quite as brisk as this one. Catch the free shuttle boat from the Congress St bridge; don't forget to tip the captain.

In a Pig's Eye (☎ 978-741-4436; 148 Derby St; meals $12-15) This dark, friendly pub boasts an eclectic menu of burgers and beef stroganoff, homemade soups and tasty salads, and 'Pig's Eye Favorites' like steak tips or pork chops. Despite the small space, it has live music (usually acoustic) a few nights a week.

Finz (☎ 978-774-8485; 76 Wharf St; sandwiches $8, meals $18-25; ☼ lunch & dinner) The highlight here is the gracious, spacious dining room with three walls of windows overlooking Salem Harbor. The kitchen keeps customers sated, especially with the char-grilled halibut. The seductive raw bar and carefully chosen wine list are added perks.

Grapevine (☎ 978-745-9335; 26 Congress St; meals $21-27; ☼ dinner) Dine alfresco in the lovely flower-filled courtyard or tuck into the romantic dining room. This Mediterranean gem is frequently rated among Boston's best restaurants. The menu changes seasonally but pasta, seafood and meats are always artfully prepared and presented.

Drinking & Entertainment

Dodge St (☎ 978-745-0139; www.dodgestreet.com; 7 Dodge St; ☯ live music 10pm) Food is served here, but most people come to suck down a few beers and get their groove on. There's live music, usually rock and blues. If you must eat here, get the ribs.

Salem Beer Works (☎ 978-745-2337; 178 Derby St) Part of the Boston Beer Works family, this microbrewery serves 15 different brews on tap, as well as a full menu of pub grub, sandwiches and more filling fare. The specialty seems to be things fried, which undoubtedly encourages more beer-drinking. Other fun perks include pool tables and outdoor seating.

Rockafellas (☎ 978-745-2411; www.rockafellasof salem.com; 231 Essex St; sandwiches $7-11, meals $18-20; ☯ 11:30am-midnight Sun-Wed, 11:30am-1am Thu-Sat) With live entertainment Wednesday through Sunday, this lively restaurant and lounge draws an upscale crowd to kick back and enjoy the semiswanky setting. Music ranges from acoustic to reggae to rock and blues. The menu is all-American, with lots of steaks and sandwiches.

Getting There & Around

Salem lies 20 miles northeast of Boston, a 35-minute drive on MA 1A (longer during rush hour). Both the Newburyport and Rockport lines of the **MBTA commuter rail** (☎ 617-722-3200, 800-392-6100; www.mbta.com) run from Boston's North Station to Salem Depot ($5.25, 30 minutes). Trains run every 30 minutes during the morning and evening rush hours, hourly during the rest of day, and less frequently on weekends. The MBTA buses 450 or 455 from Boston's Haymarket Sq (near North Station) take longer than the train and cost no less.

MARBLEHEAD

First settled in 1629, Marblehead's Old Town is a maritime village with winding streets, brightly painted colonial and Federal houses, and 1000 sailing yachts bobbing at moorings in the harbor. As indicated by the number of boats, this is the Boston area's premier yachting port and one of New England's most prestigious addresses, and has been for a long time; it was incorporated in 1649. Citizens of Marblehead boast that their town was the 'birthplace of the navy'

because the Marblehead schooner *Hannah* (1775) was the first ship to be commissioned by General George Washington in the Revolutionary War.

Orientation & Information

MA 114 – locally called Pleasant St – passes through modern commercial Marblehead en route to the Marblehead Historic District (Old Town), with its network of narrow, winding, one-way streets. Old Town is difficult to navigate by car and parking can be a challenge. This is definitely a place to explore on foot. Pick up a map from the Marblehead Chamber of Commerce information booth. Many restaurants and historic buildings are clustered around the intersection of Pleasant and Washington Sts. From here, State St heads south to the town's main dock and Marblehead Harbor.

For tourist information:

Marblehead Chamber of Commerce (www.marble headchamber.org) main office (☎ 781-631-2868; 62 Pleasant St; ☯ 9am-5pm Mon-Fri); information booth (☎ 781-639-8469; cnr Pleasant, Essex & Spring Sts; ☯ noon-5pm Mon-Fri, 10am-5pm Sat & Sun)

Spirit of New England (www.visitmarblehead.com) Useful tourist information.

Sights & Activities
ABBOTT HALL

Every American is familiar with *The Spirit of '76*, the patriotic painting (c 1876) by Archibald M Willard. It depicts three American Revolution figures – a drummer, a fife player and a flag bearer. The painting hangs in the selectmen's meeting room in **Abbott Hall** (☎ 781-631-0000; Washington Sq, Washington St; admission free; ☯ 9am-4pm, longer hr in summer), home of the Marblehead Historical Commission. The redbrick building with a lofty clock tower is the seat of Marblehead's town government, and houses artifacts of Marblehead's history, including the original title deed to Marblehead from the Nanapashemet Native Americans, dated 1684.

HISTORIC HOUSES

The Marblehead Historical Society operates the Georgian **Jeremiah Lee Mansion** (☎ 781-631-1768; www.marbleheadmuseum.org; 161 Washington St; admission $5; ☯ 10am-4pm Tue-Sat Jun-Oct, gardens open year-round), which was built in 1768 on the order of a prominent merchant. It is now a museum with period furnishings, and collections of toys and children's furniture, folk art and nautical and military artifacts.

Across the street, the historic **King Hooper Mansion**, built in 1728, is the home of the Marblehead Arts Association (below).

GALLERIES & ART SPACES

Artists & Authors (☎ 781-631-0400; 108 Washington St; ☾ 10am-5pm Mon-Sat, noon-5pm Sun) Offering 'rare books/fine art'. That means thousands of antiquarian books and hundreds of signed prints. Occasional shows feature contemporary artists.

JOJ Frost Folk Art Gallery (☎ 781-631-1768; 170 Washington St; ☾ 10am-4pm Tue-Sat Jun-Oct, Tue-Fri Nov-May) A historical and artistic exhibit of paintings by local artist JOJ Frost, depicting life in 19th-century Marblehead.

Marblehead Arts Association (☎ 781-631-2608; www.marbleheadarts.org; 8 Hooper St; ☾ noon-4pm Tue-Sat, 1-5pm Sun) Housed in the King Hooper mansion, four floors of exhibit space have shows changing monthly. Besides rotating exhibits, this facility hosts lectures, classes, receptions and occasional performance pieces by local artists.

PARKS

Steps from State St Landing, hilltop **Crocker Park** provides lovely views of the harbor, not to mention opportunities for swimming and picnicking. Stroll west on Front St from the main town dock.

If instead you walk east on Front St, you will reach **Fort Sewall**, perched on a rocky rise at the mouth of the harbor. The 17th-century fort expanded during the American Revolution and is now a pleasant park.

From Pleasant St (MA 114) just south of Marblehead's center, Ocean Ave leads east over a causeway and onto Marblehead Neck, a 2-sq-mile swath of land that juts into the ocean. It is mostly residential and very fancy, with only a few points of public access to the water. On the southeastern side of Marblehead Neck, a short walk takes you to **Castle Rock**, with views of the Boston Ship Channel and Boston's Harbor Islands. At the northern tip of Marblehead Neck, **Chandler Hovey Park**, by Marblehead Light, offers views of Cape Ann and the islands of Salem Bay. The **Audubon Bird Sanctuary** (Ocean Ave; admission free; ☾ dawn-dusk) is not on the water, but it is a peaceful place for a stroll.

Sleeping

Marblehead's dozens of B&Bs cater mostly to weekend visitors (which means you can expect to find higher prices on Saturday and Sunday). None of them have more than a few rooms, so reservations are essential. You will find a complete list of B&Bs at the Chamber of Commerce, which can also help you with reservations. Prices listed here include breakfast.

our pick **Harbor Light Inn** (☎ 781-631-2186; www.harborlightinn.com; 58 Washington St; r from $145, ste from $195; P 🅿 🖵 wi-fi 🐾) This handsome place near the Old Town House is a bit larger than the other accommodation options, but that doesn't mean it is any less romantic, especially as many rooms are fitted with fireplaces and private sundecks.

Marblehead Inn (☎ 781-630-0000; www.marbleheadinn.com; 264 Pleasant St; ste $99-164 Sun-Thu, $164-299 Fri & Sat; P 🅿 🖵 wi-fi ♿) This 1872 Victorian has 10 guest suites, equipped with kitchenette, Victorian furniture, Jacuzzi tubs and working fireplaces.

Seagull Inn (☎ 781-631-1893; www.seagullinn.com; 106 Harbor Ave; ste $165-250; P 🅿 🖵 wi-fi) This sun-filled inn on Marblehead Neck has three luxury suites, complete with Shaker furniture, cherry floors, original artwork and ocean views. Nearby beach access and a glorious garden are added perks. Take Ocean Ave across the Causeway and fork left on Harbor Ave.

Two cheaper places with shared facilities:

Seventeen Chestnut St (☎ 781-631-0941; www.17chestnutstreet.com; 17 Chestnut St; r with shared/private bathroom $80/135; ☾ Thu-Sun only; 🅿) The white frilly rooms here have common access to the elegant formal living room and cozy dining room.

Pink House on Gerry (☎ 781-631-3685; www.pinkhouseongerry.com; 5 Gerry St; r $80-95; P) A British-run B&B with floral decor, original artwork and lovely gardens.

Eating & Drinking

Crosby's Market (☎ 781-631-1741; 118 Washington St; deli $2-7; ☾ 9am-9pm) Visit this large, upscale market in Old Town for all of your picnic needs, including wine and beer. Its extensive deli is rife with the scent of freshly baked pumpernickel, dill pickles and roasted veggie salad.

Barnacle (☎ 781-631-4236; 141 Front St; meals $5-14; ☾ lunch & dinner) Perched on a rocky outcropping at the harbor's edge, the Barnacle is what waterside dining is meant to be. Specialties include steaming hot clam chowder and lobsters straight off the boat. Excellent outdoor seating.

Foodie's Feast (☎ 781-639-1104; 114 Washington St; meals $8-12; ☽ 8am-5pm; **V**) This sweet little café serves 'legendary' scones and rock cakes for breakfast or satiating soups and sandwiches for lunch. The turkey black bean chili gets rave reviews.

Maddie's Sail Loft (☎ 781-631-9824; 15 State St; meals $8-18; ☽ lunch & dinner) The place to come for local color. Set in a historic house, old-timers pack into this little pub to wolf down fried seafood and swill some beers. It's one block inland from State St Landing.

Landing (☎ 781-631-1878; 81 Front St; meals $9-40; ☽ lunch & dinner) The atmosphere is staid, but the setting is the draw at this classic seafood restaurant overlooking the harbor. Choose from the full-service restaurant or the pub, which has lighter fare. Either way, don't expect anything too exciting: just sit back and enjoy the view.

Pellino's (☎ 781-631-3344; 261 Washington St; meals $16-25; ☽ dinner) 'Quaint' is the operative word at this tiny family-run trattoria. The constantly changing menu of regional Italian treats and the excellent wine list make this a North Shore favorite.

Getting There & Away

From Salem, follow MA 114 southeast 4 miles to Marblehead, where it becomes Pleasant St. MBTA buses 441/442 and 448/449 run between Boston's Haymarket Sq (near North Station) and Marblehead. For information on MBTA trains to neighboring Salem, see p149. From Salem's train station, you can take a taxi (about $12) to Marblehead.

GLOUCESTER

Founded in 1623 by English fisherfolk, Gloucester is among New England's oldest towns. This port on Cape Ann has made its living from fishing for almost 400 years, and inspired books and films like Rudyard Kipling's *Captains Courageous* and Sebastian Junger's *The Perfect Storm*. And despite recent economic diversification, this town still smells of fish. You can't miss the fishing boats, often operated by Italian or Portuguese immigrants, festooned with nets, dredges and winches, tied to the wharves or motoring into the harbor with clouds of hungry seagulls hovering above.

Orientation & Information

Washington St runs from Grant Circle (a rotary out on MA 128) into the center of Gloucester at St Peter's Sq, an irregular brick plaza overlooking the sea. Rogers St, the waterfront road, runs east and west from the plaza; Main St, the business and shopping thoroughfare, is one block inland. East Gloucester, with the Rocky Neck artists' colony, is on the southeastern side of Gloucester Harbor.

Cape Ann Chamber of Commerce (☎ 978-283-1601, 800-321-0133; www.capeannvacations.com; 33 Commercial St; ☽ 8am-5:30pm Mon-Fri, 10am-6pm Sat, 10am-4pm Sun) South of St Peter's Sq.

Gloucester Cooperative Bank (☎ 978-283-8200; 160 Main St; ☽ 8:30am-3:30pm Mon-Wed, 8:30am-7pm Thu, 8:30am-5pm Fri, 8:30am-1pm Sat)

Post Office (15 Dale Ave; ☽ 8am-5pm Mon-Fri, 8am-noon Sat)

Sights & Activities

ROCKY NECK ART COLONY

For more than a century, Cape Ann's rocky coast and fishing fleet have attracted artists

---

A PERFECT STORM

In 1991 the fishing boat *Andrea Gail* headed out to sea and immortality, when it encountered the perfect storm. With dawn breaking and George Clooney at the helm, the Gloucester fisherman never looked better, even though disaster loomed just ahead. In a way, this Hollywood image captures more than just the tragic fate of the crew of the *Andrea Gail*, as the proud Gloucester fishing industry itself struggles against seemingly insurmountable forces.

With the fishing industry in decline, gritty Gloucester is looking to clean itself up as a tourist destination. A part of the old docks is now open to visitors. Whale-watching boats bob in place of the fishing trawlers along the pier. And Clooney's *The Perfect Storm* has created, perhaps, the perfect opportunity, attracting a stream of film fans who want to have a beer at the Crow's Nest and study the roll call of 'those who have gone to the sea in ships.' Peering out at the quiet harbor, the mystique of the stoic Gloucester fisherman survives.

AROUND BOSTON

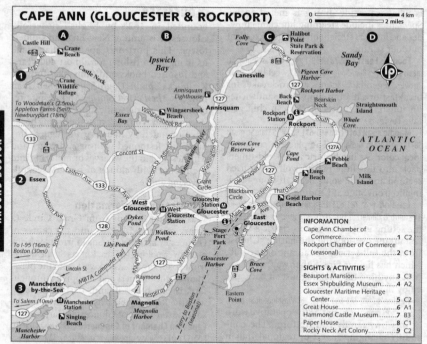

CAPE ANN (GLOUCESTER & ROCKPORT)

INFORMATION
Cape Ann Chamber of
  Commerce..1 C2
Rockport Chamber of Commerce
  (seasonal)..2 C1

SIGHTS & ACTIVITIES
Beauport Mansion..............................3 C3
Essex Shipbuilding Museum..............4 A2
Gloucester Maritime Heritage
  Center..5 C2
Great House......................................6 A1
Hammond Castle Museum.................7 B3
Paper House.......................................8 C1
Rocky Neck Art Colony......................9 C2

like Winslow Homer and Fitz Hugh Lane. This legacy endures, as Gloucester still boasts a vibrant artists community. The narrow peninsula of Rocky Neck, jutting into Gloucester Harbor from East Gloucester, offers inspiring views of the ocean and the harbor. Between WWI and WWII, artists began renting little seaside shacks from local fisherfolk, which they used as studios. Today these same shanties, considerably gentrified, constitute the **Rocky Neck Art Colony** (☎ 978-282-0917; www.rocky neckartcolony.org), displaying the work of local artists. The association operates the cooperative **Bryan Gallery** (☎ 978-282-0917; 53 Rocky Neck Ave; ⏰ 11am-7pm Mon-Wed, 10am-8pm Thu-Sat, noon-6pm Sun May-Oct) in a beautiful space overlooking Smith Cove.

Visit the first Thursday of the month, from June to October, for **Nights on the Neck**. Many galleries host receptions with refreshments, live performances and other entertainment. Follow Main St east and south around the northeastern end of Gloucester Harbor to East Gloucester then turn onto Rocky Neck Ave and park in the lot on the right (parking further on in the village proper is nearly impossible in high summer).

GLOUCESTER MARITIME HERITAGE CENTER

Visit Gloucester's **working waterfront** (☎ 978-281-0471; www.gloucestermaritimecenter.org; Harbor Loop; ⏰ 10am-5pm daily Jun-Aug, Sat & Sun Sep-Oct; ⛵) and see the ongoing restoration of wooden boats, watch the operation of a marine railway that hauls ships out of the water, and compare the different kinds of fishing boats that were used over the years. **Sea Pocket Lab** is a hands-on outdoor aquarium with exhibits on local marine habitats. It is a great chance for kids to get down and dirty with sea stars, sea urchins, snails, crabs and seaweed. The **Stellwagen Bank Marine Sanctuary Exhibit** is an excellent introduction for whale-watchers heading out on an excursion. From the Grant Circle rotary, take Washington St to its terminus then turn left on Rogers St to Harbor Loop.

Be sure not to leave Gloucester without paying your respects at **St Peter's Sq**. Here stands Leonarde Craske's famous statue, *The Gloucester Fisherman,* often called 'The Man at the Wheel.' The statue is dedicated to 'They That Go Down to the Sea in Ships, 1623–1923.'

CAPE ANN HISTORICAL MUSEUM

This tiny **museum** (☎ 978-283-0455; www.capeannhis toricalmuseum.org; 27 Pleasant St; adult/student/senior $6.50/4.50/6; ☿ 10am-5pm Tue-Sat, 1-4pm Sun Mar-Jan) is a gem – particularly for its impressive collection of paintings by Gloucester native Fitz Hugh Lane. Exhibits also showcase the region's granite quarrying industry and – of course – its maritime history. The museum is in the heart of downtown Gloucester, just north of Main St.

BEAUPORT MANSION

The lavish 'summer cottage' of interior designer Henry Davis Sleeper is known as **Beauport Mansion** (☎ 978-283-0800; www.historic newengland.org; 75 Eastern Point Blvd, Eastern Point; admission $10; ☿ 10am-4pm Mon-Fri mid-May–mid-Sep, daily mid-Sep–mid-Oct), or the Sleeper-McCann mansion. Sleeper toured New England in search of houses about to be demolished and bought up selected elements from each: wood paneling, architectural elements and furniture. In place of unity, Sleeper created a wildly eclectic but artistically surprising – and satisfying – place to live. Now in the care of the Society for the Preservation of New England Antiquities, Beauport is open to visitors. Beauport also holds afternoon teas, evening concerts and other special events.

SAILING

The 65ft **Schooner Thomas E Lannon** (☎ 978-281-6634; www.schooner.org; Rogers St; adult/senior/child $35/30/25) is the spitting image of the Gloucester fishing schooners. It leaves on two-hour sails from the Seven Seas wharf.

Festivals & Events

St Peter's Festival (www.stpetersfiesta.org) Honoring the patron saint of fisherfolk, this carnival at St Peter's Sq takes place on a weekend in late June. Besides rides and music, the main event is the procession through the streets of a statue of St Peter. Customarily, the cardinal of the Catholic Archdiocese of Boston attends to bless the fishing fleet.

Horribles Parade Takes place every year on the evening of July 3. By tradition, children dress up in fanciful costumes (from horrible to hùmorous) and compete for prizes. Politicians and local businesses enter floats, and various bands perform.

Sleeping

Cape Ann Campsite (☎ 978-283-8683; www.capeann campsite.com; 80 Atlantic St; per car incl 2 people $26-30,

per extra person $8, electricity $6-10; ☿ May-Oct) If you want to pitch your pup on 50 wooded, hilltop acres, this is the place for you. Two hundred unique campsites, with lots of shade and privacy.

Crow's Nest Inn (☎ 978-281-2965; www.crowsnest gloucester.com; 334 Main St; s/d $55/65) If you want to awake to the sound of fishermen's cries and the smell of salt air, and you don't mind the most basic of bunks, stay at the Crow's Nest, the inn associated with the pub made famous by *The Perfect Storm*.

Accommodations of Rocky Neck (☎ 978-283-1625; www.rockyneckaccommodations.com; 43 Rocky Neck Ave; r Sun-Thu $110, Fri & Sat $125; Ⓟ) You don't have to be an artiste to live the bohemian life in Gloucester. The colony association offers light-filled efficiencies – all equipped with kitchenettes – at the Rocky Neck Artist Colony. The rooms are sweet and simple, most with beautiful views of Smith Cove.

Julietta House (☎ 978-281-2300; www.juliettahouse .com; 84 Prospect St; r $125-199; Ⓟ ✖ ▢ wi-fi) Steps from Gloucester Harbor, this grand Georgian house has five spacious and elegant rooms with period furnishings and private bathrooms. Breakfast is not included, so you'll have to duck out to Two Sisters (p154).

Cape Ann Motor Inn (☎ 978-281-2900; www.cape annmotorinn.com; 33 Rockport Rd; r/ste $145/250; Ⓟ) A great location halfway between Rockport and Gloucester, and right on Long Beach. All rooms feature glass sliding doors that open onto private balconies with ocean views. Kitchenettes are also available.

From the terminus of MA 128, take Bass Ave east to Atlantic Rd to find the following sea-view options in East Gloucester.

Atlantis Motor Inn (☎ 978-283-0014, 800-732-6313; www.atlantismotorinn.com; 125 Atlantic Rd; r $155-185; Ⓟ ✖ ▢ wi-fi ▧) The standard rooms at this large motel-style facility are spruced by ocean views and private terraces.

Ocean View Resort & Inn (☎ 978-283-6200, 800-315-7557; www.oceanviewinnandresort.com; 171 Atlantic Rd; r $160-325; Ⓟ ✖ ▢ wi-fi ▧) An innovative combination of inn and resort. Quaint, comfortable rooms and great facilities are housed in lovely Tudor mansions.

Eating

You really can't go wrong at any of the local lobster shacks.

Virgilio's Italian Bakery (☎ 978-283-5295; 29 Main St; sandwiches $4-8; ☿ 9am-5pm) Primarily a take-out joint, Virgilio's has excellent sandwiches

GOING TO THE BANK

The oldest seaport in the country, Gloucester supported a thriving fishing industry for more than three centuries. Generation after generation of Gloucester fishermen plied the Atlantic Grand Banks for groundfish such as cod, haddock and flounder. In the days of sail, they used baited lines and salt to preserve the catch. Gloucester boasted one of the largest fleets in the world, with over 400 boats and an extensive processing and support industry along the waterfront.

In the 1900s the industry shifted to steam trawlers with rigged netting. The ships and nets became bigger and bigger, and more and more numerous. Gloucester boats were slow to catch up to the changing technology. As early as 1930 biologists cautioned against over-fishing and warned against the long-term dangers of the new techniques. But it took several decades before the industry started being regulated.

To protect the industry, the US government extended its claim of coastal waters from 12 to 200 miles. The measure enabled Gloucester to make a brief recovery in the 1980s, but it was not to last. The relentless use of industrial trawling drag nets has now destroyed much of the bottom habitat that sustained the Atlantic groundfish. When the government acted next, it was to curtail the allowable take with the hope of recovery. As the stocks of groundfish dwindled, it was the Gloucester fisherman becoming an endangered species.

With the fishing industry in decline, gritty Gloucester is looking to clean itself up as a tourist destination. It is perfectly situated to do so, thanks to the proximity of **Stellwagen Bank** (www .stellwagen.noaa.gov), 842 sq miles of open ocean rich in marine life. The area was declared a National Marine Sanctuary in 1992 to conserve the area's biological diversity and to facilitate research and other beneficial activity. Today it's a destination for whale-watching, diving and managed fishing.

Whale-watching cruises usually depart several times a day in summer, but only once a day or perhaps only on weekends in April, May, September and October. Reservations are recommended. Try the following outfits:

Cape Ann Whale Watch (☎ 978-283-5110, 800-877-5110; www.caww.com; Rose's Wharf, 415 Main St; adult/child/senior $41/27/36) Cruises depart from Rose's Wharf, east of Gloucester center (on the way to East Gloucester).

Capt Bill & Sons Whale Watch (☎ 978-283-6995, 800-339-4253; www.captainbillswhalewatch.com; 33 Harbor Loop; adult/child/senior $41/25/35) The boat leaves from behind Captain Carlo's Seafood Market & Restaurant.

Seven Seas Whale Watch (☎ 978-283-1776, 800-238-1776; www.7seas-whalewatch.com; Rogers St; adult/ child/senior $42/26/36) Seven Seas vessels depart from Rogers St in the center of Gloucester, between St Peter's Sq and the Gloucester House Restaurant.

Yankee Whale Watch (☎ 978-283-0313, 800-942-5464; www.yankeefleet.com; 75 W Essex Ave/MA 133; adult/child/senior/student $41/26/35/36) The Yankee fleet ties up at the dock next door to the Gull Restaurant on MA 133 (MA 128 exit 14).

and other Italian treats. Try the famous St Joseph sandwich – like an Italian sub on a fresh-baked roll. Pick one up and head down to the waterfront for a picnic.

Two Sisters Coffee Shop (☎ 978-281-3378; 27 Washington St; meals $8-10; ☽ breakfast & lunch) This local place is where the fisherfolk go for breakfast when they come in from their catch. They are early risers, so you may have to wait for a table.

Maria's Pizza (☎ 978-283-7373; 35 Pearl St; pizzas $10-15; ☽ lunch & dinner) Gloucester's favorite pizzeria is across from the train station. Crunchy-crust pizza, fried seafood and thick clam chowder will sate any appetite.

Bring your own beer from the 'packy' across the street.

Dog Bar (☎ 978-281-6565; 65 Main St; meals $12-22; ☽ dinner) Go around to the rear entrance to sample the eclectic menu and cold drinks at Dog Bar. From the simple (not-so-sloppy joes) to the sophisticated (smoked whiskey shrimp cocktail), just about everything here would be appealing to your dog, who might also appreciate the outdoor seating. There are plans to open an upscale restaurant in the front of the building.

Elliott's at the Blackburn (☎ 978-282-1919; 2 Main St; meals $15-25; ☽ lunch & dinner) Exposed brick and polished wood make for a very cozy spot.

Come for old-fashioned comfort food with a modern twist, like lobster mac and cheese, buffalo bolognese or fig pizza.

Franklin Cape Ann (☎ 978-283-7888; 118 Main St; meals $15-20; ☑ 5pm-midnight) The North Shore branch of a South End favorite in Boston (see p109), this cool place has an urban atmosphere and an excellent, modern New American menu.

Duckworth's Bistrot (☎ 978-282-4426; 197 E Main St; meals $20-30; ☑ dinner Tue-Sun) Half-portions and wines by the glass (or carafe) mean that Duckworth's won't break your bank. But the menu of fresh seafood and local produce means you will dine like a gourmand.

Drinking & Entertainment
BARS & CLUBS
Crow's Nest (☎ 978-281-2965; www.crowsnestgloucester.com; 334 Main St; ☑ 11am-1am) The down-and-dirty fisherfolk bar made famous in *The Perfect Storm*. But this is the real deal, not the set the movie folks threw up for a few weeks during filming. Come early if you want to drink with the fish crews. It gets crowded with tourists in summer.

LIVE MUSIC
Madfish Grille (☎ 978-281-4554; 77 Rocky Neck Ave; ☑ noon-1am) On a wharf at Rocky Neck, the Madfish is a hopping bar that attracts a young, cruisey crowd. Between Memorial Day and Labor Day, it hosts live music Wednesday through Sunday (weekends only in spring and fall). The kitchen turns out excellent, creative dishes.

Rhumb Line (☎ 978-283-9732; www.therhumbline.com; 40 Railroad Ave; ☑ 11:30am-1am) This club across from the train station is the best place on Cape Ann to hear live music, with performances almost nightly. Acts range from mellow acoustic and blues to high-energy rock, with the occasional open-mike night.

THEATER
Gloucester Stage Company (☎ 978-281-4099; www.gloucesterstage.com; 267 E Main St) This company stages excellent small-theater productions of classics and modern works.

Getting There & Away
You can reach Cape Ann quickly from Boston or North Shore towns via four-lane Rte 128, but the scenic route on MA 127 follows the coastline through the prim villages of Prides Crossing, Manchester-by-the-Sea and Magnolia. Alternatively, take the Rockport line of the **MBTA commuter rail** (☎ 617-722-3200, 800-392-6100; www.mbta.com) from Boston's North Station to Gloucester ($7.25, one hour).

ROCKPORT
At the northern tip of Cape Ann, Rockport is a quaint contrast to gritty Gloucester. Rockport takes its name from its 19th-century role as a shipping center for granite cut from the local quarries. The stone is still ubiquitous: monuments, building foundations, pavements and piers remain as a testament to Rockport's past.

That's about all that remains of this industrial history, however. A century ago, Winslow Homer, Childe Hassam, Fitz Hugh Lane and other acclaimed artists came to Rockport's rugged shores, inspired by the hearty fisherfolk who wrested a hard, but satisfying, living from the sea. Today Rockport makes its living from tourists who come to look at the artists. The artists have long since given up looking for hearty fishermen because the descendants of the fishers are all running boutiques and B&Bs.

Orientation & Information
Rockport is just up Rte 127 from Gloucester (or Rte 127A if you prefer the scenic route). The center of town is Dock Sq, at the beginning of Bearskin Neck. Parking in Rockport is difficult on summer weekends. Unless you arrive very early, you'd do well to park at one of the lots on MA 127 from Gloucester and take the shuttle bus to Rockport's center.

Rockport Chamber of Commerce (☎ 978-546-6575, 888-726-3922; www.rockportusa.com; 22 Broadway; ☑ 9am-5pm Mon-Sat Apr-Oct, 11am-2pm Mon, Wed & Fri Nov-Mar) On T Wharf just off Mt Pleasant St. A seasonal branch is located 1 mile out of town on Rte 127.

See Cape Ann (www.seecapeann.com) Cape Ann's online information booth.

Toad Hall Bookstore (☎ 978-546-7323; 51 Main St) Socially responsible reading: buy your books here and the shop donates some of its income to environmental projects.

Sights & Activities
DOCK SQUARE & BEARSKIN NECK
Dock Sq is the hub of Rockport. Visible from here, the red fishing shack decorated with colorful buoys is known as **Motif No 1**. So many artists of great and minimal talent have been

painting and photographing it for so long that it well deserves its tongue-in-cheek name. Actually, it should be called Motif No 1-B, as the original shack vanished during a great storm in 1978 and a brand-new replica was erected in its place. Check out the **gallery** on Bearskin Neck that sells renditions of Motif No 1 as portrayed by an impressionist, expressionist, cubist, Dadaist and just about every other artistic school.

Bearskin Neck is the peninsula that juts into the harbor, lined with galleries, lobster shacks and souvenir shops. The name Bearskin Neck apparently comes from a historic account of a young boy who was attacked by a bear. In an attempt to save the boy, his uncle, Ebenezer Babson, went after the bear with the only weapon he had available at the time – his fish knife. Babson managed to kill the bear and save the child, and then he skinned the bear and laid the pelt on the rocks to dry. The legend lives on in rhyme: 'Babson, Babson, killed a bear, with his knife, I do declare.'

BIKING, FISHING & KAYAKING

North Shore Kayak Outdoor Center (☎ 978-546-5050; www.northshorekayak.com; 9 Tuna Wharf; kayaks per day $30-45, bikes per day $16) Also offers tours.

Rockport Castaway Charters (☎ 978-546-3959; www.rockportcastaways.com) Offers half- and full-day fishing trips.

Festivals & Events

The **Rockport Chamber Music Festival** (☎ 978-546-7391; www.rcmf.org; 35 Main St) hosts at least 16 concerts by internationally acclaimed performers. The festival recently purchased the Haskins Building on Main St, which will be transformed into a magnificent performance space facing the open ocean.

Sleeping

Every year B&Bs open around Cape Ann, bringing a new level of character and value to accommodations. You can search out this emerging market at www.capeannvacations .com or www.innsofrockport.com. Breakfast is included unless otherwise indicated.

Lantana House (☎ 978-546-3535, 800-291-3535; www.thelantanahouse.com; 22 Broadway; r $99-115; P ⚌ ☐ wi-fi ⚟) Conveniently located, Lantana House features spacious rooms with floral bedspreads and lace curtains. The wide, airy porch and sundeck are wonderful places

to have breakfast in the morning or a rest in the afternoon.

Inn on Cove Hill (☎ 978-546-2701; www.innoncovehill .com; 37 Mt Pleasant St; r $100-150, ste $165; P) This is a Federal-style house built in 1791 with, so they say, pirates' gold discovered nearby. It has been lovingly restored down to the tiniest detail. Doubles have wide-plank hardwood floors, ornate moldings and canopy beds. The location, a block from Dock Sq, is hard to beat.

Sally Webster Inn (☎ 978-546-9251, 877-546-9251; www.sallywebster.com; 34 Mt Pleasant St; r $110-140; P) This handsome brick colonial, built in 1832, offers eight rooms with early-American decor. Many have working fireplaces, and all have authentic architectural details and period furniture. Well-groomed flowerbeds and cool ocean breezes make the terrace a wonderful respite.

Tuck Inn (☎ 978-546-7260, 800-789-7260; www.tuck inn.com; 17 High St; r $113-143, ste $173; P ⚌ ☐ wi-fi ⚟) Despite the unfortunate name, this inn offers excellent value. The renovated 1790s colonial home has nine rooms and a four-person suite. Elegant communal rooms feature period decor. Local artwork and homemade quilts are some of the little touches that make the rooms special. The breakfast buffet – complete with fresh, seasonal fruit salads, and fresh-baked muffins and pastries – will be a highlight of your stay.

Bulfinch House (☎ 978-546-9656; www.bulfinchhouse .com; 96 Granite St; r $135-175; P ⚌ ☐ wi-fi) This classic Federal-style home was designed by Massachusetts' most famous architect, Charles Bulfinch. The house maintains an old-fashioned feel throughout, with lace curtains and floral linens. All five rooms have private bathroom and water views, while two have access to a grand porch. It's about 1 mile north of Rockport's center on Rte 127.

Addison Choate Inn (☎ 978-546-7543, 800-245-7543; www.addisonchoateinn.com; 49 Broadway; r $149-179; P ⚌ ⚟) This Greek revival residence stands out among Rockport's historic inns. The traditional decor includes canopy beds, wide plank hardwood floors and period wallpaper. The two suites (with kitchenettes) in the carriage house are particularly appealing, with cathedral ceilings and exposed beam ceilings.

Captain's Bounty Motor Inn (☎ 978-546-9557; www .captainsbountymotorinn.com; 1 Beach St; r $155-190; P) The draw here is the prime location, right on

Front Beach and only a few minutes' stroll from Dock Sq. The 24 rooms are simple, but they all have lovely views of the dawn over the beach and local lobstermen checking their traps.

Bearskin Neck Motor Lodge (☎ 978-546-6677; www.rockportusa.com/bearskin; 64 Bear Skin Neck; d $159-169; **P**) The only lodging on Bearskin Neck is this motel-style lodge near the end of the strip. Needless to say, every room has a great view and a balcony from where you can enjoy it. Otherwise, the rooms are pretty plain and probably overpriced. Breakfast not provided.

Eating & Drinking

Dock Sq has several cafés, while Bearskin Neck is crowded with ice-cream stores, cafés and cozy restaurants – and plenty of seafood. Many places reduce hours or close completely for the winter. Rockport is a dry town, meaning that alcohol is not sold in stores and rarely in restaurants, and there are no bars. However, you can bring your own bottles, and most restaurants will open and serve them for a corkage fee.

Pigeon Cove Lobster Co (☎ 978-546-3000; Granite St) If your lodging includes kitchen facilities, consider the ultimate New England culinary experience: buying your lobsters live and boiling them yourself. Head to Pigeon Cove for live lobsters straight from the trap and piping-hot, award-winning clam chowder. This is where the fishers are unloading their daily catch from their boats and – if you wish – into your pot. You can expect to pay $6 to $8 per pound for hard-shell lobsters, and slightly less for soft-shell.

Helmut's Strudel (☎ 978-546-2824; 69 Bearskin Neck; desserts $2-5; ☺ breakfast & lunch) For coffee or tea and dessert, try this bakery, almost near the outer end, serving various strudels, filled croissants, pastries, cider and coffee. Four shaded tables overlook the yacht-filled harbor.

Top Dog (☎ 978-546-0006; Bearskin Neck; dogs $4-8; ☺ 11am-4pm Mon-Thu, 11am-7pm Fri & Sat, longer hr in summer) More than a dozen kinds of dogs, from a German Shepherd (with fresh sauerkraut) to a Chihuahua (with jalapenos, salsa and cheese).

ourpick Roy Moore Lobster Company (☎ 978-546-6696; 29 Bearskin Neck; meals $5-20; ☺ lunch & dinner) This takeout kitchen has the cheapest lobster-in-the-rough on the Neck. Your beast comes on a tray with melted butter, a fork and a wet wipe for cleanup. You can

sit in the back with the fishing boats on a few tables fashioned from lobster traps, or head next door to the restaurant for a bit of refinement. Don't forget to bring your own beer or wine.

Brackett's (☎ 978-546-2797; 25 Main St; meals $6-18; ☺ lunch & dinner Fri-Wed, closed Nov-Mar) Locals swear by this cozy little dining nook. The casual pub atmosphere, ocean views and daily specials draw a consistent crowd. The specialties of the house are scrod, shrimp, crab and scallop casseroles, rich in sherry and cream. This is one of the few places in Rockport that serves alcohol.

Ellen's Harborside (☎ 978-546-2512; 1 Wharf Rd; meals $10-15; ☺ breakfast, lunch & dinner) By the T-wharf in the center of town, Ellen's has grown famous serving a simple menu of American breakfasts, chicken, ribs and lobster since 1954. You get decent portions, fresh food and low prices. Consider the award-winning clam chowder.

You can buy liquor outside Rockport at the following places:
Lanesville Package Store (☎ 978-281-0293; 1080 Washington St/MA 127, Lanesville; ☺ 8am-9pm Mon-Sat, noon-6pm Sun)
Liquor Locker (☎ 978-283-0630; 287 Main St, Gloucester; ☺ 8am-10pm Mon-Sat, noon-5pm Sun)

Getting There & Around

MA 127/127A loops around Cape Ann, connecting Magnolia and Gloucester to Rockport. Driving the entire loop is worth it for the seaside scenery in East Gloucester, Lanesville and Annisquam. Alternatively, take the **MBTA commuter rail** (☎ 617-722-3200, 800-392-6100; www.mbta.com) from Boston's North Station to Rockport ($7.75, one hour). The **Cape Ann Transportation Authority** (CATA; ☎ 978-283-7916) operates bus routes between the towns of Cape Ann.

AROUND CAPE ANN
HAMMOND CASTLE MUSEUM
Dr John Hays Hammond, Jr (1888–1965) was an electrical engineer and inventor who amassed a fortune fulfilling defense contracts. With this wealth, Hammond pursued his passion for collecting European art and architecture. His eccentric home is a **medieval castle** (☎ 978-283-2080; www.hammondcastle.org; 80 Hesperus Ave, Magnolia; admission $7; ☺ 10am-4pm daily Jul-Aug, Sat & Sun Apr-Jun) which he built to house all his treasures, dating from the Romanesque,

---

A LESSON IN RECYCLING

In 1922, long before there was any municipal recycling program, Elis F Stenman decided that something useful should be done with all those daily newspapers lying about. He and his family set to work folding, rolling and pasting the papers into suitable shapes as building materials. Twenty years and 100,000 newspapers later, they had built the **Paper House** (☎ 978-546-2629; 52 Pigeon Hill St; admission by donation; ☽ 10am-5pm Apr-Oct), which is located inland from Pigeon Cove on Cape Ann.

The walls are 215 layers thick, and the furnishings – table, chairs, lamps, sofa, even a grandfather clock and a piano – are all made of newspaper. Some pieces even specialize: one desk is made from Christian Science Monitor reports of Charles Lindbergh's flight, and the fireplace mantel is made from rotogravures drawn from the Boston *Sunday Herald* and the New York *Herald Tribune*. The text is still legible on all of the newspapers so there is built-in reading material (literally).

---

medieval, Gothic and Renaissance periods. Furnishings are eclectic and interesting, including a magnificent 8200-pipe organ in the Romanesque Great Hall. Despite his genius with electrical things, it was not Dr John, but rather Laurens Hammond (unrelated), who invented the electric organ.

Hammond Castle overlooks several spectacular natural features. Painted by Fitz Huge Lane and many other artists over the years, Rafe's Chasm is a cleft in the rocky shoreline that is characterized by turgid and thrashing water. Near it is **Norman's Woe**, the reef on which the ship broke up in Longfellow's poem 'The Wreck of the Hesperus.'

HALIBUT POINT RESERVATION
Only a few miles north of Dock Sq along MA 127 is **Halibut Point Reservation** (☎ 978-526-8687; www.thetrustees.org; admission free; ☽ dawn-dusk; P $2). A 10-minute walk through the forest brings you to yawning, abandoned granite quarries, huge hills of broken granite rubble, and a granite foreshore of tumbled, smoothed rock perfect for picnicking, sunbathing, reading or painting. The surf can be strong here, making swimming unwise, but natural pools are good for wading or cooling your feet. A map is available at the entrance.

GOOSE COVE RESERVOIR
Much of the interior of Cape Ann is given over to reservations to preserve the unique ecological habitat of this area. Goose Cove is an Essex County reservation on the eastern side of the Cape. It consists of 26 acres of woodland, rocky shoreline and tidal mudflats. This beautiful area is home to many types of herons, ducks and egrets, not to mention mammals, like fishers and otters. The parking lot is off Washington St (Rte 127) heading north from Gloucester to Lanesville. Trails lead from the parking lot to the water's edge.

BEACHES
Cape Ann has several excellent beaches that draw thousands of Boston-area sun-and-sea worshippers on any hot day in July or August. All of these beaches get crowded, especially on weekends, so try to arrive early.

One of the loveliest North Shore beaches is **Wingaersheek Beach**, a wide swath of sand surrounded by Ipswich Bay, the Annisquam River and lots of sand dunes. Facilities include showers, toilets and refreshments. At low tide a long sandbar stretches for more than half a mile out into the bay, providing a clear view of the Annisquam lighthouse at its tip. Take Rte 128 to Exit 13. Turn left on Concord St and right on Atlantic St. Parking costs weekend/weekday $25/20.

Good Harbor Beach is a spacious, sandy beach east of East Gloucester off MA 127A on the way to Rockport. Parking is very limited here, which has its advantages and disadvantages. Fortunately, the parking lot fills up before the beach does, so if you get here early enough, you will enjoy the minimal crowds all day long. If you are late, you will be turned away at the parking lot, which charges weekend/weekday $25/20.

There are two lovely, small beaches at **Stage Fort Park** (☎ 978-281-9785): the picturesque Half-Moon Beach and the more remote Cressy's Beach. The latter is a bit of a trek from the parking lot, but worth it to get away from the other bathing beauties. The park itself is an attractive, well-maintained recreation area with picnic tables, playgrounds and hiking trails. Parking costs $10.

IPSWICH & ESSEX
pop 16,254

Heading up the North Shore from Cape Ann, Ipswich and Essex are pretty New England towns surrounded by rocky coast and sandy beaches, extensive marshlands, forested hills and rural farmland.

Ipswich is one of those New England towns that is pretty today because it was poor in the past. Because it had no harbor, and no source of waterpower for factories, commercial and industrial development went elsewhere in the 18th and 19th centuries. As a result, Ipswich's 17th-century houses were not torn down to build grander residences. Today the town is famous for its ample antique shops and succulent clams. Home of novelist John Updike, it is also the setting for some of his novels and short stories like *A&P*, which is based on the local market.

Sights & Activities

ESSEX SHIPBUILDING MUSEUM

This unique **museum** (Map p152; ☎ 978-768-7541; www.essexshipbuildingmuseum.org; 66 Main St, Essex; adult/child/senior $7/5/6; ☻ noon-4pm Wed-Sun) was established in 1976 as a local repository for all of the shipbuilding artifacts of the local residents. Most of the collections of photos, tools and ship models came from local basements and attics, allowing Essex to truly preserve its local history. Most of the collections are housed in the town's 1835 school house (check out the **Old Burying Ground** behind it). The historical society also operates the **Waterline Center** in the museum shipyard, a section of waterfront property where shipbuilding activities have taken place for hundreds of years. The historic Essex-built schooner, **Evelina M Goulart**, is moored here.

From Rte 128, take exit 15 and turn left on School St (which becomes Southern Ave). Take a left onto Rte 133; the museum and shipyard are on the right-hand side after crossing a causeway and a bridge.

CRANE ESTATE

One of the longest, widest, sandiest beaches in the region is **Crane Beach** (Map p152; ☎ 978-356-4354; www.thetrustees.org; Argilla Rd, Ipswich; admission $2; ☻ 8am-dusk), with 4 miles of fine-sand barrier beach on Ipswich Bay. It is set in the midst of the Crane Wildlife Refuge, so the entire surrounding area is pristinely beautiful. Five miles of trails traverse the dunes. The only downside is the pesky greenhead flies that buzz around (and bite) in late July and early August. Parking costs weekend/weekday $22/15.

Above the beach, on **Castle Hill** (Map p152; ☎ 978-356-4351; 290 Argilla Rd, Ipswich; per car $8; ☻ 8am-dusk) sits the 1920s estate of Chicago plumbing-fixture magnate Richard T Crane. The 59-room Stuart-style **Great House** (adult/child $10/5; ☻ 10am-4pm Thu, 10am-1pm Fri & Sat Jun-Sep) is the site of summer concerts and special events. It's open for tours in summer, but only a few days a week. The lovely landscaped grounds, which are open daily, contain several miles of walking trails.

APPLETON FARMS

One of the country's oldest continuously operating farms, **Appleton Farms** (off map p152; ☎ 978-356-5728; www.thetrustees.org; 219 County Rd, Ipswich; admission free; ☻ 8am-dusk) is now maintained and operated by the Trustees of Reservations. Four miles of trails wind along old carriageways, past ancient stonewall property markers and through acres of beautiful grasslands. The store sells fresh, organically grown produce, not to mention tantalizing jams, spreads and sauces made with said produce.

From MA 128 take MA 1A north. Turn left on Cutler Rd and drive 2 miles to the intersection with Highland Rd, where parking is available.

KAYAKING

Explore the tidal estuaries of the Essex River with **Essex River Basin Adventures** (☎ 978-768-3722; www.erba.com; 1 Main St, Essex; tours $42-58). Tours include basic kayak instruction, as well as plenty of opportunities for bird-watching. Romantics will have a hard time choosing between a sunset paddle and a moonlight paddle.

Sleeping & Eating

Inn at Castle Hill (☎ 978-412-2555; http://innatcastle hill.thetrustees.org; 280 Argilla Rd, Ipswich; r $175-385 May-Oct; ℗ ⌘ ▭ wi-fi) On the grounds of the Crane Estate, this inn is an example of understated luxury. In the midst of acres of beautiful grounds, the inn boasts 10 rooms, each uniquely decorated with subtle elegance. Turndown service, plush robes and afternoon tea are some of the very civilized perks; and who can resist that wraparound veranda and its magnificent views of the surrounding sand dunes and salt marshes?

Woodman's (☎ 978-768-6057, 800-649-1773; 121 Main St/MA 133, Essex; meals $7-25; ☉ lunch & dinner) This roadhouse is the most famous spot in the area to come for clams, anyway you like 'em. The specialty is Chubby's original fried clams and crispy onion rings. But this place serves everything from boiled lobsters to homemade clam cakes to a seasonal raw bar. Friendly, family service and tried-and-true seafood make it one of the classic New England eateries. It's on MA 133 on the way to Ipswich from Rockport (exit 14 from MA 128).

Getting There & Away

Ipswich is on the Newburyport line of the **MBTA commuter rail** (☎ 617-222-3200, 800-392-6100; www .mbta.com). Trains leave Boston's North Station for Ipswich ($6.75, 50 minutes) about 12 times each weekday and five times on Saturday (no trains Sunday).

NEWBURYPORT

pop 17,000

Newburyport's heyday was during the late 18th century, when this town at the mouth of the Merrimack River prospered as a shipping port and silversmith center. Not too much has changed in the last 200 years, as Newburyport's brick buildings and graceful churches still show off the Federal style that was popular back in those days. Today the center of this town is a model of historic preservation and gentrification. Visitors enjoy creative restaurants, pubs, museums and entertainment. Newburyport is also the gateway to the barrier Plum Island, a national wildlife refuge with some of the best bird-watching in New England.

Orientation & Information

All major roads (MA 113, US 1 and US 1A) lead to the center of the town's commercial and historic district, around the junction of Water and State Sts. The **Greater Newburyport Chamber of Commerce** (☎ 978-462-6680; www.newbury portchamber.org; 38 Merrimac St; ☉ 9am-5pm Mon-Fri, 10am-4pm Sat, noon-4pm Sun) runs a seasonal information booth in Market Sq from June to October.

Sights & Activities

CUSTOM HOUSE MARITIME MUSEUM

The 1835 granite Custom House is an excellent example of Classic Revival architecture, built by Robert Mills (of Washington Monument fame). It now houses the **Maritime Museum** (☎ 978-462-8681; www.themaritimesociety.org; 25 Water St; adult/senior & child $7/5; ☉ 11am-4pm Tue-Sat, noon-4pm Sun), which exhibits artifacts from Newburyport's maritime history as a major shipbuilding center and seaport. Seafaring folk will have a field day in the Moseley Gallery with its collection of model clipper ships.

CUSHING HOUSE MUSEUM & GARDEN

This 21-room Federal home houses the **Historical Society of Old Newbury** (☎ 978-462-2681; www.newburyhist.com; 98 High St; adult/child $5/2; ☉ 10am-4pm Tue-Fri, noon-4pm Sat May-Oct). The home is decked out with fine furnishings and decorative pieces from the region. Collections of portraits, silver, needlework, toys and clocks are all on display, not to mention the impressive Oriental collection from Newburyport's early Chinese trade. The society offers guided tours, exhibits, special events and lectures. The last tour begins one hour before closing.

GALLERIES & ART SPACES

Churchill Gallery (☎ 978-462-9891; www.thechurch illgallery.com; 6 Inn St; ☉ 10am-5pm Mon-Sat, 12:30-5pm Sun) Exhibits landscapes, still lifes and figurative paintings by emerging artists.

Firehouse Center for the Arts (☎ 978-462-7336; www.firehouse.org; 1 Market Sq; ☉ noon-5pm Wed-Sun) This restored 1823 firehouse contains an art gallery, a 190-seat theater and a restaurant. The theater offers year-round concerts, plays and children's theater, with top performers from around New England.

Newburyport Art Association (☎ 978-465-8769; www.newburyportart.org; 65 Water St; ☉ 11am-5pm Tue-Sat, 1-5pm Sun) Hosts exhibitions, lectures and performances by member artists.

Walsingham Gallery (☎ 978-499-4411; www.the walsinghamgallery.com; 47 Merrimac St; ☉ 10am-4pm Mon, Wed & Thu, 10am-6pm Fri-Sat, noon-5pm Sun) This stark Federalist building – a former sea-merchant's warehouse – holds interesting exhibits of artists from New England and beyond.

PARKER RIVER NATIONAL WILDLIFE REFUGE

The 4662-acre **sanctuary** (☎ 978-465-5753; www .parkerriver.org; Plum Island; per car/bike or pedestrian $5/2; ☉ dawn-dusk) occupies the southern three-quarters of Plum Island. More than 800 species of birds, plants and animals reside in its many ecological habitats, including beaches, sand dunes, salt pans, salt marshes, freshwater impoundments and maritime forests.

There are several observation areas that are excellent for spotting shorebirds and waterfowl, including herons and egrets. Large portions are closed because they provide an important habitat for the endangered piping plover. Inland, there are freshwater impoundments, as well as an extensive swamp and forest. During spring and fall, you can observe migrating songbirds, including magnificent wood-warblers in the woods. In winter the refuge is a good place to see waterfowl, the rough-legged hawk and snowy owl. Several miles of foot trails allow access to much of the area. Observation towers and platforms punctuate the trails at prime bird-watching spots.

PLUM ISLAND BEACHES

A barrier island off the coast of Massachusetts, Plum Island has 9 miles of wide, sandy beaches surrounded by acres of wildlife sanctuary. These are among the nicest beaches on the North Shore, if you head to the furthest points on the island. **Sandy Point** (☎ 978-462-4481; Plum Island; ☼ dawn-8pm), on the southern tip, is a state park that is popular for swimming, sunning and tidepooling. Parking is available at the Parker River Wildlife Refuge (opposite), Sandy Point or in private parking lots. Note: beaches in the refuge are generally closed April to June because of nesting piping plover, but you can go to the public beaches at the north end of the island, where there is a community of vacation homes.

WATER ACTIVITIES

Newburyport Whale Watch (☎ 800-848-1111; www.newburyportwhalewatch.com; 54 Merrimac St; adult/child/senior $40/25/35) Offers bird- and whale-watching tours, as well as cruises to the Isle of Shoals.

Plum Island Kayak (☎ 978-462-5510; www.plumislandkayak.com; 38 Merrimac St; s/tandem per day $55/75; ☼ 9am-5pm Mon-Wed, 9am-8pm Thu-Sun Apr-Oct) Rent a kayak and explore Plum Island on your own, or join one of several tours during the day (and night) exploring the islands, mud bars, salt marshes and shorelines. Expect to see lots of birds. Special moonlight paddles and trips to the Isle of Shoals are also popular.

Sleeping

Like many historic North Shore towns, Newburyport has become full of B&Bs. Several motels and hotels are located in nearby towns. For a complete list of places to stay and website links, check out www.new

buryportchamber.org. Breakfast is included unless otherwise indicated.

Essex Street Inn (☎ 978-465-3148; www.essexstreetinn.com; 7 Essex St; r $115-145, ste $185-235; P 🖥 👪) This Victorian inn was built as a lodging house in 1880. Today it's an elegant inn: the 17 rooms are all nicely decorated in 19th-century style (some with fireplaces). It's not without modern comforts, however. Several of the more expensive rooms feature whirlpools.

Newburyport B&B (☎ 978-463-4637; www.newburyportbedandbreakfast.com; 296 High St; s $115-125, d $140-160; P 🛇 🐾) This grand Georgian colonial has 16 lovely rooms, all graced with a stately elegance. The light-filled sunroom, formal dining room and fancy parlor are all open for guests to enjoy. The grounds include landscaped English gardens surrounding a brick patio.

Clark Currier Inn (☎ 978-465-8363; www.clarkcurrierinn.com; 45 Green St; r $145-175, ste $195; P 🛇 🖥 wi-fi) Travelers in search of a genteel experience can luxuriate in this 1803 Federal mansion, with its period sitting room, library, fish pond and gazebo. Details like a Franklin stove and canopy beds make this place extra charming.

Garrison Inn (☎ 978-499-8500; www.garrisoninn.com; 11 Brown Sq; d $170-240; 🖥 wi-fi👪) Once a private mansion, this gracious, red-brick building is a lovely boutique hotel with 24 spacious rooms featuring exposed brick walls, cathedral ceilings and spiral staircases. The restaurant on site, David's Tavern, is acclaimed for its menu of eclectic American haute cuisine.

blue (☎ 978-465-7171; www.blueinn.com; 20 Fordham Way, Plum Island; d from $200) In a drop-dead gorgeous location on a beautiful beach, this sophisticated inn is quite a surprise on unassuming Plum Island. Room decor features high ceilings, fresh white linens and streaming sunlight. Private decks and in-room fireplaces are a few of the perks you will find, not to mention a bottle of wine chilling for your arrival.

Eating & Drinking

The Grog (☎ 978-465-8008; 13 Middle St; meals $12-17; ☼ lunch & dinner) The Grog has been a Newburyport tradition for over 30 years. Named for the English Navy's traditional ration of rum and water, this place serves its own traditional rations of New England seafood, grilled meats and Mexican favorites; you will not leave hungry. Downstairs, the pub has live music playing Wednesday through

Sunday, making this a popular pick-up spot for 20-somethings.

The Rockfish (☎ 978-465-6601; 35 State St; meals $12-20; ☼ lunch & dinner) The downstairs pub is a great place for people-watching. In warm weather take a table by the large, streetside open windows. Snarf some spicy rockfish cakes, suck on a cold beer, network with the locals, and watch the evening strollers sashay up and down State St.

Starboard Galley (☎ 978-465-9005; 55 Water St; meals $20-25; ☼ lunch & dinner) This waterfront place is a classic seafood restaurant, with big portions, boatloads of lobster and delicious mussels drowning in garlic. The decor is drab, but you can eat on the porch and catch a glimpse of the water on the other side of the parking lot.

Black Cow Tap & Grill (☎ 978-499-8811; 54 Merrimac St; meals $20-30; ☼ lunch & dinner) The Black Cow's waterfront setting is unbeatable; and you can't miss it in the center of town near the tourist information kiosk. A huge dining room has big windows so everyone can enjoy ocean views while eating the creatures that came out of it.

Getting There & Away

From Boston follow I-95 north. Take exit 57 and follow signs to downtown Newburyport. There are free parking lots on Green and Merrimack Sts. Alternatively, the **MBTA commuter rail** (☎ 800-392-6100; www.mbta.com) runs a line from North Station to Newburyport ($7.75). There are more than 10 trains daily on weekdays, and there's six on weekends.

C&J Trailways (☎ 800-258-7111; www.cjtrailways .com; Storey Ave) runs about 12 buses daily from Logan International Airport (one way/round trip $19/34) and Boston's South Station (one way/round trip $14/24). Round-trip fares are significantly cheaper if you return on the same day.

SOUTH SHORE

The South Shore is equally blessed with historic sites and natural beauty. Seeing firsthand the challenges faced by the Pilgrims who first landed at Plymouth Rock is a vivid reminder of the value of religious tolerance and stubborn endurance – both at the core of the nation's foundation. Generations later, these values were lived out by founding father

John Adams and his son John Quincy Adams. Finally, the South Shore offers one of Boston's most accessible retreats just minutes from the city – the inviting Blue Hills.

QUINCY
pop 88,025

Like all good New England towns, Quincy, about 10 miles south of Boston, is not pronounced the obvious way: say '*Quin*-zee' if you want to talk like the locals.

Quincy was first settled in 1625 by a handful of raucous colonists who could not stand the strict and stoic ways in Plymouth. History has it that this group went so far as to drink beer, dance around a maypole and engage in other festive Old English customs, which enraged the Puritans down the road. Nathaniel Hawthorne immortalized this history in his fictional account, *The Maypole of Merrimount*. Eventually, Myles Standish arrived from Plymouth to restore order to the wayward colony.

Quincy was officially incorporated as its own entity in 1792, named after Colonel John Quincy, a respected local leader and ancestor of revolutionary Josiah Quincy and First Lady Abigail Adams.

What makes Quincy notable – and earns this town the nickname 'The City of Presidents' – is that it is the birthplace of the second and sixth presidents of the United States: John Adams and John Quincy Adams. The collection of houses where the Adams family lived now comprises the Adams National Historic Park.

In more recent history, Quincy is the birthplace of the Dropkick Murphys (see p41).

Orientation & Information

The **Adams National Historic Park Visitor Center** (☎ 617-70-1175; www.nps.gov/adam; 1250 Adams St; ☼ 9am-5pm mid-Apr–mid-Nov) is directly opposite the T-station. Tours of the national park start here, and plenty of information about the surrounding area is also available.

Sights & Activities
ADAMS NATIONAL HISTORIC PARK

The Adams family sights are accessible by guided **tours** (adult/child $5/free; ☼ 9am-3pm mid-Apr–mid-Nov), which depart from the Adams National Historic Park Visitor Center. Every half-hour, trolleys travel to the **John Adams and John Quincy Adams Birthplaces**, the oldest

---

WORTH THE TRIP: BLUE HILLS

The Native Americans who lived in this region called themselves 'the people of the great hills.' But when Europeans saw the coastline from their ships, they noticed the blue-grey hue of the slopes in the morning light and dubbed them the Blue Hills – 22 hills in a chain that stretches across the Boston South Shore suburbs.

Blue Hills Reservation (☎ 617-698-1802; www.mass.gov/dcr/parks/metroboston/blue.htm; 695 Hillside St, Milton; ☉ dawn-dusk) is a state park that encompasses over 7000 acres in the region. A network of 125 miles of trails crosses the hills, including several routes to the summit of Great Blue Hill, the highest peak at 635ft. The rocky summit enjoys fantastic city-skyline views – not what you expect in the midst of the wilderness.

The Massachusetts Audubon Society operates a **Trailside Museum** (☎ 617-333-0690; adult/child/senior $3/1.50/2; ☉ 10am-5pm Wed-Sun) that focuses on the flora and fauna of the reservation, including some live animals. **Houghton's Pond** is pleasant for fishing and swimming. Any way you wish to escape the city – rock climbing, cross-country skiing, mountain biking, ice skating – it's all possible.

The Blue Hills Reservation is 8 miles south of Boston in Milton. From Boston, take I-93 south to exit 3, Houghton's Pond. Turn right on Hillside St and take it to Houghton's Pond or reservation headquarters. Alternatively, take the Red Line 'T' to Ashmont Station and the high-speed line to Mattapan, from where the Canton & Blue Hills bus goes to the Trailside Museum and Great Blue Hill on Rte 138.

---

presidential birthplaces in the United States. These two 17th-century saltbox houses stand side by side along the old Coast Rd, which connected Plymouth to Boston. The houses are furnished as they would have been in the 18th century, so visitors can see where John Adams started his law career, started his family, and wrote the Massachusetts Constitution (which was later used as the basis for the US Constitution).

From here, the trolley continues to **The Old House**, also called Peacefields, which was the residence of four generations of the Adams family from 1788 to 1927. The house contains original furnishings and decorations from the Adams family, including the chair in which John Adams died on July 4, 1826, the 50th anniversary of the Declaration of Independence (and, spookily, the same day that Thomas Jefferson died on his estate in Virginia). On the grounds, the spectacular two-story library and the lovely formal gardens are highlights.

UNITED FIRST PARISH CHURCH & HANCOCK CEMETERY
John and Abigail Adams and John Quincy and Louisa Catherine Adams are all interred in the basement of the handsome granite **United First Parish Church** (☎ 617-773-0062; www.ufpc.org; 1306 Hancock St; adult/child/senior & student $4/free/3; ☉ 9am-5pm mid-Apr–mid-Nov), in Quincy Center.

The church was built in 1828 by Alexander Parris, who was also responsible for designing Quincy Market (p83) in Boston.

Reverend John Hancock (father to the famous patriot) had been the preacher at the old wooden meeting house that previously stood on this spot. In 1822, John Adams established a fund to replace the wooden church with the fine granite structure that stands today.

Across the street, **Hancock Cemetery** is the final resting place of many notable Quincy residents, including most of the Quincy and Adams families. The Adams family vault, near the street, was the original site of the graves of the presidents and their wives, before they were interred in the Presidential Crypt. A map to Hancock Cemetery is available at the United First Parish Church.

QUINCY HISTORICAL SOCIETY
While Quincy is famous as the birthplace of John Adams, it is less known that it is the birthplace of John Hancock. On the site of the Hancock house now stands the building of the former Adams Academy, also founded by the Adams fund. The gothic revival building houses the **Quincy Historical Society** (☎ 617-773-1144; www.quincyhistory.org; 8 Adams St; adult/child/senior & student $3/free/1.50; ☉ 9am-4pm Mon-Fri year-round, noon-3pm Sat mid-Apr–mid-Nov). Exhibits address Native American history, economic development

related to shipbuilding and granite production and other famous Quincy families.

Sleeping

Presidents City Inn (☎ 617-479-6500; www.presidentscity motel.com; 845 Hancock St; d $85-100) The old saying rings true: you get what you pay for. This place is cheap and convenient, but don't expect anything beyond the basics. About a mile north of Quincy Center and a half-mile from the Wallaston T-stop, this traditional roadside motor inn is an affordable alternative to staying in Boston. It has 36 straightforward rooms, some with kitchen appliances.

Adams Inn (☎ 617-328-1500; www.bwadamsinn .com; 29 Hancock St; d $119; 🏊) This Best Western property enjoys a pleasant waterside location on the south side of the Neponset Bridge (about three miles from Quincy Center). That means easy access to the Riverwalk, which offers trails for jogging and strolling. Rooms are innocuous, but comfortable. Look for perks like free local calls, complimentary breakfast, and transportation to Logan International Airport.

Eating & Drinking

Craig's Cafe (☎ 617-770-9271; 1354 Hancock St; meals $8-10; 🕑 6am-4pm) Perfect for a light lunch or a packed picnic, this simple café serves soups, salads and sandwiches with a smile. Folks behind the counter seem to know most of the patrons by name.

Little Q Hot Pot (☎ 617-773-5888; 1585 Hancock St; meals $20-25) If you are longing for something exotic in all-American Quincy, stop by to try Mongolian hot pots. This healthy, do-it-yourself restaurant lets you pick out your ingredients – meats, veggies and noodles – to cook in a seasoned broth.

There are no shortage of pubs around Quincy Center, including **The Four's** (☎ 617-471-4447; 15 Cottage Ave), the **Half Door** (☎ 617-472-8600; 1516 Hancock St) and **Bad Abbots** (☎ 617-774-1434; 1546 Hancock St). Bad Abbots is the best for pub grub, while the Half Door gets kudos for live music and outdoor seating.

Getting There & Away

The easiest way to reach the Adams National Historic Park from Boston is to take the Red Line to Quincy Center (Braintree line). The **MBTA Harbor Express** (☎ 617-222-6999; www.harborex press.com) also operates a high-speed catamaran that travels between Long Wharf in Boston

and Quincy Terminal (adult/child/senior $6/ free/3, 90 minutes, every half-hour).

If you are traveling by car, drive south from Boston on I-93 to exit 12 and follow the signs over the Neponset Bridge. Take Hancock St into Quincy Center.

PLYMOUTH
pop 51,700

Plymouth calls itself 'America's Home Town.' It was here that the Pilgrims first settled in the winter of 1620, seeking a place where they could practice their religion as they wished, without interference from government. An innocuous, weathered ball of granite – the famous Plymouth Rock – marks the spot where they first stepped ashore in this foreign land, and many museums and historic houses in the surrounding streets recall their struggles, sacrifices and triumphs.

Orientation & Information

'The rock,' on the waterfront, is on Water St at the center of Plymouth, within walking distance of most museums and restaurants. Main St, the main commercial street, is a block inland. Some lodgings are within walking distance, but most require a car.

Destination Plymouth (☎ 508-747-7533; www.visit-plymouth.com; 170 Water St; 🕑 9am-5pm Apr-Nov, 9am-8pm Jun-Aug) Located at the rotary across from Plymouth Harbor; provides assistance with B&B reservations.

Eastern Bank (☎ 508-746-3600; 36 Main St; 🕑 8am-3pm Mon-Wed, 8am-5pm Thu-Fri, 8:30am-noon Sat) Has a 24-hour ATM.

Plymouth Guide Online (www.plymouthguide.com) Lots of information about tourist attractions and local events.

Post Office (6 Main St; 🕑 8:30am-5pm Mon-Fri, 8:30am-noon Sat)

Yankee Book & Art Gallery (☎ 508-747-2691; 10 North St; 🕑 11am-5pm Mon-Sat, noon-4pm Sun) Offers a selection of books on Pilgrim history.

Sights & Activities
PLYMOUTH ROCK

We don't really know that the Pilgrims landed on Plymouth Rock; it's not mentioned in any early written accounts. But the story gained popularity during colonial times. In 1774, 20 yoke of oxen were harnessed to the rock to move it – splitting the rock in the process. Half of the cloven boulder went on display in Pilgrim Hall from 1834 to 1867. The sea and wind lashed at the other half,

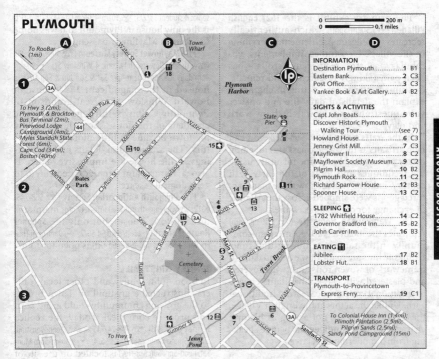

PLYMOUTH

INFORMATION	
Destination Plymouth	**1** B1
Eastern Bank	**2** C3
Post Office	**3** C3
Yankee Book & Art Gallery	**4** B2

SIGHTS & ACTIVITIES	
Capt John Boats	**5** B1
Discover Historic Plymouth	
Walking Tour	(see 7)
Howland House	**6** C3
Jenney Grist Mill	**7** C3
Mayflower II	**8** C2
Mayflower Society Museum	**9** C2
Pilgrim Hall	**10** B2
Plymouth Rock	**11** C2
Richard Sparrow House	**12** B3
Spooner House	**13** C2

SLEEPING	
1782 Whitfield House	**14** C2
Governor Bradford Inn	**15** B2
John Carver Inn	**16** B3

EATING	
Jubilee	**17** B2
Lobster Hut	**18** B1

TRANSPORT	
Plymouth-to-Provincetown	
Express Ferry	**19** C1

and innumerable small pieces were chipped off and carried away by souvenir hunters over the centuries.

By the 20th century the rock was an endangered artifact, and steps were taken to protect it. In 1921 the reunited halves were sheltered in the present granite enclosure. In 1989 the rock was repaired and strengthened to withstand weathering. And so it stands today, relatively small, broken and mended, an enduring symbol of the quest for religious freedom.

MAYFLOWER II

Plymouth Rock reveals little about the Pilgrims' journey and arrival, but **Mayflower II** (☎ 508-746-1622; www.plimoth.org; State Pier; adult/child/ senior $8/6/7; ☼ 9am-5pm Apr-Nov) offers incredible insights. It is a replica of the small ship in which they made the fateful voyage. Actors in period costume are often on board, recounting harrowing tales from the journey.

As you climb aboard, you have to wonder how 102 people – with all the household effects, tools, provisions, animals and seed to establish a colony – could have lived together on this tiny vessel for 66 days, subsisting on hard, moldy biscuits, rancid butter and brackish water as the ship passed through the stormy north Atlantic waters. But they did, landing on this wild, forested shore in the frigid months of December 1620 – testimony to their courageous spirit and the strength of their religious beliefs.

A combined ticket to Mayflower II and Plimoth Plantation is available for adult/ child/senior $25/15/22 and is valid on two consecutive days.

PLIMOTH PLANTATION

During the winter of 1620–21, half of the Pilgrims died of disease, privation and exposure to the elements. But new arrivals joined the survivors the following year; and by 1627 – just before an additional influx of Pilgrims founded the colony of Massachusetts Bay – Plymouth Colony was on the road to prosperity. **Plimoth Plantation** (☎ 508-746-1622; www.plimoth.org; MA 3A; adult/child/ senior $21/12/19; ☼ 9am-5:30pm Apr-Nov) provides excellent educational and entertaining insight into what was happening in Plymouth during that period.

The primary exhibit is the **1627 English Village** (🕙 9:30am-5pm), which authentically recreates the Pilgrims' settlement. Everything in the village – costumes, implements, vocabulary, artistry, recipes and crops – has been painstakingly researched and remade. Costumed interpreters, acting in character, explain the details of daily life and answer your questions as you watch them work and play.

In the **crafts center** (🕙 9:15am-5pm), you can help artisans as they weave baskets and cloth, throw pottery and build fine furniture using the techniques and tools of the early 17th century. Exhibits explain how these manufactured goods were shipped across the Atlantic in exchange for colonial necessities.

The **Wampanoag Homesite** (🕙 9:30am-5pm) replicates the life of a Native American community in the same area during that time. Homesite huts are made of wattle and daub (a framework of woven rods and twigs covered and plastered with clay); inhabitants engage in traditional crafts while wearing traditional garb. Unlike the actors at the English Village, these individuals are not acting as historic characters, but are indigenous people speaking from a modern perspective.

PILGRIM HALL
Claiming to be the oldest continually operating public museum in the country, **Pilgrim Hall** (☎ 508-746-1620; www.pilgrimhall.org; 75 Court St; adult/child/senior $6/3/5; 🕙 9:30am-4:30pm Feb-Dec) was founded in 1824. Its exhibits are not reproductions, but the real things the Pilgrims and their Wampanoag neighbors used in their daily lives, from Governor Bradford's journal to Constance Hopkins' beaver hat to Myles Standish's rapier. Monumental paintings in the museum's collection depict scenes of everyday Pilgrim life.

HISTORIC HOUSES
As New England's oldest European community, Plymouth has its share of fine old houses, some very old indeed. The oldest is the **Richard Sparrow House** (☎ 508-747-1240; www.sparrowhouse.com; 42 Summer St; adult/child $2/1; 🕙 10am-5pm Thu-Tue), built by one of the original Pilgrim settlers in 1640. Today the house contains a gallery that exhibits interesting art by local artists.

The 1667 **Howland House** (☎ 508-746-9590; www.pilgrimjohnhowlandsociety.org; 33 Sandwich Ave; adult/child/

senior & student $4/2/3; 🕙 10am-4:30pm late May–mid-Oct) is the only house in Plymouth that was home to a known Mayflower passenger.

The **Mayflower Society Museum** (☎ 508-746-2590; www.themayflowersociety.com; 4 Winslow St; 🕙 10am-4pm daily Jul-Aug, 10am-4pm Sat & Sun Jun & Sep-Oct) is housed in the magnificent 1754 house of Edward Winslow, the great-grandson of Plymouth Colony's third governor. The grandeur of the house shows how wealthy the town became in little more than a century. The architectural details and furnishings in the house are impressive. There is also a library and archives dedicated to genealogical research.

The **Plymouth Antiquarian Society** (☎ 508-746-0012; www.plymouthantiquariansociety.org) maintains three historic houses, but only the **Spooner House** (27 North St; adult/child $4.50/2; 🕙 9am-6pm Thu-Fri, 9am-noon Sat mid-Jun–mid-Oct) is open for tours.

JENNEY GRIST MILL
In 1636, John Jenney and other local leaders constructed a gristmill on Town Brook, so the growing community could grind corn and produce corn meal. Today, the replica **Jenney Grist Mill** (☎ 508-747-4544; www.jenneygristmill.org; 6 Spring Lane; adult/child $6/4; 🕙 9:30am-5pm Mon-Sat, noon-5pm Sun Apr-Nov) is located on the site of the original gristmill, still grinding corn the old-fashioned way. Tours of the gristmill tell the Jenney family's story and demonstrate the process of grinding whole corn into corn meal.

MYLES STANDISH STATE FOREST
About six miles south of Plymouth, this 16,000-acre **park** (☎ 508-866-252; Cranberry Rd, South Carver) is the largest public recreation area in southeastern Massachusetts. It contains 15 miles of biking and hiking trails and 16 ponds – two with beaches. It's a wonderful wilderness for picnicking, fishing, swimming and camping.

Tours
Capt John Boats (☎ 508-746-2643, 800-242-2469; www.captjohn.com; Town Wharf; 🕙 tours Apr-Oct) Offers loads of options to get you out on the water: whale-watching and 'floating classroom' cruises (adult/child/senior $37/25/33); all-day fishing trips (two-day package $200); and harbor cruises (adult/child/senior from $14/10/12). All tours are offered at least once daily in summer.
Discover Historic Plymouth Walking Tour (☎ 508-747-4544; www.jenneygristmill.org; 6 Spring

Lane; adult/child $10/8; ✆ 10am & 5pm) The miller from Jenney Grist Mill (in costume and in character) leads this one-hour tour of historic Plymouth, including Plymouth Rock, the Burial Ground, and the sites of many original Pilgrim buildings.

Sleeping

Pinewood Lodge Campground (☎ 508-746-3548; www .pinewoodlodge.com; 190 Pinewood Rd; sites without/with electricity $31/33, cabins $94-122; ✆ May-Oct) Off US 44 in Plymouth, this campground offers 300 shady campsites, yet it is among the closest to the town center. It's located on a freshwater lake, which is ideal for fishing and swimming. There are also cozy lakeside log cabins available for rental.

Sandy Pond Campground (☎ 508-759-9336; www .sandypond.com; 834 Bourne Rd; sites without/with electricity $32/35; ✆ mid-Apr–Sep) This establishment has 80 campsites with water and electricity (25 for tents), two sandy beaches and hiking trails. From Boston take MA 3 south to exit 3, bear right, then turn left onto Long Pond Rd and follow signs.

Governor Bradford Inn (☎ 508-746-6200, 800-332-1620; www.governorbradford.com; 98 Water St; d $109-145; 🐾) Named for William Bradford, the second governor of Plymouth Colony and author of the primary historical reference about the Pilgrims, *Of Plimoth Plantation*. This inn does not have much historical value, but it's conveniently located smack-dab in the middle of town. Ninety-four rooms are fully equipped with the necessities, while the more expensive rooms enjoy harbor views.

1782 Whitfield House (☎ 508-747-6735; www .whitfieldhouse.com; 26 North St; r $120, ste $170-220) This gracious Federal house is in the heart of historic Plymouth. It has only four rooms – each uniquely decorated with the utmost attention to detail. Whether it's a working fireplace, a four-poster bed or hand-stenciled wall paintings, you're bound to find something that charms you. An elegant living room and dining room and shady deck are all accessible to guests. Breakfast included.

Colonial House Inn (☎ 508-747-4274; 207 Sandwich St; www.thecolonialhouseinn.com; d $125-150) About a mile south of Plymouth center, this pleasant house has five guestrooms and one loft apartment, all of which are spacious and comfortable with a hint of elegance. The setting is pleasant for its views of the inner harbor and its location across from the salt marshes. This is the sister property of Pilgrim Sands, so guests

have access to the resort's private beach and swimming pool.

Pilgrim Sands (☎ 508-747-0900, 800-729-7263; www .pilgrimsands.com; 150 Warren Ave; d $155-195, apt $309; 🐾) This mini resort is a good option for families as it's right on a private beach and directly opposite Plimoth Plantation. Rooms with an ocean view are slightly pricier, but the other rooms look out over Plimoth Plantation, which has its own charm. Rates decrease outside of summer months.

John Carver Inn (☎ 508-746-7100, 800-274-1620; www.johncarverinn.com; 25 Summer St; d from $159; 🐾) This 85-room inn is a boon for families: special packages allow kids to stay for free and include entry to local sights. Best of all, the indoor Pilgrim-theme swimming pool (complete with a *Mayflower* replica!) will keep your little ones entertained for hours. All rooms feature tasteful, traditional colonial decor, while the fancier ones boast four-poster beds and fireplaces.

Eating

Fast-food shops line Water St opposite the *Mayflower II*. For better food at lower prices, walk a block inland to Main St, the attractive thoroughfare of Plymouth's business district, where restaurants are open year-round.

Jubilee (☎ 508-747-3700; 22 Court St; meals $8-15; ✆ lunch & dinner) Soups, salads, pastas and mains with international panache attract a stream of regular customers for lunch and dinner. Look for weekly specials, signature sandwiches and friendly service.

Lobster Hut (☎ 508-746-2270; Town Wharf; meals $10-20; ✆ lunch & dinner) Right on the town wharf, five short blocks north of *Mayflower II*, the seaside Lobster Hut has big plates of fried clams, fish-and-chips, and – of course – lobster salad, fried lobster tail, boiled lobsters etc. There is seating inside, but it's much more enjoyable to take a place on the deck and catch a harbor breeze.

Roobar (☎ 508-746-4300; 10 Cordage Park Circle; meals $25-40; ✆ 4pm-1am) Part of a chain of trendy restaurants that has opened on the South Shore, Roobar defies almost all expectations of dining in Plymouth. You can still get seafood, but it's served in innovative ways: shrimp and sea scallops in a coconut curry broth; pan-seared halibut served with a modern version of succotash. Pizzas and pastas round out the American menu. The atmosphere is hip, happening and definitely noisy.

AROUND BOSTON

Getting There & Away

Plymouth is 41 miles south of Boston via MA 3; it takes an hour with some traffic. From Providence, it's the same distance and time, but you'll want to head west on US 44.

Buses operated by **Plymouth & Brockton** (☎ 508-746-0378, 508-778-9767; www.p-b.com; adult/child $12/6) travel hourly to South Station or Logan International Airport in Boston. Heading south, these buses continue as far as Provincetown. The Plymouth P&B terminal is at the commuter parking lot, exit 5 off MA 3. From there catch a Plymouth Area Link (PAL) bus to the center of town, about 2 miles away.

You can reach Plymouth from Boston by **MBTA commuter rail** (☎ 617-222-3200, 800-392-6100; www.mbta.com) trains, which depart from South Station three or four times a day ($7.75). From the station at Cordage Park, GATRA buses connect to Plymouth center.

Operated by the ubiquitous Capt John, the **Plymouth-to-Provincetown Express Ferry** (☎ 508-747-2400, 800-242-2469; www.captjohn.com; State Pier; adult/one-way/child/senior $37/22/27/32) deposits you on the tip of the Cape faster than a car would. From July to August, the 90-minute journey departs Plymouth at 10am and leaves Provincetown at 4:30pm. It operates Saturday and Sunday only from May to June and September.

Getting Around

The **Plymouth Area Link** (PAL; ☎ 508-747-1819; www.gatra.org; adult/child $1/0.50) links the P&B bus terminal, Plymouth station at Cordage Park and Plymouth center. Passengers can flag down a bus from anywhere on the route.

NEW BEDFORD

pop 93,700

During its heyday as a whaling port (1765–1860), New Bedford commanded as many as 400 whaling ships. This vast fleet brought home hundreds of thousands of barrels of whale oil for lighting America's lamps. Novelist Herman Melville worked on one of these ships for four years, and thus set his celebrated novel, *Moby-Dick; or, The Whale,* in New Bedford.

When petroleum and electricity supplanted whale oil, New Bedford turned to fishing, scalloping and textile production for its wealth. In recent years the New Bedford economy has floundered and parts of the city are pretty run-down. But the city center has its charms: cobblestone streets and gas lanterns recall the romance of the 19th century, while the National Historical Park designation commemorates the whaling heritage.

Orientation & Information

Downtown New Bedford is formed by grid-patterned streets stretching west from the State Pier and Fisherman's Wharf. The main streets are Union St and William St, running from east to west. Most of the museums and restaurants are around and between these pillars, within a few blocks of the waterfront.

New Bedford Office of Tourism (☎ 508-979-1745, 800-508-5353; www.newbedfordtourism.com; Wharfinger Bldg, Pier 3; ☼ 9am-5pm Mon-Fri, 10am-4pm Sat & Sun) Provides general information, including lodging and events. Pick up a self-guided brochure for the 'dock walk,' which orients you with the working harbor.

New Bedford Whaling National Historical Park Visitor Center (☎ 508-996-4095; www.nps.gov/nebe; 33 William St; ☼ 9am-5pm) Offers free walking tours three times a day in July and August. Or pick up a map of *Herman Melville's New Bedford.*

Sights & Activities

NEW BEDFORD WHALING NATIONAL HISTORICAL PARK

A 66ft skeleton of a blue whale and a smaller skeleton of a sperm whale welcome you to the **New Bedford Whaling Museum** (☎ 508-997-0046; www.whalingmuseum.org; 18 Johnny Cake Hill; adult/child/senior & student $10/6/9; ☼ 9am-5pm). This excellent, hands-on museum occupies seven buildings situated between William and Union Sts. To learn what whaling was all about, you need only tramp the decks of the *Lagoda,* a fully rigged, half-size replica of an actual whaling bark. The onboard tryworks (a brick furnace where try-pots are placed) converted huge chunks of whale blubber into valuable oil. Old photographs and a 22-minute video of an actual whale chase bring this historic period to life. Exhibits of delicate scrimshaw, and the carving of whalebone into jewelry, knick-knacks and beautiful household items, are also impressive.

The small chapel called **Seamen's Bethel** (☎ 508-992-3295; 15 Johnny Cake Hill; admission free, donations accepted; ☼ 10am-5pm Mon-Fri late May–mid-Oct), across from the Whaling Museum, was a refuge for sailors from the rigors and stresses of maritime life. Melville immortalized it in *Moby-Dick.* 'In this same New Bedford there stands a Whaleman's Chapel, and few are the moody fishermen… who fail to make a Sunday visit to the spot.'

ROTCH-JONES-DUFF HOUSE & GARDEN MUSEUM

New Bedford's grandest **historic house** (☎ 508-997-1401; www.rjdmuseum.org; 396 County St; adult/child/senior & student $5/2/4; ☽ 10am-4pm Mon-Sat, noon-4pm Sun) was designed in Greek revival style by Richard Upjohn (1802–78), first president of the American Institute of Architects. Occupying an entire city block, it was built for whaling merchant William Rotch Jr in 1834 and owned by three prominent families in the following 150 years. The house contains the furniture and trinkets of these families, tracing the progression of the house's history through the years. The grounds are absolutely lovely landscaped gardens, and include the irresistible Woodland Walk.

OTHER MUSEUMS

Antique fire trucks and fire-fighting equipment fill the 1867 firehouse known as Old Station No 4, which houses the **New Bedford Fire Museum** (☎ 508-992-2162; 51 Bedford St; adult/child $4/2; ☽ 9am-4pm Mon-Sat Jul-early Sep; ♿). It appeals to children, who love the old trucks, uniforms, pumps and fire poles.

The **New Bedford Art Museum** (☎ 508-961-3071; www.newbedfordartmuseum.org; 608 Pleasant St; adult/senior & student $3/2; ☽ noon-5pm Wed-Sun) is located at City Hall Sq. Rotating exhibits feature regional artists. The space is also used to exhibit whaling artifacts and Quaker pieces from the vast 19th-century collections of the **New Bedford Free Public Library** (☎ 508-991-6275; 613 Main St).

Festivals & Events

Feast of the Blessed Sacrament (www.portuguesefeast.com) In 1915, four Madeiran immigrants wanted to recreate the feasts that were celebrated in the country they left behind. Since then, this four-day feast on the first weekend in August has grown to be the largest Portuguese feast in the country.

Moby Dick: The Marathon (☎ 508-997-0046; www.whalingmuseum.org) A non-stop reading of the Melville classic takes place at the Whaling Museum every year on January 3. The reading commemorates the anniversary of the departure from New Bedford port of Melville's ship *Acushnet*. It starts at noon and takes about 25 hours, but you don't have to stay for the whole thing.

Whaling City Festival (☎ 508-996-3348; www.whalingcityfestival.com) This classic civic fair features amusement-park rides, food vendors, crafts and flea markets and continuous entertainment. Second weekend in July.

Sleeping

Historic New Bedford is not thick with lodging possibilities, save a few B&Bs. The New Bedford Office of Tourism can direct you to places to stay in the surrounding area.

New Bedford Days Inn (☎ 508-997-1231; 500 Hathaway Rd; r $70-100) About three miles from New Bedford's historic center, this chain hotel has the same facilities and amenities that can be found at Days Inns across the country. You know that rooms are clean and comfortable enough, but nothing fancy.

our pick **Melville House** (☎ 508-990-1566; www.melvillehouse.net; 100 Madison St; d $100-150) Herman Melville often visited his sister at this 1855 Victorian manse. Of the three guest rooms, the aptly named Herman Melville room evokes the author's memory with a penetrating portrait. A gourmet continental breakfast is served in the solarium.

Captain Haskell's Octagon House (☎ 508-999-3933; www.theoctagonhouse.com; 347 Union St; r $110-125 May-Oct) Back in the day, octagonal houses were considered to enhance health, happiness and sexual harmony. Here is your chance to check it out! This architectural oddity was built in 1847, and many original architectural details remain. Three guest rooms feature private baths with claw-foot tubs, walnut and wicker furniture, and lots of antiques. All of the rooms are slightly off in terms of shape, an endearing feature of the octagonal construction.

Orchard St Manor (☎ 508-984-3475; www.the-orchard-street-manor.com; 139 Orchard St; r $125, ste $165-250) Handmade quilts, antique furniture and private bathrooms grace every room of this elegant Georgian revival home. Besides the formal parlor, guests can also partake of a billiards room and a 'gathering room.' A homemade breakfast is served in the chestnut-paneled dining room.

Eating

Café Arpeggio (☎ 508-999-2233; 800 Purchase St; meals $6-10; ☽ 7am-8pm Mon-Fri, 8am-5pm Sat; **V**) For a quick lunch or an afternoon coffee break, stop in at this friendly café that offers a whole slew of sandwiches, with many options for vegetarians and meat-lovers alike. Either way, save room for one of the 'Splits & Sundaes' featuring locally made ice cream.

Freestone's City Grille (☎ 508-993-7477; 41 Williams St; meals $8-20; ☽ lunch & dinner) Freestone's offers 'Gay Nineties' ambiance in a reclaimed bank building, complete with a stained-glass mirror

AROUND BOSTON

LIZZIE BORDEN

Lizzie Borden took an axe
And gave her mother forty whacks.
And when she saw what she had done
She gave her father forty-one.

This children's rhyme is just one of many inconsistencies in the account of what happened in Fall River on the night of 1892. Actually, Abby Borden was assaulted with 18 blows to the head with a hatchet, while Andrew Borden received 11. Ouch. Although Lizzie Borden was acquitted of this crime, her story was rife with contradictions. That nobody else was ever accused was enough indication for Lizzie Borden to go down in popular history as America's most famous murderess.

Today, the Greek Revival Borden House in Fall River is the **Lizzie Borden Bed & Breakfast** (☎ 508-675-7333; www.lizzie-borden.com; 92 Second St; r $175-250). Decked out with period furnishings and decor, the eight rooms are named for the family members that actually stayed there. It's artfully and accurately remodeled, which makes it all the creepier. If you don't care to spend the night in the room where Abby Borden was found murdered, you can just come for a **tour** (adult/child/senior $10/5/8; 🕒 11am-3pm).

and a brass monkey. Modern American fare shows hints of Asian influence, especially in the specialty salads. This place is opposite the National Historical Park visitor center, so it's easy to find.

Candleworks (☎ 508-997-1294; 72 N Water St; meals $12-40; 🕒 lunch & dinner) In a restored brick candle factory, this chic restaurant is about as good as it gets in New Bedford. You can eat in the cool cellar or under the umbrellas on the patio: either way the setting is luxurious. Italian dishes have a modern, New England flair (lots of seafood). Live piano music fills the air in the evenings.

Getting There & Away

The heart of the old city center is the restored historic district around Melville Mall. The area is about a mile south of I-195 via MA 18 (take the downtown exit 18S).

Peter Pan Bus (☎ 888-751-8800; www.peterpanbus.com) offers bus services to Providence ($10.50) and New York ($43) from the New Bedford ferry dock. **Dattco** (☎ 800-229-4879; www.dattco.com) runs 12 buses a day to Boston South Station (adult/child $12/8) from the Southeastern Regional Transit Authority (SRTA) station at the corner of Elm and Pleasant Sts.

Ferries run from the New Bedford ferry dock to Vineyard Haven and Oak Bluffs on Martha's Vineyard. A catamaran makes the quick trip in one hour with **Martha's Vineyard Express Ferry** (☎ 866-663-3779; www.mvexpressferry.com) from 6:30am to 9:30pm (one way adult/bike/child/senior $29/5/15/25). Five ferries run in from mid-May to mid-October, more in summer. From I-195, take exit 15 to MA 18. Continue south on MA 18 to the fourth set of lights, turn left onto State Pier.

FALL RIVER

'You sank my battleship!' This cry was ne'er heard aboard the mighty USS *Massachusetts,* a hulk of a craft that survived 35 battles in WWII, gunning down almost 40 aircraft and never losing a man in combat. Today, this heroic ship sits in a quiet corner of Mt Hope Bay known as **Battleship Cove** (☎ 508-678-1100, 800-533-3194; www.battleshipcove.com; 1 Water St; adult/child/senior $14/8/12; 🕒 9am-5pm). This beaut – longer than two football fields and taller than a nine-storey building – is only one of eight historic ships that visitors can explore at Battleship Cove. The USS *Joseph P Kennedy Jr,* named for President John F Kennedy's older brother, did battle in the Korean and Vietnam Wars and is now a museum. The USS *Lionfish* is a WWII submarine still in full working condition. There are also two Patrol Torpedo (PT) boats, a landing craft, a Japanese attack boat and other craft.

Just past the battleship, the **Marine Museum** (☎ 508-674-3533; 70 Water St; adult/child & senior $5/4; 🕒 9am-5pm Mon-Sat, 9am-4pm Sun) has an extensive display of intricate ship models, including a scale model of the *Titanic* that was used in the 1950s movie on the subject.

Fall River is about 50 miles south of Boston. Take I-93 south to Route 24, then merge onto Route 79. Otherwise it's 17 miles southeast of Providence on I-195.

Cape Cod, Nantucket & Martha's Vineyard

When the weather warms up, all eyes turn toward the Cape and Islands, the top beach destination in the Northeast. Think seaside cottages, children building sandcastles and sailboats at sunset. Cape Cod, Nantucket and Martha's Vineyard are ideal places to kick off your shoes and unwind. Once you've battled the traffic to get here, slow down, poke around, stumble into the good stuff. Feel the sand between your toes, dip a paddle into a stream or cool off with an afternoon swim.

Sound too tame? Well, it's not the big city, but there's plenty of action if you know where to look. Never been splashed by a 40-ton leviathan shooting straight up out of the ocean? Whale-watching is a must for you. Hit the waves at Cape Cod National Seashore or party the night away in the carnival streets of Provincetown. For foodies the scene just keeps getting better. Yes, there are great clam shacks, but one needn't live solely on fried food and lobster rolls. Top-notch chefs have been hanging out their shingles all around the region, whipping up innovative masterpieces with fresh-off-the-boat seafood.

Naturally, in this trio of summer vacationlands each destination has its own personality. Nantucket has perfected the art of catering to wealthy urbanites while keeping intact its *Moby Dick*–era village center. Martha's Vineyard revels in diversity from its carousel-bedecked ferryport to its genteel towns. The Cape has something for every taste. The beaches, hiking trails and bike paths in the National Seashore alone could take your whole holiday. Spread the net wider and the possibilities are endless – take in the theater scene, prowl the pubs, get lost in the dunes. You could spend a summer here and just scratch the surface.

HIGHLIGHTS

- Pulling up for a double-feature dose of nostalgia at **Wellfleet Drive-In** (see boxed text, p200)
- Ogling breaching humpbacks from the deck of a **whale-watching boat** (p205 and p180)
- Pedaling to your own swimming hole on the **Cape Cod Rail Trail** (see boxed text, p188)
- Clawing your way to the best **lobster roll** (p197)
- Exploring the cobbled streets of **Nantucket** (p209)
- Clambering across the dunes at **Cape Cod National Seashore** (see boxed text, p196)

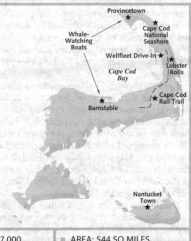

Provincetown

Whale-Watching Boats

Cape Cod National Seashore

Wellfleet Drive-In

Cape Cod Bay

Lobster Rolls

Cape Cod Rail Trail

Barnstable

Nantucket Town

| TELEPHONE CODE: 508 | POPULATION: 247,000 | AREA: 544 SQ MILES |

Orientation & Information

Cape Cod is separated from the Massachusetts mainland by the Cape Cod Canal. Two bridges span the canal – take the Bourne Bridge if you're going to Falmouth, the Sagamore Bridge to reach most other Cape destinations.

US 6, also known as the Mid-Cape Hwy, is the main west–east route across the Cape and the speediest way to get between towns. It's a four-lane highway between the Sagamore Bridge and Dennis, but peters down to two lanes as it continues on to Provincetown.

MA 28 connects the Bourne Bridge with Falmouth then veers east to run along the Cape's south shore all the way to Chatham. MA 28 is just two lanes and congested with local traffic, stop lights and strip malls. MA 6A, which runs along the north side of the Cape between Sandwich and Orleans, is also just two lanes, but delightfully scenic with lots of antique shops and small villages en route.

On Martha's Vineyard the roads are narrow but major intersections are well marked. On Nantucket, there simply aren't many roads and it would take some effort to get lost!

The **Cape Cod Chamber of Commerce** (☎ 508-362-3225, 888-332-2732; www.capecodchamber.org; US 6 at MA 132, Hyannis; ⏰ 8:30am-5pm Mon-Fri, 9am-5pm Sat, also 10am-2pm Sun in summer) provides Cape-wide information.

History

At the time of first contact with Europeans, the Cape and islands were inhabited by native people of the Wampanoag tribe. Despite skirmishes with European settlers and the eventual loss of most of their ancestral land, the Wampanoag survived as a tribe and still have a significant presence on Martha's Vineyard and Cape Cod.

English explorer Bartholomew Gosnold sailed along the Cape. Impressed by the abundant cod he saw in the surrounding waters, he named the peninsula Cape Cod. He also passed an island with abundant grape vines, which he named after his daughter Martha. In 1620 the *Mayflower* Pilgrims landed on the outer tip of Cape Cod, at what today is Provincetown, and stayed several weeks before heading on to Plymouth.

During the golden age of whaling (1750–1850) Nantucket reigned as the whaling capital of the world. Its whaling fleets and spermaceti oil factories made the island flush with riches. Nantucket's ships, which voyaged to far corners of the Pacific, were largely captained by men from Martha's Vineyard. The stately old homes that line the streets of Nantucket and Edgartown today are a legacy of that era.

The Culture

People from the Cape and Islands take pride in their regional character. Even on the Cape, people tend to see themselves as separate from other New Englanders. The pace is slower. Folks take the time to chat with neighbors, go fishing and unwind on a quiet trail. The islands take it a step further. Virtual worlds unto themselves, they're inundated with visitors in summer but insular the rest of the year. Nantucketers and Vineyarders have been known to refer to the mainland simply as 'America.' Of course you will notice qualities common with the rest of New England – to see the old Yankee work ethic in action just head down to the port and watch the fishing crews unload their catch.

Land & Climate

Nineteenth-century naturalist Henry David Thoreau referred to the Cape as 'the bared and bended arm of Massachusetts'. That indeed is its shape, with halfway-point Chatham at the elbow and Provincetown, at the end, the balled-up fist. It is surrounded by water on all sides and abounds in sandy beaches. Forget mountains – the Cape and Islands have a few modest hills, but the region is largely flat, and its edges are comprised mainly of sand dunes, salt marshes and tidal flats.

The Cape and Islands are at their peak in summer, and if you want a day at the beach this is the time to come. The weather's generally good, sunny more often than not, but sometimes humid with rainy patches. Spring and fall can also be excellent times to visit, although temperatures can be unpredictable. Winter is generally left to the locals.

Parks & Wildlife

The Cape's shining gem is the Cape Cod National Seashore (see boxed text, p196), 44,600 acres of rolling dunes and magnificent beaches that stretches along the Outer Cape from Eastham all the way to Provincetown. Explore it by foot, bicycle or kayak but whatever you do, don't miss it. Also substantial is Nickerson State Park (p189) in Brewster,

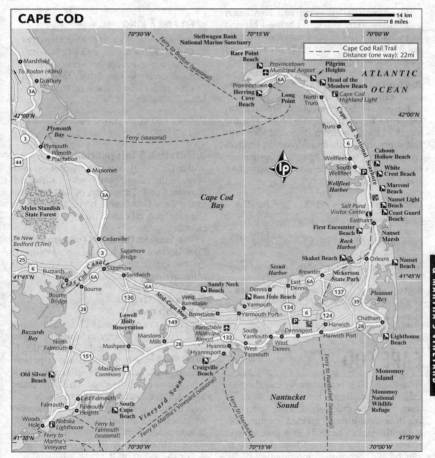

a 2000-acre forest filled with ponds and crisscrossed by wooded trails; it's the Cape's favorite campground.

Other notable sanctuaries include Monomoy National Wildlife Refuge (p192) off Chatham, Wellfleet Bay Wildlife Sanctuary (p198) in Wellfleet and Felix Neck Wildlife Sanctuary (p227) on Martha's Vineyard. These are three of the best places in the region for bird-watching.

The statewide nonprofit **Trustees of Reservations** (www.thetrustees.org) oversees some large tracts of land for historic and ecological preservation, including Cape Poge Wildlife Refuge (see Tours, p227) on Martha's Vineyard, and Coskata-Coatue Wildlife Refuge (p218) on Nantucket.

For wildlife look toward the sea. Hop on a whale-watching tour (p205) from Provincetown to get up close to frolicking humpback whales or head to the Chatham Fish Pier (p192) to spot seals basking in the sun at low tide.

Getting There & Around

You can get to Cape Cod by bus, air or boat but the vast majority of visitors arrive by car. Year-round car and passenger ferries operate from Woods Hole to Martha's Vineyard and from Hyannis to Nantucket. There are also seasonal passenger-only ferries to the islands from several Cape ports, and seasonal passenger ferry service to Provincetown from Boston and Plymouth.

The Martha's Vineyard and Nantucket authorities prefer you don't bring a car and in exchange offer extensive visitor-friendly public bus systems that make it easy to get between towns and out to the main beaches. Cape Cod buses, however, are far more restricted and you'll need your own wheels to really explore the Cape thoroughly.

Buses of the **Plymouth & Brockton Bus Company** (☎ 508-746-0378; www.p-b.com) run the length of the Cape from Boston at least four times per day, with more frequent services from Boston to the Cape's transportation hub, Hyannis. Sample one-way fares and travel times from Boston:

Destination	Price	Duration
Harwich	$22	2½hr
Hyannis	$17	1½hr
Provincetown	$27	3½hr

Within the Cape, sample bus fares and times:

Route	Price	Duration
Hyannis–Provincetown	$10	80min
Hyannis–Wellfleet	$8	50min
Wellfleet–Provincetown	$4	30min

CAPE COD

'The Cape,' as it is universally called by locals, lures vacationers hot to romp along its more than 400 miles of sparkling shoreline. It's fringed with dune-studded beaches, dotted with fishing harbors and graced with scores of old sea captain's homes, many of which have been turned into inviting B&Bs.

Cape Codders use a somewhat confusing nomenclature for the Cape's regions. The 'Upper Cape' is nearest to the mainland and includes the towns of Sandwich, Falmouth and Mashpee. 'Mid-Cape' is the midregion, including Barnstable, Dennis and Yarmouth. The 'Lower Cape' generally refers to all points east of that. Also used is 'Outer Cape,' to refer to towns from Orleans north to Provincetown.

SANDWICH
pop 20,200

The Cape's oldest town (founded in 1637) makes a perfect first impression as you cross over the canal from the mainland. Head straight to the village center, where white-

---

steepled churches, period homes and a grist mill surround a swan-filled pond.

Orientation & Information

Water (MA 130), Main and Grove Sts converge in the village center, which surrounds Shawme Pond. Tupper Rd, off MA 6A, leads to the Cape Cod Canal. If you arrive on the Cape via US 6, take exit 2 (MA 130) and you're right in town.

The **Sandwich Chamber of Commerce** (☎ 508-833-9755; www.sandwichchamber.com; 4 Water St; ⏱ 10am-4pm) is at the Thornton W Burgess Museum (opposite).

Sights & Activities
CAPE COD CANAL

Cape Cod isn't connected by land to the mainland, but it's not exactly an island, or at least wasn't until the Cape Cod Canal was dug in 1914. The 7-mile-long canal saves ships from having to sail an extra 135 miles around the treacherous tip of the Cape. The canal is also a great recreational resource bordered on both sides by trails that attract cyclists, in-line skaters, power walkers and freckle-faced kids with fishing poles. On a sunny day it looks like a scene from a Norman Rockwell painting!

For the scoop on the how, what and why of the canal, stop by the **Cape Cod Canal Visitor Center** (☎ 508-833-9678; 60 Ed Moffitt Dr; admission free; ⏱ 10am-5pm), near the Sandwich Marina, where interactive exhibits will capture the interest of kids. Follow your visit with a 10-minute walk along the canal to the beach – unlike at other beaches, car parking here is free.

Ask at the center about its free programs offered throughout the summer, including guided hikes and bike rides, beach walks and talks.

SANDWICH BOARDWALK

One of the most scenic spots at this end of the Cape is the **Sandwich Boardwalk**, which extends 1350ft across a marsh to **Town Neck Beach**. It's excellent any time of the day and a real treat under the light of a full moon. The beach itself is a bit rocky – OK for sunbathing but great for walks and beachcombing. Once you reach the beach, turn right to make a 1.5-mile loop along the shoreline and creek back to the boardwalk. There's a $10 parking fee during the day in summer, but it's free at other times. To get there, take MA 6A to the center of Sandwich; turn north onto Jarves St at the lights and then bear left onto Boardwalk Rd.

HERITAGE MUSEUMS & GARDENS
Here is fun for kids and adults alike. The 76-acre **Heritage Museums & Gardens** (☎ 508-888-3300; www.heritagemuseumsandgardens.org; cnr Grove & Pine Sts; adult/child 6-16yr $12/6; ☽ 10am-5pm Apr-Oct, 10am-5pm Sat & Sun Nov-Dec; ☝) sports a terrific vintage automobile collection, an authentic 1912 carousel (rides free with admission), fascinating folk art collections and the Cape Cod Baseball League (see boxed text, p179) Hall of Fame. It also has one of the finest rhododendron gardens in America; the best viewing is from mid-May to mid-June when thousands of rhodies blaze with color.

SANDWICH GLASS MUSEUM
Sandwich glass, now prized by collectors, had its heyday in the 19th century and this heritage is artfully displayed in the **Sandwich Glass Museum** (☎ 508-888-0251; www.sandwichglassmuseum .org; 129 Main St; adult/child 6-14yr $4.75/1; ☽ 9:30am-5pm Apr-Dec, 9:30am-4pm Wed-Sun Feb-Mar). But don't think it's just a period glass collection – there are also glass-blowing demonstrations and a cool new contemporary gallery.

DEXTER GRIST MILL
This restored **mill** (☎ 508-888-5144; Water St; adult/child 5-12yr $3/2; ☽ 10am-5pm Mon-Sat, 1-5pm Sun mid-Jun–Sep) on the edge of Shawme Pond dates to 1654 and has centuries-old gears that still grind cornmeal. Bring a camera; with its spinning waterwheel and paddling swans this is one of the most photographed scenes on the Cape.

THORNTON W BURGESS MUSEUM
A treat for young kids is the tiny **Thornton W Burgess Museum** (☎ 508-888-4668; 4 Water St; suggested donation adult/child under 13yr $2/1; ☽ 10am-4pm Mon-Sat, 1-4pm Sun May-Oct; ☝), named for the Sandwich native who wrote the *Peter Cottontail* series. Storytime on the lawn, overlooking the pond featured in Burgess'

works, can be particularly evocative – call for times.

HOXIE HOUSE
Get a feel for what life was like for early settlers by touring **Hoxie House** (☎ 508-888-1173; 18 Water St; adult/child 5-12yr $3/2; ☽ 10am-5pm Mon-Sat, 1-5pm Sun mid-Jun–mid-Oct), the oldest house on Cape Cod (c 1640). The salt box–style house has been faithfully restored to the colonial period, complete with antiques, brick fire hearth and the like.

Sleeping
Shawme-Crowell State Forest (☎ 508-888-0351, 877-422-6762; www.reserveamerica.com; MA 130 near MA 6A; campsites $14; ☽ year-round) You'll find 285 cool and shady campsites (none with hookups) in this 760-acre pine and oak woodland. It's just one mile from the Cape Cod Canal and is popular with cyclists.

Shady Nook Inn (☎ 508-888-0409; www.shadynookinn .com; 14 MA 6A; r $70-120, 2-bedroom ste $180; ☒ ☒) And shady it is – in a good way, with lots of trees. This nicely landscaped place has 29 renovated rooms that are a cut above average. All have refrigerators and some feature full kitchens. The friendly owner bakes muffins for guests in the morning.

Belfry Inne & Bistro (☎ 508-888-8550, 800-844-4542; www.belfryinn.com; 8 Jarves St; r incl breakfast $115-275) Ever fall asleep in church? Then you'll love the rooms, some with stained-glass windows, in this creatively restored former church, now an upmarket B&B. If, on the other hand, you're uneasy about the Angel Gabriel watching over you in bed, Belfry also has two other nearby inns with conventional rooms.

Eating
Brown Jug (☎ 508-888-4669; 155 Main St; ☽ 10am-5pm Tue-Sat, noon-4pm Sun) A spiffy gourmet takeout shop, for when your picnic or romantic evening requires the likes of truffle mousse pâté, caviar, artisanal breads, world cheeses and, well, you get the picture…

Marshland Restaurant (☎ 508-888-9824; 109 MA 6A; meals $5-17; ☽ 6am-8:30pm) The busiest place in town for breakfast. The chef whips up 18 varieties of muffins every morning and all the usual waffle and egg dishes as well. Lunch and dinner feature old-fashioned comfort food like grilled-cheese sandwiches and meatloaf with gravy.

Seafood Sam's (☎ 508-888-4629; Coast Guard Rd; meals $9-19; ☻ 11am-8:30pm; ♿) Opposite the Cape Cod Canal Visitor Center, Sam's is a good family choice for fish and chips, fried clams and lobster rolls. Parents will love the $4 kids' menu. Dine at picnic tables and watch the fishing boats sail by.

Bee-Hive Tavern (☎ 508-833-1184; 406 MA 6A; meals $10-27; ☻ 11:30am-9pm Mon-Sat, 8:30am-9pm Sun) This honey of a place gets packed with locals who come for tasty food at honest prices. The menu is extensive, with everything from burgers and pasta to broiled stuffed lobster. Order from the nightly specials, which always include fresh seafood, and you can't go wrong.

Belfry Inne & Bistro (☎ 508-888-8550; 8 Jarves St; meals $23-34; ☻ dinner) If you like quirky, this restaurant occupying the sanctuary of a former church is one of the Cape's more unusual fine-dining restaurants. The food is first-rate New American cuisine, with a changing menu. Ask about the three-course $25 early dinner that features such enticements as crispy duck ravioli.

FALMOUTH
pop 32,680

A traditional New England village green, lovely beaches and the quaint seaside village of Woods Hole (see boxed text, p178) are the hallmarks of the Cape's second-largest town. Falmouth puffs with pride over its favorite daughter, Katharine Lee Bates, who wrote the words to the nation's favorite patriotic hymn, *America the Beautiful*.

Orientation & Information

Falmouth sits at the southwest corner of the Cape, bordered by Martha's Vineyard Sound to the south and Buzzards Bay to the west. From Sandwich, follow MA 28 south to the town center. Further east on MA 28, the Falmouth Heights area is known for water views, beachside activities and a ferry to Martha's Vineyard. Ferries also depart from Woods Hole.

Booksmith (☎ 508-540-6064; 33 Davis Straits) A good independent bookstore, in Falmouth Plaza off MA 28.

Falmouth Chamber of Commerce (☎ 508-548-8500, 800-526-8532; www.falmouthchamber.com; 20 Academy Lane; ☻ 8:30am-5pm Mon-Fri year-round, also 10am-4pm Sat Jun-Aug) Get brochures at this office, just off Main St.

Falmouth Hospital (☎ 508-548-5300; 100 Ter Heun Dr; ☻ 24hr) One of the Cape's two main hospitals; off MA 28, just north of town.

Falmouth Post Office (☎ 800-275-8777; 120 Main St)

Falmouth Public Library (☎ 508-457-2555; 123 Katharine Lee Bates Rd; ☻ 9:30am-5:30pm Mon, Thu & Fri, 9:30am-9pm Tue & Wed, 9:30am-5pm Sat) Allows 15 minutes free internet access to non-cardholders.

Sights & Activities

MUSEUMS ON THE GREEN

The Falmouth Historical Society's **museums** (☎ 508-548-4857; 55-65 Palmer Ave; adult/child under 13yr $5/free; ☻ 10am-4pm Tue-Fri, 10am-1pm Sat mid-Jun–early Oct) are clustered in the town center. **Julia Wood House** (1790) has an early-19th-century doctor's office, **Conant House** has a room dedicated to Katharine Lee Bates, and the **Hallett Barn** is full of old tools and farm implements. Docents are on hand to show you around.

NATURE RESERVES & GARDENS

The tranquil **Ashumet Holly Wildlife Sanctuary** (☎ 508-349-2615; MA 151, East Falmouth; adult/child under 15yr $3/2; ☻ dawn-dusk), a 45-acre Mass Audubon sanctuary, offers good birding along a 1.3-mile nature trail through holly trees and around a pond.

East Falmouth's **Waquoit Bay National Estuarine Research Reserve** (☎ 508-457-0495; MA 28; ☻ 10am-4pm Mon-Fri) contains 3000 acres of barrier beach and a fragile estuary. The visitors center has information on the reserve, picnic tables overlooking the harbor and a short trail.

BEACHES

Deeply indented Falmouth has 70 miles of coastline, none finer than **Old Silver Beach** (P $20), off MA 28A in North Falmouth. The town's most popular beach attracts scores of day-trippers and families, being long and sandy and well suited to kids with its shallow sections protected by sandbars. Facilities include changing rooms and a snack bar.

For a great beach on the sound side, head to **Menauhant Beach** (P $10), off Central Ave from MA 28. It's Falmouth's longest beach, with lots of room for everyone and warm waters that invite a plunge.

Surf Drive Beach (Surf Dr; P $10) is conveniently within walking distance of Main St, and has full facilities and a good view of Martha's Vineyard.

There are lifeguards on duty at all three beaches during the summer.

BIKING

The 3.5-mile **Shining Sea Bikeway** runs along the shoreline from Falmouth center to Woods Hole (see boxed text, p178), rewarding cyclists with fine views of Martha's Vineyard en route. **Corner Cycle** (☎ 508-540-4195; 115 Palmer Ave; rental per 8/24hr $15/20; ☺ 9am-6pm) rents bicycles near the start of the bike path.

Festivals & Events

Barnstable County Fair (late Jul; www.barnstable countyfair.org; County Fairgrounds, MA 151) Weeklong old-fashioned agricultural fair with garden displays, farm animals, carnival rides, music and fireworks.
Independence Day (Jul 4) The Cape's largest fireworks display explodes over Falmouth Harbor.
Falmouth Road Race (mid-Aug) A top-class road race along the Falmouth coast, drawing international runners.
Katharine Lee Bates Poetry Fest & Birthday Party (mid-Aug) The town goes crackers for Katharine, with rhyming games, ice-cream and cake.

Sleeping
BUDGET
Sippewissett Campground & Cabins (☎ 508-548-2542; www.sippewissett.com; 836 Palmer Ave; campsites per night $28-38, cabins per week $270-775; ☺ mid-May–mid-Oct) This family-friendly 13-acre place, about 2 miles north of downtown Falmouth, has 100 wooded campsites and 15 cabins. The cabins range from one to three rooms and can hold up to eight people. Bonuses include a free shuttle to the beach and to the Vineyard ferry.

MIDRANGE
Falmouth Heights Motor Lodge (☎ 508-548-3623, 800-468-3623; www.falmouthheightsmotel.com; 146 Falmouth Heights Rd; r incl breakfast $89-189; ☒ ☒) The 28 rooms here are a cut above the competition. And you can throw your own party – the attractive grounds harbor a picnic grove with gas barbecues, and are within walking distance of the beach and Vineyard ferry.

Seaside Inn (☎ 508-540-4120, 800-827-1976; www.seasideinnfalmouth.com; 263 Grand Ave S; r in season $109-294, off-season from $59; ☒) It's not fancy but the rooms are large and clean at this well-kept little colony overlooking Nantucket Sound. Early sleepers should avoid the rooms over the on-site pub. Prices are determined by your answers to the following: Balcony? Ocean view? Kitchenette? Weekend or weekday stay?

Palmer House Inn (☎ 508-548-1230, 800-472-2632; www.palmerhouseinn.com; 81 Palmer Ave; r incl breakfast

$129-295; ☒ ☐) If you fancy time-honored elegance then treat yourself to one of the posh, antique-laden rooms in this 200-year-old Victorian-style inn in Falmouth center. Extras such as the candlelit breakfast and Jacuzzis set the tone for a romantic stay.

TOP END
Inn on the Sound (☎ 508-457-9666, 800-564-9668; www.innonthesound.com; 313 Grand Ave S; r $150-295; ☺ Apr-Oct) Falmouth's finest inn exudes a clean, contemporary elegance. It's across from the beach, and many of the 10 rooms have private decks with ocean views. Depending on your mood a gourmet breakfast is served to you on the beach, in the dining room or in bed – now *that's* pampering!

Eating
BUDGET
Clam Shack (☎ 508-540-7758; 227 Clinton Ave; dishes $3-15; ☺ 11:30am-7:30pm May-early Sep) A classic of the genre, right on Falmouth Harbor. It's tiny, with picnic tables on the back deck and lots of fried seafood, as well as burgers and hot dogs. Skip the lobster roll; frozen lobster just can't match fresh.

MIDRANGE
Peking Palace (☎ 508-540-8204; 452 Main St; meals $7-17; ☺ 11:30am-midnight) The Palace is an affordable family choice that serves the area's best Chinese fare. Standouts include the chicken stir-fried with chunks of fresh mango, the spicy Shanghai boneless duck and the sushi. Yes, you read it right – the sushi *is* good here.

Laureen's (☎ 508-540-9104; 170 Main St; meals $9-27; ☺ 8:30am-8:30pm) Join the sophisticated natives at this cheery downtown bistro specializing in Middle Eastern fare. Lunch features healthy salads and creative sandwiches made with Armenian bread that has feta cheese baked

---

WORTH THE TRIP: WOODS HOLE

This seaside village at Falmouth's southwestern tip is home to one of the most prestigious marine research facilities in the world. Research at the Woods Hole Oceanographic Institution (WHOI, pronounced 'hooey') has covered the gamut from exploring the sunken *Titanic* to global warming studies. With some 60 buildings and laboratories and 650 employees and visiting scientists, including several Nobel laureates, it's the largest oceanographic institution in the US. Founded in 1930 with funding from the Rockefeller Foundation, WHOI remains a private institution, although it receives the lion's share of its funding from the US government.

Guided 75-minute tours of **WHOI facilities** (☎ 508-289-2252; www.whoi.edu; admission free, reservation required; ⏱ 10:30am & 1:30pm Mon-Fri mid-Jun–Aug) depart from the **WHOI information office** (93 Water St; ⏱ 8am-4pm Mon-Fri year-round). You'll also gain insights into scientists' work at the **WHOI Exhibit Center** (☎ 508-289-2663; 15 School St; adult/child under 10yr $2/free; ⏱ 10am-4:30pm Mon-Sat Jun-early Sep, off-season hours vary).

The **Woods Hole Science Aquarium** (☎ 508-495-2001; 166 Water St; admission free; ⏱ 11am-4pm Tue-Sat Jun-Aug, 11am-4pm Mon-Fri Sep-May; ♿) has little flash and dazzle, but you'll find unusual sea life specimens, examples of local fish and the *Homarus americanus* (aka lobster). Kids will enjoy the touch-tank creatures.

Keeping with the nautical theme, head over to the drawbridge where you'll find **Fishmonger Café** (☎ 508-540-5376; 56 Water St; meals $11-26; ⏱ 11:30am-3pm & 5:30-9pm), with water views in every direction and an eclectic menu emphasizing fresh seafood.

---

right into it. Dinner adds on grilled meat and seafood dishes.

La Cucina Sul Mare (☎ 508-548-5600; 237 Main St; meals $9-22; ⏱ lunch & dinner) First-rate atmosphere, food and service are in-store at this innovative Italian ristorante. Begin with clams *oreganato*, then move on to the *rigatoni ala vodka* or the flavorful sole *limone*.

TOP END

Casino Wharf FX (☎ 508-540-6160; 286 Grand Ave; meals $10-32; ⏱ 11:30am-4pm & 5-9:30pm) This place is so close to the water that you could cast a fishing pole from the deck. But why bother? Just grab a deck table and let the feast begin. The ginger-wasabi tuna is a tantalizing starter, the fresh catch is always true to its name and the wine list is good but not too pricey.

Drinking & Entertainment
BARS & CLUBS

Liam Maguire's Irish Pub & Restaurant (☎ 508-548-0285; 273 Main St) Come here for Harp and Murphy's stout on tap, Irish bartenders, live music nightly and boisterous Irish songfests.

Boathouse (☎ 508-548-7800; 88 Scranton Ave) With live music and DJs nightly in summer this place packs in partying 20-somethings.

THEATER & CULTURE

In summer, Falmouth has the busiest performing arts scene on the Upper Cape.

College Light Opera Company (☎ 508-548-0668; www.collegelightopera.com; Highfield Theatre, Highfield Dr; tickets $28; ⏱ late Jun-late Aug) A well-regarded summer theater of college-age students from across the country who hope to make a career in music theater. Expect lots of Broadway and light opera staples, accompanied by a full-pit orchestra. It's consistently a sellout, so book early.

Cape Cod Theatre Project (☎ 508-457-4242; www.capecodtheatreproject.org; Falmouth Academy, 7 Highfield Dr; tickets $20; ⏱ Jul) The Theatre Project brings professional actors together with playwrights to perform staged readings of new works. Some of the plays have gone on to open off-Broadway in New York.

MASHPEE
pop 12,950

This town is home to the Mashpee Wampanoag, the Native American tribe that welcomed the Pilgrims in 1620 and soon found itself pushed to the background. In 2007 the Wampanoag culminated a long struggle by finally winning federal recognition as a tribe. The renewed sense of identity and monetary resources that followed bode well for the tribe's future. Other than the beach and a couple of Wampanoag sites, the town is largely residential neighborhoods, shopping centers and condos, just a pass-through for vacationers on their way between Falmouth and Barnstable.

Orientation & Information

Mashpee Chamber of Commerce (☎ 508-477-0792, 800-423-6274; www.mashpeechamber.com; 520 Main St/MA 130; ☺ 9am-5pm Mon-Fri) Has a seasonal booth in Mashpee Commons, the shopping complex at the corner of MA 151 and MA 28.

Sights & Activities

Mashpee's Wampanoag sights – the c 1683 **Old Indian Meetinghouse** (Meetinghouse Way) and the **Wampanoag Indian Museum** (MA 130) – are both under renovation, but well worth visiting when they reopen; call the chamber of commerce for the latest information.

The 2-mile-long sandy **South Cape Beach** (Great Oak Rd; Ⓟ $7) overlooking the Vineyard is a great place for all sorts of activities, from fishing and swimming to long beach strolls

and hikes in the surrounding woods. The extensive marsh backing the beach offers good bird-watching as well.

Festivals & Events

Native Americans from around the country join the Mashpee Wampanoag for the big three-day **Pow Wow** (☎ 508-477-0208) that includes Native American dancing, crafts, competitions and a very cool fireball game after dark.

BARNSTABLE
pop 48,000 (including Hyannis)

Sprawling Barnstable is the Cape's largest town. It comprises seven villages, each with its own unique flavor. Visitor facilities are thickest in the village of Hyannis (see p181). The rest of the town, including the south-side villages of Cotuit and Centerville and the northside villages of West Barnstable and Barnstable, are covered in this section (yes,

---

STARS OF TOMORROW

The crack of a wooden bat making contact with a curve ball. The night lights and fireflies. The rudimentary aluminum seats within spitting distance of the third baseman. The hopes and dreams of making it big-time.

If you think the major leagues have been sullied by salaries and egos, the Cape Cod Baseball League (CCBL) will renew your faith. It's the nation's oldest amateur league (founded in 1885) and remains the country's most competitive summertime proving ground. The league's slogan – 'Where the stars of tomorrow shine tonight' – isn't far from the truth. One-seventh of all players in the major leagues today played in the Cape League. Some of the best-known names include Hall-of-Famer Red Sox catcher Carlton Fisk and the late Thurman Munson. Barry Zito of the San Francisco Giants and Dodgers infielder Nomar Garciaparra are among some 200 CCBL alumni in the majors today.

There are no tickets and officially no admission charge. However, supporters do pass around the hat between innings to help defray costs. As many of the players are college students, the season runs from mid-June to mid-August. Get the full schedule online at www.capecodbaseball .org, or check the *Cape Cod Times,* which gives the games serious press.

The 10 teams and their home fields:

- **Bourne Braves** – Doran Park (Upper Cape Tech, Sandwich Rd, Bourne)
- **Brewster Whitecaps** – Stony Brook (Underpass Rd, Brewster)
- **Chatham Athletics** – Veterans Field (Depot Station, Chatham)
- **Cotuit Kettleers** – Lowell Park (Lowell St, Cotuit)
- **Falmouth Commodores** – Guv Fuller Field (Main St, Falmouth)
- **Harwich Mariners** – Whitehouse Field (Oak St, Harwich)
- **Hyannis Mets** – McKeon Field (High School Rd, Hyannis)
- **Orleans Cardinals** – Eldredge Park (MA 28, Orleans)
- **Wareham Gatemen** – Clem Spillane Field (US 6, Wareham) Just off-Cape on the mainland.
- **Yarmouth-Dennis Red Sox** – Dennis-Yarmouth Regional High School (Station Ave, South Yarmouth)

there's a Barnstable Village in the Town of Barnstable). The northside villages along MA 6A brim with historic charm, and are dotted with antique shops and colonial-era homes and churches.

Orientation & Information

Barnstable, abounding in beaches, stretches from Cape Cod Bay in the north to Nantucket Sound in the south. MA 6A, also known as Old King's Hwy, cuts across West Barnstable and Barnstable Village. MA 28, also called Falmouth Rd, leads through Cotuit to Hyannis. MA 6A doubles as Main St in Barnstable Village.

Sights & Activities

WEST PARISH MEETINGHOUSE

The country's oldest Congregational **church** (☎ 508-362-4445; 2049 MA 149; admission free; ☺ 9am-5pm Mon-Sat, noon-5pm Sun Jun-early Sep) is at exit 5 off US 6. Built in 1717, the interior, with its massive oak timbers and broad plank floors, retains its early colonial character. The bell hanging in the steeple was cast by Paul Revere.

STURGIS LIBRARY

This handsome **library** (☎ 508-362-6636; 3090 Main St/MA 6A, Barnstable Village; ☺ 10am-5pm Mon & Wed-Fri, 1-8pm Tue, 10am-4pm Sat) is a sight in itself. The building, dating to 1644, is the oldest in the country housing a public library. In the front room you'll find the 1604 Bible that belonged to Barnstable's founder, Reverend John Lothrop.

DANIEL DAVID HOUSE

This 1739 Georgian-style house, next door to the Sturgis Library, is the headquarters of the **Barnstable Historical Society** (☎ 508-362-2982; 3074 Main St/MA 6A; admission free; ☺ 1-4pm Tue-Sat mid-May–mid-Oct). Walking through the front door into the parlor with its sloping floors and antique furnishings is like stepping back in time. Cheery docents offer intriguing tidbits of local history as they guide you through the house.

CAHOON MUSEUM OF AMERICAN ART

In a house dating from 1775, this intimate **museum** (☎ 508-428-7581; 4676 Falmouth Rd/MA 28, Cotuit; adult/child under 12yr $4/free; ☺ 10am-4pm Tue-Sat Feb-Dec) focuses on the quirky works of Martha Cahoon (1905–99) and Ralph Cahoon (1910–82), wife and husband painters who lived in

this house for 37 years. His work: fanciful images like mermaids fixing dinner; hers: sly observations of American life.

SANDY NECK BEACH

The barrier beach at **Sandy Neck** (☎ 508-362-8300; off MA 6A; P $15) extends 6.5 miles along Cape Cod Bay, backed the entire way by undulating dunes and a scenic salt marsh. It's a top place for all sorts of recreational activities: a good summer swimming spot, an unbeatable year-round place for hiking and a popular destination for fishers.

The fascinating dunes, which reach heights of 100ft, provide native habitat for red foxes, endangered birds and wildflowers. From four points along the beach, paths cross inland over the dunes to a trail skirting along the salt marsh. Depending on which cross-trail you take, you can make a loop of beach, dunes and marsh in a round-trip hike of 2 to 13 miles. Even the shortest hike, which takes about 90 minutes, is rewarding. Pick up a trail map at the gatehouse, which is staffed year-round; ask about high tide, which affects the marsh trail. Parking is free from September to May.

WHALE-WATCHING

Hyannis Whale Watcher Cruises (☎ 508-362-6088, 888-287-0374; Barnstable Harbor; adult/child 4-12yr $37/20; ☺ May–mid-Oct) offers four-hour narrated trips with an onboard naturalist. On those rare occasions when you don't spot any whales, you get a free pass for your next trip.

Sleeping

Honeysuckle Hill (☎ 508-362-8418, 866-444-5522; www.honeysucklehill.com; 591 MA 6A, West Barnstable; r incl breakfast in season $179, off-season $139; 🖳 wi-fi) Here is one of the friendliest B&Bs along MA 6A. This 200-year-old inn offers comfortably elegant rooms with an upbeat period decor. Add freshly cut flowers, soft terry bathrobes and a four-course breakfast with the like of Grand Mariner French toast and things get downright cushy.

Eating

Four Seas (☎ 508-775-1394; 360 S Main St, Centerville; cone $3; ☺ 11am-9:30pm Jun–mid-Sep) It ain't summer till Four Seas opens. This local institution near Craigville Beach has been dispensing homemade ice-cream since 1934! Expect lines out the door since everyone, including the Kennedy clan whose

Hyannisport home is nearby, comes here in summer.

Whistleberries (☎ 508-362-6717; 3261 MA 6A, Barnstable; meals $5-9; breakfast & lunch Mon-Sat) This homey place in the center of Barnstable Village is just a single room, with the owner on one side of the counter baking away. Blueberry muffins, fresh salads and generous sandwiches bring in a lunch crowd.

Mattakeese Wharf (☎ 508-362-4511; 271 Mill Way, Barnstable Harbor; meals $11-27; lunch & dinner May-Oct) The food is good but it's the fine harbor view that sets this place apart. Grab a table on the waterfront deck and watch the sailboats glide by as you dine on classic New England seafood.

Drinking & Entertainment

Barnstable Comedy Club (☎ 508-362-6333; www .barnstablecomedyclub.com; 3171 MA 6A; tickets $14-18) Despite its name, it's not a comedy club. Rather, it performs musicals and plays, and is the oldest (1922) nonprofessional theater group in Massachusetts – by some reckonings it's the oldest such group in the entire country.

HYANNIS
pop 14,200

Cape Cod's commercial hub is best known to visitors as the summer home of the Kennedy clan and a jumping-off point for ferries to Nantucket and Martha's Vineyard. The village center, especially the harborfront, has been rejuvenated, making it a pleasant place to break a journey.

Orientation & Information

The ferry terminals are opposite each other at the Ocean St and South St Docks. From either terminal it's a five-minute walk to Main St and the **Hyannis Transportation Center** (cnr Main & Center Sts), from where buses depart.

Cape Cod Hospital (☎ 508-771-1800; 27 Park St) Near the center of town, this is the Cape's main hospital.

Hyannis Area Chamber of Commerce (☎ 508-362-5230, 800-449-6647; www.hyannis.com; 397 Main St; 9am-5pm Mon-Sat, noon-4pm Sun mid-May–mid-Oct, 10am-4pm Mon-Sat mid-Oct–mid-May) Provides tourism information for the Town of Barnstable.

Hyannis Public Library (☎ 508-775-2280; 401 Main St; 11am-5pm Mon, Thu & Fri, 11am-8pm Tue & Wed, also 11am-5pm Sat but closed Mon in winter) Free internet access, limited to 30 minutes.

Post office (☎ 800-275-8777; 385 Main St)

Sights & Activities
HYANNIS HARBOR

This is the real deal – a working harbor with fishing and lobster boats, ferries and yachts, surrounded by waterfront eateries and bustling with vacationers. In summer, to match the flurry of visitors, there's a flurry of activities, with local bands performing **outdoor concerts** (6pm Tue & Fri Jul & Aug) and **Shakespeare by the Sea** (5:30pm Sun Jul) at the harborfront Aselton Park.

JOHN F KENNEDY HYANNIS MUSEUM

The 35th president of the US summered in Hyannisport (an exclusive section of Hyannis, west of the town center), and this **museum** (☎ 508-790-3077; 397 Main St; adult/child 10-16yr $5/2.50; 9am-5pm Mon-Sat, noon-5pm Sun late May-Oct, 10am-4pm Thu-Sat, noon-4pm Sun Nov-Dec & mid-Feb–late May) celebrates the casual moments in JFK's life in heartwarming photographs, video presentation and artifacts.

A short drive away, a simple **memorial** to Kennedy stands at Veterans Park on Ocean St, overlooking the harbor where JFK sailed.

CAPE COD CHIPS FACTORY

These much-admired chips are of the potato, not the computer, variety, so although they won't work in your Dell, they'll taste good in your gateway. The **factory** (☎ 508-775-3358; 100 Breed's Hill Rd; admission free; 9am-5pm Mon-Fri) has a walk-through tour during which you can watch the little buggers march across the production and packaging lines. The whole visit might take you 15 minutes, and you get free samples.

BEACHES

Parking is $15 at all of the following beaches. **Sea St Beach**, off Sea St from the western end of Main St, is a narrow but decent beach with rest rooms and a bathhouse. You'll find plenty of space to lay your towel on wide **Kalmus Beach**, at the south end of Ocean St, which has the area's best windsurfing conditions. **Veterans Beach**, on Ocean St, is a popular choice for families, with picnic tables and shallow waters.

Craigville Beach, a mile-long stretch of sand on Centerville Beach Rd, is a great swimming beach that attracts a college crowd. And with 445 parking spaces, the most of any town beach, you're unlikely to get locked out even on the sunniest midsummer day. The full beach facilities include changing rooms,

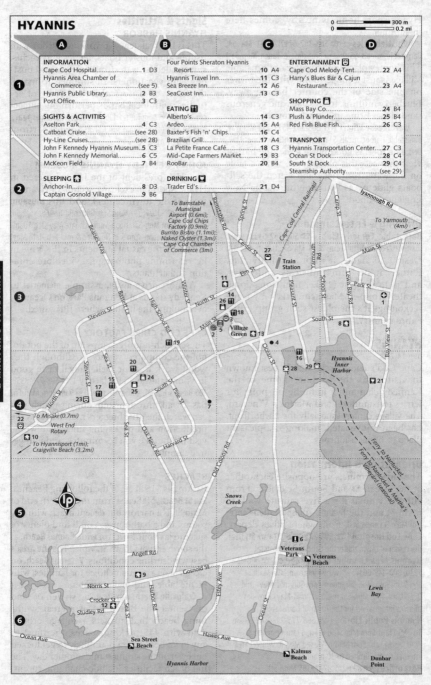

HYANNIS

INFORMATION
Cape Cod Hospital.....................1 D3
Hyannis Area Chamber of
Commerce..........................(see 5)
Hyannis Public Library...............2 B3
Post Office..............................3 C3

SIGHTS & ACTIVITIES
Aselton Park...........................4 C3
Catboat Cruise....................(see 28)
Hy-Line Cruises...................(see 28)
John F Kennedy Hyannis Museum..5 C3
John F Kennedy Memorial.........6 C5
McKeon Field.........................7 B4

SLEEPING
Anchor-In..............................8 D3
Captain Gosnold Village............9 B6

Four Points Sheraton Hyannis
Resort...............................10 A4
Hyannis Travel Inn..................11 C3
Sea Breeze Inn.......................12 A6
SeaCoast Inn........................13 C3

EATING
Alberto's...............................14 C3
Ardeo.................................15 A4
Baxter's Fish 'n' Chips.............16 C4
Brazilian Grill........................17 A4
La Petite France Café...............18 C3
Mid-Cape Farmers Market........19 B3
RooBar...............................20 B4

DRINKING
Trader Ed's...........................21 D4

ENTERTAINMENT
Cape Cod Melody Tent..............22 A4
Harry's Blues Bar & Cajun
Restaurant.........................23 A4

SHOPPING
Mass Bay Co.........................24 B4
Plush & Plunder.....................25 B4
Red Fish Blue Fish..................26 C3

TRANSPORT
Hyannis Transportation Center....27 C3
Ocean St Dock.......................28 C4
South St Dock........................29 C4
Steamship Authority.............(see 29)

showers and lifeguards, and snack bars across the street.

CAPE COD CENTRAL RAILROAD

A historic **train** (☎ 508-771-3800, 888-797-7245; www .capetrain.com; 252 Main St; adult/child under 12yr $18/14; ⊙ late May-Oct) makes a two-hour scenic run between Hyannis' Transportation Center and the Cape Cod Canal. There are two trips on most days, so you could take the early train, get off in Sandwich, mosey into the village (about a 10-minute walk) and catch the last train back.

CRUISES

Laid-back sailors will enjoy a **catboat cruise** (☎ 508-775-0222; www.catboat.com; Ocean St Dock; adult/ child $30/10; ⊙ mid-Apr–late Nov), sailing with the wind around Hyannis Harbor and out in Nantucket Sound.

Hy-Line Cruises (☎ 508-790-0696; www.hylinecruises .com; Ocean St Dock; adult/child 5-12yr $14/7; ⊙ mid-Apr–Oct) offers an hour-long harbor cruise aboard an old-fashioned steamer that circles past the compound of Kennedy family homes. Kids will prefer the Sunday afternoon 'ice-cream float,' which adds a Ben & Jerry's sundae to the view.

Festivals & Events

Independence Day celebration (Jul 4) A parade down Main St and a big fireworks bash over Hyannis Harbor.
Pops by the Sea (first Sun in Aug) This concert features the Boston Pops Orchestra and a celebrity guest conductor on the village green.

Sleeping
BUDGET & MIDRANGE

Hyannis Travel Inn (☎ 508-775-8200, 800-352-7190; www.hyannistravelinn.com; 18 North St; r incl breakfast in season $95-150, off-season $49-99; 🔁) If you want decent facilities without steep resort prices, look here. They may not be distinctive but the 83 rooms are adequate and the place has a sauna, Jacuzzi and indoor and outdoor swimming pools. It's just a block from Main St and is central to everything.

Sea Breeze Inn (☎ 508-771-7213; www.seabreezeinn .com; 270 Ocean Ave; r incl breakfast in season $98-150, off-season $70-115; 🖭 🖵 wi-fi) Some of the 14 clean, pleasant rooms here have canopy beds and sea views. If you're not traveling with your laptop you can use its guest computer for free. The beach is just steps away. There are fancier B&Bs around, but fewer with more heart.

Captain Gosnold Village (☎ 508-775-9111; www .captaingosnold.com; 230 Gosnold St; r/cottage in season from $100/250, off-season from $60/120; 🖭 🔁) A little community unto itself and just a sandal-shuffle from the beach. Choose from motel rooms or fully equipped Cape Cod–style cottages; there's a playground for the kids. The cottages vary in size and have from one to three bedrooms with the smallest sleeping four people, the largest six.

SeaCoast Inn (☎ 508-775-3828, 800-466-4100; www .seacoastcapecod.com; 33 Ocean St; r incl breakfast in season $108-138, off-season $70-98; 🖭 🖵 wi-fi) This small, two-story motel offers neat, clean rooms just a two-minute walk from the harbor in one direction and Main St restaurants in the other. OK, there's no view or pool, but the rooms are thoroughly comfy, all have kitchenettes and the price is a deal.

Anchor-In (☎ 508-775-0357; www.anchorin.com; 1 South St; r incl breakfast in season $109-259, off-season $59-139; 🖭 🖵 🔁) Bright airy rooms with harborview balconies separate this family-run hotel from all the chains back on the highway. The stylish decor and fittings here are on par with places charging twice this rate. And, if you're planning a day trip to Nantucket, the ferry is just a stroll away.

TOP END

Four Points Sheraton Hyannis Resort (☎ 508-775-7775, 800-368-7764; www.fourpoints.com/hyannis; 35 Scutter Ave; r in season $175-225, off-season $125-175; 🖭 wi-fi 🔁) The town's main resort hotel has 224 large rooms with the usual chain decor. The real appeal here lies in the facilities. The hotel boasts the area's best fitness center, both indoor and outdoor pools and an 18-hole golf course.

Eating
BUDGET

Mid-Cape Farmers Market (540 Main St; ⊙ 8am-noon Wed mid-Jun–mid-Sep) Buy fresh organic produce, Cape Cod honey, homemade bakery goods and live 'n' kickin' lobsters direct from the source at this summertime market near the corner of Main St and High School Rd.

La Petite France Café (☎ 508-775-1067; 349 Main St; sandwiches $6-7; ⊙ breakfast & lunch Mon-Sat) This star of the Hyannis café scene makes flaky croissants, superb baguette sandwiches (try the almond raisin chicken) and homemade soup du jour. And don't let the chef's accent fool you – he does a nice job with New England–style clam chowder too.

Burrito Bistro (☎ 508-771-6071; Capetown Plaza, 790 MA 132; burritos $6-9; ⏲ lunch & dinner) Forget lard, these burritos attract the health-conscious crowd with farm-fresh greens, homemade salsas and a fun international twist. The Thai burrito with satay chicken, fresh cilantro and carrots is a real taste pleaser. Free wi-fi, too.

MIDRANGE

Misaki (☎ 508-771-3771; 379 W Main St; meals $9-24; ⏲ lunch & dinner Mon-Sat) Enjoy your fresh New England seafood served up raw as first-rate sushi and sashimi at this authentic Japanese restaurant. Tempura dinners and noodle dishes round out the menu.

Ardeo (☎ 508-790-1115; 644 Main St; meals $9-26; ⏲ lunch & dinner) Can't agree on what to eat? Then Ardeo makes a perfect family choice with something for every taste. The menu ranges from pizza and Black Angus burgers to traditional Greek fare and local seafood.

Brazilian Grill (☎ 508-771-0109; 680 Main St; lunch/dinner buffet $8/15; ⏲ lunch & dinner) Celebrate the Cape's Brazilian side at this generous buffet that includes everything from rice and beans to soups, salads and stewed fish. The star is *churrasco à rodízio* (barbecued meats on skewers), which can be ordered with the buffet for $7 more.

Baxter's Fish 'n' Chips (☎ 508-775-4490; 177 Pleasant St; meals $11-37; ⏲ lunch & dinner) Baxter's serves all the seafood requisites from fried clams and fish and chips to steamed lobster. For many, though, the harborfront location with picnic tables on a floating dock is the real draw.

RooBar (☎ 508-778-6515; 586 Main St; meals $14-32; ⏲ 4pm-1am) This hip place features an exposed kitchen, high ceilings, great people-watching and innovative New American fare. Be adventurous: maybe the wood-fired spiced lamb pizza or the lobster tail in grapefruit sauce. RooBar is also known for its bar scene.

TOP END

Alberto's (☎ 508-778-1770; 360 Main St; meals $10-30; ⏲ lunch & dinner) The place for reliably good Italian food. Alberto's serves all the classics and adds in some local specialties such as fresh littleneck clams steamed in garlic marinara. The servings are generous – you won't walk away hungry. Ask about good-value sunset specials before 6pm.

Naked Oyster (☎ 508-778-6500; 20 Independence Dr; meals $22-35; ⏲ dinner) Despite the mini-mall

location, this raw bar and restaurant is thoroughly chichi. The oyster menu reads like the Oystertown phone book and the tuna tartare salad is to die for. Master chef David Kelley takes the maxim of buying local (Wellfleet oysters!) and organic to the hilt.

Drinking & Entertainment

Harry's Blues Bar & Cajun Restaurant (☎ 508-775-4188; 700 Main St; ⏲ 11:30am-1am) Hyannis' favorite dance spot serves up blues as its bread and butter, but rock, zydeco and reggae spice up the menu too.

Trader Ed's (☎ 508-790-8686; 21 Arlington St; ⏲ last call 12:30am) This is a happening place to have a drink at the marina and there's usually a DJ on weekends.

Many restaurants have popular bars. Ardeo (left) is a mellow place to go for a drink, while RooBar (left) is a more sophisticated singles scene.

Cape Cod Melody Tent (☎ 800-347-0808; www.melodytent.org; 21 W Main St) It's just that – a giant tent, seating 2300 people – but nobody sits more than 50ft from the revolving stage. Between June and August it headlines big-name acts such as Willie Nelson, the Beach Boys, Tony Bennett and Lyle Lovett.

Shopping

Main St offers a mishmash of independent shops, some funky, others classy.

Plush & Plunder (☎ 508-775-4467; 605 Main St) Fun vintage and retro clothing, with the likes of velvet hats and feather boa; shoppers have included Demi Moore and Cyndi Lauper.

Mass Bay Co (☎ 508-771-2114; 595 Main St) A good selection of quality sandals, as well as beach wear, all things Red Sox, and army/navy gear.

Red Fish Blue Fish (☎ 508-775-8700; 374 Main St) Eclectic gift shop with local handicrafts including the owner's handblown glass jewelry.

YARMOUTH & YARMOUTH PORT
pop 24,800

There are two Yarmouths, and the experience you have depends on what part of town you find yourself in. The north side of town, along MA 6A, is called Yarmouth Port – it's green and genteel with shady trees, antique shops and gracious old homes. The second Yarmouth is along MA 28 to the south,

---

CAPE COD BEACH GUIDE

The crowning glory of the Cape is its stunning beaches. Each has its own personality and there's one that is bound to fit yours. All public beaches are free to foot traffic. However, if you arrive by car most beaches charge a parking fee during the summer months and a few require parking permits issued only to town residents. If you're unsure about which beach parking areas are open to visitors, check with your accommodations or the local chamber of commerce.

Top beaches for:

- **Surfing** White Crest Beach (p198), Coast Guard Beach (p196)
- **Windsurfing** Kalmus Beach (p181), Hardings Beach (p192)
- **Sunsets** First Encounter Beach (p197), Herring Cove Beach (p204)
- **Sunrises** Nauset Beach (p194)
- **Tidal flats** Skaket Beach (p195), First Encounter Beach (p197)
- **Fishing** Race Point Beach (p204), Sandy Neck Beach (p180)
- **Families** Old Silver Beach (p176), West Dennis Beach (p187)
- **Seclusion** Long Point Beach (p204)
- **Long walks** Sandy Neck Beach (p180), Chapin Memorial Beach (p187)
- **Picnics** Grey's Beach (below), Corporation Beach (p187)
- **Sunbathing** Take your pick!

---

a flat world of mini-golf, strip malls and endless motels.

Orientation & Information

Yarmouth stretches from Nantucket Sound in the south to Cape Cod Bay in the north, sandwiched between Barnstable to the west and Dennis to the east. MA 6A, US 6 and MA 28 all run east–west through town.

Yarmouth Chamber of Commerce (☎ 508-778-1008, 800-732-1008; www.yarmouthcapecod.com; 424 MA 28, West Yarmouth; ☉ 9am-5pm daily early May–mid-Oct, 9am-5pm Mon-Fri mid-Oct–early May) The staff here are helpful.

Sights & Activities

CAPTAIN BANGS HALLETT HOUSE

This 1840 Greek Revival **house** (☎ 508-362-3021; 11 Strawberry Lane; adult/child under 12yr $3/50¢; ☉ tours 1pm, 2pm & 3pm Thu-Sun Jun–mid-Oct) was once home

---

WHY THE PINEAPPLE?

Outside the Bangs Hallett House, there's a metal spike sticking out of the hitching post. When sea captains returned from the South Seas, they brought pineapples with them as souvenirs. A pineapple sticking out of the hitching post was an indication that the captain had returned and was ready to receive visitors.

---

to a prosperous sea captain who made his fortune sailing to China and India. It's behind the post office, off MA 6A.

EDWARD GOREY HOUSE

Across from the Captain Bangs Hallett House lived the brilliant and somewhat twisted author and illustrator Edward Gorey. This **museum** (☎ 508-362-3909; 8 Strawberry Lane; adult/child 6-12yr $5/2; ☉ 11am-4pm Wed-Sat, noon-4pm Sun) in his former home has exhibits about his life and work, as well as a gift shop featuring Gorey-ana.

BEACHES

Grey's Beach, at the north end of Center St, off MA 6A, is also known as Bass Hole. It isn't very good for swimming, but a boardwalk extends over a tidal marsh and creek, offering a wonderful view of all sorts of sea life. It's great for picnics and sunsets, and the parking is free.

Long and wide **Seagull Beach** (Sea Gull Rd; **P** $15), off South Sea Ave from MA 28, is the town's best south-side beach. The scenic approach to the beach runs alongside a tidal river that provides habitat for shorebirds; bring your binoculars. Facilities include a bathhouse and snack bar.

BOATING

Great Marsh Kayak Tours (☎ 508-775-6447; 674 MA 28; tours adult/child under 14yr $45/35; ☉ May–mid-Oct) offers fun-filled 3½-hour tours that begin with a paddle lesson and then head off on a jaunt through marsh, river and open ocean.

MINI-GOLF
Two South Yarmouth courses set standards. **Bass River Sports World** (☎ 508-398-6070; 934 MA 28, South Yarmouth; mini-golf $8; ☼ 9am-6pm Apr-Oct) has a pirate-themed 'adventure golf' course, complete with an 8ft-tall skull. **Pirate's Cove** (☎ 508-394-6200; 728 MA 28, South Yarmouth; adult/child 13yr $8/7; ☼ 10am-9pm mid-Apr–Oct) has the pedigree to go with its popularity – its caves, footbridges and waterfalls were designed by Disney imagineers.

Sleeping
Village Inn (☎ 508-362-3182; www.thevillageinncape cod.com; 92 MA 6A, Yarmouth Port; r incl breakfast $90-150; ☼ May-Oct; ✖) This family-run B&B is set on 1-acre grounds and occupies a 200-year-old house that's on the National Register of Historic Places. It has lots of common space and 10 straightforward guest rooms of varying sizes. A full country breakfast is served each morning.

All Seasons Motor Inn (☎ 508-394-7600, 800-527-0359; www.allseasons.com; 1199 MA 28, South Yarmouth; r incl breakfast in season $129-185, off-season $75-149; ☐ ☒) Easily the best of the many motels along MA 28. The 114 rooms each have a refrigerator and DVD player. There are indoor and outdoor pools, saunas, a Jacuzzi, exercise room, game room and coin laundry. Nice solarium breakfast room, too.

Eating
Capt Parker's Pub (☎ 508-771-4266; 668 MA 28, West Yarmouth; meals $10-24; ☼ lunch & dinner) The Captain has won several 'best chowder' contests and serves better-than-average pub grub. House specialties include the baked stuffed scrod and the juicy prime rib. Expect to find it open even during a hurricane or heavy snow.

Inaho (☎ 508-362-5522; 157 MA 6A, Yarmouth Port; sushi from $5, meals $17-29; ☼ lunch Mon-Fri, dinner Mon-Sat) The Cape's top Japanese restaurant has excellent sushi and tempura, and a full range of other Japanese dishes. It's also got one of the most interesting designs in the region, especially the Cape-meets-Kyoto sushi bar.

902 Main (☎ 508-398-9902; 902 MA 28, South Yarmouth; meals $20-31; ☼ dinner) Proof that beautiful flowers can bloom in the oddest of places. Amid the honky-tonk of MA 28, you'll find

subdued decor and sophisticated French–New American fusion cuisine. The changing menu features the likes of warm duck confit salad, Chatham scallops with lobster risotto, and rack of lamb with truffle mashed potatoes.

DENNIS
pop 16,000
Like Yarmouth, Dennis has a distinctly different character from north to south. Dennisport, at the south side of town, runs along MA 28 and is very commercial with the expected assortment of motels, casual restaurants and mini-golf. The classier northside, the village of Dennis, runs along MA 6A with handsome old sea captain's homes sprouting a second life as inns and antique shops.

Orientation & Information
MA 134 runs north–south through town, linking MA 6A in the village of Dennis to MA 28 in Dennisport. Somewhat confusingly, MA 6A in the center of Dennis village and MA 28 through Dennisport are both locally known as Main St.

Scargo Lake and the adjacent landmark Scargo Tower are near the center of Dennis village, south off MA 6A. Sesuit Harbor, north off MA 6A, is at the eastern end of Dennis, just before entering Brewster.

Dennis Chamber of Commerce (☎ 508-398-3568; www.dennischamber.com; 238 Swan River Rd, off MA 28 at MA 134; ☼ 10am-4pm Mon-Sat Jun–mid-Oct, 9am-5pm Mon-Fri mid-Oct–May) There's also an unstaffed but well-stocked booth off MA 6A in the Cape Playhouse (see below) parking lot.

Sights & Activities
CAPE MUSEUM OF FINE ARTS
This worthwhile **museum** (☎ 508-385-4477; 60 Hope Lane off MA 6A; adult/child under 18yr $8/free; ☼ 10am-5pm Mon-Sat, noon-5pm Sun) highlights the works of Cape artists. It has been renovated and expanded, and is behind the Cape Playhouse.

CAPE PLAYHOUSE
The **Cape Playhouse** (☎ 508-385-3911, 877-385-3911; www.capeplayhouse.com; 820 MA 6A, Dennis; tickets $25-45; ☼ mid-Jun–early Sep; ♿) is the oldest operating professional summer theater (1927) in the US. Bette Davis once worked here as an usher and some of the biggest names in showbiz have appeared on its stage. It hosts a different production every 12 days, and

also presents a **Children's Theater** (tickets $8) with classics, puppetry and more.

SCARGO TOWER
Built in 1902 on the highest spot in the area – 120ft above sea level – this 38-step, stone **tower** (Scargo Hill Rd; admission free) rising above Scargo Lake gives you grand views of Cape Cod Bay. On clear days you can see all the way to Sandwich and across to Provincetown. To get here, take MA 6A to Scargo Hill Rd.

BEACHES
Parking at all of the following beaches is $15.

Wade in to the gently sloping waters at dune-backed **Chapin Memorial Beach** (Chapin Beach Rd). As with all bayside beaches in Dennis, you can walk far out onto the tidal flats at low tide. This mile-long beach is also ideal for walks under the light of the moon. To get there, take New Boston Rd opposite Dennis Public Market on MA 6A and follow the signs.

Corporation Beach (Corporation Rd), off MA 6A, is another popular bayside beach that's backed by dunes and is also one of the best equipped, with picnic space and wheelchair facilities.

West Dennis Beach (Lighthouse Rd), off MA 28, is a gorgeous mile-long beach on Nantucket Sound. It's quite popular; facilities include a snack bar and rest rooms. It's a good bet for finding a parking space on even the sunniest of days, as the parking lot extends clear down the beach, with room for 1000 cars.

If you prefer a freshwater dip, head over to **Scargo Lake** (off MA 6A), one of the Cape's 365 freshwater lakes, and one of the nicest.

BOATING
Cape Cod Waterways (☎ 508-398-0080; MA 28, Dennisport; per 90min 1-person kayak $18, 2-person kayak or canoe $29; ☷ 8am-5:30pm May–mid-Oct), near MA 134, allows you to explore scenic Swan River from the vantage point of a canoe or kayak.

Lobster Roll Cruises (☎ 508-385-1686; 356 Sesuit Neck Rd, East Dennis; cruise $27-40; ☷ Apr–Oct) provides a different setting for a lobster dinner. Take this cute boat from Sesuit Harbor on a dinner cruise, or go light with the lobster roll lunch cruise. The food, prepared by Sesuit Harbor Café (see p188), is the real deal.

BIKING
The stunningly scenic Cape Cod Rail Trail (see boxed text, p188) starts in Dennis off

MA 134. **Barb's Bike Rentals** (☎ 508-760-4723; 450 MA 134; rental per half/full day $16/24; ☷ Apr–mid-Nov) rents bicycles right at the trailhead.

Sleeping
BUDGET
Huntsman Motor Lodge (☎ 508-394-5415, 800-628-0498; www.thehuntsman.com; 829 MA 28, West Dennis; r in season $89-125, off-season $69-85; ☷ ☷) This family-run establishment has 18 simple rooms, seven efficiencies and a convenient location. The straightforward rooms are good value, clean and well maintained. Beaches, restaurants and all the ticky-tacky joys of MA 28 are just a short drive away.

MIDRANGE
Isaiah Hall B&B Inn (☎ 508-385-9928, 800-736-0160; www.isaiahhallinn.com; 152 Whig St, Dennis; r incl breakfast in season $135-185, off-season $100-155; ☷) This B&B offers 12 comfortable rooms in a 19th-century farmhouse that's set in a quiet residential neighborhood near the Cape Playhouse. The relaxing decor is antique country-style, the gardens lovely and the host charming. Prices reflect the size of the room and whether you opt for extras like balconies and fireplaces.

Scargo Manor (☎ 508-385-5534, 800-595-0034; www.scargomanor.com; 909 MA 6A, Dennis; r in season $175-250, off-season $125-175; wi-fi) A real winner. The yard abuts pretty Scargo Lake, and the rest of the house is pretty too. Each of the six rooms has its own sweet character. The water-view Hydrangea room, for example, boasts a skylight perfect for stargazing from bed. And guests are free to paddle away on the owners' canoe, rowboat or kayaks.

TOP END
Lighthouse Inn (☎ 508-398-2244; www.lighthouseinn.com; Lighthouse Rd, West Dennis; s incl breakfast $92-132, d incl breakfast $168-322; ☷) This oceanfront inn originated as a lighthouse in 1855 and has been owned by the same family since the 1930s – entering it is like stepping back in time. Accommodations are spread around 9 acres of grassy grounds. Children's programs mean free time for moms and dads. Outdoor activities include tennis and shuffleboard.

Eating
BUDGET
Kream 'n' Kone (☎ 508-394-0808; 961 MA 28 at MA 134, West Dennis; meals $5.50-18; ☷ lunch & dinner) A shrine to fried seafood, but it doesn't stop there. The

---

UP FOR A PEDAL?

The mother of all Cape bicycle trails, the **Cape Cod Rail Trail**, runs 22 glorious miles through forest, past cranberry bogs and along sandy ponds ideal for a dip. A poster boy for the rail-to-trails movement, the trail follows an abandoned railway route given a second life as a bike path in the 1970s. A $6.4 million upgrade completed in 2007 has smartened it up nicely, removing some hazardous road crossings and making it one of the finest bike trails in all of New England. The path begins in Dennis on MA 134 and continues through Nickerson State Park in Brewster, into Orleans and across the Cape Cod National Seashore all the way to South Wellfleet. There's a hefty dose of Olde Cape Cod scenery en route and you'll have opportunities to detour into the villages for lunch or sightseeing. If you've got time to do only part of the trail, begin at Nickerson and head for the National Seashore – the landscape is unbeatable. Bicycle rentals are available at the trailhead in Dennis (p187), at Nickerson State Park (see Biking, opposite) and opposite the National Seashore's visitors center (p197) in Eastham – there's free car parking at all three sites.

---

burgers are huge, the clam rolls justifiably famous, and the chowder holds its own.

MIDRANGE

Swan River Restaurant & Fish Market (☎ 508-394-4466; 5 Lower County Rd, Dennisport; meals $8-22; ☼ lunch & dinner; ⚹) If you're on the south side, this is the place for fresh seafood. Right on the water, it started as a fish market and still has its connection to the sea. It's all about the day's catch – go with whatever is on the chalkboard. The $5 kids' menu is a real family pleaser.

Blue Moon Bistro (☎ 508-385-7100; 605 MA 6A, Dennis; meals $10-32; ☼ lunch Wed-Sat, dinner Tue-Sun) This owner-run bistro specializes in upscale Mediterranean cuisine such as burgundy braised lamb with saffron risotto. At lunch think blue-cheese burgers or Cajun chicken panini, and save room for the crème brûlée.

Clancy's of Dennisport (☎ 508-394-6900; 8 Upper County Rd, Dennisport; meals $11-24; ☼ lunch & dinner) Sit out on the deck and enjoy country-style food with a terrific view of Swan River. The broad menu includes everything from burgers to baked stuffed shrimp and hearty steaks.

Sesuit Harbor Café (☎ 508-385-6134; 357 Sesuit Neck Rd, Dennis; meals $12-24; ☼ 7am-8pm) This is what Cape Cod's all about: a little shack at the Sesuit Harbor marina with freshly caught seafood served at picnic tables on the edge of the water. The scrumptious lobster rolls, like everything else, are always fresh. BYOB.

TOP END

Red Pheasant (☎ 508-385-2133; 905 MA 6A, Dennis; meals $22-35; ☼ dinner) This former ship's chandlery is over 200 years old, so you can feel as

elegant as your surroundings as you tuck into fricassee of escargot, roast duckling, rack of lamb or other delicious creations. And on chilly nights when the fireplace is stoked up, it's magic.

Drinking & Entertainment

Cape Cinema (☎ 508-385-2503; www.capecinema.com; 820 MA 6A, Dennis; tickets $8) Set on the grounds of the Cape Playhouse, this vintage movie theater shows foreign and independent films. It's a real art house: the entire ceiling is covered in a trippy art deco mural depicting the heavens painted by famed American artist Rockwell Kent.

Clancy's of Dennisport (☎ 508-394-6900; 8 Upper County Rd, Dennisport; ☼ 11:30am-1am) This riverside pub and restaurant is one pretty place to enjoy a drink.

Shopping

Scargo Pottery (☎ 508-385-3894; 30 Dr Lords Rd S, Dennis) Regarded as makers of some of the best pottery on the Cape. This extended-family operation offers a change from the omnipresent antique shops along MA 6A. It's just east of Scargo Lake, off MA 6A.

BREWSTER

pop 10,100

Brewster's backbone, the handsome Old King's Hwy (MA 6A), is known for its antique shops, pottery studios and art galleries amid old sea captain's homes. There's also an excellent natural history museum, an equally exceptional state park, and fine restaurants way out of proportion to the town's small size.

Orientation & Information

Everything of interest is on or just off MA 6A (also called Main St), which runs the length of the town. Nickerson State Park occupies most of eastern Brewster.

Brewster Chamber of Commerce (☎ 508-896-3500; www.brewstercapecod.org; 2198 MA 6A; ☷ 9am-3pm Jun-Aug, 10am-2pm Mon-Sat May & Sep–mid-Oct) Inside Brewster Town Hall.

Sights & Activities

NICKERSON STATE PARK

The 2000-acre oasis of **Nickerson State Park** (☎ 508-896-3491; 3488 MA 6A; admission free; ☷ 8am-8pm) has eight ponds with sandy beaches ideal for swimming and boating, as well as excellent biking and walking trails. Bring along a fishing pole to catch your own trout dinner or just pack a lunch and enjoy the park's picnic facilities.

Jack's Boat Rentals (☎ 508-896-8556; Cliff Pond; boat rental 1st/additional hr $20/12; ☷ 9am-6pm), within the park, rents canoes, kayaks and sailboats.

CAPE COD MUSEUM OF NATURAL HISTORY

This family-friendly **museum** (☎ 508-896-3867; www.ccmnh.org; 869 MA 6A; adult/child 3-12yr $8/3.50; ☷ 9:30am-4pm daily Jun-Sep, noon-4pm Wed-Sun Oct-May; ☊) offers fascinating exhibits on the Cape's flora and fauna and has a boardwalk trail across a salt marsh to a remote beach. The museum also sponsors naturalist-led walks, talks and kids' programs.

BREWSTER HISTORICAL SOCIETY MUSEUM

This **museum** (☎ 508-896-9521; 3171 MA 6A; admission free; ☷ 1-4pm Thu-Sat Jul-Sep) shows just how fine a small-town historical museum can be. Intriguing displays include an old barbershop, treasures brought back by sea captains, colonial tools and other bits of Brewster's centuries-old history.

Behind the museum, where parking is free, a pleasant half-mile **trail** leads through a wooded conservation area out to the **beach**.

TIDAL FLATS

When the tide goes out on Cape Cod Bay, the flats – basically giant sandbars – offer opportunities to commune with crabs, clams and gulls, and to take in brilliant sunsets. Best access to the tidal flats is via the Point of Rocks or Ellis Landing Beaches. Parking stickers are required during the summer and cost $15 per day.

BREWSTER STORE

The **Brewster Store** (☎ 508-896-3744; 1935 MA 6A at MA 124; ☷ 6am-6pm), in the heart of town, is a sight in itself. This old-fashioned country store has managed to stay in operation since 1866, and much of it has barely changed since. Penny candy is still sold alongside the local newspaper. Pop upstairs to see some interesting town memorabilia.

STONY BROOK GRIST MILL

This town-owned **mill** (☎ 508-896-3500; 830 Stony Brook Rd; admission by donation; ☷ 10am-2pm Sat late Jun-Aug) marks one of the Cape's most tranquil, lush spots. The water wheel continues to turn and on some days corn is ground with the old millstones.

Try to visit the adjacent open-air **Herring Run** (admission free), in the pond above the mill, when thousands of herring are migrating from the ocean to fresh water to spawn between mid-April and early May.

BIKING

The Cape Cod Rail Trail (see boxed text, opposite) runs through town and across Nickerson State Park. Several places rent bicycles, none more convenient than **Barb's Bike Rental** (☎ 508-896-7231; MA 6A; rental half/full day $16/24; ☷ 9am-6pm late May-early Oct), which has a kiosk at the rail trail parking lot near the entrance to Nickerson.

Sleeping

Nickerson State Park (☎ 508-896-3491, reservations 877-422-6762; 3488 MA 6A; campsites $17, 4-/6-person yurts $30/40; ☷ late May–mid-Oct) Head here for Cape Cod's best camping with 418 wooded campsites and six yurts; it often fills, so reserve your spot early. You can make reservations up to six months in advance.

Old Sea Pines Inn (☎ 508-896-6114; www.oldseapinesinn.com; 2553 MA 6A; r incl breakfast $80, with bathroom $105-185; wi-fi) It's a bit like staying at grandma's house: antique fittings, floral wallpaper, clawfoot bathtubs. This former girls' school dates to 1840 and the inn's 21 rooms retain a simple yesteryear look. No TV, but there are rocking chairs on the porch.

Old Manse Inn (☎ 508-896-3149, 866-896-3149; www.oldmanseinn.com; 1861 MA 6A; r incl breakfast in season $140-275, off-season $125-225; ☒ wi-fi) Everything about this cozy inn is inviting, from the warm hospitality to the tasteful decor. The c 1801 inn, a former sea captain's home, has a handy setting in the center of town. Start your day with a homecooked breakfast of goodies like blueberry pancakes or eggs florentine – this place is a class act.

Eating

Most Brewster restaurants reduce their hours in the off-season, depending on the flow of customers.

Cobie's (☎ 508-896-7021; 3256 MA 6A; meals $8-23; ☺ lunch & dinner mid-May–Sep) Just off the Cape Cod Rail Trail, this bustling roadside clam shack dishes out fried seafood that you can crunch and munch at outdoor picnic tables. On weekends it has lobster too.

our pick Brewster Fish House (☎ 508-896-7867; 2208 MA 6A; meals $11-31; ☺ lunch & dinner) It's not a real eye-catcher from the outside, but inside it's absolute heaven for seafood lovers. Start with the fabulous lobster bisque, naturally sweet with chunks of fresh lobster. From there it's safe to cast your net in any direction, though you may not want to let the flaky sea bass get away. Just 11 tables, and no reservations, so think lunch or early dinner to avoid long waits.

Chillingsworth (☎ 508-896-3640; 2449 MA 6A; bistro mains $17-35, fixed-price dinner $65-70; ☺ dinner) The place to celebrate milestone anniversaries. The standard here is the seven-course, fixed-price French dinner, with the cost depending upon what you select for the main course. Or take it light and dine à la carte on the restaurant's sunny bistro side.

Drinking & Entertainment

Woodshed (☎ 508-896-7771; 1993 MA 6A; cover $5) Locals hang out at this rustic bar and restaurant in the town center. It hosts local rock bands nightly in summer, weekends only the rest of the year.

Cape Rep Theatre (☎ 508-896-1888; www.caperep .org; 3397 MA 6A; tickets $20-25, children's programs $10; ☺ Tue-Sat summer, Thu-Sun spring & fall; ♿) Creative productions are held in both a 135-seat indoor theater and a natural outdoor amphitheater. Programs include musicals, drama and Seussical children's fare.

HARWICH
pop 12,400

Things move a little slower here in Harwich, and that's OK. It has good beaches, fine restaurants and one of the Cape's most photographed spots – lovely Wychmere Harbor. It also has a summertime ferry to Nantucket.

Orientation & Information

Harwich faces Nantucket Sound, with a little stretch reaching around Chatham to poke a toe in Pleasant Bay to the east. Most of what you'll need is along MA 28, through the communities of West Harwich and Harwich Port. Wychmere Harbor sits right along MA 28.

Harwich Information Center (☎ 508-432-1165, 800-442-7942; www.harwichcc.com; cnr 1 Schoolhouse Rd & MA 28; ☺ 9am-5pm Mon-Fri, 11am-4pm Sat & Sun late May–mid-Oct, reduced hours rest of year) This helpful tourist office provides all the expected lodging and dining info.

Sights & Activities
BROOKS ACADEMY MUSEUM

The Harwich Historical Society's **museum** (☎ 508-432-8089; 80 Parallel St, Harwich; admission free; ☺ 1-4pm Wed-Fri late Jun-Aug, 1-4pm Thu & Fri Sep–mid-Oct) is where to learn about the turkey-side dish, the cranberry, which was first successfully cultivated in Harwich.

CAPE COD LAVENDER FARM

These **lavender fields** (☎ 508-432-8397; Island Pond Trail, off MA 124, Harwich; ☺ 10am-5pm) on Harwich's north side blend seamlessly with the surrounding conservation land. Stroll around the fields and shop for fragrant lavender marmalade, body oils and soaps.

BEACHES

Harwich has fine beaches, although many of them restrict parking to residents. But fret not. To get to one of the prettiest, park your car for free at the municipal lot behind the tourist office and then walk five minutes to the end of Sea St, which terminates at **Sea St Beach**.

Sleeping

Beach Breeze Inn (☎ 508-432-2101, 800-942-9845; www .beachbreezeinn.com; 169 MA 28, West Harwich; r incl breakfast in season/off-season from $139/75; ☺ Apr-Nov; ♨) Despite the name, it's on the main road, not the beach, but the rooms are nicely fitted at this mom and pop motel. Everything is neat as a pin. With either two queen beds or one king bed in the rooms, there plenty of space to rest your head.

our pick Sandpiper Beach Inn (☎ 508-432-0485, 800-433-2234; www.sandpiperbeachinn.com; 16 Bank St, Harwich Port; r incl breakfast in season $180-285, off-season $150-210; ♨) If you want to be on a gorgeous beach with nothing but sand separating you from the ocean, stop the search here. A classic cedar-shingle exterior and restrained white and sea-blue interior match flawlessly with the setting. You could pay much more to be in this neighborhood, but you'd be wasting your money.

Wequassett Inn (☎ 508-432-5400, 800-225-7125; www.wequassett.com; Pleasant Bay, East Harwich; r in season/off-season from $445/170; ☼ Apr-Nov; ▢ ☑) The priciest lodging on the Cape offers pretty much anything you could ask of a full-service resort: flower-filled gardens, tennis, fitness center, volleyball, private boat launch, fine dining and boat rentals.

Eating

Mason Jar (☎ 508-430-7600; 544 MA 28, Harwich Port; sandwiches $5-6; ☼ 9am-5pm Tue-Sun) Harwich's shop of note for fancy sandwiches, soups, pastries, and lemonade made to order. Take your booty to the beach or sit at one of the café tables on the sidewalk patio.

Bonatt's Restaurant & Bakery (☎ 508-432-7199; 537 MA 28, Harwich Port; meals $9-14; ☼ breakfast & lunch) People flock to this unpretentious place in the center of town for sweet breakfast treats. The melt-a-way, a jam-filled Danish drenched in icing, is the house special. Or add a little protein with the crab cake Benedict and lunchtime steak sandwiches.

Brax (☎ 508-432-5515; 705 MA 28, Harwich Port; meals $20-27; ☼ lunch & dinner) Head to this casual gem for water-view dining and fresh seafood at honest prices. You'll be tempted by the likes of grilled Cajun swordfish and pistachio-encrusted halibut but don't miss the awesome lobster rolls.

Cape Sea Grille (☎ 508-432-4745; 31 Sea St, Harwich Port; meals $21-41; ☼ dinner) Sit on the glass-enclosed porch of this old sea captain's house and savor some of the Cape's finest seafood. The crispy oysters and the seared lobster pancetta are justifiably famous. Landlubbers in the party won't be disappointed with the pepperanade fillet mignon.

Drinking & Entertainment

Harwich Junior Theatre (☎ 508-432-2002; www.hjt capecod.org; 105 Division St, West Harwich; tickets $14-20; ☼ year-round; ♿) It's a children's summer theater (the country's oldest), and in the off-season also stages fare for grown-ups.

Brax (☎ 508-432-5515; 705 MA 28, Harwich Port) Grab yourself a seat on the outdoor deck overlooking Saquatucket Harbor for the best drink-with-a-view in town.

CHATHAM
pop 6650

The patriarch of Cape Cod towns, Chatham has a genteel reserve that is evident along its shady Main St; the shops are upscale, the lodgings tony. That said, there's something for everyone here – families flock to town for seal-watching, birders migrate to the wildlife refuge. And then there are all those beaches. Sitting at the 'elbow' of the Cape, Chatham boasts an amazing 60 miles of shoreline along the ocean, sound and countless coves and inlets.

Orientation & Information

MA 28 leads right to Main St, where the lion's share of shops and restaurants are lined up. Chatham is a town made for strolling; you'll find free parking along Main St and in the parking lot behind the Chatham Squire.

Chatham Chamber of Commerce (☎ 508-945-5199, 800-715-5567; www.chathaminfo.com; cnr MA 28 & MA 137; ☼ 9am-4pm Mon-Sat) Stop here for the latest info as you enter town.

Eldredge Public Library (☎ 508-945-5170; 564 Main St; ☼ 10am-5pm Mon, Wed, Fri & Sat, 1-9pm Tue & Thu) Has free internet access for up to 30 minutes.

Visitor booth (533 Main St; ☼ 10am-5pm Mon-Sat, noon-5pm Sun in summer) Operated by the chamber of commerce in the town center.

Yellow Umbrella Books (☎ 508-945-0144; 501 Main St) This independent store sells a fine selection of used and new books.

Sights & Activities
CHATHAM LIGHT

For dramatic vistas of sand and sea, head to the lighthouse viewing area on Shore Rd, where there's free 30-minute parking. The landmark lighthouse dates to 1878 and its light is visible 15 miles out to sea. Free 20-minute tours of the lighthouse are given between 1pm and 3:30pm on Wednesday from May to October; no reservations are taken, so just show up.

ATWOOD HOUSE MUSEUM

If you have time for just one historical **museum** (☎ 508-945-2493; 347 Stage Harbor Rd; adult/child under 12yr $5/free; ☼ 1-4pm Tue-Sat early Jun–mid-Oct, 10am-4pm Tue-Sat Jul & Aug) on the Cape, make it this one. In addition to the usual antiques you'll find a gallery of 130 portraits of Chatham townsfolk painted in the 1930s and '40s by Alice Stallnecht. The real prize, however, is a collection of finely carved duck decoys created by local resident Anthony Elmer Crowell (1862–1952). Known to collectors as the Rembrandt of decoy makers, Crowell's pieces have sold for more than $1 million each.

CHATHAM RAILROAD MUSEUM

This kid-friendly **museum** (www.chathamrailroad museum.com; 153 Depot Rd; admission by donation; 🕑 10am-4pm Tue-Sat mid-Jun–mid-Sep) in Chatham's original 1887 railroad depot will delight train buffs with its 1910 caboose and memorabilia. The Victorian building itself is an architectural treasure worth a visit.

FISH PIER

In the mid to late afternoon, head to the **Chatham Fish Pier** (Shore Rd), about 1 mile north of Chatham Light, to watch the fishing fleet unload its daily catch. Park in the upper parking lot and walk down behind the fish market.

BEACHES

Chatham doesn't come up short on sand. For the warmer waters of Nantucket Sound, the long and sandy **Hardings Beach** (Hardings Beach Rd) is the prize. To reach it, take Bank Hill Rd from MA 28. Parking costs $15. **Oyster Pond Beach** (cnr Pond St & Stage Harbor Rd), on a calm inlet, is smaller but the swimming is good and parking is free.

Directly below Chatham Light on Shore Rd are the long, wide sands of **Lighthouse Beach**. So many people come here to see the lighthouse view that the parking is limited to 30 minutes; it's only a 15-minute walk from Main St, however, where on-street parking is allowed.

Want to really get away from it all? The offshore barrier beaches of **North Beach** and **South Beach** offer miles of uninhabited sands ideal for sunbathing, ocean dips and long walks. The Atlantic sides have surf, while the Chatham-facing bay sides offer calm waters. There's no shade or facilities, so bring water, snacks and sunscreen. **Beachcomber** (☎ 508-945-5265; Crowell Rd; adult/child under 12yr $12/8; 🕑 10am-5pm) operates a water taxi to North Beach, while **Rip Ryder** (☎ 508-945-5450; Wikis Way; adult/child under 10yr $15/10; 🕑 7:30am-5pm) drops passengers at South Beach.

MONOMOY NATIONAL WILDLIFE REFUGE

This 7600-acre **wildlife refuge** (www.fws.gov/north east/monomoy), occupying the uninhabited North Monomoy and South Monomoy Islands, is a haven for shorebirds and seabirds. Nearly 300 species nest here and 10 times that number pass through on migrations. It's one of the most important ornithological stops on the Atlantic seaboard, and you'll be well rewarded for making the effort to reach it. **Outermost Harbor Marine** (☎ 508-945-5858; 83 Seagull Rd; boat tour adult/child $25/15) offers a 1½-hour Monomoy wildlife tour, or it can just shuttle you over and come back to pick you up later for $20, allowing you to explore on your own. It's off Morris Island Rd.

SEAL-WATCHING

Gray and harbor seals gather in great numbers in Chatham's waters and haul out on the shoals. There are a couple of ways to see them. The free way is to just go down to the Chatham Fish Pier (left) when the tide is low and look due east to spot seals up on the sandbars. To get closer to the action join a tour with **Beachcomber** (☎ 508-945-5265; Crowell Rd; adult/child 3-15yr $22/16; 🕑 late May–mid-Oct), which leaves from Chatham Fish Pier.

WATER SPORTS

The waters off Chatham are decent for windsurfing and kayaking and the friendly folks at **Monomoy Sail & Cycle** (☎ 508-945-0811; 275 MA 28/Orleans Rd, North Chatham; per day rental sailboard or kayak $45) can set you up.

BIKING

An extension of the Cape Cod Rail Trail (see boxed text, p188) ends at Chatham, and the town's side streets and shady lanes are well suited to bicycling. **Chatham Cycle** (☎ 508-945-8981; 193 Depot St; per day $24; 🕑 9am-5pm) rents quality bikes.

Sleeping
BUDGET & MIDRANGE

Bow Roof House (☎ 508-945-1346; 59 Queen Anne Rd; r incl breakfast $90-100) It's hard to find places like this anymore. this homey, six-room, c 1780 house is delightfully old-fashioned in price and offerings, and within easy walking distance of the town center and beach. Except for a few later-day conveniences like the addition of private bathrooms, the house with its exposed beams and central fireplaces looks nearly the same as it did in colonial times.

Chatham Highlander (☎ 508-945-9038; www .chathamhighlander.com; 946 Main St; r $119-199; 🗙 🛋) The rooms here, about 1 mile from the town center, are straightforward but large, clean and well maintained. All have a refrigerator, and some a microwave. Unlike some stodgier resorts in town that cater to an older set, this motel welcomes families – kids will love the pair of pools.

Carriage House Inn (☎ 508-945-4688, 800-355-8868; www.thecarriagehouseinn.com; 407 Old Harbor Rd; r incl breakfast $140-255; 🐾) An affordable choice by Chatham standards. The rooms in this B&B are tidy, the queen beds comfy and the breakfast home-cooked. Some of the rooms have fireplaces, and other warm touches – eg free use of beach gear – add to its popularity.

Pleasant Bay Village (☎ 508-945-1133, 800-547-1011; www.pleasantbayvillage.com; 1191 MA 28/Orleans Rd; r incl breakfast in season $155-265, off-season $125-175; 🐾 🐾) It's not central but that's its charm. Covering 6 acres at the north side of Chatham, this soothing place is set amid gardens and a Japanese-style carp pond. The rooms are spread across several low-rise buildings in traditional Cape Cod style. Request one of the rear building studios for the best digs.

TOP END

Hawthorne (☎ 508-945-0372; www.thehawthorne.com; 196 Shore Rd; r in season $230-320, off-season $175-225; 🕑 mid-May–mid-Oct; 🐾 🖥) It's all about location. The 27 rooms are standard grade but the view from the balcony is a million-dollar stunner, all ocean and sand. Grab a towel – the backyard here is your own private beach. One more perk: you can reserve a kitchenette unit for the same price as the regular motel rooms.

our pick Captain's House Inn (☎ 508-945-0127, 800-315-0728; www.captainshouseinn.com; 369 Old Harbor Rd; r incl breakfast in season from $265, off-season $180; 🐾 wi-fi 🐾) Everything about this place, set in a 1839 Greek Revival house, is gracious and inviting. The decor is sumptuous, every guest room has a fireplace, and a gourmet breakfast is served in style overlooking a bubbly fountain. Bring your own champagne.

Chatham Bars Inn (☎ 508-945-0096, 800-527-4884; www.chathambarsinn.com; 297 Shore Rd; r in season/off-season from $350/200; 🐾 🐾) This grande dame resort comprises 215 pricey rooms, and cottages on or near the beach. Its 25 acres include an oceanside heated pool, tennis, golf and a private beach. You can always visit just for a drink on the expansive verandah.

Eating
BUDGET & MIDRANGE

Chatham Cookware Café (☎ 508-945-1250; 524 Main St; pastries $2, sandwiches $7; 🕑 6:30am-4pm) No, it's not a place to buy pots and pans, but rather the favorite downtown spot for a coffee fix, homemade muffins and sandwiches made to order. Order at the counter and take your goodies straight out the back, where you'll find a leafy garden deck.

Larry's PX (☎ 508-945-3964; 1591 Main St; meals $6-14; 🕑 5am-4pm Jun-Aug, 6am-2pm Sep-May) True local flavor with Formica tables, fishermen's hours and service with a sassy smile. Join the townies for omelettes and fried seafood. The waitresses' T-shirts read 'Order what you want; Eat what you get.' The sign on the door says 'Sorry, we're open.' Gotta love that.

Marion's Pie Shop (☎ 508-432-9439; 2022 Main St; items $6-20; 🕑 8am-6pm Mon-Sat, 8am-5pm Sun, reduced hours in winter) Wild blueberry and strawberry-rhubarb rate high among the sweet pies, and savory pies such as chicken, beef or clam will satisfy your hungry crew. Deli goods too – it makes a good stop on the way to the beach.

TOP END

Impudent Oyster (☎ 508-945-3545; 15 Chatham Bars Ave; meals $10-32; 🕑 lunch & dinner) An eclectic menu, from its namesake fresh-shucked oysters to Japanese-influenced fare, makes this a real pearl – don't miss the drunken oysters in sake. The daily specials at this place come fresh off the boat.

Vining's Bistro (☎ 508-945-5033; 595 Main St; meals $21-32; 🕑 dinner) Parents (and others) seeking a quiet night away from the kids can slip away to this sophisticated bistro. It's chef-driven, with an open kitchen, and the innovative menu includes the likes of lime-cilantro crab cakes and pan-roasted scallops with smoked bacon.

Drinking & Entertainment

Chatham Squire (☎ 508-945-0945; 487 Main St) The town's favorite watering hole is both a family-friendly pub and an easygoing, boisterous bar full of happy locals. Got an old car license plate on you? It'll find a home with the hundreds of others decorating the walls.

Chatham Bars Inn (☎ 508-945-0096; 297 Shore Rd) Join the tony set here for a martini with a fabulous ocean view.

Monomoy Theatre (☎ 508-945-1589; 776 Main St; tickets $18-29; 🕑 mid-Jun–Aug) Ohio University students stage musicals, Shakespeare and

---

THE ORIGINAL FRENCH CONNECTION

Today's multibillion-dollar telecommunications industry owes a debt of gratitude to Cape Cod's Atlantic shore. The first cable connection between Europe and the US was established in 1879 by the French Telegraph Company on a windswept bluff in Eastham. When conditions there proved inhospitable, the station was moved to Orleans in 1890, and until the mid-20th century the French Cable Station transmitted communications via a 3000-mile-long cable between Orleans and Brest, France. Charles Lindbergh's arrival in Paris and Germany's invasion of France were among the messages relayed. The **French Cable Museum** (☎ 508-240-1735; cnr Cove Rd & MA 28; admission free; ⊗ 1-4pm Thu-Sun Jul & Aug, 1-4pm Fri & Sat Jun & Sep) in Orleans contains all the original equipment, and staff help explain everything.

A side note: up the road in South Wellfleet, the Marconi Wireless Station was the first place in the US to transmit messages across the Atlantic Ocean *without* wires and cables. In 1903 President Theodore Roosevelt used Guglielmo Marconi's invention to send 'most cordial greetings' to King Edward VII in England. Little remains at that site (p198) today except for interpretive plaques and a small model.

---

contemporary plays at this well-known playhouse. They've been at it since 1957.

Kate Gould Park (Main St; admission free) If you're in town on a Friday night, don't miss the summertime band concerts held under the stars at Kate Gould Park; they're an atmospheric throwback to an earlier era.

Shopping

Main St is lined with interesting shops and galleries.

Blue Water Fish Rubbings (☎ 508-945-7616; 505 Main St) Classy cotton beachwear and T-shirts are painted by a Chatham artist using rubbings of actual fish, lobsters and seashells. Very cool.

Yankee Ingenuity (☎ 508-945-1288; 525 Main St) Full of surprises, from Elvis-painted Russian nesting dolls and quirky glass jewelry to elegant pottery and dramatic photos of the Cape. Best of all, the fun comes in all price ranges.

Munson Gallery (☎ 508-945-2888; 880 Main St) One of the oldest continuously operating galleries in the country (opened in 1860), it represents established and up-and-coming American artists.

ORLEANS

pop 6350

To many, Orleans is simply the place where MA 28 and US 6 converge and US 6 heads north to Provincetown. Others know there are lots of good restaurants in town, that Nauset Beach is exceptional and that Nauset Marsh has a rich ecosystem worth exploring. When the tides are high you can paddle through the marsh by canoe – the shallow waters pulsate with all sorts of sea life from schools of tiny fish and crabs to rare migratory seabirds.

Orientation & Information

US 6, MA 6A and MA 28 converge at the rotary at the north edge of town, which marks the border with Eastham. Main St intersects with MA 6A and MA 28 in central Orleans, forming a triangle in the town center. Town Cove is just east of the intersection of routes 28 and 6A. Atlantic-facing Nauset Beach is about 3 miles east of Orleans center; Rock Harbor and Skaket Beach are on the bay side about 1.5 miles west of the town center.

Orleans Chamber of Commerce (☎ 508-255-1386, 800-865-1386; www.capecod-orleans.com; cnr MA 6A & Eldredge Park Way; ⊗ 10am-6pm Mon-Sat, 10am-2pm Sun Jun-Sep)

Snow Library (☎ 508-240-3760; 67 Main St; ⊗ 10am-5pm Mon, Thu & Fri, 10am-8pm Tue & Wed, 10am-4pm Sat) Internet access.

Sights & Activities

ROCK HARBOR

This picturesque fishing pier on the bay side of town is a quiet place when the tides are out, but when the fishing boats are in it's a hub of activity. If you want to cast a line yourself, you can hop on a charter boat from here. **Rock Harbor Charter Fleet** (☎ 508-255-9757; www.rockharborcharters.com; half-day trip per person $140; ⊗ mid-May–mid-Oct) operates from a shed in the parking lot and coordinates 14 fishing boats.

BEACHES

One of the Cape's best beaches for walking, sunning or bodysurfing is **Nauset Beach** (Beach Rd,

East Orleans; (P) $15). Dune-backed and gloriously wide and sandy, this barrier beach extends for miles along the open Atlantic. Free concerts are held at 7pm Monday in July and August and there's a clam shack and full facilities.

On the bay side, calm **Skaket Beach** (West Rd, off MA 6A; (P) $15) is popular with families. Kids love to wade in the shallow waters. Its generous sands triple in size when the tide goes out, and at low tide you can walk the flats all the way to Brewster and back.

BOATING

Goose Hummock Outdoor Center (☎ 508-255-2620; www.goose.com; MA 6A; canoe rental per 3hr $30, kayak rental per 3hr s $25-35, d $45; ⊙ 8am-6pm), right on Town Cove, rents canoes and kayaks for use on the protected and calm waters of Pleasant Bay and Nauset Marsh. It also offers kayak instruction and kayak tours.

BIKING

The Cape Cod Rail Trail (see boxed text, p188) goes through Orleans. **Orleans Cycle** (☎ 508-255-9115; 26 Main St; per day $20; ⊙ 9am-5pm) rents bikes.

Sleeping

Ship's Knees Inn (☎ 508-255-1312; www.shipskneesinn.com; 186 Beach Rd, East Orleans; r incl breakfast in season $110-215, off-season $75-165; ✖ ▯ wi-fi ▯) This place packs in a lot: the amenities are solid, the period decor is appealing and, best of all, it's within walking distance of Nauset Beach. The 16 rooms have antique themes along with modern conveniences such as cable TV and refrigerators, and there's a tennis court on the grounds.

Cove (☎ 508-255-1203, 800-343-2233; www.thecoveorleans.com; 13 MA 28; r in season $119-209, off-season $64-129; ▯ wi-fi ▯) The ideal choice for those who want to be on the water but within strolling distance of the town center. Every room has a refrigerator, microwave and HBO, but it's extras like the free boat tour of Town Cove that separate it from the pack. For the best water view, request rooms 20 to 24.

Nauset Beach-Side Motel & Cottages (☎ 508-255-3348; www.capecodtravel.com/nausetbeachside; 223 Beach Rd, East Orleans; r in season/off-season from $158/90; ⊙ Apr-Oct) Nothing fancy at this old-fashioned motel – the walls are a bit scuffed, the furniture a bit worn, but blimey, you're just steps from beautiful Nauset Beach. Short-term visitors get the motel rooms, some of which have kitchens. Knotty-pine-paneled cottages rent by the week (Saturday to Saturday) starting at $1095.

Eating

Orleans Farmers Market (11 Old Colony Way; ⊙ 8am-noon Sat Jun–mid-Oct) Buy fresh organic produce, Cape Cod honey and homemade baked goods direct from the source at this outdoor market.

Hot Chocolate Sparrow (☎ 508-240-2230; 5 Old Colony Way; sandwiches $5-7; ⊙ 6:30am-late) The Cape's finest coffee bar brews the headiest espresso around. Or for a cool treat on a hot day, try the 'frozen hot chocolate.' Panini sandwiches, homemade pastries and fresh-from-the-oven cinnamon buns make the perfect accompaniments. Smoothies and ice-cream too.

Sir Cricket's Fish & Chips (☎ 508-255-4453; 38 MA 6A; meals $8-22; ⊙ lunch & dinner) This hole-in-the-wall is the town's hot spot for fried seafood. It's mostly takeout but there are a few tables. Take a look at the wooden chairs, which are hand-painted with vintage Orleans scenes.

Academy Ocean Grille (☎ 508-240-1585; cnr 2 Academy Pl & MA 28; meals $10-34; ⊙ lunch & dinner Tue-Sun) This outstanding seafood restaurant is a bit like eating in someone's dining room, except with seafaring decor and more tables. Think crab cakes with citrus-caper beurre blanc, sole Française and swordfish with a basil glaze.

Abba (☎ 508-255-8144; cnr West Rd & Old Colony Way; meals $20-36; ⊙ dinner) Feeling adventurous? This fine-dining restaurant offers superb pan-Mediterranean fare with a hint of Thai thrown in. Start with steamed local mussels in basil-coconut milk and move on to the spiced-rubbed rack of lamb or the curry-cream scallops with grilled eggplant.

Drinking & Entertainment

Land Ho! (☎ 508-255-5165; 38 MA 6A) The place to see and be seen and to get a feel for local flavor. Good drinks, pub grub and atmosphere.

Academy of Performing Arts (☎ 508-255-1963; www.apacape.org; 120 Main St; tickets $10-18; ⊙ year-round) This community playhouse stages dramas, musicals and children's theater in the 1873 former town hall.

EASTHAM

pop 5500

Home to the Cape's oldest windmill, some well-known lighthouses and much of the Cape Cod National Seashore, Eastham is one of the Cape's quietest towns. Don't be fooled

CAPE COD NATIONAL SEASHORE

Extending some 40 miles around the curve of the Outer Cape, the **Cape Cod National Seashore** (www.nps.gov/caco) encompasses the Atlantic shoreline from Orleans all the way to Provincetown. Under the auspices of the National Park Service, it's a treasure trove of unspoiled beaches, dunes, salt marshes, nature trails and forests. Thanks to the backing of President John F Kennedy this vast area was set aside for preservation in the 1960s, just before a building boom hit the rest of his native Cape Cod. Access to the park sights is easy – everything of interest is on or just off US 6.

The National Seashore's **Salt Pond Visitor Center** (☎ 508-255-3421; cnr US 6 & Nauset Rd, Eastham; admission free; ☷ 9am-4:30pm Sep-Jun, 9am-5:30pm Jul & Aug) is the place to start and has a great view to boot. There are first-rate exhibits and short films about the Cape's geology, history and ever-changing landscape. The helpful staff can provide maps to the park's numerous trails, both hiking and biking, some of which begin right at the visitors center. Check out the daily schedule of interpretive ranger walks, talks, stargazing, campfire programs, etc; most are free.

The Province Lands Visitor Center (p204) in Provincetown is smaller but has similar services.

Beach parking permits cost $15 per day or $45 per season and are valid at all National Seashore beaches, so you can use the same permit to spend the morning at one beach and the afternoon at another.

by the bland commercial development along US 6 – slip off the highway and you'll find a world of beaches, marshes and trails.

Orientation & Information

Eastham is just 3 miles wide from bay to ocean, and 6 miles long. US 6 runs through the center of Eastham, and is dotted with shops, lodgings and restaurants its entire length,

Eastham Chamber of Commerce (☎ 508-255-3444; www.easthamchamber.com; cnr US 6 & Governor Prence Rd; ☷ 10am-5pm mid-May–early Oct, 9am-6pm Jul & Aug) Maintains an information booth just north of the Fort Hill turnoff.

Sights & Activities

Don't miss the commanding view of expansive Nauset Marsh from **Fort Hill** (Governor Prence Rd, east off US 6). It's a favorite place to be at dawn, but the view is lovely any time of the day. And bring your walking shoes for the 2-mile **Fort Hill Trail**, which leads down the hill toward the coast and then skirts inland to meander along raised boardwalks over an enchanting red maple swamp. It's one of the nicest walks in the National Seashore, especially in fall.

Near Fort Hill sits the **Captain Penniman House** (☎ 508-255-3421; Governor Prence Rd; admission free; ☷ 1-4pm Tue-Thu Jul & Aug), a mid-19th-century sea captain's house topped with a widow's walk and fronted by an awesome whale-jawbone gate. Ask at the Salt Pond Visitor Center about access at other times.

The **Old Schoolhouse Museum** (☎ 508-255-0788; cnr Nauset Rd & US 6; admission free; ☷ 1-4pm Mon-Fri Jul & Aug), across from the Salt Pond Visitor Center, features a small exhibit on author Henry Beston's year in a cottage on Coast Guard Beach.

Eastham's landmark **windmill** (cnr US 6 & Samoset Rd; admission free; ☷ 10am-5pm in summer) is the oldest structure in town, although it was actually built in Plymouth, MA in 1680.

BEACHES

All roads lead to **Coast Guard Beach** (Ⓟ $15). The main road from the Salt Pond Visitor Center deposits you here, as do biking and hiking trails. And it's for good reason – this grand beach backed by a classic coast guard station is a real pleaser that attracts everyone from beach strollers to hard-core surfers. Bird-watchers flock here for the eagle-eye view of Nauset Marsh. Facilities include rest rooms, showers and changing rooms. In summer, when the small beach parking lot fills up, a shuttle bus runs from a staging area near the visitors center.

Cliff-backed **Nauset Light Beach** (Ⓟ $15), north of Coast Guard Beach, is also the stuff of dreams. Its features and facilities are similar to Coast Guard Beach, but there's a large parking lot right at the beach. **Nauset Lighthouse**, a picturesque red-and-white striped tower, guards the shoreline. And don't miss the **Three Sisters Lighthouses**, a curious trio of 19th-century lighthouses saved from an eroding sea cliff and moved to a wooded clearing just five minutes' walk up Cable Rd from Nauset Light Beach.

First Encounter Beach (P $15), where Samoset Rd meets Cape Cod Bay, is an excellent location to watch the sunset. With its vast tidal flats and kid-friendly, calm, shallow waters, it offers a night-and-day contrast to the National Seashore beaches on Eastham's wild Atlantic side. While it's a thoroughly pleasant scene today, the beach takes its name from a more checkered history – it was on these shores that the first arrows and musket fire exchange took place between Native Americans and the Pilgrims.

SURFING

If you're ready to ride the waves, **Little Overhead** (☎ 508-240-1455; 4900 US 6; 2hr surf lesson $80; ☻ 10am-5pm) can set you up with everything you need from surfboard sales and rentals to surfing lessons for those new to the sport.

BIKING

Eastham has both the Cape Cod Rail Trail (see boxed text, p188) and a connecting National Seashore bike trail, the latter traversing a dramatic salt marsh en route to Coast Guard Beach. Rent bikes at **Little Capistrano Bike Shop** (☎ 508-255-6515; Salt Pond Rd; rental per 4/8hr adult $15/19, child $10/15; ☻ Apr–mid-Nov).

Sleeping

Hostelling International Eastham (Mid-Cape; ☎ 508-255-2785; www.capecodhostels.org; 75 Goody Hallett Dr; dm $25-30, r $69-90; ☻ late May-early Sep) With just eight cabins and 50 dorm beds this place fills quickly. The aging cabins are basic (a bit like camping), but they offer a rare chance to stay in a fine neighborhood on a budget.

Cove Bluffs Motel (☎ 508-240-1616; www.covebluffs.com; cnr US 6 & Shore Rd; r/studio in season $90/105, off-season $50/65; ☻) A home-away-from-home kind of place whose spacious grounds include a basketball court and hammocks strung from the trees. You can opt for a motel-style room, but if you swing for the studios to add on a kitchen, it'll save a bundle on restaurant bills.

Midway Motel & Cottages (☎ 508-255-3117, 800-755-3117; www.midwaymotel.com; 5460 US 6, North Eastham; r in season $108-116, off-season $60-68; ☻ Feb-Oct) The 11 tidy units here are set back a bit from the highway and shaded by pine trees. Each is set up a little differently; some have full kitchens, others just fridge and microwave. There are also

cottages with up to three bedrooms that rent by the week in summer for around $1000.

Inn at the Oaks (☎ 508-255-1886, 877-255-1886; www.innattheoaks.com; 3085 US 6; r incl breakfast in season $130-290, off-season $115-270; ☻ ☐ wi-fi) This historic inn, across from the Salt Pond Visitor Center, offers 18 antique-filled guest rooms. There's a room for every taste; some have fireplaces, others open up into family suites. The owners are very accommodating – there's a play area for kids and the place is pet-friendly too.

Eating

Box Lunch (☎ 508-255-0799; 4205 MA 6; sandwiches $5-7; ☻ lunch & dinner) The specialty at this Cape favorite is the 'rollwich,' a rolled pita-bread sandwich thick with yummy fillings. Many varieties have cute names for Pilgrims and ingredients like turkey, stuffing and cranberry.

Friendly Fisherman (☎ 508-255-6770; 4580 US 6; meals $10-20; ☻ lunch & dinner Jun-Sep) This simple eatery, attached to a fish market, has outdoor picnic tables and serves great lobster rolls; they're huge, overflowing with sweet chunks of claw and tail meat, and with just enough mayo to hold it all together. The fried clams here are impressive, too.

Arnold's Lobster & Clam Bar (☎ 508-255-2575; 3580 US 6; meals $10-24; ☻ lunch & dinner May–mid-Oct) Fried seafood is the staple but health-conscious diners will also find baked cod, scallops and lobster on the menu. Everything is fresh and at night this place adds on a raw bar, which separates it from the other counter-service seafood shacks along the highway.

Entertainment

First Encounter Coffee House (www.firstencounter.org; 220 Samoset Rd; tickets $15; ☻ 8pm 2nd & 4th Sat of the month) The little yellow Chapel of the Pines hosts acoustic and folk performances put on by this long-running organization.

WELLFLEET

pop 2750

This town lures visitors with its art galleries, lovely beaches and famous Wellfleet oysters. Actually, there's not much Wellfleet doesn't have, other than crowds. It's a delightful throwback to an earlier era, from its drive-in movie theater to its unspoiled town center, which has barely changed in appearance since the 1950s.

Orientation & Information

Wellfleet is about 6.5 miles long from north to south. Like Eastham to the south and Truro to the north, Wellfleet is bisected by US 6. Most of the land east of US 6 is part of the Cape Cod National Seashore. To get to the town center, turn west off US 6 at either Main St or School St.

Oceans of Books (☎ 508-349-6996; 50 Kendrick Ave) An institution (locals know it simply as 'the bookstore') and a marvel. It's been here since the 1930s and is jam-packed with used books, vintage magazines and comics, some of which are as old as the store.

Wellfleet Chamber of Commerce (☎ 508-349-2510; www.wellfleetchamber.com; 1410 US 6; ☒ 9am-6pm daily late May-early Sep, 10am-4pm Fri-Sun mid-May–mid-Oct) Next to the South Wellfleet post office at Lecount Hollow Rd.

Wellfleet Public Library (☎ 508-349-0310; 55 W Main St; ☒ 2-8pm Mon, Wed & Thu, 10am-8pm Tue, 10am-5pm Fri & Sat) Has free internet and wi-fi access.

Sights & Activities

ART GALLERIES

You won't have any trouble finding art galleries in central Wellfleet – there are more than 20 galleries selling fine art and hand-crafted items. Most are within a 10-minute walk of each other on the adjoining Main, Bank and Commercial Sts, but there are galleries sprinkled throughout the town. Pick up the Wellfleet Art Galleries Association map, which has descriptive listings. Hours vary; some are open year-round, others from mid-May to mid-October. Many galleries host receptions with snacks and drinks on Saturday nights in July and August.

Some galleries you shouldn't miss:

Blue Heron Gallery (☎ 508-349-6724; 20 Bank St) A zenlike gallery with museum-quality art.

Left Bank Gallery (☎ 508-349-9451; 25 Commercial St) Locally and nationally known artists.

Nicholas Harrison Gallery (☎ 508-349-7799; 25 Bank St) Fine American crafts, clothing and glass.

WELLFLEET HISTORICAL SOCIETY MUSEUM

This **museum** (☎ 508-349-9157; 266 Main St; admission free; ☒ 10am-4pm Tue & Fri, 1-4pm Wed, Thu & Sat late Jun-early Sep) harbors a fascinating mishmash of odds and ends from a vintage bank teller cage to Native American artifacts. **Walking tours** (adult/child under 12yr $3/free) of the town can be taken either with a guide at 10:15am Tuesday and Friday or with an audiotape at your own leisure.

WELLFLEET BAY WILDLIFE SANCTUARY

Mass Audubon's 1100-acre **sanctuary** (☎ 508-349-2615; www.wellfleetbay.org; West Rd, off MA 6; adult/child $5/3; ☒ 8:30am-5pm late May–mid-Oct, Tue-Sun rest of year) boasts walking trails that cross tidal creeks and salt marshes and lead to Cape Cod Bay. The most popular is the Goose Pond Trail (1.5 miles round-trip), which goes from the nature center to the beach and offers splendid opportunities for spotting a wide variety of marine and bird life. The sanctuary also offers guided walks, talks and workshops.

BEACHES

Marconi Beach (P $15), off US 6, is a narrow Atlantic beach backed by sea cliffs and sand dunes. It's part of the Cape Cod National Seashore (see boxed text, p196); facilities include changing rooms, rest rooms and showers. Not much remains of the Marconi Wireless Station (see boxed text, p194), but there is a model of the station as it looked it 1903 when the first transatlantic wireless message was sent from this site.

The adjacent town-run beaches of **Cahoon Hollow Beach** and **White Crest Beach** along Ocean View Dr offer some of the Cape's top surfable waves. Backed by steep dunes these long, untamed Atlantic beaches also make for memorable beach walks. Parking at either costs $15.

BIKING

The northern end of the Cape Cod Rail Trail (see boxed text, p188) is at Lecount Hollow Rd near its intersection with US 6. You can rent bikes at **South Wellfleet General Store** (☎ 508-349-2335; cnr US 6 & Lecount Hollow Rd; bike rental per half/full day $12/20; ☒ 5:30am-6pm), right near the trailhead, and pedal south.

Festivals & Events

During the **Wellfleet OysterFest** (www.wellfleetoysterfest.org; ☒ mid-Oct) the town hall parking lot becomes a food fair, with a beer garden and an oyster shucking contest, and, of course, bellybusters of the blessed bivalves. The festival is so popular that it's hard to believe it started only in 2000.

Sleeping

Even'Tide Motel (☎ 508-349-3410, 800-368-0007; www.eventidemotel.com; 650 US 6; r in season from $110, off-season from $75, cottages per week $1200-2600; ☒ Apr-Oct;

TURTLES & BIRDS & SEALS, OH MY

Bob Prescott, director of Mass Audubon's Wellfleet Bay Wildlife Sanctuary, has the enviable job of directing one of the Cape's most spectacular nature sanctuaries. He spends his days keeping track of wildlife on the property's trails and beaches. This interview was postponed a bit while he went looking for a turtle fitted with a radio transmitter that had stopped transmitting. Bob wasn't born on Cape Cod – rather he's 'a summer kid that never left.' He's been with the sanctuary for 25 years.

What's special about Wellfleet Bay Wildlife Sanctuary (opposite)? I think most people really enjoy the diversity of habitat; starting at the nature center, out through pine woods to a freshwater pond, then a brackish water pond, along the side of a salt marsh to a coastal heathland community, out across a boardwalk to a barrier beach. In a loop like that you could see 50 species of birds along with a variety of wildflowers. It's a nice opportunity on a single property to see a wide variety of things.

If friends were visiting for the first time, what would you suggest for a 'real Cape Cod' experience? Getting out on the water in places like Pleasant Bay and Nauset Marsh (p195) captures the feeling of what the Cape was like decades ago, a hundred years ago. It's a timeless feel to be in a kayak out on the marsh. Fort Hill (p196) is a must – you get such a tremendous view of the Atlantic and Nauset Marsh. If it's in the spring I might go up to Pilgrim Heights (p201) to see the migrating hawks and walk out through the dunes.

What do you do on your days off? I generally try to get out and walk around different places. Of course I like the National Seashore (see boxed text, p196). In the summer I mostly get out on the water – I have a sailboat – that's about the only place you can really get away.

How would you rate the Cape's wildlife? Especially on the Outer Cape, there's just a tremendous amount of wildlife here. Whale-watching is a great pastime. I recommend the Dolphin Fleet (p205) out of Provincetown. It's just a great day – all visitors really should do that. Birding places change with the season. People can call and ask us about the best birding sites at any time. We do birding tours to South Beach (p192) in Chatham, and so does Outermost Harbor Marine (p192). And then there's the thrill of seeing seals inside Chatham Harbor, where kayakers can paddle up close and families with kids can see them on a calm-water boat tour (p192).

As related to Glenda Bendure and Ned Friary

(☒ ☒) This 31-room motel, set back from the highway in a grove of pine trees, also has nine cottages that can accommodate four to eight people each. Other pluses include in-room fridges, a large indoor pool, picnic facilities and a playground.

Stone Lion Inn of Cape Cod (☎ 508-349-9565; www .stonelioncapecod.com; 130 Commercial St; r incl breakfast in season $155-170, off-season $95-120; ☒ wi-fi) Built in 1871 by a sea captain, this fetching Victorian is the finest place in Wellfleet to tuck in. Wide pine floors, antique decor and handcrafted furnishings set the tone. A full breakfast is served and the in-town location is handy for exploring on foot.

Eating

Mac's Seafood Market (☎ 508-349-9611; Wellfleet Town Pier, cnr Commercial & Kendrick Sts; meals $8-18; ☒ lunch & dinner) Head here for fish-market-fresh seafood at bargain prices. Fried fish standards join the likes of oyster po' boys, sushi rolls and grilled striped bass dinners. You order at a window and chow down at picnic tables overlooking Wellfleet Harbor.

Juice (☎ 508-349-0535; 6 Commercial St; meals $8-18; ☒ breakfast, lunch & dinner; Ⓥ) Liquids get high billing at this café serving fair-trade coffee and organic juices. The innovative menu covers the spectrum from Wellfleet shellfish to veggie fajitas and pesto pizzas.

Wicked Oyster (☎ 508-349-3455; 50 Main St; meals breakfast & lunch $8-31; ☒ breakfast, lunch & dinner) The 'in' crowd hangs out here for grilled organic salmon, seared tuna and, of course, Wellfleet oysters. Although the chef works his magic at dinner, you can also start your day here with a wicked omelette or stop by for a lunchtime sandwich.

Moby Dick's (☎ 508-349-9795; US 6, opposite Gull Pond Rd; meals $9-20; ☒ lunch & dinner; ☒) There's often a line out the door at this roadside eatery, but you'll be rewarded for your wait with some of the best fried clams, onion rings and chowder

---

PEGGY SUE, IS THAT YOU?

For an evening of nostalgia, park at **Wellfleet Drive-In** (☎ 508-349-7176; US 6; adult/child 5-11yr $7.50/4.50; ☺ May–mid-Oct), one of a dwindling number of drive-in theaters surviving in the USA. Built in the 1950s, before the word 'cinemaplex' became part of the vernacular, everything except the movie being shown on the giant screen is true to the era. Yep, they still have those original mono speakers that you hook over the car window, there's an old-fashioned snack bar and, of course, it's always a double feature. Plastic – what's that? It's cash-only at the gate.

OK, there are a few accommodations to modern times. So as to not block anyone's view, the lot is now divided into two sections: one for SUVs, the other for cars. And you don't *need* to use those boxy window speakers – you can also listen by tuning your stereo car radio to FM 89.3. But other things remain unchanged. Bring bug spray and a blanket!

Another time-honored throwback is **Wellfleet Flea Market** (☎ 508-349-2520; US 6; per car $3; ☺ 7am-4pm Wed, Thu, Sat & Sun in summer, 7am-4pm Sat & Sun in spring & fall), held during the day at the drive-in. This is the largest flea market on the Cape, hosting 300 dealers, and covering antiques to newly made objects, treasures to junk.

---

at this end of the Cape. Parents will like the kids' menu.

Bookstore & Restaurant (☎ 508-349-3154; 50 Kendrick Ave; meals $10-22; ☺ breakfast, lunch & dinner) This place raises its own oysters and little-neck clams, harvested at low tide in the waters right across the street – can't get fresher than that. Sit out on the deck and enjoy the view. The menu covers a broad gamut from fish sandwiches to seafood Alfredo and prime rib.

Drinking & Entertainment

Wellfleet Harbor Actors Theater (WHAT; ☎ 508-349-9428; www.what.org; tickets $10-29; ☺ year-round) The Cape's most celebrated theater always has something going, either at its original harborside location (1 Kendrick Ave) or its new state-of-the-art Julie Harris Stage (2357 MA 6). Contemporary, experimental plays staged here are always lively, occasionally bawdy and often the subject of animated conversation.

CAPE COD'S ATLANTIS

In the early 1800s, 60-acre Billingsgate Island stood in the bay off Wellfleet, with a fishing community of 30 homes, a whale-oil rendering plant, a school and a lighthouse. But in the mid-1800s the island was split in half by beach erosion, and by 1900 the island was abandoned except for the lighthouse keeper. Billingsgate and its lighthouse completely disappeared beneath the waves in 1942; and now it's visible only at very low tide as a shoal off northern Wellfleet.

Beachcomber (☎ 508-349-6055; Cahoon Hollow Beach, Ocean View Dr; ☺ late May-early Sep) The Cape's coolest hangout, in a former lifesaving station right on the beach, 'Da Coma' is *the* place to have a drink or rock the night away. And some really good bands – like Weezer and They Might Be Giants – sometimes pop in.

TRURO
pop 2100

Squeezed between Cape Cod Bay on the west and the open Atlantic on the east, narrow Truro abounds with water views. An odd collection of elements coexist peacefully here: strip motels along the highway, trophy homes in the hills and dales west of US 6, and undeveloped forests and beaches to the east.

Orientation & Information

To reach Truro's historic sites, which are on the ocean side, take Highland or South Highland Rds off US 6. Or for fun just take any winding road east or west of US 6. Then let yourself get a little lost, and soak in the distinctive scenery.

Truro Chamber of Commerce (☎ 508-487-1288; www.trurochamberofcommerce.com; cnr US 6 & Head of the Meadow Rd, North Truro; ☺ 10am-4pm Fri & Sat late May–mid-Oct, 10am-4pm daily Jul & Aug)

Sights & Activities

Cape Cod Highland Light (☎ 508-487-1121; Light House Rd; admission $4; ☺ 10am-5:30pm May-Oct) sits on the Cape's highest elevation (a mere 120ft!), dates to 1797 and casts the brightest beam on the New England coast. Admission includes a 10-minute video, an exhibit in the Keeper's

House and a climb up the lighthouse's 69 steps to a sweeping vista. Children must be at least 51in tall to make the climb.

The adjacent **Highland House Museum** (☎ 508-487-3397; Light House Rd; adult/child under 12yr $4/free; 10am-4:30pm Jun-Sep) focuses on Truro's farming and maritime past. It's packed with all sorts of vintage goodies from antique dolls to shipwreck salvage.

Pilgrim Heights, on the north side of town and east of US 6, has two short trails with broad views. Both start at the same parking lot and each takes about 20 minutes to walk. If you're doing just one, opt for the **Pilgrim Spring Trail**, which makes a loop to the spring where the Pilgrims purportedly first found fresh water after landing in the New World in 1620. It also has an overlook with an ideal vantage for spotting hawks that hunt for rodents in the marsh below.

Part of the Cape Cod National Seashore, **Head of the Meadow Beach** (Head of the Meadow Rd, off US 6) is a wonderfully wide, dune-backed beach. Facilities are limited, but there are lifeguards in summer. At low tide it's possible to catch glimpses of old shipwrecks that met their fate on the shoals. There are two entrances: the National Seashore beach (parking $15) is to the left, while the town-managed beach (parking $10) is to the right.

Sleeping

North of Highland Camping Area (☎ 508-487-1191; www.capecodcamping.com; 52 Head of the Meadow Rd, North Truro; campsites $30; late May–mid-Sep) Campers will be pleasantly surprised to find that little Truro harbors one of the most secluded campgrounds on all of Cape Cod, with 237 sites spread around 60 forested acres. And you don't have to worry about setting up your tent next to an RV – this place is geared to tent camping.

Hostelling International Truro (☎ 508-349-3889; www.capecodhostels.org; N Pamet Rd, North Truro; dm incl breakfast $30-35; late Jun-early Sep) Budget digs don't get more atmospheric than at this former coast guard station perched amid undulating dunes. It's so remote that wild turkeys are the only traffic along the road. And it's but a stroll to a quiet beach. There are just 42 beds, so book early to avoid disappointment.

Days' Cottages (☎ 508-487-1062; www.dayscottages.com; 271 Shore Rd/MA 6A, North Truro; cottages in season $170, off-season $100; May-Sep) The 23 identical cottages here, lined up like ducks along the beach, are an architectural landmark and have been operating since 1931. You can't get closer to the water – each cottage is just inches from the shoreline. That said, they're very basic inside, with a small kitchen, living room and two bedrooms each with a double bed. Rates cover up to four people.

Eating

Village Café (☎ 508-487-5800; 4 Highland Rd, North Truro; light eats $2-7; breakfast & lunch) Grab yourself a seat under one of the red parasols and watch the traffic trickle by at this pleasant little place in the center of North Truro. Perhaps a strawberry croissant and shot of espresso to jump-start the day. Lunch dips into Portuguese kale soup and an array of sandwiches.

Dutra's Market (☎ 508-487-0711; cnr MA 6A & Highland Rd, North Truro; sandwiches $5-6; 8am-8pm Mon-Sat, 8am-3pm Sun) This little town grocery store carries all the basics including liquor and freshly made sandwiches to go.

Terra Luna (☎ 508-487-1019; 104 Shore Rd/MA 6A, North Truro; meals $19-28; dinner; V) Deceptively nondescript from the outside, this surprisingly hip bistro exhibits local art on barnboard walls and creative New American and Mediterranean cooking. Perhaps a juicy coffee-rubbed steak with Yukon gold potatoes, or go vegan with the pine nut lasagna.

PROVINCETOWN
pop 3500

This is it: as far as you can go on the Cape, and more than just geographically. The region's most lively resort town is a world unto itself. Fringe writers and artists began making a summer haven in Provincetown a century ago, and in later years this sandy outpost has morphed into the hottest gay and lesbian destination in the Northeast. Flamboyant street scenes, brilliant art galleries and unbridled nightlife paint the town center. But that's only half the show. Provincetown is fringed with quiet sand dunes, where you can walk without another soul in sight, and an untamed coastline with glorious beaches.

Orientation

Provincetown's commercial center runs along Cape Cod Bay. Outside the town center, it's

lonelyplanet.com

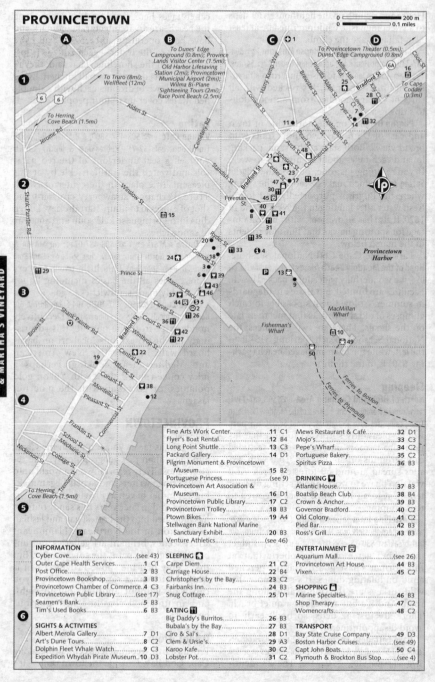

PROVINCETOWN

the dunes of the Cape Cod National Seashore all the way to the Atlantic.

Commercial St, with the lion's share of restaurants, galleries and shops, runs parallel to the harbor for the entire length of the town. It's narrow and crowded with pedestrians, so do most of your driving along the more car-friendly Bradford St, which is parallel to Commercial St a block inland.

Ferries arrive at either MacMillan Wharf or the adjacent Fisherman's Wharf in the center of town. If you're driving, you'll enter Provincetown on US 6, parallel to the town center. The airport is 2.5 miles from the town center via Conwell St.

Information

BOOKSTORES

Provincetown Bookshop (☎ 508-487-0964; 246 Commercial St) Excellent owner-run bookstore.
Tim's Used Books (☎ 508-487-0005; 242 Commercial St) Plenty of good reads at bargain prices.

INTERNET ACCESS

Cyber Cove (☎ 508-487-7778; 237 Commercial St; per min 40c; ⏰ 9am-9pm Mon-Sat, 10am-5pm Sun)
Provincetown Public Library (see p204) Allows 30 minutes free internet access.

INTERNET RESOURCES

In addition to the chamber of commerce (below):
Provincetown Business Guild (www.ptown.org) Oriented to the gay community.
Provincetown on the Web (www.provincetown.com) In connection with the *Provincetown Banner* newspaper.

MEDICAL SERVICES

Outer Cape Health Services(☎ 508-487-9395; Harry Kemp Way) Off Conwell St from US 6; open in summer for walk-ins, and year-round by appointment.

MONEY

Seamen's Bank (☎ 508-487-0035; 221 Commercial St) Has a 24-hour ATM.

POST

Post office (☎ 800-275-8777; 219 Commercial St)

TOURIST INFORMATION

Provincetown Chamber of Commerce (☎ 508-487-3424; www.ptownchamber.com; 307 Commercial St; ⏰ 9am-5pm Jun-Aug, 10am-4pm Mon-Sat Sep-May) The town's helpful tourist office is right at MacMillan Wharf, where the ferries dock.

Sights & Activities

PILGRIM MONUMENT & PROVINCETOWN MUSEUM

You can't miss the 253ft-tall tower of the **Pilgrim Monument & Provincetown Museum** (☎ 508-487-1310; High Pole Rd; adult/child 5-12yr $7/3.50; ⏰ 9am-7pm Jul & Aug, 9am-5pm Apr-Jun & Sep-Nov, last admission 45min before closing). Completed in 1910, it's the tallest all-granite structure in the USA. Climb the 116 stairs for a great view of town, the beaches, the spine of the Lower Cape and even Boston on a clear day. At the base of the tower is a museum featuring the landing of the *Mayflower* Pilgrims and Provincetown's history.

COMMERCIAL STREET

Provincetown's racing heart throbs from this waterfront drag. Walking down Commercial St through the town center on any given day, you may see cross-dressers, leather-clad motorcyclists, barely clad in-line skaters, same-sex couples strolling hand in hand and heterosexual tourists wondering what they've stumbled into on their way to a whale-watch.

Actually, walking down bustling Commercial St is *the* main attraction in this town.

PROVINCETOWN WHARVES

The lifeblood of this seaside town flows from the pair of commercial wharves at its very center. Most of the action is on the east-side **MacMillan Wharf**, the jumping-off point for whale-watching cruises (p205) and the site of the Expedition Whydah Pirate Museum (below). The west wharf, **Fisherman's Wharf**, sees most of the local commerce and is the place to catch fishermen unloading their catch. The town's main public parking lot sits between the two.

EXPEDITION WHYDAH

Of the more than 3000 shipwrecks off the coast of the Cape, the *Whydah* is one of the best documented. Captained by 'Black Sam' Bellamy, the *Whydah* sank in 1717 and to this day remains the only authenticated pirate ship ever salvaged. A local expedition recovered more than 100,000 items of booty – coins, jewelry, weapons – and some of these are on display at the **Expedition Whydah Pirate Museum** (☎ 508-487-8899; MacMillan Wharf; adult/child 6-12yr $8/6; ⏰ 9:30am-7pm Jun-Aug, 10am-5pm late Apr–mid-Oct). Note, however, that many of the prize pieces are being exhibited elsewhere by the National Geographic Society, which aided in the recovery. Arrrgh, matey.

PROVINCETOWN PUBLIC LIBRARY

The **library** (☎ 508-487-7094; 356 Commercial St; admission free; ✆ 10am-5pm Mon & Fri, noon-8pm Tue & Thu, 10am-8pm Wed, 10am-2pm Sat, 1-5pm Sun) is one of the most intriguing buildings in town. Built in 1860 as a church, it was turned into a museum a century later, complete with a half-scale model of Provincetown's famed race-winning schooner *Rose Dorothea*. When the museum went defunct, the town took over the building for the library. The only problem – the huge boat, which occupies the building's upper deck, was too large to remove. So it's still there, with bookshelves built around it. Pop upstairs and take a look.

CAPE COD NATIONAL SEASHORE

The **Province Lands Visitor Center** (☎ 508-487-1256; Race Point Rd; admission free; ✆ 9am-5pm May-Oct) has displays on dune ecology, short nature films and a rooftop observation deck with an eye-popping 360-degree view of the outermost reaches of Cape Cod. Although the visitors center closes at 5pm, the park stays open to midnight so you can still climb to the deck for sunset views.

The **Old Harbor Lifesaving Station** (☎ 508-487-1256; Race Point Beach; admission free; ✆ 2:30-5pm May–Oct), built in 1898, hosts exhibits about the Cape's fearless 'surfmen' who made daring rescues of distressed vessels on the treacherous coastline. If you're around in midsummer, try to catch a faithful-to-the-period **reenactment** (adult/child 7-17yr $5/2; ✆ 6pm Thu Jul & Aug) of a 1902 rescue drill.

PROVINCETOWN ART ASSOCIATION & MUSEUM

Don't miss this recently expanded **museum** (PAAM; ☎ 508-487-1750; www.paam.org; 460 Commercial St; adult/child under 12yr $5/free; ✆ 11am-8pm Mon-Thu, 11am-10pm Fri, 11am-5pm Sat & Sun Jun-Sep, noon-5pm Thu-Sun Oct-May), which is as classy as the art displayed within it. Founded in 1914 to celebrate the town's thriving art community, it boasts the works of some 500 artists who have found their inspiration on the Lower Cape.

If you're feeling inspired yourself, PAAM offers a full agenda of workshops in painting, silk-screening, sculpting and other mediums throughout the summer, most lasting three to five days.

GALLERIES & ART SPACES

It's no surprise that with the many artists who have worked here, Provincetown hosts some of the finest galleries in the region. Pick up a copy of the free *Provincetown Art Guide*, which maps out 40 galleries in the center of town and gives details on each. The vast majority are along Commercial St, and you can pick up the guide at any one of them.

Two high-quality galleries you won't want to miss include the **Albert Merola Gallery** (☎ 508-487-4424; 424 Commercial St), which showcases works by both contemporary and notable past Provincetown artists, and the **Packard Gallery** (☎ 508-487-4690; 418 Commercial St), which features the paintings and sculptures of abstract artist Cynthia Packard.

BEACHES

On the wild tip of the Cape, **Race Point Beach** (Race Point Rd; Ⓟ $15), in the Cape Cod National Seashore, is a breathtaking stretch of sand with crashing surf and undulating dunes extending as far as the eye can see. Kick off your sandals, kids – the soft, grainy sand makes a fun run. This is the kind of beach where you could walk for miles and see no one but the occasional angler casting for bluefish.

Swimmers generally head over to the relatively calmer, though equally brisk, waters of **Herring Cove Beach** (Province Lands Rd; Ⓟ $15), also part of the National Seashore. The long sandy beach is popular with everyone. Nude (though illegal) sunbathers generally head to the south section of the beach; families usually break out the picnic baskets closer to the parking lot. The entire beach faces west, making it a spectacular place to be at sunset.

Long Point Beach, home to the Cape's most remote grains of sand, is reached by a two-hour walk (each way) along the stone dike at the western end of Commercial St. There are no facilities, so bring water. Also time your walk carefully, as the dike is submerged at extreme high tide. Or do it the easy way and hop on the **Long Point Shuttle** (☎ 508-487-0898; MacMillan Wharf; ✆ 10am-5pm mid-May–Sep), which ferries sunbathers across the bay (one-way/round-trip $10/15).

THE ART OF THE DUNES

On the surface you might think there's not much ado in the dunes of the Cape Cod National Seashore, but **Art's Dune Tours** (☎ 508-487-1950, 800-894-1951; www.artsdunetours.com; 4 Standish St; day tours adult/child 6-11yr $21/16, sunset tours $32/20; ☺ 10am-dusk) will prove you wrong. These 4WD tours are surprisingly informative and scenic. And talk about local – the same family has been running these tours since 1946, so you can bet you'll get the inside scoop. The basic hour-long day tour takes you along a remote stretch of beach before heading off to explore the dunes. For more drama take the sunset tour, which adds time to get out and stroll along the beach as the fiery orb dips into the ocean. Or charter your own tour – perhaps with a little surf fishing worked in, a beach clambake or even a wedding in the dunes.

BIKING

Eight exhilarating miles of paved bike trails crisscross the forest and dunes of the Cape Cod National Seashore. The main loop trail is 5.5 miles, with spur trails leading to Herring Cove and Race Point Beaches.

Rent bicycles at **Ptown Bikes** (☎ 508-487-8735; 42 Bradford St; per day cruiser/mountain bike $15/20; ☺ 9am-6pm mid-May–mid-Sep).

BOATING & WATERSPORTS

Flyer's Boat Rental (☎ 508-487-0898; 131A Commercial St; sailboat rental per 2hr/1 day from $30/60, kayak rental per 4hr/1 day $30/50; ☺ 10am-5pm mid-May–Sep) rents watercraft of all sorts.

Venture Athletics (☎ 508-487-9442; 237 Commercial St; 4hr 1-/2-person kayak $25/45; ☺ 9am-6pm) rents kayaks and can arrange guided kayak tours if you have at least four people in your party.

WHALE-WATCHING

Provincetown is a great launch point for whale-watching. It's just 6 miles to Stellwagen Bank National Marine Sanctuary, where whales feed and frolic. Most whale-watching operators guarantee you'll see whales on the voyage, or you'll receive a certificate for a free cruise.

The environmentally oriented **Dolphin Fleet Whale Watch** (☎ 508-240-3636, 800-826-9300; www.whalewatch.com; MacMillan Wharf; 3-4hr trips adult/child 5-12yr $33/25; ☺ weather permitting Apr-Oct; ♿) is the leader. There are as many as nine tours daily in peak season. If you've got kids in tow, ask about its Saturday and Sunday deal in which the first boat out (9am) offers free passage to all youngsters under 12. Reservations advised.

Portuguese Princess (☎ 800-442-3188; MacMillan Wharf; 3-4hr trips adult/child 5-12yr $33/25; ☺ weather permitting Apr-Oct) is also top rate. It goes out five times a day and is affiliated with the Provincetown Center for Coastal Studies, those heroic folks who rescue whales when they get entangled in fishing gear.

Before heading out, stop by the **Stellwagen Bank National Marine Sanctuary Exhibit** (☎ 508-497-3622; 115 Bradford St; admission free; ☺ 10am-7pm Jun-Aug) for an audiovisual glimpse into the underwater world.

Tours

For a 40-minute narrated tour of Provincetown's major sights, board the **Provincetown Trolley** (☎ 508-487-9483; Commercial St; adult/child $10/5; ☺ frequent trips May-Oct) in front of the town hall.

The National Seashore's **Province Lands Visitor Center** (☎ 508-487-1256; tours free-$5; ☺ 9am-5pm May-Oct) offers walking tours ranging from dune walks and forays across the tidal flats to a historical walking tour of downtown Provincetown. Most tours last one to two hours. Call for schedules and reservations.

Feeling adventurous? **Wilma Bi-Plane Sightseeing Tours** (☎ 508-740-9390; www.flywilma.com; Provincetown Municipal Airport; 20-min per person ride $75; ☺ Jun-Sep) will take you ripping above Provincetown in a breezy 1920s vintage biplane – the oldest commercially operating aircraft in the USA. You'll see stunning views of P-town, the hulls of shipwrecks and the Outer Cape's curving shoreline.

See also Art's Dune Tours (boxed text, above).

Festivals & Events

The **Fine Arts Work Center** (☎ 508-487-9960; www.fawc.org; 24 Pearl St) offers talks and presentations by distinguished writers and artists throughout the year; the schedule is online.

Provincetown International Film Festival (mid-Jun) A fine excuse for Hollywood to come to Provincetown. You can count on director John Waters to show.

Provincetown Portuguese Festival (mid-Jun) A celebration of the town's Portuguese heritage. Includes the blessing of the fishing fleet and lots of home-cooked food.

Fourth of July Weekend (early Jul) P-town's weekend of gay 'circuit' dance parties, and of course an Independence Day parade and fireworks.

Carnival Week (mid-Aug) Mardi Gras, drag queens, flowery floats – this is the ultimate gay party event in this gay party town, attracting tens of thousands of revelers.

Holly Folly (early Dec) Said to be the world's only gay and lesbian Christmassy festival. Gives new meaning to 'Don we now our gay apparel.'

Sleeping

Provincetown offers nearly 100 small guesthouses without a single chain hotel to mar the view. In summer it's wise to book ahead, doubly so on weekends. If you arrive without a booking, the chamber of commerce (p203) keeps tabs on available rooms.

BUDGET

Dunes' Edge Campground (☎ 508-487-9815; www .dunes-edge.com; 386 US 6; campsites $30-38; ☺ May-Sep) Camp amid the dunes and shady pines at this family-friendly campground on the north side of US 6, between the National Seashore and town. With just 85 sites it gets booked solid in midsummer so reserve well in advance.

Cape Codder (☎ 508-487-0131; 570 Commercial St; r in season $50-75, off-season $35-60; ☺ Apr-Nov) Definitely think budget – this is a very simple place that makes no pretense to be anything more. The 14 rooms share just four bathrooms, so time yourself accordingly. The cheaper rooms are small, there are no TVs or phones in the rooms, and there's the occasional wall crack and threadbare bedspread. But heck, for these prices in this town it's a deal.

MIDRANGE

Christopher's by the Bay (☎ 508-487-9263, 877-476-9263; www.christophersbythebay.com; 8 Johnson St; r with shared/private bathroom from $100/155; ✗ wi-fi) Tucked away on a side street with a backyard koi pond, this welcoming inn is a top value. Local art on the walls and the afternoon wine and cheese reception add a homey Provincetown flavor. Rooms on the 2nd floor are the largest and snazziest, but the 3rd-floor rooms, which share a bathroom, get the ocean view.

Fairbanks Inn (☎ 508-487-0386, 800-324-7265; www .fairbanksinn.com; 80 Bradford St; r incl breakfast in season $139-275, off-season $90-165; ✗ ☐) If four-post beds and a cozy fireplace appeal then you're in for a treat at this cordial B&B centered around a 1776 sea captain's home. Choose between new garden units with fireplaces and cooking facilities or old-fashioned rooms in the main house where sloping pine floors and antique wallpaper set the tone.

Snug Cottage (☎ 508-487-1616, 800-432-2334; www .snugcottage.com; 178 Bradford St; r incl breakfast $155-240; ✗ ☐ wi-fi) Want a little crackle with your fire? This is one of the few places that has real wood-burning fireplaces rather than gas. And it's cute as a button with geraniums in the window boxes and artsy decor throughout. The handsome rooms are big, bright and sunny with extra touches like a DVD library.

ourpick Carpe Diem (☎ 508-487-4242, 800-487-0132; www.carpediemguesthouse.com; 12 Johnson St; r incl breakfast $155-255; ☐) This is one classy place to rest your head. Sophisticated yet relaxed, each room has a theme inspired by a different writer and the corner of the world they hail from. It makes for a soothing mix of smiling Buddhas, orchid sprays and thoughtful decor. Should you wish to take it to the next level the on-site spa facilities include a Finnish sauna, hot tub and massage therapy.

Race Point Lighthouse (☎ 508-487-9930; www.race pointlighthouse.net; Race Point; r $160-195; ☺ May–mid-Oct) Now *here's* a getaway. A 19th-century lighthouse amid unspoiled sand dunes in a remote corner of the National Seashore. You can book one of the three upstairs bedrooms in the lightkeeper's house. Literally on the outer tip of the Cape, this cool place is totally off the grid. Solar energy and gas run the lights and kitchen and your nearest neighbors are miles away…well, unless you count the seals and dolphins just offshore.

TOP END

Carriage House (☎ 508-487-8855, 800-309-0248; www.prov incetownguesthouse.com; 7 Central St; r with breakfast $195-350; ✗ ☐) Everything's done right from the quiet side-street location to the lovely details in the rooms – classic but not frilly. Treat yourself to cold lemonade and unwind on the deck out back, or just stroll down the street and jump into the bustling heart of Provincetown. To sweeten the deal ask about last-minute discounts.

Eating

Provincetown has one of the best dining scenes this side of Boston. Every third building on Commercial St houses some sort of eatery, so that's a great place to start.

BUDGET

Portuguese Bakery (☎ 508-487-1803; 299 Commercial St; snacks $2-5; ⊗ 7am-8pm) This century-old bakery is famous for its malasadas (fried dough served hot and sinfully drenched in sugar). For something more conventional, step up to the counter and order yourself an oversized blueberry turnover or a spicy linguica sandwich.

Mojo's (☎ 508-487-3140; MacMillan Wharf, 8 Ryder St Extension; dishes $3-15; ⊗ lunch & dinner) Provincetown's harborside clam shack serves everything from hot dogs to fried seafood, burritos and veggie options. It's strictly takeout but there are a couple of picnic tables where you can chow down and watch the action on the wharf.

Spiritus Pizza (☎ 508-487-2808; 190 Commercial St; pizza slices/pies $3/15; ⊗ 11:30am-2am) This is the place to pick up a late-night slice, or a latenight date if you haven't been lucky at one of the clubs. And it's not just about cruising; the pizzas here are first-rate. For something different try the white Greek, sauce-free with feta cheese, spinach and olives.

Big Daddy's Burritos (☎ 508-487-4432; 205 Commercial St; burritos $6-7; ⊗ lunch & dinner) It's strictly counter service, but don't let that deter you, because you're in for a treat. An innovative variety of burritos includes grilled organic tofu, Cajun catfish and curried chicken. Carry it to the oceanfront picnic deck out back for a knockout water view.

MIDRANGE

Karoo Kafe (☎ 508-487-6630; 338 Commercial St; meals $8-16; ⊗ lunch & dinner; **V**) A fun alternative to seafood is this brightly painted café in safari decor that features authentic home-style cooking from South Africa. The ostrich satay is a favorite. Or order the spicy *peri-peri* chicken for a blast of tomato, garlic, onion and chili; it comes in a vegetarian tofu version too.

Clem & Ursie's (☎ 508-487-2333; 85 Shank Painter Rd; meals $9-28; ⊗ breakfast, lunch & dinner) This colorful, counter-service roadhouse with tables decorated by local artists serves traditional New England seafood alongside Portuguese dishes. You'll find a broad menu with everything from breakfast fare and panini sandwiches to Dijon steamed mussels and a raw bar.

Bubala's by the Bay (☎ 508-487-0773; 183 Commercial St; meals $10-22; ⊗ 11am-1am) For great peoplewatching and good food head to this sidewalk café that bustles night and day. Omelettes, fish and chips, and focaccia sandwiches are main-

stays but lots of people just linger over a drink and watch the streetside parade roll by.

Pepe's Wharf (☎ 508-487-8717; 371 Commercial St; meals $11-22; ⊗ lunch & dinner) Locals and seasoned visitors head to this seafront eatery for a million-dollar view on a paper-plate budget. A burger and fries will set you back just $10 and nothing on the menu, including the fresh grilled swordfish, runs over $20.

ourpick Mews Restaurant & Café (☎ 508-487-1500; 429 Commercial St; meals $12-34; ⊗ dinner, plus brunch 11am-2:30pm Sun) A fantastic water view, the hottest martini bar in town and scrumptious food add up to Provincetown's finest dinner scene. There are two sections. Opt to dine gourmet on tuna sushi and rack of lamb downstairs where you're right on the sand or go casual with a juicy burger from the café menu upstairs.

TOP END

Ciro & Sal's (☎ 508-487-6444; 4 Kiley Ct; meals $17-37; ⊗ dinner) One of Provincetown's top choices for a romantic dinner out, this candlelit cellar restaurant specializes in local seafood with a northern Italian flair. Perhaps the baked oysters in pesto, or the fresh fish of the day with anchovies and plum tomatoes. Save room for the tiramisu.

Lobster Pot (☎ 508-487-0842; 321 Commercial St; meals $20-30; ⊗ lunch & dinner) True to its name, this bustling fish house overlooking the ocean is *the* place for lobster. Start with the superb lobster bisque and then put on a bib and crack open the perfect boiled lobster. Best way to beat the crowd is to come in midafternoon.

Drinking & Entertainment

Provincetown is awash with gay clubs, drag shows and cabaret. And don't be shy if you're straight – everyone's welcome and many shows have first-rate performers.

BARS & CLUBS

Many of the best bars and clubs cater to gay men and women (for more options, see boxed text, p208).

Governor Bradford (☎ 508-487-9618; 312 Commercial St) This local bar and restaurant, with big picture windows overlooking Commercial St, attracts a mixed crowd, has a large pub menu and varied nighttime entertainment.

Old Colony (☎ 508-487-2361; 323 Commercial St) This vestige of old Provincetown is a no-frills fishermen's haunt where filmmakers shot scenes

CAPE COD, NANTUCKET & MARTHA'S VINEYARD

LIFE IS A CABARET...

And anyone who thinks otherwise hasn't been to Provincetown.

P-town is full of little venues featuring drag (and other) performers who would be amazingly good singers, actors or comedians no matter how they dressed. Expect comedians, celebrity impersonators who make lightning-fast costume changes, and innuendo-laden, campy humor. Top lesbian-themed acts include comics Lea deLaria, Maggie Cassella and Kate Clinton.

Tickets are generally around $15 and, depending on the venue, you may be strongly encouraged to purchase a drink.

---

for *Tough Guys Don't Dance*. It's one of the few places that draws an almost exclusively straight crowd.

Many dining spots also have good bars. **Ross's Grill** (☎ 508-487-8878; 237 Commercial St) is one of the standouts overlooking the water.

THEATER & CULTURE

Provincetown boasts a rich theater history. Eugene O'Neill began his writing career here and several stars, including Marlon Brando and Richard Gere, performed on Provincetown stages before they hit the big screen. To see tomorrow's stars, take in a show while you're here. Theater prices vary with

performances, but expect to pay between $20 and $30.

Provincetown Theater (☎ 508-487-7487; www.new provincetownplayers.org; 238 Bradford St; tickets $20-29; ☺ year-round) This stellar performing arts center hosts Provincetown's leading theater troupe, the New Provincetown Players, and always has something of interest – sometimes Broadway musicals, sometimes offbeat local themes.

Provincetown Art House (☎ 508-487-9222; 214 Commercial St; ☺ year-round) The Art House has two state-of-the-art stages featuring a variety of edgy theater performances along the lines of the off-Broadway *Confessions of a Mormon Boy*.

Aquarium Mall (207 Commercial St; ☺ Wed late May-Aug) At dusk every Wednesday in summer, the town sets up a screen near the back deck of the oceanfront mall with free outdoor movies, which could be anything from Elvis to Frankenstein. Pick up a bag of popcorn and join the locals.

Shopping

Commercial St has the most creative and interesting specialty shops on the Cape. Just a tiny selection:

Marine Specialties (☎ 508-487-1730; 235 Commercial St) This cavernous shop sells kitsch and really cool stuff: flip-flops, swimsuits, beachwear and surfwear, army/navy surplus, firemen's coats, lobster traps and...

GAY & LESBIAN PROVINCETOWN

While other cities have their gay districts, in Provincetown the entire town is the gay district.

Since same-sex marriages became legal in Massachusetts in 2004 Provincetown has become the state's top gay honeymoon destination. More than 2000 couples have tied the knot here in weddings that have ranged from intimate ceremonies at the town hall to full-on, catered, flowered, music-filled affairs.

Those who haven't tied the knot will find plenty of action at the following clubs. When there's dancing or live entertainment, there's typically a cover charge of up to $10.

Atlantic House (☎ 508-487-3821; 4 Masonic Pl) Known locally as the A-House, Ella Fitzgerald sang here and generations of men have enjoyed its charms. The Little Bar is an intimate pub with a jukebox. There's also the Macho Bar and the Big Room, the town's hottest DJ dance club.

Boatslip Beach Club (☎ 508-487-1669; 161 Commercial St) Known for its wildly popular afternoon tea dances overlooking the harbor. In summer, it's packed with gorgeous guys.

Crown & Anchor (☎ 508-487-1430; 247 Commercial St) The queen of the scene, this multiwing complex has a nightclub, a leather bar and a steamy cabaret that takes it to the limit.

Pied Bar (☎ 508-487-1527; 193 Commercial St) A popular waterfront lounge that attracts both lesbians and gay men. Particularly hot place to be around sunset.

Vixen (☎ 508-487-6424; 336 Commercial St) A favorite lesbian hangout with everything from an intimate wine bar to comedy shows and nightly dancing.

Shop Therapy (☎ 508-487-9387; 346 Commercial St) Downstairs it's patchouli, tie-dye clothing and X-rated bumper stickers. But everyone gravitates upstairs, where the sex toys are wild enough to make an Amsterdam madam blush. Parents, use discretion: your teenagers *will* want to go inside.

Womencrafts (☎ 508-487-2501; 376 Commercial St) The name says it all: jewelry, pottery, books and music by female artists from across America.

Getting There & Around
AIR
From Boston, **Cape Air** (☎ 508-487-0241, 800-352-0714; www.flycapeair.com) flies several times a day to Provincetown's Municipal Airport (one-way/round-trip $90/180, 25 minutes).

BOAT
Boats connect Provincetown to Boston and Plymouth. All have schedules geared to accommodate day-trippers, with morning arrivals and late afternoon departures.

Bay State Cruise Company (☎ 617-748-1428, 877-783-3779; www.boston-ptown.com) links Provincetown's MacMillan Wharf and Boston's World Trade Center Pier with both a fast ferry (per adult/bicycle/child one-way $44/5/28, round-trip $69/10/50, 1½ hours, three times a day) and a weekend-only slower ferry (per adult/bicycle/child one-way $19/5/free, round-trip $33/10/free, three hours). It operates from mid-May to mid-October.

Boston Harbor Cruises (☎ 617-227-4321; www.boston harborcruises.com) offers a fast ferry service from Long Wharf in Boston (adult/bicycle/child one-way $45/5/35, round-trip $70/10/60, 1½ hours). There are one to three boats daily from June to mid-October, with the most frequent sailings on summer weekends, and one boat Thursday through Sunday in May.

Capt John Boats (☎ 508-747-2400, 800-225-4000; www.provincetownferry.com) runs a catamaran fast ferry, departing Plymouth at 10am and returning from Provincetown at 4:30pm (adult/bicycle/child round-trip $35/10/25, 1½ hours). There's service every day from mid-June to early September and on Friday to Sunday from late May to mid-June.

BUS
The **Plymouth & Brockton** (☎ 508-746-0378) bus, which terminates at the chamber of commerce, operates several times a day from Boston ($25, 3½ hours), stopping at other Cape towns along the way.

From late May to mid-October, **shuttle** (☎ 800-352-7155; single trip/day pass $1/3) buses travel up and down Bradford St, and to MacMillan Wharf, Herring Cove Beach and North Truro. An additional midsummer service heads out to Province Lands Visitor Center and Race Point Beach. Bike racks are available.

CAR
From the Cape Cod Canal via US 6, it takes about 1½ hours to reach Provincetown (65 miles), depending on traffic.

On-street parking is next to impossible in summer, but lot parking costs between $10 and $12 per day. Some visitors park in Truro for free and take the shuttle (see left) into Provincetown.

TAXI
Taxi fares are standardized at $4 per person anywhere within town, $6 between the airport and town. Try **Cape Cab** (☎ 508-487-2222) or **Queen Cab** (☎ 508-487-5500).

NANTUCKET

One need not be a millionaire to visit Nantucket, but it couldn't hurt. This compact island, 30 miles south of Cape Cod, grew rich from whaling in the 19th century, and recent decades have seen its rebirth as a summer playground for CEOs and society types.

It's easy to see why. Nantucket is New England at its most rose-covered, cobble-stoned, picture-postcard perfect, and even in the peak of summer there's always an empty stretch of sandy beach to be found. Outdoor activities abound, and there are fine museums, smart restaurants and fun bars.

NANTUCKET TOWN
pop 9520
Nantucket Town (called 'Town' by the locals) is the island's only real population center. Once homeport to the world's largest whaling fleet, the town's storied past is reflected in the gracious period buildings lining its leafy streets. It boasts the nation's largest concentration of houses built prior to 1850 and is the only place in the US where the entire town is a National Historic Landmark. It's a thoroughly

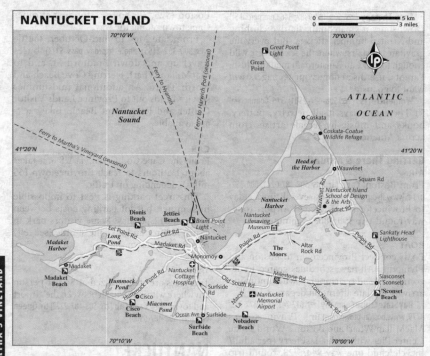

enjoyable place to just amber about and soak up the atmosphere.

Orientation
There are two ferry terminals: Straight Wharf and Steamboat Wharf. Straight Wharf becomes Main St, the main thoroughfare through the town center, while Steamboat Wharf is just a few blocks north. The majority of restaurants, inns and other visitor facilities are within a 10-minute walk of the wharves. The airport is a few miles southeast of town, via Milestone Rd.

Information
BOOKSTORES
Mitchell's Book Corner (☎ 508-228-1080; 54 Main St)
Nantucket Bookworks (☎ 508-228-4000; 25 Broad St)

EMERGENCY
Police station (☎ 508-228-1212; 20 S Water St)

INTERNET ACCESS
Bean (☎ 508-228-6215; 29 Centre St; ☺ 6:30am–10pm Mon-Sat, 9am–7pm Sun) Free wi-fi with your java.
Nantucket.net (☎ 508-228-6777; 2 Union St; per 30min $5; ☺ 10am–2pm Mon, Wed & Fri)

INTERNET RESOURCES
www.ack.net *Inquirer and Mirror,* the island's daily newspaper.
www.nantucket.net Private listings of restaurants, housing, arts and recreation.

MEDICAL SERVICES
Nantucket Cottage Hospital (☎ 508-228-1200; 57 Prospect St; ☺ 24hr) The island's only hospital.

MONEY
Pacific National Bank (☎ 508-228-1917; 61 Main St)

POST
Post office (☎ 508-228-1067; 5 Federal St)

TOURIST INFORMATION
Nantucket Island Chamber of Commerce (☎ 508-228-1700; www.nantucketchamber.org; 48 Main St; ☺ 9am-5pm Mon-Fri) Has information on the island's activities, accommodations and special events.
Visitor information kiosk (Straight Wharf; ☺ 9am-5pm Jun–mid-Oct) Step off the ferry and pick up your brochures here.
Visitor Services & Information Bureau (☎ 508-228-0925; 25 Federal St; ☺ 9am-6pm daily May-Nov,

9am-5:30pm Mon-Sat Dec-Apr) Has everything you'll need, including public rest rooms.

Sights & Activities

NANTUCKET HISTORICAL ASSOCIATION

The umbrella **Nantucket Historical Association** (NHA; ☎ 508-228-1894; www.nha.org; passes historic sites only adult/child $6/3, historic sites & Whaling Museum $18/9; all sites except Whaling Museum 10am-5pm Mon-Sat, noon-5pm Sun late May-early Sep, limited hours late Apr-late May & early Sep-mid-Oct) maintains eight historical sites covering everything from farming beginnings to the prosperous whaling days.

Its most famous property, the **Nantucket Whaling Museum** (13 Broad St; 10am-5pm Fri-Wed, 10am-8pm Thu May-mid-Oct, 11am-4pm Thu-Mon mid-Oct-mid-Dec, 11am-4pm Fri-Sun Jan-Apr), occupies a former spermaceti candle factory. The evocative exhibits include a 46ft-long sperm whale skeleton, a rigged whaleboat and assorted whaling implements.

A walk through the NHA's **Hadwen House** (96 Main St), a Greek Revival home built in 1845 by a whaling merchant, provides testimony to just how lucrative the whaling industry was in its heyday.

Built in 1686 the **Jethro Coffin House** (16 Sunset Hill) is the town's oldest building still on its original foundation. It's in a traditional 'salt box' style, with south-facing windows to catch the winter sun and a long, sloping roof to protect the home from harsh north winds.

The **Old Mill** (50 Prospect St) is America's oldest working windmill (c 1746), as game young docents will demonstrate by grinding corn (weather conditions permitting). To see where drunken sailors used to spend the night, visit the **Old Gaol** (15 Vestal St), the c 1806 jail that served Nantucket for 125 years.

MARIA MITCHELL ASSOCIATION

This **association** (www.mmo.org; 4 vestal St) is devoted to Maria (pronounced 'Mariah') Mitchell (1818–89), who was America's first female astronomer. Astronomy was no mere hobby on Nantucket: the nearly 100 whaling ships based here navigated by the stars, and the Mitchell family calibrated ships' instruments. Maria is revered for discovering a comet in the 1840s, beating some of the world's leading scientists. The following venues are run by the association.

At the **Maria Mitchell Birthplace House** (☎ 508-228-2896; 1 Vestal St; adult/child $5/4; 10am-4pm Tue-

Sat), docents tell her inspiring story. The house (1790) is interesting in its own right.

Next door, at **Vestal St Observatory** (☎ 508-228-9273; 3 Vestal St; adult/child $5/4; tours in season 11am Tue-Sat, off-season 11am Sat), student interns demonstrate principles and techniques of astronomy.

On a rolling hill out of town, the **Loines Observatory** (☎ 508-228-9273; 59 Milk St Extension; adult/child $10/6; weather permitting 9pm Mon, Wed & Fri mid-Jun–Aug, 9pm Fri Sep-May) opens to the public for nighttime viewings through a pair of telescopes.

NANTUCKET ATHENEUM

More than just a **library** (☎ 508-228-1110; 1 India St; admission free; 9:30am-8pm Tue & Thu, 9:30am-5pm Wed, Fri & Sat year-round, 9:30am-5pm Mon late May-early Sep), this stately Greek Revival edifice is a sight in itself. Just inside the front door you'll find a top-notch display of scrimshaw from Nantucket's whaling days. The 2nd-floor Great Hall, now wired for wi-fi, has hosted such notables as Ralph Waldo Emerson and abolitionist Frederick Douglass. Opinion-makers continue to speak here today.

FIRST CONGREGATIONAL CHURCH

Everyone comes to this **church** (☎ 508-228-0950; 62 Centre St; adult/child $2.50/50¢; 10am-4pm Mon-Sat mid-Jun–mid-Oct), which traces its roots to the early 1700s, for the eagle-eye's views from the top of the steeple. Well worth the 94-step climb!

AFRICAN MEETING HOUSE

This interesting **museum** (☎ 508-228-9833; cnr Pleasant & York Sts; admission by donation; 11am-3pm Tue-Sat, 1-3pm Sun Jul & Aug, by appointment rest of year) stands as testimony to the influential African American community that thrived on Nantucket in the 19th century. Built in 1820, it's the second-oldest African American meeting house in the nation.

NANTUCKET LIGHTSHIP BASKET MUSEUM

What the lighthouse is to the New England coast, the lightship was to the sea – essentially a floating lighthouse to warn of dangerous shoals or sandbars below. Sailors would stay aboard the lightships for weeks on end, and to combat boredom they created beautiful, intricate baskets that have become emblems of the island. This small **museum** (☎ 508-228-1177; 49 Union St; adult/child $4/2; 10am-4pm Tue-Sat late May–mid-Oct) highlights these craftspeople.

CAPE COD, NANTUCKET & MARTHA'S VINEYARD

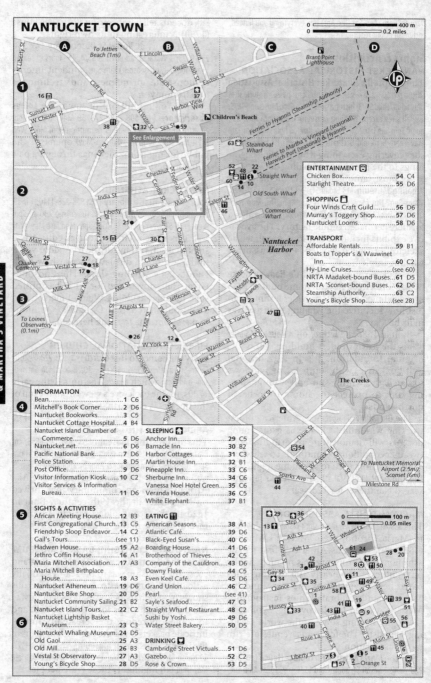

NANTUCKET TOWN

To Jetties Beach (1mi)

Brant Point Lighthouse

Children's Beach

Ferries to Hyannis (Steamship Authority)

Ferries to Martha's Vineyard (seasonal); Harwich Port (seasonal) & Hyannis

Steamboat Wharf

Straight Wharf

Old South Wharf

Commercial Wharf

Nantucket Harbor

Quaker Cemetery

To Loines Observatory (0.1mi)

The Creeks

To Nantucket Memorial Airport (2.5mi); 'Sconset (6mi)

Milestone Rd

See Enlargement

ENTERTAINMENT
Chicken Box............................54 C4
Starlight Theatre.....................55 D6

SHOPPING
Four Winds Craft Guild............56 D6
Murray's Toggery Shop............57 D6
Nantucket Looms....................58 D6

TRANSPORT
Affordable Rentals..................59 B1
Boats to Topper's & Wauwinet
 Inn......................................60 C2
Hy-Line Cruises....................(see 60)
NRTA Madaket-bound Buses....61 D5
NRTA 'Sconset-bound Buses....62 D6
Steamship Authority................63 C2
Young's Bicycle Shop..........(see 28)

INFORMATION
Bean.......................................1 C6
Mitchell's Book Corner...............2 D6
Nantucket Bookworks................3 C5
Nantucket Cottage Hospital....4 B4
Nantucket Island Chamber of
 Commerce...............................5 D6
Nantucket.net...........................6 D6
Pacific National Bank.................7 D6
Police Station...........................8 D5
Post Office...............................9 D6
Visitor Information Kiosk..........10 C2
Visitor Services & Information
 Bureau.................................11 D6

SIGHTS & ACTIVITIES
African Meeting House............12 B3
First Congregational Church....13 C5
Friendship Sloop Endeavor......14 C2
Gail's Tours........................(see 11)
Hadwen House.......................15 A2
Jethro Coffin House................16 A1
Maria Mitchell Association.....17 A3
Maria Mitchell Birthplace
 House..................................18 A3
Nantucket Atheneum..............19 D6
Nantucket Bike Shop..............20 D5
Nantucket Community Sailing 21 B2
Nantucket Island Tours...........22 C2
Nantucket Lightship Basket
 Museum...............................23 C3
Nantucket Whaling Museum..24 D5
Old Gaol...............................25 A3
Old Mill.................................26 B3
Vestal St Observatory.............27 A3
Young's Bicycle Shop..............28 D5

SLEEPING
Anchor Inn............................29 C5
Barnacle Inn..........................30 B2
Harbor Cottages.....................31 C3
Martin House Inn....................32 B1
Pineapple Inn.........................33 C6
Sherburne Inn........................34 C6
Vanessa Noel Hotel Green.....35 C6
Veranda House.......................36 C5
White Elephant.......................37 B1

EATING
American Seasons...................38 A1
Atlantic Café..........................39 D6
Black-Eyed Susan's.................40 C6
Boarding House.......................41 D6
Brotherhood of Thieves...........42 C5
Company of the Cauldron........43 C5
Downy Flake...........................44 C5
Even Keel Café.......................45 D6
Grand Union...........................46 C2
Pearl..................................(see 41)
Sayle's Seafood......................47 C3
Straight Wharf Restaurant......48 C2
Sushi by Yoshi........................49 D6
Water Street Bakery................50 D5

DRINKING
Cambridge Street Victuals.....51 D6
Gazebo..................................52 C2
Rose & Crown........................53 D5

Step La

Ash La

Ash La

Gay St

Quince St

Chestnut St

Hussey St

India St

Rose La

Liberty St

Orange St

Centre St

N Water St

Whalers Ct

Broad St

Oak St

Federal St

Cambridge

Easy St

Union St

Main St

Sparks Ave

BEACHES

A pair of family-friendly beaches shore up the options close to town. For wilder, less-frequented strands, you'll need to pedal a bike or hop on a bus.

Right in town, **Children's Beach**, along S Beach St at the north side of Steamboat Wharf, is heaven for young kids, with gentle water, a fun playground and picnic facilities. For the nonwading crowd, **Jetties Beach**, a 20-minute walk to the northwest or a short bus ride away, is the best all-round beach close to town. It's well equipped with changing rooms, a skateboard park and water sports reductions.

WATER SPORTS

Nantucket Community Sailing (☎ 508-228-6600; cnr Main & Winter Sts; rentals per hr $15-35; ◷ 9am-5pm) rents single and double kayaks, sunfish sailboats and windsurfing gear at Jetties Beach.

Feel the wind in your hair on a sail aboard the **Friendship Sloop Endeavor** (☎ 508-228-5585; Straight Wharf; sails 1hr $15, 1½hr $25-35; ◷ May-Oct), which runs numerous daily harbor sails and a sunset cruise.

BIKING

Pedaling around Nantucket is an unbeatable way to savor the island's natural beauty. Bike paths connect the town with the main beaches and the villages of Madaket and 'Sconset – no place is more than an hour's pedal away.

Several shops rent bikes for around $30 per day and provide free island maps with bike routes highlighted. Two reliable operations with well-maintained bikes are the family-run **Young's Bicycle Shop** (☎ 508-228-1151; 6 Broad St; ◷ 8:30am-5:30pm) at Steamboat Wharf, and **Nantucket Bike Shop** (☎ 508-228-1999; 4 Broad St; ◷ 8am-6pm), which has locations at both Steamboat and Straight Wharves.

Tours

A good way to get your bearings around the island is to hop on one of the 90-minute ($18) narrated van tours offered by several companies. If you just want to step off a ferry and onto the bus, Hy-Line Cruises handles tours that dovetail with ferry arrivals via **Nantucket Island Tours** (☎ 508-228-0334; Straight Wharf). Less frequent but brimming with local flavor is **Gail's Tours** (☎ 508-257-6557), run three times a day by seventh-generation Nantucketer Gail Nickerson Johnson.

ACK ATTACK

ACK! In Nantucket, the word adorns T-shirts, caps and logos. No, it's not a comment on the island's high cost of living, or reaction to the limerick 'There once was a man from Nantucket.' Instead, ACK is the code for Nantucket Airport (think nAntuCKet) and has been fondly adopted as an insider's moniker for all things Nantucket. Even the island's daily newspaper the *Inquirer and Mirror* uses www.ack.net as its website.

The town's main historical organizations offer an ever-changing variety of themed walking tours around town, most for about $10. Contact the Nantucket Historical Association (p211), Maria Mitchell Association (p211) and African Meeting House (p211) for the latest schedules.

Festivals & Event

Daffodil Festival (Apr) The island goes yellow in the last full weekend of April with three million blooms, and antique cars that make their way to 'Sconset for a tailgate picnic.
Nantucket Film Festival (mid-Jun) A good time to spot celebrities.
Independence Day Celebration (Jul 4) At high noon island firefighters duke it out – the hook and ladder trucks versus the fire pumpers. You *will* get wet. Fireworks at night.
Christmas Stroll (1st weekend Dec) Nantucket becomes the Christmas town of your fantasies, with locals dressed in 1850s garb, 150 decorated Christmas trees in the town center, the town crier and, of course, Santa Claus.

Sleeping

Unless you've got island friends with a spare room, a summer stay on Nantucket won't be inexpensive. There are no budget accommodations on the island, other than the hostel (p218), and camping is prohibited. In July and August advance reservations are a virtual necessity, but between fall and spring you can practically have the run of the place, for a fraction of the cost.

MIDRANGE

Martin House Inn (☎ 508-228-0678; www.martin houseinn.net; 61 Centre St; s in season $115, d $195-375, s off-season $95, d $130-275, all incl breakfast) In one of the finest homes in a fine neighborhood is this elegant inn, boasting soothing rooms with four-post beds and stylish period decor. And you won't have to go far for dinner since American

Seasons (opposite), one of the best restaurants in town, is right across the street. Several of the 13 rooms have a fireplace; a couple of the least expensive have shared bathroom.

Barnacle Inn (☎ 508-228-0332; www.thebarnacleinn.com; 11 Fair St; r incl breakfast $175, with shared bathroom $135) This is what old Nantucket is all about – folksy owners and simple quaint accommodations that hearken to earlier times. Rooms in this turn-of-the-19th-century inn don't have phones, TVs or air-con, but they do have good rates, particularly if you opt for shared bathroom.

Anchor Inn (☎ 508-228-0072; www.anchor-inn.net; 66 Centre St; r incl breakfast in season $195-250, off-season $85-185; ✷ wi-fi) You'll do well dropping your anchor at this former sea captain's house, built in 1806. The innkeepers are down-home friendly and the place wears its history with character, from the sloping plank floors to the old-fashioned canopy beds. The homemade apple muffins at breakfast are a star, too.

Harbor Cottages (☎ 508-228-4485; www.nisda.org; 71 Washington St; units in season per week $1100-1350, call for off-season rates) The Nantucket Island School of Design & the Arts (p218) operates these former fishermen's cottages built in the 1940s. Rustic by island standards, the simple studio and one-bedroom cottages have painted floorboards, exposed rafters and whitewashed walls. The complex is a 10-minute walk from downtown.

TOP END

Sherburne Inn (☎ 508-228-4425; 888-577-4425; www.sherburneinn.com; 10 Gay St; r incl breakfast in season $210-340, off-season $105-225; ✷) Sit in the parlor by the Victorian fireplace and share travel tips with fellow guests at this gracious inn. Built in 1838, the inn flawlessly fuses period appeal with modern amenities like central air con – no boxy air-conditioners hanging out of windows here. Rooms are cheery with comfy bedding and four-post beds. The street is quiet yet just a two-minute stroll from the town center.

Pineapple Inn (☎ 508-228-9992; www.pineappleinn.com; 10 Hussey St; r incl breakfast in season $215-325, off-season $110-250; ✷ ▣) The 12 guest rooms at this 1838 whaling captain's house have been completely restored with understated elegance. Run by restaurateurs who know fine pastries, the inn is justifiably famous for its breakfast, served with class on the patio. Everything, including the oversized beds with goose-down comforters, spells romantic.

Veranda House (☎ 508-228-0695; www.theverandahouse.com; 3 Step Lane; r incl breakfast in season $249-499, off-season $149-349) The Veranda House puts contemporary minimalism into an old New England shell, with striking results in one of the most stylish inns on the island. Fret linens, cozy comforters and orchid sprays set the tone. Request an upper-floor room for a sweeping harbor view.

Vanessa Noel Hotel Green (☎ 508-228-5300; www.vanessanoelhotelgreen.com; 33 Centre St; r in season $250-525, off-season $150-300) Go green in this 10-room hotel with organic mattresses, hemp shower curtains and a hip natural decor. And don't think spartan – this is the work of fashion designer Vanessa Noel and it's one of the artsiest places in town to lay your head.

White Elephant (☎ 508-228-2500, 800-455-6574; www.whiteelephanthotel.com; 50 Easton St; r in season/off-season from $550/250; ▣ ✷) The Elephant offers everything you'd expect of a luxury inn, from an accomplished concierge to a stellar harborfront setting. Legend has it that the builder was chided for putting up such a large hotel – it was bound to be a white elephant – and the name stuck. It is a bit oversized by island standards but to its credit it's in a typical Nantucket cedar-shingle design and no taller than the neighbors.

Eating

Nantucket has lots of exceptional restaurants, especially for fine dining. There are also some solid local eateries that are worth ferreting out.

BUDGET

Grand Union (☎ 508-228-9756; Salem St; ◷ 7am-9pm Mon-Sat, 7am-7pm Sun) If you need groceries, deli items or a ready-to-eat barbecued chicken, stop at this in-town supermarket just beyond Straight Wharf.

Downy Flake (☎ 508-228-4533; 18 Sparks Ave; meals $6-12; ◷ breakfast & lunch Mon-Sat, 6am-noon Sun) A popular stop for the island's working-class folks, this no-frills eatery on the edge of town is known for its blueberry pancakes, big omelettes and simple comfort fare. It also doubles as a bakery with homemade doughnuts and other sweet treats.

Water Street Bakery (☎ 508-228-7080; 21 S Water St; meals $7-11; ◷ lunch Mon-Sat) Gourmet on a budget? No problem at this hole-in-the-wall bakery that makes organic breads and luscious sandwiches, such as spicy grilled lamb with roasted veggies. Homemade soups and salads too. It's takeout only but there's a sidewalk bench out front.

Sayle's Seafood (☎ 508-228-4599; 99 Washington St Extension; meals $9-24; ☉ 10am-8pm) For the island's best fried clams, cheapest lobster dinners and other seafood treats, head to this combo fish market and clam shack on the south side of town. It's all takeout but there's outdoor seating where you can enjoy your feast.

MIDRANGE

Even Keel Café (☎ 508-228-1979; 40 Main St; meals $7-27; ☉ breakfast, lunch & dinner) Walk straight through the restaurant to the shady patio out back where locals and tourists in the know order up generous omelettes, wild salmon salads and the café's famous crab cakes. There's also a bakery counter with ginger scones and other pastries.

Sushi by Yoshi (☎ 508-228-1801; 2 E Chestnut St; sushi from $6, meals $11-26; ☉ lunch & dinner) The name says it all: a transplanted Japanese chef and helpers prepare sashimi, sushi and more exotic creations in this pint-sized eatery. If you've never tried it before, this is the place to order yourself a scoop of green tea ice-cream.

Black-Eyed Susan's (☎ 508-325-0308; 10 India St; meals $9-31; ☉ breakfast & lunch daily, dinner Mon-Sat) It's hard to find anyone who doesn't adore this quietly gourmet place. Snag a seat on the back patio and try the sourdough French toast, *huevos rancheros* (ranch-style eggs) or trout with sauce *marinière* (a fish broth and wine mixture). In the morning, go for the freshly squeezed orange juice. In the evening, BYOB.

Brotherhood of Thieves (☎ 508-228-2551; 23 Broad St; meals $9-26; ☉ 11:30am-1am) A longtime favorite of locals who come here for the friendly tavern atmosphere – all brick and dark woods – and the island's best burgers. Not in a burger mood? How about a fish taco made with local cod and chipotle cream, or some broiled Nantucket scallops?

Atlantic Café (☎ 508-228-0570; 15 S Water St; meals $11-20; ☉ lunch & dinner, bar to 1am; 🍴) At this nautical-themed eatery, ship figureheads hang from the walls and fishermen hang at the bar. Lots of light fare such as quahog chowder and chicken fingers, but the stars of the menu are the fresh Nantucket bluefish specials and the barbecued ribs. Although it gets boisterous

late at night, it's otherwise a family-friendly place with a kids' menu ($8).

Boarding House (☎ 508-228-9622; 12 Federal St; meals $18-37; ☉ lunch & dinner) The sidewalk patio here is perfect for people-watching, although the innovative American cuisine will vie for your attention. Linger over the likes of lobster Benedict, grilled fish with arugula, or steak-frites with béarnaise aïoli.

TOP END

American Seasons (☎ 508-228-7111; 80 Centre St; meals $25-36; ☉ dinner) This restaurant celebrates the nation's four corners. The dishes are themed by region, with an eclectic, thoughtful menu and smart staff. Let your mood swing. If you've had enough New England lobster, perhaps take on the chili-glazed salmon with crayfish, or a juicy southwestern steak.

Straight Wharf Restaurant (☎ 508-228-4499; Straight Wharf; meals $27-37; ☉ lunch & dinner) The best place for fresh-caught seafood served up with a harbor view is the deck of this hot restaurant. Boston's renowned chef couple Amanda Lydon and Gabriel Frasca command the kitchen with New American flair. The menu changes frequently, but expect your scallops or halibut to be adorned with the likes of truffle butter.

Pearl (☎ 508-228-9701; 12 Federal St; meals $37-50; ☉ dinner) Think of the most chic restaurant in your town and double the chic quotient. Now you've got some idea of the Pearl – the place really is a gem. If you're lucky enough to get a reservation, try the salt and pepper wok-fried lobster.

Company of the Cauldron (☎ 508-228-4016; 5 India St; complete dinners $56; ☉ dinner Thu-Mon) A good choice for a romantic dinner out. This intimate restaurant has attentive service and top-rated food. It's purely reserved seating times and three-course prix-fixe dinners, with the likes of lobster crepe followed by almond-crusted halibut. As the chef concentrates his magic on just one menu each evening, it's done to perfection without distraction.

Drinking & Entertainment

Gazebo (☎ 508-228-1266; Straight Wharf) Great star gazing (both kinds) at this open-air crowd-pleaser right on the wharf. You can keep one eye on who's getting off the ferry and the other on your fizzy drink.

Cambridge Street Victuals (☎ 508-228-7109; 12 Cambridge St) Dim and boisterous C-Street is the hippest bar in town. It's the place to try the crantucket mojo, made with Nantucket's native red berry, or the other homegrown favorite, Whale's Tale Pale Ale by Nantucket's Cisco Brewers.

Rose & Crown (☎ 508-228-2595; 23 S Water St) This is the place in town to go for dancing; it's a friendly bar/restaurant that clears the tables at 10pm and turns into a dancefloor. Music varies with the night, anything from jazz and blues to DJs and rock, so call ahead to see what's happening. The crowd tends to be mostly 30-somethings.

Chicken Box (☎ 508-228-5625; 14 Dave St) This former fried-chicken shack at the south end of town has evolved into a roadhouse for live jazz and blues. Actually, depending on who's on the island, these days it can cover the full spectrum, and you could hear anything from soul to trance.

Starlight Theatre (☎ 508-228-4435; 1 N Union St) Nantucket's 90-seat theater screens indie and other award-winning films. It's also a venue for live entertainment on summer weekends.

Shopping

Nantucket offers dozens of upmarket galleries, antique shops and clothing boutiques, as well as specialty shops that carry the island's signature lightship baskets.

Murray's Toggery Shop (☎ 508-228-0437; 62 Main St) Dress like a native with cotton clothing from Murray's Nantucket Reds collection – pale red shirts and shorts that trace their origins back to sailcloth. The shop itself dates to the 19th-century merchant RH Macy, who opened his first store here before heading off to New York and establishing the now-famous Macy's department store.

Four Winds Craft Guild (☎ 508-228-9623; 15 Main St) Head here for the island's largest selection of Nantucket lightship baskets. Highly prized, they command a premium, with the smallest baskets beginning at $175 and purses running into the thousands of dollars. The top-of-the-line craftsmanship is well worth a browse even it you're not buying.

Nantucket Looms (☎ 508-228-1908; 16 Federal St) Cotton blankets, mohair mufflers and cashmere throws woven on-site are just the start, all displayed so beautifully you'd think you were in an art gallery. Quality local paintings, jewelry and tapestries are sold here, too.

Getting There & Around

AIR

Cape Air (☎ 800-352-0714; www.flycapeair.com), the island's main carrier, flies from Boston, Hyannis, Martha's Vineyard and Providence to Nantucket Memorial Airport. Frequency varies with the season but in summer there are hourly flights on the busy Hyannis and Boston routes. Fares fluctuate but expect to pay about $55 one-way from Hyannis, $150 from Boston, Providence and Martha's Vineyard.

Island Airlines (☎ 508-228-7575, 800-248-7779; www.islandairlines.net) also operates from Hyannis about hourly in season with similar fares to those of Cape Air.

BOAT

The most common way to reach Nantucket is by ferry from Hyannis. Ferries also connect Nantucket to Harwich and Martha's Vineyard.

The **Steamship Authority** (☎ 508-477-8600; www.steamshipauthority.com; South St Dock, Hyannis; wi-fi), which departs from Hyannis, operates the only ferries that carry autos. Make car reservations months in advance for summer if possible. There are six ferries per day mid-May to mid-September and three per day the rest of the year (round-trip adult/bicycle/child five to 12 years $30/12/14.50, 2¼ hours). Taking your car costs $240 from November to March and $360 from April to October. If you're not taking a car, the Steamship Authority's speedier catamaran service makes five to six daily round-trips (adult/bicycle/child five to 12 years $59/12/44.50, one hour) on the same route year-round.

Hy-Line Cruises (☎ 508-778-2600, 888-492-8082; www.hylinecruises.com; Ocean St Dock, Hyannis) also offers hour-long catamaran journeys (round-trip adult/bicycle/child five to 12 years $69/12/49) between Nantucket and Hyannis. The boat makes five trips daily year-round. In addition, Hy-Line operates a passenger-only traditional ferry that's a bit slower but lots cheaper between Hyannis and Nantucket (round-trip adult/bicycle/child five to 12 years $37/12/19, 1¾ hours). There are two to three boats in each direction daily from late May to mid-September, fewer in the off-season.

Both companies offer parking in Hyannis for around $10 per calendar day.

If you're coming from the Lower Cape, it's more convenient to depart from Harwich. Morning, noon and evening passenger-only ferries operated by **Freedom Cruise Line** (☎ 508-432-8999; www.nantucketislandferry.com; Rte 28 at Saquatucket Harbor, Harwich Port) run between late June and August (round-trip adult/bicycle/child three to 12 years $57/12/44, 1⅓ hours). Outside of that period, there's only one daily ferry between late May and early October (depart Harwich at 8:50am, return 4pm), but it's conveniently scheduled for day-tripping. Advance reservations are recommended. An edge over Hyannis – parking in Harwich is free for day-trippers.

Hy-Line Cruises runs an afternoon ferry once daily in each direction between Nantucket and Oak Bluffs on Martha's Vineyard (one-way adult/bicycle/child five to 12 years $27.50/6/16) from mid-June to mid-September.

BUS
The **Nantucket Regional Transit Authority** (NRTA; ☎ 508-228-7025; www.shuttlenantucket.com) runs handy shuttle buses all over the island, connecting Nantucket Town with 'Sconset in the east, Madaket in the west and beach destinations in between. Buses have racks for up to two bikes and stop at all bike paths along their routes, so if you're biking (see p213) about, you can bus one way and pedal back.

Services run from late May to late September, with most routes operating every 30 to 60 minutes throughout the day.

Individual fares cost $1 to $2, but the best deal is the NRTA passes that cost $7/12/20 for one/three/seven days of unlimited travel.

CAR
In summer, the center of town is choked with automobiles, so it's best not to add to the congestion. However, several companies, including **Hertz** (☎ 508-228-9421, 800-654-3131), **Nantucket Island Rent A Car** (☎ 508-228-9989, 800-508-9972) and **Nantucket Windmill Auto Rental** (☎ 508-228-1227, 800-228-1227) are at the airport. In town, **Young's Bicycle Shop** (☎ 508-228-1151; 6 Broad St) and **Affordable Rentals** (☎ 508-228-3501, 877-235-3500; 6 S Beach St) both rent cars. Prices start at around $60 per day but can easily be double that in peak season.

TAXI
Taxi rides from Nantucket Town cost $10 to the airport, $20 to 'Sconset. To order a taxi, call **A-1 Taxi** (☎ 508-228-3330) or **All Point Taxi & Tours** (☎ 508-228-5779).

AROUND NANTUCKET
Siasconset ('Sconset)
Although this village is barely 7 miles from town, it thinks of itself as worlds apart. Nantucket Town may seem uncrowded and unhurried compared with the rest of the US, but 'Sconset takes it to another level.

The petite, and oh so sweet, village centers around a pair of cozy cafés, a tiny general store and a stamp-size post office. It's a wonderful place for lunch – but the secret's out, so get there early.

SIGHTS & ACTIVITIES
The **old cottages** in this seaside village are a watercolorist's dream. White picket fences, climbing roses on gray cedar shingles – you'll find some of the loveliest cottages on Broadway, near the village center. Many of them, including the Lucretia M Folger House, at the corner of Main St and Broadway, date to the 18th century. All are private homes now, so do your peeking from a respectful distance.

East-facing **'Sconset Beach** gets pounded by the open Atlantic, which has eroded much of the long, narrow beach in recent years. In fact, the erosion has been so severe that in 2007 **Sankaty Head Lighthouse**, at the north side of the village, was moved inland to prevent it from tumbling over a 90ft bluff.

SLEEPING
Summer House (☎ 508-257-4577; www.thesummerhouse .com; 17 Ocean Ave; r & cottages incl breakfast in season $600-1000, off-season $250-600; ☼ Apr-Dec; ☒) A refined getaway of low-key elegance. Stay in one of 'Sconset's signature rose-covered cottages, relax by the pool or just drink in the ocean view. Some rooms have fireplaces and Jacuzzis. A piano bar, bistro and fine-dining restaurant round out the facilities.

EATING & DRINKING
Claudette's (☎ 508-257-6622; Post Office Sq; sandwiches $9; ☼ 8am-4:30pm) Sit on the front deck of this sidewalk café and savor hearty gourmet sandwiches on whole-wheat bread as 'Sconset's beautiful people stroll by. Or should you prefer a little picnic at the beach they'll gladly wrap up your food for take out.

Sconset Café (☎ 508-257-4008; Post Office Sq; meals $11-30; ☼ breakfast, lunch & dinner) Pedal out for the Gruyère cheese omelettes, homemade quahog chowder and creative salads. Dinner turns it up another notch with the likes of lamb Dijon in a red wine marinade. You're welcome to BYOB but be prepared to dish out a $5 per person corkage fee.

Beachside Bistro (☎ 508-257-4542; 17 Ocean Ave; meals $18-40; ☺ lunch & dinner) Dine on succulent lobster rolls, chili-glazed calamari and fresh tuna sushi at this upscale open-air bistro at the Summer House resort. The fine ocean view and a good wine list perfectly complement the menu of briny seafood delights.

Wauwinet & Around

Near the northeast corner of the island, 5 miles from Nantucket Town, Wauwinet tempts travelers in search of a chic getaway.

This exclusive gated community is the departure point for tours of the **Coskata-Coatue Wildlife Refuge** (☎ 508-228-6799; www.thetrustees .org; adult/child under 12yr $40/15; ☺ tours 9:30am & 1:30pm mid-May–mid-Oct, dusk Tue Jul & Aug). Natural history tours of 2½ hours take you by over-sand vehicle to view the 1100-acre property, Nantucket's northernmost spit and the Great Point lighthouse. Tours are limited to eight people so reservations are essential.

On your way out to Wauwinet is the **Nantucket Island School of Design & the Arts** (NISDA; ☎ 508-228-9248; www.nisda.org; 23 Wauwinet Rd; ☺ year-round), which offers classes and workshops lasting from a half-day to three weeks. Just some of the offerings: painting, ceramics, quilt making and landscape design. There are also kids' classes.

The **Nantucket Lifesaving Museum** (☎ 508-228-1885; 158 Polpis Rd; adult/child 5-14yr $5/2; ☺ 12:30-4:30pm Sat & Sun May, 12:30-4:30pm daily Jun–mid-Oct) documents the lifesaving stations where 'surfmen' saved mariners from shipwrecks during the 19th and early 20th centuries. Over the years, some 700 ships have met their fate on Nantucket's dangerous shoals. Artifacts include lifesaving boats and equipment, period photos and the original Fresnel lenses from the Brant Point and Great Point lighthouses.

SLEEPING & EATING

Wauwinet (☎ 508-228-0145, 800-426-8718; www.wau winet.com; 120 Wauwinet Rd; r incl breakfast in season/off-season from $550/275; ☺ May-Oct; 🖳) The kind of place to go if you're a celebrity and want to be left alone. The Wauwinet breathes exclusivity with 32 luxuriously appointed rooms, a pampering spa, two private beaches, clay tennis courts and a fleet of boats ready to taxi guests to town.

Topper's (☎ 508-228-8768; 120 Wauwinet Rd; meals $22-37, prix-fixe dinner $85; ☺ lunch & dinner May-Oct) In a gorgeous setting at the Wauwinet inn, Topper's consistently vies for 'best island dining.' Whether in the beachside garden or indoors, you'll enjoy skillful New American cuisine such as Nantucket lobster crepes with portabella mushrooms, gracious service and a stunning wine list. Lunch is casual but dinner's a formal affair – inquire about dress codes. If you're coming from town, the inn provides a complimentary boat ride from Straight Wharf.

South Shore

The south shore communities of Surfside and Cisco consist almost entirely of private homes, but visitors head here for the long, broad beaches, which are among the island's best.

Surfside Beach, 3 miles from Nantucket Town at the end of Surfside Rd, is popular with the college and 20-something set. It has full facilities, including a snack shack and beach-accessible wheelchairs, and a moderate-to-heavy surf that can make for good body surfing. About 1 mile east of Surfside Beach is **Nobadeer Beach**, below the flight path of the airport, which attracts surfers and a young beach-party crowd.

You'll find some of the most consistently surfable waves at **Cisco Beach**, at the end of Hummock Pond Rd, where **Nantucket Island Surf School** (☎ 508-560-1020; 1hr lesson $45-65, half-day surfboard rental $25; ☺ hours vary, call ahead) handles everything you'll need for hitting the waves.

SLEEPING & EATING

HI Nantucket (☎ 508-228-0433, 888-901-2084; www .capecodhostels.org; 31 Western Ave; dm $30-38; ☺ mid-Apr–mid-Oct; 🖳) Known locally as Star of the Sea, this cool hostel has a million-dollar setting just minutes from Surfside Beach. It's housed in a former lifesaving station that dates to 1873 and is listed on the National Register of Historic Places. As Nantucket's sole nod to the budget traveler, the 49 beds here are in high demand so book as far in advance as possible.

Bartlett's Farm (☎ 508-228-4403; 33 Bartlett Farm Rd; ☺ 8am-6pm; Ⓥ) From a humble farm stand, this family operation has grown into a huge gourmet market with salads, tempting desserts and made-to-order panini sandwiches. It's the perfect place to grab everything you'll need for a lunch on the beach.

Madaket

There's not a lot to see in this western outpost, but **Madaket Beach**, at the end of the namesake bike path, is the island's ace place to watch sunsets. The strong currents and heavy surf make it less than ideal for swimming but there's some attractive beach walking to be done.

MARTHA'S VINEYARD

The largest island in New England is also one of its premier vacation destinations. Bathed in scenic beauty, Martha's Vineyard attracts wide-eyed day-trippers, celebrity second-home owners, and urbanites seeking a restful getaway. Its 15,000 year-round residents include a high percentage of artists, musicians and back-to-nature types. The Vineyard remains untouched by the kind of rampant commercialism found on the mainland – there's not a single chain restaurant or cookie-cutter motel in sight. The towns are charming, the beaches good, the restaurants chef-driven and the countryside pastoral. And there's something for every mood here – fine-dine in gentrified Edgartown one day and hit the cotton candy and carousel scene in Oak Bluffs the next.

Martha's Vineyard sits 7 miles off the south coast of Cape Cod. At its greatest extent the island is 23 miles from east to west and 9 miles from north to south. Vineyard Sound separates the island from Cape Cod, while Nantucket Sound is to the east.

The main towns and ports of entry are Vineyard Haven, Oak Bluffs and Edgartown, along the northeast section of the island. The quiet towns of West Tisbury, Chilmark and Aquinnah are collectively referred to as 'Up-Island.'

Getting around is easy by car though roads are narrow. If you don't have your own wheels, no problem – the island's extensive bus system connects every village and town on the island.

VINEYARD HAVEN
pop 3760

Although it's the island's commercial center, Vineyard Haven is a town of considerable charm. Its harbor boasts more traditional wooden schooners and sloops than any harbor of its size in New England. It's the mellowest of the three principal towns – the most 'real,' if you will – and a nice place to call home after visiting busy Oak Bluffs and Edgartown.

Central Vineyard Haven (aka Tisbury) is just four or five blocks wide and about a half-mile long. Main St is the main thoroughfare through town. Steamship Authority ferries dock at the end of Union St, a block from Main St. From the terminal, Water St leads to the infamous 'Five Corners' intersection: five roads come together and no one really has the right of way. Good luck.

Information
BOOKSTORES
Bunch of Grapes (☎ 508-693-2291; 44 Main St; 🕙 9am-6pm Sat-Thu, 9am-9:30pm Fri) The island's best bookstore.

INTERNET ACCESS
Vineyard Haven Public Library (☎ 508-696-4211; 200 Main St; 🕙 10am-5:30pm Mon, Wed, Fri & Sat, 10am-8pm Tue & Thu) Has free internet access.

MONEY
Bank of Martha's Vineyard (☎ 508-696-4400; 91 Main St) Straddles the block between the Steamship Authority terminal and Main St. Has a 24-hour ATM.

TOURIST INFORMATION
Martha's Vineyard Chamber of Commerce (☎ 508-693-0085, 800-505-4815; www.mvy.com; Beach Rd, Vineyard Haven; 🕙 9am-5pm Mon-Fri, 9am-4pm Sat) Pick up its free island-wide guide.
Visitors center (🕙 8am-8pm mid-Jun–early-Sep) This seasonal center is operated by the chamber of commerce at the ferry dock; also has the free island-wide guide.

Sights & Activities
TISBURY TOWN HALL & KATHARINE CORNELL MEMORIAL THEATER
This neoclassic **building** (51 Spring St; admission free; 🕙 8:30am-4:30pm Mon-Fri) dating to 1844 has worn many shoes. It started as a Congregational church and later morphed into the town hall. Befitting an artistic community, the town turned half of the building into a theater in 1971. Swing by to see the Vineyard-theme murals covering the walls

LIGHTHOUSES OF THE VINEYARD

What's more New England than a lighthouse? And which island has the greatest diversity of lighthouses in America? One guess.

West Chop Lighthouse

The island's last manned lighthouse sits on the west side of Vineyard Haven Harbor. The original, built in 1817, was rebuilt in its current brick form in 1838 and moved to its present location at the end of Main St in 1891. It's closed to the public, but there are walking trails around it.

East Chop Lighthouse

The original lighthouse in Oak Bluffs was privately owned, but sailing ships refused to pay the fee imposed by the owner. The US government stepped in and erected the current cast-iron structure in 1875. Until it was painted white in 1988, it was known as the chocolate lighthouse for its reddish-brown color. You can visit the **lighthouse** (☎ 508-627-4441; adult/child under 12yr $3/free; ☼ 90min before sunset-30min after sunset Sun mid-Jun–mid-Sep) during limited hours in summer.

Edgartown Lighthouse

When the lighthouse first went up at this location in 1828, it was erected on a small man-made island on Edgartown Harbor. Over time shifting sands have filled in the area between the island and the shore and now there's a land connection. You can walk over the causeway to admire this beauty up close, though the lighthouse itself is closed to the public.

Cape Poge Lighthouse

In 1801 it cost only $36 to purchase the 4 acres for the building of this lighthouse on the far corner of Chappaquiddick Island. It's a good thing the builders bought so much land. Harsh storms destroyed the lighthouse in 1838, then in 1851 and again in 1892. The current structure dates from 1922 and in 1985 it was moved by a 'sky crane' helicopter to its present site to save it from beach erosion. Visit via a Cape Poge tour (p227).

Gay Head Lighthouse

Built in 1844 with a state-of-the-art Fresnel lens, this red-brick structure on the Gay Head cliffs is arguably the most scenic lighthouse on the Vineyard. Its caretaker, the Martha's Vineyard Historical Society, opens the **lighthouse** (☎ 508-645-2111; adult/child under 12yr $3/free; ☼ 90min before sunset-30min after sunset Fri-Sun mid-Jun–mid-Sep) for two hours around sunset on summer weekends.

that depict the whaling era, the fishing village of Menemsha and the Indian tale about the Gay Head cliffs.

CHICAMA VINEYARDS

A vineyard on the Vineyard? But of course! Since 1971, the family-run **Chicama Vineyards** (☎ 508-693-0309; Stoney Hill Rd, West Tisbury; ☼ 11am-5pm Mon-Sat, 1-5pm Sun) has been producing fine wines that range from merlot to chardonnay. Free tasting tours are offered at noon, 2pm and 4pm. The vineyard is 3 miles southwest of town, off State Rd.

WATER SPORTS

Vineyard Haven has windsurfing action for all levels. Lagoon Pond, south of the drawbridge between Vineyard Haven and Oak Bluffs, has

good wind and enclosed waters suitable for beginners and intermediates. Vineyard Harbor, on the ocean side, is for advanced windsurfers. **Wind's Up** (☎ 508-693-4252; 199 Beach Rd; rentals 4hr $50-75; ☼ 9am-6pm), at the drawbridge, rents a variety of standard and high-performance windsurfing gear.

Wind's Up also rents canoes and both single and tandem sea kayaks for $45 to $55 per half-day.

For an in-town swim, or a beachside picnic, head to **Owen Park** (Owen Park Rd), on the harbor a 10-minute walk north of the ferry dock.

BIKING

Martha's Bike Rentals (☎ 508-693-6593; 24 Union St; daily rentals $20; ☼ 9am-5pm) is adjacent to the ferry terminal.

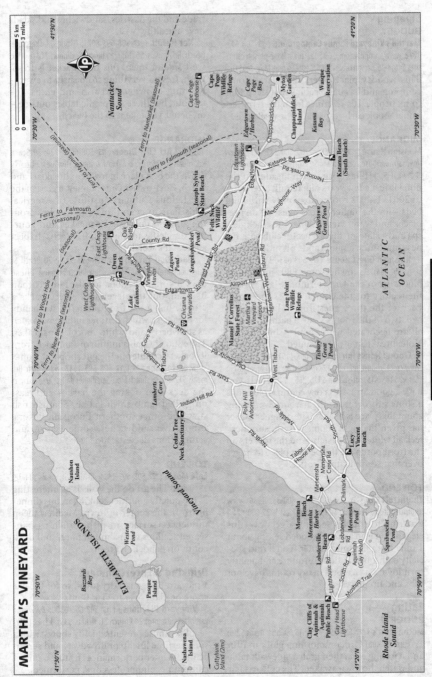

Sleeping

BUDGET

Martha's Vineyard Family Campground (☎ 508-693-3772; www.campmv.com; 569 Edgartown Rd; 2-person campsites $46, 4-/6-person cabins $120/140; ☽ mid-May–mid-Oct) This woodsy place offers the island's only camping and has basic cabins that sleep four to six people. It's 1.5 miles from the ferry terminal. Book early, especially for weekends.

MIDRANGE

Mansion House (☎ 508-693-2200, 800-332-4112; www.mvmansionhouse.com; 9 Main St; r incl breakfast $109-459; ✱ wi-fi ⚡) It has a Victorian facade but the hotel is just a few years old, rebuilt after a fire in 2001. The 32 rooms are comfy with king beds – for the higher-priced ones add on fireplaces and water views. Amenities include a spa and a state-of-the-art health club with fitness machines, a sauna and 75ft indoor pool.

Kinsman Guest House (☎ 508-693-2311; 278 Main St; r $110-125) An owner-run 1880s house four blocks from the ferry terminal. It was once the rectory for the church across the street. Each of the three guest rooms has a queen bed, two of the rooms share a bathroom, and all are decorated with Laura Ashley florals. Note: breakfast is not included.

Crocker House Inn (☎ 508-693-1151, 800-772-0206; www.crockerhouseinn.com; 12 Crocker Ave; r incl breakfast in season $185-415, off-season $115-265; ✱ wi-fi) If you have a good arm, this cozy century-old inn is a stone's throw from the harbor. Everything about this place is likable. The designer owner has given the eight rooms a fresh, summery feel, all whites and pastels. And the rockers on the front porch are the perfect place to linger over that second cup of coffee.

TOP END

Thorncroft Inn (☎ 508-693-3333, 800-332-1236; www.thorncroft.com; 460 Main St; r incl breakfast $225-600; ✱) Catering to couples seeking a getaway, this elegant inn is in a quiet, wooded setting about 1 mile from the town center. You'll find specialty bathrobes, antique furniture and nightly turndown service, and many rooms have hot tubs and fireplaces.

Eating

BUDGET

Mocha Mott's (☎ 508-693-3155; 15 Main St; items $2-6; ☽ 6am-7:30pm) Order a morning glory muffin and a jolting java, then grab a sidewalk table and watch the town awaken. The coffee is fair trade and the pastries, sandwiches and salads have a healthy twist.

Net Result (☎ 508-693-6071; Tisbury Marketplace, Beach Rd; meals $6-14; ☽ lunch & dinner) On the west side of town, this fish market is fresh, fresh, fresh. Everything from sushi to award-winning chowder and fish and chips. It's takeout, but there are picnic tables outside – or, better yet, take it to the beach.

MIDRANGE

our pick Art Cliff Diner (☎ 508-693-1224; 39 Beach Rd; meals $7-16; ☽ breakfast & lunch Thu-Tue) Hands down the best place in town for breakfast and lunch. Chef-owner Gina Stanley, a grad of the prestigious Culinary Institute of America, adds flair to everything she touches from the almond-encrusted pancakes and gourmet omelettes to the fresh fish tacos. Expect a line – it's worth the wait.

Black Dog Tavern (☎ 508-693-9223; 20 Beach St Extension; meals $8-36; ☽ breakfast, lunch & dinner) These days it's more famous for its T-shirts than its food, but this legendary eatery packs a crowd. Just a jog from the ferry, it's handy for breakfast, which features indulgences such as strawberry-and-white-chocolate pancakes. Time short? Grab a muffin or sandwich from its bakery counter in the gift shop out front.

Mediterranean (☎ 508-693-1617; 52 Beach Rd; meals $12-37; ☽ lunch Mon-Sat, dinner daily; Ⓥ) Sit on the deck overlooking the harbor and feast on grilled lamb shish kabob, Spanish fish stew and other southern European flavors. Innovative sandwiches, some vegan, and scrumptious desserts, too.

TOP END

Café Moxie (☎ 508-693-1484; 48 Main St; meals $31-38; ☽ dinner) The art on the walls is as interesting as the quietly gourmet cooking in this dinner bistro in the center of town. Mediterranean influences surface in dishes such as pan-seared scallops with almond puree and duck confit on dandelion greens.

Drinking & Entertainment

Vineyard Haven is a dry town, so for the bar scene head on over to Oak Bluffs.

Vineyard Playhouse (☎ 508-696-6300; www.vineyardplayhouse.org; 24 Church St; tickets $35) The 120-seat Playhouse presents quality shows, with a summertime lineup of Broadway and screen actors. Winter performances feature a mix of community and professional performers.

TIP FOR TIPPLERS

It may be called Martha's *Vineyard,* but alcohol can be sold only in the towns of Edgartown and Oak Bluffs. The rest of the island is 'dry.' If you'd like a beer or wine with your meal in a dry town, most restaurants will allow you to bring your own, but phone ahead to make sure of their policies.

Capawock Movie House (☎ 508-627-6689; 37 Main St; adult/child $8/6) Walking through the door is like stepping back a century at this classic 1912 cinema. It offers a healthy dose of art films.

Shopping

Vineyard Haven, and especially Main St, features a variety of fine art, jewelry and clothing shops. Here are a couple not to miss:

Shaw Cramer Gallery (☎ 508-696-7323; 56 Main St) Among the art galleries in town, this one stands out for its wide array of fine crafts, art glass and designer items.

Midnight Farm (☎ 508-693-1997; 18 Water Cromwell Rd) This shop reflects the taste of singer Carly Simon, a longtime Vineyard resident and the shop's co-owner. Look for gauzy clothing, art books, and rustic yet comfortable housewares.

Getting There & Around

AIR

Martha's Vineyard Airport (MVY; ☎ 508-693-7022), in the center of the island about 6 miles south of Vineyard Haven, has year-round service to Boston, Hyannis and Nantucket, and seasonal service to Providence. Check **Cape Air** (☎ 508-771-6944, 800-352-0714; www.flycapeair.com) for fares and schedules.

BOAT

Ferries operated by the **Steamship Authority** (☎ 508-477-8600; www.steamshipauthority.com) run from Woods Hole to Vineyard Haven every hour or two throughout the day, a 45-minute voyage (round-trip adult/child five to 12 years/bike/car $14/7.50/6/130). If you're bringing a car book as far in advance as possible.

BUS

The **Martha's Vineyard Transit Authority** (☎ 508-693-9440; www.vineyardtransit.com; 1-/3-day pass $6/15) operates a network of buses from the Vineyard Haven ferry terminal to villages throughout the island. It's a practical way to get around and you can even reach out-of-the-way destinations such as the Gay Head cliffs by bus.

CAR

Adventure Rentals (☎ 508-693-1959; 7 Beach Rd) rents mopeds, 4WDs and regular cars. Expect to pay around $65 for a moped, $100 for a car and $175 for a Jeep, though on busy summer weekends the prices will climb even higher. Be aware that Vineyarders disdain mopeds – and accidents are common.

TAXI

For a taxi, call **All Island Taxi** (☎ 508-693-TAXI) or **Harbor Taxi** (☎ 508-693-9611).

OAK BLUFFS
pop 3720

For most visitors this ferry-port town, where the lion's share of boats arrive, is their introduction to the island. This is the island's summer fun center – a place to wander with an ice-cream cone in hand, poke around souvenir shops and revel into the night.

Orientation & Information

All the ferries dock in the same general vicinity in the town center, the Steamship Authority boats along Seaview Ave and the other ferries along Circuit Ave Extension. The two roads connect together as a single loop. The area between the two docks is filled with shops, eateries and bike and moped outlets.

Bank of Martha's Vineyard (☎ 508-693-0095; cnr Oak Bluffs & Seaview Aves) Near the ferry docks; has a 24-hour ATM.

Information booth (☎ 508-693-4266; cnr Circuit & Lake Aves; ⏲ 9am-5pm late May–mid-Oct) The town hall staffs this convenient booth near the carousel.

Martha's Vineyard Hospital (☎ 508-693-0410; 1 Hospital Rd; ⏲ 24hr) At the west side of Oak Bluffs, just off the Vineyard Haven–Oak Bluffs Rd.

Sights & Activities

CAMPGROUNDS & TABERNACLE

Oak Bluffs started out in the mid-19th century as a summer retreat by a revivalist church, whose members enjoyed a day at the beach as much as a gospel service. They first camped out in tents, then soon built some 300 wooden cottages, each adorned with whimsical filigree trim.

A PROUD HERITAGE

African Americans have deep, proud roots on the Vineyard. Arriving as slaves in the late 1600s, they broke the yoke here long before slavery ended on the mainland. In 1779 a freed slave named Rebecca Amos became a landowner when she inherited a farm from her Wampanoag husband. Her influence on the island was widespread – Martha's Vineyard's only black whaling captain, William Martin, was one of her descendants.

It was during the Harlem Renaissance that African American tourism to the Vineyard really took off. Writer Dorothy West, author of *The Wedding*, was an early convert to the island's charms.

The cadre of African Americans gathered on the Vineyard during the 1960s was so influential that political activist Joe Overton's Oak Bluffs home became known as the 'Summer White House' of the Civil Rights movement. His guest list ranged from Malcolm X to Jackie Robinson and Harry Belafonte. It was at Overton's home that Martin Luther King Jr worked on his famous 'I Have A Dream' speech.

These days, Oak Bluffs is a prime vacation destination for East Coast African American movers and shakers. Filmmaker Spike Lee owns a house on the island, as does uber-lawyer lobbyist Vernon Jordan, who introduced Bill Clinton and his family to the island during Clinton's White House years.

Oak Bluffs' African American connection was explored in Matty Rich's 1994 movie, *The Inkwell,* starring Jada Pinkett Smith.

You can learn more about the Vineyard's black heritage online at www.mvheritagetrail.org.

From bustling Circuit Ave, slip into the alley between the Secret Garden and the Tibet store and you'll feel like you've dropped down the rabbit hole. Suddenly it's a world of gingerbread-trimmed houses adorned with hearts and angels and Candyland colors. Is this Pleasantville? Can you live forever?

These brightly painted cottages – known as the Campgrounds – surround emerald-green **Trinity Park** and its open-air **Tabernacle** (1879), where the lucky descendants of the Methodist Campmeeting Association still gather for community sing-alongs and concerts.

You can walk inside one of the cottages at the **Cottage Museum** (☎ 508-693-7784; 1 Trinity Park; adult/child $2/50¢; ☼ 10am-4pm Mon-Sat, 1-4pm Sun Jun-Oct), which is filled with Campmeeting Association history and artifacts.

FLYING HORSES CAROUSEL

Take a nostalgic ride on this national historic **landmark** (☎ 508-693-9481; cnr Lake & Circuit Aves; rides $1.50; ☼ 10am-10pm daily late May-early Sep, 11am-4:30pm Sat & Sun late Apr-late May & early Sep–mid-Oct; ♿), which has been captivating kids of all ages since 1876. Featuring the USA's oldest continuously operating merry-go-round, these antique horses have manes of real horse hair, and if you stare deep into their glass eyes you'll see neat little silver animals inside.

BEACHES

Beginning just south of the Steamship Authority's ferry terminal a narrow strip of sandy beach runs unbroken for several miles. Right in town, **Oak Bluffs Town Beach** is easily reached on foot. Or continue 1 mile further south to **Joseph Sylvia State Beach** on Beach Rd, which has calm waters suitable for families. It's also referred to as Bend-in-the-Rd Beach as you move toward Edgartown.

BIKING

A scenic **bike trail** runs along the coast connecting Oak Bluffs, Vineyard Haven and Edgartown – it's largely flat so makes a good pedal for families. More experienced riders might want to bike the 20 miles to Aquinnah.

Step off the ferry and you'll find a slew of wheelers and dealers renting mopeds and bicycles. Keep walking until you reach **Anderson Bike Rentals** (☎ 508-693-9346; 1 Circuit Ave Extension; per day $15; ☼ 9am-6pm), an established family-run operation with well-maintained bikes at honest prices.

Tours

Two-hour historical walking **tours** (☎ 508-693-0525; adult/child under 12yr $10/free; ☼ 10am Tue & Thu Jul & Aug) of the Campgrounds (p223) meet at the Trinity Park Tabernacle and include admission to the Cottage Museum. Or pick up a free copy of the 'Historic Walking Tour of Oak Bluffs' brochure from the tourist office and explore this fanciful town at your own pace.

Festivals & Events

It's all about lights. If you're lucky enough to be in Oak Bluffs on the third Friday in August, you'll see the island's most spectacular **fireworks** display. The Wednesday of that same week is **Illumination Night**, when the town gathers at Trinity Park for the lighting of thousands of Japanese lanterns.

Sleeping

BUDGET

Nashua House (☎ 508-693-0043, 888-343-0043; www .nashuahouse.com; 30 Kennebec Ave; r with shared bathroom in season $99-149, off-season $69-89; 💽 wi-fi) The Vineyard the way it used to be – no phones, no TV, no in-room bathroom. Instead you'll find suitably simple and spotlessly clean accommodations at this small 1873 inn in the center of town. Restaurants and pubs are just beyond the front door.

MIDRANGE

Narragansett House (☎ 508-693-3627, 888-693-3627; www.narragansetthouse.com; 46 Narragansett Ave; r incl breakfast in season $125-185, off-season $85-185; 💽 wi-fi) This charming place is comprised of two adjacent Victorian gingerbread-trimmed houses, on a quiet residential street that's just a stroll from the center. It's old-fashioned without being cloying and unlike other places in this price range all the rooms have private bathrooms.

Surfside Motel (☎ 508-693-2500, 800-537-3007; www.mvsurfside.com; 7 Oak Bluffs Ave; r in season $150-235, off-season $80-160; 💽) It's a block from the ferry terminal and across from the carousel, so this motel ranks high on convenience with a buzz of action just steps away. There's nothing brilliant about the place, but the rooms are adequate, the beds comfortable and the price right. Ask for a top-floor room to avoid hearing people walking above you.

TOP END

Oak House (☎ 508-693-4187, 800-245-5979; www.vine yardinns.com; 75 Seaview Ave; r incl breakfast & afternoon tea in season $225-350, off-season $180-245; 💽 May-Oct; 💽) Aptly named – the handsome rooms have oak furniture, oak walls, even oak ceilings! Built in 1872 as a summer mansion for the governor, this grand Victorian inn faces

Nantucket Sound and offers fine water views from most rooms.

Eating

BUDGET

MV Bakery (☎ 508-693-3688; 5 Post Office Sq; baked goods $1-3; 💽 7am-5pm) This simple joint serves inexpensive coffee, famous apple fritters and cannoli, but *the* time to swing by is from 9pm to midnight, when you can go around to the back door and buy hot, fresh doughnuts straight from the baker.

MIDRANGE

Slice of Life (☎ 508-693-3838; 50 Circuit Ave; meals $9-23; 💽 breakfast, lunch & dinner; **V**) The look is casual, the fare is gourmet. At breakfast, kick-ass coffee, portabella omelettes and fab potato pancakes. At dinner the roasted cod with sun-dried tomatoes is a savory favorite. And the desserts – decadent crème brûlée and luscious lemon tarts – are as good as you'll find anywhere.

Sharky's Cantina (☎ 508-693-7501; 31 Circuit Ave; meals $9-20; 💽 11am-12:30am) The best bang for your buck for Mexican fare on the island. And the menu doesn't skimp – you can order anything from a $7 burrito to a sizzling fajita plate with the works. Mex beers and frozen margaritas for the grown-ups, and a kids' menu for the tots.

Giordano's (☎ 508-693-0184; 107 Circuit Ave; meals $11-20; 💽 lunch & dinner) Just minutes from the ferry dock Gio's is a local institution that started as a modest clam bar in the 1930s. It's since morphed into a multifaceted family restaurant that serves everything from perfecto fried clams to hand-tossed pizzas and full pasta dinners. No credit cards.

TOP END

Sweet Life Café (☎ 508-696-0200; 63 Circuit Ave; meals $32-46; 💽 dinner) New American cuisine with a French accent is offered by this stylish bistro, which provides the town's finest dining. Local oysters in mango cocktail sauce, wild mushroom strudel and innovative beef and seafood dishes top the charts.

Drinking & Entertainment

Offshore Ale Co (☎ 508-693-2626; 30 Kennebec Ave) This popular microbrewery is the place to enjoy a pint of Vineyard ale and hear good bands on the weekends. If you're looking for the town's best burger, pop by anytime.

Lampost (☎ 508-693-9847; Circuit Ave) Head to this combo bar and nightclub for the island's hottest dance scene. The music is mostly hip-hop, reggae and funk.

Two historic cinemas, **Island Cinema** (☎ 508-627-6689; 1 Circuit Ave; adult/child $8/6) and **Strand Theatre** (☎ 508-627-6689; 13 Oak Bluffs Ave; adult/child $8/6), sit opposite each other in the town center.

Getting There & Around

Car and passenger ferries operated by the **Steamship Authority** (☎ 508-477-8600; www.steamshipauthority.com) run from Woods Hole to Oak Bluffs five times per day (round-trip adult/child five to 12 years/bike/car $14/7.50/6/130, 45 minutes).

From Falmouth Harbor, the passenger ferry **Island Queen** (☎ 508-548-4800; www.islandqueen.com; 75 Falmouth Heights Rd, Falmouth) sails to Oak Bluffs at least seven times daily in summer (round-trip adult/child three to 12 years/bike $15/7/6).

From Hyannis, **Hy-Line Cruises** (☎ 508-778-2600, 800-492-8082; www.hylinecruises.com; Ocean St Dock, Hyannis) operates a slow ferry (round-trip adult/bike/child five to 12 years $37/12/19, 1½ hours) once daily to Oak Bluffs and a high-speed ferry (adult/bike/child five to 12 years $59/12/43, 55 minutes) five times daily.

Pick up public buses in front of Ocean Park, 200 yards south of the terminal.

EDGARTOWN

pop 3780

Perched on a fine natural harbor, Edgartown has a rich maritime history and a patrician air. At the height of the whaling era it was home to more than 100 sea captains whose fortunes built the grand old homes that still line the streets today. Edgartown is where islanders head for a night of fine dining, and where well-heeled vacationers come for a weekend getaway.

Orientation & Information

All roads into Edgartown lead to Main St, which extends down to the harbor. Water St runs parallel to the harbor. The bus terminal is on Church St, near its intersection with Main St.

Edgartown Books (☎ 508-627-8463; 44 Main St; 9:30am-6pm) An in-town indie bookstore.

Edgartown National Bank (☎ 508-627-0035; cnr Main & Water Sts) Has a central location.

Edgartown Public Library (☎ 508-627-4221; 10am-5pm Mon & Thu, noon-8pm Tue & Wed, noon-5pm Fri & Sat) Has free internet access.

Edgartown Visitors Center (29 Church St; 8:30am-6pm May-Jun & Sep–mid-Oct, 8:30am-10pm Jul & Aug, shorter hours off-season) This operation at the bus terminal has rest rooms and a post office.

Sights & Activities
MARTHA'S VINEYARD MUSEUM

This intriguing **museum** (☎ 508-627-4441; www.marthasvineyardhistory.org; 59 School St; adult/child 6-15yr $7/4; 10am-5pm Tue-Sat mid-Jun–mid-Oct, shorter hours off-season), part of the Martha's Vineyard Historical Society, has a fascinating collection of whaling paraphernalia and scrimshaw. And don't miss the lighthouse display, which includes the huge Fresnel lens that sat in the Gay Head Lighthouse (see boxed text, p220) until electrical power arrived in 1952.

HISTORIC BUILDINGS

The **Martha's Vineyard Preservation Trust** (☎ 508-627-8619; www.mvpreservation.org) manages a trio of vintage buildings clustered together on Main St. Prominent among them are the **Old Whaling Church** (cnr Main & Church Sts), a former Methodist meetinghouse built in 1843 that combines New England simplicity with majestic Greek Revival columns. On the same block is the stately **Dr Daniel Fisher House** (99 Main St), an 1840 mansion that once housed the island's wealthiest resident (no, he didn't make his fortune from his medical practice, but owned the whale-oil refinery). In the yard behind it is the 1672 **Vincent House**, built in the traditional Cape style and one of the island's oldest houses.

The trust is open subject to the ability of volunteer docents, so hours are irregular; call for tours and information.

BEACHES

Simply walk along N Water St in the direction of the Edgartown Lighthouse (see boxed text, p220) to reach a pair of beaches on the northeast side of town. **Lighthouse Beach**, running north from the lighthouse, makes a good vantage to watch boats putting into Edgartown Harbor. **Fuller St Beach**, extending north from Lighthouse Beach, is frequented by college students and summer workers taking a break between shifts.

But the in-town beaches are just kids' stuff – for the real deal head to **Katama Beach** (also called South Beach), off Katama Rd, on the outskirts of Edgartown. The beach stretches for three magnificent miles; rough surf is the norm on the ocean side but there are protected salt ponds on the inland side.

FELIX NECK WILDLIFE SANCTUARY

Mass Audubon's **Felix Neck Wildlife Sanctuary** (☎ 508-627-4850; Edgartown–Vineyard Haven Rd; adult/ child 3-12yr $4/3; ☺ dawn-dusk), 3 miles northwest of Edgartown center, is a birder's paradise with miles of trails skirting fields, marshes and ponds. Because of the varied habitat this 350-acre sanctuary harbors an amazing variety of winged creatures, including ducks, oystercatchers, wild turkeys, ospreys and red-tailed hawks. Bring your binocs.

BIKING

The best bike trails on the Vineyard start in Edgartown. You can pedal on a dedicated bike route along the coastal road to Oak Bluffs; take the bike trail that follows the Edgartown–West Tisbury Rd as far as the youth hostel and then skirts up and around Manuel F Correllus State Forest, the island's largest conservation tract; or take the shorter bike path south to Katama Beach.

Several companies rent bikes in Edgartown, including **Wheel Happy** (☎ 508-627-5928; 8 S Water St & 204 Upper Main St; rental per day $20; ☺ 9am-5pm), a full-service shop with well-maintained bikes. It has two in-town locations and will also deliver to your guesthouse.

Tours

The **Trustees of Reservations** (☎ 508-693-7662; www.thetrustees.org; tours adult $20-35, child under 15yr $12-18; ☺ late May–mid-Oct) offers a variety of tours of remote Cape Poge Wildlife Refuge, which runs along the entire east side of Chappaquiddick Island. Some tours go to the century-old Cape Poge Lighthouse on Chappaquiddick's northern tip, others concentrate on the barrier beach ecology, exploring by kayak.

Felix Neck Wildlife Sanctuary (above) also offers nature tours of all sorts, from family canoe trips to marine discovery outings.

Sleeping

BUDGET

Upscale Edgartown doesn't offer budget accommodations, but the island's hostel (p229) is just a 20-minute bus ride away on the Edgartown–West Tisbury Rd.

MIDRANGE

Edgartown Inn (☎ 508-627-4794; www.edgartowninn .com; 56 N Water St; r $100-200; ☺ mid-Apr–Oct; ✴) The best bargain in town with 20 straightforward rooms spread across three adjacent buildings. The oldest dates to 1798 and claims Nathaniel Hawthorne and Daniel Webster among its earliest guests. Rooms have changed only a bit since then (no phone or TVs), but most have a private bathroom.

Edgartown Commons (☎ 508-627-4671, 800-439-4671; www.edgartowncommons.com; 20 Pease's Point Way; studio in season $195, off-season $100; ✴) A family favorite, this older complex offers 35 unassuming units ranging from studios to multi-bedroom apartments. All have kitchens and the grounds include barbecue grills, picnic tables and a playground. The central location is within easy walking distance of the bus terminal and restaurants.

Harborside Inn (☎ 508-627-4321, 800-627-4009; www.harborsideinn.com; 3 S Water St; r $160-390; ✴ wi-fi ✴) The views here, overlooking Edgartown Harbor, are stunning. The Harborside seamlessly fuses a pair of 19th-century mansions with newer hotel flanks. The rooms are cushy without being frilly and the resort-class amenities include a sauna and heated outdoor pool. Arriving by yacht? Tie up at the inn's private dock.

TOP END

Victorian Inn (☎ 508-627-4784; www.thevic.com; 24 S Water St; r incl breakfast $200-385; ✴ wi-fi) Four-post beds, freshly cut flowers and a gourmet multicourse breakfast are just part of the appeal at this upscale inn right in the heart of town. And, yes, it's Victorian – listed on the National Register of Historic Places.

Eating

BUDGET

Among the Flowers Café (☎ 508-627-3233; 17 Mayhew Lane; meals $6-13; ☺ breakfast & lunch) Join the locals on the garden patio for omelettes, homemade soups, waffles, sandwiches, crepes, even lobster rolls ($15). Although everything's served on paper or plastic, it's still kinda chichi.

Espresso Love (☎ 508-627-9211; 17 Church St; meals $7-14; ☺ 6:30am-6pm, to 11pm mid-Jun–Aug) Serves the richest cup o' Joe in town, sweet cinnamon rolls and good sandwiches – perhaps a curried chicken with walnuts and currants? The shady courtyard is the perfect place to enjoy lunch on a sunny day and the location near the bus terminal is handy.

MIDRANGE

Seafood Shanty (☎ 508-627-8622; 31 Dock St; meals $13-37; ☽ lunch & dinner) If you want a knockout harbor view this place reaches over the water with a wall of windows in all directions. Lunch focuses around burgers and fish sandwiches while dinner digs deeper into your pockets with the usual surf 'n' turf selections.

Alchemy (☎ 508-627-9999; 71 Main St; meals $14-17; ☽ lunch & dinner) The smartest place to have lunch? Snatch one of the sidewalk tables at this bistro, order a cool glass of chardonnay and take it from there. The asparagus crab salad won't disappoint. Or spice it up with the tuna tacos in a lime crème fraîche.

TOP END

Atria (☎ 508-627-5850; 137 S Main St; meals $32-50; ☽ dinner) Islanders in the know consider this stylish chef-owned restaurant the island's finest. The innovative cuisine dances playfully between French haute cuisine and Asian-inspired fare with everything from ahi tuna tempura to Vineyard lobster in beurre blanc.

Drinking & Entertainment

Newes from America (☎ 508-627-4397; 23 Kelley St) In one of the oldest buildings in town, this Colonial-style pub makes a good stop for a quiet drink and has decent pub grub as well.

Seafood Shanty (☎ 508-627-8622; 31 Dock St) For a drink with a view, head to the waterfront deck bar at this harborside restaurant.

Wharf (☎ 508-627-9966; Main St) This year-round bar with dancing nightly in summer is popular with the under-25 preppy set and pick-up scene.

Outerland (☎ 508-693-1137; www.outerlandmv.com; 17 Airport Rd) You'll find some of the best bands on the island playing at this happening nightclub adjacent to Martha's Vineyard Airport. It's the place to see and be seen.

Getting There & Around

The public bus terminal, where all buses from Edgartown depart, is in the town center on Church St. Pick up a schedule and a day pass ($6) and the whole island is yours to explore. Some key buses: bus 8 will take you to Katama (South) Beach, bus 13 to Oak Bluffs and Vineyard Haven – both leave every half-hour.

UP-ISLAND

The western side of the island – comprising the towns of West Tisbury, Chilmark and Aquinnah – is a patchwork of rolling hills, small farms and open fields frequented by wild turkeys and deer. Soak up the scenery, take a hike, pop into a gallery, stop at a farm stand and munch, lunch and beach.

West Tisbury
pop 2490

The island's agricultural heart has a white church, calm ponds and a vintage general store, all evoking an old-time sensibility. West Tisbury also has some worthwhile artists' studios and galleries sprinkled throughout.

SIGHTS & ACTIVITIES

Part food shop, part historic landmark, **Alley's General Store** (☎ 508-693-0088; State Rd; ☽ 7am-6pm) is a favorite local gathering place, and has been since 1858.

The 1859 **Grange Hall** (State Rd) is a historic meetinghouse, most visited these days for regular farmers markets (opposite). This post-and-beam structure is also a venue for concerts, lectures and other events.

Wildlife Sanctuaries

The **Cedar Tree Neck Sanctuary** (☎ 508-693-5207; Indian Hill Rd; admission free; ☽ 8:30am-5:30pm), off State Rd, has an inviting 2.5-mile hike across native bogs and forest to a coastal bluff with views of Cape Cod.

Long Point Wildlife Refuge (☎ 508-693-7392; off Edgartown–West Tisbury Rd; adult/child under 16yr $3/free; ☽ 9am-5pm; **P** $10) offers good birding and a mile-long trail to a remote beach.

Polly Hill Arboretum (☎ 508-693-9426; 809 State Rd; adult/child under 12yr $5/free; ☽ dawn-dusk, visitors center 9:30am-4pm) is a 60-acre celebration of woodlands and wildflower meadows.

Art Galleries

You can't miss the **Field Gallery** (☎ 508-693-5595; 1050 State Rd), a field of large white sculptures by local artist Tom Maley (1911–2000) that playfully pose while tourists mill around them. There's an indoor gallery, too, with works by artists of local and national renown.

In business since 1954 but hardly old-school, the **Granary Gallery** (☎ 508-693-0455; Old County Rd) stocks everything from photos by Margaret Bourke-White to fanciful paintings by local artists.

Master craftspeople turn sand into fragile and colorful creations at the **Martha's Vineyard Glass Works** (☎ 508-693-6026; 683 State Rd). If you can stand the heat, you can watch them.

SLEEPING & EATING

HI Martha's Vineyard (☎ 508-693-2665; www.capecod hostels.org; Edgartown–West Tisbury Rd, West Tisbury; dm $30-38; ☒ Apr–early Oct; ⧠) Reserve early for one of the 72 beds at this very popular purpose-built hostel in the center of the island. It's got everything you'd expect of a top-notch hotel: a solid kitchen, a volleyball court, bike delivery, no curfew and no lockouts. The public bus stops out front and it's right on the bike path. What more could you ask for?

Fella's (☎ 508-693-6924; 479 State Rd; sandwiches $5-7; ☒ 7am-8pm) Next to the West Tisbury Post Office, this modest café is operated by one of the island's top caterers. A couple of public bus routes make connections just outside the door, so it's a convenient place to stop for a sandwich or a slice of pizza.

West Tisbury Farmers Market (State Rd) Head to the Grange Hall in the center of West Tisbury on Wednesday and Saturday from 9am to noon for fresh-from-the-farm produce.

Chilmark & Menemsha
pop 850

Occupying most of the western side of the island between Vineyard Sound and the Atlantic, Chilmark is a place of pastoral landscapes and an easygoing atmosphere. Chilmark's chief destination is the picture-perfect fishing village of Menemsha, where you'll find shacks selling seafood fresh off the boat.

SIGHTS & ACTIVITIES

If the fishing village of **Menemsha** looks familiar to you, get out your DVD player: it was one of the locations for the movie *Jaws*. Nowadays, it's a relaxing outpost in which to browse. Basin Rd borders a harbor of fishing boats on one side and dunes on the other, ending at the public **Menemsha Beach**. Sunsets here are spectacular.

A little **bike ferry** (☎ 508-645-3511; one-way $5; ☒ mid-Jun–early Sep, phone for hours) takes people and their bikes across the cut to Lobsterville Beach (p230).

Lucy Vincent Beach, off South Rd about half a mile before the junction with Middle Rd, is one of the loveliest stretches of sand on the island, complete with dune-backed cliffs and good, strong surf. The far end of it is popular for nude bathing.

The 50ft catamaran **Arabella** (☎ 508-645-3511; Menemsha Harbor; daytime/sunset cruise $75/50; ☒ mid-Jun–late Sep) makes a 7-mile daytime sail to Cuttyhunk Island and a shorter sunset sail around the Gay Head cliffs.

SLEEPING & EATING

Menemsha Inn & Cottages (☎ 508-645-2521; www .menemshainn.com; North Rd; r incl breakfast in season $240-310, off-season $145-190; ☒ May-Oct) Enjoy fresh country air at this inn on 14 acres of secluded woods and gardens. The 27 units, spread across 17 buildings and cottages, range from simple rooms to luxurious water-view suites. There's a path between the inn and Menemsha Beach.

Bite (☎ 508-645-9239; 29 Basin Rd; meals $7-18; ☒ 11am-dusk) It's a fried-food fest, with fried fish and chips, oysters and clams. Forget those wimpy clam strips – big, fat bellies are the specialty at this pint-size clam shack. Take it to the beach or eat here at picnic tables.

Larsen's Fish Market (☎ 508-645-2680; 38 Basin Rd; market prices; ☒ 9am-7pm) Tourists flock to Homeport, Menemsha's largest restaurant, but if you want the freshest seafood at a fraction of the price keep driving to the end of the beach where you'll find boats unloading their catch at this harborside fish market. The staff will shuck you an oyster and steam you a lobster and you can take them out the back door and eat on a harborside bench.

Aquinnah (Gay Head)
pop 350

Apart from its isolation, the chief attraction of Aquinnah is the windswept cliffs that form a jagged face down to the Atlantic, astonishing in the colorful variety of sand, gravel, fossils and clay that reveal 100,000 centuries of geology.

Aquinnah was known as Gay Head until the 1990s. That time coincided with an increased consciousness of the native Wampanoag people, and it's here more than anywhere else on the island that you'll notice Wampanoag influence.

SIGHTS & ACTIVITIES

Aquinnah's chief draw, the **Clay Cliffs of Aquinnah**, also known as the Gay Head cliffs, were formed by glaciers more than 100 million years ago. Rising 150ft from the ocean, they're dramatic any time of day but at their very best in the late afternoon light when they glow in an amazing array of colors. The cliffs are a National Historic Landmark owned by the Wampanoag Native Americans. To protect them from erosion, it's illegal to bathe in the mud pools that form at the bottom of the cliffs, climb the cliffs, or remove clay from the area.

The 51ft, c 1856 brick **Gay Head Lighthouse** (see boxed text, p220) stands regally at the top of the bluff.

Aquinnah Public Beach (P $15) is a whopping 5 miles long. Access is free, although parking is not. From the parking lot, it's a 10-minute walk to the beach. You can hang out just below the multicolored cliffs, or walk 1 mile north along the shore to an area that's popular with nude sunbathers.

Just across from Menemsha Harbor, **Lobsterville Beach** (Lobsterville Rd) is popular with families because of the gentle surf and shallow water. Parking is restricted on Lobsterville Rd, so the best way to get there is to take the bike ferry from Menemsha (p229).

SLEEPING & EATING

Outermost Inn (☎ 508-645-3511; www.outermostinn .com; 81 Lighthouse Rd; r incl breakfast $280-390, prix-fixe dinner $75; ☼ mid-May–mid-Oct) Be a guest of Hugh Taylor, musician James Taylor's younger brother, at this attractive estate house near Gay Head Lighthouse. The hilltop setting and ocean views are grand and the Taylors make you feel right at home. Dinner, prepared by the inn's highly regarded chef, is open to the public, but call ahead for reservations.

Central Massachusetts & the Berkshires

Drive around the back roads of central Massachusetts and you'll soon realize that you've come across a very special place. The rolling hills of the Berkshires rise out of farming valleys growing apples, pumpkins and corn. Set within the rural hills and forests are a collection of main street towns supporting a wealth of culture powerhouses occupying relaxed digs inside barns and fields, including a world-class dance festival, illustrious symphony orchestra and lots of summer theater. While extreme skiers may head north to Vermont, the kinder, gentler slopes of the Berkshires promise a ski vacation the whole family can enjoy – and with fewer people fighting over the same patch of land.

Move further east and you'll find the exemplary college towns of the Pioneer Valley, particularly Northampton with its outspoken lesbian community. Here you can catch a band, find a good meal and explore bookstores set within the town's surprisingly urbane and picturesque center. The surrounding countryside contains yet more farmland and the slow current of the broad Connecticut River; along its banks are historic towns dating from the earliest days of Massachusetts Bay Colony.

In the heart of the commonwealth lies Worcester, a postindustrial mess and New England's third-largest city, home to an excellent art museum, concert hall and, most importantly, an outstanding collection of old-school diners.

CENTRAL MASSACHUSETTS & THE BERKSHIRES

HIGHLIGHTS

- Experiencing the best of the contemporary art world in the factory complex of **MASS MoCA** (p271)
- Achieving meta irony by going number two at your favorite museum in Worcester, the **American Sanitary Plumbing Museum** (see boxed text, p235)
- Taking a late-night pit stop for custard and coffee while driving across Massachusetts at **Boulevard Diner** (see boxed text, p237)
- Browsing for whatever at the incredibly picturesque **Montague Bookmill** (p255) bookstore and café.
- Listening to world-class symphonies while getting drunk on a nice patch of grass at **Tanglewood** (see boxed text, p266)

★ MASS MoCA
★ Montague Bookmill
★ Tanglewood
American Sanitary Plumbing Museum ★
Boulevard ★ Diner

▪ TELEPHONE CODE: 508, 413	▪ POPULATION: 1.6 MILLION	▪ AREA: 4293 SQ MILES

Information

There are three regional tourist offices providing information. For the Berkshires, contact the **Berkshires Visitors Bureau** (☎ 413-743-4500, 800-237-5747; www.berkshires.org; 3 Hoosac St, Adams; ☼ 8:30am-5pm Mon-Fri). The **Greater Springfield Convention & Visitors Bureau** (☎ 413-787-1548, 800-723-1548; www.valleyvisitor.com; 1441 Main St, Springfield; ☼ 9am-5pm Mon-Fri) helps with Springfield and the Pioneer Valley. The **Central Massachusetts Convention and Visitors Bureau** (☎ 508-753-2920; www.worcester.org; 30 Worcester Center Blvd, Worcester; ☼ 8:30am-5pm Mon-Fri) handles Worcester, Sturbridge and surrounds.

History

The history of the western half of Massachusetts hinges upon its rivers. The Connecticut River – the largest river in New England – attracted early settlers in the 1630s because it was not only navigable, but also passed through a fertile valley. The industrial period in the mid-19th-century caused several mill towns to develop along the Connecticut and its tributaries, in particular the Deerfield River. Some, such as Shelburne Falls and the Montague Bookmill, survive as small-scale throwbacks to another time. Worcester, at the head of the Blackstone River, owes its large population and acres of empty brick buildings to the industrial revolution and was once a center of innovation and creation.

While manufacturing no longer exists as a viable part of the economy, another 19th-century tradition remains very strong – the many liberal arts colleges and universities strewn across the landscape. There are nine alone in Worcester, and the so-called 'five colleges' of the Pioneer Valley have given it true intellectual cache. These colleges, often enjoying pretty real estate near colonial churches and commons, have liberalized the area and helped to cement the pastoral Berkshires' role as a cultural beacon in the woods.

The Culture

Stereotyping people in central and western Massachusetts is easily done. Think of its places as a function of population and colleges. The small cute towns with schools charging a lot for tuition tend to attract plenty of liberal-minded people who like to compost. Small cute towns with fewer colleges (the Berkshires) tend to have more SUVs (sport-utility vehicles) and SUV-sized baby strollers. The bigger cities are mostly remnants of the industrial revolution, and contain government workers, suits and blue-collar types trying to find jobs. Since Worcester has nine colleges, a few people living there are also generally liberal-minded.

Land & Climate

Massachusetts' climate does not dramatically differ from that of the rest of the region: winters can be bitterly cold and gloriously snowy, with summers ranging from pleasantly warm to uncomfortably hot.

The peak leaf-peeping window is around the first two weeks of October. Call Massachusetts' **foliage hotline** (☎ 800-227-6277) for specifics.

Parks & Wildlife

Dozens of parks and forests pepper central and western Massachusetts. In season it will normally cost you $2 per car to park at 'scenic areas' and $5 per car to visit inland swimming beaches. Out of state campsites cost $12 to $15. Check out **MassParks** (www.mass.gov/dem/forparks.htm) for more information about activities and amenities, plus trail maps. You can also call **MassLive** (☎ 413-442-8928) for maps to all the region's trails.

Both Skinner State Park (p246) on top of Mt Holyoke in Hadley and Mt Tom State Reservation in Holyoke offer incredible views of the Connecticut River valley, starring the switchbacking river itself. The parks are popular spots for picnicking and trail walking.

Take in the sweeping vistas of the surrounding five states from atop Mt Greylock State Reservation (p272), the tallest point in the state. You can hike part of the way to the top, or you can drive all the way. The Appalachian Trail passes over its ridge. The Connecticut River Greenway State Park runs the length of the state, with eight river access points for pure boating – or simply river lounging – pleasure.

Getting There & Around

In Connecticut, Bradley International Airport (see p246) serves Springfield and the Pioneer Valley towns.

Peter Pan Bus Lines (☎ 800-343-9999; www.peterpanbus.com) and **Bonanza Bus Lines** (☎ 888-751-8800; www.peterpanbus.com) run buses nationally and to many points in New England.

The **Pioneer Valley Transportation Authority** (PVTA; ☎ 413-781-7882; www.pvta.com) provides bus services to the Five College area (the central part of the Pioneer Valley). The

CULTURE & FESTIVALS

■ **Aston Magna** (☎ 413-528-3595; www.astonmagna.org; tickets from $30, student rush tickets $10; summer & winter series) Listen to Bach, Brahms and Buxtehude and other early classical music in venues around Great Barrington.

■ **Bankside Festival** (☎ 413-637-3353; www.shakespeare.org) Well-done Shakespearian plays are performed outdoors in a bucolic context (see p265).

■ **Berkshire Opera Company** (☎ 413-644-9988; www.berkshireopera.org; tickets $40-90) Enjoy full-dress productions of classic and modern operas at the Mahaiwe Performing Arts Center in Great Barrington and at other venues in the southern Berkshires.

■ **Berkshire Theatre Festival** (☎ 413-298-5576; www.berkshiretheatre.org; late Jun-early Sep) Stop by for experimental summer theater in an old playhouse.

■ **Big E** (☎ 413-737-2443; www.thebige.com; Sep) You will probably want to hang out with some carnies and make fun of the Connecticut pavilion (see p243).

■ **Brimfield Antique Show** (www.brimfieldshow.com; mid-May–early Jul & early Sep) The world's biggest outdoor antique extravaganza would like you to buy some 19th-century tooth powder (see p239).

■ **Jacob's Pillow** (☎ 413-243-0745; www.jacobspillow.org; mid-Jun–early Sep) Most cities' best troupes can't top the stupefying and ground-breaking dance of Jacob's Pillow. They also covet its barn (see p264).

■ **Tanglewood** (☎ 413-637-1600; www.tanglewood.org) For many, the Berkshire's most famous festival and its outstanding orchestral music is reason enough to return every year (see boxed text, p266).

■ **Williamstown Theatre Festival** (☎ 413-597-3399; www.wtfestival.org; late Jun-late Aug) If you've seen better summer theater, then you're dead and heaven apparently has different seasons (see p269).

Northampton–Amherst route has the most frequent service. **Berkshire Regional Transit Authority** (BRTA; ☎ 413-499-2782; www.berkshirerta.com) runs buses between major Berkshire towns.

The Massachusetts Turnpike (I-90) and MA 2 are the major east–west roads connecting Boston with central and western Massachusetts. Mass Pike is a toll road between Boston and Springfield.

Amtrak's (☎ 800-872-7245) *Lake Shore Limited* departs Boston, stopping at Framingham, Worcester, Springfield and Pittsfield before reaching Albany (NY). Its *Vermonter* runs from St Albans, VT to Washington, DC, stopping in Amherst and Springfield.

CENTRAL MASSACHUSETTS

Also referred to as Worcester County, central Massachusetts marks a boundary between Boston's suburbs to the east and vast swatches of farm and hill country to the west. The city of Worcester (say 'Wooster') dominates the area, offering museums and relic-diners to discerning travelers. Another big draw is the recreated 'colonial' village of Sturbridge, where you can suspend belief and maybe travel back in time with some costumed actors.

WORCESTER
pop 175,500

Welcome to 'Worm Town,' as locals affectionately call their city. A wealthy and important manufacturing center during the industrial revolution (the place invented and produced barbed wire, the modern envelope and more), Worcester has struggled mightily since factories began shutting down after WWII, with scant urban renewal victories in recent years. The result is an odd destination: on the one hand, a city with exemplary museums devoted to art and toilets; but on the other a disintegrating cityscape that is simultaneously bleak and (sort of) beautiful. The city's nine small colleges inject youth and creativity into Worcester's nightlife and cultural scene,

CENTRAL MASSACHUSETTS & THE BERKSHIRES

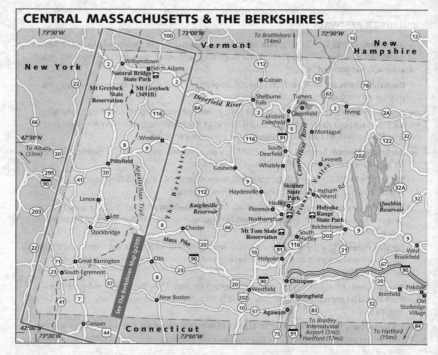

though the best draw might be the numerous historic diners (see boxed text, p237) that have slung blue-collar eggs for generations.

Orientation & Information

The clock tower on the Worcester Telegram and Gazette building marks the center of town. Main St, four blocks west of I-290, is a central drag, connecting downtown to Clark University. One block to the east, downtown's Commercial St runs parallel for a few blocks and contains several sights, with the huge DCU Center (formerly the Centrum Center) hulking nearby. The rest of the city sprawls in a confusing mess of streets, and a map will greatly help exploration efforts.

Central Massachusetts Convention and Visitors Bureau (☎ 508-753-2920; www.worcester.org; 30 Worcester Center Blvd; ☑ 8:30am-5pm Mon-Fri) Free internet access; it's across the street from the DCU Center, which sometimes provides discount coupons for many Worcester attractions. You can print these out from www .massmuseums.org/coupons.html.

Public library (☎ 508-799-1655; 3 Salem Sq; ☑ 9am-9pm Tue-Thu, 9am-5:30pm Fri & Sat) Downtown, it has free internet access.

Sights & Activities

WORCESTER ART MUSEUM

During Worcester's golden age, its captains of industry bestowed largesse upon the town and its citizens. The **Worcester Art Museum** (☎ 508-799-4406; www.worcesterart.org; 55 Salisbury St; adult/senior & student/child under 18yr $10/8/free, Sat mornings free; ☑ 11am-5pm Wed-Fri & Sun, 10am-5pm Sat; ☑ ☒) off Park and Main Sts (follow the signs) remains a generous and impressive bequest.

This small museum has a comprehensive collection, ranging from ancient Chinese, Egyptian and Sumerian artifacts to European masterworks and contemporary American pieces. Edward Hick's *Peaceable Kingdom* is perhaps the most easily recognizable, but you can also see Paul Gauguin's *Brooding Woman* and Rembrandt's *St Bartholomew*. Several pieces of Paul Revere silver have recently been acquired as well. The museum's collection of more than 2000 photographs spans the history of the medium.

MECHANICS HALL

This **hall** (☎ box office 508-752-5608, 508-752-0888; www.mechanicshall.org; 321 Main St; ☒) took shape

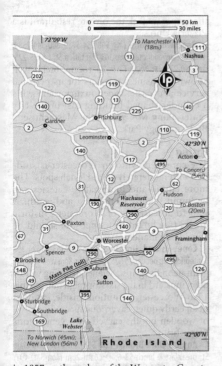

in 1857 on the orders of the Worcester County Mechanics Association, a group of artisans and small business owners that typified Worcester's inventive and industrial strength in the mid-19th-century. Boasting superb acoustics and housing the historic Hook Organ, Mechanics Hall is regarded as the finest standing pre-Civil War concert hall in the US. Notable speakers have included Henry David Thoreau, Charles Dickens, Mark Twain and Theodore Roosevelt. Restored in 1977, the hall is still used for concerts (Yo-Yo Ma, jazz), lectures

and recording sessions, some of them free. Call for information on visiting hours.

HIGGINS ARMORY MUSEUM

John Woodman Higgins, president of the Worcester Pressed Steel Company, loved good steel. Medieval armorers made piles of it – thus this collection of more than 100 full suits of armor for men, women, children and even dogs. The collection became so big (over 5000 pieces) that in 1929 Higgins built a special armory, the **Higgins Armory Museum** (☎ 508-853-6015; www.higgins.org; 100 Barber Ave; adult/senior/child 6-16yr $9/8/7; ☯ 10am-4pm Tue-Sat, noon-4pm Sun; P ♿ ☂), for it all. You'll find the art deco building with interior neo-Gothic accents off W Boylston St (MA 12). Kids will like the Quest Gallery, where they can try on 'castle clothing' and replica suits of armor.

ECOTARIUM

At this **museum** (☎ 508-929-2700; www.ecotarium .org; 222 Harrington Way; adult/child $10/8; ☯ 10am-5pm Tue-Sat, noon-5pm Sun; P ♿ ☂) and 'center for environmental exploration,' there is an array of exhibits to intrigue young minds. However, the most exciting offerings (tree-canopy walks, planetarium shows, and rides on the one-third size model steam train) cost an extra few bucks.

AMERICAN ANTIQUARIAN SOCIETY

The documents in this **research library** (☎ 508-755-5221; www.americanantiquarian.org; 185 Salisbury St; admission free; ☯ 9am-5pm Mon-Fri), a few blocks from the art museum, comprise the largest single collection of printed source materials relating to the first 250 years of US history, and covering all aspects of colonial and early American culture, history and literature. Free tours run each Wednesday at 3pm.

HOLY CRAP!

See if you can resist making this pun (or worse) when you visit the **American Sanitary Plumbing Museum** (☎ 508-754-9453; 49 Piedmont St; admission free; ☯ 10am-2pm Tue & Thu, closed Jul & Aug), the world's only known museum devoted to the subject. Withstanding the urge will probably challenge all of your mental strength.

Begun by Charles Manoog in 1979 (by day a fellow running a plumbing parts distribution business), this family-operated museum contains a legitimately fascinating and well-displayed collection of artifacts. Ogle toilet paper from the 19th century, learn what people used to use corn cobs for (predictable and gross), see wooden pipes from a 17th-century city, and enjoy the sight of dozens of ancient toilets – some beautiful, others bizarre, and all bound together in their efforts to mask one of life's most common odors.

BLACKSTONE RIVER BIKEWAY

When it is finished in the next five years, the **Blackstone River Bikeway** (☎ 508-234-9090; www.black stoneriverbikeway.com) will offer a mostly off-road bike trail from Union Station in Worcester to Providence, RI, 45 miles to the south. The trail laces through historic mill villages and farmland, following remnants of the historic Blackstone River Canal as well as a railroad right-of-way. Until the bikeway is complete, you can follow the trail on marked roads. Visit the website for updates and maps.

Sleeping

Worcester's hotels serve DCU Center arena concertgoers and high-tech firms on the outskirts of the city. This demand has jacked up the rates at the few hostelries that exist within the city limits. You will find more economical tourist lodgings and charming B&B options outside of Worcester. In addition to the Putnam House B&B, you might stay around Sturbridge, 20 miles to the southwest (see p239). The Plaza and Hilton are centrally located downtown.

ourpick Putnam House B&B (☎ 508-865-9094; www.putnamhousebandb.com; 211 Putnam Hill Rd, Sutton; r/ste $70/85) Run by British expats Margaret (a bird-watcher) and Martyn (a geography professor) Bowden, this hilltop farmstead dates to 1737 and shows its age exceedingly well. Restored by master carpenters, it has walk-in fireplaces, exposed beams and an enormous red centennial barn. The hosts exemplify the term, preparing generous breakfasts to your dietary restrictions. Caution: Dr Bowden has particularly strong opinions about soccer (he coaches a champion squad of local girls). Find the place 10 miles southeast in Sutton. Cash or check only.

Crowne Plaza (☎ 508-791-1600; www.crowneplaza .com; 10 Lincoln Sq; r $139-169; P ⊠) While rooms at this modern hotel won't overwhelm you with interesting design, some of them have decent views over Main St. The best face toward the stately art museum. An interior court contains a small flowering garden surrounding an indoor/outdoor pool.

Hilton Garden Inn (☎ 508-753-5700; www.worcester .stayhgi.com; 35 Major Taylor Blvd; r $139-169; P ⊑ ⅅ) Pros: because it opened in 2007, modest rooms come with new beds. Cons: views overlook a busy thoroughfare and a large concrete parking structure from rooms with generic (albeit up-to-date) decor. To enhance the corporate feel, the on-site restaurant is a Pizzeria Uno's.

Beechwood Hotel (☎ 508-754-5789, 800-344-2589; www.beechwoodhotel.com; 363 Plantation St; r $195-225, ste $240-275; P ⅅ) This 73-room hotel is well known to business travelers for its personal service and pastel-toned luxury rooms. It's a cylinder-shaped building east of the city center along MA 9 near the Massachusetts Biotechnology Park.

Eating

The core of downtown Worcester is studded with moderately priced lunch spots. The more ethnic and imaginative eateries can be found slightly to the west and south. A visit to at least one of Worcester's historic diners (see boxed text, opposite) should be considered mandatory.

Coney Island Hot Dog (☎ 508-753-4362; 158 Southbridge St; hot dogs $1.25; ⊙ 10am-8pm Wed-Mon) A giant neon fist grips a wiener dripping yellow neon mustard in the six-story sign outside this 1918 Worcester institution. Inside, eat dogs in an eerily quiet, cavernous space chock-full of wooden booths carved with generations of graffiti.

Annie's Clark Brunch (☎ 508-756-1550; 934 Main St; breakfast & lunch $3-6; ⊙ 6am-2pm Mon-Sat) On the edge of Clark University's campus, this greasy spoon attracts students, professors, neighborhood Joes and a gravedigger. Nearly everyone dining here is on a first-name basis with Annie, the proprietor so connected with the community that Clark University recently awarded her an honorary degree. Inside, find dusty pictures of regulars from the last 20 years and an eyebrow-raising number of pigs.

Lucky's Cafe (☎ 508-756-5092; 102 1/2 Grove St; sandwiches $4-6; dinner meals $15-20; ⊙ 7am-2pm Mon-Fri, 5-9pm Fri & Sat, brunch Sun) Inside a sprawling brick manufacturing complex begun in 1831, this modest joint's remarkable soups (white bean escarole with tomato) would cost twice as much in another city. A loyal lunch crowd fills the dozen tables, though weekend BYOB dinners (pork chops, Portuguese fish stew) have recently been added.

Sano Café (☎ 508-753-1896; 232-4 Chandler St; meals $8-15; ⊙ 9am-8pm Mon-Fri, 9am-6pm Sat, 11am-5pm Sun; V) An offshoot both physically and philosophically of the Living Earth food store, this tiny café has a menu featuring healthy fare. Everything, including the meat, is as organic

---

WORCESTER DINERS

Worcester, New England's largest rustbelt city, might look a bit like a black eye, but its occasionally brutal postindustrial landscape has nurtured a great American icon: the diner. Here, you'll find a dozen old relics tucked behind warehouses, underneath old train trestles, or steps from dicey Irish bars. Some of them are the product of the former Worcester Lunch Car Company, which produced 650 prefabricated beauties from 1906 to 1961. Models from the '30s tend to incorporate rich wood-trim and tiling and look like old train cars. Those from the '50s shoot for a sleek 'streamlined' aesthetic, incorporating sheets of gleaming metal into their exteriors.

Following is a list of Worcester's finest. For another option, try Ralph's (p238).

Boulevard Diner (☎ 508-791-4535; 155 Shrewsbury St; meals $4-9; closed 3pm Sun-10am Mon, otherwise 24hr) Reason enough to live in Worcester, this old dining car looks much like it did in 1936. Experience red Formica tables, dark wooden booths, old iceboxes and a big painting of a yellow-jacketed dude who has long stared from the doorway. Food-wise, enjoy eggs, plus a menu of Italian specialties including meatballs, veal and eggplant parmesan. Wistful memories of fabulous grapenut custards haunt college students' dreams decades after leaving Worcester.

George's Green Island Diner (☎ 508-753-4189; 162 Millbury St; eggs etc $2-6; 4:30pm-11:30am Sun-Thu, 11pm-11:30am Fri & Sat) Inside this spare diner, sit at the counter to behold the world's eighth wonder: a grill in constant use that never dirties. Just how George Army's spatula cooks up all that meat, egg and potato without a stain remains a mystery, but you'll be too distracted by kielbasa and liver and onions to notice. It's in a tough-looking Irish neighborhood. Coffee costs 55¢!

Corner Lunch (☎ 508-799-9866; 133 Lamartine St; meals $4-11; 6am-2pm Mon-Sat, 7am-1pm Sun) Here, you'll find a sweet prefab built by DeRaffelle in the 1950s. The exterior contains plenty of silvery metal panels and a big neon sign. Inside, there are fries, club sandwiches, meatloaf and eggs. While the food is bland, the seating is not – it's a patchwork of duct tape and glittery gold Naugahyde. It sits a block from the Miss Worcester Diner.

---

as possible. Eat nori, smoothies, fresh juice combinations, beef and lots of vegan stuff.

Sole Proprietor (☎ 508-798-3474; 118 Highland St; lunch $8-15, dinner $20-35; lunch & dinner) Overlook the cheesy name and head under the neon marquee for fresh, honest seafood at moderate prices in an upscale, linen-clad dining room. Eat lobster, Dijon and horseradish bluefish, maple-glazed scallops and ocean catfish with bok choy and parmesan crust.

One Love Café (☎ 508-753-8663; 800 Main St; dinner $9-18; noon-8pm Tue, noon-10pm Wed-Sun; **V**) Fill up on organic Jamaican and West Indian food at this cozy, art-filled hole-in-the-wall. Depending on your appetite, you can get 'big tings' or 'likkle tings.' Try the pungent *escov-eitched porgies* (fish in a spicy vinaigrette) and hot jerk.

Drinking & Entertainment

Pick up the free weeklies **Worcester Magazine** (Womag; www.worcestermag.com), or the more student-targeted **Pulse** (www.thepulsemag.com) for arts and entertainment listings.

BARS & CLUBS

Bars in Worcester are plentiful and rough. If adventurous, troll Salisbury St near Worcester Polytechnic Institute (WPI) for some college hangouts. Expect a lot of boys, though, since 74% of WPI students are male science geeks. Otherwise, Ralph's (p238) is king.

Moynagh's Tavern (☎ 508-753-9686; 25 Exchange St) This authentic Irish-American pub of the first order is the oldest bar in Worcester, which means it's beaten up and working class. Babe Ruth once bowled here when the place was a bowling alley. The after-work crowd of regulars likes to play keno (a televised lottery game) and the bartender looks at out-of-state IDs with suspicion.

Irish Times (☎ 508-797-9599; 244 Main St; from 11:30am) Set in a 19th-century three-story building, this place emulates a Dublin pub, with dark paneling, high ceilings and the scent of Caffrey's. On weekends the upstairs is a disco where the DJ spins out techno and dance tunes. The dinner patrons are largely urban professionals who come for the fish and chips.

MB Lounge (☎ 508-799-4521; 40 Grafton St; from 5pm Mon-Thu, 3pm Fri-Sun) Depending on the night, this queer lounge runs the gamut from casual neighborhood bar to bass-thumping dance club to Sunday piano bar. The decor could use some updating, but hey, that only makes

CENTRAL MASSACHUSETTS & THE BERKSHIRES

it typical of the rest of Worcester. Expect beers and a pool table.

LIVE MUSIC
Don't forget about Mechanics Hall (p234) for popular tunes, jazz and classical concerts.

Ralph's Chadwick Square Diner (☎ 508-753-9543; www.ralphsdiner.net; 95 Prescott St; burgers $6.50; ☽ 4pm-2am Tue-Sat) This old green diner attached to a rock club serves chili, burgers, booze and nothing else. Come for some sweet gigs, mostly local and often talented. The place attracts college kids and townies wearing prescription safety glasses. The stellar jukebox contains a homemade disc simply labeled 'really good songs.'

Palladium (☎ 508-797-9696, 800-477-6849; www.thepalladium.net; 261 Main St; tickets $10-35) This mid-sized general admission club only books all-ages shows, and some of them have aired on MTV. The offerings range from hip-hop to metal to hardcore to rock. Recent performers have included The Roots, Dashboard Confessional, Taking Back Sunday and 50 Cent.

DCU Center (☎ 508-755-6800; www.dcucenter.com; 50 Foster St) This huge venue (formerly known as the Centrum Center), attracts nationally known rock groups and other big-crowd acts. Care for a monster truck show?

THEATER & CULTURE
Cinema 320 (☎ 508-793-7477; www.cinema320.com; Jefferson Academic Center, cnr Main & Downing Sts; tickets $5) This independent operation, on the campus of Clark University, screens an incredible array of acclaimed and hard-to-find films, many of them foreign. The school is about 2 miles south of the town center on Main St.

Java Hut (☎ 508-752-1678; javahutma.com; 1073a Main St at Webster Sq; ☽ 11am-1am) Aside from featuring Worcester's only manual espresso machine, Java Hut also hosts slam poetry and folk singers most nights.

Getting There & Away
Worcester stands at the junction of four interstate highways. About an hour's drive will bring you here from Boston, Providence, Springfield or Hartford, CT.

Peter Pan Bus Lines (☎ 800-343-9999; www.peterpanbus.com; Union Station, 2 Washington Sq) has direct services between Worcester and Amherst ($18, two hours, four daily), Boston ($8, one hour, thirteen daily), Lenox ($30, 2½ hours,

three daily) and Springfield ($17, one hour, five daily). Bonanza, operated by Peter Pan and also at Union Station, runs bus services to Providence, RI ($13, 70 minutes, one daily).

Amtrak trains (☎ 508-755-0356, 800-872-7245) stop here en route between Boston and Chicago. **MBTA** (☎ 617-722-3200, 800-392-6099; www.mbta.com) runs commuter trains to/from Boston ($7.75, 80 minutes, 10 daily midweek, five daily weekends). Trains for both rails leave from Union Station at Washington Sq.

STURBRIDGE
pop 7800

Sturbridge can leave a bittersweet taste in the traveler's mouth – here is one of the most visited attractions in New England and one of the rudest examples of how far US culture has traveled in less than 200 years in search of the Yankee dollar.

The town kept much of its colonial character until after WWII. When the Mass Pike (I-90) and I-84 arrived in the late 1950s and joined just north of the town, commerce and change came all at once. To take advantage of the handy highway transportation, the town became host to one of the country's first 'living museums' – Old Sturbridge Village (OSV). The concept of the living museum was new when OSV started. Inevitably, in the community's effort to preserve a working example of a traditional Yankee community within the borders of OSV, it generated a mammoth attraction on whose borders motor inns, fast-food chains, gas stations and roadside shops have sprouted up.

Orientation & Information
There are actually three Sturbridges. The first one you see is the commercial strip along US 20 (Main St) just south of I-90 exit 9, which has most of the town's motels and restaurants. The second is Sturbridge as it used to be, best seen at the town common, backed by the Publick House Historic Inn (p240), on MA 131 half a mile southeast of US 20. The third is Old Sturbridge Village, entered from US 20.

Sturbridge can be outrageously busy with visitors in summer and during the fall foliage season. Traffic increases exponentially during the three times per year when the Brimfield Antique Shows are held in Brimfield, 6 miles west of town along US 20.

Sturbridge Area Tourist Association Information Office (SATA; ☎ 508-347-2761, 800-628-8379; www

.sturbridge.org; 380 Main St/US 20; ☉ 9am-5pm) Opposite the entrance to Old Sturbridge Village.

Sights & Activities

OLD STURBRIDGE VILLAGE

During the first half of the 20th century, brothers Albert and J Cheney Wells lived in Southbridge and carried on a very successful optics business. They were enthusiastic collectors of antiques – so enthusiastic that by the end of WWII their collections left no free space in their homes.

The brothers bought 200 acres of forest and meadow in Sturbridge and began to move old buildings from the region to this land. **Old Sturbridge Village** (OSV; ☎ 508-347-3362; www.osv .org; US 20; adult/senior/child 3-17yr $20/18/5; ☉ 9:30am-5pm daily May-Oct, 9:30am-4pm daily Nov & Dec, Sat & Sun only Jan-Apr) opened in 1946, creating a mythic version of a New England town from around the 1830s, with 40 restored structures filled with the Wells' antiques. Rather than labeling the exhibits, this museum has 'interpreters' – people who dress in costume, ply the trades and occupations of their ancestors and explain to visitors what they are doing. Expect to spend at least three hours here.

Although many historians find the layout of the village less than accurate, attention to detail is high. The country store displays products brought from throughout the world by New England sailing ships. Crafters and artisans ply their trades with authentic tools and materials. The livestock has even been back-bred to approximate the animals – smaller, shaggier, thinner – that lived on New England farms a century-and-a-half ago. The OSV library has more than 20,000 manuscripts and books describing various aspects of early-19th-century life in the region.

Admission is good for two days within a 10-day period. Food services in the village include the tavern, with buffet and à la carte service for full meals, light meals and snacks. There is also a picnic grove with grills and a play area.

HYLAND ORCHARD & BREWERY

This **orchard and brewery** (☎ 508-347-7500; www .hylandbrew.com; 195 Arnold Rd; admission free; ☉ noon-7pm Tue-Sun, shorter hours in winter) is a 150-acre family-owned farm and craft brewery that produces its Sturbridge Amber Ale and a handful of other beers with well water. Try them all at the tasting bar. Lest you think this is no place for

the kids, note that the brewery has a petting farm, pond, playground, ice-cream parlor and café. In the fall, pick apples while local folk and rock bands pick stringed instruments. To find Hyland, go west on Main St/US 20 to Arnold Rd, turn right and go 2 miles north on Arnold Rd to the farm.

ICON EXHIBIT

Since WWII it has been illegal to export icons from Russia, so the collection of 60 rare works preserved at the **icon exhibit** (☎ 508-347-7338; 16 Church St; admission free, donations accepted; ☉ 10am-4pm) at the St Anne Shrine is a treasure. Monsignor Pie Neveu, a Roman Catholic Assumptionist bishop, ministered to a diocese in Russia from 1906 to 1936. While at his post, Bishop Neveu collected valuable Russian icons, a hobby no doubt made easier by the collapse of the old order and the advent of secularist communism. The collection was further augmented by acquisitions brought to the USA by the Assumptionist fathers who served as chaplains at the US embassy in Moscow between 1934 and 1941. The collection was installed at the St Anne Shrine in 1971. The shrine is just off US 20 at the western end of Sturbridge.

BRIMFIELD ANTIQUE SHOW

Six miles west of Sturbridge along US 20 is the **Brimfield Antique Show** (www.brimfieldshow.com; US 20 in Brimfield; ☉ 6am-dusk), a mecca for collectors of antique furniture, toys and tools. More than 6000 sellers and 130,000 buyers gather to do business in 23 farmers' fields here; it's the largest outdoor antiques fair in North America, and possibly the world. The town has numerous shops open year-round, but the major antiques and collectibles shows are held in early to mid-May, early July and early September, usually from Tuesday through Sunday. The more 'premium' fields charge an admission fee of around $6, but most are free.

Contact the Sturbridge Area Tourist Association Information Office for more details, and be sure to make advance hotel reservations.

Sleeping

Even though Sturbridge is packed with places to stay, many lodgings fill up on Friday and Saturday nights in summer and, especially, in fall. When the Brimfield Antique Show (above) is in progress, local lodging prices rise substantially and advance reservations are necessary.

Staying in an inn or B&B remote from US 20 and the wheels of commerce is how many travelers preserve that jaunt-in-the-country feeling. In fact, if it's fresh air and tranquility you're seeking, the best option may be to get out of town completely and stay at a farm B&B. The Sturbridge Area Tourist Association Information Office can help with member B&Bs, and can assist with same-day reservations if you stop in at the information office. Also try **Heritage Corridor Bed & Breakfast Group** (www.heritagecorridorbb.com). If you're looking for more central lodging, look through the motel brochures at SATA – some include coupons that are good for special rates or discounts.

All lodgings listed here offer parking.

Wells State Park (☎ 508-347-9257, reservations 877-422-6762; Mountain Rd/MA 49; campsites $10-12) This campground offers 60 wooded sites – some lakefront – on its 1470 acres, with flush toilets and showers. You can reserve your site in advance with a two-night deposit. It's north of I-90.

America's Best Value Inn (☎ 508-347-7327; www.sturbridgecoach.com; 408 Main St; d $60-85; 🖭) This quiet motel scored a prime location – within spitting distance of Old Sturbridge Village, but set back from US 20 on a small hill. Typical rooms contain the usual motel flourish: locked coat hangers, florid bedspreads and ugly 'federal style' furniture.

Nathan Goodale House (☎ 413-245-9228; 11 Warren Rd/MA 19N, Brimfield; d $80) In a large and simple Victorian Italianate house, this B&B has tall sash windows and a substantial porch. Find it and its three tasteful rooms (two have private bathrooms) in residential Brimfield.

Commonwealth Cottage B&B (☎ 508-347-7708; www.commonwealthcottage.com; 11 Summit Ave; d $95-145) The owners of this lovingly tended Queen Anne–style building, just a few blocks off Main St, serve up hearty country breakfasts. In the three cozy rooms a multitude of patterns vie for supremacy (country quilts, active wallpaper, curtains with loud prints).

Sturbridge Country Inn (☎ 508-347-5503; www.sturbridgecountryinn.com; 530 Main St; r $99-129, ste $149-189; 🖭) This inn was formerly a stately Greek Revival mansion. Its nine rooms have been gutted and transformed into pink-themed realms of gas fireplaces, whirlpool baths and tackiness. There's a bit of traffic noise in the front rooms. It's about 1 mile west of Old Sturbridge Village.

Publick House Historic Inn (☎ 508-347-3313, 800-782-5425; www.publickhouse.com; MA 131 on the Common; 🖭) Here is Sturbridge's most famous historic inn, the 1771 Publick House, which faces the village common, half a mile away from the mania of US 20. Three separate buildings make up the property: Country Motor Lodge ($69 to $100) looks like it sounds (generic and boring); while Chamberlain House ($140 to $165) offers six suites with decor that is almost nice. Your best bet is the Publick Inn itself ($89 to $125), with its canopy beds and 18th-century decor.

Lying along a 1-mile stretch of US 20 just off exit 9 is a procession of chain hotels and motels. Rates can vary by season, but doubles generally fall in the range of $70 to $110.

Days Inn (☎ 508-347-3391; 66-68 Haynes St; 🖭) Off I-84 exit 1 in a quiet, wooded area.

Super 8 (☎ 508-347-9000; 358 Main St) Many rooms have views of Cedar Lake.

Eating

US 20 is awash with fast-food outlets, breakfast joints and independent restaurants that offer lunch and dinner.

Micknuck's (☎ 508-347-0116; 570 Main St; ☽ 8am-7pm Mon-Fri, 9am-6pm Sat & Sun) Tucked into the corner of this market is a deli counter serving massive gourmet sandwiches, a bag of chips and a superb deli pickle all for under $6. You can stock up on picnic standards like potato and pasta salads, too.

Rom's (☎ 508-347-3349; 179 Main St/MA 131; lunch $8-16, dinner $13-20; ☽ lunch & dinner) Rom's is a roadside institution that seats 500 and serves big portions of traditional Italian-American fare (and drinks) for moderate prices. Locals flock to the all-you-can-eat buffets (Friday night and Sunday morning). It's across the street from the Sturbridge Plaza shopping center.

Ugly Duckling Loft (☎ 508-347-2321; 520 Main St; meals $16-36; ☽ 11am-11pm) The Ugly Duckling is a popular, boisterous spot with a hefty menu of burgers and salads with mains that run the gamut from Swedish meatballs to stuffed sole. It's the less upscale and more fun sister of the downstairs Whistling Swan restaurant, and there's often live music on weekends.

Salem Cross Inn (☎ 508-867-2345; 260 W Main St/MA 9, West Brookfield; lunch $8-17, dinner $22-35; ☽ lunch & dinner Tue-Fri & Sun, dinner only Sat) If you haven't had your fill of colonial reenactment at OSV, head to this inn, built in 1705 and set on 600 lovely acres in West Brookfield. The calf's liver with bacon and caramelized onions is a house specialty ($15). Besides offering traditional New England meals, the inn hosts special events like the 'Fireplace Feast' and 'Herb Sampler.' Its Hexmark Tavern (dinner Tuesday to Friday) has less fancy fare for less fancy prices and the lunch menu incongruously offers 'Mediterranean wraps' and other items the colonists never heard of. Follow US 20 (2 miles west of Old Sturbridge Village) to MA 148 north; 7 miles along, turn left onto MA 9 and go 5 miles.

Publick House (☎ 508-347-3313, 800-782-5425; www .publickhouse.com; MA 131 on the Common; meals $25-40; ☙ lunch & dinner Mon-Sat, dinner only Sun) This classic country inn features a formal dining room with old fireplaces and hearths. Enjoy dishes such as apricot-glazed roast chicken or try pan-seared scallops with fennel. It's a staid joint, and while the food is fine, it isn't quite as good as the history. Reservations recommended.

Cedar Street Restaurant (☎ 508-347-5800; 12 Cedar St; meals $26-40; ☙ dinner Mon-Sat) With a partially modern, partially classical dining room dressed in shades of off-white, you might feeling like you're dining in a photo spread for a lesser version of *Martha Stewart Living*. In it you'll consume bouillabaisse in a saffron sauce, mushroom risotto, racks of lamb, and booze from a generous wine menu.

Getting There & Away
Most travelers arrive in Sturbridge and Old Sturbridge Village by car. Take exit 3b from I-84 and follow route 20 west into town.

PIONEER VALLEY

With the exception of gritty Springfield, the Pioneer Valley offers a gentle landscape of college towns (notably Shelburne Falls and Montague), farms and old mills that have been charmingly converted into modern use. Northampton is the biggest town with the most going on, and is a favorite destination for lesbians.

SPRINGFIELD
pop 154,000

Crap. You're in Springfield. Before sticking out your thumb or pressing down on the accelerator, be aware that if you manage to look past the depressing scene that has unfolded before you there are a few interesting sights, plus one of the best cheap Italian lunch experiences you could wish for (see p244).

Downtown Springfield contains a few reminders of the 19th-century wealth and might that once caused the city to blossom. These are a handful of quality museums, a grand symphony hall and the stately Romanesque Revival buildings that surround Court Sq. While most of the business types who work here flee promptly at 5pm, Springfield's downtown unexpectedly supports a lively night scene. Up the hill you'll find a major Civil War armory.

As all local grade-schoolers know, basketball originated in Springfield, and that explains how the Hall of Fame got to be here. Springfield is also the birthplace of Theodor Geisel, aka Dr Seuss (see boxed text, p244).

Orientation & Information
Take I-91 exit 6 northbound or exit 7 southbound, follow it to State St (east) then Main St (north), and you'll be at Court Sq in the heart of Springfield; this is a good place to start your explorations. Museum Quadrangle is a few blocks northeast, and the Tower Square complex, which includes the Marriott Hotel as well as a clutch of shops and restaurants, is two blocks northwest.

Greater Springfield Convention & Visitors Bureau (☎ 413-787-1548, 800-723-1548; www.valleyvisitor.com; 1441 Main St; ☙ 9am-5pm Mon-Fri) A block-and-a-half northwest of Court Sq.

Springfield City Library (☎ 413-263-6828; cnr State & Chestnut Sts; ☙ 11am-8pm Mon & Wed, 9am-6pm Tue, Thu & Fri, noon-4pm Sun) Also downtown; has free internet access.

Sights & Activities
MUSEUM QUADRANGLE
The **Springfield Museums** (☎ 800-625-7738; www .springfieldmuseums.org; 21 Edwards St; adult/senior & student/child 6-17yr/child under 6yr $10/7/5/free; ☙ noon-4pm Wed-Fri, 11am-4pm Sat & Sun; ☘) surround Museum Quadrangle, two blocks northeast of Court Sq. Look for Merrick Park, at the entrance to the quadrangle, and Augustus Saint-Gaudens' statue *The Puritan*.

One ticket grants entrance to all four museum. Access to the grounds, and to the Dr Seuss Sculpture Garden (see boxed text, p244), is free and they are open 9am to 8pm.

SPRINGFIELD

In addition to life-size bronzes of Seuss' active imagination there are informative plaques posted outside each museum, which explain the history and architecture of the buildings and describe the offerings housed inside.

The **George Walter Vincent Smith Art Museum** (☙ 11am-4pm Tue-Sun) is the gift of a man who amassed a fortune manufacturing carriages and then spent his money on works of art and artifacts. The exterior windows were designed by the Tiffany Studios. Inside there are fine 19th-century American and European paintings, textiles, ceramics and works in several other media. The Japanese armor collection is among the finest outside of Asia.

The art deco-style **Museum of Fine Arts** (☙ 11am-4pm Tue-Sun) has more than 20 galleries filled with lesser paintings of the great European masters and the better works of lesser masters. One of the best known pieces is Erastus Salisbury Field's *The Rise of the American Republic,* which is above the main stairway. In the impressionist and expressionist galleries, look for artworks by Edgar Degas, Gauguin, Camille Pissarro, Pierre-Auguste Renoir and Georges Rouault. In the contemporary gallery there are works by George Bellows, Lyonel Feininger, Georgia O'Keeffe and Picasso. Modern sculptors featured include Leonard Baskin and Richard Stankiewicz. There are also exemplary Japanese woodblock prints.

The **Springfield Science Museum** (☙ 10am-5pm Tue-Sat, 11am-5pm Sun; ☙) possesses a respectable, if slightly outdated, range of natural history and science exhibits – the Dinosaur Hall has a full-size replica of a *Tyrannosaurus rex,* the African Hall teaches about the evolution of peoples, animals and ecology, and the Seymour Planetarium has shows daily (adult/child $3/2).

The **Connecticut Valley Historical Museum** (☙ 11am-4pm Tue-Sun) explains how Springfield didn't always suck. It also tells of the role played by the Connecticut River back when it was an 18th-century thoroughfare shaping the surrounding cultural and physical landscapes. The museum's permanent holdings focus on the decorative and domestic arts of the Connecticut River valley from 1636 to the present, with collections of furniture, pewter and glass. Rotating exhibits might discuss

Dr Seuss or the history of the Rolls-Royce in Springfield. The museum's **Genealogy and Local History Library** holds the Ellis Island passenger records and an impressive number of records on French Canadians.

INDIAN MOTOCYCLE MUSEUM & HALL OF FAME

When Americans hear 'motorcycle,' they are most likely to think 'Harley-Davidson.' But Springfield-based Indian was the first (1901), and was, many say, the best. Up until it disbanded in 1953, the Indian Motocycle Company produced its bikes here in a sprawling factory complex. (The 'r' in motorcycle was dropped as a marketing gimmick.) Through the merger of several bike companies, the Indian Motorcycle Corporation was created in 1999 to jumpstart the manufacture of Indians again, but it's widely accepted that the new bikes don't hold a candle to the originals.

The last of the company's buildings is now the dusty **Indian Motocycle Museum & Hall of Fame** (☎ 413-737-2624; 33 Hendee St; admission $5; ☾ 10am-4pm Mar-Nov, 1-4pm Dec-Feb), with the largest, finest collection of Indian bikes and memorabilia in the world. There are other makes as well, and lots of funky period mementos. All of the machines are in working order (note the oil-drip pans underneath), and are taken out and run three times a year. If you like bikes, don't miss this place.

To find the museum, take I-291 exit 4 (St James Ave), then follow the signs north on Page Blvd to Hendee St. You'll find the museum in a low, brick building in an industrial area.

NAISMITH MEMORIAL BASKETBALL HALL OF FAME

Though the emphasis at the **basketball hall of fame** (☎ 413-781-6500; www.hoophall.com; 1000 W Columbus Ave; adult/senior/child 5-15yr/child under 5yr $17/14/12/free; ☾ 10am-5pm Sun-Fri, 9am-5pm Sat Jun-Sep, 10am-4pm Mon-Fri, 10am-5pm Sat & Sun Oct-May; ⚿) seems to be more hoopla than hoops – an abundance of multiscreened TVs and disembodied cheering – true devotees to the game will be thrilled to shoot baskets, feel the center-court excitement in a wraparound cinema and learn about the sport's history and great players.

One touted figure is James Naismith (1861–1939), inventor of the game, who came to Springfield to work as a physical education instructor at the International YMCA Training School (later Springfield College). Naismith wanted to develop a good, fast team sport that could be played indoors during the long New England winters. Sometime in early December of 1891, he had the idea of nailing two wooden peach baskets to opposite walls in the college gymnasium. He wrote down 13 rules for the game (12 of which are still used), and thus basketball was born.

In September, some fans attend induction ceremonies (tickets $35 to $75) honoring yesterday's greatest stars.

SPRINGFIELD ARMORY NATIONAL HISTORIC SITE

The **national historic site** (☎ 413-734-8551; www.nps.gov/spar; 1 Armory Sq, Federal St; admission free; ☾ 9am-5pm Tue-Sun) preserves what remains of the USA's greatest federal armory, which was built under the command of General George Washington during the American Revolution. During its heyday in the Civil War, it turned out 1000 muskets a day. Springfield Technical Community College now occupies many of the former firearm factories and officers' quarters, but exhibits in several of the old buildings, including the Main Arsenal, recall the armory's golden age quite effectively.

On the site, the **Benton Small Arms Museum** holds one of the world's largest collections of firearms, including lots of Remingtons, Colts, Lugers and even weapons from the 1600s. For some weird weaponry, don't miss the Organ of Rifles.

The Armory is a 10-minute walk northeastward from Court Sq along State St past Museum Quadrangle. If you are driving, take I-291 exit 3 to Armory St and follow it to Federal St.

Festivals & Events

In mid-September, sleepy West Springfield explodes into activity with the annual Eastern States Exposition, or the **Big E** (☎ 413-737-2443, ticket orders only 800-334-2443; www.thebige.com; 1305 Memorial Ave/MA 147; adult/child 6-12yr $15/10). The fair goes on for two weeks, with farm exhibits and horse shows, carnival rides and parades, mass consumption of food on sticks, a petting zoo, and performances from the likes of Jessica Simpson and the Peking Acrobats. In addition, each of the six New England states hosts a large pavilion with its own exhibits.

CENTRAL MASSACHUSETTS & THE BERKSHIRES

DR SEUSS NATIONAL MEMORIAL SCULPTURE GARDEN

The writer and illustrator responsible for such nonsensically sensible classics as *The Cat in the Hat*, *Norton Hatches an Egg* and *Yertle the Turtle* was born Theodor Seuss Geisel in 1904 in Springfield. Geisel credits his mother for inspiring his signature rhyming style; she would lull him and his sister to sleep by chanting pie lists she remembered from her bakery days back in Germany.

After graduating from Dartmouth College, Geisel made his living primarily as a political cartoonist and ad man. His first children's book, *And to Think That I Saw It on Mulberry Street*, was rejected by dozens of publishers before one bit. Geisel's first major success came with the publication of *The Cat in the Hat*, which he wrote after reading Rudolf Flesch's *Why Johnny Can't Read*, an article that asserted children's books of the day were boring and 'antiseptic,' and called upon people like Geisel (and, er, Walt Disney) to raise the standard of primers for young children. By the time he died in 1991, Geisel had published 44 books and his work had been translated into more than 20 languages. His classic *Green Eggs & Ham* is still ranked as one of the top-selling English language books to date.

In 2002 the **Dr Seuss National Memorial Sculpture Garden** (☎ 800-625-7738; www.catinthehat .org) was completed, featuring bronze pieces made by Geisel's step-daughter, the sculptor Lark Grey Dimond-Cates. Among the works in the middle of the Springfield Quad are a 10ft-tall 'book' displaying the entire text of *Oh! The Places You'll Go!* – the archetypal graduation gift – and an impish-looking Geisel sitting at his drawing board, the Cat standing by his shoulder. In the opposite corner of the quad, the squat figure of the Lorax looks beseechingly up at passersby, his famous environmental warning engraved at his feet: 'Unless.'

All shows are free once you're in the fairgrounds, but rides cost extra. There's a parking fee, but for about the same price and less hassle you can catch a shuttle that departs from the Greater Springfield Convention & Visitors Bureau. Hotels fill up when the Big E is in session, particularly on Friday and Saturday nights. Admission is a bit cheaper on weekdays.

Sleeping

Most of Springfield's more inexpensive motels, including **Red Roof Inn** (☎ 413-731-1010; www .redroof.com; 1254 Riverdale St; r $50-80; P ⊠ wi-fi ☐) and **Hampton Inn** (☎ 413-732-1300; www.hampton springfield.com; 1011 Riverdale St; r $89-139; P ⊠ wi-fi ☐) are in West Springfield off I-91 exit 13, near the intersection with US 5.

Lathrop House (☎ 413-736-6414; www.dianamara henry.com/lathrop; 188 Sumner Ave; r $125; P wi-fi) Within city limits but 2 miles from downtown, this B&B is one of many fine 19th-century homes lining traffic-heavy Sumner Ave. It has huge columns, two porches and a kosher kitchen.

Naomi's Inn (☎ 413-732-3998; www.naomisinn .net; 20 Springfield St; r $135; P ⊠ wi-fi) While the house itself appears nice with a broad porch and shady trees, it overlooks a rather depressing hospital compound. Rooms are ample and comfortable, though the furniture selected for them could be a little more graceful. You'll find a lot of new things trying to look old.

The city center contains only two hotels. These stare each other down on either side of Boland Way a block northwest of Court Sq and next to a freeway that practically passes through each hotel's lobby. Both are generic, comfortable and oriented toward business travelers.

Springfield Marriott Hotel (☎ 413-781-7111, 800-228-9290; www.marriott.com; 2 Boland Way; d $129-179; ⊠ wi-fi ☒ ☐)

Sheraton-Springfield Monarch Place (☎ 413-781-1010, 800-426-9004; www.sheraton.com; Boland Way at Columbus Ave; d $129-179; ⊠ wi-fi ☒ ☐) Has a quality on-site athletics facility.

Eating

Downtown Springfield has a scarcity of truly noteworthy restaurants. The greatest concentration of lunch places, pubs and bistros are in the vicinity of Court Sq and Union Station.

Mom & Rico's (☎ 413-732-8941; 899 Main St; dishes $3-6; ⏰ 8:30am-5:30pm Mon-Fri, 8:30am-3:30pm Sat) Both Rico and his mom will likely be here, bantering in rapid-fire Italian. Enjoy tortellini soup, eggplant parmesan grinders, and lot of stuff made from the meats and cheeses hanging helter-skelter behind the deli counter. On hand are lots of imported Italian specialties and tons of clutter – much of it bocce ball paraphernalia (Rico is a fierce advocate, and champion, of this sport, which is similar to bowls). Best deal in New England? Maybe: get a ham sandwich for $1.43. The price hasn't been raised since 1976.

Dolce Notte (☎ 413-734-4000; 304 Worthington St; sandwiches $4-6; 8am-8pm Mon-Wed, 9am-3am Thu-Sat) At the intersection with Dwight St, this small coffeehouse and deli serves espresso to people sitting at the five stools lining the bar. Good for a quick stop, its easy-to-clean tile floor and sterile decor (and lack of space) encourage you to not linger. Because of late weekend hours, it's a logical post-bar-hopping destination.

Student Prince Café & Fort Restaurant (☎ 413-788-6628; 8 Fort St; lunch $7-16, dinner $14-22; lunch & dinner) The Student Prince has been scratching those schnitzel and sauerkraut itches since 1935 and shows no signs of slowing down. Even if you're not in the mood for heavy starches, come by anyway to take in the stained-glass decor and the impressive bierstein collection (one was owned by a Russian czar). Disappointingly, the beer menu isn't as expansive as one would expect.

Sitar Restaurant (☎ 413-732-8011; 1688 Main St; lunch $6-9, dinner $13-22; lunch Mon-Sat, dinner from 5pm; **V**) Enter the glass-windowed storefront under some faded yellow signage to find an aromatic room serving up a popular lunch buffet to a loyal following. Slow weekdays, Fridays and Saturdays pull a decent crowd eating the usual favorites from a menu that draws from Persian, Indian and Hindi cuisine.

L'uva (☎ 413-734-1010; 1676 Main St; meals $25-35) Praised equally for its food and the depth and breadth of its wine menu, L'uva shines brightly amid the city's dim dining scene. The overwhelmingly purple color scheme reflects its name (Italian for 'the grape'). Eat different kinds of steak (sirloin, rib eye, fillet) and fish (tilapia, tuna, sea bass).

Drinking & Entertainment

The area around Union Station has been an entertainment district for 100 years, and it's brimming with pubs and clubs (some seedy, some not) that draw large crowds. Take a walk down Worthington St and you'll find a bunch of options crammed into two blocks, one of them likely to suit your taste.

Pick up a copy of the free **Valley Advocate** (www .valleyadvocate.com) for entertainment listings.

DRINKING & LIVE MUSIC

Smith's Billiards (☎ 413-734-9616; 207 Worthington St; from 5pm) This historic pool hall opened in 1902. It looks tough from the street, but head upstairs to find a friendly joint with cool light fixtures. A vast beer selection ensures that you don't shoot too well. On Mondays it's all-you-can-play for only $5.

Theodore's (☎ 413-736-6000; 201 Worthington St; cover free–$10) Truly great blues and jazz acts get booked in this cavernous bar serving an extensive menu of good barbecue and pub food. Though it looks a little too manufactured (condiments come in shiny galvanized buckets covered in Coors ads), it's still lively and fun. The kitchen will serve you spicy ribs until midnight on Friday and Saturday.

Hippodrome (☎ 413-787-0600; www.hdrome.com; 1700 Main St) The Hippodrome began life as the Paramount Theater in 1926 and was reborn as a nightclub in 1999 after years of neglect. Some nights (often Thursday and Friday) the place serves as a dance club. Other evenings may feature an 'extreme fighting' match or a Nickelback show.

Pub (☎ 413-734-8132; 382 Dwight St at Worthington St) This gay bar offers the standard weekly menu of karaoke and boys' nights. It keeps a dark tavern in the basement (referred to as the Quarry Saloon) for the leather-and-Levi's set to hang out and look tough.

THEATER & CULTURE

The **Symphony Hall** (☎ 413-788-7033; www.citystage .symphonyhall.com; 34 Court St; tickets $25-50) is an imposing edifice that resembles a Greek Temple. Enter this relic next to City Hall to hear concerts by the reputable **Springfield Symphony Orchestra** (☎ 413-733-2291). Otherwise, you might watch Gallagher smash watermelons or see some off-off-off-Broadway takes on theatrical classics (eg *Annie, Hairspray*).

CityStage (☎ 413-788-7033; www.citystage.symphony hall.com; 1 Columbus Center; tickets $28-40) Run by the same outfit that stages shows at Symphony Hall. Come here for comedians musicals and concerts (such as *The Producers, Almost Heaven – Songs of John Denver*) in a far less impressive building.

MassMutual Center (☎ 413-787-6610; 1277 Main St) A major venue for conventions, exhibits and big rock concerts, your best bet is to catch a Falcons hockey match. The American Hockey League squad boasts nine straight losing seasons (at time of press) and is an affiliate of the

Edmonton Oilers, which plays a mere 3000 miles away.

Getting There & Around
Springfield is served by the **Bradley International Airport** (☎ 860-292-2000) 15 miles to the south. **Valley Transporter** (☎ 413-253-1350, 800-872-8752; www.valleytransporter.com) sends shuttles to the airport for around $35 per person one way.

Peter Pan Bus Lines (☎ 413-781-2900, 800-343-9999; www.peterpanbus.com; 1776 Main St at Liberty St) and its affiliate, Bonanza, together serve New England and beyond. The bus station is a 10-minute walk northwest of Court Sq. Buses go to Amherst ($8, 45 minutes, six daily), Boston ($22, two hours, eight daily), Worcester ($17, one hour, five daily) and elsewhere, including Providence, RI; Hartford, CT; New Haven, CT; and Manchester, NH.

The **Pioneer Valley Transportation Authority** (PVTA; ☎ 413-781-7882; www.pvta.com; 1776 Main St), in the Peter Pan terminal, runs 43 routes to 23 communities in the region. Downtown, the 'Green 3' route connects State St and Liberty St via Main St.

Amtrak's (☎ 800-872-7245; www.amtrak.com) *Lake Shore Limited*, the once-a-day train running between Boston and Chicago, stops at Springfield's **Union Station** (☎ 413-785-4230; 66 Lyman St), which is a 10-minute walk northwest of Court Sq, as does the once-a-day *Vermonter*, which runs between St Albans, VT and Washington, DC.

SOUTH HADLEY
pop 17,000

The southernmost of the Five College towns, South Hadley's tiny center contains a gazeboed green with attendant brick church. Overlooking this sight is the Village Commons, a new urbanist open-air shopping mall. While the scene is cute, most visitors just get out to stretch their legs. If you're hungry or tired, you'll have a far better time satisfying your human needs in Northampton or Amherst.

The PVTA routes of 38, 39 and B43 ($1.50 per ride) run between all five colleges.

Odyssey Book Shop (☎ 413-534-7307; 9 College St; 🕑 10am-8pm Mon-Fri, 10am-6pm Sat, noon-5pm Sun) With a sophisticated selection of new and used volumes.

South Hadley Chamber of Commerce (☎ 413-532-6451; www.southhadleyguide.com; 362 N Main St)

Sights & Activities
Those who stay longer probably do so because their daughter or girlfriend goes to **Mount Holyoke College** (☎ 413-538-2222; www.mtholyoke .edu; on MA 116), the nation's oldest women's college (founded 1837; in South Hadley center). Bucolic and small, current enrollments average about 2000 students. The great American landscape architect Frederick Law Olmsted laid out the center of the parklike 800-acre campus in the late 1800s. It easily ranks as one of the most beautiful colleges in the country. Among Mt Holyoke's 19th-century legacies is a hand-crafted organ in the chapel, one of the last built by New England's master organ maker, Charles B Fisk. The campus maintains a half-dozen gardens that are open for strolling from dawn to dusk. These contain the glass **Talcott Greenhouse** (admission free; 🕑 9am-4pm Mon-Fri, 1-4pm Sat & Sun), dating back to 1898.

When Albert Bierstadt donated his painting *Hetch Hetchy Canyon* to the college in 1876, the **College Art Museum** (☎ 413-538-2245; Lower Lake Rd; admission free; 🕑 11am-5pm Tue-Fri, 1-5pm Sat & Sun; ♿) was born. One of the oldest teaching museums in the country, it maintains particular strengths in 19th- and 20th-century American paintings and Asian art.

The mountaintop **Skinner State Park** (☎ 413-586-0350; admission free, parking Sat & Sun $2; 🕑 dawn-dusk) is at the summit of Mt Holyoke, at a rather modest-sounding height of 942ft. But that's high enough to earn the visitor panoramic views of the Connecticut River and its oxbow curve, the fertile valley and the distant smudge of Mt Greylock to the west. It's north of South Hadley off MA 47 in Hadley. The **Summit House** (🕑 10am-5pm Sat & Sun) used to be the evening drinking spot for 19th-century hunters. There are hiking trails and a picnic area.

Nearby **Holyoke Range State Park** (☎ 413-586-0350; admission free; 🕑 10am-6pm) is a few miles north of South Hadley on MA 116. It has over 30 miles of marked trails, with hikes ranging between 0.75 of a mile and 5.4 miles on the Metacomet-Monadnock Trail (see boxed text, opposite).

Eating
Should your blood sugar drop precipitously, you'll find about six options in Village Commons, including **Tailgate Picnic Deli & Market** (☎ 413-532-7597; 7 College St; 🕑 6:30am-8pm Mon-Sat, 7am-5pm Sun) for gourmet sandwiches,

METACOMET-MONADNOCK TRAIL

The Metacomet-Monadnock Trail (or M&M Trail in local parlance) is 117 miles of a 200-mile green-way and footpath that traverses some of the most breathtaking scenery in western Massachusetts. It extends from Connecticut along the Connecticut River valley to New Hampshire's Mt Monadnock and beyond.

In Connecticut the trail takes its name from Metacomet (the Native American leader who waged war on the colonists in 1675). It enters Massachusetts near the Agawam/Southwick town line to become Massachusetts' Metacomet-Monadnock Trail. From the state line, the trail proceeds north up the Connecticut River valley through public and private lands, ascends Mt Tom, then heads east along the Holyoke Range, through Skinner State Park and Holyoke Range State Park, before bearing north again.

After entering New Hampshire, the trail ascends Mt Monadnock (see p427), where it joins the Monadnock-Sunapee Greenway.

The easiest access to the trail for day hikes is in the state parks, where leaflets and simple local trail maps are available. For longer hikes, it's good to have the *Metacomet-Monadnock Trail Guide*, published by the Appalachian Mountain Club. Trail excerpts are posted on the website of the **Appalachian Mountain Club Berkshire Chapter** (www.amcberkshire.org/mmtrail).

an assortment of coffees and convenience store items.

Thirsty Mind (☎ 413-538-9303; 19 College St) At this coffeehouse you can settle down with a cappuccino and possibly some live music, too. Its design evokes the inside of a whale, but cleaner and bluer (note: this evocation is not intentional).

Food 101 (☎ 413-535-3101; 19 College St; meals $15-30) Serves up precisely made classics such as shrimp scampi and steak in an upscale room full of stemware and linens. Good tiramisu.

Entertainment

To sample from the dizzying cultural platter served up by the five colleges, pick up a copy of the *Five College Calendar* in any café or on any campus, or take a look online at http://calendar.fivecolleges.edu. Most of the lectures, plays, and musical and dance performances are free.

Tower Theater (☎ 413-533-3456; 19 College St) Shows first-run films and the occasional art-house flick.

Musicorda Summer Festival (☎ 413-538-3040; Chapel Auditorium on Mount Holyoke campus; tickets $10-20) Lovers of chamber music shouldn't miss this festival, at which promising young musicians perform alongside the masters in several concert series over a six-week period.

NORTHAMPTON

pop 29,000

In a region famous for its charming college towns, you'll be hard-pressed to find any-thing more appealing than the crooked streets of downtown Northampton. Old red-brick buildings, buskers and lots of pedestrian traffic provide a lively backdrop as you wander into record shops, restaurants, cafés, rock clubs and bookstores. Move a few steps outside of the picturesque (and sizable) commercial center and you'll stumble onto the bucolic grounds of Smith College, whose lake and buildings are well worth exploring.

These days, the presence of college students and their professors gives the town a distinctly liberal political atmosphere. The lesbian community is famously large and outspoken, making Northampton a favorite destination for the gay community.

Orientation & Information

The center of town is at the intersection of Main St (MA 9) and Pleasant St (MA 5). Main St is where you'll find the core of restaurants, cafés, banks and shops, although most lodgings are on the outskirts. Smith College is on the west end of town, where Main St curves right and turns into Elm St.

Greater Northampton Chamber of Commerce (☎ 413-584-1900; www.northamptonuncommon.com; 99 Pleasant St; ☼ 9am-5pm Mon-Fri, 10am-2pm Sat & Sun May-Oct)

Sights & Activities

SMITH COLLEGE

Founded 'for the education of the intelligent gentlewoman' in 1875 by Sophia Smith, **Smith College** (☎ 413-584-2700; www.smith.edu) is the largest women's college in the country, with 2700 students. The verdant 125-acre campus along Elm St holds an eclectic architectural mix of nearly 100 buildings, as well as Paradise Pond. Notable alums of the college include Sylvia Plath, Julia Child and Gloria Steinem.

Visitors are welcome at the **Lyman Conservatory** (☎ 413-585-2740; 🕑 8:30am-4pm), a collection of Victorian greenhouses good for seeing odd things bloom. Another campus treat is the **Smith College Museum of Art** (☎ 413-585-2760; Elm St at Bedford Tce; adult/senior/student/child 6-12yr $5/4/3/2; 🕑 10am-4pm Tue-Sat, noon-4pm Sun). This 25,000-piece collection is strong in 17th-century Dutch and 19th- and 20th-century European and North American paintings, including fine works by Degas, Winslow Homer, Picasso and James Abbott McNeill Whistler.

While most will be very pleased with themselves after a stroll around **Paradise Pond** with its pretty Japanese **tea hut**, ambitious others might consider taking a guided campus tour arranged by the **Office of Admissions** (☎ 413-585-2500; on the hour 10am-3pm Mon-Fri, 9-11am Sat).

THORNES MARKETPLACE

You can't miss this urban mall – it's the green-awninged behemoth taking up a large chunk of Main St. Formerly a department store, it now houses an array of clothing and shoe boutiques, dorm-accessory shops, a music store and a natural foods market.

DINOSAUR FOOTPRINTS

Around 190 million years ago, the Pioneer Valley area was a subtropical swamp inhabited by carnivorous, two-legged dinosaurs, and a large cluster of their **footprints** (☎ 413-684-0148; Rte 5, Holyoke; admission free; 🕑 dawn-dusk) is preserved in situ on the west bank of the Connecticut River. The prints here, some 134 in all, represent three distinct species. In the early 1970s, paleontologist John Ostrom studied the tracks and – based in part on the fact that the majority of the trackways head west – came to the radical conclusion that some species of dinosaurs traveled in packs.

From Northampton, go south on Pleasant St/US 5 for about 5 miles. The small parking lot is on the left-hand side.

BIKING

The **Norwottuck Rail Trail** runs 8.5 miles along MA 9 from Northampton and Hadley and Amherst. Access the trail via the Elwell Recreation Area on Damon Rd where it crosses MA 9. See boxed text, p252, for details on the Amherst end, including bike rentals.

Sleeping

While the B&B phenomenon is strong in the Pioneer Valley, there are few actually in Northampton, although there are several around nearby Amherst. Contact the **Amherst Area Chamber of Commerce** (☎ 413-253-0700; www .amherstarea.com; 409 Main St at Railroad St, Amherst; 🕑 9am-5pm Mon- Fri) for a list.

It's usually easy to find a room during the summer. At other times of the year, room price and availability depend on the college's schedule of ceremonies and cultural events. If you're planning a visit during mid-May Commencement Week, book as far in advance as possible.

Historic College Inn (☎ 413-584-3300; www.historic collegeinn.com; 74 Bridge St; d $95-125; P) Once a parsonage (built in 1866), this B&B and its big porch also has a modern addition in the back. Rooms come with tall ceilings, hardwood floors and spare decoration. It sits on a noisy stretch of MA 9 and is a two-minute walk into town.

Autumn Inn (☎ 413-584-7660; www.hampshire hospitality.com; 259 Elm St/MA 9; r incl breakfast $109-139; P 🖳 wi-fi 🐾) Santa should not bring gifts to whoever designed this barn and raised-ranch combination. Despite the weird facade, the rooms are pretty comfortable. It's next to the Smith Campus, a 15-minute walk into town.

Hotel Northampton (☎ 413-584-3100; www.hotel northampton.com; 36 King St; d $160-210; P wi-fi 🐾) This old-timer is perfectly situated in the center of town and has been the town's best bet since 1927. Some rooms are airy, but others rely too much on mass-produced quilts for atmosphere. Even so, there is a quiet grandeur to the place and mailing a postcard via an antiquated letterbox system always feels good.

Eating

Whatever cuisine or ambience you're in the mood for, there's probably a restaurant to match. For the scoop on the area's eating scene, check out www.valleydin ingguide.com.

BUDGET

Haymarket Café (☎ 413-586-9969; 185 Main St; items $3-7; 🕑 11:30am-9pm; V) Need a place where you can read an entire book in one go? Then try lounging around this beautiful bohemian café. The main level (tall ceilings, and covered in gilt-framed art) offers espresso, fresh juice and spinach-gorgonzola salads from its vegetarian menu. The basement is lined with used books.

Sylvester's (☎ 413-586-5343; 111 Pleasant St; meals $5-7; ☯ 7am-2:30pm; ♿) Arguably the best breakfast spot in town (though you're strongly advised to first try Lone Wolf (p253) in Amherst. Sylvester's feels like a diner and is flooded with natural light thanks to some big windows. Bring a toothbrush and order the blueberry chocolate-chip pancakes.

Herrell's Ice Cream (☎ 413-586-9700; Thornes Marketplace at Old South St; cones $2-4; ☯ noon-11:30pm; ♿) Steve Herrell has been scooping out gourmet ice-cream since 1980. Some of the more unexpected concoctions are key lime, cardamom, Earl Grey and Twinkie, though he also serves coffee, chocolate and vanilla flavors.

Pizzeria Paradiso (☎ 413-586-1468; 12 Crafts Ave; pizzas $7-15; Ⓥ) The rainbow flag out front beckons patrons to this brightly colored joint with ample outside seating. Enjoy traditional white and red pies and choose from an extensive list of toppings – several kinds of mushrooms, 11 cheeses, capers, anchovies, arugula and more.

MIDRANGE

Paul and Elizabeth's (☎ 413-584-4832; 150 Main St; lunch $6-10, dinner $10-20; ☯ lunch & dinner Mon-Sat; ♿ Ⓥ) This airy and plant-adorned restaurant, known locally as P&E's, sits on the top floor of Thornes Marketplace and is the town's premier natural foods restaurant. It serve vegetarian cuisine and seafood, often with an Asian bent and with seasonal specials. Eat pan-fried spinach ravioli, tuna kebabs or egg custards flavored with grain coffee.

India House (☎ 413-586-6344; 45 State St; dinner $15-25; ☯ 5-9:30pm Tue-Thu & Sun, 5-10pm Fri & Sat; Ⓥ) Dishes this good aren't supposed to exist on earth, yet here they are. For legitimately inspired food made with local produce and meats, enter Indian House for tandoori, korma and curried fish in mango sauce. The smell of spice immediately hits you upon entry.

Amanouz (☎ 413-585-9128; 44 Main St; meals $6-11; ☯ 8am-10pm Mon-Thu, 8am-11pm Fri-Sun) This lovable hole-in-the-wall is the place in town for Moroccan and Mediterranean fare. Try one of its specials such as Moroccan sardine salad ($7). But why can't it make decent falafel?

Osaka (☎ 413-587-9548; 7 Old South St; lunch $8-10, dinner $12-25; ☯ 11:30am-11pm Mon-Thu, 11:30am-midnight Fri & Sat, 12:30-11pm Sun) Osaka's modern and wooden dining room is airy and bright, and serves a wide menu of à la carte sushi as well as hibachi, udon, donburi and tempura. The enclosed porch makes for good summertime seating.

TOP END

Mulino's (☎ 413-586-8900; 41 Strong Ave; meals $13-23; ☯ dinner) This family-style trattoria serves big portions of robust Italian mains. It's part of the classy triune that includes the more upscale Brasserie 40-A on the 1st floor and the Bishop's Lounge – with smoking deck – on the 3rd floor.

Eastside Grill (☎ 413-586-3347; 19 Strong Ave; meals $16-28; ☯ dinner 4-10pm) This is a steak 'n' seafood kind of place with strong Cajun overtones – its vast menu carries items like Louisiana fried oysters and chicken étouffée. The few nods to vegetarians include butternut ravioli. Weekends can be extremely busy, and it doesn't take reservations. It's a half-block south of Main St.

Drinking & Entertainment

Northampton is the center of nightlife for the Five College area. For listings of what's happening, pick up a copy of the **Valley Advocate** (www.valleyad vocate.com).

BARS & CLUBS

Dirty Truth (☎ 413-585-5999; 29 Main St; ☯ 4pm-2am Mon-Fri, 1pm-2am Sat & Sun) Slide into a high-top under some decent contemporary art to choose from 50 draft beers available from an impressive chalkboard menu. Some come from monasteries you may have never heard of before. The mussels in wine sauce and other upscale bar food taste good.

Diva's (☎ 413-586-8161; www.divasofnoho.com; 492 Pleasant St; cover free-$5; ☯ Tue-Sat) Though you can find girl-on-girl action in just about every square inch of Northampton, you might consider dropping by Diva's, the city's main gay-centric dance club that keeps its patrons sweaty thanks to a steady diet of thumping house music. There's an outdoor area if it all gets too much.

Ye Ol' Watering Hole & Beer Can Museum (☎ 413-584-9748; 287 Pleasant St) This shitty dive distinguishes itself from other shitty dives by virtue of its 'Beer Car Museum' with hundreds of empties. Cheap drinks, three pool tables and a video game in bad repair.

Northampton Brewery (☎ 413-584-9903; 11 Brewster Ct; ☿ 11:30am-1am Mon-Sat, noon-1am Sun) The oldest operating brewpub in New England enjoys a loyal summertime following thanks to its generously sized outdoor deck. In the winter the place is more sedate.

Packard's (☎ 413-584-5957; 14 Masonic St) Hit this pub off Main St for five billiard tables on the 3rd floor, dartboards or the numerous nooks and crannies in which to huddle. Plenty of microbrews can keep you company.

LIVE MUSIC

For online schedules for the Iron Horse, Calvin Theatre and Pearl Street, go to www.iheg.com. To order tickets by phone, call ☎ 413-586-8686.

Iron Horse Music Hall (☎ 413-584-0610; 20 Center St; tickets $7-25) The town's prime venue for folk, rock, jazz and 'other' books bands like Mates of State, Enter the Haggis and Caribou. Look for the small storefront half a block off Main St with the line of people waiting to get in.

Calvin Theatre (☎ 413-584-1444; 19 King St; tickets $20-75) Performers from Billy Bragg and Ryan Adams to the St Petersburg Ballet Theatre perform in the intimate setting of a gorgeously restored movie house.

Pearl Street (☎ 413-584-7771; 10 Pearl St; tickets $10-20) Don't worry, it only looks condemned. At the corner of Strong Ave across the street from the Tunnel Bar, Pearl Street draws in acts like Do Make Say Think and Josh Ritter.

You can usually find live rock or acoustic on Friday and Saturday nights in several spots around town, including the Northampton Brewery (above).

THEATER & CULTURE

New Century Theatre (☎ 413-587-3933; www.new centurytheatre.org; general admission/student rush $28/14; ♿) One of the best regional theater companies in the US stages works by playwrights such as Wendy Wasserstein and RR Gurney. Performances are held at the Mendenhall Center on the Smith College campus. The troupe also performs well-designed and well-acted children's shows (eg *The Frog Princess, Rumpelstiltskin*).

Academy of Music Theatre (☎ 413-584-8435; www .academyofmusictheatre.com; 274 Main St) This gracious, balconied theater is one of the oldest movie houses in the USA (1890), and one of the most

beautiful. It shows first-run independent films and books theatrical and opera troupes.

Pleasant Street Theater (☎ 413-586-0935; www .pleasantstreettheater.com; 27 Pleasant St) The setting isn't as glamorous as the Academy's, but it screens more films (eg *Becoming Jane, Darkon*).

Getting There & Around

See p232 for information on air, bus and train services.

Pioneer Valley Transit Authority (PVTA; ☎ 413-586-5806; www.pvta.com) provides bus services (with bike racks) to the entire Five College area, with the Northampton–Amherst route having the most frequent service (ride/daily pass $1/3). There's a bus stop in front of John M Green Hall at Smith College on Elm St, and others at several spots on Main St.

AMHERST
pop 34,000

Want another quintessential college town? This one is home to famous Amherst College, a pretty 'junior ivy' that lies near the town green, as well as the University of Massachusetts and the small liberal arts Hampshire College (these total about 30,000 students). Around the green you'll find a few busy streets containing several leftist restaurants and shops, as well as lots of people in tweed reading books on the grass.

The town centers of Amherst and Northampton are separated by only a few miles, making the sights in one convenient to the other. If trying to choose between the two, you'll find Northampton to be bigger and livelier with better nightlife and more shopping opportunities.

Orientation & Information

Amherst lies at the intersection of MA 116 and MA 9. At its center is the town common, a broad New England green framed by churches and inns.

Amherst Area Chamber of Commerce (☎ 413-253-0700; www.amherstarea.com; 409 Main St at Railroad St; ☿ 9am-5pm Mon-Fri) Less than half a mile east of Pleasant St. The chamber also maintains a summer information booth on the common facing S Pleasant St.

Sights & Activities

The most exciting thing to do is poke around the center of town, browsing through used bookstores and hanging out on the green.

Should you grow bored, there are a few other treats in store.

EMILY DICKINSON MUSEUM

During her lifetime, Emily Dickinson (1830–86) published only seven poems – usually she would just stuff her finely crafted pieces, written on scraps of paper and old envelopes, into her desk. But after her death, more than 1000 of her poems were discovered and published, and her verses on love, death, nature and immortality have made her one of the most important poets in the US.

Dickinson was raised in the strict household of her father, a prominent lawyer. When he was elected to the US Congress, she traveled with him to Washington and Philadelphia, then returned to Amherst and this house to live out the rest of her days in near seclusion. Some say she was in love with the Reverend Charles Wadsworth, a local married clergyman. Unable to show her love, she withdrew from the world into a private realm of pain, passion and poignancy.

The **museum** (☎ 413-542-8161; www.emilydickinson museum.org; 280 Main St; admission adult/senior & student/child 6-18yr $8/7/5) consists of two buildings, the Dickinson Homestead and the Evergreens, the house next door where her brother Austin lived with his family. The admission price includes a 75-minute tour of both houses. Hours vary throughout the year, so call to confirm.

ERIC CARLE MUSEUM OF PICTURE BOOK ART

Co-founded by the author and illustrator of *The Very Hungry Caterpillar*, this superb **museum** (☎ 413-658-1100; www.picturebookart.org; 125 W Bay Rd; adult/student/child $7/5/5; 10am-4pm Tue-Fri, 10am-5pm Sat, noon-5pm Sun;) celebrates book illustrations from around the world with rotating exhibits in three galleries, as well as a permanent collection. All visitors (grownups included) are encouraged to express their own artistic sentiments in the hands-on art studio. In honor of the aforementioned caterpillar, the café's cookies have holes through their middles.

AMHERST COLLEGES

Founded in 1821, **Amherst College** (☎ 413-542-2000; www.amherst.edu) has retained its character and quality partly by maintaining its small size (1650 students). The main part of the campus lies just south of the town common.

The information booth, on the edge of the town common and closed in winter, has a map and brochure for self-guided walking tours, or you can ask questions at **Converse Hall**.

The region's most innovative center of learning is **Hampshire College**, 3 miles south of Amherst center on MA 116. Students here don't pick a major in the regular sense of the word; rather, the school emphasizes multidisciplinary, student-initiated courses of study. Contact the **admissions office** (☎ 413-582-5471; www.hampshire.edu) to schedule a tour.

The enormous and hulking **University of Massachusetts at Amherst** (UMass; ☎ 413-545-0111; www.umass.edu) helps you to understand the distinction between public and private higher education in the US. Founded in 1863 as the Massachusetts Agricultural College, it's now the keystone of the public university system in Massachusetts. About 24,000 students study at the sprawling campus. It houses the **Fine Arts Center** (☎ 413-545-2511; Haigis Mall; tickets $5-12), a monstrous concrete building that hosts nearly 100 performing arts events per year in its main hall.

ATKINS FARMS COUNTRY MARKET

This **farm produce center** (☎ 413-253-9528; 1150 West St/MA 116 & Bay Rd; admission free; 7am-8pm;) and local institution, about 3 miles south of Amherst, offers maple sugar products in spring, garden produce in summer and apple-picking in the fall. Other activities, such as a scarecrow-making workshop in October, take place throughout the year. A deli/bakery sells picnic supplies. It keeps shorter hours in winter.

SWIMMING

Two miles north of town, **Puffers Pond** makes for excellent swimming, and has a wooded, secluded beach area that fills with students and locals on a warm day. Nature trails meander through the area as well. To get there, take East Pleasant St to Sand Hill Rd and then right on State St.

Sleeping

Be aware of the college schedules when planning a visit. Visitors are well advised to book as far in advance as possible if planning a trip for late August or mid-May. The Amherst Area Chamber of Commerce (opposite) has a list, which includes phone numbers and prices, of more than two dozen member B&Bs.

NORWOTTUCK RAIL TRAIL

The **Norwottuck Rail Trail** (nor-wah-tuk; www.hadleyonline.com/railtrail) is a foot and bike path that follows the former Boston & Maine Railroad right-of-way from Amherst to Hadley to Northampton, a total distance of 8.5 miles. For much of its length, the trail parallels MA 9, passing through open farms and crossing the broad Connecticut River on a historic 1500ft-long bridge. Parking and access to the trail can be found on Station Rd in Amherst, at the Mountain Farms Mall on MA 9 in Hadley and at Elwell State Park on Damon Rd in Northampton. You can rent bikes for the day from **Valley Bicycles** (☎ 413-584-4466; 8 Railroad St), right on the rail trail in Hadley.

White Birch Campground (☎ 413-665-4941; www .whitebirchcamp.com; 214 North St, Whately; campsite/RV site $27/30; ☺ May-Nov) Follow MA 116 North through Sunderland to South Deerfield, then go southwest to Whately, where you'll find this family-oriented (showers, horseshoe pitch) campground with 60 sites, some secluded.

Horace Kellogg Homestead (☎ 413-253-4988; www .hkhbb.com; 459 South Pleasant St; d incl breakfast $85) The owners of this 1828 clapboarded farmhouse let out two rooms decorated with some swing-and-a-miss decor: indoor wicker, ostentatious four-post bed, throw pillows. Find it 1 mile south of the green on MA 116.

Amherst Motel (☎ 413-256-8122; www.amherstmotel .com; 408 Northampton Rd/MA 9; d $70-100; P ✕ ⌧) Hello 1979! This motel is on the south side of MA 9, 1 mile west of the Amherst town common. Rooms are simply furnished but clean.

University Lodge (☎ 413-256-8111; 345 N Pleasant St/MA 116; d $70-100; P ✕) The attraction of this 20-room motel is the location: only a few blocks north of the town common in the heart of Amherst's restaurant district. Expect an ugly decor of dark carpet and unfortunate bedspreads.

Allen House Inn (☎ 413-253-5000; www.allenhouse .com; 599 Main St; d incl breakfast $135-175; P ✕ wifi) This is a prim, faithfully restored Queen Anne-style Victorian house with seven rooms, all with private bathroom. It is over half a mile east of Pleasant St. Main St has some traffic noise during the day.

Amherst Inn (☎ 413-253-5000; www.allenhouse .com; 257 Main St; d incl breakfast $135-175; P ✕ wi-fi) A stately, blue three-story Victorian with Tudor detailing and tall chimneys, this slightly haunted-looking B&B sits in the midst of some old shade trees with fine garden landscaping. It's a bit closer to town than Allen House Inn, but with the same traffic noise.

Lord Jeffrey Inn (☎ 413-253-2576, 800-742-0358; www.lordjefferyinn.com; 30 Boltwood Ave; d $169-239; P ✕ wi-fi ⌧) This is the classic college-town inn: colonial, collegiate and cozy, with lovely quilts; walk into the lobby on a snowy day and you're bound to smell a wood fire. The inn has 48 rooms and faces the town common. If you're an Amherst parent determined to stay here during graduation, make reservations as soon as that acceptance letter arrives. Really. Wheelchair rooms don't have roll-in showers.

Eating

Being a college town, Amherst has many places peddling pizza, sandwiches, Chinese takeout, burritos and fresh-brewed coffee. Competition is fierce and quality is high.

BUDGET

Black Sheep Café (☎ 413-256-1706; 79 Main St; sandwiches $3-7; ☺ 7am-8pm; ⓥ) This mainstay makes generous deli sandwiches (hot corned beef with Swiss cheese and coleslaw), bakes fresh bread and has a huge display of tarts éclairs and other sweets. Expect a long line for coffee in the morning and a casual side room full of café tables and rough flooring.

Antonio's Pizza by the Slice (☎ 413-253-0808; 31 N Pleasant St; slices $1.50-3; ☺ 10am-1am) Amherst's most popular pizza place features excellent slices made with a truly vast variety of toppings, flavorings and spices. Bizarro as some offerings are, the place comes across as authentic – old brick building, white and red awning.

Freshside (☎ 413-256-0296; 39 S Pleasant St; meals $5-12; ☺ 10am-9:30pm; ⓖ ⓥ) Enjoy seaweed tea rolls, rice dishes, coconut curry tofu soup and cellophane noodle salads with mint, peanuts and cabbage in a spacious Asian joint with some sidewalk seating overlooking the green. Disjointed service.

Lone Wolf (☎ 413-256-4643; 63 Main St; breakfast $5-10, lunch $6-9; ☯ breakfast & lunch; **V**) Thanks to the friendly attentive wait staff and its use of local, organic ingredients, the Lone Wolf has earned itself a strong fan base, especially among vegans, for its superb breakfasts (huevos rancheros, crepes, blintzes, benedicts).

MIDRANGE & TOP END

Amherst Chinese Food (☎ 413-253-7835; 62 Main St; lunch $7-10, dinner $10-20; ☯ lunch & dinner; **V**) All the produce at 'AmChi,' as the locals call it, is raised organically by proprietor Tso-Cheng Chang, who also grows the orchids that beautify his restaurant. Enjoy top-notch dishes and Chang himself, whose thick spectacles recall his earlier profession as a scientist.

Judie's (☎ 413-253-3491; 51 N Pleasant St; lunch $11-15, dinner $10-25; ☯ from 11:30am Tue-Sun; ♿ **V** ♨) Judie's is an Amherst institution that attracts grandmas, students, blue-collar types and just about everyone else to its oddball dining room (interior clapboarded walls, cheesy cart holding hot fudge sauce) where you can eat food that's way tastier than the space (trout, pasta, burgers, mushroom risotto).

Windowed Hearth (☎ 413-253-2576; 30 Boltwood Ave; meals $22-37; ☯ dinner Wed-Sun) This restaurant is in the Lord Jeffery Inn, facing the common, and is where folks go when they crave a stuffy meal with their parents. Pecan-crusted duck breast and tenderloin tips typify the offerings in the formal colonial dining room complete with fireplace. Also in the inn is the more downscale, kid-friendly Elijah Boltwood's Tavern (open 7am to 11pm).

Drinking & Entertainment

Although a lot of the college crowd head to nearby Northampton to get their party on, you can find nightlife in Amherst.

Moan & Dove (☎ 413-256-1710; 460 West St; ☯ 3pm-1am Mon-Fri, 1pm-1am Sat & Sun) The folks at this small, dark saloon near Hampshire College sure know their beer, and their 150 bottled and 20 draft beers are top-notch – try a Belgian lambic, the only type of commercially available beer made with wild yeast. For non-beer snobs, Schlitz and the like are available, as is a big barrel of peanuts.

Black Sheep Café (☎ 413-253-3442; 79 Main St; no cover) Welcome to the town's most popular folk club. Live music is performed Thursday through Sunday, and not necessarily at night.

If lucky, you might knock back some coffee and a bagel while a bluegrass band helps you through Sunday morning.

Amherst Brewing Company (☎ 413-253-4400; www.amherstbrewing.com; 24-36 N Pleasant St; no cover) The Amherst Jazz Orchestra has been playing here every other Monday night for a decade. Otherwise, drink some fine beer and maybe catch rock or karaoke. Try its Heather Ale, made with heather flowers in place of hops. This joint is popular with students.

Amherst Cinema Arts Center (☎ 413-256-1991; www.amherstcinema.org; 28 Amity St) This facility screens lots of art flicks, psychedelic science fiction anime, a bit of mainstream stuff and lots of films from Sundance and Cannes. It has baby-friendly screenings every Tuesday and events when directors (such as Pedro Costa) will stop in to discuss their work.

Fine Arts Center (☎ 413-545-2511; www.umass.edu/fac; UMass campus; tickets $5-45) The university's entertainment auditorium has a full program of classical and world-music concerts, theater, opera and ballet.

Getting There & Around

Amtrak (☎ 800-872-7245) runs its daily *Vermonter* between New York and Montreal, with a stop at Amherst **depot** (13 Railroad St) just off Main St, half a mile east of the common. The depot is unattended and seating is by reservation only, so book ahead.

Peter Pan's Amherst Center Bus Terminal (☎ 413-256-0431; 79 S Pleasant St) is just south of Main St, offering direct or connecting rides throughout New England and as far south as Washington, DC.

UMass Transit Service (☎ 413-586-5806) runs free buses along MA 116/Pleasant St between the town center and the UMass campus.

The **Pioneer Valley Transportation Authority** (PVTA; ☎ 413-586-5806; www.pvta.com) provides bus services to the entire Five College area, with the Northampton–Amherst route having the most frequent service (ride/day pass $1/3). Buses stop on main streets of both towns and at Haigis Mall on the UMass campus.

DEERFIELD

pop 4750

While the modern commercial center is in South Deerfield, it's Historic Deerfield 6 miles to the north that history buffs swarm to, where zoning and preservation keep the rural village looking like a time warp to the

Book your stay at lonelyplanet.com/hotels

18th-century – sleepy, slow and without much to do other than look at the museum.

Orientation & Information

The main (OK, the only) street of Historic Deerfield is simply called the Street, and it runs parallel to MA 5/10. Follow the signs from I-91.

Hall Tavern Information Center (the Street; 9:30am-4:30pm) In town, across from the Deerfield Inn. It has maps, brochures and an audiovisual presentation that gives you an overview of Historic Deerfield Village.

Historic Deerfield (☎ 413-775-7214; www.historic -deerfield.org; PO Box 321, Deerfield, MA 01342) For information before you arrive.

Sights & Activities

HISTORIC DEERFIELD VILLAGE

The main street of **Historic Deerfield Village** (☎ 413-774-5581; www.historic-deerfield.org; the Street; adult/child 6-21yr $14/5, single house $7/5; 9:30am-4:30pm) escaped the ravages of time and now presents a noble prospect: a dozen houses dating from the 1700s and 1800s, well preserved and open to the public. It costs nothing to stroll along the Street, or you can take a half-hour tour of each building individually. Guides in the houses provide commentary.

The **Wright House** (1824) has collections of American period paintings, Chippendale and Federal furniture and Chinese export porcelain. There's also the **Henry N Flynt Silver & Metalware Collection** (1814). Furnishings in **Allen House** (1720) were made in the Pioneer Valley and Boston. The **Family Discovery Center**, with hands-on activities for kids and a full-sized house on display showing the construction process step-by-step, should be open by the time you read this.

The **Stebbins House** (1799–1810) was the home of a rich land-owning family, and is furnished with typical luxury items of the time. In the **Barnard Tavern**, many of the exhibits are touchable, which makes this a favorite with kids. The rooms of the **Wells-Thorn House** (1717–51) are furnished according to period, from colonial times to the Federal period.

The **Dwight House**, built in Springfield in 1725, was moved to Deerfield in 1950. It now holds locally made furniture and, interestingly, an 18th-century doctor's office. **Sheldon House** (1743) was the 18th-century home of the Sheldons, wealthy Deerfield farmers. Contrast its furnishings with those in the Stebbins House, built and furnished a half-century later.

Be sure to visit the **Flynt Center of Early New England Life**; thousands of pieces not on display in the houses are numbered and stored here. Visitors can punch an item's number into a computer and print out its history.

MEMORIAL HALL MUSEUM

Here's the **original building** (☎ 413-774-3768; cnr Memorial St, US 5 & MA 10; adult/under 21yr $6/3; 9:30am-4:30pm May-Oct) of Deerfield Academy (1798), the prestigious preparatory school in town. It's now a museum of Pocumtuck Valley life and history. Puritan and Native American artifacts include carved and painted chests, embroidery, musical instruments and glass-plate photographs (1880–1920).

Check out the Indian House Door, a dramatic relic from the French and Indian Wars. In February 1704, Native Americans attacked the house of the Sheldon family, hacked a hole through the center of the door and did in the inhabitants with musket fire.

MAGIC WINGS BUTTERFLY CONSERVATORY & GARDENS

If you have young kids in tow, this **butterfly garden** (☎ 413-665-2805; www.magicwings.com; 281 Greenfield Rd/US 5 & MA 10, S Deerfield; adult/senior/student & child $10/9/7; 9am-6pm summer, closes 5pm rest of year;) is sure to be a highlight for them. Everywhere you turn in this 8000-sq-ft, tropically outfitted glass conservatory you're faced with a fluttering curtain of colorful things and numerous species.

CONNECTICUT RIVER

For a junket on the Connecticut River, catch a riverboat cruise on the *Quinnetukit II*. A lecturer fills you in on the history, geology and ecology of the river and the region during the 12-mile, 1½-hour ride, and you'll pass under the elegant French King Bridge. Cruises are run by the **Northfield Mountain Recreation & Environmental Center** (☎ 800-859-2960; on MA 63 north of MA 2; adult/senior/child under 15yr $10/9/5; cruises 11am, 1:15pm & 3pm Wed-Sun). To get to the departure point, take I-91 north to exit 27, then MA 2 east, then MA 63 north. Call for reservations.

Sleeping & Eating

Barton Cove Campground (☎ 413-863-9300; 90 Millers Falls Rd; campsite $22) Barton Cove has 27 family campsites on a mile-long wooded peninsula on the Connecticut River, and offers showers

CENTRAL MASSACHUSETTS & THE BERKSHIRES

WORTH THE TRIP: LEVERETT PEACE PAGODA

The world could certainly do with a little more peace these days, and a group of monks, nuns and volunteers are doing their part from the top of a hill outside the pea-sized town of Leverett.

There are over 80 so-called peace pagodas all over the globe, and their mission is simple – to spread peace. The **Leverett Peace Pagoda** (☎ 413-367-2202; www.peacepagoda.org; 100 Cave Hill Rd) was the first in the Western Hemisphere, and is run by members of the nonproselytizing Nipponzan Myohoji sect of Buddhism. But no matter what your spiritual inclination, a visit to this peace pagoda – with its stunning views of the lush valley below – will leave you feeling profoundly serene.

The centerpiece of the area is actually not a pagoda at all, but a stupa – a 100ft-tall white bell-shaped monument to Buddha, meant to be circumambulated, not entered. The grounds' temple was destroyed by fire in 1987, and the dedication of the new temple – built with donated materials and through the sweat of volunteers – took place in October 2005.

To get to the peace pagoda from Amherst, take MA 9 west until MA 116 north, then turn onto MA 63 north and follow it for about 6.5 miles. Turn right onto Jackson Hill Rd and then another right onto Cave Hill Rd. Park about half a mile up the road. The last half-mile is accessible only by foot. Due to the quiet, introspective nature of the area, visits by young children should be carefully considered.

---

and kayak rental as well. The nature trail takes you to dinosaur footprints and nesting bald eagles. It's off MA 2 in Gill: take I-91 exit 27, then MA 2 east for 3 miles and look for the sign on the right.

Deerfield Inn (☎ 413-774-5587, 800-926-3865; www.deerfieldinn.com; the Street, Deerfield; d incl breakfast $170-210; ♿) This establishment, right at the head of Historic Deerfield's main street, has 23 modernized, spacious rooms each with private bathroom. The inn, built in 1884, was destroyed by fire and rebuilt in 1981. The inn's dining room (mains $19 to $30) uses local, sustainably grown ingredients when possible, though served on furniture that looks mass-produced and out of character.

There's not a terrible lot for your stomach to get excited about in Deerfield. More enticing fare can be had a bit further north in Shelburne Falls or back down in the Five College area.

Sienna (☎ 413-665-0215; 6b Elm St; meals $32-40; ☀ dinner Wed-Sun) One of the only shining beacons in South Deerfield. The small seasonal menu exemplifies exquisite preparation and presentation (venison sirloin with bread pudding, duck breast). The restaurant's spare lines and persimmon-colored walls contribute to the elegant and romantic atmosphere. To get there from Historic Deerfield, take I-91 south, exit 25. Turn left onto MA 116, cross over I-91 and at the first light make a right onto MA 5 south. At the next set of lights make a left onto Elm St.

MONTAGUE BOOKMILL

On an unassuming road in the sleepy town of Montague you'll find the **Montague Bookmill** (☎ 413-367-9206; www.montaguebookmill.com; 440 Greenfield Rd; ☀ 10am-6pm Sun-Wed, 10am-8pm Thu-Sat), a converted cedar gristmill from 1842 whose multiple rooms contain plenty of used books (many academic and esoteric) and couches on which to read them. Its westward-facing walls are punctuated by large windows that overlook the beautiful sight of the roiling Sawmill River and its waterfall. There are also some outside decks over the water where you can take your coffee.

Though the book mill is the biggest draw, several other ventures make it even easier to while away day and night in the vicinity. The **Lady Killigrew Café** (☎ 413-367-9666; ☀ 10am-10pm Wed & Thu, 10am-midnight Fri-Sun; wi-fi **V**), featuring the same amazing riverside view, offers affordable sandwiches, particularly eggy breakfast ones, coffee wine and beer. The **Night Kitchen** (☎ 413-367-9580; meals $15-30; ☀ 5:30-9pm Wed-Sun; **V**) sources locally grown ingredients to whip up regional dishes with a creative touch.

Several antique and craft shops are open Wednesday through Sunday.

To get there from Shelburne Falls (read carefully), take MA 2 east and stay on it until the town of Turners Falls, on the other side of I-91. At the lights by the Turners Falls Bridge, take a right onto Main Rd, over the water. After the bridge, take a left onto 3rd

St, which quickly turns into Unity St. When Unity St forks, bear right onto Turners Falls Rd. Follow this road a little more than 4 miles, into Montague. Turn right onto Greenfield Rd.

SHELBURNE FALLS
pop 2000

This artisan community's main drag (Bridge St) is tiny and charming, only three blocks long and with turn-of-the-20th-century building stock. Forming the background are mountains, the Deerfield River and a pair of picturesque bridges that cross it – one made of iron, the other covered in flowers. People come mainly to visit some interestingly formed glacial potholes.

Shelburne Falls is just off MA 2 (the so-called Mohawk Trail) on MA 116.

Visitors center (☎ 413-625-2254; www.shelburnefalls .com; 75 Bridge St; ☽ 10am-4pm Mon-Sat, noon-3pm Sun May-Oct) Helps with accommodations in the area, especially B&Bs.

Sights & Activities

Shelburne Falls lays on the hype a bit thick, yet one can't deny that its **bridge of flowers** makes for a photogenic civic centerpiece. One paid gardener and a host of volunteers have been maintaining it since 1929. More than 500 varieties of flowers, scrubs and vines flaunt their colors on the 400ft-long span from early spring through late fall. Access to the bridge is from Water St and there's no charge to walk across.

The Native Americans called this area Salmon Falls, and the fishing here was so fine that warring tribes made an agreement that they wouldn't fight each other within one day's walk of the falls. These days, the geologically fascinating **glacial potholes** are drawing visitors. Ever since the end of the last Ice Age, stones trapped swirling in the riverbed have been grinding into the rock bed below, creating more than 50 near-perfect circles. The largest known glacial pothole in the world is here, with a diameter of 39ft.

These days, a hydroelectric dam controls the flow of the Deerfield River over the potholes, so it's possible that on your visit the water will be completely obscuring the holes. Either way it's worth a look – if the flow is a trickle, you see the circles; if it's raging, you'll feel like you're at Niagara Falls. The potholes are at the end of Deerfield Ave.

Sleeping & Eating

Johnson Homestead B&B (☎ 413-625-6603; www .thejohnsonhomestead.com; 79 E Buckland Rd; d $75-110) Three rooms are let in this charming 1880s farmhouse situated on 80 bucolic acres, a 10-minute drive southwest of town. No credit cards accepted, but you might get some fresh apple pie for breakfast.

High Pocket Farm B&B (☎ 413-624-8988; www .highpocket.com; 38 Adams Place Rd, Colrain; d $100) Nestled on more than 500 acres about 10 miles north of town is this special B&B. After a phenomenal farm breakfast, guests have the option of taking a guided horseback ride for an additional $70. Three rooms are let, all with private bathroom, and the view from the outdoor hot tub is incredible. Kids will like the game room, complete with Ping-Pong table. Two-night minimum.

Inn the Village B&B (☎ 413-768-9177; www.innthevil lage.com; 17 High St; r $130) Rooms are full of light and slightly frilly in this simple 1880s Victorian with a landscape mural running alongside stairs that curve to the 2nd floor. You'll find it on a quiet tree-lined side street (you can hear the crickets) close to the center of town.

Tusk 'n' Rattle (☎ 413-625-0200; 10 Bridge St; tapas $4-10, meals $9-24; ☽ lunch & dinner Thu-Mon; Ⓥ) This cheerful basement restaurant serves tapas items that are more international than Spanish. Choose from fried plantains, vegetable samosas and Moorish chicken kebabs. Mains might be seared catfish simmered in mustard or black bean burritos.

Café Martin (☎ 413-625-2795; 24 Bridge St; meals $12-16; ☽ lunch & dinner Tue-Sat, brunch Sun; ☉ Ⓥ) Intimate, casual and something like a bistro; enter to eat spinach and mushroom marsala, vegetable lo-mein, maple-glazed salmon or other dishes from a scattershot menu.

Drinking & Entertainment

While Shelburne Falls is truly sleepy, you'll find a pair of low-key places to pass part of an evening.

Mocha Maya's (☎ 413-625-6292; 417 Bridge St; ☽ 7am-6pm Sun-Wed, 6am-11pm Thu-Sat; ☉) Serves espresso and little mounds of cookies (so full of seeds that they taste healthy) to people listening to Thursday night folk sessions.

West End Pub (☎ 413-625-6246; 16 State St; ☽ 3-11pm Thu-Mon) This small place is good for a drink. It has a fantastic deck jutting out above the Deerfield River and directly overlooking the bridge of flowers.

Shopping

Stop by the visitors center for a complete list of the artisans, from potters to quilters to weavers, that call Shelburne Falls home. Or just meander through town.

On your way to the potholes, you won't be able to miss the crowd of people staring at the craftspeople shaping molten liquid in the open studio of **North River Glass** (Deerfield Ave; ☺ 10am-5:30pm). Next door you can browse through the gallery of their work in all shapes and colors. If you're a sucker for handmade, strong-smelling candles, keep walking a few more steps to **Mole Hollow Candles** (☎ 877-226-3537; ☺ 10am-5:30pm). Bargains are to be had in its 'seconds' section.

Lamson-Goodnow factory outlet (☎ 413-625-9816; ☺ 10am-5pm Mon-Sat, noon-5pm Sun) Across the river and down Conway St to the left is this factory outlet, with a wide range of finely crafted kitchen knives and barbecue accessories. The company, established in 1837, is the oldest cutlery manufacturer in the country.

THE BERKSHIRES

Few places in America combine culture with rural countryside as deftly as the Berkshire hills, home to Tanglewood, Jacobs Pillow and the Massachusetts stretch of the Appalachian Trail. Extending from the highest point in the state – Mt Greylock – southward to the Connecticut state line, the Berkshires have been a summer refuge for more than a century, when the rich and famous arrived to build summer 'cottages' of grand proportions, many of which now survive as inns or performance venues. On summer weekends when the sidewalks are scorching in Boston and New York, crowds of city dwellers jump in their cars and head for the Berkshire breezes.

For further information on this region, check out the following resources:

Berkshire Chamber of Commerce (☎ 413-499-4000; www.berkshirechamber.com; 75 North St, Suite 360, Pittsfield, MA 01201)

Berkshire Community Radio (WBCR 97.7FM) Broadcasts music, news and commentary on the southern Berkshire region.

Berkshire Grown (www.berkshiregrown.org) Online or print directory of pick-your-own orchards, farmers markets and restaurants offering organic local ingredients (see boxed text, p260).

Berkshires Visitors Bureau (☎ 413-743-4500, 800-237-5747; www.berkshires.org; 3 Hoosac St, Adams, MA 01220; ☺ 8:30am-5pm Mon-Fri) Can help with accommodations and activities planning.

Berkshires Week (www.berkshireeagle.com/berkshires week) The online version of the free newspaper has a calendar of events.

iBerkshires (www.iberkshires.com) Online daily newspaper.

See the Berkshires (www.berkshires.com) Recommendations for dining, lodging, activities, car rental, plus a trip planner.

Southern Berkshire Lodging (☎ 413-528-4006; www.berkshirelodging.com) Emphasis on the higher-end inns.

GREAT BARRINGTON & AROUND
pop 7400

Main St used to consist of Woolworth's, hardware stores, thrift shops and a run-down diner. These have given way to artsy boutiques, antique shops, coffeehouses and restaurants, so much so that locals are beginning to call their town 'Little SoHo,' perhaps to appeal to the many city travelers who are now stopping to shop and eat at the best selection of restaurants in the region. But beware: the town's popularity makes for traffic jams on summer weekends.

Orientation & Information

The Housatonic River flows through the center of town just east of Main St/US 7, the central thoroughfare. Most lodgings and restaurants are on Main St/US 7, or MA 23/41 southwest of the town. However, the finest accommodations (most of which are B&Bs) are on small roads outside town in the farmlands.

Great Barrington is 146 miles west of Boston off I-90 and New York City is 150 miles to the south.

Information kiosk (☎ 413-528-1510, 800-269-4825; www.greatbarrington.org; 362 Main St; ☺ 10am-6pm Tue-Sun) The Southern Berkshire Chamber of Commerce maintains this small kiosk, which has maps, brochures, restaurant menus and accommodations lists.

Public library Provides 15 minutes of free internet access, at the north end of Main St.

Sights & Activities

Most of your time in town will be spent strolling along the pedestrian-scaled Main St, with its mild bustle, handful of shops and dozen or so restaurants. You might even find something of a nightlife.

SCENIC DRIVE: THE MOHAWK TRAIL

A sea of color famously takes hold of the hillsides of northwestern Massachusetts in the fall. Head west on MA 2, from Greenfield to Williamstown on the 63-mile-long road known as the **Mohawk Trail**, and you'll encounter a delectable buffet of cheesy tourist traps, great art, fabulous food and gorgeous scenery. Begun as a Native American footpath, the byway became a popular trade route among colonial and tribal settlements. It is now recognized as one of the most scenic roads in the US.

The lively **Deerfield River** slides alongside flat, western sections of the route, with roaring, bucking stretches of white water that turn leaf-peeping into an adrenaline sport for kayakers.

The road winds ever upward. At the **Western Summit**, the landscape sprawls out in a colorful tapestry. To the left, **Mt Greylock** looms as the highest point in Massachusetts. North Adams rests in the seam of the valley along the Hoosic River. To the right is Bald Mountain and views into Vermont.

Ease around the famous, steep **hairpin curve** where horses once strained to haul nitro-glycerin used for blasting the famous railway tunnel. On one brutally cold winter, as a load overturned and an expected explosion never came, a discovery was made: if frozen, the volatile substance could be safely transported.

Nearby **Natural Bridge State Park** is home to some of the most contorted and spectacular results of the eternal battle of water versus stone, resulting in a chasm 60ft deep and 475ft long worn through solid, white marble. And don't miss stopping in **Shelburne Falls** (p256) for lunch, shopping or hanging out at the potholes.

In **North Adams** (p271), fresh new businesses and the sprawling **Mass MoCA** (p271) visual and performing arts center are carving artful niches amid historic buildings and businesses that speak eloquently of other eras.

The road up **Mt Greylock** (p272) is long and steep, with gasp-inducing views. The view from the summit tower stretches well into New Hampshire, Vermont, New York and Massachusetts.

After an hour or two's rest in small-town America, you might consider a hike in the hills. Ten miles south of Great Barrington along US 7 and MA 7A toward Ashley Falls is **Bartholomew's Cobble** (☎ 413-229-8600; adult/child 6-12yr $5/1; ☼ 9am-5pm mid-Apr–mid-Oct), a 'cobble' being a high, rocky knoll of limestone, marble or quartzite. The highly alkaline soil of this 329-acre reservation supports an unusual variety of trees, flowers, moss and especially ferns. Six miles of hiking trails provide routes for enjoying the cobble and the woods, which are set beneath a flyway used by over 200 species of birds. Try the Ledges Trail that weaves along the Housatonic River.

Another option on US 7, less than 5 miles north of Great Barrington center, is **Monument Mountain** (☎ 413-298-3239; admission free), which has two trails to the summit of Squaw Peak. Nathaniel Hawthorne wrote that Monument's summit resembled 'a headless sphinx wrapped in a Persian shawl.' On August 5, 1850, Hawthorne climbed the mountain with Oliver Wendell Holmes and Herman Melville, thus sealing a lifelong friendship.

If you hop in the car and drive, you're bound to find several farms where you can pick seasonal produce at harvest times, which can be overwhelmingly beautiful in the fall. One spot is **Windy Hill Farm** (☎ 413-298-3217; 686 Stockbridge Rd/US 7; ☼ 7am-5pm), about 5 miles north of Great Barrington, where more than a score of apple varieties, from pucker-sour to candy-sweet, are yours for the autumn picking. Summer is blueberry season.

Sleeping

Although a good half-hour drive from Lenox and Tanglewood, Great Barrington is nonetheless a popular place for people to stay in the summer. There are well over 50 inns and B&Bs within a 10-mile radius of Great Barrington. For links and a full list, log onto www.great barrington.org or contact the **Berkshire Lodgings Association** (☎ 413-298-4760, 888-298-4760; www.berk shirelodgings.com). All B&Bs prefer a minimum of two nights' stay, though ask about single nights. If staying a week or longer it may be worth renting a vacation apartment. Through **Berkshire Pied-à-Terre** (☎ 413-274-6926; www.berk shire-pied-a-terre.com; per week around $900) you can set

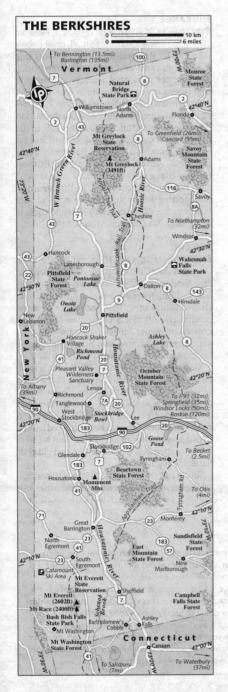

THE BERKSHIRES

yourself up in a hardwood-floor downtown apartment with equipped kitchen.

BUDGET

Beartown State Forest (☎ 413-528-0904; 69 Blue Hill Rd, Monterey; campsites $8-10) It's mostly backpackers who stay at this quiet campground, 8 miles east of Great Barrington via MA 23. It has 12 basic sites that overlook 35-acre Benedict Pond. (Number 11 is the most secluded.) Recreational vehicles (RVs) may have trouble getting up the winding road.

Mt Washington State Forest (☎ 413-528-0330; East St, Mt Washington; campsites $8-12) The forest contains the glorious Bash Bish Falls (see boxed text, p261) as well as 30 miles of trails. Some 15 wilderness campsites are available for the adventurous, with plenty of mountainous terrain and the Appalachian Trail steps away.

Briarcliff Inn (☎ 413-528-3000; 506 Stockbridge Rd; d $55-165; P ✹) Positioned on a far more scenic stretch of US 7 than the motels in town, this one stands directly across from Monument Mountain. The dark rooms are OK in a pinch, but the place is kind of depressing. The overly manicured yard looks almost like a plant version of Candy Land.

MIDRANGE & TOP END

Race Brook Lodge (☎ 413-229-2916; www.rblodge.com; 864 S Undermountain Rd/MA 41, Sheffield; r summer $130-200, winter $85-155; P ✹ ✹ ✹) At the base of Mt Race, sleep in the lodge (once an old red barn and your best bet), a cottage or the coach house. Rooms come with wide plank boards, exposed beams and rustic charm. The surrounding landscape truly charms, particularly when the colors turn in fall. Take the trail behind the lodge to the mountain's summit and a ridge walk. Rooms purposefully have no TV or phone.

Wainwright Inn (☎ 413-528-2062; www.wainwrightinn.com; 518 S Main St; r $149-199, ste $175-275; P ✹ ✹) This Victorian house with two wraparound porches has grandly spacious parlors on the 1st floor. Most of the eight guest rooms come with working fireplaces. Breakfast is a decadent experience. The inn is a short walk from the center of town on a busy road.

Howden Farm (☎ 413-229-8481; www.howdenfarm.com; 303 Rannapo Rd, Sheffield; r $140-200; P ✹ ✹) Set on a 250-acre pumpkin farm overlooking distant low-rising mountains, the four rooms in the white clapboarded home have sweeping views over fields and beyond. Ample breakfast is furnished by the farm itself.

Old Inn on the Green & Gedney Farm (☎ 413-229-7924, 800-286-3139; www.oldinn.com; MA 57, New Marlborough; d $235-260; **P**) Once a relay stop on a post road, the Old Inn, c 1760, is exactly what most people picture when they think New England country inn. The dining rooms are lit entirely by candlelight, and there are fireplaces and private bathrooms in each of the five rooms. In the summer, dinner is served outside on the garden terrace. A half mile up the road is Gedney Farm, with 16 guest rooms in a converted barn.

Eating & Drinking

Fare in the restaurants in the town center of Great Barrington ranges from Middle Eastern food to sushi to breakfast eggs. For up-to-date entertainment listings, pick up a copy of the free *Berkshires Week* at most cafés, bars and restaurants.

BUDGET

La Chosa (☎ 413-528-6380; 284 Main St; burritos $3-7; ⌚ 10am-10pm Sun-Thu, noon-10pm Fri & Sat) In the same arcade as Café Helsinki, this is the spot for filling Mexican takeout. Be sure to throw down the extra quarter to have one of the fiery hot sauces added to your burrito. On weekend nights you can often catch live rock here. Cash only.

Martin's (☎ 413-528-5455; 49 Railroad St; breakfast $4-10; ⌚ 7am-9pm; **V**) Eat breakfast all day on blond wooden chairs (country, not modern) over a black and white linoleum floor. Other telling accoutrements: pinkish paper placemats and the possible company of a gregarious high school soccer team. Sandwiches served, as well as tofu scrambles.

MIDRANGE

Baba Louie's (☎ 413-528-8100; 284 Main St; 14in pizzas $11-15; ⌚ 11:30am-9:30pm; **V**) Small, cozy Baba's is known for its wood-fired pizza with organic sourdough crust and guys with dreadlocks. The interior is painted a peach-orange tone that would look appropriate in New Mexico.

Café Helsinki (☎ 413-528-3394; 284 Main St; meals $6-20; ⌚ lunch & dinner Mon & Tue, Thu-Sat, brunch Sun) Plop down on an overstuffed sofa at this café in the back of the Barrington House Atrium and eat Scandinavian and Eastern European comfort food – dishes such as the Mad Russian (potato latkes with gravlax and sour cream) and 'Finnish' barbecue ribs. In the evenings, outstanding folksy and bluesy musical acts take over the adjoining Club Helsinki (tickets $7 to $35). No cover on Mondays.

TOP END

Bizen (☎ 413-528-4343; 17 Railroad St; rolls $7-18; ⌚ lunch & dinner) This popular, mostly organic Japanese restaurant features a small sushi bar, sashimi, tempura and a room for *kaiseki* (the seasonal meal that accompanies a tea ceremony). All meals are served on pottery created by owner Michael Marcus. The simple room is separated into nooks with paper lanterns and tatami mats.

Castle St Café (☎ 413-528-5244; 10 Castle St; meals $17-40; ⌚ dinner Wed-Mon) The piano in the back of this café just off Main St once belonged to Nat King Cole, who owned a summer home in Tyringham. Chef and owner Michael Ballon cooks up grilled Cornish hens, sautéed calves' livers, and local shad roe. Pastas and burgers are less expensive. Come for jazz on Friday or Saturday nights.

Allium (☎ 413-528-2118; 42/44 Railroad St; meals $25-40) For an upscale date, try the New American cuisine (wood-grilled pork, house-cured

---

THINGS FROM FARMS

Undeniably, part of the joy of a drive through the Berkshires – or any part of rural New England, for that matter – is stumbling unexpectedly on a small farm stand and stopping to chat for a while with the farmer who grew those apples or blueberries herself.

But if you don't want to leave it all to chance, or are curious about which restaurants in the region stock their kitchens with farm-fresh vittles, pick up or check out online the **Berkshire Grown** (☎ 413-528-0041; www.berkshiregrown.org), a guide to locally grown food and flowers, as well as other hand-crafted or hand-raised goodies such as cheeses, maple syrup and meats.

The seasonally published directory lists pick-your-own farms, farmers markets, and member restaurants like Castle St Café (below) in Great Barrington and Red Lion Inn (p263) in Stockbridge. Special events – agricultural fairs, farm dinners, and garden tours – are announced as well.

WORTH THE TRIP: BASH BISH FALLS

Twelve miles south of South Egremont, right on the New York state line, is **Bash Bish Falls** (☎ 413-528-0330), the largest waterfall in the state. Plunging down a 1000ft gorge, the waterfall's torrent is bifurcated by a massive boulder just above its pool. The falls are a popular spot for landscape painters to set up their easels.

To get there, follow MA 41 south out of Great Barrington and turn right onto Mt Washington Rd and go about 8 miles, following signs for the Catamount Ski Area. Then follow signs to the falls, taking East St, then West St and finally bumpy Bash Bish Falls Rd, deep in the Mt Washington State Forest. Stop at the first parking area you come to on your left if you're up to taking the shorter but steeper trail down to the falls. If you (or your young kids) are not, keep going a mile further down the road to the next parking area. This trail takes about 20 minutes but is much more level.

---

salmon) in this elegant room, which manages to combine a repurposed barn door, pretty jigsaw-esque panel of wooden shingles, flower boxes and modern Scandinavian influences without being heavy-handed. Bravo design team.

ourpick **John Andrews Restaurant** (☎ 413-528-3469; Rte 23, Egremont; meals $28-45; ⏱ from 5pm Thu-Tue) Chef Dan Smith turns out organic mountain lamb, a daily risotto and a fine Italian/New American menu with most items grown on nearby farms. The place occupies a clapboarded 19th-century home overlooking a garden. Prix-fixe specials on Thursdays are absolutely worth the 6 mile trek west from Great Barrington. Good wine selection.

Getting There & Away
Most travelers arrive by car on route 7, which runs through the center of town. Otherwise, **Peter Pan buses** (☎ 888-751-8800; www.peterpanbus.com) can drop you off in the center of town.

TYRINGHAM
pop 350
The village of Tyringham, several miles north of Monterey, is the perfect destination for an excursion into the heart of the countryside. While you'll find a handful of sights upon arrival, half the pleasure is driving or biking on the unpopulated roads that lead here. These snake over gentle hills and pass old houses and remnants of farmsteads.

Once the home of a Shaker community (1792–1874), Tyringham is now famous for its **Gingerbread House**, an architectural fantasy designed at the beginning of the 20th century by sculptor Henry Hudson Kitson, whose best-known work – a statue of Capt Parker as the minute man – graces the Lexington Green

(see p132). The fairy-tale thatched-roofed cottage, once Kitson's studio, almost commands you to stop your car and admire it.

If you fall in love with Tyringham, you can spend the night at **Sunset Farm B&B** (☎ 413-207-1959; www.sunsetfarminn.com; 74 Tyringham Rd; r $90-110, apt $150). Situated on a hillside overlooking one of the first Shaker settlements in the Berkshires, this casual B&B commands a view of the Tyringham Valley. All five rooms feature hand-sewn quilts and Shaker furniture.

STOCKBRIDGE
pop 2250
Take a good look down Stockbridge's wide Main St. Notice anything? More specifically, notice anything missing? Not one stoplight stutters the view, not one telephone pole blights the picture-perfect scene – it looks very much the way Norman Rockwell might have seen it.

In fact, Rockwell did see it – he lived and worked in Stockbridge during the last 25 years of his life. The town attracts summer and fall visitors en masse, who come to stroll the streets, inspect its shops and sit in the rockers on the porch of the grand old Red Lion Inn. And they come by the busload to visit the Norman Rockwell Museum on the town's outskirts. All that fossilized picturesqueness bears a price – thanks to grumpy town selectmen who want to keep things boring, there is next to nothing to do at night.

Stockbridge makes a convenient Tanglewood home base, with more affordable lodging options than Lenox.

Orientation & Information
Stockbridge is a 7-mile drive from Great Barrington to the south and Lenox to the

north. Main St in Stockbridge is MA 102. The central district is only a few blocks long.

Information kiosk In summer, volunteers sometimes staff a kiosk next door to the library on Main St.

Stockbridge Lodging Association (☎ 413-298-5200; www.stockbridgechamber.org; ⊙ 9am-5pm Mon, Wed & Fri) For accommodations information.

Sights & Activities
NORMAN ROCKWELL MUSEUM
Norman Rockwell (1894–1978) was born in New York City, and he sold his first magazine cover illustration to the *Saturday Evening Post* in 1916. In the following half-century he did another 321 covers for the *Post*, as well as illustrations for books, posters and many other magazines on his way to becoming the most popular illustrator in US history. His sense of humor can be seen in *Triple Self Portrait* (1960), where an older Rockwell looks in a mirror, only to paint a much younger version of himself.

The **museum** (☎ 413-298-4100; www.nrm.org; MA 183; adult/student/child $12/7/free; ⊙ 10am-5pm; ♿) has the largest collection of Rockwell's original art and also hosts exhibitions of other wholesome, feel-good artists such as David Macaulay, of *The Way Things Work* fame. The grounds contain Rockwell's studio (not wheelchair accessible), too, which was moved here from behind his Stockbridge home. Audio tours are available for an extra fee. The rolling, manicured lawns give way to picturesque views, and there are picnic tables set in a grove near the museum.

To find the museum follow MA 102 west from Stockbridge and turn left (south) on MA 183.

CHESTERWOOD
This pastoral 22-acre plot was 'heaven' to its owner Daniel Chester French (1850–1931), the sculptor best known for his statue *The Minute Man* (1875) at the Old North Bridge in Concord and his great seated statue of Abraham Lincoln in the Lincoln Monument in Washington, DC (1922). French lived in New York City but spent most summers after 1897 here at **Chesterwood** (☎ 413-298-3579; www.chesterwood.org; 4 Williamsville Rd; adult/child $12/5; ⊙ 10am-5pm May-Oct), his gracious Berkshire estate.

French's more than 100 great public works, mostly monumental, made him a wealthy man. His house and studio are substantially as they were when he lived and worked here,

with nearly 500 pieces of sculpture, finished and unfinished, in the barnlike studio. The space and the art have a way of beguiling even those who aren't sculpture enthusiasts.

Tours of the residence and studio leave about every hour. Follow MA 102 west from Stockbridge and turn left onto Glendale Middle Rd, proceed through Williamsville Rd and turn left; the museum is on the right.

NAUMKEAG
This 1885 grand Berkshire 'cottage' on Prospect Hill was the summer house of attorney, diplomat and notable art collector Joseph Hodges Choate; it's crammed with Oriental carpets, Chinese porcelain and other luxury goods. The stunning gardens are the result of 30 years of devoted work on the part of prominent landscape architect Fletcher Steele and the Choate family. The Choates settled on the name Naumkeag mistakenly thinking it meant 'haven of peace' – it's actually Algonquian for 'fishing place.'

You can take a **guided tour** (☎ 413-298-8146; www.thetrustees.org; 5 Prospect St; adult/child 6-12yr $10/3, gardens only $8/3; ⊙ 10am-5pm Jun–mid-Oct) of the house and gardens. Follow Pine St from the Red Lion Inn (opposite) to Prospect St.

STOCKBRIDGE CEMETERY
Most notable about this pleasant burying ground on the west end of Main St is the so-called **Sedgwick Pie**. When Judge Theodore Sedgwick, the head of a prominent Stockbridge family, died in 1813, he had himself buried in the center of a large plot, around which in concentric circles his and his wife's descendants would be laid to rest as well. Legend goes that the Sedgwicks wanted to see no one but other Sedgwicks when the day of reckoning came, but modern-day family members refute this. Might-as-well-be family members include the servant Mum Bet – whom Judge Sedgwick helped free from slavery – as well as the family dog. The pie lies in the northeast corner.

WEST STOCKBRIDGE
Though not nearly as picturesque as Stockbridge, West Stockbridge still retains its historic charm. Old country stores and the 19th-century train station stand next to new galleries and art studios. This is a great place to stay during Tanglewood season

(see boxed text, p266), because Lenox is less than a 15-minute drive away on rarely used backcountry roads.

Any baker worth his salt knows that the choice of vanilla can mean the difference between so-so cookies and oh-so cookies. **Charles H Baldwin & Sons Extracts** (☎ 413-232-7785; www.baldwinextracts.com; 1 Center St; ◷ 9am-5pm Mon-Sat, noon-3pm Sun) has been producing top-quality vanilla extract along with a score of other good-smelling extracts and oils since 1888, all made on-site. Baldwin's is worth a stop if only for the explosion of nostalgia and novelty gifts that cover every surface of the tiny storefront.

Sleeping

Card Lake Inn (☎ 413-232-0272; www.cardlakeinn.com; 29 Main St/MA 102, West Stockbridge; r incl breakfast $130-210; wi-fi) A former stagecoach stop with old pitching floors. The 11 rooms in this canary-yellow inn shoot for a 'country' or 'shaker' look with furniture that needs a bit more coordination. The place is above a tavern.

Red Lion Inn (☎ 413-298-5545; www.redlioninn .com; 30 Main St/MA 102; d $120-155, incl bathroom $210-270; ▣ wi-fi ☝) This huge, white frame hotel is at the very heart of Stockbridge. Founded in 1773, it was completely rebuilt after a fire in 1897. Many rooms in the main building have fireplaces, old print wallpaper, moldings and white linens.

Williamsville Inn (☎ 413-274-6118; www.williamsvil leinn.com; MA 41, West Stockbridge; d $190-240; ◲ wi-fi ▥) This 1797 farmhouse has wood floors, exposed beams, fireplaces and refreshingly understated decor in its 16 rooms. Renting out the Sarah Hale and Susan B Anthony rooms together is an excellent choice for families – they're within spitting distance of a tree swing and playground. In summer a three-night stay is required. The dining room (meals $33 to $45, open for dinner Friday and Saturday) specializes in German cuisine. The inn is 5 miles south of West Stockbridge toward Great Barrington.

Eating

Elm St Market (☎ 413-298-3634; 4 Elm St; items $3-6; ◷ breakfast & lunch) Just off Main St, this quaint market has a deli counter (order Reuben sandwiches), and a few tables (where you can eat them). Oldies play over the stereo, but the internet station in the back belies its throwback character as does the tacky sign out front.

Caffe Pomo d'Oro (☎ 413-232-4616; 6 Depot St, West Stockbridge; breakfast $6-15, lunch $10-15; ◷ 8am-3pm) This airy, casual café in the 1838 light-yellow railroad station is where local artisans lunch on omelettes, large sandwiches, freshly made soups, gnocchi, and creative mains such as smoked trout fillet with horseradish.

Once Upon a Table (☎ 413-298-3870; 36 Main St; meals $19-35; ◷ lunch & dinner) This bright spot in the Mews shopping arcade serves upscale fare on its glass-enclosed porch. The menu changes often and features reliably delicious treats such as pecan-crusted rainbow trout, gumbo and fine dessert pastries.

Red Lion Inn (☎ 413-298-5545; www.redlioninn.com; 30 Main St; ☝) The Red Lion is Stockbridge's premier place for dining. Besides the formal dining room (dinner $35 to $40, open 7am to 10pm), where you can indulge in a roasted native turkey while sitting under a crystal chandelier, there's the Widow Bingham Tavern (meals $12 to $25), a rustic colonial pub that serves gourmet sandwiches and many variations on cow.

Lion's Den (☎ 413-298-1654; meals $8-14; ◷ dinner Mon-Thu, lunch & dinner Fri-Sun) Downstairs at the Red Lion Inn, this cocktail lounge serve daily pub specials (meatloaf with mushroom gravy). Folk, jazz or bluegrass music is featured many nights. In fair weather you can dine in the courtyard out back.

LEE
pop 5850

Welcome to the towniest town in the Berkshires, where the population largely consists of townies. A main street, both cute and gritty, runs through the center, curving to cross some railroad tracks. On it you'll find a hardware store, bar and a few places to eat including a proper diner favored by politicians desiring photo-ops with the commoners. Most travelers pass through Lee simply because it's near a convenient exit off the Mass Pike. The main draw is the prestigious Jacob's Pillow dance festival and a few outlets malls on the periphery.

Lee, just off exit 2 of I-90 and 134 miles from Boston, is the gateway to Lenox, Stockbridge and Great Barrington, less than a 10-minute drive away (except on busy summer weekends when the traffic can be maddening). US 20 is Lee's main street, and leads to Lenox.

Lee Chamber of Commerce (☎ 413-243-0852; www.leechamber.org; PO Box 345, Lee, MA 01238-0345;

(⏰ 10am–4pm Tue–Sat) Maintains an information booth on the town green in summer.

Sights & Activities

Founded by Ted Shawn in an old barn in 1932, **Jacob's Pillow** (☎ 413-243-0745; www.jacobspillow.org; PO Box 287, Lee, MA 01238-0287; shows free–$55; ⏰ performances mid-Jun–early Sep) is one of the premier summer dance festivals in the USA. Through the years, Alvin Ailey, Merce Cunningham, the Martha Graham Dance Company and other leading interpreters of dance have taken part. A smorgasbord of free shows and talks allows even those on tight budgets to join in the fun. The festival theaters are in the village of Becket, 7 miles east of Lee along US 20 and MA 8.

Most out-of-towners who venture to the Berkshires head to the Mt Greylock State Reservation (see p272) to see the state's highest peak, and thus leave **October Mountain State Forest** (☎ 413-243-1778), a 16,127-acre state park and the largest tract of green space in Massachusetts, to the locals. Hidden amid the hardwoods, Buckley Dunton Reservoir – a small body of water stocked with bass and pickerel – is a great spot for canoeing. For hikers, a 9-mile stretch of the Appalachian Trail pierces the heart of the forest through copses of hemlocks, spruces, birches and oaks. To get there from Lee, follow Rte 20 west for 3 miles and look for signs.

If all the cute Berkshire boutiques are getting to you, score some deals at **Prime Outlets** (☎ 413-243-8186; 50 Water St/US 20; ⏰ 10am–9pm Mon-Sat, 11am–6pm Sun), with chain retailers including Timberland, the Gap and London Fog.

Sleeping & Eating

For a comprehensive list of area accommodations visit www.leelo dging.org.

October Mountain State Forest (☎ 877-422-6762; Center St; campsites $12-14) This state forest campground, near the shores of the Housatonic River, is for campers only and has 47 sites with hot showers. To find the campground, turn east off US 20 onto Center St and follow the signs.

Jonathan Foote 1778 House (☎ 413-243-454; www.1778house.com; 1 East St; r $135-225; wi-fi) An old Georgian farmhouse set in spacious grounds with shady maple trees and stone walls. Stay here for antiquated fireplaces, appropriately decorated rooms and hearty breakfasts. The resident golden retriever is a nice fellow.

Motels in Lee are clustered around I-90 exit 2, on heavily trafficked Rte 7. They include **Sunset Motel** (☎ 413-243-0302; 150 Housatonic St; 🚗), with very basic rooms, but quiet; and **Pilgrim Inn** (☎ 413-243-1328; 165 Housatonic St), which has laundry facilities. Prices at both places range from $50 in off-season to $170 in high season.

Joe's Diner (☎ 413-243-9756; 63 Center St; items $3-10; ⏰ 24hr) There's no better slice of blue-collar Americana in the Berkshires than Joe's Diner, at the north end of Main St. Norman Rockwell's famous painting of a policeman sitting at a counter talking to a young boy, *The Runaway* (1958), was inspired by this diner. Every politician who's ever run for office in Massachusetts has stopped at Joe's to get their picture taken and put on the wall. Pancakes and omelettes cost $4.

While the diner is the main draw, you'll also find a Chinese joint and a health food store in the center of town.

LENOX
pop 5150

This gracious, wealthy town is a historical anomaly: its charm was not destroyed by the industrial revolution, and then, prized for its bucolic peace, the town became a summer retreat for wealthy families with surnames like Carnegie, Vanderbilt and Westinghouse, who had made their fortunes by building factories in other towns. While Lenox's illustrious past remains tangibly present, it has thankfully developed a bit of a commercial center and is dynamic enough to actually have a grocery store.

Lenox offers two superstar attractions: the Tanglewood Music Festival, which is an incredibly popular summer event, and the Kripalu Center for yoga and spiritual reflection. Just past Tanglewood is the Stockbridge Bowl, a cerulean lake.

Orientation & Information

It's easy to get around Lenox on foot, though some of its many inns are a mile or two from the center. Tanglewood is 1.5 miles west of Lenox's center along West St/MA 183. Church St contains the best eateries.

Bookstore (☎ 413-637-3390; 9 Housatonic St; ⏰ 9am–6pm Mon-Sat, 10am–3pm Sun) The place to stop for maps, atlases or summer novels.

Lenox Chamber of Commerce & Information Center (☎ 413-637-3646; www.lenox.org; 5 Walker St,

Lenox, MA 01240; ☼ 10am-4pm Tue-Sat) A clearinghouse of information.

Sights & Activities

KRIPALU CENTER

Shadowbrook, the former summer home of Andrew Carnegie, overlooks Stockbridge Bowl and is now one of America's finest **yoga centers** (☎ 413-448-3400; www.kripalu.org; PO Box 793, West St/MA 183, Lenox MA 01240). Kripalu accommodates some 300 students, who come to study yoga, meditation and holistic therapies within peaceful surroundings. You can't show up for a drop-in class – rather, book into a three-day 'retreat and renewal' program. Family programs are offered as well.

THE MOUNT

Almost 50 years after Nathaniel Hawthorne left his home in Lenox (now part of Tanglewood), another writer found inspiration in the Berkshires. Edith Wharton (1862–1937) came to Lenox in 1899 and proceeded to build her palatial estate, the Mount. When not writing, she would entertain friends including Henry James.

Besides such novels as *The Age of Innocence*, Wharton penned *The Decoration of Houses*, which helped legitimize interior decoration as a profession in the USA. She summered at the Mount for a decade before moving permanently to France.

You can tour the **Mount** (☎ 413-637-1899; www .edithwharton.org; 2 Plunkett St; adult/student/child under 12yr $18/5/free; ☼ 9am-5pm May-Oct), which is on the outskirts of Lenox at US 7.

BERKSHIRE SCENIC RAILWAY MUSEUM

This **museum** (☎ 413-637-2210; www.berkshiresce nicrailroad.org; Willow Creek Rd; admission free; ☼ 10am-4pm Sat & Sun May-Oct; ♿) of railroad lore is set up in Lenox's 1902 vintage railroad station. Its two elaborate model-railroad displays are favorites with kids. On summer weekends, rides on a 1950s diesel locomotive connect Lenox and Stockbridge (adult/senior/child four to 14 years $15/14/8, 2½-hour round-trip).

The museum is 1.5 miles east of Lenox center, via Housatonic St.

SHAKESPEARE & COMPANY

Another enjoyable feature of a Berkshires summer is taking in a show by **Shakespeare & Co** (☎ 413-637-1199; www.shakespeare.org; 70 Kemble St; tickets $15-38; ☼ plays Tue-Sun). The repertoire also includes Shakespeare's plays and contemporary performances, such as *The Secret of Sherlock Holmes* and Tom Stoppard's *Rough Crossing*. The summertime **Bankside Festival** (☎ 413-637-3353) stages plays, demonstrations and talks that are held outdoors at the south end of the property and free to all. It's named for Elizabethan London's seedy Banksyde district, and not after some lame financial house. The company is also in the process of building the world's first historically accurate replica of London's Rose Playhouse, complete with surrounding Elizabethan village. Right now it's just got some bleachers and a tent. Huzzah?

BIKING & SKIING

Kennedy Park, just north of downtown Lenox on US 7, is popular with mountain bikers in the summer and cross-country skiers in the winter. You might also explore the Berkshires' many miles of stunning back roads or paddle down the Housatonic River. The **Arcadian Shop** (☎ 413-637-3010; 91 Pittsfield Rd/US 7; ☼ 10am-6pm Mon-Sat, 11am-5pm Sun) rents high-end mountain, road and children's bikes ($35 to 45), kayaks ($35), skis ($20) and snowshoes ($20). Rates are per day.

PLEASANT VALLEY WILDERNESS SANCTUARY

This 1300-acre **wildlife sanctuary** (☎ 413-637-0320; www.massaudubon.org; 472 W Mountain Rd; adult/child $4/3; ☼ dawn-dusk) has 7 miles of pleasant walking trails through forests of maples, oaks, beeches and birches. It's not uncommon to see beaver here if you come at dawn or dusk. A nature center is open daily, and you can arrange canoe trips on the Housatonic from here. To reach the sanctuary, go north on US 7 or MA 7A. Three-quarters of a mile north of the intersection of US 7 and MA 7A, turn left onto W Dugway Rd and go 1.5 miles to the sanctuary.

Sleeping

Lenox has no hotels and only a few motels, but it does have lots of inns. The Tanglewood festival means that many inns require a two- or three-night minimum stay on Friday and Saturday nights in summer. Many thrifty travelers opt to sleep in lower-priced towns like Great Barrington. But if you can afford them, Lenox's inns provide charming digs

TANGLEWOOD MUSIC FESTIVAL

In 1934 Boston Symphony Orchestra conductor Serge Koussevitzky's dream of a center for serious musical study came true with the acquisition of the 400-acre **Tanglewood Estate** (☎ 413-637-1600; www.tanglewood.org; 297 West St/MA 183; Ⓖ) in Lenox. People including Leonard Bernstein and Seiji Ozawa then arrived as young musicians to study at the side of great masters.

Today, the Tanglewood Music Festival is among the most esteemed music events in the world. Symphony, pops, chamber music, recitals, jazz and blues are performed from late June through early September. Performance spaces include the 'Shed,' which is anything but – a 6000-seat concert shelter with several sides open to the surrounding lawns – and the Seiji Ozawa Concert Hall.

The Boston Symphony Orchestra concerts on Friday, Saturday and Sunday in July and August are the most popular events. Most casual attendees – up to 8000 of them – arrive three or four hours before concert time, staking out good listening spots on the lawn outside the Shed or the Concert Hall, then relaxing and enjoying elaborate picnics until the music starts.

Contemporary star performers including Midori, Itzhak Perlman, Yo-Yo Ma and Andre Watts. Popular performers such as James Taylor, Harry Connick Jr, Wynton Marsalis (in jazz mode), and the Joshua Redman Quartet have given Tanglewood concerts.

The **visitors center** (☹ 10am-4pm Jul & Aug, Sat & Sun Jun & Sep-Oct) can help with any questions. The grounds are open year-round for strolling, with free walking tours being offered on Wednesdays at 10:30am and Saturdays at 1:30pm in summer.

Tickets

Tickets range from $20 per person for picnic space on the lawn to more than $90 for the best seats at the most popular concerts. If you hold lawn tickets and it rains, you get wet. There are no refunds or exchanges. If you arrive about three hours before concert time, you can often get lawn space; Shed and Concert Hall seats should be bought in advance.

and memorable stays. Log onto www.lenox .org for a list and links.

Most inn rooms have private bathroom, and include a full breakfast and perhaps afternoon tea. Few Lenox inns accept children under 12 years, or pets.

BUDGET & MIDRANGE

Walker House (☎ 413-637-1271; www.walkerhouse .com; 64 Walker St; d Mon-Fri $110-150, Sat & Sun $135-210) Bohemian owners run this casual B&B out of an early-19th-century home with eight rooms with hardwood floors. Many contain fireplaces (powered by Duraflame logs, not actual wood) and incredibly vivid wallpaper – where does someone find a green that bright? Also on hand are friendly cats and a few pianos.

Summer White House (☎ 413-637-4489; www .thesummerwhitehouse.com; 17 Main St; r $180-200) Run by a crooner from the big band era (Frank Newton, ladies and gentlemen), find ample rooms with four-post beds, family pictures and some pleasant pieces of Americana. The dining room has a quiet grandeur with a large well-set table, fireplace and big picture window set under a coffered wooden ceiling. It was built by the Wharton family.

Birchwood Inn (☎ 413-637-2600, 800-524-1646; www.birchwood-inn.com; 7 Hubbard St; r $130-225, ste $160-245) This mansard-roofed house dating from 1767 is now an accommodating inn with fine views of the town. The 11 spacious rooms all have private bathrooms and about half feature fireplaces.

Motel-wise, **Days Inn** (☎ 413-637-3560; www .daysinn.com; 194 Pittsfield Rd; d $70-140) and **Econo Lodge** (☎ 413-637-4244; www.econolodgeberkshires .com; 130 Pittsfield Rd; d in summer $110-190; Ⓟ) stand on US 7 outside the village to the east.

TOP END

Whistler's Inn (☎ 413-637-0975; whistlersinnlenox.com; 5 Greenwood St; r $150-250) This well-preserved 'English Tudor' estate (1820) contains large diamond-paned windows (some touched with stained glass), fireplaces, sherry decanting in the library and airy rooms with furniture that might seem stuffy and expensive if it didn't look so lovingly worn. Plantings and a sunken garden surround the house, which is opposite an old graveyard. When they tell you it's

For information in fall or winter, call ☎ 617-266-1492 in Boston; otherwise, call Tanglewood directly on ☎ 413-637-1600. Tickets may be purchased at the box office at Tanglewood's main entrance on West St, or through Ticketmaster, which can be reached on ☎ 413-733-2500 in the Berkshires and ☎ 800-347-0808 from other areas.

Children
Lawn tickets for children under 12 are free, thanks to a grant from the TDK company. An adult can score up to four free children's tickets per performance. Adults accompanying kids under five years old are asked to sit with them in the back half of the lawn, and kids this age aren't allowed in the Shed or the Seiji Ozawa Concert Hall during concerts at all.

Eating
Many people pack picnics to eat on the lawn (wine allowed), or buy a prepacked basket available at the gourmet markets in the area.

With a few days' notice you can have a bagged lunch, boxed meal or picnic basket from the **Tanglewood Cafe** (☎ 413-637-5240), but this costs more than (and is not as enjoyable as) picking out your own goodies. The café also serves eat-in lunches. At the grille near the theatre, you'll find hamburger-and-pizza-type fare, and ice-cream and beverage vendors roam the grounds.

Getting There & Parking
Tanglewood is easy to find – just follow the car in front of you! From Lenox center, head west on West St/MA 183 for about 1 mile, and the main entrance will be on your left. Ample concert parking is available, but remember that parking – and, more importantly, unparking – 6000 cars can take time. It's all organized very well and runs smoothly, but you'll still have to wait a while in your car during the exodus. If your lodging is close, consider walking.

---

haunted they mean it – he's nice but plays around with the plumbing.

Gateways Inn (☎ 413-637-2532; www.gateways inn.com; 51 Walker St; r $100-295, ste $230-450) Once the home of Harley T Procter (of Procter & Gamble), the place supposedly aspires to look like a bar of Ivory soap (not even close). The staid clapboarded structure offers super-clean, good-looking rooms that are perhaps a bit fussy (why the bust of Thomas Jefferson?). The owners are unfailingly gracious. Gay-friendly, too.

Blantyre (☎ 413-637-3556; www.blantyre.com; Blantyre Rd; r from $550; ⬛) If money's no object, this is the place for you. This ivy-covered imitation Scottish Tudor mansion sits on 85 acres of grounds dotted with four tennis courts, croquet lawns, hot tub and sauna. Accommodations are available in 25 rooms, suites and cottages; continental breakfast is included. Three miles west of I-90 exit 2 along US 20.

Eating & Drinking
Good news: there are a bunch of places to eat, by Berkshire's standards. Bad news: few

are great and your taste buds are better off in Great Barrington.

Carol's Restaurant (☎ 413-637-8948; 8 Franklin St; breakfast $6-12; ☾ 7am-4pm, closed Wed) This is where Old School meets New Age and you can get a psychic reading with your morning pancakes. James Taylor's favorite omelette – stuffed with tomato, feta and spinach – is physically and spiritually satisfying.

Homer's Variety (☎ 413-637-3066; 27 Housatonic St; ice-cream $2.25; ☾ 6am-6pm) At this old-school convenience store on Church St, you can buy doughnuts (a handwritten sign proclaims 'this is a magic donut machine') or some gumballs from the oversized dispenser. The real draw, however, is the homemade ice-cream in five flavors (including tiramisu and chocolate) plus some otherworldly lemon ice.

Lenox Coffee (☎ 800-946-3978; 52 Main St; ☾ 7am-7pm Mon-Sat, 8am-7pm Sun; wi-fi ⬛) For a wide selection of single origin coffee as well as some loose teas, stop in at this small café for a blast of air-conditioning and some tasty pastries. If there is a daytime hangout spot, this is it.

Nejaime's Wine Cellar (☎ 413-637-2221; 60 Main St; ☾ 9am-9pm Mon-Sat) You can order a

Tanglewood picnic basket here ($45 for two people), or just pick up a few bottles and some gourmet cheeses to get started on your own creation. There's another shop (☎ 413-448-2274, 444 Pittsfield Rd/US 7) heading north out of town.

Bistro Zinc (☎ 413-637-8800; 56 Church St; meals $22-45; ☾ lunch & dinner, bar until late) The post-modern decor here is all metal surfaces and light woods, with doors made of wine crates. The tin ceiling and parquet floors add to the LA feel. The cuisine features tempting New French offerings like lamb loin with baby carrots. If the food doesn't appeal, you can always just slip in after dinner for a glass of wine and style points.

Gateways Inn & Restaurant (☎ 413-637-2532; 51 Walker St; meals $24-30; ☾ lunch Sat & Sun, dinner daily, closed Mon in winter) Its elegant, terracotta–toned dining room is known as the place to go in town for an anniversary or birthday dinner. The rack of lamb is the chef's signature dish. Epicurean Tanglewood picnics for two are $50.

Drinking & Entertainment

La Terrazza (☎ 413-637-2532; 51 Walker St) The bar of Gateways Inn offers a stunning 225 single malt scotches and at least 90 kinds of grappa. It's not even funny how awesome you'll feel after a proper exploration. The bar also serves light meals in elegant digs.

Rumpy's (☎ 800-253-0917; 16 Church St) While the Federal-style inn upstairs is overpriced and forgettable, its red walled pub below deck comes with dim lighting and restaurant furniture from the '70s. Some call it the cruise ship of Lenox, others are just reminded of 'Twin Peaks.' Either way, folk and jazz acts play most Friday and Saturday nights.

Getting There & Away

The nearest airports are Bradley International and Albany International. **Peter Pan Bus Lines** (☎ 800-343-9999) operates between Lenox and Boston ($34, four hours, two daily). Amtrak trains stop in nearby Pittsfield. If you're driving, Lenox is 15 miles north of Lee and the same distance from I-90 on US 7.

PITTSFIELD

pop 43,500

The lame jokes about the name of this town are easy to make and also accurate. Welcome to the service city of the Berkshires, where the trains stop and where one finds the biggest stores. Travelers pause here for the Hancock Shaker Village and the nearby Crane Museum of Papermaking. For help understanding the desolate downtown, contact the **Berkshire Visitors Bureau** (☎ 413-743-4500; www.berkshires.org) in Adams or the **Berkshire Chamber of Commerce** (☎ 413-499-4000; www.berkshirechamber.com; 75 North St, Suite 360).

The Shakers were among the earliest of the numerous millennial Christian sects that flourished in the fertile climate of religious freedom in the New World. **Hancock Shaker Village** (☎ 413-443-0188; www.hancockshakervillage.org; US 20; adult/child under 18yr $15/free; ☾ 9:30am-5pm), 5 miles southwest of Pittsfield on US 20, gives you a studied look at the peaceful, prayerful Shaker way of life.

The village was known as the City of Peace and was occupied by Shakers until 1960. At its peak in 1830, the community numbered some 300 souls. Preserved as a historic monument, the village still gives you an insightful look at what the work-focused principles of Shakerism accomplished.

Twenty of the original buildings at Hancock Shaker Village are carefully restored and are open to view, most famously the **Round Stone Barn** (1826). During the summer, visitors wander around on their own and interpreters in the historic buildings demonstrate the Shaker way of life. The rest of the year, guided tours are given once or twice daily. Call for details and reservations.

Since 1879 every single American bill has been printed on paper made by the Crane Company, based in the small mill town of Dalton. This 'Champagne of papers' is made from 100% cotton rag rather than wood, and so is wonderfully strong and creamy as well as environmentally sound. The **Crane Museum of Papermaking** (☎ 413-684-6481; Housatonic St, Dalton; admission free; ☾ 1-5pm Mon-Fri Jun-Oct), housed in the original stone mill room built in 1844, traces the history of Zenas Crane's enterprise, which is still family-run after seven generations. The videos – on Crane's papermaking process and on counterfeit detection – are fascinating. To get here from Pittsfield, take MA 9 northeast for 5 miles.

While there aren't many places of interest to eat, **Elizabeth's** (☎ 413-448-8244; 1264 East St; meals $23-30; ☾ dinner Wed-Sun; ♿) is a shocking exception. Don't be put off by its location across the street from a vacant General Electric plant, nor by its deceptively casual interior – chefs travel from New York and Boston to sample Tom and Elizabeth Ellis' innovative Italian dishes. Elizabeth's is a blue-porched house on the right-hand side, about 2 miles down East St. When the road jogs, stay right (not over the bridge).

Pittsfield is 7 miles north of Lenox on US 7 at the intersection with MA 9. Peter Pan and Bonanza buses operate out of the **Pittsfield Bus Terminal** (☎ 413-442-4451; 57 S Church St). Amtrak trains on the Lake Shore Limited line stop here, going to Albany or Boston.

WILLIAMSTOWN
pop 8200

Home to Williams College, a top liberal arts college, this small town lies nestled within the heart of the Purple Valley, so named because the surrounding mountains often seem shrouded in a lavender veil at dusk. In it you'll find plenty of green spaces on which to lie and a friendly town center (two blocks long) where everyone congregates. You'll also find an excellent art museum, though if you came for art remember that MASS MoCA (p271) is just a few miles to the east.

Orientation & Information

US 7 and MA 2/Main St intersect on the western side of town. The small central commercial district is off Main St on Spring St. Other businesses, including motels, are on US 7 and MA 2 on the outskirts of town. The marble-and-brick buildings of Williams College fill the town center.

Milne Library (1095 Main St/MA 2; ☑ 10am-5:30pm Mon-Fri, 10am-4pm Sat) Across the street from the Williams Inn, has internet and wireless access.

Water St Books (☎ 413-458-0249; 26 Water St; ☑ 9:30am-6pm Mon-Sat, noon-5pm Sun) This is the Williams College bookstore, with a friendly staff that know both books and the area.

Williamstown Chamber of Commerce (☎ 413-458-9077; williamstownchamber.com; 100 Spring St) Dispenses information.

Sights & Activities
CLARK ART INSTITUTE

The **Sterling & Francine Clark Art Institute** (☎ 413-458-9545; www.clarkart.edu; 225 South St; admission Jun-Oct $12.50, Nov-May free; ☑ 10am-5pm Tue-Sun Sep-Jun, Mon only Jul & Aug; ☐) is a gem among US art museums. Even if you're not an avid art lover, don't miss it.

Robert Sterling Clark (1877–1956), a Yale engineer whose family had made money in the sewing machine industry, began collecting art in Paris in 1912. He and his wife eventually housed their wonderful collection in Williamstown in a white marble temple built expressly for the purpose. The collections are particularly strong in the Impressionists. Mary Cassatt, Winslow Homer and John Singer Sargent represent contemporary American painting. From earlier centuries, there are excellent works by Hans Memling, Jean-Honoré Fragonard and Francisco de Goya. One of the most well-known sculptures on display is Degas' famous *Little Dancer of Fourteen Years*.

The institute is less than 1 mile south of the information booth at the intersection of US 7 and MA 2.

WILLIAMS COLLEGE MUSEUM OF ART

The Clark Art Institute's sister museum is the excellent **Williams College Museum of Art** (☎ 413-597-2429; www.wcma.org; Main St btwn Water & Spring Sts; admission free; ☑ 10am-5pm Tue-Sat, 1-5pm Sun; ☐). Around half of its 12,000 pieces comprise the American Collection, with substantial works by notables such as Edward Hopper (*Morning in a City*), Winslow Homer and Grant Wood, to name only a few. The photography collection is equally strong, with representation by Diane Arbus, Man Ray and Alfred Stieglitz. The pieces representing ancient and medieval cultures are less numerous but equally distinguished. The museum also hosts traveling exhibits and stages its own shows with works from community and regional artists.

To find the museum, look for the huge bronze eyes embedded in the front lawn on Main St.

WILLIAMSTOWN THEATRE

Shining stars of the theater world descend upon small Williamstown every year from the third week in June to the third week in August. While many summer-stock theaters offer cheese, the **Williamstown Theatre Festival** (☎ 413-597-3399, tickets 413-597-3400; www.wtfestival.org; ☐) bucks the trend, and was the first summer theater to win the Regional Theatre Tony Award.

The festival mounts the region's major theatrical offerings, and tickets are usually inexpensive. Kevin Kline, Richard Dreyfuss and Gwyneth Paltrow are but a few of the well-known thespians who have performed here. Besides the offerings on the Main Stage and Nikos Stage, there are cabaret performances in area restaurants and a family-oriented free festival runs for two weeks on the campus of the Buxton School.

HIKING & BIKING

Williamstown and environs, with rolling farmland and quiet country roads, are excellent for biking. Route 43, along the Green River, is one of the prettier roads. **Mountain Goat** (☎ 413-458-8445; www.themountaingoat.com; 130 Water St; bikes per day $25; ☷ 10am-6pm Mon-Sat, noon-5pm Sun) rents bicycles as well as hiking, camping and fly fishing gear.

When Boston and Main Railroad gave up on the corridor between Lanesborough and Adams in 1990, citizens agitated to have it recast as a universally accessible walk/bike path, and thus the 11-mile **Ashuwillticook Rail Trail** (☎ 413-442-8928) was born. The trail closely follows the Hoosic River and the Cheshire Reservoir through glorious wetlands, with many benches along the way and a handful of rest facilities. The southern access is by the Berkshire Mall at the intersection of MA 9 and MA 8 between Pittsfield and Dalton, and parking is available at both ends.

Sleeping
BUDGET & MIDRANGE

Many B&Bs have a two-night minimum on Friday and Saturday nights and some require a three-night stay on holidays and during special college events. You'll find a score of hotels and motels on the outskirts of town on MA 2 east, US 7 north.

Clarksburg State Park (☎ 413-664-8345, 877-422-6762; 1199 Middle Rd; campsites $12) Follow MA 8 north from North Adams to reach these 50 campsites near the lovely and swimmable Mauserts Pond. There are pit toilets but no showers.

Maple Terrace Motel (☎ 413-458-9677; www.maple terrace.com; 555 Main St; d $93-128; ☒) The Maple Terrace is a small, 15-room place on the outskirts to the east of town. The motel itself is a big old house with rather elegant units behind it. In winter ask about discounted lift tickets to Jiminy Peak ski resort.

River Bend Farm B&B (☎ 413-458-3121; www.wind sorsofstonington.com; 643 Simmons Rd; d $120; ☷ Apr-Oct) A Georgian tavern since revolutionary times, River Bend Farm owes its painstaking restoration to hosts Judy and Dave Looms. Four doubles share two bathrooms here. Just off US 7 on the north side of the little bridge over the Hoosic River, it's a favorite among European travelers. No credit cards.

Steep Acres Farm B&B (☎ 413-458-3774; 520 White Oaks Rd; s $80, d $100-160, all incl breakfast) The gregarious Gangemi family welcomes travelers to its 30-acre hilltop farm just 2 miles north of Williamstown. From here there are spectacular views of both the Berkshires and the Green Mountains of Vermont. Furnishings and decor feature a 'country' motif (simple elegance), and three of the four rooms have a private bathroom. Kick back at the trout and swimming ponds (complete with beach toys). Reserve *far* in advance.

Williamstown B&B (☎ 413-458-9202; www.williams townbandb.com; 30 Cold Spring Rd; d incl breakfast $150-210) This meticulously maintained, four-room Victorian B&B has the perfect porch from which to watch the town's folk stroll by. All rooms have private bathroom, and breakfast is a lovely production. No credit cards, but checks are accepted.

TOP END

Guest House at Field Farm (☎ 413-458-3135; www .thetrustees.org; 554 Sloan Rd; r incl breakfast $175-250; ☒) This was the country estate of Lawrence and Eleanore Bloedel, collectors of 20th-century art. Built in 1948, in spare, clean-lined post-WWII style on 300 acres of woods and farmland facing Mt Greylock, the estate was willed to the Trustees of Reservations, which now operates it. All five rooms express big-time modernity. Some rooms feature fireplaces and private patios. The grounds contain a pond, 4 miles of walking trails and tennis courts.

Harbour House Inn (☎ 413-743-8959; www.harbour houseinn.com; 725 N State Rd/US 8, Cheshire; d incl breakfast $120-170) This seven-room inn is about 15 miles southeast from Williamstown and 17 miles north from Lenox, but it's worth mentioning because of its spectacular location, on the back side of Mt Greylock. Part of a 200-year-old farm, the Harbour House is now an elegant manor house. The three-room, 3rd-floor Summit View suite ($260) lives up to its name.

Eating & Drinking

For coffee or a light meal, wander along Spring St, the main shopping street. Other areas of town, notably Water St, have restaurants serving more substantial lunches and dinners.

Tunnel City Coffee (☎ 413-458-5010; 100 Spring St; ⏰ 7am-6pm) A bustling den of cramming students and mentoring professors. Besides liquid caffeine, some seriously delicious desserts like triple-layer mousse cake will get you buzzing. The shop's name is a reference to North Adams, where the beans are roasted.

Pappa Charlie's Deli (☎ 413-458-5969; 28 Spring St; dishes $4-8; ⏰ 8am-8pm) Here's a welcoming breakfast spot where locals really do ask for 'the usual.' The stars themselves created the lunch sandwiches that bear their names. The Richard Dreyfuss is a thick pastrami and provolone number. Or order a Politician and get anything you want on it. Downstairs is an organic juice and coffee bar.

Hot Tomatoes Pizza (☎ 413-458-2722; 100 Water St; pizzas small $8-12, large $14-20; ⏰ lunch & dinner summer, closed Sun rest of year) Simply the best pizza in town. You won't find any sad-looking salads or second-rate pastas here – these folks stick to what they know best: thin-crust Neapolitan-style pizzas. It's takeout only, but you can head to the riverside picnic tables in the back yard.

Jae's Inn (☎ 413-458-8032; 777 Cold Spring Rd; meals $13-25; ⏰ 11:30am-9pm Sun-Thu, 11:30am-10pm Fri & Sat; Ⓥ) For top-notch appetizers (duck confit spring roll; marinated octopus) and fresh sushi. This Asian joint serves dishes inspired by the cuisines of Japan, Thailand and elsewhere. Eat stir-fries, things from clay pots and great Korean stuff. It's on MA 7 south of town.

Mezze Bistro & Bar (☎ 413-458-0123; 16 Water St; meals $22-25; ⏰ dinner) This chic eatery decorated with touches of red velvet is your best bet for glimpsing actors from the Williamstown Theatre after a performance. Roasted red snapper with creamed corn and chanterelles is one of the more American-style mains. Later at night, it's the closest Williamstown gets to having a gay bar.

Entertainment

During the academic year, call **Concertline** (☎ 413-597-3146) of the Williams College Department of Music for information on concerts, recitals and performances.

In the summer the **Williamstown Chamber Concerts** (☎ 413-458-8273) group stages concerts at the Clark Art Institute.

Images Cinema (☎ 413-458-1039; www.imagescinema .org; 50 Spring St; adult/senior & student $9/5) is a single-screen, nonprofit arts institution screening indie and foreign flicks.

Getting There & Away

Williamstown's bus station is in the lobby of the **Williams Inn** (☎ 413-458-2665; Main St), close to the intersection of US 7 and MA 2, and is serviced infrequently by **Bonanza Bus Lines** (☎ 800-556-3815).

Boston lies 145 miles to the east; Lenox is 29 miles south on US 7.

NORTH ADAMS
pop 13800

At first glace, North Adams' beautiful and bleak 19th-century downtown seems out of sync with the rest of the Berkshires. But those who allow their gaze to settle will be confronted with an exemplary contemporary art museum of staggering proportions.

Welcome to **MASS MoCA** (☎ 413-662-2111; www.massmoca.org; 87 Marshall St; adult/student/child 6-16yr $12.50/9/5; ⏰ 10am-6pm Jul & Aug, 11am-5pm Wed-Mon Sep-Jun), which sprawls over 13 acres of downtown North Adams, or about one-third of the entire business district. After the Sprague Electric Company packed up in 1985, more than $31 million was spent to modernize the property into 'the largest gallery in the United States,' which now encompasses 220,000 sq feet and over 25 buildings, including art construction areas, performance centers and 19 galleries. One gallery is the size of a football field, large enough to exhibit the work of Ann Hamilton and Tim Hawkinson.

In addition to carrying the bread-and-butter rotation of description-defying installation pieces, the museum has evolved into one of the region's key venues for evening cabaret, documentary films, lectures and avant-garde dance performances.

Though the rest of town appears to be largely a culinary wasteland, the MASS MoCA campus offers two fine spots to grab a bite. **Lickety Split** (☎ 413-663-3372), a pretty café near the main lobby, serves breakfast, sandwiches, espresso and hot dishes. It stays open late when there is an evening show. Otherwise, try **Cafe Latino** (☎ 413-662-2004; meals $13-25; ⏰ 11am-3pm Mon-Sat, 5-9pm Tue-Sat) for rice and beans, fish tacos and pork chops in a half-space-age and half-wood room.

While many sleep in nearby Williamstown, you might try **Savoy Mountain State Forest** (☎ 413-663-8469; Central Shaft Rd/MA 116; campsite/cabin $12/25), a wooded campground with 45 sites and four very rustic log cabins in one of the best state parks for mountain biking. There are showers and flush toilets. Head south on MA 8 and east on MA 116.

Near MASS MoCA, is the **Porches** (☎ 413-664-0400; www.porches.com; 231 River St; r $155-235; ♿) whose new rooms combine well-considered color palettes, ample lighting and French doors into a pleasant sleeping experience. Thanks to a grant, it often puts up artists installing artworks at the museum.

MT GREYLOCK STATE RESERVATION

At a modest 3491ft, the state's highest peak can't hold a candle altitude-wise to its western counterparts, but a climb up the 92ft-high **War Veterans Memorial Tower** at its summit rewards you with a panorama stretching up to 100 verdant miles, across the Taconic, Housatonic and Catskill ranges, and over five states. The mountain sits in an 18-sq-mile forest of fir, beech, birch, maple, oak and spruce that also includes Mt Prospect, Mt Fitch, Mt Williams and Saddle Ball Mountain. Wildlife includes bears, bobcats, deer, porcupines, raccoons and birds such as hawks, grouse, thrushes, ravens and wild turkeys. Even if the weather seems drab from the foot, a trip to the summit may well lift you above the gray blanket, and the view with a layer of cloud floating between tree line and sky is simply magical.

The **Mt Greylock State Reservation** (☎ 413-499-4262; www.mass.gov/dcr/parks/mtGreylock; ☀ visitors center 9am-9pm Jun-Aug, shorter hours otherwise) has some 45 miles of hiking trails, including a portion of the Appalachian Trail. Frequent trail pulloffs on the road up – including some that lead to waterfalls – make it easy to get at least a little hike in before reaching the top. The **Hopper** is a stunning V-shaped wedge of 200-year-old spruce trees that fills a valley between Mts Greylock, Williams and Prospect and Stoney Ledge.

There a few primitive campsites in the park that are not accessible by car; call for information and reservations.

Bascom Lodge (☎ 413-743-1591; 1 Summit Rd; dm/r $36/98; ☀ mid-May–mid-Oct), a truly rustic mountain hostelry, was built as a federal work project in the 1930s at the summit of Mt Greylock. It can provide beds for 34 people, and hearty meals are available, though not included in the price. At time of press it was under renovation, and will reopen in 2009.

You can get to Greylock from either Lanesborough (follow the signs 2 miles north of town) or North Adams (from MA 2 west, and again, follow the signs). Either way, it's 10 slow miles to the summit. The Greylock visitors center is halfway up via the Lanesborough route. There's a $2 fee to park at the summit.

Rhode Island

The smallest of the united states, Rhode Island might only take 45 minutes to drive across but it packs over 400 miles of coastline into its tiny boundaries. Quite a lot of this coastline takes the form of white sandy beaches, arguably the finest places for ocean swimming in the Northeast. Otherwise there are islands to explore, seaside cliffs to walk along, and isolated lighthouses where you can either indulge in brooding melancholia or maybe hold someone's hand.

Rhode Island contains two cities of note. Providence, both a capital city and college town, is a lively place brimming with restaurants, bars and nightlife, in particular a strong experimental rock scene. Here you'll find top-notch art museums, old-school Italian-American neighborhoods and several independent movie theaters, all set within a beautiful and walkable urban fabric. It's the most dynamic city in New England after Boston.

Newport lingers as an old seaside town crammed full of cobblestone streets, wooden buildings from the colonial era and a pile of over-the-top, gilded-age mansions, the city's biggest attraction. Ever since the Vanderbilt family and associated pals set up shop at the end of the 19th century, Newport has functioned as a summertime resort. In season, you'll find thousands upon thousands of tourists who come to experience a tangibly historic place with a party atmosphere.

HIGHLIGHTS

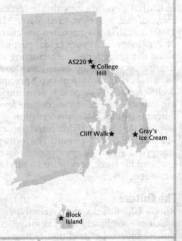

- Enjoying the close proximity of a picturesque town (booze) and a pristine beach (swim) at **Block Island** (p306)
- Wiping ocean spray from your glasses while standing between the roaring Atlantic and gilded-age mansions on the **Cliff Walk** (p297)
- Watching faux-argumentative band-mates french each other at **AS220** (p292) after throwing fake hotdogs at a yawning robot-attired audience
- Drinking a coffee cabinet at **Gray's Ice Cream** (p305) after a leisurely drive around Little Compton
- Exploring the seriously charming streets of 18th-century **College Hill** (p279)

AS220 ★
★ College Hill

Cliff Walk ★
★ Gray's Ice Cream

★ Block Island

■ TELEPHONE CODE: 401	■ POPULATION: 1.08 MILLION	■ AREA: 1045 SQ MILES

RHODE ISLAND

Orientation & Information

Rhode Island Tourism Division (☎ 401-273-8270; www.visitrhodeisland.com; 315 Iron Horse Way, Suite 101, Providence, RI 02908; ⏰ 8:30am-4:30pm Mon-Fri) This office will send you booklets and maps on places in Rhode Island and will update you on special events. They are better for pre-planning; tourists don't often walk through the door.

History

Ever since it was founded in 1636 by Roger Williams, a religious outcast from Boston, Providence has enjoyed an independent frame of mind. Williams' guiding principle, the one that got him ostracized from Massachusetts, was that all people should have freedom of conscience. He put his liberal beliefs into practice when settling Providence, remaining on friendly terms with the local Narragansett Native Americans after purchasing from them the land for a bold experiment in tolerance and peaceful coexistence.

Williams' principles would not last long. As Providence and Newport grew and merged into a single colony, competition and conflict with area tribes sparked several wars, leading to the decimation of the Wampanoag, Pequot, Narragansett, and Nipmuck peoples. Rhode Island was also a prolific slave trader and its merchants would control much of that industry in the years after the Revolutionary War (Rhode Island, by the way, was the first colony to formally declare independence from England, in May 1776).

The city of Pawtucket birthed the American industrial revolution with the establishment of the water-powered Slater Mill in 1790. Industrialism impacted the character of Providence and surrounds, particularly along the Blackstone River, creating urban density. As with many small East Coast cities, these urban areas went into a precipitous decline in the 1940s and '50s as manufacturing industries (textiles and costume jewelry) faltered. In the 1960s, preservation efforts salvaged the historic architectural framework of Providence and Newport. The former has emerged as a lively place with a dynamic economy and the latter, equally lively, survives as a museum city.

The Culture

Rhode Island lacks clear stereotypes with which one might succinctly describe its culture. A blue-collar tradition remains, with unionized electricians and plenty of fisher-men hunting for cod and lobster. But their accents, while similar to Boston's, aren't as, ahem, wicked obvious. You'll also find a military community (Newport is home to a naval base), plenty of professionals raising rents in Providence, and the smart aura of Brown.

One way that Rhode Island, in particular Providence, stands out from other New England states is its unusually large Portuguese-American community. Otherwise, you'll find a lot of people scratching their heads over how exactly they are distinct from their neighbors in Southeastern Massachusetts and even more people glad to live in a more interesting state than Connecticut, widely considered to be supremely dull.

Land & Climate

There isn't all that much land. What little exists is relatively flat (the highest point in the State is Jerimoth Hill, which rises in its unimpressive way to 812ft). The main landmass is divided by the Narragansett Bay. In this bay and in the Rhode Island Sound are more than 30 islands, the largest ones serviced by a network of ferries and bridges.

Like Massachusetts and Connecticut, Rhode Island experiences muggy, hot summers. The state enjoys a coastal climate, which partially mitigates summertime heat in places near the ocean. In cooler months, Rhode Island's southern locale makes it warmer than the northern states. Thus the autumn leaves turn a few weeks later than in Vermont.

Parks & Wildlife

Tiny Rhode Island hasn't the space to contain very many parks, and those that exist aren't particularly large. Contact the **Rhode Island Division of Parks & Recreation** (☎ 401-222-2321; www .riparks.com) for more information.

The Rhode Island Division of Parks & Recreation manages a collection of beaches (see p311) facing the Atlantic Ocean. The department has also developed a series of scenic bicycle trails that crisscross the state, often following old rail lines. These trails are free of automobile traffic. For route information and maps visit the website of the **Rhode Island Department of Transportation** (www.dot.state.ri.us/ WebTran/bikeri.html).

Block Island, dubbed 'one of the last great places in the Western Hemisphere' by the Nature Conservancy, enjoys excellent bird sanctuaries and wildlife preserves. Here, about

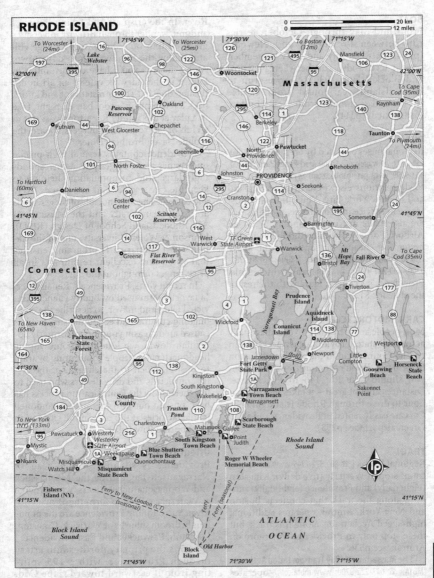

25 miles of trails wind past undisturbed brush, wildflowers and nesting birds.

Getting There & Around

By American standards, Providence has excellent transportation options. Elsewhere in the state, things can be tricky unless you have your own wheels.

AIR

The state's major airport, TF Green State Airport (p293) in Warwick, is a 20-minute drive from downtown Providence and a 45-minute drive from Newport. Tiny as Rhode Island is, you can save time by flying to Block Island from the Westerly State Airport (p310) rather than taking a ferry.

BOAT

From mid-May through October, ferries run between Providence and Newport (p294). Between July and early September, season ferries also run between Newport and Block Island (p305). Ferries run to Block Island year-round from Galilee (p310) and seasonally from New London, Connecticut (p311).

BUS

Regional buses operated by **Greyhound** (☎ 800-231-2222; www.greyhound.com) and **Peter Pan** (☎ 800-343-9999; www.peterpanbus.com) will connect you to destinations elsewhere in New England and to New York City. You'll find the most frequent service in Providence, though stops are also made in Newport and at TF Green Airport. For travel within Rhode Island, the better and cheaper bus option is the **Rhode Island Public Transit Authority** ((RIPTA; ☎ 401-781-9400, 800-221-3797; www.ripta.com), which links Providence's Kennedy Plaza with the rest of the state for $1.25.

CAR & MOTORCYCLE

Most people arrive by car. I-95 cuts diagonally across the state, providing easy access from coastal Connecticut to the south and Boston to the north. If you're coming from Worcester, you should take Rte 146 to Providence. Distances are not great – it takes less than an hour to drive through Rhode Island on I-95. Cars are easily rented in Providence and at TF Green airport (see p293).

TRAIN

Regional **Amtrak** (☎ 800-872-7245; www.amtrak.com) trains stop in Westerly (five daily), Kingston (eight daily) and Providence (eight daily) running along the track that connects Boston and New York. Amtrak operates additional high-speed Acela trains along this track, but these stop only in Providence. For more on Amtrak, see p536.

The **Massachusetts Bay Transportation Authority** (MBTA; ☎ 617-222-3200; www.mbta.com) operates an inexpensive commuter train between Providence and Boston (p294).

PROVIDENCE

pop 175,000

Rhode Island's capital city, Providence presents its visitors with some of the finest urban strolling this side of the Connecticut River. In the crisp air and falling leaves of autumn, wander through Brown University's green campus on 18th-century College Hill and follow the Riverwalk into downtown. Along the way you'll have opportunities to lounge in the sidewalk café of an art-house theater, dine in a stellar restaurant and knock back a few pints in a cool bar. At night, take in a play at the Trinity Repertory, pass out in a club or eat some 3am burgers aboard the mobile Haven Brothers Diner.

Providence contains several high-profile universities and colleges plus a correspondingly large student population, helping to keep the city's social and arts scenes lively and current. The most notable of these schools are Brown University and the Museum of Art, Rhode Island School of Design (RISD). Johnson & Wales University, one of the nation's best culinary arts programs, ensures that you'll find excellent restaurants in all price ranges throughout the city.

In recent years, Providence's 'Renaissance' (a favorite term used by Buddy Cianci, convicted felon and mayor, to describe the city's ongoing cultural and economic success) has caused an increasing number of formerly bohemian downtown lofts to become yuppie headquarters for people commuting by train to Boston, much to the chagrin of the artists, musicians and drug dealers who used to live there. Now the gentrification process has been pushed out into the many abandoned textile factories at the edge of the city and in neighboring Pawtucket.

Orientation

Providence is situated at the head of Narragansett Bay astride the Moshassuck and Woonasquatucket Rivers, which merge at Waterplace Park to form the Providence River. Surrounding Providence are the populous bedroom suburbs of Warwick, Cranston, Johnston, Pawtucket and East Providence.

I-95 is the primary north–south artery through Providence, with I-195 splitting from it eastward toward Cape Cod. Take exit 22 (Downtown) from I-95 or the Wickenden St exit from I-195 to reach Kennedy Plaza and the Amtrak train station. For the Italian neighborhood and restaurant district of Federal Hill, take exit 21 of I-95 (Atwells Ave/Broadway).

Kennedy Plaza, with the Providence Biltmore hotel and City Hall on its southwestern

PROVIDENCE

0 — 500 m
0 — 0.3 miles

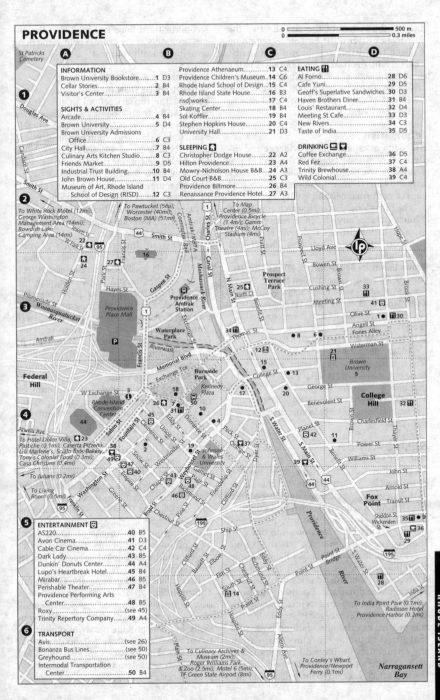

side, is the center of the city. East of the Providence River is the East Side, containing College Hill, RISD and Brown University. Federal Hill, the Italian neighborhood to the west, has dozens of good restaurants and pastry shops along its main axis, Atwells Ave. The heart of the city is compact and easy to explore on foot.

Information

The daily newspaper for Providence and indeed all of Rhode Island is the *Providence Journal* (www.projo.com). 'Lifebeat,' a daily arts and entertainment section, includes listings of performances and events.

The Providence *Phoenix*, which appears on Thursday, is the city's free alternative weekly, with nightclub listings and reviews. Find it in record stores and cafés on Thayer and Wickenden Sts.

Brown University Bookstore (☎ 401-863-3168; 244 Thayer St; ☽ 9am–6pm Mon-Fri, 10am–6pm Sat, 11am–5pm Sun) Providence's most comprehensive bookstore.

Cellar Stories (☎ 401-521-2665; 111 Mathewson St; ☽ 10am–6pm Mon-Sat) Tall dusty shelves crammed full of used volumes.

Map Center (☎ 401-421-2184; 671 N Main St; ☽ 9:30am–5:30pm Mon-Fri, 9:30am–1:30pm Sat) If you want more maps than the visitor's center can provide (some local, some esoteric) as well as a small selection of guidebooks, try this center.

Visitor's Center (☎ 401-751-1177; 1 Sabin St; ☽ 9am–5pm Mon-Sat) Stop by for maps and glossy print propaganda.

Sights & Activities

THE ARCADE

Designed in 1828, the **Arcade** (☎ 401-598-1199; 65 Weybosset St; ☽ 10am–5pm Mon-Fri, 11am–4pm Sat; ⬇), America's first enclosed shopping center, uses a form developed in Paris and London. Greek Revival in design, the airy, tile-floored passage, its marble steps worn into bows by the passage of bygone feet, has shops and cafés on three floors. It looks like a temple from the outside, while inside it is much like a street – a straight corridor leads to a second entry on Washington St. Bounding the sides of this corridor are ornamented, parallel facades three stories tall, today containing the inexpensive eateries and clothing boutiques that attract a bustling lunchtime crowd from the surrounding business district. Roofed in glass, the interior is awash in natural light. For the best effect, hike up to the galleries on the second or third floor and look over the old cast-iron rails at the crowds below, the floor creaking beneath your feet.

MUSEUM OF ART, RHODE ISLAND SCHOOL OF DESIGN (RISD)

Perhaps the top art school in the United States, **RISD** (☎ 401-454-6300; www.risd.edu) leaves an imprint on Providence that is easily felt. From public statuary to film performances to indecipherable screen-printed flyers stapled to College Hill telephone poles, creativity oozes palatably from it across the small cityscape. Though some experience the pleasure of RISD by putting together portfolios that will eventually be rejected by the admissions committee, others earn style points simply by visiting the school's many galleries.

The extraordinary collections at their **museum** (☎ 401-454-6500; www.risd.edu/museum .cfm; 224 Benefit St; adult/child/student/senior $8/2/3/5; ☽ 10am–5pm Wed, Thu, Sat & Sun, 10am–8pm Fri; ⬇ ⬇) include 19th-century French paintings; classical Greek, Roman and Etruscan art; medieval and Renaissance works; and examples of 19th- and 20th-century American painting, furniture and decorative arts. Kids love staring at the mummy, and older-types will be impressed to see the works of Manet, Matisse and Sargent. The museum stays open until 9pm on the third Thursday of the month; on those days, admission is free after 5pm. It's also free the last Saturday of the month and Sundays from 10am to 1pm.

RISD maintains several fine galleries. **Sol Koffler** (☎ 401-454-6141; 169 Weybosset St; admission free; ☽ noon–8pm; ⬇) serves as the main exhibition space for graduate students, where you can see work in a range of media. Hours vary on the weekend. Another design showcase is **risd|works** (☎ 401-277-4949; www.risdworks .com; 10 Westminster St; ☽ 10am–6pm Mon-Sat), a shop displaying an assortment of goods (jewelry, photographic prints, flatware, coffee tables, children's books) made by faculty and alumni.

If you like nice kitchens, the **Culinary Arts Kitchen Studio,** (☎ 401-454-6201; www.risd.edu/ce_cu linary.cfm; Metcalf Refectory, Angell St; single day course $65) offers classes that will not only refine your skills, but also provide plenty of opportunities to shove freshly made delights down your esophagus. These courses are held only a few times each semester, and you should enroll prior to class.

RHODE ISLAND

A few times a year (several weeks in May and shortly before Christmas), RISD hosts massive art shows where you can buy paintings, ceramics, household goods and more designed by students and other RISD affiliates. Consult RISD's website for times and locations.

BROWN UNIVERSITY

Dominating the crest of the College Hill neighborhood on the East Side, the campus of **Brown University** (☎ 401-863-2378; www.brown .edu) exudes Ivy League charm. **University Hall**, a 1770 brick edifice used as a barracks during the Revolutionary War, sits at its center. To explore the campus, start at the wrought-iron gates opening from the top of College St and make your way across the green toward Thayer St.

Free tours of the campus leave five times daily on weekdays, and on Saturday morning from mid-September to mid-November, beginning from the **Brown University Admissions Office** (Corliss Brackett House, 45 Prospect St).

RHODE ISLAND STATE HOUSE

Designed by McKim, Mead and White in 1904, the **Rhode Island State House** (☎ 401-222-2357; Smith St; admission free; ⏰ 8:30am-4:30pm Mon-Fri; ♿) rises above the Providence skyline, easily visible from the highways that pass through the city. Modeled in part on St Peter's Basilica in Vatican City, this very white building not only has the world's fourth-largest self-supporting marble dome, it also houses one of Gilbert Stuart's portraits of George Washington, which you might want to compare to a dollar bill from your wallet. Inside the public halls are the battle flags of Rhode Island military units and a curious Civil War cannon, which sat here for a century loaded and ready to shoot until someone thought to check whether it was disarmed.

The giant half-naked guy standing on top of the dome is *The Independent Man*, continuously struck by lightning.

COLLEGE HILL

East of the Providence River, College Hill, headquarters of Brown University and RISD, contains a dense and large population of wood-framed houses, largely from the 18th-century. Among the (relatively) quiet tree-lined streets of this residential neighborhood, you'll find the two campuses and a lot of folks

walking around with blue hair, tweed jackets or thick glasses. The cheap eateries and used record stores that nourish the college-types are located on **Thayer St**, College Hill's main commercial drag, which is also a second home to teenage loiterers from the suburbs and, in the evenings, a motorcycle gang. For details of the architecture in this area, check out the boxed text on below.

PROVIDENCE ARCHITECTURE

Come to Providence and you'll find an urban assemblage of unsurpassable architectural merit – at least in the States. It's the only American city to have its *entire* downtown listed on the National Registry of Historic Places. The beaux-arts **City Hall** (25 Dorrance St) makes an imposing centerpiece to Kennedy Plaza, and the stately white dome of the **Rhode Island State House** (left) remains visible from many corners of the city. The **Arcade** (opposite) is modeled after Parisian antecedents. These impressive buildings, along with the art deco **Industrial Trust building** (Fleet bldg; 55 Exchange Pl) – note the third story friezes of industrial progress on the Westminster Street facade – are only a few of many showcase buildings. The more ordinary 19th-century brick structures that fill in the space between their more famously designed neighbors work together to create an extraordinary landscape of harmonious scale, beauty and craftsmanship.

Immediately east of downtown, you'll find College Hill, where you can see the city's colonial history reflected in the multihued 18th-century houses that line **Benefit Street** on the East Side. These are, for the most part, private homes, but many are open for tours one weekend in mid-June during the annual **Festival of Historic Homes** (p289). Benefit St is a fitting symbol of the Providence renaissance, rescued by local preservationists in the 1960s from misguided urban-renewal efforts that would have destroyed it. Its treasures range from the 1708 **Stephen Hopkins House** (☎ 401-421-0694; 15 Hopkins St; donations accepted; ⏰ 1-4pm Wed-Sat May-Oct, otherwise by appt), named for the ten-time governor and Declaration of Independence signer, to the clean Greek Revival lines of William Strickland's 1838 **Providence Athenaeum** (☎ 401-421-6970; www.providenceathenaeum.org; 251 Benefit St; admission free; ⏰ 9am-7pm Mon-Thu, 9am-5pm Fri & Sat, 1-5pm Sun, shorter hrs Jun-Labor Day). This is a library of the old school, with plaster busts and oil paintings filling in spaces not occupied by books. Edgar Allen Poe used to court ladies here.

Also on College Hill, the brick **John Brown House** (☎ 401-273-7507; www.rihs.org; 52 Power St; adult/child/senior & student $8/4/6; ☷ tours begin at 1:30 & 3pm Tue-Fri, 10:30am noon 1:30pm & 3pm Sat Apr-Dec), called the 'most magnificent and elegant mansion that I have ever seen on this continent' by John Quincy Adams, was built in 1786.

FEDERAL HILL

Among the most colorful of Providence's neighborhoods is fervently Italian Federal Hill (when Tony Soprano's crew needed a special job done, they came here to enlist the aid of a geriatric, blind hit man). It's a great place to wander, taking in the aromas of sausages, peppers and garlic from neighborhood groceries such as **Tony's Colonial Food** (☎ 401-621-8675; 311 Atwells Ave). Many of Providence's best restaurants are on Atwells Ave, a street you can easily identify by looking for a large, floodlit pineapple suspended from a concrete arch spanning the traffic below.

FOX POINT

Immediately south of College Hill is Fox Point, the waterfront neighborhood where the city's substantial Portuguese population resides. Though gentrification has taken place with influxes of Brown University professors and students and artists from RISD, you can still find an old-world style grocery like the **Friends Market** (☎ 401-861-0345; 126 Brook St) tucked in among the trendy coffeehouses, salons and galleries. Most activity in Fox Point centers on Wickenden St with its restaurants, art supply store, incredible eyeglass shop (Gregory's Optical) and several home-furnishing boutiques.

CULINARY ARCHIVES & MUSEUM

Johnson & Wales' oddity of a **museum** (☎ 401-598-2805; www.culinary.org; 315 Harborside Blvd; adult/child/student $7/2/3; ☷ 10am-5pm Mon-Sat; **P** &) displays about 300,000 objects connected in some way to the culinary arts. Ogle a cookbook collection dating back to the 15th century, resist fingering presidential cutlery and peruse over 4000 menus from around the world.

ROGER WILLIAMS PARK & ZOO

In 1871, Betsey Williams, great-great-great-granddaughter of the founder of Providence, donated her farm to the city as a public park.

Today this 430-acre expanse of greenery, only a short drive south of Providence, includes lakes and ponds, forest copses and broad lawns, picnic grounds, a **Planetarium and Museum of Natural History** (☎ 401-785-9457; admission $4; ☷ 10am-5pm), an operating **Victorian Carousel** (ride $1.25; ☷ 10am-4pm), greenhouses and Williams' cottage.

Perhaps the park's most significant attraction is the **Roger Williams Park & Zoo** (☎ 401-785-3510; www.rogerwilliamsparkzoo.org; 1000 Elmwood Ave; adult/senior & child over 3 $12/6; ☷ 9am-5pm, longer hrs summer, shorter hrs winter; **P** & &). The zoo is home to more than 600 animals (polar bear, giraffes, lemurs) and performs some interesting conservation work, such as a study of the endangered American burying beetle. This little fellow eats dead animals and needs their carcasses to store his brood in. To reach the park, go south from Providence on I-95 to exit 17 (Elmwood Ave). If you are heading north from Connecticut or from the Rhode Island beaches, take exit 16.

PROVIDENCE CHILDREN'S MUSEUM

If you like to watch younger kids freak out, this well-designed, hands-on **museum** (☎ 401-273-5437; www.childrenmuseum.org; 100 South St; admission $6.50; ☷ 9am-6pm Tue-Sun, daily Apr–Labor Day; **P** & &) genuinely delights most of its guests. Try walking into a giant kaleidoscope, doing experiments with water fountains, pretending to be a veterinarian or playing with marionettes made by some renowned puppeteers. It's intended for kids aged one to 11.

PARKS

The landscaped cobblestone paths of the **Riverwalk** lead along the Woonasquatucket River to **Waterplace Park's** (Memorial Blvd) central pool and fountain, overlooked by a stepped amphitheater where outdoor artists perform in warm weather. Take a look at the historical maps and photos mounted on the walls of the walkway beneath Memorial Blvd. Waterplace Park also serves as a nucleus for WaterFire (p289).

A great spot from which to get an overview of the city, **Prospect Terrace Park** is a small pocket of green space off Congdon St on the East Side. In warm weather, you'll find students throwing Frisbees, office workers picnicking and, if you arrive at the transitional point

(Continued on page 289)

EXPLORING NEW ENGLAND

Come to New England for action and adventure, to mount seemingly insurmountable peaks and to swoosh down snow-covered slopes, to feel the ocean breeze and taste the salty air. Come to New England to tantalize your tastebuds, for seafood so succulent and syrup so sweet that only grunts of satisfaction do descriptive justice. Come for history and high culture, to ponder the creations of artists and visionaries, and to see the ways in which they are changing the world.

Mountains

New England undulates with the rolling hills and rocky peaks of the ancient Appalachian Mountains, from the beautiful birch-covered Berkshires in Western Massachusetts, to the lush Green Mountains in Vermont, to the towering White Mountains that stretch across New Hampshire and Maine.

1 Mt Washington, New Hampshire
At 6288ft, this is New England's highest peak. To reach the top, choose between three challenging hiking trails (p458), the auto road (p457) or the old-fashioned cog railway (p456). From the top, you'll enjoy high winds and incredible vistas.

2 Stowe, Vermont
This winter wonderland (p395) will get your heart racing with miles of downhill slopes and the country's most extensive network of cross-country tracks. If you don't want to go that fast, strap on a pair of snowshoes and set out on the upper trail system, which boasts clean air and magnificent views.

3 Acadia National Park, Maine
Acadia National Park (p508) is where the mountains meet the sea. Take tea at Jordan Pond House (p509) or catch the sunrise from the summit of Cadillac Mountain (p508).

4 Appalachian Trail
The storied AT passes through five New England states and 730 miles, giving ample opportunities for hikers to hop on and tackle a piece of it, even if they are not up for the thrill of thru-hiking. See p24 for suggestions.

5 Mt Greylock, Massachusetts
The highest mountain in Massachusetts (p272) boasts some 45 miles of hiking trails, a valley filled with age-old spruce trees, several waterfalls and a summit overlooking five states.

6 Litchfield Hills, Connecticut
Giving way to serious mountains further north, the Litchfield Hills (p348) are blanketed with forests, splashed with lakes and dotted with quiet villages. A plethora of picture-perfect back roads and a lack of tourists make it ideal for a country drive.

7 Mt Monadnock, New Hampshire
The 'mountain that stands alone' (p427) towers over the flats of southern New Hampshire, offering miles of well-marked trails for hiking or cross-country skiing and spectacular vistas in all directions.

Sea

Nearly 5000 miles of coastline means that New Englanders are into water sports. Souls that long for the sea will surely be satisfied – opportunities for fishing, swimming, surfing, sailing and sunbathing are unlimited. So pack your sunglasses and your sunscreen and settle in for some quality time on the open ocean.

❶ Windjammer Sailing, Maine
Sail around Penobscot Bay on a beautiful schooner, powered only by the wind in the sails. Camden, Maine (p497) is the center of windjammer country; cruises also depart from Rockland (p495).

❷ Cape Cod National Seashore
The eastern shoreline of Cape Cod – all 42 sq miles of dunes, beach and sky – is protected from development, providing endless opportunities for sunning, swimming, biking and bird-watching (p196).

❸ Whale-watching
Nothing matches the thrill of spotting a breeching humpback or watching a pod of dolphins play in the boat's wake. Educational and informative whale-watching cruises are offered from Boston (p84), Plymouth (p166), Provincetown (p205) and Gloucester (p154).

❹ Block Island, Rhode Island
Teeming with birds and beachcombers, this windswept island (p306) is small enough to get around by bicycle, but large enough that you can find an empty stretch of sand any time of year.

Food

A pile of pancakes drenched in maple syrup; fresh farm produce and sharp cheddar cheese; lobsters, oysters and shellfish straight from the sea; exotic dishes with influences from Portugal, Italy or Asia: such are some of the epicurean delights that foodies will find in New England.

❶ Maine Lobster

Nowhere is more closely associated with a crustacean than Maine. The mighty lobster was once so plentiful it was fed to prisoners and used for fertilizer; now the state symbol is deservedly esteemed as a delicacy (p464).

❷ Boston's South End

At the other end of the spectrum, Boston's trendiest neighborhood (p109) is packed with restaurants and bars, outdoing each other with hip, contemporary flair and fabulous fusion cuisine.

❸ Maple Syrup, Vermont

It takes almost 40 gallons of sap to produce a quart of maple syrup, which explains why it tastes so sinfully sweet. Come to Vermont in the cold of March or April to see how it's done (p359).

❹ Boston's North End

Boston's oldest neighborhood (p106) evokes the Old World, its narrow cobblestone streets lined with restaurants, pastry shops and cafés, emitting sounds of Italian and scents of olive oil and oregano.

❺ Wellfleet Oysters, Cape Cod

Few foods are as celebrated as this briny bivalve, which hails from Cape Cod (p197). With a squirt of lemon and a dash of cocktail sauce, they slide down smooth and sexy. And yes, of course oysters are an aphrodisiac!

❻ Vermont Cheese

In Vermont, always known for its high-quality dairy products, farmers have recently turned their attention to producing interesting artisanal cheeses, in addition to old-fashioned favorites like sharp cheddar and Colby (p359).

❼ Ben & Jerry's Ice Cream, Vermont

I scream, you scream, we all scream for Chubby Hubby, Chunky Monkey, Cherry Garcia and Phish Food. Get yours straight from the source in Waterbury, Vermont (p401).

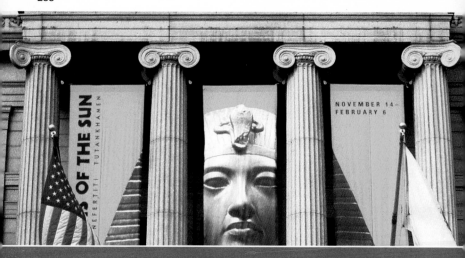

Art

New England has an eye for art. Generations of sketchers, painters and sculptors have been inspired by the sun-tinged sky hanging over the sea, the boats bobbing at their moors in the harbor, the majesty of the ancient mountains covered in fall foliage or snow white, and the historic events that transpired here.

❶ Boston, Massachusetts
New England's cultural capital is home to two world-class museums – the Museum of Fine Arts (p88) and the Institute of Contemporary Arts (p85) – as well as a thriving community of artists in the Seaport District (p84), South Boston (p86) and Jamaica Plain (p89).

❷ DeCordova Museum & Sculpture Park, Massachusetts
This wonderful, whimsical place (p140) in Lincoln has lovely, landscaped grounds studded with sculptures by national and local artists. It often launches thematic shows, tying together its interior art and outdoor sculpture.

❸ Provincetown Art Association & Museum, Massachusetts
Celebrating the town's rich artistic heritage and vibrant contemporary scene, this museum (p204) is small but stellar. The collection includes works by more than 500 artists who were, at some point or another, local.

❹ Mass MoCA
One of the few museums that is measured not in square feet but in acres. Occupying a former electrical power plant in North Adams, this cutting-edge exhibition space (p271) also hosts world music, film and avant-garde dance and music performances.

(Continued from page 280)

between day and the arrival of night, sunsets. The monumental statue facing the city is that of Providence founder Roger Williams, whose remains were moved to this site in 1939.

BIKING

Starting at India Point Park on the Narragansett Bay waterfront in Providence, the scenic **East Bay Bicycle Path** winds its way for 14.5 miles south along a former railroad track. The mostly flat, paved path follows the shoreline to the pretty seaport of Bristol. State parks along the route make good spots for picnics.

Unfortunately there is no central place to rent a bike. The closest shop is **Providence Bicycle** (☎ 401-331-6610; 725 Branch Ave; per day $20; ⏰ from 9:30am Sun-Fri). Call for directions.

ICE-SKATING

The outdoor **Skating Center** (☎ 401-331-5544; www.providenceskating.com; 2 Kennedy Plaza; adult/child $6/3, skate rental $4; ⏰ 10am-10pm Mon-Fri, 11am-10pm Sat & Sun mid-Nov–mid-Mar; ⏰) occupies prime downtown real estate. While the Biltmore and Fleet Building provide a nice architectural backdrop, you might have to skate to some seriously loud pop songs. College students skate for three bucks on Wednesday nights.

Festivals & Events

Festival of Historic Homes (☎ 401-831-7440; www.ppsri.org) Tour some of the East Side's fabulous 18th-century homes during this annual shindig in June.
Rhode Island International Film Festival (☎ 401-861-4445; www.film-festival.org) For six days in mid-August, cool-kids from RISD and beyond screen hundreds of independent shorts and feature-length films.

Gallery Night (☎ 401-490-2042; www.gallerynight.info) Held every third Thursday of the month from March to November from 5pm to 9pm. Twenty-five galleries around the city open their doors for free viewings.

Sleeping

Providence, devoid of hostels, can be hard on your wallet. The summer months represent peak season, while the big universities' parents' weekends and graduations fill rooms up to a year in advance.

BUDGET

Camping areas are outside the city, but since Rhode Island is small, they aren't all that far away. The two spots below are a half-hour's drive from Providence.

George Washington Management Area (☎ 401-568-2248; US Hwy 44; residents/out-of-staters sites $14/20, shelter $35; ⏰ mid-April–early Oct) Enjoy ample-sized and well-spaced tent and RV sites (plus two shelters) set in a fine wooded area. A small sandy beach on the freshwater Bowdish Reservoir provides a decent swim, though the lifeguard protected area is the size of a pot holder. Best to sneak off. Find the grounds 2 miles east of the Connecticut state line in West Glocester (15 miles and 30 minutes west of Providence).

Bowdish Lake Camping Area (☎ 401-568-8890; www.bowdishlake.com; US Hwy 44; tent sites $25-40; ⏰ May–mid-Oct) If the state-operated campground is full, try this much larger neighboring private campground, which also has a beach on the lake. The 450 sites range in price, depending upon location and facilities. Wooded sites cost more then a tent pitch in a common field.

As usual, inexpensive motels lurk on the outskirts of town near interstate exits, about 5 miles from the city center. Ugly Warwick,

---

WATERFIRE

Particularly during summer, much of downtown Providence transforms into a carnivalesque festival thanks to an exceedingly popular public art installation called **WaterFire** (☎ 401-272-3111; www.waterfire.com). At this event, 100 flaming braziers anchored into the city's rivers illuminate the water, viewed by thousands of pedestrians strolling on bridges and finely landscaped riverside parks. All the gazing and making out is accompanied by live (and canned) music, outdoor stages hosting theatrical performances, public ballroom dancing (you can join in) and a few ostentatious gondolas that drift by the pyres. Even cynical readers will have to admit the spectacle is both charming and good-looking, though all that overt romance has been known to arch a few eyebrows.

WaterFire occurs about 15 times a year from May to October and begins at sunset. Occasionally there's a lighting around Christmas or the New Year.

COFFEE MILK & CABINETS

In 1993, two popular beverages battled each other for the honor of becoming Rhode Island's official state drink: coffee milk and Del's frozen lemonade.

Though Del's tastes great, no one really doubted that coffee milk would come out on top. Rhode Island kids have guzzled this mixture of coffee syrup and milk since before the Great Depression. To try it, head to a grocery store, pick up a bottle and go to town.

While we've got your attention, please note this crucially important distinction: in Rhode Island, a milkshake is traditionally syrup and milk blended together without ice cream. Rhode Islanders call the version with ice cream a 'cabinet' or 'frappe.' (The term 'cabinet' is pretty much specific to Rhode Island, while 'frappe' gets thrown around by folks as far away as Boston.)

---

a town of strip malls to the south, contains many chains, including **Motel 6** (☎ 401-467-9800; www.motel6.com; 20 Jefferson Blvd; d $70-80; P). For an old-school experience, try taking a plain wood-paneled room in the **White Rock Motel** (☎ 401-568-4219; www.whiterockmotel.com; 750 Putnam Pike, US Hwy 44, Glocester; d $60), built in 1949. It's family run and on a stretch of a state highway that runs through farm country 13 miles west of Providence.

MIDRANGE

Radisson Hotel Providence Harbor (☎ 401-272-5577; www.radisson.com; 220 India St; r $129-159; P 💻) Hard to find, and separated from the rest of the city by I-195, the south side of the hotel affords views over India Point Park and the water. The rooms on the north look directly at the freeway. All rooms are comfortable, though the decorator muffed up the furniture-bedding combinations.

Mowry-Nicholson House B&B (☎ 401-351-6111; www.providence-inn.com; 57 Brownell St; r Mon-Fri $129, Sat & Sun $159; P) This B&B features a large porch that wraps around a bright blue Victorian home with simple antique furniture, handmade quilts and newly finished hardwood floors. Check-in is at Christopher Dodge House.

Christopher Dodge House (☎ 401-351-6111; www .providence-inn.com; 11 W Park St; r Mon-Fri $130-150, Sat & Sun $160-180; P) Staid on the outside and with impressive 11ft ceilings inside, rooms in this B&B, have fireplaces or stoves (burning gas, not wood) and biggish windows.

Old Court B&B (☎ 401-751-2002; www.oldcourt .com; 144 Benefit St; r Mon-Fri $155, Sat & Sun $185) Well-positioned among the historic buildings of College Hill, this three-story, 1863 Italianate home has worn wooden floors, old fireplaces and stacks of charm. Enjoy excellent wallpaper, good jam at breakfast and occasional winter discounts.

Hilton Providence (☎ 401-831-3900; www.hilton .com; 21 Atwells Ave; r $150-200; P 💻 🔊 ♿) While this bleak 13-story tower adjoins the concrete infrastructural spaghetti of I-95 (take exit 21), its 274 business-oriented rooms are conveniently located between downtown and Federal Hill. Generic, comfortable rooms were recently renovated.

Hotel Dolce Villa (☎ 401-383-7031; www.dolcevilla ri.com; 63 DePasquale Sq; suite $159-199; P 💻 ♿) Three of this hotel's 15 suites have balconies perched directly over Federal Hill's DePasquale Sq, a lively plaza covered with terrace seating for nearby restaurants. Slick, contemporary rooms overwhelm visitors with whiteness – everything from bedding to furniture to the tile floors gleams in a bright, colorless void. Gay friendly and full kitchens.

Providence Biltmore (☎ 401-421-0700, 800-294-7709; www.providencebiltmore.com; 11 Dorrance St; r $179-209; P 💻 ♿) The granddaddy of Providence's hotels, the Biltmore dates to the 1920s. The lobby, both intimate and regal, nicely combines dark wood, twisting staircases and chandeliers, while well-appointed rooms stretch many stories above the old city. Ask for a room on a high floor.

TOP END

Renaissance Providence Hotel (☎ 401-276-0010; www.renaissanceprovidence.com; 5 Avenue of the Arts; r $239-259; P ♿) Built as a Masonic temple in 1929, this monster stood empty for 77 years before it opened in 2007 as a hotel. Some rooms overlook the State House (through small windows) and are decorated in forceful colors that attempt, with limited success, to evoke Masonic traditions. The graffiti artist who once tagged the vacant building was hired to do his thing to an over-the-top 'Masonic' hotel bar.

Eating

Both RISD and Johnson & Wales University have top-notch culinary programs that annually turn out creative new chefs who liven up the city's restaurant scene. The large student population on the East Side assures that plenty of good, inexpensive places exist around College Hill and Fox Point. To experience old Providence, head over to the restaurant district along Atwells Ave in Federal Hill.

In addition to the listings below, check out the Red Fez (p292), AS220 (p292) and Cable Car Cinema (p293). For a quick and mediocre lunch, don't forget the Arcade (p278).

BUDGET

Scialo Bros Bakery (☎ 401-421-0986; 257 Atwells Ave; sweets $1-3; ☖ 7:30am-7pm Mon-Thu & Sat, 7:30am-8pm Fri, 7:30am-5pm Sun) Since 1916, the brick ovens at this relic have turned out top-notch butterballs, *torrone* (a nougat and almond combo), amaretti and dozens of other kinds of Italian cookies and pastries. Avoid the mediocre cannoli.

Cafe Yuni (☎ 401-272-3585; 10 Traverse St; 2-piece nigiri $3-5; ☖ noon-10pm Mon-Fri, 12:30-9:30pm Sat) Serving substantial pieces of fish, Cafe Yuni draws a loyal following with its fresh sushi and polite, charming service. The small restaurant also serves udon noodles, stir-fries and *japachae* (stir-fried potato noodles with vegetables).

Pastiche (☎ 401-861-5190; 92 Spruce St; cake $3-6; ☖ 8:30am-11pm Tue-Thu, 8:30am-11:30pm Fri & Sat, 10am-10pm Sun) Awash in soothing colors and warmed by a fire in winter, Pastiche offers a seasonal dessert menu. In summer, you might try the apricot almond chiffon cake, or pick up a favorite such as mascarpone tortes or chocolate layer cake.

Louis' Restaurant (☎ 401-861-5225; 286 Brook St; breakfast $3-7; ☖ from 7am; ☖) Wake up early to watch bleary-eyed students and carpenters eat strawberry banana pancakes and drink drip coffee at their favorite greasy spoon long before the rest of College Hill shows signs of life. The place is loaded with bad art (crayon on paper menus) and the faded pictures of numerous regulars.

Geoff's Superlative Sandwiches (☎ 401-751-9214; 235 Thayer St; sandwiches $4-7; ☖ from 11am; ☑) A longtime favorite with students and junior faculty, Geoff's offers a massive menu of creative sandwiches, including meatless reuben (melted swiss, spinach, carrots, sauerkraut), pastrami, kosher meat and lots of things with celery salt. Find scant seating, checked linoleum floor, and a big barrel of pickles.

Haven Brothers Diner (Washington St; meals $5-10; ☖ 5pm-3am) Parked next to City Hall, this diner sits on the back of a truck that has rolled into the same spot every evening for decades. Climb up a rickety ladder to get hamburgers, hot dogs, fries, cabinets (milkshake with ice-cream), lobster salad and little else. Everyone who has lived in Providence for a year or more is likely to have eaten here at least once.

Caserta Pizzeria (☎ 401-621-3618; 121 Spruce St; large pizza $11-16; ☖ 9:30am-10:30pm Tue-Thu & Sun, 9:30am-11:30pm Fri & Sat; ☖) This Federal Hill icon serves some of the best Neapolitan pizza you'll taste. For many, dining at one of its cheap Formica tables is reason enough to visit Rhode Island. It's so popular with local Italian Americans that you need to order several days in advance if you want a pie on Christmas Eve. Cash only.

MIDRANGE

Meeting St Café (☎ 401-273-1066; 220 Meeting St; sandwiches $8-12, meals $12-15; ☖ 8am-11pm; ☑) For enormous sandwiches and lox-oriented breakfasts, head to this College Hill delicatessen. Dinner equals vegetarian lasagna, shish kabobs or good burgers. Enormous oatmeal cookies, voted best in Rhode Island by several polls, measure about 10in diameter.

Taste of India (☎ 401-421-4355; 230 Wickenden St; meals $10-22; ☖ 11:30am-2:30pm & 5-10pm Mon-Sat, noon-9pm Sun; ☑) The bustling lunch crowd at this Indian joint comes for a tasty buffet ($7), curries and a top-notch mango *lassi* (yoghurt drink) made with strong rose water. The room contains cheap carpets, plastic plants and nooks for privacy.

Julian's (☎ 401-861-1770; 318 Broadway; brunch $6-12, meals $15-25; ☖ 9am-1am; ☖ ☑) A messy combination of neon, exposed brick and ductwork, come here for tattooed cooks preparing a stellar brunch (served until 5pm) with changing blackboard specials (goat cheese, caper, tomato and mushroom hash) along with several benedicts and lots of vegan options. The dinner menu offers seared yellowfin, small sides and alcohol.

TOP END

Casa Christine (☎ 401-453-6255; 145 Spruce St; meals $24-30; ☖ 11:30am-1:45pm & 5-7:30pm Tue-Fri, 3:45-7:30pm Sat) Locals in the know find their way

RHODE ISLAND

to this family-run dining room on a drab backstreet near Caserta Pizzeria (p291) to fill up on heaps of home-cooked veal, chicken and fish. Enjoy the hearty Italian fare in a small room covered with an odd pastel mural of a not-that-intense Bacchanalia. BYOB.

New Rivers (☎ 401-751-0350; 7 Steeple St; meals $25-45; ☽ 5:30-10pm) The seasonal menu of this New America bistro features dishes such as rabbit loin with sweet pea sauce, roasted sole or beef tenderloin with mushrooms and pearl onions. The good-looking room combines soft lighting with rich red walls, making it a fine place to peruse a well-conceived wine list. Monday to Thursday there's a $26 prix fixe.

our pick Al Forno (☎ 401-273-9760; 577 S Main St; meals $35-50; ☽ 5-10pm Tue-Fri, 4-10pm Sat; ℗) Our most recent visit featured scallops with blackened bacon so perfect that they were celestial – without doubt a constellation out there bears a resemblance. Also enjoy boar loin with cranberry potatoes and green beans, fare from local farms, and incredible desserts (limoncello cake with candied citrus peel). Budget-minded folks can order wood-fired pizzas ($20) big enough for two to split. While people tend to dress up a bit, the room and garden terrace are somewhat casual. Make a reservation.

Drinking
CAFÉS
Coffee Exchange (☎ 401-273-1198; 201 Wickenden St; ☽ 6:30am-11pm; ▣) Drink very strong coffee at one of many small tables covering a scratched wooden floor. Nearby, thick layers of flyers are tacked onto boards and a large roaster lurks behind cases displaying the 40 kinds of beans available. In warm weather, take your brew on an open-air deck.

BARS
Red Fez (☎ 401-272-1212; 49 Peck St; ☽ 4pm-1am Tue & Wed, 4pm-2am Thu-Sat) Packed full of Hasbro copywriters who work on the packaging for Transformers action figures, this dark, spooky bar makes stiff drinks and fantastic grilled cheese sandwiches. What little light exists is red, by which short RISD girls with interesting hair draw crap on napkins. Upstairs is cooler than downstairs.

Wild Colonial (☎ 401-621-5644; 250 S Water St) Come inside the basement level of a 19th-century warehouse to find a spacious tavern with a pool table and two dart boards.

A patchwork of walls appears to use every masonry device available, from giant rocks to cobblestones to crumbling brick – so crumbing that you can look through a gaping hole behind the bar to see an office beyond.

Lili Marlene's (☎ 401-751-4996; 422 Atwells Ave) If you dribbled on your pants in the bathroom, fear not – this bar is so dark that no one will notice the humiliating mark. Here, Atwells Ave looses the Italian feel and becomes either a Victorian parlor or a bordello with imitation tiffany lamps casting a faint glow on red walls set above rich wainscoting. Sit at the bar or in leather booths.

Trinity Brewhouse (☎ 401-453-2337; 186 Fountain St; ☽ 11:30am-2am) This brewhouse serves only its own hop-heavy Irish/British–style beer. There's entertainment most nights, and the kitchen, serving sandwiches (some vegetarian), burgers, shepherd's pie and grilled sausages closes at midnight.

Entertainment
LIVE MUSIC
Refer to the 'Lifebeat' section in the *Providence Journal* or the *Phoenix* for listings of performers, venues and schedules.

Lupo's Heartbreak Hotel (☎ 401-331-5876; www.lupos.com; 79 Washington St; cover $10-20) Providence's legendary music venue, Lupo's occupies digs in a converted theater, whose age adds historic charm. It hosts national acts (Bloc Party, Tiger Army, Blonde Redheads) in a relatively small space.

AS220 (☎ 401-831-9327; www.as220.org; 115 Empire St; admission free-$10; ☽ from 3pm) A longstanding outlet for all forms of Rhode Island art, AS220 (say 'A-S-two-twenty') books experimental bands (Lightning Bolt, tuba and banjo duos), hosts readings and provides gallery space for a very active community. If you need a cup of coffee, vegan cookie or spinach pie, it also operates a café and bar.

Living Room (☎ 401-521-5200; www.myspace.com/livingroomri; 23 Rathbone St) You'll want to be careful – some nights amazing indie acts make tracking down this hard-to-find joint worth the effort. But on others you might be exposed to some local high-school punks trying to piece together their first set.

CLUBS
Roxy (☎ 401-831-7699; 79 Washington St; www.roxyri.com; ☽ 10pm-2am Thu & Sat) In the same building as Lupo's (above), stop by this popular meat

market for the usual hits on a loud sound system. Expect liberal use of laser lighting and, depending on the night, paid dancers wearing tiny, uncomfortable outfits. Ironically, there is a dress code for guests (no sneaks, baggy clothes etc).

Mirabar (☎ 401-331-6761; 35 Richmond St; ☉ 3pm-1am Sun-Thu, 3pm-2am Fri & Sat) This venerable bar for gay fellows attracts devoted regulars, many on a first-name basis with the bartenders. It's got two floors – the second, a sort of promenade, overlooks the action of the main level's dance floor.

Dark Lady (☎ 401-831-4297; 124 Snow St) If Mirabar isn't your scene, there are half a dozen other queer joints on or near Richmond St, such as Dark Lady, for dancing, drag and karaoke.

THEATER & CULTURE

Trinity Repertory Company (☎ 401-351-4242; www .trinityrep.com; 201 Washington St; tickets $30-60) Trinity performs classic and contemporary plays (*Some Things are Private, A Christmas Carol*) in the stunning and historic Lederer Theater downtown. It's a favorite try-out space for Broadway productions, and it's not unusual for well-known stars to turn up in a performance. Student discounts available.

Cable Car Cinema (☎ 401-272-3970; www.cablecar cinema.com; 204 S Main St; tickets $8.50; ☉ from 7:30am; ☕) This theater screens offbeat and foreign films. Inside, patrons sit on couches and sometimes listen to a lovable weirdo sing 'Teddy Bears Picnic' before the show. The attached sidewalk café brews excellent coffee, and serves sandwiches and baked goods. It's a good place to hang out, even if you aren't catching a flick.

Avon Cinema (☎ 401-421-2866; www.avoncinema .com; 260 Thayer St; tickets $9.25) On College Hill, Avon's single screen features foreign films, cult classics and experimental movies in an old single-screen movie house from 1938.

Perishable Theater (☎ 401-331-2695; www.perish able.org; 95 Empire St; tickets from $5) This small theater programs experimental plays as well as improv comedy groups. It conducts an annual Women's Playwriting Festival and the Fledgling Festival, where you can see up-and-coming artists involved in burlesque puppetry and oddities of the stage.

Providence Performing Arts Center (☎ 401-421-2997; www.ppacri.org; 220 Weybosset St; tickets $30-60) This popular venue for touring Broadway musicals is in a former Loew's Theater dat-

ing from 1928. It has a lavish art deco interior. See *Spelling Bee,* Disney's *High School Musical* or the East Village Opera Company.

Gamm Theatre (☎ 401-723-4266; www.gammtheatre .org; 172 Exchange St, Pawtucket) Several smaller theater companies stage contemporary and avant-garde productions, in particular this intimate space, whose often intelligent and exquisitely acted experimental and mainstream plays make the drive to Pawtucket worthwhile.

SPORTS

Dunkin' Donuts Center (☎ 401-331-6700; 1 LaSalle Sq; ☉ box office 10am-6pm Mon-Fri, 10am-4pm Sat) This arena is the place to see sporting events such as the Providence College Friars (a basketball squad) and Providence Bruins, occasional big-name music groups, and boat shows.

Pawtucket Red Sox (☎ 401-724-7300; www.pawsox .com; tickets $6-10) This Triple-A (minor league) farm team for the Boston Red Sox plays all spring and summer at McCoy Stadium in Pawtucket, just north of Providence. A night here, complete with hot dogs and peanuts, is a favorite way for baseball addicts to get a fix without the hassle and cost of driving to (and parking at) Fenway Park in Boston. You'll also sit much closer to the field than in a big league park. Take I-95 north to exit 27, 28 or 29 and follow signs to the stadium.

Providence Bruins (☎ 401-331-6700; www.provi dencebruins.com) Another farm team for Boston, this hockey squad plays a regular schedule at the Dunkin' Donuts Center (above) in the fall and winter.

Getting There & Around

Providence is small, pretty and walkable, so once you arrive you'll probably want to get around on foot.

AIR

TF Green State Airport (☎ 401-737-8222; www.pvdair port.com) is in Warwick, about 20 minutes south of Providence. Green is served by most major airlines.

Aero-Airport Limousine Service (☎ 401-737-2868) runs a shuttle to most downtown Providence hotels about once an hour for $9 one way. Taxi services include **Airport Taxi** (☎ 401-737-2868) and **Checker Cab** (☎ 401-273-2222). RIPTA buses 12, 20 and 66 ($1.25, 20 to 30 minutes) run to Kennedy Plaza in Providence. Service is frequent on weekdays until 11pm. On Saturday and Sunday it is significantly reduced.

RHODE ISLAND

BOAT

From May through October, RIPTA operates the scenic **Providence/Newport Ferry** (adult/child $8/free, 65 minutes, five to six daily) from Newport to Conley's Wharf in Providence.

BUS

All long-distance buses and most local routes stop at the central **Intermodal Transportation Center** (Kennedy Plaza; ☑ 6am-8pm). **RIPTA** (☎ 401-781-9400, 800-221-3797; www.ripta.com), Greyhound and Peter Pan (☎ 401-751-8800, 888-751-8800; www.peterpanbus.com; Kennedy Plaza) all have ticket counters inside, and there are maps outlining local services.

RIPTA operates two 'trolley' routes. The Green Line runs from the East Side through downtown to Federal Hill. The Gold Line runs from the Marriott Hotel south to the hospital via Kennedy Plaza, and stops at the Point St Ferry Dock.

Bonanza Bus Lines (☎ 401-751-8800, 888-751-8800; www.peterpanbus.com; Kennedy Plaza), operated by Peter Pan, connects Providence and TF Green State Airport with Boston's South Station ($15, 70 minutes, 12 daily) and Boston's Logan International Airport ($22, 75 minutes, 12 daily).

Greyhound (☎ 401-454-0790, 800-231-2222; www.greyhound.com; Kennedy Plaza) buses depart for Boston ($8.75, 70 minutes, five daily), New York City ($25, four to 5½ hours, six daily), Foxwoods Resort Casino, Connecticut ($19, one hour, five daily) and elsewhere.

CAR & MOTORCYCLE

With hills, two interstates, and two rivers defining its downtown topography, Providence can be a confusing city to find your way around. Expect one-way streets and curving roads. Parking can be difficult downtown and near the train station. For a central lot, try the huge garage of the Providence Place Mall and get a merchant to validate your ticket. On the East Side, you can usually find street parking easily.

Most major car-rental companies have offices at TF Green State Airport in Warwick. **Avis** (☎ 401-521-7900; www.avis.com; Providence Biltmore, 1 Dorrance St; ☑ 8am-6pm Mon-Fri, 8am-4:30pm Sat, 9am-5pm Sun) has an office downtown as well.

TRAIN

Eight **Amtrak** (☎ 800-872-7245; www.amtrak.com; 100 Gaspee St) trains connect Providence with Boston ($16, 50 minutes) and New York ($65 to $85, 3½ hours). Additional high-speed Acela trains, also operated by Amtrak, make runs to Boston ($30, 45 minutes) and New York ($83 to $115, 2¾ hours); they shorten your trip and have slightly more comfortable seats. The Boston run is a rip-off.

The **MBTA commuter rail** (☎ 617-222-3200, 800-392-6100; www.mbta.com) connections to Boston ($7.75, 70 minutes, 15 midweek, fewer on weekends) use the same track as Amtrak. Watch the same scenery on a harder seat for half the price.

NEWPORT
pop 26,500

Newport's status as a favorite summertime destination stretches back to the 19th century, when America's most fabulously wealthy industrialists erected an unequalled collection of obscenely sumptuous mansions overlooking the Atlantic. Though Vanderbilt and his pals are long dead, their 'cottages' linger in excellent condition and are the area's premier attraction. Also competing for your attention are a series of music festivals – classical, folk, jazz – which are among the most important in the US.

For those that detest opulent homes and good tunes, the city's crooked colonial streets make for excellent strolling and feature several of New England's most beautiful and oldest religious buildings. The nearby harbor remains one of the most active and important yachting centers in the country. Thames St, the principal commercial drag, teems with restaurants, bars and massive weekend crowds, day and night. Indeed, the town is packed all summer with young day-trippers, older bus tourists, foreign visitors and families whose cars pack the narrow streets, bringing traffic to a standstill.

Orientation & Information

Newport occupies the southwestern end of Aquidneck Island. Adjoining it to the north is Middletown with its many strip malls. Most cheap motels and guesthouses are in Middletown, while the more expensive inns, B&Bs and hotels are in Newport proper.

Downtown Newport's main north-south commercial streets are America's Cup Ave and Thames (that's 'thaymz,' not 'temz')

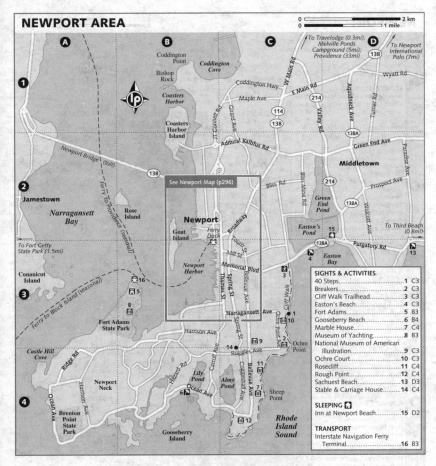

NEWPORT AREA

SIGHTS & ACTIVITIES	
40 Steps	1 C3
Breakers	2 C3
Cliff Walk Trailhead	3 C3
Easton's Beach	4 C3
Fort Adams	5 B3
Gooseberry Beach	6 B4
Marble House	7 C4
Museum of Yachting	8 B3
National Museum of American Illustration	9 C3
Ochre Court	10 C3
Rosecliff	11 C4
Rough Point	12 C4
Sachuest Beach	13 D3
Stable & Carriage House	14 C4

SLEEPING	
Inn at Newport Beach	15 D2

TRANSPORT	
Interstate Navigation Ferry Terminal	16 B3

St, just in from the harbor. There are public toilets at the entrance to the parking lot at Bowen's Wharf.

Walking or biking around town is the best way to go; see p301 for rental information. If driving in the summer, you'll find parking particularly difficult and expensive, see p305.

Newport Gateway Transportation & Visitors Center (Map p296; ☎ 800-976-5122; www.gonewport .com; 23 America's Cup Ave; ◷ 9am-5pm) is operated by the Newport County Convention & Visitors Bureau. They don't make room reservations, but they post a list of B&Bs, inns and hotels with vacancies and you can call those for free from a bank of special phones. They've got free maps.

Sights & Activities
In addition to all those mansions, don't forget to take a stroll down the Cliff Walk (p297) or watch esoteric sports (see p305). While walking around downtown, be sure to notice the lanterns on Pelham St (Map p296), the first street in the USA illuminated by gas (1805).

BANNISTER'S & BOWEN'S WHARF
These wharves typify Newport's transformation from working city-by-the-sea to a tourist destination. While much of the experience of downtown and Thames St involves shopping and eating within a cobblestone context, it is at Bowen's Wharf that you'll feel commercialism most tangibly. Fishing boats and pleasure vessels sit around the periphery of

RHODE ISLAND

NEWPORT

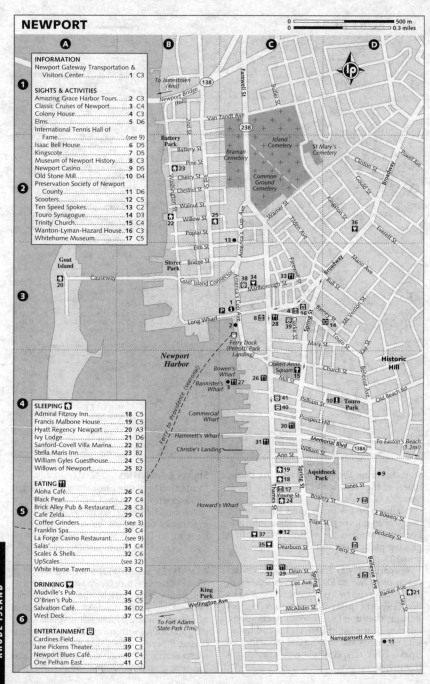

0   500 m
0   0.3 miles

INFORMATION
Newport Gateway Transportation &
Visitors Center.........................1 C3

SIGHTS & ACTIVITIES
Amazing Grace Harbor Tours......2 C3
Classic Cruises of Newport.........3 C4
Colony House..........................4 C3
Elms......................................5 D6
International Tennis Hall of
Fame.................................(see 9)
Isaac Bell House.......................6 D5
Kingscote...............................7 D5
Museum of Newport History.......8 C3
Newport Casino.......................9 D5
Old Stone Mill.......................10 D4
Preservation Society of Newport
County.............................11 D6
Scooters...............................12 C5
Ten Speed Spokes...................13 C2
Touro Synagogue....................14 D3
Trinity Church........................15 C4
Wanton-Lyman-Hazard House..16 C3
Whitehorne Museum...............17 C5

SLEEPING
Admiral Fitzroy Inn..................18 C5
Francis Malbone House.............19 C5
Hyatt Regency Newport 20 A3
Ivy Lodge..............................21 D6
Sanford-Covell Villa Marina......22 B2
Stella Maris Inn......................23 B2
William Gyles Guesthouse........24 C5
Willows of Newport.................25 B2

EATING
Aloha Café.............................26 C4
Black Pearl............................27 C4
Brick Alley Pub & Restaurant.....28 C4
Cafe Zelda............................29 C6
Coffee Grinders...................(see 3)
Franklin Spa..........................30 C4
La Forge Casino Restaurant.......(see 9)
Salas'..................................31 C4
Scales & Shells......................32 C6
UpScales...........................(see 32)
White Horse Tavern.................33 C3

DRINKING
Mudville's Pub........................34 C3
O'Brien's Pub.........................35 C5
Salvation Café........................36 D2
West Deck............................37 C5

ENTERTAINMENT
Cardines Field........................38 C3
Jane Pickens Theater...............39 C3
Newport Blues Café.................40 C4
One Pelham East.....................41 C4

RHODE ISLAND

CLIFF WALK

A narrow footpath that snakes for 3.5 miles along the eastern edge of a peninsula, the Cliff Walk (Map p295) provides one of the finest excuses for exercise you'll encounter. From its northernmost point, beach traffic and noise will recede behind you as you make your way south. Just steps to your left, a cliff – your faithful companion for the duration of your walk – drops dramatically to a foaming, bubbling Atlantic, which swells against rocky outcroppings. While a short stone wall occasionally protects you from an accidental plunge, often the only barrier is grass, flowers and squat bushes dotted with orange beach plums. For much of the first half mile, a tall hedge will impede your view to the right, with momentary breaks providing glimpses of large estates hinting at what's to come.

It all becomes clear when you arrive at the '40 Steps,' a stone staircase (sometimes used as a casting platform by fishermen) that leads from the top of the cliff to the crashing water below. Here, the hedge drops away, offering a clear view of the walk's first robber-baron-era mansion, Ochre Court (p298). Continue south and you'll experience the Breakers (below), Beechwood, Marble House (p299) and Rough Point (p298). Between these gargantuan monuments to 19th-century excess, you'll see smaller private 'cottages' mysteriously hiding behind protective walls.

The Cliff Walk begins off Memorial Blvd just west of Easton's Beach, and goes south and then west to the intersection of Bellevue and Coggeshall Aves. Strolling its entire length in one direction takes about an hour. The most convenient access point is on Narragansett Ave, which terminates near the Cliff Walk at the 40 Steps. Here, you can park for free from 6am to 9pm (there's a four-hour limit). Many favor this entry point because it shaves the first half-mile off the walk (which is pretty, but lacks mansions).

---

fudge shops, places selling sculpture made of shells, and lots of clothing stores (some local, some chain) all housed in an outdoor mall on a former wharf meant to blend into the old city by virtue of the liberal use of grey shingles. The shear number of people hanging out here lends it the air of excitement.

Nearby Bannister's Wharf is a smaller-scale version of the same thing.

NEWPORT MANSIONS

During the 19th century, the wealthiest New York bankers and business families chose Newport as their summer resort. This was pre-income tax America, their fortunes were fabulous and their 'summer cottages' – actually mansions and palaces – were fabulous as well. Most mansions are on Bellevue Ave, and they frequently turn up as settings for films like *The Great Gatsby* and PBS series featuring actors with British accents.

Many of the mansions are under the management of the **Preservation Society of Newport County** (Map p296; ☎ 401-847-1000; www.newportmansions.org; 424 Bellevue Ave), which offers combination tickets that save you money if you intend to visit several of its 11 properties. Tickets to all mansions can be purchased at the **Newport Gateway Transportation & Visitors Center** (Map p296; ☎ 800-976-5122; www.gonewport.com; 23 America's Cup Ave; ☺ 9am-5pm) or at properties run by the preservation society. A few mansions are still in private hands and aren't open to visitors.

One of the best ways to see the mansions is by bicycle (see p301). Cruising along Bellevue Ave at a leisurely place allows you to enjoy the view of the grounds, explore side streets and paths, and ride right up to the mansion entrances without having to worry about parking or holding up traffic.

Your stunning alternative to biking is to saunter along the famed Cliff Walk (above), a narrow pedestrian path that runs along the edge of a range of steep bluffs. The ocean surges on one side, while the mansions rise in grandeur on the other.

The only mansions described here not managed by the Preservation Society are Ochre Court and Rough Point.

The Breakers

Most magnificent of the Newport mansions is the **Breakers** (Map p295; ☎ 401-847-1000; www.newportmansions.org; 44 Orche Point Ave; adult/child $16/4; ☺ 9am-6pm mid-Apr–Jan, 10am-5pm Sat & Sun Jan–mid-Apr; P &), a 70-room Italian Renaissance megapalace inspired by 16th-century Genoese palazzos. Richard Morris Hunt did most of the design, though he imported craftsmen from around the world to perfect the sculptural and decorative programs. The building was completed in 1895 and sits next to Ochre Court at Ochre Point, on a supremely grand oceanside site. The furnishings, most made expressly for the Breakers, are all original. The content of the tour is well conceived and presented. Don't miss the **Children's Cottage** on the grounds.

The Breakers' grand **Stable & Carriage House** (53 Coggeshall Ave), also designed by Hunt, is inland several blocks, on the west side of Bellevue Ave. It is now a museum of Vanderbilt family memorabilia, much of which provides a detailed look at the lifestyle of one of the USA's wealthiest families at the turn of the century.

Rough Point

In 1889, Frederick W Vanderbilt built **Rough Point** (Map p295; ☎ 401-849-7300; www.newportrestoration .com; 680 Bellevue Ave; admission $25; ☺ 10am-2:40pm Tue-Sat mid-Apr–early-Nov; ⓟ ⓖ) in the tradition of English manorial estates on a rocky piece of land jutting out into the ocean. Later purchased by the tobacco baron, James B Duke, the mansion fell into the hands of Duke's only daughter, Doris (aged 13 years). She left the estate to the Newport Restoration Society upon her death.

While the splendor of the grounds alone is worth the price of admission, Rough Point also houses much of Doris Duke's impressive art holdings, including medieval tapestries, furniture owned by French emperors, Ming Dynasty ceramics, and paintings by Renoir and Van Dyck. These and other extraordinary objects formed the backdrop of Duke's daily life and remain as they were at the time of her death. Particularly interesting is a glassed-in sunroom containing just about the only pedestrian furniture (the couch appears to be from a department store). This room simultaneously cleanses your visual palette while at the same time reminding you how extravagant everything else is. Also on hand are mannequins wearing some of Duke's eight decades of bizarro clothing.

Purchase tickets to Rough Point at Newport's visitor center or online. As parking is limited at Rough Point, many visit the estate using the courtesy shuttle from the visitor center.

The Elms

Nearly identical to the Château d'Asnières built near Paris in 1750, the **Elms** (Map p296; ☎ 401-847-1000; www.newportmansions.org; 367 Bellevue Ave; adult/child $11/4; ☺ 10am-6pm mid-Apr–Jan, 10am-5pm Sat & Sun Jan–mid-Apr; ⓟ ⓖ ⓗ) offers a 'behind-the-scenes' tour which will have you snaking through the basement operations, servants' quarters and up onto the roof. Along the way you'll learn about the activities of the army of servants and the architectural devices that kept them hidden from the view of those drinking port in the formal rooms. Taking the regular tour in addition to the behind-the-scenes variant will give you the best idea about how a Newport mansion functioned, though a double tour is exhausting.

The place was designed by Horace Trumbauer in 1901. Of all the mansions, The Elms easily possess the most lavish gardens – enjoy symmetrical flower beds around fountains, specimen trees and a sunken garden.

Ochre Court

Designed by Richard Morris Hunt and built in 1892, **Ochre Court** (Map p295; ☎ 401-847-6650; 100 Orche Point Ave; admission free; ☺ 9am-4pm Mon-Fri) offers a grand view of the sea from its soaring three-story grand hallway. Elsewhere find a rainbow of stained glass, pointed arches, gargoyles and other emblems of an architecture inspired by a medieval (and mythical) French Gothic. Ochre Court is now the administration building of Salve Regina University, and as such provides an interesting example of the repurposing of a Newport mansion. You can visit much of the main floor anytime during opening hours. In summer there are guided tours.

Isaac Bell House

One of the earliest Bellevue mansions (1883), this subtly grand wooden home (Map p296; ☎ 401-847-1000; www.newportmansions.org; 70 Perry St; adult/child $11/4; ☺ 10am-6pm mid-Apr–Jan; ⓟ) not only exemplifies 'shingle style' architecture (the thing is covered in graying cedar scales) but, if you compare it to the stone behemoths that would soon arrive in Newport, helps you to understand the changing forms of the city's grandest buildings. While places like the Breakers overpower you with palatial spaces and over-the-top materials, this McKim, Mead and White structure feels more livable, graceful and American (most other mansions imitate European palaces).

Rosecliff

Stanford White designed **Rosecliff** (Map p295; ☎ 401-847-1000; www.newportmansions.org; 548 Bellevue Ave; adult/child $11/4; ⊙ 10am-6pm mid-Apr–Jan; P ⓖ) to look like the Grand Trianon at Versailles, and its palatial ballroom (Newport's largest) and landscaped grounds quickly became the setting for some truly enormous parties. Houdini, the magician, entertained at one. Rosecliff was built for Mrs Hermann Oelrichs, an heiress of the Comstock Lode silver treasure. If the building seems oddly familiar during your visit, that might be because it has appeared in films such as *The Great Gatsby*, *Amistad* and *High Society*.

Other Mansions

Designed by Richard Morris Hunt and built in 1892 for William K Vanderbilt, the younger brother of Cornelius II, the gaudy **Marble House** (Map p295; ☎ 401-847-1000; www.newportmansions.org; 596 Bellevue Ave; adult/child $11/4; ⊙ 10am-6pm mid-Apr–Jan; P ⓖ ⓕ) – built of many kinds of garishly colored marble – is the mansion that most closely resembles a prostitute. The whorish building receives its inspiration from the palace of Versailles and comes complete with custom furnishings styled after the era of Louis XIV. Check out the bright red and green Chinese Teahouse, perched on a seaside cliff, which contrasts oddly with the stern gray stone of the Marble House's exterior.

An Elizabethan fantasy complete with Tiffany glass, **Kingscote** (Map p296; ☎ 401-847-1000; www.newportmansions.org; 253 Bellevue Ave; adult/child $11/4; ⊙ 10am-5pm mid-Jun–mid-Sep; P) was Newport's first 'cottage' strictly for summer use, designed by Richard Upjohn in 1841 for George Noble Jones of Savannah, Georgia. It was later bought by China-trade merchant William H King, who gave the house its name.

INTERNATIONAL TENNIS HALL OF FAME

To experience something of the American aristocracy's approach to 19th-century leisure, visit this **museum** (Map p296; ☎ 401-849-3990; www.tennisfame.com; 194 Bellevue Ave; adult/child 16 yrs & under/senior/family $9/5/7/23; ⊙ 10am-5pm) where you'll learn about eight centuries of tennis exploits. It lies inside the historic Newport Casino building (1880), which served as a summer club for Newport's wealthiest residents. The US National Lawn Tennis Championships (forerunner of today's US Open Tennis Tournament) was held here in 1881.

If you brought your whites, playing on one of its 13 grass courts (closed in winter) remains a delightful throwback to earlier times ($90 for one or two people per 90 minutes). Otherwise, grab a drink in the rear bar of the La Forge Casino Restaurant (see p303), also inside the Casino, where some tables are courtside (no charge to sit here other then the cost of food and booze).

NATIONAL MUSEUM OF AMERICAN ILLUSTRATION

Well worth the pain it takes to arrange a visit (one needs advance reservations for time-specific tours), this acclaimed **museum** (Map p295; ☎ 401-851-8949; www.americanillustration.org; 492 Bellevue Ave; admission $25; ⊙ 10am-4pm) features an impressive collection of Maxfield Parrish's impossibly luminous works in color, NC Wyeth prints, Norman Rockwell's nostalgia and the illustrations of other American graphic heavy weights. The goods are displayed within the palatial Vernon Court (yet another mansion, this one from 1898) set within Olmstead-designed grounds. No kids under 12.

WHITEHORNE MUSEUM

A few decades ago, colonial Newport was decaying and undervalued. Enter Doris Duke, who used her huge fortune to preserve many of the buildings that now attract people to the city. One of them is this **Whitehorne** (Map p296; ☎ 401-324-611; 416 Thames; adult/child $10/4; ⊙ 11am-4pm Mon Thu & Fri, 10am-4pm Sat & Sun May 1–Oct 30), a Federal period estate, which visitors view through hourly guided tours. Rooms contain a collection of extraordinary furniture crafted by Newport's famed cabinetmakers, including pieces by Goddard and Townsend.

MUSEUM OF YACHTING

Want to look at some boats? Head inside this bad boy **museum** (Map p295; ☎ 401-847-1018; www.moy.org; Fort Adams State Park; adult/senior & child under 12 $5/4; ⊙ 10am-5pm mid-May–Oct) for a collection of model yachts, a handful of craft being restored by an onsite restoration school and pictures of the New York Yacht Club winning the America's Cup regatta for 130 consecutive years until Australia ruined sporting history's longest winning streak in 1983.

RHODE ISLAND

HISTORIC HOMES & BUILDINGS

For some serious timber framing, visit the oldest surviving house in Newport, **Wanton-Lyman-Hazard House** (Map p296; ☎ 401-846-0813; 17 Broadway; adult/child $4/3; ☺ tours 10am-2pm Tue, Thu & Sat mid-Jun–Aug), constructed circa 1697. Used as a residence by colonial governors and well-to-do residents, it's now a museum of colonial Newport history operated by the Newport Historical Society. Tours depart from **Colony House** (Washington Sq). It's open other times by appointment.

A curious stone tower of uncertain provenance, some people believe the **Old Stone Mill** (Map p296; Touro Park, off Bellevue Ave) was built by Norse mariners before the voyages of Columbus, making it the oldest-existing structure in the US. Others say it's a windmill's base, built by an early governor of the colony. Whatever myth you believe, it is set in a grass park and enjoying a picnic in its shadow won't hurt your day.

HOUSES OF WORSHIP

Touro Synagogue (Map p296; ☎ 401-847-4794; www.tourosynagogue.org; 85 Touro St; ☺ tours 10am-5pm Sun-Wed & Fri Jul-Sep, shorter hrs Oct-Jun), designed by Peter Harrison (who did King's Chapel in Boston), is one of the most architecturally distinguished buildings from the colonial period. Its large glass windows illuminate an interior that treads the line between austere and lavish. Built by the nascent Sephardic Orthodox Congregation Yeshuat Israel in 1763, it has the distinction of being North America's oldest Jewish synagogue. Inside, a letter to the congregation from President George Washington, written in 1790, hangs in a prominent spot. There's a historic cemetery just up the street. The synagogue opens for worship only on Saturday.

The **Trinity Church** (Map p296; ☎ 401-846-0660; cnr Spring & Church Sts; ☺ 10am-4pm mid-Jun–early Sep, 1-4pm May & mid-Sep–mid-Oct, 10am-1pm mid-Oct–mid-Jun), on Queen Anne Sq, follows the design canon of Sir Christopher Wren's Palladian churches in London. Built in 1725 and 1726, it has a fine wineglass-shaped pulpit, tall windows to let in light and traditional box pews to keep out drafty air.

STATE PARKS

Fort Adams (Map p295; ☎ 401-841-0707; www.fortadams.org; tours adult/child $10/5; ☺ tours mid-May–Oct from 10am-4pm), built between 1824 and 1857, crowns a rise at the end of the peninsula which juts northward into Newport Harbor. Like many American coastal fortresses, it had a short, practical life as a deterrent and a long life as a tourist attraction. It's the centerpiece of **Fort Adams State Park** (Map p295; ☎ 401-847-2400; www.riparks.com/fortadams; admission free; ☺ 6am-11pm), the venue for the Newport jazz and folk festivals and special events. A beach, picnic and fishing areas and a boat ramp are open daily. The Museum of Yachting (p299) and the ferry to Block Island are here as well.

At the opposite end of the peninsula, **Brenton Point State Park** (Map p295; ☎ 401-849-4562 summer only; Ocean Ave; ☺ dawn-dusk), due south of Fort Adams on Ocean Ave, is a prime place for standing on rocky outcroppings to watch the ocean crash about you and for flying kites.

BEACHES

Newport's public beaches are on the eastern side of the peninsula along Memorial Blvd. All are open 9am to 6pm in summer and charge a parking fee of $10 per car ($15 on weekends).

Easton's Beach (First Beach; Map p295; ☎ 401-848-6491) is the largest (a 0.75 mile long stretch of sand), with a pseudo-Victorian pavilion containing bathhouses and showers, a snack bar and a large carousel. It's within walking distance of Newport's center. You can rent umbrellas, chairs and surf boards at the pavilion.

A note to surfers: while it's true that one of Rhode Island's three decent breaks is a vigorous paddle away, the rideable waves head straight for a rocky cliff. So don't mess up, because you might die. The brave like the spot, for danger keeps the water more or less empty.

East of Easton's Beach along Purgatory Rd lies **Sachuest Beach** (Second Beach; Map p295; ☎ 401-846-6273), named for the nearby wildlife sanctuary. It's prettier and cleaner than Easton's Beach and has showers, a snack bar and a lovely setting, overlooked by the neo-Gothic tower of St George's prep school.

Third Beach (off Map p295; ☎ 401-847-1993) is a short distance east of Second Beach. Popular with families because it is protected from the open ocean, Third Beach also appeals to windsurfers because the water is calm and the winds steady.

Other 'pocket' beaches exist along Ocean Ave, but most of these, such as Bailey's Beach, are private. An exception is **Gooseberry Beach** (Map p295; 9am-5pm; admission Mon-Fri $15, Sat & Sun $20), which has calm waters, white sand and a restaurant.

BIKING

Newport is a fine town for biking, with only a few gentle slopes. A scenic and satisfying ride is the 10-mile loop around Ocean Ave, which includes Bellevue Ave and its many beautiful mansions.

Both the following stores offer free use of helmets and locks:

Scooters (Map p296; ☎ 401-849-4400; 476 Thames St; rental per day/week $19/65; 9am-7pm Mon-Sat, 9am-6pm Sun) You can rent wheels with a baby seat for $8.50 per hour. Motor scooters cost $39/50/61/89 for one/two/three/eight hours.

Ten Speed Spokes (Map p296; ☎ 401-847-5609; 18 Elm St; rental per hr/day/week $5/25/75; 9am-7pm Mon-Sat, 9am-6pm Sun) Rents Specialized brand mountain bikes and hybrids.

Tours

If you'd rather go on your own, the Historical Society has erected 26 self-guided walking-tour signs on the sidewalks of Historic Hill (Map p296) describing many of the prominent and historic buildings found there.

Amazing Grace Harbor Tours (Map p296; ☎ 401-847-9109; www.oldportmarine.com; Oldport Marine at America's Cup Ave; adult/child $13/8; mid-May–mid-Oct) Offers narrated harbor tours departing several times daily; among other sights, you'll see Hammersmith Farm, Jacqueline Kennedy's summer home.

Classic Cruises of Newport (Map p296; ☎ 401-847-0299; www.cruisenewport.com; Bannister's Wharf; adult/child $18/12; mid-May–mid-Oct) Runs excursions on the *Rum Runner II*, a Prohibition-era bootlegging vessel. The narrated tour will take you past mansions and former speakeasies.

Newport History Tours (☎ 401-846-0813; www.newporthistorical.org; tours $8; 10am Thu-Sat May-Sep) Will guide you on a walking tour of Historic Hill. Periodically, the society offers African-American and religious heritage tours, where you'll learn why Cotton Mather called Newport 'a sewer of religious contagion.' Tours begin at the Museum of Newport History (127 Thames St).

Festivals & Events

During your visit, you may find special events involving polo, yachts, flowers and horticulture, yachts, Irish music, clam chowder, yachts, traditional crafts, soapbox racers, tennis, beer and yachts. For the full schedule, see www.gonewport.com.

If you plan to attend any of the major festivals described below, make sure you reserve accommodations and tickets in advance (tickets usually go on sale in mid-May).

Newport Music Festival (☎ 401-846-1133; www.newportmusic.org; tickets $35-55) In mid-July, this internationally regarded festival offers classical music concerts in many of the great mansions. Order tickets well in advance.

International Tennis Hall of Fame Championships (☎ 401-849-3990; www.tennisfame.org/championship; daily tickets $30-50) For a week in July, the sport's top athletes come to humiliate each other on the famed grass courts.

Newport Folk Festival (☎ 401-847-3700; www.newportfolk.com; day pass $55-75, child under 12 $5) In early August, big-name stars and up-and-coming groups perform at Fort Adams State Park and other venues around town. Recent acts include Linda Ronstadt, Wilco, and the Allman Brothers Band. Zero shade exists at Fort Adams – bring sunscreen.

JVC Jazz Festival/Newport (☎ 401-847-3700; www.festivalproductions.net; adult $30-100, child $5) This classic draws top performers like Dave Brubeck and Dizzy Gillespie. It usually takes place on a mid-August weekend, with concerts at the Newport Casino and Fort Adams State Park. Popular shows can sell out a year in advance.

Newport International Boat Show (☎ 401-846-1115; www.newportboatshow.com; adult/child $16/free) Held in late September, this is the biggest and best known of Newport's many boat and yacht shows.

Sleeping

Expensive in summer (particularly on weekends) and discounted off season, the cozy inns and harbor side hotels in the center of town often require a two-night minimum on summer weekends, and a three-night minimum on holidays.

As rooms can be scarce in summer, you might want to use a reservation service. **Anna's Victorian Connection** (Map p295; ☎ 401-849-2489; 5 Fowler Ave, Newport, RI 02840) will make a reservation at any one of 200 hostelries in Rhode Island and southeastern Massachusetts at no cost to you. Otherwise **B&B of Newport** (Map p295; ☎ 401-846-5408, 800-800-8765; www.bbnewport.com; 33 Russell Ave, Newport, RI 02840) and **Taylor-Made Reservations** (☎ 800-848-8848; www.citybythesea.com), whose website is more informative, together represent about 400 establishments in the Newport area. If you arrive without a reservation, go to the visitor center and ask to see its list of vacancies.

Most motels lie several depressing miles to the north in Middletown on RI 114 (W Main Rd) and RI 138 (E Main Rd). RIPTA bus 63/Purple Line can take you to downtown Newport, saving you the expense and bother of parking.

BUDGET

Fort Getty State Park (off Map p295; ☎ 401-423-7264; tent/RV sites $20/40; ☑ mid-May–Sep) This pleasant park lies on Conanicut Island in Jamestown, with 100 RV sites, 25 tent sites on a grassy field, a dock for fishing and a view of the squat Dutch Lighthouse. Follow RI 138 over the Newport Bridge. Take the Jamestown exit, bearing right at the yield sign. Turn left onto Conanicus Ave. Continue for about 6 miles and go right onto Hamilton Ave. Continue to Mackerel Cove Beach and take the first right onto Fort Getty Rd.

Melville Ponds Campground (off Map p295; ☎ 401-682-2424; 181 Bradford Ave; tent/RV sites $22/30; ☑ Apr-Oct) This family-friendly municipal campground has 57 tent sites and 66 RV sites. The tenting spots are wooded, though a bit small and cramped, and have picnic tables. It's in Portsmouth, 10 miles north of Newport's center. To find it, take RI 114 to Stringham Rd (the turn is not prominent, though there is a small sign), go to Sullivan Rd, then head north to the campground.

William Gyles Guesthouse (Map p296; ☎ 401-369-0243; www.newporthostel.com; 16 Howard St; per bed Mon-Fri $32, Sat & Sun $59) Welcome to Rhode Island's only hostel. Run by an informal and knowledgeable host, book one of her four beds as early as you can. The tiny guesthouse contains fixings for a simple breakfast, a laundry machine and spare, clean digs in a dormitory room.

Travelodge (off Map p295; ☎ 401-849-4700, 800-862-2006; www.travelodge.com; 1185 W Main Rd/RI 114, Middletown; r $45-120; ☒) Located near an Applebee's and an Ihop on a strip-mall, you'll be living the asphalt high-life at this supremely generic motel about 5 miles north of Newport. A plus: it often provides the cheapest private room in town.

MIDRANGE

Stella Maris Inn (Map p296; ☎ 401-849-2862; www.stellamarisinn.com; 91 Washington St; r $155-225; ☒) This quiet, stone-and-frame inn has numerous fireplaces, heaps of black-walnut furnishings, Victorian bric-a-brac and some floral

upholstery. Rooms with garden views rent for less than those overlooking the water. Good breakfast muffins.

Inn at Newport Beach (Map p295; ☎ 401-846-0310; www.innatnb.com; cnr Memorial Blvd & Wave Ave; d $179-249; ☒) An imposing, wooden, beachside hotel featuring excellent views over Eaton's Beach and the distant Cliff Walk, you'll find that some rooms have ample bay windows, while others have frustratingly small fenestration. Rooms contain refrigerators, yellow bedspreads, microwaves, and a border of tacky, cheerful sailboats. You'll endure a 3-mile hike to get to downtown Newport.

our pick Sanford-Covell Villa Marina (Map p296; ☎ 401-847-0206; www.sanford-covell.com; 72 Washington St; r $200-275; ☒ ☒) This Victorian 'stick-style' place was perhaps Newport's most lavish house when a cousin of Ralph W Emerson built it in 1869. Restored by a team of historians from RISD and beyond in the 1980s, every detail enjoys period accuracy. Outside, kick back on the water-front wraparound veranda or admire a saltwater swimming pool. Rooms vary in size, and some have shared bathrooms. The most expensive provide water views. One of them contains the oldest bathtub in the States.

Admiral Fitzroy Inn (Map p296; ☎ 401-848-8000, 866-848-8780; www.admiralfitzroy.com; 398 Thames St; r Mon-Fri $200, Sat & Sun $300; ☒) Though named for Fitzroy (he invented the barometer and sailed with Darwin) and though old maps and paintings of 19th-century vessels imply a personal connection to the man, it remains unclear how much time the admiral spent in this 1854 building (none?). The place is appropriately nautical and fronts a busy stretch of Thames St near the Harbor. While noise from emptying bars can be disruptive, the rooftop terrace makes up for it with sweeping water views.

TOP END

Francis Malbone House (Map p296; ☎ 401-846-0392, 800-846-0392; www.malbone.com; 392 Thames St; d May-Oct $255-315, Nov-Apr $165-240; ☒ ☐) This grand brick mansion was designed by the Touro Synagogue's architect and built in 1760 for a shipping merchant. Now beautifully decorated and immaculately kept with a lush garden in back, it is one of Newport's finest inns. Some guest rooms have working fireplaces, as do the public areas. Breakfast and afternoon tea are included.

Ivy Lodge (Map p296; ☎ 401-849-6865, 800-834-6865; www.ivylodge.com; 12 Clay St; r $239-289/299-399; P ☐) The masculine entry hall of this mansion will make you glad to open your wallet. Three stories tall, entirely covered in handcrafted wood and with voyeuristic landings at each level, all rooms (immaculate, but carpeted) revolve around this central piece and its Moorish fireplace. Other points earned for creative breakfasts (both sweet and savory dishes), a huge wraparound porch, and a quiet setting near the even bigger homes on Bellevue Ave.

Willows of Newport (Map p296; ☎ 401-846-5486; www.thewillowsofnewport.com; 8 Willow St; r with breakfast $199-278; P) The four rooms of the Willows feature poetry, mints and canopy beds, breakfast in bed included; check out the 'French Victorian secret garden,' full of frog statuary, wooden cartoon bunnies and massive pink bird feeders. Over-the-top icons of romance abound. Some love it, others shudder and wince.

Hyatt Regency Newport (Map p296; ☎ 401-851-1234; www.hyatt.com; 1 Goat Island; r $239-269; P ☐ ☒ ☒) Yes, it's a chain hotel, but it enjoys a location so fine that we mention it anyway. Situated on the small Goat Island in Newport's harbor, most (but not all) views are stunning. Some rooms overlook downtown, others the Newport Bridge or a nearby lighthouse. The place is modern and in fine shape with firm beds, clean rooms and sturdy furniture bought in bulk.

Eating

From June through September, reserve your table for dinner in advance, then show up on time or lose your spot. Many Newport restaurants don't accept credit cards; ask about payment when you reserve. Don't forget about the Newport Blues Café (p304). The richest selection of restaurants in all price ranges is undoubtedly along lower Thames St, south of America's Cup Ave.

BUDGET

Aloha Café (Map p296; ☎ 401-846-7038; 18 Market Sq; breakfast & lunch $2-6; ☒ 7:30am-2:30pm Mon-Fri) Inside the old brick Seaman's Church Institute, locals and fishermen sit at one of a few tables or at the bar to enjoy dirt cheap coffee, eggs, meatball sandwiches, BLTs and soup. The wood-paneled room has a map mural of Narragansett Bay from the 1930s with iconographic rabbits and whales.

Coffee Grinders (Map p296; ☎ 401-847-9307; 33 Bannister's Wharf; snacks $2-4; ☒ from 8am) Enjoy espresso and a pastry on some benches at this small shingled shack at the end of Banisters Wharf. You'll be surrounded by water, with great views over yacht activity and crustaceans being unloaded at the Aquidneck Lobster Company.

Franklin Spa (Map p296; ☎ 401-847-3540; 229 Spring St; breakfast & lunch $3-10; ☒ 6am-2pm Mon-Wed, 6am-3pm Thu-Sat, 7am-1:30pm Sun) This old-school joint slings hash, eggs and grease for cheap. Enjoy your freshly squeezed orange juice, homemade turkey noodle soup or coffee cabinet at a Formica-topped table on a worn white-and-red tiled floor.

Salas' (Map p296; ☎ 401-846-8772; 345 Thames St; meals $8-22; ☒ from 5pm; ☝) Above Percy's Bistro but with a separate entrance, this Newport institution for the hearty, hungry and thrifty serves simple and tasty Italian and seafood dishes, plus a children's menu. Huge plates of pasta in red-clam sauce are sold by weight, and you're likely to be a little sentimental for the place after eating their fantastic clam boil.

MIDRANGE

Black Pearl (Map p296; ☎ 401-846-5264; Bannister's Wharf; tavern meals $11-22, commodore meals $31-46 ☒ noon-1am) For a bowl of superb clam chowder seasoned with lots of dill, enter the good-looking black-beamed tavern of this old reliable, covered in old maps and nautical charts. They've also got hearty corned beef sandwiches, fish and pot pie. Attached to the tavern is the more formal Commodore's Room, where you can eat oysters, steaks and racks of lamb. A Hot Dog Annex supplies cheap snacks.

La Forge Casino Restaurant (Map p296; ☎ 401-847-0418; 186 Bellevue Ave; meals $12-30; ☒ 11:30am-9:30am; P ☝) This joint stands out for one reason only: seats in the back are not only inside the famed Newport Casino, some of them practically sit on an enclosed grass court. If you eat here (Irish-themed decor), avoid the front room. Passable food ranges from burgers and calamari to more expensive entrees. Some forego solids and stick to booze – the bar's open till midnight.

Brick Alley Pub & Restaurant (Map p296; ☎ 401-849-6334; 140 Thames St; meals $10-25; ☒ 11:30am-10pm Mon-Fri, 11am-10:30pm Sat & Sun) This centrally located, ever-popular place has a huge menu of snacks, sandwiches, bar food, Mexican specialties and a salad bar, as well as Newport's most elaborate drinks list. A large patio holds many yellow umbrellas and brightly colored Adirondack chairs. The pub is not a chain, but it feels like one.

TOP END

Cafe Zelda (Map p296; ☎ 401-849-4002; 528 Thames St; meals $10-35; ⏲ from 11:30am Thu-Mon, from 3pm Tue & Wed; V) This bistro's wainscoting, lit by dim, frosted lamps, rises above the unfortunately carpeted floor. Enjoy a seasonal menu, which might offer hanger steak, pork chops with littlenecks, lamb or wild mushroom risotto. A cozy and popular bar is in a separate space next door.

Scales & Shells (Map p296; ☎ 401-846-3474; 527 Thames St; meals $20-35; ⏲ from 5pm; ♿) Enter this half-casual, broad, noisy room for small linen-clad tables set with grated parmesan and Tabasco sauce tended by waitresses in T-shirts. The decor is marked by an open kitchen and a blackboard menu. Have your squid, swordfish or lobster mesquite grilled for a change. In summer, a swamped U-shaped bar serves a huge waiting crowd.

UpScales (Map p296; ☎ 401-847-2000; 527 Thames St; meals $23-40; ⏲ from 6pm) Scales & Shells' more genteel 2nd-floor dining room has higher prices and more gentlemen in pressed pants. Come early or make a reservation; there's often a two-hour wait in summer.

White Horse Tavern (Map p296; ☎ 401-849-3600; 26 Marlborough St; meals $15-50; ⏲ from 11:30am) If you'd like to eat at a tavern opened by a 17th-century pirate that once served as an annual meeting place for the colonial Rhode Island General Assembly, try this historic, gambrel-roofed beauty. It opened in 1687, and is one of America's oldest taverns. Menus for dinner (at which men should wear a jacket) might include baked escargot, truffle-crusted Atlantic halibut or beef Wellington.

Drinking

This is a resort town, and in July and August it teems with crowds looking for a good time, which is why Thames St often feels like either a cobblestone obstacle course or an out-of-control sorority party. For what's going on, check out the 'Lifebeat' section in the *Providence Journal*.

Mudville's Pub (Map p296; ☎ 401-849-1408; 8 W Marlborough St; ⏲ noon-1am) With a back porch sitting about 10ft from the foul line of Cardines Field's outfield (see opposite), this bar fills many local sports fans with pub food and beer. It even sponsors a team (the Mudville Nine) that plays in a local league.

O'Brien's Pub (Map p296; ☎ 401-849-6623; 501 Thames St; ⏲ noon-1am) For a beer in a flimsy plastic cup, grab a seat under one of the many umbrellas on the patio or try to find a spot at the bar (crowded on Sunday night). You'll hear a lot of heavy New England accents, will probably meet guys who recently lived in a fraternity and maybe mouth the words to *Don't Stop Believin'*.

Salvation Café (Map p296; ☎ 401-847-2620; www.salvationcafe.com; 140 Broadway; ⏲ 5-11pm) Combining an outdoor Tiki lounge, corduroy velvet couches, stylish Formica tables and wood-paneled walls, this bar and restaurant is a good place for a hipster drink. It's a bit removed from town, so there are fewer tourists.

West Deck (Map p296; ☎ 401-847-3610; 1 Waites Wharf) With lots of open-air seating at the end of a wharf, the West Deck attracts big crowds ordering bottles of beer from two separate bars. Most evenings you can find Rhode Island's preferred form of entertainment – lame cover acts playing the tunes of stereotypical bands from the last half of the 1980s. The crowd ranges from young guns to dudes with overdeveloped retirement plans.

Entertainment

LIVE MUSIC

Newport Blues Café (Map p296; ☎ 401-841-5510; www.newportblues.com; 286 Thames St) This popular rhythm and blues bar and restaurant draws top acts to an old brownstone that was once a bank. It's an intimate space with many enjoying quahogs, house smoked ribs or pork loins at tables adjoining the small stage. Dinner is offered 6pm to 10pm, the music starts at 9:30pm. Two-for-one dinner specials on Monday and Tuesday.

One Pelham East (Map p296; ☎ 401-847-9460; 1 Pelham St; ⏲ from 6pm) This bar attracts droves of customers (ranging from meat market guys to older dudes with shorts suspended from sailing themed belts), even off season. Don't miss Bruce Jacques, a solo performer who combines shtick, crappy covers and bad costume changes so successfully that he has become a Monday night mainstay. Expect live music, perceptive bartenders and disgusting bathrooms. Two thumbs up!

THEATER

Jane Pickens Theater (Map p296; ☎ 401-846-5252; www.janepickens.com; 49 Touro St; adult/senior $8/6) This nicely restored one-screen art house used to be an Episcopalian church, built around 1834. Simple, pretty and old, the theater contains an organ and balcony. They screen both popular and art films, such as *Evening*, filmed in Newport and Tiverton.

SPORTS

Cardines Field (Map p296; ☎ 401-845-6832; cnr America's Cup Ave & Marlborough St; tickets $1-4) Likely the third-oldest-standing baseball field in the US (after Wrigley Field in Chicago and Fenway Park in Boston), this relic, home to the **Newport Gulls** (www.newportgulls.com), allows you to see some surprisingly skilled ball for cheap. Because of the seating's close proximity to the field and because the games are sparsely attended, you can easily hear the players trash-talk each other. According to local legend, Babe Ruth once played a game here.

Newport International Polo (off Map p295; ☎ 401-846-0200; www.newportinternationalpolo.com; Rt 138, Portsmouth; adult $10-15, child free) Tranquilly set amid the stone barns and walls of the 100-acre Glen Farm (established in the 1600s), bring a picnic basket for a fieldside tailgate and watch the US team take on Egypt, Jamaica and other Olympic-caliber squads. Crowds aren't large and you'll be close enough to hear snorting horses and walloping mallets. The season runs from May to September.

Getting There & Around

If you need a lift to TF Green Airport ($25, 45 minutes) in Warwick, **Cozy Cab** (☎ 401-846-2500, 800-846-1502) provides a shuttle service. Reservations are recommended.

While most everyone drives to Newport in their own car, some favor the summertime ferries. **RIPTA** (☎ 401-781-9400, 800-221-3797; www.ripta.com) runs a boat from Providence to Perrotti Park Landing near the Newport Gateway Transportation & Visitor Center (adult/child $8/free, 65 minutes, five to six times daily). From July to early September, **Interstate Navigation** (☎ 401-783-4613; www.blockislandferry.com) ferries depart from a dock near Fort Adams to Old Harbor in Block Island (one way/round-trip $10/15, two hours, one daily).

Bonanza Bus Lines (☎ 401-846-1820; 800-343-9999; www.peterpanbus.com), at the Newport Gateway Transportation & Visitors Center (p295), operates buses to Boston ($20, 1¾ hours, four to five daily).

RIPTA sends bus 60 between Providence and Newport ($1.25, one hour) almost every hour. For the South Kingstown Amtrak station, take No 60 ($1.25, 90 minutes, five buses Monday to Friday, three on Saturday). Most RIPTA buses arrive and depart from the **Newport Gateway Transportation & Visitors Center** (Map p296; 23 America's Cup Ave). Also stop at the center for help with local bus services around Newport.

Parking is tough in Newport. The very lucky might find free parking on the street, though most non-metered spots are reserved for Newport residents. The most convenient garage is at the Newport Gateway Transportation & Visitors Center, which gives you the first half-hour for free, the next for $2 and each additional half-hour for $1, up to $15.25 per day.

TIVERTON & LITTLE COMPTON

The town of **Tiverton** stretches alongside the wide Sakonnet river, with views of distant sailing vessels and Aquidneck Island. The further south you explore on Rte 77, the prettier the landscape gets with ramshackle farm stands appearing to sell fresh produce and rolling fields extending in all directions.

On the north stretch of Rte 77, you'll find gray-shingled **Evelyn's** (☎ 401-624-3100; 2335 Main Rd, Tiverton; fish $5-18; ⏱ 11am-8:30pm Wed-Mon early Apr–Sep) a traditional roadside eatery from another era. Park on the crushed shell driveway and eat amazing lobster rolls (cool, mildly spiced claw and tail meat on a hotdog bun). The place sits next to a blue inlet with a handful of bobbing dinghies.

A rare traffic light marks Tiverton's 'Four Corners,' where you can stop at **Gray's Ice Cream** (☎ 401-624-4500; 16 East Rd Tiverton; ice-cream $3-5) for a coffee cabinet (milkshake with ice-cream), as beachgoers have been doing since 1923. Otherwise, drop in at the **Provender** (☎ 401-624-8084; cnr Main & Neck Rds; sandwiches $6-8) for a hearty sandwich on fresh bread or some cookies.

Continue south into **Little Compton** and the smell of the sea will soon emerge. Here, large wood-framed homes become older, grayer and statelier just as an increasing number of stone walls crisscross the green landscape. If you found Tiverton appealing, you'll probably wet yourself at the classic sight of Little Compton's **Common** with its white steeped

RHODE ISLAND

church and graveyard. Adjacent to it are a pizza place, café and hardware store.

Though many are content just driving or biking around town, a pair of **beaches** also competes for your attention. To find them, turn right after arriving at the Common's church, continue to Swamp Rd and make a left. Make a second left onto South Shore Rd, at the end of which you'll find South Shore Beach and, your reward, **Goosewing Beach**. Lovely, remote, ocean-facing Goosewing is the only good public beach in Little Compton. Access can be tricky. Due to an ongoing wrangle between the town and the Nature Conservancy over control of the beach, parking and lifeguard coverage are perennially in question. Still, since the dispute began it has been possible to get onto Goosewing by the unusual means of parking at the town beach called **South Shore** ($10) and walking across a small tidal inlet to the more appealing Goosewing. What makes it so appealing is immediately apparent: the long sand beach with its wide-open ocean view is backed by rolling farmland that's almost a throwback to another era. With no facilities to speak of, Goosewing is not convenient, but you won't forget a summer's day spent here.

GALILEE & POINT JUDITH

Rhode Island's port for car ferries to Block Island is at Galilee State Pier, at the southern end of RI 108 in the village of Galilee, near Point Judith. Galilee – sometimes called Point Judith in ferry schedules – is a real workaday fishing town with docks for fishing craft and a dock for the ferries.

Colloquially known as Sand Hill Cove, the **Roger W Wheeler Memorial Beach**, just south of Galilee, is the spot for families with small children. Not only does it have a playground and other facilities, it also has an extremely gradual drop-off and little surf because of protection afforded by the rocky arms of a breakwater called the Point Judith Harbor of Refuge. Roger W Wheeler Memorial Beach is just south of Galilee.

All-day parking in Galilee costs $10 to $15 in any of several lots.

Fishermen's Memorial State Park (☎ 401-789-8374; www.riparks.com; 1011 Point Judith Rd, RI 108; tent sites RI residents/nonresidents $14/20) in Galilee is so popular that many families return year after year to the same site. There are only 180 campsites at Fishermen's, so it's wise to reserve early by requesting the necessary form from the park

management or the **Division of Parks & Recreation** (☎ 401-222-2632; 2321 Hartford Ave, Johnston, RI 02919).

The **Portside Restaurant & Chowder House** (☎ 401-783-3821; 321 Great Island Rd; 8:30am-8pm), the **Top of the Dock Restaurant** (☎ 401-789-7900; 294 Great Island Rd; 11am-10pm) and other eateries are good for a drink or snack while you're waiting for the boat. See p310 for ferry details.

At **Champlin's Seafood** (☎ 401-783-3152; 256 Great Rd; dishes $3-15; 11am-9pm summer, shorter hrs off-season), order a lobster roll, stuffed clams, scallops or one of many sea critters breaded and fried, and hang out on its 2nd-floor deck, which sits inches from the harbor's channel. The swaying masts of rusty fishing vessels keep you company.

Also at the port, **George's of Galilee** (☎ 401-783-2306; cnr Sand Hill Cove & Great Rds; meals $4-20; 11:30am-11pm summer, shorter hrs off-season) has a takeout window where hordes of sandy people line up for clam cakes that are crisp on the outside, doughy on the inside and studded with bits of clam. On some summer evenings, a bad two-piece band plays cheesy covers (actually, to answer your question, we do not like piña coladas) out of amps that should be turned down.

BLOCK ISLAND
pop 800

From the deck of the summer ferry, you'll see a cluster of mansard roofs and gingerbread houses rising picturesquely from the commercial village of Old Harbor, where little has changed since about 1895. Yes, they've added lights and toilets, but – especially if you remain after the departure of the masses on the last ferry – the scale and pace of the island will seem distinctly pre-modern.

The island's attractions are simple. Stretching for several miles to the North of Old Harbor is a lovely beach, long enough to find a quiet spot even on a busy day. Otherwise, bike or hike around the island's rural, rolling farmland, pausing to admire a stately lighthouse or one of the many species of birds that make the island their home. During off-season, the island landscape has the spare, haunted feeling of an Andrew Wyeth painting, with stone walls demarcating centuries-old property lines and few trees to interrupt the ocean views. At this time, the island's population dwindles to a few hundred.

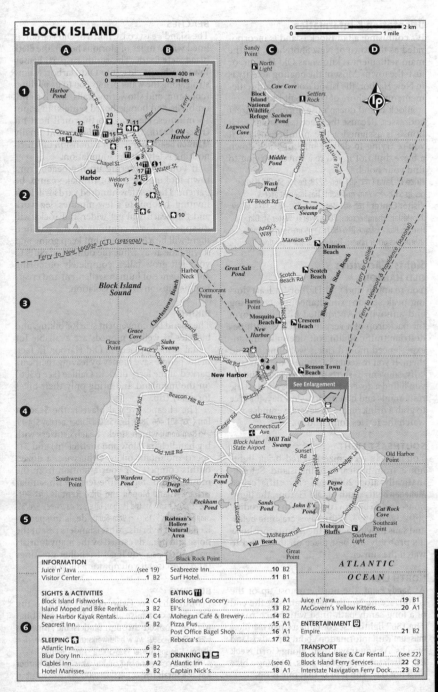

BLOCK ISLAND

Orientation & Information

It's confusing: all of Block Island is incorporated as the town of New Shoreham, but the main settlement is known as Old Harbor, or just 'the town.' Most of the boating activity is in New Harbor, the island's other main settlement, on the shore of Great Salt Pond.

Block Island doesn't use normal US street addresses. Because the place is so small, each house is assigned a fire number, useful if you're trying to deliver mail or track down a blaze, but not if you're a traveler trying to find your hotel.

Juice n' Java (☎ 401-466-5220; Dodge St, Old Harbor; per hr $10; ⊗ 7am-midnight) Has internet access.

Visitor Center (☎ 401-466-2982, 800-383-2474; www .blockislandchamber.com; PO Drawer D, Water St, Old Harbor, Block Island, RI 02807; ⊗ 9am-5pm summer, shorter hrs other times). Find it near the ferry dock.

Sights & Activities

OLD HARBOR

You're apt to find Old Harbor (at least during peak season) simultaneously charming and annoying. Antiquated buildings form the backdrop of a very lively scene, with pedestrian traffic spilling off sidewalks and inexperienced moped riders wobbling around them. If you're keen to acquire some saltwater taffy, souvenir T-shirts or some beach sandals, you'll find a dozen crowded shops amid all the restaurants and hotels. On a slow day, it's nice to grab a drink on one of several verandas and watch the ferries come and go.

SOUTHEAST LIGHT

You'll likely recognize this red-brick lighthouse from postcards of the island. Set dramatically atop 200ft red-clay cliffs called **Mohegan Bluffs** south of Old Harbor, the lighthouse had to be moved back from the eroding cliff edge in 1993. With waves crashing below and sails moving across the Atlantic offshore, it's probably the best place on the island to watch the sunset.

NORTH LIGHT

At **Sandy Point**, the northernmost tip of the island, scenic North Light stands at the end of a long sandy path lined with beach roses. The 1867 lighthouse contains a small **maritime museum** with information about famous island wrecks. As you travel there along Corn Neck Rd, watch for lemonade stands. If riding a bike on a hot day, you'll pray that one is open.

BEACHES

The island's east coast, north of Old Harbor, is lined with 3 miles of glorious beach, the **Block Island State Beach**. The southern part, **Benson Town Beach**, sits closest to Old Harbor; a slow stroll along the water brings you to its pavilion (changing and showering stalls, snack stand, umbrella and boogie board rentals) in about 15 minutes. Heading north, you'll next hit **Crescent Beach**, then **Scotch Beach** and finally **Mansion Beach**, named for a mansion of which nothing is left but the foundation.

If you're wandering up the beach from town looking for a spot to make camp, be patient. The first few hundred yards will look inviting, but put in a few minutes' leg work and the beach will get wider and rocks will disappear. If you continue to the pavilion there will be a big crowd, but keep going and it will fade away while the dunes and cliffs to your left grow taller, completely obscuring any evidence of human settlement and creating the illusion of near isolation.

BIKING

The island is a convenient size for biking, and bicycles as well as mopeds are available for rental at many places in Old Harbor. In fact, many people save money by leaving their cars parked at the ferry dock in Galilee (see p306) on the mainland and bring only their bikes for a day trip.

The cheapest rental place is the **Seacrest Inn** (☎ 401-466-2882; High St, Old Harbor; per day $14-19; ⊗ 8am-6pm), which stocks beach cruisers with big handlebars (slow and inefficient) and 21-speed mountain bikes. Otherwise, a dozen outfits compete for your attention from the moment you step off the ferry, with similar prices. **Island Moped and Bike Rentals** (☎ 401-466-2700; Chapel St, Old Harbor; bike per day/week $20/35, moped per day $115; ⊗ 9am-6pm), deals in specialized brand hybrids. Most islanders resent the noise and hazards caused by the many tourists on mopeds, so you'll get friendlier greetings (and exercise) if you opt for a bicycle.

BOATING

Fishing charters (who doesn't want to tug in a shark or a false albacore?) on small boat may be booked through **Block Island Fishworks** (☎ 401-466-5392; www.bifishworks.com; Ocean Ave, New Harbor; 4-person charter $325-500; ⊗ from 9am).

If you're canoeing or kayaking, **New Harbor Kayak Rentals** (☎ 401-466-2890; Ocean Ave, New Harbor) will launch you into a nearby series of calm, interconnected saltwater ponds which then lead into the Great Salt Pond.

HIKING & BIRD-WATCHING

The island provides some great places to hike: **Rodman's Hollow Natural Area** (entrance off Cooneymus Rd), in the south of the island, is a 100-acre wildlife refuge laced with trails that end at the beach – perfect for a picnic.

The **Clay Head Nature Trail** (off Corn Neck Rd), to the north, follows high clay bluffs along the beachfront, then veers inland through a maze-like series of paths cut into low vegetation that attracts dozens of species of bird.

Bird-watching opportunities abound, especially in spring and fall when migratory species make their way north or south along the Atlantic Flyway. The island's verdant landscape and many freshwater ponds provide ample habitat. The **Nature Conservancy** (☎ 401-466-2129) leads visitors on guided nature walks in some refuges. Call for times.

Sleeping

Camping is not allowed on the island, but there are some 35 cozy B&Bs and small guest-house-style inns. You should know, however, that many places have a two- or three-day minimum stay in summer (especially on weekends and holidays) and that advance reservations are essential. Many places close between November and April. Peak season runs roughly from mid-June to Labor Day. Off-season prices can be far cheaper than those listed below.

The visitor center near the ferry dock keeps track of vacancies, and its staff will try to help you should you make the mistake of arriving without a reservation.

Gables Inn (☎ 401-466-2213; Dodge St, Old Harbor; r $125-185, off-season $55-100) A wood-framed Victorian, the friendly Gables features high beds and small rooms with a variety of lace and wallpaper, often of a vivid floral pattern. Guests have free access to beach supplies (towels, chairs, coolers, umbrellas) and a parlor of velvet furniture. No water view.

Surf Hotel (☎ 401-466-2241; Dodge St, Old Harbor; r $200, with shared bathroom $110-150) A classic 19th-century hotel, one side of this hotel faces the bustle of Old Harbor's main drag, the other the ocean. You'll find multiple porches on several levels – one practically juts into the harbor – and a rooftop cupola.

The overly-cluttered lobby contains a jumble of taxidermy, dark Victorian furniture, busy wallpaper and people playing scrabble. Rooms can be very small and haven't been updated in forever. Spend the extra 10 bucks and get an ocean view.

Seabreeze Inn (☎ 401-466-2275; www.blockisland.com/seabreeze; Spring St, Old Harbor; r $190-260, with shared bathroom $120-160; **P**) Some rooms in these charming hillside cottages have uninterrupted views over a tidal pond and the ocean beyond. Others face inward towards a garden, though turn your head and you'll catch a glimpse of the blue. Inside, airy rooms have plenty of windows, cathedral ceilings and no electronic distractions like TVs and clocks. Expect plenty of simplicity, beauty and maybe your own porch with plantings that rustle in the night wind.

Atlantic Inn (☎ 401-466-5883, 800-224-7422; www.atlanticinn.com; High St, Old Harbor; d $189-269, off-season $165-205) This 1879 establishment overlooks the town center from a gentle perch on a grassy hilltop. The views over ocean and town are commanding and beautiful. The gracefully appointed Victorian inn features a wide porch, Adirondack chairs strewn across a spacious lawn, 21 rooms (some are kind of small) and a well-stocked bar (p310).

Blue Dory Inn (☎ 401-466-5891, 800-992-7290; www.blockislandinns.com; Dodge St, Old Harbor; d $225-325, off-season $65-95) With 14 small rooms, this cozy place sits at the edge of Old Harbor overlooking a stretch of beach. Decorated in Victorian style, it oozes 'romantic' flourishes (fresh flowers, girly bedding, saccharinely named rooms). There's a great porch, and it's open all year. Cookies baked daily.

Hotel Manisses (☎ 401-466-2421, 800-626-4773; www.blockislandresorts.com; Spring St, Old Harbor; r $220-370, off-season $65-115) With its high Victorian 'widow's walk' turret and small but lushly furnished guest rooms, the Manisses combines sophistication with Block Island's relaxed brand of country charm. It's part of a family accommodations business that includes the 1661 Inn, 1661 Guest House, Dewey Cottage, Dodge Cottage, Nicholas Ball Cottage and Sheffield House, all within a short walk from Old Harbor, so one call gets you information on dozens of rooms ranging in price depending upon the room, the building and the season. Open year-round.

Eating

Block Island specializes in fish, shellfish and more fish. Generally, cheap food = fried fish; expensive food = nonfried fish. Most places are open for lunch and dinner during the summer; many close off-season. Make a dinner reservation in the high season or risk hour-long waits.

Pizza Plus (☎ 401-466-939; Ocean Ave, Old Harbor; slice $2; 11am-2pm) It's not the best pizza, but it will do. Especially if you're trying to find something that doesn't have fish in it. The very daring might try their 'breakfast pizza,' which is a pizza crust filled with eggs and topped with meat, peppers and onion. But then the very daring never possessed great wisdom, did they?

Rebecca's (☎ 401-466-5411; Water St, Old Harbor; sandwiches $4-7, fried fishes $6-13; 7am-2am Thu-Mon, 7am-8pm Tue & Wed) This snack stand serves burgers, chowder, grilled cheese sandwiches, grease and deep-fried sea monster (aka fried clams, fried fish, fried scallops etc) to hungry tourists seated at picnic tables under umbrellas.

Post Office Bagel Shop (☎ 401-466-5959; Bridgegate Sq, Old Harbor; food $2.50-9; 6:30am-3pm; V) Order at the counter and grab a seat on the umbrella-shaded patio. Fine sandwiches are served on bagels and sourdough, though the top-shelf baked sweets should grab your eye. Perfect granola bars come warm, chewy and with the taste of coconut emerging subtly past pumpkin seeds and oats.

Mohegan Café & Brewery (☎ 401-466-5911; Water St, Old Harbor; burgers $7-9, meals $8-26; 11:30am-10pm) Besides brewing its own beer, this place serves fish-and-chips, tex-mex stuff (nachos and burritos), and fresh shark with Cajun seasoning under a pressed-tin roof. It's a dark-wood pub with a few model ships lying around. Food tends to be filling and hit-or-miss.

Hotel Manisses (☎ 401-466-2421; Spring St; meals $20-37; 5:30-9:30pm) Dine in either the Gatsby Room, a tall-ceilinged space with old light fixtures and wicker, or on a fine patio surrounded by flowers and bubbling statuary. The menu features local seafood, vegetables from the hotel's garden and sautéed frog legs. Have flaming coffees and outrageous desserts in the parlor.

our pick Eli's (☎ 401-466-5230; Chapel St, Old Harbor; meals $21-40; from 5:30pm; V) Locally caught sea bass specials (tender fillets over scallions grapes and beans) taste so fresh and mildly salty and sweet that its memory will haunt you for weeks. For real. The room is cramped, crowded and casual with lots of pine wood and a bit of well-conceived art. Try beet gnocchi and angel food cake with seasonal berries.

For alcohol and snacks, **Block Island Grocery** (☎ 401-466-2949; Ocean Ave, Old Harbor; 8am-10pm Mon-Sat, 8am-8pm Sun) is the biggest market.

Drinking

Though Block Island quiets down after the last ferry leaves, you can still find some stuff to do at night.

Atlantic Inn (☎ 401-466-5883; High St, Old Harbor) Enjoy a cocktail on the Atlantic's grassy hilltop with panoramic water view. Thanks to a bit of distance, things here are way more low-key and slow-paced than spots in the middle of town. So grab a rocking chair, put on a tweed jacket (not required) and arrive an hour before sunset. If peckish, eat a cheese plate ($12).

McGovern's Yellow Kittens (☎ 401-466-5855; Corn Neck Rd; from noon) Just north of Old Harbor, McGovern's Yellow Kittens attracts New England–area bands and keeps rowdy patrons happy with pool, table tennis and darts. It's been called Yellow Kittens since 1876.

Captain Nick's (☎ 401-466-5670; Ocean Ave, Bar Harbor; from 5pm) With a patch over one eye, this youngster offers drinks, good times and liquid treasure. It's got live music six days a week, sometimes acoustic, often rock. Please don't forget your bandana.

Juice n' Java (☎ 401-466-5220; Dodge St, Old Harbor; 7am-midnight; V) This popular coffee shop also serves smoothies – something you'll be very thankful for after last night's encounter with 2lb of lobster and butter. Also on offer are healthy sandwiches, many of them vegetarian. The colorfully painted room provides internet access.

Entertainment

Empire (☎ 401-466-2555; cnr High & Water Sts, Old Harbor) The main event for those avoiding the sauce is this single-screen movie house inside a former roller-skating rink.

Getting There & Around

New England Airlines (☎ 401-800-243-2460) provides air service between Westerly State Airport, on Airport Rd off RI 78, and Block Island State Airport (one way/round-trip $45/76; 12 minutes).

Interstate Navigation (☎ 401-783-4613; www .blockislandferry.com) operates 'traditional' car-

and-passenger ferries from Galilee State Pier, Point Judith, to Old Harbor, Block Island ($17 same day round-trip, one hour, eight times daily mid-June to early September). Cars and bikes are carried for $90 and $6 round-trip. Reservations are needed for cars, but not passengers and bikes. In winter, service is infrequent with perhaps one to three daily departures. They also run a 'high-speed' passenger ferry ($30 round-trip, 30 minutes, six daily June to September) to/from Galilee. Reservations are recommended.

In the summer, Interstate runs boats from Newport's Fort Adams Dock (one way/round-trip $9/13, two hours, one daily) to Old Harbor. It takes bikes but not cars.

Block Island Ferry Services (☎ 860-444-4624; www.goblockisland.com) offers service from New London, CT, to New Harbor (round-trip $37 to $42, one hour, four daily).

All ferries charge half-price for child fares. You don't need a car to get around Block Island and, aside from hotel parking lots, there aren't many places to put one. You'll save a ton of money by leaving it behind, and, besides, you don't really want to screw with the island's pristine ecology.

Block Island Bike & Car Rental (☎ 401-466-2297; Ocean Ave, New Harbor) rents cars, or you can hire a taxi. There are usually several taxis available at the ferry dock in Old Harbor and in New Harbor. See p308 for moped and bike rentals.

SOUTH COUNTY AREA BEACHES

Grab an umbrella, a blanket and four rocks. Not much beats a well-chosen piece of sandy turf on a sunny August day in South County. The sandy shore extends virtually uninterrupted for several dozen miles, and much of it is open to the public. Some beaches teem with thousands of well-oiled young bodies, smooshed together like an overstuffed drawer full of hand-knitted sweaters. Others are more subdued, where visitors can thin themselves into relative privacy across a long landscape.

Those afraid of melanoma or disconcerted by the chilly water temperatures in June and early July should take heart that many of the beaches lie near a series of massive salt ponds. These salt ponds are home to multitudes of waterfowl and shellfish, and some (such as Trustom Pond in South Kingstown) have been designated national wildlife refuges. They make for excellent bird-watching.

You're likely to see herons, egrets and sandpipers hunting for lunch, and, at low tide, clams squirting from beneath the muddy sand.

Orientation

The stretch of beach that runs from Point Judith to Watch Hill directly faces the Atlantic and has a different kind of geography from the portion that runs north from Point Judith to Narragansett, which faces Narragansett Bay.

The Atlantic-facing stretch is a wide apron of pristine sand separating huge salt ponds such as Quonochontaug and Ninigret from the surfy, generally seaweed-free open ocean. These beaches, which trace the coast like a necklace looped with tidal salt ponds, are similar in nature and, geologically speaking, are all the same beach.

The beaches that front the Narragansett Bay are smaller and divided from one another. Many are in coves dramatically surrounded by huge boulders. These are particularly lovely early and late in the day, when the sun slants on the granite, stage-lighting the scene. They generally have better surf.

Information

Narragansett Chamber of Commerce (☎ 401-783-7121; www.narragansettri.com/chamber; The Towers, RI 1A, PO Box 742, Narragansett, RI 02882; ⏰ 9am-4pm) For information on the town of Narragansett and its vicinity.

Rhode Island Division of Parks & Recreation (☎ 401-222-2321; www.riparks.com) For information on all of Rhode Island's state beaches.

South County Tourism Council (☎ 401-789-4422, 800-548-4662; www.southcountyri.com; 4808 Tower Hill Rd, Wakefield; ⏰ 9am-5pm Mon-Fri) For information on the South County area, including beaches and attractions, contact this office.

Sights & Activities

The following patches of sand (listed from east to west) represent only a partial list of stone-skipping possibilities. At all of them, a parking tariff is imposed from late May to the end of September. At state beaches, Rhode Island residents pay $6 on weekdays and $7 on weekends for each car. Nonresidents pay $12 or $14. Town beaches charge similar rates.

NARRAGANSETT TOWN BEACH

Narragansett tends to be crowded because it's an easy walk from the beachy town of Narragansett Pier. It's the only beach in Rhode Island that charges a per-person admission fee ($4) on top of a parking fee ($5). Still, people – surfers in particular – adore it.

SCARBOROUGH STATE BEACH
Scarborough (sometimes written as 'Scarboro') is the prototypical Rhode Island beach, considered by many the best in the state. A massive, castle-like pavilion, generous boardwalks, a wide and long beachfront, and great, predictable surf make Scarborough special. It tends to attract a lot of teenagers, but it's large enough that other people can take them or leave them. On a hot summer day, expect extra hordes of beachgoers.

SOUTH KINGSTOWN TOWN BEACH
A sandy beach that epitomizes the South County model, the Town Beach provides a small pavilion with restrooms and changing rooms. There's convenient parking in nearby Wakefield.

BLUE SHUTTERS TOWN BEACH
A Charlestown-managed beach, this is also a good choice for families. There are no amusements other than nature's, but there are convenient facilities, a watchful staff of lifeguards, generally mild surf and smaller crowds.

MISQUAMICUT STATE BEACH
With good surf and close proximity to the Connecticut state line, Misquamicut draws huge crowds. It offers families low prices and convenient facilities for changing, showering and eating. Another plus is that it's near an old-fashioned amusement area, **Atlantic Beach Park** (☎ 401-322-0504; 321-338 Atlantic Ave, Misquamicut), which ranges between charming and derelict. Here you'll find plenty to enjoy or avoid – water slides, miniature golf, batting cages, kiddie rides, arcade games and, for a lucky few, tetanus shots. Misquamicut is situated just south of Westerly.

Sleeping
For extra listings, contact **B&B Referrals of South Coast Rhode Island** (☎ 800-853-7479; ⏰ 11am-7pm), a collective group of 22 places in and around the southern coast. The phone is staffed by someone with an up-to-date list of vacancies.

BUDGET
Burlingame State Park Campsites (☎ 401-322-7337; www.riparks.com; off US 1 N, Charlestown; tent sites RI residents/nonresidents $14/20; ⏰ mid-April–mid-Oct)

This lovely campground has more than 750 spacious wooded sites near crystal-clear Watchaug Pond, which provides a good beach for swimming. The park occupies 2100 acres. First-come, first-served is the rule, but you can call ahead to check on availability. Your stay is limited to two weeks.

Worden's Pond Family Campground (☎ 401-789-9113; 416a Worden's Pond Rd, South Kingstown; sites $30; ⏰ May–mid-Oct) This pleasantly wooded family-owned campground, with 75 tent sites and 125 RV sites, provides access to a calm pond where you can fish and swim. They've got coin-operated showers, a playground and pits for playing the game of horseshoes. From US Hwy 1, follow RI 110, and turn at the second left (Worden's Pond Rd); from there it's less than a mile to the campground.

MIDRANGE & TOP END
Grandview B&B (☎ 401-596-6384, 800-447-6384; www.grandviewbandb.com; 212 Shore Rd/RI 1A, Westerly; r $90-120, off-season $85-95) Within the town limits of Westerly, yet close to the beach town of Weekapaug, this modestly furnished guesthouse boasts a stone porch and a knowledgeable proprietor full of friendly tips about the area. Charming as the place is, rooms in the front catch a bit of traffic noise.

Admiral Dewey Inn (☎ 401-783-2090, 800-457-2090; www.admiraldeweyinn.com; 668 Matunuck Beach Rd, South Kingstown; r $110-160) Near the beachy town of Matunuck, this 1898 National Historic Register building with 10 rooms offers reasonable rates and a two-minute walk to the beach. Most of the rooms in the gray-shingled inn have water views, and there's a broad porch that catches the ocean breeze.

The Richards (☎ 401-789-7746; www.therichardsbnb.com; 144 Gibson Ave, Narragansett; r $145-175) Built of locally quarried granite, the Gothic English–manor look sets it apart from other B&Bs in Narragansett. Each room contains a working fireplace, and there's a nice garden on the grounds. It's a 10-minute drive to the University of Rhode Island. No kids under 12 are allowed.

Weekapaug Inn (☎ 401-322-0301; www.weekapauginn.com; 25 Spray Rock Rd, Weekapaug; s/d with all meals $325/450) A classic with its wraparound porch and lawn sloping down to Quonochontaug Pond (a saltwater tidal pool), this vast shingled inn caters to a rather sedate crowd, many of whom have been regulars for decades. Expect croquet, shuffleboard, tennis and no phones or (gasp!) liquor license. The inn's setting, with its own private ocean beach, is one of the loveliest in New England. Men must wear jackets to dinner. Cash or checks only.

Eating

Not surprisingly, seafood is the order of the day in South County. Most spots are casual and beachy; shorts and T-shirts are far more common than suits and ties. Nearly every beach has its collection of clam shacks and snack shops good for a quick lunch. For a more elaborate meal, you might head to Newport, Providence or drop by Point Judith. In addition to the following, consider the Fantastic Umbrella Factory's café (see right).

84 High Street Café (☎ 401-596-7871; 84 High St, Westerly; meals $16-35; ☽ 11am-late Mon-Sat, 9am-3pm Sun) For big plates of Mediterranean fare (mostly Italian), this restaurant and lounge provides one of the few good kitchens outside of Newport and Providence. Enjoy tortellini and spicy sausage with linguini over a red sauce with ground rib eye. The lounge serves booze (there are TVs for sports) and hosts local bands on Thursday and Friday nights.

Coast Guard House (☎ 401-789-0700; 40 Ocean Dr, Narragansett; meals $20-30; ☽ lunch & dinner Mon-Fri) For an upscale dinner, this place has long been a Rhode Island favorite, serving pasta, seafood stew and crab cakes. It occupies a dramatic seaside site (waves crash enthusiastically against the building during storms), and practically abuts the stunning Narragansett Towers, two heavy stone towers connected by a bold bridge spanning Ocean Dr, built in the 1880s.

Basil's Restaurant (☎ 401-789-3743; 22 Kingstown Rd, Narragansett; meals $25-40) Since long before the emergence of so-called new American cuisine, this family-run joint has served classics such as beef stroganoff, crispy duck in orange sauce, filet mignon and wiener schnitzel to men wearing jackets on the Narragansett Pier.

Drinking & Entertainment

Quiet, seaside South County is not noted for its nightlife, but there are a couple of places in the area where folks can stay up past 9pm.

Theatre-by-the-Sea (☎ 401-782-8587; www.theatre bythesea.com; Cards Pond Rd, South Kingstown; tickets $39-49) Located in a scenic area close to the beaches of Matunuck, this venue offers a summer schedule of likable musicals and plays in one of the oldest barn theaters in the US.

FANTASTIC UMBRELLA FACTORY

A sprawling collection of 19th-century farm buildings and elaborate, unkempt gardens, the **Fantastic Umbrella Factory** (☎ 401-364-6616; RI 1A, Charlestown), a former commune, got its start as one of Rhode Island's strangest stores in 1968. You can find almost anything in a series of shacks and sheds filled with a wide variety of gift items: from flower bulbs and perennials to greeting cards, toys, handmade jewelry and scads of stuff hippies favor like drums and hemp clothing. Their café serves quality sandwiches and carrot cake. Exotic birds and farm animals walk all over the place, much to the delight of children.

Ocean Mist (☎ 401-782-3740; www.oceanmist.net; 145 Matunuck Beach Rd, South Kingstown; ☽ to 1am) For live music (rock, blues, reggae), try this lively bar. The deck extends over the beach, where you might glimpse a midnight loner casting for blue fish should it get too loud for you inside. They've got pub food and pool tables.

Shopping

Benny's (☎ 401-783-5170; 688 Kingstown Rd, Wakefield) People in Rhode Island couldn't live without Benny's, an odd chain of small department stores where the strangely service-minded clerks will invariably ask you if need help finding anything. It's hands-down the best place to buy cheap beach supplies (chairs, towels, plastic flip-flops, coolers). While the experience is impossible to describe, those who regularly visit Benny's over a year begin to see it as the living symbol of the state's common culture.

Getting There & Away

Though the Shore Route Amtrak trains between Boston and New York stop in Westerly, you really need a car to efficiently get to the beaches. Distances are not great: Westerly to Wakefield is only about 21 miles. Traffic to and from the South County beaches can be horrendous on hot summer weekends. Come early, stay late.

WATCH HILL
pop 2000

One of the tiniest summer colonies in the Ocean State, Watch Hill occupies a spit of land at the southwesternmost point of Rhode

Island, just south of Westerly. Drive into the village along winding RI 1A, and the place grabs you: huge, shingled and Queen Anne summerhouses command the rolling landscape from their perches high on rocky knolls. These houses show the wealth of their owners with subtle good taste; though they were built around the turn of the century, contemporaneously with Newport's mansions, they aren't flashy palaces. Perhaps partly because of that, Watch Hill's houses are still in private hands, while Newport's became white elephants, rescued only as tourist attractions.

Visitors spend their time at the beach and browsing in the shops along Bay St, the main street, a mere two blocks long. If you haven't yet hit puberty or if you've brought children, an ice-cream cone from St Clair's Annex and a twirl on the Flying Horses Carousel provide immediate gratification and fodder for fond memories. There is next to nothing to do at night.

Orientation

Summertime parking in tiny Watch Hill is a real hassle. Most curb parking is vigorously reserved for town residents. If you're lucky, you can snag a free spot (strict three-hour limit) on Bay St. Otherwise, expect to shell out $10 to $15 at one of several lots.

Watch Hill is at the end of Watch Hill Rd, 6 miles south of Westerly and 12 roundabout miles east of Stonington, CT, by car.

Sights & Activities

The antique **Flying Horses Carousel** (Bay St; ride $1; ⏲ 11am-9pm Mon-Fri, 10am-9pm Sat & Sun) at the end of Bay St dates from 1883. Besides being among the few historic carousels still in operation in the country, it boasts a unique design: its horses are suspended on chains so that they really do 'fly' outward as the carousel spins around. Yes, riders can grab for rings (a brass one equals a free ride), and, no, you can't ride if you're over 12 years old.

For a leisurely beach walk, the half-mile stroll to **Napatree Point**, at the westernmost tip of Watch Hill, is unbeatable. With the Atlantic on one side and the yacht-studded Little Narragansett Bay on the other, Napatree is a protected conservation area, so walkers are asked to stay on the trails and off the dunes.

The nearest state beach to Watch Hill is Misquamicut State Beach (p312), 3 miles to the east along RI 1A, but there is a fine free **beach** right in Watch Hill, in front of a construction

site for the Ocean House Hotel. It stretches for several pretty miles from the Watch Hill lighthouse all the way to Misquamicut, with the open ocean crashing on one side and large, gray-shingled homes rising behind grassy dunes on the other. Access to the beach is by a right-of-way off Bluff Ave near Larkin Rd. The closest parking is on Bay St. There are no facilities on the beach and neighboring property owners are vigilant about restricting beachgoers to the public area below the high-tide line. There's also the small **Watch Hill Beach** (adult/child $6/4; ⏲ 10am-7pm Mon-Fri, 9am-6pm Sat & Sun) behind the Flying Horses Carousel.

Sleeping

There aren't many good options directly in Watch Hill, which is why you might consider the Grandview B&B (see p312), about 5 miles away.

Watch Hill Inn (☎ 401-348-6300; www.watchhillinn .com; 38 Bay St; r $165-250, off-season $100-150; ⓟ ✿) The wood-floored rooms of this mostly modern inn contain Victorian-ish furnishings and overlook the bobbing boats floating in the harbor across the street. It sells out early and hosts a lot of wedding parties.

Eating

In addition to the following, you'll find an espresso joint and a pizza place on Bay St. There isn't much else.

Bay St Deli (☎ 401-596-6606; 112 Bay St; sandwiches $6-9; ⏲ 8am-8pm) Stop by this deli for takeout prepared items and specialty sandwiches (roast beef and munster cheese on pumpernickel or a wrap of tabbouleh, cucumber, tomato and sprouts) good for picnics.

St Clair's Annex (☎ 401-348-8407; 41 Bay St; cones from $2; ⏲ 7:45am-9pm) This ice-cream shop, across the street from the deli, has been run by the same family for more than a century, and features several dozen flavors of homemade ice-cream. If you don't feel like a frozen treat, they've got breakfast omelets, hot dogs and lobster salad.

Olympia Tea Room (☎ 401-348-8211; 74 Bay St; meals $12-40; ⏲ from 11am) The most atmospheric restaurant in town, the Olympia is an authentic 1916 soda-fountain-turned-bistro. Varnished wooden booths, pink walls, black-and-white checkered tiles on the floor and the antique marble-topped soda fountain help to ease calf livers, broiled flounder and little necks and sausages past your esophagus.

Connecticut

Lurking on the southern fringes of New England, Connecticut is often regarded as a mere stepping stone to the 'real thing.' Ironically, the comparative lack of tourist interest has saved Connecticut (CT) from the overexposure of some of the more 'New Englandy' states. Well-preserved towns on the Long Island Sound exude a variety of charms – from Stonington to rejuvenated New London to the sophisticated university city of New Haven. Coastal villages are home to watermen who still ply the Sound for lobsters and oysters. Their harvest can be savored at countless restaurants and sea shacks.

To be sure, many visitors are drawn to the justifiably popular Mystic Seaport Museum, a re-creation of a working 19th-century whaling village, or to gamble at Foxwoods, the largest casino on the planet, but these don't begin to scratch the surface. Three-quarters of Connecticut is rural, and the Litchfield Hills, with lakes, vineyards and hiking trails, and the Quiet Corner, with its orchards and rolling meadows, capture Connecticut as it has been for centuries. Equally pristine scenery began luring artists to the Connecticut River Valley in the 1900s, and if you follow the river up from Old Lyme, it's easy to sense what inspired them. Continue along the river past colonial Essex and the eccentric Gillette Castle and you'll arrive in Hartford. Long maligned for its grim corporate atmosphere, the capital is home to several intriguing historic sights and a world-class museum that will beg your attention – much like Connecticut itself.

HIGHLIGHTS

- Marveling at the eccentric **Gillette Castle** (p341) – and the spectacular views of the Connecticut River below

- Seducing lady luck (or at least trying) at **Foxwoods Resort Casino** (p324), the largest casino on earth

- Admiring fine art at **Yale** (p332), the Wadsworth Atheneum (p344) in **Hartford**, the Florence Griswold Museum (p339) in **Old Lyme** or the Bruce Museum (p338) in **Greenwich**

- Scarfing down lobster or juicy bivalves at down-home sea shacks like Abbott's Lobster in the Rough (p323) in **Noank** or Captain Scott's Lobster Dock (p328) in **New London**

- Whiling away the afternoon on the 12-mile stretch of MA 169 between **Woodstock** and **Brooklyn** (p329) picking apples, browsing greenhouses and poking around antique shops

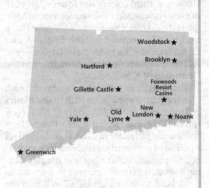

Woodstock ★

Brooklyn ★

Hartford ★

Foxwoods Resort Casino ★

Gillette Castle ★

Yale ★   Old Lyme ★   New London ★   ★ Noank

★ Greenwich

■ TELEPHONE CODE: 860, 203   ■ POPULATION: 3.5 MILLION   ■ AREA: 4845 SQ MILES

Orientation & Information

A virtual square, Connecticut is bordered by New York State to the east, Massachusetts to the north, Rhode Island to the west and the Long Island Sound in the south. Its capital, Hartford, lies almost smack in the center, and is bisected by the Connecticut River, which gives out in the Sound.

Connecticut Office of Tourism (☎ 860-256-2800; www.ctvisit.com; 755 Main St, Hartford, CT 06103) Get a free, comprehensive *Connecticut Vacation Guide* by mail, or at a Welcome Center (at Bradley International Airport Terminals A and B and on major highways entering the state).

Connecticut's Cultural Gateway (www.ctculture .org) Offers a statewide activities calendar, a directory of museums and other resources.

Nutmeg B&B Agency (☎ 860-236-6698, 800-727-7592; www.nutmegbb.com) For booking B&Bs. There's a 12% hotel tax levied on all accommodations charges; figure it in when calculating your lodging costs.

Visit Connecticut (www.visitconnecticut.com) Breaks down the state into regions and offers links to lodging, tours, fairs, activities and transportation.

History

A number of Native American tribes (notably the Pequot and the Mohegan, whose name for the river became the name of the state) were here when the first European explorers, primarily Dutch, appeared in the early 17th century. The first English settlement was at Old Saybrook in 1635, followed a year later by the Connecticut Colony, built by Massachusetts Puritans under Thomas Hooker. A third colony was founded in 1638 in New Haven. After the Pequot War (1637), the Native Americans were no longer a check to colonial expansion in New England, and Connecticut's English population grew. In 1686, Connecticut was brought into the Dominion of New England.

The American Revolution swept through Connecticut, leaving scars with major battles at Stonington (1775), Danbury (1777), New Haven (1779) and Groton (1781). Connecticut became the fifth state in 1788. It embarked on a period of prosperity, propelled by its whaling, shipbuilding, farming and manufacturing industries (from firearms to bicycles to household tools), which lasted well into the 19th century.

The 20th century brought world wars and the depression but, thanks in no small part to Connecticut's munitions industries, the state was able to fight back. Everything from planes to submarines was made in the state, and when the defense industry began to decline in the 1990s, the growth of other businesses (such as insurance) helped pick up the slack.

The Culture

Given its proximity to New York City, it's unsurprising that the southwestern part of Connecticut has become a bedroom community of the metropolis, more a part of the Tri-State Area than New England. But moving away from New York, you'll encounter communities that are staunchly independent with deep local roots.

The northeast (Litchfield Hills; p348) and northwest (the Quiet Corner; p329) are given over to farming and haven't changed much in the past century. And while the coast along the Long Island Sound has been built up by industry since WWII, its small towns still look to the sea.

And yet Nutmeggers (CT residents) are never too far from New York or Boston to feel isolated. Able to enjoy the rural life with access to the city, they have the best of both worlds.

Land & Climate

Despite its population density, almost two-thirds of Connecticut is covered by forest, park or farmland. Rolling hills define much of the terrain (particularly the Litchfield Hills in the northwest), but there are no real mountains.

As with the rest of New England, Connecticut is truly a four-season destination, and its climate does not dramatically differ from that of the rest of the region; winters are generally cold and snowy, with summers ranging from pleasantly warm to scorching and humid.

In terms of autumnal colors, the Litchfield Hills, the northeast Quiet Corner and the state's southwest strip tend to peak over the first two weeks of October. Hartford and its central environs follow a week or so later. Call Connecticut's **foliage hotline** (☎ 800-282-6863) for specifics.

Parks & Wildlife

The state has a bevy of wonderful – and often wonderfully undervisited – parks to hike, fish, swim and camp in. For camping options, including private campgrounds, grab a free copy of the *Connecticut Camp-ground Directory* at any Welcome Center. Many sites are designated as parks but are known more for their

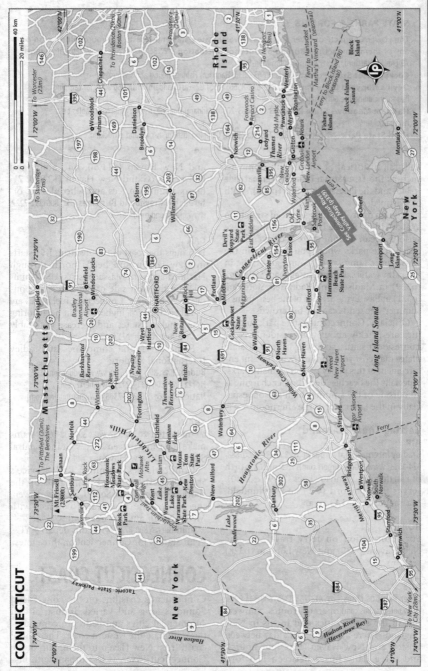

CONNECTICUT

STATE PARKS & FORESTS

The Lower Connecticut River Valley has several state parks and forests. For more information on any of them, contact the **Bureau of Outdoor Recreation** (☎ 860-424-3200; http://dep.state.ct.us/rec; 79 Elm St, Hartford; ☟ 8:30am-4:30pm Mon-Fri).
Cockaponset State Forest (☎ 860-663-2030; Haddam) Fishing, hiking and swimming.
Devil's Hopyard State Park (☎ 860-873-8566; off CT 82, East Haddam) With 860 acres for camping and hiking, including the 60ft Chapman Falls.
Haddam Meadows State Park (☎ 860-663-2030; Haddam) Boating, fishing and picnic tables on the riverbank.
Hurd State Park (☎ 860-526-2336; East Hampton) Camping, fishing, hiking and picnicking.

---

cultural, historical or simply fun elements, such as the **Essex Steam Train & Riverboat Ride** (p340) and the **Dinosaur State Park** (p348), south of Hartford.

Though many Nutmeggers head straight to Watch Hill in Rhode Island when they crave serious ocean action, there are several fine beach state parks where you can take in the sunset over Long Island Sound and frolic in the calm waters. **Hammonasset Beach State Park** (p329) in Madison and **Rocky Neck State Park** (p321) in East Lyme are two of the best, though summer weekends can see big crowds.

Officially, Connecticut's state park authorities are prickly about your resident versus nonresident status, so displaying out-of-state plates may cost you a few extra bucks. But enforcement of this policy is spotty – many parks, especially the beaches, don't bother charging at all outside of the summer high season, especially in the latter half of the afternoon.

Getting There & Around

AIR

Bradley International Airport (☎ 860-292-2000, 888-624-1533; www.bradleyairport.com), 12 miles north of Hartford in Windsor Locks (I-91 exit 40), serves the Hartford (CT) and Springfield, Massachusetts (MA) area.

BOAT

For information on ferry travel, see the New Haven (p335) and New London (p328) sections.

BUS

Peter Pan Bus Lines (☎ 413-781-3320, 800-343-9999; www.peterpanbus.com) operates routes connecting all the major cities and towns in New England. There are five buses a day between Boston and New Haven ($30, four hours), and three daily buses between Hartford

and New Haven ($11.50, one hour) and between NYC and New Haven ($24.50, 2½ hours). Similar prices and schedules are offered by **Greyhound Bus Lines** (☎ 800-231-2222; www.greyhound.com).

CAR

I-95 hugs the coast of Connecticut. I-91 starts in New Haven and heads north through Hartford and into Massachusetts. US 7 shimmies up the west side of the state, backboning the Berkshires. Connecticut fuel prices are usually at least 5% higher than in neighboring New England states and increase noticeably as you approach NYC.

Some car rental companies at Bradley International Airport:
Budget (☎ 800-527-0700; www.budget.com)
Hertz (☎ 800-331-1212; www.hertz.com)
National (☎ 800-217-7368; www.nationalcar.com)

TRAIN

Metro-North (☎ 212-532-4900, 800-638-7646) trains make the run between NYC's Grand Central Station and New Haven.

Connecticut Commuter Rail Service's **Shore Line East** (☎ 800-255-7433) travels up the shore of Long Island Sound. At New Haven, the Shore Line East trains connect with Metro-North and Amtrak routes.

Amtrak (☎ 800-872-7245) trains depart NYC's Penn Station for Connecticut on three lines.

CONNECTICUT COAST

Connecticut's coastline on the Long Island Sound is long and varied. Industrial and commercial cities and bedroom communities dominate the western coast. The central coast, from New Haven to the mouth of the Connecticut River, is less urban, with historic towns and villages. The eastern coast is centered on Mystic, whose maritime history comes to life at Mystic Seaport Museum.

MYSTIC

pop 4000

A skyline of masts greets you as you round the corner on US 1 heading west into town. They belong to the vessels bobbing ever so slightly in the postcard-perfect harbor. There's a sense of self-satisfied calm and composure in the air – until suddenly a heart-stopping steamer whistle blows, followed by the cheerful cling of a drawbridge bell. You know you've arrived in Mystic. You're sure not alone.

Mystic was a classic whaling town centuries before the Mystic Seaport Museum became such a popular tourist attraction, and the town remains a fine place to stroll, shop, dine and slurp ice cream. In addition to the museum, the town is home to the excellent Mystic Aquarium. Less than 10 miles north is the state's official biggest draw, the Foxwoods and Mohegan Sun casinos.

Orientation

Take I-95 exit 90 for the Mystic Seaport Museum and town center. The museum is a mile south of the highway off CT 27 (Greenmanville Ave); the center of the town is less than a mile further south. Old Mystic is a separate town to the north of I-95.

The Mystic River Bascule Bridge (1922), known locally as 'the drawbridge,' carries US 1 across the Mystic River at the center of the town. It's a familiar ritual in Mystic to wait while the drawbridge is raised for river traffic. There are restaurants on both sides of the bridge; most of the ice-cream shops are on the west side, where you'll also find high-end clothing boutiques and establishments with names like 'Framers of the Lost Art.'

Information

Bank of America (54 W Main St) Has an ATM.
Bank Square Books (☎ 860-536-3795; 53 W Main St; ☼ 10am-6pm Mon & Tue, 10am-9pm Wed-Sat, 11:30am-6pm Sun) This bookstore keeps a good stock of local-interest titles, plus the usual suspects. (Note the carving in the shape of a whale on the sidewalk just outside the store.)
Information kiosk (Roosevelt St; ☼ 9am-5pm Mon-Fri) This small kiosk is in the train station.
Library (☎ 860-536-7721; 40 Library St; ☼ 10am-9pm Mon-Fri, 9am-1pm Sat) This branch offers internet access for 25¢ per 20 minutes.

Mystic & Shoreline Visitors Information Center (☎ 860-536-1641; www.mysticinfo.com; 27 Coogan Blvd; ☼ 9am-6pm Mon-Sat, 9am-4:30pm Sun summer, 9am-4:30pm daily off-season) The best stop for tourist information in town, located next to the Olde Mistick Village.
Mystic Chamber of Commerce (☎ 860-572-9578; www.mysticchamber.org; 14 Holmes St, Schooner's Wharf) This chamber of commerce is another resource for travelers.

Sights & Activities

MYSTIC SEAPORT MUSEUM

From simple beginnings in the 17th century, the village of Mystic grew to become one of the great shipbuilding ports of the East Coast. In the mid-19th century, Mystic's shipyards launched clipper ships, many from the George Greenman & Co Shipyard, now the site of **Mystic Seaport Museum** (☎ 860-572-0711; www.mystic seaport.org; 75 Greenmanville Ave/CT 27; adult/6-17yr/senior $17.50/12/15.50; ☼ 9am-5pm Apr-Oct, 10am-4pm Nov-Mar; ♿). Today, the museum covers 17 acres and includes more than 60 historic buildings, four tall ships and almost 500 smaller vessels. Some buildings in the museum were originally here, but, as with Old Sturbridge Village in Massachusetts (p239), many were transported from other parts of New England and arranged to recreate a resemblance to the past. Interpreters staff all the buildings and are all too glad to discuss their crafts and trades. Most illuminating are the demonstrations scattered throughout the day, on such topics as ship-rescue procedures, oystering and whale-boat launching. See p321 for a list of festivals held here.

Visitors can board the *Charles W Morgan* (1841), the last surviving wooden whaling ship in the world; the *LA Dunton* (1921), a three-masted fishing schooner; or the *Joseph Conrad* (1882), a square-rigged training ship. The museum's exhibits include a replica of the 77ft schooner *Amistad*, the slave ship on which 55 kidnapped Africans cast off their chains and sailed to freedom. (In the Steven Spielberg movie *Amistad*, the museum was used to stage many of the scenes that actually took place in colonial New London.)

At the Henry B duPont Preservation Shipyard, you can watch large wooden boats being restored. Be sure not to miss the Wendell Building, which houses a fascinating collection of ships' figureheads and carvings. Close by is a small 'museum' (more like a playroom) for children seven and under. The Seaport also includes a small boat shop, jail, general store,

CONNECTICUT

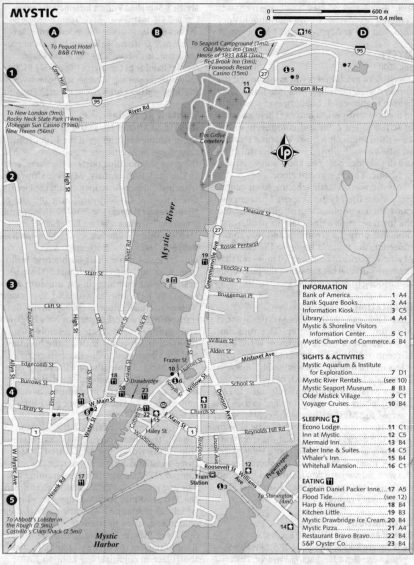

MYSTIC

INFORMATION
Bank of America	1 A4
Bank Square Books	2 A4
Information Kiosk	3 C5
Library	4 A4
Mystic & Shoreline Visitors Information Center	5 C1
Mystic Chamber of Commerce	6 B4

SIGHTS & ACTIVITIES
Mystic Aquarium & Institute for Exploration	7 D1
Mystic River Rentals	(see 10)
Mystic Seaport Museum	8 B3
Olde Mistick Village	9 C1
Voyager Cruises	10 B4

SLEEPING
Econo Lodge	11 C1
Inn at Mystic	12 C5
Mermaid Inn	13 B4
Taber Inne & Suites	14 C5
Whaler's Inn	15 B4
Whitehall Mansion	16 C1

EATING
Captain Daniel Packer Inne	17 A5
Flood Tide	(see 12)
Harp & Hound	18 B4
Kitchen Little	19 B3
Mystic Drawbridge Ice Cream	20 B4
Mystic Pizza	21 A4
Restaurant Bravo Bravo	22 B4
S&P Oyster Co	23 B4

chapel, school, pharmacy, sail loft, shipsmith and ship chandlery – all the sorts of places that you'd expect to find in a real shipbuilding town of 150 years ago.

If the call of the sea beckons during your visit, the **Sabino** (☎ 860-572-5315; adult/6-12yr $5.25/4.25), a 1908 steamboat, takes visitors on excursions up the Mystic River from May to October. The boat departs from the museum hourly on the half-hour.

MYSTIC AQUARIUM & INSTITUTE FOR EXPLORATION
This state-of-the-art **aquarium** (☎ 860-572-5955; www.mysticaquarium.org; 55 Coogan Blvd; adult/3-17yr/senior $22/17/20; ☀ 9am-6pm Mar-Nov, 10am-4pm Mon-

Fri, 9am-6pm Sat & Sun Dec-Feb;) boasts more than 6000 species of sea creatures (including three beluga whales), an outdoor viewing area for seals and sea lions (even below the waterline), a penguin pavilion and the 1400-seat Marine Theater for dolphin shows. There's even an 'immersion' theater that involves a live underwater web feed of places like the Monterey Bay Marine Sanctuary. The aquarium is home to the research and exhibition center for the Institute for Exploration, a leader in the field of deep-sea archaeology. Use I-95 exit 90 to get to the museum.

OLDE MISTICK VILLAGE
Just south of I-95, this pseudo-colonial **village green** (☎ 860-536-4941; www.oldmysticvillage .com; Coogan Blvd; 10am-6pm Mon-Sat, 11am-5pm Sun) is centered on a Congregational church and surrounded by over 60 shops selling sportswear, gifts, crafts, jewelry and Lladró porcelain. Visitors unimpressed by the array can find refuge in the cinema.

BOATING, KAYAKING & BIKING
There's no shortage of outfits ready to whisk you away on a watery adventure. **Voyager Cruises** (☎ 860-536-0416; www.voyagermystic.com; 15 Holmes St) offers half-day or sunset cruises (adult/child $36/26) or harbor cruises (adult/child $25/15) on the authentic 19th-century replica schooner *Argia*.

You can rent bikes, kayaks (lessons are available) and canoes for whole or half days from **Mystic River Rentals** (☎ 860-572-0123; Holmes St; 8am-6pm summer). You'll find them right next door to Voyager Cruises.

Festivals & Events
Mystic Seaport Museum (www.mysticseaport.org) puts on its share of festivals, check the website for details and see p319 for more information.
Annual Lobsterfest At the end of May
Annual Antique & Classic Boat Rendezvous Late July
Coastweeks Regatta Mid-September
Chowderfest Early October
Lantern Light Tours Mid-December.

Sleeping
Mystic offers a multitude of motels and inns, many of which post photographs and links at www.mysticmore.com. In July and August, most lodgings fill up every day. Consider alternatives in nearby communities such as Stonington, New London or Groton.

BUDGET
Most of Mystic's motels cluster near I-95 exit 90, particularly on CT 27 (Greenmanville Ave/Whitehall Ave) north and south of the interstate. Several other good choices lie east of the center of Mystic along US 1.

Rocky Neck State Park (☎ 860-739-5471; CT 156, Niantic; sites $15) Though there are several state parks nearer, the closest with camping is at this well-developed park with showers, a beach for swimming, hiking, fishing, horseback riding and several concession stands. Take exit 72 off the I-95.

Seaport Campground (☎ 860-536-4044; www.sea portcampground.com; CT 184, Old Mystic; tent sites $33, RV sites without/with hookups $36/38; Apr–mid-Sep;) Seaport has 130 RV sites, a swimming pool, a separate tenting area and services from free hot showers to miniature golf.

MIDRANGE & TOP END
Taber Inne & Suites (☎ 860-536-4904, 866-466-6978; www.taberinne.com; 66 Williams Ave; d $85-295, townhouses $275-375;) Popular with families, Taber offers quite a range of comfortable accommodations, from 28 pleasant motel-type rooms through to luxurious one- and two-bedroom townhouses. Guests get full access to the Mystic Health Club, including the sauna and indoor pool.

Econo Lodge (☎ 860-536-9666; 251 Greenmanville Ave/CT 27; d $89-169; wi-fi) On CT 27, this slightly shabby motel has 56 rooms on two floors, all equipped with refrigerators and microwaves.

Whaler's Inn (☎ 800-243-2588, 860-536-1506; www .whalersinnmystic.com; 20 E Main St; d $89-249; wi-fi) Right by the drawbridge in the center of Mystic, this establishment consists of an 1865 Victorian house, a contemporaneous inn and a more modern motel structure known as Stonington House. Room rates vary depending upon the number and size of beds. Ask about seasonal packages that include, for example, admission to the Seaport Museum, dinner for two or a schooner cruise.

Whitehall Mansion (☎ 860-572-7280, 800-572-3993; 40 Whitehall Ave/CT 27; d incl breakfast $89-250;) This grand colonial house dates from 1771. Each of the five rooms, one of which is wheelchair accessible, has a fireplace, whirlpool bath and a queen-size canopy bed. Evening wine and cheese are included. You'll find the mansion just to the north of I-95 at the Mystic exit, next to the rather drab-looking Residence Inn. (Whitehall guests share many of Residence's amenities, like the health facilities and indoor pool.)

Pequot Hotel B&B (☎ 860-572-0390; www.pequotho telbandb.com; 711 Cow Hill Rd; d $95-175; P) This lovely piece of property was once a stagecoach stop and now has three luxury guest rooms with bathroom (two with fireplaces). There are cats and a friendly dog in residence, too.

Inn at Mystic (☎ 860-536-9604, 800-237-2415; www .innatmystic.com; cnr US 1 & CT 27; d $95-295; P ⌘) Humphrey Bogart and Lauren Bacall spent their honeymoon at this hilltop Georgian mansion decorated with colonial-style furniture and antiques. It's easy to see why. Quarters range from simple, clean motel-style units to luxury chambers, complete with fireplaces and whirlpool baths. From the inn's hilltop setting, lawns sweep down to a boat dock and tennis court, and guests are free to use the boats, kayaks and putting greens. The Flood Tide restaurant here (see opposite) is justifiably well regarded.

Red Brook Inn (☎ 860-572-0349, 800-290-5619; cnr CT 184 & Wells Rd; d incl breakfast $129-189; P) Three miles from town, the Red Brook Inn, on seven woody acres, offers guests a choice of two buildings: the Haley Tavern (1740) with seven guest rooms and the Red Crary Homestead (1770) with three. One can retire to the Gentlemen's Parlor or the Ladies' Parlor in the evening, or the more inclusive Old Tavern room. Breakfast is included and it's a hearty one.

House of 1833 B&B (☎ 860-536-6325, 800-367-1833; 72 N Stonington Rd/CT 201; d summer $99-179, winter $129-249; P ⌘) This Greek Revival mansion has five luxury guest rooms that are heavy on the florals and the pink tones. Avail yourself of the tennis court, outdoor pool and bikes. Music from the baby grand piano accompanies your complimentary two-course breakfast.

Old Mystic Inn (☎ 860-572-9422; www.oldmysticinn .com; 52 Main St, Old Mystic; d $155-205; P ⌨ wi-fi) Situated in quiet Old Mystic, north of I-95, this cheerful, red B&B has eight guest rooms, six with working fireplaces (but specify if you want gas or wood-burning), and two with whirlpool tubs. Most rooms have four-post beds, and two of the rooms are named after

famous New England authors, Mark Twain and Robert Frost.

Mermaid Inn (☎ 860-536-6223; www.mermaidin nofmystic.com; 2 Broadway Ave; d $175-195; P) This charming Italianate B&B with a pronounced mermaid theme sits on a quiet street within walking distance of the town center. Its three rooms each have a private bathroom (with bidet and granite baths), TV and special touches like fresh flowers and Italian chocolates. In warm weather, guests enjoy breakfast on the porch.

Eating

There are several places to grab a snack or sit down to a full meal within Mystic Seaport Museum, but most of Mystic's restaurants are in or near the town center, close to the drawbridge.

BUDGET

Mystic Drawbridge Ice Cream (2 W Main St; ⌚ lunch & dinner) Strolling through town is best done with an ice-cream cone in hand, specifically one from here. Some of the more quirky flavors like pumpkin pie and southern peach are seasonal, but on any given day there will be something innovative to try, like the gooeylicious Sticky Fractured Finger (pieces of butterfingers in caramel ice cream).

Kitchen Little (☎ 860-536-2122; 135 Greenmanville Ave; meals $7-14; ⌚ breakfast & lunch) Join various staff of Mystic Seaport Museum for breakfast and grab a seat at one of the tables on the back patio overlooking the water to trawl through the lengthy, egg-heavy menu. Try the Mystic Melt, featuring crabmeat and cream cheese scrambled with eggs on raisin toast. No credit cards accepted.

Harp & Hound (☎ 860-572-7778; 4 Pearl St; meals $7-15; ⌚ lunch & dinner) Tucked in a colonial building on the west side of the drawbridge, this local pub offers up a respectable selection of Irish and Scottish malts and ales, and thoughtfully serves some non-liquid sustenance like shepherd's pie to line one's stomach. Stop in for the traditional Irish music if you're in town on a Sunday evening.

Mystic Pizza (☎ 860-536-3737; 56 W Main St; meals $8-20; ⌚ lunch & dinner) If the name sounds familiar, it's because it was the title of one of Julia Roberts' first films. The place might have inspired the movie, but sadly, the pizza, salads and grinders will inspire only the movie's most devoted fans.

MIDRANGE

our pick **Captain Daniel Packer Inne** (☎ 860-536-3555; 32 Water St; meals $10-32; ⊙ lunch & dinner) This friendly place occupies a 1754 historic house on the west side of the bridge, complete with low-beam ceiling and creaky floorboards. Locals rave about the ocean views as well as the restaurant's imaginative American cuisine; favorites include the petite filet mignon with Gorgonzola sauce and walnut demi-glace and the shrimp and scallops Provençale.

S&P Oyster Co (☎ 860-536-2674; 1 Holmes St; meals $11-22; ⊙ lunch & dinner; ♿) In warm weather, this is the perfect place to sit on the patio overlooking the river and savor helpings of fresh oysters, mussels, or clams. The large serving of fish and chips is the number one main at lunch and dinner, and can be complemented by New England– or Rhode Island–style clam chowder. There's a children's menu, too. You can dock your boat here while you eat.

our pick **Abbott's Lobster in the Rough** (☎ 860-536-7719; 117 Pearl St, Noank; meals $18-32; ⊙ lunch & dinner May-Aug, noon-7pm Fri-Sun Sep-Oct) Lobster lovers should check out Abbott's, on the waterfront in neighboring Noank. Order your lobster (or other seafood) at the window, get a number, pick out a table by the water and, when your number is called, pay and dig in. New England doesn't get much better than this on a warm summer night. Just down the road is Abbott's sister business, Costello's Clam Shack, open similar hours. To reach both from Mystic, take Water St/Rte 215 southwest. When you reach a stop sign take a left (Mosher Ave) and stay right when it divides. Turn left onto Main St and right onto Pearl. BYOB beer or wine.

Restaurant Bravo Bravo (☎ 860-536-3228; cnr E Main & Holmes Sts; meals $19-25; ⊙ lunch & dinner) This low-lit eatery with a lively bar scene serves up nouvelle Italian food – flavorsome and inventive pastas, seafood and beef – in a sleek, modern setting. The wine selection is wide, and the champagne risotto with lobster and asparagus is truly wonderful.

TOP END

Flood Tide (☎ 860-536-8140; cnr US 1 & CT 27; meals $25-38; ⊙ breakfast, lunch & dinner) Reserve a window table with a view overlooking the grounds of the inn at Mystic or grab a seat by the wood-fired oven for the upscale yet informally presented fare here. The house pâté is exquisite, the seafood fresh and steaks attentively prepared. The Sunday brunch is a sumptuous affair worth the trip even if you're not staying at the Inn.

Getting There & Away

Amtrak (☎ 800-872-7245) trains between NYC and Boston on the shore route stop at Mystic's **train station** (12 Roosevelt St), less than a mile south of Mystic Seaport Museum.

Mystic is 9 miles east of New London and Groton. The best route by car is I-95.

STONINGTON

pop 1030

Five miles east of Mystic on US 1, Stonington stands out as one of the most appealing towns on the Connecticut coast. Many of the town's 18th- and 19th-century houses were once sea captains' homes.

It's best to explore this historic town – actually a 'borough,' Connecticut's oldest – on foot. Compactly laid out on a peninsula that juts into Long Island Sound, Stonington is rife with streetscapes of period architecture. The short main thoroughfare, Water St, features shops selling high-end antiques, colorful French Quimper porcelain and upscale gifts. There are also a couple of waterfront restaurants and delis. At the southern end of Water St is the 'point' or tip of the peninsula, with a park and tiny beach.

Sights & Activities

The best way to get a good look at the town is to walk down Water St (one way, southbound) toward its southern end, climb the lighthouse tower for a panoramic view and then head back north on Main St, the other major north–south street, one block east of Water St.

Included in the Old Lighthouse Museum ticket (see p324) is admission to the 16-room **Captain Nathaniel Palmer House** (☎ 860-535-8445; 40 Palmer St; ⊙ 10am-4pm Wed-Mon), one of the finest houses in town and the former home of the first American to see the continent of Antarctica (at the tender age of 21, no less).

Stonington is one of two towns in the country with an official shop for **Quimper Faïence** (☎ 860-535-1712, 800-470-7339; 141 Water St; ⊙ 10am-5pm Mon-Sat), the colorfully painted dinnerware handmade in France since the 17th century. The folk-art plates, cups, mugs, platters, figurines and utensils are popular collector's

TAKING A GAMBLE AT FOXWOODS

Rising above the forest canopy of Great Cedar Swamp, north of Mystic, the gleaming towers of the mammoth **Foxwoods Resort Casino** (☎ 800-752-9244; www.foxwoods.com) are an alien vision in turquoise and lavender.

Under treaties dating back centuries, Native Americans have territorial and legal rights separate from those enjoyed by other citizens of the US. In recent times, these tribes have used the courts and the Congress to elaborate these treaty rights into a potent vehicle for addressing longstanding discrimination against them and its resulting poverty.

One such group, the 700-member Mashantucket Pequot Tribal Nation, known as 'the fox people,' kept a tenuous hold on a parcel of ancestral land in southeastern Connecticut. The tribe had dwindled to insignificant numbers through assimilation and dispersion, but a few souls refused to abandon the reservation. Living in decrepit trailers dragged onto the land, they fought a dispiriting legal battle against attempts to declare the reservation abandoned.

Their tenacity paid off in 1986 when they reached an agreement with the Connecticut state government that allowed the Pequots to open a high-stakes bingo hall. In 1992, again under an agreement with the state, the tribe borrowed $60 million from a Malaysian casino developer and began to build Foxwoods.

The resort features the world's largest bingo hall, nightclubs with free entertainment, cinemas, rides and video-game and pinball parlors for children. There are about 1400 luxury **guest rooms** (reservations ☎ 800-369-9663) in three hotels (the Grand Pequot Tower, Great Cedar Hotel and Two Trees Inn).

Visitors to Foxwoods interested in the tribe behind the casino should definitely set aside a few hours to see the **Mashantucket Pequot Museum & Research Center** (☎ 860-396-6838, www.pequotmuseum.org; adult/6-15yr/senior $15/10/13; 10am-4pm). This ultramodern museum devoted to an ancient people features dioramas, films and interactive exhibits, highlighted by a very effective simulated glacial crevasse and a recreated 16th-century Pequot village. The free observation tower affords a good view of the reservation. Shuttles run every 20 minutes between the museum and Foxwoods.

To reach Foxwoods, take I-95 to exit 92, then follow CT 2 west; or take I-395 to exit 79A, 80, 81 or 85 and follow the signs for the 'Mashantucket Pequot Reservation.'

The **Mohegan Sun Casino** (☎ 888-226-7711; www.mohegansun.com), at I-395 exit 79A, is a smaller version of Foxwoods operated by the Mohegan tribe on its reservation.

---

items. Prices are not low, but then again, each Quimper (pronounced 'kamm-*pehr*') piece is one of a kind, by definition.

Moving along Water St, closer to the point the houses become plainer and simpler, many dating from the 18th century. These were the residences of ships' carpenters and fishermen.

Before the end of the point, near the small Du Bois Beach, is the **Old Lighthouse Museum** (☎ 860-535-1440; 7 Water St; adult/6-12yr $5/3; 10am-5pm Tue-Sun May-Oct). The surprisingly short, octagonal-towered granite lighthouse was moved to its present location in 1840 and deactivated 50 years later. Now it's a museum that recounts British assaults on the harbor during the American Revolution and the War of 1812, which were both repelled, as well as hosting exhibits on whaling, Native American artifacts, curios from the China trade, 19th-century oil portraits, wooden boats, weaponry, toys and decoys. Climb the staircase to the top for a view of the Sound, including Block and Fishers Islands.

The 1809 **Captain Amos Palmer House** (cnr Main & Wall Sts) was the home of the mother and children of artist James McNeill Whistler and later of poet Stephen Vincent Benét. (The house is not open to the public.)

The **Portuguese Holy Ghost Society building** (Main St), built in 1836, is a reminder of the contributions made to Stonington by the Portuguese who signed on to Stonington-bound whalers during the 19th century and eventually settled in the village. Today, their descendants still form a significant part of Stonington's population, though the small village's ever-increasing appeal to wealthy New Yorkers seeking summer homes is pricing the locals out of the real-estate market.

Sleeping

Stonington is the area's quaintest place to stay; see the Mystic (p321), New London (p327) or Groton (p326) sections for cheaper options.

Stonington Motel (☎ 860-599-2330; 901 Stonington Rd/US 1; d $55-90; ⅋) This motel's 12 well-used but clean rooms have cable TV, microwaves and fridges, and some are wheelchair accessible. Inquire about weekday discounts.

ourpick Randall's Ordinary (☎ 860-599-4540; www .randallsordinary.com; 41 Norwich/Westerly Rd, North Stonington; d $80-400) Extraordinary would better describe this 17th-century farmhouse, which reputedly was a stop on the underground railroad. Today's visitors will find an inn with exposed beams, modern conveniences and an excellent restaurant (see right). In the main house there are three guest rooms; 12 more are in the barn. The inn's 250 acres sit 8.4 miles northeast of the center of Stonington along CT 2, a third of a mile north of I-95 (exit 92).

Orchard Street Inn (☎ 860-535-2681; www.orchard streetinn.com; 41 Orchard St; d $125-175) This quiet, unpretentious inn is within easy walking distance of everything in town. The butter-yellow guest cottage houses three rooms, each with a patio and separate entrance. To get there, turn left from Water St at Noah's restaurant and then left onto Orchard. Children 14 and over are welcome.

Inn at Stonington (☎ 860-535-2000; www.innatston ington.com; 60 Water St; d $135-435) Let yourself be pampered at this elegant, modern 18-room inn, complete with evening wine and cheese. Most rooms are equipped with a Jacuzzi and all have fireplaces, while guests can enjoy free use of kayaks, bikes and the town's private beach. It's worth paying a bit more for a seaside room. Children 15 and older are welcome.

Eating

You will see Stonington's few restaurants as you proceed south on Water St.

Noni's Deli (☎ 860-535-0797; 143 Water St; meals $6-10; ⅋ 8am-4pm) This Irish-themed deli is perfect for scoring picnic supplies before heading to the point at the southern end of Water St, or you can eat on the cozy front patio. Try the Galway (crab-cake sandwich) for $4.

Water St Café (☎ 860-535-2122; 142 Water St; meals $9-27; ⅋ lunch & dinner) North of Grand St, this crimson-walled café with exposed beams boasts a menu that is creative and moderately priced – a rare combination. One recent spe-cial was the satisfying Vietnamese fried cod salad with sesame orange dressing.

Skipper's Dock (☎ 860-535-0111; 66 Water St; meals $10-37; ⅋ lunch & dinner; ⅋) This casual, kid-friendly seafood restaurant with a waterside deck is *the* place to order steamers, lobster or what is locally known as a clam boil – the works, including clams, corn, lobster, fish and sausage. A jazz brunch enlivens the Sunday scene.

Noah's (☎ 860-535-3925; 115 Water St; meals $19-24; ⅋ 7am-9pm Tue-Sun) Noah's is a popular, informal place on Church St, with two small rooms topped with original stamped-tin ceilings and oil paintings of Stonington on the walls. Besides Americana standards like asparagus quiche, there are some unexpected dishes like Chinese noodles with chicken.

Randall's Ordinary (☎ 860-599-4540; 41 Norwich/ Westerly Rd, North Stonington; ⅋ May-Dec) Hearth cooking in the authentic colonial manner is the specialty at Stonington's finest eatery. There is just one dinner seating for a fixed-price menu ($39 not including drinks, tax and tip) of slow-simmered soups, beef, fish, chicken or venison, hearth-baked cornbread and colonial-style desserts, served by costumed waitstaff. Reservations are essential.

GROTON
pop 39,400

Proud to be nicknamed the Submarine Capital of America, Groton is home to the US Naval Submarine Base, the first and the largest in the country, and General Dynamics Corporation, a major naval defense contractor. Unsurprisingly, both are vigorously off-limits to the public, but you can get into the spirit of things with a visit to the Historic Ship Nautilus & Submarine Force Museum (below) and the US Coast Guard Academy (see p327) inNew London.

Orientation

Located halfway between Boston and New York, Groton is perched on the east bank of the Thames River (that's 'thaymz,' not 'temz'), just across the bridge from New London. Fishers Island Sound lies just south of town. Take exit 85 off the I-95 for Thames St, the town's main artery.

Sights & Activities

On the Naval Submarine Base, the **Historic Ship Nautilus & Submarine Force Museum** (☎ 860-694-3174,

800-343-0079; 1 Crystal Lake Rd; admission free; 9am-5pm Wed-Mon, 1-5pm Tue mid-May–Oct, 9am-4pm Wed-Mon Nov–mid-May) is home to *Nautilus*, the world's first nuclear-powered submarine and the first sub to transit the North Pole. The brief audio tour of *Nautilus* is fascinating primarily for military enthusiasts. Other museum exhibits feature working periscopes and sounds of the ocean.

Fort Griswold State Park (860-445-1729; cnr Monument St & Park Ave; admission free; 10am-5pm late May–early Sep, 10am-5pm Sat & Sun early Sep–mid-Oct) is centered on a 134ft obelisk that marks the place where colonial troops were massacred by Benedict Arnold and the British in 1781 in the Battle of Groton Heights. The battle saw the death of colonial Colonel William Ledyard and the British burning of Groton and New London. Monument House features the Daughters of the American Revolution's collection of Revolutionary and Civil War memorabilia.

Sleeping

For a complete list and links to accommodations in eastern Connecticut, consult www .mysticmore.com. For camping not far from Groton, see p321.

Thames Inn & Marina (860-445-8111; 193 Thames St; d $69-100) Though it prefers guests staying a week or longer, this inn will let rooms, all with fully equipped kitchens, for the night as well. There's a coin-operated laundry.

Groton Inn & Suites (860-445-9784, 800-452-2191; www.grotoninn.com; 99 Gold Star Hwy/CT 184; d $80-200) Groton Inn, at I-95, has over 100 rooms, including 39 apartments, six efficiencies and 29 deluxe suites. Visitors also get a restaurant, bar and fitness center.

Eating

Flanagan's (860-445-6511; 360 CT 12; breakfast, lunch & dinner) Highly popular with officers from the naval base, this congenial Irish spot serves up wraps, salads, sandwiches, steaks and burgers. However, it's the filling portions of fish 'n' chips that really make the place stand out.

Paul's Pasta Shop (860-445-5276; 223 Thames St; 11am-9pm Tue-Sun) When the smell of fresh tomato sauce lulls you into this ultra-casual eatery, you'll most likely find Paul himself standing right behind the counter. All pasta dishes, be it spaghetti and meatballs or linguini primavera, are $7, but for house specialties like Paul's wife Dorothy's five-cheese

lasagna you'll have to cough up an extra $2. The back door peers down over the river.

NEW LONDON
Pop 26,200

During its golden age in the mid-19th century, New London was home to some 200 whaling vessels. But until recently, the city seemed somewhat exhausted from its trip through the 20th-century industrial wringer. Though there's still a palpable grittiness about the place, the slew of 'vacant' signs are making way for ones reading 'coming soon.' To wit, Pfizer (the world's largest pharmaceutical company) moved its research and development headquarters to town, while the Hygienic Art complex has brought the arts into fresh focus in this town where playwright Eugene O'Neill spent his childhood summers (see opposite).

Orientation & Information

Nestled on the west side of the Thames facing Groton, downtown New London is right off I-95 (use exit 84 if driving west, 83 if driving east). Its shops and restaurants line Bank St southwest of the Amtrak train station near the waterfront.

For information try the following:

Connecticut East Convention & Visitor's Bureau (860-444-2206, 800-863-6569; www.mysticmore.com; 470 Bank St; 8:30am-4:30pm Mon-Fri)

New London Chamber of Commerce (860-443-8332; 105 Huntington St; 8:30am-4:30pm Mon-Fri)

Visitor Center (860-444-7264; 228 Eugene O'Neill Dr; 10am-4pm summer) Offers helpful maps and brochures.

Sights & Activities

A well-laid-out walking tour starts along the restored pedestrian mall called the **Captain's Walk** (State St). The tiny **Nathan Hale Schoolhouse** (860-443-7949; Union Plaza; admission free; 11am-4pm Wed-Sun mid-May–mid-Oct) is one of the many Connecticut schoolhouses that bear the name of this peripatetic pedagogue. Hale (1755–76) is famous for his patriotic statement, 'I only regret that I have but one life to lose for my country,' as he was about to be hanged for treason by the British without trial. He taught in this schoolhouse before enlisting in the Connecticut militia.

Nearby is the 1833 **Custom House Maritime Museum** (860-447-2501; 150 Bank St; adult/child $5/3; 1-5pm Tue-Sun), the oldest operating customhouse in the country. Its front door is made from the wood of the USS *Constitution*.

On Huntington St right next to the St James' Church, **Whale Oil Row** features four identical white mansions (Nos 105, 111, 117 and 119) with imposing Doric facades built for whaling merchants in 1830. They're now private businesses not open to the public, but the exterior is impressive.

Of the two **Hempsted Houses** (☎ 860-443-7949; 11 Hempstead St; adult/child $5/2; ☸ noon-4pm Thu-Sun May-Oct), the wood-framed older one (1678) is one of the best-documented 17th-century houses in the country. Maintained by the descendants of the original owners until 1937, it is one of the few 17th-century houses remaining in the area, having survived the burning of New London by Benedict Arnold and the British in 1781. The house is insulated with seaweed, of all things.

Further downtown, you'll find a lovely strip of more **historic houses** on Starr St, between Eugene O'Neill Dr and Washington St.

Monte Cristo Cottage (☎ 860-443-0051; 325 Pequot Ave; adult/senior & student $7/5; ☸ noon-4pm Thu-Sat, 1-3pm Sun mid-Jun–early Sep) was the boyhood summer home of Eugene O'Neill, America's only Nobel Prize–winning playwright. Near Ocean Beach Park in the southern districts of the city (follow the signs), the Victorian-style house is now a research library for dramatists. Many of O'Neill's belongings are on display, including his desk. You might recognize the living room: it was the inspiration for the setting for two of O'Neill's most famous plays, *Long Day's Journey into Night* and *Ah, Wilderness!* Theater buffs should be sure to visit the **Eugene O'Neill Theater Center** (www.oneill theatercenter.org) in nearby Waterford, which hosts an annual summer series of readings by young playwrights.

The **Lyman Allyn Art Museum** (☎ 860-443-2545; www.lymanallyn.org; 625 Williams St; adult/senior & student $5/4; ☸ 10am-5pm Tue-Sat, 1-5pm Sun; ☝) is a neoclassical building with exhibits that span the 18th, 19th and 20th centuries, including impressive collections of early American silver and Asian, Greco-Roman and European paintings. Among the highlights are the American impressionists gallery and the charming doll and toy exhibit. There's also a self-guided children's art park on the grounds.

At the southern end of Ocean Ave is **Ocean Beach Park** (☎ 860-510-7263; 1225 Ocean Ave; ☝), a popular beach and amusement area with waterslides, a picnic area, miniature golf, an arcade, a swimming pool and an old-fashioned boardwalk. The parking fee ($9 on weekdays, $13 on weekends) includes admission for everyone in your car, or else it's $5 for adults and $3 for kids. After Labor Day (early September), weekdays are free.

Visitors can stroll the grounds of the **US Coast Guard Academy** (☎ 860-444-8270; 15 Mohegan Ave; admission free; ☸ 11am-5pm), one of the four military academies in the country. Pick up a self-guided walking tour booklet at the museum.

GALLERIES & ART SPACES

Done up in a Greek Revival style replete with a sculpture garden, mural plaza, fountains and a large performance area, **Hygienic Art** (☎ 860-443-8001; www.hygienic.org; 79 Bank St; ☸ 11am-3pm Thu, 11am-6pm Fri & Sat, noon-3pm Sun) is centered on a gallery featuring exhibits in many media. It hosts poetry readings, film screenings and other events. The gardens and amphitheater are open during daylight hours.

Golden Street Gallery (☎ 860-444-0659; 94 Golden St; ☸ 3-7pm Thu-Fri, noon-7pm Sat) features rotating exhibits by local artists, with a focus on painting and printmaking.

Ya-Ta-Hey (☎ 860-443-3204; www.yahtaheygallery .com; 279 State St; ☸ 11am-5pm Mon-Sat) presents sculpture, painting, pottery and jewelry by contemporary Native American artists.

Sleeping

Radisson Hotel New London (☎ 860-443-7000, 800-333-3333; www.radisson.com; 35 Governor Winthrop Blvd; d $99-169; ☐ wi-fi ☒) Restaurant, bar, health club and a free shuttle to area casinos are all part of the package at the Radisson. Within walking distance from the train station and ferry terminal.

ourpick **Lighthouse Inn Resort** (☎ 860-443-8411, 888-443-8411; www.lighthouseinn-ct.com; 6 Guthrie Pl; r $99-150, ste $185-369; ☐ wi-fi) This four-star hotel at the southern end of Montauk Ave offers a variety of deluxe rooms in two buildings – one is a finely restored 1902 mansion and the other is the Carriage House, whose rooms are the least expensive of the bunch. The resort owns a private beach just for guests, Timothy's restaurant (p328) and the 1902 Bar which slakes the evening thirsts of guests.

Queen Anne Inn B&B (☎ 860-447-2600, 800-347-8818; www.queenannebnb.com; 265 Williams St; d incl breakfast $115-175; ☐) All eight rooms at this friendly, antique-laden B&B have their own TV, phone and DSL access. The least expensive room has its bathroom down the hall. Queen Anne isn't quite within walking distance of Bank St but it's convenient from the interstate.

Eating

New London is short on fancy restaurants, but you'll find a number of cafés and bars along Bank St.

Recovery Room (☎ 860-443-2619; 443 Ocean Ave; meals $9-18; ☽ lunch & dinner Mon-Sat, dinner Sun) The family-run Recovery Room has New London's best pizza – thin crusted and one-sized – with a variety of topping options some of which (barbecue chicken or sour cream) you might want to pass on. Makes for a good stop en route from a day at Ocean Beach Park (p327).

our pick Captain Scott's Lobster Dock (☎ 860-439-1741; 80 Hamilton St; meals $10-20; ☽ lunch & dinner May-Oct) The Coast Guard knows a thing or two about the sea, and you'd be remiss if you didn't follow students of its academy to *the* place for seafood in the summer. The setting's just a series of picnic tables by the water, but you can feast on succulent (hot or cold) lobster rolls, followed by steamers, fried whole-belly clams, scallops or lobsters.

Bang Kok City (☎ 860-442-6970; 123 State St; meals $12-22; ☽ lunch & dinner Mon-Sat) The amiable servers here can guide you through the large menu, and the spice level is under your control. Use it. Try their memorable *tom yam kong* (spicy shrimp soup) and leave space for custard dessert. Under the same roof is Little Tokyo (☎ 860-447-2388) where a filling yakitori bento lunch is $8.

Timothy's (☎ 860-443-8411; meals $12-30; ☽ lunch & dinner) Blessed with a stunning view of the Sound and decorated with hand-carved chandeliers, this dining room at the Lighthouse Inn Resort (p327) promises gracious food in equally gracious surroundings, and excellently named chef Timothy Grills delivers. The menu is seasonal with a focus on seafood, starring such dishes as lobster at dinner. Try the sautéed salmon medallions with roasted onions served on jasmine rice ($20).

Drinking

Dutch Tavern (☎ 860-442-3453; 23 Green St) Raise a cold one to Eugene O'Neill at the Dutch, the only surviving bar in town that the playwright frequented (though back in the day it was known as the Oak). It's a good honest throwback to an earlier age, from

the tin ceiling to the century-old potato salad recipe.

Frank's Place (☎ 860-443-8833; 9 Tilley St) For a quarter-century, Frank's has provided the area's gay community with a comfortable place to eat, drink, play pool and sing karaoke. No matter what the evening's entertainment may turn out to be, there's never a cover charge. Its birdcage room is not something you see every day.

Getting There & Away

New London's transportation center is the **Amtrak train station** (cnr Water & State Sts); the bus station is in the same building and the ferry terminal (for boats to Long Island, Block Island and Fishers Island) is next door.

BOAT

The **Cross Sound Ferry** (☎ 860-443-5281, 516-323-2525; www.longislandferry.com; 2 Ferry St) operates car ferries and high-speed passenger ferries year-round between Orient Point, Long Island, NY and New London, a 1½-hour run on the car ferry, 40 minutes on the high-speed ferry. From late June through Labor Day, ferries depart each port every hour on the hour from 7am to 9pm (last boats at 9:45pm). Off-season, boats tend to run every two hours. For high-speed ferries, the one-way rates are adult/child $16/7.75. The rates for car ferries are adult/child $10.50/5. Cars cost $39, bicycles $2. Call for car reservations.

The **Fishers Island Ferry** (☎ 860-442-0165; www.fiferry.com; adult/child $22/16 mid-May–mid-Sept, $16/12 mid-Sept–mid-May, cars $26-40) runs cars and passengers from New London to the wealthy summer colony at Fishers Island, NY several times a day year-round.

In summer, there are daily boats between New London and Block Island, Rhode Island (p306; adult/child $21/10).

CAR & MOTORCYCLE

For New London, take I-95 exit 84, then go north on CT 32 (Mohegan Ave) for the US Coast Guard Academy, or take I-95 exits 82, 83 or 84 and go south for the city center. CT 32 will also whisk you north to Mohegan Sun Casino (p324). The center of the commercial district is just southwest of the Amtrak station along Bank St. Follow Ocean Ave (CT 213) to reach Ocean Beach Park and Harkness Memorial State Park.

WORTH THE TRIP: THE QUIET CORNER

Perhaps nowhere else in New England will you find such an undeveloped green valley so close to major urban areas. Dubbed the Quiet Corner, the furthest patch of northeast Connecticut is known (when it's known at all) for farmland, rolling meadows, reasonably priced antiques and most significantly, an air of timelessness. The 12 miles of CT 169 between Brooklyn and Woodstock induces sighs of contentment and frequent pullovers. To get to 169 from New London, take I-395 north for about 32 miles. There are a few highlights listed here, but off-guidebook exploration is strongly encouraged.

From I-395, take US 6 W to Danielson, where family-run **Logee's Greenhouses** (☎ 860-774-8038; www.logees.com; 141 North St, off CT 12; ☼ 9am-5pm Mon-Sat, 11am-5pm Sun) has been in the beautifying business since 1893. Stroll through seven greenhouses brimming with over 1000 tropical and subtropical varieties, from bougainvilleas to begonias.

Heading west on US 6 again will bring you to Brooklyn, home of the oldest **agricultural fair** in the US, held during the third weekend in August.

Dinner at the **Golden Lamb Buttery** (☎ 860-774-4423; 499 Wolf Den Rd, Brooklyn; lunch $20, dinner $65; ☼ lunch Tue-Sat, dinner Fri & Sat) isn't just a meal – it's an experience. Guests mingle over drinks, head off for a hayride and then settle into an award-winning prix-fixe dinner. You'll need to reserve several weeks in advance. Even if you can't squeeze in a visit to the 1000-acre farm, be sure to drive the few miles up Wolf Den Rd and be rewarded with views of pastoral perfection.

Back on CT 169 heading north, stop at the old-fashioned **Woodstock Orchards** (☎ 860-928-2225; 494 CT 169, Woodstock; ☼ 9am-6pm) to pick your own blueberries (late summer) and apples (fall). Stock up on jams, fresh cider and honey at the farm stand.

For detailed area information, contact **Northeast Connecticut's Quiet Corner** (☎ 860-779-6383; www.ctquietcorner.org).

TRAIN

Amtrak (☎ 800-872-7245) trains between New York and Boston on the shore route stop at New London.

HAMMONASSET BEACH STATE PARK

Though not off the beaten path by any means, the two full miles of flat, sandy beach at **Hammonasset Beach State Park** (☎ 860-566-2304, 877-668-2267; I-95 exit 62; residents $7-9, out-of-staters $10-14 in summer; ☼ 8am-sunset) handily accommodate summer crowds. This is the ideal beach at which to set up an umbrella-chair, crack open a book and forget about the world. The surf is tame, making swimming superb; restrooms and showering facilities are clean and ample; and a wooden boardwalk runs the length of the park. There is no entry charge in the off-season.

Stroll the boardwalk all the way to Meigs Point at the tip of the peninsula and visit the **Nature Center** (☎ 203-245-8743) before heading out on a trail that meanders through saltwater marshes. Excellent bird-watching here.

Hammonasset is a Native American word for 'where we dig holes in the ground,' alluding to agricultural practices. These days it's more likely to refer to the holes of tent stakes.

The **campground** (☎ 860-566-2304, 877-668-2267; 1288 Boston Post Rd; sites $15) here offers Connecticut's only beach camping. It's on the coast between Madison and Clinton, and despite its 558 sites, is often full in high summer. Reserve early.

NEW HAVEN
pop 124,500

Much maligned for decades as a decayed urban seaport notable only for being an uneasy home to the venerable Yale University, Connecticut's second-largest city has risen from its ashes to become an arts mecca. New Haven is still an important port – as it has been since the 1630s – but today manufacturing, health care and telecommunications also help power New Haven's economy. At the city's center stands tranquil New Haven Green, bordered by graceful colonial churches and Yale. Ethnic restaurants, theaters, museums, pubs and clubs dot the city and make the Yale University area almost as lively as Cambridge's Harvard Sq – but with better pizza.

Orientation
Entering New Haven along I-95 or I-91 (which joins I-95 right in the city), take I-95 exit 47 for

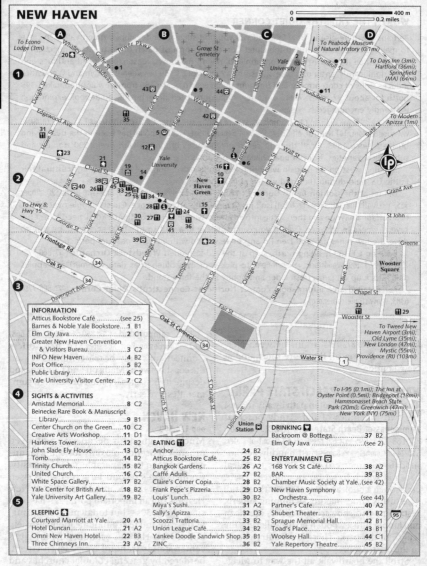

NEW HAVEN

CT 34, the Oak St Connector, to reach New Haven Green, the city center, with Yale to its west. From the Wilbur Cross Parkway, take exit 57, 59 or 60 and follow the signs to the center.

Most hotels and sights are within a few blocks of the green. The bus and train stations are near I-95 in the southeast part of the city. Street parking downtown can be a frustrating proposition.

Parking lots are everywhere – strings of them line Crown, George and State Sts.

Information

BOOKSTORES

Atticus Bookstore Café (☎ 203-776-4040; 1082 Chapel St; ⏰ 7:45am-midnight) A favorite bookstore and café (see p333).

Barnes & Noble Yale Bookstore (☎ 203-777-8440; 77 Broadway; ☺ 9am-9pm Mon-Sat, noon-6pm Sun) Not only sells a rich collection of books, but also Yale sweat-shirts and souvenirs.

INTERNET ACCESS
Elm City Java (☎ 203-776-2248; 77 Whitney Ave; ☺ 7am-8pm Mon-Thu, 7am-midnight Fri, 10am-6pm Sat & Sun, shorter hrs in summer) Offers free internet (with purchase) on four iMacs, and is a wi-fi hotspot.

Public library (☎ 203-946-8130; 133 Elm St; ☺ noon-8pm Mon, 10am-8pm Tue-Thu, 1-5pm Fri, 10am-5pm Sat) Free access though hours fluctuate throughout the year.

MONEY
Scads of ATMs line Church St, especially at the intersections with Elm and Grove Sts.

POST
Post office (206 Elm St; ☺ 8am-5pm Mon-Fri, 8am-noon Sat) At the intersection with High St.

TOURIST INFORMATION
Greater New Haven Convention & Visitors Bureau (☎ 203-777-8550, 800-332-7829; www.newhavencvb .org; 169 Orange St; ☺ 8:30am-5pm Mon-Fri) Centrally located downtown.

INFO New Haven (☎ 203-773-9494; www.infonewha ven.com; 1000 Chapel St; ☺ 10am-9pm Mon-Sat, noon-5pm Sun) Downtown bureau offers maps and helpful advice.

Yale University Visitor Center (☎ 203-432-2300; www.yale.edu/visitor; cnr Elm & Temple Sts; ☺ 9am-4:30pm Mon-Fri, 11am-4pm Sat & Sun) Located on the north side of the green. Supplies free campus maps and a self-guided walking-tour pamphlet ($1). For information on guided tours, see right.

Sights & Activities
NEW HAVEN GREEN
New Haven's spacious green has been the spiritual center of the city since its Puritan fathers designed it in 1638 as the prospective site for Christ's Second Coming. Since then it has held the municipal burial grounds – graves were later moved to Grove Street Cemetery – several statehouses and an array of churches, three of which still stand. The 1816 **Trinity Church** (Chapel St) is Episcopal and resembles England's Gothic York Minster, featuring several Tiffany windows. The Georgian-style 1812 **Center Church on the Green** (United Church of Christ), a fine New England interpretation of Palladian architecture, harbors many colonial tombstones in its crypt. The 1814 **United Church** (also United Church

of Christ), at the northeastern corner of the green, is another Georgian-Palladian work.

Across Church St, the 14-foot bronze **Amistad Memorial** stands in front of City Hall on the spot where 55 kidnapped African slaves who had sought their freedom were imprisoned in 1839 while awaiting one of a series of trials that would ultimately release them.

GROVE STREET CEMETERY
Three blocks north of the green, this **cemetery** (227 Grove St; ☺ 8am-4pm) holds the graves of several famous New Havenites behind its grand Egyptian Revival gate, including rubber magnate Charles Goodyear, the telegraph inventor Samuel Morse, lexicographer Noah Webster and cotton-gin inventor Eli Whitney. It was the first chartered cemetery in the country in 1797 and the first to arrange graves by family plots. Around the turn of the century, Yale medical students would sneak in at night to dig up bodies for dissection, but you can simply join the free walking tour at 11am on Saturdays.

YALE UNIVERSITY
Each year, thousands of high-school students make pilgrimages to Yale, nursing dreams of attending the country's third-oldest university, which boasts such notable alums as Noah Webster, Eli Whitney, Samuel Morse, and Presidents William H Taft, George HW Bush, Bill Clinton and George W Bush. You don't need to share the students' ambitions to take a stroll around the campus, which evokes the university's illustrious history and impact on American life.

In 1702, James Pierpont founded a collegiate school in nearby Clinton. In 1717 it went to New Haven in response to a generous grant of funds by Elihu Yale. The next year the name was changed to Yale in his honor, and by 1887 it had expanded its offerings to such an extent that it was time to rename it Yale University. Phelps Gate on College St opens onto the campus, which is crowded with old Gothic buildings and dominates the northern and western portions of downtown New Haven. Tallest of its spires is 216ft **Harkness Tower**, from which a carillon peals at appropriate moments throughout the day. Among the more compelling paces to visit is the state-of-the-art **Beinecke Rare Book & Manuscript Library** (admission free; ☺ 8:30am-8pm Mon-Thu, 8:30am-5pm Fri, 10am-5pm Sat), the world's largest building devoted to

CONNECTICUT

YALE UNIVERSITY MUSEUMS

The **Yale Center for British Art** (☎ 203-432-2800; ycba.yale.edu; 1080 Chapel St; admission free; ⊙ 10am-5pm Tue-Sat, noon-5pm Sun), at the corner of High St, holds the most comprehensive collection of British art outside the UK. The permanent collection represents the 16th to mid-19th centuries most significantly, while the work of more modern artists is often on exhibition. Of note is the fact that the galleries are not only arranged chronologically, but also by theme, such as 'Ideal Landscape' or the 'Conversation Piece,' and artist, such as JMW Turner or Joseph Wright of Derby. The museum is housed in the last building designed by American architect Louis Kahn

Kahn's first public commission, the outstanding **Yale University Art Gallery** (☎ 203-432-0600; artgallery.yale.edu; 1111 Chapel St; admission free; ⊙ 10am-5pm Tue-Sat, 1-6pm Sun) was restored in 2006 to align it with the architect's original vision. The oldest university collection in the country includes masterworks by Frans Hals, Peter Paul Rubens, Manet, Picasso and van Gogh, plus American silver from the 18th century and art from Africa, Asia, the pre- and post-Columbian Americas and Europe.

The **Peabody Museum of Natural History** (☎ 203-432-5050; www.yale.edu/peabody; 170 Whitney Ave; adult/child 3-18/senior $7/5/6; ⊙ 10am-5pm Mon-Sat, noon-5pm Sun), five blocks northeast of the green along Temple St, has a vast collection of animal, vegetable and mineral specimens, including wildlife dioramas, meteorites and minerals. The Great Hall of Dinosaurs illuminates the museum's fossil collection against the backdrop of the Pulitzer Prize–winning mural *The Age of Reptiles*. Parking is available.

rare books, which includes a 1455 Gutenberg Bible among its 600,000 manuscripts.

Conversely, the **Tomb** (64 High St) is not open to the public. This is the home of Yale's most notorious secret society, the Skull & Bones Club, founded in 1832, and its list of members reads like a 'who's who' of high-powered judges, financiers, politicians, publishers and intelligence officers. Stories of bizarre initiation rites and claims that the Tomb is full of stolen booty like Hitler's silverware and the skulls of Apache warrior Geronimo and Mexican general Pancho Villa further fuel popular curiosity.

Stop at the visitors center (p331) and pick up a free campus map or a walking-tour brochure. For a free one-hour student-guided walking tour, arrive slightly before 10:30am or 2pm weekdays or at 1:30pm on weekends.

GALLERIES & ART SPACES

In a stately 1905 building, the **John Slade Ely House** (☎ 203-625-8055; www.elyhouse.org; 51 Trumbull St; admission free; ⊙ 11am-4pm Wed-Fri, 2-5pm Sat & Sun, closed Aug) puts on four shows a year in a variety of media.

A new arrival on the scene, the **White Space Gallery** (☎ 203-495-1200; www.whitespacegallery.com; 1020 Chapel St; admission free; ⊙ 10am-6pm Mon-Sat) is geared toward serious collectors and features hand-signed lithographs by surrealists such as Dalí and Chagall.

Specializing in the visual arts, the three-story **Creative Arts Workshop** (☎ 203-562-4927; www.creativeartsworkshop.org; 80 Audobon St; admission free; ⊙ 9am-5pm Mon-Fri) offers classes as well as exhibitions in two galleries.

Festivals & Events

New Haven Folk Alliance (www.ctfolk.com) sponsors September's **New Haven Folk Festival** (tickets around $24) and various one-off concerts throughout the year.

In summer, the New Haven Green hosts the free concert series **Music on the Green** (www.infonewhaven.com/freeconcerts), which has featured the likes of Soul Asylum and Regina Belle, while the **New Haven Symphony Orchestra** (www.newhavensymphony.com) draws crowds with periodic opera performances.

Sleeping

BUDGET

Hotel Duncan (☎ 203-787-1273; 1151 Chapel St; s $44-50, d/ste $60/70) Though the shine has rubbed off this fin-de-siècle New Haven gem – with stained carpets, unstable water pressure and exfoliating towels – it's the enduring features that still make a stay here a pleasure, like the handsome lobby and the hand-operated elevator with uniformed attendant. There are 65 rooms let on a long-term basis plus 35 for nightly rental; eight suites are available. Rooms all the way down on the left side tend to be quietest. Check out the wall in the manager's office filled with autographed pictures of celebrity guests like Jodie Foster and Christopher Walken.

Days Inn (☎ 203-469-0343, 800-544-8313; www.day sinn.com; 270 Foxon Blvd; d $56-64; P 🖳 wi-fi) A few miles north of the city, this inn has 58 rooms, all with cable TV with HBO. To get there, take I-91 exit 8.

Econo Lodge (☎ 203-387-6651; 877-424-6423; www .econolodge.com; 100 Pond Lily Ave; d $69-150; P 🐾) This inn is just off the Wilbur Cross Parkway (exit 59), several miles to the northeast of town, and has 125 rooms. You get a fitness center and Jacuzzi along with a well-furnished motel unit.

MIDRANGE

Courtyard Marriott at Yale (☎ 203-777-6221; www .marriott.com; 30 Whalley Ave; d from $109; P 🖳 wi-fi🐾) This hotel has 160 rooms (the higher rooms afford good views), all sporting fridges, granite baths and safes. Make sure to ask about discounts.

Omni New Haven Hotel (☎ 860-772-6664; www .omnihotels.com; 155 Temple St; d $118-199; P 🖳 wi-fi 🔗) At this enormous, 306-room hotel you get all the smart amenities you'd expect, including a 24-hour fitness center and a restaurant on the top floor. Ask for a room with a view of either the Sound or the Green. Several wheelchair-accessible rooms are available.

ourpick Inn at Oyster Point (☎ 203-773-3334, 860-978-3778; www.oysterpointinn.com; 104 Howard Ave; s/d $109/119; P 🖳 wi-fi) About five minutes from downtown, this converted 19th-century oysterman's house on the shore contains six sumptuous rooms tastefully and thematically appointed (eg the Italian suite, the Provençal Room). New Haven's best bed and breakfast, the inn is also gay friendly.

TOP END

Three Chimneys Inn (☎ 203-777-1201, 800-443-1554; 1201 Chapel St; d incl breakfast $195-215; P 🖳) A stay in one of the 11 rooms in this sumptuously restored four-storey 1874 Victorian 'painted lady' promises to be memorable, with just-so touches at every turn – what with morning coffee over the *New York Times*, afternoon wine and cheese, and fireside port and sherry in the evening, why even bother venturing into town?

Eating

Chapel Sq, the area just south of campus roughly between York and Church Sts, con-stitutes a restaurant zone with cuisines from every part of the globe. New Haven is known as the pizza capital of New England, if not the entire East Coast, and its best parlors can be found along Wooster St.

BUDGET

Yankee Doodle Sandwich & Coffee Shop (☎ 203-865-1074; 258 Elm St; dishes $2-6; 🕑 breakfast & lunch Sat-Tue, breakfast, lunch & dinner Wed-Fri) The family-run Doodle is a classic '50s hole-in-the-wall American lunch counter – Formica coun-tertop, chrome and plastic stools, real foun-tain soda – with prices to match. Despite the name, burgers and breakfast are the draws here. The defunct cigarette machine in the corner is kept around for purely nostalgic reasons – it was installed on the day JFK was shot. When Yale's not in session, Doodle's hours are sharply curtailed.

Louis' Lunch (☎ 203-562-5507; 261-263 Crown St; burgers $4.50; 🕑 lunch Tue & Wed, lunch & dinner Thu-Sat, closed Aug) This squat, brick number claims to be the place where the hamburger was in-vented – well, almost. Around 1900, when the vertically grilled ground beef sandwich was first introduced at Louis', the restaurant was in a different location. It still uses the historic vertical grills, and serves a few non-burger items as well. Ask for ketchup and feel the disdain rain down upon you. Credit cards aren't accepted.

Atticus Bookstore Café (☎ 203-776-4040; 1082 Chapel St; dishes $5-8; 🕑 breakfast, lunch & dinner) You don't have to be a student to chow down at this spot – named after the first-known publisher – but you're sure to be surrounded by them. This recently renovated café has been serving strong coffee and from-scratch soups, sandwiches and pastries amid the stacks for two decades. An ideal place to refuel before or after a trip to the nearby Yale museums.

ourpick Frank Pepe's Pizzeria (☎ 203-865-5762; 157 Wooster St; dishes $5-20; 🕑 4-10pm Mon, Wed & Thu, 11:30am-11pm Fri & Sat, 2:30-10pm Sun) Pepe's serves immaculate pizza fired in a coal oven, just as it has since 1925, in frenetic white-walled surroundings. Prices vary depending on size and toppings; the large mozzarella pizza runs at $12. No credit cards.

Modern Apizza (☎ 203-776-5306; 874 State St; pizza $6-18; 🕑 lunch & dinner Tue-Sat, 3-10pm Sun) Lots of locals believe that this place serves up pies as good as, if not better than, Frank Pepe's and

Sally's – and without the throngs. Despite the name, it's been tossing dough since 1934.

Claire's Corner Copia (☎ 203-562-3888; 1000 Chapel St; meals $7-10; ⏰ breakfast, lunch & dinner; Ⓥ) Bright, airy and always packed, this has been the best vegetarian restaurant in town for over thirty years. The soups, salads and quiches are excellent, though the sandwiches can be a bit anemic. Try something off the Mexican section of the menu or just come for a sweet treat, like the Lithuanian coffeecake ($3.60).

Bangkok Gardens (☎ 203-789-8684; 172 York St; meals $7-13; ⏰ lunch & dinner) Just off Chapel St, this large, white-linened establishment is the center's most popular Thai eatery. The Golden Bay appetizer, fried tofu pouches stuffed with shrimp and veggies, is exquisite. At lunch, big plates of pork, beef and chicken with vegetables are inexpensive and best topped off with an order of fried ice cream. Try to get a seat on the sun porch.

Sally's Apizza (☎ 203-624-5271; 237 Wooster St; pizza $7-15; ⏰ dinner Tue-Sun) A nearby challenger to Pepe's; the white-clam pie ($10) is legendary for good reason, but all pies share the same thin, crispy crust. Sally's is closed most of September, and doesn't take credit cards.

our pick Anchor (☎ 203-865-1512; 272 College St; meals $10-18; ⏰ lunch & dinner) Sure, you can score the standard pub-grub burgers here, but you're much better off strolling in later in the evening. The clientele represents a real cross-section of folks. Throw some tunes on the jazz-heavy jukebox, get a drink from the full bar and settle into your black-leather banquette booth. No plastic accepted.

MIDRANGE

Caffé Adulis (☎ 203-777-5081; 228 College St; meals $11-27; ⏰ dinner) This jewel of a place offers Eritrean-Ethiopian cuisine in a sophisticated but unerringly friendly package. One of the many house specialties is the shrimp *barka* (pan-seared jumbo shrimp with coconut, tomato and dates over basmati rice, $19). The wine list is reason enough to linger late into the evening – the bar is open until 1am.

Scoozzi Trattoria (☎ 203-776-8268; 1104 Chapel St; meals $11-30; ⏰ lunch & dinner) At York St, next to the Yale Repertory Theatre, this basement trattoria serves trendy Italian fare with strong New American cuisine accents. The little pizzettes and other appetizers like mussels and calamari sautéed with red grapes are favorites with the before- and after-theater crowd, who

combine them with wine by the glass to make a light supper. Weather permitting, there's outdoor dining in an intimate courtyard. Reservations recommended.

TOP END

Miya's Sushi (☎ 203-777-9760; 68 Howe St; meals $13-36; ⏰ lunch & dinner) Superlative sushi – probably the best in the state – is prepared in this low-key spot by chef Bun Lai, two-time winner of the Taste of the Nation Award. Sushi appetizers sport alluring names like the Concubine's Delight (smoked salmon and goats cheese wrapped in tempura eggplant), but the true star is the *kaiseki* ($30), a truly exceptional prix-fixe meal highlighted by several inventive sashimi arrangements, which must be ordered in advance.

ZINC (☎ 203-624-0507; 964 Chapel St; meals $14-31; ⏰ dinner Mon, lunch & dinner Tue-Sat) Whenever possible, this trendy bistro's ingredients hail from local organic sources, but the chef draws inspiration from all over, notably Asia and the Southwest. There's a constantly changing 'market menu,' but for the most rewarding experience, share several of the small plates for dinner, like the smoked duck nachos or the *prosciutto Americano crostini*. Reservations recommended.

Union League Café (☎ 203-562-4299; 1032 Chapel St; meals $22-31; ⏰ lunch Mon-Fri, dinner Mon-Sat) Here's an upscale French bistro in the historic Union League building. Expect a menu featuring continental classics like *cocotte de joues de veau* (organic veal cheeks with sautéed wild mushrooms, $25) along with those of nouvelle cuisine. If your budget won't stretch to dinner, slip in for a sinful dessert like *crêpe soufflé au citron* (lemon crepes) washed down with a glass from the exquisite wine list. Date place par excellence.

Drinking

Backroom @ Bottega (☎ 203-562-5566; 954 Chapel St; cover after 10pm $5) With live acts on Thursday, local DJs on weekends, cheap martinis ($7) and Italian small plates, this spot draws a mix of college kids, locals and assorted nighthawks.

Elm City Java (☎ 203-776-2248; 77 Whitney Ave; ⏰ 7am-8pm Mon-Thu, 7am-midnight Fri, 10am-6pm Sat & Sun, shorter hrs in summer) This café hosts local acts every Thursday evening, and all the bands you hear over the stereo system are New Haven–based. Better yet, the coffee is fair-trade organic.

Entertainment

As a college town and a city of some size, New Haven has amassed an unusual number of quality theater, dance and musical companies, most of which offer substantial discounts to seniors and students – be sure to ask. On any given night you'll be spoilt for choice, from acoustic coffeehouse warbling to symphonic spectacles.

Pick up a copy of the free weeklies *New Haven Advocate* (www.newhavenadvocate .com) and *Play* (www.playnewhaven.com) for up-to-the-minute entertainment listings. The latter is geared more toward the student set.

CLUBS

BAR (☎ 203-495-1111; www.barnightclub.com; 254 Crown St; cover $4-8) This club encompasses the Bru Room (New Haven's first brew pub), the Front Room, the video-oriented BARtropolis Room and various other enclaves. Taken in toto, you're set for artisinal beer and brick-oven pizza, a free pool table and excellent live music or DJs spinning almost every night of the week. Check the *Haven Advocate* for specifics.

Partner's Café (☎ 203-776-1014; www.partnerscafe .com; 365 Crown St; cover $3; ⊗ 5pm-1am Fri & Sat) An anything-goes crowd packs it into the three floors at Partner's. There are pool tables, quiet alcoves for conversation, and thumping house music upstairs. M&M Fridays sees male dancers and midnight pizza. Every Sunday is karaoke night and the boys get the run of the place each Tuesday. Happy hour, which knocks $1 off cocktails and beer, is 5pm to 8pm.

168 York St Cafe (☎ 203-789-1915; www.168york streetcafe.com; 168 York St; ⊗ 3pm-1am summer, from 11am in-season) This bar-restaurant isn't too far off its own billing as a gay *Cheers*. Sunday and Thursday nights will get you $1 domestic beers, while daily happy hours between 4pm and 7pm knock a dollar off all drink prices.

Toad's Place (☎ recording 203-624-8623, office 203-562-5589; www.toadsplace.com; 300 York St; cover free-$25) Toad's is arguably New England's premier music hall, having earned its rep hosting the likes of the Rolling Stones, U2 and Bob Dylan. These days, an eclectic range of performers work the intimate stage, including They Might Be Giants and Martin & Wood.

THEATER & CLASSICAL MUSIC

New Haven Symphony Orchestra (☎ 203-776-1444, 800-292-6476; www.newhavensymphony.org; cnr College & Grove Sts; tickets $10-55) Yale's Woolsey Hall is home to most performances by this orchestra, whose season runs from October through April. The Pops series performs on Friday evenings.

Chamber Music Society at Yale (☎ 203-432-4158; www.yale.edu/music/concerts/cms; 470 College St; tickets $25-32) This Yale society sponsors concerts from such eminent ensembles as the Guarneri String Quartet at 8pm Tuesday evenings from September through April in the Morse Recital Hall of Sprague Memorial Hall.

Yale Repertory Theatre (☎ 203-432-1234; www.yale edu/yalerep; 1120 Chapel St; tickets $38-45) Performing in a converted church, this Tony-winning repertory company has mounted more than 90 world premiers and performs classics and new works featuring graduate students of the Yale School of Drama (Meryl Streep and Sigourney Weaver are alums) as well as professionals. From September to May, a full and varied program is offered.

Long Wharf Theatre (☎ 203-787-4282, 800-782-8497; www.longwharf.org; 222 Sargent Dr; tickets $30-60; ⊗ Oct-Jun) This nonprofit regional theater mounts productions from the likes of Tom Stoppard and Eugene O'Neill in a converted warehouse. It's at I-95 exit 46, on the waterfront.

Shubert Theater (☎ 203-562-5666, 800-228-6622; 247 College St; tickets $18-55; ⊗ Sep-May) Dubbed 'Birthplace of the Nation's Greatest Hits,' since 1914 the Shubert has been hosting ballet and Broadway musicals on their trial runs before heading off to the Big Apple. They have expanded their repertoire to include events such as 'An Evening with David Sedaris.'

Other concerts are hosted by the **Yale School of Music** (☎ 203-432-4158; www.yale.edu/schmus), mostly free of charge, and on occasion by the **Yale Collection of Musical Instruments** (☎ 203-432-0822; www.yale.edu/musicalinstruments; tickets $10-20).

Getting There & Around

AIR

Bus G of **Connecticut Transit** (☎ 203-624-0151) gets you to **Tweed New Haven Airport** (☎ 203-466-8833; www.flytweed.com; I-95 exit 50), from where several commuter airlines can take you to Boston or New York.

BOAT

The **Bridgeport & Port Jefferson Steamboat Company** (☎ CT 888-443-3779, Long Island 631-473-0286; www.bpjferry.com; 102 W Broadway, Port Jefferson,

NY) operates its daily car ferries year-round between Bridgeport, 10 miles southwest of New Haven, and Port Jefferson on Long Island about every 1½ hours. The one-way 1½-hour voyage costs $15.75 for adults, $11 for seniors, and is free for children 12 and under. The fee for a car is $44.50 not including passenger fares, depending on the number of passengers. Call to reserve space for your car.

BUS

Peter Pan Bus Lines (☎ 800-343-9999; www.peterpanbus .com) connects New Haven with NYC ($24.50, 2½ hours, four daily), Hartford ($11.50, one hour, four daily), Springfield ($21, two hours, four daily) and Boston ($30, four hours, five daily), as does **Greyhound Bus Lines** (☎ 203-772-2470, 800-221-2222; www.greyhound.com), inside New Haven's **Union Station** (☎ 203-773-6177; 50 Union Ave).

Connecticut Limousine (☎ 800-472-5466; www .ctlimo.com) runs buses between New Haven and NYC's airports (La Guardia and JFK, plus Newark) for around $50 per person.

CAR & MOTORCYCLE

Avis and **Hertz** rent cars at Tweed New Haven Airport. Both can be reached by calling ☎ 203-466-8833. New Haven is 141 miles southwest of Boston, 36 miles south of Hartford, 75 miles from New York and 101 miles from Providence via interstate highways.

TRAIN

Metro-North (☎ 212-532-4900, 800-223-6052, 800-638-7646) trains make the 1½-hour run between NYC's Grand Central Terminal and New Haven's **Union Station** (☎ 203-773-6177; 50 Union Ave), at I-95 exit 47, almost every hour from 7am to midnight on weekdays, with more frequent trains during the morning and evening rush hours. On weekends, trains run about every two hours. Shore Line East runs **Commuter Connection buses** (☎ 203-624-0151) that shuttle passengers from Union Station (in the evenings) and from State St Station (in the mornings) to New Haven Green.

Frequent **Amtrak trains** (☎ 800-872-7245) run from NYC's Penn Station to New Haven's Union Station, but at a higher fare than Metro-North. **Shore Line East** (☎ 800-255-7433) travels up the shore of Long Island Sound. At New Haven, the trains connect with Metro-North and Amtrak routes.

NORWALK
pop 84,000

Straddling the Norwalk River and encrusted with the salt spray of the Long Island Sound, Norwalk is fiercely proud of its maritime tradition. The area supported a robust oystering industry in the 18th and 19th centuries, but overharvesting in the early 1900s threatened the supply. Thanks to careful regulation, Norwalk is again the state's top oyster producer.

The past decade has seen the rebuilding of the crumbling waterfront in South Norwalk, where a clutch of innovative restaurants has set up shop around Washington, Main and Water Sts, earning the area the nickname 'SoNo.' New Yorkers can get from Manhattan to Norwalk in about an hour, and be kayaking around the Norwalk Islands soon after.

For tourist and accommodation information try **Fairfield County's Convention & Visitors Bureau** (☎ 203-853-7770, 800-866-7925; www.visitfair fieldcountyct.com; Mathews Park, 297 West Ave; ☉ 9am-5pm), located in a small stone building.

In mid-September, the **Oyster Festival** is a big deal, with skydivers, fireworks, bands and plenty of the slippery guys themselves.

Sights & Activities
MARITIME AQUARIUM

This **aquarium** (☎ 203-852-0700; www.maritimeaquar ium.org; 10 N Water St, S Norwalk; adult/2-12yr/senior $11/9/10; ☉ 10am-5pm, 10am-6pm summer; ☑) focuses on the marine life of the Long Island Sound, including sand tiger sharks, loggerhead turtles and harbor seals, whose daily feedings at 11:45am, 1:45pm and 3:45pm are a real treat. IMAX movies are also shown throughout the day for an additional fee. For a more hands-on experience, take a 2½-hour cruise on the research vessel *Oceanic* (per person $20.50). Cruises depart at 1pm daily in July and August, and on weekends in April through June and September.

STEPPING STONES MUSEUM FOR CHILDREN

This well-crafted **museum** (☎ 203-899-0606; www .steppingstonesmuseum.org; Mathews Park, 303 West Ave; admission $8; ☉ 10am-5pm summer, closed Mon & Tue morning off-season; ☑) is bursting with interactive, instructive fun, from the weather cycle to gravity to the principles of conservation. The Toddler Terrain is a hit with the under-three crowd. Across the parking lot from the museum is **Devon's Place**, a playground designed with mentally and physically challenged children in mind, but it holds appeal for all.

LOCKWOOD-MATHEWS MANSION MUSEUM

This is one of the best surviving Second Empire–style country houses in the nation, so it's no wonder the 62-room **mansion** (☎ 203-838-9799; www.lockwoodmathewsmansion.org; Mathews Park, 925 West Ave; adult/student/under 12yr $8/$5/free; ☺ noon-5pm Wed-Sun) was chosen as the set for the 2004 version of *The Stepford Wives*. The 2nd floor houses the Music Box Society International's permanent collection of music boxes, viewable (and listenable) only if you're on a tour. They leave every hour on the hour.

NORWALK ISLANDS

The Norwalk Islands lie a half-mile off the coast of SoNo, and are the playground of a menagerie of gawk-worthy coastal birds. Admission to the historic **Sheffield Island Lighthouse**, activated in 1868, is included in the price of the summer-only **ferry** (GW Tyler Lighthouse Ferry; ☎ 203-838-9444; adult/4-12yr/3yr & under $16/12/5). Or if you want to take matters into your own hands, you can kayak there. The **Small Boat Shop** (☎ 203-854-5223; www.thesmallboatshop.com; 144 Water St; ☺ 10am-5pm Mon-Sat, 10am-3pm Sun) leads two-hour, four-hour and all-day trips to the islands in the summer.

Sleeping

our pick **Silvermine Tavern** (☎ 203-847-4558, 888-693-9967; www.silverminetavern.com; 194 Perry Ave; s $80, d $115-150; 💻 wi-fi) Standing by the gorgeous tree-lined waterfall here, you couldn't feel further away from I-95, only a 15-minute drive away. All of its antique-laden rooms have private bathrooms, and the restaurant (see right) is terrific. From the center of SoNo, head north on Main St and turn left onto CT 123. Bear right onto Silvermine Ave, and turn right onto Perry Ave.

Main Street Inn (☎ 203-972-2983; 190 Main St, New Canaan; s $90-125, d $115-160) A short drive from Norwalk, this restored Victorian with modern touches lets three spankingly clean rooms. Morning coffee and muffins are included.

Eating

Jeremiah Donovan's (☎ 203-838-3430; 138 Washington St, S Norwalk; sandwiches $5-10; ☺ 11:30am-1am Mon-Sat, noon-6pm Sun; 👶) Head to this Victorian-era former saloon if all the SoNo gourmet chic is getting to you (or your kids). Alongside the tuna melts and Reubens on rye, JD dishes out hearty daily specials. Vintage photos of prize fighters festoon the place.

our pick **Bistro du Soleil** (☎ 203-855-9469; 120 Washington St; meals $7-37; ☺ lunch & dinner) It's difficult to pigeonhole family-run Soleil's cuisine, and really, there's no need. Stylish yet warm, this bistro deftly executes everything from *langoustine* (shellfish) quesadillas to free-range New Zealand petite lamb chops to fillet of ostrich. The rotating art exhibits ensure a feast for the eyes to rival the one on your plate.

Shacojazz Art Cafe (☎ 203-853-6124; 21 N Main St, S Norwalk; meals $9-17; ☺ 11:30am-9:30pm Tue-Sat, 1-9pm Sun) Had it up to here with clam chowder? Try something a little different at this Afro-Caribbean shop-cum-eatery. A small bowl of the delicious peanut soup is $4, though be warned that its ingredients include fish broth and, er, gizzard.

Silvermine Tavern (☎ 203-847-4558, 888-693-9967; 194 Perry Ave; meals $12-36; ☺ lunch & dinner Wed-Sun) Gracious dining is de rigueur in this wood-accented dining room. Warm up on the crisp duck spring rolls ($8) before tackling the pecan-crusted fillet of brook trout ($22), or opt for one of the juicy burger creations. If the weather is fine, be sure to secure seating on the deck overlooking the mill pond. If it's not, try to snag a fireside table.

Wasabi Chi (☎ 845-358-7977; 2 South Main St; meals $16-57; ☺ lunch Tue-Thu, dinner Tue-Sun) In a sleek, dark-lit setting suggesting a club lounge, Wasabi Chi conjures up creative and elegantly presented Japanese food. Try a lobster martini (lobster, avocado and caviar in a martini glass) or savor the pan-seared duck in a sweet chili sauce with deep-fried yam slices. The inside-out rolls are exceptionally good.

Pasta Nostra (☎ 203-854-9700; 116 Washington St; meals $25-40; ☺ dinner Thu-Sat) You can feel the love at this black-and-white-tiled restaurant, where chef Joe Bruno has been wowing diners since 1984 with his handmade pastas and exquisite attention to detail. Freshness being paramount, even the meat is butchered on site. Reservations required.

Getting There & Away

Norwalk is about 32 miles south of New Haven on I-95. There are dozens of weekday

CONNECTICUT

WORTH THE TRIP: UNITED HOUSE WRECKING, INC.

Even if you're one of those folks who reflexively yawns – or gags – at the thought of 'going antiquing,' the extraordinary **United House Wrecking, Inc.** (☎ 203-348-5371; www.unitedhousewrecking.com; 535 Hope St, Stamford; ⏰ 9:30am-5:30pm Mon-Sat, noon-5pm Sun) is well worth a visit. Upon pulling into the parking lot you may be greeted with a 15ft-tall Pinocchio standing with a 12ft Statue of Liberty, flanked by dozens of lampposts or scores of cherubic garden sculptures. Inside, the 35,000-sq-ft warehouse holds vintage chandeliers, stained glass, furniture and classy knickknacks of all sorts. No room in the car for that one-of-a-kind fireplace mantle? No worries – they ship world-wide. (Hyperactive children and accident-prone adults may want to wait outside with Pinocchio.)

To get there from I-95 heading south, take exit 9 and turn right at the light onto US 1. Take your first right (Courtland Ave) and then turn left onto Glenbrook Rd. At the light go straight onto Church St and then turn right onto Hope St.

---

trains between NYC's Grand Central Terminal and the South Norwalk Station (and all the stops in between), and a train about every hour on the weekends.

GREENWICH
pop 62,000

For those with money to burn, Greenwich beckons with a main street lined with the likes of Tiffany & Co, Sacks Fifth Avenue and Kate Spade, along with some charming but still pricey non-chain establishments, especially in the home furnishing and kids-wear categories. Luckily for the rest of us, Greenwich also holds within its compact downtown a notable museum and an enticing town common (which is a wi-fi hot spot). Being only 28 miles from Grand Central Terminal, less than an hour by train, makes Greenwich a very doable day trip from NYC. If you're driving, avoid heading north for Greenwich anywhere around evening rush hour, or south into town during the morning commute – its proximity to NYC spells traffic nightmare.

Norwalk's **Fairfield County's Convention & Visitors Bureau** (☎ 203-853-7770, 800-866-7925; www.visitfairfieldcountyct.com; Mathews Park, 297 West Ave, Norwalk; ⏰ 9am-5pm) carries information on Greenwich. **Diane's Books** (203-869-1515; 8 Grigg St; ⏰ 9am-5pm Mon-Sat) boasts the largest selection of family books in the country.

The **Bruce Museum** (☎ 203-869-0376; www.bruce museum.org; 1 Museum Dr; adult/student & senior $7/6; ⏰ 10am-5pm Tue-Sat, 1-5pm Sun) serves up a bit of everything, but there's no suffering from cultural indigestion. Sculpture, photography and painting by impressionists from Cos Cob's art colony (notably Childe Hassam) meld smoothly into exhibits on natural sci-

ence and anthropology. The Bruce is also home to a variety of traveling exhibitions.

For a quick and delicious bite, you can't do better than **Meli-Melo** (362 Greenwich Ave; crepes $3-15; ⏰ lunch & dinner). Meaning 'hodge-podge' in French, Meli-Melo serves salads, soups and sandwiches, but its specialty is undoubtedly buckwheat crepes. Try a wild combination like smoked salmon, chive sauce, lemon and daikon ($9.50). The French onion and French lentil soups are, appropriately, superb.

Head to **Restaurant Jean-Louis** (☎ 203-622-8450; 61 Lewis St; meals $33-43; ⏰ lunch & dinner Mon-Fri, dinner Sat) for a meal that neither your taste-buds nor your wallet will forget soon. Jean-Louis and Linda Gerin – chef and manager, respectively – have garnered accolades for their 'nouvelle classique,' with dishes like pan-seared ostrich thigh fillet with polenta and cognac sauce. The five-course tasting menu is the ideal way to taste a variety of offerings, and the prix-fixe lunch menu is a bargain at $29.

CONNECTICUT RIVER VALLEY

Snaking its way from the Long Island Sound up through Connecticut and into Massachusetts before forming the border between Vermont and New Hampshire, the Connecticut River covers over 400 miles. It is easily New England's longest river. Mercifully, it escaped the bustle of industry and commerce that marred many of the northeast's rivers, and the fact that it's largely navigable 50 miles inland was one of the reasons the

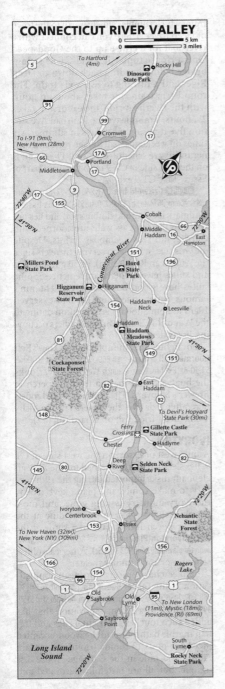

CONNECTICUT RIVER VALLEY

colony, and then the state, prospered in the days before highways.

Surprisingly shallow near its mouth, its lack of depth led burgeoning industry to look for better harbors elsewhere, and the lower valley was far more likely to witness the establishment of artist colonies than of factories. Today, well-preserved historic towns grace the river's banks, notably Old Lyme, Essex, Ivoryton, Chester and East Haddam. Together, they enchant visitors with gracious country inns, fine dining, antique stores, and train rides and river excursions that allow authentic glimpses back into provincial life on the Connecticut.

Hartford, the state's capital and largest city, seems to be rediscovering the river these days, with new parks and walkways landscaped along its banks. Most visitors come for its world-class museum and historical homes, however, and the city hasn't quite shaken off its reputation as a grim, workaday city rather than a tourist destination.

OLD LYME
pop 7500

Near the mouth of the Connecticut River and perched on the smaller Lieutenant River, Old Lyme (I-95 exit 70) was home to some 60 sea captains in the 19th century. Since the early 20th century, however, Old Lyme has been known as the center of the Lyme Art Colony, which embraced and cultivated the nascent American Impressionist movement. Numerous artists, including William Chadwick, Childe Hassam, Willard Metcalfe and Henry Ward Ranger, came here to paint, staying in the mansion of local art patron Florence Griswold.

Her house, which her artist friends decorated with murals (often in lieu of paying rent), is now the **Florence Griswold Museum** (☎ 860-434-5542; www.flogris.org; 96 Lyme St; adult/child/senior & student $8/4/7; ☼ 10am-5pm Tue-Sat, 1-5pm Sun) and contains a fine selection of both Impressionist and Barbizon paintings. The estate consists of her Georgian-style house, the Krieble Gallery, the Chadwick studio and Griswold's beloved gardens.

The neighboring **Lyme Academy of Fine Arts** (☎ 860-434-5232; lymeacademy.edu; 84 Lyme St; admission free; ☼ 10am-4pm Tue-Sat, 1-4pm Sun) features rotating drawing, painting and sculpture exhibits by students.

ourpick **Bee & Thistle Inn** (☎ 860-434-1667, 800-622-4946; www.beeandthistleinn.com; 100 Lyme St, Old

Lyme; d incl breakfast $130-194), a butter-yellow 1756 Dutch Colonial farmhouse, makes it easy to see where the artists' inspiration came from when you stay here. The well-tended gardens stretch down to the Lieutenant River, and all 11 antique-filled rooms feature a canopy or a four-post bed. Its romantic dining room with an intimate porch alcove is the perfect setting for superlative New American cuisine. Lunch and dinner (meals $25-42) are served Wednesday to Sunday, often enhanced by a harpist. Although the menu changes, you can expect dishes like Szechuan pepper and ginger seared rare tuna with wasabi mashed potatoes or premium Hereford filet mignon with a prosciutto and Cotswold cheese salad. Reservations essential.

ESSEX
pop 6800

Tree-lined Essex, established in 1635, stands as the chief town of the region and features well-preserved Federal-period houses, legacies of rum and tobacco fortunes made in the 19th century. Essex was also the birthplace of the modern production of witch hazel, a traditional folk medicine. Today, the town has the genteel, aristocratic air of historical handsomeness, and prides itself on the fact that it is the oldest-known continuously operating waterfront in the country.

Coming into the town center from CT 9, you'll eventually find yourself on Main St. The centerpiece of Essex both physically and socially is the 1776 **Griswold Inn**, a hostelry since the time of the Revolutionary War. 'The Gris' is both an inn and a restaurant (see right), and its taproom is the place to meet the townsfolk.

At the end of Main St is the riverfront and the newly renovated **Connecticut River Museum** (☎ 860-767-8269; www.ctrivermuseum.org; adult/6-12yr/senior $7/4/6; ☉ 10am-5pm Tue-Sun, 10am-4pm Jan-Apr), next to Steamboat Dock. Its meticulous exhibits recount the history of the area. Included among them is a replica of the world's first submarine, the *American Turtle*, a wooden barrel-like vessel built here by Yale student David Bushnell in 1776 and launched at nearby Old Saybrook. Don't miss the ships in bottles exhibit on the top floor.

The best way to experience the river here is to take the **Essex Steam Train & Riverboat Ride** (☎ 860-767-0103, 800-377-3987; www.essexsteamtrain .com; 1 Railroad Ave; train only adult/child $17/9, train & riverboat cruise $26/13). A steam engine powers the

train, which rumbles slowly north to the town of Deep River. There you can connect with a riverboat for a cruise up to the Goodspeed Opera House (opposite) and CT 82 swing-bridge before heading back down to Deep River and returning to Essex via train. The round-trip train ride takes about an hour; with the riverboat ride, the excursion takes 2½ hours. Trains leave the Railroad Ave station five times on weekdays in summer, six times on weekends. Fall foliage runs and dinner trains are scheduled as well. The depot is on the west side of CT 9 from the main part of Essex. Take CT 9 exit 3A.

ourpick Griswold Inn (☎ 860-767-1776; www.gris woldinn.com; 36 Main St; r $100-220, ste $160-370) is Essex's landmark lodging and dining spot, and lies not far from the river. Its walls are adorned with Currier and Ives steamboats prints. Despite the Gris' age (it has been serving travelers since the American Revolution), its 30 guest rooms and suites have modern conveniences. Some suites have wood-burning stoves. The inn's famous buffet-style Hunt Breakfast (served 10am to 2pm Sunday) is a tradition dating to the War of 1812, when British soldiers occupying Essex demanded to be fed.

For lighter fare, the aptly named **Crow's Nest Gourmet Deli & Pizza** (☎ 860-767-3288; Pratt St; dishes $1.50-8; ☉ breakfast & lunch Wed-Mon) overlooks the boatyard and marina from its perch at Brewer's Shipyard. The yachting crowd roosts here after a day on the water. Try the 'fishy swah,' deep-fried fish on a hard roll ($7).

IVORYTON

A mile west of Essex, on the west side of CT 9, lies sleepy Ivoryton, named for the African elephant tusks imported during the 19th century to make combs and piano keys. Today the ivory industry is long gone, and most people visit Ivoryton to stay or dine at the Copper Beech Inn or take in a show at the 1908 **Ivoryton Playhouse** (☎ 860-767-8348; www .ivorytonplayhouse.com; 103 Main St), America's oldest self-supporting summer theater.

Yankee charm meets European sophistication at the **Copper Beech Inn** (☎ 860-767-0330, 888-809-2056; www.copperbeechinn.com; 46 Main St; d $150-395), thanks to a recent renovation that has added such touches as Oriental rugs and Italian marble bathrooms to the wood-accented inn. Each of its 13 rooms – four in the Main House and nine in the Carriage House – is unique, but all are tastefully decorated and brimming with sumptuous touches like extra-fluffy white bathrobes and fresh flowers. Nine feature Jacuzzis. Reserve well in advance, and contact the inn to find out about weekend package deals (lodging plus dinner or an evening at the Goodspeed Opera House).

For dinner (or Sunday lunch), take a cocktail in the 'conservatory,' then enjoy such contemporary French dishes as rabbit 'two ways' ($31), with apples and mustard glazing, in one of the inn's three dining rooms (closed Monday). The inn's wine cellar boasts more than 5000 bottles. Meals cost $30 to $40.

CHESTER
pop 4000

Cupped in the valley of Pattaconk Brook, Chester is another sedate river town. A general store, post office, library and a few shops pretty much account for all the activity in the village. Most visitors come either for fine dining or to browse in the antique shops and boutiques on the town's charming main street.

From Chester, an eight-car **ferry** (☎ 860-443-3856; car/pedestrian $3/1) crosses the Connecticut River to Hadlyme daily April through November. Crossing eastbound, the ferry drops you at the foot of Gillette Castle (right) in East Haddam.

The **Connecticut River Artisans** (☎ 860-526-5575; www.ctartisans.com; 5 W Main St; ☯ 11am-6pm daily Jul-Aug & Nov-Dec, Wed-Sun Jan-Jun & Sep-Oct) is a co-op featuring one-of-a-kind art and craft pieces including clothing, folk art, furniture, jewelry, paintings, photographs and pottery. The building is adjacent to the Mill House art gallery, which presents changing exhibits.

The original **Inn at Chester** (☎ 860-526-9541, 800-949-7829; 318 W Main St/CT 148; d $135-300) was a farmhouse built in 1776. Several buildings were added during the 20th century to produce a colonial-style inn with modern conveniences in its 44 rooms. To reach the inn from the center of Chester, follow CT 148 west for 4.4 miles and go past CT 9 exit 6 and Killingworth Reservoir to the inn, which is right on the Chester–Killingworth town line.

our pick **River Tavern** (☎ 860-526-9417; 23 Main St; meals $17-30; ☯ lunch & dinner Wed-Mon) has invariable crowds waiting for a table – clearly they're onto something. This wood-accented bistro with a bar and dining-room menu serves up impeccable food with a variety of inflections. The menu changes, but if it's in season you

should definitely order shad, caught from the Connecticut River. Soufflé desserts are to die for and must be ordered with the rest of the meal as they take time to prepare.

With its wrought-iron gate, lacy white curtains and flower-filled window boxes beneath multi-paned windows, the tiny **Restaurant du Village** (☎ 860-526-5301; 59 Main St; meals $30-34; ☯ dinner Wed-Sun) is a gem featuring a predominantly French wine list and Alsatian-influenced dishes like roast duckling with citrus and balsamic vinegar or sautéed veal sweetbreads with a morel mushroom.

EAST HADDAM
pop 8700

Two first-rate attractions mark this small town on the east bank of the Connecticut. Looming on one of the Seven Sisters hills above the ferry dock is **Gillette Castle** (☎ 860-526-2336; 67 River Rd; adult/6-11yr $5/3; ☯ 10am-4:30pm), a turreted, bizarre-looking, 24-room mansion made of fieldstone. Completed in 1919 by eccentric actor William Gillette, it was modeled on the medieval castles of Germany's Rhineland. Gillette made his name and his considerable fortune on stage in the role of Sherlock Holmes. He created the part himself, based on the famous mystery series by Sir Arthur Conan Doyle, and in a sense he made his castle part of the Holmes role as well: an upstairs room replicates Conan Doyle's description of the sitting room at 221B Baker St, London. Following Gillette's death in 1937, his dream house and its surrounding 125 acres were designated a state park – a development that would doubtless have pleased its creator, whose will gave instructions that it not fall into the clutches 'of some blithering saphead who has no conception of where he is.'

North of Gillette Castle stands the **Goodspeed Opera House** (☎ 860-873-8668; www.goodspeed.org; CT 82 at the bridge; tickets $26-66; ☯ performances Wed-Sun Apr-Dec), an 1876 Victorian music hall renowned as the only theater in the country dedicated to both the preservation of old and the development of new American musicals. The shows *Man of La Mancha* and *Annie* premiered at the Goodspeed before going on to national fame.

Also in East Haddam is the **Nathan Hale Schoolhouse** (☎ 860-873-9547; Main St; admission free; ☯ by appointment), behind St Stephen's Church in the center of town. Hale (see p326) taught in this one-room building from 1773 to 1774.

CONNECTICUT

WORTH THE TRIP: AVERY'S BEVERAGE CO, NEW BRITAIN

It doesn't get much more authentic than **Avery's** (☎ 860-224-0830; www.averysoda.com; 520 Corbin Ave, New Britain; ◷ 8:30am-5:30pm Tue & Wed, 8:30am-7pm Thu, 8:30am-6pm Fri, 8:30am-3pm Sat). Its 30-plus flavors of sodas and seltzers are still made with 1950s technology in the original red barn where it all started back in 1904. The water is pure well and the sugar is pure cane – no high-fructose corn syrup here. Standbys like Birch Beer and Black Cherry share the stage with concoctions like Half & Half and Pineapple.

If your group is at least four strong, be sure to call ahead to arrange a make-your-own-soda tour ($11.50 per group). You'll go upstairs to the Mixing Room and create three bottles of soda to your exact flavor specifications and then watch the conveyor-belt machine downstairs add the water and CO_2 and affix the cap.

Sodas are sold by the case (within which you can mix and match flavors), but there are some single bottles available for 75¢ a pop.

From Hartford, drive west on I-84 for about 11 miles, and merge onto CT 72 via exit 35. Take exit 7 and turn slightly right onto Corbin Ave.

From the path to the schoolhouse, you can see the church's 9th-century bell, originally built for a Spanish monastery and the oldest in the New World.

HARTFORD

pop 124,400

Despite the slow exodus of the insurance companies (the industry started here) that earned Hartford the unfortunate reputation as the 'filing cabinet of America,' few specifically visit Connecticut's capital and largest city. The loss is theirs, for while Hartford is by no means a vacation spot on its own, those passing through or pausing from a lengthier journey will be surprised at how much the city has to offer, with several engaging historical sights and a terrific art museum.

Orientation

On its hilltop perch, the pseudo-Gothic Connecticut State Capitol is visible from most of the interstate highways entering the city. The tallest building, with a brilliant laser beacon shining atop it at night, is the Travelers Tower.

The easiest way to take in most of the Hartford attractions – the Wadsworth Atheneum, Old State House and Center Church – is on foot. The houses of literary figures Mark Twain and Harriet Beecher Stowe are a few miles west of the town center off Farmington Ave. There are tons of downtown garages for parking, but for the most bang for your buck, head to the huge outdoor **Morgan St Garage** (Talcott St), between Market St and Columbus Blvd.

Information

Bookworm (☎ 860-233-2653; 968 Farmington Ave, West Hartford; ◷ 9:30am-6pm Mon-Sat, noon-4pm Sun) This is on the shady main street of West Hartford.

Cosí Café (☎ 860-521-8495; 970 Farmington Ave, West Hartford; ◷ 7am-10pm) This is a wi-fi hot spot.

Gallows Hill Bookstore (☎ 860-297-2191; 300 Summit St; ◷ 9am-7pm Mon-Fri, 7am-2pm Sat during school term) You'll find well-stocked shelves at this bookstore on the campus of Trinity College.

Greater Hartford Welcome Center (☎ 860-244-0253; www.connectthedots.org; 45 Pratt St; ◷ 9am-5pm Mon-Fri) The bulk of tourist services can be found at this centrally located office.

Library (☎ 860-695-6300; 500 Main St; ◷ 10am-8pm Mon-Thu, 10am-5pm Sat) The central library is at Arch St and has free internet access.

Sights & Activities

TRAVELERS TOWER

Score the best views of the city and the Connecticut River from the observation deck of the 34-story **Travelers Tower** (☎ 860-277-4208; 740 Main St), named after its tenant, the Travelers Insurance Company, and once the tallest in New England. The observation deck is free, but only open from May through October, and you have to climb 70 steps along a spiral staircase from the elevator to the deck.

Keep your eyes peeled for Amelia, a peregrine falcon who since 1997 has made her nest on a ledge on the 21st floor. She – along with her mate and their succession of fluffy hatchlings – have inspired peregrine-lovers to establish a website (http://falconcam.travelers .com) devoted to the birds.

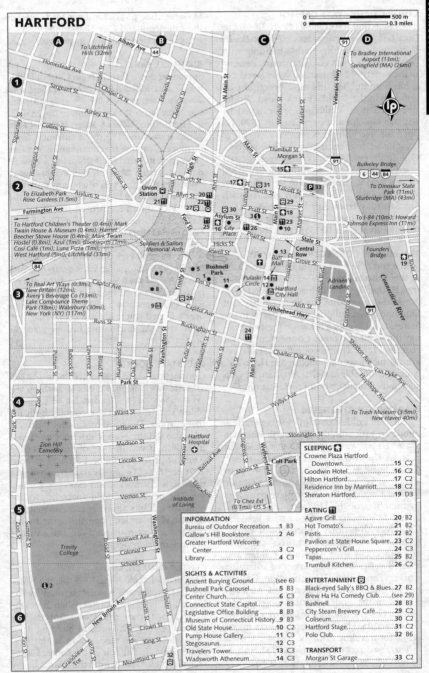

HARTFORD

SLEEPING 🛏
Crowne Plaza Hartford
  Downtown.....................................15 C2
Goodwin Hotel................................16 C2
Hilton Hartford...............................17 C2
Residence Inn by Marriott............18 C2
Sheraton Hartford..........................19 D3

EATING 🍴
Agave Grill......................................20 B2
Hot Tomato's..................................21 B2
Pastis..22 B2
Pavilion at State House Square......23 C2
Peppercorn's Grill...........................24 C3
Tapas..25 B2
Trumbull Kitchen.............................26 C2

ENTERTAINMENT 🎭
Black-eyed Sally's BBQ & Blues......27 B2
Brew Ha Ha Comedy Club..........(see 29)
Bushnell..28 B3
City Steam Brewery Café................29 C2
Coliseum..30 C2
Hartford Stage.................................31 C2
Polo Club...32 B6

TRANSPORT
Morgan St Garage...........................33 C2

INFORMATION
Bureau of Outdoor Recreation......1 B3
Gallow's Hill Bookstore..................2 A6
Greater Hartford Welcome
  Center...3 C2
Library...4 C3

SIGHTS & ACTIVITIES
Ancient Burying Ground...........(see 6)
Bushnell Park Carousel..................5 B3
Center Church...............................6 C3
Connecticut State Capitol.............7 B3
Legislative Office Building 8 B3
Museum of Connecticut History...9 B3
Old State House............................10 C2
Pump House Gallery......................11 C3
Stegosaurus...................................12 C3
Travelers Tower.............................13 C3
Wadsworth Atheneum....................14 C3

CONNECTICUT STATE CAPITOL

The **Connecticut State Capitol** (☎ 860-240-0222; cnr Capitol Ave & Trinity St; admission free; ☼ 8am-5pm Mon-Fri) is an imposing white-marble building with Gothic details and a gold-leaf dome. Because of the variety of architectural styles it reflects, it has been dubbed 'the most beautiful ugly building in the world' (Frank Lloyd Wright dismissed it as 'ridiculous'). Designed by Richard Upjohn and completed in 1879, it's open for free visits that take in a myriad of civic items, highlighted by the hall of flags. One-hour guided tours, also free, depart hourly from the **Legislative Office Building** (Capitol Ave, near Broad St), from 9:15am to 1:15pm on weekdays (also 2:15pm in July and August). On Saturday from April to October, they depart hourly from the southwest entrance (Capitol Ave) from 10:15am to 2:15pm.

MUSEUM OF CONNECTICUT HISTORY

While you're up on Capitol Hill, have a look at this **museum** (☎ 860-757-6535; www.cslib.org/museum; 231 Capitol Ave; admission free; ☼ 9am-4pm Mon-Fri, 9am-3pm Sat) housed in the State Library and Supreme Court Building just across from the State Capitol. Nationally known for its genealogy library, it also holds Connecticut's royal charter of 1662, a prime collection of Colt firearms (which were manufactured in Hartford), coins and the table at which Abraham Lincoln signed the Emancipation Proclamation.

WADSWORTH ATHENEUM

The nation's oldest continuously operating, public art museum, the **Wadsworth Atheneum** (☎ 860-278-2670; www.wadsworthatheneum.org; 600 Main St; adult/6-17yr/senior & student $10/5/8; ☼ 11am-5pm Wed-Fri, 10am-5pm Sat & Sun) houses more than 40,000 pieces of art in a castle-like Gothic Revival building. On display are paintings by members of the Hudson River School, including some by Hartford native Frederic Church; 19th-century impressionist works; furniture from the 18th century; sculptures of Connecticut artist Alexander Calder; and a small yet outstanding array of surrealist works. The Amistad Foundation Gallery has an outstanding collection of African-American art and historical objects; the Matrix Gallery features works by contemporary artists. The Atheneum is also a major venue for traveling exhibits.

There's a decent café here too, and a free shuttle runs between the museum and the Morgan St Garage (see p348). On Burr Mall between the Atheneum and City Hall stands Calder's massive red steel sculpture **Stegosaurus**.

BUSHNELL PARK

Spreading down the hill from Capitol Hill is the 37-acre **Bushnell Park** (☎ 860-522-3668; www.bushnellpark.org; admission free; ☼ dawn-dusk), designed by Jacob Weidenmann in the 1850s.

The Gothic **Soldiers & Sailors Memorial Arch**, which frames the Trinity St entrance, commemorates Civil War veterans and offers fine views from its turrets, unfortunately accessible only on a **tour** (☎ 860-232-6710; tours by donation; ☼ noon Thu May-Oct). If you're a botany buff, take the **self-guided tree tour** (☎ 860-232-6710) of the park. Pick up a brochure at the Memorial Arch or call the number. The Tudor-style **Pump House Gallery** (1947) features art exhibits and a summer concert series.

The **Bushnell Park Carousel** (☎ 860-585-5411; rides 50¢; ☼ 11am-5pm Tue-Sun mid-May–Aug, Sat & Sun mid-Apr–mid-May & Sep; ⚐) is a 1914 merry-go-round designed by Stein and Goldstein, with 48 horses and a 1925 Wurlitzer band organ. Even if you're not game for a ride, stop by to read the fascinating history placards on display.

OLD STATE HOUSE

Connecticut's 1756 **Old State House** (☎ 860-522-6766; www.ctosh.org; 800 Main St; admission free; ☼ 11am-5pm Tue-Fri, 10am-5pm Sat; ⚐) is the oldest state capitol in the country built for that purpose. Designed by Charles Bulfinch, who also did the Massachusetts State House in Boston, it was the site of the trial of the *Amistad* prisoners. Gilbert Stuart's famous 1801 portrait of George Washington hangs in the senate chamber it was expressly painted for. The newly expanded space houses interactive exhibits aimed at kids, as well as a **Museum of Curiosities**, open the same hours, that features a two-headed calf and a variety of mechanical devices.

CENTER CHURCH

This **church** (☎ 860-249-5631; 675 Main St; admission free; ☼ by appointment) was established by the Reverend Thomas Hooker when he came to Hartford from the Massachusetts Bay Colony in 1636. The present building dates from 1807 and was modeled on St Martin's-in-the-Fields in London. In the **Ancient Burying Ground** (☼ 10am-4pm) behind the church lie the remains of Hooker and Revolutionary War patriots Joseph and Jeremiah Wadsworth. Some headstones date from the 17th century. Adjacent to the church is Carl Andre's **Stone Field sculpture**, which to some is a powerful minimalist statement. To others, it's exactly what it sounds like – a field of rocks.

MARK TWAIN HOUSE & MUSEUM

For 17 years, encompassing the most productive period of his life and the most tragic (two of his children died here), Samuel Langhorne Clemens (1835–1910) and his family lived in this striking orange-and-black brick Victorian **house** (☎ 860-247-0998; www.marktwainhouse.org; 351 Farmington Ave; adult/6-16yr/senior $13/8/11; ⊙ 9:30am-5:30pm Mon-Sat, noon-5:30pm Sun, closed Tue Jan-Mar), which then stood in the pastoral area of the city called Nook Farm. Architect Edward Tuckerman Potter lavishly embellished it with turrets, gables and verandas, and some of the interiors were done by Louis Comfort Tiffany. Though Twain maintained that it was difficult to write in the house, it was here that he penned some of his most famous works, including *The Adventures of Tom Sawyer, The Adventures of Huckleberry Finn* and *A Connecticut Yankee in King Arthur's Court*. A tour is part of the admission fee. The museum center further supplements visitors' appreciation through thoughtfully selected photos, films, artifacts and manuscripts.

HARRIET BEECHER STOWE HOUSE

Next door to the Twain house is the **house** (☎ 860-525-9317; www.harrietbeecherstowe.org; 73 Forest St; adult/6-12yr/senior $8/4/7; ⊙ 9:30am-4pm Tue-Sat, noon-4:30pm Sun) of the woman who wrote the antislavery book *Uncle Tom's Cabin*. Upon meeting Stowe, Abraham Lincoln is alleged to have said, 'So this is the little lady who made this big war.' Built in 1871, the Stowe house reflects the author's strong ideas about decorating and domestic efficiency, as she expressed in her bestseller *American Woman's Home*, which was nearly as popular as the phenomenal *Uncle Tom's Cabin*. The house is light-filled, with big windows draped in plants.

Tickets include admission to the adjoining **Katharine S Day House**, named for Stowe's grandniece, who sought to preserve the memory of her great-aunt's community spirit and works. The house has 1880s decor as well as changing exhibits.

ELIZABETH PARK ROSE GARDENS

Known for its fine collection of 15,000 rose bushes, **Elizabeth Park** (☎ 860-722-6514; Prospect Ave; admission free; ⊙ dawn-dusk daily, greenhouses 8am-3pm Mon-Fri) at Asylum Ave is a 100-acre – and 100-year-old – preserve on the Hartford-West Hartford town line. More than 900 varieties such as climbers, American Beauties, ramblers and heavily perfumed damasks cover the grounds. June and July are the months to see the roses in full flower, but they bloom, if less profusely, well into fall. Besides roses, the park tends a tall dahlia display, herb gardens and greenhouses. The landscaped paths make for excellent jogging trails.

Sleeping

There are no B&Bs in the city, but there are a number in the surrounding countryside. Call **Nutmeg B&B Agency** (☎ 860-236-6698, 800-727-7592; www.nutmegbb.com) for a list and profile of Hartford area B&Bs.

Just outside the center of Hartford are many of the usual chain motels, usually offering the best-value accommodations. Hartford's city-center luxury hotels charge high rates on weekdays and lower rates on weekends. The suburban motels' rates go up on weekends.

BUDGET

Mark Twain Hostel (☎ 860-523-7255, 800-909-4776; www.hiayh.org; 131 Tremont St; dm member/nonmember $24/27, r $48) This rickety Victorian-style building in the city's West End has clean-enough beds, and guests can use the fully equipped kitchen and laundry facilities. It's just off Farmington Ave (I-84 exit 46), a 25-minute walk from downtown and Union Station. Cash preferred. Call for pick-up service.

Howard Johnson Express Inn (☎ 860-875-0781; www.hojo.com; 451 Hartford Turnpike, Vernon; d incl breakfast from $65; ☒) This 64-room lodge at I-84 exit 65 is northeast of the city in Vernon, on the way to Boston. Each room has a fridge and microwave, and there's a 24-hour restaurant for your snack-attack pleasure.

MIDRANGE

Sheraton Hartford (☎ 860-528-9703; www.sheraton.com; 100 E River Dr; d Sun-Thu $149, Fri & Sat $89; ☐ wifi ☒) Across the river in East Hartford (I-84 West exit 54, I-84 East exit 53, I-91 North exit 29, I-91 South exit 30, CT 2 exit 4), you find a fitness center, restaurant and lounge. The

A TRASHY MUSEUM

On the whole, we are woefully ignorant of what happens to that juice container once we toss it into the recycling bin. The fascinating **Trash Museum** (☎ 860-247-4280; www.crra.org; 211 Murphy Rd, Stratford; admission free; ☒ 10am-4pm Tue-Sat Jul & Aug, noon-4pm Wed-Fri Sep-Jun; ☒) educates us on the entire process, from consumption to collection, cleaning, sorting and reselling, with side exhibits on landfills and composting. The best part, however, is standing on the upstairs observation deck to witness the recycling trucks dumping their loads (overwhelmingly milk-carton white with some Tide-red highlights), and watching the monstrous sorting, cleaning and crushing machine do its thing.

Though the museum is geared towards the under-12 set, adults will find it enlightening. To get there from Hartford, take I-91 south and get off at exit 27. Turn left off the ramp onto Airport Rd, and after bearing right at the split, take a left onto Murphy Rd. The museum is housed in the Connecticut Resources Recovery Authority Visitors Center.

spacious rooms boast lush ribbed carpets and ergonomically designed workstations.

Hilton Hartford (☎ 860-728-5151, 800-325-3535; www.hilton.com; 315 Trumbull St; d Sun-Thu $165, Fri & Sat $85; ☐ wi-fi ☒) Connected to the Civic Center by an elevated skyway, this ultra-modern 22-story hotel is one of Hartford's most centrally located. It has 392 well-appointed rooms and 10 suites, some of which overlook the Capitol. Work out in the state-of-the-art health facility and then relax in the whirlpool and sauna.

Crowne Plaza Hartford Downtown (☎ 860-549-2400; www.ichotels.com; 50 Morgan St; d Sun-Thu $159-189, Fri & Sat $135; ☐ wi-fi ☒ ☒) This imposing white block of a building on the city's north side houses 350 luxury guest rooms and is flush with guest services, including shuttle service to Bradley Airport ($15), an outdoor pool and an onsite restaurant. Some rooms are wheelchair accessible.

Residence Inn by Marriott (☎ 860-524-5550, 800-331-3131; www.residenceinn.com; 942 Main St; d Sun-Thu $189, Fri & Sat $144; ☐ wi-fi) Overlooking the Connecticut River, this 100-unit hotel is housed in a stately 19th-century brownstone close to downtown. Each room and suite has a full kitchen, voicemail and cable TV. There's an exercise facility too.

TOP END

Goodwin Hotel (☎ 860-246-7500, 800-922-5006; www.goodwinhotel.com; 1 Haynes St; d Sun-Thu $199-218, Fri & Sat $129-299; ☐ wi-fi) Easily the fanciest hotel in Hartford, this five-story, 124-room, 1881 redbrick building looks austerely historic on the outside, but as soon as you enter the four-story lobby it's apparent the interior has been entirely remodeled to appeal to modern tastes. There are 11 suites, some of which

are duplexes. Staff serve afternoon tea in the lobby. The Pierpont Restaurant, with its deeply burnished walls and continental fare, is well regarded.

Eating

BUDGET

Pavilion at State House Square (10 State House Sq, Ste 90; dishes $4-12; ☒ lunch; Ⓥ) Across from the Old State House on Main St, this vastly popular food court has a dozen vendors selling ethnic and vegetarian lunches in the airy interior courtyard of a high-rise office palace. Try the pad thai ($4.25) at Bangkok or the veggie lasagna at the Natural ($6.25).

Tapas (☎ 860-525-5988; 126 Ann St; meals $9-12; ☒ lunch & dinner Mon-Fri, dinner Sat) Crowds pack this storefront bistro at lunch and happy hour for good reason. You can sit at high tables or stand at wall counters and rub shoulders with three neighbors while eating blackened chicken tapas ($8) or souvlaki ($7). They brag that their food's so fresh, they don't even have a freezer.

MIDRANGE

Hot Tomato's (☎ 860-241-9100; 1 Union Pl; meals $11-30; ☒ lunch & dinner Mon-Fri, dinner Sat & Sun) Locals love this place with its café deck overlooking Bushnell Park and the State Capitol. The interior is postmodern chrome. Try the simple but delicious linguini *vongole* ($19).

Luna Pizza (☎ 860-233-1625; 999 Farmington Ave, West Hartford; pizzas $12-20; ☒ lunch & dinner) The pizzas that come out of the brick oven are divine – crispy and thin-crusted – and the mozzarella is fresh. Luna's space is reminiscent of an upmarket cafeteria, and jazz musicians play on the weekends. Try the salmon, onions and caper pizza. Amazingly, they offer single slices, too.

ourpick Agave Grill (☎ 860-882-1557; 100 Allyn St; meals $14-22; ☽ lunch & dinner Mon-Sat, dinner Sun) Dine amid colorful murals at this warm and breezy Mexican spot that's found an unlikely niche a block from Union Station. Ten different margaritas pack a variety of punches, but don't let them distract from such innovative fare as grilled chicken glazed in mango sauce or lobster enchiladas – just like your Connecticut *abuela* used to make it.

Peppercorn's Grill (☎ 860-547-1714; 357 Main St; meals $14-22; ☽ lunch & dinner Mon-Sat) Modern American interpretations of traditional Italian dishes are the specialty at this restaurant between Capitol Ave and Buckingham St. In this family-run place, you might find anything from veal *saltimbocca* ($18) to a zesty dish of ravioli with scallops and lobster ($19).

Trumbull Kitchen (☎ 860-493-7417; 150 Trumbull St; small dishes $5-12, meals $17-24; ☽ lunch & dinner Mon-Fri, dinner Sun) At this slick downtown eatery you can get bites of anything from dim sum, tapas, stone pies or (and?) fondue. The bar stays open later on the weekend, the longer to sample the impressive cocktail list.

TOP END

Pastis (☎ 860-278-8852; 201 Ann St; meals $19-32; ☽ lunch & dinner Mon-Fri, dinner Sat) A great date place, this French-American bistro wins you over with its intimate tables, candlelight, lace curtains and French acoustic music. The mains, classics like coq au vin, are well done, if not swoon-worthy. Try the seared scallops with saffron rice or the steak-frites (both $20).

Azul (☎ 860-233-1726; 124 LaSalle Rd, West Hartford; meals $22-30; ☽ lunch & dinner Mon-Sat, dinner Sun) With its black-clad waiters and relentless sound system, Azul specializes in high-class, presentation-oriented Nuevo Latino dishes like Chilean salmon with ginger chili compote in banana leaf. However, it offers enough Americanized dishes to satisfy the unadventurous. You'll want to spiff up for dinner here.

Entertainment

Pick up a free copy of the *Hartford Advocate* (www.hartfordadvocate.com) for up-to-the-minute entertainment listings.

BARS & CLUBS

City Steam Brewery Café (☎ 860-525-1600; 942 Main St; ☽ 11:30am-1am Mon-Thu, 11:30am-2am Fri & Sat, noon-10pm Sun) This big and boisterous place has plenty of yummy beers on tap. The Naughty Nurse Pale Ale is a bestseller, but be sure to check out their seasonals. The café is also home to the **Brew Ha Ha Comedy Club**, where you can yuk it up with comedians seen on Conan O'Brien and at the Improv. Shows are $15 on Friday and Saturday nights and $5 on Thursdays. You must pay for tickets with your credit card.

Chez Est (☎ 860-525-3243; 458 Wethersfield Ave; cover free-$5; ☽ 3pm-1am Sun-Thu, 3pm-2am Fri & Sat) South of Colt Park, Chez Est has a cozy, mixed crowd. On Mondays, there's no cover and free pool after 8pm; Wednesday means karaoke.

Polo Club (☎ 860-278-3333; 678 Maple Ave; cover $5-8; ☽ 8pm-2am Thu-Sat) While this place seems to cater more to curious straight couples who come to watch the drag-queen shows than to gay men themselves, it's a fun place to lounge around with a martini in hand, feeling fabulous.

LIVE MUSIC

Black-eyed Sally's BBQ & Blues (☎ 860-278-7427; www.blackeyedsallys.com; 350 Asylum St; cover $4-8; ☽ 11:30am-10pm Mon-Fri, 5-11pm Sat) This blues palace drags in local and national acts. The walls are covered with graffiti, some penned by visiting bands. There's live music Wednesday through Saturday, and Sunday and Monday are all-you-can-eat BBQ nights (meals cost $17 to $20).

THEATER & CLASSICAL MUSIC

Bushnell (☎ 860-987-5900; www.bushnell.org; 166 Capitol Ave; tickets $20-45), hosting over 500 events a year, plays a major role in the state's cultural life. Its historic building is where you go for most ballet, symphony, opera and chamber music performances. For current shows contact the **Greater Hartford Arts Council** (☎ 860-525-8629; www.letsgoarts.org). For events in Bushnell Park, call ☎ 860-543-8570. The well-respected **Hartford Symphony** (☎ 860-244-2999; www.hartfordsymphony.org; tickets $30-60) stages performances year-round.

Hartford Stage (☎ 860-527-5151; www.hartfordstage.org; 50 Church St; tickets $20-60) Contemporary as well as classic dramas play from September to June. Venturi & Rauch designed the striking theater building of red brick with darker red zigzag details.

Real Art Ways (RAW; ☎ 860-232-1006; www.realartways.org; 56 Arbor St; suggested donation $3; ☽ 2-10pm Mon-

Fri, 2pm-midnight Sat & Sun) Contemporary works in all kinds of media find an outlet at this consistently offbeat and adventurous gallery/cinema/performance space/lounge. Evening events at RAW usually cost between $5 and $12. You can sip wine or beer while watching the new drag-queen documentary or the latest export from the new Brazilian cinema.

Hartford Children's Theater (☎ 860-249-7970; www.hartfordchildrenstheatre.org; 360 Farmington Ave; tickets $12-16; ⑤) This theater puts on several productions a year, like *Charlotte's Web* and the *Wizard of Oz*. Both children and adults make up the casts.

Getting There & Around

By car, interstates connect Hartford to Boston (102 miles), New Haven (36 miles), New York (117 miles) and Providence (71 miles). The cheapest downtown parking is at the **Morgan St Garage** (cnr Talcott & Market Sts).

See p318 for information on air travel via Bradley International Airport in Windsor Locks, and intercity bus services. The city bus service, **Connecticut Transit** (☎ 860-525-9181; www.cttransit.com), can shuttle you from the airport to downtown Hartford for $1.10 on its Bradley Flyer.

By train, **Amtrak** (☎ 800-872-7245) connects Hartford to New York and Boston.

In Hartford, centrally located **Union Station** (☎ 860-247-5329; 1 Union Pl), at Spruce St, is the city's transportation center and the place to catch trains, airport shuttles, intercity buses and taxis.

For cabs, check the taxi stand outside Union Station, or call **Yellow Cab Co** (☎ 860-666-6666).

LAKE COMPOUNCE THEME PARK

If the kids are in dire need of a rollercoaster and funnel-cake infusion, **Lake Compounce Theme Park** (☎ 860-583-3300; www.lakecompounce.com; 822 Lake Ave, Bristol; adult/child $33.95/24.95; ⑤ 11am-8pm daily mid-Jun–Aug, Sat & Sun May & Sep; ⑤) is the ticket. This 100-acre lakeshore amusement park in the town of Bristol, 18 miles southwest of Hartford at the junction of CT 61 and CT 132, boasts two rollercoasters (one of which, Boulder Dash, is an excellent wooden specimen), a whitewater raft ride, historic steam train, interactive haunted house and many other amusements. Clipper Cove, with a 300-gallon water bucket, and Splash Harbor Water Park with its pools and waterslides, are perfect for a steaming sum-

---

MUSIC FESTIVALS

The **Greater Hartford Festival of Jazz** (www.jazzhartford.org) is held in Bushnell Park over the third weekend in July. You can also treat yourself to the sweet sounds of the summer-only **Monday Night Jazz Series**, the oldest jazz series in the country. For bluegrass lovers, East Hartford's early August **Podunk Bluegrass Festival** (www.podunkbluegrass.net) promises a knee-slappin', foot-stompin' good time.

---

mer's day. The 180ft free-fall 'swing' will thrill even the most jaded of extreme- sports enthusiasts.

Admission includes unlimited access to most rides and amusements. The child's price applies to kids under 52in (133cm). There's a $5 parking charge.

DINOSAUR STATE PARK

Connecticut's answer to Jurassic Park, **Dinosaur State Park** (☎ 860-529-8423; www.dinosaurstatepark.org; 400 West St; adult/6-13yr $5/2; ⑤ 9am-4:30pm Tue-Sun) lets you view dinosaur footprints left 200 million years ago on mudflats near Rocky Hill, 10 miles due south of Hartford along I-91. The tracks hardened in the mud and were only uncovered by road-building crews in the early 20th century. Today, they're preserved beneath a geodesic dome and you can tour an 80ft-long diorama that shows how the tracks were made.

Outside, there are several on-site dino prints where visitors can make plaster casts. The casting site is free, open from May through October, and the park provides everything you need but the plaster of paris, 25 pounds of which is recommended to make several decent-sized casts.

The park also has a picnic area and 2 miles of interesting nature trails. Take I-91 exit 23, then go a mile east. No credit cards accepted.

LITCHFIELD HILLS

The rolling hills in the northwestern corner of Connecticut take their name from the historic town of Litchfield at their heart. Sprinkled with lakes and dotted with forests and state parks rich in waterfalls, this region offers an abundance of tranquility. Only a handful of inns and campgrounds provide for travelers, an intentional curb on development that guarantees the preservation of the area's rural character. Quite a few celebrities from the entertainment industry keep a low profile on their farms and country estates on the back roads here.

Contact the **Litchfield Hills Visitors Bureau** (☎ 860-567-4506; www.litchfieldhills.com; PO Box 968, Litchfield, CT 06759) for its excellent booklet *Touring by Car, Foot, Boat & Bike*, which includes a map of the area and dozens of detailed itineraries. It also maintains a listing of over 40 hard-to-find inns and B&Bs in the region.

LITCHFIELD
pop 8500

The centerpiece of the region is Litchfield, Connecticut's best-preserved late-18th-century town, and the site of the nation's first law school. The town itself converges on a long oval green, and is surrounded by lush swaths of protected land just aching to be hiked through and picnicked on.

Founded in 1719, Litchfield prospered from 1780 to 1840 (by 1810 it was the state's fourth largest town) on the commerce brought through the town by stagecoaches en route between Hartford and Albany. In the mid-19th century, railroads did away with the coach routes, and industrial water-powered machinery drove Litchfield's artisans out of the markets, leaving the town to languish in faded gentility. This development proved to be Litchfield's salvation, as its grand 18th-century houses were not torn down to build factories, Victorian mansions or malls.

Orientation & Information

The town green is at the intersection of US 202 and CT 63. An 18th-century milestone stands on the green as it has since stagecoach days, when it informed passengers that they had another 33 miles to ride to Hartford, or 102 to NYC.

Locals staff an **information booth** (☾ 9:30am-4pm daily Jun–mid-Sep, Sat & Sun mid-Sep–Nov) on the town green.

Sights & Activities

A walk around town starts at the information kiosk, where you should ask for the walking-tour sheets. Just north across West St is the town's **historic jail**. Stroll along North St to see the fine houses. More of Litchfield's well-preserved 18th-century houses are along South St. Set well back from the roadway across broad lawns and behind tall trees, the houses take you back visually to Litchfield's golden age.

In 1775, Tapping Reeve established the English-speaking world's first law school at his home, which is now the **Tapping Reeve House & Law School** (☎ 860-567-4501; www.litchfield historicalsociety.org/lawschool.html; 82 South St; adult/under 14yr/senior & student $5/free/3; ☾ 11am-5pm Tue-Sat, 1-5pm Sun mid-May–Nov). When attendance overwhelmed his own house, he built the meticulously preserved one-room schoolhouse in his side yard. John C Calhoun and 130 members of Congress studied here. One of the school's many notable graduates was Aaron Burr, who, while serving as vice-president of the US under Jefferson, killed Alexander Hamilton in a duel in 1804. Admission to the history museum is included in the ticket.

The **Litchfield History Museum** (☎ 860-567-4501; www.litchfieldhistoricalsociety.org; 7 South St; ☾ 11am-5pm Tue-Sat, 1-5pm Sun mid-May–Nov; &) features a small permanent collection, including a modest photographic chronicle of the town and a dress-up box with colonial clothes for children to try on, plus some local-interest rotating exhibits.

As a boy, Sherman P Haight Jr would go fox-hunting on the land where he now makes wines from vinifera and French-American hybrid grapes. **Haight Vineyards** (☎ 860-567-4045, 800-325-5567; www.haightvineyards.com; 29 Chestnut Hill Rd; admission free; ☾ 10:30am-5pm Mon-Sat, noon-5pm Sun), the state's first winery, grows varieties such as chardonnay, Riesling, Seyval Blanc, Vidal Blanc and Vignoles. Winery tours and free tastings are available, and the vineyard holds occasional wine and cheese pairings. The vineyard is 1 mile southeast of Litchfield off CT 118.

The **White Memorial Conservation Center** (☎ 860-567-0857; www.whitememorialcc.org; US 202; admission free; ☾ dawn-dusk) is made up of 4000 supremely serene acres. Two dozen trails (0.2 miles to 6 miles long) crisscross the center, including swamp paths on a raised boardwalk. There's also a **nature museum** (☎ 860-567-0857; adult/child $5/2.50; ☾ 9am-5pm Mon-Sat, noon-5pm Sun). For visually impaired visitors, all the information in the museum is presented in braille as well. The center is 2 miles west on 202 from Litchfield.

Topsmead State Forest (☎ 860-567-5694; CT 118, admission free; ☻ 8am-sunset) was once the estate of Edith Morton Chase. You can visit her grand Tudor-style summer home (open for free guided tours on alternate weekends during summer months, hours vary) complete with its original furnishings. Then spread a blanket on the lawn and have a picnic while enjoying the view at 1230ft. Topsmead is 2 miles east of Litchfield.

You can hike and swim at **Mount Tom State Park** (☎ 860-868-2592; US 202; resident per car $6-7, nonresident per car Jun-Aug $7-10; ☻ 8am-sunset), 3.5 miles west of Bantam. The not-even-1-mile tower trail leads to the stone Mt Tom Tower at the summit.

If your spirit is still craving some quiet contemplation, walk the seven-circuit labyrinth at **Wisdom House Retreat Center** (☎ 860-567-3163; www.wisdomhouse.org; 229 E Litchfield Rd; suggested donation $5). Call to arrange a visit, and a volunteer will prepare you for the experience by sharing some background on the labyrinth. Bringing young children isn't recommended.

Sleeping

Hemlock Hill Camp Resort (☎ 860-567-2267; 118 Hemlock Hill Rd; tent sites $22-28, RV sites $27-46; ☻ May–late Oct; ☐ wi-fi ☻) This full-service campground, with 125 pine-shaded sites, has a stream meandering through it as well as a Jacuzzi and a bocce ball court. From Litchfield, go west along US 202 for a mile, then right on Milton Rd.

Looking Glass Hill Campground (☎ 860-567-2050; 14 Cozy Hill/Rte 202, Bantam; sites $30; ☻ Apr–early Oct) Five miles west of Litchfield, this simple, appealing place has 50 partially wooded sites, with laundromat, canoeing and room for tents.

Litchfield Hills B&B (☎ 860-567-2057; www.litchfield hillsbnb.com; 548 Bantam Rd Rte 202; d $95-120; ☐ wi-fi) One of the oldest houses in Litchfield, this deep-red colonial has charming perennial gardens that verge on the woods of the White Memorial Nature Conservation Center. It lets three wicker-centric rooms. A canoe is available for a paddle on the Bantam River across the street, and (well-behaved) children and pets are welcome.

Tollgate Hill Inn (☎ 860-567-1233; 866-567-1233; www.tollgatehill.com; 571 Torrington Rd/Rte 202; r $95-170, ste $160-195; ☐ wi-fi) About 2 miles east of town, this 1745 property used to be the main way-station for travelers between Albany and Hartford. All rooms have a private deck and pull-out couch. In the suites you get a wood-burning fireplace, canopy bed, fridge and bar. Suite 10 is a lovely option for families.

our pick Litchfield Inn (☎ 860-567-4503, 800-499-3444; www.litchfieldinnct.com; US 202; d $160-192, theme r incl breakfast $250-300; ☐ wi-fi) Two miles west of Litchfield, set in extensive grounds, this establishment with 32 rooms looks like an upscale motel. Many of the theme rooms, like the Irish Room of Mami O'Rourke and the lavender Lady Agnew (Dennis Hopper slept here) have four-poster beds. The inn's restaurant Bistro East, where Dick Cavett spottings are not unheard of, has an impressive wine selection and stick-to-yer-arteries fare like gorgonzola-crusted steak. The restaurant is closed on Monday.

Eating & Drinking

Aspen Garden (☎ 860-567-9477; 51 West St; dishes $6-16; ☻ lunch & dinner; ☻) Aspen Garden serves a good selection of light meals with Greek accents: salads, sandwiches and baklava. It's got a kid's menu for the kids, and a beer menu for you. In good weather, sit at an umbrella-shaded table on the brick terrace.

our pick 3W & Blue Bar (☎ 860-567-1742; 3 West St; meals $9-30; ☻ lunch & dinner) Seemingly lifted en masse from Soho, this swinging eatery features a 'blue bar' and trance music that's hard to tune out. Submit to the suggestive bamboo and red-lantern decor by ordering an Asian-inspired dish like sesame-crusted tuna. Or just go all the way with some sushi; the Dynamite roll – with shrimp, spicy tuna, salmon and avocado – is, well, dynamite ($12).

Market Square Café (☎ 860-567-4882; 33 West St; meals $10-32; ☻ lunch & dinner) This is the best place in town to pick up deli-esque picnic provisions, and it also makes for an unpretentious lunch and dinner spot, focusing on steaks and seafood.

West St Grill (☎ 860-567-3885; 43 West St; meals $11-29; ☻ lunch & dinner Wed-Sun) Easily the poshest eatery in the town center, this sophisticated city grill and tavern changes its menu seasonally, but always serves creative New American cuisine with Irish inflections (the chef hails from Ireland). If you're lucky, the salmon fillet burger will be on offer. There are several sidewalk tables and a pub scene after 9pm.

Bohemian Pizza & Ditto's Bar (☎ 860-567-3980; 432 Bantam Rd/Rte 202; pizzas $12-19; ☻ lunch & dinner Tue, Wed, Fri & Sat, dinner Mon) Litchfield lets its hair down at Boho's, where for dinner you can try the crisscross pizza – portobello mushrooms, andouille sausage, grilled chicken and caramelized onions – and chill in one of the fauxcowskin booths. As the sun sets, the pizza joint and the adjacent dive bar (open late) dissolve into one loud, friendly mess. Shoot some free pool while being serenaded by the locals who play (almost) nightly.

Tollgate Hill Restaurant (☎ 866-567-1233; 571 Torrington Rd/Rte 202; meals $19-34; ☯ lunch & dinner Wed-Sat, dinner Sun) After a cocktail in the cozy Captain William Bull Tavern, ease into the dining room in the Tollgate Hill Inn, which has maintained its spare, wide-planked ambience, presenting no unwelcome distraction from the sophistication of its fare. The menu is small but imaginative, with mains like olive oil poached salmon over a horseradish mash.

Getting There & Away

If you're traveling by car, Litchfield lies 34 miles west of Hartford and 36 miles south of Great Barrington, MA, in the Berkshires.

No buses stop in Litchfield proper, but **Bonanza Bus Lines** (☎ 800-556-3815) will get you to Torrington, the closest major town, from NYC ($20, 2½ hours), via Danbury and Waterbury. From Torrington to Litchfield, you really need your own wheels.

LAKE WARAMAUG

Of the dozens of lakes and ponds in the Litchfield Hills, Lake Waramaug, north of New Preston, stands out. Gracious inns dot its shoreline, parts of which are a state park. Public transportation isn't frequent in the area and really the only way to get here is by car.

As you make your way around the northern shore of the lake on North Shore Rd, you'll come to the **Hopkins Vineyard** (☎ 860-868-7954; www.hopkinsvineyard.com; 25 Hopkins Rd, New Preston; ☯ 10am-5pm May-Dec). The wines, made mostly from French-American hybrid grapes, are eminently drinkable – their low-oak Chardonnay wins frequent awards. They host wine tastings, and the view of the lake from the wine bar is worth a little splurge, particularly when the foliage changes in the fall. Call ahead to find out opening times in the off-season.

Next door to the winery, **Hopkins Inn** (☎ 860-868-7295; www.thehopkinsinn.com; 22 Hopkins Rd, New Preston; d $90-190) has a variety of lodging options, from rooms with shared bathrooms to lakeview apartments, most decorated in light

florals. Its fine restaurant (meals $14 to $28) specializes in contemporary Austrian cuisine. In good weather, sit on the terrace with your wienerschnitzel, catch the cooling west wind and vistas overlooking the lake and hills and imagine you're in the Alps. The restaurant is closed January through March.

Around the bend in the lake is the **Lake Waramaug State Park** (☎ 860-868-0220, 877-688-2267; 30 Lake Waramaug Rd; sites $13) with 77 campsites, both wooded and open, and many lakeside. The sites usually get booked well in advance. There's a snack bar in the park. Fishing is the main lure here.

KENT
pop 3000

During the summer and fall, weekenders (often starting on Thursday) throng to Kent's small but respected clutch of art galleries and to its gourmet chocolatier. The small town on the banks of the Housatonic River (about 7 miles west of Warren on CT 341) is also a popular stop for hikers on the Appalachian Trail, which intersects CT 341 about 2 miles northwest of town.

You can take a train from NYC to Wingdale, NY, and catch a taxi or take a bus to Danbury and take a taxi, but the area is best accessible by car.

Pierre and Susan Gilissen have brought to Kent a little slice of Belgium, and for this they are to be commended. In a butter-yellow Victorian they preside over the **Salon de Thé** (☎ 860-927-3681; 1 Bridge St; ☯ lunch Thu & Sun, dinner Fri & Sat), where, after donning your best manners, you can come for lunch, tea or a 'savory dinner' ($30 minimum and reservations strongly recommended). Next door in the carriage house is the **Belgique Patisserie & Chocolatier** (☎ 860-927-3681; ☯ 9am-6pm Thu-Sat, 10am-6pm Sun), selling unfathomably rich chocolates, pralines, tarts, cocoa and ice cream.

Rotating exhibits of contemporary and local artists are on display at the **Bachelier-Cardonsky Art Gallery** (☎ 860-927-3357; www.bacheliercardonsky.com; North Main St; ☯ 11am-5pm Sat & Sun), operated by the former owner of the Paris-New York-Kent Gallery, which put Kent on the art scene in the mid-'80s. The recently opened **Ober Gallery** (☎ 860-927-5030; www.obergallery.com; 14 Old Barn Rd; ☯ noon-5pm Wed & Thu, 11am-5pm Fri-Sun) offers changing exhibits in a variety of media by German, Russian and New York–based artists.

OUTDOOR CONNECTICUT

New England's three northern states – Vermont, New Hampshire and Maine – are justly noted for their outdoor activities, but that doesn't mean that Connecticut can't compete.

Northwest Connecticut's Housatonic River is particularly good for canoeing, kayaking, rafting and tubing. With the spring floods, the white water can reach Class III. Expect to pay about $90 for guided white-water rafting during the spring run-off, and about $25 for unguided rafting the rest of the year. Here are of some of the more well-established companies:

Clarke Outdoors (☎ 860-672-6365; www.clarkeoutdoors.com; 163 US 7, West Cornwall; 2-person canoeing $49-54, kayaking per person $40, rafting adult $24-27, under 16yr $14-17; ☺ 10am-5pm Mon-Fri, 9am-6pm Sat & Sun) This outfit can equip you with a canoe, kayak or raft for a 10-mile run down the Housatonic River. It also leads white-water rafting trips during spring's high water. Guided rafting trips are an additional $80.

Farmington River Tubing (☎ 860-693-6465; www.farmingtonrivertubing.com; CT 44, New Hartford; tubing $18-20) Tube down 2.5 miles of the Farmington River. Only cash payments are accepted.

Huck Finn Adventures (☎ 860-693-0385; www.huckfinnadventures.com; PO Box 137, Collinsville, CT 06022; tubing $18-20) Huck Finn has a similar tubing service. They also offer a guided tour through the Lost Park River, miles of spacious tunnels buried under Hartford.

The northwest is also home to many ski resorts, one of the best being **Mohawk Mountain** (☎ 860-672-6100, 800-895-5222; www.mohawkmtn.com; 46 Great Hollow Rd, Cornwall), with a 650ft vertical drop.

More traditional, though still quirky, **Sloane-Stanley Museum** (☎ 860-927-3849; US 7; adult/child/senior & student $4/2/3; ☺ 10am-4pm Wed-Sun May-Oct) is a barnful of early American tools and implements – some dating from the 17th century – lovingly collected and arranged by artist and author Eric Sloane. The museum is about 2 miles north of town on the left.

At **Kent Falls State Park**, about 5 miles north of town, the water drops 250ft over a quarter mile before joining up with the Housatonic River. Hike the easy trail to the top of the cascade, or just settle into a sunny picnic spot at the bottom.

Just before you reach Kent Falls, you may notice a menagerie of life-sized metal animals grazing off to your right. This is the **studio** (☎ 860-927-3420; www.deniscurtisssculptor.com) of sculptor Denis Curtiss, which is open for browsing most weekends – call to confirm.

You can rent bikes at **Bicycle Tour Company** (☎ 888-711-5368; 9 Bridge St; per day $25) or they can customize a guided ride for you around the area.

NORTH TO NORFOLK

If you have your own car, there's no shortage of postcard-perfect country roads to explore in the Litchfield Hills, but just one delightful stretch is from Cornwall Bridge taking CT 4 west and then CT 41 north to Salisbury.

From May through September, race-car drivers (including celebs like Paul Newman) go at it at **Lime Rock Park** (☎ 860-435-0896; www.lime rock.com; 497 Lime Rock Rd, Lakeville; adult/student & senior $6/3). If you've never been to a race, Lime Rock is a picturesque setting for your first time. The speedway is west of US 7 along CT 112.

The lovely, tranquil, 14-room historic property at **Cornwall Inn** (☎ 860-672-6884, 800-786-6884; www.cornwallinn.com; 270 Kent Rd/US 7, Cornwall Bridge; r $99-139, ste incl breakfast $129-209; ☒ ☐ wi-fi) consists of the six-room inn and the more rustic-flavored eight-room lodge. All the recently refurbished rooms feature down comforters and cable TV. Fill up on straightforward country cuisine at the restaurant (meals $12 to $31), open for dinner Thursday to Sunday, which features a different fish dish each week.

At first glance the one-story **Inn at Iron Masters** (☎ 860-435-9844; www.innatironmasters.com; 229 Main St/US 44, Lakeville; d incl breakfast $100-180; ☒) looks suspiciously like a Florida motel, but the rooms are more elegant, the grounds feature gardens and gazebos, and there's a large common fireplace for chilly evenings.

Housatonic Meadows State Park (☎ 860-927-3238; US 7) is famous for its 2-mile-long stretch of water set aside exclusively for fly-fishing. Its **campground** (☎ 860-672-6772, 877-688-2267; sites $13; ☺ mid-Apr–mid-Oct) has 97 sites on the banks of the Housatonic.

Blackberry River Inn (☎ 860-542-5100, 800-414-3636; www.blackberryriverinn.com; 538 Greenwoods Rd/Rte 44, Norfolk; r & ste incl breakfast $135-249; ☒) has amiable staff, an exceptional breakfast, and grounds – complete with open trails – begging to be explored. The inn offers a range of rooms and suites in three buildings; a suite earns you a fireplace, Jacuzzi and sun porch. The least expensive rooms have shared bathroom. Tea is served daily.

our pick **Norfolk Pub & Restaurant** (☎ 860-542-5716; US 44, Norfolk; meals $8-24; ⏱ lunch & dinner Tue-Sun) claims the 'widest selection of the finest beers in the world,' which we can't confirm, but they do indeed serve excellent suds, especially those hailing from Belgium and England. Happily, their solids stand up to their liquids – smart pub grub with some twists. Try the spicy crab cakes with Thai chili sauce ($15.50). Take note of the chair made of antlers in the corner.

Tea-lovers will want to check out Mary O'Brien's shop **Chaiwalla** (☎ 860-435-9758; 1 Main St/US 44, Salisbury; items $3-10; ⏱ 10am-6pm Wed-Sun) in Salisbury, which serves a variety of tea, especially unblended Darjeelings, as well as traditional accompaniments. Try Mary's famous tomato pie.

Vermont

Nestled in the northeast corner of New England, Vermont is the region's only state without an Atlantic coastline, but the Green Mountains that give the state its name (from the French *verts monts)* more than make up for this lack of ocean playground. Each year, crowds flock to the celebrated slopes of Killington, Mt Snow and Stowe for the finest skiing and snowboarding on the East Coast. These same mountains help form the Long Trail, a hiking path that courses the length of the state and lures countless repeat visitors – especially during the autumn months, when the state erupts in a blaze of spectacular foliage.

Much of Vermont is serene farmland, yielding up the state's famous maple syrups and cheeses as well as the fresh produce that make it home to some of the nation's finest restaurants. This attention to quality can also be savored at Vermont's microbreweries; their fine craft brews help stoke the nightlife in bars up and down the state.

But above all, Vermont is home to the eccentric and the unexpected. From a puppet museum lurking in a massive barn and an old mill converted into a first-class restaurant; to llamas grazing in the backyard of a rural bed-and-breakfast and the only state capital without a McDonald's. So, arm yourself with a good map, leave the main roads to the masses, and find your own charmed back-way along the capillary network of dirt roads that hug the banks of squiggling rivers, lead through tunnels of trees and lure you to unexpected discoveries.

VERMONT

HIGHLIGHTS

- Gawking at the spellbinding puppets in the **Bread & Puppet Museum** (p405) in the Northeast Kingdom
- Soaring over Quechee Gorge in a hot-air **balloon ride** (p377)
- Savoring an immaculate meal at **Pangea** (p369) in North Bennington, **L'Amante** (p394) in Burlington, **Simon Pearce** (p378) in Quechee or the **Blue Moon Café** in Stowe (p400)
- Slithering down any of the state's many and varied slopes, from expansive **Killington** (p378) – the 'Beast of the East' – to well-preserved, cooperatively owned **Mad River Glen** (p384)
- Losing yourself along the celebrated **Long Trail** (p371), which runs the length of the state
- Quaffing Vermont's fine and distinctive **microbrews** (p366)

■ TELEPHONE CODE: 802	■ POPULATION: 619,100	■ AREA: 9613 SQ MILES

Orientation & Information

Vermont is bordered along the Connecticut River by New Hampshire to the east, by New York State to the west, the Canadian province of Quebec to the north and Massachusetts to the south. The capital, Montpelier, is about two-thirds of the way up the state and its largest city, Burlington, lies on Lake Champlain in the northwest.

DeLorme's *Vermont Atlas & Gazetteer* ($19.95) is the best map of the state.

Vermont Chamber of Commerce (☎ 802-223-3443; www.vtchamber.com) Additional information on hotels, restaurants and other tourist services.

Vermont Division of Tourism and Marketing (☎ 802-828-3236; www.vermontvacation.com; 6 Baldwin St, Montpelier, VT 05633-1301) Producers of a free, detailed road and attractions map and camping guide, this organization also maintains a fabulous Welcome Center on I-91 near the Massachusetts (MA) state line, another on VT 4A near the New York state line and another on I-89 near the Canadian border.

Vermont Ski Areas Association (☎ 802-223-2439; www.skivermont.com) Helpful information for planning ski trips. For daily ski condition reports (in winter only), call ☎ 802-229-0531.

Vermont State Parks (☎ 802-241-3655; www.vt stateparks.com) Complete camping and parks information.

History

Vermont was home to the indigenous Abenaki peoples when the first French explorers appeared in the 16th century. In 1609 Samuel de Champlain claimed the region surrounding the lake that now bears his name as part of New France, naming it *les Verts Monts* (the Green Mountains). More colonists soon arrived from France, as well as from Britain (settling further south in Bennington and Brattleboro).

Unsurprisingly, the French and Indian War (1754–63) exacerbated tensions between the two, including two battles at the French fort of Fort Carillon – renamed Fort Ticonderoga after the British victory in the second skirmish in 1759. Britain received Vermont as part of the Treaty of Paris four years later.

As British settlers poured into the territory, it was claimed by the Massachusetts Bay Colony, the Province of New York and the Province of New Hampshire. In 1741 King George II invalidated Massachusetts's claim, but the conflict between New Hampshire and New York persisted. In the 1770s the Green Mountain Boys were formed by Ethan Allen to fight for the rights of the New Hampshire settlers against the New Yorkers and, ultimately, the British.

While the sole battle of the American Revolution to take place in Vermont was the comparatively insignificant Hubbardton in 1777, Vermonters played a very major role that same year in the Battle of Bennington, which actually took place over the border in New York. A major victory, it was a significant turning point in the war. In 1791 Vermont became the 14th state of the new Union.

The Culture

Much of Vermont is farmland, marked by small communities that are tight yet surprisingly welcoming. Indeed, an increasing portion of the population is made up of out-of-staters, many of whom are come for the spring, summer and fall. A fair number are artists seeking peace or (if they move to the Northeast Kingdom) seclusion. More than a few hippies moved here in the 60s and 70s and soon blended in. All of which gives off a relaxed vibe (unless you're visiting one of the bigger ski resorts during the winter) that makes Vermont all the more alluring.

Land & Climate

Because Vermont has such varying elevations and terrains, it's hard to generalize about its climate and how it might affect your trip. But there are a few things that a traveler can count on. In the winter expect bitter cold and a number of snowstorms that drop at least 5in in one fell swoop. Freezing rain is common. Springtime is fleeting and doesn't really arrive until well into May. Summertime is glorious, and although it can be hazy, the humidity is rarely oppressive. Autumn, when leaves turn ablaze with color, is the peak season – with blue-sky days followed by (hopefully) crisp nights.

If climatic conditions are likely to seriously affect your travel schedule, contact the **highway department** (☎ 802-828-2648) and listen to **An Eye on the Sky** (http://fairbanksmuseum.org/eye.cfm), aired on Vermont Public Radio (at the lower end of your FM dial). These reports provide frequent and utterly entertaining, informative discourses on the wheres and whys of Mother Nature's whims.

Parks & Wildlife

With more than 150,000 acres of protected forest set aside in more than 50 state parks,

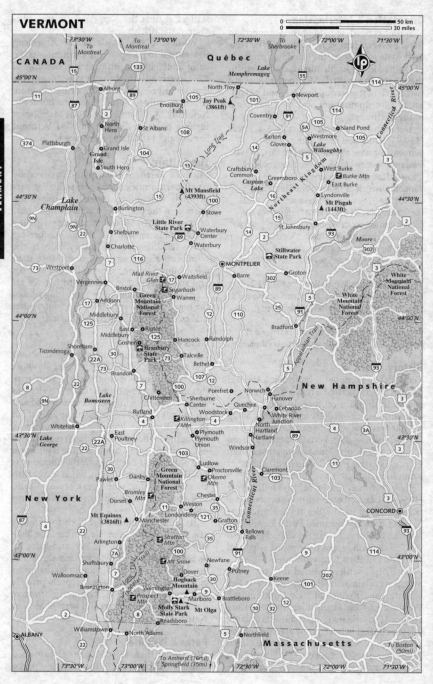

Vermont ain't called the Green Mountain State for nothing! Finding an exceptional and often underutilized state park in Vermont is about as easy as breathing. See the various Activities sections (and budget Sleeping options for camping) throughout this chapter for details. Whether you're interested in swimming, hiking, snowshoeing, cross-country skiing, camping or fishing, you'll find plenty of places that fit the bill. For complete information contact the **Vermont State Parks** (☎ 802-241-3655; www.vtstateparks.com) or the **Department of Forests, Parks & Recreation** (☎ 802-241-3665).

Speaking of green mountains, the wild and undeveloped Green Mountain National Forest, which runs right up the center of the state, covers more than 850,000 acres and boasts more than 900 miles of hiking trails. The Appalachian Trail and Long Trail call these woods home. A person could get delightfully (and metaphorically) lost for days here.

Getting There & Around

AIR

Vermont's major airport is in **Burlington** (☎ 802-863-2874; www.burlingtonintlairport.com), but there is also a small commercial airport in **Rutland** (☎ 802-786-8881; www.flyrutlandvt.com). Burlington is served by Continental, Delta, JetBlue, Northwest, United and US Airways, while Rutland receives flights from Cape Air, a small regional carrier.

BOAT

Lake Champlain Transportation Company (☎ 802-864-9804; www.ferries.com) runs ferries between Plattsburgh, New York and Grand Isle; between Port Kent, New York and Burlington; and between Essex, New York and Charlotte. **Fort Ti Ferry** (☎ 802-897-7999; www.middlebury.net/tiferry) runs from Larrabees Point in Shoreham to Ticonderoga Landing, New York, from late May through October.

BUS

Vermont Transit (☎ 802-864-6811, 800-552-8737; www.vermonttransit.com) connects major Vermont towns and makes forays to Manchester and Keene, New Hampshire; Boston; and Albany. **Greyhound** (☎ 800-231-2222; www.greyhound.com) operates four buses daily between Burlington and Montreal (one way $27.50, three hours).

CAR

Vermont is not particularly large, but it is mountainous. Although I-89 and I-91 provide speedy access to certain areas, the rest of the time you must plan to take it slow and enjoy the winding roads and mountain scenery. Having said that, I-91 north of St Johnsbury offers expansive vistas, as does I-89 from White River Junction to Burlington.

TRAIN

Amtrak (☎ 800-872-7245; www.amtrak.com) is relaxing, albeit inconvenient. The *Ethan Allen* departs New York City and stops in Fair Haven and Rutland. From New York City to Rutland costs $54 one way and takes 5½ hours. The *Vermonter* heads from New York City to Brattleboro, Bellows Falls, Windsor, White River Junction, Randolph, Montpelier, Waterbury, Burlington-Essex Junction and St Albans. If you're a cyclist, you can buy one ticket on the *Vermonter* and get on and off as many times as you like, as long as you reserve a space for yourself and your bicycle ahead of time.

SOUTHERN VERMONT

Tidy white churches and inns surround village greens throughout historic southern Vermont, a region that's home to several towns that predate the American Revolution. In summer the roads between the three 'cities' of Brattleboro, Bennington and Manchester roll over green hills; in winter, they wind their way toward the ski slopes of Mt Snow, southern Vermont's cold-weather playground. For those on foot, the Appalachian Trail passes through the Green Mountain National Forest here, offering a colorful hiking experience during the fall foliage season.

BRATTLEBORO

pop 12,000

Perched at the confluence of the Connecticut and West Rivers, Brattleboro is a little gem that reveals its facets to those who stroll the streets and prowl the dozens of independent shops and eateries. An energetic mix of aging hippies and the latest crop of pierced and tattooed hipsters fuels the town's sophisticated eclecticism, keeping the downtown scene percolating and skewing its politics decidedly leftward.

VERMONT

VERMONT

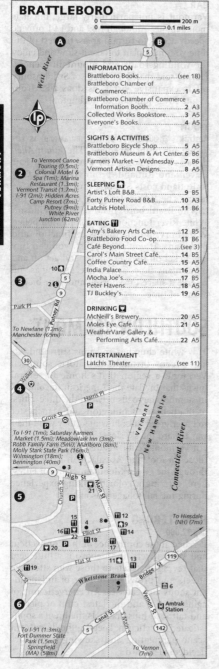

BRATTLEBORO

INFORMATION
Brattleboro Books.........................(see 18)
Brattleboro Chamber of
Commerce.................................1 A5
Brattleboro Chamber of Commerce
Information Booth.......................2 A3
Collected Works Bookstore........3 A5
Everyone's Books..........................4 A5

SIGHTS & ACTIVITIES
Brattleboro Bicycle Shop...........5 A5
Brattleboro Museum & Art Center.6 B6
Farmers Market – Wednesday....7 B6
Vermont Artisan Designs..............8 A5

SLEEPING
Artist's Loft B&B.........................9 B5
Forty Putney Road B&B.............10 A3
Latchis Hotel..............................11 B6

EATING
Amy's Bakery Arts Cafe.............12 B5
Brattleboro Food Co-op.............13 B6
Café Beyond.............................(see 3)
Carol's Main Street Café............14 B5
Coffee Country Cafe..................15 A5
India Palace...............................16 A5
Mocha Joe's...............................17 B5
Peter Havens............................18 A5
TJ Buckley's...............................19 A6

DRINKING
McNeill's Brewery......................20 A5
Moles Eye Cafe..........................21 A5
WeatherVane Gallery &
Performing Arts Café................22 A5

ENTERTAINMENT
Latchis Theater.........................(see 11)

The Whetstone Brook runs through the south end of town, where a wooden stockade dubbed Fort Dummer was built to defend Vermont's first Colonial settlement (1724) against Native Americans. The town received its royal charter a year later, named for Colonel William Brattle Jr of the King's Militia, who never set foot in his namesake.

At the Old Town Hall (location of the current Main Street Gallery), many celebrated thinkers and entertainers held forth on the concerns of the day, including Oliver Wendell Holmes, Horace Greeley and Will Rogers. Rudyard Kipling married a Brattleboro woman in 1892, and while living here he wrote *The Jungle Book*.

Orientation & Information

Brattleboro proper is east of I-91; West Brattleboro is west of the highway. While most of the action is easily found in the downtown commercial district, the surrounding hillsides are well salted with farms, cheesemakers and artisans, all awaiting discovery on a pleasant back-road ramble.

Brattleboro Books (☎ 802-257-7777; 34-36 Elliot St; 🕑 10am-6pm Mon-Sat, 11am-5pm Sun) One of a trove of bookstores in Brattleboro offering a long list of store-sponsored readings and events. This is a used-book junkie's dream, with endless aisles containing more than 75,000 used, out-of-print and even new titles.

Brattleboro Chamber of Commerce (☎ 802-254-4565; www.brattleborochamber.org; 180 Main St; 🕑 9am-5pm Mon-Fri, 10am-2pm Sat)

Brattleboro Chamber of Commerce Information Booth (☎ 802-257-1112; 🕑 9am-5pm Thu-Mon early May-late Oct) On the town green just north of downtown.

Collected Works Bookstore & Café Beyond (☎ bookstore 802-258-4900, café 802-246-1063; www .collectedworksbooks.com; 29 High St; 🕑 8am-6pm Mon-Thu, 8am-8:30pm Fri, 9am-6pm Sat, 9am-5:30pm Sun) Here you can browse Zen titles, women's literature and art books, then snuggle into the comfy chairs. Hanging out in its fantastic café is always a prime activity.

Everyone's Books (☎ 802-254-8160; 25 Elliot St; 🕑 9:30am-5:30pm Mon-Thu, 9:30am-8pm Fri, 9:30am-7pm Sat, 11am-5pm Sun) Sells unusual publications, rabble-rousing political literature and an audacious selection of radical T-shirts and bumper stickers.

Sights & Activities

BRATTLEBORO MUSEUM & ART CENTER

Located in a 1915 railway station, this **museum** (☎ 802-257-0124; www.brattleboromuseum.org; 10 Vernon St; adult/student/senior/under 6yr $4/2/3/free; 🕑 11am-5pm

EATING VERMONT

Over a fifth of Vermont's surface is given over to farmland, and the quality of the produce is among the finest in the country. If you're interested in a farm stay, check out www.vtfarms.org for a list of 20 or so places. Visitors who prefer to sample local produce from the comfort of a restaurant will not be disappointed.

Maple sugaring

Ranking first among states in maple production, Vermont produces over 400,000 gallons of the sweet stuff – 36% of America's entire output. This is particularly impressive considering almost 40 gallons of sap must be tapped from maple trees for a mere quart of syrup. Demonstrations can be seen and samples tasted at the Robb Family Farm (below), Shelburne Farms (p389), Maple Grove Farms (p404), or innumerable roadside farms in the spring.

Cheesemaking

Local cheesemakers have been around since colonial times in Vermont, but it's only in the last few decades that artisanal cheese has come into vogue and become available in a wider range. Sheep and goat's milk are now used in addition to cow's milk, adding variety to the traditional staples of cheddar and Colby. The Vermont Cheese Council (www.vtcheese.com) lists 37 farms for visiting on its Cheese Trail, but if you're less ambitious you should check out Sugarbush Farm (p375), Shelburne Farms (p389) or the Grafton Village Cheese Company (p363).

Wed-Mon) hosts a wealth of inventive exhibits by local artists in a variety of media. It also boasts a rotating multimedia exhibition program of contemporary art.

MAPLE SUGARING

The 400-acre **Robb Family Farm** (☎ 888-318-9087; www.robbfamilyfarm.com; 827 Ames Hill Rd; 10am-5pm Mon-Sat & 1-5pm Sun in season) has been run by the same family for about a century. Maple-sugaring demonstrations take place from late February to early April. There are fun hay or sleigh rides ($7/5 per adult/child, $30 minimum spend required, reservations essential), which usually end with a marshmallow roast. The farm is located west of I-91 on VT 9; take a left on Greenleaf St (which becomes Ames Hill Rd), head 3 miles and look to the right.

GALLERIES & ART SPACES

Vermont Artisan Designs (☎ 802-257-7044; www.vtartisans.com; 106 Main St; seasonal) is a contemporary crafts gallery selling outstanding creations by Vermont artists. Don't miss it.

On the first Friday of each month, join the immensely popular **Gallery Walk** (☎ 802-257-2616; www.gallerywalk.org; 5:30-8pm). Since the early 1990s, galleries and businesses have opened their walls to artists from an ever-increasing geographic reach and renown. A free monthly publication, available throughout town and

on the website, maps the locations for this self-guided tour.

COVERED BRIDGES

Windham County has 30 covered bridges and the Brattleboro Chamber of Commerce (opposite) distributes information about them.

BRATTLEBORO FARMERS MARKET

Offering an excellent crash course in Vermont food, the **market** (www.brattleborofarmersmarket.com; 10am-2pm Wed early Jun–mid-Oct, 9am-2pm Sat early May–mid-Oct) boasts as many as 70 local vendors selling cheese, free-range beef and lamb, honey, pastries, maple syrup and fruit. Live music and a lively crafts scene round out the experience. The Saturday market is just west of town by the Creamery Bridge, while the Wednesday market is held in the Merchants Bank Building parking lot off Main St.

BIKING

Brattleboro Bicycle Shop (☎ 802-254-8644, 800-272-8245; www.bratbike.com; 165 Main St; bike hire daily $20) rents hybrid bicycles and dispenses plenty of advice about where to use them. It doesn't have racks or kids' bikes, though.

CANOEING & KAYAKING

Vermont Canoe Touring (☎ 802-257-5008; Veterans Memorial Bridge, 451 Putney Rd; late May–mid-Oct) rents kayaks and canoes. While away an afternoon by bird-watching in the estuaries or visiting an unofficial nude sunbathing spot up the White River.

Sleeping

You have the option of cheap camping, moderately priced motels that line Putney Rd (US 5) north of Brattleboro and VT 9 west of town, or more upscale inns and B&Bs in and around downtown.

BUDGET

Fort Dummer State Park (☎ 802-254-2610; www .vtstateparks.com/htm/fortdummer; 517 Old Guilford Rd; campsites/lean-to sites $14/21; ☺ late May-early Sep) This great 217-acre park has 51 sites (10 of them lean-to shelters), hot showers and nature trails. From I-91 exit 1, go north a few hundred yards on US 5. Then go a half-mile east on Fairground Rd, then a mile south on Main St to Old Guilford Rd. There are no RV hookups here.

Hidden Acres Camp Resort (☎ 802-254-2098, 866-411-2267; www.hiddenacresvt.com; 792 US 5, Dummerston; RV sites/campsites $40/27; ☺ May–mid-Nov; ☒) This area has 40 open and wooded sites (12 just for tents), a large recreational vehicle (RV) safari field, a game room, a rec hall and miniature golf. It's about 3 miles north of I-91 exit 3.

Colonial Motel & Spa (☎ 802-254-5040, 800-239-0032; www.colonialmotelspa.com; 889 US 5; r $60-95, ste $140; ☒ ☒) Some of the 73 units in this place north of the town center are suites and some also have a kitchen. As for the spa part of the name, it includes Jacuzzis, saunas and steam rooms, and a cramped space with a handful of exercise machines.

MIDRANGE & TOP END

Latchis Hotel (☎ 802-254-6300; www.latchis.com; 50 Main St; s $65, d $115, ste $180; wi-fi) Located in the epicenter of downtown, you can't beat the location of these 30 reasonably priced rooms and suites. The hotel's art deco overtones are refreshing and wonderfully surprising for New England.

our pick **Artist's Loft B&B** (☎ 802-257-5181; www .theartistsloft.com; 103 Main St; ste $138-158) In the heart of downtown, this B&B has only one room, but what a room! Innkeepers (and artists) Patricia Long and William Hays rent a spacious 3rd-floor suite (the size of a large one-bedroom apartment) that overlooks the Connecticut River and the seasonally changing canvas of Wantastiquet Mountain.

Meadowlark Inn (☎ 802-257-4582, 800-616-6359; meadowlarkinnvt.com; Orchard St; d $155-225; wi-fi) You'll find exquisite peace here, where you can relax on the porch or escape to one of the eight thematically decorated rooms. The innkeepers are culinary-school graduates and serve breakfast and treats just like you wish your mamma used to.

Forty Putney Road B&B (☎ 802-254-6268, 800-941-2413; www.fortyputneyroad.com; 192 Putney Rd; d incl full breakfast $159-219; ☐ wi-fi) This 1930 B&B with a small cheery pub is a sweet spot just north of town. It has a glorious backyard and a tiny pub, four rooms plus a cute, separate, self-contained cottage. Overlooking the West River estuary, it also offers boat and bike rentals that are just a five-minute walk away. Request a room at the back if you want peace and quiet.

Eating

If you are self-catering, **Brattleboro Food Co-op** (☎ 802-257-0236; 2 Main St; ☺ breakfast, lunch & dinner) is the perfect place to load up your picnic basket with ready-made eats and treats. It also offers whole-food groceries, a juice bar, organic produce, and an incredible cheese department stocked with local varieties. Another great place for picnic fixings is **Carol's Main Street Café** (☎ 802-254-8380; 73 Main St; ☺ 7am-5pm Mon-Fri, 7am-4pm Sat) – those in the know come for turkey specials on Monday and Friday, tacos on Wednesday and hamburgers on Thursday. Or you can explore delectables from an amazing variety of gourmet hot and salad dishes sold by the pound.

BUDGET

Coffee Country Cafe (☎ 802-257-0032; 12 Harmony Pl; coffee $1.25, pastry $1.75; ☺ 7am-6pm Mon-Fri, 8am-6pm Sat, 9am-4pm Sun) This informal place attracts everyone from tongue-studded teenagers to 65-year-old farmers. Drop in for some good java and hot baked goods.

Mocha Joe's (☎ 802-257-7794; 82 Main St; coffee $1.25, pastry $2.00; ☺ 7am-8pm Mon-Thu, 7am-11pm Fri & Sat, 7:30am-7pm Sun) Before your eyes spy this ultrahip, subterranean space, your nose will locate the exceptionally rich brews.

Amy's Bakery Arts Cafe (☎ 802-251-1071; 113 Main St; dishes $3-8.50; ☺ 8am-6pm Mon-Sat, 10am-5pm Sun) Of the many bakeries in town that inspire poetic accolades, this one garners the most. Enjoy breakfast breads, pastries and coffee with views of the river and local art.

Lunchtime offerings include salads, soups and sandwiches.

MIDRANGE

Café Beyond (☎ 802-246-1063; 29 High St; breakfast & lunch $6-8, meals $14-20; ✦ 8am-3pm Sun-Wed, 8am-3pm & 5-9pm Thu-Sat; ▣) Head to the Collected Works Bookstore for full meals with international flair. The Thai and Colombian chefs here offer an inspired world-ranging menu. Additionally, the fabulous bookstore, meeting space and seating designed for lingering draw a wild cross-pollination of, well, lingerers.

Marina Restaurant (☎ 802-257-7563; 28 Springtree Rd; dishes $6-22; ✦ lunch & dinner) This fun, refreshing local favorite blends fantastic food, spirited atmosphere and a sublime location on the banks of the West River. Food is reasonably priced and features all-natural beef filet mignon ($21.95) and daily seafood specials.

India Palace (☎ 802-254-6143; 69 Elliot St; meals $8-38; ✦ lunch & dinner) This is *the* place for northern Indian cuisine, especially tandoori; lunchtime curries are a bargain, best sampled with a mango *lassi*.

TOP END

ourpick **Peter Havens** (☎ 802-257-3333; 32 Elliot St; meals $30-40; ✦ dinner Tue-Sat) This intimate, 10-table local institution features an incredible menu bursting with culinary mastery. Fresh seafood dishes share the roster with venison, duck, tenderloin and pasta dishes (which can be modified for vegetarians). Brimming with intimate and artsy atmosphere, Peter Havens also has a full (eight-seat) bar.

TJ Buckley's (☎ 802-257-4922; 132 Elliot St; meals $32-37; ✦ dinner Thu-Sun) This upscale but classic and authentic 1927 diner seats just 18 souls, but those lucky 18 are in for an exceptional dinner. The menu of four mains changes nightly, and locals rave that the food here is Brattleboro's best. Reservations are strongly recommended; credit cards are not accepted.

Drinking & Entertainment

WeatherVane Gallery & Performing Arts Café (☎ 802-246-2560; 19 Elliot St; ✦ 8am-2am; ▣) This great hangout is where you'll find the kind of cool, witty guy behind the counter that you always see in movies. Slide into one of the giant booths and enjoy light fare (dishes $1 to $10), a full bar and live music. The latter is usually bluesy/folky, but can also be wild and ear-splitting on select nights.

Moles Eye Cafe (☎ 802-257-0771; cnr Main & High Sts; cover Fri & Sat nights $5; ✦ 4pm-midnight Mon-Thu, 11:30am-1am Fri & Sat) This popular, subterranean hangout in an oak-paneled café has live entertainment on Friday and Saturday nights and good meals at moderate prices (dishes from $7 to $11) served until 9pm. Thursday's open mic is usually a blast.

McNeill's Brewery (☎ 802-254-2553; 90 Elliot St; ✦ 4pm-2am Mon-Thu, 2pm-2am Fri-Sun) This classic pub, inhabited by a lively, friendly local crowd, features 15 beers on tap. The place flows with award-winning suds, including three naturally carbonated, cask-conditioned brews.

Latchis Theater (☎ 802-254-6300; www.latchis.com; 50 Main St) The nicely restored, art deco Latchis Building houses this theater where you can see mainstream and indies on three screens nightly.

Getting There & Away

Vermont Transit (☎ 800-552-8737; www.vermonttransit.com) runs one daily bus between Brattleboro and Middlebury ($25 to $27, three hours) via Rutland, where there are connecting buses northward. The bus stops behind the **Citgo station** (☎ 802-254-6066) at the intersection of US 5 and I-91.

The **Amtrak** (☎ 800-872-7245; www.amtrak.com) *Vermonter* train stops in Brattleboro. The trip from New York City to Brattleboro costs $52 to $57 one way.

By car, it takes 1¼ hours (40 miles) to traverse scenic VT 9 from Brattleboro to Bennington. From Northampton, MA, it takes less than an hour (40 miles) straight up I-91 to reach Brattleboro.

While Brattleboro is very easy to get around on foot, you can call **Brattleboro Taxi** (☎ 802-254-6446) for transportation beyond its limits.

AROUND BRATTLEBORO

The Lower Connecticut and West River valleys of southern Vermont are home to a warren of pristine villages worth exploring.

Marlboro

pop 1000

At first sight, this village 8 miles west of Brattleboro is pretty but unremarkable: a white church, a white inn, a white village office building and a few white houses. But to chamber-music lovers, Marlboro looms very large as the home of the **Marlboro Music Fest** (☎ 215-569-4690, 802-254-2394; www.marlboromusic.org;

135 S 18th St, Philadelphia, PA 19103; tickets $5-35) held on Saturdays and Sundays from early July to mid-August. The festival was founded in 1951 and directed for many years by the late Rudolf Serkin, and attended by Pablo Casals. The small Marlboro College comes alive with enthusiastic music students and concertgoers, who consistently pack the small, 700-seat auditorium. Many concerts sell out almost immediately, so it's essential to reserve seats, by phone or mail, in advance. All seating is reserved.

Marlboro is a short distance off the so-called Molly Stark Trail (VT 9), a road named for the wife of General Stark, the hero of the American Revolution's Battle of Bennington.

Head west from Marlboro on VT 9 until you get to Augur Hill Rd, where a nice detour awaits. Take this side road for about 8 miles to South Newfane. It's a hard-packed spur road that leads past classic farms, alongside little Rock River and through the woods. Take the right split for South Newfane, through a covered bridge dating to 1870 and past the Williamsville General Store. If you're still having fun, backtrack a few miles and take VT 30 north to Newfane proper.

Otherwise, stay on VT 9, which brings you to the top of **Hogback Mountain** (2410ft), where you'll find the **Southern Vermont Natural History Museum** (☎ 802-464-0048; www.vermontmuseum.org; adult/5-12yr/senior $5/2/3; ☽ 10am-5pm late May-late Oct), an interesting little place that features mounted specimens of more than 600 New England birds and mammals as well as a small center devoted to live raptors.

At the high point of VT 9, there's a lookout and the family-owned **Skyline Restaurant** (☎ 802-464-3536; dishes $7-10; ☽ 7:30am-9pm summer, 7:30am-3pm Mon & 7:30am-9pm Fri-Sun winter), where you can dine on homemade soups, a 'Monte Cristo' (a grilled triple-decker sandwich made with Swiss cheese, ham and turkey drizzled with maple syrup) and traditional New England comfort foods, all with the backdrop of a marvelous '100-mile' view, which – weather permitting – takes in the Berkshires.

Newfane
pop 1700
Vermont is rife with pretty villages, but Newfane is near the top of everyone's list. All the postcard-perfect sights you'd expect in a Vermont town are here: tall old trees, white high-steepled churches, excellent inns and gracious old houses. In spring Newfane is busy making maple sugar; in summer, the town buzzes around its flea market; fall lures leaf-peepers; and winter brings couples seeking cozy rooms in warm hideaways. A short stroll exposes Newfane's core: you'll see the stately **Congregational church** (1839), the **Windham County Courthouse** (1825), built in Greek Revival style, and a few antique shops.

Newfane is on VT 30, just 12 miles northwest of Brattleboro, and 19 miles northeast of Wilmington.

Just outside of town, **West River Lodge** (☎ 802-365-7745; www.westriverlodge.com; 117 Hill Rd; r incl full breakfast $75-140) features English riding workshops (it has its own stables) and eight farmhouse accommodations to fit your family's needs. Some bathrooms are shared.

Visitors with panache stop in Newfane just long enough for a meal or a night at **Four Columns Inn** (☎ 802-365-7713, 800-787-6633; www.four columnsinn.com; 21 West St; r incl full breakfast $165-235, ste $$265-385; wi-fi), a 1830s Greek Revival inn on the common that has 15 rooms and an excellent dining room serving outstanding New American cuisine. Accommodations range from elegant, 'simple' country rooms to luxurious suites with gas fireplaces and Jacuzzis. The sylvan property surrounding the inn is excellent for hiking or snowshoeing.

Townshend State Park (☎ 802-365-7500; www .vtstateparks.com/htm/townshend; VT 30; campsites $14; ☽ mid-May–mid-Oct), tucked deep into the forest about 3 miles north of Newfane, is one of the state's better places to camp, with 34 tent sites. Hiking trails include the sometimes steep, challenging path to the summit of Bald Mountain (1680ft), a rocky climb that rises 1100ft in less than a mile. Other trails within Townshend State Park are easier. There's swimming and boating at the nearby Army Corps of Engineers' Recreation Area at Townshend Dam. The West River is good for canoe trips.

Weston
pop 640
On the eastern side of the Green Mountains, Weston is another of Vermont's pristine towns. Its common is graced with towering maples and a bandstand, and is home to an acclaimed summer theater. Weston also draws fans from far and wide to its famed **Vermont Country Store** (☎ 802-463-2224; www.ver

montcountrystore.com; VT 100), a time warp from a simpler era when goods were made to last, and quirky products with appeal (but not a mass-market appeal) had a home. Here you'll discover taffeta slips, Tangee lipstick, three kinds of shoe stretchers with customizable bunion and corn knobs, personal care items and clothing. Some of the products have survived from past decades and many have become indispensable – once you've been introduced to them.

The **Weston Playhouse** (☎ 802-824-5288; www .westonplayhouse.org; tickets $22-26; ☜ performances late Jun-early Sep), Vermont's oldest professional theatre, occupies an old church on the town common and backs onto the West River. It enjoys a good reputation for musicals and drama; if you're in the area, try to obtain tickets. Arrive early for a show or to dine on light fare 'Downstairs at the Playhouse.'

Grafton
pop 650

Right next to Newfane on that shortlist of must-see villages, Grafton lies at the junction of VT 121 and VT 35, only about 15 miles north of Newfane. Grafton is graceful, but it's not that way by accident. In the 1960s the private Windham Foundation established a restoration and preservation program for the entire village, and it has been eminently successful.

Head a half-mile south of the village to find mouthwatering and nose-tingling cheddars at the **Grafton Village Cheese Company** (☎ 802-843-2221; www.graftonvillagecheese.com; 533 Townshend Rd; admission free; ☜ 8am-4pm Mon-Fri, 10am-4pm Sat & Sun), which you can sample while watching them being made. The maple-smoked and stone-house cheddars regularly win awards at international cheese festivals.

Set up high on 200 acres, just outside of Grafton off Middletown Rd, is the **Inn at Woodchuck Hill Farm** (☎ 802-843-2398; www.wood chuckhill.com; r $99-155, ste $175-280). This restored 1790s farmhouse offers 10 guest rooms and suites filled with lovely antiques as well as complimentary Grafton cheddar and crackers; the studio suite with a private deck is particularly coveted. Relax in the sauna in the woods next to the pond – itself great for swimming, fishing and canoeing. Or tire yourself by hiking or cross-country skiing the farm's private network of trails. Prices vary according to amenities and the size of the room.

The **Old Tavern at Grafton** (☎ 802-843-2231, 800-843-1801; www.old-tavern.com; cnr VT 35 & Townshend Rd; r incl full breakfast $150-245, ste $195-400; ☜ May-Mar), the double porch of which is Grafton's landmark, has played host to such notable guests as Rudyard Kipling, Theodore Roosevelt and Ralph Waldo Emerson. While the original brick inn is quite formal, many of the 47 guest rooms and suites – scattered around houses within the village – are less so. The inn has tennis courts, a sand-bottomed swimming pond and cross-country skiing trails. The dining room is New England formal and the cuisine is refined New American with a seasonal menu, but the café fare is lighter and less formal.

Putney
pop 2700

Where do hippies go when they grow up? This village answers that question – one look at the general-store bulletin board tells you all you need to know about the craftspeople who populate Putney, and their grassroots involvement in local affairs. Pick up a quick bite at the **general store** in the center of town or at the **Putney Food Co-op**, just south of the village on US 5. Putney is 10 miles north of Brattleboro via I-91.

In a retrofitted school bus, **Curtis' Barbeque** (☎ 802-387-5474; US 5; dishes $4-8; ☜ 10am-dusk Wed-Sun Apr–mid-Oct) dispenses some of the best ribs and barbecue chicken north of the Mason-Dixon line. Wash it down with one of Curtis' own bottled sodas.

WILMINGTON
pop 2300

Wilmington is the gateway to Mt Snow, one of New England's best ski resorts and an excellent summertime mountain-biking and golfing spot. Many restaurants and stores cater to families, who are the resort's main clientele.

Orientation & Information

The state's central north–south highway, VT 100, goes north from Wilmington past Haystack and Mt Snow. VT 9, the main route across southern Vermont, is Wilmington's main street. The **Mt Snow Valley Region Chamber of Commerce** (☎ 802-464-8092; www.visitvermont.com; West Main St, PO Box 3 Wilmington VT 05363; ☜ 10am-5pm) maintains a village office.

Sights & Activities

The terrain at **Mt Snow** (☎ 802-464-3333, 800-245-7669; www.mountsnow.com) is varied, making it popular with families. High season runs from late December through February. The resort has 132 trails (20% beginner, 60% intermediate, 20% expert) and 23 lifts, plus a vertical drop of 1700ft and the snowmaking ability to blanket 85% of the trails. Area cross-country routes cover more than 60 miles. As if that weren't enough, you can also undertake snowmobile tours and winter mountain tubing.

Come summer, Mt Snow has lots of hiking possibilities, and hosts one of the best mountain-biking schools in the country. All this activity surely warrants a stop at its full-service **Grand Summit Spa** (☎ 802-464-1100, ext 6006), which provides a range of services from sports to Swedish massage, and from energy balancing to reflexology.

To reach Mt Snow/Haystack from Wilmington, travel 10 miles north of town on VT 100. The free bus service, **MOO-ver** (☎ 802-464-8487), transports skiers from Wilmington to the slopes of Mt Snow for free at least every hour between 7am and 5pm.

Sleeping
BUDGET
Molly Stark State Park (☎ 802-464-5460; www.vtstate parks.com/htm/mollystark; VT 9; RV sites/campsites $21/14; ☙ late May–mid-Oct) This 160-acre state park, named for the wife of American Revolution general John Stark, is about 3 miles east of Wilmington. From this park's 23 sites and 11 lean-tos, a trail leads to the fire tower on Mt Olga, which affords spectacular views. There are no RV hookups available here, but other facilities include a playground, picnic pavilion and hot showers.

MIDRANGE
Vintage Motel (☎ 802-464-8824, 800-899-9660; vintage motel.net; VT 9; d $85-$95, ste $200; wi-fi 🛋) A mile west of the town center, the Vintage Motel has 16 tidy units, including three economy rooms with pull-out beds that are great for families. There is also a grand suite with a fireplace and three double beds. The motel sits on 17 acres with direct access to a formal network of snowmobile trails, as well as a big 2-acre pond on the premises.

Nutmeg Inn (☎ 802-464-3351, 800-277-5402; www .nutmeginn.com; VT 9; incl breakfast d $89-149, ste $179-234) Just west of Wilmington, this renovated 18th-century farmhouse has 10 rooms and four suites with antiques and reproduction pieces. Breakfasts are ample, and the owners

are constantly baking goodies. Ask for the Grand Deluxe King Suite, with skylights and a marble bath.

Trail's End (☎ 802-464-2727, 800-859-2585; www .trailsendvt.com; 5 Trail's End Lane; r incl full breakfast mid-Dec–mid-Mar $130-200, mid-Mar–mid-Dec $110-180; 🛋) Set on 10 acres 4 miles north of Wilmington, Trail's End has a country-home feel. In addition to 15 cozy rooms and suites (many with wood-burning fireplaces) and a game room with a billiard table, it also has a pond stocked with trout and catfish, and clay tennis courts. Take VT 100 north from town to E Dover Rd, which leads to Smith Rd and then Trail's End Lane.

Red Shutter Inn (☎ 802-464-3768, 800-845-7548; www.redshutterinn.com; VT 9; incl full breakfast d $165-195, ste $305) Dating from 1894, this grand old house, restored by innkeepers Lucylee and Gerard Gingras, has seven rooms and two suites, each with unique decor. The recently renovated carriage house welcomes guests in its three rooms or the cozy suite. If you want to stay in and eat, Thursday evening is Italian night; Sunday features a hearty English menu.

TOP END
our pick White House of Wilmington (☎ 802-464-2135, 800-541-2135; www.whitehouseinn.com; VT 9; incl full breakfast d $185-235, ste $285; 🛋) Local legend says that it's haunted by the ghost of the wife of the lumberman who built it in 1915. Whether that's true or not, this white Colonial Revival mansion perched on a hill on the eastern outskirts of town boasts great cross-country trails and 25 luxury rooms – all adding up to a particularly romantic stay. Guest rooms, some with a balcony and fireplace, are divided between the main house and the cottage. The restaurant here is one of the best in the area.

Snow Goose (☎ 802-464-3984, 888-604-7964; www .snowgooseinn.com; VT 100, West Dover; incl full breakfast d $185-295, ste $335-410; wi-fi) Only a mile from the ski slopes, this elegant, romantic inn on three sylvan acres has 13 large rooms and suites with large Jacuzzis, fireplaces and private decks overlooking the forest. Breakfasts are sumptuous (the Snow Goose bacon is seasoned on site); complimentary hors d'oeuvres are served by the fire in winter.

Eating
Cup N' Saucer (☎ 802-464-5813; VT 100; dishes $2-6; ☙ breakfast & lunch) Judging from the muddy pickups in the parking lot, locals make up a

large percentage of this joint's clientele. They flock here for burgers and hot, open-faced turkey sandwiches. Then again, the pancakes are great and breakfast is served all day. The circular counter is decidedly old-fashioned.

ourpick Dot's (dishes $3-15.95; ☺ breakfast, lunch & dinner) Main St (☎ 802-464-7284); Mt Snow (☎ 802-464-6476; VT 100, Mt Snow) Probably the last place you'd expect to find outstanding chili, this down-home diner with pine paneling and a long Formica counter serves up a spicy Jailhouse Chili coated in a layer of melted cheese that's renowned throughout New England. With locations in the village and in Dover nearer the slopes, Dot's is justly popular with locals and skiers in search of cheap sustenance like steak and eggs for breakfast.

Silo (☎ 802-464-2553; VT 100, West Dover; meals $6-25; ☺ lunch & dinner) This serious steak house is good for large skiing parties who all want something different – from stuffed shrimp to chicken pot pie to Caesar salad to pastas, pizzas and sandwiches. In the winter, Silo offers entertainment, DJs, dancing and 10¢ wings (from 4pm to 6pm).

Poncho's Wreck (☎ 802-464-9320; 10 S Main St; meals $8-28; ☺ dinner daily, lunch Sat & Sun) A favorite with the après-ski crowd since 1972, casual Poncho's has an extensive menu with plenty of Mexican dishes, steaks and nightly seafood specials. To keep patrons jolly, it also offers a wide selection of margaritas and live entertainment on winter and holiday weekends.

Alonzo's (☎ 802-464-2355; W Main St; meals $12-24; ☺ dinner) Within the Crafts Inn, Alonzo's specializes in Italian food, including homemade pastas and grilled dishes. You can create your own grill special – or perhaps be tempted by something along the lines of andouille sausage or teriyaki steak?

White House of Wilmington (☎ 802-464-2135, 800-541-2135; VT 9; meals $28-35; ☺ dinner daily, brunch Sun; Ⓥ) Stylish dining in a stylish setting with a fireplace, wood paneling and views of the Deerfield Valley. Dishes include homemade crab cakes, roasted Vermont duckling (topped with oranges and blueberries) and a daily vegetarian special, complemented by an acclaimed wine list. Sunday's brunch stars the lobster omelette (in season).

Drinking & Entertainment

Maple Leaf Malt & Brewing (☎ 802-464-9900; 3 North Main St; ☺ lunch & dinner) Ignore the fruit-flavored offerings and sample the well-crafted ales,

lagers and stouts at this local microbrewery, which serves up good burgers.

Wilmington Pub (☎ 802-464-9900; 7 South Main St; ☺ lunch & dinner) The pub karaoke evenings can get a bit raucous but the crowd mellows for its basement Mo' Jazz Café.

Getting There & Away

Wilmington is 21 miles west of Brattleboro (a drive of 45 minutes on the winding road) and 20 miles east of Bennington (40 minutes).

BENNINGTON
pop 15,600

Bennington is a mix of historic Vermont village (Old Bennington), workaday town (Bennington proper) and college town (North Bennington). It is also home to the famous Bennington Monument that commemorates the crucial Battle of Bennington during the American Revolution. Had Colonel Seth Warner and the local 'Green Mountain Boys' not helped weaken British defenses during this battle, the colonies might well have been split. Robert Frost, one of the most famous American poets of the 20th century, is buried in Bennington, and a museum in his old homestead pays eloquent tribute. As it's located within the bounds of the Green Mountain National Forest, there are many hiking trails nearby, including the granddaddies of them all: the Appalachian and Long Trails.

Orientation & Information

Most businesses, lodgings and restaurants are in downtown Bennington at the convergence of US 7, VT 7A and VT 9, but the Bennington Monument, Bennington Museum and prettiest houses are in Old Bennington, a mile west on VT 9. The actual site of the Battle of Bennington is in Walloomsac, New York, 6 miles west of the monument. The tranquil little village of Arlington is about 10 miles away via VT 7.

Bennington Area Chamber of Commerce (☎ 800-229-0252, 802-447-3311; www.bennington.com; 100 Veterans Memorial Dr, US 7; ☺ 9am-5pm Mon-Fri, 9am-4pm Sat & Sun mid-May–mid-Oct) Offers current and historical information and a self-guided walking tour of historic Old Bennington.

Bennington Bookshop (☎ 802-442-5059; 467 Main St; ☺ 9am-5:30pm Mon-Thu & Sat, 9am-9pm Fri, noon-4pm Sun) At more than 80 years of age, one of Vermont's oldest independent bookstores.

Sights & Activities

BENNINGTON MUSEUM

Head half a mile west from downtown Bennington on VT 9 for this **museum** (☎ 802-447-1571; www.benningtonmuseum.com; W Main St, VT 9; adult/student & senior/under 12yr $8/7/free; ⏲ 10am-5pm Thu-Tue). The museum's outstanding collection of early Americana includes furniture, glassware and pottery (made in Bennington), colonial paintings, dolls, military memorabilia and the oldest surviving American Revolutionary flag in the world. The museum is especially noted for its rich collection of paintings by Anna Mary Moses (1860–1961), better known as 'Grandma Moses.' She started painting her lively, natural depictions of farm life at the age of 70 and continued until she was 100.

OLD BENNINGTON

The charming hilltop site of Colonial Old Bennington is studded with 80 Georgian and Federal houses (dating from 1761 – the year Bennington was founded – to 1830).

The **Old First Church** (1 Monument Circle) was built in 1806 in Palladian style. Its churchyard holds the remains of five Vermont governors, numerous American Revolution soldiers and poet Robert Frost (1874–1963), the best-known, and perhaps best-loved, American poet of the 20th century. In nearby Shaftsbury, visit the new Robert Frost Stone House Museum (opposite). One of his farms, Frost Place (p447), is near Franconia, NH,

and another is in Ripton, VT (p381), near Middlebury College's Bread Loaf School of English. His gravestone here bears the epitaph 'I had a lover's quarrel with the world.'

Across from the church, the ramshackle 1764 **Walloomsac Inn** (cnr Monument Ave & VT 9) was a working hostelry up until the 1980s, complete with Victorian-era plumbing and spartan appointments. It's now closed.

Up the hill to the north, the **Bennington Monument** (☎ 802-447-0550; www.bennington.com/chamber/walking/monumentdescription; 15 Monument Circle; adult/child $2/1; ⏲ 9am-5pm mid-Apr–Oct 31) offers impressive views from the obelisk, which was built between 1887 and 1891. An elevator whisks you two-thirds of the way up the 306ft tower (purchase tickets at the nearby gift shop).

BENNINGTON BATTLEFIELD HISTORIC SITE

To reach the actual battle site 6 miles away, follow the 'Bennington Battlefield' signs from the monument, along back roads, through a historic covered bridge (there are two others nearby) to North Bennington, then go west on VT 67 to the Bennington Battlefield Historic Site. Admission is free, and picnic tables are provided under welcome shade.

PARK-MCCULLOUGH HOUSE MUSEUM

Just off VT 67A in North Bennington, look for the **Park-McCullough House Museum** (☎ 802-442-5441; www.parkmccullough.org; 1 Park St; adult/student/senior/under 12yr $8/5/7/free; ⏲ 10am-4pm mid-May–

VERMONT'S MICROBREWERIES

The same easy access to fresh ingredients and commitment to local craftsmanship that enhances the state's restaurants also fuel its microbreweries – as does a simple, honest love of beer. Boasting more craft breweries per capita than any other state (roughly one beermaker for every 28,000 people), Vermont pours an acclaimed and diverse array of beers.

Several offer free tours (and samples):

- **Magic Hat Brewing Co** (p389; ☎ 802-658-2739; www.magichat.net; South Burlington)
- **Otter Creek Brewing** (p382; ☎ 802-388-0727; www.ottercreekbrewing.com; Middlebury)
- **Harpoon Brewery** (☎ 802-674-5491; www.harpoonbrewery.com; Windsor)

Others operate pubs that are well worth the visit:

- **Long Trail Brewing** (p377; ☎ 802-672-5011; www.longtrail.com; West Bridgewater) Just west of Woodstock.
- **Vermont Pub & Brewery** (p394; ☎ 802-865-0500; www.vermontbrewery.com; Burlington)
- **Maple Leaf Malt and Brewing** (p365; ☎ 802-464-9900; Wilmington)
- **McNeill's Brewery** (p361; ☎ 802-254-2553; Brattleboro)

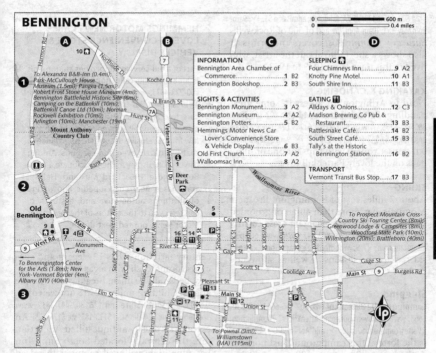

BENNINGTON

INFORMATION	
Bennington Area Chamber of Commerce	**1** B2
Bennington Bookshop	**2** B3

SIGHTS & ACTIVITIES	
Bennington Monument	**3** A2
Bennington Museum	**4** A2
Bennington Potters	**5** B2
Hemmings Motor News Car Lover's Convenience Store & Vehicle Display	**6** B3
Old First Church	**7** A2
Walloomsac Inn	**8** A2

SLEEPING	
Four Chimneys Inn	**9** A2
Knotty Pine Motel	**10** A1
South Shire Inn	**11** B3

EATING	
Alldays & Onions	**12** C3
Madison Brewing Co Pub & Restaurant	**13** B3
Rattlesnake Café	**14** B2
South Street Café	**15** B3
Tally's at the Historic Bennington Station	**16** B2

TRANSPORT	
Vermont Transit Bus Stop	**17** B3

VERMONT

---

mid-Oct, 10am-4pm Sat & Sun Dec). Built in 1865, this 35-room mansion holds period furnishings and a fine collection of antique dolls, toys and carriages. Tours depart on the hour, with the last one departing at 3pm. The house is also open for Victorian tea (by reservation) and seasonal celebrations.

BENNINGTON CENTER FOR THE ARTS

About half a mile west of the Old First Church, this **arts center** (☎ 802-442-7158; www .benningtoncenterforthearts.org; cnr Gypsy Lane & VT 9; adult/senior & student/under 12yr $7/6/free; ⏰ 10am-5pm Tue-Sun) has one gallery called the Great Outdoors, which is home to wind sculptures and fanciful metal whirligigs that respond to the breezes. Inside, other galleries feature fine art, Native American art and artifacts and several rotating exhibits by contemporary artists.

The only one of its kind, the center's **Covered Bridge Museum** reveals the evolution and intricacies of these bridges, of which just over 100 still stand in Vermont. If inspired, you can design your own with the help of a computer.

BENNINGTON POTTERS

The artisans at this **pottery** (☎ 802-447-7531, 800-205-8033; www.benningtonpotters.com; 324 County St; ⏰ 9:30am-6pm Mon-Sat, 10am-5pm Sun) are maintaining a strong tradition of local handmade stoneware manufacturing that dates back to the 1700s. Take a self-guided tour through the manufacturing area, which reveals how much hand work still goes into the company's mass-produced items.

ROBERT FROST STONE HOUSE MUSEUM

When he moved his family to Shaftsbury (4 miles north of Bennington), Frost was 46 years old and at the height of his career. This modest **museum** (☎ 802-447-6200; www.frostfriends.org; 121 VT 7A, Shaftsbury; adult/under 18yr $5/2.50; ⏰ 10am-5pm Tue-Sun May-Dec) opens a window into the life of the poet, with one entire room dedicated to his most famous work, 'Stopping by Woods on a Snowy Evening,' which he penned here in the 1920s.

NORMAN ROCKWELL EXHIBITION

In nearby Arlington, a 10-mile drive north, a Hudson Gothic church houses this **exhibition**

(☎ 802-375-6423; VT 7A, Arlington; admission $1; ☷ 9am-5pm May -Oct, 10am-4pm Nov-Apr) of 500 of Rockwell's *Saturday Evening Post* covers and prints. It also shows a short film about the artist, who lived in this town from 1939 to 1953.

KAYAKING & CANOEING

Head to Arlington for access to some great paddling. **Battenkill Canoe Ltd** (☎ 802-362-2800, 800-421-5268; www.battenkill.com; 6328 VT 7A; tandem canoe or kayak daily $48-60, single $30-35; ☷ 9am-5:30pm May-Oct) can set you up with trips for one or more days on the lovely Battenkill River.

SKIING

About 7 miles east of Bennington, Prospect Mountain has more than 40km of groomed trails. The **Prospect Mountain Cross-Country Ski Touring Center** (☎ 802-442-2575; www.prospect mountain.com; VT 9, Woodford; ☷ 9am-5pm) offers ski rentals and lessons as well as snowshoe rentals.

Sleeping

Camping on the Battenkill (☎ 802-375-6663, 800-830-6663; www.campvermont.com/battenkill; VT 7A, Arlington; RV sites/campsites $28/20; ☷ mid-Apr–mid-Oct) Fishing is the forte at this campground just north of Arlington, which boasts 100 sites split between forest, meadow and open areas. Call early to reserve the popular riverside sites. Multiday stays are required during peak periods.

Greenwood Lodge & Campsites (☎ 802-442-2547; www.campvermont.com/greenwood; VT 9, Prospect Mountain; RV sites/campsites $25/20, dm $23, r $45-50; ☷ mid-May-late Oct) Nestled in the Green Mountains in Woodford, this 120-acre space with three ponds holds one of Vermont's best-sited hostels. Accommodations include 17 budget beds and 40 campsites. You'll find it easily, 8 miles east of Bennington on VT 9 at the Prospect Mountain Ski Area. Facilities include hot showers and a game room. Credit cards are not accepted.

Knotty Pine Motel (☎ 802-442-5487; www.knot typinemotel.com; 130 Northside Dr, VT 7A; r $63-95) On VT 7A in a commercial strip just off US 7, this friendly, family-run motel has a fairly convenient location and 19 country-style rooms paneled in knotty pine (surprise!).

Alexandra B&B-Inn (☎ 802-442-5619, 888-207-9386; www.alexandrainn.com; Orchard Rd, VT 7A; r $109-169; wi-fi) About 2 miles north of Bennington, with a view of the monument, this 19th-

---

HEMMINGS MOTOR NEWS CAR LOVER'S CONVENIENCE STORE & VEHICLE DISPLAY

Part of a full-service Sunoco gas station, this is an absorbing **collection** (☎ 802-442-3101, 800-227-4373; www.hemmings.com; 222 Main St; ☷ 10am-3pm May-Oct) of classic cars, muscle cars, toy cars, vintage trucks, road signs and arcane automobilia (been looking high and low for that elusive dashboard hula dancer?) that will dazzle even non-car buffs. Among the cars on display in the back lot are a 1910 Buick and a 1965 Ford Mustang. Helpful staff has a near-encyclopedic knowledge of all things automotive and, if stumped, can refer you to the editors of the *Hemmings Motor News*, printed next door.

---

century farmhouse has 12 elegant and spacious rooms, each with a gas fireplace, four-post bed and fine linen. Breakfasts are ample affairs. Children under 12 are not welcome.

** our pick** **South Shire Inn** (☎ 802-447-3839; www .southshire.com; 124 Elm St; d $130-185, ste $175-225) An extremely plush, antique-filled Victorian inn, the centrally located South Shire Inn has nine high-ceilinged rooms with raised plastic moldings, some of which have fireplaces. Complimentary afternoon teas held in the mahogany library enhance the sense of luxury here, which is remarkable given the reasonable prices.

Four Chimneys Inn (☎ 802-447-3500; www .fourchimneys.com; 21 West Rd; d $125-165, ste 225-275) The only B&B in Old Bennington, Four Chimneys is a grand white 1910 mansion set amid 11 acres of verdant manicured lawns on which guests can play bocce. All 11 spacious, conservative rooms have television and private bath, and some have a fireplace as well as a porche. The restaurant offers fine dining and has seated such guests as Walt Disney, Richard Burton and Elizabeth Taylor.

Eating & Drinking

South Street Café (☎ 802-447-2433; South St; ☷ breakfast, lunch & dinner Mon-Sat, 9am-5pm Sun) Sink into a chair and sip a cuppa in this pleasant, tin-ceilinged café. Soups, sandwiches or quiche top out at $3.25. Located in Bennington's center, it's an oasis for coffee, tea and bakery treats.

Rattlesnake Café (☎ 802-447-7018; 230 North St; meals $8-16; ✷ dinner Tue-Sun) At this artsy, local Mexican joint, a hefty bean-and-cheese burrito will set you back $8, but it – and any of the wide range of inventive margaritas – will be worth every *peso*.

Madison Brewing Co Pub & Restaurant (☎ 802-442-7397; 428 Main St; meals $8-22; ✷ lunch & dinner) This pleasant, airy pub features standard fare ranging from sandwiches and burgers to steak and pasta. As an added bonus, it always has six to eight of its own brews on tap. There's nothing like really fresh beer.

Tally's at the Historic Bennington Station (☎ 802-447-1080; 150 Depot St; meals $9-27; ✷ lunch & dinner) Set in a beautifully restored 100-year-old train station, this spacious restaurant features an extensive menu of prime rib, fish, pasta, salad and children's dishes.

our pick **Pangea** (☎ 802-442-7171; 1 Prospect St, North Bennington; meals $11-23; ✷ dinner Tue-Sun) Whether you opt for the airy dining room, the intimate lounge or the small terrace, you'll be served with exceptional food. The menu uses fresh ingredients and appropriates a variety of international influences – try the Thai shrimp on organic udon noodles in a curry peanut sauce or the Provence rubbed Delmonico steak topped with gorgonzola. This is one of the finer restaurants in the state.

Alldays & Onions (☎ 802-447-0043; 519 Main St; dishes $3-9, meals $13-21; ✷ breakfast, lunch & dinner Mon-Sat, brunch Sun) For lunch, create your own sandwich or try one of this excellent eatery's inventive offerings (like the Neil, with hot pastrami, tortellini and melted cheese). At night, try the special 'chicken Alldays' – roasted breast meat with blue cheese.

Getting There & Away

Vermont Transit (☎ 802-864-6811, 800-552-8737; www.vermonttransit.com), which stops at 126 Washington Ave, runs two daily buses from Bennington to Manchester ($10, 30 minutes); the same buses continue on to Middlebury and Burlington.

Bennington is 40 miles west of Brattleboro via VT 9 and 19 miles south of Manchester via US 7.

MANCHESTER

pop 4300

Manchester has been a fashionable resort town for almost two centuries. These days, the draw is mostly winter skiing and upscale outlet shopping (there are more than 100 shops). From mid-September to mid-November one of Vermont's biggest fall festivals, the **Stratton Arts Festival**, an arts and crafts extravaganza showcasing works by Vermont artists, takes place at nearby Stratton Mountain.

Two families put Manchester on the map. The first was native son Franklin Orvis (1824–1900), who became a New York businessman but returned to Manchester to establish the Equinox House Hotel (1849). Franklin's brother, Charles, founded the Orvis Company, makers of fly-fishing equipment, in 1856. The Manchester-based company now has a worldwide following.

The second family was that of Abraham Lincoln (1809–65). His wife Mary Todd Lincoln (1818–82) and their son Robert Todd Lincoln (1843–1926) came here during the Civil War, and Robert returned to build a mansion – Hildene – a number of years later.

Orientation & Information

US 7 bypasses the town to the east; VT 7A goes right through the town's center.

Manchester has a split personality. When the locals say 'Manchester' or 'Manchester Village,' they're referring to the southern part of the town, a beautiful, dignified, historic Vermont village centered on the huge, venerable, posh Equinox hotel.

'Manchester Center,' a few miles north along VT 7A, used to be called Factory Point, but this name didn't fit well with Manchester's resort image so it was changed. Manchester Center has several moderately priced inns and inexpensive-to-moderate restaurants, but the area is devoted mostly to upscale outlet stores – Mark Cross, Giorgio Armani, Polo etc.

Manchester and the Mountains Regional Chamber of Commerce (☎ 800-362-4414, 802-362-2100; www.manchestervermont.net; 5046 Main St, Suite 1, Manchester Center; ✷ 10am-5pm Mon-Sat year-round, 10am-2pm Sun late May–mid-Oct) Maintains an information office on the village green in Manchester Center. Staff help visitors find rooms and have printouts for hikes of varying difficulty within the Green Mountain National Forest.

Northshire Bookstore (☎ 802-362-2200; www .northshire.com; Main St; ✷ 10am-7pm) An enormous independent bookstore with comfy nooks everywhere. It shares a huge hangout space with the attached java-and-munchies joint, Spiral Café.

VERMONT

Spiral Café (☎ 802-362-9944) Offers wireless internet access and two computers with free usage.

Sights

HILDENE

The wife and children of Abraham Lincoln had tragic lives. Mary went mad and only one of four sons lived to adulthood. That son was Robert Todd Lincoln, who served on General Grant's staff during the Civil War. He later became a corporate lawyer in Chicago, president of the Pullman Palace Car Company, and secretary of war and minister (ambassador) to Great Britain. Robert Todd Lincoln's 24-room Georgian Revival mansion, which he named **Hildene** (☎ 802-362-1788; www.hildene.org; VT 7A; adult/child $12/4; ☽ 9:30am-4:30pm mid-May–Oct, 11am-3pm Thu-Mon Nov & Dec), is a national treasure. He enjoyed the house until his death in 1926, and his great-granddaughter lived in the house until her death in 1975. Soon after, it was converted into a museum, and filled with many of the Lincoln family's personal effects and furnishings. These include the hat Abraham Lincoln probably wore when he delivered the Gettysburg Address, and remarkable brass casts of his hands, the right one swollen from shaking hands while campaigning for presidency. Free tours of Hildene depart every 30 minutes. Be alert for the 1000-pipe Aeolian organ, which springs to life during tours.

Hildene also has a packed concert and lecture-series calendar; check its website for up-to-date listings. It also makes a great place to cross-country ski and snowshoe until about mid-March.

SOUTHERN VERMONT ARTS CENTER

In addition to excellent outdoor sculpture gardens, the **Southern Vermont Arts Center** (☎ 802-362-1405; www.svac.org; West Rd; adult/child $8/3; ☽ galleries 10am-5pm Tue-Sat, noon-5pm Sun) has a full program of concerts from June through August. Its 10 galleries of classic and contemporary art feature touring shows of sculpture, paintings, prints and photography. Lectures and jazz concerts are held in the 430-seat Arkell Pavilion. After enjoying the museum and surrounding trails, consider staying for a light lunch at its Garden Cafe.

AMERICAN MUSEUM OF FLY FISHING & ORVIS

The **museum** (☎ 802-362-3300; www.amff.com; 4070 VT 7A; adult/child $5/3; ☽ 10am-4pm), next door to Orvis, has perhaps the world's best display of fly-fishing equipment. This includes fly collections and rods used by Ernest Hemingway, Bing Crosby and several US presidents, including Herbert Hoover. If you can believe it, the latter penned the tome *Fishing for Fun & to Wash Your Soul*.

If you're hooked, head across the parking lot to **Orvis** (☎ 802-362-3750; www.orvis.com), on the west side of VT 7A. Try out a rod in the trout ponds on the grounds of this famous fishing, hunting and general outdoor sporting outfitter, or inquire about its fly-fishing schools and free seminars. Across another parking lot is a warehouse filled with sale items, and the rod-building shop (with free tours at 10am Monday to Friday).

MT EQUINOX

To reach 3816ft **Mt Equinox** (☎ 802-362-1114; www.equinoxmountain.com; car & driver $7, each additional passenger $2; ☽ 9am-dusk May-Oct as the snow allows), follow VT 7A south out of Manchester and look for Skyline Dr. From Manchester to the summit is just 5 miles via this private toll road that winds seemingly up to the top of the world. It's believed that the mountain's name is a corrupted Native American phrase meaning 'place where the very top is.' Rather than drive, you could undertake the five-plus-hour hike (2918ft elevation gain) on Burr and Burton, and Lookout Rock Trails, which will take you to the summit and back. Hiking information is available at the Equinox hotel and resort (p372), where the trail begins.

Activities

BROMLEY MOUNTAIN

Approximately 5 miles from town, 3284ft **Bromley Mountain** (☎ 802-824-5522, 800-865-4786; www.bromley.com; VT 11, Peru; per ride $3.50-7.50, book of 10 rides $55; ☽ 9am-5pm Jun-Oct, 8:30am-4:30pm Nov-Apr, closed May) is a small family-oriented resort featuring 43 downhill ski runs and 10 chairlifts. In summer, you can try the Alpine Slide (the longest run in North America), a climbing wall, trampolines, a water slide, a children's adventure park and more. Chairlifts whisk hikers and sightseers up to trails. The Long/Appalachian Trail runs right through Bromley. In mid-August, the **UX Open** (www.uxopen.com) – a play-off for the wildest golf game in the country – takes place on these brush-hogged slopes.

THE LONG, LONG TRAIL

America's first long-distance hiking trail, Vermont's Long Trail, is a 264-mile mountainous corridor that runs the length of the state from Massachusetts to Canada.

Backpackers have been hiking the south-to-north ridge of the Green Mountains since 1930, when the Green Mountain Club finished clearing the length of the trail. Today, the club has over 9500 members and maintains the trail system, which covers 440 miles when you include the 175 miles of side trails.

And what an impressive network of trails it is. Often only 3ft wide, the Long Trail crosses streams, skirts ponds, and weaves up and down mountains on open ridges to bare summits that offer exceptional vistas of the entire state. Wave after wave of hillside gently rolls back to a sea of green dotted with the occasional pasture or meadow. A little less than half of the trail is located inside the **Green Mountain National Forest** (☎ 802-747-6700).

The trail is best taken from south to north so that you don't have to read the *Guide Book of the Long Trail* backwards. Another fine companion, *The Long Trail End-to-Ender's Guide*, is packed with nitty-gritty details on equipment sales and repairs, and mail drops and B&Bs that provide trailhead shuttle services. Both guides are published by the **Green Mountain Club** (☎ 802-244-7037; www.greenmountainclub.org; 4711 Waterbury-Stowe Rd, Waterbury Center, VT 05677; 🕑 9am-5pm Mon-Fri Nov-Mar, 9am-5pm daily Jun-Aug).

For shelter, the Green Mountain Club maintains more than 60 lodges and lean-tos along the trail. Hikers can easily walk from one shelter to the next in a day because the rest stops were built at 5- to 7-mile intervals. However, it is imperative that you bring a tent in case a shelter is full. Although the trail is wonderful for a trip of several days, it is also popular for day hikes.

For more information, contact the Green Mountain Club.

STRATTON MOUNTAIN

Stratton Mountain (☎ 800-843-6867, 802-297-2200; www.stratton.com; VT 30, Bondville) is an all-season playground about 16 miles east of Manchester. For downhill skiing and snowboarding (mid-November through April, conditions permitting), it has 90 trails and 100 acres of glade and tree skiing terrain, 13 lifts (including a summit gondola) and a vertical drop of more than 2000ft on a 3875ft mountain. There are also 20 miles of cross-country trails. Summer activities include golf, tennis, squash, swimming, hiking, horseback riding, mountain biking and tons more.

HIKING & BIKING

The **Appalachian Trail** passes just east of Manchester, and in this area it follows the same route as Vermont's Long Trail (above). Shelters pop up about every 10 miles; some are staffed from June to early October. Good day hikes include one to the summit of Bromley Mountain and another to Stratton Pond. For details and maps, contact the **USFA Green Mountain National Forest** (☎ 802-362-2307; www.fs.fed.us/r9/gmfl; 2538 Depot St, VT 11/30), about 3 miles east of Manchester Center. The chamber of commerce also has detailed printouts.

About a mile from Manchester Center, **Battenkill Sports Bicycle Shop** (☎ 802-362-2734, 800-340-2734; cnr US 7 & VT 11/30; 🕑 9:30am-5:30pm) rents road, mountain and hybrid bikes for as little as $25 daily, including helmet, lock, trail recommendations and map. It also does repairs.

Sleeping

BUDGET

Camping on the Battenkill River (p368) is just south of Manchester on VT 7A.

Casa Blanca Motel (☎ 802-362-2145, 800-254-2145; www.casablancamotel.com; 5927 VT 7A; cottages $62-92; 🖳 wi-fi 🖳) This tidy collection of cottages on the northern fringes of town has 12 units that have been renovated in different themes.

Aspen Motel (☎ 802-362-2450; 5669 VT 7A; r $70-125; 🖳 🖳) A sprawling place north of Manchester, the Aspen has a social room with a fireplace and 24 rooms, including one cottage suite with a fireplace. Has fine views of the Green Mountains to the east and Mt Equinox to the west.

MIDRANGE

Barnstead Innstead (☎ 802-362-1619; www.barnstead inn.com; 349 Bonnet St; s $99, d $120, ste $150-160; wi-fi 🖳) Barely a half-mile from Manchester Center, this converted 1830s hay barn exudes charm in a good location. The 14 rooms have refrigerators and homey braided rugs, while the porch features wicker rockers for watching the world pass by.

our pick Seth Warner Inn (☎ 802-362-3830; www
.sethwarnerinn.com; 2353 VT 7A; r incl full breakfast $130-140)
Named after the colonel who, along with his Green Mountain Boys, was instrumental in winning the Battle of Bennington, this five-room inn dates back to 1800. Its rooms have exposed beams and country quilts, antiques, period restoration and the occasional moose straying through the backyard. No children under 10.

Johnny Seesaw's Country Inn & Restaurant (☎ 802-
824-5533, 800-424-2729; www.jseesaw.com; 3574 VT 11; incl
full breakfast d $160, ste $180, 2-r cottage $400) Two hundred yards north of Bromley Mountain, this rustic, laid-back lodge has a huge, circular, stone fireplace in the common/dining room. While the cottage and its 18 guest rooms are basic, the tales told around the fire are tall and unforgettable. Just imagine what Charles Lindbergh said when he stayed; he heads the cast of characters who have visited. On a more prosaic note, you can catch live (usually acoustic) music Friday through Sunday, or play tennis on the inn's clay court.

TOP END

Inn at Manchester (☎ 802-362-1793, 800-273-1793;
www.innatmanchester.com; 3967 VT 7A; r incl full breakfast
$155-235, ste $195-295; wi-fi) This restored inn and carriage house offers 13 rooms and five suites to a loyal clientele. There's a big front porch, afternoon teas with fresh-baked goodies, an expansive backyard and comfortable common rooms, one with a wee pub.

Inn at Ormsby Hill (☎ 802-362-1163, 800-670-2841;
www.ormsbyhill.com; 1842 VT 7A; r incl full breakfast $195-
435) Just southwest of Manchester, Ormsby Hill is arguably one of the most welcoming inns in all of New England. Fireplaces, two-person Jacuzzis, flat-screen TVs, antiques, gracious innkeepers and 2.5 acres of lawn are among features that draw repeat guests to its 10 rooms. The inn's absolutely bountiful breakfast offerings are without equal.

1811 House (☎ 802-362-1811; www.1811house.com;
3654 VT 7A; s $140, d $210-260, ste $300; wi-fi) This refined Federal house, surrounded by 7 acres of lawns and gardens, was built in the 1770s and has served as an inn since 1811. In addition to 13 antique-filled rooms with oriental rugs and wood-burning fireplaces, its engaging

little pub (open to the public, 5:30pm to 8pm) features dark wood walls and low beams hung with pewter tankards and assorted antique swords. It's the perfect place to linger over a single malt from its impressive selection of 93 scotches.

Equinox (☎ 802-362-4700, 800-362-4747; www
.equinoxresort.com; 3567 Main St, VT 7A; r $229-509, ste
$469-1200; wi-fi) One of Vermont's most famous resorts, this grand property smack in the center of town boasts 183 elegant rooms, an 18-hole golf course, two tennis courts, a state-of-the-art fitness center and full-service spa. Other activities include falconry, archery, off-road driving and snowmobiling. Room rates vary with the view and season. While the presidential suites boast two bathrooms and period furnishings, the lap of luxury is truly found in the Dormy House – a duplex suite with a mirrored Jacuzzi, slate flooring and a patio with a private barbecue.

Eating

BUDGET

Mrs Murphy's Donuts & Coffee Shop (☎ 802-362-
1874; VT 11/30 E; dishes $3; 5am-6pm Mon-Sat, 5am-
4pm Sun) Pull up to the U-shaped counters at Manchester's favorite down-home, basic diner, which serves fresh doughnuts and bacon-and-egg 'tuck-ins' throughout the day – and that's about it, but be sure to order more than one doughnut, or you'll regret it.

Little Rooster Cafe (☎ 802-362-3496; VT 7A; dishes
$6-9; breakfast & lunch Thu-Tue) This colorful spot serves dishes like Asian vegetables with noodles, and chicken or grilled portobello focaccia. It's very popular with locals and shoppers so be prepared to wait for a table.

Up for Breakfast (☎ 802-362-4204; 4935 Main St;
dishes $6-14; 7am-noon) This artsy nook serves breakfast dishes ranging from cheddar omelette to wild turkey hash (a regional specialty). Sit at the tiny counter to catch the action in the kitchen.

Garden Cafe (☎ 802-366-8297; West Rd; dishes
around $10; lunch Tue-Sat May–mid-Oct) Gaze out over the sculpture garden in the indoor and outdoor café at the Southern Vermont Arts Center, featuring an array of sandwiches and salads.

MIDRANGE

Forty Nine Forty (☎ 802-362-9839; 4940 Main St; all-
day menu $5-9, meals $12-21; lunch & dinner; V) In addition to good-noshing appetizers, this

pleasant, bright bistro serves veggie burgers, Black Angus burgers and grilled Tuscan cheese sandwiches all day. The evening meals are simple, with grilled chicken, stir-fry or pasta *Alfredo*.

Dormy Grill (☎ 802-362-4700; Gleneagles Golf Course, Union St; meals $13-17; ☒ 11:30am-4pm & 5:30-8pm Thu-Sun summer) Reserve a table overlooking the links and chow down on American bistro fare, like buffalo wings, crab cakes or the Equinox Steak 'Cobb' Salad (guajillo-marinated hanger steak, blue cheese, buttermilk onion rings and romaine lettuce). The mountain view is alluring but watch out for stray golf balls.

TOP END

Black Swan (☎ 802-362-3807; 4384 VT 7A; meals $19-27; ☒ dinner Thu-Tue) This 1834 brick Colonial house is divided into small, charming dining rooms with candlelight and working fireplaces. Continental cuisine is served with a West Coast accent, and everything at the Black Swan is imaginatively presented and spectacularly delicious.

our pick **Ye Olde Tavern** (☎ 802-362-0611; 214 N Main St; meals $20-28; ☒ lunch & dinner) Hearth-side dining at candlelit tables enhances the experience at this gracious roadside 1790s inn. The menu is wide-ranging, but the 'Yankee favorites' like traditional pot roast cooked in the tavern's own ale and New England scrod (baked with Vermont cheddar) seal the deal.

Bistro Henry (☎ 802-362-4982; VT 11/30; meals $23-30; ☒ dinner Tue-Sun) This casual, chef-owned bistro serves creative modern cuisine highlighting fresh seafood, aged meats and fresh vegetables. Its acclaimed wine selection features eclectic and hard-to-find labels.

Mistral's (☎ 802-362-1779; 10 Toll Gate Rd; meals $29-38; ☒ dinner Wed-Mon) Nestled deep in the woods (off VT 30 and VT 11 east of town) and overlooking Bromley Brook, Mistral's offers fine dining on Norwegian salmon or roast duck in an incredibly intimate setting.

Getting There & Away

Vermont Transit (☎ 802-864-6811, 800-552-8737; www .vermonttransit.com) runs daily buses (number varies seasonally) from Manchester to Middlebury ($16, two hours) and onward to Burlington and Montreal. The bus stop is at **Village Valet** (☎ 802-362-1226; 4945 Main St).

From Manchester Village, take the back road (West Rd) north to VT 30 to Dorset.

Manchester is 32 miles (one hour with traffic) south of Rutland via US 7, but it's far more scenic to head north on VT 30 through Dorset and onward to Middlebury.

AROUND MANCHESTER

Manchester's a terrific base for visiting quintessential Vermont towns, whether they are pristine like Dorset or more workaday like Pawlet.

Dorset

pop 2050

Six miles northwest of Manchester along VT 30, Dorset resembles a prototypical Vermont village, with its stately inn, lofty church and village green. The difference between this and other Vermont villages, however, is that in Dorset the sidewalks, the church and lots of other buildings are made of creamy marble.

Settled in 1768, Dorset became a farming community with a healthy trade in marble. The **quarry**, about a mile south of the village center, supplied much of the marble for the grand New York Public Library building and numerous other public edifices, but it's now filled with water. It's a lovely place to picnic.

If your interest in marble is piqued, stop in at the **Danby Marble Company** (☎ 802-293-5425; VT 7; ☒ May-Oct & mid-Nov–Dec), on the VT 7 north of Danby. The town is the site of what's billed as 'the largest underground marble quarry in the world.' Perhaps you're in need of some marble cut to your specifications? They make everything here from bookends to chessboards to vases.

More than a century ago the village of Dorset became known as a summer playground for well-to-do city folks. Today, in addition to the village's pristine beauty, the **Dorset Playhouse** (☎ 802-867-5777; www.dorsetplayers .org; Cheney Rd) draws a sophisticated audience. In summer the actors are professionals; at other times they're community players.

Innkeepers Jean and Jim Kingston greet travelers at the tidy 1800s **Dovetail Inn** (☎ 802-867-5747, 888-867-5747; www.dovetailinn.com; VT 30; incl continental breakfast d $125, ste $195), which faces the village green. Breakfast is served in the comfort of the 11 well-kept guest rooms.

Vermont's oldest continuously operating inn (in business since 1796), the **Dorset Inn** (☎ 802-867-5500, 877-367-7389; www.dorsetinn.com; cnr Church & Main Sts; s incl full breakfast $100-145, r $145-225;

VERMONT

wi-fi) is still going strong. Just off VT 30 facing the village green, this traditional but updated inn has 31 renovated guest rooms. The front-porch rockers provide a nice setting for watching the comings and goings of this sleepy Vermont town. Opt for rates that include dinner, as the chef-owned restaurant is highly regarded.

Just north of East Dorset, the 430-acre **Emerald Lake State Park** (☎ 802-362-1655; www .vtstateparks.com; US 7; RV sites/campsites $23/14; ⌚ late May–mid-Oct) has 105 sites, including 32 lean-tos. You can swim and canoe on the 80ft-deep lake and hike through the mountains; some trails connect with the Long Trail.

Peltier's (☎ 802-867-4400; VT 30) has been an institution since 1816. It sells all manner of edible Vermont items, especially high-end gourmet goodies and picnic fixings. Staff will even prepare almost any kind of fish on request.

Pawlet
pop 1400

Heading north along VT 30 you'll pass through the blink-and-you'll-miss-it village of Pawlet. Stop at the fine old-fashioned **Mach's General Store** (☎ 802-325-3405; VT 30; ⌚ 10am-5pm), which generates its electricity from an adjacent stream passing through a gorge. You can see all this from inside the store, thanks to a glass counter.

The village consists of a few little shops and the **Station Restaurant** (☎ 802-325-3041; ⌚ 6am-3pm), formerly a 1905 railroad station in another town: the structure was converted into a classic diner, moved to Pawlet and situated above this babbling brook. Complete with swivel stools and counter, it's also atmospheric thanks to hook-hung cups bearing the names of regulars.

Continuing north, take a quick detour into **East Poultney** on VT 140 from VT 30. The traditional town green, lined with a fine church and 18th- and 19th-century houses, has a classic old general store.

CENTRAL VERMONT

Vermont's heart features some of New England's most bucolic countryside. Cows begin to outnumber people just north of Rutland, Vermont's second-largest city. Lovers of the outdoors make frequent pilgrimages to central Vermont, especially to the resort areas of Killington, Sugarbush and Mad River Glen, which attract countless skiers and summer hikers. For those interested in indoor pleasures, antique shops and art galleries dot the back roads between picturesque covered bridges.

WOODSTOCK & QUECHEE VILLAGE
pop 3300

Chartered in 1761, Woodstock has been the highly dignified seat of scenic Windsor County since 1766. It prospered in this role. The townspeople built many grand houses surrounding the oval village green, and four of Woodstock's churches can claim bells cast by Paul Revere. Senator Jacob Collamer, a friend of Abraham Lincoln's, once observed, 'The good people of Woodstock have less incentive than others to yearn for heaven.'

Today Woodstock is still very beautiful and very wealthy. Spend some time walking around the green, surrounded by Federal and Greek Revival homes and public buildings, or along the Ottauquechee River, spanned by three covered bridges. The Rockefellers and the Rothschilds own estates in the surrounding countryside, and the well-to-do come to stay at the grand Woodstock Inn & Resort. Despite its high-tone reputation, the town also offers some reasonably priced lodgings and meal possibilities.

About five minutes east of Woodstock, small, twee Quechee Village is home to Quechee Gorge, Vermont's answer to the Grand Canyon, as well as several outstanding restaurants and working farms.

Many nearby state parks (see p376) offer hiking trails and lakes good for swimming, boating and canoeing.

Orientation & Information

Woodstock, off US 4, is part of the Upper Connecticut River Valley community that includes Hanover and Lebanon, in New Hampshire, and Norwich and White River Junction, in Vermont. People think nothing of driving from one of these towns to another to find accommodations, a meal or an amusement. Quechee lies further east along US 4.

Woodstock Area Chamber of Commerce (☎ 802-457-3555; www.woodstockvt.com; 18 Central St; ⌚ 9:30am-5pm May-Oct) Has a small information booth on the village green that can be quite helpful, particularly with accommodations. Parking places are at a premium in Woodstock, and enforcement is strict, so obey the regulations.

Yankee Bookshop (☎ 802-457-2411; 12 Central St; ☯ 10am-5pm) Great for local guidebooks, maps, and books in general. It's particularly strong in works by local authors and publishers.

Sights & Activities

BILLINGS FARM & MUSEUM

After your walk around Woodstock pay a visit to this **farm museum** (☎ 802-457-2355; www .billingsfarm.org; VT 12; adult/child/student/senior $10/3/8/9; ☯ 10am-5pm daily May-Oct, 10am-4pm Sat & Sun Nov-Feb), less than a mile north of the village green, at River Rd. Railroad magnate Frederick Billings founded the farm in the late 19th century and ran it on sound 'modern' principles of conservation and animal husbandry. In 1871 he imported cattle directly from Britain's Isle of Jersey, and the purebred descendants of these early bovine immigrants still give milk on the farm today. Life on the working farm is a mix of 19th- and 20th-century methods, all of which delight curious children. Call for details about the daily demonstrations, audio-visual shows and special programs.

MARSH-BILLINGS-ROCKEFELLER NATIONAL HISTORICAL PARK

This **mansion & park** (☎ 802-457-3368; www.nps.gov /mabi; Elm St; tours adult/senior/child $8/$4/free; ☯ 10am-4pm late May-Oct), off VT 12, focuses on the relationship between land stewardship and environmental conservation. Tours are run every 30 minutes. While there is an admission fee to the mansion, the 20 miles of trails and carriage roads are free for exploring and the view across the valley from 1250ft-high Mt Tom warrants the trek. In the winter the roads and trails are groomed for snowshoeing and cross-country skiing. Some start on the far side of the Ottauquechee from the village green, along the east edge of the cemetery. When the mansion is closed, the Woodstock Inn & Resort has a walking-trail pamphlet.

QUECHEE GORGE

Lurking beneath US 4, less than a mile east of Quechee Village, the **gorge** is a 163ft-deep scar that cuts about 3000ft along a stream that you can view from a bridge or easily access by footpaths from the road. A series of undemanding trails cut away from the stream, none of which should take you over an hour.

VERMONT INSTITUTE OF NATURAL SCIENCE

Learn all about raptors and other birds of prey at the **Vermont Institute of Natural Science** (☎ 802-457-2779; www.vinsweb.org; VT 4; adult/child $8/6.50; ☯ 9am-5pm May-Oct, 10am-4pm Nov-Apr), just before you reach Quechee coming from Woodstock. It houses two dozen species of raptors, ranging from the tiny, 3oz saw-whet owl to the mighty bald eagle. The birds that end up here have sustained permanent injuries that do not allow them to return to life in the wild. The three self-guided nature trails are delightful for hikes in summer or for snowshoeing in winter.

SUGARBUSH FARM

While this working **farm** (☎ 802-457-1757; www .sugarbushfarm.com; 591 Sugarbush Farm Rd; admission free; 8am-5pm Mon-Fri, 9am-5pm Sat & Sun) at the end of a bucolic road also collects maple sap, cheddar is the king. See how it's made and sample their 14 varieties – from the mild sage cheddar to the jalapeño and cayenne pepper variety to the prize-winning hickory and smoked cheddar. Wax-coated bars of the curd are sold and travel well.

HIKING & BIKING

Bike Vermont (☎ 800-257-2226; www.bikevermont .com; 6-day trip per person spring $1060, summer $1145, fall $1310) operates six-night bike tours in the area, including inn-to-inn tours.

   Woodstock Sports (☎ 802-457-1568; 30 Central St; ☯ 8:30am-5:30pm Mon-Sat) and **Cyclery Plus** (☎ 802-457-3377; 490 Woodstock Rd, US 4; ☯ 10am-5pm Mon-Sat) rent mountain and speed bicycles and provide maps of good local routes. Full-day rentals are $25.

SKIING & SNOWBOARDING

In 1934 Woodstockers installed the first mechanical ski tow in the USA, and skiing is still important here. **Suicide Six** (☎ 802-457-6661, 800-448-7900; www.woodstockinn.com; VT 12, Pomfret; ☯ mid-Dec–Mar), 3 miles north of Woodstock, is known for challenging downhill runs. The lower slopes are fine for beginners, though. There are 23 trails (30% beginner, 40% intermediate, 30% expert) and three lifts.

   The full-service **Woodstock Ski Touring Center** (☎ 802-457-6674; www.woodstockinn.com; VT 106), just south of town, rents equipment and has 50 miles of groomed touring trails, including one that takes in 1250ft Mt Tom.

VERMONT

EXPLORING BEYOND THE GORGE

Getting to the middle of nowhere is easy in Vermont. While the rumpled green countryside offers endless miles of solitude, just about any blob of blue on the map will serve as an escape hatch as well – though few as perfectly as **North Hartland Lake**.

Within minutes of Quechee Village, you can scoot your boat off the North Hartland Lake Recreation Area ramp. Trees and meadows swallow virtually every shred of evidence of the existence of anyone beyond you and whoever else is plying these tranquil waters.

You head into the various nooks and rivulets of the 215-acre lake, and just beyond sight of the beach, a noisy great-blue heron rookery occupies the tops of the pines on the north shore. Around the bend an eagle may just be pulling this afternoon's catch out of the water. You'll see an occasional shallow-domed muskrat lodge, and turtles soaking up the sun on floating logs. Keep an eye out for browsing deer on the clearings of the north shore. Follow the left channel as the lake turns swampy, and the channel on either side of a small island leads to the mouth of **Quechee Gorge**. Park your boat and scramble onto the ledgy outcrop for a rewarding picnic and swimming break. Check out the stunning view up the gorge, with the US 4 bridge appearing delicate and distant. Be aware that the water level can rise quickly during dam releases, so keep an ear cocked for the alarm that sounds this occasional event. Take the walking trail from the VT 4 bridge at the gorge, head away from the dam and, at all the forks, keep veering right, or toward the lake, for a lovely ramble (this will make it easier to find your way back, as well).

From VT 4 head south on Hartland/Quechee Rd for 1.5 miles, then left on Clay Hill Rd for just shy of 3 miles to reach the parking area of the **North Hartland Lake Recreation Area** (☎ 802-295-2855; 112 Clay Hill Rd, Hartland; per person/car $1/4; ☒ 8am-8pm Apr-Oct).

With a kiosk just east of the Quechee Gorge bridge, and a main location behind Quechee Inn, Main St (from VT 4, go right after the covered bridge, and the inn is half a mile on the left), **Wilderness Trails** (☎ 802-295-7620; www.wildernesstrailsvt.com) rents boats at $25 per day from May to October. It also rents bikes. From December to March it rents cross-country skis and snowshoes – and be sure to ask about its moonlight bonfire trips to the lake. It also offers fly-fishing instruction for $135 per person, plus $30 for each additional person (with a maximum of four people per group). Fishing licenses ($15) are required for this and are supplied by the company. A shuttle service to the North Hartland Lake, or the Connecticut or White Rivers, adds $10 per person to the cost.

Sleeping

BUDGET

Thetford State Park (☎ 802-785-2266; www.vtstateparks .com; Academy Rd, Thetford; RV sites/campsites $21/14; ☒ mid-May–mid-Oct) You'll find 16 sites (two lean-tos) plus hiking trails and a playground here. From I-91 exit 14 go a mile west on VT 113 to Thetford Hill, then a mile south on Academy Rd.

Quechee Gorge State Park (☎ 802-295-2990, 886-2434; www.vtstateparks.com/htm/quechee; 190 Dewey Mills Rd, White River Junction; RV sites $21-23, campsites $14-16; ☒ mid-May–mid-Oct) Eight miles east of Woodstock and 3 miles west of I-89 along US 4, this 611-acre spot has 54 pine-shaded sites (with seven lean-tos) that are a short stroll from Quechee Gorge.

Silver Lake State Park (☎ 802-234-9451, 886-2434; www.vtstateparks.com; RV sites $23-25, campsites $16-18; ☒ mid-May–mid-Oct) This 34-acre park (off VT

12 in Barnard) is 10 miles north of Woodstock and has 47 sites (with seven lean-tos), a beach, boat and canoe rentals and fishing.

MIDRANGE

Applebutter Inn (☎ 802-457-4158, 800-486-1374; www .applebutterinn.com; 7511 Happy Valley Rd, Taftsville; d incl breakfast $100-215) Just 3 miles east of Woodstock and set on 12 extraordinary acres with one of Vermont's most picturesque barns, the Applebutter is an 1854 Federal-style house with six guest rooms and a wonderful old kitchen. The house is furnished with period pieces and Oriental rugs that partly cover the wide-plank floors.

our pick **Ardmore Inn** (☎ 802-457-3887, 800-497-5692; www.ardmoreinn.com; 23 Pleasant St; r incl full breakfast $135-195) Congenial centrally located inn in a stately 1867 Greek Revival building that features five antique-laden rooms with oriental rugs and private marble bathrooms. The owners are especially helpful and the breakfasts are seemingly never-ending.

Shire Motel (☎ 802-457-2211; www.shiremotel.com; 46 Pleasant St; d $148-178; 💻) Within walking distance of the town center on US 4, this place has 42 comfortable rooms (some with fireplaces) and some luxury suites. It's located on the Ottauquechee River, which visitors can mull over from rockers on a wraparound porch.

TOP END

Village Inn of Woodstock (☎ 802-457-1255, 800-722-4571; www.villageinnofwoodstock.com; 41 Pleasant St; r incl full breakfast $150-320) This lovely Victorian mansion, situated on a 40-acre estate, has eight guest rooms. Most feature four-post feather beds, down comforters and period details like oak wainscoting and tin ceilings. Enjoy the cozy tavern with its stained-glass windows and full bar. Chefs David and Evelyn prepare a breakfast you're sure to remember fondly.

Parker House Inn (☎ 802-295-6077; www.theparkerhouseinn.com; 1792 Main St, Quechee; d incl full breakfast $195-275) A Victorian-style redbrick house built in 1857 for former Vermont senator Joseph Parker, this antique-laden inn features seven large guest rooms. The downstairs parlors have been converted into dining rooms, but a small sitting room remains for your use on the 2nd floor. A riverside porch just begs to be part of your day. It's just 100 yards from one of the Ottauquechee River's covered bridges and a waterfall.

MORE THAN HOT AIR

While the Quechee-Woodstock general area affords no end of outdoor activities, none is likely to prove as memorable as a balloon ride. **Balloons Over New England** (☎ 800-788-5562; www.balloonsovernewengland.com) do it in style, with 'champagne' trips that last 2½ to three hours for $245 per person. **Balloons of Vermont** (☎ 802-291-4887; www.vtballooning.com) launch from behind the Simon Pearce Glass factory and restaurant and serve a continental breakfast for $245 per person, for 2-½-hour trips. Needless to say, the world below is particularly beautiful during the fall foliage and you should be sure to reserve well in advance.

Woodstock Inn & Resort (☎ 802-457-1100, 800-448-7900; www.woodstockinn.com; 14 The Green; r $199-299, ste $454-559; wi-fi 💻) One of Vermont's most luxurious hotels, this resort has extensive grounds, a formal dining room, an indoor sports center and 144 guest rooms and suites. A fire blazes in the huge stone fireplace from late fall through spring, making this famous inn even more welcoming. Facilities include an 18-hole golf course, tennis courts, cross-country skiing and a fitness center.

Eating & Drinking

BUDGET

If you have a picnic lunch, take it to the George Perkins Marsh Man and Nature Park, a tiny hideaway right next to the river on Central St, across the street from Pane e Salute.

Mountain Creamery (☎ 802-457-1715; 33 Central St; dishes $4-6; ⏰ 7am-3pm) In addition to serving Woodstock's most scrumptious apple pie, it offers sandwiches, salads, soups and other yummy picnic fare. The house-made ice cream is particularly revered.

Long Trail Brewing Company (☎ 802-672-5011; cnr US 4 & VT 100A; meals $8-12; ⏰ 10am-6pm Mon-Sat, 1-5pm Sun) Halfway between Killington and Woodstock, the brewer of 'Vermont's No 1 Selling Amber' draws crowds for its grub as well as beer. Weather permitting, you can sit on the patio by the river, have a sandwich or burger and wash it down with a cold hearty stout or a fruity blackberry wheat ale. There are free tours of the brewery.

MIDRANGE

Pane e Salute (☎ 802-457-4882; 61 Central St; meals $6-22, prix fixe $39; ⏰ breakfast & lunch Thu-Sun year-round, call for winter dinner times) Specialties include authentic Italian pastries and the best cup of espresso this side of the Connecticut River. Expect buttery panettone, rolls filled with ricotta, pear and chocolate, and Florentine coffee cake. In the evening, you'll be rewarded with classic northern Italian dishes, complemented by an extensive wine list.

Skunk Hollow Tavern (☎ 802-436-2139; Hartland Four Corners; meals $10-26; ⏰ dinner Wed-Sun) Fear not – there are no skunks on the menu at this tiny 200-year-old tavern 8 miles south of Woodstock, with worn wooden floors that ooze history. You can have burgers or fish-and-chips ($8) at the bar or head upstairs, where it's more intimate, to enjoy rack of lamb ($24). The same menu is available upstairs and downstairs. It's a treat when there's live music (Wednesday and Friday) and the band takes up half the room.

Prince & the Pauper (☎ 802-457-1818; 24 Elm St; meals $23-26, bistro menu $13-19, prix fixe $38; ✆ dinner) Woodstock's elegant New American bistro serves a sublime three-course prix-fixe menu. You might order applewood-smoked ruby trout with grilled corn cake and crème fraîche from the menu. Depending on your appetite, lighter bistro fare is always an enticing option as well.

TOP END

Simon Pearce Restaurant (☎ 802-295-1470; The Mill, Main St, Quechee; meals $13-31; ✆ lunch & dinner) Be sure to reserve a window table in the dining room suspended over the river in this converted brick mill. Local ingredients are used to inventive effect here to produce such delicacies as crab and cod melt or the seared chicken (with roasted corn mascarpone polenta). The restaurant's beautiful stemware is blown by hand in the Simon Pearce Glass workshops, also in the mill. This place is difficult to leave.

Parker House Inn (☎ 802-295-6077; 16 Main St, Quechee; meals $24-34; ✆ dinner) Catching much of the overspill of Simon Pearce next door, the slightly pricier Parker House serves modern French fare in the front room or out on the terrace overlooking the waterfall. The menu is seasonal, but look for the likes of cornmeal-crusted salmon (with homemade blueberry chutney) or balsamic-glazed sea scallops.

Jackson House Inn (☎ 802-457-2065; 114-3 Senior Lane, US 4; prix fixe $55; ✆ dinner daily Jul-Oct, Wed-Sun Nov-Jun) Expect tranquility, exquisite views of Mt Tom and premier cuisine at the Jackson House. The prix-fixe menu might feature scallops and stone crab or duck in phyllo, followed by a main dish of pepper-crusted tuna or a juicy little squab lightly caramelized with maple syrup. The chef also offers a 10-course tasting menu at $95, a true treat for your tastebuds. End with the pumpkin *brûlée*, steamed lemon pudding or tarte tatin.

Shopping

Old Mill Marketplace (☎ 802-672-1331; VT 4, Bridgewater; ✆ 10am-6pm) The three-story converted 1820s mill has space for some 20 local craftspeople selling soap, pottery, furniture, jewelry and more. The Hillbilly Flea Market in the basement is an upscale treasure trove open from Thursday to Sunday.

Simon Pearce Glass (☎ 802-295-2771; www.simonpearce.com; 1760 Main St, Quechee; ✆ store 9am-4pm, glassblowing 9am-9pm) At this exceptional studio and shop visitors can watch artisans produce distinctive pieces of original glass.

Getting There & Away

Vermont Transit (☎ 802-864-6811, 800-552-8737; www.vermonttransit.com) buses stop at nearby **White River Junction** (☎ 802-295-3011; Sykes Ave). If you take the bus to White River Junction on your way to Woodstock, you will need to take a taxi (drivers wait at the bus station) from there to Woodstock, a distance of 16 miles.

Amtrak (☎ 800-872-7245; www.amtrak.com) runs the *Vermonter* train, which stops at nearby White River Junction.

It's a straight shot (two hours, 89 miles) via US 4 east to I-89 north to Burlington from Woodstock. It'll take a mere half-hour (20 miles) to reach Killington via US 4 west.

KILLINGTON MOUNTAIN
pop 1100

The largest ski resort in the east, Killington spans seven mountains, highlighted by 4241ft Killington Peak, the second highest in Vermont. It operates the largest snowmaking system in North America and, while upwards of 20,000 people can find lodging within 20 miles, its numerous outdoor activities are all centrally located on the mountain.

Orientation & Information

Officially, the mountain town is Killington Village, but there's really not a lot there besides a post office. All the action can be found along Killington Rd on the way up the mountain.

Killington Central Reservations (☎ 800-621-6867; www.killington.com; US 4; ✆ 8am-9pm Nov-May) The best place to go for accommodations advice and help. Check in advance for info on package deals.

Killington Chamber of Commerce (☎ 802-773-4181; www.killingtonchamber.com; US 4 W; ✆ 9am-5pm Mon-Fri, occasionally 10am-2pm Sat) Conveniently located on US 4.

Sights & Activities
KILLINGTON RESORT

Vermont's prime **ski resort** (☎ 802-422-3261, 800-621-6867; www.killington.com) is enormous, yet the East Coast's answer to Vail runs efficiently enough (it has five separate lodges, each with a different emphasis, as well as 32 lifts) to avoid overcrowding.

WORTH THE TRIP: THE COOLIDGE HOMESTEAD

'I have never been hurt by what I have not said,' remarked Calvin Coolidge (1872–1933) – and you can quote him on it. The 30th president of the USA was born in Plymouth, Vermont, and attended Amherst College in Massachusetts. He opened a law practice in 1898, in Northampton, Maine, and then ran for local office. Following election, Coolidge served as state senator, lieutenant governor and governor of Massachusetts. Elected vice-president on the Warren Harding ticket in 1920, he assumed the presidency upon Harding's death in 1923. Vice-president Coolidge was visiting his boyhood home in Plymouth when word came of Harding's death. His father, the local justice of the peace, administered the presidential oath of office by kerosene lamp at 2:47am on August 3, 1923.

Known for his simple, forthright style and honesty, Coolidge was notoriously tight-lipped. Once, his hostess at a dinner party told him that she'd made a bet 'that I could get more than two words out of you.' Coolidge replied, 'You lose.' Such terseness was reflected by the passiveness of his presidency. He had the good fortune to preside over a time of great prosperity – the Roaring Twenties. His laissez-faire business policies were well accepted but contributed to the stock-market crash of 1929. He declined to run for another term as president in 1928, although he probably would have won. Instead he retired to Northampton to write articles for newspapers and magazines.

Thus, the burden of blame for the Great Depression fell hard on the shoulders of the 31st president, Herbert Hoover, who had engineered many of the Coolidge administration's successes as its Secretary of Commerce. Hoover had only been in office a matter of months when the stock market crashed. In 1931, when many banks failed and a quarter of the nation's workers were unemployed, former president Coolidge reflected (with characteristic understatement), 'The country is not in good shape.'

The tranquil and perfectly manicured **Coolidge homestead** (☎ 802-672-3773; www.historicvermont.org/coolidge; VT 100A; adult/6-14yr/family $7.50/2/20; ☒ 9:30am-5pm late May–mid-Oct) is open for tours. You can check out the birthplace, Wilder Barn, now a farmers museum. Wilder House, once the home of Coolidge's mother, has become a lunchroom. Calvin Coolidge is buried in the local cemetery.

K-1 Lodge boasts the Express Gondola, which transports up to 3000 skiers per hour in heated cars along a 2.5-mile cable and is the highest lift in Vermont. **Snowshed Lodge** is an ideal base for adults looking for lessons or refresher courses. Free-ride enthusiasts should check out **Bear Mountain Lodge** for pipe action, tree skiing or rail jibbing, not to mention Outer Limits, the steepest mogul run in the East. **Ramshead Lodge** caters to children and families, as well as those looking for easier terrain, while **Lodge** is the home of the Skyeship Gondola, a two-stage gondola with quick and direct access to the Skye Peak. Each of the lodges has food courts, restaurants, bars and ski shops.

SKIING & SNOWBOARDING

Typically the ski season runs from early November through early May, enhanced by the largest snowmaking system in America. Two hundred runs snake down Killington's seven mountains (4241ft Killington Peak, 3967ft Pico Mountain, 3800ft Skye Peak, 3610ft Ramshead Peak, 3592ft Snowdon Peak, 3295ft Bear Mountain and 2456ft Sunrise Mountain), covering some 1215 acres of slopes. Of these, a quarter are considered easy, a third moderate and the rest difficult, most infamously **Outer Limits**, a very steep double black diamond run.

Snowboarders will find six challenging parks, including superpipes with 18ft walls.

HIKING & MOUNTAIN BIKING

Killington facilities are also used for other outdoor activities, notably excellent hiking and biking.

Mountain Bike & Repair Shop (☎ 802-422-6232; Killington Rd; ☒ Jun–mid-Oct) rents mountain bikes for $50 daily; helmets and trail maps are included. Serious riders will want to take the 1.25-mile K-1 gondola ride to the summit of Killington Mountain and find their way down along the 45 miles of trails. Mountain-bike trail access costs $8 daily or $30 for trail and gondola access. Inquire about guided tours and packages.

As for hiking, the Mountain Bike & Repair Shop has an excellent (free) map of 14 self-guided nature hikes. Hikers can ride the gondola to the top (adult/child/senior/family $9/5/5/20) and hike down. If you want to ride up and down, the gondola costs $13/8/8/31 per adult/child/senior/family.

Sleeping

For details of condo and house rentals and hotels, the Killington Resort (p378) really finds the best deals.

Gifford Woods State Park (☎ 802-775-5354, 886-2434; www.vtstateparks.com; Gifford Woods Rd, Killington; RV sites $21-23, campsites $14-16; ☉ late May–early Oct) A half-mile north of US 4 and VT 100, this park has 48 campsites (including 21 lean-tos) set on 114 acres. Added bonuses are the playground, hiking trails and fishing in Kent Pond.

Inn of the Six Mountains (☎ 802-442-4302, 800-228-4676; www.sixmountains.com; 2617 Killington Rd; d incl full breakfast $80-309; wi-fi) Well situated a third of the way up the mountain, this 99-room hotel features all the modern conveniences in addition to a Jacuzzi, exercise rooms, tennis courts and an onsite masseuse.

our pick Inn at Long Trail (☎ 802-775-7181, 800-325-2540; www.innatlongtrail.com; 709 US 4; incl full breakfast d $99-115, ste $130) The first hotel expressly built (in 1938) as a ski lodge, the inn is also temporary home to hikers pausing along the nearby Long Trail. The rustic decor makes use of tree trunks (the bar is fashioned from a single log), and the 14 rooms are cozy.

Eating

The mountain has more than 100 restaurants; you won't go hungry.

Sunup Bakery (☎ 802-422-3865; 2250 Killington Rd; dishes $2-9; ☉ breakfast & lunch) Fresh muffins and bagels are baked daily along with yummy breakfast sandwiches, great soy lattes and an emphasis on friendly (ie not fast) service. It makes great box lunches to go.

Choices Restaurant (☎ 802-422-4030; Glazebrook Center, Killington Rd; dishes $13-22; ☉ lunch & dinner Wed-Sun, brunch Sun) Can't decide what you're in the mood for? Grazers happily munch away on appetizers here, while serious eaters find plenty of satisfying main dishes on the huge menu. Meals range from soups and salads to pastas, steaks and a raw bar.

Casa Bella Inn (☎ 802-746-8943; VT 100; meals $15-23; ☉ dinner) Chef-owner Franco Cacozza, who turned this former stagecoach stop into a pleasant restaurant, offers a traditional menu of authentic Italian dishes. They're complemented by a good cellar filled with Italian wines.

Sushi Yoshi (☎ 802-422-4241; 1915 Killington Rd; meals $14-32; ☉ lunch & dinner) A gourmet Chinese restaurant that has successfully added Japanese food to its repertoire, Sushi Yoshi is one of the more exotic restaurants on the main drag. Its eight hibachi tables are extremely popular.

our pick Vermont Inn (☎ 802-775-0708; US 4; meals $15-24; ☉ dinner) Popular with skiers and one of the mountain's best value dining options, the inn offers rack of lamb, local veal and variations on the steak theme. The varied menu changes nightly and is served next to a cozy fireplace in winter. A good children's menu is available year-round and early specials are offered until 6:30pm in the summer.

Casey's Caboose (☎ 802-422-3795; Killington Rd; dishes $16-27; ☉ lunch Sat & Sun, dinner daily) Families should head here, where the atmosphere is great, the buffalo wings are free during happy hour and there's a good children's menu.

Drinking & Entertainment

With 25 clubs, and lively bars in many restaurants, Killington is where the après-ski scene rages. Many of these nightspots are on the 4-mile-long Access Rd. Check out these:

Jax Food & Games (☎ 802-422-5334) Combines an indoor gameroom-bar with an outdoor deck for cracking atmosphere.

McGrath's Irish Pub (☎ 802-775-7181; US 4; ☉ from 11:30 mid-Jun–mid-Apr) At the Inn at Long Trail. Has live Irish music on winter weekends.

Outback Pizza (☎ 802-422-9885) The lively outdoor patio and music acts draw an exuberant crowd.

Pickle Barrel (☎ 802-422-3035; ☉ from 4pm) Showcases great rock and roll bands.

Wobbly Barn (☎ 802-422-3392; ☉ from 3:30pm) Has dancing, blues and rock and roll.

Getting There & Away

Vermont Transit (☎ 802-864-6811, 800-552-8737; www.vermonttransit.com) buses stop at the **Deli** (☎ 802-775-1599) on US 4 in Killington. The ride from Sherburne to Rutland costs $5.50 one way (30 minutes). Once you're in Rutland, you can catch buses to Burlington, Brattleboro or Bennington.

VERMONT

THE ROAD ROBERT FROST TRAVELED

In 1920 Robert Frost moved from New Hampshire to Vermont seeking 'a better place to farm and especially grow apples.' For almost four decades, Frost lived in the Green Mountain State, growing apples and writing much of his poetry in a log cabin in Ripton, a beautiful hamlet set in the Vermont mountains 10 miles southeast of Middlebury on VT 125, where he kept a summer home.

Today the Ripton area in the Green Mountain National Forest has been officially designated Robert Frost Country. In addition to a picnic area and a memorial drive named after the poet, this area encompasses the **Robert Frost Interpretive Trail** and the **Bread Loaf School of English**, which Frost helped found while teaching at Middlebury College. Roughly 0.75 miles, the circular trail is marked by half a dozen of his poems, while the surrounding woods and meadows are highly evocative of his work. To get here from Ripton, take VT 125 east for 2 miles and look for the trail on the right side of the road.

The eight-room **Chipman Inn** (☎ 802-388-2390, 800-890-2390; www.chipmaninn.com; VT 125; r incl full breakfast $105-145; ⏱ Dec-Mar & May-Oct), a beautiful Federal house built in 1828, is big on Frostiana and also on the peace and quiet that Robert Frost sought. The warming hearth and woodstove are key in wintertime. Since guests dine at communal tables, there is a palpable sense of camaraderie here. Children aged 12 and over are welcome.

RUTLAND
pop 17,000

Rutland is Vermont's second-largest city (after Burlington). US 7 bypasses the center of Rutland, and you should probably do the same. If you need to find a big hardware store, automobile dealership, airport or hospital, Rutland will do. Otherwise, move on.

In the 19th century, Rutland was important as a railroad town. The trains shipped Vermont marble out and the manufactured goods of the world in. But the city's main railroad station was torn down in the 1960s and replaced by a nondescript shopping mall, leaving Rutland without even a visual memory of its heyday.

The **Vermont State Fair** (www.vermontstatefair .net) takes place here in the first week of September. It's a fun monster of an old-fashioned country fair, with exhibits, livestock, carnival rides, food booths and lots of priceless local color.

About five minutes out of Rutland on US 4, the **Norman Rockwell Museum of Vermont** (☎ 802-773-6095; 654 US 4; adult/5-15yr/senior $4.50/2.50/4 ⏱ 9am-5pm Jun-Nov;) presents a small collection of the artist's magazine covers and portraits.

MIDDLEBURY
pop 8200

Prosperity resides at the crossroads, and Middlebury obviously has its share. Aptly named, Middlebury stands at the nexus of eight highways and as a result the center of town is always busy with traffic. Middlebury was permanently settled at the end of the 18th century. In 1800 Middlebury College was founded, and it has been synonymous with the town ever since. Poet Robert Frost (1874–1963) owned a farm in nearby Ripton and co-founded the renowned Bread Loaf School of English at Middlebury College.

Despite Middlebury's history of marble quarrying, most buildings in the town's center are built of brick, wood and schist. Middlebury College, however, contains many buildings made with white marble and gray limestone.

Orientation & Information

Middlebury stands on hilly ground straddling Otter Creek. Main St (VT 30) crosses the creek just above the Otter Creek Falls. The town green and Middlebury Inn are on the north side of the creek; Frog Hollow (a small shopping complex in an old mill) and Middlebury College are to the south.

Addison County Chamber of Commerce (☎ 802-388-7951; www.midvermont.com; 2 Court St; ⏱ 9am-5pm Mon-Fri year-round, noon-4pm Sat late Jun–mid-Oct) On the north side of the creek facing the town green, this place is ensconced in a grand mansion and dispenses plenty of information.

Vermont Book Shop (☎ 802-388-2061; 38 Main St; ⏱ 8:30am-5:30pm Mon-Sat, 11am-4pm Sun) Features a thorough selection of Vermont and Frost titles.

Sights & Activities

MIDDLEBURY COLLEGE

For Middlebury College tours, contact the **admissions office** (☎ 802-443-3000; www.middlebury college.com) in Emma Willard House, on the south side of S Main St (VT 30). Within the Center for the Arts, the **Middlebury College Museum of Art** (☎ 802-443-5007; www.middlebury.edu/arts/museum; S Main St, VT 30; admission free; ☀ 10am-5pm Mon-Fri, noon-5pm Sat & Sun) presents rotating exhibits as well as its fine permanent collections of Cypriot pottery, 19th-century European and American sculpture, and works by such luminaries as Man Ray, Pablo Picasso and Salvador Dalí.

HENRY SHELDON MUSEUM

This 1829 Federal-style brick **mansion-turned-museum** (☎ 802-388-2117; www.henrysheldonmuseum .org; 1 Park St; adult/6-18yr/senior/under 6yr $5/3/4.50/free; ☀ 10am-5pm Tue-Sat year-round, 11am-4pm Sun fall, winter & spring, tours May-Oct) owes its existence to Henry Sheldon, a town clerk, church organist, storekeeper and avid collector of 19th-century Vermontiana. His collection runs the gamut from folk art and furniture to paintings and bric-a-brac, but is highlighted by an upstairs room devoted to such curios as a cigar holder made of chicken claws and Sheldon's own teeth.

OTTER CREEK BREWING

One of New England's best, the **brewery** (☎ 802-388-0727, 800-473-0727; 85 Exchange St; ☀ 10am-6pm Mon-Sat, tours 1pm, 3pm & 5pm Mon-Sat) makes a rich Stovepipe Porter, Copper Ale and other specialty microbrews, including its organic Wolaver's line. Free informative guided tours of the brewing process from grain to glass and samples are offered.

FROG HOLLOW CRAFT CENTER

In a small converted mill right by the waterfalls, this outstanding Vermont **state craft center** (☎ 802-388-3177; 1 Mill St; ☀ 10am-5:30pm Mon-Sat, noon-5pm Sun) has an exhibition and sales gallery showing works by many local artisans. It's always worth stopping here.

UNIVERSITY OF VERMONT MORGAN HORSE FARM

In 1789 Justin Morgan and his thoroughbred Arabian colt, named Figure, came to Vermont from Springfield, MA. The colt grew to a small bay stallion, and the hardy farmers and loggers of Vermont looked upon him as pretty but not particularly useful. Morgan, however, proved to them the horse's surprising strength, agility, endurance and longevity. Renamed Justin Morgan after his owner, the little horse became the USA's first native breed, useful for heavy work, carriage draft, riding and even war service.

You can see 70 registered Morgans and tour their stables and the farm grounds at the **University of Vermont's Morgan Horse Farm** (☎ 802-388-2011; Horse Farm Rd; adult/child/teenager $5/2/4; ☀ 9am-4pm May-Oct), about 3 miles from Middlebury. Drive west on VT 125, then north onto Weybridge St (VT 23) to the farm.

ATWOOD ORCHARDS

The countryside surrounding Middlebury is rife with apple farms, and these **orchards** (☎ 802-897-5592; Barnum Hill, Shoreham; ☀ 9am-5:30pm Jul–mid-Oct) have branches ripe for the pickin' in September and October. Pick cherries or enjoy pre-ordered peaches in July. To find this orchard, head west on VT 125, then south on VT 22A; it's 3 miles south of Shoreham village.

HIKING & BIKING

Undulating with rolling hills and farms, the pastoral countryside around Middlebury makes for great biking. **Bike Center** (☎ 802-388-6666; www.bikecentermid.com; cnr 74 Main St & Frog Hollow; equipment rental per hr/day/weekend $5/20/35; ☀ 9:30am-5:30pm Mon-Sat year-round, 1-4pm Sun summer) has plenty of equipment and information on regional biking.

There are lots of good day hikes in the region. Contact the **Green Mountain National Forest District Office** (☎ 802-388-4362; US 7; ☀ 8am-4:30pm Mon-Fri) for free, detailed printouts of 30 or so hikes.

Sleeping

BUDGET

There is little camping in or very close to Middlebury, but several places are within an easy drive.

DAR State Park (☎ 802-759-2354; www.vtstateparks .com/htm/dar; VT 17; RV sites/campsites $21/14; ☀ mid-May–early Sep) About 17 miles northwest of Middlebury, DAR enjoys a choice shore location right on Lake Champlain between West Addison and Chimney Point. The park has 70 campsites (including 24 lean-tos) as well as boating, fishing and a playground.

Branbury State Park (☎ 802-247-5925; www.vt stateparks.com/htm/branbury; VT 53; RV sites $23-25, campsites

$16-18; ◷ May–mid-Oct) About 10 miles south of Middlebury on Lake Dunmore, this place has 39 sites (including six lean-tos) on 96 acres. Hiking trails lead to spectacular views.

Blue Spruce Motel (☎ 802-388-4091, 800-640-7671; www.midvermont.com/bluespruce; US 7; d $55-135, ste $75-185) A mere 3 miles south of the town center, Blue Spruce has 22 comfortable rooms and suites (which are more like mini apartments, some of which can sleep four). Free continental breakfast.

MIDRANGE

Middlebury Inn (☎ 802-388-4961, 800-842-4666; www .middleburyinn.com; 14 Court House Sq, VT 7; r incl breakfast $88-375) This inn's fine old main building (1827) has beautifully restored formal public rooms with wide hallways, and its charming guest rooms have all the modern conveniences. The adjacent Porter Mansion, with 10 Victorian-style rooms, is full of architectural details. The inn opposes the green and overlooks the bandstand, but many of the 75 guestrooms are less desirable modern motel units in the back. Complimentary tea is served daily from 2:30pm to 4:30pm.

Swift House Inn (☎ 802-388-9925; www.swift houseinn.com; cnr Stewart Lane & US 7; incl continental breakfast d $135-195, ste $255-265) This grand white Federal mansion was built in 1814, served as the family estate of philanthropist Jessica Stewart Swift and is surrounded by fine formal lawns and gardens. In addition to 21 luxurious rooms, the inn boasts suites featuring a fireplace, sitting area and Jacuzzi. Other welcome luxuries include a steam room and sauna, a cozy pub, a library, a sun porch and gracious amenities.

Waybury Inn (☎ 802-388-4015, 800-348-1810; www .wayburyinn.com; VT 125, East Middlebury; r incl full breakfast $140-180, ste $225-250) A favorite of Robert Frost, this former stagecoach stop has a popular pub and 14 sumptuous guest rooms. The inn's exterior was used in the 1980s TV show *Newhart* to evoke *the* traditional New England inn (though Bob's never actually been here). In the summer, laze away an afternoon in the swimming hole underneath the nearby bridge; in winter, warm yourself in the pub.

TOP END

our pick Inn on the Green (☎ 802-388-7512, 888-244-7512; www.innonthegreen.com; 19 S Pleasant St; r incl continental breakfast $199-229, ste $299-329; wi-fi) Lovingly restored to its original stateliness, this 1803 Federal-style home offers seven spacious rooms in the house and four more-modern rooms in an adjoining carriage house.

Eating

BUDGET

Greenfield's Mercantile (☎ 802-388-8221; 46 Main St; smoothies $2; ◷ 9am-5pm Mon-Sat, 11am-4pm Sun) Get your smoothies and hemp cookies here. Great combination, eh? And while you're at it, pick up anything else made of hemp.

Otter Creek Bakery (☎ 802-388-3371; 14 College St; sandwiches $4-5; ◷ 7am-6pm Mon-Sat, 7am-3pm Sun) This bakery, with some outdoor seating, is popular for takeout pastries, strong coffee and creative sandwiches. Traveling with a pooch? It'll lick your face if you buy it an Otter Creek dog biscuit.

Storm Cafe (☎ 802-388-1063; 3 Mill St; lunch $3-8, dinners to go $6-13; ◷ 11:30am-6pm Tue-Sat) In the basement of Frog Hollow Mill, this creekside café has soups, salads, sandwiches and the like. The blackboard menu highlights more substantial dishes like vegetarian lasagna to take away for a late-afternoon picnic or early dinner. In good weather, sit on the terrace overlooking Otter Creek to enjoy what some consider to be the most imaginative menu in town.

Mister Up's (☎ 802-388-6724; 25 Bakery Lane; dishes $6-14; ◷ 11:30am-midnight) Exceptionally popular with Middlebury College undergrads, Mister Up's serves up burgers, steak and seafood, with a portobello sandwich or two thrown in for good measure. You can dine outside on the riverside deck or inside the brick and stained-glass greenhouse. The bar is a mecca for town nightlife.

MIDRANGE

Tully & Marie's (☎ 802-388-4182; 5 Bakery Lane; meals $8-22; ◷ 11:30am-midnight; **V**) Overlooking Otter Creek, this small art-deco eatery presents a menu of New American fare with Asian, Mexican and Italian inflections with plenty of delicious vegetarian and vegan dishes. At lunch, try the Indian curry soup with chickpeas or a Vermont maple-smoked pork BBQ. Dinner ranges from pad thai to steak to pan-blackened tuna. Wednesday offers a build-your-own-burrito option.

Fire & Ice (☎ 802-388-7166; 26 Seymour St; meals $10-31; ◷ lunch Tue-Sun, dinner daily) In a setting rich in stained glass and mahogany, quirky Fire & Ice (the name comes from a Frost poem) is locally known for its hearty seafood and steaks (notably the steak Rockport – filet mignon with lobster tail in a hollandaise sauce). The salad bar is something to behold: featuring over 50 items, it is made from an old motorboat.

TOP END

our pick Christophe's on the Green (☎ 802-877-3413; 5 North Green St, Vergennes; meals $30; ✈ dinner Tue-Sat May-Oct, Thu-Sat Nov-Apr) Consistently winning major culinary awards, Christophe's is located in a former hotel in Vergennes, 15 miles north of Middlebury. Christophe himself has devised a delectable French menu, featuring such dishes as sautéed calf's liver in a mustard-seed crust, or braised rabbit with mushrooms. Couples can splurge on the six-course taster's menu for $205 ($130 without the wine pairings that accompany each course).

Getting There & Away

Vermont Transit (☎ 802-864-6811, 800-552-8737; www .vermonttransit.com) operates two buses daily on the Burlington–Rutland–Albany route, which stops in Middlebury. It takes an hour to ride from Middlebury to Burlington ($12). You can connect at Albany with buses for New York City and at Burlington with buses for Montreal, Canada. The bus stops at the Middlebury Village Depot. Note: you need a passport to cross into Canada.

By car, it takes about the same amount of time (an hour) to get from Middlebury to either Warren/Waitsfield or Burlington.

MAD RIVER VALLEY & SUGARBUSH
pop 1700 (Warren); 1690 (Waitsfield)
North of Killington, VT 100 is one of the finest stretches of road in the country – a bucolic mix of rolling hills, covered bridges, white steeples and farmland so fertile you feel like jumping out of the car and digging your hands in the soil. Forty-five miles (or an hour) north of Killington, you'll land in the Mad River Valley, a virtual advertisement for Vermont. Nestled in the valley are Waitsfield and Warren, two villages that exude a certain timelessness, as well as two major ski areas, Sugarbush and Mad River Glen. Both feature the New England skiing of yore, a time when trails were cut by hand and weren't much wider than a hiking path.

Orientation & Information
The 'gap roads' that run east to west over the Green Mountains offer some of the most picturesque views of the region. VT 73 crosses the Brandon Gap (2170ft) from Brandon to Rochester and Talcville. VT 125 crosses the Middlebury Gap from East Middlebury (2149ft) to Hancock. A narrow local road crosses Lincoln Gap (2424ft) from Bristol to Warren. (The Lincoln Gap road is closed in wintertime due to heavy snowfall.)

VT 17 crosses the Appalachian Gap (at 2356ft) from Bristol to Irasville and Waitsfield, and this route offers the best views of all.

Sugarbush Chamber of Commerce (☎ 802-496-3409, 800-828-4748; www.madrivervalley.com; General Wait House, VT 100, Waitsfield; ✈ 9am-5pm Mon-Fri) Assists with lodging and the latest skiing info; has additional hours on Saturday (10am to 5pm) during the summer, fall and winter tourism seasons.

Sights & Activities
SUGARBUSH
Lincoln Peak (3975ft) and Mt Ellen (4083ft) are the main features of **Sugarbush** (☎ 802-583-6300; www.sugarbush.com). The two peaks were linked only a dozen years ago by a chair. In all, the two afford skiers 111 trails, many of which hurtle through a rolling tapestry of maple, oak, birch, spruce, pine and balsam. This is particularly evident as you ski Paradise, Castlerock or the backcountry runs in between, which braid through the forest. There are 508 acres for skiing here overall, and snowboarding is also available.

The resort is popular with groups, many of whom come up for weekend jaunts. Sugarbush has a definite sense of newness to it. The slopeside Clay Brook Luxury Hotel & Residences was built in 2006 to complement the recently renovated Sugarbush Inn. Lounges, shops and restaurants are available at each, and golf, tennis and a variety of other activities are available when the snow melts.

MAD RIVER GLEN
Subaru wagons with Vermont license plates often have bumper stickers that present this dare: 'Mad River Glen, Ski It If You Can.' Bumper stickers don't lie. This is the nastiest lift-served ski area in the east, a combination of rocks, ice, trees – and snow, of course. Unlike Sugarbush, cooperatively owned **Mad River Glen** (☎ 802-496-3551; www.madriverglen.com) is largely averse to change. Snowboarding isn't even permitted here, in an effort to keep the slopes as near as possible to the mountain's gnarled primal state (telemark skiing is

allowed, however). Very little artificial snow-making is used.

Such is Mad Glen's commitment to preservation that it still operates the only **single chair lift** in the country. Restoration (rather than a cheaper replacement) is planned for this vintage 1948 model and, at the time of writing, three-quarters of the necessary $1.54 million had been raised.

CROSS-COUNTRY SKIING

Local ski touring centers feature more than 100 miles of groomed cross-country trails. Call the Sugarbush Chamber of Commerce for information. One of the biggest ski touring centers is **Ole's Cross Country Ski Center** (☎ 802-496-3430; www.olesxc.com; 2355 Airport Rd, Warren; ☯ noon-5pm when not snowing, 9am-5pm when snowing).

OTHER ACTIVITIES

Canoeing and kayaking are prime on the Mad River (along VT 100) and White River (along VT 100 near Hancock) in April, May and early June, and on the larger Winooski River (along I-89) in the spring, summer and fall.

Clearwater Sports (☎ 802-496-2708; www.clearwatersports.com; VT 100, Waitsfield; canoe rentals per day $40-60, bike rentals per day $25, 4hr canoeing & kayaking trips incl lessons per person $58; ☯ 9am-6pm) rents canoes (price depends on whether you need a shuttle service), kayaks, river-floating tubes, in-line skates, bicycles, snowshoes, telemark demo gear and many other types of sports equipment. Clearwater also organizes sea-kayak tours, family overnight tours and one-day guided canoeing and kayaking trips.

Sugarbush Soaring (☎ 802-496-2290; http://sugarbush.org; 20-30min rides 1 person $100-115, 2 people $120-160; ☯ May-Oct), off VT 100, offers an unconventional activity. You take off from Warren-Sugarbush Airport in a glider towed by a conventional aircraft. After gaining altitude, you cast off the tow rope and soar quietly through the skies above the mountains and river valleys, kept aloft by updrafts of warm air. A glider can accommodate one or two passengers, but the two-person craft has a weight restriction of 300lb.

Vermont Icelandic Horse Farm (☎ 802-496-7141; N Basin Rd, Waitsfield; rides full day with lunch/half day without lunch $135/70; ☯ year-round, riding tours by appointment), 1000 yards south of the town common, takes folks on half-day or full-day jaunts year-round. Icelandic horses are fairly easy to ride, even for novices.

Sleeping

Because the Sugarbush area is primarily active in the winter ski season, there are no campgrounds nearby. Many accommodations are condos marketed to the ski trade. The largest selection of condos is rented by **Sugarbush Village** (☎ 800-451-4326; www.sugarbushvillage.com), right at the ski area. Rentals cost about $90 to $550 per day, depending on condo size and location, and your date of arrival and length of stay.

Hyde Away (☎ 802-496-2322, 800-777-4933; www.hydeawayinn.com; VT 17, Waitsfield; incl full breakfast d $79-129, ste $189) This 1830 farmhouse, sawmill and barn boasts its own mountain-bike touring center, hiking, and snowshoeing trails. The 12 rooms, suites and bunks range from one- and two-person rooms to a suite that sleeps five. Some rooms have private bathrooms, while some are basic bunk rooms with shared bathroom.

Inn at Mad River Barn (☎ 802-496-3310, 800-631-0466; www.madriverbarn.com; VT 17, Waitsfield; incl full breakfast s $50, d $115; 🐾) One of the last old-time Vermont lodges. Betsy Kratz operates this 1940s ski lodge and rents 15 rooms, some of which are in the annex with queen-size beds, steam bathrooms and TVs. The charm of the old lodge is preserved with a massive stone fireplace, deep leather chairs and a deck overlooking landscaped gardens. A pool hidden in a birch grove welcomes guests in summer.

our pick Waitsfield Inn (☎ 802-496-3979; www.waitsfieldinn.com; VT 100; d incl full breakfast $129-179; wi-fi) This converted parsonage features 14 tastefully decorated rooms as well as various nooks and dining areas to help you unwind. All rooms have private baths and some have four-post beds.

Inn at Round Barn Farm (☎ 802-496-2276, 800-721-8029; www.roundbarninn.com; 1661 E Warren Rd, Waitsfield; incl breakfast d $195-255, ste $325; wi-fi 🐾) This premier, elegant inn gets its name from the adjacent 1910 round barn, one of the few authentic examples remaining in Vermont. The decidedly upscale inn features 12 antique-furnished guest rooms with mountain views, gas fireplaces, canopy beds and antiques. All overlook the meadows and mountains. In winter guests leave their shoes at the door to preserve the hardwood floors. The country-style breakfast is huge.

Eating

Skiers' taverns abound in this area. Restaurants are quite busy in the ski season, but a bit sleepy at other times.

Warren Store (☎ 802-496-3864; Main St, Warren; dishes $4-6; ☺ 8am-6pm or 7pm) This atmospheric country store serves the area's biggest and best sandwiches. Eat on the deck overlooking the waterfall in the summer (except when there are swarms of bees).

American Flatbread (☎ 802-496-8856; VT 100, Waitsfield; flatbreads $9-18; ☺ dinner Fri & Sat) For excellent pizza pies cooked in a primitive wood-fired oven, no one does it better. In fact, the Revolution Flatbread is so good that it's distributed to grocery stores throughout New England and even from Chicago to Florida. Dine in or take out.

ourpick **John Egan's Big World Pub and Grill** (☎ 802-496-3033; VT 100, Waitsfield; dishes $10-17; ☺ 5pm-closing) Don't let the exterior decor fool you. Extreme skier John Egan has hired a renowned chef from New England Culinary Institute and the venison and lamb dishes are arguably the finest in the Green Mountain state. That makes foodies happy, but John Egan's is also a brewpub at heart, a hangout for skiers who heartily consume the house brew, Egan's Extreme Ale.

Rositas Mexican (☎ 802-583-3858; Sugarbush Access Rd, Warren; meals $14-20 ☺ dinner daily May-Oct, Thu-Tue Nov-Apr) Great burritos, salads, shrimp in tequila and homemade desserts are featured at this fun place, found across from the bridges. Juan Gorilla's cantina and sports bar is just downstairs.

Common Man (☎ 802-583-2800; 3209 German Flats Rd, Warren; meals $16-29; ☺ dinner Tue-Sun) Despite its proletarian name, this fancy favorite specializes in French, Italian and a smattering of other European cuisines. It's rather like dining around the Continent without leaving Vermont, especially since it's housed in a restored 19th-century barn hung with chandeliers and sporting an open-hearth fire. Menus change often, but the food is always outstanding. Homemade pastas join the signature dishes like Vermont venison with mushrooms and red wine. The wine cellar is impressive.

Spotted Cow (☎ 802-496-5151; Bridge St Marketplace, Waitsfield; meals $11-30; ☺ lunch Tue-Sun year-round, dinner Tue-Sun winter) Locals rave about the Spotted Cow, owned by Bermudian Jay Young. You can't go wrong with a bowl of the Bermudian fish chowder ($6), but then again, the smoked chicken salad at lunch and the pan-fried rainbow trout at dinner are excellent, too. Just because it's small

doesn't mean it's not superb. Find it just off VT 100.

Getting There & Away

Area bus and train travel is impractical because the nearest Vermont Transit and Amtrak stations are in Waterbury, 14 miles north of Waitsfield (see p401 for details).

From Waitsfield, it's 22 miles (40 minutes) to Stowe via VT 100, about the same if you're taking a detour to Montpelier (via VT 100 north to I-89 south).

BURLINGTON & NORTHERN VERMONT

Home to the state capital, Montpelier, northern Vermont also contains the state's largest city, Burlington. Never fear, though: this area still features all of the rural charms found elsewhere. Even within Burlington, café-lined streets coexist with scenic paths along Lake Champlain. Further north, the pastoral Northeast Kingdom offers a full range of outdoor activities, from skiing to biking, in the heart of the mountains.

BURLINGTON

pop 40,000

Vermont's largest city would be a small city in most other states, but Burlington's size is one of its charms. With the University of Vermont (UVM) swelling the city by 13,400 students, and a vibrant cultural and social life, Burlington has a spirited, youthful character. And when it comes to nightlife, this is Vermont's epicenter.

The city's location adds to its appeal. Perched on the shore of Lake Champlain, Burlington is less than an hour's drive from Stowe and other Green Mountain towns. In fact, the city can be used as a base for exploring much of northwestern Vermont, where each season brings its own festivals and events.

Orientation & Information

Take I-89 exit 14 to reach the city center; or take exit 13 to I-89 west to head for Shelburne and the motel strip that runs along US 7, south of Burlington. Downtown is easily negotiated on foot, though parking can be a big problem. The heart of the city is the Church St Marketplace and the adjacent pedestrian

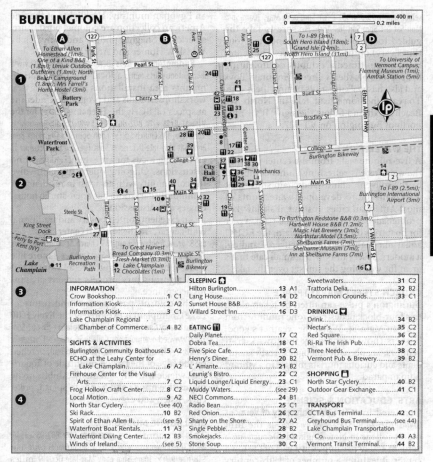

BURLINGTON

mall, where an amble is always a pleasure and often a wonderful surprise. Five blocks west along College St is the city's nice Waterfront Park and recreation path.

One of the best resources for getting a comprehensive idea of what's going on in the area is *Seven Days* (www.sevendaysvt.com). This hip, free tabloid is found in stacks just about everywhere around town.

Crow Bookshop (802-862-0848; www.crowbooks .com; 14 Church St; 10am-9pm Mon-Wed, 10am-10pm Thu-Sat, 11am-6pm Sun) A great source of used, new, remaindered and out-of-print books. It's nicely arranged, with many temptations.

Information kiosks (802-434-4569; www.bluemap .com; 10am-5pm daily mid-Jun–late Aug, 10am-5pm Sat & Sun mid-May–mid-Jun & late Aug–mid-Oct)

One at the lake end of College St and another on Church St.

Lake Champlain Regional Chamber of Commerce (802-863-3489; 60 Main St; 8:30am-5pm Mon-Fri, 10am-6pm Sat, 10am-5pm Sun late May–early Sep, longer hr summer & fall) Although staff at the Main St branch provide information, they seem to prefer you to pick up brochures at the rest stop just north of the Williston exit on I-89, or at the airport location (open 9am-midnight).

Sights
ETHAN ALLEN HOMESTEAD
American Revolution hero Ethan Allen, often referred to as 'Vermont's godfather,' lived in this 18th-century Colonial **homestead** (802-865-4556; www.ethanallenhomestead.org; adult/child/

senior/family $5/3/4/15; ☼ 1-5pm daily May, 10am-5pm Mon-Sat & 1-5pm Sun Jun-Apr). Be sure to take the guided tour (included in entrance fee; tour times vary) of the historic house. The center features multimedia exhibits documenting the exploits of Allen's Green Mountain Boys and also has walking trails behind the house. To reach the homestead, take the North Ave Beaches exit and follow the signs. It's 1 mile north of Burlington on VT 127.

THE WATERFRONT

A five-minute walk from the center of town, the **waterfront** is refreshingly unencumbered by the souvenir stands and chain stores that crowd the more developed waterfronts of most American cities. Instead, it's a low-key promenade with a 7.5-mile bike path, a pier for boat trips on Lake Champlain, the ECHO aquarium (right) and the Discovery Landing, a modern observatory with a small café that's great for watching the sun set over the lake.

CHURCH STREET MARKETPLACE

Burlington's pulse can often be taken along this four-block pedestrian zone running from Pearl to Main St. When the weather's good, buskers (now licensed by the town), craft vendors, soapbox demagogues, restless students and curious tourists mingle in a vibrant human parade.

ARTS, EDUCATION & SCIENCE

Chartered in 1791, the **University of Vermont** (UVM; ☎ 802-656-3131; www.uvm.edu) is the fifth oldest college in New England. Occupying a verdant 460-acre campus just east of the town center, it features a number of 18th-century buildings, but it's the youthful vigor of its 10,700-student body that has the greatest impact on Burlington life. From fall to spring, the main event at the Gutterson Field House is hockey, which consistently draws sellout crowds to watch the UVM Catamounts; call ahead for information on getting tickets to these thrillers. Also on campus and worth a look-see are art museums, theaters and science centers.

Fleming Museum (☎ 802-656-2090; www.fleming museum.org; 61 Colchester Ave; adult/student & senior/family $5/3/10; ☼ noon-4pm Tue-Fri & 1-5pm Sat & Sun May-Aug, 9am-4pm Tue-Fri & 1-5pm Sat & Sun Sep-Jun) at the UVM boasts a collection of over 20,000 objects from a variety of civilizations, ranging from African masks, Indian drums and samurai armor to

an Egyptian mummy. Highlights of the fine American collection are colonial portraiture, a series of Stieglitz photos and canvases by Winslow Homer and Andy Warhol.

Burlington City Arts (BCA; ☎ 802-865-7166; www.burlingtoncityarts.com), a local arts organization, mounts area installations and runs classes, workshops, studios and programs. Under the auspices of BCA, the **Firehouse Center for the Visual Arts** (☎ 802-865-7165; www.burlingtoncityarts.com/fcva; 135 Church St; ☼ noon-5pm Sun-Thu, noon-8pm Fri & Sat May-late Oct, noon-5pm Tue-Sun late Oct-Apr) is an exciting locus for art exhibits, classes and discussions. Ongoing open studios involve the community with an artist in residence. A community darkroom has open-studio hours, classes and discussions.

An excellent contemporary and traditional craft center, **Frog Hollow Craft Center** (☎ 802-863-6458; www.froghollow.org; 85 Church St; admission free; ☼ 10am-6pm Mon-Sat, noon-5pm Sun) feels more like a museum gallery than the retail store that it is. A rigorous jury process screens artisans for acceptance.

The colorful past, present and future of Lake Champlain is explored at the lively **ECHO at the Leahy Center for Lake Champlain** (☎ 802-864-1848; www.echovermont.org; College St; adult/3-17yr/senior $9/6/8; ☼ 10am-5pm Fri-Wed, 10am-8pm Thu), perched on the edge of the lake. A multitude of aquariums wiggle with life and many exhibits invite inquisitive minds and hands to splash, poke, click, listen and crawl.

SHELBURNE MUSEUM

This extraordinary **museum** (☎ 802-985-3346; www.shelburnemuseum.org; US 7; adult/under 6yr/6-14yr $18/free/9; ☼ 10am-5pm early May-late Oct), 9 miles south of Burlington off US 7, occupies 45 acres near the former Vanderbilt/Webb estate. HO and Louisine Havemeyer were patrons of the arts and collectors of European and old masters paintings. Their daughter Electra's interests, however, tended toward Americana. Electra Havemeyer Webb (1888–1960) amassed a huge, priceless collection of American works of art and craft that she put on display in the numerous buildings of the museum. Indeed, the buildings themselves are exhibits. Many were moved here from other parts of New England to ensure their preservation.

The collections – 150,000 objects housed in 39 buildings – include folk art, decorative arts, impressionist masterpieces and New England architecture. Items include a sawmill (1786), a covered bridge (1845), a lighthouse (1871), a luxury private rail coach (1890), a classic round barn (1901), a railroad station complete with locomotive (1915), the Lake Champlain side-wheeler steamship *Ticonderoga* (1906), and a circus building and 1920s carousel.

A minimal visit takes three hours, but you can easily (and pleasantly) spend all day here. Sustenance is available from the museum café or from a more elaborate restaurant and eateries in Shelburne village.

A local bus run by **Chittenden County Transportation Authority** (CCTA; ☎ 802-864-2282; www.cctaride.org) travels the route from Burlington's Cherry St terminal along US 7 south to the Shelburne Museum frequently on weekdays and four times on Saturday. There is no Sunday service. The adult fare is $1 and it's 50¢ for children and seniors.

SHELBURNE FARMS

In 1886 William Seward Webb and Lila Vanderbilt Webb built a little place for themselves in the Vermont countryside on Lake Champlain. The 1400-acre farm, designed by landscape architect Frederick Law Olmsted (who also designed New York's Central Park and Boston's Emerald Necklace), was both a country house for the Webbs and a working farm. The grand, 24-bedroom English-style country manor (completed in 1899), now an inn (p392), is surrounded by working farm buildings inspired by European romanticism.

Today, you can tour **Shelburne Farms** (☎ 802-985-8686, 802-985-8442; www.shelburnefarms.org; off US 7; adult/3-17yr/senior $6/4/5; ☼ cheesemaking, tours, inn & farmyard 9am-5:30pm mid-May–mid-Oct, walking trails only 10am-5pm mid-Oct–mid-May) and buy some of the cheese, maple syrup, mustard and other items produced here. You can also hike the walking trails and visit the animals in the children's farmyard. The guided 1½-hour tours begin at 9:30am, 11:30am, 1:30pm and 3:30pm from mid-May through October (costing an additional $3). The walking trail and children's farmyard close at 4pm.

The farm is 8 miles south of Burlington, off US 7.

MAGIC HAT BREWERY

You can drink in the history of one of New England's most dynamic microbreweries on the fun, free, 20-minute **Artifactory Tour** (☎ 802-658-2739; www.magichat.net; Bartlett Bay Rd; ☼ tours hourly 3-5pm Wed-Fri, noon-3pm Sat late May-early Sep, no tour Wed Jun-early Sep) and learn all the nuances of the beermaking process. Afterwards, sample four of 16 beers on tap.

Activities

See p394 for details of local shops supplying gear for outdoor activities.

WALKING & BIKING

The **Burlington Recreation Path**, a popular 7.5-mile route for walking, biking, in-line skating and general perambulating, runs along the waterfront through the Waterfront Park and Promenade. Rent bikes at **Ski Rack** (☎ 802-658-3313; www.skirack.com; 85 Main St; bike rental 1/4/24hr $10/16/22; ☼ May-Nov). You can also rent in-line skates, roller-skis, tandems, trailer bikes, snowshoes and skis (of course). Catch Tour de France action here on a big-screen TV.

Another spot to rent bikes (between mid-May and mid-November) is **North Star Cyclery** (☎ 802-863-3832; www.northstarsports.net; 100 Main St; bike rental 1/4/8hr $12/18/24).

Local Motion (☎ 802-652-2453; www.localmotion.org; 1 Steele St; bike rentals per 4/24hr $18/24; ☼ 10am-6pm mid-May–mid-Oct), a nonprofit group located at the trailside center, is spearheading an effort to link Burlington to Montreal via Burlington's own Island Line Trail and Canada's Route Verte. It offers bike rentals, maps, gifts, tours and refreshments. The 13-mile Island Line Trail combines with the waterfront bike path, beginning just south of the Burlington Boathouse and ending on the narrow Colchester causeway that juts 5 miles out into the lake.

BOATING & WATERSPORTS

Approximately 120 miles long and 12 miles wide, **Lake Champlain** is the largest freshwater lake in the country after the Great Lakes. Consistently good wind, sheltered bays, lack of boat traffic, hundreds of islands and scenic anchorages combine to make this immense lake one of the top cruising grounds in the northeast.

You can charter boats of 30ft to 41ft from **Winds of Ireland** (☎ 802-863-5090, 800-458-9301; www.windsofireland.net; Burlington Boathouse, College St; ☼ late May-early Sep, trips 11:30am, 2:30pm & dusk) for anywhere from a half-day to a week. The company of a sailing guide will cost you $25 per hour.

THERE'S SOME MAGIC BREWING...

Todd Haire received formal training from the Siebel Institute of Technology in Chicago and 10 years ago he went to work at Magic Hat Brewery in South Burlington, Vermont. He is now master brewer at Magic Hat. We spoke to Todd about his dream job.

What's behind the name 'Magic Hat'? A million and one theories abound. Some go by the story that when our founder Alan Newman was living on a commune and he, or anyone in the group, was short on coin, a hat would be passed around. Miraculously, said hat would always return with enough cash to buy whatever was needed. Others believe that, when the founders of the brewery were trying to name this place, they tossed their respective ideas into a hat with the goal of randomly selecting one. As it turned out, that hat was equally magic and the gang abandoned the idea of drawing a name out in favor of making the hat itself the brewery's namesake.

What makes Magic Hat distinctive? Our mission is to brew the best-tasting beers on the planet, but we also take an offbeat approach to our beers. Our wheat beer isn't called Magic Hat Hefeweizen, it's called Circus Boy; our flagship #9 is 'not-quite-a-pale-ale.' So, what does a not-quite-pale ale taste like? Well – you have to try it to find out.

We're seriously committed to the performing arts – something you don't see every day in the beer world. Every year, we sponsor hundreds of performances, and we have invented our own events for the sake of sharing visual tricks and treats. Take the Summer Variety Show Tour with the sexy Bindlestiff Family Cirkus burlesque troupe, our annual Night of the Living Dead fall freak show (and the birthday party we throw for ourselves and a few hundred – okay, maybe even a thousand or so – of our closest friends), and of course the Magic Hat Mardi Gras Parade. We do everything with aplomb and take great pride in our over-the-top approach to beer and life.

Which is your favorite brew? Oh, that's like asking a parent to choose a favorite kid! Our most widely available beer is #9, an ale that swirls across the palate and asks more questions than it answers. Also Circus Boy (the Hefeweizen) is alive with an unfiltered and unfettered American-style wheat taste that is an ideal drink no matter the time of year. We also produce a line of SeasonAles that are brewed to be in touch with the calendar: Roxy Rolles in the winter, hIPA in the spring, Hocus Pocus for summer and Jinx in the fall.

As related to Richard Koss

Rent all manner of boats at **Waterfront Boat Rentals** (☎ 802-864-4858, 877-964-4858; www .waterfrontboatrentals.com; Perkins Pier; canoes 1/2/4/8hr $15/25/40/60, kayaks $10/20/30/50, double kayaks $15/$25/$40/$60, rowboats 1/2/4hr $10/20/30; ☒ 10am-dusk May-Oct). Skiffs are priced depending on the size and horsepower as well as the rental duration.

Interested in river trips, tours, camps and instructional classes? Or how about double kayaks and canoes? **Umiak Outdoor Outfitters** (☎ 802-865-6777; www.umiak.com; North Beach, Institute Rd; kayak hire per 1/4/8hr $12/24/32; ☒ 11am-6pm Jun-late Aug) can fulfill all these needs; for the rest you're on your own.

The departure point for hourly and daily boat cruises and boat rentals is **Burlington Community Boathouse** (☎ 802-865-3377; www .enjoyburlington.com; foot of College St; ☒ mid-May–mid-Oct), a popular hangout fashioned after Burlington's original 1900s yacht club. Traveling with your own yacht? Transient dock space is available. The boathouse is easy to spot on the waterfront's 8-mile recreational path.

There's no finer way to enjoy Lake Champlain than to set out on a multiday paddling trip on **Lake Champlain Paddlers' Trail** (☎ 802-658-1414; www.lakechamplaincommittee.org). Paddlers are encouraged to join the eco-friendly Lake Champlain Committee ($40 per year), for which they receive an essential guidebook that details the trails, campsites and rules of the nautical road.

In addition to lunch and dinner cruises, the **Spirit of Ethan Allen II** (☎ 802-862-8300; www.soea.com; Burlington Boathouse, College St; ☒ mid-May–mid-Oct) plies the lake with a 1½-hour, scenic, narrated day cruise (adult/child $12/6), and a 2½-hour sunset cruise (adult/child $17/13) at 6:30pm.

DIVING
Ever since the 18th-century French and Indian War, 120-mile-long Lake Champlain has been a major thoroughfare from the St Lawrence Seaway to the Hudson River. During the

American Revolution and the War of 1812, numerous historic battles were fought on the lake to control this navigational stronghold. In the latter half of the 19th century, commercial vessels replaced gunboats. Many of these military and merchant ships sank to the lake's deep, dark bottom as a result of a cannonball or temperamental weather.

The misfortunes of these vessels make lucky finds for scuba divers. Two hundred wrecks have already been discovered, including the 54ft American Revolution boat *Philadelphia*, pulled from the waters in 1935 (and now sitting in the Smithsonian Institution in Washington, DC). Unfortunately, many of the earlier wrecks are far too deep for scuba divers, but six of the commercial vessels that lie on the lake's floor have been preserved by the state of Vermont as an underwater historical site.

All divers must obtain a free permit, available at the Burlington Boathouse, with limited permits available on first-come basis.

Waterfront Diving Center (☎ 802-865-2771, 800-238-7282; www.waterfrontdiving.com; 214 Battery St; ☼ 9am-6pm Mon-Fri & 9am-5pm Sat mid-Oct–early May, 9am-6:30pm Mon-Fri & 8:30am-5:30pm Sat & Sun early May–mid-Oct) offers rentals, charters, instruction and a full line of snorkeling, swimming, scuba and underwater photography gear.

Festivals & Events
On the first Friday of each month, year-round, there's the **First Friday ArtWalk** in town. In early April, nearby St Albans hosts the **Vermont Maple Festival**. In late May, the state's proud dairy heritage is celebrated at the **Vermont Dairy Festival**, held in nearby Enosburg Falls. In late August and early September, the week-long **Champlain Valley Fair** dominates nearby Essex with musical acts, farm stalls and art exhibits. Early October brings the annual **Applefest**, a celebration of all things apple (including a cider-pressing contest) to South Hero.

In Burlington proper, look for the **Discover Jazz Festival** and the **Chew-Chew Festival** of food and music in June; a patriotic civic celebration on the **Fourth of July**; the **Vermont Brewers Festival** by the waterfront in July; the **Champlain Shakespeare Festival** from July through August; and a very big and festive **First Night** celebration – a winter festival featuring a parade, an ice- and snow-sculpture exhibition, music and lots more – on

December 31. Contact the chamber of commerce for details.

Sleeping
Burlington's budget and midrange motels are on the outskirts of town. It's not usually necessary to reserve in advance, but if you call ahead on the day you intend to stay and ask for the 'same-day rate' you may get a discount. Many of the chain motels lie on Williston Rd east of I-89 exit 14; there's another cluster along US 7 north of Burlington in Colchester (take I-89 exit 16). Perhaps the best selection, though, is along Shelburne Rd (US 7) in south Burlington.

BUDGET
Mrs Farrell's Home Hostel (☎ 802-865-3730; dm $17.50, r $40; ☼ Apr-Oct) This six-bed hostel is about 3 miles from town and is quiet and tidy. Reservations are essential. Reserve at least 24 hours in advance (calls are taken between 4pm and 6pm) and then arrive by 5pm. Host Nancy Farrell will give you directions to the hostel when you call.

North Beach Campground (☎ 802-862-0942, 800-571-1198; 60 Institute Rd; RV sites/campsites $30/20; ☼ May–mid-Oct; wi-fi) This great place should be the first choice for tent campers. Right on Lake Champlain, it has 67 tent sites and 69 RV sites with hookups on 45 acres of woods and beach near the city center. To find it, get to Burlington's waterfront, then head north along Battery St and North Ave (VT 127), turning left on Institute Rd.

Northstar Motel (☎ 802-863-3421; www.northstarmotelvt.com; 2427 Shelburne Rd; r incl breakfast $30-70; wi-fi) These plain, tidy rooms (32 in all) are neat as a pin and the staff are wonderful. The very nice continental breakfast is served in a comfortable, sunny common area.

Hartwell House B&B (☎ 802-658-9242; www.vermontbedandbreakfast.com; 170 Ferguson Ave; r incl breakfast $70-90; ☐ ☎) Linda Hartwell offers two clean rooms (with shared bathroom) in her welcoming home situated in a residential neighborhood just five minutes' drive from the center of town. A pool is available in good weather, as is the deck for continental breakfasts.

MIDRANGE & TOP END
One of a Kind B&B (☎ 802-862-5576, 877-479-2736; www.oneofakindbnb.com; 53 Lakeview Tce; r with shared bathroom $95, ste with private bathroom $135; wi-fi) Located

in a quiet neighborhood just to the north of downtown, this sweet, peaceful and creatively renovated 1910 house overlooks Lake Champlain and the Adirondacks. Carry your generous breakfast – including croissants and assorted local cheeses – into the backyard and savor the lake views.

Sunset House B&B (☎ 802-864-3790; www.sunsethousebb.com; 78 Main St; r $99-149) Within easy walking distance of the waterfront and downtown, this hostel-like B&B features four tidy guestrooms. Bathrooms are shared, and there's a small common kitchen.

Inn at Shelburne Farms (☎ 802-985-8498; www.shelburnefarms.org; 1611 Harbor Rd; r with shared bathroom $100-190, with private bathroom $210-385; ☆ mid-May–mid-Oct) One of the top 10 places to stay in New England, the inn, 7 miles south of Burlington off US 7, was once the summer mansion of the wealthy Webb family. Relive their opulent lifestyle by taking tea (served every afternoon), or chill out playing billiards or relaxing in one of the common areas, complete with elegant, original furnishings from this gracious, welcoming country manor. If you're feeling more energetic, the hiking trails are a not-to-be-missed highlight. The 24 guest rooms vary in size and appointment, which is reflected in the rates.

Hilton Burlington (☎ 802-658-6500, 800-996-3426; 60 Battery St; r $119-289; ☐ wi-fi ☕) Formerly the Wyndham, this recently renovated 257-room, business-class hotel with stellar lake views offers just what you'd expect for this price: upscale rooms, a workout facility with an indoor pool and Jacuzzi, an airport shuttle and executive suites with a whole host of other amenities. An onsite café and bistro offer meals throughout the day.

Willard Street Inn (☎ 802-651-8710, 800-577-8712; www.willardstreetinn.com; 349 S Willard St; r incl full breakfast $130-230, ste $230; wi-fi) Perched on a hill within easy walking distance of UVM and the Church St Marketplace, this mansion, fusing Queen Anne and Georgian Revival styles, was built in the late 1880s. It has a fine-wood and cut-glass elegance, yet radiates a welcoming warmth. Many of the 14 guest rooms overlook Lake Champlain. The sublime breakfasts might include cranberry-walnut French toast.

Burlington Redstone B&B (☎ 802-862-0508; www.burlingtonredstone.com; 497 S Willard St; r incl full breakfast $145-185) This wonderful old stone house is tastefully appointed with period antiques and owned by an avid gardener – you can stroll through her lakeside perennial patches set on a hill. All rooms (actually suites) boast lake views you'll never tire of.

our pick **Lang House** (☎ 802-652-2500, 877-919-9799; www.langhouse.com; 360 Main St; r $145-245) Burlington's most elegant B&B occupies a centrally located, tastefully restored 19th-century Victorian house with 11 spacious rooms, some with fireplaces. Breakfasts are truly sumptuous affairs in an alcove-laden room decorated with old photographs of the city. Reserve in advance to get one of the 3rd-floor rooms with views of the lake.

Eating

Most eateries are in and near the Church St Marketplace. But if you explore just a little bit further out, your tastebuds will be richly rewarded.

BUDGET

Uncommon Grounds (☎ 802-865-6227; 42 Church St; dishes $2-5; ☆ 7am-10pm Mon-Thu, 8am-11pm Fri & Sat, 9am-9pm Sun) Take your newspaper, order a cup o' Joe and a muffin, grab a sidewalk table and people-watch in good weather. And muse about how good life is.

Radio Bean (☎ 802-660-9346; 8 N Winooski Ave; sandwiches & bakery items $2-6; ☆ 8am-midnight) This is the social hub for the arts and music scene. A low-power FM radio station (105.9) beams over the airwaves from this Dutch-style coffeehouse. Espressos, beer and wine keep things jumping, and grilled sandwiches and baked goods feed the soul. Live performances nightly include jazz, acoustic music and poetry readings.

Liquid Lounge/Liquid Energy (☎ 802-860-7666; 57 Church St; drinks $3-6; ☆ 9am-6pm; ☐) By day, order wheatgrass concoctions, veggie tonics and other enhanced nutritional drinks, and enjoy them in front of TVs, DSL internet stations or your own wireless gizmo. Undo all that healthy stuff with beer or wine at night.

Muddy Waters (☎ 802-658-0466; 184 Main St; dishes $3-6; ☆ 7:30am-6pm Mon, 7:30am-midnight Tue-Sat, 10am-10pm Sun) Besides serving all kinds of coffee, Muddy Waters offers juice concoctions, light eats (soup, chili, lasagna, hummus and veggies, and baked goodies), Guinness and a couple of McNeill's brews (from Brattleboro), so you can enjoy a pint in the cool glow of your laptop (bedecked with a 'Stop bitching, start a revolution' sticker, of course) as you write your novel.

Dobra Tea (☎ 802-951-2424; 80 Church St; dishes $3-7; ☯ 11am-10pm Mon-Thu, 11am-11pm Fri & Sat, noon-10pm Sun) This Czech-owned tearoom offers over 50 varieties, some seasonal, all hand-selected directly from their regions of origin. Sit at a table, an up-ended tea box, or on cushions around a small, low pedestal. When weather permits and the urge calls, hookah pipes ($12) are available at sidewalk tables.

Stone Soup (☎ 802-862-7616; 211 College St; dishes $3-7; ☯ 7am-7pm Mon & Sat, 7am-9pm Tue-Fri; **V**) Stone Soup is a big lunchtime hit with local vegetarians. Homemade soups (about $3), the salad bar and sandwiches with home-baked bread (about $6.50 per pound) are quite popular.

Red Onion (☎ 802-865-2563; 140½ Church St; dishes $3-7; ☯ 7:30am-8pm Mon-Fri, 10am-8pm Sat, 11am-8pm Sun) Expect lines at lunch, even in the blustery days of winter, at this popular spot offering deeply gorgeous baked goods. Tempting specials include the Red Onion sandwich: turkey, sun-dried tomato mayo, green apples, red onion, smoked Gruyère and bacon.

Great Harvest Bread Company (☎ 802-660-2733; 382 Pine St; sandwiches $3.50-4.50; ☯ 7am-6pm Mon-Fri, 8am-5pm Sat) A soft, yeasty scent surrounds you and an array of samples tempts you the minute you enter this sunny, airy, baking paradise a five-minute walk south of the town center. The monthly bread specialties are always imaginative. Great Harvest mills its own flour and offers a delectable variety of grilled panini.

Fresh Market (☎ 802-863-3968; 400 Pine St; sandwiches $5.50; ☯ 7am-7pm Mon-Sat, 10am-5pm Sun) Come for the amazing local cheese selection, 21 flavors of olives, and beautifully prepared foods such as enormous sandwiches, sushi, pies and salads. This mid-sized, bustling health-food grocer a five-minute walk south of the town center offers a tiny produce department and gourmet items, making it the place to stock up for a picnic or a gourmet feast.

Henry's Diner (☎ 802-862-9010; 115 Bank St; dishes under $8; ☯ 6am-6pm Mon-Fri, 6am-4pm Sat & Sun) A Burlington fixture since 1925, this diner has daily specials for around $5. The food is simple (you can get breakfast all day), the atmosphere homey and pleasant, the prices unbeatable.

MIDRANGE

Smokejacks (☎ 802-658-1119; 156 Church St; meals $6-26; ☯ lunch & dinner) No argument among locals as to the best burger in town – it's Smokejacks Big Bold Burger, made from local Angus beef and flipped over an oakwood grill. Fresh fish and specialties like applewood-smoked duck breast are also available, while the cheese list features some of America's finest small-farm cheeses.

Shanty on the Shore (☎ 802-864-0238; 181 Battery St; meals $8-25; ☯ lunch & dinner) With its fine lake views, this combo seafood market and eatery serves fresh lobster, fish and shellfish. The raw bar is exquisite, the outdoor deck is wonderful in the summer, and the array of potent drinks enhances the sunset.

Single Pebble (☎ 802-865-5200; 133-135 Bank St; meals $9-14; ☯ 11:30am-1:45pm & 5-11pm Mon-Fri, 5-11pm Sat & Sun) The brainchild of a local chef who mastered Szechuanese and Cantonese cuisine living in China, this spacious restaurant sprawls over two adjoining clapboard houses and offers up sumptuous MSG-free fare to the strains of traditional Chinese music. The dim sum is particularly satisfying – be sure to try the mock eel.

Sweetwaters (☎ 802-864-9800; 120 Church St; meals $9-20; ☯ lunch & dinner) Drenched in heavily nouveau-Victorian decor, this local watering hole attracts the young and upwardly mobile. In the evening the glass-enclosed patio is loud with chatter and redolent of nachos and chicken wings; the beverage of choice is an exotic beer.

NECI Commons (☎ 802-862-6324; 25 Church St; meals $9-22; ☯ lunch & dinner daily, brunch Sun) Operated by Montpelier's New England Culinary Institute students. You can expect dishes such as rotisserie chicken, roasted turkey breast and sea bass. They're all served at a long, welcoming wooden counter, a bar, banquettes, booths and quiet tables. Stop by for gourmet lunchtime picnic fare. A lighter bistro menu is also available (2pm to 4pm weekdays).

Five Spice Cafe (☎ 802-864-4045; 175 Church St; meals $10-19; ☯ lunch & dinner) This café is incredibly popular for Sunday dim-sum brunches (11am to 2:30pm, $2 to $3 per dish), but it'll be worth the wait. The café also serves excellent dishes from China, India, Indonesia, Thailand and Vietnam.

Daily Planet (☎ 802-862-9647; 15 Center St; meals $13-22; ☯ 4-10pm; **V**) Popular with locals for its vegetarian fare and relaxed, inviting atmosphere, Daily Planet offers a changing menu of creative dishes like potato-crusted salmon with Moroccan vegetable sauté, or Thai shrimp salad.

VERMONT

VERMONT

Trattoria Delia (☎ 802-864-5253; 152 St Paul St; meals $14-28; ⏰ 5-10pm) A longtime favorite, this dimly lit Italian restaurant with a large stone fireplace serves homemade pastas and specialties like osso buco ($26.50) and couples them with selections from their award-winning wine list.

TOP END

Leunig's Bistro (☎ 802-863-3759; 115 Church St; meals $21-30; ⏰ 11am-11pm Mon-Fri, 9am-11pm Sat & Sun) 'Live well, laugh often and love much' advises the sign over the bar at this stylish French-style brasserie with an elegant, tin-ceilinged dining room, and you'd do well to heed it. As Piaf and fellow *chanteuses* provide the tunes, the kitchen serves up such treats as Graham crackerfried duck with frog legs or an exquisite steak-frites.

our pick **L'Amante** (☎ 802-863-5200; 126 College St; meals $22-27; ⏰ 5:30-11pm Mon-Sat) Sleek yet engagingly informal, low-lit L'Amante serves upscale Northern Italian cuisine such as an irresistible *salumi* appetizer and swordfish with saffron-encrusted risotto cake. The wine list is extensive enough for all price ranges, and meals can be topped off with a glass of homemade grappa.

Drinking & Entertainment

The *Burlington Free Press* carries a special weekend entertainment section in its Thursday issue, and the free, energetic tabloid *Seven Days* tells all with a sly dash of attitude. Otherwise, head to the center of Burlington nightlife, Church St Marketplace, thick with restaurants and sidewalk cafés.

Nectar's (☎ 802-658-4771; www.liveatnectars.com; 188 Main St) Indie darlings Phish got their jump-start here, and the joint still rocks out with the help of aspiring acts. Grab a vinyl booth or chill at the bar and, if you feel you're hearing the next big thing, jump on the bandwagon.

Vermont Pub & Brewery (☎ 802-865-0500; 144 College St; dishes $5-15; ⏰ 11:30am-1am Sun-Wed, 11:30am-2am Thu-Sat) This large pub's specialty and seasonal brews are made on the premises. Try the Burly Irish Ale, the highly popular Dogbite Bitter and Mick's Smoked Stout. There's plenty of British pub fare – cock-a-leekie pie ($5.99) or fish and chips ($9.99) – to accompany the pints.

Red Square (☎ 802-859-9909; 136 Church St; ⏰ 4pm-2am Mon-Fri, 5pm-2am Sat & Sun) With a stylish Soho-like ambience, this is where Vermonters in the know go to sip martini or wine, munch on good bar food (including sandwiches) and listen to Burlington's best roadhouse music.

Drink (☎ 802-951-9463; www.wineworks.net; 133 St Paul St; ⏰ from 4:30pm Tue-Sat) You've heard of wines by the glass? Well, this mod place with an adjoining wine shop also offers them by the ounce, all the better for teaching your palate a lesson, while an armada of inventive mojitos will sink those in search of stiffer treatment. Small plates of New England delicacies (like scallops wrapped in bacon, and mini crab cakes) complement the drinks admirably.

Three Needs (☎ 802-658-0889; 207 College St; ⏰ 4pm-2am) Whatever *your* needs, this small college hangout doles out award-winning suds from its microbrewery. The crowd gravitates toward the pool table in the back, which can get pretty raucous on weekends.

Ri-Ra The Irish Pub (☎ 802-860-9401; 123 Church St; ⏰ 11:30am-2am) Want authenticity? This Irish pub was restored in Ireland, dismantled and shipped to the US. Order a pint of what is arguably the state's best Guinness or a dram of *uisce beatha* (Irish whiskey). Check out folk music on Wednesday and Sunday, a DJ on Friday and bands on Saturday night.

Shopping

Lake Champlain Chocolates (☎ 802-864-1807; www.lakechamplainchocolates.com; 750 Pine St; ⏰ 9am-6pm Mon-Sat, noon-5pm Sun, tours hourly 9am-2pm Mon-Fri) The aroma of rich chocolate is intoxicating as you make your way past the gift shop (if you can) to the glass wall overlooking the small factory here. No, you can't run through the chocolate waterfall, but you'll probably savor some samples during one of the tour's several taste tests. Back in the store, you can purchase an array of chocolate truffles, bars, coins and placesetting snowmen or gift baskets. The café serves coffee drinks and its own luscious ice cream.

Outdoor Gear Exchange (☎ 802-860-0190, 888-547-4327; www.gearx.com; 152 Cherry St) This place rivals major outdoor-gear chains for breadth of selection, and definitely trumps them on price for a vast array of used, closeout (clearance) and even new gear and clothing. You name the outdoor pursuit and staff can probably outfit you.

North Star Cyclery (☎ 802-863-3832; www.northstarsports.net; 100 Main St; ⏰ 10am-6pm Mon-Sat, noon-5pm Sun) Head to this friendly, laid-back local favorite for an unusually complete selection

of clothing, gear and bikes specifically designed for women. Don't worry, guys; there's
plenty here for you too. For winter fun, it
offers Nordic skis, snowshoes and outer-
wear. It's open for slightly longer hours in
the summer.

Getting There & Around

A number of national carriers serve **Burlington
International Airport** (☎ 802-863-2874; www.burling
tonintlairport.com), 3 miles east of the city center.
You'll find major car-rental companies at
the airport.

Vermont Transit (☎ 802-864-6811, 800-552-8737;
www.vermonttransit.com), based in Burlington, provides bus service to major Vermont towns,
as well as to Manchester and Keene (NH),
Albany (New York) and Boston (MA). The
main terminal (☎ 802-864-6811; 345 Pine St) also
serves **Greyhound** (☎ 800-231-2222; www.greyhound
.com), which operates buses daily between
Burlington and Montreal (one way $27.50,
about 1¼ hours).

The **Amtrak** (☎ 800-872-7245; www.amtrak.com)
Vermonter train stops in Essex Junction, 5
miles from Burlington. The station is served
by local buses run by **Chittenden County Transportation Authority** (CCTA; ☎ 802-864-2282; www
.cctaride.org).

By car, it takes 4½ hours (230 miles) to
reach Burlington from Boston; take I-93 to
I-89. It's another 1¼ hours (102 miles) from
Burlington to Montreal.

Lake Champlain Transportation Co (☎ 802-864-
9804; www.ferries.com; King St Dock) runs car ferries connecting Burlington with Port Kent,
New York, at least nine times daily from late
May to mid-October; there's no service off-
season. The one-way voyage takes 70 minutes and costs $13.25 for a car and driver,
and $3.75/1.50 for each additional adult/child
aged six to 12.

The company also operates ferries connecting Charlotte, VT with Essex, New York
(south of Burlington) for as long as the lake
stays unfrozen; and 24-hour, year-round service from Grand Isle, VT (north of Burlington)
to Plattsburgh, New York.

The CCTA operates buses from its Cherry St
terminal to Burlington International Airport.
Buses depart Cherry St every half-hour or so,
less often on Sunday. There are no services
on major holidays. Fares to the airport and
around town are $1 for adults, amd 50¢ for
children aged six to 18 and seniors.

A free College St shuttle bus runs a loop
route from the Waterfront Park near the
Burlington Boathouse, stopping at Battery St,
St Paul St, Church St Marketplace, Winooski
Ave, Union St and Willard St, ending at the
UVM campus. In summer, shuttle buses run
every 10 minutes from 11am to 6pm.

STOWE

pop 4700

In a cozy valley where the West Branch River
flows into the Little River and mountains
rise to the sky in all directions, the quintessential Vermont village of Stowe (founded in
1794) bustles quietly. A high concentration
of local artisans shares gallery space with
those of world renown. A bounty of inns
and eateries lines the thoroughfares almost
all the way up through stunning Smuggler's
Notch, halted at the border of the Green
Mountain National Forest where the highest
point in Vermont, Mt Mansfield (4393ft),
towers in the background. More than 200
miles of cross-country ski trails, some of the
finest mountain biking and downhill skiing in the east, and world-class rock and
ice climbing make this a natural mecca for
adrenaline junkies and active families. If
the *Sound of Music* is one of your favorite
things, there's also a lodge built by Maria
Von Trapp, which offers activities and accommodations (see p400).

Orientation & Information

Stowe is 10 miles north of I-89 on VT 100,
and its heart lies at the intersection of VT 100
(Main St) and Mountain Rd (VT 108), which
leads up to a dramatic, rocky gorge called
Smuggler's Notch (the road may be closed in
winter, but Smuggler's Notch Resort is open
year-round). Many of the village's hotels and
restaurants crowd Mountain Rd to the edge of
the Green Mountain National Forest.

Bear Pond Books (☎ 802-253-8236; Main St, Old
Depot Bldg; ⏰ 9am-6pm Sep-Jun, 9am-9pm Jul & Aug)
Browse the vast offerings of books about Vermont and
by Vermonters, as well as those on just about any other
subject you'd care to contemplate.

Stowe Area Association (☎ 802-253-7321, 800-
247-8693; www.gostowe.com; 51 Main St; ⏰ 9am-8pm
Mon-Sat & 9am-5pm Sun Jun–mid-Oct, 10am-6pm
Mon-Fri & 9am-5pm Sat & Sun mid-Oct–May) This
association is well organized and can help you plan your
trip, including making reservations for rental cars and
local accommodations.

VERMONT

STOWE & AROUND

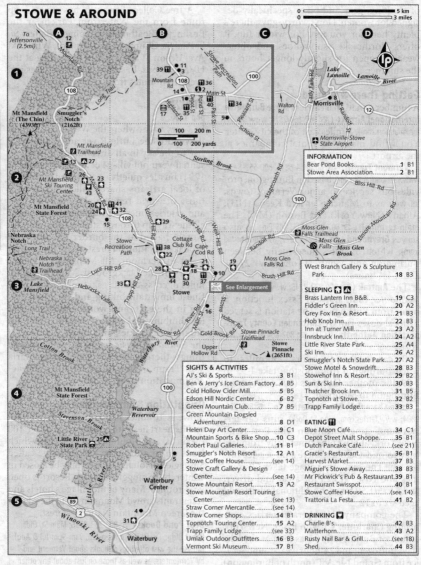

0 — 5 km
0 — 3 miles

INFORMATION
Bear Pond Books......................................1 B1
Stowe Area Association.........................2 B1

West Branch Gallery & Sculpture
   Park..18 B3

SLEEPING
Brass Lantern Inn B&B..........................19 C3
Fiddler's Green Inn...............................20 A2
Grey Fox Inn & Resort........................21 B3
Hob Knob Inn..22 B3
Inn at Turner Mill.................................23 A2
Innsbruck Inn...24 A2
Little River State Park.........................25 A4
Ski Inn..26 A2
Smuggler's Notch State Park.............27 A2
Stowe Motel & Snowdrift...................28 B3
Stowehof Inn & Resort........................29 B2
Sun & Ski Inn...30 B3
Thatcher Brook Inn..............................31 B5
Topnotch at Stowe...............................32 B2
Trapp Family Lodge..............................33 B3

SIGHTS & ACTIVITIES
AJ's Ski & Sports.....................................3 B1
Ben & Jerry's Ice Cream Factory.......4 B5
Cold Hollow Cider Mill.........................5 B5
Edson Hill Nordic Center.....................6 B2
Green Mountain Club............................7 B5
Green Mountain Dogsled
   Adventures...8 D1
Helen Day Art Center............................9 C1
Mountain Sports & Bike Shop..........10 C3
Robert Paul Galleries...........................11 B1
Smuggler's Notch Resort....................12 A1
Stowe Coffee House..................(see 14)
Stowe Craft Gallery & Design
   Center.................................(see 14)
Stowe Mountain Resort......................13 A2
Stowe Mountain Resort Touring
   Center.................................(see 13)
Straw Corner Mercantile..........(see 14)
Straw Corner Shops.............................14 B3
Topnotch Touring Center...................15 A2
Trapp Family Lodge.....................(see 33)
Umiak Outdoor Outfitters..................16 B3
Vermont Ski Museum...........................17 B1

EATING
Blue Moon Café....................................34 C1
Depot Street Malt Shoppe..................35 B1
Dutch Pancake Café...................(see 21)
Gracie's Restaurant..............................36 B1
Harvest Market......................................37 B3
Miguel's Stowe Away............................38 B3
Mr Pickwick's Pub & Restaurant......39 B1
Restaurant Swisspot............................40 B1
Stowe Coffee House....................(see 14)
Trattoria La Festa.................................41 B2

DRINKING
Charlie B's..42 B3
Matterhorn...43 A2
Rusty Nail Bar & Grill................(see 18)
Shed...44 B3

Sights & Activities

STOWE MOUNTAIN RESORT

The great **Stowe Mountain Resort** (☎ 802-253-7311; www.stowe.com; Mountain Rd) encompasses two major mountains, Mt Mansfield (which has a vertical drop of 2360 ft) and Spruce Peak (1550ft). It offers 48 beautiful trails, 16% of which are earmarked for beginners, 59% for middle-of-the-roadies and 25% for hard-core backcountry skiers – many of whom get their adrenaline rushes from the 'front four' runs: Starr, Goat, National and Lift Line.

The resort also features eight restaurants, three lodges, a Children's Adventure Center (offering classes), the 33-room **Inn at the Mountain** (☎ 800-253-4754; www.stowe.com/lodging

---

VERMONT SKI MUSEUM

Located in an 1818 meeting house that was rolled to its present spot by oxen in the 1860s, this **museum** (☎ 802-253-9911; www.vermontskimuseum.org; 1 S Main St; suggested donation $3-5; ☯ noon-5pm Thu-Tue) is an inspired tribute to skiing history. It holds much more than an evolution of equipment (including 75 years of Vermont ski lifts) and a chance to chuckle at what was high slopeside fashion in the '70s. A huge screen shows ski footage so crazy that you can hardly keep your footing. The most moving exhibit tells the tale of the famous 10th Mountain Division of skiing troops from WWII – it inspires wonder at how they held out with the (then cutting-edge) canvas- and leather-based gear.

VERMONT

/inn) and several condo options. The true nexus of Stowe Mountain is Cliff House restaurant (p400), accessible by an eight-passenger gondola at an elevation of 3625ft. It affords spectacular views of the Green Mountains as well as Stowe Village.

SMUGGLER'S NOTCH RESORT
Consistently less crowded than Stowe, family-oriented **Smuggler's Notch Resort** (☎ 800-451-8752; www.smuggs.com; VT 108; ☒), just over the Notch, was founded in 1956. Spread over Sterling (3010ft), Madonna (3640ft) and Morse (2250ft) mountains, the resort offers incredible alpine and cross-country skiing (78 trails and 14 miles' worth), dogsled rides (reservations strongly recommended), a lit tubing hill, nightly family entertainment, and the only learn-to-ski program for two- to five-year-olds in the country.

CROSS-COUNTRY SKIING & SNOWSHOEING
Stowe boasts the second-largest cross-country skiing network in the country (200 miles of groomed and backcountry trails), which links a handful of ski areas, including four of the top ski touring centers in the state, connected via groomed trails as well as tough backcountry ski runs.
Edson Hill Nordic Center (☎ 802-253-7371; www.edsonhillmanor.com; 1500 Edson Hill Rd)
Green Mountain Club (☎ 802-244-7037; www.greenmountainclub.org; 4711 Waterbury-Stowe Rd, Waterbury Center, VT 05677)
Stowe Mountain Resort Touring Center (☎ 802-253-7311, 800-253-4754; www.stowe.com; Mountain Rd)
Topnotch Touring Center (☎ 802-253-6433; www.topnotch-resort.com; 4000 Mountain Rd)
Trapp Family Lodge (☎ 802-253-8511, 800-826-7000; www.trappfamily.com; 700 Trapp Hill Rd)

Within Stowe's wide network of trails that traverse mountains and skirt lakes is the long-est cross-country ski trail in the United States, a 300-mile-long route that runs the length of Vermont. Known as the **Catamount Trail**, it starts in southern Vermont at Readsboro and ends at North Troy on the Canadian border. In between lies some of the finest skiing in the east, from backcountry trails on Mt Mansfield to 11 ski touring centers (some within the Green Mountain National Forest), including **Blueberry Hill** (☎ 802-247-6735, 800-448-0707; www.blueberryhillinn.com; Ripton Rd, Goshen) and **Mountain Top Inn & Resort** (☎ 802-483-2311, 800-445-2100; www.mountaintopinn.com; Mountaintop Rd, Chittenden). Contact the **Catamount Trail Association** (☎ 802-864-5794; www.catamounttrail.org) for more information.

If snowshoeing is more your speed, purchase or rent a pair at **Umiak Outdoor Outfitters** (☎ 802-253-2317; www.umiak.com; 849 S Main St; ☯ 9am-6pm). Umiak guides lead popular snowshoeing jaunts, lit by the sun, headlamp or moonlight, for $12 (for a half-hour trip) to $48 (day trip ending with sugar-on-snow, hot cider and Cabot cheese at a remote cabin).

HIKING
The 5½-mile **Stowe Recreation Path** (www.gostowe.com) offers a great in-town escape, as the trail rambles through woods, farms and hillsides. Walk, bike, skate, ski or swim in one of the swimming holes along this meandering yet well-kept course just above the village and east of Mountain Road.
Green Mountain Club (☎ 802-244-7037; www.greenmountainclub.org; 4711 Waterbury-Stowe Rd, Waterbury Center, VT 05677), 5 miles south of Stowe, was founded in 1910 to maintain the Long Trail. The club publishes some excellent hikers' materials, available here or by mail. Staff also lead guided hiking, biking, boating, skiing and snowshoeing day trips. For more information on the Long Trail and trail guidebooks, see p371.

The Green Mountain Club recommends the following day hikes around Stowe:

Moss Glen Falls (easy, one mile, 45 minutes) Follow VT 100 for 3 miles north of Central Stowe and bear right onto Randolph Rd. Go 0.3 miles and turn right for the parking area, then walk along the obvious path to reach a deep cascade and waterfalls.

Mt Mansfield (difficult, 7 miles, five hours) Follow VT 108 west from Stowe to the Long Trail parking area, 0.7 miles past Stowe Mountain Resort ski area. Mt Mansfield is thought by some to resemble a man's profile in repose. Follow the Long Trail to the 'chin,' then go south along the summit ridge to Profanity Trail; follow that aptly named route to Taft Lodge, then take the Long Trail back down.

Nebraska Notch (moderate difficulty, 3.2 miles, 2½ hours) Take VT 100 south of Stowe and turn west onto River Rd, which becomes Moscow Rd. Continue for 5.8 miles to the Lake Mansfield Trout Club. The trail follows an old logging road for a while and then ascends past beaver dams and grand views to join the Long Trail at Taylor Lodge.

Stowe Pinnacle (moderate difficulty, 2.8 miles, three hours) Follow VT 100 south of Stowe and turn east onto Gold Brook Rd, proceeding for 0.3 miles; cross a bridge and turn left to continue along Gold Brook Rd. About 1.6 miles later, you come to Upper Hollow Rd; turn right and go to the top of the hill, just past Pinnacle Rd, to find the small parking area on the left. The hike to Stowe Pinnacle, a rocky outcrop offering sweeping mountain views, is short but steep.

BIKING

Several bike shops can supply you with wheels for light cruising or backwoods exploration. Rent bikes from the **Mountain Sports & Bike Shop** (☎ 802-253-7919; www.mountainsportsvt.com; 580 Mountain Rd; recreation path bikes per 2hr/day $11/25, mountain bikes per 4 hr/day $20/30). **AJ's Ski & Sports** (☎ 802-253-4593, 800-226-6257; www.ajssports.com; Mountain Rd; in-line skate rental per hr/half day/full day $7/16/24) rents in-line skates as well as bikes. Opening hours for both these places vary with the seasons: phone before visiting.

CANOEING & KAYAKING

Umiak Outdoor Outfitters (☎ 802-253-2317; www .umiak.com; 849 S Main St; per half/full day canoes $34/42, kayaks $24/32; ☾ 9am-6pm) rents canoes and sport kayaks and will shuttle paddlers and boats to the river and then pick them up at the put-out ($28/38 for a two-/four-hour trip per person, which includes transportation and boat rental).

DOGSLEDDING

Learn about the fine art of dogsledding with **Green Mountain Dogsled Adventures** (☎ 802-888-8911, 802-793-6220; www.dogsledvt.com; 535 Bryan Pond Rd, Morrisville; adult/3-15yr $145/95; ☾ tours by appointment) and meet the dog team that will hurtle you 6 to 8 miles (in 2½ to three hours) over hill and dale through deep woods. These pups are training for the 1000-mile Alaskan Iditorod, so you know they pack some speed. After helping harness the team, you can ride the runners or relax on the sled. Afterwards, warm up in the cabin and head out again for a ski or snowshoe in some of the wildest yet most serene land around. Reservations are required and availability of tours depends on the weather.

GALLERIES & ART SPACES

Stowe has no shortage of galleries and fine craft shops with artists of local and international renown. Within the **Straw Corner Shops** (cnr Main St & Mountain Rd) offerings are surreal, traditional, contemplative, sometimes prankish and always finely hewn. Look for the **Straw Corner Mercantile** (☎ 802-253-3700; 57 Mountain Rd; ☾ 10am-6pm), featuring folk art, Americana, prints and artsy home accessories; and **Stowe Craft Gallery & Design Center** (☎ 802-253-4693, 877-456-8388; www .stowecraft.com; 55 Mountain Rd; ☾ 10am-6pm), which offers some of the most adventurous, eclectic and surreal works of art and craft.

Don't miss the winding, sculpture-filled paths along the river's edge at the **West Branch Gallery & Sculpture Park** (☎ 802-253-8943; www.chris tophercurtis.com; ☾ 11am-6pm Tue-Sun). A captivating collection of contemporary sculpture, paintings, photography and fountains fill this gallery and sculptural park, found 1 mile up Mountain Rd from Stowe village.

In the heart of the village, the **Helen Day Art Center** (☎ 802-253-8358; www.helenday.com; School St; ☾ noon-5pm Tue-Sun Jun–mid-Oct & Dec, noon-5pm Tue-Sat mid-Oct–Nov & Jan-May) is a gently provocative community art center with rotating traditional and avant-garde exhibits. It also sponsors 'Exposed,' an annual townwide outdoor sculptural show that takes place from mid-July to mid-October.

On your way up Mountain Rd, pause to take a gander at **Robert Paul Galleries** (☎ 800-873-3791; www.robertpaulgalleries.com; 394 Mountain Rd; ☾ 10am-6pm Mon-Sat, 10am-5pm Sun), with its acclaimed collection of painting, photography and sculpture.

Sleeping

Stowe has a wide variety of lodging, with dozens of inns, motels and B&Bs; many are along Mountain Rd. The **Stowe Area Association** (☎ 802-253-7321, 800-247-8693; www.gostowe.com) helps with reservations.

BUDGET

Smuggler's Notch State Park (☎ 802-253-4014; www.vtstateparks.com; 6443 Mountain Rd; campsites $14-23; ☙ late May–mid-Oct) This 35-acre park, 8 miles northwest of Stowe, is perched up on the mountainside. It has 81 tent and trailer sites and 20 lean-tos and walk-in sites. RV hookups are not available.

Little River State Park (☎ 802-244-7103; www.vtstateparks.com; Little River Rd, Waterbury; campsites $16-25; ☙ late May–mid-Oct) Just north of I-89, this place has 81 campsites (including 20 lean-tos) next to Waterbury Reservoir (sorry, there's no beach), on which you can canoe, kayak, fish and swim. Head 1.5 miles west of Waterbury on US 2, then 3.5 miles north on Little River Rd. RV hookups are not available.

Inn at Turner Mill (☎ 802-253-2062, 800-992-0016; www.turnermill.com; 56 Turner Mill Lane; r $70-110) Hidden on 9 acres next to Notch Brook, this streamside inn is just a sweet 1-mile ski from Stowe's lifts. It's a rustic place with only two rooms and two small apartments, but it makes up for lack of quantity with the innkeepers' encyclopedic knowledge of local outdoor activities.

Fiddler's Green Inn (☎ 802-253-8124, 800-882-5346; www.fiddlersgreeninn.com; 4859 Mountain Rd; r $90) This 1820s farmhouse less than a mile from the lifts has rustic pine walls, a fieldstone fireplace and seven guest rooms geared to outdoor enthusiasts. Not surprisingly, guests congregate around the hearth; it's all quite homey.

Sun & Ski Inn (☎ 802-253-7159, 800-448-5223; www.stowesunandski.com; 1613 Mountain Rd; d $109-133, ste $165-375; ☙) A nicely landscaped inn adjacent to the recreation path – the 25-room lodge has a fireplace, Jacuzzi and sauna.

Ski Inn (☎ 802-253-4050; www.ski-inn.com; 5037 Mountain Rd; r incl full breakfast & dinner winter $110, incl continental breakfast summer $55-65) The Catamount Trail runs right through the 28-acre property of this traditional inn, which was opened in 1941 just after the first chairlift was built in the area. It features 10 clean and simple rooms (some with shared bathroom) and a homey common area. You can cross-country ski, hike and mountain bike right out the back door. Catch the Stowe Mountain shuttle at the end of the driveway and you can alpine and Nordic ski back to the inn at the end of the day.

MIDRANGE

Hob Knob Inn (☎ 802-253-8549, 800-245-8540; www.hobknobinn.com; 2364 Mountain Rd; r incl breakfast $75-235; ☙ Jun-Aug & Dec-Apr) The 21 large rooms here (some with fireplace, some with efficiency kitchens) are set back from the road on 10 acres. The rustic cabin on a nearby knoll has a huge fieldstone fireplace.

Innsbruck Inn (☎ 802-253-8582, 800-225-8582; www.innsbruckinn.com; 4361 Mountain Rd; r incl breakfast $79-219 winter; wi-fi ☙) A modern interpretation of a traditional Alpine inn (with a health spa and heated outdoor pool); the 24 rooms and efficiencies here are comfy and well equipped. Inquire about the five-bedroom chalet.

Grey Fox Inn & Resort (☎ 800-544-8454; www.stowegreyfoxinn.com; 990 Mountain Rd; d $94-154, ste $255-487; ☙ ☙) Just off the Recreational Path, the Grey Fox has a good mix of old and new accommodations, the main offerings of which are in a former ski lodge. Amenities on the 9-acre property include a fitness room, bike rentals, Jacuzzi and a bar, and a full breakfast at the attached Dutch Pancake Café is included.

Brass Lantern Inn B&B (☎ 802-253-2229, 800-729-2980; www.brasslanterninn.com; 71 Maple St, VT 100; r incl full breakfast $99-199) Just north of the village, this beautifully renovated inn has nine spacious antique-laden rooms with handmade quilts. Six feature fireplaces and views of Mt Mansfield.

our pick **Stowe Motel & Snowdrift** (☎ 802-253-7629, 800-829-7629; www.stowemotel.com; 2043 Mountain Rd; d $110-175, ste $175-210; ☙ ☙) In addition to 21 efficiencies, suites and houses, this motel set on 16 acres offers such amenities as a tennis court, hot tubs, badminton and lawn games. You can also borrow bicycles to use on the recreation path.

TOP END

Stowehof Inn & Resort (☎ 802-253-9722, 800-932-7136; www.stowehofinn.com; 434 Edson Hill Rd; r incl full breakfast $210-500; ☙) In addition to a dramatic hillside location, this rustic 46-room inn has a very good dining room, sauna, Jacuzzi, outdoor hot tub, and 30 acres of hiking and cross-country ski trails. Rooms are divided into three categories: classic (decorated with antiques), traditional (appointed in an 'Alpine' manner) and premier (rooms at the top with great views and fireplaces).

Topnotch at Stowe (☎ 802-253-8585, 800-451-8686; www.topnotchresort.com; 4000 Mountain Rd; d $230-$350, ste

$500-785; wi-fi) Stowe's most lavish resort, with 92 rooms, really is top notch. Amenities include a bar, fine dining, indoor and outdoor tennis courts, a skating rink and a touring center. The spa is legendary, with a waterfall Jacuzzi and luxurious pampering services.

Trapp Family Lodge (☎ 802-253-8511, 800-826-7000; www.trappfamily.com; 700 Trapp Hill Rd; r $245-520; wi-fi) Off Luce Hill Rd from Mountain Rd, with wide-open fields and mountain views, this is *the* spot for taking a twirl and pretending you're Julie Andrews. At the Austrian-style chalet, built by Maria von Trapp of *The Sound of Music* fame, there are 96 motel and lodge rooms, and time-share units. The 2700-acre spread offers excellent hiking, snowshoeing and cross-country skiing.

Eating

As with any resort area, food here can be expensive and the atmosphere predictable. However, there are some great finds here as well.

BUDGET

Depot Street Malt Shoppe (☎ 802-253-4269; 57 Depot St; dishes $3-7; 11:30am-9pm) Burgers and old-fashioned malteds reign at this fun, 1950s-themed restaurant. The egg creams hit the spot in any season.

Harvest Market (☎ 802-253-3800; 1031 Mountain Rd; sandwiches $4-8; 7am-7pm) This one-stop gourmet purveyor dishes out cold mains by the pound, wonderful Vermont cheeses, wood-fired flatbreads, salads and sandwiches. Don't even try to leave without something from its dessert section.

Stowe Coffee House (☎ 802-253-2189; 57B Mountain Rd; dishes $5-7; 8am-6pm) What's art without coffee? After a browse through the nearby art galleries, drop into this coffee house, which serves homemade baked goods and specialty lattes. Lunch offerings include wraps, grilled sandwiches, homemade soups, pasta, salads and quiches.

Dutch Pancake Café (☎ 802-253-8921; 900 Mountain Rd; dishes $6-10; 8am-12:30am) Located within the Grey Fox Inn, this Dutch-owned eatery decked in Delft tiles makes more than 80 kinds of *pannekoeken* (Dutch pancakes); some have a Southern American twist with sausage and gravy.

MIDRANGE

Gracie's Restaurant (☎ 802-253-8741; Main St; meals $7-25; lunch & dinner) Behind Carlson Real Estate, Gracie's has dog-themed specialties, such as a Mexican plate called 'South of the Border Collie.' Or stick to big burgers, hand-cut steaks, Waldorf salad and garlic-laden shrimp scampi. Try its famous 'Doggie Bag' dessert: a white-chocolate bag filled with chocolate mousse and hot fudge.

Mr Pickwick's Pub & Restaurant (☎ 802-253-7064; 433 Mountain Rd; meals $7-27; 8am-midnight) The respectfully teasing bartender at this pub and eatery in Ye Olde England Inne keeps the crowd on high perk. An old-world feel is fully manifested, and this is the place to try ye olde bangers-and-mash or ostrich tenderloin. Otherwise, indulge in the Chef's Tasting Dinner ($60 per person, reservations required).

Miguel's Stowe Away (☎ 800-245-1240, 802-253-7574; 3148 Mountain Rd; meals $9-22; dinner) This Mexican farmhouse cantina became so popular that it launched its own line of chips and salsa that's sold around the country. You'll find Tex-Mex, gringo and creative Mexican dishes like salmon with a mango poblano sauce ($19).

Trattoria La Festa (☎ 802-253-8480; 4080 Mountain Rd; meals $11-22; dinner Mon-Sat) Just north of Topnotch at Stowe, this trattoria has very good Italian fare made by Italian chefs. Check out its spaghetti *pescatore*, which is chock-full of mussels, clams and shrimps for $18.50.

Cliff House (☎ 802-253-3665; 5781 Mountain Rd; meals $17-19; lunch daily, dinner Fri & Sat in summer) While the view atop Stowe Mountain is worth the visit alone, the food (made largely from local produce) is quite a revelation. Try the crepe of the day, the house burger (made from Wood Creek Farm beef) or the lamb skewer. You won't be in a rush to descend.

Restaurant Swisspot (☎ 802-253-4622; 128 Main St; meals $19-26; lunch & dinner) In addition to the selection of pastas and meat dishes, this cozy spot in the village offers an impressive array of fondues, running from the bizarre (scallop and beef or whole peeled shrimp) to the more traditional.

TOP END

ourpick **Blue Moon Café** (☎ 802-253-7006; 35 School St; meals $19-31; dinner daily Dec-Mar & May-Oct, Fri-Sun Nov & Apr) In a converted house with a little sun porch, this intimate bistro is one of New England's top restaurants. Mains change weekly, but the contemporary cuisine is usually sublime. Look for crab cakes, salmon dishes, or steak with chipotle and ji-cama. The cheese plate, compiled from local varieties, is exquisite.

Drinking

Charlie B's (☎ 802-253-7355; 1746 Mountain Rd; ☼ noon-1am) If you're searching for a standard après-ski scene with a bit more class, check out this place, at the Stoweflake Inn and Resort.

Shed (☎ 802-253-4364; 1859 Mountain Rd; ☼ 11:30am-10pm Sun-Thu, 11:30am-11pm Fri & Sat) This little microbrewery always has six fresh beers on tap and a crowd of locals tucking into pub fare.

Rusty Nail Bar & Grill (☎ 802-253-6245; www.rusty nailbar.com; 1190 Mountain Rd; ☼ 11:30-1am) You wonder where the wild things are? They're here, hanging around three bars, plenty of pool tables and a dance floor, where they groove to live bands dishing everything from alt rock to jazz funk to calypso. The martini bar has some local renown. Oh yeah, there's food too, with an inventive menu.

Matterhorn (☎ 802-253-8198; 4969 Mountain Rd; cover free-$15; ☼ 5pm-late daily late Nov–mid-Apr, Thu-Sat mid-Apr–late Nov) At the top of Mountain Rd, this place is always hopping, beginning at 5pm when skiers start to hobble off the slopes. Bands play Friday and Saturday nights during ski season.

Getting There & Around

Vermont Transit (☎ 802-864-6811, 800-552-8737; www .vermonttransit.com) buses stop at Waterbury, 10 miles south of Stowe. There is one daily bus from Burlington to Waterbury ($8, 30 minutes). From Waterbury, you can call **Peg's Pick Up** (☎ 800-370-9490) for the short drive into Stowe ($20 per person).

The **Amtrak** (☎ 800-872-7245; www.amtrak.com) *Vermonter* train stops daily at Waterbury. Some hotels and inns will arrange to pick up guests at the station.

By car, it's 36 miles (45 minutes) to Burlington from Stowe; head south on VT 100, then north on I-89.

If you don't have your own vehicle, the Stowe Trolley runs every half-hour daily during ski season from Stowe village, along Mountain Rd, to the ski slopes. Pick up a schedule and list of stops at your inn or the Stowe Area Association's information office.

WATERBURY & AROUND

Although there's little to detain you in Waterbury, 10 miles south of Stowe on VT

100, it does have an Amtrak station and serves as an excellent base for the legions of visitors to Ben and Jerry's Ice Cream Factory as well as the nearby Cold Hollow Cider Mill.

In 1978 Ben Cohen and Jerry Greenfield took over an abandoned gas station in Burlington and, with a modicum of training, launched the outlandish flavors that forever changed the way ice cream would be made. While a tour of **Ben & Jerry's Ice Cream Factory** (Map p396; ☎ 802-882-1240; www.benjerry.com; VT 100N, Waterbury; adult/senior/under 12yr $3/2/free; ☼ 9am-6pm Jun, 9am-9pm Jul-late Aug, 9am-7pm late Aug-late Oct) is no over-the-top Willie Wonka experience, there is a campy video that follows their long, strange trip to corporate giant – albeit a very nice giant with an inspiring presence of community building and environmental leadership. After chowing your (very teeny) free scoops, linger a while in the final hallway, which is festooned with mementos of the past 30 years of changing the world one scoop at a time. Behind the factory, a mock cemetery holds 'graves' of Cool Britannia, Holy Cannoli and other flavors that have been laid to rest. The factory is 1 mile north of I-89.

Several miles north of Ben & Jerry's on VT 100N, **Cold Hollow Cider Mill** (Map p396; ☎ 802-244-8771, 800-327-7537; www.coldhollow.com; VT 100; ☼ 8am-7pm Jul–mid-Oct, 8am-6pm mid-Oct–Jun) shows how it makes its famous cider doughnuts (guaranteed love at first bite). The cider itself tastes so crisp and fresh you'd swear there was a spigot coming right out of the apple. The gift shop is packed with the most inventive gourmet goodies selection in town, including corn relish, horseradish jam and piccalilli.

A cone's throw from Ben & Jerry's, the **Thatcher Brook Inn** (☎ 802-244-5911; www.thatcher brook.com; VT 100N at exit 10; incl continental breakfast d $135-175, ste $399) has 24 rooms, all with private bathrooms, in a renovated 1899 Victorian mansion. The luxury suite offers a Jacuzzi and a fireplace.

MONTPELIER & BARRE
pop 8000

Montpelier (pronounced mont-*peel*-yer) would qualify as a large village in some countries. But in sparsely populated Vermont it is the state capital – the smallest in the country. You may want to visit Montpelier for a good meal or if you are intensely interested in Vermont history and affairs.

VERMONT

Montpelier's smaller neighbor Barre (pronounced *bar*-ee), which touts itself as the 'granite capital of the world,' is a 10-minute drive from the capital.

Orientation & Information

Montpelier lies at the confluence of the Winooski and North Branch rivers. As it's quite small, it's easy to find the golden dome of the State House and then locate the town's two other major sights: the museum and the gallery. Barre lies ten miles east of Montpelier along Rte 302.

Bear Pond Books (☎ 802-229-0774; 77 Main St; ☻ 10am-5:30pm Mon-Fri, 10am-9pm Sat & Sun)

Information kiosk (State St; ☻ summer) Opposite the post office.

Vermont Chamber of Commerce (☎ 802-223-3443, 877-887-3678; www.centralvt.com; ☻ 9am-5pm Mon-Fri) Distributes a wealth of information.

Sights

STATE HOUSE

The front doors of the **State House** (☎ 802-828-2228; www.vtstatehouse.org; State St; admission & tours free; ☻ 8am-4pm Mon-Sat, tours every 30min 10am-3:30pm Mon-Fri, 11am-2:30pm Sat Jul–mid-Oct) are guarded by a massive statue of American Revolutionary hero Ethan Allen. The gold dome was built of granite quarried in nearby Barre in 1836. You can wander around the building during weekday business hours, or take one of the free tours.

VERMONT HISTORICAL SOCIETY

Next door to the State House, the Pavilion Building houses an excellent **museum** (☎ 802-828-2291; http://vermonthistory.org; State St; adult/student & senior $5/3; ☻ 10am-4pm Tue-Sat, noon-4pm Sun May-Oct) that recounts Vermont's history with exhibits, films and re-creations of taverns and Native American settlements.

TW WOOD ART GALLERY

This **gallery** (☎ 802-828-8743; 36 College St; Tue-Sat adult/under 12yr $2/free, Sun admission free; ☻ noon-4pm Tue-Sun), at E State St on the Vermont College campus, was founded in 1895 by Thomas Waterman Wood (1823–1903), a native of Montpelier, who gained a regional reputation for his portraits and genre paintings. The museum has a large collection of Wood's art as well as Depression-era paintings. Changing exhibits, especially of arts created in Vermont, fill the main gallery.

ROCK OF AGES QUARRIES

The world's largest **granite quarries** (☎ 802-476-3119; www.rockofages.com; 773 Quarry Hill Rd; ☻ early May-Oct), 4 miles southeast of Barre off I-89 exit 6, cover 50 acres. The granite vein that's mined here is a whopping 6 miles long, 4 miles wide and 10 miles deep. The beautiful, durable, granular stone, formed more than 330 million years ago, is used for tombstones, building facades, monuments, curbstones and tabletops.

Visit the onsite **Rock of Ages Visitor Center** (admission free, tours adult/child/senior $4/1.50/3.50; ☻ 8:30am-5pm Mon-Sat, 10am-5pm SunMay-Oct, 8:30am-5pm daily mid-Sep–mid-Oct). The quarry tour includes a short video and historical exhibits. This 35-minute guided minibus tour of an active quarry heads off-site. At the onsite **Rock of Ages Manufacturing Division** (tours free; ☻ every 45min 9:15am-3:30pm Mon-Sat, 10:15am-3:30pm Sun May–mid-Oct), you can watch granite products being made – some with an accuracy that approaches 25-millionths of an inch.

HOPE CEMETERY

Where do old granite carvers go when they die? In Barre, they end up in Hope Cemetery, just a mile north of US 302 on VT 14. To granite carvers, tombstones aren't dreary reminders of mortality but artful celebrations of the carver's life. And what celebrations! A carver and his wife sit up in bed holding hands, smiling for eternity; a granite cube balances precariously on one corner. Other gravestones reproduce the deceased's favorite soccer ball or even a small airplane. If a cemetery can ever be amusing, this one is. It's open to the living all the time.

COVERED BRIDGES

Vermont is rife with these classic beauties, but you generally don't get two (and almost three) for the price of one. From Montpelier, take VT 12 southwest to Northfield Falls to the intersection of Cox Brook Rd, where two covered bridges straddle a river within walking distance of each other. **Station Bridge** and **Newell Bridge** both span a section of the river that's about 100ft across. **Upper Bridge** is a bit further up Cox Brook Rd. Fittingly, a general store marks the intersection where these timeless icons remain as sentinels.

Sleeping

our pick **Betsy's Bed & Breakfast** (☎ 802-229-0466; www.betsysbnb.com; 74 E State St; d incl full breakfast $70-140;

wi-fi) This restored Victorian house on an inclined road leading to Vermont College has 12 gracefully appointed rooms and suites decorated with period antiques. Updated amenities include phone and TV; the suites even have kitchens. Despite the feeling of seclusion, you are a quick walk from the middle of town.

Inn at Montpelier (☎ 802-223-2727; www.innat montpelier.com; 147 Main St; incl continental breakfast d $147-171, ste $210; wi-fi) Good enough for repeat visitor Martha Stewart, this first-rate, 19-room inn, made up of two refurbished Federal houses right in the heart of town, boasts deluxe rooms with fireplaces. Hosts Rita and Rick Rizza have renovated these stately houses and furnished them luxuriously. Coffee in wicker rocking chairs on the wraparound veranda is the perfect tonic for a lazy afternoon.

Eating
As home to one of the country's finest cooking schools, the **New England Culinary Institute** (NECI; ☎ 802-223-6324; ww.neci.edu), Montpelier is an excellent place to stop for a meal. NECI runs three restaurants in town: La Brioche, Main St Bar & Grill and the Chef's Table. Depending on the student chefs of the day, you can either have one of the best meals in New England at an affordable price or a damn good attempt. Be a guinea pig and support someone's learning curve.

La Brioche (☎ 802-229-0443; 89 Main St; sandwiches $5; 6:30am-7pm Mon-Fri, 7:30am-5pm Sat & Sun) NECI's first restaurant is a casual bakery and café offering soups and sandwiches on homemade bread, among other things. It starts running out of sandwich fixings at about 2pm, so you'd better time it right if you're hungry. Eat in or take out.

our pick **Sarducci's** (☎ 802-223-0229; 3 Main St; meals $8-18; lunch Mon-Sat, dinner daily) If you don't feel like tossing the dice and risking a meal made by students, head to this reliable standby. With tables overlooking the river (unfortunately reservations aren't taken) in an old railroad station, its menu features Italian dishes like pastas, personalized wood-oven pizzas and eggplant parmigiana. The restaurant feels spacious and the lunch portions are very generous.

Main St Bar & Grill (☎ 802-223-3188; 118 Main St; Sun brunch $17, meals $9-17; brunch Sun, lunch & dinner daily) NECI's signature restaurant is a multilevel spot boasting an open window to the kitchen – this allows you to watch first-year student chefs at work. The fare may feature almond-crusted trout or leg of venison. Sunday brunch is an excellent all-you-can-eat affair.

Chef's Table (☎ 802-229-9202; 118 Main St; meals $17-31; dinner Tue-Sat) Since this upstairs, upscale restaurant is run by second-year NECI students, the food is generally somewhat more accomplished than at the Main St Bar & Grill. Specials change nightly but you'll usually find some variant of veal chops, lamb dishes and rosemary-seared swordfish.

Getting There & Away
Vermont Transit (☎ 802-864-6811, 800-552-8737; www.vermonttransit.com) runs four buses daily between Boston and Burlington, stopping in Montpelier at the **main terminal** (☎ 802-223-7112; 1 Taylor St). Tickets from Boston to Montpelier cost $43 (four hours); Montpelier to Burlington costs $12 (one hour).

The **Amtrak** (☎ 800-872-7245; www.amtrak.com) *Vermonter* train stops in Montpelier on its way to St Albans. The fare from Brattleboro to Montpelier is $23 to $35, depending on the day of the week.

From Montpelier to Burlington, it's an easy drive on I-89 (38 miles, 45 minutes).

NORTHEAST KINGDOM
When Senator George Aiken noted in 1949 that 'this is such beautiful country up here. It ought to be called the Northeast Kingdom of Vermont,' locals were quick to take his advice. Today, the Northeast Kingdom connotes the large wedge between the Quebec and NH borders. Less spectacular than spectacularly unspoiled, the landscape is a sea of green hills, with the occasional small village and farm spread out in the distance.

Here, inconspicuous inns and dairy cows contrast with the slick resorts and Morgan horses found in the southern part of the state; the white steeples are chipped, the barns in need of a fresh coat of paint. In a rural state known for its unpopulated setting (only Wyoming and Alaska contain fewer people), the Kingdom is Vermont's equivalent to putting on its finest pastoral dress, with a few holes here and there. It's a region that doesn't put on any airs about attracting tourists, and locals speak wryly of its 'picturesque poverty.'

Orientation & Information
While St Johnsbury is easily reached by I-91 or I-93 (a three-hour drive from Boston through

New Hampshire), the rest of the Northeast Kingdom is incredibly spread out. Use I-91 as your north–south thoroughfare, and then use smaller routes like VT 5A to find dramatically sited Lake Willoughby, or VT 14 to find picturesque Craftsbury Common. Other favorite villages include Greensboro, nestled upon the shores of Caspian Lake; Barton, near pristine Crystal Lake; and Lyndonville, 10 miles north of St Johnsbury, which boasts five covered bridges.

Northeast Kingdom Chamber of Commerce
(☎ 802-748-3678; www.vermontnekchamber.org; 357 Western Ave, St Johnsbury; ❤ 8:30am-5pm mid-Jun–mid-Oct) Runs a convenient information booth at Courthouse Park on Main St, as well as the St Johnsbury location, with plentiful regional information.

Sights
ST JOHNSBURY ATHENAEUM
Home to the country's oldest art gallery still in its original form, the **athenaeum** (☎ 802-748-8291; www.stjathenaeum.org; 1171 Main St, St Johnsbury; admission $5; ❤ 10am-8pm Mon & Wed, 10am-5:30pm Tue, Thu & Fri, 9:30am-4pm Sat) was founded in 1871 when Horace Fairbanks gave the town a library. Comprising some 9000 finely bound books of classic world literature, the library was soon complemented by the gallery, built around its crown jewel, Albert Bierstadt's 10ft-by-15ft painting, *Domes of the Yosemite*. The rest of the collection consists of works by such Hudson River School painters as Asher B Durand, Worthington Whittredge and Jasper Cropsey as well as dozens of copies of old masters. Bierstadt is said to have returned to the gallery every summer until his death to touch up his masterpiece.

FAIRBANKS MUSEUM & PLANETARIUM
In 1891, when Franklin Fairbanks' collection of stuffed animals and cultural artifacts from across the globe grew too large for his home, he built the **Fairbanks Museum of Natural Science** (☎ 802-748-2372; www.fairbanksmuseum.org; 1302 Main St, St Johnsbury; adult/child/senior/family $5/3/4/12; ❤ 9am-5pm Mon-Sat, 1-5pm Sun, closed Mon mid-Oct–mid-Apr). This massive stone building with a 30ft-high barrel-vaulted ceiling still displays more than half of Franklin's original collection. Over 3000 preserved animals in glass cases can be seen, including a 1200lb moose shot in Nova Scotia in 1898, an American bison from 1902 and a Bengal tiger. There are planetarium shows

at 1:30pm ($3 per person), and also in July and August at 11am.

MAPLE GROVE FARMS
Actually a factory, the **farms** (☎ 802-748-5141; www.maplegrove.com; 1052 Portland St or US 2) about half a mile east of St Johnsbury have been making maple candy for almost a century and are the world's largest producers of the saccharine stuff. Stop by to see how the molding process works and satisfy your sweet tooth – the popularity of the Santa Claus–shaped candies transcends all seasons.

CRAFTSBURY COMMON
Even if you don't plan on skiing at the Craftsbury Outdoor Center (below), you should take a drive over to **Craftsbury Common**, where you'll find what may be Vermont's most spectacular village green. White clapboard buildings surround a rectangular lawn that hasn't changed one iota from the mid-19th century.

Activities
Not surprisingly, this sylvan countryside is the perfect playground for New England outdoor activities. Almost any such pursuit is at its best in the Northeast Kingdom.

SKIING
When it's balmy in Boston in winter, you can still expect a blizzard at Vermont's northernmost ski resort, **Jay Peak** (☎ 802-988-2611; www.jaypeakresort.com; VT 242), 8 miles north of Montgomery Center. Bordering Quebec, Jay gets more snow than any other ski area in New England (about 350in of powder). Being so far north, Jay also sees far more Quebeckers than New Yorkers. Black-diamond lovers enjoy the steeper tree runs off the tram, while novices find the trails in Bonaventure Basin to their liking. Add the natural off-trail terrain, and you have some of the most challenging backcountry snowboarding and skiing runs in America.

Burke Mountain (☎ 802-626-3305; www.skiburke.com), off US 5 in East Burke, is relatively unknown to anyone outside the Northeast Kingdom. Locals enjoy the challenging trails and empty lift lines. Burke has 33 trails (30% beginner, 40% intermediate, 30% expert) and four lifts, including one quad chair and one lift with a vertical drop of 2000ft.

Cross-country skiers are bound to end up at the full-service **Craftsbury Outdoor Center** (☎ 802-

THE BREAD & PUPPET MUSEUM

Rolling though the Northeast Kingdom, it's easy to become jaded at the sight of yet another barn. One in Glover definitely warrants a detour – not for its livestock but for the cosmological universe of the **Bread & Puppet Museum** (☎ 802-525-3031; www.breadandpuppet.org; 753 Heights Rd, Glover), lurking within.

Formed in New York City by German artist Peter Shumann in 1963, the Bread & Puppet Theater is a collective-in-training that presents carnivalesque pageants, circuses, and battles of Good and Evil with gaudy masks and life-size (even gigantic) puppets. The street theater of its early performances gave voice to local rent strikes and anti–Vietnam War protests as well as an epic parade down Fifth Ave in the early eighties to protest nuclear proliferation. By then, it had moved its operation to Glover, where it currently occupies two barns.

The first barn is a two-floor space crammed with puppets and masks from past performances. The high-ceilinged top floor is especially arresting, with its collection of many-headed demons, menacing generals, priests, bankers, everyday people and animals, and an array of gods (some as large as 15ft). A second barn features performances in July and August – Bread & Puppet is on tour the rest of the year – for which Schumann bakes the bread that gives the enterprise half its name. Regular shows are on Friday evening and Sunday afternoon, but it's well worth checking the website to see if anything special is cooking.

To get to the Bread & Puppet Museum, take I-91 to exit 24, then take a right onto VT 122 and continue 13 miles.

586-7767; www.craftsbury.com; Lost Nation Rd), 3 miles from Craftsbury Common. The 80 miles of trails – 50 of them groomed – roll over meadows and weave through forests of maples and firs, offering an ideal experience for all levels.

Nearby, **Highland Lodge** (☎ 802-533-2647; www.highlandlodge.com; Craftsbury Rd, Greensboro) has 40 miles of trails that slope down to the shores of Caspian Lake.

MOUNTAIN BIKING

On VT 114 off I-91, **East Burke** is a terrific place to start a mountain-bike ride. In the summer of 1997 John Worth, co-owner of East Burke Sports, and several other dedicated locals linked together more than 200 miles of single and double tracks and dirt roads to form a network they call the **Kingdom Trails**. Riding on a soft forest floor dusted with pine needles and through century-old farms makes for one of the best mountain-biking experiences in New England. **East Burke Sports** (☎ 802-626-3215; www.eastburkesports.com; VT 114; bikes per day $20-30) rents bikes and supplies maps.

HIKING

Hiking through the stunning beauty of **Lake Willoughby** will leave even a jaded visitor in awe. Sandwiched between Mt Hor and Mt Pisgah, cliffs plummet more than 1000ft to the glacial waters below and create, in essence, a landlocked fjord. The scenery is best appreci-

ated on the hike (three hours) to the summit of **Mt Pisgah**. From West Burke, take VT 5A for 6 miles to a parking area on the left-hand side of the road, just south of Lake Willoughby. The 2-mile (one-way) **South Trail** begins across the highway. It's about a 30-minute drive from St Johnsbury to Mt Pisgah.

Sleeping

The Northeast Kingdom offers some of the most affordable lodgings in the state. The best accommodations are at small inns on family-run farms or by the shores of a hidden lake.

BUDGET

Stillwater State Park (☎ 802-584-3822; www.vtstateparks.com; Groton; RV sites/campsites $21/14; ◯ mid-May–mid-Oct) Near to Ricker Pond State Park, off VT 232, Stillwater has 107 sites and a prime swimming spot on the northwestern shores of Lake Groton.

Rodgers Country Inn (☎ 802-525-6677, 800-729-1704; 582 Rodgers Rd, West Glover; r per person incl breakfast & dinner per day/week $45/250) Not far from the shores of Shadow Lake, Jim and Nancy Rodgers offer five guest rooms in their 1840s farmhouse. Hang out on the front porch and read, or take a stroll on this 350-acre former dairy farm. This inn appeals to people who really want to feel what it's like to live in rural Vermont.

Craftsbury Bed & Breakfast (☎ 802-586-2206; 414 Wiley Hill Rd, Craftsbury Common; d incl full breakfast $60-80)

Set in a farmhouse atop Wylie Hill, this B&B with shared bathrooms offers expansive views of rolling farmland. It's just down the road from the historic village green and close to the Craftsbury Outdoor Center for mountain biking and cross-country skiing. Innkeeper Margy Ramsdell's cinnamon apple pancakes send guests out ready to tackle their day. Reservations are required.

MIDRANGE

our pick **Craftsbury Inn** (☎ 802-586-2848, 800-336-2848; www.craftsburyinn.com; Craftsbury Village; incl full breakfast s $60-90, d $90-130) A charming B&B with 10 cozy rooms across from the village general store, half a mile east of Crafstbury Common. Breakfasts on the back porch are hearty affairs, enlivened by the occasional sighting of one of the llamas the owners keep with their farm.

Inn on Trout River (☎ 802-326-4391, 800-338-7049; www.troutinn.com; 241 Main St, Montgomery Center; r per person incl full breakfast $69-96) One of the better places to stay if you plan on skiing Jay Peak, which is ten minutes away. This village house was built by a lumber baron over a century ago, and features 10 guest rooms, one suite and two restaurants (one fancy and one a pub).

Village Inn of East Burke (☎ 802-626-3161; www.villageinnofeastburke.com; VT 114, East Burke; r incl full breakfast $75-85) Innkeepers Lorraine and George Willy treat guests like family in this good-value B&B at the base of Burke Mountain's ski area. The inn has six very clean rooms, an outdoor Jacuzzi, a guest kitchen and a living-room fireplace. From the wonderful 5-acre garden out back, you can follow a trail that leads to a waterfall. (If only life could always be this simple.)

Willoughvale Inn (☎ 802-525-4123, 800-594-9102; www.willoughvale.com; VT 5A, Westmore; r incl continental breakfast d $103-263, ste $135-245, cottages $179-350) Overlooking the majestic granite cliffs of Mt Hor and Mt Pisgah, this inn sits on the northern shores of Lake Willoughby. It features eight spacious rooms, two suites and four cottages. In summer, cast off from the small beach and kayak (rented for a small fee) on the cool waters of the lake. In winter, rent snowmobiles and head up into the hills.

TOP END

Highland Lodge (☎ 802-533-2647; www.highlandlodge.com; Greensboro; incl breakfast & dinner d $137-180, ste $255-295; ⊙ late Dec–mid-Mar & May–mid-Oct) This 11-room lodge (with additional cottages) is perched on a hill over Caspian Lake, off VT 16, and all guest rooms have a view of the lake. A trail leads to a private beach and canoe-rental shop. Wintertime guests can enjoy an extensive cross-country skiing network.

Inn at Mountain View Farm (☎ 802-626-9924, 800-572-4509; www.innmtnview.com; 3383 Darling Hill Rd, East Burke; r incl full breakfast d $155-195, ste $275) Built in 1883 as a gentleman's farm, this splendid place now houses a 14-room inn. Rooms reflect the charm of a spacious, comfortable farmhouse with details like hand-held European shower, fainting couch (what's that, you say?) and chintz touches. The farm's 440 acres are ideal for mountain biking, cross-country skiing or simply taking a long stroll on the hillside.

Wildflower Inn (☎ 802-626-8310, 800-627-8310; www.wildflowerinn.com; 2059 Darling Hill Rd, Lyndonville; incl full breakfast s $200, ste $230, 2-r ste $305; ⊙ Dec–Mar & May–Oct; 🐾) This is a perennial favorite with families. Maybe it's because owners Jim and Mary O'Reilly have eight children and their home is littered with toys. Or perhaps it's the hayrides, mountain-bike trails, petting zoo with sheep and goats, playground, tennis courts and heaps of other onsite activities. Besides the cozy sitting rooms with fireplaces, the inn has 10 rooms and 11 suites.

Eating

Although, the region is not replete with restaurants, it does offer some fine dining with surprisingly inexpensive tabs.

Miss Lyndonville Diner (☎ 802-626-9890; US 5, Lyndonville; dishes $2-11; ⊙ breakfast, lunch & dinner) Five miles north of St Johnsbury and popular with locals, this place also offers friendly and prompt service. Large breakfasts are cheap; sandwiches cost a bit more, but the tasty dinners (like roast turkey with all the fixings) are a real steal.

Bagel Depot (☎ 802-748-1600; 1216 Railroad St, St Johnsbury; bagels $3-9; ⊙ breakfast & lunch) This Creamery Building eatery serves the freshest bagels in the Northeast Kingdom. Add a cup of Green Mountain Coffee to kick-start your morning or come back for daily lunch specials.

Anthony's Diner (☎ 802-748-3613; 50 Railroad St, St Johnsbury; dishes $3-15; ⊙ breakfast, lunch & dinner Mon-Sat, breakfast & lunch Sun) While hanging around the large counter, try the mountain-size Vermont woodsman burger. The homemade soups, chowders and desserts are a deserved source of pride.

ourpick Elements (☎ 802-748-8400; 98 Mill St, St Johnsonbury; dishes $7-23; ⊙ lunch Tue-Fri, dinner Tue-Sat) The setting in a former mill complements the novel menu, which uses local ingredients whenever possible. Try the polenta lasagna with eggplant over roasted vegetables, or trout cakes with tomato jam, wasabi and crème fraîche. Try to share so that you sample several dishes. Dried cranberries go into the corn-bread pudding for dessert – a unique treat. Almost everything is made on the premises.

Candlepin Restaurant (☎ 802-525-6513; VT 5; meals $8-18; ⊙ breakfast, lunch & dinner) A roadside diner, just north of Barton, with surprisingly good fare, the Candlepin serves up juicy burgers and Vermont roast turkey. The pies are especially worth sticking around for.

Cucina di Gerardo (☎ 802-748-6772; 213 Railroad St, St Johnsbury; meals $9-24; ⊙ lunch & dinner) This Creamery Building place serves hearty Italian fare like mussels marinara and fancy gourmet pizzas.

River Garden Cafe (☎ 802-626-3514; VT 114, East Burke; meals $10-24; ⊙ lunch & dinner Tue-Sun, brunch Sun)

This place is true to its name: you'll enjoy the back porch (open year-round) and summer patio within earshot of the river. This local favorite offers salads, pastas, filet mignon and stir-fried dishes served in a casually elegant atmosphere. For lunch, try the Green Mountain pizza ($7) topped with Vermont goat cheese, mozzarella, pesto and tomato sauce. As you might have guessed, breads and desserts are homemade.

Willoughvale Inn (☎ 802-525-3234; VT 5A, Westmore; meals $17-26; ⊙ lunch & dinner) Even if you don't stay here, at least have a meal in its glass-enclosed dining room overlooking Lake Willoughby. Hearty American fare, including prime rib and turkey, prevails. Then again there's always a giant burger or lasagna.

Getting There & Away

By car, St Johnsbury is 39 miles (about 45 minutes) from Montpelier via US 2 east, or 76 miles (1½ hours) if you're coming directly from Burlington. The only way to get around the Northeast Kingdom is by car.

New Hampshire

Among artists, poets and the occasional free spirit or two, New Hampshire has long been a place of a great inspiration. Boasting jagged mountains, scenic valleys and forest-lined lakes, this proud, rugged state is no stranger to natural beauty. Thoreau, Robert Frost, and the sculptor Augustus Saint-Gaudens were but a few of the talented Americans who were moved by the beauty of this former English colony, and created some of their greatest works here.

Inspiration, of course, claims no master, and the great bounty of the state belongs not only to art colonies and famous writers – both still present in New Hampshire – but to anyone who takes the time to visit. Those who do will have some choices to make: great outdoor adventure lurks in all corners of the state, from kayaking the hidden coves of the Lakes Region to trekking the upper peaks surrounding Mt Washington. Seasonal pursuits include fantastic skiing and snowshoeing in winter, magnificent walks through autumn's fiery colors and swimming in crisp mountain streams in summer. New Hampshire's villages and historic towns likewise make for some memorable exploring. Jewel-box colonial settlements such as Portsmouth offer a window into 18th-century New England, while small-town culture lives on in charming villages such as Keene and Peterborough.

New Hampshire is the most politically conservative state in New England with a libertarian streak that runs deep. This was, after all, the last state in New England to institute a smoking ban in its bars and restaurants (in 2007) and its citizens still cling with pride to the famous words uttered by General John Stark, victor at the crucial Battle of Bennington: 'Live free or die.'

HIGHLIGHTS

- Watching fog blanket the 18th-century homes and cobbled lanes of **Portsmouth** (p411), New Hampshire's loveliest colonial town

- Strolling the shoreline of Winnipesaukee outside **Wolfeboro** (p436), a charming lakeside village with a heart of gold

- Gazing at thousands of leering jack-o'-lanterns at the quirky pumpkin festival in **Keene** (p424), a picture-book town in the shadow of Mt Monadnock

- Skiing, hiking, kayaking and reconnecting with the great outdoors amid the alpine beauty of the **White Mountains** (p439)

- Walking in the footsteps of a great poet and taking in autumn's dazzling colors in bucolic **Franconia** (p447)

White Mountains
★ Franconia ★

Wolfeboro ★

Portsmouth ★

★ Keene

- TELEPHONE CODE: 603   - POPULATION: 1.3 MILLION   - AREA: 8968 SQ MILES

Orientation & Information

New Hampshire's tiny coastline, sandwiched between Maine and Massachusetts is just 18 miles long. More impressive is the vast White Mountain region in the central north. In roughly the center of the state is enormous Lake Winnipesaukee and the surrounding lakes region, while south of the waters lie Concord, the state capital, and Manchester, the largest 'city' in New Hampshire. Both towns are situated along the Merrimack River.

Some state information sites:

New Hampshire Division of Parks & Recreation
(☎ 603-271-3556; www.nhparks.state.nh.us) Offers information on a statewide bicycle route system and a very complete camping guide.

New Hampshire Division of Travel & Tourism
(☎ 603-271-2665; www.visitnh.gov) Information including ski conditions and fall foliage reports.

History

Nomadic Abenaki tribes were the first settlers in the area, thriving on bountiful streams and forests, where they survived on fish, venison, turkey and other wild fowl, along with corn, squash, pumpkin and wild fruits and berries. Indigenous place names live on in the state, while the Abenaki themselves do not. The Europeans scouted the area in the early 1600s and first settled (around present-day Durham) in 1631. The economy of the early royal colony was based on timber and shipbuilding, with settlements largely confined to the coast until after the French and Indian Wars.

New Hampshire was among the earliest colonies (along with Rhode Island) to declare its independence, and it was the first to establish its own government. It contributed substantial troops to both the American Revolution and the Civil War. Following the latter, New Hampshire's economy leaned toward industrial production, with a steady influx of immigrants (largely from Québec and Ireland) and a boom in textile manufacturing. In 1915 it boasted of having the largest producing textile mills in the world. As the local economy grew the forests shrank, with large tracts of woodlands channeling through the sawmills. Luckily, in 1911 the first of the conservation laws was passed, eventually leading to the creation of the vast White Mountain National Forest.

Manufacturing continued apace until the Great Depression dealt the deathblow and the state began the slow process of diversifying its economy. Since the 1980s the local economy has flourished, with an influx of high-tech and financial firms.

Today New Hampshire is known for the angst it brings to hopeful presidential contenders. Every four years – as it did in 2008 – the state hosts the country's first primary election (both Democratic and Republican). Since candidates who do poorly in New Hampshire usually quit, this gives the tiny state an enormous role in deciding who will rule the world's richest country – a role most Hampshirians rather enjoy.

The Culture

New Hampshire natives take pride in the fact that they 'live free or die.' Sometimes this motto takes some curious twists, like the insistence on not having a seatbelt law or a helmet law for motorcyclists ('live free *and* die' seems more apt in these instances). New Hampshirians also sneer at handgun laws and other statutes they feel will limit them in some way. Because of this libertarian streak, they normally vote Republican, though this trend is changing in recent years. Some credit Democratic success with the blundering of the Bush administration, while others chalk it up to the influx of outsiders (liberals!) moving into their state. Although blue bloods aren't particularly welcomed by many New Hampshirians, who can blame them for wanting to live here? At last count, the state ranked near the top in median income, with a high quality of life; it has no urban blight (because there really aren't any cities here) and no state or sales tax. On the downside, the state is woefully homogenous (a whopping 98% white) and it does have sky-high property taxes (mostly because it doesn't have state or sales taxes).

Land & Climate

New Hampshire comprises 9304 sq miles, and is sometimes called the 'mother of rivers' since five of the great New England rivers originate in its hills. The state has 1300 lakes or ponds and 40 rivers, totaling more than 40,000 miles. It boasts the most impressive mountains in New England, with 48 peaks reaching over 4000ft, the highest of which is famed Mt Washington.

The climate of New Hampshire is usually similar to that of the rest of New England,

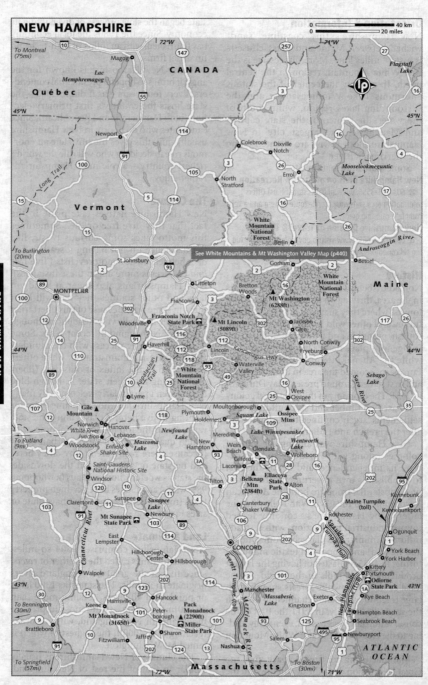

NEW HAMPSHIRE

See White Mountains & Mt Washington Valley Map (p440)

with the exception of the mountain peaks, where conditions are notoriously volatile and can be severe, even when the weather in the lowlands is fine.

Parks & Wildlife

The feather in New Hampshire's cap is the White Mountain National Forest (WMNF; p439), which covers nearly 800,000 acres in New Hampshire and Maine. Hiking trails, skiing slopes, campgrounds, swimming beaches and a few carefully controlled auto roads provide access to this gigantic natural playground.

Aside from the WMNF, New Hampshire has a small but well-run network of state parks, including Franconia Notch, Crawford Notch and Echo Lake, along with the entire seacoast.

Wildlife in the region includes 300 species of vertebrates, with another 120 species of annual migrants. Moose are the state's biggest mammals, present in the North Woods, while black bear are found (but rarely seen) in all ten New Hampshire counties. Other fine-furred friends include muskrat, porcupine, white-tailed deer. beaver, coyote, snowshoe hare, harbor seal, bobcat, the endangered lynx and a host of voles, shrews and chipmunks. There's some fine bird-watching throughout the state, particularly in the White Mountains, with 38 year-round species and 110 species in the summer months when neotropical birds such as the wood thrush and blue warbler breed here. In the winter, keep an eye out for the great gray owl and the northern hawk owl. On the coast you might spot osprey, heron, egrets and the endangered bald eagle. Squam Lake is famous for its loons.

Getting There & Around

AIR

Manchester Airport (☎ 603-624-6556; www.flyman chester.com) is the state's largest airport with direct flights to 15 other American cities as well as Toronto. The smaller **Lebanon Municipal Airport** (☎ 603-298-8878; www.flyleb.com) serves Hanover.

BUS

Concord Trailways (☎ 603-228-3300, 800-639-3317; www.concordtrailways.com) operates a bus route to and from Boston South Station and Logan International Airport, with stops in Manchester, Concord, Meredith, Conway, North Conway, Jackson, Pinkham Notch, Gorham and Berlin. Another route runs through North Woodstock/Lincoln, Franconia and Littleton.

Dartmouth Coach (☎ 603-448-2800, 800-637-0123; www.dartmouthcoach.com) offers services from Hanover, Lebanon and New London to Boston South Station and Logan International Airport (also in Boston).

Vermont Transit (☎ 800-451-3292; www.vermont transit.com) operates a route connecting Boston and Portsmouth, with continuing services to Portland, Bangor and Bar Harbor, ME.

CAR & MOTORCYCLE

The New Hampshire Turnpike (along the seacoast), Everett Turnpike (I-93) and Spaulding Turnpike (NH 16) are toll roads. For road conditions, call ☎ 800-918-9993.

PORTSMOUTH & THE SEACOAST

New Hampshire's coastline stretches just 18 miles, but provides access to the captivating coastal town of Portsmouth and a length of attractive beaches, sprinkled around rocky headlands and coves. The shore along these parts has substantial commercial development, with well-regulated access to its state beaches and parks.

PORTSMOUTH

pop 23,000

Perched on the edge of the Piscataqua river, Portsmouth is one of New Hampshire's most elegant towns, with a historical center set with tree-lined streets and 18th-century colonial buildings. Despite its early importance in the maritime industry, the town has a youthful energy, with tourists and locals filling its many restaurants and cafés. Numerous museums and historic houses allow visitors a glimpse into the town's multilayered past, while its proximity to the coast brings both lobster feasts and periodic days of fog that blanket the waterfront.

Still true to its name, Portsmouth remains a working port town and its economic vitality has been boosted by the Naval Shipyard (actually located across the river in Maine) and by the influx of high-tech companies.

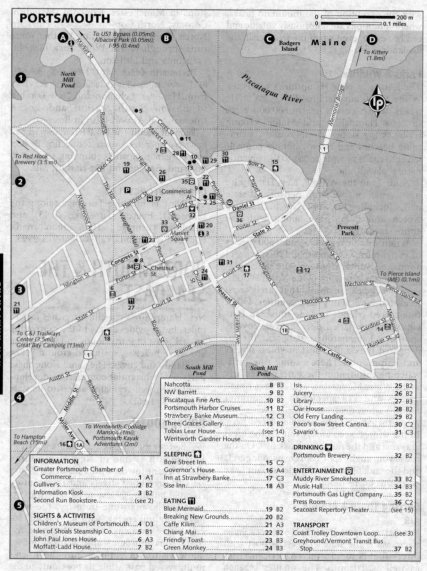

PORTSMOUTH

0 ——————— 200 m
0 ——————— 0.1 miles

Orientation

Historic Portsmouth is surrounded on three sides by water. To the northwest is the North Mill Pond, to the northeast is the Piscataqua River and to the southeast is the South Mill Pond. Market St, reached via I-95 exit 7, is the main commercial street.

Information

Greater Portsmouth Chamber of Commerce

(☎ 603-436-1118; www.portsmouthchamber.org; 500 Market St/I-95 exit 7) Also operates an information kiosk in the city center at Market Sq.

Gulliver's (☎ 603-431-5556; 7 Commercial Alley; ☽ 10am-5pm Mon-Sat, noon-5pm Sun) A large selection of maps and travel guidebooks, including an excellent section on New England.

Second Run Bookstore (☎ 603-431-2100; 7 Commercial Alley; ☯ 10am-5pm Mon-Sat, noon-5pm Sun) An independent bookstore above Gulliver's.

Sights
MARKET SQUARE
The heart of Portsmouth is this picturesque **square** (☎ 603-436-3680; cnr Congress & Pleasant Sts), set neatly beneath the soaring white spire of the North Church. Within a few steps of the square are open-air cafés, colorful storefronts and tiny galleries with banjo-playing buskers entertaining the tourists and locals that drift past on warm summer nights.

PRESCOTT PARK
Overlooking the Piscataqua River, this small, grassy **park** (☎ 603-436-3680; cnr Congress & Pleasant Sts) makes a pleasant setting for a picnic. More importantly, it's the leafy backdrop to the **Prescott Park Arts Festival** (☎ 603-436-2848; www.prescottpark .org), which means free music, dance, theater and food festivals throughout the summer. Separate one-day music festivals showcase jazz, folk and Americana; other highlights include the clam-chowder and chili festivals.

STRAWBERY BANKE MUSEUM
Spread across a 10-acre site, the **Strawbery Banke Museum** (☎ 603-433-1100; www.strawberybanke.org; 14 Hancock St; adult/child/family $15/10/40; ☯ 10am-5pm Mon-Sat, noon-5pm Sun May-Oct, 10am-2pm Sat & Sun Nov-Apr) is an eclectic blend of period homes that date back to the 1690s. Costumed guides recount tales that took place among the 40 buildings (10 furnished). Strawbery Banke includes Pitt Tavern (1766), a hotbed of American revolutionary sentiment, Goodwin Mansion (a grand 19th-century house from Portsmouth's most prosperous time) and Abbott's Little Corner Store (1943). The admission ticket is good for two consecutive days.

ALBACORE PARK
Just north of the old town center, this park serves as maritime museum and host to the **USS Albacore** (☎ 603-436-3680; http://ussalbacore.org; 600 Market St; adult/child/family $5/3/10; ☯ 9:30am-5pm daily Jun-Oct, 9:30am-4.30pm Thu-Mon Nov-May), a 205ft-long US Navy submarine, now open to the public. The *Albacore* was launched from the Portsmouth Naval Shipyard in 1953 and, with

a crew of 55, it was piloted around the world for 19 years without firing a shot.

CHILDREN'S MUSEUM OF PORTSMOUTH
Ensconced in an old meeting house, this exciting **museum** (☎ 603-436-3853; www.childrens-museum .org; 280 Marcy St; adult/senior/child $6/5/6; ☯ 10am-5pm Tue-Sat, 1-5pm Sun, plus 10am-5pm Mon Jun-Aug) has changing exhibits, toys and experiments for children aged between one and 10 years old. As you might expect, many displays elucidate the region's maritime history in an engaging way.

HISTORIC HOUSES
Several of Portsmouth's grand old houses have been beautifully preserved. If you visit, don't miss the lovely landscaped grounds, most of which are bursting with blooming gardens.

The **John Paul Jones House** (☎ 603-436-8420; www.portsmouthhistory.org; 43 Middle St; adult/child $8/ free; ☯ 11am-5pm May-Oct) was a boardinghouse when America's first great naval commander resided in Portsmouth. Jones, who uttered, 'I have not yet begun to fight!' during a particularly bloody engagement with the British, is believed to have lodged here during the outfitting of the *Ranger* (1777) and the *America* (1781). The marvelous Georgian mansion with gambrel roof is now the headquarters of the **Portsmouth Historical Society**.

The 1760 **Wentworth Gardner House** (☎ 603-436-4406; www.wentworthgardnerandlear.org; 50 Mechanic St; adult/child $5/2; ☯ 1-4pm Tue-Sun Jun-Oct) is one of the finest Georgian houses in the USA. Elizabeth and Mark Hunking Wentworth were among Portsmouth's wealthiest and most prominent citizens, so no expense was spared in building this home, which was a wedding gift for their son. Next door, the **Tobias Lear House** (☯ 1-4pm Wed; adult/child $5/2) is a hip-roofed colonial residence that was home to the family of George Washington's private secretary.

Originally owned by an influential ship captain, the Georgian **Moffatt-Ladd House** (☎ 603-436-8221; 154 Market St; adult/child $6/2.50; ☯ 11am-5pm Mon-Sat & 1-5pm Sun Jun-Oct) was later the home of General William Whipple, a signer of the Declaration of Independence. The 18th-century chestnut tree and the old-fashioned **gardens** (admission $2) behind the house are delightful.

The 42-room **Wentworth-Coolidge Mansion** (☎ 603-436-6607; www.wentworthcoolidge.org; 375 Little

Harbor Rd; adult/child $7/3; ⏰ 10am-3pm Sat & Sun May-Jun, daily Jul-Aug), south of the town center, was home to New Hampshire's first royal governor and served as the colony's government center from 1741 to 1766. The lilacs on its grounds are descendants of the first lilacs planted in America, which were brought over from England by Governor Benning Wentworth.

GALLERIES & ART SPACES

Portsmouth has a small collection of galleries around the historical center, featuring the oil paintings, watercolors and woodblock prints of local and international artists. Simultaneous receptions at the following key galleries – and Portsmouth's other major galleries – are held on the second Friday of each month from 5pm to 8pm. For a complete list, visit www .artroundtown.org, or pick up a brochure at the chamber of commerce.

Nahcotta (☎ 603-433-1705; www.nahcotta.com; 110 Congress St)

NW Barrett (☎ 603-431-4262; www.nwbarrett.com; 53 Market St)

Piscataqua Fine Arts (☎ 603-431-4110; www.dongor vettgallery.com; 23 Ceres St)

Three Graces Gallery (☎ 603-436-1988; www.three gracesgallery.com; 105 Market St)

Activities

CRUISES

From mid-June to October the **Isles of Shoals Steamship Co** (☎ 603-431-5500, 800-441-4620; www .islesofshoals.com; 315 Market St, Barker Wharf; adult $20-33, child $10-23) runs an excellent tour of the harbor and the historic Isles of Shoals aboard a replica 1900s ferry. This is a deservedly popular voyage, especially the midday trip, which docks at Star Island for three hours. Look into the all-day whale watches and shorter sunset and dinner cruises.

Cruises on the *Heritage*, run by **Portsmouth Harbor Cruises** (☎ 603-436-8084, 800-776-0915; www .portsmouthharbor.com; Ceres St Dock; adult $12-20, child $8-13) go around the harbor or to the Isles of Shoals. One unique option is cruising up an inland river and through the Great Bay tidal estuary. This cruise is particularly popular in fall when the foliage is colorful.

KAYAKING

Portsmouth Kayak Adventures (☎ 603-559-1000; www.portsmouthkayak.com; 185 Wentworth Rd, Witch Cove Marina; tours $40-59, kayak rental per half/full day $40/59; ⏰ 9am-5pm) offers a range of peaceful kayaking

tours out on the harbors near Portsmouth, including a sunset tour, a moonlight tour and a combined kayaking-yoga-on-the-beach experience. Those with experience can rent a kayak and explore the waterways on their own. To get there, take Miller Ave (1A) south and turn left onto Wentworth Rd. It's the first building on the left.

Tours

Harbor Trail (☎ 603-436-3988; Market Sq; adult/child/ senior $8/5/7; ⏰ 10:30am & 5:30pm Thu-Sat & Mon, 1:30pm Sun Jul-Oct) A guided walking tour of the historic downtown and waterfront.

Legends & Ghosts (☎ 207-439-8905; www.neweng landcuriosities.com; tours $12-25) New England Curiosities runs a variety of walking tours, visiting old graveyards, an abandoned prison, the 'haunted' pubs of Portsmouth and other locales where history and mystery collide. Call or check their website for meeting places and times.

Red Hook Brewery (☎ 603-430-8600; www.redhook .com; 35 Corporate Dr) For the chance to see the crafting of a fine ale, book one of Red Hook's free daily tours. On site is also the Cataqua Public House (open from noon to 10pm Monday to Saturday and noon to 8pm on Sunday), which serves pub fare alongside the signature brews. Call for tour schedule and directions.

Sleeping

Many of Portsmouth's motels and hotels cluster at I-95 exits 5 and 6, around the Portsmouth (Interstate) traffic circle. Most camping areas are privately run, inland from the seacoast and very busy in the summer.

Great Bay Camping (☎ 603-778-0226; www.greatbay camping.com; 56 NH 108, Newfields; campsites/RV sites $25/30; ⏰ May-Sep) About 13 miles from Portsmouth, this family-oriented campground has numerous RV sites along a tidal river and a handful of more peaceful tent sites.

Bow Street Inn (☎ 603-431-7760; www.bowstreetinn .com; 121 Bow St; r incl breakfast Nov-Mar $99-150, May-Oct $150-180; Ⓟ) In a brick building overlooking the river, this cozy inn is just upstairs from the Seacoast Repertory Theater. The ten rooms have floral bedspreads and brass bedsteads, with some rooms boasting harbor views.

Inn at Strawbery Banke (☎ 603-436-7242, 800-428-3933; www.innatstrawberybanke.com; 314 Court St; r incl breakfast Nov-Mar $110-115, Apr-Oct $145-150; Ⓟ) Set amid the historic buildings of Strawbery Banke, this colonial charmer has seven small but attractive rooms, each uniquely set with quilted bedspreads, brass or canopy beds and wood floors in all but one room. The fabulous breakfast spread includes homemade pastries, quiches and pancakes with local maple syrup.

Governor's House (☎ 603-427-5140, 866-427-5140; www.governors-house.com; 32 Miller Ave; r Nov-Mar $145-195, Apr-Oct $175-235; P ⌨ wi-fi) This stately Georgian house is named for New Hampshire governor Charles Dale, who lived here in the mid-20th century. It has only four wood-floored guest rooms, each exquisitely fitted out with unique period furnishings, a private bathroom with hand-painted tiles and elegant decor. Little luxuries like down comforters, terry bathrobes and an outdoor hot tub help to make this one of Portsmouth's gems.

Sise Inn (☎ 603-433-1200, 877-747-3466; www.sise inn.com; 40 Court St; incl breakfast r/ste Nov-Apr $119/149-189, May-Oct $199/239-279; P ⌨ wi-fi) A short walk from the city center, this elegant, Queen Anne-style inn dates from 1881, and beautiful common areas with original wood details and antiques. Its 28 large, carpeted rooms and six suites feature period furnishings coupled with modern comforts, like telephones and VCR or DVD players; some of the larger suites have Jacuzzi bathtubs.

Eating
BUDGET

Breaking New Grounds (☎ 603-436-9555; Market Sq; pastries $2-3; ⏰ 6:30am-10:30pm) Smack in the heart of town, this buzzy café serves excellent coffee and lattés. Arrive early for plump muffins and a sunny table on the square.

Caffe Kilim (☎ 603-436-7730; 163 Islington St; coffee $2-3.75; ⏰ 7am-9pm Mon-Sat, 7am-8pm Sun May-Oct, shorter hr Nov-Apr) Portsmouth's most atmospheric café is a short stroll from the historic center and features rich espresso, blends (try the Dancing Goats) and Turkish coffee. As in their former Daniel St locale, you can still haggle over rugs while sipping hot tea, just like in Istanbul.

Juicery (☎ 603-431-0693; 51 Hanover St; juices $4-5; ⏰ 9am-8pm Mon-Sat, 10am-6pm Sun May-Oct, shorter hr Nov-Apr; V) Refuel with fresh-squeezed organic juices and all-natural nondairy smoothies. Organic wraps, salads and chili are also available for take-out.

Savario's (☎ 603-427-2919; 278 State St; ⏰ noon-2pm & 5-8pm Mon-Fri) This tiny, family-run takeout pizza shop serves tasty pizzas and calzones, and remains something of a Portsmouth secret – despite winning 'best in town' awards for its homemade pies.

Friendly Toast (☎ 603-430-2154; 121 Congress St; meals $7-9; ⏰ 7am-11pm Mon-Thu, 7am Fri-9pm Sun; V) Fun, whimsical furnishings set the scene for filling sandwiches, omelettes, Tex-Mex and vegetarian fare at this retro diner. The breakfast menu is huge and is served around the clock – good thing since weekend morning waits can be long.

MIDRANGE

Poco's Bow Street Cantina (☎ 603-431-5967; 37 Bow St; meals $11-21; ⏰ lunch & dinner) Southwestern dishes arrive with New England flair at this lively waterfront spot. Blackened red snapper, fish tacos and jerk chicken quesadillas are among the mouthwatering favorites.

Chiang Mai (☎ 603-433-1289; 128 Penhallow St; meals $10-21; ⏰ lunch Tue-Sat, dinner Tue-Sun) For a break from seafood and New England fare, head to this simply furnished but locally popular Thai restaurant, which serves satisfying curries and noodle dishes.

Old Ferry Landing (☎ 603-431-5510; 10 Ceres St; meals $8-22; ⏰ 11:30am-8pm mid-Apr–mid-Sep) In a truly nautical setting overlooking the harbor, this place dishes up moderately priced seafood favorites like lobster rolls and haddock sandwiches. Several other no-nonsense seafood eateries clutter the same street.

ourpick Blue Mermaid (☎ 603-427-2583; 409 The Hill; meals $9-22; ⏰ lunch & dinner) A few blocks from the center, Blue Mermaid serves a delectable mix of Caribbean-inspired fare, including wood-grilled seafood, salads and polenta cakes. The setting of dark-wood floors, jewel-toned tiles and a turquoise-textured ceiling give a fun and funky vibe to the place. In the summer the outdoor deck's a great spot for refreshing margaritas.

Green Monkey (☎ 603-427-1010; 86 Pleasant St; meals $20-32; ⏰ dinner) This well-received newcomer to the dining scene serves expertly prepared fusion fare, including Moroccan bouillabaisse, macadamia-encrusted mahi-mahi (dolphin fish), and other sizzling grilled fish and meats in a stylish, downtown setting.

TOP END

Isis (☎ 603-431-1178; 106 Penhallow St; meals $24-30, brunch $8-10; ⏰ lunch daily, dinner Thu-Sat) Isis earns solid reviews for its excellent Sunday brunch (gingerbread pancakes, crabmeat Benedict, brie and portobello mushroom omelettes

NEW HAMPSHIRE

and other decadent fare). At other times, the stylish but minimalist dining room serves fresh eclectic food, including slow-roasted salmon and wild-mushroom ravioli.

Library (☎ 603-431-5202; 401 State St; meals $12-35; ☣ lunch Mon-Sat, dinner Thu-Sun, brunch Sun) Within a palatial and opulent home built by a prominent judge in 1785, the Library is among New Hampshire's top steakhouses, serving juicy prime rib and rack of lamb in a dapper wood-paneled dining room. There's also a wood-paneled English pub where you can enjoy burgers and lighter fare.

Oar House (☎ 603-436-4025; 55 Ceres St; meals $11-34; ☣ lunch & dinner) One of Portsmouth's best seafood restaurants, this elegant place has a dark cozy interior with an inviting wine bar, as well as an outdoor deck (across the street) overlooking the harbor. Classic dishes like broiled haddock, sautéed scallops and baked stuffed lobster come expertly prepared.

Drinking & Entertainment
BARS & CLUBS
Portsmouth Gas Light Company (☎ 603-430-9122; 64 Market St; ☣ 11:30am-10pm, club until 1am) This multi-story complex gathers a youthful crowd on weekends, who come for live music on the outdoor patio, with DJs picking things up on the 3rd floor later in the night. There's also an inviting pub and a basement brick-oven pizzeria.

Portsmouth Brewery (☎ 603-431-1115; 56 Market St; ☣ 11:30am-midnight) Classically set with tin ceilings and exposed brick walls, this airy brewpub serves excellent homegrown pilsners, porters and ales – a fine accompaniment to decent, if not overly dazzling, pub fare.

LIVE MUSIC
Portsmouth is a local mecca for music as well as dining. Several clubs feature ever-changing schedules of local and national acts playing rock, folk, jazz, R&B and so on.

Press Room (☎ 603-431-5186; 77 Daniel St; ☣ 4pm-midnight Mon-Fri, noon-midnight Sat) Nightly live music ranges from jazz to blues to folk. There is a long menu of bar food in case the jamming makes you hungry.

Muddy River Smokehouse (☎ 603-430-9582; 21 Congress St) Barbecue and bands (at 8pm from Tuesday to Saturday) compete at this lively Market Sq venue. With swamp-theme murals and rustic wood furniture, the dining room tries to recreate the bayou.

THEATER & CULTURE
Music Hall (☎ 603-436-2400; www.themusichall.org; 28 Chestnut St; tickets $20-60) For a small town theater, this venue hosts a surprising array of performances, including dance, theater, opera and other music. Musicians, comedians and theater companies from around the country make appearances here.

Seacoast Repertory Theater (☎ 603-433-4472; www.seacoastrep.org; 125 Bow St; tickets $22-30) This theater is housed in a cool, reconverted building on Portsmouth's industrial riverfront and stages numerous musicals, while also hosting the occasional comedian.

Getting There & Around
Portsmouth is equidistant from Boston and Portland, Maine. It takes about 1¼ hours to travel the 57 miles via I-95 in either direction.

Greyhound/Vermont Transit (☎ 603-433-3210; 800-552-8737; www.vermonttransit.com) runs several daily buses on a route connecting Boston and Portsmouth with Portland, Bangor and Bar Harbor, Maine. Portsmouth to Boston costs $16 one way. Buses stop either on Hanover St (between High and Fleet Sts) or at the **C&J Trailways Center** (☎ 603-430-1100; www.cjtrailways.com; 185 Grafton Dr), located 3.5 miles west of downtown (off NH-33). C&J Trailways buses run similar routes at like prices.

Once in Portsmouth, the **Coast Trolley Downtown Loop** (☎ 603-743-5777; per ride $0.50, 3-day pass $2; ☣ 8:45am-8:45pm Mon-Sat, 11:45am-8:45pm Sun Jun-Sep) provides shuttle service between public parking lots, Market Sq and the major historic sights around town. Pick up a schedule and route map at the Market Sq information kiosk.

HAMPTON BEACH & AROUND
pop 20,200

Littered with summer clam shacks, ramshackle motels, fried dough stands and noisy arcades full of pudgy children, Hampton Beach isn't the classiest stretch of New England coastline. It does, however, boast New Hampshire's only sandy beach, a wide, inviting stretch of shore that gives pasty sun-seekers their fix. North of Hampton Beach, white-trash paradise peters into the rolling greenswards and serpentine private drives of Rye, whose oceanfront mansions and sprawling 'summer cottages' show a radically different side of the coastline.

Orientation & Information

Highway NH 1A runs up the seacoast from Salisbury, Massachusetts in the south, over the New Hampshire border and all the way up to Portsmouth, just south of the Maine border. En route, the seaside highway traverses Seabrook Beach, Hampton Beach and Rye Beach. Each of these towns has a commercial center that lies further inland along US 1 (which parallels NH 1A), but for most visitors the main attraction of this region is the beach.

Hampton Beach Area Chamber of Commerce
(☎ 603-926-8718; www.hamptonbeach.org; 169 Ocean Blvd, Hampton Beach) Offers information on tourist attractions.

New Hampshire Seacoast Regional Office
(☎ 603-436-1552; 1730 Ocean Blvd, Rye; ☯ 10am-5pm Mon-Fri May-Sep) Administers the state parks in the region – meaning all the beaches.

Seacoast, NH (www.seacoastnh.com) The insider's guide to 'America's smallest seacoast.'

Sights & Activities

HAMPTON BEACH STATE PARK

The beach actually begins south of the state line, on the north bank of the Merrimack River at Salisbury Beach State Reservation in Massachusetts. Take I-95 exit 56 (MA 1A) and head east to Salisbury Beach, then north along NH 1A to **Hampton Beach State Park** (☎ 603-926-3784) a long stretch of sand shielded by dunes. Facilities include changing rooms, toilets and a snack bar. Parking is $10 per day.

North of the state park, where NH 1A becomes Ocean Blvd, the town of Hampton is both beach and honky-tonk playground. In summer this vast main beach is crowded with all of humanity. At the center of the strip the **Hampton Seashell** (☎ 603-926-8717, 603-926-5000) is a band shell with an amphitheater, as well as public toilets, a first-aid station and the chamber of commerce information center. Across the boulevard, the Hampton Beach casino (p418) has live entertainment, video games, fast-food stands and souvenir shops. Beach admission is free, but you'll have to feed quarters to the parking meters ($1.50 per hour).

In the residential neighborhoods north of Hampton Beach you'll find a few less crowded and less spectacular beaches. Ten minutes north of Hampton Beach, **North Hampton State Beach** (☎ 603-436-1552) is not nearly as wide but is quieter than its grand southern neighbors. It has all the same facilities, including metered parking.

RYE BEACHES

As NH 1A enters Rye, parking along the road is restricted to vehicles with town parking stickers, but **Jenness State Beach** (☎ 603-436-1552) has a small metered parking lot that's open to the general public. Further north near **Rye Harbor** you're allowed to park along the roadway. Climb over the seawall of rubble and rocks to get to the gravel beach. It lacks facilities, but it is much less crowded than anything further south. Continuing northward, **Wallis Sands State Beach** (☎ 603-436-9404) has a wide sandy beach with views of the Isles of Shoals. Besides the bathhouses, there are grassy lawns for children's games and a large parking lot ($10), making this the top spot for families with smaller kids.

ODIORNE POINT STATE PARK

At the northern tip of the seacoast, just before NH 1A turns westward to Portsmouth, lies the underutilized **Odiorne Point State Park** (☎ 603-436-1552; admission adult/child $3/free). It lacks a beach, but instead offers seaside strolls and forested trails, as well as sweet hidden spots for picnicking and fishing. It is also the site of the **Seacoast Science Center** (☎ 603-436-8043; www.seacoastsciencecenter.org; 570 Ocean Blvd, Rye; adult/child $1/free; ☯ 10am-5pm). Undersea videos, huge aquariums and a hands-on 'touch tank' are the highlights of this family favorite. The center hosts lots of special activities such as trail walks, lighthouse tours and concerts.

SURFING

Diehard surfers ride the waves at Hampton Beach from June to October. The **Cinnamon Rainbows Surf Co** (☎ 603-929-7467; www.cinnamonrainbows.com; 931 Ocean Blvd, North Beach, Hampton; lesson per hr with equipment $50, surfboard & wetsuit rental per day $35) offers lessons and equipment rental.

FISHING, WHALE-WATCHING & CRUISING

You can arrange a variety of aquatic excursions at Rye Harbor, including fishing and lobstering tours, trips to the Isles of Shoals and whale-watching excursions.

Al Gauron Deep Sea Fishing (☎ 603-926-2469; www.algauron.com; State Pier, Hampton Beach; adult/child/senior

2hr trips $18/13/15, day trips $50/40/42) offers fishing trips, lasting from two to 12 hours (full-day trips go from 8:30am to 4:30pm, July to August). Whale watches and other cruise packages are also available.

Daily whale-watching cruises, as well as relaxing cruises to the Isles of Shoals and a Sunset Fireworks cruise, are hosted by **Granite State Whale Watch** (☎ 603-964-5545, 800-964-5545; www.granitestatewhalewatch.com; Ocean Blvd, Rye; adult/child/senior whale-watching $27/18/23, other cruises $20/14/17).

Sleeping

Hampton Beach and – to a lesser degree – Rye have no shortage of roadside motels, scattered along NH 1A. Wherever you stay, you'll need reservations during summer months.

Tidewater Campground (☎ 603-926-5474; 160 Lafayette Rd, Hampton; campsites/RV sites $28/35; ☻ mid-May–mid-Oct; ☒) A prime spot for families, this private 40-acre campground offers 100 sites for tents and RVs, including shaded spots near the ocean. It's near the intersection of US 1 and NH 101.

Wakeda Campground (☎ 603-772-5274; www.wakedacampground.com; 294 Exeter Rd, Hampton Falls; campsites/RV sites $30/33) Eight miles northwest of Hampton Falls you'll find 400 secluded sites amid 180 acres of towering pine trees.

Lamie's Inn & Tavern (☎ 603-926-0330; www.lamiesinn.com; 490 Lafayette Rd, Hampton; r $130-150; ☐) To escape the din and tack of Hampton Beach, head inland to this colonial manor in downtown Hampton. Thirty-two graceful rooms feature exposed brick walls, four-post beds and lace curtains. The Old Salt, the inn's restaurant, has a cozy dining room and fresh seafood.

Ashworth By the Sea (☎ 603-926-6762, 800-345-6736; www.ashworthhotel.com; 295 Ocean Blvd, Hampton; r $169-239; ☒) This sizable 105-room hotel has trim, modern rooms with striped carpeting, flat-screen TVs and small perks like in-room coffeemakers; many have private balconies and ocean views. Several on-site restaurants provide a nice alternative to fried dough and pizza.

Eating

Sizzling oil is the ingredient of choice in snack shops lining NH 1A. More appealing are seasonal lobster pounds dotting the seacoast along US 1 and NH 1A.

Brown's Seabrook Lobster Pound (☎ 603-474-3331; NH 286; meals $12-22; ☻ lunch daily mid-Apr–mid-Nov,

Fri-Sun mid-Nov–mid-Apr) In Seabrook, just south of Hampton Beach, this year-round pound overlooks a marsh and serves freshly boiled crustaceans. Bring your own beer and wine and take a seat at one of the picnic tables on the deck.

Galley Hatch (☎ 603-926-6152; 325 Lafayette Rd/US 1, Hampton; sandwiches $8, meals $17-24; ☻ lunch & dinner) Located in Hampton proper, Galley Hatch is a longtime favorite for its wide menu of fresh fish, sandwiches, steaks, pastas, pizzas and veggie dishes. There's a bakery attached and a cinema next door.

our pick Saunders at Rye Harbor (☎ 603-964-6466; Rye Harbor, NH 1A, Rye; meals $20-28; ☻ lunch & dinner) Nicely set over the water, this classic seafood restaurant serves lobster and other fresh catches, as well as unique dishes such as feta-crusted salmon and sea scallops baked with mushrooms. The outdoor deck makes a lovely spot for a sundowner.

Carriage House (☎ 603-964-8251; 2263 Ocean Blvd, Rye; meals $20-32; ☻ 5-10pm) Set in a tastefully decorated Cape Cod house, the elegant Carriage House serves tasty fresh seafood, salads, pastas and grilled meats.

Drinking & Entertainment

Casino Ballroom (☎ 603-929-4100; www.casinoballroom.com; Ocean Blvd, Hampton Beach) Besides arcade rides and miniature golf, the casino stages rock and R&B bands – five or 10 years after they were popular. Megadeth, Chris Isaak and the Indigo Girls have all played here recently.

La Bec Rouge (☎ 603-926-5050; www.labecrouge.com; 73 Ocean Blvd, Hampton Beach) Essential stomping ground for partying Hamptonites, La Bec Rouge features eclectic local bands (rock, blues, reggae) playing in its basement pub and nice ocean views from its outdoor deck.

Getting There & Around

There is no public transportation servicing the Hampton Beach area. Once you arrive, however, ditch your car and utilize the free **Beach Trolley** (☻ noon-9:30pm Jun-Aug), which circles the beach. Convenient stops include the chamber of commerce, the Ashworth Hotel and La Bec Rouge.

EXETER

pop 15,000

One of New Hampshire's most beautifully preserved small towns, Exeter boasts an impressive assortment of colonial homes and a proud history dating back to its founding in 1638. The town's specially designated meetinghouse, unique in these parts, played a crucial role in 1774, when British Governor John Wentworth dissolved the provincial assembly that met in Portsmouth in an attempt to prevent the election of a continental congress. The revolutionary councils then began to gather at the meetinghouse in Exeter, which effectively became the seat of government. Exeter later served as the capital of New Hampshire during 14 crucial years, when the first New Hampshire constitution was adopted and the US Constitution was ratified. Although Exeter is a staunchly Democratic town, the Republican party was founded here in 1853. Today, however, it's better known for being home to the elite Phillips Exeter academy.

Exeter's early history is still widely celebrated, thanks in part to the **American Independence Museum** (☎ 603-772-2622; www.independencemuseum.org; 1 Governor's Lane; adult/student $5/3; ☼ 10-4pm Wed-Sat mid-May–Oct), which maintains the town's collections inside the historic **Ladd-Gilman House**. Among the highlights of this National Landmark Property are the furnishings and possessions of the Gilman family, who lived here from 1720 to 1820, along with a document archive, including two original drafts of the US Constitution and personal correspondence of George Washington, Pierre L'Enfant and other notables. The museum also maintains **Folsom Tavern** (Spring St), which was once an important meeting place for George Washington and his revolutionary officers.

Exeter is one of the few places in New England that is utterly quiet on the Fourth of July. This is because Exeter celebrates Independence Day two weeks after the rest of the country. On the second Saturday after the 4th, the spirited **Revolutionary War Festival** brings out the whole town (seemingly) dressed up in colonial garb. The procession led by George Washington and the reading of the Declaration of Independence take center stage. But there are loads of other events, from colonial cooking to militia drills to gunpowder races. And an annual charity road race and a night of rock and roll music are reminders that re-enactments are fun, but this is, after all, the 21st century.

A mile or so outside of town, the **Exeter Elms** (☎ 603-778-7631; www.exeterelms.com; 188 Court St, Exeter; tent/RV $30/33) campground offers sites along the idyllic Exeter River, with access for fishing and canoeing.

In the center of town the **Inn by the Bandstand** (☎ 603-772-6352; www.innbythebandstand.com; 4 Front St; r incl breakfast $150-230; wi-fi) is a colonial gem with nine cozy, uniquely furnished rooms. Features in various rooms include fireplaces, Jacuzzi bathtubs, four-post beds and goose-down comforters.

Exeter has a small selection of attractive restaurants along Water St, several of which have outdoor tables overlooking the river. **Blue Moon Café** (☎ 603-778-6850; 8 Clifford St; meals $8-12; ☼ 9am-7pm Mon-Fri, 9am-5pm Sat; **V**) serves fresh-baked goods and delicious organic fare in a pleasant setting one block from Water St. The **Green Bean** (☎ 603-778-7585; 33 Water St; meals $8-9; ☼ 11am-3pm Mon & Sat, 11am-7pm Tue-Fri; **V**) serves tasty fresh salads, soups and sandwiches, best enjoyed on the shaded brick patio at this tidy little bistro. Student favorites include the turkey-cranberry sandwich and the gorgonzola-and-walnut salad.

To reach Exeter, take I-95 to exit 2, then NH 101 west. Turn left on Portsmouth Ave (NH 108) and right on Water St.

MERRIMACK VALLEY

Although New Hampshire is noted more for mountains than cities, the state does have its urban distractions. Manchester, a historic mill city, and Concord, the state's tidy capital, are pleasant – if not overly exotic – places to spend a day. Both sit along the mighty Merrimack River, which has dominated their economies since their founding.

MANCHESTER
pop 110,000

Once home to the world's largest textile mill, Manchester is an intriguing riverside town that still retains, both historically and culturally, a bit of its blue-collar roots. Exploiting the abundant water power of the Merrimack River, the massive Amoskeag mills made the city into a manufacturing and commercial powerhouse in the early 19th century up until its bankruptcy in the 1930s. Nowadays the iconic brick mill houses a museum, an arts center, a college, several restaurants and a changing array of local businesses.

Although manufacturing still plays a role in Manchester's economy, the city has undergone radical changes since its early laboring days. Attracted by low taxes and a diverse work force, the high-tech and financial industries have long since moved in, bringing city culture on their heels. Manchester has opera, several orchestras, a growing gallery and dining scene and the state's most important art museum.

Orientation & Information

Manchester stretches along the east bank of the Merrimack River. If you enter Manchester from I-93, you miss the view that defines the city's history: the redbrick swath of the great Amoskeag textile mills stretching along the east bank of the river for over a mile. To get the view, follow I-293 along the river's west bank. After you've passed the mills, exit via the Amoskeag Bridge or the Queen City Bridge to enter the town. The heart of Manchester lies along Elm St (US 3), running north–south through the business and commercial district. Many hotels and motels are clustered at the interstate exits. Despite its size, Manchester's downtown is compact and walkable.

Greater Manchester Chamber of Commerce (☎ 603-666-6600; www.manchester-chamber.org; 889 Elm St, Manchester, NH 03101) Provides tourist information.

Sights & Activities

One of the best ways of discovering the city's past is by following one of the self-guided walking tours distributed by the Chamber of Commerce. The Millyard stroll leads past the old towers, hidden canals and workers tenements of Amoskeag to a scenic overlook along the rushing Merrimack.

CURRIER MUSEUM OF ART

New Hampshire's premier **fine-arts museum** (☎ 603-669-6144; www.currier.org; 201 Myrtle Way) has an excellent collection of 19th- and 20th-century European and American art, including painting, decorative arts, photography and sculpture. At the time of research Currier was closed for an expansion that will add 30,000 sq ft to the galleries. The museum is six blocks east of Elm St along Beech St (follow the signs).

The Currier also operates the marvelous Frank Lloyd Wright **Zimmerman House** (tours adult/child $11/8), the only residence in New England designed by the acclaimed architect that is open to the public (reservations required). Call for the latest schedule. The house is closed from January to March.

AMOSKEAG MILLS

These former textile mills, impressive brick buildings with hundreds of tall windows, stretch along Commercial St on the Merrimack riverbank for almost 1½ miles. Other mills face the buildings from across the river in West Manchester. For almost a century (1838–1920), the Amoskeag Manufacturing Company was the world's largest textile manufacturer. The mills employed up to 17,000 people a year (out of a city population of 70,000). Many mill employees lived in the trim brick tenements stretching up the hillside eastward from the mills. The restored tenements are still used as housing.

Today, Mill No 3 houses the **Millyard Museum** (☎ 603-622-7531; www.manchesterhistoric.org; cnr Commercial & Pleasant Sts; adult/child/senior/student $6/2/5/5; ☼ 10am-4pm Tue-Sat). The museum hosts exhibits, walking tours and other programs that trace the history of Manchester, from the Amoskeag Indians who dwelled in this region, to the Amoskeag Mills that developed it.

Upstairs in the same building, the **SEE Science Center** (☎ 603-669-0400; www.see-sciencecenter.org; 200 Bedford St; admission $5; ☼ 10am-3pm Mon-Fri, noon-5pm Sat & Sun) has hands-on science exhibits on lunar gravity, sound waves, static electricity and other kid-focused crowd pleasers.

Sleeping

Most lodgings here are for business travelers, so prices are often lower on weekends. There are many hotels near the airport.

Bear Brook State Park (☎ 603-485-9869, reservations 603-271-3628; NH 28, Allenstown; campsites $23; ☼ mid-May–mid-Oct) Halfway to Concord, this 10,000-acre park has 95 sites (but no hook-ups for RVs), which are remotely located on the shore of Beaver Pond. There's hiking and swimming in the park. Take US 3 north, turn right onto NH 28 and follow the signs.

Stephen Clay Homestead (☎ 603-483-4096; www.stephenclaybedandbreakfast.com; 193 High St, Candia; r incl breakfast with shared/private bathroom $98/135) Located 12 miles northeast of Manchester, this cozy B&B has three comfortable rooms, each with floral duvets and other frilly touches. There are fireplaces throughout the colonial house and 3 acres of gardens and fruit trees surrounding the property. It's located off NH 27 in Candia.

Center of New Hampshire Radisson (☎ 603-625-1000; www.radisson.com; 700 Elm St; r Nov-Apr $129, May-Oct $179; P ☐ wi-fi ☻) Sporting 250 rooms, this huge conference facility has an excellent down-town location near Veterans' Park. For a chain hotel, this Radisson isn't bad, with subdued, attractively set rooms and an excellent fitness center. Parking is available for $6 a day.

Ash Street Inn (☎ 603-668-9908; www.ashstreetinn .com; 118 Ash St; r incl breakfast $139-189; wi-fi) Steps from the Currier Museum of Art, this fantastic Victorian home has five comfortable and cozy rooms. They feature ornamental fireplaces, wood floors and stained-glass windows – originals from the house's construction in 1885. Plush robes and afternoon tea add to the pampering.

Eating

Elm St (US 3) and nearby Lowell St are good places to browse for a meal.

Lala's Hungarian Pastry (☎ 603-647-7100; 836 Elm St; meals $9-12; ☻ 7am-5pm Mon & Tue, 7am-8pm Wed-Sat) No-nonsense Lala's serves wondrous Hungarian pastries, as well as savory ethnic luncheon specials like chicken goulash and schnitzel in a cozy old-world setting.

Cotton (☎ 603-622-5488; 75 Arms Park Dr; meals $10-23; ☻ lunch Mon-Fri, dinner daily) For artfully prepared food in sophisticated surroundings, this elegant restaurant near the river and the Amoskeag mills wins hands down. Cotton serves wood-grilled salmon, wild-mushroom risotto, seafood pesto linguine and other upscale bistro fare alongside 40 wines by the glass.

Consuelo's Taqueria (☎ 603-622-1134; 36 Amherst St; meals $6-8; ☻ 11am-8pm Mon-Wed 11am-9pm Thu & Fri, noon-9pm Sat) Yet another facet of Manchester's growing multiculturalism, Consuelo's whips up satisfying tacos, burritos and quesadillas in a friendly, low-key environment.

Drinking & Entertainment

Wild Rover (☎ 603-669-7722; 21 Kosciuszko St; ☻ noon-1am; wi-fi) One of the best places in town for a pint is this inviting Irish-style pub, with exposed brick walls, outdoor tables and filling burgers, wraps and bangers-and-mash. Stop in (or avoid like the plague!) Wednesday and Thursday night, when Wild Rover hosts its evening sing-along.

Verizon Wireless Arena (☎ 603-644-5000; www.veri zonwirelessarena.com; 555 Elm St) Manchester's biggest shows and events are held at this arena, a few blocks south of the commercial center. The lucky few might catch a boxing or hockey match, the circus, or even a horse show.

Strange Brew Tavern (☎ 603-666-4292; 88 Market St; ☻ 4pm-1am) This welcoming pub boasts 61 beers on tap, the largest selection in the state (it claims)! More importantly, it offers live music seven nights a week and no cover charge. The mixed local crowd is friendly and fun.

Opera New Hampshire (☎ info 603-647-6564; box office 603-668-5588; www.operanh.org; Palace Theatre, 80 Hanover St; tickets $40-75, student $10-75) Manchester stages a full season of contemporary and classic operas at the downtown Palace Theatre.

New Hampshire Fishercats (☎ 603-641-2005; www.nhfishercats.com; 1 Line Dr; tickets $4-12) New Hampshire's minor-league baseball team is the farm team for the Toronto Blue Jays, but it attracts its own loyal fans. Since 2005 the team has been playing in a brand new stadium on the waterfront west of Granite St.

Getting There & Away

Fast growing but still not too large, **Manchester Airport** (☎ 603-624-6539; www.flyman chester.com), off US 3 south of Manchester, is a civilized alternative to Boston's Logan International Airport.

Concord Trailways (☎ 603-228-3300, www.concord trailways.com) runs frequent daily buses to Logan International Airport ($15, 1½ hours) and South Station ($11, one hour) in Boston, as well as north to Concord ($5, 30 minutes). Buses depart from the **Manchester Transportation Center** (☎ 603-668-6133; 119 Canal St).

Driving from Boston to Manchester via I-93 and the Everett Turnpike takes an hour. It's another 30 minutes from Manchester to Concord via I-93.

CONCORD
pop 43,000

New Hampshire's capital is a trim and tidy city with a wide Main St dominated by the striking State House, a granite-hewed 19th-century edifice topped with a glittering dome. The stone of choice in 'the granite state' appears in other fine buildings about Concord's historical center, cut from the still-active quarries on Rattlesnake hill, just north of town. Aside from cutting stone, the local citizens are involved in a wide range of activities including government, light manufacturing, craftwork and education. While not the most dazzling of towns, Concord has a pleasant, easy-going vibe, with a handful of interesting sites (a presidential home, a history museum and a

---

NEW HAMPSHIRE'S FAVORITE STONE

Even though it lost its 'Great Stone Face' in 2003 (see p446), New Hampshire will forever be known as 'the granite state'. This refers not merely to the tough, take-no-bullshit attitude of the locals, but also to the enormous granite quarries, which still yield vast amounts of this very solid stone. They've also played a pivotal role in some of the country's most important structures. New Hampshire granite was used in Boston's Quincy Market, the Brooklyn Bridge, the Pentagon and even the Library of Congress.

---

planetarium). It's also a fine base for exploring the idyllic Canterbury Shaker village, 15 miles north of town.

Orientation & Information

I-93 passes just east of the city center, and US 3 is Main St, where you'll find everything worth visiting. Take I-93 exit 14 or 15 for Main St. The **Greater Concord Chamber of Commerce** (☎ 603-224-2508; www.concordnhchamber .com; 40 Commercial St) is quite helpful but keeps unreliable hours. There's also a small, seasonal information kiosk in front of the State House on N Main St.

Sights

STATE CAPITOL

The state legislature still meets in the original chambers of the handsome 1819 **State House** (☎ 603-271-2154; 107 N Main St; admission free; ☒ 8am-4pm Mon-Fri). It's the longest such tenure in the USA. A self-guided tour brochure is available to point out the building's highlights, including the **Memorial Arch** and the various monuments around the grounds. The **Hall of Flags** holds the standards that state military units carried into battle. Portraits and statues of New Hampshire leaders, including the great orator Daniel Webster, line its corridors and stand in its lofty halls.

MUSEUM OF NEW HAMPSHIRE HISTORY

The New Hampshire Historical Society operates this intriguing two-story warehouse **museum** (☎ 603-228-6688; www.nhhistory.org; 6 Eagle Sq/N Main St; adult/child/senior/family $5.50/3/4.50/17; ☒ 9:30am-5pm Tue-Sat & noon-5pm Sun year-round, 9:30am-5pm Mon Jul-Oct & Dec). The chronological displays here

illuminate such arcane subjects as the milk delivery in New England. One of the most compelling exhibits considers the state's famous residents, from Shaker 'eldresses' to Robert Frost to President Franklin Pierce. The museum also has beautiful 19th-century landscape paintings of the White Mountains. The handsome building itself – granite again – and the small park outside are rather successful examples of urban renewal.

PIERCE MANSE

Franklin Pierce (1804-69), 14th president of the US, is the only man from New Hampshire to be elected to this office. His Concord home, known as the **Pierce Manse** (☎ 603-225-4555; www .piercemanse.org; 14 Horseshoe Pond Lane; adult/child/senior $5/2/4; ☒ 11am-3pm Tue-Sat mid-Jun–mid-Sep), is now a museum. The Greek Revival house was completed in 1839 and served as his family home from 1842 to 1848, between his Senate and presidential terms. The son of a two-term New Hampshire governor, Pierce served in both Congress and the Senate, and harbored little presidential ambition during his tenure. He retired from the US Senate to practice law in Concord, maintaining an interest in politics but having little desire to engage in further public service. During the Democratic Party's convention of 1852, however, there were so many strong candidates for the presidency that none could achieve a majority vote. On the 49th ballot, Pierce, a compromise candidate, became the party's nominee, and he went on to win the presidential election. The house is located at the north end of N Main St.

CHRISTA MCAULIFFE PLANETARIUM

This **planetarium** (☎ 603-271-7827; www.starhop.com; 2 Institute Dr; adult/child/senior $8/5/7; ☒ 10am-5pm Mon-Sat, noon-5pm Sun) honors the New Hampshire schoolteacher chosen to be America's first teacher-astronaut. McAuliffe and her fellow astronauts died in the tragic explosion of the Challenger spacecraft on January 28, 1986. Hour-long shows examine topics such as space travel to Mars and the power of the sun. The popular 'Tonight's Sky' takes visitors on a tour of the constellations and planets visible that month.

CANTERBURY SHAKER VILLAGE

Members of the United Society of Believers in Christ's Second Appearing were called

---

WORTH THE TRIP: LAKE SUNAPEE

Lake Sunapee is a worthwhile detour any time of year. In summer, head to **Lake Sunapee State Park** (☎ 603-763-5561; Newbury; adult/child $3/1; 🕑 dawn-dusk daily Sat & Sun mid-May–mid-Jun, daily mid-Jun–mid-Oct), off NH 103, for hiking, picnicking, swimming and fishing. The wide sandy beach has a pleasant grassy sitting area. Canoes and kayaks are available for rental. From I-89 take exit 9, NH 103 to Newbury. In winter, alpine skiing is the attraction at **Mt Sunapee Resort** (☎ 603-763-2356; www.mtsunapee.com; Newbury; adult/child/senior/teen Mon-Fri $60/36/45/45, Sat & Sun $64/40/53/53; 🕑 9am-4pm). Mt Sunapee boasts a vertical drop of 1510ft – the biggest in southern New Hampshire. It's not much to compete with Cannon or Loon Mountain, but offers some challenging skiing all the same. Other facilities including rental, lessons and childcare are available.

Coming from Hanover or Concord, take exit 12A off I-89 and turn right on Rte 11. In the town of Sunapee, turn left onto Route 103B. Coming from the south, take exit 9 and follow NH 103 through Bradford and Newbury to Mt Sunapee.

'Shakers' because of the religious ecstasies they experienced during worship. This particular Shaker community was founded in 1792 and was actively occupied for two centuries. Sister Ethel Hudson, last member of the Shaker colony here, died in 1992 at the age of 96.

The **Canterbury Shaker Village** (☎ 603-783-9511; www.shakers.org; 288 Shaker Rd; adult/child/family $15/7/37; 🕑 10am-5pm daily May-Oct, 10am-4pm Sat & Sun Nov & Dec, closed Jan-Apr) is now preserved as a nonprofit trust to present Shaker history. The lone surviving Shaker community, at Sabbathday Lake, ME, still accepts new members.

Canterbury Shaker Village has 'interpreters' in period garb who perform the tasks and labors of community daily life: fashioning Shaker furniture and crafts (for sale in the gift shop) and growing herbs and producing herbal medicines. The guided tour takes you to an herb garden, meetinghouse (1792), apiary (bee house), ministry, 'Sisters' shop (a crafts shop run by Shaker women), laundry, horse barn, infirmary and schoolhouse (1826).

The **Shaker Table** (☎ 603-783-4238; meals $15-32; 🕑 11:30am-4pm, 5-9pm Fri & Sat, 9am-4pm Sun) serves a lovely lunch and a sumptuous candlelight dinner. The menu changes seasonally, but it features regional specialties and organic produce from the garden on-site, not to mention sinful desserts. Dinner and brunch reservations are recommended. The Canterbury Shaker Village is 15 miles north of Concord on MA 106. Take I-93 to exit 18.

Sleeping

Holiday Inn (☎ 603-224-9534; www.holidayinn.com; 172 N Main St; r $108-154; 🖳 🕭) The only full-service hotel in the heart of Concord's historic downtown, this comfortable 122-room hotel has all of the expected amenities, including a fitness center, a restaurant and a business center. Book online for the best deals.

our pick **Centennial Inn** (☎ 603-227-9000, 800-360-4839; 96 Pleasant St; r $149-189; **P** wi-fi) Recently renovated, this turn-of-the-20th-century turreted manse has 32 luxurious rooms and suites. Stylish minimalism prevails, with subdued earth tones, deluxe bedding, trim furnishings, black-and-white artwork on the walls and vessel-bowl sinks in the granite bathrooms. Several rooms are set in the turret, while the best have private outdoor porches. The Centennial and its fine restaurant lie about 1 mile west of Main St.

Eating

Most restaurants catch the legislative lunch crowd across from the State House on N Main St at Park St.

Bread & Chocolate (☎ 603-228-3330; 29 S Main St; sandwiches $5-7; 🕑 7:30am-6pm Mon-Fri, 8am-4pm Sat) This exceptional European-style bakery is a local favorite for its decadent pastries as well as satisfying homemade sandwiches.

In a Pinch Cafe (☎ 603-226-2272; 146 Pleasant St; meals $6-8; 🕑 7am-3pm Mon-Sat) Located east of the center near the Centennial Inn, this popular joint serves good sandwiches, soups and salads. Grab some picnic fare or relax on the sun porch.

55 Degrees (☎ 603-224-7192; 55 N Main St; meals $7-20; 🕑 dinner Tue-Sat) In a former silversmith's shop, this elegant newcomer serves delectable cuisine amid exposed-brick walls trimmed with artwork and old-world touches. The menu features excellent cheeses, quinoa and roasted-walnut salad, seared sea-scallops, roasted duck and other tempting choices. It's matched by a decent wine list.

Hermanos Cocina Mexicana (☎ 603-224-5669; 11 Hills Ave; meals $10-16; ☾ lunch & dinner) Just off Main St in an unlikely historic brick building, Hermanos serves authentic and creative Mexican dishes, from pork *taquitos* (minitacos) to chimichangas (filled, deep-fried tortillas). Head to the upstairs bar for excellent margaritas and catch some live jazz (from 6.30pm to 9pm Sunday to Thursday).

Capitol Grille (☎ 603-228-6608; 1 Eagle Sq; sandwiches $6-8, meals $14-19; ☾ 11am-1am Tue-Sat, 11am-midnight Sun) This warm, inviting restaurant and bar has tasty pub fare, with a decent selection of sandwiches, soups and salads. The other specialty here is a juicy steak, hand-cut and aged in house. In the evening the lounge often hosts karaoke, live music, or less fussily a sporting event on TV.

Getting There & Away

Concord Trailways (www.concordtrailways.com) has a frequent daily service from the **Trailways Transportation Center** (☎ 603-228-3300, 800-639-3317; 30 Stickney Ave, I-93 exit 14) to Manchester ($5, 30 minutes) and Boston ($13.50, 1½ hours).

MONADNOCK REGION

In the southwestern corner of the state the pristine villages of Peterborough and Jaffrey Center (2 miles due west of Jaffrey) anchor Mt Monadnock (moh-NAHD-nock; 3165ft). 'Mountain That Stands Alone' in Algonquian, Monadnock is relatively isolated from other peaks, which means hikers to the summit are rewarded with fantastic views of the surrounding countryside. The trail, however, is anything but lonely. Monadnock is one of the most climbed mountains in the world.

For a list of inns and B&Bs in the Monadnock region, visit www.nhlod ging.org.

KEENE
pop 24,000

A classic New England town, Keene is a charming settlement of historic homes and manicured streets, with a strong community feel. Its pleasant but lively Main St is lined with shops, cafés and restaurants, and crowned by a small, tree-filled plaza with fountain at one end. At the opposite end of

Main St lies the elegant redbrick campus of Keene, which brings a bit of youth and its artistic sensibilities to the town.

Greater Keene Chamber of Commerce (☎ 603-352-1303; 48 Central Sq; ☾ 9am-5pm Mon-Fri) Dishes up information.

Toadstool Bookshop (☎ 603-352-8815; Colony Mill Marketplace; ☾ 10am-9pm Mon-Sat, 11am-6pm Sun) Offers new and used books, music and magazines.

Sights

At the west end of Main St, **Keene State College** (☎ 603-358-2276; www.keene.edu; 229 Main St) accounts for almost one-quarter of the town's population. The **Thorne Sagendorph Art Gallery** (☎ 603-358-2720; www.keene.edu/tsag; Wyman Way; admission free; ☾ noon-4pm daily, closed Mon Jun-Aug) housed at Keene State College plays a crucial role in supporting the arts in this rural region. Its spacious skylit halls showcase rotating exhibits of regional and national artists. Sagendorph hosts an annual exhibit focusing on New Hampshire native artists. The small permanent collection includes pieces by the many national artists that have been drawn to the Monadnock region since the 19th century

Near the college is the **Horatio Colony House Museum** (☎ 603-352-0460; www.horatiocolonymuseum .com; 199 Main St; admission free; ☾ 11am-4pm May-mid Oct) a marvelous 1806 Federal-style house filled with the eclectic period furnishings and artwork collected by the eccentric Colony family. Thirty-minute guided tours through the house highlight the extraordinary collection.

Sleeping & Eating

Carriage Barn Guest House (☎ 603-357-3812; www .carriagebarn.com; 358 Main St; s/d incl breakfast $65/75 Nov-Apr, $79/89 May-Aug, $100/110 Sep-Oct) Opposite Keene State College, this welcoming B&B has four frilly guest rooms and lovely common areas including a pine-floored parlor full of antiques and a deck overlooking lilac trees.

EF Lane Hotel (☎ 603-357-7070; www.eflane.com; 30 Main St; r/ste $139/209; wi-fi) In a picture-perfect Main St location, the EF Lane Hotel has 40 attractive rooms, each uniquely furnished in a classic style, insuring you won't get the cookie-cutter experience. There are plenty of creature comforts (individual climate control, high-speed internet connections) and a good restaurant on the first floor.

Lindy's Diner (☎ 603-352-4273; 19 Gilbo Ave; sandwiches $4-6, meals $8-14) Just off Main St, Lindy's

HAVE PUMPKIN, WILL TRAVEL

One of New Hampshire's quirkiest annual gatherings, the **Keene Pumpkin Festival** (www.pumpkin festival.org) brings some 80,000 visitors to the tiny town of Keene (more than three times its population), who come for the magnificent tower of jack-o'-lanterns rising high above Central Sq.

The event started in 1991 when local merchants, eager to keep shoppers in the area on weekend nights, displayed hundreds of pumpkins around Main St. Since then the event has exploded as, each year on the third Saturday in October, Keene attempts to better its record of nearly 29,000 in 2003. (This was a Guinness world record for the most jack-o'-lanterns lit in the same place at the same time until Boston copied the event and trumped Keene with 30,000 or so in 2006.) In addition to gazing into the eyes of the plump, artfully carved orange fruit, visitors can enjoy a craft fair, a costume parade, seed-spitting contests and fireworks. Live bands play on the surrounding streets as local merchants dish up clam chowder, fried sausages, mulled cider and plenty of pumpkin pie.

Following the festival, all those brightly lit gourds become pearls before swine as area farmers spread a feast before their pumpkin-loving piggies. If you plan to go, don't forget your pumpkin.

is a jewel-box–sized diner serving a big menu of comfort food to the students and worker folk who flock here. In the summer you can enjoy steak sandwiches and country fried chicken at picnic tables out front, or grab a booth inside and peruse the choices on your private juke box.

Luca's (☎ 603-558-3335; 10 Central Sq; meals $17-22; ☾ lunch Mon-Fri, dinner daily) A handsome Mediterranean gem overlooking Central Sq, Luca's serves excellent thin-crust pizzas, tasty salads and gourmet sandwiches at lunch, while dinner sees a tempting array of pastas, grilled fish and pan-seared beef tenderloin. There's outdoor seating during the summer.

Entertainment

Colonial Theater (☎ 603-352-2033; www.thecolonial .org; 95 Main St) After 80 years, this classic Main St theater is still going strong. From August to May the Colonial stages a diverse line-up of off-Broadway musicals, African and Eastern dance troupes and jazz ensembles.

Shopping

Colony Mill Marketplace (☎ 603-357-1240; 222 West St; ☾ 10am-9pm Mon-Sat, 11am-6pm Sun) Set in a former woolen mill, this redbrick complex houses craft and antique shops, a bookstore, a chocolate shop and several attractive restaurants.

Getting There & Away

If you are stuck without wheels, **Vermont Transit** (☎ 603-436-0163, 800-552-8737; www.vermonttransit.com) serves **Keene bus terminal** (☎ 603-352-1331; 6 Gilbo

Ave) from Boston ($29, 2 hours 20 minutes) and Brattleboro ($12, 30 minutes).

PETERBOROUGH & AROUND
pop 6000

The picturesque town of Peterborough is a charming village of redbrick houses and tree-lined streets, with the idyllic Nabanusit River coursing through its historic center. Nestled between Temple Mountain to the east and Mt Monadnock to the west, Peterborough is a gateway to some captivating countryside, and its restaurants and B&Bs draw plenty of visitors in their own right.

Peterborough is something of an arts community, an impression left deeply by the nearby **MacDowell Colony** (www.macdowellcolony .org). Born in the early 1900s, the country's oldest art colony has attracted a diverse and dynamic group of poets, painters, composers and playwrights. Aaron Copland composed parts of *Appalachian Spring* at the colony; Virgil Thomson worked on *Mother of Us All;* Leonard Bernstein completed his Mass; and Thornton Wilder wrote *Our Town*, a play that was openly inspired by Peterborough. Milton Avery, James Baldwin, Barbara Tuchman and Alice Walker are but a few of the luminaries that have passed this way.

More than 200 poets, composers, playwrights, architects, filmmakers, painters and photographers still come to Peterborough each year. They come for inspiration from the serene beauty of the countryside, from each other, and from the MacDowell legacy of creative collaboration that endures to this day.

The colony is open to visitors just once a year, during the second weekend in August.

Orientation & Information

The heart of Peterborough is Depot Sq.
Greater Peterborough Chamber of Commerce (☎ 603-924-7234; www.peterboroughchamber.com; ☺ 9am-5pm Mon-Fri year-round, 10am-3pm Sat Jun-Oct) At the intersection of NH 101 and NH 123.
Toadstool Bookshop (☎ 603-924-3543; 12 Depot St; ☺ 10am-6pm Mon-Fri, 10am-5pm Sat, 10am-4pm Sun; wi-fi) Also has a café with wireless access.

Sights & Activities

MARIPOSA MUSEUM

'Please touch!' implores this **museum** (☎ 603-924-4555; www.mariposamuseum.org; 26 Main St; adult/child $5/3; ☺ noon-5pm Mon-Fri, 11am-4pm Sat & Sun, closed Mon & Tue Sep-May), which exhibits folk art and folklore from around the world. It's a wonderful place for kids, who are invited to dive into the collections to try on costumes, experiment with musical instruments, play with toys and make their own art. Periodic performances feature musicians and storytellers who lead interactive performances.

SHARON ARTS CENTER

Based in Sharon, about 8 miles south of Peterborough on NH 123, this **arts center** (☎ 603-924-2787; 20-40 Depot St; admission free) also has an annex gallery in Depot Sq. It displays fine arts and crafts by some of the region's many artists. To reach the arts center, head east on NH 101 and turn right on Elm Hill Rd/NH 123. It's four miles further, on the right.

MILLER STATE PARK

New Hampshire's oldest state park is **Miller State Park** (☎ 603-924-3672; www.nhparks.state.nh.us; NH 101; adult/child $3/1; ☺ 6am-6pm daily Jun-Oct, Sat & Sun May, Nov & Dec). Miller is the site of Pack Monadnock, a 2290ft peak (not to be confused with its better-known neighbor, Mt Monadnock). It has three easy-to-moderate paths to the summit of Pack Monadnock; you can also access the 21-mile Wapack trail here. The park has an auto road to the summit, and is located about 4.5 miles east of Peterborough along NH 101.

Sleeping

Greenfield State Park (☎ 603-271-3628; campsites $24; ☺ mid-May–mid-Oct) Twelve miles northeast of Peterborough, off NH 136, this 400-acre park has 257 pine-shaded campsites, with fine swimming and hiking, as well as canoe and kayak rental.

Apple Gate B&B (☎ 603-924-6543; 199 Upland Farm Rd; s incl breakfast $80-95, d incl breakfast $85-100) This 1832 colonial is nestled among apple orchards and its four cozy guest rooms are each named after a variety of apple. It has an incredible parlor with crackling fireplace and a reading room warmed by a wood stove. Breakfast is a romantic treat, served by candlelight.

Little River B&B (☎ 603-924-3280; www.littleriverbedandbreakfast.com; 184 Union St; r incl breakfast $90-125; wi-fi) Splendidly set along the Nubanusit River, this familial B&B has four comfortable, simply decorated rooms, two of which overlook the river. Attractive common areas (including an outdoor deck steps from the river) add to the charm.

OUR PICK Hannah Davis House (☎ 603-585-3344; www.hannahdavishouse.com; 186 Depot Rd; s incl breakfast $85-165, d incl breakfast $95-175) This excellent B&B features six rooms and suites decorated with great attention and flair. Fluffy down comforters, canopy beds, shiny hardwood floors and claw-foot tubs are de rigueur. The cheapest rooms are small and modestly furnished, while the priciest rooms are spacious with private wood-burning fireplaces. Breakfast features homemade pastries, granola and apple sauce, in addition to eggs.

Eating & Drinking

Nonie's (☎ 603-924-3451; 28 Grove St; meals $5-8; ☺ 6am-2pm Mon-Sat, 7am-1pm Sun) A longtime Peterborough favorite, Nonie's serves excellent breakfasts as well as fresh bakery items. In the summer grab a table in the tiny front garden.

Twelve Pine (☎ 603-924-6140; Depot St; meals $9-14; ☺ 8am-7pm Mon-Fri, 9am-7pm Sat, 9am-4pm Sun) Housed in a former train station, this casual, sweet-smelling café has a good deli selection where you assemble a fresh salad, homemade sandwiches and a nice coffee-and-juice bar. There's outdoor seating.

Acqua Bistro (☎ 603-924-9905; Depot Sq; meals $18-28; ☺ 4-10pm Tue-Sat, 11am-10pm Sun) One of the best restaurants in the region, Acqua Bistro serves a small but seductive menu of haute bistro fare, including pan-seared duck breast with tropical fruit salsa, ginger-crusted salmon and delightful thin-crust pizzas.

Outdoor tables are beautifully set near the river's edge. Sunday brunch is stellar.

Entertainment

Harlow's Pub (☎ 603-924-6365; www.harlowspub.com; 3 School St; ☷ 4-10pm Tue-Sat) This local pub features a good selection of draught beers, including New England brews, with live music throughout the month. Harlow's serves Mexican and pub fare, but the real reason to come here is its communal-loving wooden bar.

Peterborough Folk Music Society (☎ 603-827-2905; www.pfmsconcerts.org; Peterborough Players, Hadley Rd; tickets $17-22) This active group attracts nationally known folk musicians to perform in a wonderful barn-style theater about 3½ miles from Peterborough center. Recent shows have included the inimitable Jonathan Edwards, Ellis Paul and April Verch.

Getting There & Away

Peterborough is located at the intersection of US 202 and NH 101. No public transportation is available.

JAFFREY CENTER

Two miles due west of bigger less-interesting Jaffrey, Jaffrey Center is a tiny, picture-perfect village of serene lanes, 18th-century homes and the dramatic white-steepled meetinghouse. For a fascinating stroll detailing the historical and architectural highlights of the village, pick up a walking-tour brochure at the **Jaffrey Chamber of Commerce** (☎ 603-532-4549; www.jaffreychamber.com; Main St, Jaffrey, cnr NH 124 & NH 202; ☷ 10am-4pm Mon-Fri). The old **textile mills** along the river now house offices and shops. Other intriguing sites include the frozen-in-time **Little Red School House** and the **Melville Academy**, which houses a one-room museum of rural artifacts. Both are open from 2pm to 4pm on weekends in summer. For a deeper look at local history, wander the **Old Burying Ground** behind the meetinghouse. Jaffrey Town Green often hosts free concerts on Wednesday nights in summer. Try to catch the Temple Band, the oldest town band in the country.

Sleeping & Eating

Emerald Acres Campground (☎ 603-532-8838; 39 Ridgecrest Rd; campsites $20-28; ☷ May–mid-Oct) Off NH 124, these 52 sites sit amid the pine trees adjacent to Cheshire Pond. The campground is ideal for families who enjoy fishing, swimming and boating.

Benjamin Prescott Inn (☎ 603-532-6637, 888-950-6637; www.benjaminprescottinn.com; NH 124; incl breakfast r $85-130, ste $125-175) In East Jaffrey, this classic mid-19th-century farmhouse has 10 country-style guest rooms that have been meticulously restored. Expansive views of the surrounding 500-acre dairy farm and fields are icing on the cake.

Inn at Jaffrey Center (☎ 603-532-7800; www.theinn atjaffreycenter.com; 379 Main St; r $110-160 Jun-Oct, $75-110 Nov-May) This family affair features 11 unique guest rooms, each with its own color scheme and decorative style. Beautifully maintained grounds and wide porches grace the exterior of the home, while the interior has a warm and welcoming dining room. The bistro serves hearty homemade country fare.

Grand View (☎ 603-532-9880; www.thegrandviewinn .com; 580 Mountain Rd; r $100-250; ☒) This 19th-century country mansion is located at the base of Mt Monadnock and has trailheads to the summit. When you finish your hike, indulge in a massage or soak in the Jacuzzi at the Grand View's spa; then fall into your king-size bed in one of nine luxurious rooms. Prices vary according to the room size.

Aylmer's Grille (☎ 603-532-4949; 21 Main St, Jaffrey; meals $12-28) This handsome little restaurant serves creative American cuisine with Eastern accents. Grilled tamari salmon, saffron linguine, shrimp and tomato tart are all nicely prepared, and there are wine suggestions with every main course.

Kimball Farm (☎ 603-532-5765; NH 124; ☷ 11am-10pm May-Oct) This dairy has achieved more than local fame for its sinfully creamy ice cream that comes in 40 flavors and unbelievable portion sizes. It also serves sandwiches and seafood specials – mostly of the deep-fried variety.

Getting There & Away

Jaffrey is located at the intersection of US 202 and NH 124, while quaint Jaffrey Center is 2 miles west on NH 124. No public transportation is available.

MT MONADNOCK STATE PARK

This commanding 3165ft **peak** (☎ 603-532-8862; www.nhstateparks.org; NH 124; adult/child $3/1) can be seen from 50 miles away in any direction and is the area's spiritual vertex. Complete with a visitor center (where you can get good hiking information), 12 miles of ungroomed cross-country ski trails and over 40 miles of hiking trails (6 miles of which reach

---

SCENIC DRIVE: MONADNOCK VILLAGES

The region surrounding Mt Monadnock is a web of narrow winding roads connecting classic New England towns, and one could easily spend a few days exploring this picturesque countryside. South of the mountain, **Fitzwilliam**, on NH 119, has a town green surrounded by lovely old houses and a graceful town hall with a steeple rising to the heavens.

Harrisville, northwest of Peterborough via NH 101, is a former mill village that looks much as it did in the late 1700s, when the textile industry in these parts was flourishing. Today its brick and granite mill buildings have been converted into functionally aesthetic commercial spaces.

Hancock, north of Peterborough on NH 123, is another quintessential New England village. The town's showpiece is one of the oldest continuously operating inns in New England: **Hancock Inn** (☎ 603-525-3318, 800-525-1789; www.hancockinn.com; 33 Main St, Hancock; r incl breakfast $180-290). New Hampshire's oldest inn has 15 rooms, each with its own unique charms. Dome ceilings (in rooms that used to be part of a ballroom), fireplaces and private patios are some of the features. The cozy dining room is open for breakfast and dinner. Room prices vary according to size and features.

Hillsborough Center, 14 miles north of Hancock on NH 123, is another classic, not to be confused with Hillsborough Lower Village and Upper Village. Steeped in the late 18th and early 19th century, the trim little town boasts a number of art studios.

Walpole, northwest of Keene along NH 12, is another gem. Locals descend from surrounding villages to dine at **Burdick Chocolate** (☎ 603-756-9058; 47 Main St, Walpole; meals $14-30; ✆ noon-2:30pm Mon-Sat, 5:30-9pm Tue-Sat, 10am-2pm Sun). Originally a New York City chocolatier, Burdick moved the operation to this tiny New Hampshire village and opened a sophisticated café to showcase its desserts. Besides rich chocolaty indulgences, the lively bistro has a full menu of creative new American dishes, plus artisanal cheeses and top-notch wines.

---

the summit), this state park is an outdoor wonderland. The White Dot Trail (which turns into the White Cross Trail) from the visitor center to the bare-topped peak is about a 3½-hour hike round-trip.

Well placed for a sunrise ascent up the mountain, the **Monadnock State Park campground** (☎ 603-532-8862, reservations 603-271-3628; NH 124; campsites $23; ✆ year-round) has 28 peaceful, well-shaded sites. From November until mid-May there is no water and the road in may not be plowed.

To reach Peterborough and Jaffrey from Manchester, head south then east on NH 101. Expect the 40-mile trip to take about 1½ hours. It also makes sense to visit the region on the way to or from Brattleboro, VT.

UPPER CONNECTICUT RIVER VALLEY

The Connecticut River, New England's longest, is the decisive boundary between New Hampshire and Vermont. The Upper Connecticut River Valley extends roughly from Brattleboro, VT, in the south to Woodsville, NH in the north, and includes

towns on both banks. The river has long been an important byway for explorers and traders. Today it is an adventure destination for boaters and bird-watchers, canoeists and kayakers. The region's largest population center is Lebanon, while the cultural focal point is prestigious Dartmouth College in Hanover.

HANOVER & AROUND
pop 11,300

Hanover is the quintessential New England college town. On warm days, students toss Frisbees on the wide college green fronting Georgian ivy-covered buildings, while locals and academics mingle at the laid-back cafés, restaurants and shops lining Main St. Dartmouth College has long been the town's focal point, giving the area a vibrant connection to the arts.

Dartmouth was chartered in 1769 primarily 'for the education and instruction of Youth of the Indian Tribes.' Back then, the school was located deep in the forests where its prospective students lived. Although teaching 'English Youth and others' was only its secondary purpose, in fact Dartmouth College graduated few Native American youths and was soon attended al-

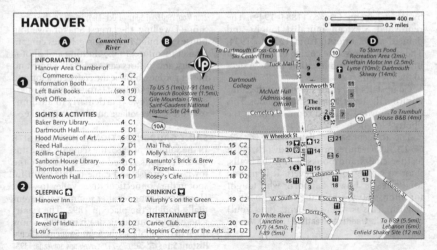

most exclusively by colonists. The college's most illustrious alumnus is Daniel Webster (1782–1852), who graduated in 1801 and went on to become a prominent lawyer, US senator, secretary of state and perhaps the USA's most esteemed orator.

Hanover is part of a larger community which includes Lebanon in New Hampshire, as well as Norwich and White River Junction in Vermont. When looking for services (especially accommodations), consider all of these places, not just Hanover. Unless otherwise stated, items in this section are in Hanover proper.

Each February, Dartmouth celebrates the weeklong **Winter Carnival** (☎ 603-646-3399; www .dartmouth.edu/~sao), featuring special art shows, drama productions, concerts, an ice-sculpture contest and other amusements. It is organized by the Student Activities Office.

Orientation & Information

To visit Hanover is to visit Dartmouth College, for the college dominates the town. The central reference for everything is the green, the broad lawn bounded by Wheelock, N Main, Wentworth and College Sts. Many services are along Main St, which runs for several blocks south from the green.

Hanover Area Chamber of Commerce (☎ 603-643-3115; www.hanoverchamber.org; 216 Nugget Bldg, Main St) For tourist information. Also maintains an information booth on the village green, staffed from July to mid-September.

Left Bank Books (☎ 603-643-4479; 9 S Main St; 🕑 9.30am-5pm Mon-Sat, noon-5pm Sun) A small, cozy used bookstore above a café.

Norwich Bookstore (☎ 802-649-1114; 291 Main St, Norwich; 🕑 9am-6pm Mon-Sat, noon-5pm Sun) An unusually good bookstore, especially for a small town.

Sights

DARTMOUTH COLLEGE GREEN

The green is the focal point of the campus, both physically and historically. Along the east side of the green, picturesque **Dartmouth Row** (College St) consists of four harmonious Georgian buildings: **Wentworth**, **Dartmouth**, **Thornton** and **Reed**. Dartmouth Hall was the original college building, constructed in 1791. Just north of Dartmouth Row, **Rollins Chapel** (College St) is a fine example of Richardsonian architecture and a peaceful place to collect your thoughts.

Throughout the year undergraduate students lead free guided **walking tours** (☎ 603-646-2875; www.dartmouth.edu; 2nd fl, McNutt Hall) of the Dartmouth campus. Reservations are not required, but call to confirm the departure times, which change seasonally.

BAKER BERRY LIBRARY

On the north side of the green is the college's central library, **Baker Berry Library** (☎ 603-646-2560; 🕑 8am-midnight Mon-Thu, 8am-10pm Fri, 10am-10pm Sat, 10am-midnight Sun). The reserve corridor on the lower level houses an impressive mural called *Epic of American Civilization*, painted by José Clemente Orozco (1883–1949). The renowned Mexican muralist taught and painted at Dartmouth from 1932 to 1934. The mural follows the course of civilization in the Americas from the time of the Aztecs to the present.

Go upstairs and enjoy the view of the campus from the **Tower Room** on the 2nd floor. This collegiate wood-paneled room is one of the library's loveliest.

The adjacent **Sanborn House Library** (☎ 603-646-2312) also features ornate woodwork, plush leather chairs and books lining the walls, floor to ceiling, on two levels. It is named for Professor Edwin Sanborn, who taught for almost 50 years in the Department of English. This is where students (and you!) can enjoy a **traditional teatime** (⏱ 4pm Mon-Fri) each afternoon.

HOOD MUSEUM OF ART

Shortly after the university's founding in 1769 Dartmouth began to acquire artifacts of artistic or historical interest. Since then the collection has expanded to include nearly 60,000 items, which are housed at the **Hood Museum of Art** (☎ 603-646-2808; www.hoodmuseum .dartmouth.edu; 6034 E Wheelock St; admission free; ⏱ 10am-5pm Tue & Thu-Sat, 10am-9pm Wed, noon-5pm Sun). The collection is particularly strong in American pieces, including Native American art. One of the highlights is a set of Assyrian reliefs from the Palace of Ashurnasirpal that date to the 9th century BC. Special exhibits often feature contemporary artists.

ENFIELD SHAKER SITE

Set in a valley overlooking Mascoma Lake, the Enfield Shaker site dates back to the late 18th century and grew into a small but prosperous community of Shaker farmers and craftspeople in the early 1800s. At its peak, some 300 members (divided into several 'families') lived in Enfield, farming 3000 acres of land. They built a handful of impressive wood and brick buildings in the area took in converts, orphans and children of the poor – who were essential for the Shaker future, since sex was not allowed in the pacifist rule-abiding community. By the early 1900s the community had gone into decline, with the last remaining family moving out in 1917.

The **Enfield Shaker Museum** (☎ 603-632-4346; www.shakermuseum.org; 447 NH 4A; adult/child $7.50/3; ⏱ 10am-5pm Mon-Sat, noon-5pm Sun Jun–mid-Oct; noon-

2pm Mon, Wed & Fri-Sun mid-Oct–May) is set in the Great Stone Dwelling, the largest Shaker dwelling house ever built. Exhibition galleries contain Shaker furniture, tools, clothing and photographs, and visitors can explore the herb and flower gardens, browse the crafty gift shop and hike to the Shaker Feast Ground, which offers spectacular views (particularly in autumn) over the former village and Mascoma Lake.

SAINT-GAUDENS NATIONAL HISTORIC SITE

In the summer of 1885, the sculptor Augustus Saint-Gaudens rented an old inn near the town of Cornish and came to this beautiful spot in the Connecticut River Valley to work. He returned summer after summer, and eventually bought the place in 1892. The estate, where he lived until his death in 1907, is now open to the public as the **Saint-Gaudens National Historic Site** (☎ 603-675-2175; www.nps.gov/saga; 139 St Gaudens Rd, Cornish; adult/child $5/free; ⏱ buildings 9am-4:30pm May-Oct, grounds 9am-dusk year-round).

Saint-Gaudens is best known for his public monuments, such as the Sherman Monument in New York's Central Park and the Adams Memorial in Rock Creek Park in Washington DC. Perhaps his greatest achievement was the Robert Gold Shaw Memorial across from the State House in Boston. Recasts of all of these sculptures are scattered around the beautiful grounds of the estates.

In addition to seeing Saint-Gaudens' work, the National Historic Site allows visitors to tour his home and wander the grounds and studios, where artists-in-residence sculpt. The visitor center shows a short film about the artist's life and work. The site is just off NH 12A in Cornish.

Activities
HIKING

Just over the river in Norwich, about 7 miles from Hanover, **Gile Mountain** is a popular destination for Dartmouth students looking for a quick escape from the grind. A half-hour hike – and a quick climb up the **fire tower** – rewards adventurers with an incredible view of the Connecticut River Valley and the White Mountains beyond.

Cross the river into Norwich and take Main St through town to Turnpike Rd. Stay left at the fork and straight on Lower Turnpike Rd, even as it turns to gravel. Look for the old farmhouse on the right and the sign for parking on the left.

SKIING

The **Dartmouth Cross Country Ski Center** (☎ 603-643-6534; Occum Pond; day pass $7, ski rental per day adult/child $13/9, snowshoe rental per day $10/7; ◷ 9am-7pm Mon-Fri, 9am-5pm Sat & Sun) maintains over 15 miles of groomed trails in the immediate vicinity of Dartmouth campus for wintertime fun. Head northeast on Lyme Rd to reach the center. Trails are on the golf course and at Storrs Pond.

With two challenging mountains, minimal crowds and reasonable prices, **Dartmouth Skiway** (☎ 603-795-2143; http://skiway.dartmouth.edu; 39 Grafton Turnpike, Lyme; one-day lift ticket adult/child/senior Mon-Fri $20/18/20, Sat, Sun & holidays $40/25/20) is one of New Hampshire's best skiing value areas. Take NH 10 north to Lyme. Fork right at the white church and continue 3 miles to the Skiway. You can also take a shuttle bus from campus to the Skiway ($4 one way).

Sleeping

Regional accommodations (in Hanover, Lebanon and White River Junction) are in greatest demand during the fall foliage season, when virtually all the rooms are reserved. Special events at the college also create demand.

Storrs Pond Recreation Area (☎ 603-643-2134; www.storrspond.com; NH 10; campsites/RV sites $25/30; ◷ mid-May–mid-Oct; ⌘) In addition to 37 woodsy sites next to a 15-acre pond, this private campground has tennis courts and two sandy beaches for swimming. From I-89 exit 13, take NH 10 north and look for signs.

Norwich Inn (☎ 802-649-1143; www.norwichinn.com; 325 Main St, Norwich, VT; r $100-200; wi-fi) Just across the Connecticut River in Norwich, Vermont, this historic inn has 16 attractive inn rooms, seven more basic motel rooms, four vestry apartments and an atmospheric dining room. They are all decorated with Victorian antiques and traditional country furniture. Room prices vary according to size and amenities. The brewpub, Jasper Murdock's Alehouse, will whet your whistle while you are here.

Chieftain Motor Inn (☎ 603-643-2550; www.chieftaininn.com; 84 Lyme Rd; r incl breakfast $120-140; ⌨ wi-fi ⌘) This 22-room inn has large rooms overlooking the Connecticut River, with some rooms sporting pine-paneling and cheery quilts. Canoes are available for guest use, and numerous hiking trails are nearby. The inn sits along NH 10 North.

Trumbull House B&B (☎ 603-643-2370, 800-651-5141; www.trumbullhouse.com; 40 Etna Rd; r incl breakfast $165-300; ⌨ wi-fi) Four miles east of Dartmouth, this luxurious, family-friendly B&B is set in a colonial house, built in 1919, with five handsome guest rooms of varying sizes and amenities and a peaceful cottage, set amid 16 acres of verdant countryside. A hiking path links it to the Appalachian Trail.

Hanover Inn (☎ 603-643-4300, 800-443-7024; www.hanoverinn.com; cnr Wheelock & Main Sts; r from $275) Owned by Dartmouth College, Hanover's loveliest guesthouse has nicely appointed rooms with elegant wood furnishings and sleek modern bathrooms. It has a wine bar and an award-winning restaurant on site.

Eating

Lou's (☎ 603-643-3321; 30 S Main St; meals $7-9; ◷ breakfast & lunch) A Dartmouth institution since 1947, this is Hanover's oldest establishment, always packed with students meeting for a coffee or perusing their books. From the retro tables or the Formica-topped counter, order typical diner food like eggs, sandwiches and burgers. The bakery items are also highly recommended.

Rosey's Cafe (☎ 603-643-5282; 15 Lebanon St; sandwiches $7; ◷ 8:30am-6pm Mon-Sat, 10am-5pm Sun) Rosey's serves up excellent panini sandwiches with ingredients such as eggplant, feta, pesto, tomato and basil. The artsy space is a choice setting to linger over frothy cappuccinos, especially if you snag a seat on the patio.

Molly's (☎ 603-643-2570; 43 S Main St; meals $10-15; ◷ 11.30am-10pm) Wood-paneled walls, black-and-white photos and quirky decor form the backdrop to Molly's tasty bistro fare. Fish and chips, wood-fired mac and cheese, burgers and salads are some of the ample offerings. Menus hidden inside old LP covers – a nice touch.

Mai Thai (☎ 603-643-9980; 44 S Main St; lunch buffet $8.50, meals $10-16; ◷ 11:30am-10pm Mon-Sat) This popular 2nd-floor place has an excellent-value lunch buffet and pleasantly upscale environs. Six kinds of curry and five different versions of pad Thai make this a spicy delight.

Jewel of India (☎ 603-643-2217; 27 Lebanon St; meals $8-14; ◷ lunch & dinner) In a classic New England house, this casual restaurant serves a wide selection of classic Indian dishes. The place is popular and the food is decent, but it's probably not the best Indian fare you've ever tasted.

NEW HAMPSHIRE

Ramunto's Brick & Brew Pizzeria (☎ 603-643-9500; 9 E South St; pizzas $8-20; ◷ 11am-midnight Mon-Sat, noon-midnight Sun) The longtime favorite in town, Ramunto's recently moved its headquarters to a new space, but still serves up nicely seasoned pizzas. You can grab a slice and watch the game or enjoy a slice a freshly baked pie alfresco on the front patio.

Drinking & Entertainment

Murphy's on the Green (☎ 603-643-4075; 11 S Main St; ◷ 11am-12:30am) This classic collegiate tavern is where students and faculty meet over pints of ale (with ten beers on tap) and satisfying pub fare (mains $8 to $15) served until 10pm. Stained-glass windows and church-pew seating enhance the cozy atmosphere.

Hopkins Center for the Arts (☎ 603-646-2422; www .hop.dartmouth.edu; 6041 Lower Level Wilson Hall, Dartmouth College) A long way from the big-city lights of New York and Boston, Dartmouth hosts its own entertainment at this outstanding performing arts venue. The season brings everything from movies to live performances by international companies.

Canoe Club (☎ 603-643-9660; www.canoeclub.us; 27 S Main St) Not your typical college nightlife scene, this upscale pub features live music seven nights a week – usually jazz, folk and a little bit of bluegrass. An excellent menu (mains $15 to $24) of organic fare such as shellfish stew and spice-rubbed lamb with curried vegetables adds to the appeal.

Getting There & Around

Short-haul 'commuter' subsidiaries of some major airlines link **Lebanon Municipal Airport** (☎ 603-298-8878), 6 miles south of Hanover, with Boston, New York and Philadelphia.

It's a three-hour drive to Hanover from Boston; take I-93 to I-89 to I-91. From Hanover to Burlington, Vermont (VT), it's an additional 2½ hours north via I-89. **Vermont Transit** (☎ 802-864-6811, 800-552-8737; www.vermont transit.com) has direct buses from Hanover to Logan International Airport ($38.50, three hours) and Manchester International Airport ($21, three hours). There is also a service to Burlington, VT (two hours) and Montreal, Québec (four hours).

Dartmouth Coach (☎ 603-448-2800; www.dart mouthcoach.com) operates five daily shuttles from Hanover to Logan International Airport and South Station in Boston (adult/child one way $35/25, three hours).

Advance Transit (☎ 802-295-1824; www.advance transit.com) provides a free service to White River Junction, Lebanon, West Lebanon and Norwich. Bus stops are indicated by a blue-and-yellow AT symbol.

LAKES REGION

Vast Winnipesaukee is the centerpiece of one of New Hampshire's most popular holiday destinations, with an odd mix of natural beauty and commercial tawdriness. Here, forest-shrouded lakes with beautiful sinuous coastlines stretch for hundreds of miles. The roads skirting the shores and connecting the lakeside towns, however, are a riotous spread of uninspiring Americana: shopping malls, amusement arcades, auto dealerships, go-cart tracks, clam shacks, junk-food outlets and boat docks.

Lake Winnipesaukee has 183 miles of coastline, more than 300 islands and excellent salmon fishing. Catch the early morning mists off the lakes and you'll understand why the American Indians named it 'Smile of the Great Spirit.' The prettiest stretches are in the southwest corner between Glendale and Alton (on the shoreline Belknap Point Rd), and in the northeast corner between Wolfeboro and Moultonborough (on NH 109). Stop for a swim, a lakeside picnic or a cruise. Children will enjoy prowling the video arcades, bowl-a-dromes and junk-food cafés of Weirs Beach.

LACONIA & AROUND

pop 17,200

The largest town of the Lakes Region, Laconia has a host of important services (including a hospital) and a small, quaint downtown. Laconia is also the gateway to hiking or skiing on Belknap Mountain (2384ft) and swimming at Ellacoya State Beach. Most visitors, however, whiz through Laconia en route to other destinations. Neighboring Gilford, in the shadow of Belknap Mountain, is joined at the hip to Laconia, while towns near the lake like Glendale and Alton are the bigger draw with pine-shaded guesthouses and cottages overlooking the idyllic waterfront.

Orientation & Information

Laconia lies along NH 106, which is also Main St. The less trafficked downtown area lies around Main St/106 and Daniel Webster

NEW HAMPSHIRE

Hwy/11A. Heading north of town along NH 106 leads past Opechee Bay to the east and Winnnisquam Lake to the west.

Greater Laconia-Weirs Beach Chamber of Commerce (☎ 603-524-5531; www.laconia-weirs.org; 383 S Main St, Laconia; ☻ 8:30am-5pm Mon-Fri, noon-4pm Sat) Maintains an information office in the old railroad station in the center of town.

Lakes Region Association (☎ 603-744-8664, 800-605-2537; www.lakesregion.org; NH 104, New Hampton) An online business directory with information about skiing, hiking trails, scenic drives, covered bridges and leaf-peeping, as well as local service providers.

Lake Winnipesaukee Home Page (www.winnipesaukee.com) A great independent site with lots of resources, web cams and news.

Sights & Activities
BELKNAP MILL
America's oldest unaltered textile mill, the **Belknap Mill** (☎ 603-524-8813; www.belknapmill.org; 25 Beacon St; free admission; ☻ 9am-5pm Mon-Fri) is handsomely set along the Winnipesaukee River in downtown Laconia. The four-story 19th-century brick mill houses an industrial knitting museum and galleries that hold changing exhibitions throughout the year.

ELLACOYA STATE PARK
Many lakeshore lodgings have water access, but if your place does not, head for **Ellacoya State Park** (☎ 603-293-7821; adult/child $3/1; ☻ late May–mid-Oct), which has a 600ft-wide beach with lovely views across to the Sandwich and Ossipee mountains. This is an excellent place for swimming, fishing and canoeing.

HIKING
At 2384ft, Belknap Mountain is the highest peak in the Belknap Range, with numerous hiking trails. The most direct route to the summit is from the Belknap Carriage Rd in Gilford. From NH 11A, take Cherry Valley Rd and follow the signs for the Belknap Fire Tower. Three marked trails lead from the parking lot to the summit of Belknap Mountain, a one-hour trek. The white-blazed trail leads to the summit of nearby Piper Mountain (2030ft).

Within the Belknap Mountain State Forest, the **Mt Major Summit Trail** is a good 2-mile trek up that 1780ft peak. The summit offers spectacular views of all corners of Lake Winnipesaukee. The trailhead is a few miles south of West Alton on NH 11; park just off the road.

SKIING
When the snow covers the ground, Belknap Mountain becomes **Gunstock** (☎ 800-486-7862; www.gunstock.com; NH 11A, Gilford; lift tickets adult/child/senior/teen Fri-Sun $56/36/46/46, Tue-Thu $48/28/38/28; ☻ 1-4pm Tue-Fri, 9am-4pm Sat & Sun), a ski area with 45 downhill runs on a vertical drop of 1400ft. There are seven lifts, as well as a ski school, day-care facilities and night skiing between 4pm and 9pm Tuesday to Thursday, and 4pm and 10pm Friday and Saturday. Most mountain trails are intermediate, with more advanced than beginner trails. A few hills are dedicated to tubing (two/four hours $15/20) – no equipment and no skill required! Over 30 miles of cross-country trails follow the wooded paths around Gilford. Rental skis are available, as are snowboards and snowshoes.

FESTIVALS & EVENTS
In mid-June, the raucous **Motorcycle Week** (www.laconiamcweek.com) draws two-wheeled crowds to the **New Hampshire International Speedway** (☎ 603-783-4931; www.nhis.com; NH 106, Loudon), south of Laconia. Races, shows and other spectacles create quite a scene. Bikers are everywhere.

Sleeping
Gunstock (☎ 603-293-4341, 800-486-7862; www.gunstock.com; NH 11A, Gilford; campsites/RV sites $27/35; ☻ year-round) The ski area has a large campground that is open when the slopes are closed. It is a woodsy setting in the midst of mountains and lakes. Water hookups are not available in winter, but there are heated bathrooms and drinking water nearby. Gunstock also has some cabins ($70) that sleep five people.

Inn at Smith Cove (☎ 603-293-1111; www.innatsmithcove.com; 19 Roberts Rd, Gilford; r incl breakfast $90-180) This elegant Victorian inn has nine uniquely appointed rooms with wonderful lake views and three quaint cottages with a garden setting. A spacious piazza and landscaped grounds lead down to a private beach and boat docks on Lake Winnipesaukee. Prices vary according to room size and amenities.

Ferry Point House B&B (☎ 603-524-0087; www.ferrypointhouse.com; 100 Lower Bay Rd, Winnisquam; r $110-155) Overlooking Lake Winnisquam, this picturesque Victorian B&B has nine cozy, uniquely furnished rooms set with antiques. Rooms range in size from small to spacious, some have lake views and one has a large Jacuzzi bathtub. The B&B is about 7 miles south of Laconia, reached via NH3.

NEW HAMPSHIRE

Belknap Point Motel (☎ 603-293-7511, 888-454-2537; www.bpmotel.com; 107 Belknap Point Rd, Gilford; r $120-140) Just northwest of Ellacoya State Park, these 16 lakeside motel rooms and apartments are an excellent choice. The waterfront location yields views of the Ossipees to the east, the foothills of the White Mountains to the north, and Mt Washington in the distance on clear days.

Bay Side Inn (☎ 603-875-5005; www.bayside-inn .com; NH 11D, Alton Bay; r $150-185) Eighteen attractive guest rooms right on the Winnipesaukee waterfront. Guests enjoy a private beach that is an excellent setting for fishing and swimming. Motorboats (with skis) and kayaks are available for rental. Two-bedroom efficiency suites (and weekly rates) are available for longer-term guests.

Eating

Las Piñatas (☎ 603-528-1405; 9 Veterans Sq, Laconia; meals $11-15; ☻ lunch & dinner) This friendly, family-run restaurant serves tasty chile rellenos, nachos, enchiladas and other Tex-Mex fare amid colorful ambience. On warm days the outside tables make a fine setting for frozen margaritas.

Nadia's Trattoria (☎ 603-524-8688; 1402 Lakeshore Rd, Gilford; meals $17-22; ☻ 4:30-9pm May-Aug, Tue-Sun Sep-Apr) One of New Hampshire's finest Italian restaurants. The menu features delectable antipasti, homemade pasta and fresh seafood. Save room for a sweet treat crafted by Bindi, the master Italian pastry chef.

Getting There & Around

Driving from Laconia to North Conway, take US 3 to NH 25 to NH 16 (1½ hours, 50 miles). **Concord Trailways** (☎ 603-228-3300, 800-639-3317; www.concordtrailways.com) runs a route between Boston and Berlin. Pick it up at the Evans Expressmart/Exxon gas station in Tilton or the Munce's Konvenience/Citgo gas station in New Hampton. Buses go south to Concord ($6.50, one hour), Manchester ($9.50, 1½ hours), Boston ($18.50, 2½ hours) or Logan International Airport ($24, 2½ hours). Heading north, you can go to North Conway (1½ hours), Jackson (1½ hours), Pinkham Notch (two hours) or all the way up to Gorham and Berlin.

The **Greater Laconia Transit Agency** (☎ 603-528-2496, 800-294-2496; all-day pass adult/child $2/1; ☻ Jul-early Sep) runs shuttle trolleys through town to Weirs Beach and Meredith.

WEIRS BEACH

Called 'Aquedoctan' by its Native American settlers, Weirs Beach takes its English name from the weirs (enclosures for catching fish) that the first white settlers found along the small sand beach. Today Weirs Beach is the honky-tonk heart of Lake Winnipesaukee's childhood amusements, famous for video-game arcades and fried dough. The vacation scene is completed by a lakefront promenade, a small public beach and a dock for small cruising ships. A water park and drive-in theater are also in the vicinity. Away from the din on the waterfront, you will notice evocative Victorian-era architecture – somehow out of place in this capital of kitsch.

Weirs Beach is just north of Laconia at the convergence of US 3 and NH 11.

Information

Greater Laconia-Weirs Beach Chamber of Commerce (☎ 603-524-5531; www.laconia-weirs.org; US3) Useful for same-day accommodations; located south of Weirs Beach.

Sights & Activities

WINNIPESAUKEE SCENIC RAILROAD

The touristy **scenic railroad** (☎ 603-745-2135; www .hoborr.com; adult/child 1hr $11/9, 2hr $12/10; ☻ 11am-5pm daily Jun-Aug, Sat & Sun May & Sep-Oct) departs Weirs Beach and Meredith for a one- or two-hour lakeside ride aboard '20s and '30s train cars. The train travels to Lake Winnipesaukee's southern tip at Alton Bay before making a U-turn. Kids might wish to ride in the ice-cream parlor car.

CRUISES

The classic **MS Mount Washington** (☎ 603-366-5531; www.cruisenh.com; adult/child $22/12) steams out of Weirs Beach on relaxing 2½-hour scenic lake cruises at 10am and 12:30pm from mid-May to mid-October. Special events include the Sunday champagne brunch cruise and Friday Theme Cruises ('70s Dance Fever, Lobsterfest, etc) running throughout the summer ($40 to $50 per person).

The same company also operates the MV *Sophie C*, a veritable **floating post office** (adult/child $22/12). This US Mail boat delivers packages and letters to quaint ports and otherwise inaccessible island residents on 1½-hour runs at 11am and 2pm Monday to Saturday. The **MV Doris E** (adult/child from $15/7) offers cruises of Meredith Bay and northern Lake Winnipesaukee from 10:30am to 7:30pm from late June to August.

Both leave from Weirs Beach and the *Doris E* also stops at Meredith.

Sleeping

Some of the nicer moderately priced area motels lie on US 3 (Weirs Blvd) between Gilford and Weirs Beach.

Paugus Bay Campground (☎ 603-366-4757; 96 Hilliard Rd; campsites/RV sites $34/38; ☷ mid-May–mid-Oct) Off US 3, Paugus has 170 wooded sites overlooking the lake. The campground has a private beach as well as other recreation facilities.

Sun Valley Cottages (☎ 603-366-4945; www.sunvally .com; NH 3; r $90-130; ⬚) Nestled amid tall windswept pines, Sun Valley rents out 14 simply furnished cottages with kitchenettes. Most of the rooms are pine-paneled and half of the cottages have fireplaces. A pool and Jacuzzi add to the appeal.

Baytop Motel (☎ 603-366-2225; www.baytop.com; 1025 Weirs Blvd; r $90-170; ⬚) Just 0.5 miles south of Weirs Beach, these traditional motel rooms overlook the lake. Rooms are nicely decorated and well equipped with refrigerators, microwaves and coffee-makers. Extra perks include a Jacuzzi and a Ping-Pong table.

Lighthouse Inn B&B (☎ 603-366-5432; www .lighthouseinnbb.com; 913 Scenic Rd; r incl breakfast Jun-Sep $150-200, Oct-May $100-160; wi-fi) Set on five acres of fields and forest, this charming B&B has attractively designed guestrooms, all with fireplaces and homey touches. Complimentary tea is served in the afternoon and the breakfasts are superb.

Eating

Cruise Lakeside Dr for an abundance of snack shops.

Weirs Beach Lobster Pound (☎ 603-366-2255; 70 N Endicott St; meals $9-17; ☷ mid-May–mid-Oct; ⬚) A Weirs Beach institution, this place serves a broad menu, including clam chowder, lobsters, barbecue and more. Popular children's menu.

Getting There & Around

Weirs Beach is located on the west side of Lake Winnipesaukee. From I-93 take exit 20 (from the south) or 24 (from the north) to US 3. See opposite for information on transportation around the Lakes Region.

MEREDITH & AROUND

pop 6900

More upscale than Weirs Beach, Meredith is a lively lakeside town with a long commercial strip stretching along the shore. Its few backstreets are set with attractive colonial and Victorian homes. US 3, NH 25 and NH 104 converge here.

The MS *Mount Washington* (Monday only; see opposite) and the Winnipesaukee Scenic Railroad (see opposite) all stop at Meredith Town Docks . **Meredith Chamber of Commerce** (☎ 603-279-6121; www.meredithcc.org; US 3 at Mill St, Meredith; ☷ 9am-5pm Mon-Fri year-round, 9am-5pm Sat, 9am-2pm Sun May-Oct) can answer other questions.

Unless otherwise stated, items in the following section are in Meredith proper.

Sleeping

Long Island Bridge Campground (☎ 603-253-6053; Moultonboro Neck Rd; campsites/RV sites $23/25; ☷ mid-May–mid-Oct) Thirteen miles northeast of Meredith near Center Harbor, this camping area overlooking the lake has popular tent sites and a private beach. Waterfront sites are more expensive. In July and August, there is a three-day minimum stay. Follow NH 25 east for 1.5 miles from Center Harbor, then go south on Moultonboro Neck Rd for 6.5 miles.

White Lake State Park (☎ 603-323-7350; West Ossipee; campsites with/without water views $32/24; ☷ mid-May–mid-Oct) White Lake, 22 miles northeast of Meredith off NH 16, has 200 tent sites on over 600 acres, plus swimming and hiking trails. This state park boasts some of New Hampshire's finest swimming in the pristine glacial lake.

Tuckernuck Inn (☎ 603-279-5521, 888-858-5521; www.thetuckernuckinn.com; 25 Red Gate Lane; r incl breakfast $119-155) Tuckernuck has five cozy, quiet rooms (one has a fireplace) with stenciled walls and handmade quilts. From Main St, head inland along Water St, then turn right (uphill) onto Red Gate Lane.

Meredith Inn B&B (☎ 603-279-0000; www.mere dithinn.com; Main St; d incl breakfast $130-190) This delightful Victorian inn has eight rooms outfitted with antique furnishings and luxurious bedding; several rooms also have Jacuzzis, gas fireplaces or walk-out bay windows.

Inns at Mill Falls (☎ 603-279-7006, 800-622-6455; www.millfalls.com; 312 Daniel Webster Way; r $130-310; ⬚) Four different properties (the original Inn at Mill Falls, Chase House, Bay Point and Church Landing) front Lake Winnipesaukee at different points around Meredith Bay, all offering designer-decorated rooms with lovely water views. Church Landing is particularly appealing, as every room has a fireplace, and there's an enticing spa and top-notch restaurant on site. Rooms in Mill Falls are less expensive, as this property is not on the water, but across busy Daniel Webster Way.

Eating
Abondante (☎ 603-279-9931; 30 Main St; meals $8-10; 9am-5pm Mon-Sat, 9am-3pm Sun) This sweet-smelling bakery in the heart of Meredith has a tantalizing selection of pastries, cakes and pies, plus fresh salads and tasty sandwiches for lunch (try the grilled portobello panini). You can enjoy them on the patio. At dinnertime, the like-named restaurant in back (☎ 603-279-7177) serves classic Italian cuisine (mains $16 to $22).

Mame's (☎ 603-279-4631; 8 Plymouth St; meals $10-25; lunch & dinner; wi-fi) Tucked inside an 1825 brick mansion on one of Meredith's back streets, Mame's serves a broad selection of seafood and classic American fare among its pine-floored, antique-filled dining rooms. Roast prime rib, baked scallops and lobster crab cakes are top dinner choices, while sandwiches, salads and flat-bread pizzas round out the lunch menu. Mame's also serves a decadent Sunday brunch.

Lakehouse (☎ 603-279-5221; cnr US 3 & NH 25, Church Landing; meals $18-26; 5:30-9:30pm) Within the Inn at Church Landing, this classy restaurant is part of the statewide 'Common Man' family of restaurants. The wide-ranging menu focuses on seafood and steaks, usually prepared with some creative international twist. Enjoy your dinner on the breezy lakeside deck.

Getting There & Away
Concord Trailways (☎ 603-228-3300, 800-639-3317; www.concordtrailways.com) stops in Meredith at a **Mobil gas station** (☎ 603-279-5129) on NH 25 on a route between Boston and Berlin. You can take this bus to Concord ($10, one hour), Manchester ($12.50, 1½ hours), Boston South Station ($21.50, 2½ hours), and Logan International Airport ($27, 2½ hours).

WOLFEBORO
pop 6700
Wolfeboro is an idyllic town where children still gather around the ice-cream stand on warm summer nights and grassy lakeside park gathers young and old to weekly concerts. Named for General Wolfe, who died vanquishing Montcalm on the Plains of Abraham in Québec, Wolfeboro (founded in 1770) claims to be 'the oldest summer resort in America.' Whether that's true or not, it's certainly the most charming, with pretty lake beaches, intriguing museums, cozy B&Bs and a worthwhile walking trail that courses along several lakes as it leads out of town.

Wolfeboro is on the eastern shore of Lake Winnipesaukee, at the intersection of NH 28 with the lakeside NH 109.

Wolfeboro Chamber of Commerce information booth (☎ 603-569-2200; www.wolfeborochamber.com; 32 Central Ave; 10am-5pm Mon-Sat, 11am-3pm Sun Jul–mid-Oct, 10am-3pm Mon-Fri, 9am-noon mid-Oct–Jun) Located inside the old train station.

Sights & Activities
WENTWORTH STATE BEACH
If your lodging or campsite does not have access to the lake, head to this small **beach** (☎ 603-569-3699; NH 109; adult/child $3/1; dawn-dusk daily Jun-Aug, Sat & Sun May) on the serene Wentworth Lake. Much smaller but much less developed than Winnipesaukee, Wentworth Lake offers all the same opportunities for swimming, picnicking, hiking and fishing.

LIBBY MUSEUM
At the age of 40, Dr Henry Forrest Libby, a local dentist, began collecting things. In 1912 he built a home for his collections, which later became the eccentric little **Libby Museum** (☎ 603-569-1035; www.wolfeboro.com/libby; NH 109, Winter Harbor; adult/child $2/1; 10am-4pm Tue-Sat, noon-4pm Sun Jun-Sep). Starting with butterflies and moths, the amateur naturalist built up a private natural history collection. Other collections followed, including Abenaki relics and early-American farm and home implements. It lies 3 miles north of Wolfeboro.

OTHER MUSEUMS
The **Clark House Museum Complex** (☎ 603-569-4997; 233 S Main St; 10am-4pm Wed-Fri, 10am-2pm Sat Jul-Aug) is Wolfeboro's eclectic historical museum, comprising three historic buildings: the 1778 Clark family farmhouse, an 1805 one-room schoolhouse and a replica of an old firehouse. The buildings contain relevant artifacts (such as fire engines!), furniture and the like. Admission was free when we were there but a fee was being considered.

For a Rosie-the-riveter and baked-apple-pie look at WWII, visit the **Wright Museum** (☎ 603-569-1212; www.wrightmuseum.org; 77 Center St; adult/student/child $6/3/free; 10am-4pm Mon-Sat, noon-4pm Sun).

Interactive exhibitions feature music, documentary clips, posters and other American paraphernalia relating to the war. There are also uniforms, equipment and military hardware (including a 42-ton Pershing tank), meticulously restored by the museum.

Wolfeboro is an appropriate place for the **New Hampshire Boat Museum** (☎ 603-569-4554; www.nhbm.org; 397 Center St; adult/student/child $5/3/ free; ☻ 10am-4pm Mon-Sat, noon-4pm Sun). Nautical types will appreciate the collection of vintage watercraft, motors, photographs and other memorabilia.

WALKING TOURS
Wolfeboro is a pretty town with some good examples of New England's architectural styles, from Georgian through Federal, Greek Revival and Second Empire. It also has an excellent multiuse trail starting near the information office: The **Cotton Valley Trail** runs for 12 miles along a former railroad. It links the towns of Wolfeboro, Brookfield and Wakefield and passes by two lakes, climbs through Cotton Valley and winds through forests and fields around Brookfield.

CRUISES, DIVING & KAYAKING
The **MS Mount Washington** stops in Wolfeboro as part of its 2½-hour cruise around Lake Winnipesaukee, at 11:15am on Tuesday, Wednesday, Friday and Saturday. See p434 for details.

For bigger adventures across and into the deep blue, stop in **Dive Winnipesaukee** (☎ 603-569-8080; www.divewinnipesaukee.com; 4 Main St), which rents kayaks ($35 per day) and offers a range of diving courses in the frigid lake.

Sleeping
Wolfeboro Campground (☎ 603-569-9881; www.wolfeborocampground.com; 61 Haines Hill Rd; campsites/RV sites $24/27; ☻ mid-May–mid-Oct) Off NH 28, and about 4.5 miles north of Wolfeboro, this campground has 50 private, wooded sites.

Tuc' Me Inn B&B (☎ 603-569-5702; www.tucmeinn.com; 118 N Main St; r incl breakfast $139-179; wi-fi) Just north of Wolfeboro Inn, this unfortunately named B&B has seven pretty rooms. Their various charms include handmade quilts, four-post beds, cathedral ceilings and private porches. Breakfast at this chef-owned inn is delightful, featuring seasonal fresh fruit, rum-raisin French toast, cranberry pancakes or orange-glazed waffles.

Topsides B&B (☎ 603-569-3834; www.topsidesbb.com; 209 S Main St; r incl breakfast weekday $129, weekend $175-195; ☻ Apr-Oct; wi-fi) Just a short walk to the center of town, this handsome new addition to Wolfeboro has five elegant, classically furnished rooms with wood floors. Several have lake views.

Wolfeboro Inn (☎ 603-569-3016, 800-451-2389; www.wolfeboroinn.com; 90 N Main St; r incl breakfast $190-270; wi-fi) The town's best-known lodging is right on the lake with a private beach. One of the region's most prestigious resorts since 1812, it has 44 very comfortable, individually decorated country-style rooms in the main inn and in a modern annex. Facilities include a restaurant and pub, Wolfe's Tavern.

Eating
Bailey's (☎ 603-569-3612; Railroad Ave; ice cream $2-3) This old-time fave has scooped ice cream for generations of families, and is still the most popular gathering spot in the summer. There are more than 20 different flavors; feel free to mix and match, but the servings are huge!

Strawberry Patch (☎ 603-569-5523; 50 N Main St; meals $7-12; ☻ 7am-2pm Mon-Sat year-round, & 7am-1pm Sun Mar-Oct) The extensive menu here includes a litany of entirely homemade items: Belgian waffles, eggs with hollandaise sauce, crab omelettes and numerous strawberry concoctions.

Cider Press (☎ 603-569-2028; 30 Middleton Rd; meals $14-20; ☻ 5-9:30pm Tue-Sun) Off NH 28 south of town, this cozy spot is deservedly popular, with rustic barn-board walls, fireplaces and antiques. As for the cuisine, it roams from baby back-ribs to grilled salmon. Don't overlook the creative blackboard specials.

Wolfe's Tavern (☎ 603-569-3016; 90 N Main St; meals $16-20) The bar menu at the rustically colonial Wolfeboro Inn ranges from burgers and grilled meats to pasta and seafood. Terrace tables are set outside in good weather.

51 Mill (☎ 603-569-3303; 51 Mill St; meals $10-24; ☻ lunch & dinner) Perched right on the lake, tastefully decorated 51 Mill serves delicious seafood, excellent salads, grilled meats and creative American fare. Crab cakes, seared sea scallops and rack of lamb go nicely with the wine selections. Grab an outdoor lakeside table in back for splendid al fresco dining.

Entertainment
The local organization **Wolfeboro Folk** (☎ 603-522-8697; www.wolfeborofolk.com; tickets $15-25) attracts some of the country's top folk musicians. In

NEW HAMPSHIRE

the summer, concerts take place north of Wolfeboro at **Moody Mountain Farm** (100 Pork Hill Rd, off NH 28). Concerts in spring and fall are held at **Tumbledown Farm** (295 Governor Wentworth Rd, off NH 109) in Brookfield. You can also reserve a pre-concert dinner (around $15 per person), which features locally sourced, often organic products.

Getting There & Away

Wolfeboro is located on the east side of Lake Winnipesaukee. From I-93, take US 3 to its intersection with NH 11. Follow this road south as it skirts the lake. Pick up NH 28 in Alton and head north.

SQUAM LAKE

Northwest of Lake Winnipesaukee, Squam Lake is more tranquil, more tasteful and more pristine than its big sister. It is also less accessible, lacking any public beaches. Nonetheless, if you choose your lodging carefully, you can enjoy Squam Lake's natural wonders, just like Katherine Hepburn and Henry Fonda did in *On Golden Pond*. With 67 miles of shoreline and 67 islands, there are plenty of opportunities for fishing, kayaking and swimming.

Orientation & Information

Holderness is the area's main town, at the southwest corner of the lake. Little Squam Lake is a much smaller branch further southwest. US 3 follows the south shore of Squam Lake to Holderness. The road then turns west, skirting the north shore of Little Squam Lake before rejoining I-93 at Ashland.

Holderness Chamber of Commerce (☎ 603-968-7536; NH 3, Holderness; ☯ 9am-4pm Mon-Fri, 10am-3pm Sat).

Squam Lakes Area Chamber of Commerce (☎ 603-968-4494; www.squamlakeschamber.com)

Sights & Activities

SQUAM LAKES NATURAL SCIENCE CENTER

To get up close and personal with the wildlife that lives in the Lakes Region, visit the **Squam Lakes Natural Science Center** (☎ 603-968-7194; www.nhnature.org; NH 113, Holderness; adult/child/senior $13/9/11; ☯ 9:30am-4:30pm May-Nov). Four different nature paths weave through the woods and around the marsh. The highlight is the **Gephart Trail**, leading past trailside enclosures that are home to various creatures including bobcat, fisher (a kind of marten), mountain lion, a great

horned owl and a bald eagle. The nearby **Kirkwood Gardens**, featuring many species of New England native shrubs and flowers, are specially designed to attract birds and butterflies. The center also organizes **nature cruises** (combination tickets adult/child/senior $30/20/25) around Squam Lake.

CRUISES

Squam Lake Tours (☎ 603-968-7577; www.squamlaketours.com; US 3, Holderness; ☯ tours 10am, 2pm & 4pm May-Oct) visits the singing loons and wondrous Church Island and allows visitors to see the famed sights from *On Golden Pond*, including Thayer Cottage and Purgatory Cove.

Squam Lakes Natural Science Center Tours (☎ 603-968-7194; www.nhnature.org; NH 113, Holderness; adult/child/senior $20/16/18) offers pontoon-boat cruises that observe the loons and eagles, visit sites from *On Golden Pond* or watch the sun set over the lake. Combination tickets for the center and tour are available; see left.

Squam Lakes Camp Resort (☎ 603-968-7227; www.squamlakesresort.com) rents out 16-foot canoes (per day $49) and pontoon boats of varying sizes ($120 to $280 per day).

Sleeping & Eating

Cottage Place on Squam Lake (☎ 603-968-7116; www.cottageplaceonsquam.com; US 3, Holderness; r $110, cottages $95-140) The cozy, comfortable Cottage Place fronts Squam Lake, offering a private beach, a swimming raft and docking space for boats. There is a wide variety of accommodations, including lakefront cottages and motel suites. Weekly rentals are encouraged in summer.

Squam Lake Inn (☎ 603-968-4417; www.squamlakeinn.com; cnr Shepard Hill Rd & US 3 Holderness; r $150-175; wi-fi) This century-old Victorian farmhouse has eight rooms, all decorated in vintage New England style with quilts on the beds, antique furnishings and a local 'Lakes' theme. A mahogany deck and wrap-around porch overlook woodsy grounds.

Manor on Golden Pond (☎ 603-968-3348; www.manorongoldenpond.com; US 3, Holderness; r $210-395, cottage $445, ste $460; wi-fi ⬚) This luxurious B&B is perched up on Shepard Hill, overlooking serene Squam Lake. Elegant rooms (some with fireplaces and Jacuzzis), gourmet breakfasts and a lovely private beach make this one of the lake region's finest retreats. Extra perks include clay tennis courts, a full service spa and an excellent dining room.

Holderness General Store (☎ 603-968-3446; US 3, Holderness; meals $7-10; ☷ 7am-9pm) This gourmet grocery store and bakery serves excellent breakfast and lunch sandwiches, homemade fudge and other goodies. You'll also find wines, sake, marinated meats and veggies (ready for grilling), pasta salads and marvelous scones.

Walter's Basin (☎ 603-968-4412; US 3, Holderness; meals $15-28; ☷ lunch & dinner) Lake trippers are encouraged to dock their boats and come in for a meal at this casual, waterfront spot. Located on Little Squam Lake near the bridge, the friendly restaurant features stuffed haddock, turkey dinner, macaroni and cheese and other comfort fare.

Getting There & Away

Concord Trailways (☎ 603-228-3300, 800-639-3317; www.concordtrailways.com) stops in Center Harbor, on the east side of Squam Lake, en route from Boston to Berlin. The bus stop is at Rob's Gas Depot/Citgo gas station, on US 25. This bus will take you to Concord ($10, one hour), Manchester ($12.50, 1½ hours), Boston South Station ($21.50, 2½ hours), and Logan International Airport ($27, 2½ hours). Heading north, it goes to North Conway, Pinkham Notch, Gorham and Berlin.

WHITE MOUNTAIN REGION

Covering one quarter of New Hampshire (and part of Maine), the vast White Mountains area is a spectacular region of soaring peaks and lush valleys, and contains New England's most rugged mountains. There are numerous activities on offer including hiking, camping, skiing and canoeing. Much of the area – 780,000 acres – is designated as the White Mountain National Forest (WMNF), thus protecting it from overdevelopment and guaranteeing its wondrous natural beauty for years to come. Keep in mind, however, that this place is popular: six million visitors flock here every year, making it the nation's second most-visited park after the Great Smoky Mountains. Parking at National Forest trailheads costs $3/5/20 per day/week/season. Purchase parking permits at any of the visitor centers in the area.

WATERVILLE VALLEY & AROUND
pop 270

In the shadow of Mt Tecumseh, this beautiful valley was developed as a complete mountain resort community. Condominiums and golf courses are carefully set on picture-perfect Corcoran's Pond, surrounded by miles of downhill and cross-country ski trails, hiking trails, bike routes and in-line skating paths. The result is a harmonious – although rather sterile – resort with lots of organized sports activities.

Orientation & Information

Town Sq is the valley's main service facility, with a post office, bank, information office, laundry, restaurants and shops. This is also the locale of the main accommodations office, where you will check in to your condo.

Waterville Valley (☎ 800-468-2553; www.waterville.com) For all the information you need about snow conditions and skiing facilities.

Waterville Valley Region Chamber of Commerce (☎ 603-726-3804, 800-237-2307; www.watervillevalleyregion.com; 12 Vintinner Rd, Campton; ☷ 9am-5pm) Provides tourist information and is easily visible on NH 49.

Activities

In summer, Snow's Mountain offers cross-country and downhill mountain biking trails (for hiking too). You can take a chairlift to the mountaintop from the **Adventure Center** (☎ 603-236-4344; 1 Ski Area Rd; www.waterville.com; lift $9), which also rents bikes. There are 30 miles of other trails in the valley, but you'll need to buy a trail pass ($6 per day). Mountain bikes cost $32 per day ($57 for a full suspension bike). Waterville's **Ice Arena** (☎ 603-236-4813; Town Square Complex; adult/child $5/4) is a good place to practice your triple axles. It's open most of the year. Hours change frequently; check www.watervillevalley.org/wvnh_icearenas.html for current schedules.

Skiing (lift ticket adult/student/child & senior $59/49/35) is excellent but pricey in the valley. There are 11 lifts and 52 trails on the mountain.

Sleeping & Eating

There is no cheap lodging in Waterville Valley resort, although if you're camping, you'll find some rustic campsites along Tripoli Rd. Campton, 13 miles southwest, has inexpensive lodgings.

All Waterville Valley lodging options have on-site restaurants.

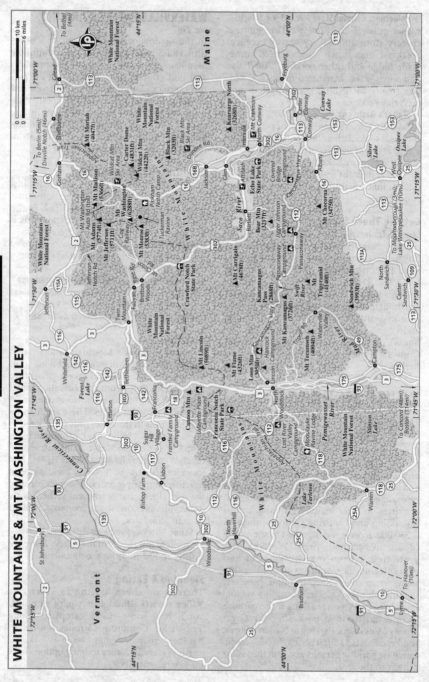

TRIP PLANNER: WHITE MOUNTAINS

Whether you're keen on outdoor adventure or simply intent on enjoying some inspiring landscape, the White Mountains won't disappoint. There are 1200 miles of hiking trails (including 100 miles of the Appalachian Trail) and 48 peaks over 4000ft. For hiking, the **Franconia Notch State Park** (p445) has many trailheads as well as spectacular sights such as the Flume Gorge. Although this place gets packed, the more challenging the hike, the thinner the crowds. There's also an aerial tramway from the park that goes up Cannon Mountain. The **Kancamagus Hwy** (p443), a scenic road set along a wandering river, is another popular place for hiking, and it has many campsites along the road. For more extensive info on hikes, pick up the excellent *White Mountain Guide* ($24.95, available online and in some New Hampshire bookstores) published by the **Appalachian Mountain Club** (www.outdoors.org). **North Woodstock & Lincoln** (below) can be a bit of a tourist circus, but are gateway to kid adventures like the scenic railway and exploring boulder caves; you can also arrange kayaking and zip-line tours here. Winter sports enthusiasts have a few options, including the downhill runs at **Cannon Mountain** (p447) near Franconia Notch State Park or **Loon Mountain** (p444), just off the Kancamagus Hwy. **Waterville** (p439) offers access to ice-skating and cross-country skiing. Wherever you go, be prepared for bad weather. The mountains have their own weather pattern, with fierce winds and strong storms that can appear out of nowhere. Those more interested in literary delights shouldn't miss a visit to the idyllic **home of Robert Frost** (p447), near some charming B&Bs in the area. For a complete list of activities in the mountains, see p445.

Waterville Campground (☎ 877-444-6777; Tripoli Rd; campsite $16; ☷ year-round) Waterville has 26 very basic sites run by the United States Forest Service (USFS) that are nicely wooded and extremely peaceful. Most are first-come, first served, but several can be reserved in advance. To get there take I-93 exit 331 via the unpaved Triopli Rd.

Russell Pond Campground (☎ 888-226-7764; 603-536-1310; Tripoli Rd; campsite $20; ☷ mid-May–mid-Oct) Four miles off I-93, this beautifully located campground has 86 campsites, many pondside, with flush toilets and pay showers.

Snowy Owl Inn (☎ 603-236-8383, 800-766-9969; www.snowyowlinn.com; 4 Village Rd; r incl breakfast $135-230, ste/apt $160-400; wi-fi ☒) This handsome resort was built to look like a country inn, albeit a large one, with 85 rooms and suites in a range of styles. This place is among the more cozy options in the area, thanks in part to the three-story hearth in the main lobby where afternoon wine and cheese are served. If you can lure yourself in from the slopes, the indoor octagonal pool and accompanying spas are very enticing.

Valley Inn (☎ 603-236-8425, 800-343-0969; www.valleyinn.com; Tecumseh Rd; r Sep–mid-Dec, $90-190, Jan-Jul $120-230; ☒) The Valley Inn consists of a mix of condominiums and hotel-style rooms that range from small and sparsely furnished to large and lavish (the best have a balcony, private sauna or fireplace). All prices include

use of the resort facilities, from tennis courts and health club to mountain-bike trails and a golf course.

Coyote Grill (☎ 603-236-4919; NH 49; meals $17-27; ☷ 5-9pm) Above the White Mountain Athletic Club, this bistro serves creative American fare. Gazpacho, roasted beet salad, New York strip (top loin steak) and herb-roasted salmon are some of the popular dishes you can enjoy to mountain views in the rustic dining room.

Getting There & Away
Driving from Boston to Waterville Valley is a straight three-hour shot via I-93. Take exit 28 (Campton) off I-93 and continue 13 miles northeast on NH 49. Scenic Tripoli Rd (unpaved, closed in winter) pushes northward 27 miles from the valley to Lincoln, which takes another 45 minutes via I-93.

NORTH WOODSTOCK & LINCOLN
pop 1200 (Woodstock), 1330 (Lincoln)

Not the prettiest towns in the White Mountains, these neighboring settlements gather a mix of adventure seekers and drive-by sightseers en route to the Kancamagus Hwy (NH 112). North Woodstock has a busy but small-town feel with battered motels and diners lining the main street and a gurgling river running parallel to it. Lincoln has less charm, and is essentially one long strip mall en route to the Kancamagus.

Orientation & Information

These two towns are located at the convergence of I-93 (just south of Franconia Notch) and NH 112 (otherwise known as the Kancamagus Hwy). Each is located on a separate branch of the shallow, boulder-strewn Pemigewasset River. Both are pretty much one-street towns.

For tourist information try the **Lincoln/Woodstock Chamber of Commerce** (☎ 603-745-6621; www.lincolnwoodstock.com; Kancamagus Hwy, Lincoln, NH 03251; ⏲ 9am-5pm Mon-Fri). It's located above the Laconia Savings Bank.

Sights & Activities

CLARK'S TRADING POST & THE WHALE'S TALE

Just north of North Woodstock on US 3, **Clark's** (☎ 603-745-8913; www.clarkstradingpost.com; US 3, Lincoln; adult/child 3-5yr/senior $15/6/14; ⏲ 10am-6pm Jun–mid-Oct) has been a traditional family stop since 1928. If the children are bored from too much time in the car, Clark's has an old-fashioned photo parlor, water-bumper boats, a magic house and a gift shop. Admission includes a 30-minute excursion on a narrow-gauge steam locomotive. The featured attraction is the Bear Show, a sad spectacle starring a team of North American black bear.

LOST RIVER GORGE & BOULDER CAVES

More adventurous kids will enjoy exploring the **Lost River Gorge & Boulder Caves** (☎ 603-745-8031; www.findlostriver.com; NH 112, Kinsman Notch; adult/child $12/8; ⏲ 9am-5pm May-Oct), a network of caverns and crevices formed by glaciers millions of years ago. Each cave has its own title and story, from the Bear Crawl to the Dungeon. Climbing, crawling and squeezing is required. This place is west of North Woodstock on NH 112.

TRAIN RIDES

Hobo Railroad (☎ 603-745-2135; www.hoborr.com; Kancamagus Hwy, Lincoln; adult/child $11/9) is a scenic, 1½-hour train ride from Lincoln south to Woodstock. Seasonal themes include foliage trains and Santa trains that follow the same route.

Travel in the first-class dining car of the 1924 Pullman-Standard Victorian Coach **Cafe Lafayette** (☎ 603-745-3500; www.nhdinnertrain.com; NH 112; adult/child from $65/45). The dining car has been completely and beautifully restored and decorated with dark wood, stained glass and brass

fixtures. The train rides along a spur of the Boston and Maine railroad for two hours, while you indulge in a five-course meal.

ZIP-LINE

Alpine Adventure (☎ 603-745-9911; www.alpinezipline.com; 41 Main St, Lincoln; $85) offers high-speed thrills on their zip-line course on Barron Mountain (10 minutes from Lincoln). The 2000ft course has seven platforms, ranging between 15ft and 65ft in height, and the whole trip lasts two hours including transportation there and back. You must weigh between 70lb and 240lb to participate.

Tours

Outback Kayak (☎ 603-745-2002; www.outbackkayak.net; Main St, US 3, North Woodstock; kayak tour $49) Provides kayak and snowmobile rental and tour packages. Kayak rental without a guide costs $29.

Pemi Valley Excursions (☎ 603-745-2744; www.i93.com/pvsr; NH 112, Lincoln) Located across from McDonald's. Tours include a twilight Moose Tour (adult/child $20/14), which runs from June to October and tracks moose and other wildlife with a 95% success rate, albeit in a 33-passenger bus. Various Horseback Trail Rides (one hour $40 to $50, two hours $80) along the banks of the Pemigewasset River are also offered.

Sleeping

For the United States Forest Service (USFS) campgrounds along the Kancamagus Hwy east of Lincoln, see p439.

Lost River Valley Campground (☎ 603-745-8321, 800-370-5678; www.lostriver.com; NH 112; campsites/RV sites $25/29, cabins $50-65; ⏲ mid-May–mid-Oct) This excellent 200-acre campground is on the site of a turn-of-the-century lumber mill, and the water wheel still churns. Many of the 125 sites are on the river, which also offers fishing and hiking possibilities. To get there, take exit 32 off I-93 and turn right onto NH 112.

Franconia Notch Motel (☎ 603-745-2229, 800-323-7829; www.franconianotch.com; 572 US 3, Lincoln; r $55-80) A tidy place with 18 attractive rooms and cottages facing the Pemigewasset River. It's a friendly, family-run place that caters to a lot of international visitors.

Riverbank Motel & Cottages (☎ 603-745-3374, 800-633-5624; www.riverbankmotel.com; NH 3A; r $55-100; ☒) In a peaceful, riverside setting just outside of North Woodstock, this inexpensive option has 11 motel rooms and four cottages. Accommodations are simple, though all but the cheapest rooms have small kitchen units. The cabins also have fireplaces.

Wilderness Inn (☎ 603-745-3890, 800-200-9453; www.thewildernessinn.com; cnr US 3 & NH 112; r incl breakfast $65-175) Just south of the junction, this former lumber-mill–owner's house has seven lovely guest rooms, ranging from small to suite size, as well as a family-size cottage overlooking Lost River. Each is individually decorated with stenciled walls and cozy furnishings, and all but one has wood floors. Breakfasts are marvelous.

Econo Lodge at Loon (☎ 603-745-3661; 800-762-7275; www.econolodgeloon.com.com; US 3, Loon Mountain; r incl breakfast $80-160, cottage $120-250; ☒) This large nicely outfitted lodge caters to skiers and snowmobilers, who appreciate the sauna, Jacuzzi and spa. Fifty-three rooms – many with kitchenettes – offer decent value, while cottages add space and coziness to the equation.

Woodstock Inn (☎ 603-745-3951, 800-321-3985; www.woodstockinnnh.com; US 3, North Woodstock; r with shared bathroom $65-105, r incl breakfast $94-184) This Victorian country inn is North Woodstock's centerpiece. It features 33 individually appointed rooms, each with modern amenities but old-fashioned style. For dinner, you have your choice of a microbrewery (right) and an upscale restaurant, with outdoor seating on the lovely flower-filled patio.

Woodward's Resort (☎ 603-745-8141, 800-635-8968; www.woodwardsresort.com; US 3; r $100-175; ☒) Just north of North Woodstock, Woodward's has lovely landscaped grounds and lots of facilities, including a sauna, hot tub and tennis court. Rooms are spacious, modern and attractive.

Eating

Peg's Restaurant (☎ 603-745-2740; Main St, North Woodstock; meals $6-10; ☽ 5:30am-4pm Jul-Oct, 5:30am-2pm Nov-Jun) Locals flock to this no-frills eatery for hearty early breakfasts and late-lunch sandwiches such as roast turkey and meat loaf with gravy. Lunch specials, kids' specials and the infamous 'Hungry Man's Special' make everyone feel pretty special.

Nachos (☎ 603-745-8820; 179 Main St, Lincoln; meals $12-15; ☽ noon-9pm) This newcomer to the dining scene features addictive Tex-Mex fare. Burritos, chimichangas, tacos and, of course, ubiquitous margaritas – best enjoyed on the sunny patio. Service unfortunately can be patchy.

Woodstock Station & Brewery (☎ 603-745-3951; Main St, North Woodstock; meals $12-18; ☽ noon-10pm) Formerly a railroad station, this eatery tries to be everything to everyone. In the end, with more than 150 items, it can probably satisfy just about any food craving, but pasta, sandwiches and burgers are the safest orders. The beer-sodden rear tavern here is one of the most happening places in this neck of the woods.

Gypsy Café (☎ 603-745-4395; NH 112, Main St, Lincoln; sandwiches $6-9, meals $14-18; ☽ 11am-9pm Tue-Sun) This charming little café serves an eclectic assortment of cuisine from around the world. Favorite dishes include hummus, falafel sandwiches, pesto pasta and piping hot enchiladas. In the midst of a relative culinary void, this is a gem.

Fratello's (☎ 603-745-2022; Kancamagus Hwy, Lincoln; meals $12-22; ☽ 5-10pm) Inside an uninspiring strip mall, this classic Italian restaurant features a lengthy menu of brick-oven pizzas, traditional pasta dishes and chicken, veal and seafood plates. The dining room is bright and welcoming, thanks to the wall of windows. The upstairs lounge has entertainment on weekends.

Drinking & Entertainment

Truant's Tavern (☎ 603-745-2239; 96 Main St, North Woodstock; meals $12-17; ☽ 11.30am-10pm) This popular place has live music, pool tables and darts, and serves hearty pub fare, including sandwiches, burgers, fish and chips, and even blackened swordfish salad.

Papermill Theatre (☎ 603-745-2141; www.papermilltheatre.org; NH 112, Inn Season Resorts, Lincoln; adult/child $27/18) This local theater stages musicals and plays, as well as regular performances of children's theater throughout the summer.

Getting There & Away

It's about 3¼ hours (140 miles) from Boston to Lincoln via I-93. **Concord Trailways** (☎ 603-228-3300, 800-639-3317; www.concordtrailways.com) runs buses between Boston and Littleton that stop at **Munce's Konvenience/Shell gas station** (☎ 603-745-3195; Main St, Lincoln). Catch one to Concord ($13.50, 1½ hours), Manchester ($21, two hours), Boston South Station ($29, three hours) or Logan International Airport ($35, three hours).

KANCAMAGUS HIGHWAY

The winding Kancamagus Hwy (NH 112) between Lincoln and Conway runs right through the WMNF and over Kancamagus Pass (2868ft). Unspoiled by commercial development, the

NEW HAMPSHIRE

WORTH THE TRIP: MOOSILAUKE RAVINE LODGE

About 50 miles north of Hanover and 15 miles west of North Woodstock, the **Moosilauke Ravine Lodge** (☎ 603-764-5858; moosilauke.ravine.lodge@dartmouth.edu; dm $20-24, linens $8; meal $7-12; ☼ May-Oct) is a rustic lodging owned and maintained by the Dartmouth Outing Club, but open to the public. The lodge is set in the midst of wooded hills and pristine countryside. Thirty miles of hiking trails connect the lodge to the summit of Mt Moosilauke and other trailheads. Accommodations at Moosilauke are basic bunks and shared baths, but the price is right. Delicious, hearty meals are served family-style in the dining hall.

For information on hiking, regional history and trail maps visit www.mtmoosilauke.com. To reach Moosilauke, take NH 118 west from Woodstock. From Hanover, take NH 10A north to NH 25. Head north on NH 25 and turn right at the junction with NH 118. Moosilauke Ravine Lodge is north of NH 118; follow the signs from the turn-off.

---

paved road offers easy access to USFS campgrounds, hiking trails and fantastic scenery.

Though the Kancamagus Hwy was paved only in 1964, its name dates to the 17th century. The route is named for Chief Kancamagus ('The Fearless One'). In about 1684 Kancamagus assumed the powers of *sagamon* (leader) of the Penacook Native American tribe. He was the third and the final *sagamon*, succeeding his grandfather, the great Passaconaway, and his uncle Wonalancet. Kancamagus tried to maintain peace between the indigenous peoples and European explorers and settlers, but the newcomers pushed his patience past breaking point. He finally resorted to battle to rid the region of Europeans, but the tide of history was against him and in 1691 he and his followers were forced to escape northward.

Orientation & Information

The Kancamagus Hwy (NH 112) runs for 35 miles from Lincoln to Conway. Since there are no services along the highway, the towns are convenient for picking up picnic supplies before hitting the trails.

Conway Village Chamber of Commerce (☎ 603-447-2639; www.conwaychamber.com; 250 Main St, NH 16, Conway; ☼ 9am-5pm Apr-Oct) The eastern gateway to the scenic highway.

White Mountains Attractions Association (☎ 603-745-8720; www.visitwhitemountains.com; 200 Kancamagus Hwy; ☼ 8:30am-5pm Apr-Oct) You can pick up detailed hiking brochures for area trails here. It's about a mile west of Conway.

Activities

HIKING

The WMNF is laced with excellent hiking trails of varying difficulty. For detailed trail-by-trail information, stop at any of the WMNF ranger stations or the White Mountains Attractions Association.

The trailhead for the 2.9-mile **Lincoln Woods Trail** (elevation 1157ft) is located on the Kancamagus Hwy, 5 miles east of I-93. Among the easiest and most popular in the forest, the trail ends at the Pemigewasset Wilderness Boundary (elevation 1450ft).

The easy **Wilderness Trail** begins where the Lincoln Woods Trail ends, and it continues for 6 miles to Stillwater Junction (elevation 2060ft). You can follow the Cedar Brook and Hancock Notch Trails to return to the Kancamagus Hwy, which is some miles east of the Lincoln Woods trailhead parking lot.

LOON MOUNTAIN

For winter fun, skiers should head to **Loon Mountain** (☎ 603-745-8111; www.loonmtn.com; adult/child/teen $67/47/57; ☼ 9am-3:45pm Mon-Fri, 8am-3:45pm Sat & Sun). Almost 20 miles of trails crisscross this 3050ft mountain, which boasts a 2100ft vertical drop. Skis, snowboards etc are available for rental. At night the trails open up for **tubing** (walk-up/lift $9/15; ☼ 6-9:40pm Wed-Sun).

Loon Mountain offers its fair share of summer fun as well. A **gondola** (adult/child/senior $9.50/5.50/8; ☼ 9:30am-5:30pm late Jun–mid-Oct) allows guests to soar to the summit. The facility also offers mountain-bike rentals (adult/child per day $36/32) and a climbing wall (single/double climb $7/12).

Sleeping

The **Village of Loon Mountain** (☎ 603-745-3401, 800-228-2968; www.vrivacations.com; Kancamagus Hwy; r $140-170, ste $160-200; 🐾) resort includes a lodge with basic, modern suites that sleep at least four people, as well as condos right on the mountainside, so you can ski out the door to

---

WHITE MOUNTAINS ACTIVITIES GUIDE

With so much to do, and so much ground to cover (786,000 acres), the White Mountains can be a little daunting for the intrepid adventurer. The following is our roundup of what to do where and includes both the eastern and western side of the mountains.

- **Hiking** Franconia Notch State Park (p446), Kancamagus Hwy (opposite), Moosilauke Ravine (opposite), Crawford Notch State Park (p456), Mt Washington (p458), Pinkham Notch (p457)
- **Skiing** Loon Mountain (opposite), Waterville Valley (p439), Cannon Mountain (p447), Black Mountain (p454), Attitash (p454), Mt Washington Resort (p456), Wildcat Mountain (p458), Mt Cranmore (p451)
- **Kayaking** Echo Lake (p446), Lincoln (p442), Saco River (p451)
- **Rock Climbing** Echo Lake State Park (p451)
- **Mountain Biking** Waterville Valley (p439), Franconia Notch State Park (p446)
- **Zip-line** Lincoln (p442)
- **Scenic Drives** Kancamagus Hwy (p443), NH 26 (Colebrook–Dixville Notch–Milan) NH 112 and NH 118 (North Woodstock–Warren), NH 2 (Jefferson–Shelburne), NH 117 (Lisbon–Sugar Hill–Franconia), Waterville Valley Loop
- **Train Rides** Lincoln (p442), North Conway (p451), Mt Washington Cog Railway (p456)

NEW HAMPSHIRE

the chair lift. Recreational facilities are unlimited here, with tennis courts, horseback riding, hiking and biking on offer.

The heavily wooded USFS campgrounds east of Lincoln along the Kancamagus Hwy are primitive sites (mostly with pit toilets only) but are in high demand in the warm months. It is not possible at every campground, but **advance reservations** (☎ 877-444-6777; www.reserveusa .com) are highly recommended where they are accepted (as indicated). Otherwise, arrive early, especially on weekends.

The following campgrounds are listed from west to east (Lincoln to Conway):

Hancock Campground (☎ 603-744-9165; campsites $20; ❤ year-round) Four miles east of Lincoln, it has 56 sites near the Pemigewasset River and the Wilderness Trail.

Passaconaway Campground (☎ 603-477-5448; campsites $18; ❤ mid-May-Oct) This is 12 miles west of Conway, and has 33 sites on the Swift River, which is good for fishing.

Jigger Johnson Campground (☎ 603-477-5448; campsites $20; ❤ late-May-Oct) Ten miles west of Conway, it has 75 sites, flush toilets and pay hot showers. There are nature lectures on summer weekends.

Covered Bridge Campground (campsites $18; ❤ mid-May-Oct) Six miles west of Conway, this place has 49 sites, some of which can be reserved. And yes, you do cross the Albany Covered Bridge to reach the campground.

FRANCONIA NOTCH STATE PARK

Franconia Notch, a narrow gorge shaped over the eons by a wild stream cutting through craggy granite, is a dramatic mountain pass. This was long the residence of the infamous Old Man of the Mountain, a natural rock formation that became the symbol of the Granite State. Tragically, the Old Man collapsed in 2003, which does not stop tourists from coming to see the featureless cliff that remains. Despite the Old Man's absence, the attractions of Franconia Notch are many, from the dramatic hike down the Flume Gorge to the fantastic views of the Presidentials.

Orientation & Information

The most scenic parts of the notch are protected by the narrow Franconia Notch State Park. Reduced to two lanes, I-93 (renamed the Franconia Notch Parkway) squeezes through the gorge. Services are available in Lincoln and North Woodstock to the south and in Franconia and Littleton further north. Both branches of the **Franconia Notch Visitor Center** Flume Gorge (☎ 603-745-8391; www.flumegorge .com; I-93 exit 34A) Lafayette Place (☎ 603-823-9513) have lots of information about the state park and surrounding area. The Flume also has a cafeteria and gift shop.

Sights & Activities

FLUME GORGE & THE BASIN

To see this natural wonder, take the 2-mile self-guided nature walk that includes the 800ft boardwalk through the **Flume** (☎ 603-745-8391; www.flumegorge.com; I-93 exit 34A; adult/child

THE SOUL OF AN OLD MAN

Geologists estimate that the Old Man of the Mountain had gazed out over Profile Lake for more than 12,000 years. That's why it was such a shock when, on May 3, 2003, he crumbled down the mountainside.

The collapse of the Old Man of the Mountain was no surprise to those in the know. In fact, the Appalachian Mountain Club had reported on his precarious state as early as 1872. Everybody recognized that it wouldn't do to have the stoic symbol of New Hampshire drop off the side of the mountain, so attempts to anchor the top-heavy face began in 1916 and continued for the next four generations. But Mother Nature could not be thwarted. Every year snow and rain were driven into the cracks and caverns. As temperatures dropped the water expanded, exacerbating the cracks. The gradual process of wear and tear finally upset the balance and the Old Man crumbled.

Following his destruction, some have claimed the state will soon find a 'new' Old Man to replace him, and contenders sprout up every few months; but for purists this is out of the question. New Hampshire residents seem determined not to forget the iconic old sourpuss. His visage still adorns their license plates – and may long remain in their hearts.

6-12yr $10/7; (☾ 9am-5pm mid-May–mid-Oct), a natural cleft (12ft to 20ft wide) in the granite bedrock. The granite walls tower 70ft to 90ft above you, with moss and plants growing from precarious niches and crevices. Signs along the way explain how nature formed this natural phenomenon. A nearby covered bridge is thought to be one of the oldest in the state, perhaps erected as early as the 1820s.

The **Basin** is a huge glacial pothole, 20ft in diameter, that was carved deep into the granite 15,000 years ago by the action of falling water and swirling stones. The Basin offers a nice (short) walk and a cool spot to ponder one of nature's minor wonders.

OLD MAN HISTORIC SITE

In the wake of the Old Man's collapse in 2003 (above), the state of New Hampshire is struggling over the future of this **historic site** (I-93 exit 34B) that once held the symbol of the state. Proposals ranging from interactive museums to state-wide sculpture contests are being debated at all levels. In the meantime, the museum at the Old Man Historic Site was closed indefinitely at the time of research. You can still pull off at the viewing platform (follow signs for 'Old Man Viewing') and use your imagination.

CANNON MOUNTAIN AERIAL TRAMWAY

Just north of the Old Man Historic Site, a **tramway** (☎ 603-823-8800; www.cannonmt.com; adult/child round-trip $11/7, one way $9; ☾ 9am-5pm late May–mid-Oct) shoots up the side of Cannon Mountain, offering a breathtaking view of Franconia Notch and the surrounding mountains. In 1938 the first passenger aerial tramway in North America was installed on this slope. Thankfully, it was replaced in 1980 by the current, larger cable car, capable of carrying 80 passengers up to the summit of Cannon Mountain in five minutes – a 2022ft, 1-mile ride. Alternatively, visitors can hike up the mountain and take the tramway down. Look for the New England Ski Museum in the base station.

ECHO LAKE

Despite its proximity to the highway, this little **lake** (adult/child $3/1, ☾ 10am-5:30pm late Jun-Aug) at the foot of Cannon Mountain is a pleasant place to pass an afternoon – swimming, kayaking or canoeing (rentals $10 per hour) in the crystal clear waters. And many people do. The small beach gets packed, especially on weekends.

HIKING & BIKING

The park has good hiking trails; most are relatively short, but some may be steep. For a casual walk or bike ride, you can't do better than the 8-mile paved **Recreation Trail** that wends its way along the Pemigewasset River and through the notch. Bikes are available for rental at the Franconia Sports Shop (p448). Pick up the trail in front of the Flume Gorge Visitor Center.

Other recommended hikes:

Bald Mountain & Artists Bluff Trail Just north of Echo Lake, off NH 18, this 1.5-mile loop skirts the summit of Bald Mountain (2320ft) and Artists Bluff (2368ft), with short spur trails to the summits.

Kinsman Falls On the Cascade Brook, these falls are a short 0.5-mile hike from the Basin via the Basin Cascade Trail.

Lonesome Lake Trail Departing from Lafayette Place and its campground, this trail climbs 1000ft in 1.5 miles to Lonesome Lake. Various spur trails lead further up to several summits on the Cannon Balls and Cannon Mountain (3700ft to 4180ft) and south to the Basin.

Mt Pemigewasset Trail This trail begins at the Flume Visitor Center and climbs for 1.4 miles to the 2557ft summit of Mt Pemigewasset (Indian Head), offering excellent views. Return by the same trail or the Indian Head Trail, which joins US 3 after 1 mile. From there, it's a 1-mile walk north to the Flume Visitor Center.

SKIING

The slopes at **Cannon Mountain Ski Area** (☎ 603-823-7771; www.cannonmt.com; I-93 exit 2; adult/child & senior/teen Mon-Fri $45/25/25, Sat & Sun $54/30/39) enjoy a prime geographic position to receive and retain the 150in of snow that falls annually. It has 55 runs (nine novice, 26 intermediate and 20 expert) making up 22 miles of trails (it's longest run is 2.3 miles), with a vertical drop of 2146ft. The slopes are equipped with an aerial tramway, three triple and two quad chairlifts, two rope tows and a wonder carpet (a moving walkway for beginners). Other facilities include three cafeterias, a nursery, a ski school and a ski shop with rental equipment.

Sleeping

Lafayette Place Campground (☎ 603-271-3628; campsites $18; ☽ year-round) This popular campground has 97 wooded tent sites that are in heavy demand in summer. Reservations are accepted for 88 of the sites. For the others, arrive early in the day and hope for the best. Many of the state park's hiking trails start here.

FRANCONIA TOWN & AROUND

pop 1040 (Franconia), 2500 (Bethlehem)

A few miles north of the notch via I-93, Franconia is a tranquil town with splendid mountain views and a poetic attraction: Robert Frost's farm. As a rule, the further the distance from the highway, the more picturesque and pristine the destination. Accordingly, the little town of **Bethlehem** and the tiny village of **Sugar Hill** are delightful. One could easily while away an afternoon driving down country roads, poking into antique shops, browsing farm stands and chatting up the locals at divey diners.

Orientation & Information

NH 18, NH 116 and NH 117 meet at the center of Franconia, marked by a prominent local prep school, Dow Academy. NH 18 is Main St. Sugar Hill is a few miles west along tranquil NH 117. Bethlehem is north along NH 142.

Both the **Bethlehem Chamber of Commerce** (☎ 888-845-1957; www.bethlehemwhitemtns.com; 2182 Main St, Bethlehem; ☽ 11am-4pm Jun-Oct, variable Nov-Feb, closed Mar-May) and the **Franconia Notch Chamber of Commerce** (☎ 603-823-5661, 800-237-9007; www.franconianotch.org; Main St, Franconia; ☽ 11am-5pm Tue-Sun mid-May–mid-Oct; wi-fi), which is southeast of the town center, provide tourist information.

Sights & Activities

Robert Frost (1874–1963) was America's most renowned and best-loved poet in the mid-20th century. For several years he lived with his wife and children on a farm near Franconia, now known as the **Frost Place** (☎ 603-823-5510; Ridge Rd; suggested donation adult/child/senior $4/2/3; ☽ 1-5pm Sat & Sun late May-Jun, 1-5pm Wed-Mon Jul–mid-Oct). The years spent here were some of the most productive and inspired of his life. Many of his best and most famous poems describe life on this farm and the scenery surrounding it, including 'The Road Not Taken' and 'Stopping by Woods on a Snowy Evening.'

The farmhouse has been kept as faithful to the period as possible, with numerous exhibits of Frost memorabilia. In the forest behind the house there is a 0.5-mile **nature trail**. Frost's poems are mounted on plaques in sites appropriate to the things the poems describe, and in several places the plaques have been erected at the exact spots where Frost composed the poems. To find Frost's farm, follow NH 116 south from Franconia. After exactly a mile, turn right onto Bickford Hill Rd, then left onto unpaved Ridge Rd. It's a short distance along on the right. See the boxed text, p448, for more background.

The **Sugar Hill Sampler** (☎ 603-823-8478; www.sugarhillsampler.com; NH 117, Sugar Hill; admission free; ☽ 9:30am-5pm Sat & Sun mid-Apr–mid-May, 9:30am-5pm mid-May-Oct, 10am-4pm Nov-Dec, closed Jan–mid-Apr) was originally a collection of heirlooms amassed by the Aldrich family over the many years they have lived in Sugar Hill. The collection has expanded to include all sorts of local memorabilia dating from 1780, all housed

ROBERT FROST: THE GREAT AMERICAN POET

Jim Schley is a writer, editor, performer and activist. He's also the Executive Director of the Frost Place (p447), which he describes as 'a historic site and a haven for some of the nation's most accomplished contemporary poets.'

What makes the Frost Place so special? The Frost Place house and barn and their surrounding meadows and woods have an uncanny atmosphere, as if very little changed by the passage of time. This was where some of the most beautiful, most complex poems in the English language were written; yet it's also a very modest place. It was somewhere that an intensely determined and sensitive artist could concentrate and, despite everything, this is still a place of contemplation.

Does Frost's spirit live on? My job doesn't require me to be reverential toward Robert Frost, and when I was hired I was by no means an expert on his life and achievements. But over the past couple of years I've immersed myself in Frost's work, and I'd now describe myself as awed by the breadth and scale of Frost's accomplishment.

As a working writer, I'm more aware than ever of the technical aspects of Frost's artistry, and as a human being I find I love many of his poems more as I grow older and acquire more life experience. He was a great lyric poet, a great dramatic poet and a great philosophical poet. He was also a man who struggled to be altogether awake in the world and to create a resilient body of work that stands alongside the achievements of his literary forebears. I think of him as our Yeats – the most important American poet in the first half of the 20th century.

Frost had connections to New Hampshire, where you work, and Vermont, where you live. Any great rivalries between the two states? There are all kinds of rivalries between New Hampshire and Vermont, some silly and some expressive of more deep-rooted natural and cultural distinctions. Frost wrote an extended meditation celebrating the unique nature (including human nature) of New Hampshire, which he concluded with the line, 'At present I am living in Vermont.' So he too partook of that jocular competition. And there are several communities and colleges that claim Frost. Franconia's claim is based on how long he lived here then visited, from 1915 through the late 1930s, and how auspicious this locale was for his poetry, since he went from being virtually unknown when he arrived in New Hampshire to nationwide acclaim by the time he sold the house now known as the Frost Place in 1920 to move to Amherst, MA, for a teaching position.

Some people think Frost is one of those poets you study only in elementary school. Do you agree? The majority of our museum visitors are adults, and it's obvious that many of them still have profound relationships with his poems, originating in childhood. Teachers at all levels enjoy using Frost's work in the classroom, because in many instances the surface of a poem is clear, memorable and accessible. Personally I've seen that Frost's strongest poems grow more complicated as one lives longer and has more life experience. Before I was a parent, for instance, I couldn't discern the full enormity of feeling and understanding in Frost's poems about family life. And Frost's family suffered such tragedies – mental illness, untimely death, poverty. Only one of Elinor and Robert's six children outlived their father.

What's your favorite Frost poem? The poems that consistently affect me are 'To Earthward,' 'The Death of the Hired Man,' 'The Witch of Cöos,' 'After Apple Picking' and 'Directive.' Also 'Home Burial.' I couldn't name fewer. And by tomorrow I'd name more.

As related to Regis St. Louis

in an old barn built by the Aldrich ancestors themselves. This place also has a store, selling homemade arts and crafts and edibles.

Franconia Sports Shop (☎ 603-823-5241; www.franconiasports.com; Main St, Franconia; road/mountain bike per day $19/25) offers bike rental. **Northern Land Guide Service** (☎ 603-869-2634; www.northernguideservices

.com; 134 Maple St, Bethlehem) provides services for birding, hiking and wildlife photography.

Sleeping

Peak season in Franconia is during early fall (late September to mid-October), when the leaves turn fiery colors, and traffic clogs the

---

WILD AT HEART

One of the great unsung festivals of this corner of New Hampshire is the summertime Lupine (LOO-puhn) Festival. You've probably heard about the spectacular (and crowded) fall foliage season. Well, in June the hillsides and valleys of the Franconia region are carpeted with purples, blues and pinks, as this spring-blooming wildflower blossoms. Framed against the mountains and dotted with butterflies, the vast carpets of flowers are a spectacular sight. The **Fields of Lupine Festival** celebrates the annual bloom with garden tours, art exhibits and concerts throughout the month. It's a big event but with a fraction of the leaf-peeping crowds. The Franconia Chamber of Commerce even publishes its own Lupine festival guidebook, on sale in early May ($5). Other festival events include horse-drawn wagon rides through the lupine fields, tours of local inns, open-air markets, night-time astronomy tours and craft shows. For more on the fest, visit www .harmanscheese.com/lupine.html or www.franconianotch.org.

---

roads. Expect prices to rise and rooms to book out months in advance.

BUDGET

Fransted Family Campground (☎ 603-823-5675; www.franstedcampground.com; NH 18; campsites/RV sites from $30/36; ◷ May-Oct) Two miles northwest of Franconia Notch State Park, this wooded campground caters more to tenters (70 sites) than RVers (40 sites). Many sites are along a stream.

Pinestead Farm Lodge (☎ 603-823-8121; www .pinesteadfarmlodge.com; 2059 Easton Rd/NH 116; r $40-60) Among the possible accommodations in Franconia is this rarity: a working farm. The family rents 11 clean, simple rooms with shared bathroom and communal kitchen-sitting rooms. Hosts Bob and Kathleen Sherburn (whose family has been renting rooms since 1899) have an assortment of cattle, chickens, ducks and horses. If you come in March or April, you can watch maple sugaring.

our pick Kinsman Lodge (☎ 603-823-5686; www .kinsmanlodge.com; 2165 Easton Rd/NH 116, Franconia; s/d incl breakfast from $50/85) This lodge – built in the 1860s – has nine rooms (with shared bathroom) that are comfortable but not pretentious. They are all on the 2nd floor, while the 1st floor consists of cozy common areas and an inviting porch. Homemade breakfasts here are superb.

MIDRANGE & TOP END

Horse & Hound Inn (☎ 603-823-5501; www.horseand houndnh.com; 205 Wells Rd, Franconia; s/d incl breakfast from $90/105) This pleasant country inn offers eight frilly rooms set in a cozy 1830 farmhouse. Some rooms are set with antiques, while others – those with rosy curtains and floral

bedspread – can be a bit over the top, but it's good value for the area.

Sugar Hill Inn (☎ 603-823-5621, 800-548-4748; www .sugarhillinn.com, NH 117, Sugar Hill; r incl breakfast $115-170, ste $195-295; wi-fi) This restored 1789 farmhouse sits atop a hill lined with sugar maples ablaze in autumn and offering panoramic views any time of year. Sixteen acres of lawns and gardens and 15 romantic guest rooms, not to mention the delectable country breakfast, make this a top choice. Room and suite prices vary according to amenities.

Franconia Inn (☎ 603-823-5542, 800-473-5299; www .franconiainn.com; NH 116, Franconia; r incl breakfast $111-215, ste $166-280) This excellent 34-room inn, just 2 miles south of Franconia, is set on a broad, fertile, pine-fringed river valley. You'll find plenty of common space and well-maintained, traditional guest rooms. The 107-acre estate has prime cross-country ski possibilities and summertime hiking and horseback riding. Prices vary based on features and room size.

Bishop Farm (☎ 603-838-2474; www.bishopfarm .com; 33 Bishop Cutoff, Lisbon; r incl breakfast $130-160; wi-fi) This family-run, newly refurbished farmhouse has seven attractively designed rooms done in a trim, contemporary look (but with old-fashioned touches like claw-foot tubs). The house is set on 19 forested acres, which means snowshoeing and cross-country skiing in the winter and mountain biking or hiking in the summer. The front porch is an idyllic spot for enjoying the scenery. It's located 9 miles west of Franconia, just off US 302.

Sunset Hill House (☎ 603-823-5522; www.sunsethill house.com; 231 Sunset Hill Rd, Sugar Hill; r incl breakfast $150-300) This 'Grand Inn,' as it is called, lives up to its moniker. All 28 rooms have lovely views of either the mountains or the golf course next door. The pricier rooms feature Jacuzzis, fireplaces and private decks, but all the rooms are lovely. The dining room is a formal affair, but there is also a more casual tavern.

Eating

Many of Franconia's inns offer fine dining, including the Horse & Hound, Sugar Hill Inn, Franconia Inn and Sunset Hill House.

Harman's Cheese & Country Store (☎ 603-823-8000; www.harmanscheese.com; 1400 NH 117, Sugar Hill; ◷ 9:30am-5pm) If you need to pack a picnic for your hike – or if you simply wish to stock up on New England goodies before heading home – don't miss this country store, boasting delicious cheddar cheese (aged for at least two years), maple syrup, apple cider (in season) and addictive spicy dill pickles.

Polly's Pancake Parlor (☎ 603-823-5575; NH 117, Sugar Hill; meals $9-16; ◷ 7am-3pm May–mid-Oct) Attached to a 19th-century farmhouse 2 miles west of Franconia, this local institution offers pancakes, pancakes and more pancakes. They're excellent, made with home-ground flour and topped with the farm's own maple syrup, eggs and sausages. Polly's cob-smoked bacon is excellent, and sandwiches and quiches are also available.

our pick **Cold Mountain Cafe & Gallery** (☎ 603-869-2500; www.coldmountaincafe.com; 2015 Main St, Bethlehem; sandwiches $7-8, meals $11-18; ◷ 11am-3pm & 5:30-9pm Mon-Sat) Hands down the best restaurant in the region, this casual café and gallery has an eclectic, changing menu, featuring gourmet sandwiches and salads at lunch and rich bouillabaisse, seafood curry and rack of lamb at dinner. Everything is prepared with the utmost care and nicely presented, but the atmosphere is very relaxed. Be prepared to wait for your table (outside, since the place is cozy). There's live music from time to time.

Entertainment

Colonial Theater (☎ 603-869-3422; www.bethlehemcolonial.org; Main St, Bethlehem; live shows $15-25) This classic theater in downtown Bethlehem needs some renovation (slowly under way), but the auditorium is a historic place to hear the jazz, blues and folk musicians that pass through this little town. Recent performers have included Aztec Two Step and George Winston. The venue also serves as a cinema showing independent and foreign films.

Getting There & Away

Concord Trailways buses (☎ 603-228-3300, 800-639-3317; www.concordtrailways.com) stop at **Kelly's Foodtown** (☎ 603-823-7795) in the center of Franconia. They go south to Lincoln (25 minutes), Concord ($33, two hours), Manchester ($28, 2½ hours), Boston South Station ($19, 3½ hours) and Logan International Airport ($16, 3½ hours).

MT WASHINGTON VALLEY

Dramatic mountain scenery surrounds the tiny villages of this popular alpine destination, providing an abundance of outdoor adventures. There's great hiking, skiing, kayaking and rafting, along with idyllic activities like swimming in local creeks, overnighting in country farmhouses and simply exploring the countryside. Mt Washington Valley stretches north from Conway, at the eastern end of the Kancamagus Hwy, and forms the eastern edge of the White Mountain Range. The valley's hub is North Conway, though any of the towns along NH 16/US 302 (also called the White Mountain Hwy) can serve as a White Mountain gateway. The valley's namesake is – of course – Mt Washington, New England's highest peak (6288ft), which towers over the valley in the northwest. For an overview of outdoor activities in the White Mountains see p445.

NORTH CONWAY & AROUND
pop 2200

Gateway to mountain adventure, North Conway is a bustling one-street town lined with motor inns, camping supply stores, restaurants and other outfits designed with the traveler in mind. Although most people are just passing through, North Conway does have its charm, with outdoor concerts in the summertime, cozy cafés and nearby inns with historic charm.

Unless otherwise stated, items in the following section are in North Conway proper.

Orientation & Information

Most of the time, traffic moves at a glacial pace along the long Main St. If your aim is to get around North Conway, take West Side

NEW HAMPSHIRE

Rd, which follows the Saco River between Conway and Glen.

Met (☎ 603-356-2332; Schouler Park, Main St; per hr $8, wi-fi) A coffee house with high-speed internet connections and computers available.

Mt Washington Valley Chamber of Commerce (☎ 603-356-3171; www.mtwashingtonvalley.org; Main St) Just south of the town center. Provides tourist information.

New Hampshire State Information Office (cnr NH 10 & US 302, Intervale; ☿ 10am-5:30pm Mon-Thu, 7am-11pm Fri-Sun) Two miles north of North Conway center.

Sights & Activities

CONWAY SCENIC RAILROAD

The **Notch Train** (☎ 603-356-5251, 800-232-5251; www.conwayscenic.com; adult/infant/child mid-Jun–mid-Sep $42/6/26, mid-Sep–mid-Oct $47/10/30), built in 1874 and restored in 1974, now offers New England's most scenic journey. The spectacular five-hour trip passes through Crawford Notch and terminates at Fabyan Station near Bretton Woods. Accompanying live commentary recounts the railroad's history and folklore. Reservations required.

Alternatively, the same company operates the antique steam **Valley Train**, which makes a shorter journey south through the Mt Washington Valley, stopping in Conway (adult/child $12.50/9) and Bartlett (adult/child $20/13.50). Sunset trains, dining trains and other special events are all available.

ECHO LAKE STATE PARK

Two miles west of North Conway via River Rd, this placid **mountain lake** (☎ 603-356-2672; River Rd; adult/child $3/1; ☿ dawn-dusk Sat & Sun May, daily Jun-Aug) lies at the foot of White Horse Ledge, a sheer rock wall. A scenic trail circles the lake. There is also a mile-long auto road and hiking trail leading to the 700ft-high Cathedral Ledge, with panoramic White Mountains views. Both Cathedral Ledge and nearby White Horse Ledge are excellent for rock climbing. This is also a fine spot for swimming and picknicking, but there's no camping.

SKIING

Mt Cranmore Resort (☎ lodging 603-356-5543, snow report 800-786-6754; www.cranmore.com; lift ticket adult/child & senior/teen $47/26/36; ☿ 9am-4pm Sun-Fri, 8:30am-9pm Sat), on the outskirts of North Conway, has a vertical drop of 1200ft, 40 trails (36% beginner, 44% intermediate and 20% expert), nine lifts and 100% snowmaking ability. There's also a terrain park, tubing and abundant facilities for non-skiers (including a Jacuzzi, swimming pool, climbing wall and indoor and outdoor tennis courts).

CLIMBING & KAYAKING

Eastern Mountain Sports Climbing School (EMS Climbing School; ☎ 603-356-5433, 800-310-4504; www.emsclimb.com; Eastern Slope Inn, Main St) sells maps and guides to the WMNF, and rents camping equipment, cross-country skis and snowshoes. Year-round, the climbing school offers classes and tours, including one-day ascents of Mt Washington, and the grueling Presidential Range traverse. Climbing lessons cost between $150 and $220 per day, depending on how many are in a group (three maximum).

Saco Bound Inc (☎ 603-447-2177; www.sacobound.com; 2561 E Main St, US 302, Center Conway; rental per day $25.50) rents out canoes and kayaks and organizes guided canoe trips, including the introductory trip to Weston's Bridge ($20) and overnight camping trips. **Eastern Slope Campground** (☎ 603-447-5092; NH 16, Conway; rental per day kayaks $18-25, canoes $25-40) also rents kayaks and canoes; and can provide transportation up the Saco River ($10 to $20 per person) so you can have a leisurely paddle downriver (either 5.5 miles or 7.5 miles).

Festivals & Events

Just over the state border in Maine, the annual county **Fryeburg Fair** (☎ 207-935-3268; www.fryeburgfair.com; adult/child $8/free, parking $5) is one of New England's – if not the country's – largest and best-known agricultural events. Held every year in early October, the week-long fair features harness racing, ox pulling, wreath-making and judging of just about every kind of farm animal you can imagine. There is also plenty of music, food and other fun.

Throughout the summer **Cranmore Resort** (www.cranmore.com) hosts free outdoor concerts, showcasing blues, classical, jazz and show tunes. It's a fun family affair (bring your own picnic or buy food on the grounds) that sometimes ends with fireworks over the mountain.

Sleeping

There are dozens of regional inns and affordable B&Bs, 15 of which belong to the organization **Country Inns in the White Mountains** (☎ reservations 603-356-9460; www.countryinnsinthewhite mountains.com), with another dozen listings at **Bed & Breakfasts Inn Mt Washington Valley** (www.bbinns mwv.com). As elsewhere in New Hampshire, rates vary wildly between seasons, with lower prices in winter and spring, and higher rates in summer and autumn's foliage season.

BUDGET

Conway, North Conway and Glen are riddled with commercial campgrounds.

Saco River Camping Area (☎ 603-356-3360; www .sacorivercampingarea.com; NH 16, North Conway; campsites/ RV sites from $25/27; ☒ May–mid-Oct; wi-fi ☒) A riverside campground, away from the highway, with 140 wooded and open sites. Canoe and kayak rental available.

Beach Camping Area (☎ 603-447-2723; www.the beachcampingarea.com; 98 Eastern Slope Tce/NH 16, Conway; campsites/RV sites $25/32; ☒ mid-May–mid-Oct) Some of these 124 forested sites are on the Saco River.

Eastern Slope Camping Area (☎ 603-447-5092; www.easternslopecamping.com; NH 16, Conway; camp-sites $27-39; ☒ late May–mid-Oct; wi-fi ☒) Eastern Slope has mountain views, 260 well-kept sites, long beaches on the Saco River and lots of facilities.

Albert B Lester Memorial HI-AYH Hostel (☎ 603-447-1001; www.conwayhostel.com; 36 Washington St, Conway; dm $20-23, d $38-48 incl breakfast; ☐) Set in an early 1900s farmhouse, New Hampshire's only youth hostel is this 43-bed place off Main St (NH 16) in Conway. The environmentally conscientious hostel has five bedrooms with bunk beds and four family-size rooms, and guests can use the kitchen. Excellent hiking and bicycling opportunities are just outside the door, and canoeists can easily portage to two nearby rivers. Our only gripe is the location, which puts you 5 miles south of the action in North Conway. This place is smoke and alcohol-free.

Cranmore Inn (☎ 603-356-5502, 800-526-5502; www .cranmoreinn.com; 80 Kearsarge St, North Conway; incl breakfast s $79-104, d $94-119; ☒) The Cranmore has been operating as a country inn since 1863, and it has been known as reliably good value for much of that time. Traditional country decor predominates, meaning lots of floral and frills. Prices for rooms vary according to amenities.

MIDRANGE & TOP END

Merrill Farm Resort (☎ 603-447-3866, 800-445-1017; www.merrillfarmresort.com; 428 NH 16; r incl breakfast $80-170; ☒) Set on 7 acres of countryside, the Merrill Farm Resort's 60 rooms vary between plain motel-style, spacious duplex suites and unique old-fashioned rooms with homey floral touches. The whole place exudes country charm, making for a pleasant overnight in the mountains.

1785 Inn (☎ 603-356-9025, 800-421-1785; www .the1785inn.com; NH 16, Intervale; r incl breakfast with shared bathroom $69-139, with private bathroom $89-179; ☒) This colonial hostelry has a deservedly renowned dining room, 17 individually decorated guest rooms and lovely Victorian-style common areas with two fireplaces. Six acres of beautiful grounds include opportunities for hiking and cross-country skiing. It is 2 miles north of the center of North Conway near the New Hampshire state information center.

Spruce Moose Lodge (☎ 603-356-6239, 800-600-6239; www.sprucemooselodge.com; 207 Seavey St, North Conway; r $70-210) Located a five-minute walk from town, Spruce Moose has charming rooms set inside a spruce-green 1850s home. Styles vary from classic, pine-floored rooms with dark-wood furnishings to cheery, modern, carpeted quarters. There are also attractive wood-floored cottages with country charm and cozy bungalows with Jacuzzi tubs.

Cabernet Inn (☎ 603-356-4704, 800-866-4704; www .cabernetinn.com; NH 16; d incl breakfast $90-235) This 1842 Victorian cottage is north of North Conway center, near Intervale. Each of the 11 guest rooms has antiques and queen beds, while pricier rooms also have fireplaces or Jacuzzis. Two living rooms with fireplaces and a shady deck are open for guests to enjoy and relax in. The large gourmet kitchen is the source of a decadent country breakfast.

Wyatt House Country Inn (☎ 603-356-7977, 800-527-7978; www.wyatthouseinn.com; NH 16, North Conway; d incl breakfast $89-229) You'll be pampered with fresh-baked breakfast goods (served by candle-light), afternoon tea and evening sherry. Rooms are uniquely decorated with lots of lace, ruffles and flowers, and furnished with antiques; some have private decks overlooking the serene Saco River.

Stonehurst Manor (☎ 603-356-3113, 800-525-9100; www.stonehurstmanor.com; NH 16; r $110-200; ☒) Spacious, gracious Stonehurst, 1 mile north of North Conway, has 25 luxury rooms (many with fireplaces) in a manor house filled with stained glass and oak paneling. The motel annex is less interesting. All rooms have access to 33 acres of landscaped grounds, including tennis courts and beautiful gardens.

Red Elephant Inn (☎ 603-356-3548; www.victorian harvestinn.com; 28 Locust Lane, North Conway; r $110-225) Set on a quiet street behind the Red Jacket Mountain View Inn, this lovely Victorian is a hidden gem. The eight rooms are individually decorated in colorful, eclectic themes with telling names like Southeast Asia, Country Quilts and Desert Cat.

White Mountain Hotel & Resort (☎ 603-356-7100, 800-533-6301; www.whitemountainhotel.com; 2660 West Side Rd, North Conway; r $120-210; wi-fi ⚛) This handsome 80-room hotel has trim modern rooms with a classic look. Most have fine mountain views. Amenities here include a year-round heated pool and Jacuzzi, a golf course and tennis courts, and the elegant dining room serves excellent meals.

Kearsarge Inn (☎ 603-356-8700; www.kearsargeinn .com; 42 Seavey St, North Conway; r $119-259) Just off Main St in the heart of North Conway, this lovely inn is the perfect setting if you want an intimate experience near the center of town. The inn is a 'modern rendition' of the historic Kearsarge House, one of the region's first and grandest hotels. Each of the 15 rooms and suites offers a choice of king- or queen-size beds, gas fireplaces, period furnishings and Jacuzzis. The innkeepers also operate the lively Steakhouse next door, Decades.

Buttonwood Inn (☎ 603-356-2625; www.button woodinn.com; Mt Surprise Rd; r incl breakfast $125-270) Two miles northeast of North Conway, this lovely inn has 10 nicely furnished rooms that don't overwhelm with the floral or country-kitsch theme. Wood floors, modern furnishings and a neat and trim look with farmhouse touches prevail. The Buttonwood is set in an 1820s farmhouse overlooking 6 acres.

Eating

Many inns – especially those north of the town center and in Jackson (see p454) – have elegant dining rooms with excellent, traditional menus. The following places are all in North Conway, unless otherwise stated.

Met (☎ 603-356-2332; Main St; ☾ 7am-9pm; pastries $2-3; wi-fi) Just north of Schouler Park, this small coffeehouse is the best place in town for a cup of coffee or a pastry. You can sink into a plush sofa, or grab a table out front in the summer and enjoy the passing people parade. Artwork (all for sale) decorates the walls and baristas play an eclectic mix of world tunes and jazz.

Peach's (☎ 603-356-5860; 2506 White Mountain Hwy, Main St; meals $6; ☾ 7am-2:30pm) Away from the in-town bustle, this little house is an excellent option for soups, sandwiches and breakfast. Who can resist fruit-smothered waffles and pancakes and fresh-brewed coffee, served in somebody's cozy living room?

Café Noche (☎ 603-447-5050; 147 Main St, Conway; meals $11-14; ☾ 11:30am-9pm) This festive café has some of the best Mexican food north of the Massachusetts border. The bar features a huge selection of tequilas and over 25 types of margarita!

Shalimar of India (☎ 603-356-0123; 27 Seavey St; meals $8-15; ☾ 11am-2:30pm Tue-Sun & 5pm-10pm daily; Ⓥ) Featuring exposed-brick walls and lantern-like ceiling lamps, this friendly Indian restaurant serves many traditional dishes. Aside from tandooris, kormas and curries, Shalimar has a children's menu that radically redefines cuisine from the subcontinent: meatballs and chicken nuggets, anyone?

Moat Mountain Smokehouse & Brewing Co (☎ 603-356-6381; 3378 White Mountain Hwy; sandwiches $7-8, meals $14-22; ☾ lunch & dinner) Come here for a plate of BBQ ribs, a bowl of beefy chili or a juicy burger. Wash it down with one of eight brews made on site. The friendly bar also has a pool table and dart boards, so it's a fun place to hang around.

Horsefeathers (☎ 603-356-2687; Main St; meals $14-22; ☾ 11:30am-10:30pm) The most popular gathering place in town has an encyclopedic menu featuring pasta, salads, sandwiches, burgers, bar snacks and main-course platters.

Bellini's (☎ 603-356-7000; 1857 White Mountain Hwy; meals $16-24; ☾ 5pm-10pm Wed-Sun) Come here for Italian cuisine served in huge portions at moderate prices. The menu includes all the classics, from eggplant parmigiana to a 13oz sirloin steak.

Getting There & Around

Concord Trailways (☎ 603-228-3300, 800-639-3317; www.concordtrailways.com) runs a daily route between Boston and Berlin, which stops in North Conway at the Eastern Slope Inn. The bus stops in Concord ($16.50, 2½ hours) and Manchester ($19.50, three hours) before heading south to Boston ($28, four hours).

Once you're in town, leave your car behind and hop on the new **village trolley** (☎ 877-986-7267; www.wmtransit.com; one way $2; ☾ every 30min 8am-10pm Mon-Thu, 8am-11.30pm Fri & Sat, 8am-7pm Sun), which runs along North Conway's main street from the North Conway Grand to Settlers Green.

JACKSON & AROUND
pop 890

This quintessential New England village is 7 miles north of North Conway. Take NH 16 and then cross the Ellis River via the historic red covered bridge. In addition to being a picture-perfect postcard destination, Jackson village is Mt Washington Valley's premier cross-country ski center.

Glen is 3 miles south of Jackson; unless otherwise stated, items in the following section are in Jackson proper.

Jackson Area Chamber of Commerce (☎ 603-383-9356; www.jacksonnh.com; Jackson Falls Marketplace; ⏰ 9am-4pm Mon-Fri year-round, 9am-1pm Sat Jul-Feb) Has loads of local insight; ask here about scenic walks in the area.

Sights & Activities

One of the best ways to spend a sun-drenched afternoon in Jackson is taking a swim in **Jackson Falls** on the Wildcat River just outside of town. You'll have marvelous mountain views as you splash about. To get there, take the Carter Notch Rd (NH 16B) 0.5 miles north of town.

Easily the area's most intriguing shop, **Raven** (☎ 603-383-8026; Jackson Village Rd; ⏰ 10am-6pm Wed-Mon) is a small two-story cottage packed with wildly designed clocks, antique lamps, recycled glass ornaments, jewelry and other curios. In back, the even more fantastical garden has a tiny pathway skirting beside fountains, faerie sculptures, Buddha heads and assorted gnomes. It's worth a look even if you're not in the market for an elfin lawn ornament.

In nearby Glen, **Storyland** (☎ 603-383-4186; www.storylandnh.com; NH 16; adult/child under 4yr $23/free; ⏰ 9am-5pm daily mid-Jun-early Sep, Sat & Sun late May–mid-Jun & early Sep–mid-Oct) is a delightful 30-acre theme and amusement park aimed at the three- to nine-year-old crowd. The rides, activities and shows are small-scale and well done – a refreshing break from the mega-amusements in other places.

Jackson is famous for its 93 miles of cross-country trails. Stop at the **Jackson Ski Touring Foundation Center** (☎ 603-383-9355; www.jacksonxc .org; 153 Main St; day passes adult/child/senior $17/8/12) for passes and to inquire about lessons and groomed trails. You can rent skis or snowshoes there (per day ski/snowshoe from $16/12).

Black Mountain Ski Area (☎ 603-383-4490, snow report 800-475-4669, lodging reservations 800-698-4490; www .blackmt.com; NH 16B, Jackson; adult/senior & teen/student Sat & Sun $32/22/25, Mon-Fri $22/17/22) is a smaller ski area with a vertical drop of 1100ft. Forty trails – equally divided between beginner, intermediate and expert slopes – are served by four lifts. This a good place for beginners and families with small children.

West of Glen, you can play and stay at **Attitash** (☎ 603-374-2368, snow report 877-677-7669, lodging reservations 800-223-7669; www.attitash.com; US 302; adult/child & senior/teen Sun-Fri $59/37/47, Sat & holidays $65/45/51; ⏰ 8am-4pm). The resort includes two mountains, Attitash and Bear Peak, which offer a vertical drop of 1750ft, 12 lifts and 70 ski trails. Half the trails are intermediate level, while the other half are equally divided between expert and beginner level.

From mid-June to mid-October the chairlifts at Attitash whisk you to the top of the **Alpine Slide** (per ride $15, one-day pass adult/child $35/15), a long track that you schuss down on a little cart. It's an exhilarating ride safe for all ages. It also has a **climbing wall, mountain-bike rental & trails** (full-day rental adult/child from $40/20) and (for anyone over 8 years old) **guided horseback riding** ($49 per person) from mid-June to mid-October.

Sleeping

Covered Bridge Motor Lodge (☎ 603-383-9151, 800-634-2911; www.jacksoncoveredbridge.com; NH 16; d incl breakfast $80-250) Appropriately, this comfortable 32-room motel is located just south of Jackson's covered bridge. Rooms have – variously – kitchenettes, private balconies and views of a lovely gurgling brook. There's a common Jacuzzi for a nice soak after a day of skiing or hiking.

Village House (☎ 603-383-6666, 800-972-8343; www .villagehouse.com; NH 16A; d $110-140; 🖳 wi-fi 🐾) This large village house and renovated barn have nine comfy rooms, all furnished simply and stylishly. Rooms have private bathrooms and kitchenettes. Management is 'hands-off' so guests take care of themselves, but they don't lack for privacy.

Wildcat Inn & Tavern (☎ 603-383-4245, 800-228-4245; www.wildcattavern.com; 3 Main St; r incl breakfast $100-220) This centrally located village lodge has a dozen cozy rooms with private bathrooms and antique furnishings. The cottage ($200 to $325) – known as the 'Igloo' – sleeps up to six. One of Jackson's best restaurants is on site.

Inn at Jackson (☎ 603-383-4321; www.innatjackson .com; cnr Main St & Thornhill Rd; r $130-250) Enter this charming red farmhouse through the grand foyer where you will be greeted by enticing aromas wafting from the kitchen. Romantic rooms feature fireplaces and four-post beds, and an outdoor Jacuzzi is open to all guests. Breakfast is served on the sun porch or in the dining room next to the fire.

Wentworth (☎ 603-383-9700; www.thewentworth .com; NH 16B; r $110-355; ⚑) This grand country inn is on the edge of Jackson Village, beside a gorgeous public golf course. It is an elegant affair, with 51 spacious rooms, a gracious lobby and dining room and outdoor facilities such as tennis courts. The best rooms have fireplaces, outdoor hot tubs or gorgeous antique furnishings.

Snowflake Inn (☎ 603-383-8259; www.thesnow flakeinn.com; 95 Main St; r incl breakfast $180-350) A handsome addition to Jackson, this elegant, all-suites inn has spacious rooms, all with fireplaces and two-person Jacuzzis (in the rooms themselves). There are plenty of modern creature comforts including 400-count triple sheeting, flat-screen TVs and lavish sitting areas. An on-site spa adds to the charm.

Eating & Drinking
Many of Jackson's inns have excellent (and expensive) dining rooms.

Jackson Village Bakery (☎ 603-383-6425; Jackson Falls Marketplace, NH 16B; sandwiches $6-7; ☒ 7am-4pm; wi-fi) Next door to the Chamber of Commerce, this simple, friendly café is a popular local spot for its pastry items, wraps and sandwiches.

Shannon Door (☎ 603-383-4211; NH 16; meals $11-16; ☒ 4-9pm Sun-Thu, 4-11pm Fri & Sat) This long-running Irish pub (around since the 1950s) serves shepherd's pie, but most of its menu is non-Gaelic in flavor: delicious thin-crust pizzas, steak *au poivre* (with pepper) and baked manicotti, to name a few options. It also has 14 beers on tap, a welcoming crowd and live entertainment (folk bands and such) Thursday through Sunday.

Red Fox's (☎ 603-383-4949; 49 NH 16; meals $12-22; ☒ brunch Sun, lunch Sat & Sun, dinner daily) For wood-grilled steaks, barbecue pork and char-grilled burgers, casual, family-friendly Red Fox's is the place to go. You'll also find wood-fired pizzas, fresh salads and a couple of seafood dishes thrown in for good measure.

Thompson House Eatery (☎ 603-383-9341; 193 Main St, NH 16B; meals $10-32; ☒ lunch Thu-Mon, dinner nightly) Casual but cool, the Thompson House is a local favorite for creative new American cuisine. The seasonal menu is big on organic locally grown produce, which is also for sale at the farm stand outside. Eat on the porch, with light filtering through the stained-glass windows, or at the friendly bar.

White Mountain Cider Co (☎ 603-383-9061; US 302, Glen; snacks $2-6) If you are packing a picnic for your day hike, stop at this country store. Besides cider, you'll find gourmet coffee, cider doughnuts, apple pie and a whole range of specialty New England products. Next door is a more formal restaurant that's open for dinner (mains from $18 to $28), serving expertly prepared cuisine (pan-seared sea-scallops, butternut risotto, roasted haddock) in an elegant 1890s farmhouse.

Getting There & Away
Concord Trailways (☎ 603-228-3300, 800-639-3317) runs a daily bus between Boston ($29, four hours) and Berlin, making a stop in Jackson at the **J-Town Deli** (☎ 603-383-8259, 95 Main St).

CRAWFORD NOTCH & BRETTON WOODS
US 302 travels west from Glen, then north to Crawford Notch (1773ft), continuing on to Bretton Woods. Before 1944 the area was known only to locals and wealthy summer visitors who patronized the grand Mt Washington Hotel. When President Roosevelt chose the hotel as the site of the conference to establish a new global economic order after WWII, the whole world learned about Bretton Woods.

The mountainous countryside is still as stunning now as it was during those historic times, the hotel is almost as grand and the name still rings with history. At the very least, stop to admire the view of the great hotel set against the mountains. Ascending Mt Washington on a cog railway powered by a steam locomotive is dramatic fun for all, and a must for railroad buffs.

Information
Complete information about hiking, biking and camping in the area is available from **AMC Highland Center** (☎ 603-466-2727; www.amc-nh.org; Crawford Notch; ☒ 9am-5pm Mon-Sat), including maps and trail guides. Daily activities and guided hikes are offered.

Sights & Activities

MT WASHINGTON COG RAILWAY

Purists walk, the lazy drive, but certainly the quaintest way to reach the summit of Mt Washington is to take this **cog railway** (☎ 603-278-5404, 800-922-8825; www.thecog.com; adult/child/senior/child under 4yr $59/39/54/free). Since 1869 coal-fired, steam-powered locomotives have followed a 3.5-mile track up a steep mountainside trestle for a three-hour round-trip scenic ride, with two daily departures (weekend departures only from late April to late May). Reservations are highly recommended. On weekends from late November through March the train runs a shorter, one-hour round-trip up to Kroflite Kamp at 4100ft (adult/child $31/26).

Instead of having drive wheels, a cog locomotive applies power to a cogwheel (gear wheel) on its undercarriage. The gears engage pins mounted between the rails to pull the locomotive and a single passenger car up the mountainside, burning a ton of coal and blowing a thousand gallons of water into steam along the way. Up to seven locomotives may be huffing and puffing at one time here, all with boilers tilted to accommodate the grade, which at the 'Jacob's Ladder' trestle is 37% – the second-steepest railway track in the world.

The base station is 6 miles east of US 302. Turn east in Fabyan, just northwest of the Mt Washington Hotel (between Bretton Woods and Twin Mountain). Also, remember that the average temperature at the summit is 40°F in summer and the wind is always blowing, so bring a sweater and windbreaker.

CRAWFORD NOTCH STATE PARK

In 1826 torrential rains in this steep valley caused massive mud slides that descended on the home of the Willey family. The house was spared, but the family was not – they were outside at the fatal moment and were swept away by the mud. The dramatic incident made the newspapers and fired the imaginations of painter Thomas Cole and author Nathaniel Hawthorne. Both men used the incident for inspiration, thus unwittingly putting Crawford Notch on the tourist maps. Soon visitors arrived to visit the tragic spot – and they stayed for the bracing mountain air and healthy exercise.

From the Willey House site, now used as a **state park visitor center** (☎ 603-374-2272; ☼ dawn-dusk mid-May–mid-Oct), you can walk the easy 0.5-mile Pond Loop Trail, the 1-mile Sam Willey Trail and the Ripley Falls Trail, a 1-mile hike from US 302 via the Ethan Pond Trail. The trailhead for Arethusa Falls, a 1.3-mile hike, is 0.5 miles south of the Dry River Campground on US 302.

SKIING

Mt Washington Resort at Bretton Woods includes a **ski station** (☎ 603-278-3320; www.bretton woods.com; adult/child/teen/senior Mon-Fri $59/35/47/25, Sat & Sun $69/41/55/69; ☼ 8:30am-4pm) with a vertical drop of 1500ft. Seven different chair lifts serve 88 different trails, most of which are intermediate. The Ski & Snowboard school offers childcare and ski lessons for kids. All equipment is available for rental.

The resort also maintains a 62-mile network of trails for **cross-country skiing** (day-pass adult/child & senior/teen $17/10/14). The trails traverse the resort grounds, crossing open fields, wooded paths and mountain streams. Ski rental and lessons are also available.

Sleeping & Eating

In addition to offering lavish accommodations, the Mt Washington Hotel has an extensive breakfast buffet and dress-up dinners, and there are restaurants at both the Bretton Arms Inn and the Lodge.

BUDGET & MIDRANGE

Dry River Campground (☎ 603-374-2272; US 302; campsites $23; ☼ late May–mid-Oct) Near the southern end of Crawford Notch State Park, this quiet state-run campground has 36 tent sites with a nicely kept bathhouse, showers and laundry facilities. Thirty of the sites can be reserved in advance.

Crawford Notch General Store & Campground (☎ 603-374-2779; www.crawfordnotchcamping.com; US 302; campsites $20-30, cabins $50-110; ☼ May–mid-Oct) This handy all-purpose place sells camping supplies and groceries to use at its lovely wooded sites. You'll also find small, rustic, but rather handsome wooden cabins. Some of the sites are on the Saco River, and there's good swimming right in front.

Above the Notch (☎ 603-846-5156; www.above thenotch.com; NH 302; r $78-93) For lower-price lodging, you'll have to drive a fair bit away from the Mt Washington Hotel. This classic drive-up motel is a simple, friendly place, with clean basic rooms. It's conveniently located next to Bretton Woods ski resort and the Cog Railway.

Lakes of the Clouds Hut (☎ 603-466-2727, 800-262-4455; www.outdoors.org; dm adult/child $87/53; Jun–mid-Sep) Advance reservations are essential for this AMC hut located near the summit of Mt Washington.

Lodge at Bretton Woods (☎ 603-278-1000, 800-314-1752; www.mtwashington.com; US 302; r $115-175;) Operated by the Mt Washington Resort, this modern place (with 50 spacious rooms) actually enjoys the best view of the Mt Washington Hotel and its mountain backdrop. It has a motor-inn layout and an inexpensive diner, Darby's, on site.

AMC Highland Center (☎ 603-466-2727; www.outdoors.org; Crawford Notch; dm adult/child $77/44, s/d incl breakfast & dinner with private bathroom per person $191/135) The newest AMC (Appalachian Mountain Club) lodge is set amid the splendor of Crawford Notch, an ideal base for hiking Mt Washington and many other trails in the area. The grounds are beautiful, rooms are basic but comfortable, meals are hearty and guests are all outdoor enthusiasts. Discounts are available for AMC members. The center also has loads of information about hiking in the region.

TOP END

Mt Washington Hotel (☎ 603-278-1000, 800-258-0330; www.mtwashington.com; US 302; r incl breakfast & dinner $270-340;) Arguably the grande dame of New England lodging, this magnificent 200-room hotel has imposing public rooms, 27 holes of golf, 12 clay tennis courts, an equestrian center and other amenities, all on thousands of acres. It is steeped in history, and you can feel it as you wander the elegant halls. Daily tours are available.

Bretton Arms Inn (☎ 603-278-1000, 800-258-0330; www.mtwashington.com; US 302; r incl breakfast $80-220) People have been staying here for almost a century. On the same estate as the Mt Washington Hotel, this 34-room manse was built as a grand 'summer cottage' in 1896, but it has been an inn since 1907. It offers a more intimate and more folksy atmosphere.

PINKHAM NOTCH

Pinkham Notch is known for its wild beauty even though useful facilities for campers and hikers make it one of the most popular activity centers in the White Mountains. Wildcat Mountain and Tuckerman Ravine

offer good skiing, and an excellent system of trails provides access to the natural beauties of the Presidential Range, especially Mt Washington. For the less athletically inclined, the Mt Washington Auto Rd provides easy access to the summit.

Orientation & Information

NH 16 goes north 11 miles from North Conway and Jackson to Pinkham Notch (2032ft), then past the Wildcat Mountain ski area and Tuckerman Ravine, through the small settlement of Glen House and past the Dolly Copp Campground to Gorham and Berlin.

The nerve center for hiking in the Whites, the **AMC Pinkham Notch Camp** (☎ 603-466-2727; www.outdoors.org; Pinkham Notch, NH 16; 6:30am-10pm) provides extensive information, maps, lectures and guided hikes, as well as a cafeteria and lodging.

Sights & Activities

MT WASHINGTON AUTO ROAD

The **Mt Washington Summit Road Company** (☎ 603-466-3988; www.mt-washington.com; car & driver $20, per additional adult/child $7/5; 8am-4pm May-Oct, longer hr summer, closed Nov-Apr) operates an 8-mile-long alpine toll road from Pinkham Notch to the summit of Mt Washington. The entrance is off NH 16, 2.5 miles north of Pinkham Notch Camp. The toll includes an audio tour on CD. If you'd rather not drive, you can take a 1½-hour **guided tour** (adult/child/senior $26/11/23; 8:30am-5pm), which allows you 30 minutes on the summit. In severe weather the road may be closed (even in summer).

PINKHAM NOTCH CAMP

Guided nature walks, canoe trips, cross-country ski and snowshoe treks and other outdoor adventures out of Pinkham Notch Camp are organized by the **AMC** (☎ 603-466-2727, 800-262-4455; www.outdoors.org), which also operates a summer hiker's shuttle that stops at many trailheads along US 302 in Pinkham Notch.

The *AMC White Mountain Guide*, on sale here or online from the AMC website, includes detailed maps and the vital statistics of each trail.

The AMC maintains hikers' 'high huts' providing meals and lodging. Carter Notch Hut is located on Nineteen-Mile Brook Trail, and Lakes of the Clouds Hut (left) is sited on Crawford Path. For those hiking the

NEW HAMPSHIRE

THESE LEGS CLIMBED MT WASHINGTON!

Mt Washington's summit is at 6288ft, making it the tallest mountain in New England. The **mountain** (www.mountwashington.com) is renowned for its frighteningly bad weather - the average temperature on the summit is 26.5°F. The mercury has fallen as low as -47°F, but only risen as high as 72°F. About 256in (more than 21ft) of snow fall each year. (One year, it was 47ft.) At times the climate can mimic Antarctica's, and hurricane-force winds blow every three days or so, on average. In fact, the highest wind ever recorded was here during a storm in 1934, when gusts reached 231 mph.

If you attempt the summit, pack warm, windproof clothes and shoes, even in high summer, and always consult with AMC hut personnel. Don't be reluctant to turn back if the weather changes for the worse. Dozens of hikers who ignored such warnings and died are commemorated by trailside monuments and crosses.

In good weather, the hike is exhilarating. The only disappointment is exerting hours of effort, exploring remote paths, following caroms and finally reaching the summit, only to discover a parking lot full of cars that motored up. Don't feel bad – just treat yourself to a 'This car climbed Mt Washington' bumper sticker.

Tuckerman Ravine Trail

The Tuckerman Ravine Trail starts at the Pinkham Notch Camp (p457) and continues for 4.2 thigh-burning, knee-scrambling miles to the summit. It takes most relatively fit hikers just over four hours to get to what feels like the top of the world, a bit less time for the trip down. To Tuckerman Ravine itself, the trail is fairly protected, but the steep, rocky headwall and barren cone are exposed to the dependably moody weather. It's a brute of a hike, but what a prize. If your knees can't take the descent, AMC offers a shuttle bus ($26) back to Pinkham Notch Camp.

Ammonoosuc Ravine Trail

This trail, via the AMC's Lakes of the Clouds Hut (elevation 5000ft), is one of the shortest hiking routes to the summit. It's also one of the best routes during inclement weather because it is protected from the worst winds, and, if the weather turns very nasty, you can take shelter in the AMC hut. For overnight lodging and meals, see opposite.

The trail starts at a parking lot on Base Station Rd, near the entrance to the Mt Washington Cog Railway (elevation 2560ft), and climbs easily for 2 miles up the dramatic ravine to Gem Pool. From Gem Pool, however, the climb is far more strenuous and demanding, with a sharp vertical rise to the AMC hut.

Jewell Trail

This trail is more exposed than the Ammonoosuc Ravine Trail and should be used only in good conditions. The last 0.7 miles is above the tree line and very windy. The Jewell Trail starts at the same parking lot as the Ammonoosuc Ravine Trail but follows a more northeasterly course up a ridge. At 2.8 miles, the trail rises above the timberline and climbs 3.5 miles by a series of switchbacks to meet the Gulfside Trail. The Gulfside continues to the summit.

Appalachian Trail, the Zealand and Carter huts are open year-round. For lodging and meals at the camp, see opposite.

SKIING

With a vertical drop of 2112ft, **Wildcat Mountain** (☎ 603-466-3326, 800-255-6439, snow report 800-754-9453; www.skiwildcat.com; NH 16, Pinkham Notch; adult/child & senior/teen $59/29/49) tops out at 4415ft. Just north of Jackson, Wildcat's 225 acres include 47 downhill ski trails (25% beginner, 45% intermediate,

30% expert), four lifts and 90% snowmaking capacity. The longest run is 2.75 miles.

The cirque at **Tuckerman Ravine** has several ski trails for purists. What's pure about it? No lifts. You climb up the mountain then ski down. Purists posit that, if you climb up, you will have strong legs that won't break easily in a fall on the way down. Tuckerman is perhaps best in spring, when most ski resorts are struggling to keep their snow cover, since nature conspires to keep the ravine in shadow much of the time. Park in the Wildcat Mountain lot for the climb up the ravine.

WILDCAT SKYRIDE

Wildcat Mountain's summertime **Gondola Skyride** (adult/child/senior $13/7/12; ☻ 10am-5pm mid-May–mid-Oct) was the first of its kind in the USA. It operates in summer just for the fun of the ride and the view.

Sleeping & Eating

Dolly Copp Campground (☎ 603-466-3984; NH 16; campsites $20; ☻ mid-May–mid-Oct) This USFS campground is 6 miles north of the AMC camp and has 176 primitive sites. Reservations are accepted at a few sites, but most are first-come first-served.

Joe Dodge Lodge (☎ 603-466-2727, 800-262-4455; NH 16; dm $43/25, dm incl meals adult/child $71/39; ☻ year-round) The AMC camp at Pinkham Notch incorporates this lodge, with dorms housing more than 100 beds. Reserve bunks in advance. Discounts are available for AMC members.

Getting There & Away

Concord Trailways (☎ 603-228-3300, 800-639-3317; www.concordtrailways.com) runs a daily route between Boston ($31 to $36, four hours) and Berlin, stopping at Pinkham Notch Camp.

GREAT NORTH WOODS

Not too many people make it all the way up here, north of Berlin. There are two scenic routes north of the Notches and Bretton Woods. If you've been feeling like you can't see the forest for the trees, nothing beats US 2 from the Vermont/New Hampshire state line to the Maine/New Hampshire state line. The expansive but looming mountain views are unparalleled. Alternatively, if you really want to get remote, or are heading to the outposts of Maine, take NH 16 north from Gorham to Erol. This route runs parallel to the birch-lined Androscoggin River.

Assuming you're out at dawn or dusk, you should be able to catch a glimpse of a moose in the **Northern Forest Heritage Park** (☎ 603-752-7202; www.northernforestheritage.org; 961 Main St/NH 16, Berlin; adult/child $15/8). The park currently offers 90-minute boat tours along the Androscoggin River, departing at 3pm and 5pm Tuesday to Saturday from late May to mid-October.

You'll have an even better chance of spotting the land-roaming behemoths on one of the Moose Tours sponsored by the town of **Gorham** (☎ 603-466-3103; www.gorhamnh.org; 20 Park St, Gorham; adult/child $20/15). These three-hour, 21-passenger van tours are led by naturalist guides, who claim a 96% success rate at spotting moose. Tours leave twice weekly at 5.30am and three or four times weekly at 6.30pm. Call for the latest schedule.

Nestled in a dramatic and narrow valley, the elegant, 15,000-acre resort **Balsams** (☎ 603-255-3400, in New Hampshire 800-255-0800, in the rest of US & Canada 800-255-0600; www.thebalsams.com; NH 26, Dixville Notch; r $190-260; ☻), with 212 rooms, has been hosting guests since 1866. The all-inclusive price gives unlimited use of two golf courses, putting greens, tennis courts, a lake, boats, hiking and mountain-biking trails and all other resort services. Room prices vary according to the size, view, and amenities. Other activities include shuffleboard, badminton, croquet, horseshoes, table tennis and billiards. Even if you don't stay, it's worth a drive to check out this rare bird.

NEW HAMPSHIRE

Maine

Blessed with one of America's most magnificent coastlines, Maine looms large over New England. Countless islands, deep-water harbors, and wild, glacier-carved bays create the dramatic beauty of Maine's rocky shores – which, if smoothed from end to end, would stretch more than 3500 miles. Planted along this seascape are fishing villages, summer resorts and picture-book colonial towns, with a thickly settled southern coast and wilder untouched scenery to the northeast. A suitable introduction to Maine is the old city of Portland, whose atmospheric downtown boasts a growing restaurant and gallery scene. East of there, the Midcoast offers a mix of old shipbuilding villages, academic settlements and pretty harbor towns. Further east lies Acadia National Park, a spectacular island of mountains, lakes, fjord-like estuaries and coves. Beyond it stretch the little-visited peninsulas and jagged cliffs running east to Canada.

While the coast is the fame of Maine, inland travel offers ample reward. This is, after all, 'the pine state' with forests covering 90% of the land. Thousands of lakes and ponds fill the vast wilderness, with moose and bald eagles far outnumbering humans. Maine's own stretch of White Mountains provide alpine appeal, luring snow-seekers to slopes near Bethel and Rangeley, while further east lies the cloud-piercing summit of Mt Katahdin.

Adventure comes in many forms in Maine, from racing white-water rapids to kayaking tranquil coves along the coast; there's hiking, bird-watching, mountain-biking and rock-climbing, with plenty of bucolic B&Bs in which to recover after the day is done. Perhaps best of all are the wondrous fruits of the sea. The lobsters fished from Maine waters have no equal anywhere on earth: other attractions aside, a lobster feast is reason enough to linger here.

HIGHLIGHTS

- Exploring the galleries, restaurants and bars on the atmospheric back streets of Portland's **Old Port District** (p474)

- Hiking up Cadillac Mountain, followed by a dip in Echo Lake in **Acadia National Park** (p508)

- Photographing the cliffs of **Monhegan Island** (p493), whose dramatic scenery has inspired countless artists

- Strolling the peaceful, historic lanes of **Castine** (p498), a marvelous colonial village on the sea

- Seeing the sun rise over the magnificent cliffs of **Quoddy Head State Park** (p512, the eastern-most point in America

| ■ TELEPHONE CODE: 207 | ■ POPULATION: 1.3 MILLION | ■ AREA: 35,387 SQ MILES |

Orientation & Information

Maine is the northernmost state in the continental United States, and the behemoth of New England, roughly equal in size to the other five states combined. To the north and west, Maine borders Canada and to the southwest New Hampshire (NH), with whom it shares a portion (53,000 acres) of the White Mountains.

Good sources of information include the following:

DeLorme's Maine Atlas & Gazetteer (www.delorme .com) The best map of the state, bar none.

Maine Office of Tourism (☎ 207-287-5711, 888-624-6345; www.visitmaine.com; 59 State House Station, Augusta) These folks maintain information centers on the principal routes into the state – Calais, Fryeburg, Hampden, Houlton, Kittery and Yarmouth. Each facility is open 9am to 5pm, with extended hours in the summer.

Maine Tourism Association (www.mainetourism.com) Links all Chamber of Commerce offices in Maine.

Maine Website (www.maine.gov) The state's official website.

Portland Press Herald (www.pressherald.mainetoday .com)

History

Maine's first inhabitants were descendants of Ice Age hunters, a hardy lot comprising dozens of tribes before the arrival of Europeans. They were collectively known as the Wabanaki ('people of the dawn'), and numbered perhaps 20,000 in Maine when the English set up Popham colony at the tip of the Phippsburg peninsula in 1607. Unlike Jamestown (Virginia), which was founded in the same year, the early Maine settlement failed and dispersed.

Over the next several generations, other English settlements sprang up in the Province of Maine, though settlers there faced enormous hardship from harsh winters and attacks by Native Americans. Adding insult to injury, Maine lost its sovereignty when Massachusetts took over the failing colony in 1692.

Bloody battles raged for many generations, destroying entire villages in Maine, with settlers facing attacks from Native Americans, the French and later the British. This didn't end until after the War of 1812, when the British finally withdrew from Maine. After ridding itself of the royal yoke, Maine focused on freeing itself from its Boston rulers, and in 1820 it gained its independence, becoming the 23rd state in the union.

The 19th century was one of tremendous growth for the new state, with the emergence of new industries. Timber brought wealth to the interior, with Bangor becoming the lumber capital of the world in the 1830s. Fishing, shipbuilding, granite quarrying and farming were also boom industries, alongside manufacturing, with textile and paper mills employing large swaths of the population.

Unfortunately, the boom days were short-lived, with a collapse on land (sawmills couldn't compete with larger, more accessible forests out west) and on sea (brought on by devastating overfishing) as nearly every major industry in Maine foundered. By the turn of the century, population growth stagnated and Maine became a backwater.

Ironically, Maine's rustic, undeveloped landscape would later become part of its great appeal to would-be visitors. Maine soon emerged as a summer cottage destination around the time the slogan 'Vacationland' (which still adorns Maine license plates) was coined in the 1890s. Today, tourism accounts for 15% of the state's economy (compared to the 6% average elsewhere in New England).

The Culture

Mainers are a tough breed. Their ancestors experienced many years of hardship, while today's generation continues to endure some of New England's fiercest winters and some of its least optimistic economic prospects. Among other things, this has led to a tenacious pride in being a 'native' – which means not only being born (and spending one's entire life) in Maine, but coming from a family that lived here at least a generation prior to one's birth. It's also set up a bit of antagonism with growing numbers of folk 'from away' who have summer homes in Maine, and are often blamed (rightly, it turns out) for driving up the price of real estate, which in turn has forced natives off their land.

Mainers trace their stock back to various waves of immigration, with large groups of Irish arriving during the potato famines of the 1840s. Significant numbers of Scots, Finns, Swedes and French Canadians have also planted their roots in the northern state. Meanwhile, the real Maine natives were mostly wiped out during the colonial days, with only five tribes remaining today – the Abenaki (southwest), Penobscot (south-central),

MAINE

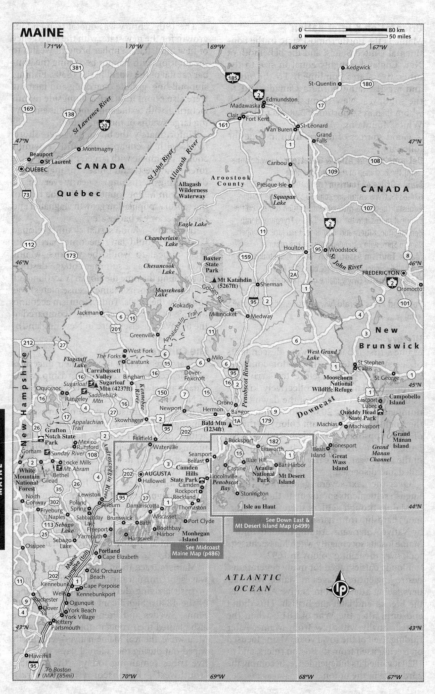

Passamaquoddy (southeast), Maliseet (north-central) and Mi'kmaq (north).

Land & Climate

Covered by glacial ice some 25,000 years ago, Maine is a geographic adolescent. The glaciers, which finally receded about 12,000 years ago, certainly left their mark on the state. Maine boasts nearly 6000 lakes and ponds (the largest of which is Moosehead Lake, p519), close to 5000 salt-water islands and another 5000 rivers and streams. Its highest point is 5267ft-tall Mt Katahdin (Penobscot for 'greatest mountain', p519), with another 10 mountains surpassing 4000ft (and over 100 above 3000ft). These lie in the White Mountain Region, which covers northwestern Maine.

Maine's best known region is the coastal lowland, which runs from 10 to 40 miles inland from the Atlantic Ocean with sandy beaches in the south, jagged inlets in the center and rugged cliffs in the north. Further into the interior lie the eastern New England uplands which, as far as Mainers are concerned, means fertile farmland, where local crops – particularly potatoes – flourish.

In summer coastal Maine tends to be more temperate and less humid than inland Maine because of ocean breezes, but in the winter those same winds can turn awfully bitter. The interior receives its share of snow and arctic blasts. Spring is fleeting and arrives late, and as such, the tourist season on the coast doesn't really open for business in earnest until May. In the fall, blue-sky days tend to be crisp, providing the prefect backdrop to the reds and golds of autumn. Fog in Maine is as iconic as its coastal brethren the lighthouse, and it can arrive at any time along the seascape. It tends to come thicker and more frequently the further east you travel.

Parks & Wildlife

Maine has an excellent assortment of state parks, suitable for every conceivable outdoor activity. It also boasts New England's only national park, **Acadia National Park** (p508), an extremely popular getaway in the summer.

The state's 35 parks are overseen by the **Bureau of Parks & Lands** (☎ 207-287-3821; www.maine.gov/doc/parks) and staff will send you an information pack that describes each in detail. For camping at these parks, call the central **reservation hotline** (☎ 207-624-9950, 800-332-1501).

About 275 miles of the 2150-mile Appalachian Trail runs through Maine, and it is perhaps most easily accessible via Grafton Notch State Park (p517), although the hiking is tough here. Its northern terminus is Baxter State Park (p519) and the summit of Mt Katahdin. The White Mountain National Forest (p517) also has dramatic sections of protected land in northern Maine, although most people tend to think that the forest stops at the New Hampshire border.

Maine has abundant wildlife in its thick forests. Foremost is the moose, a magnificent animal standing six to seven feet tall at the shoulder and weighing up to 1200lb. There are an estimated 30,000 in the state. Other animals present in the state include harbor seals, black bear, beaver, fox, eastern coyotes, skunks, otter, snowshoe hares, white-tailed deer, porcupines and red squirrels. More than 400 bird species have been spotted in Maine, including the osprey, bald eagles, snowy egret, peregrine falcon and puffins.

Getting There & Around

AIR

Portland International Jetport (☎ 207-874-8877; www.portlandjetport.org) is the state's main airport, but a number of airlines serve **Bangor International Airport** (☎ 866-359-2264; www.flyba ngor.com).

BOAT

Maine State Ferry Service (☎ 207-596-2202; www .maine.gov/mdot/opt/ferry/maine-ferry-service.php) operates boats to several larger islands. **Bay Ferries** (☎ 877-359-3760; www.catferry.com) offers services to Yarmouth in Nova Scotia (Canada) from Bar Harbor (p508), while its Cat Ferry runs from Portland (p482).

BUS

Concord Trailways (☎ 800-639-3317; www.concordtrail ways.com) operates daily buses between Boston and many Maine towns (including Bangor, Bar Harbor, Bath, Belfast, Brunswick, Camden/Rockport, Damariscotta, Ellsworth, Lincolnville, Portland, Rockland, Searsport, Waldoboro and Wiscasset). Some of these connect with the Maine State Ferry Service to islands off the coast.

From Bangor, **SMT/Acadian** (☎ 800-567-5151; www.smtbus.com) and **Cyr Bus Lines** (☎ 800-244-2335;

MAINE

THE GREAT AMERICAN LOBSTER

Once considered a food fit only for prisoners and indentured servants, the American lobster has come a long way in the last 200 years. Early settlers fished for lobster – along with cod, hake and other sustenance – but it wasn't until the 19th century, that entrepreneurs envisioned the lobster as a lucrative enterprise. In the 1850s Upham S Treat of Prospect, Maine, set up a cannery in Eastport and began procuring fresh lobster to be cooked, canned then sold to stores across the country for 5¢ a pound. His venture soon caught on, and within 30 years dozens of canneries sprang up along the Maine coast. To meet the enormous demand (5lb of lobster yielded roughly 1lb of meat), more and more fishermen switched to lobstering, and by 1880, more than 10 million pounds of lobsters were passing through the canneries each year. In those days, the supply seemed limitless, and it wasn't uncommon for boats to return with 500 lobsters a day, with some specimens weighing as much as 50lb. Yet, the halcyon days wouldn't last.

The late 19th century was also a boom time for wealthy northeasterners who came to summer in Maine. Eager to sample the exotic fish of Maine, these newcomers soon cultivated a taste for fresh lobster, which would eventually spell the end for the canneries.

Unfortunately, by then the damage had already been done, and the lobster population was on a downward spiral. Despite more and more fishermen entering the lobster trade, the yield fell from 25 million pounds in 1890 to 11 million by 1900. By 1920, it was down to five million pounds, and scientists predicted the total collapse of the lobster stock, just as hake, halibut, mackerel and later cod were fished to utter depletion in Maine waters.

Given the drastic circumstances, Maine Fish commissioner Horatio Crie sponsored a drastic conservation law in the 1930s, which would protect not just undersized lobsters but large lobsters as well, since females carried exponentially more eggs the bigger they grew. It took several generations, but the lobster population has made a tremendous recovery, up from 20-million-pound yields in the 1970s to over 60 million pounds in 2007. For Maine this amounts to a $260 million industry.

Scientists have offered various theories regarding the lobster's return, including the decimation of cod and other species that eat lobster, though the management by local fishermen also remains a significant factor. Lobstering in Maine remains a small-scale enterprise, with no corporate conglomerates trolling the waters, but rather long-time lobstermen, who often come from several generations of lobstermen. Locals manage the waters themselves, and outsiders who encroach on another's territory or are suspected of overfishing often receive none-too-subtle hints to back off (leaving a glove in an empty cage or even cutting lines, resulting in the loss of pricey equipment).

For more insight into Maine's best-loved export, check out *The Lobster Coast* by Colin Woodard or *The Lobster Chronicles*, by Linda Greenlaw.

www.cyrbustours.com) operate buses along various routes.

CAR & MOTORCYCLE

Except for the Maine Turnpike (I-95 and I-495) and part of I-295, Maine has no fast, limited-access highways. Roads along the coast flood with traffic during the summer tourist season. As a result, you must plan for more driving time when traveling in Maine.

Note: moose are a particular danger to drivers in Maine, even as far south as Portland – they've been known to cripple a bus and walk away. Be especially watchful in spring and fall and around dusk and dawn, when the moose are most active.

TRAIN

Amtrak's (☎ 800-872-7245; www.amtrak.com) *Downeaster* makes four or five trips daily between Boston, Massachusetts, and Portland, Maine.

SOUTHERN MAINE COAST

Maine's southern coast embodies the state slogan 'vacationland,' with busy commercial strips, sandy beaches and resort towns that get packed in the summer months. Despite the crowds, there are some charming features to this coast. While Kittery is a long, commercial strip mall, Ogunquit has a lovely beach, and is Maine's gay Mecca. Further north, lies historic York Village, and less comely York Beach. Beyond, the Kennebunks are small historic settlements with lavish mansions (some of which are B&Bs) near pretty beaches and rugged coastline. Although you'll have to use your imagination, the southern coast is deeply associated with the works of American artist Winslow Homer, who spent his summers in Prout's Neck (just south of Portland), which still has some magnificent scenery.

KITTERY
pop 10,100

The only reason most travelers visit Kittery is to shop. The busy roads leading from New Hampshire are lined with shopping malls and vast parking lots. While there's no natural beauty among the concrete, there are some deals if you feel like browsing the many outlet malls.

To escape the mayhem, head south to the pretty back roads along the coast. Founded in 1623, Kittery is one of Maine's oldest settlements, and here you'll find historic homes, manicured parks and some enticing lobster restaurants if you follow ME 103 a few miles out of town to Kittery Point.

Sights & Activities
OUTLET SHOPPING

In the space of about a mile there are upwards of 120 **outlet shops** (☎ 207-439-4367, 888-548-8379; www.thekitteryoutlets.com; 9am-9pm Mon-Sat, 10am-6pm Sun) lining US 1 in Kittery. Of all the stores, the **Kittery Trading Post** (☎ 888-587-6246; www.kittery tradingpost.com; 9am-9pm Mon-Sat, 10am-6pm Sun) is the most interesting retail spot. Opened in 1926, this was the town's original outpost and still sells a wide range of outdoor clothing and gear.

RIVER TOURS

For a cruise along the Piscataqua, **Cap & Patty** (☎ 877-439-8976; www.capandpatty.com; Town Dock, Pepperell Rd; adult/child $12/8; Tue-Sun Jun–mid-Oct) offers river tours, taking in the lighthouses, forts and the Navy yard around the basin. Tours last approximately 80 minutes and are offered six times per day in the summer.

Sleeping & Eating
Portsmouth Harbor Inn & Spa (☎ 207-439-4040; www .innatportsmouth.com; 6 Water St; r with breakfast in-season/

off-season $170-220/110-200) Kittery's most charming guesthouse lies across the street from the Piscataqua River and within walking distance of Portsmouth, NH. It has five somewhat small rooms, each uniquely designed (antique four-post beds, hardwood floors, water views are some of the attributes). The spa provides many services.

Cap'n Simeon's (☎ 207-439-3655; 99 Pepperell Rd; meals $12-22; lunch & dinner) To escape the mediocrity of chain restaurants along US 1, head south to Kittery's harbor. Cap'n Simeon's serves hearty plates of seafood (haddock, lobster, sea scallops) as well as quiche, salads and, yes, fried fare.

Getting There & Away

From Portsmouth, NH, it's a mere 3 miles to Kittery via US 1 or I-95 across the Piscataqua River.

THE YORKS
pop 16,200

York Village, York Harbor and York Beach collectively make up the Yorks. **York Village**, the first city chartered in English North America, has a long and interesting history and well-preserved colonial buildings in the village center. **York Harbor** was developed more than a century ago as a posh summer resort, and it maintains some of that feeling today. **York Beach** was where the masses came in summer, and its mass-culture roots still show in its large number of recreational vehicle (RV) parks and humdrum commercial development.

For visitor information, stop by the helpful **Greater York Chamber of Commerce** (☎ 207-363-4422; www.gatewaytomaine.org; Stonewall Ln, York; 9am-5pm Mon-Sat, 10am-4pm Sun), just off US 1.

Sights & Activities
COLONIAL YORK

Historic York was called Agamenticus by its pre-colonial Native American inhabitants. British colonials settled York in 1624, and it was chartered as a city in 1641. The **Old York Historical Society** (☎ 207-363-4974; www.oldyork .org; 207 York St, York Village; adult 1 bldg/all bldgs $5/10, child $3/5; 10am-5pm Mon-Sat Jun-Oct) is proud of the town's historic buildings and has preserved several of them as a museum of the town's history. Tickets are sold at **Jefferds' Tavern Visitor Center** (Lindsay Rd, York Village), off US 1A.

MAINE

The historic buildings include the **School House**, dating from the mid-18th century. The **Old Gaol** (jail) gives a vivid impression of crime and punishment two centuries ago. The **Emerson-Wilcox House** is a museum of New England decorative arts and the **Elizabeth Perkins House** was a wealthy family's summer home. The **John Hancock** warehouse preserves the town's industrial and commercial history, while the **George Marshall Store** houses a changing selection of contemporary art exhibitions.

If you have children, you may want to visit **York's Wild Kingdom** (☎ 207-363-4911, 800-456-4911; www.yorkzoo.com; US 1, York Beach; adult/child $18.25/14.25; ☺ 10am-6pm late May–mid-Sep; ♣), the state's largest zoo.

OUTDOOR ACTIVITIES

Harbor Adventures (☎ 207-363-8466; www.harbor adventures.com; Town Dock No 2, York Harbor) offers a chance to explore this scenic coastline by sea kayak or by mountain bike. Popular kayaking options include the two-hour harbor tour ($39), the sunset tour ($34) and the lobster luncheon ($67), which consists of paddling along Chauncey Creek and around Kittery Point peninsula before docking for crustaceans.

Sleeping & Eating

Dockside Guest Quarters (☎ 207-363-2868, 888-860-7428; www.docksidegq.com; 22 Harris Island Rd, York; r with breakfast in summer $134-216, off-season $98-125; ☺ daily Jun-Oct, Sat & Sun Apr-May & Nov-Dec, closed Jan-Mar) This quintessential guesthouse has the best views of any accommodations in York. In all, there are 26 nicely furnished rooms dispersed between the main 19th-century inn and the more modern cottages. There's also a glassed-in dining room overlooking the harbor that serves traditional seafood.

Inn at Tanglewood Hall (☎ 207-351-1075; www .tanglewoodhall.com; 611 York St, York Harbor; r with breakfast Jul & Aug $160-250, off-season $95-195; ☺ Apr-Nov) This lovely B&B boasts six sweetly furnished rooms with feather beds and abundant country charm. Several rooms have gas fireplaces and private porches. The wraparound veranda provides a peaceful vantage point overlooking the gardens.

Fox's Lobster House (☎ 207-363-2643; Nubble Point, York Beach; meals $19-24; ☺ 11:30am-9pm Jun-Oct) Although there's a broader selection of restaurants in Ogunquit, Fox's has history

(it's been around since 1966) and is worth seeking out for scrumptious lobster, fresh seafood dishes and homemade blueberry pie. It's beautifully set on the waterfront with views of Nubble lighthouse.

Getting There & Away

From Kittery, it's another 6 miles up US 1 or I-95 to York. York Harbor is about one mile east of York via US 1A; York Beach is 3 miles north of York via US 1A.

OGUNQUIT & WELLS

Known to the Abenaki tribe as the 'beautiful place by the sea,' **Ogunquit** (pop 1300) is justly famous for its 3-mile sandy beach. Wide stretches of pounding surf front the Atlantic, while warm back-cove waters make an idyllic setting for a swim. In the summer, the beach draws hordes of visitors from near and far, increasing the town's population exponentially.

Prior to its resort status, Ogunquit was a shipbuilding center in the 17th century. Later it became an important arts center, when the Ogunquit art colony was founded in 1898. Today, Ogunquit is the northeastern-most gay and lesbian Mecca in the US, adding a touch of open San Francisco culture to a more conservative Maine one. For more information, visit www.gayogunquit.com.

Neighboring **Wells** (pop 10,040) to the northeast is little more than an eastward continuation of Ogunquit Beach, with a long stretch of busy commercial development. Wells has good beaches, though, and many relatively inexpensive motels and campgrounds.

Orientation & Information

The center of Ogunquit, called Ogunquit Sq, is the intersection of Main St (US 1), Shore Rd and Beach St. The town stretches southeast down Shore Rd to Perkins Cove, and northeast to Wells. Parking in town lots costs $6 per day during the busy summer months.

Ogunquit Chamber of Commerce (☎ 207-646-2939; www.ogunquit.org; ☺ 9am-5pm Mon-Fri & Sun, 10am-6pm Sat) Located on US 1, near the Ogunquit Playhouse and just south of the town's center.

Ogunquit Memorial Library (☎ 207-646-9024; 166 Shore Rd, Ogunquit; ☺ 9am-noon & 2-5pm Tue-Sun) Get online for free inside this marvelous 19th-century fieldstone building.

Sights & Activities

MARGINAL WAY & PERKINS COVE

Ogunquit's well-known coastline footpath, **Marginal Way**, starts southeast of Beach St at Shore Rd. Named because it follows the 'margin' of the sea, the path and right-of-way were ceded to the town in the 1920s after its owner, Josiah Chase, sold off his valuable sea-view property. The scenic walk is slightly more than a mile. If you don't want to walk back, you can hop on the summertime trolley.

Marginal Way ends near **Perkins Cove**, a picturesque inlet dotted with sailboats and lobstering boats. A narrow pedestrian bridge spans the harbor and leads to a handful of attractive restaurants, art galleries and boutiques.

OGUNQUIT MUSEUM OF AMERICAN ART

Beautifully set overlooking the shore, this **museum** (☎ 207-646-4909; 543 Shore Rd, Ogunquit; adult/child/teen/senior $7/free/4/5; ⏰ 10:30am-5pm Mon-Sat, 2-5pm Sun Jul-Oct), houses an exquisite collection of paintings, sculpture and photography made by American artists. Standouts are works by Reginald Marsh, Charles Demuth and Robert Henri; the museum also has two changing exhibitions each summer, which in the past have included works by Jamie Wyeth and Ansel Adams.

WILDLIFE RESERVES

The **Wells National Estuarine Research Reserve** (Laudholm Farm; ☎ 207-646-1555; www.wellsreserve.org; 342 Laudholm Farm Rd, Wells; adult/child $2/1; ⏰ 7am-sunset) has 1600 acres of protected coastal ecosystems, with 7 miles of hiking and cross-country ski trails past woodlands, fields, wetlands, beaches and dunes. Its diverse habitats make it a particularly intriguing place for birdwatchers. To get there, take US 1, 1.5 miles north of Wells and turn right onto Laudholm Rd.

Named after the famous environmentalist, the **Rachel Carson Wildlife Refuge** (☎ 207-646-9226; www.fws.gov; 321 Port Rd; admission free; ⏰ dawn-dusk) consists of 9000 acres of protected coastal areas. There are four trails scattered in the non-contiguous refuge, the most popular being the 1-mile interpretive Carson Trail that passes tidal creeks and salt marshes, and is a great spot for seeing migratory birds. It's located off ME 9, at the northern edge of Wells.

WELLS AUTO MUSEUM

Lover of a well-made touring car should pay a visit to this fanciful **museum** (☎ 207-646-9064; Post Rd/US 1, Wells; adult/child $6/3; ⏰ 10am-5pm late May–mid-Oct). Here you'll find a collection of restored classic cars powered by steam, electricity and gasoline. There's over 70 cars on hand, representing 45 different makes, including Rolls-Royce, Stutz, Cadillac, Packard, Pierce Arrow and Knox.

OGUNQUIT PLAYHOUSE

This 1933 **theater** (☎ 207-646-5511; www.ogunquit playhouse.org; 10 Main St, Ogunquit; tickets $35-50; ⏰ performances May-Sep) hosts four or five musicals annually in the 750-seat theater. Well-known performers occasionally perform in the cast, although the productions are high quality even without them.

BEACHES

A sublime stretch of family-friendly coastline, **Ogunquit Beach** (or Main Beach to the locals) is only a five-minute walk along Beach St, east of US 1. Walking to the beach is a good idea in the summer, because the lot fills up early (and it costs $4 per hour to park). The 3-mile beach fronts Ogunquit Bay to the south; on the west side of the beach are the warmer waters of the tidal Ogunquit River.

Footbridge Beach, 2 miles to the north near Wells, is actually the northern extension of Ogunquit Beach. It's reached from US 1 by Ocean St and a footbridge across the Ogunquit River. Another way to access the beach is via Eldridge Rd in Wells – follow the sign for Moody Beach.

Little Beach, near the lighthouse on Marginal Way, is best reached on foot.

KAYAKING

Excursions in Maine (☎ 207-363-0181; www.excursionsinmaine.com; 1740 US 1, Cape Neddick; ⏰ mid-Jun–Sep) offers scenic half-day kayak tours ($60) as well as overnight trips with two days of paddling ($250). If you're proficient, you can rent kayaks for $35 to 45 per day.

CRUISES

Finestkind (☎ 207-646-5227; www.finestkindcruises.com; Perkins Cove, Ogunquit; adult $12-28, child $7-28; ⏰ 9:30am-3pm May-Oct) offers many popular trips including a 50-minute lobstering trip, a sunset cocktail cruise and a two-hour cruise aboard the twin sailed *Cricket*.

MAINE

Silverlining (☎ 207-646-9800; Perkins Cove, Ogunquit; adult $40; ☷ May-Oct) Offers four two-hour sails daily on a 42ft Hinckley sloop (single-masted sailboat), cruising the tranquil and rocky shoreline near Ogunquit.

Sleeping
BUDGET
Pinederosa Camping Area (☎ 207-646-2492; www .pinederosa.com; 128 Captain Thomas Rd, Wells; sites $25-40; ☷ mid-May–mid-Sep; ☲) This secluded campground has 162 sites, most of which are heavily wooded, and some of which overlook the Ogunquit River. Because it's far from Ogunquit, a shuttle runs to and from the beach from 9am to 5pm daily in the summer. To reach the campground, take US 1 for a mile northwest of Ogunquit center and turn just south of the Falls at Ogunquit Motel onto Captain Thomas Rd.

Moon Over Maine (☎ 207-646-6666, 800-851-6837; www.moonovermaine.com; 22 Berwick Rd, Ogunquit; r with breakfast $90-170, off-season $60-140; ☐ wi-fi) Up the hill from Key Bank, Moon Over Maine is an 1839 Cape-style house with an outdoor hot tub and nine nicely furnished rooms. The best have wood floors and French doors leading onto a shared balcony.

MIDRANGE & TOP END
Norseman (☎ 207-646-2823, 207-646-9093, www.ogun quitbeach.com; 135 Beach St, Ogunquit; r with breakfast $170-340, off-season $60-130; ☲) Ideally positioned right on the beach, the Norseman has carpeted rooms with beamed ceilings and trim furnishings. Rooms open onto shared balconies overlooking either the beach or the back cove.

Ogunquit Beach Inn (☎ 207-646-1112; www.ogun quitbeachinn.com; 67 School St, Ogunquit; r with breakfast $139-169, off-season $89-159; ☷ Mar-Jan; ☐ wi-fi) This gay- and lesbian-friendly B&B has handsome rooms with colorful decor, large beds and modern amenities such as DVD players. Some rooms are a bit small, while the best room has wood floors and private decks.

Nellie Littlefield House (☎ 207-646-1692; www.nellie littlefieldhouse.com; 27 Shore Rd, Ogunquit; r with breakfast $188-238, off-season $89-185; ☲) This beautifully restored Victorian dates from 1889 and offers 11 attractive rooms, some of which are set with antiques and period furnishings. Four rooms have private decks with ocean views.

Rockmere Lodge (☎ 207-646-2985; www.rockmere .com; 150 Stearns Rd, Ogunquit; r with breakfast $155-225, off-season $99-179) Set in an 1890s shingle man-

sion, Rockmere enjoys splendid views over the ocean from its hillside perch. It has eight rooms, each uniquely decorated, and several overlook the ocean. Some tend toward floral extravagance, while others are classically furnished with antiques. On the grounds are flower gardens, fountains and a pond.

Eating
Caffe Prego (☎ 207-646-7734; 44 Shore Rd, Ogunquit; meals $9-14; ☷ 8:30am-10pm mid-May–mid-Oct) Unmatched for people watching, Prego is a sleek and stylish café serving excellent cappuccinos, creamy gelato, pizzas and panini. Look for a table on the inviting front patio.

Blue Water Inn (☎ 207-646-5559; 111 Beach St, Ogunquit; meals $12-22; ☷ lunch & dinner) Nicely set along the water, this casual spot has a covered patio where you can enjoy lobster, blackened tuna and other seafood dishes. The sandwiches, salads and burgers are also quite popular.

Gypsy Sweethearts (☎ 207-646-7201; 30 Shore Rd, Ogunquit; meals $19-31; ☷ dinner Tue-Sun) In the heart of town, Gypsy Sweethearts serves unique dishes such as lobster quesadilla, cranberry-marinated pork tenderloin and sea scallops with tropical fruit compote. It's set in a cozy dining room, with an outdoor deck for warm evenings.

Clay Hill Farm (☎ 207-361-2272; 220 Clay Hill Rd, Cape Neddick; meals $24-35; ☷ lunch & dinner) This award-winning restaurant is set in an elegantly restored 18th-century farmhouse and serves new American cuisine. Rack of lamb with fennel salad, organic trout, roasted Cornish hen and sesame-crusted scallops are among the changing menu selections. It's located 5 miles north of Ogunquit, off US 1.

Arrows (☎ 207-361-1100; Berwick Rd, Ogunquit; meals $44-48; ☷ dinner Wed-Sun Jan-Mar & Jun-Oct, Sat & Sun Apr-May & Nov-Dec) One of the best restaurants in this part of Maine, Arrows features imaginative dishes such as herb-coated yellowfin tuna with Maine clams, potato pierogi and crispy prosciutto (that's one dish). Arrows is 4 miles west of Ogunquit; reservations and jackets for men are recommended.

Drinking & Entertainment
Front Porch (☎ 207-646-4005; Ogunquit Sq, Ogunquit; ☷ from 6pm Wed-Sun mid-May–mid-Oct) This kitschy fun piano bar attracts a mixed crowd to its many off-key singalongs, and is a dapper

setting for a cocktail. There's tasty seafood served in the new adjoining restaurant.

Beachfire (☎ 207-646-8998; 658 Main St, Ogunquit; ☽ 5pm-1am Wed-Mon) This new spot has an upstairs and a downstairs bar, a sizzling firepit out front, and live music (folk, jazz, R&B) on Friday and Saturday nights (no cover).

Club Inside OUT (☎ 207-646-6655; www.clubinsideout .com; 237 Main St, Ogunquit; ☽ 5pm-1am Mon-Fri, noon-1am Sat & Sun) Ogunquit's biggest entertainment complex is a big ball of gay fun, comprising a dance club, a cocktail lounge and a rooftop café with a full menu. Check the website for upcoming events.

Getting There & Around

Ogunquit lies 70 miles northeast of Boston off I-95 on US 1. Portsmouth, NH, is just 17 miles southwest of Ogunquit along the coast. Portland is 35 miles to the northeast.

In the summer, 'trolleys' (more like disguised buses, $1) circulate through Ogunquit every 10 minutes, from 8am to 11pm. Leave the driving to them in this horribly congested town; they'll take you from the center to the beach or Perkins Cove.

THE KENNEBUNKS

pop 14,900

Together, the towns of Kennebunk, Kennebunkport and Kennebunk Beach make up the Kennebunks. **Kennebunkport**, the most famous of the three towns, is beautiful, historical and absolutely packed in summer. Walk anywhere in the town to see the pristine 100- and 200-year-old houses and mansions, manicured lawns and sea views. Even in fall, visitors converge on Kennebunkport to browse the art galleries, overnight in its gracious inns and drive along the ocean to admire the view. Ocean Ave presents the most dramatic vistas, but the back streets, inland from the Kennebunk River and the sea, are less busy.

Orientation & Information

The epicenter of Kennebunkport activity is Dock Sq, just over the bridge on the east side of the Kennebunk River. South of Dock Sq is the historic district, with many fine old mansions, some of which are now inns. Ocean Ave heads south from Dock Sq to the sea, then northeast to Walkers Point and the Bush compound (the vacation residence of

the elder former president George Bush). Continue northeast on Ocean Ave to reach Cape Porpoise, a charming hamlet.

Kennebunk Lower Village lies on the west side of the Kennebunk River Bridge.

Kennebunkport Information & Hospitality Center (☎ 207-967-8600; www.visitthekennebunks.com; Union Sq, Kennebunkport; ☽ 9am-9pm Sat & Sun mid-May–mid-Oct, 10am-9pm Mon-Fri Jun-Sep) This center has helpful staff who might be able to find you accommodations.

Kennebunk-Kennebunkport Chamber of Commerce Information Center (☎ 207-967-0857; www .visitthekennebunks.com; 17 Western Ave/ME 9, Kennebunk Lower Village; ☽ 9am-5pm Mon-Fri, 11am-3pm Sat & Sun Jun-Aug, 9am-5pm Mon-Sat Sep & Oct, 9am-5pm Mon-Fri Nov-May) This center occupies the yellow building adjacent to a gas station.

Sights & Activities

SEASHORE TROLLEY MUSEUM

Trolleys, the light-rail systems that provided most urban transportation a century ago, are the focus of this **museum** (☎ 207-967-2712; www .trolleymuseum.org; 195 Log Cabin Rd, Kennebunkport; adult/child $8/5.50; ☽ 10am-5pm daily Jun-Sep, Sat & Sun May & Oct). There are over 250 streetcars (including one named Desire), as well as antique buses and public transit paraphernalia. Head north on North St from Dock Sq to reach Log Cabin Rd.

BEACHES

Kennebunkport proper has only one beach, **Colony Beach**, which is dominated by the Colony Hotel. But Beach Ave and Sea Rd (west of Kennebunk River and then south of Kennebunk Lower Village) lead to three good public beaches: **Gooch's Beach**, **Middle Beach** and **Mother's Beach**, known collectively as **Kennebunk Beach**. Beach parking permits cost $10 daily, $20 weekly and $50 seasonally.

BIKING & KAYAKING

To pedal the back roads outside of town, stop by **Cape-able Bike Shop** (☎ 207-967-4382; www.cape ablebikes.com; 83 Arundel Rd, Kennebunkport; bike per half/full day $17/22; ☽ 9am-6pm Mon-Sat, 8am-3pm Sun Apr-Oct), an outfit that rents cruisers and mountain bikes, in adult and child sizes. New in 2007, Cape-able also offers kayak tours, from half-day adventures ($60) to two-hour full-moon paddles ($40). If you're just renting a bike, stop in their handily located **Outpost** (Western Ave, Kennebunk Lower Village; Jun–mid-Sep), across the bridge from Dock Sq.

MAINE

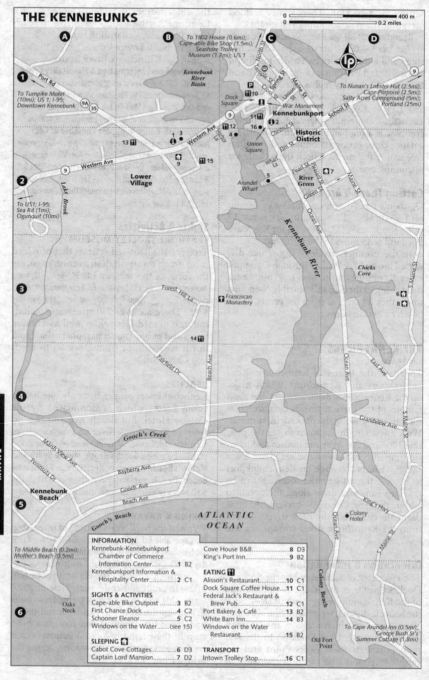

THE KENNEBUNKS

0 ———————— 400 m
0 ———————— 0.2 miles

To 1802 House (0.6mi);
Cape-able Bike Shop (1.5mi);
Seashore Trolley
Museum (1.7mi); US 1

Port Rd

To Turnpike Motel
(10mi); US 1; I-95;
Downtown Kennebunk

Kennebunk
River
Basin

Dock
Square

War Monument

Kennebunkport

To Nunan's Lobster Hut (2.5mi);
Cape Porpoise (2.5mi);
Salty Acres Campground (5mi);
Portland (25mi)

Western Ave

Union
Square

Historic
District

Western Ave

Lower
Village

To US1; I-95;
Sea Rd (1mi);
Ogunquit (10mi)

Lake Brook

Arundel
Wharf

River
Green

Kennebunk River

Chicks
Cove

Forest Hill La

Franciscan
Monastery

Fairfield Dr

Beach Ave

Grandview Ave

Gooch's Creek

Marsh View Ave

Bayberry Ave

MAINE

Peninsula Dr

Gooch Ave

Beach Ave

Kennebunk
Beach

Gooch's Beach

ATLANTIC
OCEAN

King's Hwy

Colony
Hotel

Ocean Ave

Colony Beach

To Middle Beach (0.2mi);
Mother's Beach (0.5mi)

Oaks
Neck

Old Fort
Point

To Cape Arundel Inn (0.5mi);
George Bush Sr's
Summer Cottage (1.8mi)

INFORMATION
Kennebunk-Kennebunkport
  Chamber of Commerce
  Information Center............1 B2
Kennebunkport Information &
  Hospitality Center............2 C1

SIGHTS & ACTIVITIES
Cape-able Bike Outpost 3 B2
First Chance Dock..................4 C2
Schooner Eleanor...................5 C2
Windows on the Water.......(see 15)

SLEEPING
Cabot Cove Cottages...........6 D3
Captain Lord Mansion............7 D2

Cove House B&B..................8 D3
King's Port Inn......................9 B2

EATING
Alisson's Restaurant..............10 C1
Dock Square Coffee House....11 C1
Federal Jack's Restaurant &
  Brew Pub........................12 C1
Port Bakery & Café.............13 B2
White Barn Inn..................14 B3
Windows on the Water
  Restaurant......................15 B2

TRANSPORT
Intown Trolley Stop............16 C1

CRUISES

Schooner Eleanor (☎ 207-967-8809; Arundel Wharf, Kennebunkport; cruises $40) is a splendid 55ft schooner offering two-hour sails off Kennebunkport (season and weather dependent). Stop by Arundel Wharf for schedules and reservations.

First Chance (207-967-5507, 800-767-2628; www .firstchancewhalewatch.com; 4 Western Ave, Kennebunk; cruises adult/child $18/12; ☻ May-Oct) offers a 1½-hour lobster-boat cruise departing every two hours from 10am to 6pm as well as a four-hour whale-watching voyage that departs at 9am and 2:30pm (adult/child $40/25). Board the vessels in Kennebunk Lower Village, next to the Kennebunk River Bridge.

Courses

Several times per year, **Windows on the Water** (☎ 207-967-3313; www.windowsonthewater.com; 12 Chase Hill Rd, Kennebunkport), one of Kennebunkport's best restaurants (p472), offers a three-course cooking demonstration (per person $50) hosted by chef John Hughes.

Sleeping

Although accommodations in Kennebunkport are not cheap, the quality is high, with some beautiful guesthouses around town.

BUDGET

Salty Acres Campground (☎ 207-967-2483; www .saltyacrescampground.com; ME 9, Kennebunkport; sites $25-38; ☻ mid-May–mid-Oct) This campground, 5 miles northeast of Kennebunkport near Cape Porpoise, has 225 tent and trailer sites, many with electricity and water hook-ups.

Turnpike Motel (☎ 207-467-8222; www.turnpikemo tel.com; 77 Old Alewife Rd, Kennebunkport; r $79-119, off-season $49-69) This family run, two-story motel has 24 reasonably priced rooms, all of which have been renovated recently. Rooms are simple but bright, with a few cheery touches and modern bathrooms.

MIDRANGE

King's Port Inn (☎ 207-967-4340; www.visitkennebunk port.com; Western Ave, Kennebunkport; r with breakfast $149-249, off- season $99-139; wi-fi) A short stroll to the center of town, the King's Port Inn has 33 spacious, nicely maintained rooms designed in an elegant country style. The best rooms have four-post beds, fireplaces and two-person Jacuzzi tubs.

Cove House B&B (☎ 207-967-3704; www.covehouse .com; 11 S Maine St, Kennebunkport; r with breakfast $150) A small but comfortable inn overlooking Chick's Cove on the Kennebunk River, this B&B has spacious rooms with wood floors, Oriental carpets and antique furnishings.

1802 House (☎ 207-967-5632; www.1802inn.com; 15 Locke St, Kennebunkport; r with breakfast $189-259, off-season $109-169; wi-fi) In a lovely neighborhood just north of Dock Sq, the 1802 House has six attractive rooms amid a restored 19th-century farmhouse. Rooms have either brass or four-post beds, and several rooms have fireplaces or two-person Jacuzzi tubs. The decor throughout this friendly place aims for country charm.

Cabot Cove Cottages (☎ 207-967-5424, 800-962-5424; www.cabotcovecottages.com; 7 S Maine St, Kennebunkport; r with breakfast $175-325; ☻ late May–mid-Oct; wi-fi) In an idyllic setting overlooking the Kennebunk River, these 16 cottages are a splendid alternative to a hotel or B&B. Each cottage is handsomely designed with modern furnishings, a full kitchen and loads of amenities. Kayaks are available for paddling along the serene tidal cove.

TOP END

Cape Arundel Inn (☎ 207-967-2125; www.capearundelinn .com; 208 Ocean Ave, Kennebunkport; r with breakfast $295-375, off-season $125-355; ☻ Mar-Jan) Magnificently set on the ocean, this grand summer cottage has lovely, sunny rooms, most with porches and all but one boasting unobstructed ocean views. Gardens surround the 19th-century inn, and an excellent restaurant adds to its pedigree.

Captain Lord Mansion (☎ 207-967-3141; www.cap tainlord.com; 6 Pleasant St, Kennebunkport; r with breakfast $257-475, off-season $116-375) If money is no object, this former sea captain's home demands your attention. The meticulously restored rooms are more lavish than when lived in by its original occupants. You'll get fireplaces in all the rooms, classical antique furnishings, oil paintings decorating the walls and even heated bathroom tiles.

Eating

BUDGET

Dock Square Coffee House (☎ 207-967-4422; 18 Dock Sq, Kennebunkport; pastries $2-4; ☻ 7:30am-5pm Apr, May & Sep-Dec, 7:30am-10pm Jul & Aug) This tiny café is a cozy spot for coffee, tea and pastries.

Port Bakery & Café (☎ 207-967-2263; cnr Port Rd & Western Ave, Kennebunkport; ☻ 7am-6pm; ☐ wi-fi) For

MAINE

delicious, inexpensive breakfasts, this casual place is hard to beat. Daily specials include French toast piled high with blueberries, vegetarian eggs benedict and satisfying omelettes. The sunny patio is a peaceful refuge.

Alisson's Restaurant (☎ 207-967-4841; 5 Dock Sq, Kennebunkport; meals $8-14; ◷ lunch & dinner) Centrally located, Alisson's is a long-running favorite for its nicely prepared meals at good prices. You'll find traditional American and New England fare: lobster rolls, crab cakes, sandwiches, burgers and steaks.

MIDRANGE

Federal Jack's Restaurant & Brew Pub (☎ 207-967-4322; 8 Western Ave, Kennebunkport; meals $12-22; ◷ lunch & dinner) Above the Kennebunkport Brewing Co, Federal Jack's serves satisfying bistro fare, including crab-stuffed haddock, wood-roasted salmon, barbecue ribs and a range of salads, sandwiches and pizzas. Hand-crafted microbrews go nicely with the food. Free brewery tours are offered by appointment through the coffee shop downstairs.

our pick **Nunan's Lobster Hut** (☎ 207-967-4362; 9 Mills Rd, Cape Porpoise; meals $14-28; ◷ dinner) Four miles east of Kennebunkport, Nunan's cooks up some ridiculously good lobsters. Although there are a few other culinary distractions – clam chowder, blueberry pie – no one comes here for anything other than those succulent crustaceans. It's set in a long wooden shack, with black-and-white fishing photos and nautical instruments setting the stage.

TOP END

Windows on the Water Restaurant (☎ 207-967-3313; www.windowsonthewater.com; 12 Chase Hill Rd, Kennebunkport; meals $24-34; ◷ lunch Tue-Sat, dinner Tue-Sun) Just south of the bridge, this award-winning restaurant offers creative, largely organic seasonal fare. Coriander seared ahi tuna, wild shrimp and lobster ravioli and parmesan crusted rack of lamb are a few of the recent temptations offered in the attractive riverside spot.

White Barn Inn (☎ 207-967-2321; www.whitebarninn.com; 37 Beach Ave, Kennebunkport; 4-course meal $100-115; ◷ dinner) Kennebunkport's most renowned restaurant boasts country-elegant decor and fantastic New American cuisine. The menu changes weekly and features local seafood complemented by locally grown herbs, fruits and vegetables and California greens. Make reservations, and be sure to dress the part.

Getting There & Around

The Kennebunks lie halfway between Portsmouth, NH, and Portland, ME (28 miles from each city), just off I-95 on ME 9. Ogunquit is 11 miles to the southwest.

The **Intown Trolley** (☎ 207-967-3686; www.intown trolley.com; Ocean Ave; one-day pass adult/child $13/6; ◷ hourly 10am-5pm Jul & Aug, 10am-4pm spring & fall) circulates through Kennebunkport, with stops at Gooch's Beach, Middle Beach and Mother's Beach (see p469). You can ride the entire route on a 45-minute narrated tour, or hop on and off at designated stops, including along Ocean Ave.

OLD ORCHARD BEACH
pop 9700

This quintessential; New England beach playground is saturated with lights, music and noise. Skimpily clad crowds of fun-loving sun worshippers make the rounds of fast-food emporiums, mechanical amusements and gimcrack shops selling trinkets. Palace Playland, on the beach at the very center of town, is a fitting symbol, with its carousel, Ferris wheel, children's rides, fried-clam and pizza stands, and T-shirt and souvenir shops.

Old Orchard Beach has long been a favorite summer resort of Québécois, who flock south in July and August. Many signs are in French as well as English, to accommodate the Canadians.

Dozens of little motels and guesthouses line the beaches to the north and south of the town center, and all are full from late June to early September. Before and after that, Old Orchard beach slumbers.

PORTLAND

pop 63,100

Maine's biggest city is small and laid-back, with a lively waterfront, impressive late 19th-century architecture and a burgeoning restaurant and gallery scene. Its vibrant downtown near the old port is lined with handsomely restored brick buildings, where colorful cafés, shops and bars gather Maine's most bohemian crowd. Portland also has historic Victorian-filled neighborhoods to explore, a highly respected art museum and abundant green space with superb city and harbor views.

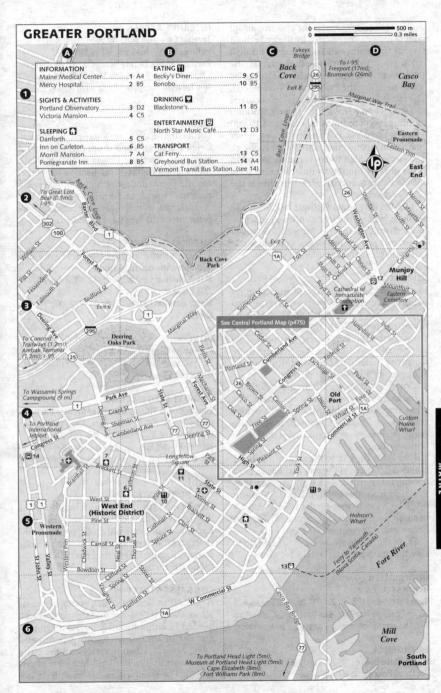

GREATER PORTLAND

0	500 m
0	0.3 miles

INFORMATION
Maine Medical Center............1 A4
Mercy Hospital.....................2 B5

SIGHTS & ACTIVITIES
Portland Observatory.............3 D2
Victoria Mansion...................4 C5

SLEEPING 🏠
Danforth..............................5 C5
Inn on Carleton....................6 B5
Morrill Mansion....................7 A4
Pomegranate Inn...................8 B5

EATING 🍴
Becky's Diner.......................9 C5
Bonobo..............................10 B5

DRINKING 🍷
Blackstone's........................11 B5

ENTERTAINMENT 🎭
North Star Music Café...........12 D3

TRANSPORT
Cat Ferry............................13 C5
Greyhound Bus Station.........14 A4
Vermont Transit Bus Station..(see 14)

Tukeys Bridge

Back Cove

To I-95; Freeport (17mi); Brunswick (26mi)

Casco Bay

Exit 8

Marginal Way Trail

Eastern Promenade

Eastern Prom

East End

Munjoy Hill

Mountfort Eastern Cemetery

Cathedral of Immaculate Conception

To Great Lost Bear (0.1mi); I-95

Back Cove Loop

Baxter Blvd

William St

Pitt St

Fessenden St

Falmouth St

Forest Ave

Bedford St

Exit 6

Back Cove Park

Exit 7

Fox St

Anderson St

Greenleaf St

Smith St

Oxford St

Washington Ave

Sheridan St

Merrill St

Lafayette St

North St

Congress St

To Concord Trailways (1.2mi); Amtrak Terminal (1.2mi); I-95

Deering Oaks Park

Marginal Way

Somerset St

Pearl St

Hampshire St

India St

See Central Portland Map (p475)

To Wassamki Springs Campground (5 mi)

Park Ave

Grant St

Sherman St

Deering Ave

State St

Forest Ave

Mechanic St

Parris St

Cedar St

Cumberland Ave

Portland St

Brown St

Casco St

Oak St

Free St

Spring St

Congress St

Center St

Exchange St

Federal St

Pearl St

Fore St

Wharf St

India St

Union St

Old Port

Custom House Wharf

To Portland International Jetport

Congress St

Cumberland Ave

Deering St

Longfellow Square

Park St

State St

Brackett St

High St

Spring St

Pleasant St

York St

Commercial St

West St

West End (Historic District)

Pine St

Bramhall St

Brackett St

Pine St

Cushman St

Clark St

Hobson's Wharf

Western Promenade

Chadwick St

Carroll St

Neal St

Thomas St

Spruce St

State St

Vaughan St

Western Prom

Bowdoin St

Clifford St

Spring St

Danforth St

W Commercial St

Ferry to Yarmouth (Nova Scotia, Canada)

Fore River

Casco Bay Bridge

Mill Cove

South Portland

St John St

Valley St

To Portland Head Light (5mi); Museum at Portland Head Light (5mi); Cape Elizabeth (8mi); Fort Williams Park (8mi)

MAINE

One of the city's icons is the phoenix, an apt symbol for a city devastated by fire and rebuilt several times since its founding by English colonists in 1632 (prior to their arrival, the settlement was known as Machigonne or 'great neck' by the indigenous Wabanaki). The latest and worst conflagration occurred in 1866, when many of the town's wooden buildings were reduced to ashes and 10,000 were left homeless. Portlanders vowed 'never again,' and rebuilt their city using redbrick and stone – which today is the backdrop to some of New England's most atmospheric cobbled streets and squares, this side of the Charles River.

The **Old Port Street Festival**, begun in the 1970s, is held on the first Sunday in June; it's marked by outdoor performances (folk, world music, rock) on various stages, a parade, kiddy rides and plenty of street food.

Orientation

Portland is set on a ridge of hills along a peninsula surrounded by Fore River, Casco Bay and Back Cove. Portland Harbor is its historical heart, with the charming back streets of the Old Port district behind it. Two promenades (well-heeled Western and more workaday Eastern) frame downtown Portland at opposite ends of the peninsula.

Congress St is the main thoroughfare through downtown, passing Portland's most imposing buildings: city hall, banks, churches and hotels. Commercial St, where many businesses are located, runs the length of the harbor.

I-95 skirts the city to the west, while I-295 makes a detour into the city and hooks back up with I-95 north of Back Cove. Approaching Portland from the south, follow I-95 to exit 6A; take I-295 to exit 4; take US 1 to US 1A heading north (aka Commercial St). Stay on Commercial St right into the Old Port.

From the north, follow I-295 to exit 7, then take the Franklin Arterial (US 1A south).

Information

BOOKSTORES
Books Etc (Map p475; ☎ 207-774-0626; 38 Exchange St; ☼ 9am-6pm Mon-Wed, 9am-9pm Thu-Sat, noon-6pm Sun) This atmospheric store is a great place for browsing.

EMERGENCY
Maine State Police (☎ 207-624-7076)
Portland Police (☎ 207-874-8300)

INTERNET ACCESS
JavaNet Café (Map p475; ☎ 207-773-2469; 37 Exchange St; ☼ 7am-10pm; ▣ wi-fi)
Portland Public Library (Map p475; ☎ 207-766-5540; 5 Monument Sq; ☼ 9am-6pm Mon, Wed & Fri, noon-9pm Tue & Thu, 9am-5pm Sat; ▣ wi-fi) Internet access is free here.

MEDIA
For a glossy look at seasonal events and galleries, restaurants and shopping, pick up the bimonthly *Portland* magazine (often free at information centers), published every other month. For a rundown on upcoming events, pick up Thursday's edition of the *Portland Press Herald*, with a handy entertainment supplement, or the free weekly *Phoenix*.

MEDICAL SERVICES
The city's major medical facilities have emergency rooms open 24 hours.
Maine Medical Center (Map p473; ☎ 207-662-0111; 22 Bramhall St)
Mercy Hospital (Map p473; ☎ 207-879-3000; 144 State St)

POST
Post office (Map p475; ☎ 800-275-8777; 400 Congress St; ☼ 7:30am-7pm Mon-Fri, 7:30am-5pm Sat) The most central post office.

TOURIST INFORMATION
Convention & Visitors Bureau of Greater Portland (Map p475; ☎ 207-772-5800; www.visitportland.com; 245 Commercial St; ☼ 8am-5pm Mon-Fri, 10am-3pm Sat mid-Oct–mid-May, 8am-5pm Mon-Fri, 10am-5pm Sat mid-May–mid-Oct)

Sights
OLD PORT DISTRICT
Handsome 19th-century brick buildings line the streets of the Old Port (Map p475), with Portland's most enticing shops, pubs and restaurants located within this five-square-block district. By night, flickering gas lanterns add to the atmosphere.

CONGRESS STREET
A once rather derelict stretch of city, Congress Street (Map p475) has undergone a much-needed facelift and today boasts a growing number of antique shops, art galleries and cafés, as well as two libraries and the city's best museum, the Portland Museum of Art (p476). The rough edges, however, have not

CENTRAL PORTLAND

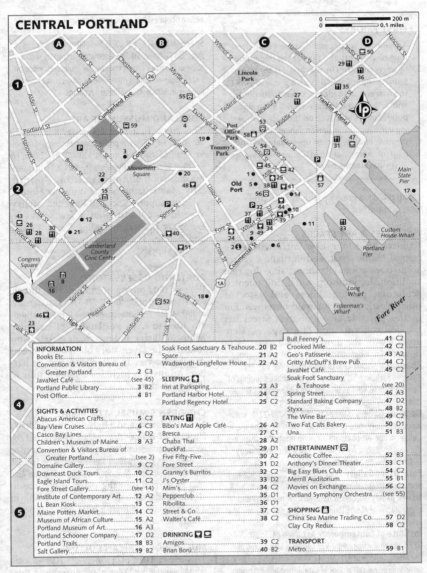

0 — 200 m
0 — 0.1 miles

MAINE

been totally effaced, so this place still has some character.

WEST END

Portland's loveliest neighborhood is the West End (Map p473), a hillside enclave of brick townhouses, elegant gardens and stately mansions, some of which date from the neighborhood's founding in 1836. This is a fairly mixed community along the gay-straight, young-elderly divide, with pockets of smaller, working class families living amid their higher mortgage–paying neighbors. In addition to cultural diversity, travelers will find some of Portland's best B&Bs here. They'll also find the scenic **Western Promenade**

FIRST FRIDAYS

As far as art is concerned, there's no better time to visit Portland than at the beginning of each month. On the first Friday (from 5pm to 8pm), you'll find a lively downtown scene as galleries open their doors and artists exhibit their works in studios, public spaces and even on the back of moving vehicles. Street performances add to the creative energy. For an up-to-date list and map of participating galleries visit www.firstfridayartwalk.com.

(Map p473), a grassy pathway with fine views over the harbor.

GALLERIES & ART SPACES

Painters have long been attracted to the rugged Maine coast, and Portland's gallery scene does a fine job showcasing this rich tradition. In addition, you'll find talented sculptors, photographers and assorted other plastic artists unafraid of reinvention in this portside city. Congress Street has the best concentration of art spaces. Here are a few of the more than 30 galleries in downtown Portland.

Abacus American Crafts (Map p475; ☎ 207-772-4880; 44 Exchange St) Displays the dreamlike paintings of Dan Merriam as well as brilliant hand-blown glass lamps, colorful weavings and finely crafted jewelry.

Domaine Gallery (Map p475; ☎ 207-772-2270; www.domainegallery.com; 223 Commercial St) Domaine specializes in fine-art photography, with prints that feature the rugged geography of Maine. You'll also find jewelry crafted by Maine artisans.

Fore Street Gallery (Map p475; ☎ 207-874-8084; www.forestreetgallery.com; 372 Fore St) This well-located gallery displays watercolors, oil paintings and photographs of Maine landscapes, all created by regional artists.

Institute of Contemporary Art (Map p475; ☎ 207-879-5792; www.meca.edu; 522 Congress St) Located at the Maine College of Art (MECA), this progressive gallery hosts impressive exhibitions of established and emerging artists in MECA's Porteous Building location.

Maine Potters Market (Map p475; ☎ 207-774-1633; www.mainepottersmarket.com; 376 Fore St) This cooperatively owned gallery features the work of 15 different ceramicists.

Salt Gallery (Map p475; ☎ 207-761-0660; www.salt.edu; 110 Exchange St) The arm of a documentary institute that isn't afraid of multimedia exhibitions. Visitors can peruse photo essays, audio recordings and works in prose and poetry.

Space (Map p475; ☎ 207-828-5600; www.space538.org; 538 Congress St) This alternative arts space shows some of Portland's most imaginative sculptures, video art, installations and other mixed-media projects. It also hosts live music, film fests and literary readings.

PORTLAND MUSEUM OF ART

The city's first-rate **art museum** (Map p475; ☎ 207-775-6148; www.portlandmuseum.org; 7 Congress Sq; adult/child/senior & student $10/4/8; free 5-9pm Fri; ⊙ 10am-5pm Tue-Sun, 10am-9pm Fri) has an outstanding collection of American artists – particularly Maine painters like Winslow Homer, Edward Hopper, Rockwell Kent and Andrew Wyeth. You'll also find a few works by European masters, including Degas, Picasso and Renoir. The temporary exhibitions are usually superb.

PORTLAND OBSERVATORY

Built in 1807 on top of Munjoy Hill, this **observatory** (Map p473; ☎ 207-774-5561; 138 Congress St; adult/child $6/4; ⊙ 10am-5pm Jun–early Oct) was originally used to warn Portlanders of incoming fishing, military and merchant vessels. Now restored, the seven-story observatory boasts panoramic views of Portland and its harbor. Admission includes a guided tour of the observatory.

CHILDREN'S MUSEUM OF MAINE

Near Congress and High Sts, the **Children's Museum of Maine** (Map p475; ☎ 207-828-1234; www.childrensmuseumofme.org; 142 Free St; admission $7, free 5-8pm Fri; ⊙ 10am-5pm Tue-Sat, noon-5pm Sun Sep-May, 10am-5pm Mon-Sat, noon-5pm Sun Jun-Aug; ⊛) gives children the place and space to climb inside an oak tree's hollow trunk in a squirrel suit or float a boat down a model Maine stream.

MUSEUM OF AFRICAN CULTURE

This **museum** (Map p475; ☎ 207-871-7188; www.museumafricanculture.org; 13 Brown St) houses over 1500 pieces of art and craftwork from sub-Saharan Africa, with a particularly impressive collection of ceremonial masks. Traditional pottery, ivory flutes and nicely executed changing exhibitions add to the portfolio. At the time of research the museum was temporarily closed in preparation for a move to its new Brown Street location.

HISTORIC BUILDINGS

Victoria Mansion (Morse-Libby House; Map p473; ☎ 207-772-4841; www.victoriamansion.org; 109 Danforth St; adult/child $10/3; 🕑 10am-4pm Tue-Sat, 1-5pm Sun late May–early Oct), just a few blocks southeast of the art museum, is an outstanding Italianate palace dating back to 1860. Inside, it's decorated sumptuously with rich furniture, frescoes, paintings, carpets, gilt and exotic woods and stone. Admission includes a 45-minute guided tour.

Wadsworth-Longfellow House (Map p475; ☎ 207-879-0427; www.mainehistory.com; 489 Congress St; adult/child/student $7/3/6; 🕑 10am-5pm Mon-Sat, noon-5pm Sun late May–late Oct), a beautifully sited brick homestead with lush gardens, was built in 1788 in the Federal style. The builder, General Peleg Wadsworth, was a hero in the Revolutionary War and the grandfather of poet Henry Wadsworth Longfellow. The poet grew up here, and the house's furnishings recall his 19th-century surroundings.

FORT WILLIAMS PARK & PORTLAND HEAD LIGHT

Head 4 miles southeast from Portland across the bay via the Casco Bay Bridge to Cape Elizabeth, where you'll find **Fort Williams Park** (off Map p473). It's worth visiting simply for the panoramas and picnic possibilities. Fortification of Portland Head began in 1873, but the installation was not dubbed Fort Williams until 1899. These days, WWII bunkers and gun emplacements (a German U-boat was spotted in Casco Bay in 1942) still dot the rolling lawns of the park. Strange as it may seem, the fort actively guarded the entrance to Casco Bay until 1964.

Right next to the park stands **Portland Head Light** (off Map p473), the oldest of Maine's 52 functioning lighthouses. It was commissioned by President George Washington in 1791 and staffed until 1989, when machines took over. The keeper's house has been passed into service as the **Museum at Portland Head Light** (off Map p473; ☎ 207-799-2661; www.portlandheadlight.com; 1000 Shore Rd; adult/child $2/1; 🕑 10am-4pm Jun-Oct, 10am-4pm Sat & Sun Apr-May & Nov–mid-Dec), which traces the maritime and military history of the region.

Activities

PORTLAND TRAILS

Thanks to the hard work of the conservation organization **Portland Trails** (Map p475; ☎ 207-775-2411; www.trails.org; 305 Commercial St), there are more than 30 miles of multi-use trails sprinkled about the Greater Portland area, with another 20 miles on the horizon. One of the most popular paths is the 3.5-mile **Back Cove Loop** (Map p473), which provides excellent water and city views northwest of the city center. This trail connects to the **Eastern Promenade** (Map p473), a 2.1-mile paved waterfront path that follows a former railway, just east of East End. For a complete rundown of trails (26 in all), with maps, visit the Portland Trails website or purchase their *Portland Trails Map & Guide* ($4.95).

SEA KAYAKING

Casco Bay Lines (Map p475; ☎ 207-774-7871; www.cascobaylines.com; 56 Commercial St; adult/child $7.25/3.60) has boats that depart hourly in the summer for a 15-minute cruise to Peaks Island. Once there, you can hook up with **Maine Island Kayak Company** (☎ 207-766-2373, 800-796-2373; www.maineislandkayak.com; 70 Luther St, Peaks Island; kayak tours half/full day $65/110; 🕑 May-Nov), a reputable outfitter that offers fine tours exploring this rocky coastline.

LL Bean (☎ 207-400-4814; www.llbean.com/ods; kiosk 180 Commercial St; adult/child $29/19; daily Jul-Aug, Sat & Sun Sep) offers 90-minute kayak tours around the bay; tours launch from the port. Sign up at their kiosk next to the Portland Lobster Company.

FOOT MASSAGES

Although you probably didn't come to Portland for a foot massage, the **Soakology Foot Sanctuary & Teahouse** (Map p475; ☎ 207-879-7625; www.soakology.com; 30 City Center; 🕑 11am-7pm Mon-Wed, 11am-9pm Thu-Sat, 11am-5pm Sun) is a great place to treat your aching gams. The first floor houses an elegant teahouse, with a salon downstairs. There are an extensive array of foot soaks ($20 to $50), scrubs, massages ($26 to $30 for 20 minutes) and reflexology treatments.

Tours

Bay View Cruises (Map p475; ☎ 207-761-0496; www.bayviewcruises-me.com; Fisherman's Wharf, 184 Commercial St; adult/child $12/8; 🕑 daily mid-Jun–Sep, Sat & Sun May–mid-Jun) Offers four different narrated harbor trips six times daily.

Casco Bay Lines (Map p475; ☎ 207-774-7871; www.cascobaylines.com; 56 Commercial St; adult $7.25-11, child $3.60-5.50) This outfit cruises the Casco Bay islands delivering mail, freight and visitors. It also offers cruises to

Bailey Island (adult/child $18.50/8.50. See p488 for more information.

Downeast Duck Tours (Map p475; ☎ 207-774-3825; www.downeastducktours.com; 177 Commercial St; adult/child $22/17; ☒ mid-May–mid-Oct; ☒) This 65-minute amphibious bus tour putters through the Old Port, before plunging into the bay for a waterside look at the port.

Eagle Island Tours (Map p475; ☎ 207-774-6498; www.eagleislandtours.com; Long Wharf, 170 Commercial St; adult/child $14/9; ☒ Jun-Sep) Runs sightseeing trips out to Eagle Island and Portland Head Light (p477).

Portland Schooner Company (Map p475; ☎ 207-766-2500; www.portlandschooner.com; Maine State Pier, Commercial St; adult/child $30/12; ☒ Jun-Aug) Offers tours aboard an elegant, early-20th-century schooner. In addition to two-hour sails, you can book overnight tours ($225 per person, including dinner and breakfast).

WALKING TOURS

Greater Portland Landmarks (☎ 207-774-5561; adult/child $7/free; ☒ Mon-Sat Jun–mid-Oct) offers 1½-hour walking tours of the city. It's a sprightly trip that'll provide you with an interesting overview of the city's history as you make your way around the Old Port, Eastern and Western Promenades, and the Portland Head Light. Trips depart at 10:30am in front of the **Convention & Visitors Bureau of Greater Portland** (Map p475; ☎ 207-772-5800; www.visitportland.com; 245 Commercial St). They also offer a tour of the historic Eastern Cemetery and of Portland's 19th-century homes (each offered once a week).

Sleeping

Portland has a healthy selection of midrange and upscale B&Bs, though very little at the budget end. The most idyllic accommodations are in the old townhouses and grand Victorians in the West End, a quiet residential neighborhood near the Western Promenade.

Wassamki Springs (Map p473; ☎ 207-839-4276; www.wassamkisprings.com; 56 Saco St, Scarborough; sites from $41, off-season from $23; ☒ wi-fi) The closest campsite to Portland lies about 9 miles west of the center, and offers shaded, not terribly private campsites, some of which overlook a pretty lake (making for a refreshing swim on hot days). To get there, take Park avenue west, which turns into ME 22, and turn right on Saco St.

Danforth (Map p473; ☎ 207-879-8755; www.danforthmaine.com; 163 Danforth St; r $100-150, off-season $85-115; ☒) Inside an elegant, ivy-covered brick building, the Danforth has seven cozy guestrooms, most of which have queen-sized beds, fireplaces and period furnishings. This is excellent value, and guests may enjoy access to the wood-paneled billiards room and the gardens.

Inn on Carleton (Map p473; ☎ 207-775-1910; www.innoncarleton.com; 46 Carleton St; r with breakfast $140-235, off-season $105-190) Inside a restored 1869 Victorian, this inn has six grandiose rooms, all with high ceilings and large windows, allowing ample light into the antique-filled rooms (the carved wooden headboards in several rooms are astounding). The English garden in back is a particularly peaceful setting in which to unwind.

Inn at Parkspring (Map p475; ☎ 207-774-1059; 800-437-8511; www.innatparkspring.com; 135 Spring St; r with breakfast $150-175, off-season $99-165; ☒) Set in an 1835 brick townhouse, the Inn at Parkspring is another West End charmer, with six comfortably decorated rooms. Four of the rooms are carpeted with modern furnishings, while two have a more classic look with hardwood floors and antique furniture.

our pick **Morrill Mansion** (Map p473; ☎ 207-774-6900; www.morrillmansion.com; 249 Vaughan St; r from $159) On the northern edge of the West End, Morrill Mansion is set in a historic 19th-century townhouse. Rooms here have wood floors, elegant bed frames and a trim, classic look. There's no chintz, floral excess or overly worn furnishings. The whole house is spotlessly maintained. The main drawback is that street noise can be a slight problem in some of the rooms, and several rooms are rather small. To be assured ample space, book the two-room Morrill suite, which also has a Jacuzzi bathtub.

Pomegranate Inn (Map p473; ☎ 207-772-1006; 800-356-0408; www.pomegranateinn.com; 49 Neal St; r with breakfast $175-265, off-season $95-165; ☒) Few innkeepers can mix modern art with antiques as skillfully as Isabel Smiles has done here. An antiques dealer and interior designer, Smiles' eclectic taste runs the gamut from faux marble columns in the living room to hand-painted walls and century-old dressers in the eight guest rooms. Large contemporary sculptures and collages are displayed in the hallways. Remarkably, they all seem to fit together.

Portland Harbor Hotel (Map p475; ☎ 207-775-9090; www.portlandharborhotel.com; 468 Fore St; r from $225) This independent hotel has a classically coiffed lobby, with a fireplace surrounded by polished wood furniture. The rooms carry on the classicism, albeit in bright, yellow tones, with elegant wooden bed frames, a striped armchair or divan and modern bathrooms. The windows face Casco Bay, the interior garden or the street. Waterside views are worth the extra cash as they tend to be much quieter than street-fronting rooms.

Portland Regency Hotel (Map p475; ☎ 207-774-4200; www.theregency.com; 20 Milk St; r from $250) With an excellent location in the heart of the Old Port, this first-rate hotel is set in the city's former armory. The large 19th-century red-brick building has classically designed rooms, an excellent spa and a host of enticing amenities to sweeten the deal.

Eating

Portland has an excellent cuisine scene, incorporating the riches from both sea and land in atmospheric dining rooms in the Old Port. The best concentration of restaurants is along tiny pedestrian Wharf Street, as well as nearby Middle, Exchange and Fore Streets. There are a growing number of restaurants on Monument Square (with outdoor tables in summertime).

BUDGET

Becky's Diner (Map p473; ☎ 207-773-7070; 390 Commercial St; meals $7-17; 4am-9pm) If you want to rub elbows with working fisherfolk, opt for breakfast or lunch at this waterfront diner. Grab a seat at the counter and let the chowing begin.

Bonobo (Map p473; ☎ 207-347-8267; 46 Pine St; slice/pizza from $2.50/12; lunch & dinner) On a pleasant residential street in the West End, Bonobo is a neighborhood favorite for its delicious thin-crust pizzas. You can eat there, or order it to go – and enjoy it on the nearby Western Promenade.

Granny's Burritos (Map p475; ☎ 207-761-0751; 420 Fore St; burritos $5.50-8; lunch & dinner; **V**) Stop here for a quick, healthy fill-up of Tex-Mex. Vegetarians have options, like the hot tempeh burrito, and Granny's also prepares tasty quesadillas. Head upstairs for local brews and live music on weekends.

DuckFat (Map p475; ☎ 207-774-8080; 43 Middle St; sandwiches $8-9; 11am-8pm Mon-Sat, noon-6pm Sun) DuckFat, an upscale fast-food spot, can't be beat for its warm panini (pressed sandwiches), rich salads, creamy milkshakes and delicious but infamous crispy fries, which are indeed fried in duck fat (do throw in truffle ketchup for fifty cents).

Chaba Thai (Map p475; ☎ 207-253-5311; 21 Forest Ave; meals $10-14; 11am-9pm Mon-Fri, 4-9pm Sat; **V**) A newcomer to Portland, Chaba Thai is a nice alternative to the creative American restaurants blanketing the Old Port. Instead, you'll find here traditional, immaculately prepared Thai dishes served in an Eastern-accented dining room.

MIDRANGE

J's Oyster (Map p475; ☎ 207-772-4828; 5 Portland Pier; dishes $6-20; lunch & dinner) Although it's a total dive, J's Oyster has the cheapest raw oysters in town, and you can enjoy them on the rugged waterside deck outside. If you'd rather not, you're well placed for something same-same but different, with more than a dozen lobster/seafood shacks on either side.

Pepperclub (☎ 207-772-0531; 78 Middle St; meals $12-18; dinner; **V**) Boasting an eclectic menu of world cuisine, this vegetarian-friendly place serves superb dishes like a Middle Eastern mezze plate, Thai lime vegetables with sesame tofu and udon, and mushroom and fresh basil lasagna.

Bibo's Mad Apple Café (Map p475; ☎ 207-774-9698; 23 Forest Ave; meals $16-28; lunch Wed-Fri, dinner Wed-Sat, brunch Sun) Bibo's has brightly painted walls decorated with eclectic artwork that set the stage for first-rate dining at this creative fusion restaurant. Tasty appetizers, good wines and flavorful salads nicely precede mains such as BBQ-rubbed steak, vegetarian pad Thai and grilled shrimp dishes.

Bresca (Map p475; ☎ 207-772-1004; 111 Middle St; meals $18-26; dinner Tue-Sat) New in 2007, Bresca is a charming, jewel-box-sized restaurant (just five tables) serving excellent creative Italian cuisine. Creamy polenta, tender roast meats and rich pasta dishes – followed by tasty gelato – make this a secret favorite in the dining scene.

Mim's (Map p475; ☎ 207347-7478; 205 Commercial St; meals $14-30; lunch & dinner daily, brunch Sun) Mim's receives mixed reviews for its eclectic cuisine, but we include it for its excellent brunch (try the eggs Benedict with crab cakes) and for the unbeatable outdoor seating – both at sidewalk level and on the upstairs patio.

Ribollita (Map p475; ☎ 207-774-2972; 41 Middle St; meals $14-20; dinner) This cozy local favorite serves satisfying Northern Italian cuisine and prides itself on its handmade pastas. Start with the caramelized onion tart and move on to shrimp carbonara. It's a tiny place, with a few tables out front, so be sure to make a reservation.

MAINE

CAFÉ CULTURE

Laid-back coffee shops and heavenly bakeries are an intrinsic part of the Portland experience. Good spots to catch up on the local gossip over cappuccino and pastries include the following.

- **Crooked Mile** (Map p475; ☎ 207-772-8708; 8 Milk St; meals $8-10; ☼ 7:30am-6pm Mon-Fri, 9am-5pm Sat; ☐ wi-fi) Just off the beaten path, this handsome café has excellent coffee and fresh baked goods, along with sandwiches, soups and wraps at lunch. On Saturdays (1pm to 3pm), you can catch live jazz.

- **JavaNet Café** (Map p475; ☎ 207-773-2469; 37 Exchange St; snacks $1.50-3.50; ☼ 7am-10pm; ☐ wi-fi) A cozy hangout for surfing the Net over a steaming cup of chai.

- **Standard Baking Company** (Map p475; ☎ 207-347-5144; 75 Commercial St; pastries $2-3.50; ☼ 7am-5pm) This Old Port favorite has fresh-baked baguettes, plump cinnamon rolls and other delights.

- **Geo's Patisserie** (Map p475; ☎ 207-699-2655; 27 Forest Ave; pastries $2.50; ☼ 7am-6pm Mon-Fri, 8am-5pm Sat; wi-fi) Geo's has a huge selection of temptations – muffins, scones, *pain au chocolat*, croissants, cakes, tortes and more.

- **Two Fat Cats Bakery** (Map p475; ☎ 207-347-5144; 47 India St; snacks $2-3.50; ☼ 9am-5pm Mon-Sat, 10am-4pm Sun) Tiny bakery serving pastries, pies and melt-in-your-mouth chocolate-chip cookies.

- **Soak Foot Sanctuary & Teahouse** (Map p475; ☎ 207-879-7625; 30 City Center; ☼ 11am-7pm Mon-Wed, 11am-9pm Thu-Sat, 11am-5pm Sun) Portland's best teahouse has an excellent selection. For massages, see p477.

Walter's Café (Map p475; ☎ 207-871-9258; 15 Exchange St; meals $11-23; ☼ lunch & dinner) This is one of Portland's best-loved bistros; a narrow storefront dining room with a high ceiling and even higher culinary aspirations. Among the temptations: mouth-watering bouillabaisse, grilled fish tacos and heirloom tomatoes and jumbo shrimp fettuccine.

TOP END

Five Fifty-Five (Map p475; ☎ 207-761-0555; 555 Congress St; meals $16-29; ☼ dinner daily, brunch Sun) One of Portland's best new chefs holds court at this handsome restaurant north of the West End. Plates here are both delicious and imaginative, including blueberry salad, scallop ceviche, smoked trout risotto and a range of desserts, artisanal cheeses and good wines.

Street & Co (Map p475; ☎ 207-775-0887; 33 Wharf St; meals $19-26; ☼ dinner) The menu here might be simple, but the seafood is the freshest in town. You'll find grilled, broiled or Cajun-style fish (tuna, salmon, swordfish), plus steamed or sautéed mussels, clams and calamari. The cramped but congenial dining rooms are usually packed, so reserve in advance.

ourpick Fore Street (Map p475; ☎ 207-775-2717; 288 Fore St; meals $20-31; ☼ dinner) Still one of Portland's best restaurants, award-winning Fore Street has a dining room of airy, exposed-brick and pine-paneling that faces an open kitchen. Owner and chef Sam Hayward has made apple-wood grilling and roasting his forte. The menu changes nightly, and features the best seasonal fruits of the land and sea.

Drinking

After dinner, Wharf Street transforms into one long bar, with a young, easily intoxicated crowd spilling onto the streets. Other places to browse for a drink are along Fore, between Union and Exchange Sts. If you're looking for something more low-key, you may want to avoid the Old Port area.

Bull Feeney's (Map p475; ☎ 207-773-7210; 375 Fore St; ☼ noon-midnight) Despite the mediocre food, Bull Feeney's remains a local favorite for its central location, warm ambience (it spills over two floors, with a crackling fire in one room) and a garrulous crowd. Live bands play Thursday through Saturday.

Great Lost Bear (off Map p473; ☎ 207-772-0300; 540 Forest Ave; ☼ noon-11pm; ☐ wi-fi) Hands down the best place in town for a draft is this cozy wood-and-brick tavern, located 2 miles north of the Old Port. At last count, GLB had over 50 beers on tap, with 15 Maine microbrews, as well as New Hampshire, Vermont and Massachusetts selections. Live music on weekends continues to draw the crowds.

MAINE

Gritty McDuff's Brew Pub (Map p475; ☎ 207-772-2739; www.grittys.com; 396 Fore St) Gritty is an apt description for this down-at-the-heels pub. You'll find a generally raucous crowd drinking excellent beers – Gritty brews their own award-winning ales downstairs.

Una (Map p475; ☎ 207-828-0300; 505 Fore St) Often voted 'best martini bar' by various local publications, Una is a trim and stylish lounge with a decent assortment of wines and a crowd that favors cocktails over beer. Also on hand are tapas, oysters and tasty lighter fare.

Brian Ború (Map p475; ☎ 207-780-1506; 57 Center St) This sometimes raucous Irish pub, between Spring and Fore Sts, is a favorite hangout for the under-30 crowd.

Amigos (Map p475; ☎ 207-772-0772; 9 Dana St; ☯ 5pm-midnight) Amigos is a fun, lively bar with an outdoor patio, a pool table, tasty Mexican fare and a mix of young and old. Good happy hour specials.

The Wine Bar (Map p475; ☎ 207-773-6667; 38 Wharf St; ☯ 5pm-midnight) Although the wine selection isn't great at The Wine Bar, we like the mellow ambience at this second-floor bar. It's a fun little Bohemian place, with black floors, velvet Elvis paintings, exposed brick walls and comfy lounge chairs.

Blackstone's (Map p473; ☎ 207-775-2885; 6 Pine St; ☐ wi-fi) Portland's oldest gay bar is still a fine place for a drink. It hosts a decent happy hour and events throughout the year. Blackstone's also serves bistro fare.

Spring Street (Map p475; ☎ 207-772-5101; 117 Spring St) This handsome gay-friendly new space brings a dash of South Beach to the Portland scene, with polished wood floors, sleek furnishings, a well-coifed crowd and a bartender who can mix a mean margarita.

Styxx (Map p475; ☎ 207-828-0822; www.styxxportland .com; 3 Spring St; admission $3-5; ☯ from 7pm Thu-Mon) Styxx throws consistently good parties, with a huge dance floor, watched over by some of the city's best DJs. There's also a billiards room and a solid lineup of events – drag nights, '80s night and Monday-night football.

Entertainment

LIVE MUSIC

In addition to the Space Gallery (p476) and the places listed in Drinking (opposite), the following venues have live music.

Big Easy Blues Club (Map p475; ☎ 207-871-8817; www.bigeasyportland.com; 55 Market St) This small music club hosts rock, jazz and blues – mostly

local bands – in addition to open-mic hip-hop nights. Most shows start at 8pm.

North Star Music Café (Map p473; ☎ 207-699-2994; www.northstarmusiccafe.com; 225 Congress St; ☯ 7am-10pm Mon-Sat, 8am-4pm Sun) There's a lot going on at this little café and music venue. A packed calendar features live bands, acoustic spoken word, even tango lessons.

Acoustic Coffee (Map p475; ☎ 207-774-0404; 32 Danforth St; ☯ 7am-9pm Mon-Sat, 9am-5pm Sun) This much-loved neighborhood café hosts live folk music as well as poetry readings.

THEATER & CULTURE

Portland Symphony Orchestra (Map p475; ☎ 207-842-0800; www.portlandsymphony.com; Merrill Auditorium, 20 Myrtle St; admission $3-5; ☯ from 7pm Thu-Mon) The Portland Symphony has a solid reputation in these parts; it's been around since 1924 and continues to perform popular classical and pop concerts, often with guest conductors or star performers sharing the limelight.

Anthony's Dinner Theater (Map p475; ☎ 207-221-2267; www.anthonysdinnertheater.com; 151 Middle St; dinner & theater $35; ☯ 7-9pm Fri & Sat) Portland's only dinner theater features five-course dinners (think homemade, family-style cooking) and costumed singing. Hits from Broadway musicals are among the favored repertoire.

Movies on Exchange (Map p475; ☎ 207-772-9600; www.moviesonexchange.com; 10 Exchange St; adult/child $7/5) Catch foreign and independent films at this theater in the heart of the Old Port. Wednesday is bargain day: all seats are five bucks.

Shopping

Going 'antiquing' in Portland largely means trolling Congress (west of Monument Square) and Fore Streets, both of which have their gems.

Clay City Redux (Map p475; ☎ 207-774-3892; 157 Middle St; ☯ 11am-6pm Mon-Sat, noon-5pm Sun) A wonderland of kitsch, Clay City stocks Mexican wrestling masks, 'good boy' morality charts from India, inflatable moose and a range of other toys, trinkets and frivolity that you won't find at your local hardware store.

China Sea Marine Trading Co (Map p475; ☎ 207-773-0081; 324 Fore St; ☯ noon-6pm) This atmospheric shop is packed to the gills with old wooden helms, sextants, telescopes, and all sorts of nautical equipment you might need if you were planning a voyage into the 19th century. You'll also find navy peacoats, mariner books,

MAINE

vintage weaponry, spooky old diving helmets and a character with a parrot on their shoulder (that's the owner).

Getting There & Away
AIR
Portland International Jetport (off Map p473; ☎ 207-774-7301; www.portlandjetport.org) is Maine's largest and most chaotic air terminal. The lines here are dreadful: arrive at least 90 minutes before a flight or risk missing it. Metro buses take you from Continental Airlines' doors to the center of town for $1.25. Take bus 5 and transfer to bus 8 to get to the Old Port.

BOAT
For passenger ferry cruises between Portland and Bailey Island, see p477.

During the summer, the **Cat Ferry** (Map p473; ☎ 207-761-4228; www.catferry.com; 468 Commercial St; adult/child/vehicle from $89/59/149; ⊙ Jun-Sep) departs Portland for Yarmouth, Nova Scotia (Canada) three to four times weekly at 8am, arriving in Canada 5½ hours later. The return trip departs Yarmouth at 4pm four or five times weekly for Portland. You must have proof of citizenship to enter Canada at Yarmouth (a passport and an alien registration or green card for foreign residents).

One important note: the international ferry terminal was deemed to contain dangerous levels of toxins (dozens of molds) in 2005. Although the city of Portland claims the building is now safe, it's well worth investigating the current status of the terminal before you spend any time in this building.

BUS
Vermont Transit (Map p473; ☎ 207-772-6587, 800-231-2222; www.vermonttransit.com; 950 Congress St), in the Greyhound terminal, runs five to six buses daily to and from Boston ($19, two hours), connecting with buses to Hartford, Connecticut ($39, 3¼ hours more) and New York City ($43, 4½ hours more).

Vermont Transit also runs three buses northeastward to Brunswick ($16, 30 minutes), and four up the Maine Turnpike to Lewiston, Augusta ($23, 1½ hours), Waterville and Bangor ($24, 3¼ hours), with one bus continuing to Bar Harbor (four hours from Portland).

Concord Trailways (Map p473; ☎ 207-828-1151, 800-639-3317; www.concordtrailways.com; Thompson Point Connector Rd) shares its terminal with Amtrak

at exit 5A off I-295. It runs 13 nonstop buses daily between Portland and Boston ($21). From Portland, two Concord Trailways buses provide local service to Brunswick ($11), Bath ($12), Wiscasset ($13), Damariscotta ($15), Waldoboro ($16), Rockland ($19), Camden/Rockport ($21), Lincolnville ($21), Belfast ($22), Searsport ($23) and Bangor ($24). The Bangor bus also connects with a Cyr Bus Lines (☎ 800-244-2335; www.cyrbustours.com) bus headed north to Medway, Sherman, Houlton, Presque Isle and Caribou.

CAR & MOTORCYCLE
Coming from the south, take I-95 to I-295 then exit 7 onto Franklin Street, which leads down to the Old Port. To bypass Portland, simply stay on I-95.

TRAIN
The **Amtrak** (☎ 800-872-7245; www.amtrak.com; 100 Thompson Point Connector Rd) *Downeaster,* making tracks between Boston and Portland, runs four to five trains daily in each direction. The trip takes about two hours ($21), making brief stops in New Hampshire at Dover ($12, one hour) and Durham ($14, 1¼ hours).

Getting Around
BUS
Portland's **Metro** (Map p475; ☎ 207-774-0351; www.gpmetrobus.com; one-way $1.25) is the local bus company, with its main terminus, 'Metro Pulse,' housed near Monument Sq.

CAR & MOTORCYCLE
Parking is a challenge downtown; for quick visits, you can usually find a metered space (two hours maximum) in the Old Port, but rarely on Commercial St. A parking garage is an easier bet. We've marked a few on the map.

AROUND PORTLAND
Freeport
pop 8200
Here, nestled amid the natural beauty of Maine's rockbound coast, is a town devoted almost entirely to shopping. More than 100 stores line the town's mile-long Main St (US 1), leading to long traffic jams during the summer. Unlike Kittery, however, Freeport is nicely laid out for walking (there are sidewalks in this town and the parking lots are hidden from sight). This – and the handful of decent

A MAN FOR ALL SEASONS

In 1911 Leon Leonwood Bean invented the Maine Hunting Shoe, now known as the 'Bean Boot.' In addition to the quality and practicality of the boot's construction, it was accompanied by a lifetime offer of replacement or repair if outdoorsmen found the item in any way unsatisfactory during the life of the boot. Bean began his successful mail order sales business with a four-page flyer describing the boots and the guarantee sent to out-of-state sportsmen. Other items for the outdoors were added, notably the often-imitated LL Bean Field Coat in 1924, popular for its rugged quality and craftsmanship. These days Bean sells over one billion dollars' worth of clothing, outdoor gear and home furnishings. And the guarantee of no questions asked and 100% satisfaction is still honored.

While the merchant's successful start began through mail order, an additional delight is a visit to the **LL Bean store** (☎ 800-341-4341; www.llbean.com; cnr Main & Elm Sts; ☽ 24hr). For close to 90 years, the store has sold Bean merchandise to the hardy, the sports-minded and the merely curious. In 1951, Bean himself removed the locks from the store doors and made the decision to stay open 24 hours a day, 365 days a year. Since then the store has only closed twice – once in 1963 when President John F Kennedy was assassinated and once in 1967 for LL Bean's funeral.

Popular with locals as well as those 'from away', the store is easily the most popular tourist attraction in Maine, with more than three million visitors each year.

Late night shopping at the 24-hour venue is a popular sport for locals and tourists alike, who down the proffered free coffee and candy before admiring huge tents, trying on the blaze-orange hunting gear or enjoying a midnight dip in the trout pond. After-dark celebrity spottings abound – particularly of John Travolta, who owns a home in nearby Islesboro.

Reflecting small town camaraderie, locals often treat LL Bean's as a community center during storms and power outages. Also, nearly all shoppers report the joys of late-night Christmas shopping without crowds. On so many levels and in so many ways, no place matches it.

restaurants thrown in – makes for a much more pleasant shopping experience.

Freeport's fame and fortune began a century ago when Leon Leonwood Bean opened a shop to sell equipment and provisions to hunters and fishermen heading north into the Maine woods. His success later brought other retailers to the area, making Freeport what it is today.

During the summer, LL Bean sponsors free **Saturday evening concerts** (www.llbean.com/events) in Freeport at Discovery Park.

ORIENTATION & INFORMATION

Take I-95 exit 19 or 20 to reach central Freeport. The downtown shopping district is along Main St/US 1. South Freeport, south off US 1, is a sleepy residential community, but its town dock has a good local eatery and bay cruises.

DeLorme Mapping Company (☎ 207-846-7100; www.delorme.com; 2 DeLorme Dr; ☽ 9.30am-6pm) Don't miss a visit to this office with its giant 5300 sq ft rotating globe, Eartha, in nearby Yarmouth at exit 17 off I-95. Maker of the essential *Maine Atlas and Gazetteer*, DeLorme also creates maps and software for every destination in the United States.

Freeport Merchants Marketing Association (☎ 207-865-1212; www.freeportusa.com; 23 Depot St; ☽ 9am-5pm Mon-Fri) Maintains an information kiosk one block south of Main St and another on Mallet St near Main.

State of Maine information center (☎ 207-846-0833) This is a large information center facing DeLorme Mapping Company at I-95 exit 17. It dispenses mountains of information on Freeport and all of Maine.

SIGHTS & ACTIVITIES
Desert of Maine

William Tuttle came to Freeport in 1797 to farm potatoes, but his deadly combination of clear-cutting and overgrazing caused enough erosion to expose the glacial **desert** (☎ 207-865-6962; www.desertofmaine.com; 95 Desert Rd; adult/child/teen $8.75/5.25/6.25; ☽ 9am-dusk May-Oct; ☖) hidden beneath the topsoil. The shifting dunes, which are 70ft deep in some areas, cover entire trees and the old farm's buildings. Admission includes a 30-minute tram tour and lots of kiddy activities. To reach the farm, take I-95 exit 19 and head west of the highway for 2 miles.

Hiking & Swimming

Overlooking the islands of Casco Bay, the **Winslow Memorial Park** (☎ 207-865-4465; Wolf Neck Rd;

admission $1.50), is a 90-acre seaside park with a short nature trail and a beach area for swimming. For directions see Sleeping (below).

Bradbury Mountain State Park (☎ 207-688-4712; 528 Hallowell Rd/ME 9, Pownal; adult/child $3/1) has several miles of forested hiking trails, including an easy 10-minute hike to a 485-foot summit. It yields a spectacular view all the way to the ocean. There's camping as well (see below). To reach it, take ME 125 and ME 136 north from Freeport, and turn left just after crossing I-95; from there, follow the state park signs.

Wolf Neck Woods State Park (☎ 207-865-4465; Wolf Neck Rd; adult/child $3/1), just outside Freeport, has 5 miles of easy hiking trails, including a scenic Shoreline Walk that skirts Casco Bay. To reach the park, take Bow Street and turn right on Wolf Neck Rd.

LL Bean Courses

In the warmer months **LL Bean Outdoor Discovery Schools** (☎ 888-552-3261; www.llbean.com/ods) offers adventure courses aimed toward beginning and intermediate kayakers and fly-fishers. Full-day courses cost between $95 and $120, and you can also sign up for overnight camping-kayaking trips, or arrange for private lessons. Very short 'walk-on adventures' ($15) are available at their store location.

Cruises

Atlantic Seal Cruises (☎ 207-865-6112; Freeport Town Wharf; adult/child $25/18; ❂ May-Oct) offers three-hour trips where the captain hauls in lobster traps, and you go in search of wild osprey and adorable seals. Pack a picnic lunch or ask about catered picnics when reserving.

Cruises depart from the Freeport Town Wharf in South Freeport. Follow US 1 to the 40ft-high Native American statue, and follow the unmarked road in front of it (South Freeport Rd). When you reach a four-way stop sign, turn right.

SLEEPING

Winslow Memorial Park (☎ 207-865-4198; sites $22-28) This choice pick is hard to beat as it's right on the ocean. Head south from Freeport along US 1, take a left at the towering Native American statue, head toward South Freeport and then turn right onto Staples Point Rd (there's a park sign) and follow it another 2 miles.

Bradbury Mountain State Park (☎ 207-688-4712; Hallowell Rd/ME 9, Pownal; sites $18) The 35 rustic

campsites here are in a beautifully wooded area. For directions see left.

Recompense Shore Campsites (☎ 207-865-9307; www.freeportcamping.com; 134 Burnett Rd; sites $21-42; ▯ wi-fi) On the other side of the bay from South Freeport, this attractive campground has 115 shaded sites, some of which are right along the water.

White Cedar Inn (☎ 207-865-9099; www.whitecedar inn.com; 178 Main St; r with breakfast $105-180; ▯ wi-fi) The former home of Arctic explorer Donald MacMillan, this Victorian houses a charming B&B, conveniently located within walking distance of the shops. It has seven rooms with brass beds, vintage-style wallpaper and a few antique furnishings.

Royalsborough Inn (☎ 207-865-6566; www.royals boroughinn.com; 1290 Royalsborough Rd, Durham; r with breakfast $130-175; ▯ wi-fi) A 10-minute drive from downtown Freeport, in rural Durham, the Royalsborough Inn is set in a restored 18th-century home. Its seven rooms have handsome wood floors, beamed ceilings and handcrafted antique furniture. Acres of fields and lovely gardens surround the place, ensuring a peaceful getaway.

James Place Inn (☎ 207-865-4486; www.jamesplace inn.com; 11 Holbrook St; r with breakfast $130-185) Built in 1880, this B&B has seven guest rooms (four of which boast Jacuzzi tubs, and one has a fireplace). All have wood floors, attractive furnishings and a delightful color scheme.

Atlantic Seal B&B (☎ 207-865-6112; 25 Main St, South Freeport; r with breakfast $175-220) Situated near South Freeport's town dock, this quiet B&B features three comfortable rooms with superb harbor views. One room has a large balcony, while another has a fireplace. Nautical accoutrements adorn the interior of the 1850 Cape-style house.

EATING & DRINKING

Isabella's (☎ 207-865-6635; 2 School St; meals $7-9; ❂ breakfast & lunch) You'll find huge cinnamon rolls and Freeport's best breakfasts at this casual town café. Healthy but tasty wraps, salads and panini make up the lunch offerings.

Gritty McDuff's (☎ 207-865-4321; 187 Lower Main St; meals $9.50-17; ❂ lunch & dinner) Two miles south of LL Bean, this all-wood tavern is the perfect setting for pub grub and, more importantly, beer. McDuff's is deservedly popular for its tasty microbrews.

Harraseeket Lobster Co (☎ 207-865-4888; 36 Main St, South Freeport; meals $10-22; ❂ lunch & dinner May-

Oct) On the town dock, Harraseeket serves some of the best lobster in town. It's a casual dockside affair; you'll feast at picnic tables overlooking the bay. Order ahead to beat the crowds.

Azure (☎ 207-865-1237; 123 Main St; meals $12-26; ☽ lunch & dinner) Seafood is the name of the game at this handsome patio restaurant. Intriguing dishes like blueberry barbecue salmon, stuffed haddock and seafood risotto are featured alongside classic Italian dishes such as lasagna bolognese and linguine with clam sauce.

Maine Dining Room (☎ 207-865-1085; 162 Main St; meals $23-38; ☽ dinner daily, brunch Sun) This upscale dining room in the Harraseeket Inn serves excellent creative cuisine including roasted vegetables over quinoa cake, pan-seared halibut with polenta and chocolate soufflé for dessert. The inn also hosts the **Broad Arrow Tavern** (meals $14-26; ☽ lunch & dinner), a wood-floored charmer with a good selection of microbrews and high-end bistro fare.

GETTING THERE & AWAY

Freeport, 15 miles north of Portland via I-295, is a mile off the interstate on US 1. For the nearest bus transport, see the Portland section, p482; buses do not stop in Freeport.

Sabbathday Lake & Poland Spring

The last active community of Shakers in the world lies just 25 miles north of Portland. Founded in the 18th century, the **Sabbathday Lake** community has a small number of devotees (perhaps four or five), keeping the Shaker tradition of prayer, simple living, hard work and fine artistry alive – check out the excellent Ken Burns documentary *The Shakers*). New members are very much welcome, but if you didn't come to sign up, you can still take a two-hour guided **village tour** (☎ 207-926-4597; www.shaker.lib.me.us; adult/child $6.50/2; ☽ 10am-4:30pm Mon-Sat late May–mid-Oct). Among the plain white, well-kept buildings of the community are a welcome center, museum, and shop selling the community's crafts. Most other buildings, including the impressive Brick Dwelling House, are not open to visitors.

A few miles to the north is the village of **Poland Spring** that's famous for its mineral water, which is now sold throughout the US. In the early 19th century, a visitor was miraculously cured by drinking water from Poland Spring. Not known to miss a good thing, the locals opened hotels to cater to those wanting to take the waters.

To reach the Sabbathday Lake village, take I-95 to exit 63, then continue along ME 26/Shaker Rd for another 12 miles. Poland Spring is 3 miles north of there, also along ME 26.

MIDCOAST MAINE

Midcoast Maine is celebrated for its exceptional natural beauty and down-to-earth residents. Seaside villages backed by thick pine forests line this dramatic coast, providing numerous opportunities for biking, hiking, sailing, kayaking and other adventures. You'll also find world-famous ports for yachting: Camden, Rockport and Rockland, from which windjammers (multimasted sailing ships) take passengers on cruises of the jagged coast.

The English first settled this region in 1607, which coincided with the Jamestown settlement in Virginia. Unlike their southerly compatriots, though, these early settlers returned to England within a year. British colonization resumed in 1620. After suffering through the long years of the French and Indian Wars, the area became home to a thriving shipbuilding industry, which continues today.

BRUNSWICK
pop 22,000

Near the banks of the meandering Androscoggin River, Brunswick (first settled in 1628) is a handsome, well-kept town set with a pretty village green and historic homes tucked along its tree-lined streets. It's home to the highly respected Bowdoin College (founded in 1794), which infuses the town with a surprising cultural presence, while the nearby Brunswick Naval Air Station brings capital to the city (though it will close in 2011).

A short drive through the city center reveals stately Federal and Greek mansions built by wealthy sea captains. Harriet Beecher Stowe wrote *Uncle Tom's Cabin* at 63 Federal St. This poignant story of a runaway slave, published in 1852, was hugely popular and fired the imagination of people in the northern states, who saw the book as a powerful indictment against

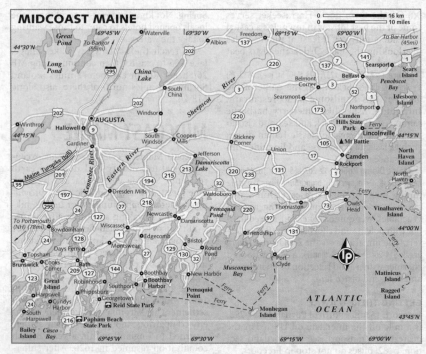

MIDCOAST MAINE

MAINE

slavery. See also Harriet Beecher Stowe's House in Hartford, Connecticut, p345.

Brunswick's green, called the Town Mall, is along Maine St. Farmers markets are set up Tuesday and Friday and there are band concerts Wednesday evening in summer. Also worth seeing are the Androscoggin Falls, once a source of hydroelectric power for 18th-century sawmills. A well-placed restaurant just across the bridge provides a waterside vantage point.

Orientation

To someone driving along US 1, the commercial center of Brunswick does not present a very attractive prospect. Turn off US 1 onto aptly named Pleasant St for Brunswick's prettier side, an attractive, tree-lined street with grand houses and magnificent gardens.

Sights

BOWDOIN COLLEGE

One of the oldest colleges in the US, **Bowdoin** (☎ 207-725-3375) is the alma mater of Henry Wadsworth Longfellow, Nathaniel Hawthorne and US president Franklin Pierce. For a cam-

pus tour, follow the signs from Maine St to Moulton Union. Smith Union is the student center, with an information desk on the mezzanine level, as well as a café, pub, lounge and small art gallery.

One worthwhile stop on campus is the **Bowdoin College Museum of Art** (☎ 207-725-3275; www.bowdoin.edu/artmuseum; admission free; 10am-5pm Tue-Sat, 2-5pm Sun), located in the quadrangle, which is strong in the works of 19th- and 20th-century European and American painters, including Mary Cassatt, Andrew Wyeth and Rockwell Kent.

The **Peary-MacMillan Arctic Museum** (☎ 207-725-3416; Hubbard Hall; admission free; 10am-5pm Tue-Sat, 2-5pm Sun) holds memorabilia from the expeditions of Robert Peary and Donald MacMillan, Bowdoin alumni who were among the first explorers to reach the North Pole.

PEJEPSCOT MUSEUMS

On the Bowdoin campus, the Pejepscot Historical Society preserves several house museums, which provide a fascinating glimpse into the past. You can visit them all for an $8 combination ticket.

MIDCOAST MAINE BY TRAIN

The **Maine Eastern Railroad** (☎ 866-637-2457; www.maineeasternrailroad.com; adult/child one-way $25/15; ☷ Fri-Sun late May–late Jun, Wed-Sun late Jun–early Nov) recently began offering a roundtrip service (twice daily, but once on Sundays) between Brunswick and Rockland, with stops at Bath and Wiscasset. The two-hour, 57-mile journey passes along lovely stretches of coastline aboard restored mid-20th-century rail cars. There's a dining car where you can enjoy wine and a light repast while watching seaside villages and rugged coastline drift slowly past.

The **Pejepscot Museum** (☎ 207-729-6606; 159 Park Row; admission free; ☷ 9am-5pm Tue-Fri, noon-4pm Sat) displays changing exhibits relating to Brunswick history, with photographs and artifacts pulled from its 50,000-piece inventory. **Skolfield-Whittier House** (☎ 207-729-6606; 161 Park Row; adult/child $5/2.50; ☷ mid-May–mid-Oct), an adjacent 17-room brick mansion, is a virtual time capsule, closed as it was from 1925 to 1982. Victorian furnishings and decor are handsomely preserved – even the spices in the kitchen racks are authentic. It's only open for tours. The **Joshua L Chamberlain Museum** (☎ 207-725-6958; 226 Maine St; adult/child $5/2.50; ☷ 10am-4pm Tue-Sat mid-May–mid-Oct) exhibits artifacts from the late owner's eventful life as college professor, Civil War hero, president of Bowdoin College and four-term governor of Maine. Tours are included with the admission fee.

Festivals & Events

During the summer **Bowdoin's Pickard Theater** (☎ 207-725-8769; www.msmt.org; cnr Park Row & Bath Rd, Bowdoin campus) hosts the Maine State Music Theater series, a run of Broadway musicals with performances from June through August.

Another summertime event is the **Bowdoin International Music Festival** (www.bowdoinfestival.org; ☷ late Jun–early Aug), featuring classical concerts held throughout town.

Sleeping & Eating

Brunswick Inn on Park Row (☎ 207-729-4914; www.brunswickinnparkrow.com; 165 Park Row; r with breakfast $125-175; ☐ wi-fi) Overlooking Brunswick's town green, this elegant guesthouse has 15 rooms ranging from small to spacious. Each is uniquely designed with modern furnishings, and several have wood floors. The wine bar on the first floor is an excellent place to enjoy a glass, particularly on the patio overlooking the park.

Sweet Leaves Tea House (☎ 207-725-1376; www.sweetleaves.com; 22 Pleasant Rd; meals $10-19; ☷ 11:30am-9pm Tue-Sat) Brunswick's most charming address opened in 2006. The bright and cheerful café-bistro serves delicious soups, salads, panini and desserts with a menu that changes daily. In addition to some 30 teas, Sweet Leaves serves beer and wine, which pair nicely with live acoustic nights and other weekly events.

Getting There & Away

Brunswick, off I-295 exit 31, is the point at which I-295 heads north and inland toward Augusta, Waterville and Bangor, and US 1 heads northeast along the coast. It's about 9 miles from Freeport, and 8 miles from Bath. For bus information, see the Portland section, p482.

BATH & AROUND

pop 9200

Called 'mouth of the big river' (Sagadahoc) by the Abenaki tribe, Bath is a small, historic Midcoast town set on a wide stretch of the Kennebec River. Red brick sidewalks and solid 19th-century buildings line its quaint Main Street, while just downhill lies a small grassy park overlooking the water. Its picturesque back streets seem a world away from the enormous Bath Iron Works a little downriver, but in fact this large complex is merely the latest incarnation of Bath's rich shipbuilding tradition.

Back in the early colonial days, the forested coasts of Maine were thick with tall trees that made flawless masts for the king's navy. Indeed, for a time the king forbade anyone to cut Maine's trees for any other purpose. In 1607, the pinnace *Virginia*, one of the earliest vessels built by Europeans on this coast, was launched into the Kennebec River at Phippsburg, south of Bath. Later, the shipyards on the Kennebec turned to building coastal freighters, then tall clipper ships and grand multimasted schooners.

Today, the ships coming out of Bath are steel frigates, cruisers and other navy craft, built at Bath Iron Works (BIW), one of the largest and most active shipyards in the US. The Maine Maritime Museum, south of the

MAINE

WORTH A TRIP: THE HARPSWELLS

Several long wooded peninsulas sprinkled with fishing villages jut southward into Casco Bay from Brunswick. Together these settlements compose the township of **Harpswell** (population 5200). If you have a few hours and want to escape the mad traffic on US 1, venture south for a meal or an overnight. There are several B&Bs, inns and motels (and enough restaurants) to provide dependable sustenance.

For the complete experience, head all the way south on ME 24 (I-95 exits 22 or 24) to **Bailey Island**, reached from Great Island and Orrs Island. You'll cross several causeways and the granite Cribstone Bridge that allows the tides to flow right through it.

The village dock on Bailey Island is a stop on the Casco Bay Lines cruise circuit (see p477). It can be more crowded than one would expect when the cruise boats tie up here for their lobster bakes. If you want a lobster lunch, try **Cook's Lobster House** (☎ 207-833-2818; 68 Garrison Cove Rd; ⊙ 11:30am-8pm), off ME 24. This place has succulent crustaceans and fantastic views, so aim for sunset.

---

shipyard, is an excellent place to learn about this 400-year-old tradition.

Orientation

Bath has an attractive, small commercial district north of US 1, along Front St. The famous ironworks sprawls to the south of US 1. Avoid driving in or out of town around 3:30pm on weekdays, when the work shift changes at the ironworks and US 1 chokes with cars.

Sights & Activities

MAINE MARITIME MUSEUM & SHIPYARD

The **museum** (☎ 207-443-1316; www.mainemaritimemu seum.org; 243 Washington St; adult/child $10/7; ⊙ 9:30am-5pm), south of the ironworks on the western bank of the Kennebec River, preserves the Kennebec's long shipbuilding tradition. In summer, the 19th-century **Percy & Small Shipyard** here still has boatwrights hard at work building wooden craft. The **Maritime History Building** contains paintings, models and hands-on exhibits that tell the tale of the last 400 years of seafaring. In the apprentice shop of the Percy & Small Shipyard, boat builders restore and construct wooden boats using traditional tools and methods.

In summer, the museum offers a variety of **boat trips and tours** ($20 to $40), ranging from 50-minute tours along the Kennebec Waterway and 3½-hour afternoon lighthouse cruises to trolley tours through the Bath Iron Works.

BEACH

The 6-mile long, sandy **Popham Beach State Park** (☎ 207-389-1335; adult/child $3/1) is one of the prettiest in the state, with views onto offshore islands and the Kennebec and Morse Rivers

framing either end. Lifeguards are on hand, but the surf is strong, with undertows and riptides. It's located off ME 209, about 14 miles south of Bath.

Sleeping

Meadowbrook Campground (☎ 207-443-4967; www .meadowbrookme.com; 33 Meadowbrook Rd, Phippsburg; sites $26; ⊙ May-Sep; ⊠) In Phippsburg, this friendly campground is well located to take advantage of pretty Popham Beach a few miles away, though you'll be sharing the grounds with many RVs.

Galen Moses House (☎ 207-442-8771; www.galen moses.com; 1009 Washington St; r with breakfast $120-260; ⊠ wi-fi) This antique-pink Victorian has six uniquely designed rooms, each colorfully decorated with antiques and period furnishings. In addition to a warm welcome, guests will enjoy the gardens, stately dining room and library, and perhaps even the attentions of the (friendly) ghost said to inhabit the house.

Fairhaven Inn (☎ 207-443-4391, 888-443-4391; www.mainecoast.com/fairhaveninn; 118 North Bath Rd; r with breakfast $80-145) This early-1800s inn is a few miles north of the city center with 16 acres of trails. Guest rooms are the model of comfort and simplicity, with quilted comforters and wooden furnishings.

our pick 1774 Inn (☎ 207-389-1774; www.1774inn .com; 44 Parker Head Rd, Phippsburg; r with breakfast $125-195) Overlooking the ocean 4 miles south of town, this gorgeous Federal-style house dates to 1774 and was the home of Maine's first US congressman. All of its rooms have wood floors with nice lighting, and the best have antique furniture.

Popham Beach B&B (☎ 207-389-2409; www.popham beachbandb.com; 4 Riverview Ave, Phippsburg; r with breakfast $150-215) Formerly a US Coast Guard station, this upscale 1880s B&B has four bright rooms directly on the sands of Popham Beach.

Eating & Drinking

Mae's Café & Bakery (☎ 207-442-8577; 160 Center St; meals $8-19; ⊗ breakfast & lunch daily, dinner Thu-Sat) Known for astonishing baked goods and desserts, Mae's also serves delicious seafood and roast meat dishes. The crab cakes are superb.

Solo Bistro (☎ 207-443-3373; 128 Front St; meals $24-30; ⊗ dinner Mon-Sat) This stylish, fairly new restaurant serves a small selection of expertly prepared dishes that change seasonally. Start off with a fresh goat cheese and tomato salad, followed by risotto or pan-seared wild salmon then raspberry cheesecake for dessert. The downstairs wine bar hosts live jazz and other events.

Kennebec Tavern (☎ 207-442-9636; 119 Commercial St; meals $24-30; ⊗ dinner Mon-Sat) Facing the river, this waterfront spot serves a huge selection of grilled meats, seafood, sandwiches and other bistro fare. The food is fine but the setting is the real attraction.

Getting There & Away

Bath is 8 miles east of Brunswick and 10 miles southwest of Wiscasset on US 1. For bus information, see the Portland section, p482.

WISCASSET

pop 3800

As the sign says, 'Welcome to Wiscasset, the Prettiest Village in Maine.' Other villages may dispute this claim, but Wiscasset's history as a major shipbuilding port in the 19th century has left it with a legacy of exceptionally beautiful houses. Set near the Sheepscot River, Wiscasset has some fine vantage points, and its tidy streets are dotted with antique shops, galleries, restaurants and a few old-fashioned inns.

Like Bath, Wiscasset was a shipbuilding and maritime trading center. Great four-masted schooners carrying timber, molasses, salt, rum and cod sailed down the Sheepscot bound for England and the West Indies, a route known as the Triangle Trade.

One caveat: as with other pretty towns astride US 1, Wiscasset has bad traffic jams in the summer.

Orientation

Wiscasset straddles Main St/US 1 and most of town is easily accessible on foot.

Sights

MAINE ART GALLERY

One of a handful of galleries in town, the **Maine Art Gallery** (☎ 207-882-7511; Federal St; admission free; ⊗ 11am-4pm Tue-Sun) is a non-profit exhibition space set in a lovely red-brick school house built in 1807. Exhibitions change monthly, with paintings, photographic works and occasional sculpture by local artists.

LINCOLN COUNTY JAIL MUSEUM

The first prison in the district of Maine opened in 1811 and surprisingly remained in operation until 1953. The hilltop structure of granite, brick and wood holds 12 tiny cells, complete with graffiti and other mementos from its earliest days. In addition, the jail functions as a **museum** (☎ 207-882-6817; 133 Federal St/ME 218; adult/child $4/free; ⊗ 11am-4pm Tue-Sat Jul & Aug), with changing exhibitions covering episodes from Wiscasset's history. It's located about a half-mile north of US 1.

CASTLE TUCKER

Wiscasset's grandest and best-situated mansion is the 1807 **Castle Tucker** (☎ 207-882-7364; cnr High & Lee Sts; adult/child/senior $5/2.50/4; ⊗ 11am-5pm Tue-Sun Jun–mid-Oct), which commands beautiful views over the countryside. Judge Silas Lee built it to resemble a mansion in Dunbar, Scotland, but he only lived here for seven years before dying. It was later sold to a sea captain, and today it remains a marvelous refuge of Victoriana, with 19th-century furnishings and wallpaper.

MUSICAL WONDER HOUSE

On the way to Castle Tucker, don't overlook this sweet **museum** (☎ 207-882-7163; www.musical wonderhouse.com; 18 High St; 45-/90-min tour $10/20; ⊗ 10am-5pm late May–mid-Oct). Its outstanding collection of antique music boxes, player pianos and early talking machines (gramophones) are displayed in period rooms.

NICKELS-SORTWELL HOUSE

This **historical mansion** (☎ 207-882-6218; www.spnea .org; cnr US 1 & Federal St/ME 218; admission $5; ⊗ 11am-5pm Tue-Sun Jun–mid-Oct) is one of the town's finest

MAINE

Federal houses (built in 1807), complete with period gardens. Tours begin on the hour and run from 11am to 4pm.

Sleeping

Wiscasset Motor Lodge (☎ 207-882-7137; www.wiscasset motorlodge.com; 596 Bath Rd/US 1; r $60-105; ☒ Apr-Oct) Southwest of the city center, this motel's comfy, knotty pine-paneled rooms and cottages are excellent value.

Highnote B&B (☎ 207-882-9628; www.wiscasset .net/highnote; 26 Lee St; r with breakfast $90) At the Highnote, you'll get a spacious room in a Victorian home, a shared bathroom and a breakfast with fruit, meat, bread and homemade scones. It's within walking distance of all the major sites, antique shops and restaurants in Wiscasset.

Marston House (☎ 207-882-6010 www.marston house.com; 101 Main St; r with breakfast $100; ☒ May-Oct; ☒ wi-fi) This B&B has two classy rooms in a late-19th-century carriage house that are styled with a hint of New England simplicity. It's a romantic setting; the hosts will even set up your room's fireplace. Breakfast is brought to your room in a wicker basket and antique jars.

Eating

Treat's (☎ 207-882-6192; 80 Main St; dishes $3-12; ☒ 10am-6pm Mon-Sat, 10am-3pm Sun) Treat's is a countrified café that prepares decadent fruit pies, homemade pastries, and other sweets to go with their tasty breads, soups, cheeses and wines. It's a great shop for picnickers.

Edna Rose Café (☎ 207-882-9951; 25 Fort Hill St; meals $9-14, ☒ noon-5pm Thu-Mon) On the ground floor of a 19th-century Methodist Church, Edna Rose is a little café and art gallery serving homemade sandwiches, salads and lighter fare. The menu changes frequently, but expect fresh ingredients and dishes made with care.

Le Garage (☎ 207-882-5409; 15 Water St; meals $9-24; ☒ noon-8pm Tue-Sun) Overlooking the wrecks of two disintegrating wooden schooners, Le Garage is a fine waterside spot for a meal. Try the walnut crusted haddock or the scallops carbonara.

Getting There & Away

Wiscasset is 10 miles northeast of Bath, 13 miles north of Boothbay Harbor and 23 miles south of Augusta. For bus transportation, see the Portland section p482.

BOOTHBAY HARBOR

pop 2300

Once a beautiful little seafarers' village on a broad ford-like harbor, Boothbay Harbor is now an extremely popular tourist resort in the summer, when its narrow and winding streets pack with visitors. Still, there's good reason to join the holiday masses. For one, the setting is indeed picturesque. Overlooking a pretty waterfront, large, well-kept Victorian houses crown the town's many knolls, and a wooden footbridge ambles across the harbor.

After you've strolled the waterfront along Commercial St and the business district along Todd and Townsend Aves, walk along McKown St to the top of McKown Hill for a fine view. Then, take the footbridge across the harbor to the town's East Side, where there are several huge, dockside seafood restaurants.

To truly appreciate Boothbay, try coming in June or September, when this summer playground isn't quite so packed.

Orientation & Information

First things first: Boothbay and East Boothbay are separate from Boothbay Harbor, the largest, busiest and prettiest of the three towns. Follow ME 27 south to the town, which you will enter along Oak St (one way) – this runs into Commercial St, the main street.

Dealing with narrow, often one-way roads and scarce parking isn't any fun. It's best to park further out and take the free shuttle into the city center. Catch the shuttle at the small mall on Townsend Ave. Once in town, hop aboard the trolley ($1) that tools around.

Boothbay Harbor Region Chamber of Commerce (☎ 207-633-2353; www.boothbayharbor.com; 192 Townsend Ave, Boothbay Harbor; ☒ 8am-5pm) There's also an information kiosk on ME 27.

Sights & Activities
COASTAL MAINE BOTANICAL GARDENS

Already a much-loved addition to Boothbay, these magnificent **gardens** (☎ 207-633-4333; www.mainegardens.org; Barters Island Rd; adult/child $10/5; ☒ 9am-5pm Mon-Fri, 9am-6pm Sat & Sun) opened in 2007 to much fanfare. Set along the waterfront, this verdant kingdom has 248 acres, with a number of groomed trails winding past exotic and native species through forest, ornamental gardens and rose gardens, with splendid views over the water. It's located on Barters Island Rd, about 1.5 miles west of Boothbay.

MAINE

BOOTHBAY RAILWAY VILLAGE

This endearing **village** (☎ 207-633-4727; www.rail wayvillage.org; ME 27; adult/child $8/4; ⏰ 9:30am-5pm mid-Jun–mid-Oct; ♿) is a historical replica of a New England town, with 27 buildings and a narrow-gauge steam-train line running through it. It's basically a nonprofit educational park, and has a collection of more than 55 antique steam- and gasoline-powered motor vehicles.

HIKING

There are over 25 miles of hiking trails in the region under the management of the **Boothbay Region Land Trust** (☎ 207-633-4333; www.bbrlt.org; 2nd fl, 1 Oak St, Boothbay Harbor). Beautiful coastal scenery consists of tidal waters, quiet coves and salt marshes backed by forests and fields. Birdwatchers should keep their eyes peeled for great blue herons, eider ducks, herring gulls and migratory birds. Stop by the office or go online for maps and trail guides.

KAYAKING

Tidal Transit (☎ 207-633-7140; www.kayakboothbay.com; 18 Granary Way, Boothbay Harbor) rents kayaks (per day $50) and also offers two- to three-hour kayak excursions across the placid bay ($35 to $40).

CRUISES

Balmy Days Cruises (☎ 207-633-2284; www.balmy dayscruises.com; Pier 8, Boothbay Harbor; ⏰ May-Oct) This outfit takes day-tripping passengers to Monhegan Island (90 minutes; adult/child $32/18; p493) or 5-acre Burnt Island ($22); you can also take a 90-minute sailboat excursion ($20).

Cap'n Fish's Boat Trips (☎ 207-633-3244, 800-636-3244; www.mainewhales.com; Pier 1, Boothbay Harbor; adult/child $35/22; ⏰ May-Oct) Cap'n Fish travels along the coast in search of whales.

Eastwind (☎ 207-633-6598; www.fishermanswharfinn .com; Pier 6, Boothbay Harbor; tours $22; ⏰ May-Oct) Hop aboard a stately 64ft windjammer for a 2½-hour sail-powered cruise; there are four trips daily.

Sleeping

Budget travelers should cruise the motels on Townsend Ave/ME 27 north of Boothbay Harbor.

Gray Homestead (☎ 207-633-4612; www.graysocean camping.com; 21 Homestead Rd, West Boothbay Harbor; sites $32; ⏰ mid-May–Oct) South of Boothbay Harbor on Southport Island, Gray Homestead has 40 wooded, oceanfront sites. There's swimming off the beach and kayak rental.

Lion d'Or (☎ 207-633-7367; www.liondorboothbay.com; 106 Townsend Ave, Boothbay Harbor; r with breakfast $70-140) A short walk to the thick of things, this 1886 Victorian has five cozy rooms, each set with queen-sized beds and homey furnishings. Four rooms have gas fireplaces.

Pond House (☎ 207-633-5842; www.pondhousemaine .com; 7 Bay St, Boothbay Harbor; r $80-115; ⏰ Mar-Jan) Pond House is an artists' retreat that has a studio in a detached barn. The main house has five simple and spacious guestrooms, decorated with antiques and artwork.

Lawnmere Inn (☎ 207-633-2544; www.lawnmereinn .com; 65 Hendricks Hill Rd/ME27, Boothbay Harbor; r $90-190; ⏰ mid-May–Oct) On Southport Island, southwest of Boothbay Harbor, Lawnmere is a nice old 31-room inn. It's set on spacious lawns at the water's edge, far from the bustle of town. Prices vary according to the view.

1830 Admiral's Quarters Inn (☎ 207-633-2474; www.admiralsquartersinn.com; 71 Commercial St, Boothbay Harbor; r with breakfast $95-215; 💻 wi-fi) The name says it all at this 19th-century former sea captain's home. Overlooking the waterfront, you'll find seven rooms, each furnished with a mix of antiques, wicker furniture and nautical accouterments, and all rooms have private entrances and open onto patios with harbor views.

Linekin Bay B&B (☎ 207-633-9900; www.linekinbay bb.com; 531 Ocean Point Rd/ME 96, Boothbay Harbor; r $105-185) This waterside B&B has four spacious, nicely furnished rooms and an extremely amiable host who enjoys cooking and baking for guests.

Topside (☎ 207-633-5404; www.topsideinn.com; 60 McKown St, Boothbay Harbor; r with breakfast $120-165; ⏰ May-Oct) Atop McKown Hill, Topside has unparalleled views of the town and the harbor. Rooms in the original sea captain's house are preferred, but all the rooms are trim and modern, with an attractive design and either wood floors or carpeting.

Five Gables Inn (☎ 207-633-4551; www.fivegablesinn .com; Murray Hill Rd, Boothbay Harbor; r with breakfast $130-225; ⏰ mid-May–Oct) This grand 125-year-old hotel with wraparound porch is set on a hill and has a large common living room and 16 guest rooms, most of which offer wonderful views of Linekin Bay.

Eating & Drinking

Center Café (☎ 207-633-6051; 7 Common Dr, Boothbay Harbor; meals $8-10; ⏰ 7am-3pm Mon-Fri, 7am-noon Sat & Sun) Center Café serves the best breakfast in

MAINE

town, with plump blueberry pancakes, rich crab cakes and all the standards. You can dine on the large porch of this country-style farmhouse. It's off ME 27, 1 mile north of Boothbay Harbor.

Lobster Dock (☎ 207-633-7120; 49 Atlantic Ave, Boothbay Harbor; meals $15-24; ❤ lunch & dinner May-Oct) Of all the lobster joints in Boothbay Harbor, this is one of the best and cheapest. It serves traditional shore dinners (steamed clams, boiled lobster and corn on the cob) as well as other seafood, but lobster is the dish.

93 Townsend (☎ 207-633-3622; 43 Oak St, Boothbay Harbor; meals $19-24; ❤ noon-10pm) One of Boothbay's top restaurants, 93 Townsend is an elegant but understated restaurant where you can sample award-winning cuisine. The menu features fresh, locally sourced ingredients, with unique dishes such as burgundy bistro steak, broiled haddock topped with lobster and coriander-crusted tuna with seaweed salad. The bar stirs up excellent martinis.

Boat Bar (☎ 207-633-5761; Granary Way, Boothbay Harbor) Located behind the Chowder House, this unpretentious spot is a great setting for a drink, particularly in the summer when you can enjoy an open-air cocktail on the water's edge.

Getting There & Away

From Wiscasset, continue on US 1 for 2 miles, and then head south on ME 27 for 12 miles through Boothbay to Boothbay Harbor. For bus information see p482.

DAMARISCOTTA & PEMAQUID

pop 2040

Another pretty waterside town with a picturesque Main Street, Damariscotta is sprinkled with historic churches and grand mansions, which attest to its prominence in early colonial days. The town is also gateway to the picturesque coastline to the south.

ME 130 goes from Damariscotta through the heart of the Pemaquid Peninsula (the longest on the coast of Maine) to Pemaquid Point, a major destination for its natural beauty; artists and dilettantes from across the globe come here to record the memorable seascape in drawings, paintings and photographs.

Although it's bypassed by the masses today, the area was well explored in the early 17th century. English explorers set foot on the Pemaquid Peninsula in the early 1600s, but France claimed the land as well: the great Samuel de Champlain came here in 1605. By the 1620s, the area had a thriving settlement with a customhouse.

Orientation & Information

Follow US 1B ('Business') to reach the center of town.

Damariscotta Region Chamber of Commerce (☎ 207-563-8340, www.drcc.org; ❤ 9am-5pm Mon-Fri) The information office is located in the Damariscotta town center, just beyond where ME 129/130 veers off to the right.

Sights & Activities

MAIN STREET

Damariscotta's Main Street is a slice of old-time Americana, with shops, cafés, bookstores and a handful of restaurants.

PEMAQUID BEACH & TRAIL

Believe it or not, there are a few stretches of sandy beach along this rockbound coast, and **Pemaquid Beach** (adult/child $2/free; ❤ summer) is one of them. As ME 130 approaches Pemaquid Neck, watch for signs on the right (west) for Pemaquid Beach and make a right onto Huddle Rd (which turns into Snowball Hill Rd). The beach is set in a park, and the water is usually very cold for swimming. (Remember, this is Maine!) The **Pemaquid Trail**, a paved dead-end road, heads south from Snowball Hill Rd just east of the Pemaquid Beach access road.

FORT WILLIAM HENRY

A quarter-mile south of Pemaquid Beach lies the remains of **Fort William Henry** (☎ 207-677-2423, 207-624-6080; adult/child $2/free; ❤ 9am-5pm late May–early Sep). A replica of a 17th century fort, this circular stone structure boasts commanding views, old foundations from the 1600s, a burial ground with interesting tombstones, an archaeological dig and a small museum.

KAYAKING

Midcoast Kayak (☎ 207-563-5732; www.midcoastkayak.com; 47 Main St, Damariscotta; kayak tours $39-99) offers an enticing selection of kayaking tours (full-moon paddles, sunset excursions) and classes, as well as rentals ($39 to $49 full day). Among the attractions on the water: Muscongus Bay, the Damariscotta River, Franklin Island Light and Damariscove Island.

MAINE

WORTH THE TRIP: PEMAQUID POINT

Along a 3500-mile coastline famed for its natural beauty, Pemaquid Point stands out because of its tortuous, grainy, igneous rock formations pounded by restless, treacherous seas.

Perched on top of the rocks in **Lighthouse Park** (adult/child $2/free; 🕑 dawn-dusk) is the 11,000-candlepower **Pemaquid Light**, built in 1827. It's one of the 61 surviving lighthouses along the Maine coast, 52 of which are still in operation. The keeper's house now serves as the **Fishermen's Museum Lighthouse** (Pemaquid Point; 🕑 10am-5pm Mon-Sat, 11am-5pm Sun), displaying fishing paraphernalia and photos, as well as a nautical chart of the entire Maine coast with all the lighthouses marked.

Sleeping & Eating

Pemaquid Point Campground (☎ 207-677-2267; www.midcoast.com/~ed; 9 Pemaquid Point Campground Rd, New Harbor; sites $25; 🕑 late Jun–early Sep) Toward Pemaquid Point off ME 130, this basic campground has 20 tent and 30 RV sites.

Oak Gables (☎ 207-563-1476; www.oakgablesbb.com; 36 Pleasant St, Damariscotta; r with breakfast $95; 🏊) Set on 11 acres overlooking the Damariscotta River, Oak Gables has four small but delightfully furnished rooms with wood floors in the main house. The grounds are an idyllic place to stroll with oak trees, and an orchard leading down to the river. It's a short walk to the cafés and shops of town.

Bradley Inn (☎ 207-677-2105, 800-942-5560; www.bradleyinn.com; 3063 Bristol Rd/ME 130, New Harbor; r with breakfast $165-235; 🕑 Apr-Oct) A few hundred yards inland from the bay, this elegant guesthouse has 16 attractive rooms decorated with Victorian furnishings and maritime artwork. The seaside spa offers a range of treatments, while the restaurant serves superb cuisine.

Schooner Landing (☎ 207-563-3380; 40 Main St, Daramiscotta; meals $14-24; 🕑 noon-8pm) Overlooking the river, Schooner's patio is the prettiest spot in town for an al fresco meal during the summer months. You'll find top-notch fish and chips, lobster and other seafood favorites at this popular restaurant.

Getting There & Away

From Wiscasset, continue on US 1 for 7 miles, and head southeast on ME 129 for 2 miles to Damariscotta. Take ME 130 south for 12 miles through New Harbor to Pemaquid Point. To get back to US 1 heading north, take ME 32 for 22 miles north through Round Pond until you reach US 1. For bus information see p482.

MONHEGAN ISLAND

pop 75

This rocky outcrop is a deservedly popular summertime destination. The small island (just 1.5-miles long by a half-mile wide) was known to Basque and Portuguese fishers and mariners before the English cruised these waters, but it came into its own as a summer resort in the early 19th century. When the cities of the eastern seaboard were sweltering in summer's heat, sea breezes cooled Monhegan and those fortunate enough to have taken refuge here.

Early in its history as a resort, Monhegan became popular with artists who admired its dramatic views and agreeable isolation. To this day, the island village remains small and very limited in its services. Residents and visitors are drawn to plain living and traditional village life. The few unpaved roads are lined with stacks of lobster traps.

With few motor vehicles on the tiny island, Monhegan is laid out for walking and has 17 miles of trails. Children, in particular, enjoy the southern tip of the island, with its wrecked ship rusting away, lots of rocks to climb, and cairn-art (stacks of stones and driftwood made into fantasy sculptures). The views from the lighthouse are excellent, and its little museum is an amusing diversion.

The island's environments – natural, social and commercial – are fragile and thus subject to strict rules: smoking and mountain biking are not allowed, and it's a good idea to carry your garbage with you when you leave (bring a bag).

Unless you've made reservations well in advance at one of the island's few lodgings, don't plan on finding a room upon arrival. Make sure you take a day excursion from Port Clyde or Boothbay Harbor (p490), and allow yourself at least a half-day to walk the trails over the rocks and around the shore. Stop at the 1824 **lighthouse museum** for a look at the keeper's former house.

Be sure to bring a sweater and windbreaker, as the voyage and the coast can be chilly even in August. Browse **Monhegan Commons** (www.monhegan.com) for more information.

MAINE

Sleeping & Eating

Accommodations are simple and basic on the island; few rooms have private bathrooms. The sparse restaurants on the island serve OK fare.

Monhegan House (☎ 207-594-7983; www.monhegan house.com; r with breakfast $70-185; ☺ May-Sep) Located in the heart of the tiny village, this guesthouse has been in operation since 1870, and offers 31 rooms decorated with antique furniture and views of either the ocean or the meadows. All but two rooms have shared bathrooms. The café serves three meals and sells freshly made baked goods.

Hitchcock House (☎ 207-594-8137; www.midcoast .com/~hhouse; r & efficiency $90-140) On Horn's Hill, the secluded Hitchcock House has four old-fashioned rooms and two efficiency units (with a kitchen) that provide basic comforts (no more) after a day exploring.

Shining Sails (☎ 207-596-0041; www.shiningsails.com; r with breakfast $100-200) Shining Sails is a friendly year-round place with a mix of comfortable rooms and more spacious kitchen-equipped apartments. Five of the rooms have ocean views and private decks. You can also rent cottages scattered about the island through Shining Sails.

Island Inn (☎ 207-596-0371; www.islandinnmonhegan .com; r with breakfast $155-340; ☺ May-Oct) A Victorian mansard-roofed summer hotel with a big front porch, this hostelry offers marvelous views and 32 small but elegant rooms (all but eight of which have a private bathroom). All three meals are available in the dining room.

Monhegan House Café (☎ 207-594-7983; meals $12-28; ☺ breakfast, lunch & dinner late May–mid-Oct) This popular, art-filled café serves decent seafood and bistro fare, and on warm evenings you can sit out on the patio overlooking the lush meadows.

Getting There & Away

During high season, **Monhegan Boat Line** (☎ 207-372-8848; www.monheganboat.com; roundtrip adult/child $30/18) runs several daily trips to Monhegan Island from Port Clyde. Schedules and fares vary according to the season; advance reservations are always a must. Parking in Port Clyde costs $4 per day.

Departing New Harbor from Shaw's Fish & Lobster Wharf on ME 32, **Hardy Boat Cruise** (☎ 207-677-2026; www.hardyboat.com; roundtrip adult/child $29/17; ☺ mid-May–mid-Oct) runs *Hardy III* twice daily for Monhegan.

You can also visit Monhegan on a day excursion from Boothbay Harbor (p490) aboard one of the boats run by **Balmy Days Cruises** (☎ 207-633-2284; www.balmydayscruises.com; roundtrip adult/child $32/18; ☺ May-Oct).

ROCKLAND
pop 7600

This thriving commercial town boasts a large fishing fleet and a proud year-round population that gives Rockland a vibrancy lacking in some other Midcoast towns. Its Main Street is a window into the city's socio-cultural diversity, with a jumble of working class diners, bohemian cafés and high-end bistros alongside galleries, old-fashioned storefronts and one of the state's best art museums.

Settled in 1769, Rockland was once an important shipbuilding center and a transportation hub for goods moving up and down the coast. Today, tall-masted sailing ships still fill the harbor, as Rockland, along with Camden, is a center for Maine's busy windjammer cruises (to join a multi-day cruise, see opposite). Rockland is also the birthplace of poet Edna St Vincent Millay (1892–1950), who grew up in neighboring Camden.

The big events in Rockland are the **Maine Lobster Festival** (www.mainelobsterfestival.com) in early August and the **North Atlantic Blues Festival** (www .northatlanticbluesfestival.com) in mid-July. Both of these are huge events, siphoning up accommodation for many miles surrounding Rockland.

Orientation & Information

Like other Maine coastal towns, Rockland lies along US 1, which becomes Maon St in the small downtown area.

For area information, stop in the **Penobscot Bay Chamber of Commerce** (☎ 207-596-0376; www .therealmaine.com; 1 Park Dr; ☺ 9am-5pm daily Jun-Sep, 9am-5pm Mon-Fri Oct-May), just off Main St. It's housed in the same building as the Main Lighthouse Museum (opposite).

Sights
FARNSWORTH ART MUSEUM & WYETH CENTER

Rockland is famous for its **Farnsworth Art Museum & Wyeth Center** (☎ 207-596-6457; www.farnsworthmu seum.org; 16 Museum St; adult/child/student & senior $10/free/8; ☺ 10am-5pm late Sep–mid-Oct, closed Mon mid-Oct–late Sep), one of the country's best small regional museums. Its collection of 5000 works is especially

---

SAILING THE HIGH SEAS

Although traveling by schooner largely went out of style at the dawn of the 20th century, adventurers can still explore the rugged Maine coast the old-fashioned way: onboard fleet sailing vessels known as windjammers. A dozen of these multi-masted vessels anchor at Rockland, and each offers trips ranging from three to 11 days around Penobscot Bay and further up the coast. Powered by the winds, travelers will explore towns and islands along the way, stopping for hiking, sightseeing, or shopping. They also take their meals on the boat (expect sunset dinners and plenty of lobster – meals are generally excellent). Bunks below decks are basic shared quarters, with shared toilets and showers; it's not recommended for high-maintenance travelers (private cabins are available on some boats). Still, the experience often rates high on any Maine itinerary.

Schooners offering trips include the following:

American Eagle (☎ 800-648-4544; www.schooneramericaneagle.com) Accommodates 26 passengers and offers four-/six-day excursions from $595/895.

Victory Chimes (☎ 207-594-0755; www.victorychimes.com) The largest in the fleet, this classic 132ft wooden vessel accommodates 40 passengers and offers four-/five-day excursions from $500/800.

Mistress (☎ 207-594-0755; www.mainewindjammercruises.com) Offers a more intimate sailing experience, with just six guests (in two-person cabins) on board this 46ft schooner. Three-/four-day excursions start at $595/695.

For a complete list of schooner companies and the rundown on vessels, schedules and prices visit **Maine Windjammer Association** (☎ 800-807-9463; www.sailmainecoast.com).

---

strong in landscape and marine artists who have worked in Maine, such as Andrew, NC and Jamie Wyeth; Louise Nevelson; Rockwell Kent; John Marin and others.

MAINE LIGHTHOUSE MUSEUM

Lovers of maritime history should pay a visit to the lighthouse **museum** (☎ 207-594-3301; www.mainelighthousemuseum.com; One Park Dr; adult/child $10/free; ✆ 9am-5pm Mon-Fri, 10am-4pm Sat & Sun; ⓐ) perched over Rockland harbor. Collections here include lighthouse artifacts (enormous jewel-like prisms), foghorns, marine instruments and ship models, with hands-on exhibits for children.

OWLS HEAD

Three miles south of Rockland, the **Owls Head Transportation Museum** (☎ 207-594-4418; www.ohtm.org; ME 73, Owls Head; adult/child $8/5; ✆ 10am-5pm Apr-Oct, 10am-4pm Nov-Mar) collects, preserves (yes, everything works!) and exhibits pre-1920s aircraft, vehicles and engines that were instrumental in the evolution of transportation. Besides its year-round exhibits, the museum hosts WWI air shows and specialty vehicle shows.

Also in Owls Head is the photogenic sight of **Owls Head Lighthouse** (ME 73, Owls Head) atop a promontory overlooking the dramatic coastline. Although the 19th-century lighthouse and keeper's cottage are off limits, you can

visit the surrounding grounds, which have short walking paths, a pebble-strewn beach and picnic tables.

Sleeping & Eating

LimeRock Inn (☎ 207-594-2257; www.limerockinn.com; 96 Limerock St; r with breakfast $110-200; ⌨ wi-fi) This eight-room mansion, built in 1890 for a local congressman, is decorated with fine mahogany furniture, rugs and king- or queen-size beds. Period furnishings with modern touches (Jacuzzi baths in some rooms) make it a Rockland favorite.

Rock City Books & Coffee (☎ 207-594-4123; 328 Main St; meals $8-9; ✆ 8am-6pm; Ⓥ) Along restaurant-strewn Main Street, Rock City serves the best cup of joe in town. Comfy chairs and a bohemian vibe make it a great spot for lounging, and local jazz bands play here throughout the summer. Tempting pastries, gourmet sandwiches and smoothies complement the caffeine.

our pick Primo (☎ 207-596-0770; 2 S Main St/ME 73; meals $21-28; ✆ dinner Thu-Mon, mid-May–Oct) Set in a Victorian home, Primo remains one of the top restaurants in the Northeast. The changing menu features creative, expertly prepared dishes of roast meats and seafood followed by superb desserts. Reserve well in advance or plan on dining in the bar (cozy ambience, same great menu and service).

MAINE

Getting There & Away

US Airways Express, operated by **Colgan Air** (☎ 800-428-4322; www.colganair.com), serves Rockland via its Boston-Bar Harbor route.

Concord Trailways (☎ 800-639-3317; www.concord trailways.com; 517A Main St) runs buses from Boston and Boston's Logan Airport to Rockland, via Portland. The trip from Boston to Rockland takes 4½ hours ($31).

CAMDEN & ROCKPORT

pop 5300

Camden and its picture-perfect harbor, framed against the mountains of Camden Hills State Park, is one of the prettiest sites in the state. Home to Maine's large and justly famed fleet of windjammers, Camden continues its historic close links with the sea. Most vacationers come to sail, but Camden also has galleries, fine seafood restaurants and back streets ideal for exploring. The adjoining state park offers hiking, picnicking and camping.

Like many communities along the Maine coast, Camden has a long history of shipbuilding. The mammoth six-masted schooner *George W Wells* was built here, setting the world record for the most masts on a sailing ship.

Alas, beauty comes at a price. The cost of Camden's lodgings and food during the summer is higher than those of many other Maine communities.

Two miles south of Camden, the sleepy harborside town of Rockport is a much smaller and more peaceful settlement that's famous for the stellar Maine Photographic workshops held there.

Orientation

Absolutely packed in the summer, US 1 snakes its way from Camden to Rockport, changing names from High to Main to Elm to Commercial Street as it goes southward.

Information

Owl & Turtle Bookshop (☎ 207-236-4769; 32 Washington St, Camden; ☼ 9am-5:30pm) One of Maine's favorite independent bookstores.

Rockport, Camden & Lincolnville Chamber of Commerce (☎ 207-236-4404; www.visitcamden .com; ☼ 9am-5pm Mon-Fri, 10am-5pm Sat year-round, noon-4pm Sun mid-May–mid-Oct) Has an information office on the waterfront at the public landing in Camden, behind Cappy's.

Sights & Activities

HISTORIC CAMDEN

Camden has range of architectural gems, including former estates dating from the early 1800s, a pretty **congregational church** (1834), an 18th-century **schoolhouse** and a plethora of striking 19th-century mansions. Many of these buildings are private residences, but you can wander the tree-lined streets of Chestnut and High Streets for a glimpse back in time. The chamber of commerce distributes a free brochure listing 30 or so historic buildings you can see on a 2.5-mile walk through town. If you have a car or bicycle, you can continue the tour into Rockport.

MAINE PHOTOGRAPHIC WORKSHOPS

One of the world's leading instructional centers in photography, film and digital media, this **institute** (☎ 877-577-7700; www.theworkshops .com; 2 Central St, Rockport) offers more than 250 workshops and master classes throughout the year, with classes for both beginners and professionals. Intensive one-week workshops (costing from $895 per week) are taught by leaders in their fields. Changing exhibitions of student and faculty work are displayed in **Union Hall** (2 Central St, Rockport; ☼ noon-8pm Mon-Wed, noon-5pm Thu-Fri, 9am-3pm Sat).

CAMDEN HILLS STATE PARK

Boasting more than 30 miles of trails, **Camden Hills State Park** (☎ 207-236-3109; adult/child $3/1; ☼ dawn-dusk) is a splendid place to take in the lovely scenery of the Midcoast. A favorite is the 45-minute (0.5 mile) climb up Mt Battie, which offers exquisite views of Penobscot Bay. Simple trail maps are available at the park entrance, just over 1.5 miles northeast of Camden center on US 1. The picnic area has short trails down to the shore.

KAYAKING & BIKING

To explore the coast at a leisurely paddle, contact **Ducktrap Kayak Rentals** (☎ 207-236-8608; US 1, Lincolnville; per day from $20; ☼ Jun-Aug), which rents kayaks and offers guided coastal kayak tours, starting at $30 per person. Both kayak and bicycle rental are available at **Maine Sport** (☎ 207-236-7120; Main St & ME 1, Camden; kayak/bike rental per day from $25/28).

ISLEBORO

From Camden, it's a five-minute drive to Lincolnville Beach from where you can take a 20-minute ferry ride to the island of **Islesboro** (for the Islesboro ferry schedule, call ☎ 207-789-5611), one of the finest places to ride a bike in Maine.

The island is relatively flat, yet hilly enough to offer majestic vistas of Penobscot Bay and long enough to feature a 28-mile bike loop. Picnic at Pendleton Point, where harbor seal and loons often lounge on the long, striated rocks.

CRUISES

Like nearby Rockland, Camden offers many windjammer cruises, from two-hour trips to multiday journeys up the coast. For overnight cruises see p495.

The following boats depart from Camden's Town Landing or adjoining Sharp's Wharf (across from the Chamber of Commerce):

Appledore (☎ 207-236-8353; www.appledore2.com; 2hr cruise $30; ☽ Jan-Oct)

Olad (☎ 207-236-2323; www.maineschooners.com; 2hr sail adult/child under 12 $29/17; ☽ May–mid-Oct)

Sleeping

For budget accommodations, troll the motels along US 1, just north of Camden.

Megunticook Campground by the Sea (☎ 207-594-2428, 800-884-2428; www.campgroundbythesea.com; 620 Commercial St/US 1, Rockport; sites $28-45; ☽ mid-May–mid-Oct) This quiet and wooded campground, 3 miles south of Camden, has good sites on the coast.

Belmont Inn (☎ 207-236-8053; www.thebelmontinn.com; 6 Belmont Ave, Camden; r with breakfast $90-175) On a quiet, residential street near the harbor, the friendly Belmont has six unique rooms with features like gas fireplaces (in three rooms), views of Mt Battie, wood floors and trim period-style furnishings. The cheapest rooms are small but good value for Camden.

Camden Maine Stay Inn (☎ 207-236-9636; www.camdenmainestay.com; 22 High St, Camden; r with breakfast $110-250) This fine Greek house (1802) sits at the base of Mt Battie. The friendly owners offer eight nicely appointed guest rooms and can share a wealth of information on the area.

Hartstone Inn (☎ 207-236-4259; www.hartstoneinn.com; 31 Elm St, Camden; r with breakfast $150-265; 🖳 wifi) This grand 1845 Victorian has a mansard roof and bright, lavishly furnished rooms with oil paintings and vintage-style wallpaper. The best rooms have four-post beds, gas fireplaces and Jacuzzi tubs. The dining room

serves top-notch five-course meals, and is open to the public.

Eating

Cappy's (☎ 207-236-2254; 1 Main St, Camden; meals $8-17; ☽ lunch & dinner) This casual, long-time favorite serves a venerable bowl of clam chowder alongside sandwiches and other light fare.

Lobster Pound Restaurant (☎ 207-789-5550; US 1, Lincolnville; meals $18-28; ☽ noon-8pm daily May-Oct) Fresh lobster is the name of the game at this highly recommended pound on Lincolnville's beach.

Francine Bistro (☎ 207-230-0083; 55 Chestnut St, Camden; meals $26-30; ☽ dinner Tue-Sat) A much-heralded newcomer to the culinary scene, Francine is a cozy, rather simply decorated bistro serving fantastic salads, seafood and grilled meats. In the summer, you can dine on the patio overlooking the harbor. Reserve well in advance or try your luck at the bar.

Getting There & Away

South of Bangor (53 miles) on US 1, Camden is 85 miles north of Portland and 77 miles southwest of Bar Harbor.

DOWN EAST

Without question, this is quintessential Maine: as you head further and further up the coast toward Canada, the peninsulas seem to become more and more narrow, jutting farther into the sea. The fishing villages seem to get smaller, and the lobster pounds closer and closer to the water.

'Down east' starts around Penobscot Bay. If you make time to drive to the edge of the shore, south off US 1, let it be here.

Officially, 'down east' also includes Blue Hill Bay and Frenchman Bay, which frame Mt Desert Island (p501). The region continues 'further down east' (p510) from Acadia all the way to the border with New Brunswick, Canada.

BUCKSPORT

pop 4970

A crossroads for highways and rail lines, Bucksport is slowly transforming itself from a mill town into a well-rounded coastal settlement. Art galleries, a marina and a handful of restaurants and inns have spruced up little Bucksport in recent years. Stop in

MAINE

WORTH THE TRIP: BELFAST & SEARSPORT

Just north of Camden on US 1 lies Belfast, a sleepy often-overlooked town, of grand architecturally eclectic houses and a diverse population mingling in the galleries and cafés of town. A pleasant seaside park and a welcome shortage of tourists make Belfast a worthwhile stop. Five miles northeast, Searsport has a fine historic district with its share of 19th-century mansions. Searsport is also home to the superb **Penobscot Marine Museum** (☎ 207-548-2529; www.penobscotmarinemuseum.org; 5 Church St & US 1; adult/child $8/3; ☾ 10am-5pm Mon-Sat, noon-5pm Sun late May–early Oct), housing Maine's biggest collection of mariner art and artifacts, which are spread through a number of historic buildings.

You can also explore Sears Island, which is the largest uninhabited island on the US's eastern seaboard. Paddle here by kayak from **Searsport Shores Camping Resort** (☎ 207-548-6059; 216 W Main St; kayak per half/full day $30/50), a mile south of Searsport, or walk the pedestrian causeway. Then hike around the island and appreciate ospreys, bald eagles and bear (be careful!) in their natural habitat.

In a landmark 1898 Victorian, the classic **Jeweled Turret** (☎ 207-338-2304; www.jeweledturret.com; 40 Pearl St, Bucksport; r with breakfast $105-150) is a B&B with seven pretty rooms, each with wood floors, big windows and elegant furnishings (for antique charm, book one of the rooms in the octagonal turret). Guests can enjoy the parlors, verandas and the evening social hour, complete with sherry and other refreshments.

Open since 1865, **Darby's** (☎ 207-338-2339; 155 High St, Belfast; lunch $9-10, dinner $9-15; ☾ lunch & dinner; **V**) is a picture-book bistro with tin ceilings and an original antique bar; paintings by local artists adorn the walls. Eclectic fare features crab-melts, Portobello sandwiches, pecan-crusted haddock and pad Thai.

---

the centrally located **Chamber of Commerce** (☎ 207-469-6818; www.bucksportbaychamber.com; 52 Main St, ME 04416; ☾ 10am-5pm Mon-Fri) for the latest.

The newest attraction in town is the **Penobscot Bridge Observatory**, an enclosed observation deck offering panoramic views from its 420ft perch above the Penobscot Narrows. The elevators that whisk you up top are on the grounds of the **Fort Knox State Historic Site** (☎ 207-469-7719; 711 Fort Knox Rd; adult/child fort & observatory $5/3, fort only $3/1; ☾ observatory 9am-5pm mid-May–Oct, fort 9am-sunset), just out of town and north of the bridge on ME 174.

Not to be confused with the US army's bullion depository in Kentucky, this Fort Knox dates from 1844, and was built as a bulwark against a British invasion. The huge granite fortress dominates the Penobscot River Narrows, which was an important gateway to Bangor, the commercial heart of Maine's rich timber industry.

Bring a flashlight if you plan a close examination, as the fort's granite chambers are unlit.

CASTINE
pop 1480

From Orland, a few miles east of Bucksport along US 1, ME 175/166 heads south to the dignified and historic village of Castine. Following an eventful history, today's Castine is charm-

ing, quiet and refreshingly off the beaten track. Almost all of its houses were built before 1900, so it's easy to get a feel for how this seaside town would have been during Maine's early settlement days. It's also the home of the Maine Maritime Academy and its big training ship, the *State of Maine* (1952), which you can visit.

In 1613, seven years before the Pilgrims landed at Plymouth, the French founded Fort Pentagöet – which later became Castine – to serve as a trading post. It was the site of battle after battle through the American Revolution, the War of 1812 and the French and Indian Wars. The French, English, Dutch and Americans all fought for a niche on this bulge of land that extends into Penobscot Bay.

Castine is a good place to appreciate pre-tourist-boom Maine. It's a gorgeous village with none of the kitsch you'd stumble across in Boothbay Harbor, Bar Harbor or Camden. Tourists that do visit, tend to be a slightly crusty East Coast crowd.

Castine is small enough to be easily traversed on foot. Pick up the free map entitled *A Walking Tour of Castine*, readily available at establishments in town.

Sights & Activities
FORTS

While Castine lacks a great stone citadel like Fort Knox, it did have some important

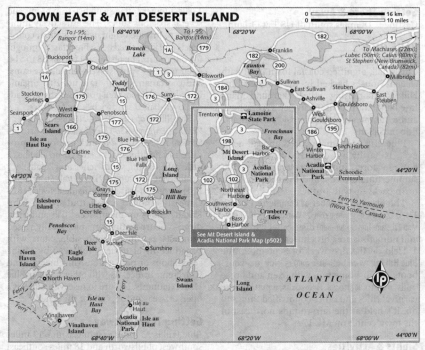

DOWN EAST & MT DESERT ISLAND

fortifications, though these are low earth-works, now park-like and grass-covered. Close to the Maine Maritime Academy campus, **Fort George** is near the upper (northern) end of Main St where it meets Battle Ave and Wadsworth Cove Rd. Look for **Fort Pentagöet** (cnr Perkins Rd & Tarratine St). The American **Fort Madison** (earlier called Fort Porter and dating to 1808) is further west along Perkins St, opposite Madockawando St.

WILSON MUSEUM
Near Fort Pentagöet this **museum** (☎ 207-326-9247; www.wilsonmuseum.org; 107 Perkins St; admission free; ☼ 2-5pm Tue-Sun Jun-Sep) holds a good collection of Native American artifacts, historic tools, farm equipment and other relics from Maine's past.

KAYAKING & BIKING
For trips out onto the water, stop by **Castine Kayak** (☎ 207-326-9045; www.castinekayak.com; Castine Wharf) which offers two-hour sunset trips ($40), full-day paddles ($105) or even overnight island-hopping excursions. Bicycle rental is also available (from $28 per day).

It's located behind Dennett's Wharf restaurant on the harbor.

Sleeping & Eating
There are very few places to stay in little Castine and most have excellent restaurants.

our pick **Castine Harbor Lodge** (☎ 207-326-4335; www.castinemaine.com; 147 Perkins St; r $95-245) Magnificently set overlooking Penobscot Bay, this 19th-century oceanfront mansion has plenty of places on the porch and broad lawn to drink in classic coastal views. The rooms, all with water views, range from small to spacious and are set with top-notch furnishings. There's a charming oyster bar and seafood restaurant on site.

Pentagöet Inn (☎ 207-326-8616, 800-845-1701; www.pentagoet.com; 26 Main St; r $115-245; ☼ May-Oct) This classic Queen-Anne Victorian, Castine's oldest summer hotel, has a tranquil wraparound porch and 16 delightful guest rooms set with antiques and period details. The Pentagöet also serves heavenly dishes, from lobster bouillabaisse to anise-dusted scallops. After dinner, you can retire to the old-world pub for a glass of port among the old photographs.

MAINE

Getting There & Away

Castine is 18 miles south of US 1 at Orland.

BLUE HILL

pop 2300

This small, dignified coastal town is set with elegant houses backed by the forested Blue Hill mountain rising in the background. Many fine handicrafts artisans live and work here, and a summer chamber music series draws fine musicians.

Blue Hill's well-manicured appeal, however, is hardly a secret, and its handful of antique stores, inns and restaurants gather summertime crowds, and the road through town backs up with traffic.

The **Blue Hill Chamber of Commerce** (☎ 207-374-3232; www.bluehillme.com; 28 Water St; ☼ 10am-4pm Mon-Fri, 9am-1pm Sat Jun-Sep) distributes a free map and numerous area brochures.

Held on the first week of September, the **Blue Hill Fair** (www.bluehillfair.com) is kick-up-your-boots, down-home fun, with oxen and horse pulls, livestock shows, fireworks, a petting zoo, carnival rides and other countrified things to do. It's held at the fairgrounds northeast of the town center on ME 172.

Sights & Activities

The **Marine Environmental Research Institute** (☎ 207-374-2135; www.meriresearch.org; 55 Main St; ☼ 9am-5pm Mon-Fri; ⚒) is an important center studying the relationship between pollution and marine life. Visitors can learn about MERI's activities in a series of changing exhibitions in the main gallery, often with hands-on exhibits for children. During the summer MERI offers two- to four-hour daily cruises (adult/child from $40/20) led by naturalists. Itineraries range from observing wildlife along the coast to exploring an uninhabited island, all with an educational focus in mind.

Sleeping & Eating

Blue Hill Farm Country Inn (☎ 207-374-5166; www.bluehillfarminn.com; ME 15; r with breakfast $70-110) Two miles north of the village, this classic 1903 farmhouse has rustic country charm in its 14 simple rooms with wood floors. Its best feature surrounds the inn: there are 48 acres of land with hiking trails.

Barncastle Inn (☎ 207-374-2300; www.barn-castle.com; 125 South St; r with breakfast $100-150; ▣ wi-fi) New in 2007, the Barncastle is a handsomely restored 1880s summer cottage with two trim rooms and several spacious suites. The attractively minimalist rooms are bright, with Egyptian cotton sheets and king-sized beds; breakfast is brought to your room. The restaurant (meals $8 to $14, open noon to 9pm) serves delicious seasonal and vegetarian-friendly fare utilizing organic ingredients. Wood-fired pizzas, satisfying salads and oven-baked sandwiches are favorites.

Blue Hill Co-op (☎ 207-374-2165; Greene's Hill Pl, cnr ME 172 & ME 176; meals $6-12; ☼ 8am-6pm Mon-Sat, 9am-5pm Sun) A great place to pick up organic produce and healthy snacks, this co-op also has a little café serving sandwiches and salads.

Arborvine (☎ 207-374-2119; 33 Main St; meals $18-24; ☼ dinner Wed-Sun summer) Inside a sweet 1823 Cape-style house, much touted chef John Hikade cooks up magnificent fish and meat dishes, incorporating organic, locally raised products as much as possible. Start with Bagaduce River oysters, followed by Maine sea scallops or pan-seared Ahi tuna and end with crème brûlée. As with other popular Blue Hill restaurants, be sure to reserve a table. It's open off-season too, call for the schedule.

Getting There & Away

Blue Hill is 23 miles east of Castine, 13 miles southwest of Ellsworth and 18 miles southeast of Bucksport.

DEER ISLE & STONINGTON

pop 1870

Rugged rock-strewn shores backed by thick forests form the backdrop to this beautiful coastal region. Traveling south along ME 15, you'll encounter views of pristine farms and magnificent harbors framed against hilly islands off in the distance. This is Deer Isle, actually a collection of islands joined by causeways and connected to the mainland by a picturesque suspension bridge near Sargentville. Although the sights are few, the exploring is highly rewarding.

The **Deer Isle-Stonington Chamber of Commerce** (☎ 207-348-6124; www.deerislemaine.com; ☼ 10am-4pm mid-Jun–early Sep) maintains an information booth a quarter-mile south of the suspension bridge.

Deer Isle Village, the first settlement you reach, has a few shops and services. It's worth exploring before continuing south (five miles) to reach Stonington, a quaint settlement, where lobstermen and artists live side by side. A few galleries and restaurants draw the odd traveler or two.

MAINE

Boats depart Stonington for Isle au Haut (right).

Sights & Activities

Seven miles to the east of Deer Isle Village, hidden at the end of Sunshine Rd, look for the exceptional and prestigious **Haystack Mountain School of Crafts** (☎ 207-348-2306; www .haystack-mtn.org; 89 Haystack School Dr, Sunshine; tours $5; ☺ tours 1pm Wed Jun-Aug), founded in 1950 and now open for one public tour per week. There are several galleries in Stonington and scattered around the island (keep your eyes peeled for signs), a testament to the fascination this beautiful seaside area holds for fine artists.

Sleeping & Eating

Boyce's Motel (☎ 207-367-2421; www.boycesmotel.com; 44 Main St, Stonington; r $55-110; ☺ summer) A cedar shake–covered hostelry that looks more like an inn, Boyce's rents simple but clean rooms by the night and cottages by the week. Rooms range from small to large, and the best have small kitchens and private decks with harbor views.

ourpick Pilgrim's Inn (☎ 207-348-6615; www.pilgrims inn.com; 20 Main St, Deer Isle Village; r with breakfast $99-209; ☺ mid-May–mid-Oct; ☐ wi-fi) Overlooking the Northwest Harbor, this handsome post-and-beam inn was built in 1793 and offers refined country charm in its 12 rooms and cottages. Pine floors and solid wood furnishings are common throughout, while some rooms have gas fireplaces and pretty views over the millpond. Inside the inn's converted barn, the Whale's Rib Tavern (meals $14 to $27, open for dinner) serves tasty plates of fish and chips, seafood casserole, steamed lobster and other versions of Maine comfort food. Reservations recommended.

Cockatoo (☎ 207-367-0900; Oceanville Rd; meals $20-30; ☺ dinner) This new addition to Deer Isle is deliciously off-the-beaten-path and serves Portuguese-inspired seafood dishes. Start with crisp codfish balls, followed by mussels over linguini or paella and wash it down with crisp *vinho verde* (semi-sparkling white wine). You can feast in the informal dining room or outside on the patio overlooking pine trees and a secluded cove below. Call for reservations and directions. To reach Cockatoo, take NH 15 a few miles north from Stonington and drive east on Oceanville Rd, following the signs.

Getting There & Away

From Blue Hill, take ME 176 west for 4 miles and then head south on ME 175/15 for 9 miles to Little Deer Isle.

ISLE AU HAUT

pop 79

Much of Isle au Haut (that's pronounced aisle-a-ho), a rocky island 6 miles long, is under the auspices of Acadia National Park (p508). More remote than the parklands near Bar Harbor, it is not flooded with visitors in summer. Serious hikers can tramp the island's miles of trails and camp for the night in the **Duck Harbor Campground** (sites $25; ☺ mid-May–mid-Oct), which has five shelters maintained by the National Park Service (NPS).

For information on hiking and camping on Isle au Haut, contact **Acadia National Park** (☎ 207-288-3338; www.nps.gov/acad). Reservations for shelters must be accompanied by payment (made after 1 April).

For a less rustic experience, the **Inn at Isle au Haut** (☎ 207-335-5141; www.innatisleauhaut.com; r with breakfast, lunch & dinner $275-350; ☺ Jun-Sep) offers four bright, cheerfully furnished rooms with antique furnishings and quilted bedspreads. Two rooms have ocean views. Meals are included in the rate and are generally excellent. Bring your own wine and alcohol. Bicycles are available for exploring the island.

The **Isle au Haut Boat Company** (☎ 207-367-5193; www.isleauhaut.com; adult/child $16/8) operates daily, year-round mail-boat trips from Stonington's Atlantic Ave Hardware Dock to the village of Isle au Haut. In summer, except on Sunday, at least three boats a day make the 45-minute crossing. On Sunday and major holidays, there's only one boat a day. Bicycles, boats and canoes (no cars) can be carried to the village of Isle au Haut for a fee. To park your car in Stonington while visiting Isle au Haut costs around $10 per day.

MT DESERT ISLAND & ACADIA NATIONAL PARK

The jewel of the Down East region, Mt Desert Island has long captivated visitors. Set with forest-covered mountains, placid lakes and dramatic coastline, this 108-sq-mile island provides many ways to experience its natural beauty. It's home to Acadia National Park,

MAINE

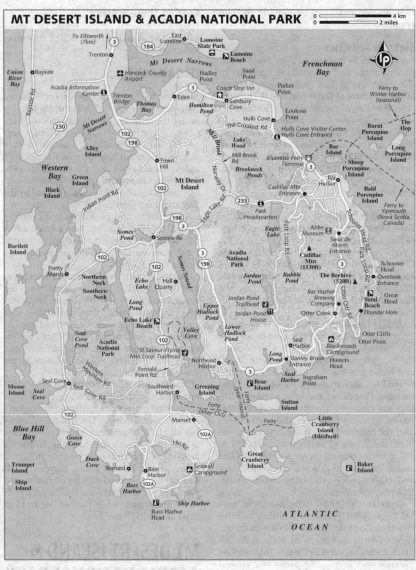

MT DESERT ISLAND & ACADIA NATIONAL PARK

New England's most biodiverse setting – some 200 species of plants, 80 species of mammals and 273 kinds of birds live here.

Adventure comes in many forms, from hiking and mountain biking the many miles of trails and unpaved roads to kayaking Acadia's scenic coves and rivers. On the northeastern shore of the island is the popular gateway of Bar Harbor, Maine's oldest summer resort.

While the coastal vistas and spruce forests are impressive, Acadia draws enormous crowds – particularly in July and August. This is, after all, the second-most-visited national park in the country (after Yosemite). Be prepared for long lines and heavily congested roads, or plan your visit for the off season.

Samuel de Champlain, the intrepid French explorer, sailed along this coast in the early 17th century. Seeing the bare, windswept granite summit of Cadillac Mountain, he called the island on which it stood l'Île des Monts Déserts. The name is still pronounced day-*zehr* almost 400 years later.

BAR HARBOR
pop 4800

Bar Harbor is a village of handsome Victorians and magnificent summer cottages, which date back to the 1890s when wealthy summer rusticators first started visiting the island. Since then, the village has grown in popularity, with a mix of historic inns and cozy B&Bs that accommodate a wider variety of visitors. The town has many restaurants, bars, shops and numerous other commercial enterprises targeted toward the summer crowds. Bar Harbor is also an essential stop-off for planning outdoor adventures. For biking, kayaking, sailing, and rock-climbing, see p509.

Bar Harbor was chartered as a town in 1796, while Maine was part of the Commonwealth of Massachusetts. In 1844, landscape painters Thomas Cole and Frederick Church came to Mt Desert and liked what they saw. They sketched the landscape and later returned with their art students. Naturally enough, the wealthy families who purchased their paintings asked Cole and Church about the beautiful land depicted in their paintings, and soon the families began to spend summers on Mt Desert. In a short time, Bar Harbor rivaled Newport, Rhode Island (RI), for the stature of its summer-colony guests. A rail line from Boston and regular steamboat service brought even more visitors. By the end of the 19th century, Bar Harbor was one of the eastern seaboard's most desirable summer resorts.

WWII damaged the tourist trade, but worse damage was to come. In 1947, a forest fire torched 17,000 acres of parkland, along with 60 palatial 'summer cottages' of wealthy summer residents, putting an end to Bar Harbor's gilded age. But the town recovered as a destination for the new mobile middle-class of the postwar years.

Bar Harbor's busiest season is late June through August. There's a short lull just after Labor Day (early September), but then it gets busy again from foliage season through mid-October.

Orientation & Information

ME 3 approaches Bar Harbor from the north and the west, and it passes right through the town. Main St is the town's principal commercial thoroughfare, along with Cottage St. Mt Desert St has many of the town's inns, just a few minutes' walk from the Town Green.

The Town Green has a free wi-fi connection if you're sporting a laptop. If not, head to **Opera House Internet** (☎ 207-288-3509; 27 Cottage St; per hr $9; 8am-11pm) to get online.

For information centers covering the local area, see p505. For information regarding Nova Scotia (Canada), stop at the **Nova Scotia Visitor Information Center** (☎ 207-288-9438; www.novascotia.com; 37 Cottage St). It's next to the Criterion Theatre. For info on getting to Nova Scotia, see Bay Ferries on p508.

Sights & Activities

Bar Harbor has its share of attractions, but it's also the base for many activities in other parts of Mt Desert Island, see p509.

DOWNTOWN

Despite the gorgeous scenery just outside of town, there's plenty of human-made distractions in Bar Harbor. Restaurants, taverns and boutique are scattered along Main Street and the intersecting roads of Mt Desert and Cottage Streets. You'll find shops selling everything from wool sweaters and fudge to camping gear, books, handicrafts and musical instruments. The following galleries are worth checking out.

Argosy Gallery (☎ 207-288-9226; www.argosygallery .com; 110 Main St) This colorful gallery displays the landscapes and still lifes of more than 36 artists, many of whom are native to the area.

Island Artisans (☎ 207-288-4214; www.islandartisans .com; 99 Main St) One of Bar Harbor's biggest galleries, this place features the works of over 100 Maine artisans, with works in paper, glass, jewelry, metalwork and ceramics.

SHORE PATH

For a picturesque view of the harbor, take a stroll along the Shore Path. This half-mile walkway first laid down in 1880 begins near Agamont Park and continues past birch-tree-lined Grant Park, with views of the Porcupine

MAINE

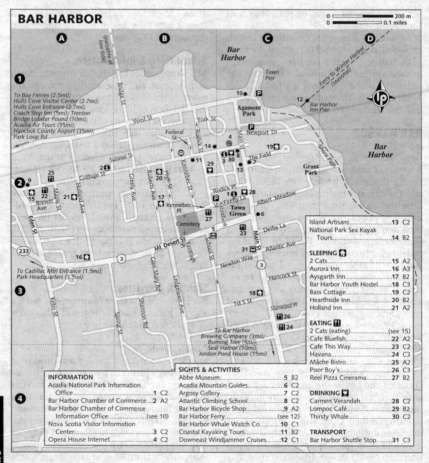

BAR HARBOR

SIGHTS & ACTIVITIES	
Abbe Museum	5 B2
Acadia Mountain Guides	6 C2
Argosy Gallery	7 C2
Atlantic Climbing School	8 C2
Bar Harbor Bicycle Shop	9 A2
Bar Harbor Ferry	(see 12)
Bar Harbor Whale Watch Co	10 C1
Coastal Kayaking Tours	11 B2
Downeast Windjammer Cruises	12 C1
Island Artisans	13 C2
National Park Sea Kayak Tours	14 B2

SLEEPING	
2 Cats	15 A2
Aurora Inn	16 A3
Aysgarth Inn	17 B2
Bar Harbor Youth Hostel	18 C3
Bass Cottage	19 C2
Hearthside Inn	20 B2
Holland Inn	21 A2

EATING	
2 Cats (eating)	(see 15)
Cafe Bluefish	22 A2
Cafe This Way	23 C2
Havana	24 C3
Mâche Bistro	25 A2
Poor Boy's	26 C3
Reel Pizza Cinerama	27 B2

DRINKING	
Carmen Verandah	28 B2
Lompoc Café	29 B2
Thirsty Whale	30 C2

TRANSPORT	
Bar Harbor Shuttle Stop	31 C3

INFORMATION	
Acadia National Park Information Office	1 C2
Bar Harbor Chamber of Commerce	2 A2
Bar Harbor Chamber of Commerce Information Office	(see 10)
Nova Scotia Visitor Information Center	3 C2
Opera House Internet	4 C2

Islands offshore and the historic mansions set back from the path. Complete the loop by returning along Wayman Lane.

ABBE MUSEUM

Across from the village green, the **Abbe Museum** (☎ 207-288-3519; www.abbemuseum.org; 26 Mt Desert St; adult/child $6/2; ☼ 10am-6pm) contains a fascinating collection of cultural artifacts related to Maine's Native American heritage. More than 50,000 objects are in the collection with pottery, tools, combs and fishing implements that span the last 2000 years. Contemporary pieces include finely wrought woodcarvings, birch-bark containers and baskets. The museum also has a smaller **branch** (☎ 207-288-2179; ME 3 & Park Loop Rd; adult/child $2/1) in a lush park-like setting at Sieur de Monts Spring, 2.5 miles south of Bar Harbor.

BAR HARBOR BREWING COMPANY

This tiny award-winning **brewery** (☎ 207-288-4592; www.barharborbrewing.com; 135 Otter Creek Dr; ☼ 10am-6pm; ♿) is one of North America's smallest, producing just 260 barrels a year. Rich-roasted ales and dark creamy stouts are brewed, bottled and delivered by a husband-and-wife team. Free tours and tastings take place during the summer (☼ 3:30-5pm Tuesday to Friday). For the kids, the brewery makes root beer and 100% natural blueberry soda. It's located along ME 3, about 3 miles south of town.

TRIP PLANNER: MT DESERT ISLAND

Formed by glaciers some 18,000 years ago, Mt Desert Island boasts great geographical variety, including freshwater lakes, dense forests, impressive mountains and picturesque valleys. Its rich natural beauty and size (the island is the third-largest on the east coast) bring a wealth of options for outdoor adventurers.

Orientation

First things first: although many people use 'Mt Desert Island' interchangeably with 'Acadia National Park' (p508), the park includes areas outside the island (such as Isle au Haut, p501, and the Schoodic Peninsula, p511). Admission to the park is $20 per vehicle, good for seven days. Unlike some other national parks, there are towns on the island, chief among them Bar Harbor (p503), with many inns, restaurants and outdoor outfitters. Quieter settlements include well-heeled Northeast Harbor (p509) and laid-back Southwest Harbor (p510).

Activities

Among the many ways to spend a day on the island, hiking ranks high, with more than 120 miles of trails; for mountain-bikers, the park offers 45 miles of unpaved, vehicle-free carriage roads. There's also plenty of water-based activity, from sailing and whale-watching trips to kayaking and canoeing. Bar Harbor is the best place to arrange an excursion. Scenic drives are an option for those who want an overview of the park; the 20-mile park loop road affords some beautiful vistas. You can also visit lighthouses or go for a swim at Echo Lake Beach or off Sand Beach. In winter, the brave few enjoy cross-country skiing and snowshoeing. Other activities include attending ranger-led programs and taking in the shops and galleries of Bar Harbor. For a rundown on adventure activities and outfitters see p509.

Sleeping

Two park campgrounds open during the warmer months. **Blackwoods** (p509; open year-round) requires reservations, while **Seawall** (p508; open late May to September) is first-come, first served. There are dozens of guesthouses throughout the park; prices are fairly high during the summer and reservations are essential. Other options for accommodations are the nearby towns of Ellsworth and Franklin (p507).

Getting Around

One other crucial point: driving. With millions of visitors each year, the roads get frustratingly crowded during the summer. Do yourself and the environment a big favor and park your car at your guesthouse or campground and take the free shuttle bus. The park runs the **Island Explorer** (www.exploreacadia.com; ☼ late Jun-Sep) along eight routes that connect visitors to hiking trails, carriage roads, island beaches, and in-town destinations. It can even carry mountain bikes.

More Information

For more information, stop by one of the following information booths:
Acadia Information Center (Map p502; ☎ 207-667-8550, 800-358-8550; www.acadiainfo.com; ☼ early May–mid-Oct) A good first stop before entering the park, with loads of information, and staff can also help with lodging. It's located on your right (ME 3) just before you cross the bridge to Mt Desert Island.
Acadia National Park Information Office (Map p504; Firefly Lane, Bar Harbor) This offers strictly walk-in service and is run by park rangers. It faces the Town Green.
Bar Harbor Chamber of Commerce (Map p504; ☎ 207-288-5103, 888-540-9990; www.barharbormaine .com; 93 Cottage St, Bar Harbor; ☼ 8am-5pm Mon-Fri Jun-Sep, 8am-4pm off-season) Offers maps, guidebooks and general information; It also maintains a small information office at 1 Harbor Pl by the Town Pier (open 9am to 5pm from mid-May to mid-October).
   Hulls Cove Visitor Center (Map p502; ☎ 207-288-3338; www.nps.gov/acad; ☼ 8am-4:30pm May-Oct) Sixteen miles south of Ellsworth on the mainland and 3 miles north of Bar Harbor, this is Acadia National Park's visitor center. Off-season, head to Park Headquarters for information, which is 3 miles west of Bar Harbor on ME 233.

CRUISES

Numerous outfits offer adventures out on the water. Keep in mind that it is often 20°F (11°C) cooler on the water than on land, so bring a jacket.

Bar Harbor Ferry (☎ 207-288-2984; www.down eastwindjammer.com; Bar Harbor Inn Pier; adult/child $30/20; ☼ mid-May–mid-Oct) Makes frequent one-hour trips to Winter Harbor, where there's great biking.

Bar Harbor Whale Watch Co (☎ 207-288-2386, 800-508-1499; www.barharborwhales.com; 1 West St; adult/child/child under 5 $49/25/8; ☼ Jun–Oct) Operates four-hour whale-watching cruises, among other options.

Downeast Windjammer Cruises (☎ 207-288-4585; www.downeastwindjammer.com; Bar Harbor Inn Pier; adult/child $32/22; ☼ May–Oct) Offers two-hour cruises on the majestic 151ft, four-masted schooner *Margaret Todd*.

Sleeping

Bar Harbor has thousands of guest rooms found in both cookie-cutter motels and Victorian charmers. Reservations are essential in the summer.

For camping in the Park, see p508. Commercial campgrounds are also located along ME 3 near Ellsworth and clustered near the entrances to the park. Numerous inexpensive motels line ME 3 from Ellsworth to Bar Harbor.

Bar Harbor Youth Hostel (☎ 207-288-5587; www .barharborhostel.com; 321 Main St; dm/r $25/80; ☐ wi-fi) In a converted home a few blocks south of the village green, this pleasant, friendly and very clean hostel has simple male and female dorm rooms, each sleeping 10, as well as a private room that sleeps four. There's a midnight curfew and daily lockout from 10am to 5pm.

Aurora Inn (☎ 207-288-3771; www.aurorainn.com; 51 Holland Ave; r $60-160; ☐ wi-fi) This simple but comfortable motel has clean rooms and a good location within walking distance of everything. Guests can use the heated pool and Jacuzzi of the nearby Quality Inn.

Holland Inn (☎ 207-288-4804; www.hollandinn.com; 35 Holland Ave; r with breakfast $55-165) This restored 1895 farmhouse, within walking distance of town, is run by personable innkeepers who offer eight comfortable rooms, space for lounging in the lush garden and a great morning repast.

Aysgarth Inn (☎ 207-288-9655; www.aysgarth .com; 50 Roberts Ave; r with breakfast $70-135) This charming six-room B&B is well located in town and provides comfortable rooms with homey touches (some with views of Cadillac Mountain, wood floors or four-post beds). The 19th-century house has a front porch for lounging, a third-floor sun deck and cozy nooks in the parlor.

Hearthside Inn (☎ 207-288-4533; www.hearthsideinn .com; 7 High St; r with breakfast $75-160) Hearthside is an elegant Victorian inn with nine inviting rooms, each set with antique and period furnishings, queen-sized beds and artwork adorning the walls. Some rooms have fireplaces, Jacuzzi tubs or a private veranda.

2 Cats (☎ 207-288-2808; www.2catsbarharbor.com; 130 Cottage St; r with breakfast $125-195) This cozy guesthouse has three bright, sunny, nicely designed rooms, each with wood floors, four-post beds, a sitting area and a private entrance. Breakfasts are spectacular with oversized cappuccinos and home-baked goodies. There's also a restaurant here, see below.

Bass Cottage (☎ 207-288-3705, 866-782-9224; www .basscottage.com; 14 The Field; r with breakfast $185-350; ☼ May–Oct) Hidden from the throngs but perfectly situated in the center of town, the 1885 Bass Cottage has 10 handsome rooms, awash with antiques and luxurious linens. They're fresh and inviting, without being weighed down by frilly decor found in many other period guesthouses.

Eating

Bar Harbor's most interesting dining possibilities are along Rodick, Kennebec and Cottage Sts.

2 Cats (☎ 207-288-2808; 130 Cottage St; meals $8-17; ☼ breakfast & lunch; Ⓥ) A splendid café with a heart of gold, 2 Cats serves delicious breakfasts (try a smoked trout omelet), smoothies and homemade muffins as well as heartier fare – vegetarian, seafood and grilled meats for lunch. You can also stay here (see above).

Poor Boy's (☎ 207-288-4148; 300 Main St; meals $13-22; ☼ dinner) This locally owned favorite spreads an enormous menu of lobster, grilled fish and chicken dishes, roast meats, pastas, salads and a dozen desserts. It's good value, and the quality is generally high.

Reel Pizza Cinerama (☎ 207-288-3828; www.reelpizza .net; 33B Kennebec Pl; pizza $13-20) This place caters to the indulgent among us who like munching on good pizza, drinking local microbrews and lounging on couches while watching a nightly flick ($6) on the big screen. Films range from indie and foreign films to the latest Hollywood fodder, with two screenings most nights (usually around 6pm and 8pm).

WORTH THE TRIP: ELLSWORTH & FRANKLIN

Just north of Mt Desert Island, the small town of Ellsworth (Map p499) is a slice of old-school Americana, with a pretty Main street lined with shops, galleries and restaurants. Nearby is the **Woodlawn Museum** (☎ 207-664-8671; www.woodlawnmuseum.com; ME 172, Ellsworth; adult/child $7.50/3; ☷ 10am-5pm Tue-Sat, 1-4pm Sun Jun-Sep, 1-4pm Tue-Sun May & Oct) located 0.25 miles south of US 1. The former home of three generations of the wealthy Black family dates from the 1820s and has marvelously preserved furnishings, decorations and family artifacts dating from 1820 to 1920. Formal gardens and a picturesque lawn surround the mansion, with a pleasant trail circling the woods.

Afterwards, treat yourself to a meal at **Cleonice** (☎ 207-664-7554; 112 Main St, Ellsworth; meals $7-22; ☷ lunch & dinner), which serves traditional and exotic Mediterranean fare using local ingredients in tasty lunchtime panini and salads, and marvelous tapas, grilled fish and seafood pastas at dinner. The landmark building has black-and-white tiled floors and tables hidden in carved wooden alcoves that lend an old-world feel to the place.

Trenton Bridge Lobster Pound (☎ 207-667-2977; ME 3, Ellsworth; meals $12-22; ☷ lunch & dinner Mon-Sat May–mid-Oct) is one of many lobster pounds in the area, and one of the oldest and best, with a pretty water-view picnic area. It lies just north of the Trenton Bridge on ME 3, about 6.5 miles south of Ellsworth on the road to Bar Harbor.

There are many charming, good-value guesthouses in the area, including the 1830s colonial **White Elephant Inn** (☎ 207-565-2020; 25 Main St/ME 182, Franklin; r with breakfast $80-120) in Franklin, about 10 miles north of Ellsworth (Map p499). Rooms tend toward bohemian exoticism with a mix of antiques and colorful tapestries, the iconic elephant present throughout the house. Guests will enjoy excellent home-cooked breakfasts. Afternoon tea is served on weekends (reservations required).

In Franklin, you're well placed for a quiet kayaking experience far from the madding crowds in Bar Harbor. The **Water's Edge** (☎ 207-460-6350; 222 W Franklin Rd/ME 182; kayak/canoe per day $30/25) rents kayaks on the shores of tranquil Egypt Bay.

Mâche Bistro (☎ 207-288-0447; 135 Cottage St; meals $16-23; ☷ dinner Tue-Sat; **V**) Bar Harbor's premier restaurant, Mâche Bistro, serves eclectic New England fare in a stylish setting. The changing menu highlights the local riches, with seafood stew, braised lamb shanks and pan-fried tempeh among recent offerings. The chef's signature dish is a luscious breast of duck glazed with orange and ginger. Specialty cocktails add to the appeal.

Café Bluefish (☎ 207-288-3696; 122 Cottage St; meals $16-23; ☷ lunch & dinner May-Oct) This intimate storefront bistro offers the fresh catch of the day served in inventive ways such as pistachio-crusted salmon, lobster strudel and Cajun-style tilapia. The café also serves roasted duck and two vegetarian dishes.

Café This Way (☎ 207-288-4483; 14 Mt Desert St; meals $16-32; ☷ breakfast & dinner May-Oct) This relaxed, quirky eatery is *the* place for breakfast, with plump Maine blueberry pancakes and eggs Benedict with smoked salmon. It also serves fairly sophisticated dinners such as Maine crab cakes, grilled sea scallops and lamb sirloin.

Havana (☎ 207-288-2822; 318 Main St; meals $18-34; ☷ dinner) This dashing restaurant serves nicely seasoned meat and seafood dishes

with a touch of Latin flair (Cuban this isn't). Sesame ginger-crusted salmon, double-cut pork chops, and appetizers like monkfish ceviche and coconut-stuffed shrimp are among the options. The small dining menu is complemented by a much larger wine list.

Drinking

Carmen Verandah (☎ 207-288-2886; 119 Main St; ☷ 11am-1am) The ridiculous name of this 2nd-floor terrace bar doesn't detract from the festive atmosphere, refreshing cocktails and dance floor that sometimes sees some action courtesy of the live music and DJs in the summer. Downstairs, there's Joe's Smoke Shop, an upscale cigar bar, and the popular, but uninspiring, outdoor restaurant Rupunini.

Lompoc Café (☎ 207-288-9392; www.lompoccafe .com; cover charge $3-10; 36 Rodick St; ☷ May-Nov) This homey restaurant and bar hosts a variety of performers playing bluegrass, indie rock, jazz and folk on the patio. Step up to the bar and order a glass of Bar Harbor Real Ale. Blueberry ale may satisfy the intrepid.

Thirsty Whale (☎ 207-288-9335; 40 Cottage St; ☷ noon-midnight) Head here to mingle with locals and lobstermen over a pint and some

MAINE

hearty, inexpensive seafood. There's often live music Wednesday through Saturday nights.

Getting There & Away

US Airways Express, operated by **Colgan Air** (☎ 800-428-4322; www.colganair.com), connects Bar Harbor and Boston with daily flights year-round. The Hancock County Airport (Map p502) is in Trenton, off ME 3, just north of the Trenton Bridge.

Vermont Transit/Greyhound (☎ 207-772-6587, 800-231-2222; www.vermonttransit.com; ☺ year-round) runs four daily buses between Boston and Bangor ($39), as well as NYC and Bangor ($49). From Bangor, you have to transfer to the pricey **Bar Harbor Shuttle** (☎ 207-479-5911; www.barharborshuttle .com; one-way from $25) to reach the island.

Bay Ferries (☎ 207-288-3395; www.catferry.com; 121 Eden St; one-way tickets $63, autos $130; ☺ Jun-Oct) operates an ultrafast car ferry, *The Cat*, providing a maritime link between Bar Harbor and Yarmouth, Nova Scotia (Canada). The voyage takes 2½ hours.

ACADIA NATIONAL PARK

The only national park in all of New England, Acadia National Park offers unrivaled coastal beauty and activities for both leisurely hikers and adrenaline junkies.

Orientation & Information

The park's main Hulls Cove entrance, which is northwest of Bar Harbor via ME 3, has the **Hulls Cove Visitor center** (☎ 207-288-3338; www.nps .gov/acad; ☺ 8am-4:30pm May-Oct), from where the 20-mile-long Park Loop Rd circumnavigates the northeastern section of Mt Desert island. It is a one-way road for much of its length. See also p505 for other information outlets.

The admission fee to the park costs $20 ($10 off-season) per vehicle and is good for seven consecutive days. The fee is collected at a booth on the Park Loop Rd, just north of Sand Beach. If you enter the park by bike or on foot, the fee is $10 ($5 off-season) per person.

You'll find other entrances to the park and the Park Loop Rd at the **Cadillac Mountain entrance** just west of Bar Harbor; the Sieur de Monts entrance just south of Bar Harbor; the **Overlook entrance** southwest of Bar Harbor; and the **Stanley Brook entrance** east of Northeast Harbor.

Cadillac Mountain (1530ft), the highest point in the park, is a few miles southwest of Bar Harbor, and can be reached by auto road.

Most of the carriage roads (closed to motor vehicles) are between Bubble Pond and Somes Sound, to the west of Cadillac Mountain.

Call the visitor center for camping, road and weather information. For park emergencies, call ☎ 207-288-3369.

MAPS & GUIDES

Free NPS maps of the park are available at the information and visitor centers (p505). Try and get a copy of the out-of-print *AMC Guide to Mt Desert Island & Acadia National Park* by the Appalachian Mountain Club, which has descriptions of all the trails, and a good trail map. More recent is *Acadia: The Complete Guide*, by Jay Kaiser, perhaps the most comprehensive guidebook to the park. You can pick up guides and maps at the visitor center and at bookshops in Bar Harbor.

Sights & Activities

Start your tour with an orienting drive along the Park Loop Rd; you can also cover this trip on the park's free Island Explorer bus system. On the portion called **Ocean Dr**, stop at **Thunder Hole**, south of the Overlook entrance, for a look at the surf crashing into a cleft in the granite. (The effect is most dramatic with a strong incoming tide.) **Otter Cliffs**, not far south of Thunder Hole, is basically a wall of pink granite rising right from the sea.

At **Jordan Pond**, there's a lovely self-guided nature trail that follows a one-mile loop around the pond. Stop for tea and popovers (a puffy, hollow muffin-like creation) at Jordan Pond House (opposite).

For a nice, easy hike, consider making the quick (20-minute) ascent of **The Beehive** near the Overlook entrance. For a slightly longer walk on the more-secluded 'backside' of the island, try the **St Saveur-Flying Mountain Loop Trail**, off Fernald Point Rd, just north of Southwest Harbor. Make sure you wear proper hiking boots to avoid an injury.

For swimming, try either **Sand Beach** or **Seal Harbor** for chilly salt water, or **Echo Lake** for fresh water. Cyclists shouldn't miss the **carriage paths** around the lake. Finish exploring atop the windy summit of **Cadillac Mountain**, which is quite popular with bands of hardy souls at sunrise.

Sleeping & Eating

There are three great and rustic campgrounds in the park: **Seawall Campground** (campsites per night

MT DESERT ISLAND ACTIVITIES GUIDE

The great outdoors are great indeed when out scaling the peaks of Mt Desert Island, kayaking its pristine coastline or mountain-biking along winding, rugged trails. Here are a few ways to take in the scenery:

- Hiking: Acadia has more than 120 miles of hiking trails, ranging from easy to challenging, and more than a dozen peaks.

- Mountain Biking: The park's 45 miles of carriage roads are excellent settings for riding. You can rent bikes at **Bar Harbor Bicycle Shop** (Map p504; ☎ 207-288-3886; www.barharborbike.com; 141 Cottage St; per day $21-35).

- Kayaking: numerous Bar Harbor–based outfits offer tours and rentals, including **National Park Sea Kayak Tours** (Map p504; ☎ 800-347-0940; www.acadiakayak.com; 39 Cottage St; half-day tour $46; ☑ May-Oct) and **Coastal Kayaking Tours** (Map p504; ☎ 800-526-8615; www.acadiafun .com; 48 Cottage St; half/full day tours $46/69).

- Rock Climbing: With all that granite, Acadia National Park is a Mecca for rock climbers. Two Bar Harbor outfits offering guided trips and instruction are the **Atlantic Climbing School** (Map p504; ☎ 207-288-2521; www.acadiaclimbing.com; 2nd fl, 67 Main St; half/full day trips $100/180; ☑ May-Nov) and **Acadia Mountain Guides** (Map p504; ☎ 207-288-8186; www.acadiamountain guides.com; 198 Main St; half-day trips $100, full-day trips $180-225; ☑ May-Oct).

- Gliding: For scenic glider and biplane trips over the island, book a flight with **Acadia Air Tours** (off Map p504; ☎ 207-667-7627; www.acadiaairtours.com; Hancock County Airport, ME 3; 20-/40-min biplane trip $225/325; glider trip per couple $179-299; ☑ May-Oct) located north of the Trenton Bridge.

- Cruises: for sailing and whale-watching trips onto the bay, see p506.

$14-20; ☑ May-Sep), rents sites on a first-come, first-served basis; **Blackwoods Campground** (☎ 207-288-3338; campsites per night $20; ☑ year-round) requires reservations in summer; and **Duck Harbor** (campsites $25), on Isle au Haut (p501), where the charge is per reservation and last for 3 to 5 days. No backcountry camping is allowed. There are also private campgrounds outside the park.

Coach Stop Inn (☎ 207-288-9886; www.coachstopinn .com; 715 Acadia Hwy/ME 3, Salisbury Cove; r $125-155) Five miles outside Bar Harbor and just 2 miles from the main entrance to Acadia National Park, this is the oldest surviving area hostelry. Built in 1804, the inn has five handsomely decorated rooms set on three acres of gardens.

Jordan Pond House (☎ 207-276-3316; www.jordan pond.com; Park Loop Rd, Seal Harbor; meals $13-23; ☑ lunch, tea & dinner mid-May–mid-Oct) Beautifully set amid the park's lush greenery (it's the only restaurant within park boundaries), this elegant teahouse serves afternoon tea and delectable popovers with strawberry jam. Best of all, it's an outdoor affair, with tables set on a broad lawn, overlooking mountain and ocean views. Dinner is similarly refined, though the food is often disappointing.

our pick **Burning Tree** (☎ 207-288-9331; 69 Otter Creek Dr/ME 3; meals $20-29; ☑ dinner) One of the best restaurants on the island, Burning Tree prepares a rich and eclectic assortment of dishes, with local seafood taking pride of place. Among the crowd pleasers: prosciutto-wrapped sea scallops, squash blossom appetizers, chili-glazed monkfish and Earl Grey ice cream. This place is popular, so do reserve a table. It's 4 miles south of town, along ME 3.

Getting There & Around

For information on getting to the island, see opposite. The free shuttle system, the **Island Explorer** (☎ 207-667-5796; www.exploreacadia.com), features eight routes that link hotels, inns and campgrounds to destinations within Acadia National Park. Route maps are available at local establishments and online.

Northeast Harbor

One of Mt Desert Island's prime vacation villages, simply called 'Northeast,' this town has a marina chock-full of yachts. It also features a tiny main street populated with art galleries and boutiques and back streets dotted with mansions, and comfortable summer hideaways that are good for a short stay. It's a tranquil spot.

MAINE

Asticou Terraces & Azalea Garden (ME 3; suggested donation $3; ⊙ 7am-7pm Jul–early Sep), designed in 1900, is simply lovely. This 200 acre garden is laced with paths, little shelters and ornamental Japanese-style bridges. Azaleas and rhododendrons bloom profusely from mid-May to mid-June. Don't neglect to wander up the garden's **Thuya Lodge** (⊙ 10am-5pm late Jun–early Sep), the depository of botanical books, where there's a reflecting pool and well-tended perennial gardens. The terraces zigzag through the woods and down to the water.

SLEEPING & EATING

Harbourside Inn (☎ 207-276-3272; www.harboursideinn.com; ME 3; r $125-295; ⊙ mid-Jun–mid-Sep) Set on a wooded hillside above the village, this 1880s shingle-style summer cottage has 14 attractive rooms and suites. Most guest rooms have a fireplace, and all are outfitted with antiques, but the real draw is the warm hospitality you'll receive.

Asticou Inn (☎ 207-276-3344; www.asticou.com; ME 3; r with breakfast Jul-Aug $225-300, off-season $130-220; ⊙ late-May–mid-Oct; ⊛) This famed summer hotel has been taking in guests since the late 1880s. It offers elegant common spaces, upwards of 50 rooms and suites, and tennis courts. The best rooms have wood floors, classical furnishings and a fireplace or private balcony.

Tan Turtle Tavern (☎ 207-276-9898; 151 Main St; meals $9-18; ⊙ lunch & dinner) You'll find an enormous menu of tasty, nicely prepared fare at this popular new restaurant on Main St. Zingy salads, fresh fish, sandwiches, burgers, chops, fajitas, barbecue and smoothies are just a few of the choices.

Red Bird (☎ 207-276-3006; 11 Sea St; meals $12-24; ⊙ lunch & dinner) This colorful, stylish place serves excellent curry chicken salads, prosciutto sandwiches and other high-end bistro fare in a pretty setting near the harbor. More substantial seafood dishes and grills are served in the evening. Reserve ahead.

Southwest Harbor & Bass Harbor
pop 2000

More laid-back and less affluent than Northeast Harbor, 'Southwest' is also quite tranquil. But that's a bit deceiving: it's also a major boat-building center and a commercial fishing harbor.

From the Upper Town Dock – a quarter-mile along Clark Point Rd from the flashing light in the center of town – boats venture out

into Frenchman Bay to the Cranberry Isles (see opposite).

A few miles south of Southwest Harbor along ME 102A lies the much photographed **Bass Harbor Head Light**, a 26ft lighthouse built in 1858. Afterwards, continue around the craggy coast and loop back down to Bernard, where you'll find Thurston's Lobster Pound (below), one of the best on the island.

SLEEPING & EATING

Penury Hall (☎ 207-244-7102; www.penuryhall.com; 374 Main St, Southwest Harbor; r with breakfast $80-115) This snug and longtime B&B, the first on Mt Desert Island, rents three rooms in an 1865 schoolhouse. If you want a real taste of old-time Maine, not to mention a filling breakfast, this is the place. The hosts are incredibly knowledgeable about area activities and lesser-known spots.

Claremont (☎ 207-244-5036; www.theclaremonthotel.com; Claremont Rd, Southwest Harbor; r $115-245; ⊙ late May–mid-Oct) The island's oldest and most graceful hotel, the Claremont has some of the most stunning views from any guesthouse in the area, where a wraparound porch and sloping broad lawns give way to boats bobbing in the ocean. Its 24 guest rooms are decorated in period cottage-style furnishings. There's a fantastic restaurant and elegant bar on site.

our pick **Thurston's Lobster Pound** (☎ 207-244-7600; Steamboat Wharf, Bernard; meals $14-22; ⊙ noon-8pm late May–Sep) Overlooking Bass Harbor in Bernard, this casual waterside spot serves amazingly fresh lobster to superb views. Among locals, Thurston's serves the best crustacean on the island.

Captain's Galley (☎ 207-244-3202; 1 Clark Point Rd, Southwest Harbor; meals $15-28; ⊙ 9am-8pm mid-May–Aug, 9am-5pm Sep–mid-Oct) For serious seafood sustenance and local atmosphere, everyone heads to this casual spot on Beal's pier. Grab a picnic table and dine on chowder, crabmeat rolls and, most importantly, lobster.

FURTHER DOWN EAST

The 'Sunrise Coast' is the moniker given by Maine's tourism promoters for the area that lies east of Ellsworth, all the way to Lubec and Eastport. But to Mainers, this is far 'down east' Maine, the area downwind and east of the rest of the state. It's much less traveled,

---

WORTH THE TRIP: ISLANDS OFF THE ISLAND

The **Cranberry Isles** (www.cranberryisles.com) are delightful, primarily because they're so off the beaten path. The 400 acre Little Cranberry, more commonly known as **Islesford**, is about 20 minutes offshore from Southwest Harbor. Diversions include a few galleries, a couple of B&Bs and the **Islesford Market** (☎ 207-244-7667; ☸ Mon-Sat mid-Jun–early Sep), where the 80-some year-rounders and 400-some summer folk gather around like it's their own kitchen. Great Cranberry Island is even more low-key; stop in at the **Seawich Café & Cranberry Store** (☎ 207-244-5336) to see who's around and what's up.

Cranberry Cove Boating Co (☎ 207-244-5882; roundtrip adult/child $22/14; ☸ May-Oct) carries passengers to and from the Cranberry Isles, departing Southwest Harbor, aboard the 47-passenger *Island Queen*, which cruises six times daily in summer.

The **Beal & Bunker Mailboat** (☎ 207-244-3575; round-trip adult/child $20/10) offers frequent year-round service between Northeast Harbor and the Cranberry Isles.

---

but more scenic and unspoiled. The region also boasts fewer settlements and thick coastal fog that creeps in for longer periods of time.

If you seek quiet walks away from the tourist throngs, traditional coastal villages with little impact from tourism, and lower travel prices, explore the 900-plus miles of coastline east of Bar Harbor.

SCHOODIC PENINSULA

Jutting into the Atlantic Ocean, the southern tip of this peninsula contains a quiet portion of Acadia National Park. It includes a 7.2-mile shore drive called Schoodic Point Loop Rd, which offers splendid views of Mt Desert Island and Cadillac Mountain. The one-way loop road is excellent for biking since it has a smooth surface and relatively gentle hills. The Fraser's Point park entrance also has a fine picnic area. Further along the loop, reached by a short walk from the road, you'll find Schoodic Head, a 400ft high promontory with fine ocean views.

North of the peninsula, the little towns of Gouldsboro and Winter Harbor host tourist services like stores and restaurants. This is definitely the quieter part of Acadia, with fewer crowds – but also fewer activities. For information on local businesses, contact the **Schoodic Peninsula Chamber of Commerce** (☎ 207-963-7658; www.acadia-schoodic.org).

Ocean Wood Campground (☎ 207-963-7194; Schoodic Point Loop Rd; sites $25-35; ☸ May–mid-Sep), a pine-filled place that's more akin to a nature reserve than a campground, is south of Birch Harbor and ME 186 and has ocean access.

Jonesport & Great Wass Island

Just off the southern tip of the Jonesport Peninsula, a few miles from the town of Jonesport, Great Wass Island is a standout, a 1540 acre reserve under the control of the **Nature Conservancy** (☎ 207-729-5181; www.tnc.org). In order to maintain the integrity of the reserve for those who most appreciate it, the way to it is not well marked. Parking at the trailhead is also limited, but the cars parked there bear license plates from many different states. This is bird-watching for the cognoscenti.

The reserve's attraction is its rocky coastal scenery, peat bogs, a large stand of jack pines, and bird life, including the amusing puffins. Try to make time for the 2-mile hike to Little Cape Point; it takes about 1½ to two hours, round-trip.

Jonesport and Beals Island are traditional Maine fishing and lobstering villages. The towns get a smattering of visitors during the summer season, most of whom come to take photographs, paint pictures and walk on Great Wass Island. Follow ME 187 to find most of these towns' services, including restaurants and lodgings.

SLEEPING & EATING

Henry Point Campground (☎ 207-497-9633; Kelly Point; sites $18-25; ☸ Apr-Nov) On the point in Jonesport, this simple campground has only portable toilets, picnic tables and one big stone fireplace. But it's surrounded by water, and the semi-shaded sites have fine coastal views. To reach it from ME 187, head southeast on Kelly Point Rd, and thereafter, when in doubt, bear right.

Harbor House on Sawyer Cove (☎ 207-497-5417; www.harborhs.com; Sawyer Sq, Jonesport; r with breakfast $100-120) This old-time Maine B&B and antique shop has two comfortably furnished rooms overlooking the harbor. This

MAINE

is a great base for exploring marvelous, untouched coastline.

GETTING THERE & AWAY

To reach Great Wass Island, follow ME 187 through Jonesport and onto the bridge (it'll be on your right). Cross the bridge and turn left. A little more than a mile further on, cross the small causeway that connects Beals Island to Great Wass Island and turn right. A small 'Nature Conservancy' sign points the way. A mile later, the paved road ends, and after another 1.5 miles on an unpaved road, you'll come to the Great Wass Island parking lot. It holds about a dozen cars. If the parking lot is full, please don't park on the road; the Conservancy sign suggests that you go away and come back some other time.

THE MACHIASES

pop 4811

Although Machias proper hosts a branch of the University of Maine, it's not a place to spend any time. However, its beautiful neighbors, East Machias and Machiasport, are worthy of some attention. Machiasport, in fact, is where the first naval engagement of the Revolutionary War took place. After the king of England received the Declaration of Independence from the colonies, he sent a frigate to Machiasport to monitor the timely collection and transportation of lumber to Portland to build his ships. But a few drunken American colonists at **Burnham Tavern** (☎ 207-255-4432; www.burnhamtavern.com; Main St, East Machias; ☺ 9am-5pm Mon-Fri Jun-Sep) decided to pay the frigate a visit before they could reach shore. After killing the English captain with a single shot to the head, they emptied the ship and burned it on the shores of Jonesport. The king's reaction to this act of rebellion? He ordered his troops to torch Portland.

Don't miss **Jasper Beach**, a bizarre mile-long beach consisting entirely of polished red jasper stones. As the waves wash in, the rocks slide against one another, creating a rather haunting song. It's one of two such beaches in the world (the other is in Japan). To reach it, head down Machias Rd toward the village of Starboard.

The **Machias Bay Area Chamber of Commerce** (☎ 207-255-4402; www.machiaschamber.org; 12 E Main St/US 1, Machias; ☺ 10am-4pm Mon-Fri Jun-Aug), next to the Irving gas station on the edge of town, provides lots of useful information.

Sleeping & Eating

Basic motels line US 1 in Machias, while more serene East Machias and Machiasport have nicer B&Bs.

Machias Motor Inn (☎ 207-255-4861; 26 E Maine St/US 1; r $58-66; ☺) Next to the landmark Helen's Restaurant, this place has 35 rooms overlooking the Machias River; there's also an indoor heated pool.

Captain Cates B&B (☎ 207-255-8812; www.captaincates.com; 309 Port Rd/ME 92, Machiasport; r with breakfast $60-95) Overlooking Machias Bay, this 1850s B&B is furnished with period antiques; six comfortable rooms share a bathroom.

Riverside Inn & Restaurant (☎ 207-255-4134; www.riversideinn-maine.com; US 1, East Machias; r with breakfast May-Oct $95-130, off-season $85-115) About 5 miles east of Machias' center, this large inn has only four guest rooms but it also has a restaurant with a good dinner menu (meals cost $19 to $24).

Getting There & Away

From Ellsworth (the gateway to Bar Harbor), Machias is 64 miles north via US 1. East Machias is 4 miles further north on US 1; Machiasport is 3 miles east of Machias on ME 92.

LUBEC

pop 1650

Perched upon a hill overlooking four lighthouses and Canada, this small fishing village makes its living off the trans-border traffic and a bit of tourism. Away from the crowds and traffic of Acadia National Park and surrounds, this is the real Downeast Maine. There's an informal **information office** in the foyer of the Eastland Motel, on the left-hand side of ME 189 as you roll into town.

Off US 1 at the end of ME 189, Lubec is sited on America's easternmost border with Canada, 60 miles south of Calais and 88 miles northeast of Mt Desert Island.

Sights & Activities

QUODDY HEAD STATE PARK

Some of the most striking scenery in Maine is found in **Quoddy Head State Park** (☎ 207-733-0911; 973 S Lubec Rd; adult/child $2/1). The 531 acre park boasts a walking trail that passes along the edge of towering, jagged cliffs. The tides here are similarly dramatic, fluctuating 16ft in six hours. Follow the fantastic 4-mile loop trail and keep an eye to the sea for migrating whales (finback, minke, humpback and right whales) which migrate along the coast in the summer. The park also boasts intriguing subarctic bogland and the much-photographed red-and-white-banded West Quoddy Light (1858).

CAMPOBELLO INTERNATIONAL PARK

Once beyond Lubec, you're in Canada, specifically on Campobello Island, home to **Roosevelt Campobello International Park** (☎ 506-752-2922; www.fdr.net; admission free; ⊗ park year-round, cottage 9am-5pm mid-May–mid-Oct). Franklin Roosevelt's father, James, bought land here in 1883 and built a palatial summer 'cottage.' The future US president spent many boyhood summers here, and he was later given the 34-room cottage. Franklin and Eleanor made brief, but well-publicized, visits during his long tenure as president.

The park hours, by the way, are given in Eastern Standard Time (which is 10am to 6pm Atlantic Standard Time); the last tour of the cottage is at 4.45pm. Border formalities (p535) are quick and easy for American citizens in cars with US license plates who are crossing into Canada just to visit the park. Travelers from other countries should have their passports (and may need visas) to cross into Canada. The **Campobello Island Chamber of Commerce** (☎ 506-752-2233; ⊗ 9am-6pm May-Oct) provides information on local services.

Sleeping & Eating

South Bay Campground (☎ 207-733-1037; ME 189; sites $20-30; ⊗ May-Oct) Just 7.5 miles off US 1, this campground has 80 wooded and open field sites as well as a sea-kayak landing. The best sites have lovely bay views.

Home Port Inn (☎ 207-733-2077; www.homeportinn.com; 45 Main St; r with breakfast $90-105; ⊗ May-Oct) This hilltop inn, constructed in 1880, has seven cozy rooms, the best with wood floors, elegant furnishings and views over Cobscook bay. Fortunately (as eating options are somewhat limited around here), the dining room serves fine dinners ($20 to $30).

Murphy's (☎ 207-733-4440; ME 189; meals $7-14; ⊗ 6am-9pm) One of the only restaurants in town, Murphy's cooks up tasty breakfasts, served all day. For lunch and dinner there's a range of vegetarian specials and a mix of American, Italian and Mexican dishes.

Getting There & Away

From Machias, head 17 miles north on US 1 then take ME 189 northeast for 11 miles to reach Lubec.

INLAND MAINE

BANGOR

pop 31,600

Bangor is inland Maine's commercial and cultural center that was once the lumber capital of the world. Its Main St is lined with sleepy antique shops and wood-paneled taverns, while the elegant Victorians along West Broadway attest to its former timber wealth in the 1800s. Only a handful of tourists make it to this largely working-class town, which may be reason enough to visit if you're coming from Bar Harbor. Among the attractions: a giant statue of Paul Bunyan (reputedly a native son), a few curious museums and periodic ghostly walking tours – an appropriate activity in the hometown of Stephen King. Look for the author's spooky mansion – complete with a bat-and-cobweb fence – along West Broadway.

The **Bangor Region Chamber of Commerce** (☎ 207-947-0307; www.bangorregion.com; 519 Main St, Bangor; ⊗ 8am-5pm Mon-Fri) is next to the 31ft statue of Paul Bunyan.

Sights & Activities

The **Bangor Museum and Center for History** (☎ 207-942-1900; www.bangormuseum.org; 25 Broad St; ⊗ 10am-4pm) houses a rambling collection of Civil War artifacts and historic clothing (some 800 gowns, dresses, hats, suits and handbags dating from 1918 to the present) as well as thousands of photographs. Check the website for current admission rates. The museum also offers guided tours (by appointment only) of the 1836 **Thomas A Hill House** (159 Union St; adult/child under 18 $5/free; ⊗ noon-3pm Tue-Sat), which is set with period furnishings.

The museum sponsors events throughout the summer, including weekly **ghost lamp tours**, excursions to the **Mt Hope Cemetery** and other activities.

Dedicated to preserving the history of Maine's transportation equipment, the **Cole Land Transportation Museum** (☎ 207-990-3600; www.colemuseum.org; 405 Perry Rd; adult/senior/child $6/free/4; ⊗ 9am-5pm May–mid-Nov) houses a wistful collection of antique vehicles, snow-removal equipment, fire trucks, logging vehicles and thousands of photographs from Maine's bygone days.

If you have kids in tow, don't miss the huge **Discovery Museum** (☎ 207-262-7200; www.mainediscoverymuseum.org; 74 Main St; admission $6.50; ⊗ 9:30am-5pm Tue-Sat, noon-5pm Sun; ♿), the largest kids' museum north of Boston. Hands-on exhibits include a nature exploration, a sound studio, an anatomical journey through the body, space exploration and travel-the-world exhibits on Peru, the Australian outback and a Ghanaian market.

The downtown, with its walkways along the wandering Kandaskeag stream and the Penobscot River, makes for some fine exploring. But for more expansive greenery, head to **Bald Mountain** (1234ft), located 12 miles southeast of Bangor in Dedham. A moderate 1.4-mile hike up this lone mountain yields spectacular views over the countryside; there's a fire tower you can climb for better views. Reach the trailhead by taking Wilson St/ME 1A southeast just past ME 46 and turn right onto Upper Dedham Rd; go 2.5 miles and veer left onto Dedham Rd; the trailhead is another 3.5 miles on the left.

Sleeping

Lots of motels are located off I-95, close to the Maine Mall, but you'll save money if you drive beyond the obvious places near the exit.

Paul Bunyan Campground (☎ 207-941-1177; www .paulbunyancampground.com; 1862 Union St; sites $20-29; ⏰ Apr-Nov) On the outskirts of Bangor, this place has 52 sites; there's not much shade or privacy, as it's really set up for RVs.

Nonesuch Inn (☎ 207-942-3631; www.bangorsfirst bedandbreakfast.com; 59 Hudson Rd/ME 221; r with breakfast $90-130; 🖳 wi-fi) Set in a handsomely restored 19th-century farmhouse, Nonesuch offers three small but nicely furnished rooms surrounded by bucolic countryside. This is still a working farm (among other things they breed appaloosas), with trails just beyond the pastures. There are also rugged river rapids across the road. Nonesuch is 6 miles north of Bangor: take ME 15/Broadway north to ME 221.

Charles Inn (☎ 207-992-2820; www.thecharlesinn.com; 20 Broad St; r with buffet breakfast $80-150) This inn offers 35 charming, tidy and renovated rooms. The staff is friendly and efficient, and the location is ideal: it's in the heart of Bangor, just steps from restaurants and shops.

Eating & Drinking

Friars Bakehouse (☎ 207-947-3770; 21 Central St; pastries $2; ⏰ 7am-3pm Wed-Fri, 8am-2pm Sat) Two Franciscan monks preside over this tiny bakery, serving fresh baked goods at breakfast and usually sandwiches and soup at lunch.

Bagel Central (☎ 207-947-1654; 33 Central St; meals $6-7; ⏰ 6am-5pm Mon-Fri, 6am-2am Sun; Ⓥ) Bagel Central bakes up 16 varieties of bagel, which are then transformed into tasty breakfast or lunch sandwiches. Omelettes and other breakfast fare are served all day.

Sea Dog Brewing Co (☎ 207-947-8004; 26 Front St; meals $9-17; ⏰ 11:30am-1am) This inviting restaurant and pub serves tasty salads, sandwiches, burgers and other pub fare as well as award-winning homemade brews. The rich porter and Old Gollywobbler brown ale are well worth a try.

Café Nouveau (☎ 207-942-3338; 86 Hammond St; meals $14-18; ⏰ lunch & dinner Tue-Sat) Tucked down a side street, Café Nouveau is an elegant wine bar that also serves tasty, creative fare. The menu features warm duck salad, lobster brioche, blackened salmon quesadillas and other seafood choices. The wine and cheese shop next door is great for assembling a picnic.

Paddy Murphy's (☎ 207-945-6800; 26 Main St; meals $10-18; ⏰ noon-10pm) One of several drinking spots overlooking West Market Square, Paddy's has good old-fashioned appeal, with a wood-lined bar, friendly faces and 16 beers on tap. There's a full menu of hearty pub fare.

Getting There & Away

Bangor International Airport (☎ 207-947-0384; www .flybangor.com) is served by regional carriers associated with Continental, Delta and US Airways.

Vermont Transit/Greyhound (☎ 207-945-3000, 800-231-2222; www.vermonttransit.com; 158 Main St; ⏰ year-round), at the Bangor Bus Terminal, runs four direct buses daily between Bangor and Boston ($39) with onward connections to New York City ($49). Buses go via Portland ($24) and Portsmouth, New Hampshire ($39). **Concord Trailways** (☎ 800-639-3317; www.concordtrailways.com; Trailways Transportation Center, 1039 Union St) has three more, as well as services along the Maine coast to Portland. For more detailed bus routes, see p482.

AUGUSTA & AROUND
pop 18,600

Although not the smallest state capital in America (an honor reserved for Montpelier, Vermont), Augusta sure feels like it. Overlooking a peaceful stretch of the Kennebec River, boaters still cast for dinner while the glittering dome of the State House looms just over the treeline. While there isn't much reason to venture here, there are several fine historic sites (a good history museum, an old wooden fort) and some antique shops and cafés in the more charming nearby town of **Hallowell**. Also in the area is **Gardiner**, another sleepy town with a few galleries and a good restaurant.

Augusta was founded as a trading post in 1628, later abandoned, then resettled in 1724 at Fort Western (later Hallowell). Lumber, shingles, furs and fish were its early world exports, sent downriver in sloops built right here. Augusta became Maine's capital in 1827, but was only chartered as a city in 1849.

Orientation & Information

Memorial Circle, near the state capitol, is this city's traffic nexus. (US 202, US 201, ME 8, ME 11, ME 17, ME 27 and ME 100 all intersect at this large traffic circle.)

Augusta's traditional commercial district sits on the eastern bank of the Kennebec River. Western Ave runs from Memorial Circle due west 1.5 miles to I-95 exit 30; most of Augusta's motels are here. Three miles northwest of town, at I-95 exit 31, you'll find the University of Maine at Augusta, the Augusta Civic Center, the Mall at Augusta, the Kennebec Valley Chamber of Commerce and more chain motels. Water St (US 201/ME 27) runs south from Memorial Circle, past the capitol, to Hallowell (2 miles) and Gardiner (7 miles).

Kennebec Valley Chamber of Commerce (☎ 207-623-4559; www.augustamaine.com; University Dr; ☽ 8:30am-5pm Mon-Fri) At I-95 exit 31.

Maine Office of Tourism (☎ 207-287-5711, 888-624-6345; www.visitmaine.com; 59 State House Station, Augusta)

Kennebec Valley Tourism Council (☎ 207-626-3188; www.kennebecvalley.org; 21 University Dr, Augusta; ☽ 8:30am-5pm Mon-Fri) Has information on rafting the Kennebec River.

Sights

STATE HOUSE

Built in 1832 and enlarged in 1909, the granite **State House** (☎ 207-287-2301; www.maine.gov; cnr State & Capitol Sts; admission free; ☽ 9am-5pm Mon-Fri) was designed by the famed Boston architect Charles Bulfinch. You can pick up a leaflet for a self-guided tour, or pick up a red courtesy phone and request a free guided tour. Park in the lot on the southwest side of the building, near the Department of Education and Maine State Museum, and enter the capitol through the southwest door.

MAINE STATE MUSEUM

By all means, take a gander within the **Maine State Museum** (☎ 207-287-2301; www.maine.gov/museum; 83 State St; adult/child $2/1; ☽ 9am-5pm Tue-Fri, 10am-4pm Sat, 1-4pm Sun), ensconced in the Maine State Library

and Archives adjacent to the State House. The museum traces Maine's history through an astounding 12,000 years and includes prehistoric arrowheads and tools, as well as impressive artifacts relating to Maine's role in ship-building, fishing, textiles and granite quarries.

OLD FORT WESTERN

Located in its own riverside park, **Old Fort Western** (☎ 207-626-2385; www.oldfortwestern.org; 16 Cony St; adult/child $6/4; ☽ 1-4pm Jun–early Sep) was originally built as a frontier outpost in 1754. The restored 16-room structure, now a museum, is New England's oldest surviving wooden fort. It's also open in the off-season – call ahead to find out the hours.

Sleeping

Maple Hill Farm B&B (☎ 207-622-2708; www.maplebb.com; 11 Inn Rd, Hallowell; r with breakfast $100-200; ☐ wi-fi) Hosted by Maine (state) Senator Scott Cowger, this late-Victorian B&B is set on 130 acres of rolling hayfields and marked by trails ripe for exploration. The eight rooms are bright and comfortable, and the best have whirlpool tubs, fireplaces and private decks. Take I-95 exit 30 for US 202 West, then immediately turn left onto Whitten Rd and follow the signs.

Eating & Drinking

The best dining options are south of the capitol in Hallowell or Gardiner. You'll reach both settlements by heading south along Water St.

A1 to Go (☎ 207-582-5586; 347 Water St, Gardiner; meals $9-12; ☽ 7am-7pm Mon-Fri, 7am-5pm Sat) In laid-back Gardiner, A1 to Go is a charming modern café serving unique and flavorful wraps (curried chicken salad, smoked salmon with capers), granola with yogurt, mango *lassi* and other organic options. The small deli and grocery is a good spot for a picnic assembly (good wines, salads and cheeses).

A1 Diner (☎ 207-582-4804; 3 Bridge St, Gardiner) Next door to A1 to Go, the more classic-looking A1 Diner serves a more traditional menu.

Higher Grounds (☎ 207-621-1234; 119 Water St, Hallowell; meals $12-17; ☽ 8am-11pm Mon-Sat) This cozy café is a relaxing spot by day, while the evening brings live acoustic music (including open mic on Tuesdays). In addition to melancholic chords, you can enjoy pizza and beer – there's a fully stocked bar.

Slate's Restaurant & Bakery (☎ 207-622-4104; 169 Water St, Hallowell; meals $14-22; ☽ bakery 7am-6pm) This much-loved Hallowell institution suffered a

MAINE

LORD OF THE LURID

Master of the macabre and recipient of the 2003 National Book Foundation Medal, Stephen King is a remarkably normal husband and father. He is also a native and lifelong resident of Maine. Born in Portland in 1947, he was the second son of Donald and Nellie King. When his father abandoned the family, his mother took the boys to live temporarily in other states. Eventually they returned to Maine, where King began his fledgling writing career by producing, along with his brother David (now an appliance repairman in New Hampshire), a mimeographed newspaper called *Dave's Rag*. They sold it for 5¢ a copy. His mother kept the family together by working at Pineland, a residential facility for the mentally challenged in Durham, Vermont.

King graduated from Lisbon Falls High School in 1966, after what he termed an undistinguished academic career. It was marked in 1965 by his first publication, a story called *I was a Teenage Grave Robber*. Let the strangeness begin. He attended the University of Maine, Orono, on scholarship and there enjoyed his first paid publication – $35 for *The Glass Floor*.

King graduated from the University of Maine in 1970 with a BA in English and a teaching certificate. He then proceeded to write while performing a variety of jobs, including pumping gas and mopping floors. He looked for teaching work and avoided the draft – thanks to high blood pressure, poor vision and flat feet – and occasionally sold short stories, mostly to men's magazines.

In 1971, he married college girlfriend Tabitha Spruce and they moved to Hermon, west of Bangor, so Stephen could teach at Hampden Academy. His grand salary of $6400 annually provided a subsistence lifestyle but not much more. Tabitha steadfastly aided King's ambition to write, even famously fishing a manuscript of *Carrie* out of the trash and encouraging him to keep working on it. Her rumored reward when King netted $200,000 from the sale of the paperback rights? He bought her a hairdryer.

Although he now splits his time between Maine and Florida, King's Bangor roots run deep and he and his wife provide scholarships for local high school students, as well as contributing to many local charities. Many of King's books and stories are set in Maine, although frequently in fictional towns. In fact, his official website, www.stephenking.com, boasts a rendering of what Maine would look like if mapped as in King's fiction.

tragic fire in 2007, leaving only its bakery intact. Rebuilding is underway, meaning you should be able to enjoy the area's best seafood and grilled dishes soon. In the meantime, stop in the cheery bakery for excellent scones and other goodies.

Getting There & Away

Augusta is 23 miles north of Wiscasset. **Greyhound** (☎ 207-622-1601; www.greyhound.com) buses stop at Augusta State Airport. Sample fares include to/from Portland ($23, 1½ hours) and to/from Bangor $27, (1½ hours).

WESTERN LAKES & MOUNTAINS

Western Maine receives far fewer visitors than coastal Maine, which thrills the outdoorsy types who love western Maine the way it is. The fine old town of Bethel and the mountain setting of Rangeley Lakes are relatively accessible to city-dwellers in the northeast. Bethel is also very close to the White Mountain National Forest in New Hampshire and Maine.

Perhaps surprisingly, the mountains of western Maine yield an abundance of gemstones, such as amethyst, aquamarine and tourmaline. Keep your eyes open for gem shops.

BETHEL

pop 2640

For a small farm town surrounded by Maine woods, Bethel, 63 miles northwest of Portland via ME 26, is surprisingly beautiful and refined. It's a prime spot to be during Maine's colorful fall foliage season and during the winter ski season. If you head west on US 2 toward New Hampshire, be sure to admire the Shelburne birches, a high concentration of the white-barked trees that grow between Gilead and Shelburne.

Part of Bethel's backwoods sophistication comes from being the home of Gould

Academy, a well-regarded prep school founded in 1836.

Information

Bethel Area Chamber of Commerce (☎ 207-824-2282; www.bethelmaine.com; 8 Station Pl; ❤ 9am-6pm Mon-Fri year-round, 10am-6pm Sat & Sun Nov-Apr) This helpful office maintains an information office in the Bethel Station building.

White Mountain National Forest (☎ 207-824-2134; 18 Mayville Rd/US 2; ❤ 8am-4:30pm Tue-Sat May-Oct, 8am-4:30 Fri & Sat Nov-Apr) The Evans Notch Ranger Station is loaded with good information about hiking, camping and every conceivable kind of area recreation.

Mouse & Bean (☎ 207-824-2366; 63 Main St; per hr $10; ❤ 7am-4pm Mon-Sat, 9am-3pm Sun; free wi-fi) To get online visit this place, which also serves sandwiches and smoothies.

Sights & Activities

Roughly 50,000 acres of the White Mountain National Forest lie inside Maine. For a dose of mountain scenery, consider a scenic drive along NH 113 from Gilead south to Stow. Stop for a picnic and panoramic views at the Cold River Outlook. Access NH 113 by heading west along NH 2. NH 113 closes in the winter.

DR MOSES MASON HOUSE

For a look at how the gentry lived in the 1800s, visit this historic federal-style **house** (☎ 207-824-2908, 800-824-2910; www.bethelhistorical.org; 10-14 Broad St; adult/child 6-12 $3/1.50; ❤ 1-4pm Tue-Sun Jul & Aug). Now the research library of the Bethel Historical Society, the house is set with period furnishings and intriguing murals painted by itinerant artist Rufus Porter in the 1830s.

HIKING & KAYAKING

Lovely scenery surrounds Bethel, with some great hiking nearby. The **Mt Will Trail** starts from US 2, east of Bethel, and ascends to mountain ledges with fine views of the Androscoggin Valley. **Grafton Notch State Park**, north of Bethel via ME 26, offers hiking trails and pretty waterfalls, but no camping. Try the park's 1.5-mile trail up to Table Rock Overlook, or the walk to Eyebrow Loop and Cascade Falls, with excellent picnicking possibilities right by the falls.

Bethel Outdoor Adventure & Campground (☎ 207-824-4224, 800-533-3607; www.betheloutdooradventure.com; 121 Mayville Rd/US 2; ❤ May-Oct) rents canoes, kayaks and bicycles, and it arranges lessons, guided trips and shuttles to and from the Androscoggin River.

SKIING

The mountains near Bethel are home to several major ski resorts.

Sunday River Ski Resort (☎ 207-824-3000; www.sundayriver.com; Sunday River Rd; lift ticket adult/child $67/47; 🎿), 6 miles north of Bethel along ME 5/26, boasts eight mountain peaks and 131 trails, with 18 lifts. It's regarded as one of the region's best family ski destinations.

Mt Abram (☎ 207-875-5003; www.skimtabram.com; Howe Hill Rd, Locke Mills; lift ticket adult/child $43/32; 🎿) is a small, family-friendly and reasonably priced ski area with 44 trails just southeast of Bethel.

Sleeping

Bethel has numerous places to stay, with motels sprinkled along US 2 to the north. If making winter reservations, ask about ski and meal packages.

The Bethel Chamber of Commerce operates the **Bethel Area Reservations Service** (☎ 800-442-5826; www.bethelmaine.com), which can help with rooms.

There are five simple public campgrounds, with well water and toilets, in the Maine portion of the White Mountain National Forest: Basin Pond, Cold River, Crocker Pond, Hastings and Wild River (sites $18 to $20). For more information, contact the **Evans Notch Visitor Center** (☎ 207-824-2134; 18 Mayville Rd/US 2; www.fs.fed.us/r9/white; ❤ 8am-4:30pm Tue-Sat May-Oct, 8am-4:30pm Fri-Sat Nov-Apr).

Stony Brook Recreation (☎ 207-824-2836; www.stonybrookrec.com; US 2, Hanover; sites $23) With 100 acres of forest along the Androscoggin River, this great camping spot is east of Bethel. Most sites offer lean-tos to provide shelter from wet weather.

Chapman Inn (☎ 207-824-2657, 877-359-1498; www.chapmaninn.com; 1 Mill Hill Rd; dm $33, r $69-109) Among the most economical lodgings in town, Chapman Inn has a 24-bed dorm and nine rooms for singles, couples and families; the cheaper rooms have shared bathrooms.

Briar Lea Inn & Restaurant (☎ 207-824-4717, 877-311-1299; www.briarleainn.com; 150 Mayville Rd/US 2; r with breakfast $90-160; 🖳 wi-fi) This 150-year-old Georgian farmhouse has six small, cozy rooms set with antique beds and colorful wallpaper. Breakfasts are good, and there's an English-style pub onsite.

Austin's Holidae House B&B (☎ 207-824-3400; www.holidae-house.com; 85 Main St; r with breakfast $100-130; 🖳 wi-fi) Highly rated by travelers, this 1902 Victorian inn has seven attractive rooms, each with wood floors, queen-sized beds (brass or four-poster) and elegant décor. It's well located in the center of town.

Victoria Inn (☎ 207-824-8060; www.thevictoria-inn.com; 32 Main St; r with breakfast $100-180; ☑ wi-fi) Under new, friendly ownership, this looming lavender mansion offers 15 clean, carpeted rooms, most of which are set with period antiques and vintage-style wallpaper. The deluxe rooms are worth the extra cost, as you'll get brighter, more spacious digs; standard rooms are small and uninspiring.

Eating & Drinking

Bethel has a growing number of decent restaurants, with enticing options for vegetarians.

Taste of Eden (☎ 207-824-8939; 188 Main St; meals $7; ☺ breakfast & lunch; Ⓥ) Amid New Age music and religious-bookstore ambience, Taste of Eden serves delicious vegetarian breakfast and lunch specials (ie veggie quesadilla, basmati rice and sweet potatoes) at excellent prices. Next door the Sassafras Market is a fine spot to assemble a picnic.

Café DiCocoa (☎ 207-824-5282; 125 Main St; meals $9-13; ☺ breakfast & lunch; Ⓥ) For tip-top coffee and espresso drinks, Café DiCocoa is a great destination. It also serves wholegrain baked goods and vegetarian lunches.

Cho Sun (☎ 207-824-7370; 141 Main St; meals $19-22; ☺ 5-9pm Wed-Sun) Serving eclectic Japanese and Korean dishes, this sophisticated restaurant provides a nice break from diner food. Seafood and curry dishes along with glazed meats, sushi and sashimi round out the menu. By summer, dine by torchlight on the outdoor deck. Reservations recommended.

Sudbury Inn (☎ 207-824-2174; 151 Main St; meals $20-32; ☺ inn dinner Thu-Sat, pub dinner nightly) This inn has a cozy dining room upstairs and a menu that generally receives positive reviews. The downstairs Suds Pub, however, is more fun and has a tavern menu (with good pizzas), a large selection of draft beers and, on some nights, live entertainment.

Sunday River Brewing Company (☎ 207-824-4253; cnr US 2 & Sunday River Rd; ☺ noon-10pm) Bethel's brewpub pours a half-dozen of its own brews (from a light golden lager to a black porter), as well as offering mediocre bar food. Live bands fire things up on weekends.

Getting There & Away

Bethel lies 70 miles north of Portland, via ME 26 (among other routes). If you're heading into the White Mountains of New Hampshire, take US 2 east from Bethel towards Gorham (22 miles) and head south to North Conway.

RANGELEY LAKE & AROUND
pop 1200

Surrounded by mountains and thick forests, the Rangeley Lake region is a marvelous year-round destination for adventurers. Gateway to the alpine scenery is the laid-back town of Rangeley, whose tidy inns and down-home restaurants makes a useful base for skiing, hiking, white-water rafting and mountain biking in the nearby hills.

During the early 20th century, the lakes in this region were dotted with vast frame hotels and peopled with vacationers from Boston, New York and Philadelphia. Though most of the great hotels are gone the reasons for coming here remain.

The **Rangeley Lakes Chamber of Commerce** (☎ 207-864-5364; www.rangeleymaine.com; 6 Park Rd; ☺ 9am-5pm Mon-Sat), just off Main Street, can answer questions.

Sights & Activities
WILHELM REICH MUSEUM

Austrian-born psychiatrist and scientist Wilhelm Reich (1897–1957) devoted his life to proving the existence of biological sexual energy in humans, which he called 'orgone energy.' Needless to say, Reich's experiments attracted a lot of attention, and things ended badly for him, with the FDA destroying his equipment and burning his books and publications; he was also sentenced to prison and died there of heart failure. To learn about his life and work, visit the **museum** (☎ 207-864-3443; www.wilhelmreichmuseum.org; 19 Dodge Pond Rd; adult/child $6/free; ☺ 1-5pm Wed-Sun Jul-Aug; 1-5pm Sun Sep), for guided tours through Reich's fieldstone mansion. The 160 acre grounds have nature trails, and there are impressive views from the roof of the Orgone Energy Observatory.

SKIING

The mountains around Rangeley offer good skiing and snowboarding options.

Sugarloaf (☎ 207-237-2000, 800-843-5623; www.sugarloaf.com; ME 16, Kingfield; lift ticket adult/child $64/43) Rangeley's most-popular ski resort has a vertical drop of 2820ft, with 133 trails and 15 lifts. This is Maine's second highest peak (4237ft).

Sugarloaf Outdoor Center (☎ 207-237-6830; www
.sugarloaf.com/nordic_center.html; ME 27/ME 16, Carrabassett
Valley; adult/child $17/10), near Sugarloaf, has 136
miles of groomed cross-country trails.

Saddleback Ski Area (☎ 207-864-5671; www.sad
dlebackmaine.com; Rangeley; lift ticket adult/child $40/30),
at 4120ft, has 40 alpine ski trails with seven
lifts and three T-bars. Call for lodging
information.

Sleeping

North Country Inn B&B (☎ 207-864-2440; www
.northcountrybb.com; 2541 Main St; r with breakfast $96-116)
Constructed by Rangeley's first multimillion-
aire, this attractive 1912 house (and former
speakeasy during Prohibition) offers excellent views over the town park and lake. Four
clean, spacious rooms have comfortable beds
and antique furnishings.

Pleasant Street Inn (☎ 207-864-5916; www.pleasant
streetinnbb.com; 104 Pleasant St; r with breakfast $125-
145; ⌨ wi-fi) The tidy Pleasant Street Inn has
five clean, comfortable, modern rooms with
quilted bedspreads and a welcome lack of
frilly decoration. It's a short stroll from here
to the town's restaurants.

NORTH WOODS

On a map, it appears as if the further north
you go in Maine, the fewer roads there are.
You'd think this is trackless wilderness. In
fact, this vast area is owned by large paper
companies that harvest timber for their
paper mills. The land is crisscrossed by a
series of rough logging roads. Logs used to
be floated down the region's many rivers,
but this practice increased the tannin levels
in the rivers and threatened the ecological
balance. Roads came with the advent of the
internal combustion engine.

Now that logs are out of the rivers, white-
water rafters are in them. The **Kennebec River**,
below the Harris Hydroelectric Station,
passes through a dramatic 12-mile gorge
that's one of the US's prime rafting locations. Outflow from the hydroelectric station is controlled, which means that there
is always water, and the periodic big releases
make for more exciting rafting.

The **Kennebec Valley Tourism Council** (☎ 800-
393-8629; www.kennebecvalley.org; 21 University Dr,
Augusta; ⌚ 8:30am-5pm Mon-Fri) will help with
information.

Maine sporting camps – those remote forest outposts for hunters, fishers and other
deep-woods types – still flourish in the most
remote regions. For information, contact the
Maine Sporting Camp Association (☎ 207-723-6622;
www.mainesportingcamps.com).

MOOSEHEAD LAKE

North of **Greenville** (population 1620),
Moosehead Lake is huge. In fact, it is the largest lake completely contained within any one
New England state. (Lake Champlain is bigger,
but it's split between Vermont, New York and
Canada). This is lumber and backwoods country, which is why Greenville is the region's
largest seaplane station. Pontoon planes will
take you even deeper into the Maine woods
for fishing trips. Though once a bustling
summer resort, Greenville has reverted to a
backwoods outpost. A few of the old summer
hotels survive, but most of the visitors today
are camping or heading through on their way
to Baxter State Park and Mt Katahdin.

For more regional information, contact the **Moosehead Lake Region Chamber of
Commerce** (☎ 207-695-2702; www.mooseheadlake
.org; ME 15, Greenville; ⌚ 9am-5pm summer, 10am-4pm
Tue-Sat winter).

Owned and maintained by the Moosehead
Marine Museum, the **SS Katahdin** (☎ 207-695-
2716; www.katahdincruises.com; adult $30-60, child $15-30;
⌚ May-Oct) is a 115ft steamboat built in 1914.
It still makes the rounds – more like three- to
eight-hour cruises – on Moosehead Lake from
Greenville's center, just like it did in Greenville's
heyday. The lake's colorful history is preserved
in the **museum** right in the center of town.

From Bangor, head south on I-95 for 23
miles, then north on ME 11/7/23 for 26 miles,
then 2 miles west on ME 16/6 and then 22
miles north on ME 15/6 to Greenville, the
gateway to Moosehead Lake.

BAXTER STATE PARK

Mt Katahdin (5267ft), Maine's tallest mountain and the northern end of the over-2000-
mile-long **Appalachian Trail**, is the centerpiece
of **Baxter State Park** (☎ 207-723-5140; www.baxter
stateparkauthority.com; 64 Balsam Dr, Millinocket; admission
per person per day $8), which boasts 46 other moun-
tain peaks, 1200 campsites and 180 miles of
hiking trails. Mt Katahdin offers the wildest,
most unspoiled wilderness adventures in New
England. Katahdin has a reputation for being
a real rock climber's mountain.

MAINE

KENNEBEC RIVER RAFTING TRIPS

The villages of **Caratunk** and **The Forks**, south of Jackman via US 201, are both at the center of the Kennebec rafting area. White-water rafting trips down the Kennebec and nearby rivers are wonderful adventures. Trips cost from $75 to $130 per person, and many trips don't require previous experience.

Numerous companies run organized rafting trips on the Kennebec, Dead or Penobscot Rivers. Trips range in difficulty from Class II (easy enough for children aged eight and older) to Class V (intense, difficult rapids, with a minimum age of 15).

Most rafting companies have agreements with local lodgings (inns, cabins and campgrounds) for your accommodations. Ask about all-inclusive packages.

A reliable area standby if you don't book through a rafting company is the **Inn by the River** (☎ 207-663-2181; www.innbytheriver.com; US 201, West Fork; r with breakfast $75-160), a modern lodge overlooking the Kennebec River, which has very comfortable rooms.

Rafting companies we recommend:

■ **Crab Apple Whitewater** (☎ 207-663-4491, 800-553-7238; www.crabapplewhitewater.com) Also runs trips on rivers in western Massachusetts.

■ **Maine Whitewater** (☎ 800-345-6246; www.mainewhitewater.com)

■ **New England Outdoor Center** (☎ 207-723-5438, 800-766-7238; www.neoc.com) Also runs canoe trips on the Allagash Wilderness Waterway.

■ **Northern Outdoors** (☎ 207-663-4466; www.northernoutdoors.com) Runs rafting, mountain-biking, fishing and sea-kayaking trips in Maine.

■ **Professional River Runners of Maine** (☎ 207-663-2229, 800-325-3911; www.proriverrunners.com) Also runs rafting trips on other rivers in the eastern US.

■ **Three Rivers Whitewater, Inc** (☎ 877-846-7238; www.threeriverswhitewater.com) Also runs rafting trips on the Rapid River.

Despite its relative inaccessibility – deep in the Maine woods over unpaved roads – Baxter hosts over 100,000 visitors every year, mostly from mid-May through mid-October. It's also open December through March for winter activities.

To fully enjoy the park, you must arrive at the park entrance early in the day – only so many visitors are allowed in on any given day. You should also be well equipped for camping and perhaps for hiking and canoeing. Campsites in the park cost $9 per person ($18 minimum) and must be reserved well in advance by contacting the park. You may also want more information from the **Maine Appalachian Trail Club** (www.matc.org) and the **Katahdin Area Chamber of Commerce** (☎ 207-723-4443; www.katahdinmaine.com; 1029 Central St, Millinocket).

If you are unable to secure a reservation at one of the park's campsites, you can usu-ally find a private campground just outside the Togue Ponds and Matagamon gates into the park. There are several in Medway (just off I-95 exit 56), in Millinocket and in Greenville.

From Bangor, head north on I-95 for 61 miles to Medway, then head 10 miles northwest on ME 11 to Millinocket and then continue another 10 miles beyond Millinocket to the southern entrance of the park. From Greenville, if you have a 4WD, take Lily Bay Rd to Kokadjo, where the road becomes a dirt logging road (Sias Hill Rd). Take this until you get to the end and make a right on paved Golden Rd. This is a gorgeous drive, and you're likely to see moose in streams if you're on Golden Rd toward dusk. However, be careful: these are logging roads! Those humongous trucks can be dangerous when coming around the bends.

Directory

CONTENTS

ACCOMMODATIONS

New England provides an array of accommodations options from simple campsites and B&Bs to midrange inns and top-end hotels. But truly inexpensive accommodations are rare. The most comfortable accommodations for the lowest price are usually found in that great American invention, the roadside motel.

For last-minute deals, check www.expedia.com, www.travelocity.com, www.orbitz.com, www.priceline.com, www.hotwire.com and www.hotels.com.

PRACTICALITIES

Electricity Voltage is 110/120V, 60 cycles.
Laundry Most accommodations have inexpensive coin-operated washers and dryers.
Newspapers The *Boston Globe,* the largest area newspaper, is available throughout New England.
Radio National Public Radio (NPR) features a level-headed approach to news and talk radio and is found between 89 and 92 on your FM dial.
TV All the major US TV networks are represented, but for the best regional coverage check out New England Cable News.
Video Video systems use the NTSC color TV standard, not compatible with the PAL system.
Weights & Measures Distances are measured in feet, yards and miles; weights are tallied in ounces, pounds and tons.

If you're traveling with children, be sure to ask about children-related policies before making reservations (see p524).

Our reviews indicate rates for single occupancy (s), double (d) or simply the room (r) or suite (ste), when there's no appreciable difference in the rate for one or two people. Unless otherwise noted, breakfast is not included, bathrooms are private and all lodging is open year-round; rates generally don't include taxes, which can add a whopping 5.2% to 12%, depending on the state (see p530).

A double room in our budget category costs $80 or less; midrange doubles cost $80 to $200; top-end rooms start at $200.

For a list of icons used in this book, check out the inside front cover. A parking icon is only employed in cities where free parking is not readily available; sometimes a fee applies, as indicated. The air-conditioning icon only appears in locations where the weather might warrant it (like Cape Cod or urban areas). The internet icon appears where establishments provide a computer terminal, while 'wi-fi' indicates wireless access; the swimming icon appears when there is a pool on the premises. Smoking is not permitted indoors for most of the destinations in this book.

A reservation guarantees your room, but most reservations require a deposit, after which, if you change your mind, the establishment will only refund your money if they're able to rebook your room within a certain period. Note the cancellation policies and other restrictions before making a deposit.

In general, the peak travel season to New England is summer and fall. High season varies slightly depending on the region within New England. For example, high season on Cape Cod and the Maine Coast is late May to early September, but in the mountains of New Hampshire, it's mid-September to mid-October. In some Vermont regions, high season means ski season (late December to late March). High-season prices are provided in our reviews, so if you are traveling off-season you can generally expect significantly reduced rates.

Holidays (p527) and school vacations always command premium prices. When demand peaks (and during special events whatever the time of year see p18), book lodgings well in advance.

B&Bs, Inns & Guesthouses

Accommodations in New England vary from small B&Bs to rambling old inns that have sheltered travelers for several centuries.

In smaller towns, guesthouses with simple rooms may charge $75 to $100 for rooms with shared bathroom and breakfast included. Others are relentlessly charming, with frilly decor and doting hosts. These fancier B&Bs charge $125 to $175 per night with private bathroom. Historic inns converted from wealthy summer homes, decorated with antique furnishings and equipped with every conceivable modern amenity cost $200 a night and up. Most inns require a minimum stay of two or three nights on weekends, advance reservations and bills paid in advance by check or in cash (not by credit card).

Many B&Bs are booked through agencies, including the following:

Bed & Breakfast Reservations (☎ 617-964-1606, 800-832-2632; www.bbreserve.com; 11A Beach Rd, Gloucester, MA 01930) Books B&Bs, historic inns and apartments in Massachusetts and northern New England.

Destinnations (☎ 207-563-2506, 800-333-4667; www.destinnations.com; 16 East Pond Rd, Nobleboro, ME 04555) A reservation and itinerary-planning service for visitors staying in New England more than a few nights.

Camping

You can buy camping equipment at many places such as Hilton's Tent City (p125) in Boston and LL Bean (p483) in Freeport.

With few exceptions, you'll have to camp in established campgrounds (there's no bivouacking on the side of the road). Make reservations well in advance (especially in July and August) for the best chance of getting a site. Private campgrounds are always more expensive ($20 to $40) and less spacious than state parks, but they often boast recreational facilities like playgrounds, swimming pools, game rooms and miniature golf.

Rough camping is occasionally permitted in the Green Mountain National Forest (p371) or the White Mountain National Forest (p439), but often it must be at established sites; it's usually free. Drive-up sites in national forests with basic services generally cost about $10. State and national park sites usually offer a few more services (like flush toilets, hot showers and dump stations for RVs). Campsites at these places cost between $14 and $26; most campgrounds are open from mid-May to mid-October.

For further camping information, contact the following:

Connecticut Bureau of Outdoor Recreation (☎ 860-424-3000; http://dep.state.ct.us/stateparks)

Maine Bureau of Parks & Lands (☎ 207-287-3821; www.state.me.us/doc/parks)

Massachusetts Department of Conservation & Recreation (☎ 617-626-1250; www.mass.gov/dcr)

New Hampshire Division of Parks & Recreation (☎ 603-271-3556; www.nhparks.state.nh.us)

Rhode Island Division of Parks & Recreation (☎ 401-222-2632; www.riparks.com)

Vermont State Parks (☎ 802-241-3655; www.vtstateparks.com)

Cottages, Cabins & Condos

Renting a cottage or condominium is not particularly easy for those who don't live in the region, but your best bet is to contact local chambers of commerce (see Information under each town) and ask for listings of available properties.

Cottages and cabins are generally found on Cape Cod, Nantucket, Martha's Vineyard and in New England's woods. They are two- or three-room vacation bungalows with basic furnishings, bathroom and kitchen. Condos are usually capable of accommodating more people than an efficiency unit (below) – some condos can sleep six, eight or even 10 people in a small multi-room apartment with kitchen and dining facilities. Rates vary greatly, from $70 to $700 per night, depending upon the location, season and size. Mountainside condos are especially popular with skiers, but they're much cheaper during the warmer months.

Efficiencies

An 'efficiency,' in New England parlance, is a hotel, motel or inn room, or one-room cabin, with cooking and dining facilities: stove, sink, refrigerator, dining table and chairs, cooking utensils and tableware. Efficiency units, which physically resemble their brethren in all but their interior amenities, are located throughout New England in all but the most upscale communities. They usually cost slightly more than standard rooms.

Hotels & Resorts

New England hotels, mostly found in cities, are generally large and lavish, except for a few 'boutique' hotels (which are small and understatedly lavish). Resorts often offer a wide variety of guest activities, such as golf, horseback riding, skiing or water sports. Prices range from $100 to $200 and up per night; ask about discounts and special packages when you make reservations. Virtually all large hotels have toll-free numbers for making reservations, but you may find better discounts by calling the hotel directly.

Hostels

Hosteling isn't as well developed in New England as it is in Europe. But some prime destinations, including Boston, Cape Cod, Bar Harbor, Martha's Vineyard, and Nantucket, have hostels that allow you to stay in $150-per-night destinations for $20 to $25. Needless to say, advance reservations are essential.

US citizens/residents can join **Hostelling International USA** (HI-USA; ☎ 301-495-1240; www.hiusa .org; 8401 Colesville Rd, ste 600, Silver Spring, MD 20910) by calling and requesting a membership form or by downloading a form from the website and mailing or faxing it. Membership can also be purchased at regional council offices and at many (but not all) youth hostels. Non-US residents should buy a HI membership in their home countries: visit www.hihostels .com to find out how. If you are not a member, you can still stay in US hostels for a slightly higher rate.

Two hosteling councils cover New England. **HI-USA Eastern New England Council** (☎ 617-718-7990; www.usahostels.org; 218 Holland St, Somerville, MA 02144) covers Eastern Massachusetts, Maine and New Hampshire. The **HI-USA Yankee Council** (☎ 860-683-2847; www.yankeehostels.org; 181 Broad St, Windsor, CT 06095) covers Connecticut, Vermont and Western Massachusetts.

New England hostels are located in the following towns:

Connecticut Hartford (p345)
Maine Bar Harbor (p506)
Massachusetts Boston (p100 or p102), Eastham(p197), Truro (p201), Martha's Vineyard (p229), Nantucket (p218)
New Hampshire Conway (p452)
Vermont Burlington (p391), Woodford (near Bennington; p368)

Motels

Motels, located on the highway or on the outskirts of most cities, range from 10-room places in need of a fresh coat of paint to resort-style facilities. Prices range from $50 to $100 and up. Motels offer standard accommodations: a room entered from the outside, with private bathroom, color cable TV, heat and air-con. Some have small refrigerators, and many provide a simple breakfast, often at no extra charge. Most provide toll-free reservation phone lines.

ACTIVITIES

For a complete discussion of the wealth, depth and breadth of ways to have fun in New England, see the New England Outdoors chapter (p58). Two activities specific to New England bear mentioning here, though. Consider cruising for a few days along the gorgeous Maine coast, among the world's finest sail-cruising areas. Traditional wooden schooners (or windjammers) use Camden (p496), Rockport (p155) and Rockland (p495) as their home ports. The other activity is whale-watching. Once known for their prowess in seeking out whales for slaughter, New England's sea captains now follow the whales with boatloads of camera-carrying summer tourists. Cruises depart from Barnstable (p180), Provincetown (p205), Boston (p84), Plymouth (p166), Gloucester (p154) and Newburyport (p161), Massachusetts; Portsmouth (p414), New Hampshire; and Kennebunkport (p471), Boothbay Harbor (p491) and Bar Harbor (p506), Maine, among other coastal towns.

BUSINESS HOURS

Unless there are variances of more than a half-hour in either direction, the following serve as the standard for opening hours for entries in this book:

Banks & Information 9am or 10am to 5pm or 6pm Monday to Friday

Eating breakfast 6 to 10am; lunch 11:30am to 2:30pm; dinner 5-10pm Monday to Sunday

Drinking 5pm to midnight, some open until 2am

Shopping 9am to 5pm Monday to Saturday, some open noon to 5pm Sunday, or until evening in tourist areas

CHILDREN

Traveling within New England with children presents no destination-specific problems. Successful travel with young children does require planning and effort – packing too much into the time available can cause problems. Include your children in the trip planning; if they've helped to work out where you will be going, they will be much more interested when they get there. Consult Lonely Planet's *Travel with Children*, which has lots of valuable tips and interesting anecdotes.

Children are not welcome at many smaller B&Bs and inns (even if they do not say so outright). In motels and hotels, children under 17 or 18 are usually free when sharing a room with their parents if no extra bedding is required. Cots and roll-away beds are usually available (for an additional fee) in hotels and resorts.

Some resorts, like the Chatham Bars Inn on Cape Cod (p193), offer camp-style programs for children three to 15 (see the Sleeping section in the relevant chapters). When places are particularly family friendly, we say so. Look for the child-friendly 🖑 icon in reviews.

Because children are seen as well as heard in New England, many restaurants have children's menus with significantly lower prices. High chairs are usually available, but it pays to inquire ahead of time.

Most car-rental companies (see p538) lease child safety seats, but they don't always have them on hand; reserve in advance if you can.

Family-friendly sights are plentiful in New England and we have peppered suggestions for where to entertain the kids throughout the regional chapters. See our Top Picks for Kids on p16. For Boston, see p95.

CLIMATE CHARTS

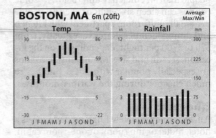

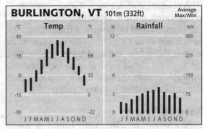

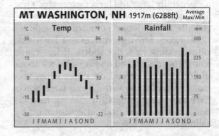

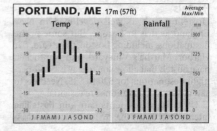

COURSES

Opportunities abound across erudite New England to educate yourself while on vacation. In Boston you can take sailing classes at Community Boating (p95), cooking classes at Cambridge School of Culinary Arts (p95) and yoga classes at Baptiste Power Vinyasa Yoga (p95).

You can also take fly-fishing classes at the famous Orvis Fly-Fishing School (p370) in Manchester, Vermont or at LL Bean (p483) in Freeport, Maine. For the artistically minded, art classes are offered at Burlington City Arts (p388) in Vermont and the DeCordova Sculpture Garden & Museum (p140) near Concord, Massachusetts.

For more on cooking courses, see p51. For information on Elderhostel (a nonprofit organization helping seniors travel and take college courses), see right.

CUSTOMS

Each visitor is allowed to bring 1 liter of liquor and 200 cigarettes duty free into the US, but you must be at least 21 years old to possess the former and 18 years old to possess the latter. In addition, each traveler is permitted to bring gift merchandise up to the value of $100 into the US without incurring any duty.

DANGERS & ANNOYANCES

New England's cities are relatively safe, but you should observe the following standard urban safety guidelines:

- Lock valuables in your hotel room or put them in the hotel safe.
- Lock your car doors and don't leave any valuables visible.
- Avoid walking alone on empty streets or in parks at night.
- Try to use ATMs only in well-trafficked areas.
- Street people and panhandlers may approach you; nearly all of them are harmless.

In rural areas, be aware of hunters during the November hunting season. 'No Hunting' signs are widely ignored and are not a guarantee of safety. For health concerns, see the Health chapter (p540).

DISABLED TRAVELERS

Travel within New England is becoming less difficult for people with disabilities, but it's still not easy. Public buildings are now required by law to be wheelchair accessible and also to have appropriate restroom facilities. Public transportation services must be made accessible to all, and telephone companies are required to provide relay operators for the hearing impaired. Many banks provide ATM instructions in braille, curb ramps are common, many busy intersections have audible crossing signals, and most chain hotels have suites for disabled guests. Even so, it's best to call ahead to see what's available.

A number of organizations specialize in the needs of disabled travelers:

Mobility International USA (☎ 541-343-1284; www .miusa.org; 132 E Broadway, Eugene, OR 97440) Advises disabled travelers on mobility issues, but primarily runs an educational exchange program.

Society for the Advancement of Travel for the Handicapped (SATH; ☎ 212-447-7284; www.sath .org; 347 Fifth Ave, ste 610, New York, NY 10016) Publishes a quarterly magazine; has various information sheets on travel for the disabled.

DISCOUNT CARDS

Yankee frugality is not a myth. Plenty of discounts are available; you just have to know when, where and whom to ask for them.

Senior Cards

Travelers aged 50 years and older can receive rate cuts and benefits at many places. Inquire about discounts at hotels, museums and restaurants *before* you make your reservation. With the America the Beautiful – Senior Pass ($10), US citizens aged 62 and over receive free admission to national parks nationwide and a 50% reduction on camping fees. Apply in person at Acadia National Park (p508), or call ☎ 877-444-6777.

Some national advocacy groups:

American Association of Retired Persons (AARP; ☎ 888-687-2277; www.aarp.org; 601 E St NW, Washington, DC 20049) Advocacy group for Americans 50 years old and older; a good resource for travel bargains. US residents can get one-/three-year memberships for US$12.50/29.50.

Elderhostel (☎ 877-454-5768; www.elderhostel.org; 11 Ave de Lafayette, Boston, MA 02111) Nonprofit organization offering seniors the opportunity to attend academic college courses and travel worldwide.

Student & Youth Cards

Most hostels in the US are members of Hostelling International–American Youth Hostels (HI-USA; see p523), which offers low-cost accommodations to card-carrying members. In college towns such as Amherst, Boston, Cambridge, Hanover or New Haven, your student ID card sometimes can get you discounts. Museums and attractions outside these cities may also give small discounts but you'll need a card to prove you're a student.

AAA Discount Cards

If you plan on doing a lot of driving in New England, consider joining your national automobile association before arriving in the US. Members of clubs affiliated with the American Automobile Association (AAA; p538) can get roadside assistance as well as discounts on lodging, car rental and sightseeing admission with membership cards.

EMBASSIES & CONSULATES
US Embassies & Consulates

Australia (☎ 02-6214 5600; http://canberra.usembassy .gov; 21 Moonah Pl, Yarralumla, Canberra, ACT 2600)

Austria (☎ 1-31339-0; http://vienna.usembassy.gov; Boltzmanngasse 16, A-1090, Vienna)

Canada (☎ 613-238-5335; http://ottawa.usembassy .gov; 490 Sussex Dr, Ottawa, Ontario K1N 1G8)

Denmark (☎ 33 41 71 00; http://denmark.usembassy .gov; Dag Hammarskjölds Allé 24, 2100 Copenhagen)

Finland (☎ 9-616-250; www.usembassy.fi; Itäinen Puistotie 14 B, 00140 Helsinki)

France (☎ 33 1 43 12 22 22; http://france.usembassy .gov; 2 Av Gabriel, 75008 Paris)

Germany (☎ 030-2385 174; www.usembassy.de; Neustádtische Kirchstrasse 4-5, 10117 Berlin)

Ireland (☎ 353 1 668 8777; http://dublin.usembassy .gov; 42 Elgin Rd, Ballsbridge, Dublin 4)

Israel (☎ 3-519-7327; www.usembassy-israel.org.il; 71 Hayarkon St, Tel Aviv 63903)

Italy (☎ 39 06 46741; www.usembassy.it; Via Vittorio Veneto 121, 00187 Rome)

Japan (☎ 03-3224-5000; http://tokyo.usembassy.gov; 1-10-5, Akasaka, Minato-ku, Tokyo)

Mexico (☎ 01-55 5080-2000; www.usembassy-mexico .gov; Paseo de la Reforma 305, Colonia Cuauhtémoc, 06500 México, DF)

Netherlands (☎ 070-310 2209; http://thehague.usem bassy.gov; Lange Voorhout 102, 2514 EJ The Hague)

New Zealand (☎ 04-462 6000; http://wellington .usembassy.gov; 29 Fitzherbert Terrace, PO Box 1190, Thorndon, Wellington)

Spain (☎ 91-587-2200; http://madrid.usembassy.gov; Calle Serrano 75, 28006 Madrid)

Sweden (☎ 08 783 53 00; http://stockholm.usembassy .gov; Dag Hammarskjölds Väg 31, SE-115 89 Stockholm)

Switzerland (☎ 031-357-7011; http://bern.usembassy .gov; Jubiläumsstrasse 93, CH-3005 Bern)

UK (☎ 020-7499 9000; www.usembassy.org.uk; 24/31 Grosvenor Sq, London W1A 1AE)

Embassies & Consulates in New England

Embassies are in Washington, DC. Some countries maintain consulates, honorary consuls or consular agents in Boston. To get the telephone number of an embassy or consulate not listed below, call directory assistance (☎ 411).

Australia Embassy (☎ 202-797-3000; www.austemb .org; 1601 Massachusetts Ave NW, Washington DC 20036)

Canada Consulate (☎ 617-262-3760; www.boston .gc.ca; 3 Copley Pl, ste 400, Boston, MA 02116)

France Consulate (☎ 617-832-4400; www.consulfrance -boston.org; 31 St James Ave, ste 750, Boston MA 02116)

Germany Consulate (☎ 617-369 4900; www.germany info.org; 3 Copley Pl, ste 500, Boston MA 02116)

Ireland Consulate (☎ 617-267-9330; www.ireland emb.org; Chase Bldg, 535 Boylston St, Boston MA 02116)

Israel Embassy (☎ 202-364-5500; www.embassyofis rael.org; 3514 International Dr NW, Washington DC 20008)

Italy Consulate (☎ 617-722-9201; www.consboston .esteri.it; 600 Atlantic Ave, 17th floor, Boston MA 02116)

Japan Embassy (☎ 202-238-6700; www.us.emb-japan .go.jp; 2520 Massachusetts Ave NW, Washington DC 20008)

Mexico Embassy (☎ 202-728-1600; www.embassy ofmexico.org; 1911 Pennsylvania Ave, Washington DC 20006)

Netherlands Embassy (☎ 877-388-2443; www .netherlands-embassy.org; 4200 Linnean Ave, Washington DC 2008)

New Zealand Embassy (☎ 202-328-4800; www .nzembassy.com/usa; 37 Observatory Circle NW, Washington DC 20008)

UK Consulate (☎ 617-245-4500; www.britainusa.com /boston; 1 Memorial Dr, 15th fl, Cambridge, MA 02142)

FESTIVALS & EVENTS

Special events never cease in New England, including holiday celebrations, harvest celebrations and cultural events. Tourist information offices and websites have complete information. See also p18 for a comprehensive Event Calendar.

FOOD

The Eating section for each destination is broken down into three price categories: budget (for meals costing $12 or less), midrange (where meals cost $12 to $23) and top end (where meals cost more than $20). These price estimates do not include taxes, tips or alcoholic beverages.

For details about New England specialties and delicacies, see (p46).

GAY & LESBIAN TRAVELERS

Out and active gay communities are visible across New England, especially in cities such as Boston (see p98), Portland, New Haven and Burlington, which have substantial gay populations, and where it is easier for gay men and women to live their lives with a certain amount of openness. Traveling outside of large cities, gay travelers should be more cautious about exhibiting their sexual preferences.

Provincetown, Massachusetts (p201) and Ogunquit, Maine (p466) are gay meccas during the summer. College and university towns like Northampton, Massachusetts (p247) and Burlington, Vermont (p386) also have lively lesbian communities year-round. Many cities have a gay or alternative newspaper such as *Bay Windows,* a Boston-based publication that lists current events and local contacts.

Other excellent national resources:

Damron Company (☎ 415-255-0404, 800-462-6654; www.damron.com) Publishes national guidebooks with listings of gay-owned or gay-friendly accommodations nationwide.

Gay Yellow Pages (☎ 212-674-0120; http://gayellow pages.com) An impressive online database organized by state.

Lambda Legal Defense Fund (☎ 212-809-8585 NYC office, 213-382-7600 LA office; www.lambdalegal.org)

National AIDS/HIV Hotline (☎ 800-227-8922; www.ashastd.org)

National Gay/Lesbian Task Force (☎ 617-492-6393; www.ngltf.org; 1151 Massachusetts Ave, Cambridge MA)

For more information about being gay in New England, see p36; for legal matters see right.

HOLIDAYS

See p18 for an Events Calendar.

New Year's Day January 1
Martin Luther King Jr Day Third Monday of January
Presidents' Day Third Monday of February
Easter In March or April
Memorial Day Last Monday of May
Independence Day July 4
Labor Day First Monday of September
Columbus Day Second Monday of October
Veterans Day November 11
Thanksgiving Fourth Thursday of November
Christmas Day December 25

LEGAL AGES

The legal age for certain activities around New England varies by state.

Driving Massachusetts 18, Connecticut 16, Rhode Island 18 Vermont 16, New Hampshire 17, Maine 16
Voting 18, in every state
Drinking 21 in every state
Heterosexual sex 16 in every state
Homosexual sex Massachusetts and New Hampshire 18, no age restriction in Connecticut, Rhode Island, Vermont and Maine

---

INSURANCE

It's expensive to get sick, crash a car or have things stolen from you in the US. For rental car insurance see p538 and for health insurance see p540. To protect yourself should items be stolen from your car, consult your homeowner's (or renter's) insurance policy before leaving home.

INTERNET ACCESS

If you bring a laptop with you from outside the US, it's worth investing in a universal AC and plug adapter. Many hotels, restaurants and cafés offer wireless access for free or for a small fee (look for 🖳 wi-fi in the reviews). See also the boxed text on p68.

Cybercafés and business centers like Kinkos offer inexpensive online computer access. See the relevant Internet Access sections (under Information) in individual chapters. For more information, also see above.

LEGAL MATTERS

If you are arrested for a serious offence, you have the right to remain silent and to have an attorney present during any interrogation, and you are presumed innocent until proven guilty. You have the right to an attorney from the very first moment you are arrested. If you can't afford one, the state must provide one for free. All persons who are arrested have the right to make one phone call. If you don't have a lawyer or family member to help you, call your embassy or consulate.

The minimum age for drinking alcoholic beverages is 21. You'll need a government-issued photo ID (such as a passport or US driver's license). Stiff fines, jail time and penalties can be incurred if you are caught driving under the influence of alcohol or providing alcohol to minors.

MAPS

Local chambers of commerce usually hand out simple maps of their towns. Detailed state highway maps are also distributed free by state governments. You can call or write to state tourism offices in advance (see p531) to request maps, or you can pick up the maps at highway tourism information offices ('welcome centers') when you enter a state on a major highway.

Hiking-trail maps are available from outdoors organizations, such as the Appalachian Mountain Club (p69). Other excellent map resources:

Delorme Mapping Company (☎ 207-846-7100; www.delorme.com) Publishes individual state maps – atlas-style books with detailed coverage of New England's backcountry roads. The Massachusetts map is done at an impressive 1:80,000 scale.

Globe Corner Bookstore (☎ 617-497-6277, 800-358-6013; www.globecorner.com; Cambridge) Place your order in person or online.

US Dept of the Interior Geological Survey (USGS; www.usgs.gov) The topographical maps are superb close-up maps for hiking.

MONEY

The dollar (commonly called a buck) is divided into 100 cents. Coins come in denominations of one cent (penny), five cents (nickel), 10 cents (dime), 25 cents (quarter) and the rare 50-cent piece (half dollar). Notes come in one-, five-, 10-, 20-, 50- and 100-dollar denominations.

See Quick Reference inside the front cover for exchange rates and p14 for information on costs.

ATMs & Cash

Automatic teller machines (ATMs) are great for quick cash influxes and can negate the need for traveler's checks entirely, but watch out for ATM surcharges. Most banks in New England charge around $1.50 per withdrawal. The Cirrus and Plus systems both have extensive ATM networks that will give cash advances on major credit cards and allow cash withdrawals with affiliated ATM cards. Look for ATMs outside banks, and in large grocery stores, shopping centers, convenience stores and gas stations.

If you're carrying foreign currency, it can be exchanged for US dollars at Logan International Airport in Boston. Many banks do not change currency, so stock up on dollars when there's an opportunity to do so.

Some banks in small vacation towns frequented by Canadian tourists will buy and sell Canadian currency; some businesses near the border will offer to accept Canadian dollars 'at par,' meaning that they will accept Canadian dollars as though they were US dollars, in effect giving you a discount on your purchase.

Credit Cards

Major credit cards are widely accepted throughout New England, including at car rental agencies and at most hotels, restaurants, gas stations, grocery stores and tour operators. Many B&Bs and some condominiums – particularly those handled through rental agencies – do not accept credit cards, however. We have noted that in our reviews when it is the case.

American Express (☎ 800-528-4800)
Diners Club (☎ 800-234-6377)
Discover (☎ 800-347-2683)
MasterCard (☎ 800-826-2181)
Visa (☎ 800-336-8472)

Tipping

Taxi drivers and baggage carriers expect tips (15% and $1 per bag, respectively). Waiters and bartenders rely on tips for their livelihoods. Tip 15% unless the service is terrible (in which case a complaint to the manager is warranted), or about 20% if the service is great. Never tip in fast-food, takeout or buffet-style restaurants where you serve yourself. Baggage carriers in airports and hotels get about US$1 per bag. In hotels with daily housekeeping, remember to leave a few dollars in the room for the staff when you check out. In budget hotels, tips are not expected, but are always appreciated.

Traveler's Checks

Traveler's checks provide protection from theft and loss. For refunds on lost or stolen traveler's checks, call **American Express** (☎ 800-992-3404) or **Thomas Cook** (☎ 800-287-7362). Keeping a record of the check numbers and those you have used is vital for replacing lost checks, so keep this information separate from the checks themselves.

Foreign visitors will have an easier time if their traveler's checks are in US dollars. Most mid-range and upscale restaurants, hotels and shops accept US dollar traveler's checks and treat them just like cash.

FIVE PHOTO TIPS

For the very complete short course on photographic ins and outs, dos and don'ts, consult Lonely Planet's *Travel Photography*. In the meantime, try these tips:

- Shoot at dusk and dawn – sure it's hard to wake up and be in the right place at the right time, but the light is more angular and dramatic.
- Include people for perspective – when you get home, your friends won't ask 'How big was that?'
- Shoot street life – shots of one building after another will test your friends' patience.
- Change perspective – get low and shoot up; get high and look down.
- Move in closer – whether it's people or places, there's almost no such thing as too close (and when there is, it's called an abstraction!).

PHOTOGRAPHY & VIDEO

There are virtually no restrictions on photography except within museums and at some musical and artistic performances.

For the traditionalists out there, both print and slide films are readily available in New England. Furthermore, every town of any size has a photo shop that stocks cameras and accessories. With little effort you should be able to find a shop to develop your color print film on the same day. If you're in New England for any length of time, have your film developed here, as summertime heat and humidity greatly accelerate the deterioration of exposed film.

With high-powered X-ray machines now at many airports, don't pack film into checked luggage or carry-on bags. Instead carry your film in a baggie to show separately to airport security officials (known as a hand check). Remember to finish off the roll in your camera and take it out, too, or those photos may end up foggy.

Photos may also be interested in Maine Photographic Workshops (p496) in Rockport, Maine and Photo Walks (p97) in Boston. For more specific photographic tips, see above.

POST

No matter how much people like to complain, the **US postal service** (☎ 800-275-8777; www .usps.gov) provides great service for the price. For 1st-class mail sent and delivered within the US, postage rates are 41¢ for letters up to 1oz (27¢ for each additional ounce) and 26¢ for standard-sized postcards. International airmail rates for letters up to 1oz are 69¢ to Canada or Mexico, 90¢ to other countries.

If you have the correct postage, drop your mail into any blue mailbox. However, to send a package weighing 16oz or more, you must bring it to a post office. Post office locations are listed in the Information sections for major towns.

You can have mail sent to you c/o General Delivery at most big post offices in New England. When you pick up your mail, bring some photo identification. General delivery mail is usually held for up to 30 days. Most hotels will also hold mail for incoming guests.

Call private shippers like **United Parcel Service** (UPS; ☎ 800-742-5877) and **Federal Express** (FedEx; ☎ 800-463-3339) for more important or larger items.

SHOPPING

New England has a lot of fine craftspeople, and quality handicrafts can be readily found in each state. Keep some money in reserve so you can spend it here.

In Connecticut, home to crafty Martha Stewart, don't miss Connecticut River Artisans (p341) in Chester or Quimper Faïence (p323) in Stonington, one of the few official shops that sells these one-of-a-kind folk-art plates, cups and figurines.

If you want to bypass Maine's outlet scene, head to Blue Hill (p500), a small town with many outstanding artisans. Or visit the Haystack Mountain School of Crafts (p501) in Deer Isle Village.

Boston has a few craft cooperatives, which are goldmines for craft-seekers. Seek out the Cambridge Artists' Cooperative (p122) and the Society of Arts & Crafts (p122), located on fashionable Newbury St. In Western Massachusetts don't miss the colorful and fragile North River Glass (p257) in Shelburne Falls.

DIRECTORY

New Hampshire offers intrepid shoppers a curious mix of mall mania and quality artisan shops. The main drag in North Conway (p450) is lined with an endless strip of outlets, while the Canterbury Shaker Village (p422) offers a quiet glimpse of old New England life, where you can watch employees fashion Shaker furniture (and then consider a purchase).

When in Rhode Island, visit the The Arcade (p278), America's first enclosed shopping center, in Providence.

Vermont crafts are more akin to fine arts than you might think, and you can easily spend a fortune on one-of-a-kind pieces. Great shopping towns include Brattleboro (stop at the Vermont Artisan Designs, p359); Middlebury (don't miss the Frog Hollow Craft Center, p382) and Burlington (p394). Manchester (p369) is famed for its upscale outlet shops, while Simon Pearce Glass (p378) in Quechee has one-of-a-kind creations and the Vermont Country Store (p362) in Weston sells things you'll find nowhere else.

Shopaholics love searching for discounted clothing, shoes, china and jewelry at the original Filene's Basement (p122) in Boston. Fall River and New Bedford (Massachusetts), North Conway (New Hampshire) and Freeport and Kittery (Maine) also have massive factory-outlet malls.

SOLO TRAVELERS
Solo travel in New England is generally safe and easy. In general, women need to exercise more vigilance in large cities than in rural areas. Everyone, though, should avoid hiking, cycling long distances or camping alone, especially in unfamiliar places. For more safety advice, see p532 and p525.

TAXES

State	Meal	Lodging	Sales
Connecticut	6%	12%	6%
Maine	7%	7%	5%
Massachusetts	5%	5.7%	5%
New Hampshire	8%	8%	n/a
Rhode Island	8%	13%	7%
Vermont	9%	9%	6%

TELEPHONE
Always dial '1' before toll-free (800, 888 etc) and domestic long-distance numbers. Remember that some toll-free numbers

may only work within the region or from the US mainland.

All phone numbers in the US consist of a three-digit area code followed by a seven-digit local number. Because of the exponential growth of telephone numbers in New England, you now must dial ☎ 1 + area code + the seven-digit number for local as well as long-distance calls in many areas, particularly in eastern Massachusetts.

Pay phones aren't as readily found at shopping centers, gas stations and other public places now that cell phones are more prevalent, but keep your eyes peeled and you'll find them. Calls made within town are local and cost 25¢ or 50¢.

To make direct international calls, dial ☎ 011 + country code + area code + number. (An exception is calls made to Canada, where you dial ☎ 1 + area code + number. International rates apply to Canada.)

For international operator assistance, dial ☎ 0. The operator can provide specific rate information and tell you which time periods are the cheapest for calling.

If you're calling New England from abroad, the international country code for the US is ☎ 1. All calls to New England are then followed by the area code and the seven-digit local number.

Cellular Phones
The US uses a variety of cell-phone systems, 99% of which are incompatible with the GSM 900/1800 standard used throughout Europe and Asia. Check with your cellular service provider before departure about using your phone in New England. Verizon has the most extensive cellular network in New England, but Cingular and Sprint also have decent coverage. Once you get up into the mountains and off the main interstates in Vermont, New Hampshire and Maine, cell-phone reception is often downright nonexistent. Forget about using it on hiking trails.

Phone Codes
See the first page of each destination chapter.

Phone Cards
These private prepaid cards are available from convenience stores, supermarkets and pharmacies. Cards sold by major telecom-

munications companies like AT&T may offer better deals than upstart companies.

TIME

New England observes daylight saving time, which involves setting clocks ahead one hour on the first Sunday in April and back one hour on the last Sunday in October. The US (excluding Alaska and Hawaii) spans four time zones. New England is on US Eastern Time.

TOILETS

Americans have many names for public toilet facilities, but the most common names are 'restroom,' 'bathroom,' or 'ladies/men's room.' Of course, you can just ask for the 'toilet.'

Restrooms can be difficult to find in the larger cities of New England. There is no public mandate stating that restaurants, hotels or public sites must open their doors to those in need, but you can usually find relief at information centers and larger hotels. The city of Boston has a few coin-operated toilets placed at key tourist destinations (25¢ for 15 minutes).

TOURIST INFORMATION

State and regional tourist offices include the following:

Connecticut Office of Tourism (☎ 800-282-6863; www.ctbound.org; 505 Hudson St, Hartford CT 06106-7106)

Greater Boston Convention & Visitors Bureau (GBCVB; ☎ 617-536-4100, 800-888-5515; www.boston usa.com; 2 Copley Place, Suite 105, Boston MA 02116)

Maine Office of Tourism (☎ 207-287-5711, 888-624-6345; www.visitmaine.com; 59 State House Station, Augusta ME 04330)

Massachusetts Office of Travel & Tourism (☎ 617-973-8500, 800-227-6277; www.massvacation.com; State Transportation Building, 10 Park Plaza, Suite 4510, Boston MA 02116)

New Hampshire Division of Travel & Tourism (☎ 603-271-2665; www.visitnh.gov; PO Box 1856, Concord NH 03302)

Rhode Island Tourism Division (☎ 401-273-8270; www.visitrhodeisland.com; 1 W Exchange St, Providence RI 02903)

Vermont Division of Tourism and Marketing (☎ 802-828-3236; www.vermontvacation.com; 6 Baldwin St, Montpelier VT 05633-1301)

Chambers of Commerce

Often associated with convention and visitors' bureaus (CVBs), these are membership organizations for local businesses including

hotels, restaurants and shops. Although they often provide maps and other useful information, they usually don't tell you about establishments that are not chamber members, and these nonmembers are often the cheapest or most independent establishments.

A local chamber of commerce usually maintains an information booth at the entrance to the town or in the town center, often open only during tourist seasons (summer, foliage season, ski season).

TOURS

For those with limited time, package tours can sometimes be the cheapest way to go. Basic ones cover airfare and accommodation, while deluxe packages include car rental, island-hopping and all sorts of activities. Active tours include Bike Vermont (p375), which operates two- to six-night bike tours and inn-to-inn walking tours. Elderhostel (p525) offers educational programs for seniors.

Throughout New England you'll find many towns with a historical society that offers walking tours. Kayaking tours, which are always fun for families and the inner child, are plentiful on inland lakes and along the coast. Always keep an eye out for quirky tours like Moose Tours in Northern Forest Heritage Park, New Hampshire (p459) or nature tours like Art's Dune Tours in Provincetown (p205).

VISAS

Since the establishment of the Department of Homeland Security following the events of September 11, 2001, immigration now falls under the purview of the **Immigration & Customs Enforcement** (www.ice.gov).

Getting into the United States can be a bureaucratic nightmare, depending on your country of origin. To make matters worse, the rules are rapidly changing. For up-to-date information about visas and immigration, check with the **US State Department** (www.unitedsta tesvisas.gov).

Most foreign visitors to the US need a visa. However, there is a Visa Waiver Program in which citizens of certain countries may enter the US for stays of 90 days or less without first obtaining a US visa. This list is subject to continual re-examination and bureaucratic rejigging. Currently these countries include Andorra, Australia, Austria, Belgium, Brunei, Denmark, Finland, France, Germany, Iceland, Ireland, Italy, Japan, Liechtenstein,

DIRECTORY

Luxembourg, Monaco, the Netherlands, New Zealand, Norway, Portugal, San Marino, Singapore, Slovenia, Spain, Sweden, Switzerland and the UK. Under this program you must have a round-trip ticket (or onward ticket to any foreign destination) that is nonrefundable in the US and you will not be allowed to extend your stay beyond 90 days.

To participate in the Visa Waiver Program, travelers are required to have a passport that is machine-readable. Depending on when your passport was issued, you may also be required to provide a digital scan of your fingerprints.

In any case, your passport should be valid for at least six months longer than your intended stay and you'll need to submit a recent photo (50.8mm x 50.8mm) with the visa application. Documents of financial stability and/or guarantees from a US resident are sometimes required, particularly for those from developing countries. Visa applicants may be required to 'demonstrate binding obligations' that will ensure their return home. Because of this requirement, those planning to travel through other countries before arriving in the US are generally better off applying for their US visa while they are still in their home country rather than while on the road.

The validity period for a US visitor visa depends on your home country. The actual length of time you'll be allowed to stay in the US is determined by the Bureau of Citizenship and Immigration Services at the port of entry.

WOMEN TRAVELERS

Contemporary women in New England can take some comfort in knowing that generations of the region's women have won respect and equality for females in business, arts, science, politics, education, religion and community service. In fact, in some communities like Nantucket, which developed as a matriarchy run by the Quaker 'gray ladies' (while the men were at sea, whaling), women still dominate commercial and community affairs.

Nevertheless, women travelers everywhere, including in New England, do face challenges particular to their gender. Avoiding vulnerable situations and conducting yourself in a commonsense manner will help you to avoid most problems. You're more vulnerable if you've been drinking or using drugs than if you're sober, and you're more vulnerable

alone than if you're with company. If you don't want company, most men will respect a firm but polite 'no, thank you.'

If despite all your precautions you are assaulted, call the police (☎ 911). Many cities have rape crisis centers to aid victims of rape. For the telephone number of the nearest center, call directory information (☎ 411 or 1 + area code + 555-1212).

The **National Organization for Women** (NOW; ☎ 202-628-8669; www.now.org; 1100 H St NW, 3rd floor, Washington DC 20005) is a good resource for a variety of information and can refer you to state and local chapters. **Planned Parenthood** (☎ 212-541-7800; www.plannedparenthood.org; 434 W 33rd St, New York NY 10001) can refer you to clinics throughout the country and offer advice on medical issues.

WORK

You will find lots of summer jobs at New England seaside and mountain resorts. These are usually low-paying service jobs filled by young people (often college students) who are happy to work part of the day so they can play the rest. If you want such a job, contact the local chambers of commerce or businesses well in advance. You can't depend on finding a job just by arriving in May or June and looking around. In winter, contact New England's ski resorts, where full- and part-time help is often welcome.

Foreigners entering the US to work must have a visa that permits it. Apply for a work visa from the US embassy in your home country before you leave. The type of visa varies, depending on how long you're staying and the kind of work you plan to do. Generally, you need either a J-1 visa, which you can obtain by joining a visitor-exchange program (issued mostly to students for work in summer camps), or an H-2B visa, when you are sponsored by a US employer.

The latter can be difficult to procure unless you can show that you already have a job offer from an employer who considers your qualifications to be unique and not readily available in the US. There are, of course, many foreigners working illegally in the country. Controversial laws prescribe punishments for employers employing 'aliens' (foreigners) who do not have the proper visas. Bureau of Citizenship and Immigration Service officers can be persistent and insistent in their enforcement of the laws.

Transportation

CONTENTS

GETTING THERE & AWAY

While the two most common ways to reach New England are by air and car, you can also get here easily by train and bus. Boston is the region's hub for air travel, but some international travelers fly into New York City to do some sightseeing before heading up to New England.

ENTERING THE COUNTRY

Despite the fact that Boston's Logan International Airport was intimately connected to the events of September 11, entering the country here is no different than entering any major US city. Be patient and pleasant and you will have no problems. As for border crossings from Canada, the worst problems you will encounter are long lines waiting in your car (see p535).

THINGS CHANGE...

The information in this chapter is particularly vulnerable to change. Check directly with the airline or a travel agent to make sure you understand how a fare (and ticket you may buy) works and be aware of the security requirements for international travel. Shop carefully. The details given in this chapter should be regarded as pointers and are not a substitute for your own careful, up-to-date research.

AIR

Because of New England's location on the densely populated US Atlantic seaboard between New York and eastern Canada, air travelers have a number of ways to approach the region.

Airports & Airlines
NEW ENGLAND

The major gateway to the region is Boston's **Logan International Airport** (BOS; ☎ 800-235-6426; www.massport.com), which offers many direct, nonstop flights from major airports in the US and abroad.

Depending on where you will be doing the bulk of your exploring, several other airports in the region receive national and international flights:

Bangor (BGR; ☎ 866-359-2264; www.flybangor.com) Serves central Maine.

Bradley International (BDL; ☎ 860-292-2000; www.bradleyairport.com) Serves Hartford, Connecticut, and Springfield, Massachusetts.

Burlington (BTV; ☎ 802-863-2874; www.burlingtonintlairport.com) Serves northern Vermont.

Manchester (MHT; ☎ 603-624-6556; www.flymanchester.com) Serves southern and central New Hampshire.

Portland Jetport (PWM; ☎ 207-774-7301; www.portlandjetport.org) Serves coastal Maine.

Green Airport (PVD; ☎ 888-268-7222; www.pvdairport.com) Serves Providence, Rhode Island.

NEW YORK CITY

Flights into metro New York may be more convenient for some travelers, who have three airports from which to choose:

JFK International (JFK; ☎ 718-244-4444; www.panynj.gov)

LaGuardia (LGA; ☎ 718-244-4444; www.panynj.gov)

Newark International (EWR; ☎ 718-244-4444; www.panynj.gov)

Tickets

Airfares to the US and New England range from incredibly low to obscenely high. See p535 for recommendations of good sites for airplane tickets, as well as rental cars and hotel reservations. If you prefer to talk to someone in person, try **STA Travel** (☎ 800-777-0112;

CLIMATE CHANGE & TRAVEL

Climate change is a serious threat to the ecosystems that humans rely upon, and air travel is the fastest-growing contributor to the problem. Lonely Planet regards travel, overall, as a global benefit, but believes we all have a responsibility to limit our personal impact on global warming.

Flying & climate change

Pretty much every form of motorized travel generates CO_2 (the main cause of human-induced climate change) but planes are far and away the worst offenders, not just because of the sheer distances they allow us to travel, but because they release greenhouse gases high into the atmosphere. The statistics are frightening: two people taking a return flight between Europe and the US will contribute as much to climate change as an average household's gas and electricity consumption over a whole year.

Carbon offset schemes

Climatecare.org and other websites use 'carbon calculators' that allow travellers to offset the level of greenhouse gases they are responsible for with financial contributions to sustainable travel schemes that reduce global warming – including projects in India, Honduras, Kazakhstan and Uganda.

Lonely Planet, together with Rough Guides and other concerned partners in the travel industry, support the carbon offset scheme run by climatecare.org. Lonely Planet offsets all of its staff and author travel.

For more information check out our website: lonelyplanet.com.

---

www.statravel.com), which has offices in major cities nation- and worldwide.

Many domestic carriers offer special fares to visitors who are not US citizens. Typically, you must purchase a booklet of coupons in conjunction with a flight into the US from a foreign country other than Canada or Mexico. In addition to other restrictions, these coupons typically must be used within a limited period of time.

Round-the-world (RTW) tickets can be a great deal if you want to visit other regions on your way to New England. Often they are the same price – or not much more expensive – than a simple round-trip ticket to the USA. RTW itineraries that include stops in South America or Africa, though, can be substantially more expensive. Two airlines with good RTW programs are **British Airways** (☎ 800-247-9297; www.britishairways.com) and **Qantas** (☎ 800-227-4500; www.qanta susa.com).

Most airlines require a 14-day advance purchase. But if you're flying standby, call the airline a day or two before the flight and make a standby reservation so that you'll get priority.

Australia

Qantas flies to Los Angeles from Sydney, Melbourne and Brisbane. United flies from Sydney to San Francisco and Los Angeles, where connecting flights are available to the East Coast. In the summertime, fares are generally around AUD$2700 to AUD$3200 (US$2000 to US$2500) for a round-trip from Melbourne or Sydney to Boston.

From Australia, a Qantas RTW ticket permits six stops in North America and the Caribbean, four stops in Europe and four stops in Asia for A$3479 (US$3159).

Canada

Boston receives daily direct and nonstop flights from most major Canadian cities on many major carriers, including Air Canada, American, Delta, Northwest and United. Canadian fares to Boston in the summertime are reasonable: you can expect to find round-trips from Halifax for about C$250 (US$264), while flights from Montreal or Toronto are twice as much, unless you find a bargain.

The Canadian Federation of Students' **Travel CUTS** (www.travelcuts.com) travel agency offers low fares and has offices in major cities throughout Canada.

Continental Europe

Many carriers offer direct services to Boston, but prices can vary substantially depending on the season and directness of routing.

SURFING FOR FARES

You have a choice when booking tickets: talk to a live agent or tap away at the computer. Frankly, your odds are better doing it yourself if you can make the time. The following websites are recommended:

■ www.kayak.com – searches hundreds of airline websites and other search engine sites to give you a cost comparison. It's also possible to do a flexible search to compare dates and routes.

■ www.expedia.com – one of the original on-line search engines, this is a reliable stand-by.

■ www.cheaptickets.com – true to its name, this one often seems to come up with the cheapest fares.

■ www.priceline.com – name your budget and Priceline will try to find you a ticket. Best for last-minute travel, when airlines are unloading empty seats and hotels are trying to fill empty rooms.

■ www.bestfares.com – name your city and this site keeps track of the cheapest flights to destinations worldwide.

From Frankfurt, Amsterdam or Paris, expect a round-trip ticket to Boston cost from €419 to €454 (US$600 to US$650) in the winter, and from €560 to €700 (US$800 to US$1000) in the summer.

When calculating costs, don't forget to add the cost of getting from New York to Boston or New England via some other mode of transportation.

New Zealand

United and Air New Zealand both fly to San Francisco and Los Angeles from Auckland (via Sydney). Fares are generally around NZ$1970 (US$1500). Connector flights are readily available to the East Coast.

From New Zealand, a RTW ticket via North America, Europe and Asia with Air New Zealand and other airlines costs NZ$3100 and up.

UK & Ireland

London is arguably the world's headquarters for bucket shops specializing in discount tickets, and they are well advertised. Two good, reliable agents for cheap tickets in the UK are **Trailfinders** (☎ 0845 058 5858; www.trailfinders.co.uk; 1 Threadneedle St, London) and **STA Travel** (☎ 0871 2300 040; www.statravel.co.uk; 33 Bedford St, Covent Garden, London).

British Airways flies (round-trip) nonstop between London and Boston for about £400 to £500 (US$800 to US$1000) in summer, and £250 to £300 (US$500 to US$600) in winter. Virgin Atlantic often offers good deals for short stays (one month maximum) with a 21-day advance purchase. Flights in winter

from London can be as low as £230 (US$450) to Boston or £190 (US$375) to New York.

Aer Lingus offers direct flights from Shannon and Dublin to Boston for about £225 to £250 (US$450 to US$500) in winter and £350 to £400 (US$700 to US$800) in summer.

USA

Competition is high among airlines flying to Boston from major US cities. With a bit of luck and flexibility, you can usually get a flight from the West Coast to Boston for about $400 round-trip. From Washington, DC, fares are in the $200 round-trip range. From Chicago, expect to spend about $300 round-trip. Savvy internet browsers can cut the cost of coast-to-coast airfares in half with a bit of flexibility.

LAND
Border Crossings

Generally, crossing the US/Canadian border is pretty straightforward. The biggest hassle is usually the length of the lines. As of 2008, all travelers entering the United States are required to carry passports, including citizens of Canada and the United States. You may also be asked to show a return plane ticket or proof of sufficient funds, but this is rare.

Bus

You can get to New England by bus from all parts of the US and Canada, but the trip will be long and may not be much less expensive than a discounted flight. Bus companies usually offer special promotional fares.

For travel between San Francisco and New England, **Green Tortoise** (☎ 415-956-7500, 800-867-8647; www.greentortoise.com) buses are relaxing and entertaining. You'll spend 12 to 14 days winding across the country via state and national parks, monuments, forests and anywhere else your fellow passengers agree to stop; flexibility is key. Fares are $599, plus a food fund payment of $171 per person.

Greyhound (☎ 800-231-2222; www.greyhound.com) is the national bus line, serving all major cities in the United States. Greyhound advertises that you can go anywhere in the US for US$99 or less with a 14-day advance purchase, US$109 if you are traveling on a weekend. Prices are significantly cheaper for shorter distance, with prices as low as US$29 to US$39 for distances less than 300 miles.

Peter Pan Buslines (☎ 800-343-9999; www.peterpanbus.com) Serves 52 destinations in the northeast, as far north as Concord (New Hampshire) and as far south as Washington, DC, as well as into western Massachusetts.

Vermont Transit (☎ 802-864-6811, 800-552-8737; www.vermonttransit.com) links destinations around New England with Boston, Montreal and New York City.

The cheapest way to get to Boston from New York City is on one of the **Chinatown Buses** (www.chinatown-bus.com; tickets $15). These are bus companies that run between the major cities on the east coast, from Chinatown to Chinatown. It's crowded, it's confusing, but it sure is cheap:

Fung Wah Bus Company (☎ 212-925-8889; www.fungwahbus.com)
Lucky Star Bus (☎ 800-881-0887; www.luckystarbus.com)

Car & Motorcycle

Interstate highways crisscross New England and offer forest, farm and mountain scenery once you are clear of urban areas and the I-95 corridor between Boston and New York. These interstate highways connect the region to New York, Washington, DC, Montreal and points south and west. See opposite for more on car and motorcycle travel in New England.

Train

The rail passenger service in the US is operated primarily by **Amtrak** (☎ 800-872-7245; www.amtrak.com). Services along the Northeast Corridor (connecting Boston, Providence, Hartford and New Haven with New York

and Washington, DC) are some of the most frequent in Amtrak's system.

Amtrak's high-speed Acela trains make the trip from New York City to Boston in three hours. One-way weekend special fares aboard Acela trains cost from $102 to $117 departing New York City, and from $164 to $184 departing Washington, DC. About 10 trains depart New York City daily for Boston's South Station.

The *Lake Shore Limited* departs Chicago each evening for Boston, making stops in Springfield, Worcester and Boston.

Amtrak offers excursion fares, seasonal discounts and rail passes good for unlimited travel during a certain period of time. Children receive discounts as well. The fares listed below are unreserved, coach class, one-way fares to Boston.

From	One-way Fare (peak/non-peak)	Duration
New York, NY	$84/102	4 hrs
Chicago, IL	$80/126	23 hrs
Washington, DC	$83/140	8 hrs
San Francisco, CA	$155/240	77 hrs

GETTING AROUND

Simply put, the best way to get around New England is by car. The region is relatively small, the highways are good and public transportation is not as frequent or as widespread as in some other countries. Still, there are the alternatives of air, train and bus.

AIR

Regional and commuter airlines connect New England's cities and resorts with Boston and New York City. The following airports receive scheduled flights:

Bangor International Airport (☎ 866-359-2264; www.flybangor.com) Serves inland and northern Maine.

Barnstable Municipal Airport (☎ 508-775-2020; www.town.barnstable.ma.us/departments/airport) Serves Cape Cod.

Bradley International Airport (☎ 860-292-2000; www.bradleyairport.com) Serves Connecticut, the Berkshires and Central Massachusetts.

Burlington Airport (☎ 802-863-2874; www.burlingtonairport.com) Vermont's major airport.

Groton/New London Airport (☎ 860-445-8549; www.grotonnewlondonairport.com) Serves the southeastern Connecticut coast.

Hancock County Airport (☎ 207-667-7329; www
.bhbairport.com) Serves Mt Desert Island and Down East.
Martha's Vineyard Airport (☎ 508-693-7022; www
.mvyairport.com) Serves the Vineyard.
Nantucket Airport (☎ 508-325-5300; www.nantuck
etairport.com) Serves Nantucket Island.
Rutland Southern Vermont Regional Airport
(☎ 802-786-8881; www.flyrutlandvt.com)
Worcester Municipal Airport (☎ 508-799-1350;
www.flyworcester.com) Serves central Massachusetts.

Regional Airlines

Cape Air (☎ 800-352-0714; www.flycapeair.com)
Flights to Cape Cod, Martha's Vineyard and Nantucket.
Colgan Air (☎ 800-428-4322; www.colganair.com)
Connects Bar Harbor and Boston year-round.
Nantucket Air (☎ 800-635-8787; www.nantucketair
lines.com) Flights from Cape Cod to Nantucket.
New England Airlines (☎ 800-243-2460; www
.block-island.com/nea) Flights to Block Island from
Westerly.

BICYCLE

Bicycling is a popular New England sport
and means of transport on both city streets
and country roads. Several of the larger cities have systems of bike paths that make
bike travel much easier and more pleasant.
Disused railroad rights-of-way have also been
turned into bike trails. The Cape Cod Rail
Trail (p188) between Dennis and Wellfleet is
a prominent example.

Bicycle rentals are available in most New
England cities, towns and resorts at reasonable
prices (often $15 to $25 per day). Many rental
shops are mentioned in this guide. For more
on bicycling, see p59.

BOAT

Boat service in New England is more ac-
curately called ferry service and it tends
to be more for pleasure excursions than
transportation. There are a couple of
exceptions though.

In Massachusetts, you can take a ferry between Boston and Provincetown on Cape Cod
(p209). For Martha's Vineyard, ferries travel
between Falmouth and Oak Bluffs (p226) and
Woods Hole and Vineyard Haven (p223). You
can reach Nantucket (p216) from Hyannis,
Harwich and Martha's Vineyard.

In Connecticut, ferries travel between
Bridgeport and Port Jefferson (Long Island,
New York, see p335); New London and Block
Island; New London and Orient Point (Long

Island); and New London and Fisher's Island
(New York, see p328).

In Rhode Island, ferries run from
Providence to Newport (p305). You can
reach Block Island by ferry from Newport or
Galilee (p310).

In Vermont, there's a ferry running from
Burlington to New York state, traversing Lake
Champlain (p395).

In Maine, you can travel by ferry between
Bar Harbor (p508) and Portland (p482) and
Yarmouth, Nova Scotia; local ferries also serv-
ice island communities such as Monhegan,
North Haven and Vinalhaven.

BUS

Buses go to more places than airplanes or trains,
but the routes still bypass some prime destinations, especially in rural places. Individual
route prices are covered under the Getting
There & Away sections of regional chapters.

Besides the national bus company,
Greyhound (see p535), there are several regional
carriers that ply routes within New England:
Concord Trailways (☎ 617-426-8080; 800-639-3317,
www.concordtrailways.com) Covers routes from Boston
to New Hampshire (Concord, Manchester, and as far up as
Conway and Berlin) and Maine (Portland and Bangor). Its
partner Dartmouth Coach goes to Hanover, New Hampshire.
C&J Trailways (☎ 603-430-1100, 800-258-7111; www
.cjtrailways.com) Provides daily service between Boston
and Newburyport (Massachusetts), as well as Portsmouth
and Dover (New Hampshire). Kids travel for free when
accompanied by a full-paying adult.
Peter Pan Bus Lines (☎ 800-343-9999; www
.peterpanbus.com) Serves 52 destinations in the northeast,
as far north as Concord (New Hampshire) and as far south
as Washington DC, as well as into western Massachusetts.
Fares are comparable to Greyhound.
Plymouth & Brockton Street Railway Co (☎ 508-
746-0378; www.p-b.com) Provides frequent service to the
South Shore and to most towns on Cape Cod, including
Hyannis and Provincetown.
Vermont Transit (☎ 800-552-8737; www.vermont
transit.com) The route from Boston goes via Manchester and
Concord (New Hampshire) to White River Junction, Montpe-
lier and Burlington (Vermont), then all the way to Montreal
in Canada. Another route runs up the coast to Newburyport
(Massachusetts); Portsmouth (New Hampshire); and
Portland, Augusta, Bangor and Bar Harbor (Maine).

CAR & MOTORCYCLE

Yes, driving is the best way to see New
England. But heads up: New England drivers are aggressive, speedy and unpredictable,

particularly around Boston and other cities. Traffic jams are common in urban areas.

As for parking, municipalities control parking by signs on the street stating explicitly what may or may not be done. Meters require multiple feedings with quarters. A yellow line or yellow-painted curb means that no parking is allowed there.

Automobile Associations

The **American Automobile Association** (AAA; ☎ 800-564-6222; www.aaa.com) provides members with maps and other information. Members also get discounts on car rentals, air tickets, some hotels, some sightseeing attractions, as well as emergency road service and towing (☎ 800-222-4357). AAA has reciprocal agreements with automobile associations in other countries. Be sure to bring your membership card from your country of origin.

Driver's License

An international driving license, obtained before you leave home, is only necessary if your country of origin is a non-English speaking one.

Fuel

Gas stations are ubiquitous and many are open 24 hours a day. Small-town stations may be open only from 7am to 8pm or 9pm. Plan on spending $2.00 to $2.80 per US gallon.

At some stations, you must pay before you pump; at others, you may pump before you pay. The more modern pumps have credit/debit card terminals built into them, so you can pay with plastic right at the pump. At 'full service' stations, an attendant will pump your gas for you; no tip is expected.

Hire

Rental cars are readily available. With advance reservations for a small car, the daily rate with unlimited mileage is about $35, while typical weekly rates are $250 to $300. (Rates for midsize cars are often only a tad higher.) Dropping off the car at a different location from where you picked it up usually incurs an additional fee. It always pays to shop around between rental companies. You can often snag great last-minute deals via the internet – check out www.kayak.com to compare rates across companies.

Having a major credit card greatly simplifies the rental process. Without one, some

agencies simply will not rent vehicles, while others require prepayment, a deposit of $200 per week, pay stubs, proof of round-trip airfare and more.

The following companies operate in New England:

Alamo (☎ 800-462-5266; www.goalamo.com)
Avis (☎ 800-321-3712; www.avis.com)
Budget (☎ 800-527-0700; www.budget.com)
Dollar (☎ 800-800-5252; www.dollarcar.com)
Enterprise (☎ 800-261-7331; www.enterprise.com)
Hertz (☎ 800-654-3131; www.hertz.com)
National (☎ 800-227-7368; www.nationalcar.com)
Thrifty (☎ 800-283-0898; www.thrifty.com)

There are a handful of smaller agencies that may offer better deals, such as **Rent-A-Wreck** (☎ 800-944-7501; www.rentawreck.com), which rents cars that may have more wear and tear than your typical rental vehicle, but are actually far from wrecks.

Insurance

Should you have an accident, liability insurance covers the people and property that you have hit. For damage to the actual rental vehicle, a collision damage waiver (CDW) is available for about $15 a day. If you have collision coverage on your vehicle at home, it might cover damages to car rentals; inquire before departing. Additionally, some credit cards offer reimbursement coverage for collision damages if you rent the car with that credit card; again, check before departing. Most credit card coverage isn't valid for rentals of more than 15 days or for exotic models, jeeps, vans and 4WD vehicles.

Road Conditions & Hazards

New England roads are very good – even the warren of hard-packed dirt roads that criss-cross Vermont. Some roads across northern mountain passes in Vermont, New Hampshire and Maine are closed during the winter, but good signage gives you plenty of warning.

Road Rules

Driving laws are different in each of the New England states, but most require the use of safety belts. In every state, children under four years of age must be placed in a child safety seat secured by a seat belt. Most states require motorcycle riders to wear helmets whenever they ride. In any case, use of a helmet is highly recommended.

The maximum speed limit on most New England interstates is 65mph, but some have a limit of 55mph. On undivided highways, the speed limit will vary from 30mph to 55mph. Police enforce speed limits by patrolling in police cruisers and in unmarked cars. Fines can cost upwards of $350 in Connecticut, and it's similarly expensive in other states.

LOCAL TRANSPORTATION

City buses, and the T (the subway/underground system) in Boston, provide useful transportation within the larger cities and to some suburbs. Resort areas also tend to have regional bus lines. See Getting Around under the relevant regional sections for more information.

Taxis are common in the largest cities, but in smaller cities and towns you will probably have to telephone a cab to pick you up. Shuttles may take travelers from their hotel to the airport.

TRAIN

Shore Line East (☎ 203-255-7433; www.shoreeastline.com) trains connect New Haven and New London. **Metro-North** (☎ 212-532-4900, 800-638-7646; www.mta.info) trains run between New York City and New Haven.

Amtrak (p536) has a few different routes to and through New England. The *Vermonter* runs through New Haven and Hartford, (Connecticut), Springfield and Amherst (Massachusetts), and then on to St Albans in Vermont.

The *Montrealer* runs to northern Vermont along the Connecticut River Valley, with stops in New Haven (Connecticut), Amherst (Massachusetts) and Essex Junction (for Burlington), White River Junction and Brattleboro (Vermont).

In Boston, **MBTA Commuter Rail** trains (☎ 800-392-6100; www.mbta.com) travel west to Concord and Lowell, north to Salem, Rockport, Gloucester and Newburyport, and south to Plymouth and Providence. See p126 for more information.

The **Maine Eastern Railroad** (☎ 866-637-2457; www.maineeasternrailroad.com) now offers a seasonal service between Brunswick and Rockland, Maine (see p487).

TRANSPORTATION

Health

CONTENTS

The North American continent encompasses an extraordinary range of climates and terrains, many of which may be encountered in New England. Because of the high level of hygiene here, infectious diseases will not be a significant concern for most travelers, who will most likely experience nothing worse than a little diarrhea or a mild respiratory infection.

BEFORE YOU GO

HEALTH INSURANCE

The United States offers possibly the finest health care in the world. The problem is that, unless you have good insurance, it can be prohibitively expensive. It's essential to purchase travel health insurance if your regular policy doesn't cover you when you're abroad.

Bring any medications you may need in their original containers, clearly labeled. A signed, dated letter from your physician that describes all medical conditions and medications, including generic names, is also a good idea.

If your health insurance does not cover you for medical expenses abroad, consider getting supplemental insurance. Make sure you find out in advance if your insurance plan will make payments directly to providers or reimburse you later for overseas health-care costs.

RECOMMENDED VACCINATIONS

No special vaccines are required or recommended for travel to New England. All travelers should be up to date on routine immunizations.

INTERNET RESOURCES

There is a large amount of travel health advice on the internet. The World Health Organization (WHO) publishes a superb book called *International Travel and Health*, which is revised annually and is available online at no cost from its website at www.who.int/ith/. Another website of general interest is MD Travel Health at www.mdtravelhealth.com, which provides complete travel health recommendations for every country; it's updated daily, also at no cost.

It's usually a good idea to consult your government's travel health website before departure, if one is available:
Australia (www.dfat.gov.au/travel/)
Canada (www.hc-sc.gc.ca/english/index.html)
UK (www.doh.gov.uk/traveladvice/index.htm)
US (www.cdc.gov/travel/)

IN THE USA

AVAILABILITY & COST OF HEALTH CARE

In general, if you have a medical emergency, the best bet is to find the nearest hospital and go to its emergency room. If the problem isn't urgent, you can call a nearby hospital and ask for a referral to a local physician, which is usually cheaper than a trip to the emergency room. You should avoid stand-alone, for-profit urgent care centers, which tend to perform large numbers of expensive tests, even for minor illnesses.

Pharmacies are abundantly supplied throughout the USA, but you could find that some medications which are available over the counter in your home country require a prescription here, and, as always, if you don't have insurance to cover the cost of these prescriptions, they can be shockingly expensive.

INFECTIOUS DISEASES

In addition to more common ailments, there are several infectious diseases that are unknown or uncommon outside North

America. Most are acquired by mosquito or tick bites.

West Nile Virus

These infections were unknown in the United States until a few years ago, but have now been reported in almost all 50 states. The virus is transmitted by culex mosquitoes, which are active in late summer and early fall and generally bite after dusk. Most infections are mild or asymptomatic, but the virus may infect the central nervous system, leading to fever, headache, confusion, lethargy, coma and sometimes death. There is no treatment for West Nile virus. For the latest update on the areas affected by West Nile, go to the US Geological Survey website (http://westnile maps.usgs.gov/).

Lyme Disease

This disease has been reported from many states, but most documented cases occur in the northeastern part of the country, especially in New York, New Jersey, Connecticut and Massachusetts. Lyme disease is transmitted by deer ticks, which are only 1mm to 2mm long. Most cases occur in the late spring and summer. The CDC has an informative, if slightly scary, web page on Lyme disease at www.cdc.gov/nci dod/dvbid/lyme/.

The first symptom is usually an expanding red rash that is often pale in the center, known as a bull's eye rash. However, in many cases, no rash is observed. Flu-like symptoms are common, including fever, headache, joint pains, body aches and malaise. When the infection is treated promptly with an appropriate antibiotic, usually doxycycline or amoxicillin, the cure rate is high. Luckily, since the tick must be attached for 36 hours or more to transmit Lyme disease, most cases can be prevented by performing a thorough tick check after you've been outdoors, as described on p542.

Rabies

Rabies is a viral infection of the brain and spinal cord that is almost always fatal. The rabies virus is carried in the saliva of infected animals and is typically transmitted through an animal bite, though contamination of any break in the skin with infected saliva may result in rabies. In the US, most cases of human rabies are related to exposure to bats. Rabies may also be contracted from raccoons, skunks, foxes and unvaccinated cats and dogs.

If there is any possibility, however small, that you have been exposed to rabies, you should seek preventative treatment, which consists of rabies immune globulin and rabies vaccine and is quite safe. In particular, any contact with a bat should be discussed with health authorities, because bats have small teeth and may not leave obvious bite marks. If you wake up to find a bat in your room, or discover a bat in a room with small children, rabies prophylaxis may be necessary.

Giardiasis

This parasitic infection of the small intestine occurs throughout North America and the world. Symptoms may include nausea, bloating, cramps, and diarrhea, and may last for weeks. To protect yourself from giardia, you should avoid drinking directly from lakes, ponds, streams and rivers, which may be contaminated by animal or human feces. The infection can also be transmitted from person to person if proper hand washing is not performed. Giardiasis is easily diagnosed by a stool test and readily treated with antibiotics.

HIV/AIDS

As with most parts of the world, HIV infection occurs throughout the United States. You should never assume, on the basis of someone's background or appearance, that they're free of this or any other sexually transmitted disease. Be sure to use a condom for all sexual encounters.

ENVIRONMENTAL HAZARDS
Bites & Stings

Commonsense approaches to these concerns are the most effective: wear boots when hiking to protect from snakes, and wear long sleeves and pants to protect from ticks and mosquitoes. If you're bitten, don't overreact. Stay calm and follow the recommended treatment.

MOSQUITO BITES

When traveling in areas where West Nile or other mosquito-borne illnesses have been reported, keep yourself covered (wear long sleeves, long pants, hats, and shoes rather than sandals) and apply a good insect repellent, preferably one containing DEET, to exposed skin and clothing. In general, adults and children over 12 should use preparations

HEALTH

containing 25% to 35% DEET, which usually lasts about six hours. Children between two and 12 years of age should use preparations containing no more than 10% DEET, applied sparingly, which will usually last about three hours. Neurologic toxicity from DEET has been reported, especially in children, but appears to be extremely uncommon and generally related to overuse. DEET-containing compounds should not be used on children under the age of two.

Insect repellents containing certain botanical products, including eucalyptus oil and soybean oil, are effective but last only 1½ to two hours. Products based on citronella are not effective.

Visit the website of the **Center for Disease Control** (CDC; www.cdc.gov/ncidod/dvbid/westnile/prevention_info.htm) for information about preventing mosquito bites.

TICK BITES

Ticks are parasitic arachnids that may be present in brush, forest and grasslands, where hikers often get them on their legs or in their boots. Adult ticks suck blood from hosts by burrowing into the skin and can carry infections such as Lyme disease.

Always check your body for ticks after walking through high grass or thickly forested areas. If ticks are found unattached, they can simply be brushed off. If a tick is found attached, press down around the tick's head with tweezers, grab the head and gently pull upwards – do not twist it. (If no tweezers are available, use your fingers, but protect them from contamination with a piece of tissue or paper.) Do not rub oil, alcohol or petroleum jelly on it. If you get sick in the following couple of weeks, consult a doctor.

ANIMAL BITES

Do not attempt to pat, handle, or feed any animal, with the exception of domestic animals known to be free of any infectious disease. Most animal injuries are directly related to a person's attempt to touch or feed the animal.

Any bite or scratch by a mammal, including bats, should be promptly and thoroughly cleansed with large amounts of soap and water, followed by application of an antiseptic such as iodine or alcohol. The local health authorities should be contacted immediately for possible postexposure rabies treatment, whether or not you've been immunized against rabies. It may also be advisable to start an antibiotic, since wounds caused by animal bites and scratches frequently become infected.

SNAKE BITES

There are several varieties of venomous snakes in the US, but unlike those in other countries they do not cause instantaneous death, and antivenins are available. First aid is to place a light constricting bandage over the bite, keep the wounded part below the level of the heart and move it as little as possible. Stay calm and get to a medical facility as soon as possible. Bring the dead snake for identification if you can, but don't risk being bitten again. Do not use the mythic 'cut an X and suck out the venom' trick; this causes more damage to snakebite victims than the bites themselves.

SPIDER & SCORPION BITES

Although there are many species of spiders in New England, the only ones that cause significant human illness are the black widow, brown recluse and hobo spiders. The black widow is black or brown in color, measuring about 15mm in body length, with a shiny top, fat body and distinctive red or orange hourglass figure on its underside. It's found throughout the US, usually in barns, woodpiles, sheds, harvested crops and bowls of outdoor toilets. The brown recluse spider is brown in color, usually 10mm in body length, with a dark violin-shaped mark on the top of the upper section of the body. It's usually found in the south and southern Midwest, but has spread to other parts of the country in recent years. The brown recluse is active mostly at night, lives in dark sheltered areas such as under porches and in woodpiles, and typically bites when trapped. Hobo spiders are found chiefly in the northwestern United States and western Canada. The symptoms of a hobo spider bite are similar to those from the bite of a brown recluse, but milder.

If bitten by a black widow, you should apply ice or cold packs and go immediately to the nearest emergency room. Complications of a black widow bite may include muscle spasms, breathing difficulties and high blood pressure. The bite of a brown recluse or hobo spider typically causes a large, inflamed wound, sometimes associated with fever and chills. If bitten, apply ice and see a physician.

Glossary

For a hilarious and informative look at Boston dialect, browse Adam Gaffin's site at www.boston-online.com/wickedv.html. See also 'Eat Your Words' on p49 for special New England culinary terms.

Abenaki – a New England Native American tribe

alpine slide – a curvy chute navigated for fun on a simple wheeled cart or, if it's a water-slide, on an inflatable cushion

AMC – Appalachian Mountain Club

ayuh – locution pronounced by some people in Maine during pauses in conversation; perhaps a distant variant of 'yes'; vaguely positive in meaning

Back Bay – a Boston neighborhood developed during the 19th century by filling in a bay in the Charles River

batholith – a mass of rock formed deep in the earth, later perhaps thrust to the surface; customarily of large-crystalled rock (such as granite) and appears as mountainous domes of rock above surrounding terrain of softer material (as Mt Monadnock in southern New Hampshire)

boondocks or **boonies** – a city-dweller's derogatory term for the countryside, especially a remote rural place, as in 'The inn is nice, but it's way out in the boonies'

Brahmin – member of Boston's wealthy, well-educated, 19th-century class; now, any wealthy, cultured Bostonian

BYO or **BYOB** – 'bring your own' or 'bring your own bottle'; designates a restaurant that allows patrons to bring their own wine or beer; see *dry town*

cabinet – milkshake with ice-cream (Rhode Island)

Cape, the – Cape Cod

CCC – Civilian Conservation Corps, the Depression-era federal program established in 1933 to employ unskilled young workers, mainly on projects aimed at the conservation of US wildlands

CCNS – Cape Cod National Seashore

chamber of commerce – a co-operative of local businesses that operates a center offering information on member businesses, including hotels, restaurants and tourist attractions

chandlery – retail shop specializing in yachting equipment

cobble – a high rocky knoll of limestone, marble or quartzite that is found in western Massachusetts

cod cheeks – soft oyster-like bits of meat found on the sides of a codfish's 'face'; a delicacy, along with cod tongues, in some parts of New England and Atlantic Canada

common – see *green*

DAR – Daughters of the American Revolution, a patriotic service organization for women

Downeast – the Maine coast, especially its more easterly reaches, roughly from Mt Desert Island to Eastport

drumlin – a low, elongated hill formed of glacial till (earth and rock debris) during the most recent ice age; a common feature of the terrain in New England

dry town – a town in which municipal ordinances prohibit the sale (but usually not the possession, consumption or service) of alcoholic beverages

efficiency (unit) – a hotel or motel room with cooking and dining facilities (hot plate or range, refrigerator, sink, utensils, crockery and cutlery); see also *housekeeping cabin/unit*

foliage season – a few weeks from late September to late October when fall colors are at their prime; see also *leaf-peeping*

frappe – see *cabinet*

gap – mountain pass with steep sides; called a 'notch' in New Hampshire

gimcrack – a small item of uncertain use, perhaps frivolous; a gizmo

glacial pond – a deep, round freshwater pond formed by glacial gouging action during the ice age; a common feature of the New England terrain (such as Walden Pond in Concord, Massachusetts)

green – the grass-covered open space typically found at the center of a traditional New England village or town, originally used as common pastureland ('the common'), but now serving as a central park; often surrounded by community service buildings such as the town hall

grinder – a large sandwich of meat, cheese, lettuce, tomato, dressing etc in a long bread roll; in other parts of the US often called a 'submarine,' 'po' boy,' 'Cuban' or 'hoagie'

half-and-half – a very light cream (between 10% and 18% butterfat), typically used in coffee

hidden drive – a driveway entering a road in such a way that visibility for approaching drivers is impaired; signs warn of them

hookup – a facility at an RV camping site for connecting (hooking up) a vehicle to electricity, water, sewer or even cable TV

housekeeping cabin/unit – a hotel or motel room or detached housing unit equipped with kitchen facilities, rented by the day, week or month; see *efficiency*

hybrid bike – cross between a road bike and a mountain bike with medium-thickness tires

Indian summer – a brief warm period, usually in late autumn, before the cold weather sets in for the winter

ironclad – a 19th-century wooden warship with iron sheathing

Islands, the – Martha's Vineyard and Nantucket islands

leaf-peeping – recreational touring (by 'leaf-peepers') to enjoy autumn foliage colors; see also *foliage season*

lean-to – a simple shelter for camping, usually without walls, windows or doors, with a steeply slanting roof touching the ground on one side

lobster roll – a hot-dog bun or other bread roll filled with lobster meat in a mayonnaise sauce and sometimes dressed with celery and lettuce

Lower (or Outer) Cape – the long, narrow extension of Cape Cod north and east from Orleans to Provincetown

maple – a tree of the genus *Acer* having lobed leaves, winged seeds borne in pairs and close-grained wood, well suited to making furniture and flooring; the sap of the sugar maple *(Acer saccharum)* is gathered, boiled and reduced to make maple syrup; see *sugar bush, sugaring off*

Mid-Cape – region of Cape Cod roughly from Barnstable and Hyannis eastward to Orleans

minuteman – a colonial militiaman pledged to be ready at a moment's notice to defend his home and village; originally organized against Native American attacks, the minutemen provided the first organized American military force in the Revolutionary War against British troops

mud season – springtime in New England when the snow melts and the earth thaws

NPS – National Park Service, a division of the Department of the Interior that administers US national parks and monuments

Nutmeggers – nickname for residents of Connecticut

OSV – Old Sturbridge Village, Massachusetts

P-Town – Provincetown, on Cape Cod, Massachusetts

package store – liquor store

pie – another name for pizza

raw bar – a counter where fresh uncooked shellfish (clams, oysters, etc) are served

redcoat – a soldier from the British side during the American Revolution

RISD – Rhode Island School of Design

rush tickets – sometimes called 'student rush' or 'rush seats,' these are discounted tickets bought at a theater or concert hall box office usually no more than an hour or two before a performance

sachem – Native American chieftain; Massasoit was sachem of the Wampanoag tribe

sagamon – similar to *sachem*

shire town – county seat, town holding county government buildings

soaring – term for glider (sailplane) rides

Southie – South Boston, a neighborhood inhabited largely by Bostonians of Irish descent with a strong sense of Irish identity

sugar bush – a grove of sugar-maple trees; see *maple*

sugaring off – the springtime (March) harvest of sap from maple trees, which is collected and boiled to reduce it to maple syrup

T, the – official nickname for the Massachusetts Bay Transportation Authority (MBTA) Rapid Transit System

tall ships – tall-masted sailing vessels

taqueria – a casual Mexican food joint

tin ceiling – late-19th- to early-20th-century decorative feature consisting of thin steel sheets ('tinplates') embossed with decorative patterns, painted and used to cover ceilings

tuck-in – a substantial, sandwich-like meal

UMass – University of Massachusetts

Upper Cape – Cape Cod region near the Cape Cod Canal and the mainland

USFS – United States Forest Service, a division of the Department of Agriculture that implements policies on federal forest lands on the principles of 'multiple use,' including timber cutting, wildlife management, camping and recreation

USGS – United States Geological Survey, an agency of the Department of the Interior responsible for, among other things, detailed topographic maps of the entire country (particularly popular with hikers and backpackers)

UMass – University of Massachusetts

UVM – University of Vermont

Vineyard, the – (pronounced 'vin-yerd'), the island of Martha's Vineyard

weir – fishnet of string, bark strips, twigs etc placed in a river current to catch fish; using weirs is the oldest-known method of fishing in the world

windjammer – a tall-masted sailing ship

WPA – Works Progress Administration; established under President Roosevelt to put artists to work during the Great Depression

Yankee – perhaps from *Jan Kees* (John Cheese), a derogatory term for English settlers in Connecticut used by 17th-century Dutch colonists in New York; an inhabitant or native of New England; one from northeastern USA; a person or soldier from the northern states during the Civil War; an American

The Authors

MARA VORHEES   Coordinating Author, Boston, Around Boston

Born and raised in St Clair Shores, Michigan, Mara traveled the world (if not the universe) before finally settling in the Hub. She now lives in Somerville with her husband and her cat. She spent several years pushing papers and tapping keys at Harvard University, but she has since embraced the life of a full-time travel writer. She is often spotted sipping Sam Seasonal in Union Square and pedaling her bike along the River Charles. Mara is a frequent contributor to the *Boston Globe* Travel. She is also the author of Lonely Planet's *Boston City Guide*, among others.

My Favourite Trip

My preferred mode of travel is bicycle, and there is no better place to ride than Cape Cod. My favorite trip starts with some waterside cycling at the base of the Cape, on the Shining Sea Bicycle Path (p177) in Falmouth or along the Cape Cod Canal (p174) in Sandwich.

The mother of Cape Cod bike trails is the Rail Trail (p188), traversing salt marshes, freshwater ponds and shady forests. In Brewster, the Rail Trail passes through Nickerson State Park (p189), its hills and dales offering an adventurous diversion. It ends in Wellfleet, where I can't resist a lobster roll from Moby Dick's (p199).

At the tip of the cape, I cycle the Province Lands network of trails through the Cape Cod National Seashore (p196), offering dunes covered in wildflowers and panoramic vistas over the ocean. I cap off my cycling extravaganza in Provincetown with a seaside dinner at Mew's Restaurant (p207).

NED FRIARY & GLENDA BENDURE   Cape Cod, Nantucket & Martha's Vineyard

Although they've traveled far and wide, when it was time to call a place home, Ned and Glenda – taken by its windswept beauty – settled on Cape Cod. Over the years, they've explored their new home from one end to the other, leaving few rocks unturned. The things they recommend they know from heart. They've searched for the best lobster roll, canoed the marshes, stayed in old sea captains' homes on Nantucket, and hiked and biked the trails. And when summer comes around, it's a rare day that passes without a dip in the sea.

THE AUTHORS

RICHARD KOSS
Vermont, Connecticut

A native New Yorker, Richard has long been enamored with New England, the motherland of his own dear mother. Childhood trips to Boston and longer forays up the coast of Maine kindled a pride in his New England roots. When he grew up to become a freelance travel writer, he leapt at the opportunity to contribute the Vermont and Connecticut chapters to Lonely Planet's *New England*. Among other guidebooks, Richard covers Jamaica for Lonely Planet.

JOHN SPELMAN
Rhode Island, The Berkshires, Central Massachusetts

John's life changed drastically when he was born in Providence, Rhode Island. Years later, he attended college in Worcester, ruining his stomach lining with the coffee and swill of countless diners. He's canoed in Maine, cried on the Appalachian and Long Trails and endorses his grandfather's policy of drinking every cabinet life provides. John is a PhD student studying architectural history at the University of Virginia and has a Masters of Design Studies from Harvard. He's written for multiple Lonely Planet titles, including *Boston* and *Philadelphia & the Pennsylvania Dutch Country*.

REGIS ST. LOUIS
Maine, New Hampshire

A freelance writer based in Manhattan, Regis takes to the mountains and rugged coastline of New England every chance he gets. On his most recent journey, Regis traveled with his dog Cosmic and camped for 41 days, swam in mountain streams in New Hampshire, ate magnificent amounts of Maine lobster and watched the sunrise over the cliffs of America's eastern-most point. Regis has contributed to more than a dozen Lonely Planet titles and his travel articles have appeared in the *Chicago Tribune*, the *Los Angeles Times* and *Vivre Voyager*, among other publications.

LONELY PLANET AUTHORS

Why is our travel information the best in the world? It's simple: our authors are independent, dedicated travelers. They don't research using just the internet or phone, and they don't take freebies in exchange for positive coverage. They travel widely, to all the popular spots and off the beaten track. They personally visit thousands of hotels, restaurants, cafés, bars, galleries, palaces, museums and more – and they take pride in getting all the details right, and telling it how it is. Think you can do it? Find out how at lonelyplanet.com.

THE AUTHORS

Behind the Scenes

THIS BOOK

This 5th edition of *New England* was written by six tried-and-true East Coasters. Mara Vorhees coordinated the book, and wrote the front and end chapters, plus the Boston and Around Boston chapters. Ned Friary and Glenda Bendure wrote the Cape Cod, Nantucket & Martha's Vineyard chapter. Richard Koss covered Vermont and Connecticut, and John Spelman wrote the Rhode Island and Central Massachusetts & the Berkshires chapters. Regis St. Louis covered New Hampshire and Maine. Gerald Easter contributed the History chapter. The 4th edition was written by Kim Grant, Mara Vorhees, Alex Hershey, Andrew Bender and John Spelman. Earlier editions of *New England* were written by Tom Brosnahan and Steve Jermanok.

This guidebook was commissioned in Lonely Planet's Oakland office, and produced by the following:

Commissioning Editor Jay Cooke
Coordinating Editor Averil Robertson
Coordinating Cartographer Diana Duggan
Coordinating Layout Designer Jacqui Saunders
Managing Editors Brigitte Ellemor, Geoff Howard
Managing Cartographer Alison Lyall
Managing Layout Designers Adam McCrow, Celia Wood

Assisting Editors Janice Bird, Monique Choy, Margedd Heliosz, Kate James, Anne Mulvaney
Assisting Cartographers Mick Garrett, Jacqueline Nguyen, Andy Rojas, Julie Sheridan, Amanda Sierp, Andrew Smith
Cover Designer Marika Mercer
Project Managers Chris Love, Fabrice Rocher

Thanks to David Burnett, Jennifer Garrett, Mark Germanchis, Lisa Knights, Glenn van der Knijff, John Mazzocchi, Darren O'Connell

THANKS
MARA VORHEES

Thank you! To Jay: for commissioning me to write about my favorite city in a year that the Olde Towne Team was still alive in October (and for your patience when the World Series started and I still had not turned in a completed manuscript). To my co-authors: for your hard work in turning out a great book. To B: for always coming along for the ride. Go Sox!

NED FRIARY & GLENDA BENDURE

A hearty thanks to everyone who chimed in on their favorite spots, especially Bryan Lantz, Bob Prescott, Patti Bangert, Julie Lipkin, Bill O'Neill and Susan Milton. And a special thanks to co-author

---

THE LONELY PLANET STORY

Fresh from an epic journey across Europe, Asia and Australia in 1972, Tony and Maureen Wheeler sat at their kitchen table stapling together notes. The first Lonely Planet guidebook, *Across Asia on the Cheap*, was born.

Travelers snapped up the guides. Inspired by their success, the Wheelers began publishing books to Southeast Asia, India and beyond. Demand was prodigious, and the Wheelers expanded the business rapidly to keep up. Over the years, Lonely Planet extended its coverage to every country and into the virtual world via lonelyplanet.com and the Thorn Tree message board.

As Lonely Planet became a globally loved brand, Tony and Maureen received several offers for the company. But it wasn't until 2007 that they found a partner whom they trusted to remain true to the company's principles of traveling widely, treading lightly and giving sustainably. In October of that year, BBC Worldwide acquired a 75% share in the company, pledging to uphold Lonely Planet's commitment to independent travel, trustworthy advice and editorial independence.

Today, Lonely Planet has offices in Melbourne, London and Oakland, with over 500 staff members and 300 authors. Tony and Maureen are still actively involved with Lonely Planet. They're traveling more often than ever, and they're devoting their spare time to charitable projects. And the company is still driven by the philosophy of *Across Asia on the Cheap*: 'All you've got to do is decide to go and the hardest part is over. So go!'

Mara Vorhees, and Jay Cooke and Alison Lyall at Lonely Planet for pulling it all together.

RICHARD KOSS

Thanks to Don Gellert and Elaine Koss for generous use of their car, The Unscathable; to Julie Kahn and David Schaye for the lowdown on the Vermont ski scene; to Anja Mutic for sage advice on Burlington; and to Bridget and Bob Lyons for sharing their knowledge of Brattleboro and its surrounding area. Also, immense gratitude to Cap'n Jay Cooke at LP for inviting me on board; to Mara Vorhees for her patience (even these acknowledgments are drifting in late) and good nature; and, as ever, to my mentor/tormentor Thomas Kohnstamm.

JOHN SPELMAN

Deepest thanks to Matt Lasner, Jenny Conathan and Jacob Leach for separating yes from no in Western Massachusetts; to Maggie Sullivan for witnessing Springfield; to Lisa for witnessing everything else; to my family and Nick Emlen for Rhode Island help; and finally to Mara and Jay at LP: I could write several love songs about how nice it is to work with you, but unfortunately I've used up my allocation of words.

REGIS ST. LOUIS

Many thanks to Jay Cooke for inviting me onboard and to the countless fishermen who kept me in lobsters all summer long. I'm also grateful to the kind travelers, innkeepers and chamber and park staff who shared excellent travel tips; in particular, I'd like to thank Michael Sharpston for first-rate conversations, Chet and Sue in Franconia, Zsuzsa in Franklin and Emily Mitchell in Deer Isle for letting me pitch a tent in her backyard during the fiercest thunderstorm I've ever seen. Warmest thanks to Francie, Brent, Greta, Augie, Lily and friends for a most memorable Cape Cod finale. Most of all, thank you, Cassandra for sharing much of the adventure and being such a splendid travel partner.

OUR READERS

Many thanks to the travelers who used the last edition and wrote to us with helpful hints, useful advice and interesting anecdotes:

Bree Aldridge, Michael Badman, Donald Bartholomew, Alison & Richard Bennett, Cathy Boys, David Brown, Juliet Challis, Nigel Clements, Zane Cornett, Christiane Cunnar, Paul Ertelt, Simon Esland, Kenneth Fergusson, Raul Flores, Mary Fry, Colleen Gray,

SEND US YOUR FEEDBACK

We love to hear from travelers – your comments keep us on our toes and help make our books better. Our well-traveled team reads every word on what you loved or loathed about this book. Although we cannot reply individually to postal submissions, we always guarantee that your feedback goes straight to the appropriate authors, in time for the next edition. Each person who sends us information is thanked in the next edition – and the most useful submissions are rewarded with a free book.

To send us your updates – and find out about Lonely Planet events, newsletters and travel news – visit our award-winning website: **www.lonelyplanet.com/contact**.

Note: we may edit, reproduce and incorporate your comments in Lonely Planet products such as guidebooks, websites and digital products, so let us know if you don't want your comments reproduced or your name acknowledged. For a copy of our privacy policy visit www.lonelyplanet.com/privacy.

Stephen Harris, Teresa Herrera, Martin Hicks, Jim Jer-Don, Mary Ellen Kitler, George & Dilys Lawrence, Mikael Lund, Chris Lyddon, Jill Mahon, Martina Miertsch, Linda Nightingale, Michael O'Brien, Colin Poyser, John Sargant, Sheryl Sirotnik, Betsy Street, Crystal Thiele, Julia Tirler, Alan Todd, E Todd, Neal Tognazzini, Meg Weber, Gisela Zigan-Wagne

ACKNOWLEDGMENTS

Many thanks to the following for the use of their content:

Globe on title page ©Mountain High Maps 1993 Digital Wisdom, Inc.

Massachusetts Bay Transportation Authority: MBTA Transit Map ©2008

Internal photographs p285 (#3) by Brandon Cole Marine Photography/Alamy; p287 Andre Jenny/ Alamy. All other photographs by Lonely Planet Images, and p281 Mark Newman; p282, p283 (#3) John Elk III; p283 (#2) Glenn van der Knijff; p284, p286 (#1) Corinne Humphrey; p285 (#2), p288 Kim Grant; p286 (#2) Angus Oborn.

All images are the copyright of the photographers unless otherwise indicated. Many of the images in this guide are available for licensing from Lonely Planet Images: www.lonelyplanetimages.com.

Index

INDEX

INDEX

000 Map pages
000 Photograph pages

GreenDex

Sustainability is increasingly key in the travel industry. But how can you know which businesses are actually eco-friendly and which are simply jumping on the environmental bandwagon?

The following attractions, accommodations, eateries and entertainment/drinking options have been selected by Lonely Planet authors because they demonstrate a commitment to sustainability. We've selected hotels, bars and restaurants for their support of local producers or their devotion to the 'slow food' cause – so they might serve only seasonal, locally sourced produce on their menus. We've also highlighted farmers markets and the local producers themselves. In addition, we've covered accommodations that we deem to be environmentally friendly, for example for their commitment to recycling or energy conservation. Attractions are listed because they're involved in conservation or environmental education.

For more tips about travelling sustainably in New England, turn to the Getting Started chapter (p15).

We want to keep developing our sustainable-travel content. If you think we've omitted somewhere that should be listed here, or if you disagree with our choices, contact us at www.lonelyplanet.com/contact and set us straight for next time. For more information about sustainable tourism and Lonely Planet, see www.lonelyplanet.com/responsibletravel.

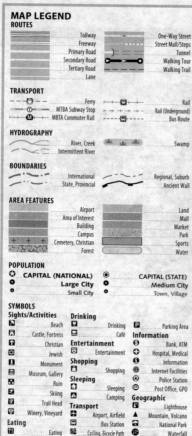

MAP LEGEND
ROUTES

Tollway	One-Way Street
Freeway	Street Mall/Steps
Primary Road	Tunnel
Secondary Road	Walking Tour
Tertiary Road	Walking Trail
Lane	

TRANSPORT

Ferry	Rail
MTBA Subway Stop	Rail (Underground)
MBTA Commuter Rail	Bus Route

HYDROGRAPHY

River, Creek	Swamp
Intermittent River	

BOUNDARIES

International	Regional, Suburb
State, Provincial	Ancient Wall

AREA FEATURES

Airport	Land
Area of Interest	Mall
Building	Market
Campus	Park
Cemetery, Christian	Sports
Forest	Water

POPULATION

✪ CAPITAL (NATIONAL)	◉ CAPITAL (STATE)
● Large City	● Medium City
○ Small City	○ Town, Village

SYMBOLS

Sights/Activities
- Beach
- Castle, Fortress
- Christian
- Jewish
- Monument
- Museum, Gallery
- Ruin
- Skiing
- Trail Head
- Winery, Vineyard

Eating
- Eating

Drinking
- Drinking
- Café

Entertainment
- Entertainment

Shopping
- Shopping

Sleeping
- Sleeping
- Camping

Transport
- Airport, Airfield
- Bus Station
- Cycling, Bicycle Path

P Parking Area

Information
- Bank, ATM
- Hospital, Medical
- Information
- Internet Facilities
- Police Station
- Post Office, GPO

Geographic
- Lighthouse
- Mountain, Volcano
- National Park
- Waterfall

Handwritten note: Econolodge #66 Rt. 4 Mennen, VT (800) 992-9067

LONELY PLANET OFFICES

Australia
Head Office
Locked Bag 1, Footscray, Victoria 3011
☎ 03 8379 8000, fax 03 8379 8111
talk2us@lonelyplanet.com.au

USA
150 Linden St, Oakland, CA 94607
☎ 510 893 8555, toll free 800 275 8555
fax 510 893 8572
info@lonelyplanet.com

UK
2nd Floor, 186 City Road,
London EC1V 2NT
☎ 020 7106 2100, fax 020 7106 2101
go@lonelyplanet.co.uk

Published by Lonely Planet Publications Pty Ltd
ABN 36 005 607 983